Encyclopedia of
ANCIENT ASIAN CIVILIZATIONS

Encyclopedia of
ANCIENT ASIAN CIVILIZATIONS

Charles F. W. Higham

☑®

Facts On File, Inc.

Encyclopedia of Ancient Asian Civilizations

Facts On File, Inc.
132 West 31st Street
New York NY 10001

Library of Congress Cataloging-in-Publication Data
Higham, Charles.
Encyclopedia of ancient Asian civilizations / Charles F. W. Higham.
p. cm.
Includes bibliographical references and index.
ISBN 0-8160-4640-9
1. Asia—Civilization—Encyclopedias. I. Title.
DS12.H5 2003
959'.1'03—dc212003048513

Facts On File books are available at special discounts when purchased in bulk quantities for businesses, associations, institutions, or sales promotions. Please call our Special Sales Department in New York at (212) 967-8800 or (800) 322-8755.

You can find Facts On File on the World Wide Web at http://www.factsonfile.com

Text design by Joan M. Toro
Cover design by Cathy Rincon
Maps by Jeremy Eagle

Printed in the United States of America

VB Hermitage 10 9 8 7 6 5 4 3 2 1

This book is printed on acid-free paper.

CONTENTS

LIST OF ILLUSTRATIONS AND MAPS

Photographs & Illustrations

Maps

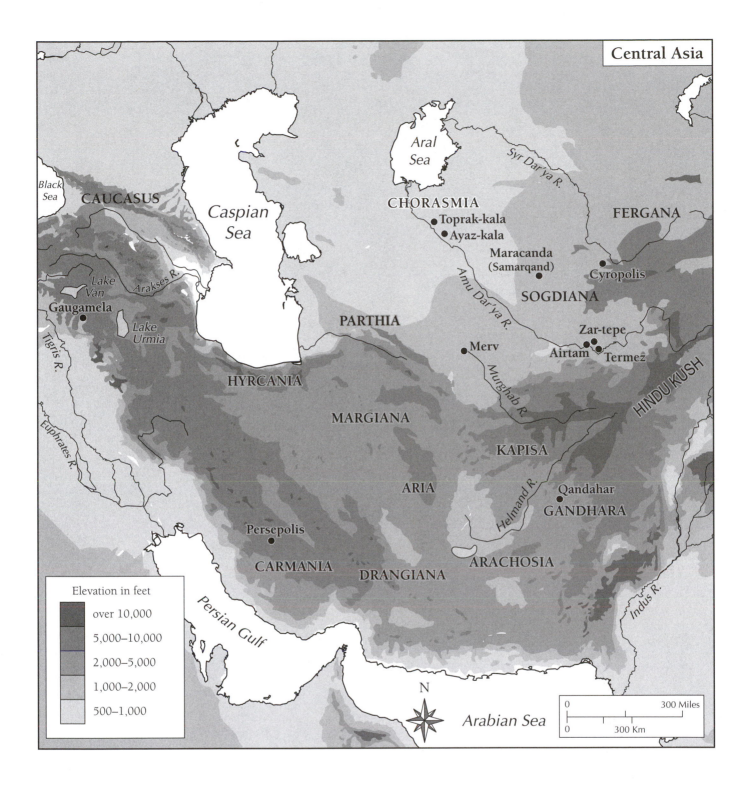

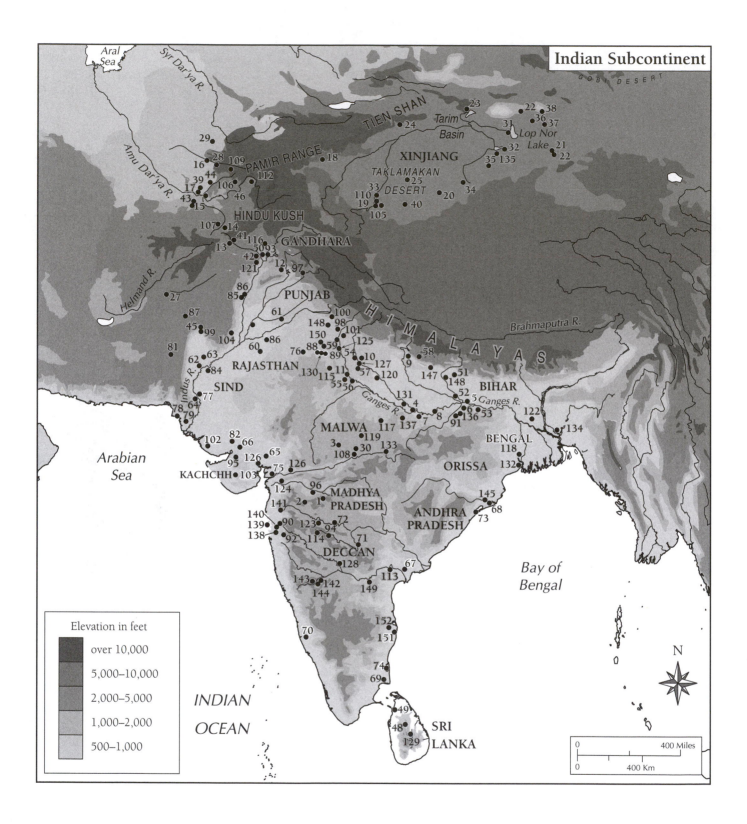

Indian Subcontinent

Aral Sea

Syr Dar'ya R.

TIEN SHAN

Tarim Basin

GOBI DESERT

Lop Nor Lake

XINJIANG

Amu Dar'ya R.

PAMIR RANGE

TAKLAMAKAN DESERT

HINDU KUSH

GANDHARA

Helmand R.

PUNJAB

HIMALAYAS

Brahmaputra R.

RAJASTHAN

Indus R.

SIND

MALWA

Ganges R.

BIHAR

Ganges R.

BENGAL

Arabian Sea

KACHCHH

MADHYA PRADESH

ORISSA

ANDHRA PRADESH

DECCAN

Bay of Bengal

INDIAN OCEAN

SRI LANKA

Elevation in feet

- over 10,000
- 5,000–10,000
- 2,000–5,000
- 1,000–2,000
- 500–1,000

N

| 0 | 400 Miles |
| 0 | 400 Km |

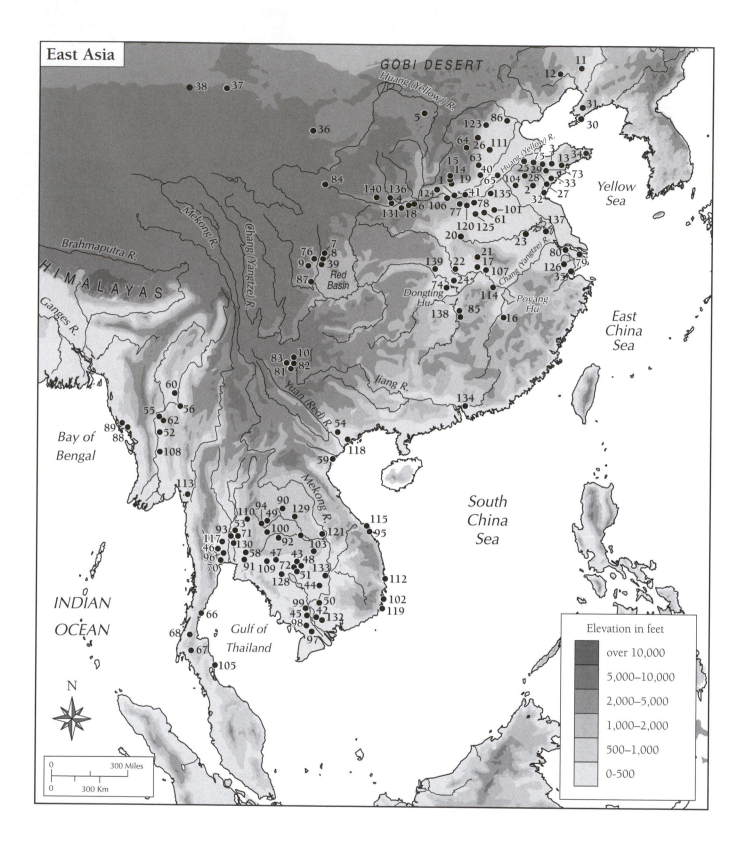

East Asia

GOBI DESERT

Huang (Yellow) R.

Huang (Yellow) R.

Yellow Sea

HIMALAYAS

Brahmaputra R.

Mekong R.

Chang (Yangtze) R.

Ganges R.

Red Basin

Chang (Yangtze) R.

East China Sea

Dongting Hu

Poyang Hu

Bay of Bengal

Jiang R.

Yuan (Red) R.

South China Sea

Mekong R.

INDIAN OCEAN

Gulf of Thailand

N

Elevation in feet	
	over 10,000
	5,000–10,000
	2,000–5,000
	1,000–2,000
	500–1,000
	0–500

0   300 Miles

0   300 Km

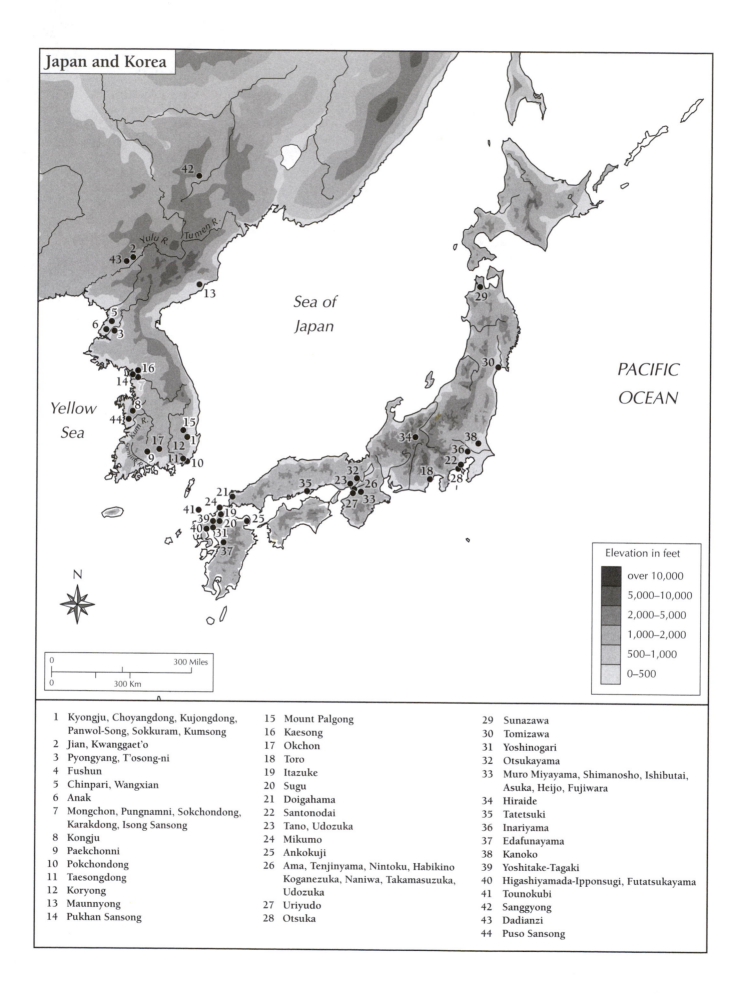

Japan and Korea

Yulu R.

Tumen R.

42

43 ● 2

13

Sea of
Japan

PACIFIC

OCEAN

5

6   3

Yellow
Sea

16
14   7
8
44   Kum R.   15
17   12   1
9   11   10

29

30

34   38
36
22
18   28

32
35   23   26
27   33
21
24
41   19
39   20   25
40   31
37

N

0   300 Miles

0   300 Km

Elevation in feet

over 10,000

5,000–10,000

2,000–5,000

1,000–2,000

500–1,000

0–500

1   Kyongju, Choyangdong, Kujongdong,
     Panwol-Song, Sokkuram, Kumsong
2   Jian, Kwanggaet'o
3   Pyongyang, T'osong-ni
4   Fushun
5   Chinpari, Wangxian
6   Anak
7   Mongchon, Pungnamni, Sokchondong,
     Karakdong, Isong Sansong
8   Kongju
9   Paekchonni
10 Pokchondong
11 Taesongdong
12 Koryong
13 Maunnyong
14 Pukhan Sansong

15 Mount Palgong
16 Kaesong
17 Okchon
18 Toro
19 Itazuke
20 Sugu
21 Doigahama
22 Santonodai
23 Tano, Udozuka
24 Mikumo
25 Ankokuji
26 Ama, Tenjinyama, Nintoku, Habikino
     Koganezuka, Naniwa, Takamasuzuka,
     Udozuka
27 Uriyudo
28 Otsuka

29 Sunazawa
30 Tomizawa
31 Yoshinogari
32 Otsukayama
33 Muro Miyayama, Shimanosho, Ishibutai,
     Asuka, Heijo, Fujiwara
34 Hiraide
35 Tatetsuki
36 Inariyama
37 Edafunayama
38 Kanoko
39 Yoshitake-Tagaki
40 Higashiyamada-Ipponsugi, Futatsukayama
41 Tounokubi
42 Sanggyong
43 Dadianzi
44 Puso Sansong

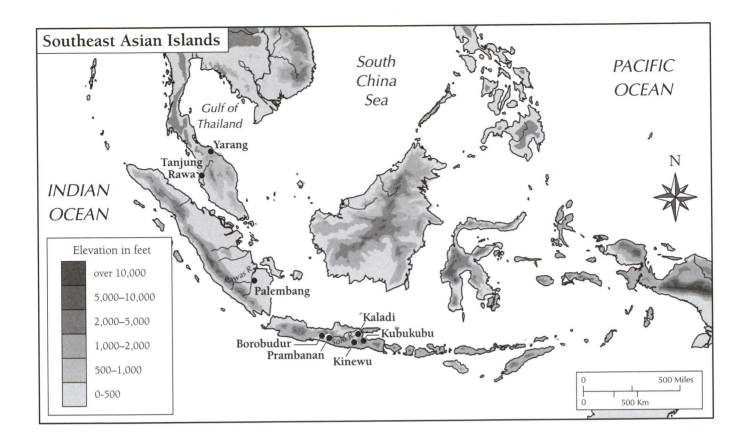

Southeast Asian Islands

INDIAN OCEAN

South China Sea

PACIFIC OCEAN

N

Gulf of Thailand

Yarang

Tanjung Rawa

Rawas R.

Palembang

Kaladi

Kubukubu

Borobudur

Solo R.

Prambanan

Kinewu

Elevation in feet

over 10,000

5,000–10,000

2,000–5,000

1,000–2,000

500–1,000

0-500

0   500 Miles

0   500 Km

INTRODUCTION

This volume concentrates on the civilizations that arose east of the Caspian Sea. These early civilizations of Asia developed over a vast territory stretching from the region of modern Afghanistan and the Aral Sea to Japan and Korea, and from Sri Lanka (former Ceylon) to the islands of Southeast Asia. These civilizations developed in the oases that bordered the arid Taklamakan Desert in western China and the tropical jungles of Java in Indonesia. Virtually every major river basin sustained one or more early states, along rivers like the Yalu, which flowed through the icy cold of a Korean winter, or the Irrawaddy and the Chao Phraya, which ran through the pervading heat of their valleys. Early Western visitors to East and Southeast Asia were invariably taken aback by the scale and power of the rulers they encountered. Even the mighty army of Alexander the Great (356–323 B.C.E.) rebelled at the prospect of advancing beyond the Beas River into India. Romans, Greeks, and Persians were keen to trade with the East but barely gained a foothold on Asian soil.

When intrepid Portuguese friars penetrated the jungles of Cambodia in the 16th century and came across a great stone city abandoned to the forest, they were so surprised that they could advance only the Roman emperor Trajan (98–117) or Alexander the Great, rather than the Cambodians, as being responsible for such magnificence. Those Portuguese, as many later archaeologists did, at once recognized the external trappings of what is now called a state society. They encountered large temples and walled cities, huge reservoirs, and inscriptions of texts in an unknown form of writing. Had the people of Angkor constructed their palaces as well as their temples in stone, the friars would also have found large, opulent, and richly ornamented domestic buildings. The discovery of palace foundations, however, had to await more recent archaeological excavation.

SIGNS OF CIVILIZATION

Great temples, roads, canals, and reservoirs, together with tombs and writing, are the hardware of civilization.

The software lies in a social system that can be discerned through the translation of writing and the inferences drawn from the archaeological record.

The central operating system of a state lies in the ruling elite. This usually takes the form of a hereditary dynasty in which the ruler, who, in Japan and Korea, was frequently a woman, often assumed godlike qualities linked with an ability to communicate with the ancestors and spirit world. Administration involved an upper class of relatives of the ruling dynasty, a bureaucracy of centrally appointed officials, or both. Power was concentrated in the capital, often located in an urban center that incorporated a palace, state temples, and quarters for specialists. Tight control over the military helped ensure the rulers' continuance in power, but in many early states, there was a perennial problem of scale, manifested in centrifugal tendencies. The farther from the center, the greater the temptation to seek independence.

One of the recurrent issues confronting the rulers of early states in Asia was the success of the harvest. Whether rice, millet, wheat, or barley, the surplus generated by the field workers was vital to the well-being of all. There is much evidence of central concern for predictable harvests, manifested in state irrigation works, deployment of increasingly efficient agricultural tools, and infrastructure for transportation. Essentially, agricultural and other surpluses were taxed and used to sustain the administrative system. In many instances this taxation encouraged a system of currency that took various forms: cowry shells and cast imitations thereof, measures of gold and silver, and coins that in India owed much to Greek prototypes.

INDIGENOUS ASIAN CIVILIZATIONS

In at least two instances it is possible to recognize an indigenous development of an Asian civilization with minimal outside influence. The origins of the Indus Valley civilization can be traced to increasing social complexity in the basin of this river and the surrounding uplands to the north and west, linked with growing maritime and overland trade with the contemporary civilizations of the Tigris and Euphrates Rivers. Here are all the classic hallmarks of an early state system: huge walled cities with elite precincts dividing the priests and aristocrats from the rest of the urban population; regular streets, granaries, craft workshops, and domestic houses; and, most intriguing perhaps to the visitor, an efficient system of latrines and drains. A written script was used by at least 3300 B.C.E., but the failure of modern scholars to read the brief texts means that the administrative and ruling system remains conjectural. Several large cities dominated, particularly Mohenjo Daro and Harappa, but there were many smaller centers, villages, and hamlets.

The end of this civilization is dated to the first half of the second millennium B.C.E., but the reasons for the decline are not yet clearly defined. Some scholars have turned for explanation to the Rig-Veda, sacred ritual hymns, which survived through oral tradition in India until first transcribed in the 14th century C.E. For millennia Hindu priests have intoned these hymns during religious ceremonies incorporating the soma ritual. This ritual involved taking the juice from the soma plant, the identity of which remains unknown. Some was then offered to the gods; the rest was imbibed by the priests. The gods worshiped include the principal Hindu deities in their early manifestations: Foremost are Agni, the god of fire; Surya, the Sun god; Rudra, god of storms; and Indra and Vishnu, the gods of war. The Rig-Veda survives in Sanskrit, an Indo-European language, and its early manifestation was once seen as evidence of warriors arriving in the Indus Valley from the northwest, warriors who destroyed the cities of the Indus. Few now hold to this view for lack of archaeological evidence. Indeed some scholars have even suggested that the Rig-Veda in essence originated in the Indus cities and actually describes events that occurred in them.

In any case the Indus civilization did not survive in a recognizable form beyond the first centuries of the second millennium B.C.E. The center of gravity in India then moved to the Ganges (Ganga)-Jamuna Basin, where a series of small competing states, known as *janapadas*, arose. The elimination and absorption of the weak led to the formation of larger states, and ultimately by the same process, the Mauryan state arose to form the first Indian empire in the fourth century B.C.E.

The second independent development of a civilization took place in China from about 2000 B.C.E. For many years, the central focus for the early Chinese state lay in the middle reaches of the Huang (Yellow) River Valley. Early Chinese histories described the states of Xia and Shang, including the names of capitals, dynasties, and kings. Archaeological research has validated these semimythical states, identified cities, recovered early written records, and opened the burials of elite leaders.

Even after nearly a century of such research, new discoveries are still crowding in. Thus a new Shang capital was found as recently as 1999 at Huanbai. Excavations have also revealed the antecedents of the first states, which reach back to the period of early farming, and extending through the increasingly complex societies of the loess land bordering the Huang River. Long-range contact with the West was manifested by the beginnings of bronze casting and the adoption of the chariot.

Of even greater significance, there is compelling new evidence for a parallel development to the south, in the lands bordering the mighty Chang (Yangtze) River. Here rice replaced millet as the subsistence base of states known as the Changjiang civilization. Already by 4000 B.C.E., walled settlements like Chengtoushan were established. The Liangzhu culture (3200 to 2000 B.C.E.) of the lower Chang River Valley presents the picture of a complex society, whose leaders were interred in opulent tombs with fine jade grave goods. The most spectacular finds are from Sanxingdui in the Sichuan Basin, a huge walled city and likely capital of the regional state of the Shu people during the second millennium B.C.E. The bronze, ivory, gold, and jade offerings recovered from two sacrificial pits reveal a society no less complex than its contemporary at Anyang, the capital of the Shang state in the Huang Valley to the north.

In north China, the Shang dynasty was replaced in 1045 B.C.E. by the Zhou rulers. The Western Zhou kings controlled a considerable area. However, their policy of sending royal relatives to rule over newly conquered regions in due course weakened the center, as regional lords assumed their own power bases and formed their own states. In addition, the states known to the Chinese as Shu and Chu continued to flourish in the Chang Valley independent of the Zhou. This policy, with the transition to the Eastern Zhou period in 770 B.C.E., led to the weakening of the royal house; as rival states entered into increasingly bellicose relationships, the state of Qin emerged as the dominant force. By 221 B.C.E., the first emperor, Qin Shihuangdi, had vanquished his last rivals. His dynasty, however, was short lived, being succeeded by the Western and then the Eastern Han. This period of empire, which ended in 220 C.E., saw the establishment of an enduring Chinese state that exercised considerable influence on its borders.

OTHER STATES IN EARLY ASIA

The development of powerful states in China and India during the first millennium B.C.E. had a potent effect on the cultures with which they came into contact. Many new states mushroomed in the wake of international trade relations, wars of undisguised imperial conquest, or exposure to new ideas and ideologies. To the northeast, the Han policy of imperial expansion during the second century B.C.E. saw the establishment of the commandery, or province, of Lelang in northern Korea. This imposition of an alien regime in the midst of already sophisticated societies was, at least in part, a stimulus for the rise of four Korean states—Koguryo, Shilla, Paekche, and Kaya. By the fourth century C.E., the Chinese had withdrawn from their foothold in the Korean Peninsula, and the rulers of these states fought among themselves. In the seventh century, the rulers of Shilla allied themselves with the Chinese Tang emperor to vanquish all rivals and to establish the first pan-Korean state, Unified Shilla.

Across the Tsushima Strait in Japan, the adoption of sophisticated techniques for rice cultivation on the Han model, together with the construction of irrigation works, underpinned emerging statelets concentrated in Kyushu and the margins of the Inland Sea. The rulers built for themselves gigantic mounded tombs, the largest of which reached a length of nearly half a kilometer. The *Nihongi,* an indigenous historical record completed in the early eighth century C.E., names a sequence of emperors and empresses, together with their capitals, temples, and palaces. Tracing these sites and opening them by excavation have yielded a rich harvest of new information. The Nara plain, east of modern Osaka, was a focus for the early Japanese state, with royal tombs and the remains of great cities at Fujiwara and Heijo, which were built along the lines of the Chinese capital of Chang'an. In 1961, a vital discovery revealed that *mokkan,* written records on wooden slips, survived at Heijo in considerable quantities. These illuminated the detailed workings of aristocratic households and court functionaries. Linked with the excavations in royal palaces and Buddhist temples, the features of the early Nara state of the eighth century have emerged clearly defined from oblivion.

With the end of the Han dynasty in the early third century, China was divided into three states. The southern kingdom of Wu had no access to the lucrative Silk Road that linked China with the West, and the emperor sent emissaries south to seek a possible maritime link with the worlds of India and Rome. To their considerable surprise, the emissaries encountered a state that they named Funan, located on the delta of the Mekong River in modern Vietnam and Cambodia. Their report, which has survived, described a palace and walled settlements, a system of taxation and laws, written records, and the presence of craft specialists. Rice was cultivated, and there was vigorous trade.

Once again, archaeology has verified these written accounts. Air photography before the Second World War revealed the outline of moated and walled cities on the flat delta landscape, linked by canals that radiated, straight as arrows, between the centers. At ground level, the French archaeologist Louis Malleret in 1944 excavated the city of Oc Eo and traced the outlines of brick temple foundations, jewelry workshops, and house foundations. Dating this city was facilitated by the dis-

covery of coins minted by Roman emperors of the second century C.E. Since the end of the war in Vietnam in 1975, research has raced ahead. Many more sites have been identified, and the inscriptions, written in Sanskrit and employing the Indian Brahmi script, record the presence of kings and queens who took Indian names and founded temples dedicated to Indian gods. Wooden statues of the Buddha have survived in the delta mud.

Funan was one of many small mercantile states that prospered by participating in a great trade network now known as the maritime Silk Road. A two-way trade with the Indian subcontinent saw gold and spices heading west, while bronzes, glass and carnelian ornaments, and novel ideas entered Southeast Asia. Along the coast of Vietnam, temples dedicated to Siva and other Hindu gods, as well as Sanskrit texts, document the rise of the Cham states. Chams spoke an Austronesian language, unlike their neighbors in Southeast Asia, and they dominated this coastal tract with its restricted river floodplains until the march to the south by the Vietnamese that ended in the 18th century. The rich soil of Java sustained kingdoms that were responsible for Borobudur, the largest Buddhist monument known, dating to the ninth century, while the demand in the west for cloves and nutmegs saw the Spice Islands of Southeast Asia prosper.

The broad floodplain of the Chao Phraya River in Thailand witnessed the rise of a state known from its inscriptions, in the Mon language, as Dvaravati. Here are large, moated centers dominated by temples dedicated to the Buddha, which rose at the same time as the Funan state to the south. Small states developed along the coast of peninsular Thailand and Malaysia, as goods were transshipped from the Gulf of Siam to the ports on the Andaman Sea. One major trading state, known as Srivijaya, arose at Palembang on the island of Sumatra. To the west, the Pyu civilization of the dry zone in modern Myanmar (Burma) bequeathed great cities at Halin, Beikthano, and Sri Ksetra. On the Arakan coast, the part of Southeast Asia most exposed to trade with India, there are reports of visits by the Buddha himself, and cities were founded at Dhanyawadi and Vesali, complete with palaces and temples.

Local origins are common to all these states that burgeoned along the maritime Silk Road. Explorations into their prehistoric ancestry reveal growing cultural complexity, as chiefs rose up and took advantage of the new opportunities afforded by international trade. Indian influence is seen in the Sanskrit and Pali languages, the Brahmi script, and Hindu gods. Beneath the surface of the Pyu, Dvaravati, Funan, and Cham civilizations lies a strong local culture. These cultures continued well into the second millennium C.E. In Cambodia the civilization of Angkor grew into a major regional power. Pagan was the center of the Burmese civilization. The Chams continued to flourish until the predatory Vietnamese began their march south.

THE SILK ROAD AND THE RISE AND FALL OF CULTURES

The Silk Road itself was a labyrinth of trackways that began with the Gansu corridor in western China. It then skirted north and south of the arid Tarim Basin, before reaching the crossroads that lay in the valleys of the Syr Dar'ya and Amu Dar'ya Rivers as they flowed north to the Aral Sea. Here it was possible to strike south into Afghanistan and India or to continue in a westerly direction, south of the Caspian Sea, to the Black Sea and the Mediterranean.

This route was an ancient one, followed, it seems, by early farmers trekking east, who founded settlements in the Tarim oases during the third millennium B.C.E. There, in the dry wastes, are 4,000-year-old cemeteries containing the remains of fair-skinned people with European features, interred with woven plaid textiles, sprigs of ephedra (a hallucinatory plant), and trousers and boots. Their descendants in all probability spoke Tocharian, an Indo-European language. It was along this route that knowledge of bronze working and the chariot reached China. The Silk Road was a conduit for the arrival of Buddhist teachings in China and ultimately Korea and Japan. At Mogao, east of the Taklamakan Desert, are some of the finest Buddhist shrines anywhere.

The Chinese Han dynasty's establishment of peaceful conditions in the second century B.C.E., always problematical where steppe horsemen might intervene, promoted the development of states along the eastern stepping stones of the Silk Road. When the archaeologist-explorers Sven Hedin and Sir Aurel Stein reached the deserts of far western China a century ago, they encountered the remains of walled cities, roads, even ancient vineyards. Letters and royal orders on wood and leather have survived, in an Indian script dating to the third century C.E. These illuminate the kingdoms of Shan-shan, Sogdiana, and Hotan and their oasis cities at Niya, Endere, Panjikent, and Lou-lan.

The crossroads of Asia, where the routes south into India bisect the Silk Road south of the Aral Sea, have seen the rise and fall of many civilizations. Under the rule of Cyrus the Great (ruled c. 585–c. 529 B.C.E.), the Achaemenid empire of Persia expanded east, incorporating the Indus Valley as its 20th province during the reign of Darius the Great in the early fifth century B.C.E. Achaemenid rule came to an end with the defeat of Darius III at the hands of Alexander the Great at the Battle of Gaugamela (modern Iraq) in 331 B.C.E., setting in motion the beginning of the Greek control of this region. Under Seleucus Nicator (356–281 B.C.E.), one of Alexander's generals and ruler of the former Persian Empire, Greek influence was profoundly felt through the foundation of cities, the construction of temples, and the minting of coins bearing the images of many Bactrian Greek kings. At Ay Khanum in Afghanistan and Sirkap in Pakistan are cities that match their contemporaries in Greece itself. This powerful wave of Hellenistic influence can be seen in the Gandharan art style as well as in theaters and mausoleums, for example, at Ay Khanum. However, the Seleucid empire was on the wane by the mid-second century B.C.E., and from its remnants arose the Parthians in the region southeast of the Caspian Sea. They briefly held sway over the great center of Merv (modern Mary in Turkmenistan), reaching down into the Indus Valley.

The Kushans, however, were to exert a major influence in this area. Moving west from China, these initially nomadic groups settled south of the Aral Sea by the end of the second century B.C.E., and under a line of potent rulers beginning with Kujula Kadphises, they came to rule a large empire south into India, with a capital at Purusapura (modern Peshawar). King Kanishka, who took the title *devaputra*, or son of god, showed a deep interest in Hinduism. By 200 C.E., Persian power resurfaced with the Sasanid dynasty under Ardashir I (224–241). Sassanian control of the strategic Merv Oasis and this central part of the Silk Road provided a welcome element of stability. By the third century C.E., a Christian monastery was founded at Merv.

From the fifth century C.E., however, the Sassanians came under mounting pressure from the Hephthalite Huns to the east, a people of shadowy origins, whose prowess as mounted cavalrymen and archers was feared. After the defeat and death of their king, Firuz, in 484, the Sassanians paid tribute in coinage to the Hephthalites, largely to keep the peace on their eastern frontier, until the reign of Khosrow I in the mid-sixth century C.E. Hephthalite territory at this juncture included Tokharistan and much of Afghanistan. They conquered Sogdiana in 509 and extended their authority as far east as Urumqi in northwest China. By 520, they controlled this area and in India came up against the western frontiers of the Gupta empire under King Bhuhagupta. Under their own king, Toramana, the Hephthalites seized the Punjab, Kashmir, and Rajputana; Toramana's successor, Mihirakula, established his capital at Sakala (modern Sialkot in Pakistan). He was a devotee of Siva, and this was a period of devastation for the venerable Buddhist monasteries in Pakistan and India, many of which were sacked and destroyed. The last Hephthalite king, Yudhishthira, ruled until about 670, when he was replaced by the Turkish dynasty known as the Shahi.

STRANDS OF EARLY ASIAN CIVILIZATIONS

The pattern underlying early Asian civilizations entails three strands. The first involves the origin and flowering of the indigenous states. Two can be identified: The earlier was centered in the Indus Basin and flourished during the fourth millennium B.C.E., before the cities were abandoned and the focus of Indian civilization moved to the Ganges (Ganga) and Yamuna Valleys. The later, and most durable, began in catchments of the two great rivers of China, the Chang and the Huang. Here there was a twin development of agriculture, with rice dominating the balmier south and millet the colder north. Again cultural complexity developed in tandem in both areas, as did the early states, Xia and Shang in the central plains of the Huang River and Changjiang in the land bordering the Chang.

The second strand involved the development of what might be termed "secondary civilizations" in areas that came under the influence of China, India, or both. While Chinese influence was strongly felt in Korea and Japan, the impact of Buddhism cannot be discounted. To the south, the states of the maritime Silk Road developed from indigenous chiefdoms, retaining their autonomy but prospering through the enriching influence of India and China. The same cross-fertilization of ideas between local inhabitants and foreign traders may be identified on the Silk Road itself.

The third and most complex contributor to the pattern of Asian civilization lies in the regions where east met west through the expansion of the Greek and Persian Empires and the intrusion of Sakas or Scythians, Kushans, and Hephthalite Huns. This region, centering on modern Afghanistan, northern Pakistan, and the basins of the Syr Dar'ya and Amu Dar'ya Rivers, is one of the most interesting areas, because of the variety of peoples, religions, languages, and cultures that came and went, each contributing and at the same time adapting to the ways of other societies.

Today Asia teems with humanity. Its billions of people speak thousands of languages. Its contribution to the development of the human species outweighs that of any other part of the globe: the domestication of rice, the largest mortuary complexes, two of the world's great religions, massive temples, cast iron, paper, silk, writing, universities, totalitarian states, the crossbow, outstanding works of art—the list is endless. The development of Asian civilizations from their first foundations is a key to understanding Asia today.

ENTRIES A TO Z

Abeyadana temple The Abeyadana temple, at PAGAN in modern Myanmar (Burma), is thought to have been inspired by the queen of King Kyanzittha (1084–1112 C.E.). It includes a large, rectangular, central temple adjoining a rectangular hall. A large brick image of the Buddha dominates the temple; some of the inner walls are embellished with frescoes of Hindu gods, such as Brahma, Vishnu, Siva, and Indra.

Abhayagiri Abhayagiri, a monastery at ANURADHAPURA in modern Sri Lanka (Ceylon), was founded by King Vattagamani Abhaya in the early first century B.C.E. It enjoyed royal patronage until the last days of Anuradhapura itself. Under King Gajabahu (114–136 C.E.), the Abhayagiri stupa (Buddhist shrine) reached the enormous height of 84 meters (277 ft.). In the fifth century C.E., it was visited by the Chinese monk FAXIAN, who described a jade image of the Buddha standing six meters (20 ft.) high. There were ceaseless ceremonials there, suggesting that MAHAYANA BUDDHISM, the high ritual form of the religion, was in favor.

abhiseka An *abhiseka* is a plaque used in consecration ceremonies for Buddhist kings in Southeast Asia. Such plaques have strong Hindu traditions, and the symbols on them are highly significant. An example in steatite was recovered in 1965 during the construction of a road from the ancient city of VESALI to the later capital of MRAUK-U in the Rakhine (formerly ARAKAN) region of western Myanmar (Burma). The steatite plaque was used as the support for a bronze vessel found at the same time. The decoration represents the universe, bounded by a wall depicted as the raised, square edge of the plaque; the four continents within are seen as lotuses at each corner. A circular frieze of lotus petals in the center represents MOUNT MERU, the home of the gods; a second circular frieze incorporates symbols of royal mystical power. These include the *srivatsa* (mother goddess) motif, a conch shell, a cornucopia and fish, all of which are deemed to bring prosperity to the kingdom. A fly whisk, elephant goad, parasol, and bull are also depicted, and all are symbols of powerful kingship. Such symbols are evident in many other contexts in Southeast Asia, not least in the reliefs depicting King SURYAVARMAN II at ANGKOR WAT in Cambodia. A peacock and a deer on the plaque represent the Sun and the Moon; a pillar and goose indicate the conjunction of heaven and Earth. These esoteric powers are deemed to enter the king's person through the lustral water contained in the bronze bowl that the plaque supports. Its closest parallels are found in the ceramic *abhisekas* found in the Dvaravati sites of central Thailand.

See also DVARAVATI CIVILIZATION.

Achaemenid empire At its height, during the fifth century B.C.E., the Achaemenid empire stretched from Albania in the west to TAXILA and the course of the Indus Valley in the east, and from the Aral Sea to Cyrene in modern Libya, including western Asia and Egypt. Founded by Cyrus the Great (r. c. 585–c. 529 B.C.E.), the empire was organized into provinces. In the east, these included, from north to south, Khwarizm south of the Aral Sea, SOGDIANA in the headwaters of the Syr Dar'ya River, Arachosia and Gedrosia in Baluchistan, and BACTRIA, Margiana, and GANDHARA in Afghanistan. The eastern conquests were stimulated by the desire of Cyrus for a stable frontier against the Scythians, as well as by an imperialist impulse to seize and exploit territory. His policy included the foundation of frontier settlements, of which Cyropolis in the valley of the Syr Dar'ya River is best known. In the late sixth century B.C.E., a succeeding king, Darius the Great (r. 522–489 B.C.E.), led a campaign in the east that is said to have reached the shores of the Aral Sea. During the ensuing several years, the Persians conquered the area of modern northern Pakistan, and soldiers from the eastern provinces were prominent in the Achaemenid army. The empire ended with the defeat of Darius III by ALEXANDER THE GREAT at the Battle of Gaugamela (modern Iraq) in 331 B.C.E.

However, the two centuries of Achaemenid rule saw much cultural interaction between the center and the east. Scythians, Bactrians, Arachosians, Gandharans, and Indians are all depicted on the reliefs of Persepolis, the Persian ceremonial center in modern south Iran. The Scythians wear their characteristic pointed caps and carry short swords; the Bactrians are seen holding cups and guiding a Bactrian camel with a bell around its neck. The Indian wears a headband and a short kilt and carries vessels in baskets slung from a wooden holder supported over the shoulders, just like those still seen in India today. This intercourse and travel exposed participants to one of the world's great empires, involving knowledge of the Aramaic script and methods of administration. Both eased the consolidation of the conquest by Alexander the Great and his forces.

Further reading: Briant, P. *From Cyrus to Alexander: A History of the Persian Empire.* Winona Lake, Ind.: Eisenbrauns, 2002; Dandamaev, M. A. *Political History of the Achaemenid Empire (Ancient Near East).* Leiden: Brill, 1997; Dusinberre, E. R. M. *Aspects of Empire in Achaemenid Sardis.* Cambridge: Cambridge University Press, 2003.

acupuncture Acupuncture has been a central part of traditional Chinese medicine for more than 2,000 years. A set of four gold needles has been recovered from the tomb of Prince Jing of Zhongshan, dated to the Western HAN DYNASTY (206 B.C.E.–9 C.E.). Three different types of needles are represented, each having its own special function. An engraving from an Eastern Han tomb in Shandong province shows a creature with a human head and arms and a bird's body performing acupuncture on a kneeling patient.

Adhyapura Adhyapura, a site located in the Mekong Valley near the border between modern Cambodia and Vietnam, is notable as the home base of a highly ranked family that provided ministers to five kings, spanning the transition from the state of FUNAN to CHENLA (c. 550 C.E.)

and beyond. One family member, named Simhadatta, was the doctor of JAYAVARMAN I of Chenla and the governor of Adhyapura in 667 C.E.

Afrasiab Afrasiab is the ancient name for Samarqand, once a province of Russian Turkestan and now the name of a city and province in Uzbekistan. The city was a major center of both the Bactrian Greeks (250 B.C.E.–10 C.E.) and of SOGDIANA in the period from 200 B.C.E. up to the Arab conquests of the eighth century C.E. In the seventh century, Afrasiab covered an area of 214 hectares (535 acres) and minted its own coinage. The Sogdians grew wealthy through irrigation agriculture and control of the SILK ROAD. Their town houses and palaces were constructed of compressed loess and mud brick, and the interior walls were coated with clay. Mural paintings are a particular feature of these stately residences. One painting reveals a delegation of HEPHTHALITE HUNS; another shows an elegant boat with waterfowl. The Sogdians, through extensive trade contacts and the remote colonies of their merchants, incorporated foreign motifs into their outstanding silver metalwork as well as their religious art. They were Zoroastrians, followers of an ancient Iranian religion, but there were also small groups of Christians and Buddhists among the inhabitants. The religious art of Sogdiana shows the adoption of local and foreign elements into Zoroastrianism, such as an Indian-style four-armed depiction of an ancient Mesopotamian goddess, Nana.

A mural from Afrasiab, from the house of a wealthy aristocrat, shows foreign ambassadors arriving at the court, probably of King Varkhuman, in about 660 C.E. An inscription states that one of the delegates was from a small state known as Chaganiyan. Others traveled from China and as far afield as Korea. The Chinese are seen presenting silks to the king. The southern wall of this same chamber shows King Varkhuman in a procession, visiting a holy shrine probably dedicated to his ancestors.

Agni Agni, the god of fire in early Indian religion, is mentioned in the Rig-Veda around 1500 to 1000 B.C.E. He had three principal manifestations: as fire itself, as lightning, and as the Sun. The crackling of a fire was the god Agni speaking. He had seven arms and rode a chariot pulled by red horses. The presence of fire altars in the INDUS VALLEY CIVILIZATION sites might indicate that Agni was already part of the pantheon in the third millennium B.C.E. The construction of a fireplace or altar, known as *agnicayana*, in SANSKRIT, was a vital part of Vedic ritual. The *agnihotri* (priest) was responsible for maintaining the sacred flame. The Rig-Veda describes Agni as the illuminator of darkness, guardian of cosmic order, and recipient of daily homage.

Agni is the Hindu god of fire. He has a long ancestry, going back to the Rig-Veda. The name of this god was chosen for India's missile armed with a nuclear warhead. This image of Agni comes from a South Indian temple panel dating to the 17th century. *(Victoria & Albert Museum, London/Art Resource, NY)*

Agnimitra (ruled c. 148–140 B.C.E.) *Agnimitra was the second king of the Sunga dynasty in the lower Ganges (Ganga) Valley of India.*
He succeeded his father Pushyamitra after a period when Agnimitra governed the Sunga province of Vidisa. There he exercised a considerable measure of independence. He was succeeded after ruling for eight years by his son Sujyeshtha.

Ahicchatra   Ahicchatra, a city in the upper Ganges (Ganga) Valley of northern India, was occupied from the fourth century B.C.E. to around 1100 C.E. According to Raymond Allchin, it was a city falling into the third size grade of Mauryan centers, with an area of between 121 and 180 hectares (300 and 450 acres). This area, however, is defined by a mud wall built during the early part of the fourth phase of the city's life at the beginning of the first century C.E. In the seventh century C.E., the site was visited by the Chinese monk XUANZANG, who described 10 Buddhist monasteries and nine Hindu temples there, in a city built on a strongly fortified location. The surrounding country, he said, produced wheat and rice and had many springs and woods.

It is clear that the site was continuously occupied for a lengthy period. Excavations undertaken in 1940–44 and again in 1963–65 followed initial work by SIR ARTHUR CUNNINGHAM, who opened a stupa and found a steatite foundation deposit containing pearls, glass, and an amber bead. The excavations examined the defenses and interior mounds and identified nine periods of occupation, beginning in the late prehistoric period and lasting until about 1100 C.E. The dating of the successive layers and defenses has been undertaken on the basis of ceramic typology and the coins recovered. The second and third phases from the base reflect a Mauryan period of occupation, followed by layers containing Kushan coins and coins contemporary with the GUPTA EMPIRE. A Gupta temple was also uncovered, designed in the form of terraces and dedicated to SIVA. It was finely decorated with terra-cotta images of the gods Gaga and Yamuna. The defenses were improved on at least two occasions with the addition of brickwork, and an interior wall was constructed to divide the city into two sectors after the construction of the Gupta temple. The city itself seems to have been deserted by about 1100 C.E.
See also MAURYA EMPIRE.

Aihole   The complex of temples at Aihole (formerly Aryapur) in southern India was the creation of the CHALUKYA DYNASTY (sixth to eighth centuries C.E.). The temples crowd in a walled precinct 500 by 500 meters (1,650 ft.) in extent on the bank of the Malprabha River in Karnataka. The Meguti temple, built in 636 C.E. by King Ravikirti, commands an eminence overlooking the site as a whole. Dedicated to JAINISM, the complex includes a notable inscription that describes the military prowess of King Pulakesin II. The earliest temple, known as Lad Khan after a villager who had used it as a cattle byre, was adorned with images of the major Hindu deities, including Vishnu, Garuda, and Surya. The Durga temple is regarded as one of the most impressive in this remarkable site. Raised on a decorated plinth, it presents a massive appearance that is due to its broad exterior columns.

Airlangga (ruled 1016–1049) *Airlangga was the king of a major East Javan trading state in modern Indonesia, known for its wealth and power.*
He rose to power after the defeat of his predecessors by the Srivijayan state, but during a period of Srivijayan weakness he had founded a capital in the vicinity of Surabaya and controlled not only the rich volcanic BRANTAS RIVER basin but increasingly also the spice trade. One of his major achievements was to dam the Brantas River to control flooding and increase the area of land under irrigation for rice cultivation. He also grew wealthy from trade, particularly with China. His court is recalled for its literary output. Airlangga considered himself to be an

incarnation of the Indic god Vishnu, and his mausoleum at Balahan incorporated a statue of him riding on Garuda, the eagle mount of the god. Before his death, he retired to become an ascetic and left his kingdom divided between two sons. Janggala was the name of the polity east of the Brantas River, but it was soon absorbed by Kederi, the kingdom on the western bank.

See also SRIVIJAYA.

Airtam   Airtam, a village on the Amu Dar'ya River 13 kilometers (8 mi.) south of TERMEZ in modern Uzbekistan, is a large, undefended settlement, whose history dates back to the fourth century B.C.E. Covering an area at least three kilometers in length, the site has been partially destroyed by river erosion. In 1932 a Russian soldier discovered a large stone slab that had formed the main part of a remarkable frieze dating to the Kushan period (70–200 C.E.). The slab has carved figures of musicians and a border of acanthus leaves. After a successful search for more pieces, the reconstructed limestone frieze was found to be seven meters (23 ft.) in length. On one side of the frieze are figures holding garlands of flowers; on the other are musicians. Both groups are thought to have been taking part in the ritual of preparing the body of the dead Buddha for cremation.

RESULTS OF LATER EXCAVATIONS

Excavations followed in the 1930s and again in 1979, when a bridge was constructed over the Amu Dar'ya River. It was found that the site had a long history, beginning with the construction of a brick temple during the BACTRIAN GREEK period. This construction extended over a distance of 50 meters (165 ft.) from east to west. On excavation, the walls survived to a height of 1.7 meters (5.6 ft.); within the buildup of sand deposited after the site's abandonment, three coins were found. Two of these belong to the second half of the reign of the Kushan king KUJULA KADPHISES and thus date the building earlier than the first century C.E. Galina Pugachenkova has suggested that this temple might have been dedicated to the local river god Okhsho, whose name survives in the name of the Vaksh River. The structure, however, was not completed, perhaps because of the troubled times associated with the invasions of nomadic SAKAS.

This destruction of Airtam was followed by a period of abandonment, before Buddhist influence entered the area under the tolerant policy of the Kushans and many temples were constructed in sites along the Amu Dar'ya River. Important constructions of this period are seen at TERMEZ, KARA TEPE, AND DALVERZIN TEPE (Uzbekistan). At Airtam this development was manifested by the Buddhist temple whose limestone frieze the soldier had discovered. On reconstruction and further analysis, it was found that there were two matching friezes, one containing images of female celestial musicians and the second with figures making offerings of flowers.

The temple was associated with at least two stupas and was surrounded by a wall that included what were thought to be a kitchen and a storage room. The plan is distinctive to this region and is matched at other sites, including DILBERJIN and Kara Tepe. Its extent was given an additional dimension when a bulldozer cut through the opening to a subterranean complex lined in brick; at least one of the chambers was probably used for meditation.

The date of the temple was not surely known until the 1979 excavation season, when the base of a stone stela was found. It was decorated with figures of a man and a woman, preserved up to the level of the knees. An inscription in the Bactrian script was incised on the base. Dated to the fourth year of the reign of King Huvishka (c. 140 C.E.), it named a certain Shodija as the benefactor who had built the large structure. The two figures on the fragmentary stela are probably Shodija and his wife. They are shod in Indian-style footwear. Even the sculptor's name is known: He was one Mirzad, who probably hailed from Persia, if his name is any guide.

Airtam declined in the third and fourth centuries, probably as a result of conflict associated with the Sassanian expansion into this region. There is much evidence of destruction, seen in the broken statue fragments, the overturned and shattered foundation inscription, and the looting of Buddhist relic chambers that contained precious offerings.

See also BUDDHISM; SASSANIAN EMPIRE; TERMEZ.

Ajanta   Ajanta, one of the most famous rock temple sites of India, is located on the outer bend of the Wagora River in Maharashtra state. The 30 caves cut into the granite were built by Buddhists between the second century B.C.E. and the seventh century C.E., and their walls are decorated with frescoes and sculpture.

The caves, concealed by forest, were discovered more than a millennium after they had been deserted in the early 19th century. Already by 1844, the directors of the East India Company had urged the British government to preserve and record these caves, and a Captain Gill was charged with the responsibility of recording the paintings there. At the same time SIR ALEXANDER CUNNINGHAM wrote that the temples would contain treasures, which should be excavated and analyzed.

The caves of Ajanta, even after extensive pillaging and destruction, are among the jewels in the crown of Buddhist art. The caves form *caitya*s (sanctuaries) and *vihara*s (monasteries), heavily carved and decorated with fresco paintings that depict scenes in the life of the Buddha. Because the Buddha experienced life in all its rich variety, the scenes evoke many aspects of life in early India beyond the strictly religious—the rhythms of the court and life in towns and villages, as well as in the monasteries themselves. The ultimate purpose of the paintings was educational, to instruct and inform pil-

The fresco painting on the walls of the Ajanta caves in India are world famous. This example from cave 1 shows servants pouring holy water over a prince before his coronation. *(© Lindsay Hebberd/CORBIS)*

grims and novices about the principal events in the life of the Buddha that led to his enlightenment, in the same way that the reliefs of the great sanctuary of BOROBUDUR in Java were a medium of instruction.

See also BAGH; BUDDHISM.

Further reading: Allchin, F. R., ed. *The Archaeology of Early Historic South Asia.* Cambridge: Cambridge University Press, 1995; Behl, B. K., Nigam, S., and Beach, M. C. *The Ajanta Caves: Artistic Wonder of Ancient Buddhist India.* New York: Harry N. Abrams, 1998; Harle J. C. *Gupta Sculpture: Indian Sculpture of the Fourth to the Sixth Centuries AD.* Oxford: Clarendon Press, 1974; Harle, J. C. *The Art and Architecture of the Indian Subcontinent.* London: Penguin Books, 1986; Pant, P. *Ajanta and Ellora: Cave Temples of Ancient India.* Columbia, Mo.: South Asia Books, 1998; Schlingloff, D. *Guide to the Ajanta Paintings: Narrative Wall Paintings.* Columbia, Mo.: South Asia Books, 1999.

Ajatasatru (c. 563–483 B.C.E.) *Ajatasatru was a king of Magadha, an ancient kingdom in the Ganges (Ganga) Valley of India and a contemporary of the Buddha.*
He expanded his kingdom and fought with other MAHA-JANAPADAS, or early states, and is said in a Buddhist text to have visited the Buddha.
See also BUDDHISM.

Akhauri   Akhauri is a Buddhist monastery at TAXILA in northern Pakistan, belonging to the early Kushan period (first century C.E.). It provides a clear example of the structure of a Buddhist foundation at that period. There is a main court entered by a portal from the north. Rooms are set around the outer courtyard wall, looking inward. There are an assembly room, two chapels, each containing a stupa, and rows of monks' cells. A smaller court with 11 cells was later added on the western side.
See also KUSHANS.

Ak-terek   In 1906, during his explorations in the western TARIM BASIN, in the area of the ancient state of HOTAN, Sir Aurel Stein discovered the site of Ak-terek, a Buddhist monument lying to the south of the Buddhist shrine at RAWAK. Smaller than the Rawak shrine, the temple of Ak-terek had been destroyed by fire and never reoccupied. This had the effect of firing the clay sculptures, while those from Rawak remained friable. The sculptures included a fine image of a seated Buddha dated stylistically to the mid-fourth century C.E. The presence of fragments of gold leaf suggested that some, at least, of the structure had been gilded.

Ak Yum   Ak Yum is a temple site located near the center of the square enclosure known as BANTEAY CHOEU, west of Angkor in Cambodia. Excavations by George Trouvé in 1935 exposed much of the central structure. The lowest platform was built of earth, with its major paths sealed in bricks. This platform measured 100 meters (330 ft.) square and rose 2.6 meters (8.5 ft.) in height. Access to the second stage was by stairs, which ascend 2.4 meters onto a brick platform. The walls were decorated with sculptures of miniature palaces. The second stage incorporates a series of brick towers embellished with sandstone false doors and lintels. An inscription on a stone sculpture near the southeast-angle tower records a donation to the god Gamhiresvara in 1001 C.E. The religious text reveals the sanctity of this temple during a period of at least two centuries.

The main sanctuary on the third tier had one entrance facing east, but the other three walls were later provided with separate portals. The original lintel dates to the end of the eighth century. Two reused inscriptions from the central tower date to 704 and 717, respectively. The latter records a foundation by the *mratan* (official) Kirtigana to the god Gamhiresvara and notes donations to the temple, which include rice, draft cattle, cloth, and workers. There can be no doubt that this area, so close to the future center of Angkor, was occupied and farmed by the early eighth century.

The central sanctuary yielded six bronze statues, two of a Hindu deity and four of the Buddha, varying between nine and 35 centimeters (14 in.) in height, as well as part of a large stone lingam, a phallic-shaped symbol of Siva. A vault led down to a subterranean chamber, the base of which was 12.5 meters below the floor of the central sanctuary. It included a brick shrine and contained two elephants in gold leaf and a statue of a standing man 1.25 meters in height. Ak Yum dates later than the early eighth century and possibly represents an enlargement of temple architecture dating to and perhaps inspired by King JAYAVARMAN II (c. 770–834 C.E.).

Alamgirpur Alamgirpur is a small settlement site located on the Hindon River, a tributary of the Jamuna River in northern India. Discovered in 1959, it is notable as a site showing the presence of the INDUS VALLEY CIVILIZATION east of the Jamuna. The site covers an area of only 60 by 50 meters (200 by 165 ft.), but excavations have uncovered the remains of late Harappan (early second millennium B.C.E.) material at the base, followed by occupation dating to the PAINTED GREY WARE phase and historic occupation. The initial occupation saw the construction of houses in mud brick, wattle and daub, and, rarely, fired brick. These houses were associated with a typical Harappan material culture that included pottery vessels bearing the Indus script, animal figurines and carts in terra-cotta, steatite beads, and small bowls of faience.

Alexander the Great (356–323 B.C.E.) *Alexander the Great, king of Macedonia, was one of the greatest military leaders known.*
He succeeded his father, Philip, at the age of 20 in 336 B.C.E., inheriting plans to conquer the ACHAEMENID EMPIRE, whose armies had previously unsuccessfully invaded Greece. In 334 B.C.E., Alexander crossed the Hellespont (Dardanelles, the strait separating Europe and Asiatic Turkey). After a series of stunning victories, he toppled the Achaemenid Empire and thus took control of its provinces or satrapies. To the east these extended as far as the Indus River. Seven years later, he marched east, with an army of 80,000, crossed the Hindu Kush Mountains, and descended onto the plains of the Indus and its tributaries. He first crossed the Indus, accepting Indian client kings on his way. He then moved farther east, crossing the Jhelum River, which the Greeks named the Hydaspes, then the Chenab, the Ravi, and finally the Beas River (the Hyphasis). The Greeks had little knowledge of the geography of India, since their sources were little more reliable than the *Indikos* of Ktesias of Knidos, written in 396 B.C.E.

At this point Alexander wished to proceed to conquer the known world, but his troops mutinied, and he returned to the Jhelum River, where a fleet of ships was under construction. With these, he sailed down the Indus River. His journey to the sea met stout resistance from the local tribe known as the Agalassoi, who mustered, it is said, more than 40,000 men. But Alexander defeated them and, on reaching the coast, divided his forces, one group traveling with the fleet and the other by land to the west. The two parties met again at modern Hormuz, in Iran, after one of the most extraordinary military campaigns.

EFFECTS OF HIS CONQUESTS

Although of brief duration, Alexander's Indian adventure had deep-seated repercussions. He was a highly educated person who took scientists and historians in his entourage to learn about and record the countries and peoples he conquered. He actively encouraged the adoption of local ways and intermarriage between Macedonians and local women. Most profoundly, he settled his veterans in new settlements, and these people established outposts of Greek culture.

Alexander died of a fever in Babylon in 323 B.C.E., and his far-flung empire was divided among his leading generals. SELEUCUS I NICATOR ruled the eastern provinces, founding the Seleucid Empire that he ruled from Babylon. BACTRIA, located between the Amu Dar'ya River and the Hindu Kush Mountains, was part of this empire from about 300 to 250 B.C.E. It then achieved independence and extended its domain to incorporate parts of modern Pakistan, including the city of Taxila. The Bactrian capital, Baktra (modern BALKH), was a noted center for trade and for BUDDHISM, which had been established there. Another Greek Bactrian foundation is located at AY KHANUM on the upper Amu Dar'ya River in Afghanistan.

Hellenistic influence originating from the campaigns of Alexander the Great continued with the foundation of non-Greek states. Thus the Scythians, or Sakas, who conquered the Bactrian states in the late second century B.C.E., adopted many Greek traditions, including coinage with Greek script, Greek titles, and Greek methods of city planning. This pattern became even more pronounced when the Parthians succeeded the Scythians as rulers of the upper Indus and its tributaries. Hellenistic influence was still to be found under the Kushans, not least in the architectural features of their city at SURKH-KOTAL in Afghanistan. The most enduring Greek influence in the region, however, was the GANDHARA school of art founded in modern Pakistan. While drawing on Buddhism for its themes, Gandharan art owed a deep artistic debt to Greek sculptural traditions.

Further reading: Fuller, J. F. C. *The Generalship of Alexander the Great.* New York: DeCapo Press, 1989; Green, P. *Alexander of Macedon.* London: Penguin Books, 1992; Worthington, I. *Alexander the Great.* London: Routledge, 2003.

Alikasudaro (late fourth–third century B.C.E.) *Alikasudaro is a king mentioned in the rock edicts of Asoka, the third king of the Maurya Empire (c. 324–c. 200 B.C.E.) in India.*
The name is thought to refer to Alexander of Epirus, a minor Greek ruler (r. 272–258 B.C.E.). The inscription helps to date ASOKA to the period between 268 and 235 B.C.E.

Allahdino Allahdino is a small settlement of the INDUS VALLEY CIVILIZATION in modern southern Pakistan. It lies 15 kilometers (9 mi.) from the Arabian Sea and covers an area of only one hectare (2.5 acres). The finds from this site reveal the degree of wealth characteristic of this civilization, even in provincial settlements. The mound rises about three meters above the surrounding countryside. Three phases of occupation have been identified since the excavations by W. Fairservis in 1976. There was no evidence for a defensive wall, but the internal layout of the houses, all of which belong in time to the mature Indus civilization of the later third millennium B.C.E., shows remarkable evidence for town planning even in a site that barely exceeds 100 meters (330 ft.) in any direction. Houses were laid out on an east-northeast to west-south-west orientation and were constructed of mud brick on stone foundations. They were equipped with stone-lined wells and drains. The presence of SEALS indicates participation in trade, and the recovery of gold and silver ornaments hints that the site was involved in the exchange of precious jewelry. This indication is highlighted by a jar containing a remarkable belt made of long carnelian beads interspersed with beads of copper, silver bead necklaces, agate beads, and items of gold.

Altyn Tepe Altyn Tepe, the site of an ancient settlement in the lower Tedzhen River Valley of Turkmenistan where the river forms the Geoksiur Oasis, was occupied as early as the fifth millennium B.C.E. This area of Turkmenistan has a long and important cultural sequence that culminated in the formation of urban communities as old as the INDUS VALLEY CIVILIZATION.

EARLIEST SETTLEMENTS

By the fifth and early fourth millennia B.C.E., this oasis region had agricultural settlements in which barley and wheat were cultivated on the basis of an IRRIGATION system, and cattle were raised. A copper industry was in place, and there is also much evidence of weaving. Evidence from Altyn Tepe has shown that during the mid-fourth millennium B.C.E., irrigation agriculture was well established, and trade relations were carrying gold and silver, carnelian, TURQUOISE, and LAPIS LAZULI to the site. The late aeneolithic period toward the end of the fourth and start of the third millennia B.C.E. saw further achievements, including the domestication of the camel, the use of wheeled carts, irrigation employing channels up to three kilometers (1.8 mi.) in length, and the construction of multiroomed houses for a protourban population. The site was now ringed by a mud-brick wall up to two meters (6.6 ft.) in height, enclosing an area of 25 hectares (62.5 acres). Figurines of terra-cotta depicted helmeted warriors.

LATER CULTURES

The culture of the oases in Turkmenistan also expanded to the east and south. At the site of Sarazm on the Zerafshan River Delta, rich burials included gold and carnelian grave offerings. The third millennium saw extraordinary cultural developments at Altyn Tepe and related sites, as trade with the Indus Valley burgeoned. During the Early Bronze Age, Altyn Tepe boasted a huge entrance gateway 15 meters (49.5 ft.) wide, with room for both pedestrians and wheeled vehicles. There was a temple precinct within; rich graves equipped with stone lamps may well have held leading priestly figures. Stamp SEALS made of terra-cotta and bronze probably indicated private ownership, and both industry and agriculture developed. There were copper foundries and specialized ceramic workshops and kilns, while grapes were added to the range of cultivated crops.

The heyday of the Indus Valley civilization saw further evidence of exchange: Two Harappan-style seals, one bearing a swastika motif and the other a brief written text, were found at Altyn Tepe, and an eagle amulet has clear Harappan parallels. Excavations indicate that there were at least three social groups, on the basis of spatially delimited grades of housing and burials. The poorer graves incorporated few ceramic offerings, and the dead were wrapped in reed mats. The rich, however, lived in fine houses and were interred in woolen shrouds, accompanied by stamps with eagle, leopard, and goat motifs; statuettes; religious symbols; and fine exotic bead necklaces and belts. Industrially the town saw specialized production of silver ornaments and mirrors, arsenic and lead bronzes, and a massive output of pottery vessels, as one kiln among many had a potential annual output of up to 20,000 vessels. By this juncture the population was in the vicinity of 7,000, and the Turkmenian oasis sites were in regular contact with the civilizations to the south.

Ama Ama, a site of the YAYOI culture on Honshu Island in Japan, covers the period from about 150 B.C.E. until 300 C.E. It is located on an eminence commanding a broad alluvial plain on the eastern shore of the Inland Sea. Because the earliest establishment of Yayoi culture did not occur on this part of the island of Honshu, the site represents the expansion of agricultural communities east from Kyushu to the area that was to become the heartland of Japanese civilization. The Yayoi culture itself was the result of a major infusion of influence, and almost certainly immigrant groups, from the mainland of Korea. It saw the adoption of wet rice cultivation, a knowledge of bronze and iron production, and intensified trade, following the long period of hunter-gatherer dominance on the archipelago, known as the Jomon culture.

The excavations at Ama revealed a long occupation period, beginning with the late phase of Early Yayoi. This site was afflicted by a major flood that laid down a thick deposit over the settlement, but it was reoccupied during Middle and Late Yayoi. The investigations have revealed that the village was defined by ditches, which, in the early period of occupation, covered an area of 70 by 110 meters. This was not a large settlement by any means, but the waterlogged conditions have preserved organic remains that reveal intensive rice cultivation as the mainstay of the economy. The wooden agricultural implements include large spades and hoes made on the site, to judge from the unfinished wooden tools and wood shavings that have survived. Friction with other communities, of which many are known in this strategic area, is suggested by the presence of bows and arrows made of stone or, in one instance, bronze. There are also stone spearheads. The rice was probably ground on milling stones, and wooden pounders have been recovered. Wood was also converted into cups and bowls, along with ceramic vessels whose styles relate to those typical of the earlier Yayoi on Kyushu sites to the west.

Burials in the settlement were found in special ditched enclosures, each probably representing a social unit at the site. The dead were interred in wooden-plank coffins, but there are insufficient findings to account for the duration of the settlement, and it is likely that poorer members of the community were buried with less ceremony beyond the confines of the village. There are many sites of the Middle and Late Yayoi phases in the vicinity of Ama, and it has been suggested that these probably represent new settlements, founded as the original population expanded. Some of these villages were significantly larger than Ama, again indicating population expansion on the basis of intensive wet rice cultivation.

Amaravati   Amaravati is a major Buddhist religious complex inspired by the rulers of the SATAVAHANA DYNASTY (late first century B.C.E.–third century C.E.), located on the Krishna River in modern Andhra Pradesh state, southern India. It is part of the ancient settlement of Dharanikota and derives its name from the temple of Amaresvara, mentioned in Amaravati period inscriptions.

It was first recognized as a major site in 1796, when a Colonel McKenzie visited it and found it still intact. However, on his return, in 1816, he found that the complex had been plundered by villagers for building material. Research at Amaravati began under Alexander Rea in the early years of the 20th century, and the results were published in 1905. Rea was able to uncover the circular pavement around the great stupa and identify the foundations to the gateways. The complex incorporated monasteries and Buddhist temples embellished with outstanding sculptured reliefs dating from the second century B.C.E. to the third century C.E.

The stupa at Amaravati was one of the largest in India, originally standing about 30 meters (99 ft.) high, with a base 50 meters (165 ft.) in diameter. Tradition has it that the stupa covers sacred relics of the Buddha himself. It probably originated during the reign of ASOKA (d. 238 or 232 B.C.E.), a king of the Maurya dynasty, and now

Amaravati was one of the great early centers of Buddhism in India. Although only the base of the great stupa survives, its splendor can still be seen in this relief carving, dating to the second century C.E. *(Scala/Art Resource, NY)*

survives as a ruined base, for the superstructure was quarried during the 18th and 19th centuries as a source of lime mortar. The original appearance of this now ruined stupa can be seen on a relief on one of the temple railings. It had a huge dome on a cylindrical base. Some of the marble reliefs were taken to the British Museum in London, England, and others were taken to Madras in India.

The reliefs depict superb narrative scenes taken from tales in the life of the Buddha that survive in the so-called *jataka* stories. The style embraced the move from representing the Buddha symbolically—for instance, by an empty throne—to depicting him in human form, and the two types of scenes are even found on the same carving. The name *Amaravati* has been given to the style of art that developed there, a style that had a wide influence, extending into Sri Lanka and Southeast Asia.

Amarendrapura   Amarendrapura refers to a city named in an important inscription from SDOK KAK THOM in Thailand, which dates to the mid-11th century. It states that JAYAVARMAN II of Angkor in Cambodia founded a city at a location named Amarendrapura. Identification of sites known only from epigraphic evidence often resembles a wild-goose chase. Some authorities have placed Amarendrapura at BANTEAY CHOEU, a large rectangular earthwork that encloses temples of the same period, such as AK YUM and Prei Kmeng, at the western end of the WESTERN BARAY at Angkor. However, Banteay Choeu is now regarded as a partially completed reservoir.

amatya The *amatya*, described as one of the vital components of a kingdom in the political treatise known as the ARTHASASTRA of KAUTILYA, were those who administered the functions of the state in India and were maintained as a civil service by the royal treasury. Kautilya wrote his treatise on statehood during the fourth century B.C.E. as an adviser to King CANDRAGUPTA MAURYA, whose kingdom was centered on the city of PATALIPUTRA (modern Patna).

Ampil Rolum This site in Cambodia is one of the most extensive of the surviving centers of the CHENLA period (550–800 C.E.). It incorporates three brick sanctuaries with fine sandstone lintels and an inscription dated to the seventh or eighth century C.E. The corpus of Chenla inscriptions records the names of a series of centers, but it is not possible to identify the precise location of all of them. In the case of Ampil Rolum, however, one inscription noted that a king with a name ending in -*aditya* (the rising sun) ruled in "this city of Bhavapura."

Amri Amri is a settlement mound located in the lower Indus Valley of India. Excavations in 1929 by N. G. Majumdar and again by J. M. Casal in 1959–62 have uncovered evidence for a long period of occupation from at least 3000 B.C.E. until the end of the INDUS VALLEY CIVILIZATION in the second millennium B.C.E. The sequence has been divided into three major phases. The first phase, with four subdivisions, provides vital evidence for cultural developments leading to the mature civilization of the Indus Valley.

Changing pottery styles provide the basis for the division of Period I, which has yielded evidence for a mud-brick wall and structures that were regularly rebuilt on earlier foundations. Some of these contain small cell-like rooms that might, as at MEHRGARH, have been grain stores. The subsistence economy was based on the cultivation of barley and domestic cattle, but the earlier phases also contain numerous gazelle bones. There was a flourishing ceramic industry, and chert was used in the manufacture of blades. Rare carnelian and marine-shell beads indicate an exchange network. Amri has given its name to the Amri-Nal phase in the early development of the Indus Valley civilization, and many further sites belonging to this phase have been found, some little more than small hamlets, others more substantial, like Amri itself.

During the fourth and last phase of Period I, there is evidence of a transitional phase to the Indus civilization. However, Amri was never a major site, and the hallmarks of exchange and manufacturing, such as SEALS, clay sealings, and weights, were rare. The last major period of occupation belongs to the so-called JHUKAR culture, traditionally dated to about 2000–1800 B.C.E.

Amri-Nal Amri-Nal is the name given to one of the four phases of the Early Harappan culture. The sites of this phase concentrate in Sind and Baluchistan in Pakistan, and radiocarbon dates place them within the period 3200–2600 B.C.E. The vast majority of the 88 sites known fall below five hectares (12.5 acres) in extent; some sites a little more than 1,000 square meters (1,200 sq. ft.) in area might have been temporary camp sites. Only a few settlements extended beyond 10 hectares, the largest, DHOLAVIRA, probably covering three times that area.

The principal exposures of archaeological material are from the eponymous sites. Excavations at AMRI, particularly the second phase of research under Jean-Marie Casal in 1959–62, revealed a sequence of superposed building phases in stone and mud brick. Some structures were domestic, but the smaller rectangular buildings are thought to have been granaries. There is also evidence for the manufacture of jewelry, including shell bangles, and a rich ceramic industry. The faunal remains reveal a marked predominance of domestic cattle bones, along with the bones of sheep and goats.

The site of Nal covers nearly six hectares. Excavations in 1925 by Harold Hargreaves followed a number of earlier investigations dating back to 1903, attracted perhaps by the outstanding ceramics from this site, decorated with animal paintings that include images of cattle and gazelles. Again stone and mud-brick structural foundations were traced, as well as evidence for the manufacture of beads in agate, carnelian, shell, and LAPIS LAZULI. Copper was also cast at the site into small tanged spearheads and chisels. Gregory Possehl has suggested that the expansion of Amri-Nal sites southeast into Gujarat in India might have been due to a predominantly pastoral economy. The practice of transhumance (seasonal movement of herders and flocks) between the river valleys and surrounding uplands in the core region is highly likely, for the two major types of pottery are present beyond their areas of manufacture. It has also been suggested that it was during this important period that irrigation began to be applied to agriculture. Some Amri-Nal sites, such as BALAKOT, have a coastal orientation.

See also INDUS VALLEY CIVILIZATION.

amrita In Indian mythology, *amrita* was ambrosia, the food of the gods, conferring immortality on those who drank it. It had very early origins, mentioned in the Hindu epics the MAHABHARATA (500 B.C.E.–400 C.E.) and the *Ramayana* (first century B.C.E.). Its legendary origin involved a battle between the Hindu gods and demons for its possession. The outcome was unsuccessful, so on the advice of Vishnu, the gods and demons cooperated by taking opposite ends of a sacred *naga* snake that was coiled around Mount Mandara. They thus spun the mountain, churning the ocean of milk below as they did so. The mountain began to collapse into the ocean, and

Vishnu descended in the guise of a turtle to support the mountain until the elixir was obtained. The battle that followed saw the gods victorious.

The CHURNING OF THE OCEAN OF MILK was a popular theme in the Hindu religion of Angkor in Cambodia and was splendidly portrayed on a relief at ANGKOR WAT. The actual city of Angkor Thom, constructed by King JAYAVARMAN VII in the early 13th century C.E., was probably a metaphorical representation of this theme. The gods and the demons are seen flanking the entrance causeways; under this metaphor, the BAYON temple in the center of the city, the resting place for the ashes of the king, represented Mount Mandara.

Ananda (fifth century B.C.E.) *Ananda, a cousin of the Buddha, became his faithful personal attendant and is said to have followed the Buddha as a shadow, ensuring that his needs were always met.*

After his enlightenment, Buddha had no permanent attendant for a period of 20 years. When aged 55, however, he selected Ananda, the only one of his close followers who had not offered his services when the Buddha let it be known that he sought such a person to assist him. Ananda accepted this demanding position subject to eight self-denying conditions, including that he was not to be permitted to share any of the special offerings of clothing or food made to his cousin or to stay in the Buddha's own quarters.

Ananda outlived the Buddha by many years, finally dying at the age of about 120. It is recorded that his death took place on a barge in the middle of the Ganges (Ganga) River, and that at his own request his body was divided into two so that the rulers of the northern and southern banks could each have a share. His remains were then covered by stupas, both of which were later visited by the Chinese monk and pilgrim XUANZANG (602–64 C.E.).

Anandacandra (ruled early eighth century B.C.E.) *Anandacandra was the king of ARAKAN (now Rakhine) in western Myanmar (Burma). He was known for his generosity to Buddhist establishments but also favored Hindu deities.*

Anandacandra is best known as the author of a major addition to an inscription from SHIT-THAUNG, which sets out the names of his 18 predecessors and describes the origin of the royal line with the god Siva. His capital was located at VESALI, a huge walled city surrounded by a moat and containing a walled palace precinct. His inscriptions record his foundation of Buddhist monasteries and reliquaries, together with donations of land, slaves, and draft animals. But he also favored Hindu deities and founded temples for their gods that bore his name. His state was strategically placed to command the passage of goods and people across the Bay of Bengal from India, and he not only received many Buddhist monks but also sent fine gifts to the monastic communities of Sri Lanka. He was the guardian of the law and, as did the Gupta kings of India, followed a policy of commuting capital sentences.

See also GUPTA EMPIRE.

Ananda temple The Ananda temple, built in the reign of King KYANZITTHA (1084–1112 C.E.), is an outstanding example of Buddhist temple building at PAGAN in modern Myanmar (Burma). It lies about 200 meters (660 ft.) to the east of the city walls. It is of a cruciform plan, each axis being 87 meters (287 ft.) long. The central shrine is covered by a gilded stupa. Many decorated plaques on the temple terraces show narrative scenes on the life of the Buddha from birth to enlightenment. The interior walls were formerly covered in frescoes depicting *jataka* stories of the Buddha's life, but these were covered later by a plain whitewash. A statue of Kyanzittha himself is also found in the temple.

There is a story that the king encountered a group of Indian monks begging for alms, and he asked them where they were from. They answered that they had traveled from a cave monastery at Nandamula Hill in India. He asked them to describe their temple and was so struck by their words that he ordered the Ananda temple to be built according to what they had said. It was completed, again according to tradition, in 1090.

Charles Duroiselle, writing in 1913, pointed to INSCRIPTIONS from the vicinity of Pagan that contained an account of the consecration of the Ananda temple. The king, the texts say, seated on the back of a magnificent elephant, arrived with members of his court. A sacred white elephant was embellished with fine trappings and gems. Another tradition, supported by the words of old songs surviving on palm-leaf documents, has it that the king entered riding his white elephant and that the architect was executed lest he build another temple to rival the Ananda.

anastylosis In Greek, *anastylosis* means "the reerection of columns." The technique was applied to the historic monuments of Indonesia under Dutch colonial rule during the 20th century. When monuments of brick, laterite, or sandstone have collapsed or have become overgrown with vegetation, the issue of restoration and conservation is a delicate one. In the case of the TA PROHM temple at ANGKOR, in Cambodia, for example, the monument was left to the mercy of the jungle, and the massive roots and tree trunks that have invaded the stones are one of the major attractions for visitors. In the fullness of time, however, the temple will inevitably be smothered and destroyed as the vegetation prizes apart the component stones.

The technique involves first the clearance of invasive vegetation and the preparation of a site plan showing the

The Ananda temple at Pagan, Myanmar (Burma), was constructed under the order of King Kyanzittha (r. 1084–1112 C.E.). The king arrived at the consecration on a sacred white elephant, and it is said that his architect was killed so that he could never build another temple to rival its magnificence. *(Borromeo/Art Resource, NY)*

location of all stones. The surviving walls are then removed, with the relative position of each stone or brick numbered for later replacement. The foundations can then be examined and, where necessary, strengthened with permanent materials. The stones are then replaced, with gaps being filled by new stones cut roughly but not finished along the lines of the original ones, their recent origin discreetly displayed.

The first major application of the *anastylosis* method in Cambodia saw the reconstruction of BANTEAY SREI under Henri Marchal. The success of this operation led to similar work at Angkor itself, particularly at NEAK PEAN and BAN-TEAY SAMREAY. *Anastylosis* is now being widely applied, as may be seen at Angkor. In Thailand the sanctuaries of PHI-MAI, MUANG TAM, Phnom Rung, and PHNOM WAN have all been conserved by this technique; perhaps the most famous of all reconstructions took place at BOROBUDUR in Java.

Anavatapta, Lake This lake, also known as Lake Ano-tatta, lying north of the Himalayas, holds an important place in Buddhist writings as having miraculous curative powers. The name means "a lake without heat or trouble." Although its location cannot be identified, it was said to be surrounded by mountains so that its waters were never exposed to the Sun or Moon. The lake, square in shape, was supposedly the source of four rivers: the Sita, Ganges (Ganga), Sindhu, and Vaksu. The Ganges is said to emerge from the golden elephant gate at the eastern end of the lake. The Sindhu (Indus) leaves the lake through the silver ox gate at the southern bank. The Vaksu (Amu Dar'ya or Oxus) originates via the horse gate at the west, and the Sita (Tarim River) begins at the lion gate on the northern bank. The lake was crystal clear, with no turbidity. Early Buddhist sources declare that the lake could be visited only by the enlightened. Early texts ascribe various qualities to its water. One describes how Queen Maya, the mother of the Buddha, was taken there to be bathed and purified. Afterward, she was dressed in divine clothes and flowers and conceived the Buddha. This scene is depicted on a sculpture at Amaravati in eastern India as early as the second century C.E. In the third century B.C.E., Emperor ASOKA had water from the lake carried to him daily for his own use and for gifts to his most learned followers. The water was also used by Asoka in royal consecration, because it was deemed to bestow divinity: He sent lake water to King Tissa of Sri Lanka for this purpose, and both kings took the title *Devanampiya* (Beloved of the gods).

It is thought that the temple of NEAK PEAN and the JAYATATAKA *baray* (reservoir) at ANGKOR in Cambodia reproduced the lake. At the temple, water emerges through the mouths of, respectively, an ox, a horse, a lion, and an elephant, the sources of the four rivers and a crucial clue in any interpretation of the purpose of the Angkorian *barays*. It is widely held that they were primarily used for irrigation, but the representation of Lake Anavatapta makes it plausible to see the Jayatataka as a means of gaining merit for the king.

See also BUDDHISM.

Anawrahta (r. 1044–1077) *Anawrahta a king of Burma, is best known for reinforcing devotion to* BUDDHISM *by attacking the ruler of the city of* THATON, *Shin Arahan, and taking sacred texts, senior monks, and members of the royal family back to Pagan.*

The king of Thaton was sent to serve in the Shwezigon temple in the city of PAGAN. Seeking other sacred Buddhist relics, Anawrahta led his forces to the cities of Prome and ARAKAN (modern Rakhine), where he made an unsuccessful attempt to seize the venerable MAHAMUNI statue of the Buddha, the only one thought to have been modeled after the actual likeness of the Buddha himself. He also had many temples and stupas, as well as irrigation works, constructed. It is recorded that he died after being gored by a buffalo.

ancestor worship

CHINA

Veneration for the ancestors has a long history in China, from the remote prehistoric past to the present. Ancestor worship during the period of the late Shang dynasty (13th–11th centuries B.C.E.) is well attested through texts inscribed on ORACLE BONES. There were three principal ways of undertaking the appropriate rituals for dead ancestors. One was by burning offerings, another by leaving offerings in water, and the third by burying sacrificial objects, including humans and animals, in the ground near the burial place of a notable ancestor or in the vicinity of an ancestral temple. Thus at the royal necropolis at

ANYANG (1200–1050 B.C.E.), thousands of sacrificial victims have been unearthed. Similar rituals have been documented at many later historic sites, such as Majiazhuang in Shaanxi province, an EASTERN ZHOU DYNASTY (770–221 B.C.E.) royal center where the ancestral temples incorporated sacrificial pits containing the remains of people, sheep, cattle, and chariots.

The association of highly ranked individuals in society with sacrificial offerings can be traced back into the prehistoric past. The LONGSHAN CULTURE (2500–1900 B.C.E.), for example, included many sites from Shandong to the upper reaches of the Huang (Yellow) River. The excavated cemeteries reveal the presence of a limited number of rich individuals, interred with objects known to have had important ritual uses later during the historic period. At the Shandong Longshan site of CHENGZI, four groups of graves were identified by rank. The excavators found that only the richest were associated with pits containing ash, complete pottery vessels, and pig bones. These pits have been interpreted as containing offerings for important ancestors.

Drums with alligator-skin covers were restricted to royal graves at Anyang (1200–1050 B.C.E.). Such a drum has been found with a rich grave at the Longshan cemetery of TAOSI (2200–2000 B.C.E.). Earlier still, at the Banshan phase YANGSHAO CULTURE site of Yangshan in Qinghai province, excavations uncovered 218 burials thought to represent an entire cemetery dated to about 2300 B.C.E. Three particularly rich graves with multiple burials included ceramic drums, as well as marble tubes and beads and ceremonial axes. These rich interments were also those around which sacrificial pits clustered. Similar associations of pits containing the remains of sacrificed animals, stone tools, and pottery vessels have been recovered at Longgangsi in southern Shaanxi province. This site belongs to the Banpo phase of the YANGSHAO CULTURE and dates to the late fifth millennium B.C.E.

SOUTHEAST ASIA

Throughout the late prehistoric period in mainland Southeast Asia, the dead were interred in patterned cemeteries structured, it is thought, on the basis of family or ancestral relationships. Proximity to the ancestors was evidently an important factor in determining where people were interred. Infants were often buried in the arms of a female or in a pottery vessel beside a woman's head or feet. With the historic period and the availability of written records, it is possible to turn to inscriptions to evaluate the role played by ancestors in determining an individual's status in society. It is known that archivists and genealogists maintained records. Thus the official Sukavarman at PREAH VIHEAR in Cambodia maintained the royal archives on leaves stored in the temple. These records traced the royal genealogy back to the mythical founders of the kingdom of ANGKOR in Cambodia. The

CHENLA period (550–800 C.E.) inscriptions reveal a wide range of local deities, both male and female, but their identification with ancestors is not specified.

With the richer textual record following the establishment of the kingdom of Angkor in 802 C.E., the fusion of ancestors with the gods is documented. There are six shrines at King INDRAVARMANI's temple of PREAH KO at HARIHARALAYA. The three towers of the front row were dedicated to Rudravarman and Prithivindravarman, representing Indravarman's maternal grandfather and father, and the central tower was dedicated to JAYAVARMAN II under his posthumous name, Paramesvara. The three sanctuaries in the second row were dedicated to the principal consorts of each lord, Narendradevi, Prithivindradevi, and Dharanindradevi. Each shrine would have contained an image of the ancestor, and it is notable that their names were combined with that of SIVA by using the suffix -esvara. Thus Rudravarman was named Rudresvara. The eight small sanctuaries placed uniformly around the base of the adjacent BAKONG pyramid probably acknowledged male and female ancestors of Indravarman, for the eastern set incorporates male figures on exterior niches, whereas the western ones have females. When his son YASHOVARMANI completed the island shrine of LOLEI in the Indtratataka reservoir, the four shrines were dedicated, respectively, to his father, maternal grandfather, mother, and maternal grandmother. Again the names of each combine that of the royal ancestor with the name of a god. The tradition was maintained when Harshavarman I, son of Yashovarmani, dedicated the temple of BAKSEI CHAMKRONG to JAYAVARMAN III, Indravarman, and his father.

As with his predecessors, RAJENDRAVARMAN's (r. 944–968 C.E.) state temple of PRE RUP was designed to honor the king and his ancestors in the context of the god Siva. The largest and centrally placed brick sanctuary housed Rajendrabhadresvara, the royal lingam, a stone phallus and object of veneration. The four subsidiary towers were dedicated first to Isvara Rajendravarmesvara, representing the king; Rajendravesvarupa, in favor of the Brahman Vishvarupa, a distant ancestor of the king; the king's aunt Jayadevi; and his predecessor Harshavarman. Worship of the dead king, according to GEORGES CŒDÈS, was ensured once his soul entered the stone image in his temple mausoleum, thus permitting contact with the ancestors of the dynasty.

Thus the temple of ANGKOR WAT should be seen as the preserve of the immortal sovereign SURYAVARMAN II (1113–50 C.E.) merged with Vishnu. The construction of temples and shrines dedicated to ancestor worship reached its zenith during the reign of JAYAVARMAN VII (1181–1219 C.E.). The BAYON was his own temple mausoleum, but he also constructed entire temple complexes for the worship of his father, mother, and one of his sons. These also housed subsidiary shrines dedicated to the ancestors of members of his court.

INDIA

Reconstructing the history of kingship in India and its link with the sacred world is necessarily based on the content of the Vedas. It appears that in the early Vedic tradition, rulers were required to take the advice of a tribal council. Indeed, some tribes had no sovereign at all. However, with the rise of settled agriculture and expansion of settlement sizes, as shown in the later Vedas, kings emerged not by council choice but through military prowess, and their ascent incorporated rituals, such as the horse sacrifice, that invoked cosmic significance. This period saw the rise of the *janapadas,* small states, in the Ganga Valley. The rise of the MAURYAN EMPIRE took place at a time when BUDDHISM was established. The emperor ASOKA, who succeeded in about 268 B.C.E., enthusiastically adopted Buddhism and had many stupas constructed to cover the relics of the Buddha and his early followers. The old Indian royal rituals, however, were revived under the great Gupta king SAMUDRAGUPTA (335–380 C.E.). These included the horse sacrifice (*ashvamedha*). It is significant that one of his coins issued at the time bore the legend "the great king of kings, an invincible hero, is going to conquer the heavens." His descendants, in recalling this renewal of cosmic and magic aspects of kingship, followed the precept in his Allahabad inscription. In it, Samudragupta announced his ascent to the role of *chakravartin,* or supreme monarch. He was described as a god, dwelling on earth. During the reign of KUMARGUPTA (415–455 C.E.), the available texts refer more to donations and land grants being made to Buddhist and Hindu temples than to monuments dedicated to divine ancestors.

CENTRAL ASIA

The veneration of ancestors played a prominent part of the ritual life among the states that flourished along the ancient Silk Road. A mural from the Sogdian center of AFRASIAB, for example, dating to the reign of King Varkhuman in about 660 C.E., shows the sovereign in a procession to visit a shrine dedicated to his ancestors. At the KUSHAN site of KHALCHAYAN, dating to the mid-first century C.E., a famous columned hall has been interpreted as a shrine dedicated to the deified royal ancestors. The site of SURKH KOTAL incorporated a temple within the fortress, dating to the reign of King KANISHKA (r. 100–126 C.E.). It, too, was dedicated to the Kushan ancestors. This king, according to the RABATAK inscription, also founded other shrines for the same purpose.

JAPAN

Appreciation of ancestors has been identified as early as the middle YAYOI phase of Japanese culture, where cemeteries were patterned on the basis of an individual's descent. This has been described as the beginning of a divine ancestorship that developed into full and powerful expression with the construction of the *kofun* burial mounds. The honored place of the ancestors in the early states of Japan is seen particularly clearly in the energy expended on their mausolea. Thus the burial mound of fifth-century ruler NINTOKU is the largest recorded in Japan, with a total length of nearly 500 meters (1,650 ft.). The energy expended in such structures emphasizes the social importance of the dead ruler as a divine being, who even in death mediated and fostered the well-being of the living community, and when the NIHONGI was completed early in the eighth-century C.E., it portrayed the *tenno*, that is, the sovereign of the NARA STATE, as having a divine ancestry. The text covers the historic period of Japan, going back to the founding period of mythical ancestors.

Andi (94–125 C.E.) *Although Andi means "peaceful emperor," the sixth emperor of the Eastern Han dynasty of China did not enjoy a peaceful reign.*
A grandson of Emperor ZHANGDI, he was only 12 on his accession in 106 C.E. During his reign the XIONGNU nomadic horsemen on the northwestern frontier were active, raiding DUNHUANG and creating unrest and disturbances among the Chinese client states along the SILK ROAD, such as SHAN-SHAN. To counter this peril, Chinese troops and administrators were sent to the threatened areas. Continuing problems that resulted from floods and droughts were alleviated by providing central granaries in the affected regions, among other measures.

Angkor   Angkor is the modern name given to a complex of cities, Hindu and Buddhist temples, and reservoirs located north of the GREAT LAKE (Tonle Sap) in northwest Cambodia. Cambodian kings had these structures erected during a period of several centuries, beginning in the eighth century C.E. and ending with the kingdom's collapse in the 15th century. The ANGKOR WAT temple is the largest religious monument known, but it is only one of the elaborate architectural works undertaken here. Relief sculptures and inscriptions on the buildings offer valuable information about religious practices and daily life.

Angkor was first encountered by Europeans in the 16th century, when Portuguese missionaries visited and described a gigantic, abandoned stone city, encroached on by the jungle. Their accounts were recorded by DIOGO DO COUTO (c. 1543–1616) and archived in Lisbon.

The Great Lake is one of the world's most productive sources of freshwater fish. During the wet season the Tonle Sap River, which connects the lake with the Mekong River, reverses its flow and backs up, greatly expanding the lake's area. In the dry season the river drains the lake, and rice can be grown in the wetlands left as the lake level falls. The lake margins are a particularly favorable place for settlement by rice farmers and fishers, and the region of Angkor is further attractive because of the perennial rivers that cross the flat floodplain from their source in the KULEN HILLS to the north.

EARLIEST OCCUPATION

There is a long history of settlement in this area, which began at least as early as the Iron Age (500 B.C.E.–200 C.E.), for evidence of prehistoric occupation of this period has been found under the temple of BAKSEI CHAMKRONG. The earliest historic occupation probably took place near the WESTERN BARAY. Several temples lie in that area, including AK YUM, Prei Kmeng, and Phnom Rung.

LATER CONSTRUCTIONS

The second major complex lies to the southeast of Angkor and is known as HARIHARALAYA, or the Roluos Group. It includes a series of temples to the south of the INDRATATAKA, a BARAY, or reservoir, of unprecedented size (3,800 by 800 meters[12,540 by 2,640 ft]). It is known from much later inscriptions that JAYAVARMAN II, the founder of the kingdom of Angkor, lived here during his declining years until his death in about 835 C.E. Most of the Roluos Group of buildings, however, were constructed during the reign of INDRAVARMAN I (877–889 C.E.). The royal center of this king incorporated two major temples, known as PREAH KO and the BAKONG. The water of the Roluos River was diverted to fill the Indratataka and was then reticulated to service the extensive moats surrounding the temples, as well as presumably the royal palace. Preah Ko is a recent name meaning "sacred ox," after the statues of the bull Nandi, SIVA's sacred mount, which guard the entrance. This temple complex is surrounded by a 50-meter (65-foot)-wide moat west of the Srah Andaung Preng, a basin 100 meters (330 ft.) square.

The open area between the moat and the wall of the second enclosure has not been investigated by archaeologists; it is thought that a rectangular platform on a north-south axis in the western precinct might well be the foundations for the royal palace. Access to the second court is effected through a laterite and sandstone *gopura*—an entrance pavilion incorporating a gateway. The area within is dominated by a platform bearing six shrines. The three towers of the front row were dedicated to Indravarman's maternal grandfather and father, the central tower dedicated to Jayavarman II. The three sanctuaries in the second row acknowledged the principal consorts of each lord. Each shrine would have contained an image of the ancestor.

While Preah Ko might have been the chapel royal, the adjacent Bakong is far larger and of different construction and design. It may have begun as a laterite structure in the reign of JAYAVARMAN III (834–877 C.E.) but was completed under Indravarman I. The first innovation is the sheer scale of the conception: The central pyramid rises in five stages within a double-moated enclosure 800 meters square. Eight small sanctuaries placed around the base of the pyramid probably acknowledged male and female ancestors of Indravarman. Still awesome today, it would have been a potent symbol of royal power and sacred ancestry.

With the death of Indravarman in 889 C.E. his son, YASHOVARMAN I (Protégé of Glory), completed the northern dike of the Indratataka and had the Lolei temple constructed on an island in the middle of the reservoir. However, he abandoned Hariharalaya in favor of a new capital centered on a low sandstone hill known as the BAKHENG. This center, known as YASHODHARAPURA, the city of Yashovarman, lies at the heart of the complex now known as Angkor. The Bakheng temple stands in the center of the new city. It was itself ringed by a moat 650 by 436 meters in extent, traversed by four gopuras. Access to the summit temple is by steep stairs, but the top of the hill has been partially leveled so that the six terraces of the sanctuary rise from the plateau as on a crown. There are numerous brick chapels at the base of the pyramid and on the terraces. The topmost tier incorporates a quincunx of temples, the largest in the center and the others at each corner. The extent of the city of Yashovarman has not been defined, although for many years a canal system to the southwest of the Bakheng was thought to be the outer moat of his massive city. This feature, however, has now been shown to be much later than his reign.

Yashovarman was responsible for the creation of the massive YASHODHARATATAKA, or Eastern Baray, the dikes of which are 7.5 by 1.8 meters (25 by 29 ft.) in extent. Inscriptions erected at each corner record the construction of this reservoir fed by the Siem Reap River, which, when full, would have contained more than 50 million cubic meters (1.75 billion ft.^{3}) of water. He also had at least four monasteries constructed south of his new reservoir, as well as temples on hills surrounding the capital.

After a brief interlude when King JAYAVARMAN IV established his capital at Koh Ker to the northeast of Angkor, his successor and older brother, King RAJENDRAVARMAN, returned to the old center and had two major state temples constructed. One is now known as Pre Rup; the other, the EASTERN MEBON, was built on an island in the center of the Yashodharatataka. The former honored the king and his ancestors in the context of the god Siva. Its five major towers rise on two laterite tiers. The largest and centrally placed brick sanctuary housed Rajendrabhadresvara, the royal lingam. The architect Kavindrarimathana designed the Eastern Mebon. Its central tower held a lingam named Rajendresvara, and the four subsidiary temples on the uppermost platform housed images of the king's forebears. Rajendravarman was succeeded by his 10-year-old son, JAYAVARMAN V. He continued to reign at Angkor, and his state temple, then known as Hemasringagiri, or "the mountain with the golden summits," was built to represent MOUNT MERU, the home of the gods. It is located just west of the Yashodharatataka.

Jayavarman V's reign was followed by a period of civil war that left the state in serious disarray. The victorious king, SURYAVARMAN I, established his court at Angkor, with the focal point of his capital the temple known as the PHIMEANAKAS. It comprises a single shrine, surrounded by narrow roofed galleries on top of three tiers of laterite of descending size. The royal palace would have been built of perishable materials and can be traced only through the excavation of its foundations. These buildings were located within a high laterite wall with five gopuras ascribed to this reign, enclosing a precinct 600 by 250 meters in extent. Today a great plaza lies to the east of this walled precinct. On its eastern side lie the southern and northern khleangs, long sandstone buildings of unknown function. The southern group belong to the reign of Suryavarman I.

Suryavarman also underlined his authority by beginning the construction of the Western Baray, the largest reservoir at Angkor, which today retains a considerable body of water. This reservoir was unusual, in that the area within the dykes was excavated, whereas the customary method of construction entailed simply the raising of earth dykes above the land surface. The Western Mebon temple in the center of the baray was built in the style of Suryavarman's successor, Udayadityavarman.

It was under the succeeding dynasty of Mahidharapura, from about 1080 C.E., that Angkor reached its present layout. Angkor Wat, the largest religious monument known, was constructed by SURYAVARMAN II (1113–50). Devoted to Vishnu, the temple still houses a large stone statue to this god, which was probably originally housed in the central lotus tower. Angkor Wat incorporates one of the finest and longest reliefs in the world, and the scenes do much to illuminate the religious and court life of Angkor during the 12th century. One scene, for example, shows the king in council; another reveals the Angkorian army on the march, while a third shows graphic scenes of heaven and hell. Very high-status princesses are seen being borne on palanquins. Within the walls of reliefs, the temple rises to incorporate five towers, representing the five peaks of Mount Meru, home of the Hindu gods.

Despite its size and fame, there are still controversies about Angkor Wat. Portuguese visitors of the 16th century described an inscription that may well have been the temple's founding document, but this has not been seen or recorded since. Whether the entire complex was sacred and had restricted access, or whether people resided within the area demarcated by an outer wall and moat, is unknown, as is the function of the temple. GEORGES CŒDÈS has argued that it was a temple and a mausoleum for the king, whose ashes would have been interred under the central shrine. More recently Eleanor Mannika has taken an exhaustive series of measurements and has argued in favor of a deep astrological significance on the basis of the dimensions of key features.

A second king of the MAHIDHARAPURA DYNASTY, JAYAVARMAN VII (1181–1219), was responsible for the construction of ANGKOR THOM, the rectangular walled city that today dominates Angkor. This moated and walled city centers on the BAYON, an extraordinary edifice embellished with gigantic stone heads thought to represent the king as a Buddha. He also ordered the construction of the Northern Baray, or reservoir, and the central island temple of NEAK PEAN, formerly known as Rajasri. According to contemporary inscriptions, visitors to this temple would wash away their sins in the water that gushed from four fountains in the form of human and animal heads. Foundation inscriptions also describe how Jayavarman VII founded and endowed two vast temple complexes, TA PROHM to his mother and PREAH KHAN to his father. Each temple also incorporated shrines dedicated to ancestors of the aristocracy.

After the death of Jayavarman VII, building activity slowed. By the 14th and 15th centuries, the Angkor state was under stress from the encroaching Thais and was abandoned in the middle years of the latter century. While much of the site was then overgrown by the jungle, Angkor Wat was never completely abandoned. It, as indeed do all other temples, retains its sanctity to this day.

ARTISTIC AND WRITTEN EVIDENCE

The physical remains of the civilization of Angkor, and the corpus of inscriptions, make it clear that there must have been many specialists engaged in regular activities. The construction of a temple even of relatively humble proportions would have called on architects and a wide range of laborers, from those who manufactured bricks to those who cut and shaped stone, as well as carpenters, plasterers to create the frescoes, painters, and gilders. Surviving bronzes, for example, for palanquin fittings and statues, indicate the presence of metal workshops, and the ornate jewelry seen on the elite in the reliefs reflects not only lapidaries but workers of gold, silver, and precious stones.

Inscriptions are one of the best sources for artisans during the pre-Angkorian period, because they list the skills of workers assigned to the temple foundations and often their numbers as well. These provide insight into tasks such as basket maker, and the mention of products reveals specialist output: gold, bronze, a copper gong, diadem, umbrellas, many types of pottery vessels, and varieties of woven cloth. Agricultural laborers were mentioned most frequently. An inscription from Lonvek records the assignment of 17 dancers or singers; 23 or 24 record keepers; 19 leaf sewers; 37 artisans, including a potter, 11 weavers, and 15 spinners; and 59 rice-field workers, of whom 46 were female.

An inscription from the reign of Udayadityavarman I shows the king confirming temple rights to indentured laborers, but reserving the right to call on them for assistance if necessary. His successor or rival, Jayaviravarman, is said to have allowed the people of Divapura to enter as artisans in the corporation of goldsmiths. King Suryavarman I ordered royal artisans of the first, second, third, and fourth categories and the people of the district of Sadya to construct for Divakarapandita and his descendants a tower, a *baray*, and a surrounding wall.

There are also scenes depicting the activities of artisans on the reliefs of the Bayon. Some are seen in the act of constructing a monument or preparing a banquet for the elite. The war vessels of the Angkorian navy must have been built by shipwrights. In 1296 the Chinese visitor ZHOU DAGUAN described the fine fabric worn by the elite, which must have been woven by specialists, as well as a range of artifacts that include parasols of oiled taffeta and palanquins with golden shafts. Archaeological excavations have also uncovered ceramic kilns at Tani, east of Angkor, and at Ban Kruat in Thailand, on a scale compatible with specialized production.

AGRICULTURAL ECONOMY

The civilization of Angkor was dependent on rice surpluses for its survival. Rice domestication commenced in the Chang River (Yangtze River Valley) in China by at least the eighth millennium B.C.E. and reached Southeast Asia during the late third millennium. B.C.E., probably as a result of population growth and the spread of farming communities. Rice is widely consumed with fish, because fish are well adapted to life in low wetlands and in rice fields themselves. But domestic cattle and pigs were also closely associated with early rice farmers.

The techniques for growing rice during the period of early states in Southeast Asia are not known in depth. There is controversy, for example, over the development of irrigation based on the vast reservoirs found at Angkor. The adoption of animal traction and the plow greatly increases production, but again, firm evidence for the beginning of plowing is not known. A relief of plowing is found on the walls of BOROBUDUR on Java, dated to the ninth century C.E., but no evidence exists for the kingdom of Angkor.

At Angkor small square field systems on the same orientation as the temples indicate that the bunded or banked system of rain-fed agriculture was employed. This system is particularly productive when the rice plants are transplanted in a pattern that allows sufficient space for each to flourish. When the Chinese diplomat Zhou Daguan visited Angkor in 1296–97, he observed that there were four crops of rice per annum. This has fueled speculation that irrigation fed by the reservoirs there allowed the cultivation of multiple crops. However, he did not mention irrigation, and no canals or other systems of reticulation have survived.

Moreover, there are four methods of cultivating rice without irrigation. Rice is a marsh plant, reliant for nutrients more on the water that percolates past its stems than on the soil in which it is rooted. Therefore, the expansion of rice cultivation requires the creation of conditions that resemble a natural swamp or the exploitation of natural wetlands. Today much of lowland Southeast Asia has been converted into rice fields by the simple expedient of building low earth banks, to retain rainwater where it falls. The water can then be reticulated through the fields by opening or closing intervening conduits. Where floodwaters rise along lake margins or river floodplains, floating rice can flourish. The rice does not in fact float, but it has the capacity to grow at the same pace as the rising flood. If water rises faster than the plant's capacity to grow, the rice dies. Such rice, which proliferates along the margins of the Great Lake in Cambodia, can be harvested by beating the rice grains into a boat. It is also possible to grow rice by retaining floodwater behind linear bunds, called *tanub* in Cambodia, and planting out the rice during the early months of the dry season. Another method is the swidden or slash-and-burn system, which involves clearing forest by burning and growing rice in the resulting fields. This system relies heavily on rainwater and cannot be sustained for more than one or two seasons because of soil exhaustion.

The inscriptions of this period do not mention irrigation or disputes surrounding access to irrigation water. On the other hand, they contain numerous allusions to the organization of labor and the provision of rice surpluses for the temples and the court center. The nobility owned estates that centered on the ancestral temple, under the authority of the king. They commanded an agricultural workforce for whom escape was severely punished. These workers were required to contribute their labor for two weeks out of four to produce the vital surpluses of rice and other agricultural products. The other two weeks were probably spent working for themselves. Agricultural surpluses were used to maintain the upper classes and the clergy and figuratively to feed the gods. Inscriptions of Jayavarman VII specify the number of villages and people assigned to the maintenance of his temple foundations. These, and the list of goods required by the king's hospitals, give some idea of the range of agricultural products then grown. In addition to rice, the list includes honey, wax, fruit, camphor, coriander, pepper, mustard, cardamom, molasses, cumin, pine resin, and ginger.

See also ANCESTOR WORSHIP.

Further reading: Cœdès, G. *Angkor: An Introduction.* Hong Kong: Oxford University Press, 1966; Giteau, M. *Khmer Sculpture and the Angkor Civilisation.* London: Thames and Hudson, 1965; Higham, C. F. W. *The Civilization of Angkor.* London: Weidenfeld and Nicholson, 2001; Jacques, C. *Angkor, Cities and Temples.* Bangkok: River Books, 1997; Mannika, E. *Angkor Wat. Time, Space and Kingship.* St. Leonards: Allen and Unwin, 1996.

The massive sculptured heads of the Bayon temple at Angkor are thought to represent King Jayavarman VII. A devout Buddhist, his ashes were probably placed within the temple after the cremation ceremonies. *(Charles Higham)*

Angkor Borei Angkor Borei, a city covering about 300 hectares (750 acres), located above the Mekong Delta in Cambodia mayonee have been the capital of a state called FUNAN.

The city had been occupied as early as the fourth century B.C.E. and was a major center. It is ringed by a brick wall and a moat. Chinese visitors to the region in the third century C.E. described a capital of a state called Funan, and Angkor Borei, which was linked to OC EO and other delta settlements by a canal, may well have been such a regal center.

Recent excavations directed by Miriam Stark have shown that the site was first occupied during the prehistoric Iron Age, with radiocarbon dates going back to the fourth century B.C.E. She has uncovered a deep Iron Age cemetery in which the dead were interred with pottery vessels among the mortuary offerings. This period was followed by an occupation whose remains yield very large quantities of thin orange pottery that dates between the first and sixth centuries C.E. The encircling walls might belong to the later part of this period. Their construction would have absorbed much energy not only in obtaining the clay but also in shaping the bricks and obtaining sufficient wood to fire them; the wall is at least 2.4 meters (8 ft.) wide and still rises in parts to a height of 4.5 meters.

There are many mounds within the walls, which represent brick temple foundations. Excavations in one such temple uncovered a statue of Vishnu dated stylistically to the seventh century C.E. There are also many rectangular ponds and reservoirs, one measuring 200 by 100 meters in extent. The site would have been a major population center. The surrounding terrain is suited today to flood-retreat farming, whereby the retreating floodwaters from the Mekong and Bassac Rivers are retained behind banks to sustain rice.

Angkorian art The art of the early Cambodian states has been divided into 15 successive, often overlapping styles on the basis of the surviving statues and decorative elements in temple architecture, such as the lintels and columns. The earliest is known as the style of PHNOM DA, which is traditionally dated to the early seventh century C.E. It is followed by the styles of SAMBOR PREI KUK (first half of the seventh century), Prei Kmeng (second half of the seventh century), Prasat Andet (end of the seventh to the start of the eighth century), and Kompong Preah (eighth century). The art styles of the kingdom of ANGKOR begin with Kulen style (first half of the ninth century), followed by the styles of PREAH KO (second half of the ninth century), BAKHENG (first half of the 10th century), KOH KER (928–944 C.E.), PRE RUP (third quarter of the 10th century, BANTEAY SREI (967–1000), Khleang (end of the 10th century), BAPHUON (11th century), ANGKOR WAT (first half of the 12th century), and BAYON (end of the 11th to the beginning of the 13th century).

Angkor Thom Angkor Thom is the name given to the city constructed at ANGKOR in Cambodia as the capital of King JAYAVARMAN VII (1181–1219). The architectural design and decoration symbolize the Hindu view of heaven. The city is three kilometers (1.8 mi.) square and thus encloses an area of 900 hectares (2,250 acres). The surrounding laterite walls stand eight meters high and are punctured by five massive gateways. The moats are crossed by bridges flanked by 54 demons and an equal number of gods, each group holding a sacred snake known as a *naga*. The gateways are particularly impressive, constructed of sandstone in the form of elephants eating lotuses, surmounted by a tower from which four giant stone faces gaze at each cardinal point of the compass. Shrines at each corner of the city record the foundation by Jayavarman VII of his capital. The BAYON, the king's temple mausoleum, is located in the center of the city, but the walls also enclose many structures built both before and after the reign of Jayavarman VII. Foremost is the BAPHUON, the temple mausoleum of UDAYADITYAVARMAN II (1050–66), the royal palace, and the PHIMEANAKAS, the chapel royal. Because all secular buildings were rendered in wood, only the temples have survived. However, excavations in the walled royal precinct have revealed large wooden post foundations. Only archaeology can validate and extend the understanding of urban life and planning. Research along these lines has begun under the direction of Jacques Gaucher in the southeastern quarter of the city, with most promising results.

The symbolism underlying the design of Angkor Thom and the Bayon has been variously interpreted. Paul Wheatley extended the idea of the gods and demons, each group holding a snake from the entrance causeways to incorporate the city as a whole and the Bayon in particular. He suggested that the *naga* was symbolically twined around the Bayon, the temple mausoleum of Jayavarman VII, which in turn represented the churning stick used to produce AMRITA, the elixir of immortality. Again, for those entering the city, the moats would have symbolized the oceans around MOUNT MERU, the walls the encircling mountain ranges.

Paul Mus preferred to see in the *naga* balustrade a symbol of the rainbow, as the bridge linking the world of humans with that of the gods, while Jean Boisselier has returned to the contemporary inscriptions in seeking the underlying symbolism of the city, stressing that it was designed to represent the capital of the god Indra. Just as Indra's capital dominated Mount Meru, so the new Angkor would be built in the center of the kingdom. The Bayon, lying as it does in the heart of the city, is in Boisselier's words, the Assembly Hall of the Gods. It was Indra who cast out the *asuras*, or demons, from heaven and then, with the fortunate intercession of an eagle or a *garuda* after an ensuing battle, repelled their attempt to return. The god then established a permanent guard against any future attacks. These defenses are represented in the form of the entrance gates to the city and the 108 guards located on the bridges spanning the moat. Close inspection of the gates reveals not only the faces of the kings guarding each cardinal point of the compass but also Indra himself, riding his three-headed elephant and holding a thunderbolt.

Angkor Thom, while reproducing heaven in stone through its profound religious symbolism, also had a vigorous secular life. In 1297, ZHOU DAGUAN visited the capital as part of a Chinese delegation. He did not mention irrigation once in his eyewitness account of the country but did describe a large and active urban population, distinguishing, for example, between the splendor of the royal palace and the superior housing enjoyed by the elite and the ordinary dwellings of the populace at large. The Bayon reliefs depict aspects of urban life, the market, the house of a Chinese merchant, and construction activity.

The temple mausoleum of Angkor Wat is one of the great religious monuments of the world. It was constructed as a temple and mausoleum for King Suryavarman II (r. 1113–1150 C.E.). *(Charles Higham)*

Angkor Wat Angkor Wat was dedicated to the Hindu god Vishnu. It is the largest religious edifice known and contains the longest continuous reliefs ever carved. It was the temple mausoleum of KING SURYAVARMAN II (1113–50 C.E.), constructed on a remarkable scale. The original name of Angkor Wat is not known. Portuguese visitors to ANGKOR in Cambodia in the late 16th century described Angkor Wat and mentioned the presence of a large stone inscription there. This has not been identified subsequently, but if it was the foundation stela of the temple, it would be most revealing. Angkor Wat was described by DIOGO DO COUTO (c. 1543–1616), historian of the Portuguese East Indies, in the following terms: "Half a league from this city is a temple called Angar. It is of such extraordinary construction that it is not possible to describe it with a pen, particularly since it is like no other building in the world. It has towers and decoration and all the refinements which the human genius can conceive of. There are many smaller towers of similar style, in the same stone, which are gilded. The temple is surrounded by a moat, and access is by a single bridge, protected by two stone tigers so grand and fearsome as to strike terror into the visitor."

A Japanese visitor in the 17th century drew a map of the monument, annotated with descriptions of surviving gilding on some reliefs. Faint traces of gilding also survive on the central towers, and ZHOU DAGUAN, who visited ANGKOR in 1296–97, described many of the temples as being golden. The first photographs of Angkor Wat, taken in the 1880s, indicate that the temple remained an object of veneration, and it is today portrayed on the national flag of Cambodia.

THE ARCHITECTURE AND SCULPTURE

The complex is surrounded by a moat 200 meters (660 ft.) wide, bounded by megalithic blocks of sandstone, each cut to fit against its neighbor, for a distance of about 10 kilometers (6 mi.). A wall, still 4.5 meters high, encloses the complex within the moat. There are four entrances, the largest on the western side, where the entrance pavilion (*gopura*) is equipped with five portals. The central doorway links the bridge across the moat with the temple via a causeway flanked by balustrades in the form of *nagas* (sacred snakes). On either side lie two small temples and two rectangular water basins. The causeway gives way to a cruciform platform and then the three galleries and central tower, which make up the heart of the complex.

The reliefs covering the walls of the third, outermost gallery illustrate a king and his court for the first time in

Angkorian history. These include a royal audience and a court progress. The king, larger than life, is seen seated on a wooden throne and wearing an elaborate crown and pectoral, heavy ear ornaments, armlets, bracelets, and anklets. He holds a dead snake in his right hand and an unidentified object in his left. He is shaded by 14 parasols and cooled by five fans and four fly whisks as he receives his ministers. Small inscriptions set into the walls state that one Virasimhavarman is offering him a scroll, while Vardhana and Dhananjaya hold their hands over their hearts to indicate loyalty and deference. A fourth minister is described as the inspector of merits and defects.

This audience is followed by the depiction of a progression down the mountainside. The king rides an elephant and is accompanied by the *rajahotar*, or royal priest. The great generals in this military parade ride on their elephants. There is Virendradhipativarman, who in 1108 had the image of the god Trailokyavijaya erected in the sanctuary of PHIMAI. He is surrounded by nine parasols. Ahead of him in the column is Jayayuddhavarman with eight parasols. His troops wear distinctive helmets with deer-head images. Rajasinghavarman has 13 parasols and two banners, but pride of place naturally goes to Vrah Pada Kamraten An Paramavishnuloka (The Sacred Feet of the Lord Who Has Gone to Live with Vishnu), the king. He has 15 parasols, five fans, six fly whisks, four banners, and, in front of his elephant, a standard of Vishnu riding Garuda. Even his elephant wears a splendid jeweled headdress. The king's presence in signaled by the sacred fire carried aloft and an orchestra of trumpets, conches, drums, and a gong. The women of the court, princesses, are carried aloft in fine palanquins as they travel through a forest. There are also serried ranks of foot soldiers and cavalry, stolid rows of Khmer and loosely drilled, longhaired troops labeled as Syem, which might indicate that they were from Siam or, alternatively, that they were dark-skinned vassals.

Many Angkorian inscriptions conclude with lines threatening punishment for those who injure the foundation and promising rewards for the faithful supporters. At Angkor Wat, the fate of the former and the heavenly abode of the latter are graphically portrayed. Again, small inscriptions in the walls describe the punishments for particular crimes, as the fate of each person is determined by Yama, god of death, who sits in judgement on a water buffalo. The crimes include theft of land, houses, animals, rice, liquor, shoes, and parasols. Incendiaries are also destined for severe punishment, as are those guilty of gluttony and greed. Punishments were indeed severe. The guilty were crushed under heavy rollers or suspended upside down from trees and beaten. On the other hand, those with a spotless life on Earth were rewarded with a delightful existence in celestial palaces.

Scenes from Hindu epics fill other sections of the gallery walls. The most impressive is undoubtedly the depiction of the CHURNING OF THE OCEAN OF MILK in search of the elixir of immortality—AMRITA—but the Battles of Lanka and Kurukshetra also bring home the nature of warfare at this period, dominated, it seems, by vicious hand-to-hand slaughter.

Progress toward the central tower involves a large columned building containing four sunken water basins and, formerly, statues of gods. Steps then lead up to a second gallery and beyond to the heart of the monument with its central tower rising up in the form of a lotus. This overlies a 27-meter-deep shaft that contained the sacred deposit of two white sapphires and two gold leaves. The demand for labor to construct a monument on this scale must have exceeded all previous experience. Not only is the weight of the stone extraordinary, but virtually every surface bears decorative carving of the highest quality, none more so than the APSARAS, heavenly maidens who welcomed the king to heaven.

INTERPRETATIONS OF THE SITE

The five central towers rising in the center of the temple represent the peaks of MOUNT MERU, the home of the gods, while the moat symbolizes the surrounding ocean. Eleanor Mannika has sought deeper symbolic structures through the medium of the monument's dimensions and relationship to the annual movements of the Sun and Moon, but this initiative has invoked some skepticism. There is also debate on the ultimate purpose of Angkor Wat. Did it incorporate residential areas, including the king's palace, or was it an entirely religious entity, designed for the worship of Vishnu? Was it built as a temple and mausoleum for Suryavarman? There is no specific allusion to his mortuary rites, but it is probable that Angkor Wat was not completed in his lifetime, for the depictions of him at court and in a progression are accompanied by his posthumous name, Paramavishnuloka, "He who has entered the heavenly world of Vishnu."

GEORGES CŒDÈS has concluded that it was a monument to the king, himself portrayed as divine, where he had communion with the gods. At death, the king's remains were placed in the central tower to animate his image. A stone container 1.4 meters long has been recovered from the central tower of Angkor. It was probably placed there to contain the king's cremated remains. Worship of the dead king would have ensued once his soul entered his stone image, thus permitting contact with the ancestors of the dynasty. A colossal stone image of Vishnu survives at Angkor Wat, and it is still worshiped. Angkor Wat should thus be seen as the preserve of the immortal sovereign merged with Vishnu, in a heaven populated by the celestial APSARDS.

See also ANCESTOR WORSHIP.

Aninditapura　Several Angkorian inscriptions in modern Cambodia refer to Aninditapura as the original region where an important group of supporters of King JAYAVAR-MAN II (c. 770 to 834) originated. Its location is not known with certainty, but it probably lay on the west bank of the Mekong River above Phnom Penh.

Ankokuji   Ankokuji is a site of the late phase of the YAYOI culture, located on the island of Kyushu in Japan, but looking east over the Inland Sea toward Honshu. The Yayoi culture covered six vital centuries of Japanese history from about 300 B.C.E., during which stimuli from the mainland in the form of wet-rice cultivation, iron and bronze metallurgy, and trading opportunities saw a late hunter-gatherer society develop into a series of small states. ANKOKUJI commanded access to rich rice soil in the form of old river meanders, which ultimately were covered in peat. The peat has preserved many wooden artifacts that reveal how plowshares, spades, and hoes were used in the cultivation of rice. Peaches, almonds, walnuts, and acorns have also survived to demonstrate the varied diet enjoyed by the inhabitants. The eminence that supported the village itself has many postholes that might represent the foundations for raised dwellings or rice stores. While no metal tools have survived, it is clear that they were used in the manufacture of the wooden implements.

Anotatta, Lake   *See* ANAVATAPTA LAKE.

Antiochus   (324–261 B.C.E.) *Antiochus I was the son of* SELEUCUS I NICATOR *and his Bactrian wife, Apama.*
Antiochus ruled from 281 to 261 B.C.E., and despite his military prowess, he had to struggle to hold the Seleucid Empire together. Before becoming king, he was viceroy of the eastern satrapies (provinces) in Central Asia west of the Syr Dar'ya River. This area was greatly valued for its agricultural products, increased through the establishment of irrigation, as well as sources of ore and precious stones. Antiochus consolidated his hold in this region by founding heavily fortified cities. One of these was located to command the strategic and rich oasis of MARY (Merv), covering an area of 225 hectares (563 acres) within its brick ramparts. Maracanda (modern Samarqand) commanded another oasis, and the rampart of Antiochus survives there. The satrap of Aria lies near Herat in the Harirud Valley, and here Antiochus restored the defenses of the capital, Artacoana.

Antiquities Protection Law   In 1930 the government of China enacted the Antiquities Protection Law. Hitherto, looting and treasure hunting had destroyed many sites, and Western and Japanese collectors and museums had been responsible for the loss of numerous national treasures. This applied in particular to the site of Xiaotun, where the ORACLE-BONE records of the Shang dynasty (1766–1045 C.E.) were found. The law stated that all antiquities below

ground belonged to the state and that no person could excavate without an official permit. The first such permit was issued in 1935 to the learned academy known as the Academia Sinica, for the excavation of ANYANG.

Laws to protect antiquities and ancient sites now apply in all countries of Asia, but traffic in collectable artworks has increased to alarming proportions. In Afghanistan, for example, state-sponsored destruction of sacred Buddhist sites under the Taliban has been followed by widespread looting of items of Gandharan art. Recently, the U.S. government has banned the import of stone carvings from the civilization of ANGKOR in Cambodia.

Anuradhapura   Anuradhapura is a huge urban complex located in the dry zone of north central Sri Lanka (Ceylon). Legendary sources claim that it was founded by the

Anuradhapura was one of the great urban centers of South Asia. Buddhism was the key religion there, and several very large Buddhist foundations were established. This statue of the Buddha comes from the Ruvanvalisaya stupa, built by King Dutthagamani (r. 161–137 B.C.E.). (*© Philip Baird/ www.anthroarcheart.org*)

third king of the Vijayan dynasty, Pandukkabhaya. This dynasty, again in oral traditions, was founded by a Prince Vijaya, who traveled from the mainland of India and found the island inhabited by demons. The city was the major city of Sri Lanka from the third century B.C.E. until it was finally abandoned in the early 10th century C.E. In the interim, two dynasties ruled from Anuradhapura. In addition to the founding line, the Lamakanna dynasty dominated from the first century C.E. until 432 and again from the seventh to the 10th century. The site was attacked more than once by forces from the mainland, leading to a break in local rule. Anuradhapura includes a walled city, surrounded by several impressive stupas with associated monasteries and several huge reservoirs. Its internal history, however, is reconstructed on the basis of archaeological research rather than the stuff of legends.

Excavations have revealed an eight-meter (26.4-in.)-deep stratigraphic buildup, divided into a sequence of major cultural phases. The problem with such deep historic sites is that to obtain any feel for the spatial planning, one most uncover enormous areas. This is increasingly uneconomic, particularly as excavation procedures have become more complex and time consuming. The history of this city is thus partial and based on a tiny area excavated, compared with the huge earlier excavations at sites such as TAXILA and MOHENJO DARO in modern Pakistan.

EARLY PHASES

The area was first settled early in the prehistoric period, and there is a later major phase ascribed to the late prehistoric Iron Age, dated from about 800 to 450 B.C.E. The next phase is called Early Historic (450–350 B.C.E.) but reveals continuity in material culture from the Iron Age. The contexts have yielded the remains of iron slag, postholes representing domestic structures on a circular plan, and a possible burial in a circular shaft, containing mortuary offerings. A particularly important feature of this period is the discovery of four ceramic shards bearing letters in the Indian BRAHMI script. It is thought that this writing system was introduced to Sri Lanka through the aegis of trade contacts with the West. It might not be coincidental that exotic shell and amethyst were also found at this juncture, dated from the period 450–350 B.C.E.

DEVELOPMENT OF THE CITY

The fourth phase, which lasted from about 350 until 275 B.C.E., is particularly important, because it provides evidence for the rapid establishment of a city. Divided into eight subphases, the site revealed an early rectangular building demarcated by the posthole foundations for a wooden structure, laid out on the cardinal points of the compass. By the fourth subphase, clay tiles entered the repertoire for building, and there is evidence that the first rampart covered a rectangular area of about 100 hectares (250 acres). There is further evidence for wide-ranging exchange in the form of carnelian from the mainland, LAPIS LAZULI from Afghanistan, ivory, cowry shells, and iron ore. One shard bears the image of a large boat fit for oceanic trade, and the first copper coins appeared.

Coins increased in quantity and motifs during the period dated from 275 B.C.E. to 150 C.E., as did exotic ceramics and objects of ivory and whalebone. Buildings were now made of brick and cut stone, and their location relative to a street suggests that the city was laid out in squares on the cardinal points. The construction of large buildings in permanent materials burgeoned during the first six centuries of the Common Era, and this is best seen in the Buddhist monuments, rather than the few foundations revealed through deep excavations. The earliest Buddhist monastery at Anuradhapura probably dates to the late third century B.C.E. It was followed by the foundation of further monasteries and associated stupas, the size and splendor of which owe much to the growing extent and efficiency of the developing irrigation network.

STUPAS

The are five major stupas at Anuradhapura. The earliest is known as the Thuparama. This was followed by two built during the reign of Dutthagamani (161–137 B.C.E.), the Mirisavati and Ruvanvalisaya, also known as the Mahastupa. These were followed by the ABHAYAGIRI and Jetavana stupas, both of which reached colossal proportions. Under King Gajabahu (114–136 C.E.), the Abhayagiri stupa reached a height of 84 meters; the Jetavana stupa, when completed, was more than 120 meters tall. The monks of the Mahavira monastery were housed in a building known as the Lovamahapaya, a multistoried edifice in which the senior or most venerable were housed in the upper floors. Palaces at Anuradhapura were built of wood and have not survived, but the texts leave no doubt as to their splendor. Sculptures played a central role in the embellishment of the shrines, seen in the ornamented pillars that surround the major monuments, and in the so-called moonstones, which were placed at the foot of the access stairs to shrines decorated with panels of animals, plant motifs, and rows of *hamsa*s, or sacred geese. Images of the Buddha date back to the first century C.E. Some of the Buddha images reached massive proportions, such as that at Avukana, which is almost 13 meters high. Painting also reached high artistic levels, as is seen at the Jetavana.

Anyang Anyang was the capital of the SHANG STATE of China from about 1200 until 1045 B.C.E. Anyang has for decades been prominent for the sudden appearance there of written records, CHARIOTS, massive royal graves, and human sacrifices. Located north of the Huang (Yellow) River in Henan province, it was recognized as a potential site of great importance in 1915, when Luo Zhenyu identified Anyang as the source of the ORACLE BONES that were then appearing on the antiquities market. These oracle bones recorded divinations made by Shang kings hitherto known only from much later historic records. Confirmation of the veracity of these records stimulated LI JI and the newly founded Academia Sinica to institute 15 seasons of research at Anyang. This research resulted in the identification of a palace area, containing the stamped-earth foundations of substantial residential compounds, as well as ancestral temples and subterranean pits containing chariot burials. In 1936, on the last day of the excavation season, a pit containing thousands of oracle bones was identified in this part of the site. The oracle texts illuminate the intimate concerns of the Shang kings, of whom nine are known to have reigned at this site, beginning with Wu Ding (1400–1200 B.C.E). The bones describe preparations for war against rival states, concern about the harvest, hunting expeditions, sacrifices to ancestors to alleviate health problems, and insight into the welfare of pregnant consorts. One such consort to Wu Ding, FU HAO, was interred in the only intact royal tomb to survive at Anyang, a find revealing the wealth of the court in its exquisite bronzes, jades, and ivories.

ANYANG TOMBS

By the end of Wu Ding's reign, Anyang covered at least 10 square kilometers (4 mi.); it extended over more than twice that area by the end of the dynasty in 1045 B.C.E. In 1933, during the eighth season of research there, the team encountered a subterranean tomb of massive size. Although it was completely looted, it opened the possibility that a royal cemetery lay in the vicinity. Unfortunately this discovery resulted in frenzied looting, as a result of which three bronze *ho* (wine vessels) were displayed in the Nezu Art Museum in Tokyo.

The next season of scientific inquiry was directed toward the area where massive bronzes were reported to have been looted, and there followed the discovery of royal graves of extraordinary dimensions. Four of these were examined, together with many smaller graves rich in mortuary offerings, including bronzes, jades, and ceramic vessels. The 11th season concentrated on the opening of the royal graves. An area of 8,000 square meters was excavated, and four massive tomb chambers, up to 13 meters deep, were cleared. These tombs had all been looted on many occasions in the past, but by means of a complete clearance undertaken professionally, many bronzes and jades of exquisite finish were recovered in the disturbed fill of the graves. Moreover, more than 400 smaller burials were encountered. Many were without heads, while some crania were found severed from the bodies. It was concluded that these graves contained the remains of sacrificial victims interred as part of the royal mortuary rituals.

Even this major program of excavation was to be exceeded in 1935, when 500 workers were employed to open an area of nearly 10,000 square meters. Three further royal graves were cleared, but once again looters had preceded the archaeologists, even as early as the Zhou dynasty (1045 to 221 B.C.E.). Nevertheless, the fine jades and bronzes that survived the sackings were unprecedented in Chinese archaeology. A further 800 smaller burials that were also excavated are seen as ancillary to the royal graves.

The seven royal graves all had the same plan. A central pit that contained the wooden tomb chamber was reached by means of four sloping corridors entering it from each side. In the case of Burial HPKM 1004, the central pit reached a depth of 12.2 meters below the ground surface and measured 15.9 by 10.8 meters at the base. The southern and longest entrance corridor was 31.4 meters long. The base of the pit contained a wooden chamber entered from the south. The space between the tomb and the sides of the pit was filled with pounded earth. The interment of the body would have been accompanied by lengthy rituals and probably the sacrifice of those found in the smaller graves in the vicinity.

In the case of Burial 1004, the excavators were fortunate to find a small part that had escaped looting. The finds provide a tiny insight into the riches that were once placed with the dead Shang kings. Two huge bronze cauldrons were found in the central pit, at a level just two meters above the top of the wooden burial chamber. These overlay a deposit of bronze weapons, including 360 spearheads and 141 helmets, which concealed the fragmentary vestiges of some form of vehicle. Jade figures of animals, including turtles, frogs, and monsters, were found in the looters' pits. In Tomb 1217, the traces of a large decorated drum were recovered.

Subsequent to these excavations, a deeper understanding of the sequence of material culture at Anyang has made it possible to group the royal graves into a sequence. There are four major phases at this royal center that are divided on the basis of the dynastic sequence. The first belongs to the early part of the reign of Wu Ding (r. c. 1200–1181 B.C.E.). The second corresponds to the reigns of Zu Geng (r. c. 1180–1171 B.C.E.) and Zu Jia (r. c. 1170–1151 B.C.E.), while the third covers the reigns of Lin Xin (r. c. 1150–1131 B.C.E.), Kang Ding (r. c. 1131–1121 B.C.E.), Wu Yi (r. c. 1120–1106 B.C.E.) and Wen Ding (r. c. 1105–1091 B.C.E.). The fourth corresponds to the Kings Di Yi (r. c. 1090–1071 B.C.E.) and Di Xin (d. c. 1045 B.C.E.). The artifacts recovered while excavating the graves make it possible to assign Graves 1001, 1550, and 1400 to the second period. Two of these lie in the western sector, and one in the eastern. Each has four entrance ramps. Graves 1002, 1004, 1217, and 1500 belong to the third period, while Graves 1003 and 1567 are the latest and belong to Period IV. Within each sector, it is possible to refine the sequence on the basis of the intercutting of the entrance ramps. Burial 1567 was not completed, and it was probably intended for the last Shang king, Di Xin. It may never have been completed because the construction coincided with the end of the dynasty. Adding the massive Burial 1400 to the rest of the graves in the western sector reveals a perfect match between the nine huge burials and the number of kings now known from the oracle-bone inscriptions.

The eastern part of the cemetery also contains rows of sacrificial pits. The oracle texts reveal that human sacrifice to the ancestors was a major part of divination, and this is reflected in the neat rows of victims' graves at the royal necropolis. Several other cemeteries for the populace at large have been investigated, and these indicate the presence of clans in which senior members were given prominence in terms of the size and quantity of mortuary offerings.

BRONZE WORKING

The presence of a substantial population is documented not only by such cemeteries, but also by the large areas dedicated to specialized production, not least the casting of large bronzes. The largest, found at Xiaomintun in Anyang, was first recognized in 1960, when excavations uncovered the molds used to cast chisels and knives. Further digging in 2000–01 revealed that this part of the ancient capital was also the focus for the production of bronze ritual vessels. These were found in the southeastern part of the workshop area, while the weapons were concentrated in the western area.

Anyang continues to be the subject of major international research, and new areas are being investigated. The most significant recent find is the walled city of HUANBEI, a probable royal capital north of the Huan River, which lies chronologically between the occupation of ZHENGZHOU and the reign of Wu Ding (1400–1200 B.C.E.). Future excavations at Huanbei have the potential to illuminate the antecedents to the last Shang capital, before the dynasty fell to the Zhou after the BATTLE OF MUYE in 1045 B.C.E.

See also XIBEIGANG.

Further reading: Chang, K.-C. *The Shang Civilization.* New Haven, Conn.: Yale University Press, 1980; Keightley, D. N. *Sources of Shang History: The Oracle Bones of Bronze Age China.* Berkeley: University of California Press, 1978; Loewe, M., and Shaugnessy, E. L., eds. *The Cambridge History of Ancient China.* Cambridge: Cambridge University Press, 1999.

Apeyatana The Apeyatana temple is one of the principal monuments of the city of PAGAN in Myanmar (Burma). It has been ascribed to King Kyanzittha (1084–1112) and is named after his queen. It is best known for the decorative paintings that depict divinities of the Mahayana School of BUDDHISM. There are also, however, Hindu deities, including Siva, Vishnu, and Ganesha.

See also MAHAYANA BUDDHISM.

apsara In early Indian mythology, an *apsara* was a celestial water nymph. Both in the Hindu and in Buddhist religions, these creatures took the form of heavenly nymphs with a particular fondness for music and dance. They welcomed to the heavenly realm men whose virtuous lives translated them to paradise at death, and many

of the *apsara* were regarded as goddesses. They are particularly prominent in the reliefs of ANGKOR WAT, Cambodia, where more than 2,000 have been recorded. These images reveal a wide range of costumes and ornaments, reflecting the luxury of the Angkorian court as much as celestial imagery. The nymphs wear elaborate headdresses, pectorals, and other ornaments, including multiple armlets and bracelets, belts, and anklets. Their distended earlobes were weighted with ear pendants, and their postures reveal that dancing then was similar to that still taught and practiced in Cambodia.

See also BUDDHISM; SURYAVARMAN II.

Arahaki-ji Also known as the Shitenno-ji, the Arahaki-ji is a Buddhist temple and monastery built at Naniwa, south of the Yodo River as it flowed toward Osaka Bay, by order of PRINCE SHOTUKU (d. 622 C.E.). In 587 C.E., the prince had vowed to build a temple if he was successful in a civil war against rival clans. During this period the

Apsaras were divine maidens. More than 2,000 carved in sandstone at Angkor Wat waited to attend on King Suryavarman II when he went to live in the world of Vishnu, a euphemism for his death. *(Charles Higham)*

leaders of the YAMATO state in Japan were heavily influenced by continental powers, particularly the PAEKCHE state of Korea and the new Sui dynasty in China. BUDDHISM was being well received, and Shotuku's fine new temple foundations were laid in 593. The structure had an exterior wall and a cloistered compound measuring 100 by 70 meters (330 by 230 ft.). The central pagoda in this compound was flanked by a gilded hall, while a lecture hall, bell tower, and monks' living quarters lay to the north of the cloisters. The temple was destroyed by Allied bombing in the Second World War, and it has been replaced by a concrete replica.

Arakan

Arakan The Arakan (now Rakhine) coast of western Myanmar (Burma) occupies a key geographic position in the maritime exchange route that developed during the early centuries C.E. It faces India across the Bay of Bengal and was thus a natural stepping stone when, for example, the Mauryan emperor ASOKA (268–235 B.C.E.) sent Buddhist missions to Southeast Asia. Tradition has it that the Buddha manifested himself in Arakan when an image of him was cast. This bronze statue, known as the MAHAMUNI (Great Sage), is now in Mandalay. Although the history of Arakan has scarcely been tested archaeologically, it is known that two major cities span the fifth to the eighth centuries C.E.

The first city, DHANYAWADI, incorporated a walled royal precinct and the hill on which the Mahamuni was housed and revered until the early 18th century, when it was removed to Mandalay. The second city, VESALI, like Dhanyawadi in a rich agricultural valley suited to rice cultivation but with access to the sea, was also ringed by a substantial brick wall and moat. The inscription from SHIT-THAUNG listed 22 kings of the Ananda dynasty who ruled this area. BUDDHISM was the dominant religion, but not to the exclusion of Hinduism. Coins were minted, and there is evidence for extensive maritime trade and wealthy urban communities.

Archaeological Survey of India The Archaeological Survey of India was founded in 1870, following a period during which SIR ALEXANDER CUNNINGHAM was the archaeological surveyor to the governor of India. Cunningham was the first director of the survey, and among his successors, SIR JOHN MARSHALL and SIR MORTIMER WHEELER stand out for their many achievements. The survey received considerable support under the viceroyalty of George, Lord Curzon in 1899. Under the direction of the survey, many major sites were excavated and published, and others were restored and maintained. These sites include TAXILA, BHITA, HARAPPA, MOHENJO DARO, and ARIKAMEDU.

Arikamedu Arikamedu, an archaeological site in India four kilometers south of Pondicherry, facing the Bay of Bengal, is located on an island opposite the bank of the Ariyankuppam River. It has been identified as the port of Podouke, cited in the first century C.E. work *PERIPLUS OF THE ERYTHRAEAN SEA*. The site was recognized as ancient and important as early as 1768, when Guillaume Le Gentil visited it and encountered substantial brick walls and pottery remains. In 1937, surface material was collected, and the site was recognized as having considerable historic importance. Excavations showed that the site was an important port for trade between India and Italy during the second and first centuries B.C.E.

Excavations under A. Aiyappan ensued in 1940, and further work was undertaken between 1941 and 1944. The site was selected for excavation by SIR MORTIMER WHEELER in 1945, after the discovery there of an intaglio containing the image of the Roman emperor Augustus and other items of possible Roman origin. Although the site had suffered considerable disturbance, Wheeler uncovered the foundations of a probable brick warehouse 45 meters (150 ft.) in length and the remains of two tanks or vats that had been used for dying cloth. The Roman remains included Arretine ware, a style of impressed red pottery from kilns at Arezzo in Italy, dating from the last decades of the first century B.C.E. and the mid-first century C.E. Amphorae, large handled vessels used for transporting wine, were also represented, and the presence of Chinese ceramics revealed the entrepôt nature of trade from this port. Trade is further confirmed by the presence of rouletted ware, a style of pottery decorated with a particular design on the base, which has been found widely distributed in India and in Bali and Vietnam to the east.

The site was examined again in 1947–50 by J.-M. Casal over three seasons, but his results were never fully published. Excavations resumed in 1989 under the direction of V. Begley, and much new information has modified the earlier view that Arikamedu was, in the words of Wheeler, an "Indo-Roman trading station." There appear to have been two areas under occupation, which jointly covered almost 500 meters (1,650 ft.) of the riverbank. The southern area has provided extensive evidence for manufacturing products of glass, shell, semiprecious stones, and metals. It might have been the principal workshop area. The northern sector includes a large brick structure thought by Wheeler to have been a warehouse. Its foundations covered pottery dated to the early first century C.E., providing evidence for the establishment of port facilities.

However, trade with the Greco-Roman world was under way by at least the first century B.C.E. and possibly even earlier, as indicated by the presence of trade amphorae that carried wine to southern India from the Greek island of Kos. An early text in the Tamil language refers to Yavanas, that is, Westerners, taking cool fragrant wine to India. A detailed examination of the exotic Western ceramics from Arikamedu reveals changing patterns of trade and the addition of a new range of imports over time. The wine originally was from the island of Kos, then from Knidos and Rhodes, but in due course, olive oil was sent east from the region of Pompeii in southern Italy and southern France, while *garum,* a type of fish oil, was imported from Spain. Other goods included Egyptian faience, Roman lamps, and glassware. Several Roman coins have been found, largely by looters.

The Roman trade with southern India lasted until the early second century C.E. before declining markedly. However, Arikamedu continued in occupation, perhaps as a result of the port facilities on a coast where safe anchorages are rare.

Arimaddanapura *See* PAGAN.

Arthasastra The *Arthasastra* (Treatise on material gain), is attributed to KAUTILYA, a minister to King CANDRAGUPTA MAURYA (325–297 B.C.E.). This king ruled the MAURYA EMPIRE from his capital of PATALIPUTRA in the lower Ganges (Ganga) Valley of India and was a contemporary of ALEXANDER THE GREAT (356–323 B.C.E). It may even have been the case that Alexander's campaign of conquest in northwest India galvanized the first Mauryan king and his court to investigate the means of combining the many MAHAJANAPADAS, or states, that then existed in the Ganges (Ganga) Valley into one effective political unit. The *Arthasastra* is thus a unique treatise that documents the political philosophy advocated in India during the late fourth century B.C.E. It describes a philosophy more in harmony with Machiavelli's than the pacifist tendency of BUDDHISM and may reflect the influence of Western absolutism under a strong king manifested in the conquests of Alexander the Great. The *Arthasastra* is thus a manual of government written by a man whose objective was to secure the safe maintenance of the kingdom by establishing the proper principles. It exercised a long and important influence both in India and in other areas, such as Southeast Asia, that exchanged goods and ideas with India.

ROYAL DUTIES

Kautilya's prescriptions for successful rule center on the duties of the king, who had a long list of responsibilities. It is interesting to note the importance placed on the gathering of intelligence, as the king was urged to have regular daily meetings with his spies. The same motive is seen in Kautilya's recommendation that the ruler allow his subjects access to his person; otherwise he would be too far removed from them and fall into the hands of a coterie of court advisers. Many other duties are also laid out: to read reports on the administration of law; to inspect army units, which are listed as the elephants, cavalry, infantry, and chariots; to plan conquests with his military leaders; and to consult the priests about the performance of rituals. Most of all, the king should display energy and resolve to all around him.

THE STATE

The treatise then turns to the seven basic components of the state. These are the king, his ministers, the territory, forts, treasury, the army, and allied states. Ministers should be well born and educated, imaginative, industrious, dignified, cultured, and determined. The boundaries of the state should be strongly defended with forts designed to make the best use of the local terrain. Several types of fort are enumerated, including those in deserts, mountains, and forests and those alongside rivers. The treasury should contain gold, silver, and precious stones. The army should be well equipped and trained, loyal, experienced in battle, and prepared to suffer pain. Allies must be loyal and able to deploy their forces rapidly. Practically speaking, Kautilya inherited the fruits of many centuries of war between the rival states of the Ganges (Ganga) Valley. His policy toward rivals was predicated on the means of destruction through the ruthless exercise of superior power. However, he also recognized that relations with other states involved shifting sands, requiring a cynical application of different policies depending on likely outcomes. If, for example, a rival state is more powerful, then the policy must be one of temporizing and duplicity until the moment is right to strike. If an alliance benefits the defeat of a joint enemy, then the ruler must forge one.

The ideal state in India of the fourth century B.C.E required 10 principal ministers to advise the king, including a chief priest, prime minister, army commander, judge, adviser on economic management, and ambassador. The chaplain had to be learned about the VEDAS and virtuous behavior but also, curiously, skilled in archery and military tactics. Considerable thought was given to the role of the army commander, and his duties disclose the nature of warfare. He had, for example, to ensure that the elephants and horses were well maintained and trained but also that camels and oxen were available. The last two animals were probably used for transport. His duties included the training of those who played military music or carried the royal standards and had experience of coded signaling. He had to evaluate the quality of the missile throwers and report on the quality of the troops, how many were growing too old for combat and which men were new and inexperienced.

A formal legal system is widely regarded as an essential component of a state, and Kautilya insisted that the judges have a thorough grounding in local customs; when hearing cases, they should take account of witnesses, relevant documents, and logical conclusions. The survival of the state ultimately turned on the production of agricultural surpluses and their proper central deployment. For overseeing this vital area of activity, the king turned to his economy minister, whose responsibilities are set out in considerable detail: How much grass is available in store, for example, and how much will be needed? What are the sources of taxation, and how much wealth has been accumulated from the various sources, such as mines, forests, and agriculture? How much has been obtained from fines or recovered from robbers?

arya   In SANSKRIT, the word *arya* means "noble." It came to be used in Sanskrit to describe a race, with particular reference to those who allegedly invaded and conquered India. The name of the country of Iran is derived from the same root word. *Arya* appears in the RIG-VEDA to distinguish between its authors and the *dasa,* or natives of the area conquered.

ashrama   An *ashrama* (ashram) is a retreat or hermitage where Hindu wise men and ascetic devotees retire and practice contemplation. A fine example of life in such a hermitage appears on a carved panel at Mamallapuram in India. Dating to the seventh to eighth centuries C.E., it shows an old holy man contemplating an image of the god Vishnu. King YASHOVARMAN (889–910) of ANGKOR in Cambodia claimed to have founded about 100 such institutions, and his surviving foundation stelae include an account of the king's ancestry and the rules for the occupants. The distribution of the inscriptions provides evidence for the extent of his kingdom. All are identical and prescribe, for example, that the ascetics had to wear white garments. Punishments were graded for those who failed to follow the regulations. No buildings have survived, presumably because they were constructed of wood, but it is known that a row of *ashrama*s was constructed along the southern margin of the YASHOD-HARATATAKA (EASTERN BARAY) at Angkor.

Asoka (268–235 B.C.E.)   *Asoka, the third king of the Maurya Empire in India, is widely regarded as the greatest of Indian kings.*
The son of Bundusara, Asoka succeeded in about 268 B.C.E. His conversion to BUDDHISM (c. 261 B.C.E.) was felt well beyond the boundaries of his empire. During the first eight years of his reign, Asoka continued on his predecessors' path by expanding his empire through force. His conquest of Kalinga, the area of modern Orissa, involved considerable loss of life, and his inscriptions record his feeling of remorse and his desire to embrace the pacifist tenets of Buddhism. The text of the 13th rock edict, a text inscribed in six places in India and Pakistan, makes his position clear. It refers to Asoka as the king beloved of the gods, who in the eighth year of his reign was responsible for the deaths of 100,000 people and the forced deportation of 150,000 others. After this holocaust, he took up the teachings of the DHARMA, the course of righteousness, and proclaimed his wish that all members of his empire live in security and peace of mind. The final lines of this edict make its principal message clear: He wished his sons and grandsons to follow his precept

not to seek new territorial gains through force and consequent miseries, but only through pacifist enlightenment.

ASOKA'S INSCRIPTIONS

Asoka is renowned for the erection of a series of pillars across his empire, linked with major Buddhist foundations. His life and philosophy are recorded in a series of inscriptions he inspired, some engraved on rocks, others on enormous stone columns erected strategically across his empire. About 10 of Asoka's columns have survived, but only two remain in their original location, at Laurya Nandangarh and Kolhua in Bihar state. Most inscriptions are in the BRAHMI script, but another script, KHAROSHTHI, was used in the northwest. Two further inscriptions from Kandahar in Afghanistan were written in Greek and Aramaic.

The columns were embellished on the capitals with Buddhist symbols, such as the lion, and inscribed texts. The first pillar text extolled the virtues of a righteous rule for all his subjects and expressed his concern for animals.

His first rock inscription declared a ban on sacrificing animals. Having outlined the daily slaughter of stock for the palace kitchens, he stated that only deer and peacocks were currently killed and that this practice would also cease. In his second rock inscription, he recorded his concern for the health and welfare of his people and described practical measures to ensure a supply of medicinal plants and of fresh water through the digging of wells by the roads, for animals as well as people. He ordered that banyan trees be planted along roads to provide shade. Every 25 kilometers (15 mi.), the traveler along the main routes would find a rest house and water basin provided by the king.

The inscriptions of Asoka impart much information on the bureaucracy with which he administered his empire. Obviously unhappy with his officials at Tosali, the capital of the newly won province of Kalinga, he wrote warning them against improper or hasty imprisonment or torture and informed them that he would send an impartial official on a tour of inspection every fifth year to ensure fair local government. He evidently maintained viceroys, because he recorded that the princes of UJJAIN and TAXILA would also send out inspectors every three years.

The 12th rock edict outlined Asoka's attitude toward different religious persuasions. He showed tolerance for all and described how, on his various provincial tours, he gave money and support to Hindu Brahmans (priests) and Buddhist foundations alike. In the seventh of his column inscriptions, he laid out his philosophy of government, putting particular stress on the search for righteousness and the welfare of all his people. He wished to ensure that this policy would endure.

ASOKA'S BUDDHIST FOUNDATIONS

The inscriptions of Asoka represent a major innovation in the advertisement of royal policy. The custom of engraving important information on stone was fortunately copied in both India and Southeast Asia, and the texts provide vital historic information. The king, however, was also a vigorous founder of religious establishments, and his monasteries are widely distributed across his realm. When the Chinese monk and pilgrim XUANZANG (602–64) visited India, he traveled to the holiest places of Buddhism. At KUSINAGARA, where the Buddha died, he saw an enormous stupa standing 60 meters (198 ft.) high, built, he said, by Asoka. Three stupas he visited at MATHURA, he said, were also built by King Asoka, and he named the monks whose remains lay beneath them. At VAISALI, Xuanxang noted that King Asoka had opened the relic chamber and removed eight of the nine fragments of bone before erecting one of his columns at the site, with a lion at the top.

The impact of Asoka's enthusiastic conversion to Buddhism was felt well beyond the boundaries of his empire. The text known as the *Sasanvamsappadika* records his decision to send three missionaries, Gavampti, Sona, and Uttara, to Southeast Asia as early as the third century B.C.E. The 13th rock edict also indicates Asoka's wide knowledge of the outside world. He mentioned the Greek rulers of BACTRIA and GANDHARA and even claimed to have converted to his path of righteousness the rulers of remote kingdoms to the west. These rulers have been identified as Antiochus II Theos of Syria (r. 261–246 B.C.E.), Ptolemy II of Egypt (r. 285–247 B.C.E.), Antigonos Gonatas of Macedonia (r. 278–239 B.C.E.), Magas of Cyrene in North Africa (r. 300–258 B.C.E.) and Alexander of Spirus in Greece (r. 272–258 B.C.E.).

Further reading: Nikam, N. A., and McKeon, R., eds. *The Edicts of Asoka.* Chicago: University of Chicago Press, 1959; Seneviratna, A., ed. *King Asoka and Buddhism.* Seattle: Pariyatti Press, 1995; Strong, J. S. *Legend of King Asoka.* Delhi: Motilal Banarsidass, 2002.

Aston, W. G. (1841–1911) *William George Aston was one of the greatest Western scholars of Japan and Japanese history and an important translator of early Japanese.*
Born in Northern Ireland, he became an official translator to the British legation in Japan. His most important contribution to understanding of early Japanese culture was his translation of the NIHONGI, the classic document that recorded the history of the archipelago until 697 C.E. This was a major undertaking because the text was then available only in early Chinese characters and early Japanese characters adapted from Chinese.

Asuka-dera The Asuka-dera, also known as the Hokoji, is the oldest recorded monumental religious structure in Japan. The Buddhist temple and monastery constructed at Asuka, the capital of the YAMATO state of Japan from 593 C.E., was built by order of Soga-na-Umako, the power behind the throne of Empress Suiko (r. 592–628).

In 593 C.E., the capital of Yamato had moved to Asuka in the southern Nara Basin on western Honshu Island. After the establishment of the Sui dynasty in China (581 C.E.), the states of Korea and Japan paid tribute to the Chinese court, and Japan in particular underwent a cultural metamorphosis known as the Asuka enlightenment. This saw the acceptance from mainland Asia of BUDDHISM and the introduction of Korean specialists in the construction of Buddhist structures based on Chinese models. During the period of civil strife that led up to Suiko's enthronement, Soga-na-Umako had called on the Buddha for support and protection at a time when Buddhist priests were valued for their powers of divination and miracle working. He promised at that time that, if politically successful, he would have a Buddhist temple constructed. Thus the Asuka-dera was conceived.

The NIHONGI, a Japanese historical text dating to 720 C.E., recorded the details of its construction. The first step was to choose an auspicious location, which was the house of a shaman, or magician. After his residence was removed in 588, construction commenced in 592 and was completed four months later. The historic records recount the temple's fine wall hangings and the bronze image of the Buddha, both of which were put in place before the temple was dedicated in 606. The shrine was lavishly patronized by the court until the palace moved farther north in the Nara Basin; the temple was badly damaged by fire in 1196.

Excavations in 1956–57 provided the plan of the principal buildings. The central court, or *garan*, within a surrounding wall, incorporated cloisters and the pagoda for housing a relic of the Buddha, as well as three symmetrically placed *kondo*, or halls, which had been gilded. The placement of these three halls to house statues and paintings of deities is unique in Japan. The central *kondo* and the pagoda were raised on square-cut stones; the other two stood on two levels of small stone foundations. A lecture hall lay beyond the northern cloister, together with a library for storing sacred texts and a bell tower.

asura In Indian mythology, an *asura* was a demon. Such creatures became an important part of the imagery of ANGKOR in Cambodia. An *asura* with a broken spear, indicating his defeat, can be seen on an early relief at the BAKONG temple. A multiple-headed *asura* also appears on the famous relief of ANGKOR WAT showing the CHURNING OF THE OCEAN OF MILK to obtain the elixir of immortality, or AMRITA. The same site also contains the relief of an *asura* locked in battle with a monkey in a scene of the Battle of Lanka, a story derived from the Indian epic the *Ramayana*. Perhaps the best known of all such images, however, are those at the entrance gates to ANGKOR THOM, where 54 statues are seen holding a multiple-headed divine snake known as a *naga*.

Atranjikhera   Atranjikhera is a prehistoric and historic settlement with a long period of occupation, on the bank of the Kali Nadi River, a tributary of the Ganges (Ganga), in northern India. The site was first identified by SIR ALEXANDER CUNNINGHAM in 1862, while he was tracing the route of the seventh-century Chinese pilgrim XUAN-ZANG. Its importance lies in the results of excavations that began in 1962, which revealed that the site was occupied from about 1200 B.C.E. to at least the third century C.E.

Spanning the prehistoric into the period of the early MAHAJANAPADAS, or states, in this region, the extensive remains of material culture reveal how iron smelting and the local forging of artifacts contributed to increasing settlement size and social complexity. The early use of iron belonged to Period III (1200–600 B.C.E.), and the output included spears, knives, and tongs, which, in addition to the presence of slag, also indicate local iron working. Iron tools would have facilitated the clearance of dense vegetation and the establishment of fields for the cultivation of rice, wheat, and barley. Domestic cattle were also kept.

Between 600 and 350 B.C.E., the period that saw the rise of the mahajanapadas, further advances were made in the manufacture of iron plowshares, hoes, and sickles. The recovery of unlined wells also indicates the possibility of IRRIGATION. The growth of city life up to the first century C.E. encompassed the construction of defensive walls within which lay substantial houses of fired bricks, granaries, a drainage system, and SEALS and coins of the KUSHAN empire. Few sites illustrate so clearly the increasing forces of social complexity during this period in the Ganges (Ganga) Valley.

Avalokitesvara   Avalokitesvara is one of the most important of the Buddhist BODHISATTVAS, beings who seek *bodhi,* or enlightenment. They form a vital component in the Mahayana school of BUDDHISM. Avalokitesvara is a metaphysical creation originating in the Buddha's expression of compassion. The precise meaning of the name is hard to express in English, but it involves the notion of the Lord of Compassion. *Avalok* in SANSKRIT means "to look out on," while *isvara* means "lord." Avalokitesvara came to command a preeminent position in Mahayana Buddhist worship as a being with all the qualities of a world savior, given the name Samanatamukha, meaning "omnipresent." Some texts even make it clear that he was regarded as being supreme over the Buddhas. His worship spread widely through the Buddhist world, including China, Japan, Tibet, Sri Lanka, and Southeast Asia.

See also MAHAYANA BUDDHISM.

Avanti   Avanti is described in Buddhist texts as one of the 16 MAHAJANAPADAS, or great states, that struggled for supremacy before the establishment of the Indian MAURYA EMPIRE (325 B.C.E.), with its capital at UJJAIN.

Ayaz-kala   Ayaz-kala is a major settlement in Khwarizm (Chorasmia), the land dominated by the Amu Dar'ya River south of the Aral Sea. Little is known of the internal history of this agriculturally rich area, with widespread IRRIGATION works. It was intermittently taken by the Sassanians and, on other occasions, strongly under the influence first of the KUSHANS, then of the HEPHTHALITE HUNS. During the fifth to seventh centuries, Ayaz-kala included a palace of the ruler of Khwarizm, a strongly walled fort, and a residential area.

Ay Khanum   Ay Khanum is an ancient Greek city occupying a naturally defended site at the junction of the Amu Dar'ya and Kokcha Rivers in northern Afghanistan. It was possibly founded in about 330 B.C.E. by ALEXANDER THE GREAT or a ruler of the early Seleucid empire and grew to be a major center under the Seleucids. Ay Khanum in Turkish means "Lady Moon" and is the name of the local village. Its original name is not known for certain, but it was probably the city known as Alexandria Oxiana, which is described in the *Geography* of Ptolemy (second century C.E.). An alternative name is Eucratidia, after King Eucratides, who is known to have ruled there in the second century B.C.E. The city was ideally placed to offer defense against any group attempting to enter BACTRIA from the northeast.

The names of BACTRIAN GREEKS who once lived in this city have survived in graffiti and inscriptions. Some family names suggest an origin in Asia Minor, but others are typical of Greece itself and of Macedonia. The settlers clearly planned for a long stay: The stone for some of the columns was quarried 50 kilometers (30 mi.) to the southwest. The major buildings were constructed of blocks of stone joined with metal dowel pins sealed with lead. Ay Khanum was a capital city, and some of the Greeks living there would have served in the administration, while others would have been provided with agricultural land. Other occupants of the city, again as indicated by family names surviving as graffiti, were native Bactrians. Greek, however, was the official language, and there is compelling evidence for regular contact with the Greek homeland. Thus Clearchus of Soli visited Ay Khanum when traveling to India about 275 B.C.E. and commissioned an inscription repeating the maxims for leading a good and worthy life, which were to be found at Delphi in Greece.

CITY PLAN

Ay Khanum has a triangular form dictated by the location of the two rivers. It is entirely walled in mud brick, with particularly massive defenses on the weak northeastern portion that lacks the precipitous river banks. An acropolis on the southeast corner was chosen as the site of the citadel. A road aligned with the northern gate bisected the city, which measures 1,800 by 1,500 meters (5,940 by

4,950 ft.). The upper section contains the citadel; the lower incorporates a large palace, a royal mausoleum, a gymnasium, and a sanctuary temple. A Greek theater lies adjacent to the main road. The palace dominates the lower part of the city and covers an area of 350 by 250 meters (1,155 by 825 ft.). It has a huge courtyard surrounded by a portico whose columns have Corinthian-style capitals. Doric columns surround a smaller court in the palace proper.

EXCAVATIONS

Excavations have revealed an audience hall, residences with kitchens and bathrooms, and a treasury. The excavators recovered a large assemblage of treasure in this last structure, including items of carnelian, agate, rubies, TURQUOISE, and pearls. The massive gymnasium would have fulfilled both educational and recreational needs. It is 350 meters long and comprises a courtyard surrounded by rooms on all sides. The theater is a fascinating structure, modeled on the classical Greek antecedents, with an audience capacity of about 5,000. Unusually, it has a royal box, again emphasizing the role of Ay Khanum as a capital city. There was also an arsenal, supporting the military function of such foundations.

Investigation of the houses revealed considerable opulence among the wealthier members of the community. Their houses were, for example, equipped with a suite of bathrooms with mosaic floors and plastered walls. The dead were interred in a cemetery beyond the city walls, but luminaries were buried within the city in temple mausolea, one of which received the remains of one Kineas, recorded as a founder of the city. The coins minted at Ay Khanum reveal that several Greek gods were worshiped, including Zeus, Apollo, and Athena. Other evidence of close relations with the West is seen in a silver medallion bearing an image of the goddess Cybele on a chariot, probably of Syrian origin, and a terra-cotta mold for manufacturing statuettes of the goddess of Demeter. Both date to the third century B.C.E.

The extensive excavations at this site also produced artifacts revealing the everyday activities of the inhabitants. The houses were equipped with milling stones of pure Greek design. There were also ink wells and wine presses, and the gymnasium had a Greek-style sundial. Statuary closely followed the Greek tradition, and ivory was carved into furniture decorations after Western models. The many bronze coins that have been discovered suggest that Ay Khanum flourished for two centuries until about 145 B.C.E., when it was abandoned and burned to the ground.

Aymonier, Étienne (1844–1929) *Étienne (E.) Aymonier, an official in the French administration in Cambodia, traveled over much of Cambodia and Thailand, recording monuments and inscriptions.*
In 1900, Aymonier published his findings in *Le Cambodge* in three volumes. These contain an inventory of all the known sites, illustrated with maps and plans. Because he was an epigrapher, he translated many of the inscriptions he found, with commentaries on their historic relevance. He was also interested in ethnography, and some of his illustrations are important records of rural Cambodian life at the end of the 19th century.
See also ANGKOR.

Ayodhya Ayodhya is a famous site, described in the Indian epic the *Ramayana* as the capital of the hero Rama himself. Excavations of this high and substantial mound have revealed a late prehistoric occupation period, dating around 700 B.C.E., in which houses were made of mud brick. Occupation continued into the historic period, during which houses were now made of fired bricks. There is a lacuna in occupation between about 400 and 1000 C.E., but this may represent limited archaeological sampling, because it is recorded that two Chinese monks, XUANZANG and FAXIAN, visited the site during those centuries. It has recently seen much friction between Hindus and Muslims over the sanctity of their respective temples.

B

Bactria Bactria is the name of a country lying between the Hindu Kush and the Amu Dar'ya River in northern Afghanistan. Strategically placed on the ancient SILK ROAD that linked Rome with India and China, the country underwent many changes in political fortunes over the centuries. It was the conduit, for example, for the transmission of Greek art in the formation of the Gandharan school from the early third century B.C.E. Beginning as a satrap of the Persian empire, it was later conquered by ALEXANDER THE GREAT during his eastern campaign in 327 B.C.E. Thereafter it was a component of the Seleucid empire but assumed independence under King Euthydemus in the late third century B.C.E. It was later conquered by the KUSHANS, Guptas, and HEPHTHALITE HUNS.

See also GANDHARA.

Further reading: Rhie, M. M. *Later Han, Three Kingdoms and Western Chin in China and Bactria to Shan-shan.* Leiden: Brill, 1999; Sarianidi, V. I. *The Golden Hoard of Bactria: From the Tillya-tepe Excavations in Northern Afghanistan.* New York: H. N. Abrams; Leningrad: Aurora Art Publishers, 1985; Sims-Williams, N., and Cribb, J. "A New Bactrian Inscription of Kanishka the Great," *Silk Road Art and Archaeology* 4 (1998): 75–142.

Bactrian Greeks The study of the Bactrian Greeks was initiated in 1738 with the publication of a book in Saint Petersburg by Theophil Bayer (1694–1738). His study was based on the historic accounts of the Greeks in Asia, as well as on a single coin of the Bactrian Greek king Eucratides. Excavations reveal a vigorous episode of Greek colonization, including the minting of Greek coins, staging of Greek plays, carving of statues in Greek style, and construction of temples for the worship of Zeus and Athena. The power of the Seleucid empire, based in Syria and founded by King SELEUCUS I NICATOR in about 305 B.C.E., was waning by the mid-third century B.C.E. It was then that Diodotus, the satrap of the Seleucid province of Bactria-Sogdiana, declared independence and had himself crowned king of an independent state. SOGDIANA soon thereafter seceded from BACTRIA and maintained its deeply imbued Seleucid culture. Bactria, however, which lies to the north of the Hindu Kush and is centered on the upper Amu Dar'ya River, remained strongly Hellenized. Its first three kings after independence were Diodotus I, Diodotus II, and Euthydemus I. The establishment of IRRIGATION works greatly expanded the agricultural wealth of the kingdom, which issued its own COINAGE and engaged in widespread trading. Euthydemus was sufficiently powerful to withstand an attempt by the Seleucid king Antiochus III to retake Bactria. King Demetrius, the son of Euthydemus, expanded the Graeco-Bactrian kingdom south of the Hindu Kush into regions known as Arachosia and Drangiana (modern Afghanistan). Eucratides (171–145 B.C.E.) succeeded Demetrius and invaded northern Pakistan. This resulted in the foundation of the city of SIRKAP at TAXILA (modern Pakistan), which follows Greek principles of town planning, and the construction of the Greek temple of Jandial just north of the main northern entrance to the city. The best-documented city of this period, however, is AY KHANUM on the upper Amu Dar'ya River in Afghanistan. Excavations there have uncovered the king's sumptuous palace, as well as a Greek theater, gymnasium, and temples. Other major cities include CHARSADA, BEGRAM, and TERMEZ.

BACTRIAN GREEK STATES

A series of Greek states was founded by petty kings in the northwest of the subcontinent apart from Taxila. Their coinage in gold and silver has provided the names of at least 30 kings, but little else is known about them. Menander (150–135 B.C.E.) is recorded as having adopted BUDDHISM, and Apollodotus led a military expedition against Gujarat. Some Indian sources claim that the Bactrian Greeks campaigned deep into the Ganges (Ganga) Valley. The Bactrian Greeks, however, swallowed too much territory over too wide an area for the maintenance of central control. While they lost their grip north of the Hindu Kush during the second century B.C.E., the area south of this mountain range fragmented into many small and competing states and, according to the numismatic evidence, more than 30 named kings, the last of whom, Strato, was ruling in about 10 C.E.

EVIDENCE FROM BACTRIAN COINAGE

In the absence of even the basic historic references to the shadowy history of the Bactrian Greek rulers, the information must be derived from archaeology and the coin issues. A detailed study of the latter has furnished the names of rulers who can be placed into a reasonable sequence, and their distribution provides some evidence for the centers from which successive kings governed. The earliest examples are square coins bearing the name of ALEXANDER THE GREAT. Bactria has furnished most examples of coins minted by Seleucus. The nature of the coins allows the identification of certain historic events, such as the establishment of King Diodotus of Bactria against Antiochus II as the power of the Seleucids waned in the east. His son, Euthydemus, who was born in Ionia and was confirmed in his rule after being defeated in battle by Antiochus II, succeeded Diodotus as ruler of Bactria. His coins are distributed into Pakistan and provide evidence for an expansion of Bactrian Greek rule into this region during his later years and the subsequent rule of his son, Demetrius, who was described by the Greek historian Strabo (about 64 B.C.E.–23 C.E.) as a conqueror of India, and by the Roman author Justin (third century C.E.) as the king of India. From the middle of the second century B.C.E., Bactrian power was on the wane, until it was extinguished as an independent entity by steppe nomad attacks, not the least from the Yuezhi. The year 145 B.C.E. is generally accepted as the terminal date for Greek rule in Bactria.

Badami Badami was the early capital of the CHALUKYA DYNASTY of India. It is located in the upper reaches of the Malprabha River in Karnataka state. Cave shrines dedicated to SIVA or Vishnu were richly ornamented with images of the Hindu gods. Cave 4 bears an inscription indicating that it was constructed in or about the year 578 C.E. There is also shrine of the Jain religion. The Malegitti-Shivalaya is a freestanding stone temple of early Chalukyan date, dedicated, as the name indicates, to the god Siva.

Bagh The site of Bagh is located in the valley of a tributary of the Narmada River in central India. It is notable for a series of caves converted into Buddhist monasteries in the sandstone bluff overlooking the river. The style of wall paintings in the caves relates this site to the same tradition as the AJANTA caves, which date from the second century B.C.E. There are nine caves at Bagh in all; Cave 2 is particularly interesting, with a large occupation hall surrounded by 20 individual cells for the monks. Each cell had a niche in the wall for a lamp. The complex included also a stupa and a shrine for worship. The third cave revealed an impressive number of wall paintings in the monks' cells, including images of the Buddha and BODHISATTVAS.

See also BUDDHISM.

Bairat Bairat is a Buddhist site in India dating to the period of ASOKA, king of the MAURYA EMPIRE (268–235 B.C.E.), although its origins lie in the preceding Iron Age. It is located north of Jaipur in Rajasthan and is renowned for the presence of two of Asoka's inscriptions, one of which is directed to the Buddhist communion, or *sangha*. The inscriptions were discovered in 1837 and 1871. One is in poor condition and cannot be fully translated. The other, located at Bijak Pahar (Inscription Hill), near the town of Bairat, records the devotion of Asoka to BUDDHISM. It also mentions seven specific Buddhist texts and is thought to be the only Asokan inscription that specifically names the Buddha.

The architectural remains include a monastery and a sanctuary, both excavated during the 1930s. A stupa stood in the center of the sanctuary, surrounded by an inner circle of wooden columns and an outer circle of brick, to form an ambulatory. There was almost certainly once an Asokan column at the site, for fragments of polished Chunar sandstone have been found. The ruins of the monastery held a hoard of coins, showing that the site was still occupied during the first century C.E.

Bakheng The Phnom Bakheng is a 60-meter (200-ft.)-high hill visible for miles around, located in the center of ANGKOR in Cambodia. It was a strategic fortress during the period of the Khmer Rouge (1975–78), as it affords distant views in every direction. King YASHOVARMAN I chose it as the location for his state temple, known as the Bakheng. It was consecrated only a year or two before the king died in 910 C.E. The temple was reached after crossing a moat and entrance pavilion, passing two stone lion guards, and ascending a steep stone stairway. The temple rose more than 14 meters (46 ft.) in height, incorporating six levels. The first five each support 12 shrines, and the uppermost platform has a central and four subsidiary shrines. These numbers have cosmological significance, for when the 60 shrines are combined with a further 44 that ring the base of the pyramid and the four subsidiary buildings on the top, the sum is 108, a figure of deep symbolic meaning. Jean Filliozat has pointed out that only 33 of these are visible when viewed from the center of any side of the monument, the number of gods in Indra's heaven. Dividing the 108 towers by 4 gives 27, the phases of the lunar cycle. The 12 towers on each level may represent the 12-year cycle of Jupiter. Paul Wheatley has explored this symbolism: "The 12 year cycle of Jupiter in multiples of five was used as a dating era from early in the fifth century A.D. Thus, while in elevation, the Bakheng was a plastic representation of MOUNT MERU, the axis of the universe, the kingdom, and the capital; in plan it constituted an astronomical calendar in stone, depicting from each of the four cardinal directions the positions and paths of the planets in the great Indian conception of cyclic time."

Bakong In 881 C.E., King INDRAVARMAN consecrated his state temple, now known as the Bakong, at HARIHAR-ALAYA, southeast of ANGKOR in Cambodia. As the contemporary INDRATATAKA does, this monument represents a quantum change in monumentality. In the words of a contemporary inscription: "In 881, the king, like a god, dispenser of riches, has erected a lingam named Indresvara, here." There are several novel features of this monument apart from its great size. The walls of the uppermost platform retain damaged reliefs, which must once have been of outstanding quality. One shows a battle between gods and demons; another incorporates goddesses. There are numerous subsidiary shrines between the two surrounding moats, which were probably constructed by high court officials. These moats are very large and had a capacity of almost a million cubic meters of water. Steps give access to the water of the innermost one. Four avenues radiate out from the moated area on the cardinal points of the compass, one of which links the temple with the Indratataka reservoir 600 meters (1,980 ft.) to the north.

The name Indresvara combines that of the king with the god Siva, indicating a submergence of the king within the deity into a single object of devotion. The text proceeds: "Here, in the court of Indravarman, causing joy to those who behold it and unreserved wonder of the celestial builder, he erected eight lingams, named by royal practice after the eight elements of Siva: earth, wind, fire, the Moon, Sun, water, ether and the sacrificer." The central temple pyramid, faced with large sandstone blocks, comprises five platforms, the uppermost rising 14 meters (46 ft.) above ground level. The shrine, which formerly housed the god Indresvara, has not survived, and a later temple has taken its place. Eight small sanctuaries placed uniformly around the base of the pyramid probably

acknowledged male and female ancestors of Indravarman, for the eastern set incorporates male figures on exterior niches, but the western ones have females.

Baksei Chamkrong This temple at ANGKOR in Cambodia was built during the reign of Harshavarman I (c. 910–922 C.E.) and dedicated to his parents. On his return to rule at Angkor, RAJENDRAVARMAN (944–968 C.E.) restored it and dedicated new statues there in 948. It lies on the northern side of the Phnom BAKHENG and has four tiers of laterite that support a brick temple. The foundation inscription describes a golden image of Siva within. B.-P. Groslier excavated an extensive area in front of the temple during the 1960s and reported the presence of prehistoric Iron Age occupation. This was confirmed in 2001, when a further excavation encountered first a brick wall and associated floor thought to antedate the temple foundation and the clay furnaces dating to the Iron Age (c. 500 B.C.E.–400 C.E.).

Balakot Balakot is a small site of the INDUS VALLEY CIVILIZATION, located on Sonmiani Bay in southern Baluchistan, an area overlapping parts of eastern Iran and southeast Pakistan. The site was a center for the production of ceramic vessels and figurines and the manufacture of shell jewelry. The cultural deposits, which rise to a height of 10 meters (33 ft.), fall into two distinct periods. The basal layers represent a variant of the AMRI-NAL early Harappan cultural phase (c. 3200–2600 B.C.E.). They have yielded LAPIS LAZULI beads, evidence for copper metallurgy, chert harvesting knives, and the bones of cattle, sheep, and goat. Houses were constructed of mud brick.

Radiocarbon dates suggest that the second major phase, which belongs to the mature Indus civilization, commenced about 2500 B.C.E. As in many other Indus settlements, there were two sections. Of these, the western is the higher. Excavations in 1973–76 revealed house construction in mud brick, with dwellings equipped with drains of fired brick and, on at least one occasion, a bathroom. Houses were laid out with streets running on a grid pattern oriented to the cardinal points of the compass. While it is likely that both the western and eastern sections of the site were walled separately, the excavations did not produce any evidence.

Typical Indus artifacts are spear- and arrowheads, gaming pieces, and steatite SEALS bearing the impression of a unicorn. The locally manufactured shell jewelry made use of the local bivalve *Meretrix*. Balakot's coastal location might well have given the inhabitants the opportunity to feed their shell ornaments into a wide-ranging trade network.

Balitung (r. c. 901–910 C.E.) *Balitung was king of central Java, in Indonesia, where most of his 31 inscriptions* *have been found, but he also exercised authority over the eastern part of the island.*

He was entitled Sri Maharaja on his inscriptions. These were largely concerned with taxation and the dedication of surpluses to the maintenance of a temple foundation, the provision of tax exemptions for villages or individuals, and the settlement of ownership disputes. In that they mention the names of officials charged with carrying out the king's wishes and the ceremonies or payments that accompanied land settlements, they provide much incidental information on social issues. Large stone inscriptions of the reign of Balitung were set up as a permanent statement, but portable copper inscriptions also recorded his enactments. Since archaeology is virtually silent on this period of Javanese history, these texts are an unparalleled source of information on the reign of this king.

Balkh   Balkh is a settlement strategically placed north of the Hindu Kush range and south of the Amu Dar'ya River and was an important staging post on the ancient SILK ROAD that linked Rome with India and China. It was occupied by or under the control of most of the major powers that successively controlled this region, including the Sasanid dynasty, whose COINAGE was minted there under the title Bahlo, their name for the city. There were also periods of BACTRIAN GREEK, Mauryan, SAKA, and KUSHAN occupation. When XUANZANG, the Chinese Buddhist pilgrim, visited BACTRIA in the seventh century C.E., he found that Balkh, the capital, was occupied by a sizable population of Buddhist monks. There are many early Buddhist foundations in the vicinity of the city, making Balkh one of the most westerly points of Buddhist expansion. One of these, the stupa known as Tope y-Rustam, is probably the same monument described by Xuanzang as Navasangharama.

See also BUDDHISM.

Balu   Balu is a small site of the INDUS VALLEY CIVILIZATION, located west of the upper reaches of the Jamuna River in India. It is thus one of the most easterly Harappan sites. It covers an area of 200 by 80 meters (660 by 264 ft.), and excavations have revealed three phases of occupation that cover the sequence of the Early, Mature, and Late Indus periods. The site was surrounded by a wall of mud brick, within which the houses were laid along streets conforming to a grid pattern. The material culture recovered includes typical artifacts of this civilization, including steatite beads, ceramics, and copper implements.

Bamboo Annals   The *Zhushu Jinian* (*Bamboo Annals*), are a set of strips of bamboo recovered from the tomb of King Xiang of Wei at Shanbiaozhen in China in 279 C.E. Long segments cut from a straight stem of bamboo were tied together with silk cords. Each strip contains 40 graphs of Chinese script, documents placed in the royal

tomb in 296 B.C.E. Such documents on BAMBOO SLIPS are a rich source of historic information, but given the fact that it is 1,700 years since this set was exhumed, and the originals are long since lost, questions have been raised as to its authenticity. One method of testing this issue is to seek incidents or events found in other sources. In the case of the *Bamboo Annals*, this test has been passed with the discovery of the inscribed text on the Xi Jia *pan*, a bronze vessel cast in the middle of the WESTERN ZHOU dynasty (late ninth century B.C.E.). Both it and the annals describe in some detail the same military campaign waged by Jifu against the Xianyun people in the fifth year of the reign of King Xuan. The Ban *gui*, another bronze vessel, was inscribed with a text describing an attack on the eastern countries by the duke of Mao, who commanded by the Zhou king, included infantry, chariots, and halberd men in his army. This campaign is also mentioned in the *Bamboo Annals*.

The annals may thus be added to the corpus of vital historic documents describing the Shang and Zhou dynasties. They include descriptions of court activities, royal progresses, wars, obituaries of leading figures, and records of harvests and of portents. One section in particular describes the fall of the Shang dynasty at the hands of KING WU of Zhou and recounts how the king survived this major event in early Chinese history by only two years.

See also SHANG STATE.

bamboo slips   Before the invention of paper in about 105 C.E. during the HAN DYNASTY, Chinese books were written on long strips of bamboo, cut lengthwise from the stem, polished, and then inscribed on the interior surface. The slips were then strung together with silk cords and could be rolled up for storage. A graph used to designate such books is found on the Shang ORACLE BONES. The texts often contain information about important events and everyday life. Those scribes in charge of the bamboo archives were described as *zuo ce; ce* is the word for the slips themselves. The word for *ce* is depicted as a set of vertical strokes linked by two horizontal lines, the former representing the bamboo and the latter the silk cords. Most of the bamboo-slip archives were found in southern China, where bamboo flourishes. Wood was also used as a medium for record keeping.

EARLIEST EVIDENCE FOR BAMBOO SLIPS

Although no bamboo slips have been found that belong to the WESTERN ZHOU DYNASTY, it is known that they existed. A bronze *jia,* or vessel, from a hoard found at Zhuangbai, dating to about 975 B.C.E., mentions a person named Zhe and his title, *zuoce,* "maker of strips." He was a court scribe. In 825 B.C.E., the Song *gui,* an inscribed bronze vessel, was cast to commemorate a court appointment under King Xuan (r. 827–782 B.C.E.). The text describes in detail the ceremonial investiture of Song to supervise warehouses, for which he was awarded a black embroidered jacket and other choice gifts from the sovereign. It then describes how he "suspended the strips from his jacket in order to withdraw." It seems that a copy of the document appointing him, written with a brush on the bamboo slips, was presented to him during the audience.

The earliest known bamboo slips are from a tomb at Leigudun in the state of Zeng and date to 433 B.C.E. This tomb was that of the marquis of Zeng, and it was richly furnished with grave goods. The coffin was made of black lacquered wood, colored with designs in gold and red. Golden vessels were also found, together with a fine golden ladle with holes to permit its use as a strainer. The bamboo-slip inventory of the contents for this tomb runs to 6,600 entries and includes a list of 43 chariots.

DISCOVERIES OF LATER SLIPS

Tombs of the CHU state are particularly abundant and date to the WARRING STATES PERIOD (475–221 B.C.E.). The Slips fall into three categories: historic texts, inventories of tomb offerings, and ritual documents. A set of slips from a tomb at Wanshan sets out prayers offered during the occupant's illness and shows Dao Gu offering prayers to the ancestors and sacrificing cattle and sheep. The tomb of Fan Chi at Tianxingguan likewise contained a record of the prayers offered and divinations made. Where such records name ancestors or kings of an ill man, they become important historic documents. The tomb inventories are also fascinating documents, particularly when a rich burial like Tomb 1 at MAWANGDUI, a suburb of Changsha, is found to contain such records. The records from Tomb 25 at the site of Yangtianhu near Changsha is particularly detailed. It includes the names of those who gave items to be buried with the deceased.

One of the most important discoveries of actual early texts is from the tomb of Xi, an archivist who lived during the reign of the first emperor of QIN, QIN SHIHUANGDI (221–210 B.C.E.). He was buried in Tomb 11 at Shuihudi and was accompanied by about 1,200 slips bearing historic texts that Xi might well have written himself. One document records, similarly to a diary, the events that took place, including references to the life of Xi between 306 and 217 B.C.E. It is fascinating to compare this history with the well known *Shijing*, written by SIMA QIAN a century after the event. Sometimes Sima Qian's dates for events were in error, while the Shuihudi text, known as the *Biannianji*, describes events that pass without mention in the *Shijing*. A second text found in the stomach area of the deceased, known as the *Yushu*, sets out the edicts issued by Teng. Teng was in charge of the Nanjun commandery in what had been part of the southern state of Chu. The text illuminates how the local people continued in their traditional ways despite the fact that they had been defeated by the Qin 50 years previously. Another set of slips from the tomb of Xi sets out the elements of the Qin legal system, including the rules governing the harmonization of the system of weights and measures across the new empire.

A text known as the *Fengzhenshi* contains an extraordinarily detailed account of the investigation of a robbery. It details the size of the hole made in a wall to gain access to someone's property, the type of tools used to make the access hole, the shape of the footprints of the alleged robber, and the sort of shoes he must have been wearing. These legal documents recall the earlier Chu texts from Tomb 2 at BAOSHAN, dated to 316 B.C.E. The Baoshan slips include reports on individual cases before the courts and were sealed in the tomb of a prominent legal officer of the Chu state. A second set from the same grave lists the burial offerings. One chamber contained the food for the deceased, another the objects used when traveling. A third set of offerings was used in the actual mortuary rituals, and the fourth lists the vehicles, including chariots, that took part in the burial procession.

Tomb 4 at Shuihudi in Hubei province dates to the late third century B.C.E. and yielded letters written home from two soldiers, Heifu and Jing in 223 B.C.E. They described a battle in which the Qin forces defeated rebels. A huge find of more than 5,000 slips was recovered from Tomb 1 at Yinqueshan, Shandong, in 1972. Dating to the second century B.C.E., they contain the text of the *Art of War* in 13 chapters, together with many other supplementary documents on war and politics.

Further reading: Shaughnessy, E. L. "On the authenticity of the *Bamboo Annals*," *Harvard Journal of Asiatic Studies* 46 (1986): 149–180.

Bamiyan Bamiyan, located northwest of Kabul, Afghanistan, is best known for the two colossal statues of the Buddha carved into the mountainside. One of these, standing 53 meters in height, was, until its destruction with dynamite by the Taliban rulers of Afghanistan in 2001, the tallest stone statue in the world. The site occupied a strategic position on the trade routes that were part of the ancient SILK ROAD. To the east were BEGRAM, HADDA, and TAXILA. A route over the Hindu Kush mountains to the north linked Bamiyan with BALKH and TERMEZ. XUANZANG, the Chinese scholar and pilgrim, described it in the seventh century as the seat of 10 monasteries and several thousand monks. In 727 the Korean Buddhist monk Heicho traveled to Bamiyan and, while not mentioning the giant Buddhas, noted the presence of temples and monks and the royal patronage of his faith. The presence of a powerful army produced peaceful conditions, and agriculture, particularly viticulture, flourished. The main products were sheep, horses, cotton, and wool.

THE STATUES

The complex dates between the third and seventh centuries C.E. Xuanzang said of one of the massive statues; "At the northeast of the royal city, there is at the corner of the mountains a rock statue of Buddha standing, 50 meters (165 ft.) high, a dazzling gold color and adorned with brilliant gems." The second colossus stood 38 meters (125 ft.) high. Both massive statues probably date to the end of the third century C.E.

Benjamin Rowland has described the methods whereby these statues were created. The body and the head were carved roughly from the living rock. The details were then formed with a mixture of mud and finely cut straw, before being covered in a lime plaster and gilded or painted. The larger of the two had finely detailed folds in the Buddha's robe, created by attaching ropes to wooden dowels cut into the rock before being covered in the manner described. Xuanzang also described a copper statue of the Buddha more than 30 meters (99 ft.) high, made of separate pieces welded together, as well as another stone image of the Buddha, more than 330 meters (1,089 ft.) long, lying down in the pose of attaining nirvana.

THE CAVES

Although Bamiyan is best known for these two statues, the sheer face of the cliffs into which these statues were cut also bears many cave chambers. Monks would have occupied some of these, but the walls of some are covered in paintings depicting events in the life of the Buddha. There are three groups of caves that extend over a distance of 1,300 meters (4,290 ft.). In the eastern group, 294 caves are known, as well as the lesser of the two giant Buddha statues. Fifty caves occupy the central group, and there are a further 323 caverns in the western series.

The caves have suffered severely over the years through neglect or wilful destruction, no more so than under the Taliban regime. One chamber only 35 meters (116 ft.) from the giant Buddha statue contained written records on birch bark scrolls, and the study of some others has allowed an assessment of the interior plans and nature of the wall paintings. Cave 24, for example, in the eastern group and probably of relatively early date, was embellished with outstanding paintings of the Buddha and BODHISATTVAS. The ceiling was painted with a bodhisattva associated with 14 images of the Buddha in a variety of seated positions. Stylistically, these paintings belong to the third or fourth century C.E.

In 1930 a French team found a cave that had been concealed by sand. Protected from the elements, the paintings and architecture within survived and were recorded at the time, although little now remains. It is not a large chamber, measuring only about four by four meters, and is unusual in having in the center the foundations of a stupa. Excavations uncovered the remains of stucco statues, including a male head. The holes in the cave walls for attaching such images revealed that there had formerly been as many as 12 statues. The painted decoration on part of the ceiling as found in 1930 depicted the seated Buddha with a halo. Four further

Buddhas flank him, while a woman offers him the gift of a string of pearls. Rows of small Buddha images, representing the thousand Buddhas, were painted below the main images, while rows of lotus petals were placed above. Similar multiple images of the Buddha remained in another cave that overlooked the giant eastern Buddha statue.

This treasury of Buddhist art and sculpture, described as the most magnificent in the world, has been devastated. Yet, in 1959, Arnold Toynbee wrote that, if "you look out across the valley in the moonlight, there is peace in the shadowy shapes of the Buddhas and caves."

Further reading: Klimburg, D. E. *The Kingdom of Bamiyan.* Naples/Rome: Buddhist Art and Culture of the Hindukush, 1987; Klimburg-Salter, D. E. *The Silk Route and the Diamond Path.* Los Angeles: UCLA Art Council, 1982; Ogura, R. *Bamiyan Art and Archaeological Researches on the Buddhist Cave Temples in Afghanistan: 1970–1978.* Chicago: Art Media Resources, 2001.

Banavasi Banavasi is a substantial urban complex located in Karnataka province, southern India. The massive walls were built of brick and were associated with a moat. There are many mounds containing the brick foundations of Buddhist structures of the SATAVAHANA period within the walled area, but clearly the site was already prominent during the MAURYA EMPIRE, because it was mentioned in an Asokan edict. The Chinese pilgrim XUANZANG visited the site in the seventh century and noted the presence of a Buddhist community there.

See also ASOKA; BUDDHISM.

Banawali Banawali is a site of the INDUS VALLEY CIVILIZATION, located only 200 meters (660 ft.) from the course of the now dried out SARASVATI RIVER in the Punjab. Excavations were undertaken during 1974–77, and three phases of occupation have been identified. The first dates between about 2500 and 2300 B.C.E. and includes the remains of the pre-Indus culture also found at KALIBANGAN in Rajastan and RAKHIGARHI, northwest of Delhi, and ascribed to the SOTHI-SISWAL phase of the Early Harappan culture. Excavations have revealed important aspects of this phase. A shard, for example, was decorated with the image of a canopied cart on spoked wheels, and the remains of a house of mud brick containing a series of hearths was uncovered. Ornaments were made of gold and faience, and several terra-cotta animal figurines have been found. Houses, complete with ovens, were made of mud brick and fired brick.

During the second phase, that of the classic Indus civilization (c. 2300–1700 B.C.E.), the site had two walled enclosures with a linking gateway. The layout is most unusual. While the outer walls and the moat form a roughly square enclosure covering an area of about 16 hectares (40 acres), the inner citadel is ellipsoid in plan, jutting out into the town from the southern wall. It is possible that this citadel housed the elite, while artisans, merchants, and other members of the community at large occupied the lower town. Excavations in the citadel have uncovered the foundations of mud-brick houses and a grid street system.

The lower town was divided into city blocks by roads and lanes. Their layout approximately followed a grid plan, although some crossroads, such as the one in front of the main northern entrance to the citadel, had roads entering it from the southeast and southwest. Intimate details of life in this area are afforded by the excavation of the mud-brick houses, which include living and storage rooms, kitchens with the remains of scorched barley, and latrines. Floors were of beaten earth, and ceramic containers were found on them, while the roofs were made of wooden beams and reeds. Rooms were grouped around courtyards and were clearly occupied by people of substance. One house complex might have belonged to a wealthy merchant, for it yielded many SEALS and weights. Another belonged to a jeweler; the excavated material included beads of LAPIS LAZULI, gold, and etched carnelian; tiny weights; and a stone that had been used for testing the purity of gold, streaked with the samples taken. Some weights were minute; the lightest was only 0.072 gram (0.0025 oz.). One structure might well have been a temple, for it had an unusual apsidal shape not found in dwellings.

The subsistence base of the inhabitants included intensive agriculture, seen in the recovery of a terra-cotta model of a plowshare. The elements of a typical Indus material culture—including weights, seals, and sealings; a wide range of beads in agate, lapiz lazuli, carnelian, FAIENCE, and ivory; and bronze razors, chisels, fishhooks, bangles, and rings—all point to occupation during the heyday of this civilization.

Phase III represents the final occupation of Banawali and dates from about 1700–1500 B.C.E. Town planning was no longer in evidence. Houses were now made of clay. There was a different ceramic tradition, but the local manufacture of jewelry continued.

Ban Biao (Pan Piao) (3–54 C.E.) *Ban Biao was a historian who began the compilation of the* Hanshu *(History of the Former Han).*
In this endeavor, he followed in the footsteps of SIMA QIAN, author of the SHIJI (*Records of the Grand Historian*), which covered Chinese history from the earliest beginnings to 100 B.C.E. Ban Biao continued the history of China to cover the second century of the HAN DYNASTY (see HANSHU). His work was continued by his son, BAN GU, and ultimately by Ban Gu's daughters.

Ban Don Ta Phet   This Iron Age cemetery is located in Kanchanaburi province of Central Thailand and has been excavated by Ian Glover. The burials are Hanshu, particularly notable for the evidence they provide for early contact between India and the people of Southeast Asia. The inhabitants of the region had easy access to the Three Pagodas Pass, which links the Chao Phraya Valley with the Bay of Bengal and India. The radiocarbon dates were determined on the basis of rice temper recovered from pottery vessels. The calibrated age ranges of four samples dated at Oxford, England, are 640–160 B.C.E., 670–190 B.C.E., 470–80 B.C.E., and 500–100 B.C.E. Taken in conjunction, these provide a mean range of 390–360 B.C.E., although the material culture of the site would be better placed two centuries later. Exotic imports were employed in mortuary rituals. The dead were interred in a cemetery bounded by a ditch, in association with carnelian, agate, glass, and bronze artifacts, all of which could have originated in India. The etched carnelian and agate beads, for example, fall within the Indian repertoire, while the origin of the glass may also be traced to South Asia. The bronze bowls have a very high tin content and were turned to an exceeding thinness on a lathe. They were decorated with scenes of women and animals. Some of the latter are exotic to Southeast Asia, but there was already a tradition of casting such high-tin bronzes in India. About 30 of the bronze bowls were finished on the inside base with a knob or boss in the center of a series of concentric circles. This feature of Indian stone and ceramic vessels provides supporting evidence for their Indian origin. The recovery of a carnelian lion with one of the burials not only points without doubt to an Indian origin, but it also provides evidence for the spread of BUDDHISM, for the Buddha was often depicted during that period in the form of a lion.

There is also much evidence for the advancement of local technological skills, particularly in the area of iron forging, for many billhooks and spears, bent or destroyed as part of the mortuary ritual, were incorporated with the dead. The recovery of a double-headed animal ornament in jade also points to exchange with the Iron Age communities of coastal Vietnam, the center for the production of these unusual ornaments. Local bronze casting also reached specialist levels, with, for example, the production of a bronze birdcage under a fighting cockerel.

Bangarh   Bangarh is a walled city site located north of the lower Ganges (Ganga) River in India, occupied from prehistoric times to the medieval period. Formerly known as Banapura, it was dominated by a large citadel covering an area of about 25 hectares (63 acres). Excavations in 1938–41 showed that the site was founded during the period of NORTHERN BLACK POLISHED WARE, dated by the presence of this style of pottery and both cast and punch-marked coins. The second occupation phase is dated to the later first millennium B.C.E. on the basis of sealings inscribed with early BRAHMI characters. The third phase includes house remains belonging to the GUPTA EMPIRE period, but the site continued in occupation until the medieval period.

Ban Gu (Pan Ku) (32–92 C.E.) *Ban Gu was a prominent member of a distinguished family of historians in China.* His father, BAN BIAO, commenced compiling the *HANSHU (History of the Former Han)*, a work Ban Gu continued. This text was the model for all future dynastic histories of China. The *History of the Later Han Dynasty* recorded the details of his life and work, which was devoted exclusively to historic scholarship. Resolved to continue his father's ambitious project, he worked on it privately. However, an informant sent a letter to the emperor Mingdi describing Ban Gu's activities, and he was arrested and incarcerated for possible sedition, while his library was impounded. His brother probably saved his life by explaining to the emperor Ban Gu's intention of writing a history of the dynasty and showing Mingdi his writings. The emperor was pleased with this information and appointed Ban Gu an official historian. Twenty years of research, in which he called on oral traditions and available documents, resulted in a history that spanned the reigns of Gaozu to the WANG MANG interregnum that ended in 23 C.E.

Ban Gu was also the author of the *BOHU TONG (Discourses in the White Tiger Hall)*. In this text, he recorded the conversations between the emperor Zhang (r. 75–88 C.E.) and his advisers on the Confucian issue of the relationship between the ruler and his subjects. After the preference for LEGALISM under the QIN dynasty and for TAOISM among the earlier Han rulers, Confucianism had a renaissance during and after the reign of Han WUDI. In this work, Ban Gu described the vital Confucian ethic of complementarity, whereby the ruler heeds the advice of his ministers for the good of the people.

Ban Khu Muang This DVARAVATI CIVILIZATION city is located in central Thailand, less than two kilometers from the Chao Phraya River. It covers an area of 650 by 750 meters (2,145 by 2,475 ft.) and incorporates many brick temple foundations. There are four phases of occupation contained within a cultural accumulation four meters (13 ft.) deep. The earliest, dated between 300 and 550 C.E., includes ceramics similar to those of the FUNAN state of the Mekong Delta. The second and third phases belong to the Dvaravati civilization and include iron spears and knives. Clay anvils indicate a local ceramic industry, for they are used to shape pottery vessels. The final phase includes late Angkorian ceramics.

Ban Non Wat Ban Non Wat is a large, moated archaeological site in the upper Mun Valley of northeast Thailand. Excavations in 2002 revealed a rare sequence of prehistoric occupation that began in the Neolithic period, approximately 2100 B.C.E., continued into the Bronze Age (1500–500 B.C.E.), and ended with Iron Age (500 B.C.E.–200 C.E.) and Historic period (200–800 C.E.) occupation. The Neolithic and Bronze Age burials revealed an unexpected level of wealth and sophistication, adding much to the understanding of the developing complexity of prehistoric societies in the region that ultimately saw the genesis of the states of CHENLA and ANGKOR.

Banteay Chmar Banteay Chmar is a huge temple mausoleum in a remote corner of northwestern Cambodia, constructed during the reign of JAYAVARMAN VII (1181–1219) to honor his son, Srindrakumaraputra, who had led a military expedition against the Chams. Four of his generals are also commemorated. The sanctuary to Arjunadeva lies to the southeast, that for Dharadevapuradeva to the northeast, Devadeva to the southwest, and Varddhanadeva to the northwest. Arjuna and Dharadevapura had died defending King Yashovarman II (1160–66) and were given high posthumous titles. The other two warriors died defending the king during a battle against the Chams and were likewise awarded a hero's funeral and high posthumous titles. The site includes first a moat and an outer walled enclosure 2.2 by 2.4 kilometers (about 1 sq. mi.) in extent, which is punctured on the eastern side by a reservoir 1.7 kilometers long and one kilometer wide. A stream fed this BARAY at its northeast corner, and water flowed into the moat at the southwest corner. The overflow then filled the moat, which runs around the outer walls. The island temple in the middle of the reservoir incorporates an oval bank in which lie four basins, two of which are curved and the other two circular. The reservoir extends by about 200 meters (660 ft.) into the eastern sector of the complex, in the center of which lies the actual temple. This extensive area between the outer wall and the moat and walls of the inner temple, which covers 448 hectares (1,120 acres), now includes only eight single-chambered shrines but presumably would have housed a considerable population.

The walls of the inner sanctum are covered in reliefs revealing scenes of battles between the Khmer and Chams. There is a naval battle and the army on the march, with leaders riding on their elephants. On one occasion, the troops stop in front of a large forest filled with monkeys. The baggage train with elephants and military supplies is depicted, and the reliefs also include APSARAS (celestial water nymphs) and an extraordinary range of gods with multiple heads and arms. A maze of shrines and passageways clusters around the central temple. An inscription states that it held an image of Srindrakumaraputra, represented as Lokesvara with the name Srindradeva. It is entirely possible that this was his funerary mausoleum.

Banteay Chmar was a temple mausoleum constructed in northwest Cambodia by Jayavarman VII of Angkor for his crown prince and for military heroes. As with other monuments of this king, who ruled from 1181 until 1219, it was embellished with huge heads carved in sandstone. *(Charles Higham)*

The site has been severely damaged by looting: In 1998 a section of wall bearing reliefs was removed by the Cambodian army for sale on the Bangkok antiquities market.

See also CHAM CIVILIZATION.

Banteay Choeu   ANGKOR in Cambodia includes many separate foundations constructed over a period of more than six centuries. Banteay Choeu may well be the oldest. From the air, a faint square enclosure is visible at the western end of the WESTERN BARAY. The water of the *baray*, or reservoir, has inundated part of the site. To the north, there is a linear dyke, which incorporates a right angle, again partially submerged. The square enclosure incorporates the temple of AK YUM, a very early example of a shrine raised on platforms of descending size. A further temple at Prei Kmeng lies toward the western limits of the enclosure. It is known that JAYAVARMAN II, founder of the kingdom of Angkor, was active in this area in the late eighth century C.E., and Banteay Choeu might have been one of his successive centers. The dykes to the north would then have constitute the *baray* to retain

water flowing from the KULEN HILLS. Excavations are necessary to obtain datable material in testing this possibility, because it has also been suggested that the site represents an unfinished *baray* rather than an early city.

Banteay Prei Nokor   Banteay Prei Nokor is a huge pre-Angokorian city located in eastern Cambodia, 40 kilometers (34 mi.) from the Mekong River. It is enclosed by an earthen wall 2.5 kilometers square (1 sq. mi.) and an outer moat. In 1936 Victor Goloubew took a series of aerial photographs of this site, in which the temples, bank, and moat stand out clearly. He also noted five reservoirs on the same axis, all outside the moat, and a road linking the site with the Mekong River to the west. Today the enclosure remains demarcated by its encircling walls and moat, while the brick shrines of Preah Theat Thom and Preah Theat Toch dominate its center. This site is particularly significant because it is thought to have been the capital of JAYAVARMAN II (c. 770–834 C.E.) before this king and his followers began their odyssey to the northwest that led to the foundation of ANGKOR. Excavations are required to pursue the possibility that it dates to this period.

Banteay Samre   The temple of Banteay Samre is often overlooked because of the attention given to its near contemporary, ANGKOR WAT. It is located just east of the EASTERN BARAY, at ANGKOR, but the absence of any inscriptions means that little is known of its origin and history. The temple is surrounded by two walled enclosures, each severed by entrance pavilions on the four sides. These *gopura*s, as well as the central shrine, were richly ornamented with reliefs. As at Angkor Wat, the scenes are largely drawn from Indian epics, including the CHURNING OF THE OCEAN OF MILK and the birth of Brahma.

Banteay Srei   Located 25 kilometers (15 mi.) northeast of ANGKOR, Banteay Srei (Citadel of the Women) is one of the most famous of all Angkorian temples because of its completeness and the beauty of its decoration. The temple, formerly known as Ishvarapura, was discovered only in 1914 and is particularly notable for its miniature

The delightful miniature temple of Banteay Srei (Citadel of the Women) lies just northeast of Angkor. It contains some of the most exquisite bas-reliefs to come from that civilization. *(Charles Higham)*

dimensions and overall decoration. The latter attracted the French writer André Malraux, who set out for Angkor in 1923 and stole some of the carvings. Fortunately, these were later retrieved, and Malraux was briefly imprisoned.

The foundation stela reveals that the temple was consecrated on 22 April 967 by Yajnyavaraha, a grandson of King Harshavarman I. He served as one of Rajendravarman's ministers and then became teacher and adviser to JAYAVARMAN V. Yajnyavaraha was a scholar and philanthropist who helped those suffering from illness, injustice, or poverty. He founded many monasteries containing statues of Siva and had reservoirs constructed as acts of merit. The king honored him with parasols of peacock feathers, golden palanquins, and other insignia of high esteem and status. A text from Banteay Srei, dating to early in the reign of JAYAVARMAN V, sets out some of the donations for functionaries of the temple, which include white rice, and established the boundaries of the estates designated to endow it. Only small parts of the original foundation survive; the temple was added to and embellished for at least three centuries after its foundation. The early brick structure can be seen today only in a wall and *gopura* (entrance pavilion). Vittorio Roveda has provided a detailed analysis of the temple's history, based largely on the decorative elements of the exterior walls. He has suggested that the eastern *gopura* was constructed in 1011 C.E. in the reign of SURYAVARMAN I. This ruler also added a pillared causeway and the western *gopura* later in his reign. Further construction followed in the 12th century, but the temple did not reach its final form, following Roveda's analysis, until the rule of King Shrindravarman in the 14th century.

Baoshan   The Baoshan cemetery, located near the CHU capital of Ying in Hubei province, China, contained five tombs of which Tomb 2 is best known through excavation. It contained the remains of Shao Tuo, a senior legal official of the Chu court, who died in 316 B.C.E. The tomb's size and contents illustrate clearly the wealth of the Chu kingdom during the period of WARRING STATES. It measures approximately 34 by 32 meters (112 by 105 ft.) and was covered by a mound 5.8 meters high and 54 meters in diameter. The central shaft descends through 14 steps of declining size to the wooden mortuary structure at the base. This set of chambers, measuring 6.3 meters square and 3.1 meters in height, was placed over a pit containing the remains of a goat and cloth woven from silk and wool. The entire wooden building was surrounded by a layer of clay to protect it from dampness and the ingress of air. Within lay the tomb chamber itself and four further rooms for placing mortuary offerings. Along with exquisite lacquerwork and bronze vessels, the most important assemblage was a series of texts written on BAMBOO SLIPS, found together with Shao Tuo's writing brush and knife for erasing errors.

Shao Tuo died at about 35 to 40 years of age and was interred in the innermost of three coffins, together with a wide range of personal goods deemed necessary for the afterlife. These included his vessels for entertaining, chariot equipment, and even a folding bed and bamboo containers that would have accompanied him on his travels around the kingdom. His inner coffin was decorated in lacquer, with images of birds and dragons depicted in vibrant colors embellished with gilt and silver. The quality of the grave offerings was very high: A footed and lidded vessel known as a *zun,* for example, was inlaid with exquisite gold and silver work. One of a pair, it contained chicken bones. A lacquer box only five centimeters (2 in.) high was decorated with a narrative scene of great detail. It shows a bureaucrat in the course of a tour, traveling by chariot. A second lidded lacquer box contained nested cups, a plate, and condiment jars. It might have been taken by Shao Tuo on his travels. The master was accompanied in his grave by figurines of his retainers more than a meter high; these individuals were fully dressed and wore wigs of real hair.

The texts were largely concerned with legal issues, although there was also an inventory of the tomb contents, as well as divinations. One set even included continuing references to his declining health. The inventory of tomb contents, found in four separate parts of the complex, included one set describing the contents of a chamber as the goods needed when traveling, suggesting that the person depicted on the lacquer box riding in a chariot might be Shao Tuo himself. Other lists described the vessels employed during the funerary rituals and others used to make sacrifices at the ancestral temple.

The texts are an invaluable source of information on the Chu legal system. The importance of maintaining a register of all adults is stated, and the penalties imposed on the local leaders who omitted young men from the list noted. There is also a poignant reference to a prisoner who escaped from the silk warehouse belonging to the royal consort and attempted to stab himself when apprehended in the street. Another text reported on a dispute over the right to use certain workers that involved Ruo, a legal official, and Jin, an aristocrat. It referred to the king of Chu as "the shining Sun."

Baphuon The Baphuon is the temple mausoleum of King UDAYADITYAVARMAN II of ANGKOR (1050–66 C.E.) in Cambodia. It lies near the center of the later city of ANGKOR THOM, just to the south of the walls of the royal palace precinct, and was described by ZHOU DAGUAN in 1297 as the tower of copper. An inscription states that the Baphuon was constructed to represent the mountain home of the gods and that it originally incorporated a golden tower containing a lingam of gold. The principal shrine has not survived, and it is possible that the stones were reemployed at a later date to construct a large image of the Buddha. The Baphuon has suffered severely from deterioration and collapse but is currently under reconstruction. It is a very large and impressive temple mausoleum, measuring 425 by 125 meters (1,402 by 412 ft.) in extent, while the central temple pyramid is 125 by 100 meters at the base. It has three levels and is particularly notable for the number of reliefs adorning some of the walls. These depict scenes from Hindu sagas, goddesses, and various animals set in individual panels.

Bara Bara is a prehistoric mound located near the headwaters of the Jamuna River in northern India, dating to between 2000 and 1600 B.C.E. Its significance lies in the pottery remains, which recall decorative motifs found on the wares from the INDUS VALLEY CIVILIZATION, such as fish, trees, and nets. The remains of mud-brick structures have also been found here. Slightly later than the Indus civilization, it might represent a rural counterpart to the major cities just after the latter went into decline.

Barabar Barabar, on the Phalgu River in northern India, is the location of Buddhist cave temples cut into the granite rock face. One dates from the reign of ASOKA, the Sudama cave temple, was cut in 252 B.C.E., and the Gopi cave belongs to the reign of Asoka's grandson, Dasaratha. The decoration on the cave walls and entrances, particularly on the LOMAS RISHI cave, imitated wooden forms.

baray Baray is a Sanskrit word for "reservoir" or "pond." *Barays* are a recurrent feature of the landscape of the kingdom of ANGKOR, in Cambodia, invariably taking a rectangular form. In certain cases their date is provided by foundation inscriptions, but most of the smaller examples are undated. They usually are components of urban and ceremonial centers, and many have an island temple in the middle; they may have symbolized the oceans encircling MOUNT MERU. Water-control measures in a region with a long dry season have prehistoric origins in Southeast Asia. At NOEN U-LOKE banks were constructed during Southeast Asia's Iron Age (200 B.C.E.–300 C.E.) to regulate and restrain the flow of water past the site. The FUNAN maritime state (150–550 C.E.) was responsible for the construction of an extensive canal network, and at its main center of ANGKOR BOREI the EASTERN BARAY covers an area of about 200 by 100 meters (660 by 330 ft.). There is a large *baray* at ISHANAPURA, a major center of the CHENLA period (550–802 C.E.), and the pre-Angkorian inscriptions record numerous reservoirs and water-control measures. BANTEAY CHOEU, west of Angkor, is located just south of a linear dyke on an east-west axis, linked with a further dyke at right angles. The rest of this feature is now submerged below the water of the later WESTERN BARAY, but in all likelihood the *baray* was used in water control.

BARAYS OF THE ANGKOR REGION

The geography of the Angkor region sees three rivers flowing south into the GREAT LAKE from the KULEN HILLS. The Banteay Choeu *baray* would have retained the water provided by the Puok River. To the east of Angkor, Indravarman had the INDRATATAKA constructed to harness the water of the Roluos River. The foundation stela of the temple of Preah Ko in 879 C.E. records, "Five days hence, I will begin digging." A second inscription states, "He made the Indratataka, mirror of his glory, like the ocean." Now dry but clearly visible from the air, this *baray* was of unprecedented size: 3,800 meters (12,540 ft.) in length and 800 meters (2,640 ft.) wide. The northern dyke and the Lolei temple in the middle of the reservoir were completed by Indravarman's successor, YASHOVARMAN I. It was the latter king who ordered the construction of the YASHODHARATATAKA, or Eastern Baray, at Angkor, the dykes of which are 7.5 by 1.8 meters (25 by 6 ft.) in extent. Inscriptions erected at each corner record this remarkable achievement, which when full would have contained more than 50 million cubic meters (1.75 billion cu. ft.) of water. The *baray* was fed by a canal linking it with the Siem Reap River, and it emptied into a canal that filled the moats of the city to the west.

The Western Baray is even larger. It was probably commenced by SURYAVARMAN I (1002–50) and completed by Udayadityavarman II (1050–66). Recent investigations reveal that it was probably built in stages, each marked by a north-south dyke as work progressed. Unlike the Eastern Baray, it was excavated below the then-ground surface. There is no doubt that the *baray* was completed at this period, for the western Mebon temple in its center has the architectural style of Udayadityavarman II's reign. This artificial island incorporates a square enclosure demarcated by a wall containing niches and decorative reliefs. Within there is a water basin with a causeway giving access to a central structure. Part of a huge bronze statue of Vishnu was found here. The Northern Baray is the last of the major reservoirs at Angkor. It was built by JAYAVARMAN VII (1181–1219). Known as the JAYATATAKA, it is 3.7 by 0.9 kilometer (2 by .5 mi.) in extent. The island in the middle housed Rajasri (NEAK PEAN), one of the most exquisite of all Angkorian temples.

BARAYS IN OTHER REGIONS

Beyond Angkor *baray*s are a feature of other major centers in Cambodia. At BANTEAY CHMAR, the outer wall of the temple complex is punctured by a reservoir 1.7 kilometers long and one kilometer wide. A stream fed this *baray* at its northeast corner, and water then flowed into the moat at the southwest corner, where ÉTIENNE AYMONIER noted the paved outlet that controlled the water level. The overflow then filled the moat running around the outer walls. There is an island temple in the center of the *baray*. The Rahal *baray* at Lingapura (KOH KER) measures 1,200 by 560 meters and was partially hewn from the rock substrate. The gigantic center of Preah Khan of Kompong Svay incorporated a *baray* 2.8 kilometers long and 750 meters wide. Where a temple complex was located on a hill, there is usually a *baray* at the base, as at PHNOM CHISOR, while *baray*s are also found at regional centers, such as PHNOM WAN, MUANG TAM, and PHIMAI in Thailand.

FUNCTION OF *BARAYS*

Despite the numerous *baray*s and some associated inscriptions, their function remains controversial. B.-P. Groslier has been prominent in arguing in favor of their central role in irrigating rice fields. He has referred to Angkor as a hydraulic city, reliant on IRRIGATION to provide sufficient rice to feed a large urban population. In his view, each successive *baray* augmented the irrigated area, and sedimentation of the system contributed to the collapse of the civilization. This view has been seriously challenged by Philip Stott, W. J. Van Liere, and Robert Acker, who argue against an irrigation theory on several grounds. The deeply incised Siem Reap River would have restricted the reticulation of water by canals. On the other hand, Christophe Pottier has recently found evidence for a canal distribution system below the *baray*s at Angkor, as well as former rice plots. However, the land available would have been insufficient to add significantly to the quantity of rice needed to sustain the population. It is also the case that no inscription relating to the *baray*s mentions irrigation, nor are there any records in available texts for disputes over the distribution of water. Yet in Sri Lanka, where *baray*s were used for irrigation, there are numerous such records. Each *baray* has a temple at the center, and there are many allusions to the religious and curative properties of the sacred water that flowed from the Kulen Hills. Again, ZHOU DAGUAN did not mention canals or the use of *baray* water for rice cultivation.

Until the possible evidence for irrigation is dated, therefore, it is considered likely that the *baray*s fulfilled a ritual and domestic purpose. The state temple mausolea were built to represent the home of the gods on MOUNT MERU, while the *baray*s and moats might represent the encircling oceans. This interpretation is supported by the clear relationship between the Neak Pean temple in the center of the Jayatataka and LAKE ANAVATAPTA. The latter is the sacred lake of BUDDHISM, located in the Himalayan region, and mythical source of four great rivers, the Ganges (Ganga), Indus, Syr Dar'ya, and Tarim. The water from each left the lake through the mouth of a horse, an ox, an elephant, and a lion. This is matched at Neak Pean, and contemporary inscriptions state that pilgrims could cross the *baray* to this temple to wash away their sins.

Bari-Kot Bari-Kot is one of a number of important Buddhist sites that has yielded examples of the Gandharan tradition of art in the Swat Valley of Afghanistan. It is probably the center named Bazira by the second-century

C.E. Greek historian Arrian, and its former name was Vajirasthana. The site is dominated by two large stupas and the remains of a *vihara* (meeting hall) and was intensively occupied during the KUSHAN period (78–200 C.E.), to judge by the many finds dating to that period identified here. The Chinese Buddhist pilgrim XUANZANG visited the site in the seventh century C.E. and described a statue of the BODHISATTVA AVALOKITESVARA.

See also GANDHARA.

Barygaza   See BROACH.

bas-reliefs

INDIA

The embellishment of temples with relief carvings has a long ancestry in India, and the practice was adopted in Southeast Asia and along the SILK ROAD probably as a result of acquaintance with Indian architectural techniques. The Great Stupa at SANCHI, for example, is surrounded by a railing incorporating four *toranas* decorated with narrative reliefs depicting events in the life of the Buddha. Some scenes also provide illuminating depictions of war. In southern India, the Virupaksha temple at PATTADAKAL includes bas-reliefs showing scenes from the *Ramayana* and *Mahabharata* on the columns. One of these depicts the Churning of the Ocean of Milk to obtain the elixir of immortality. This theme came to be particularly popular at Angkor in Cambodia. To the northwest, KHAM ZARGAR in Afghanistan is a Buddhist monastery that has yielded reliefs on schist showing the worship of a bodhisattva and the nirvana.

SOUTHEAST ASIA

SELAGIRI HILL in western Mynmar (Burma) is a location of the greatest sanctity because, according to legend, the Buddha and some followers flew there from India. Investigations on Selagiri Hill have identified a brick stupa, associated with a series of magnificent sandstone reliefs dating to the sixth and seventh centuries C.E. depicting events in the life of the Buddha.

The decoration on the exterior of temple buildings—scenes from Hindu epics and myths, representations of court and everyday life, and historical events—has a long ancestry in Cambodia. During the period of CHENLA kingdoms (550–800 C.E.), brick temples incorporated stone lintels. The surface of the brick was carved to portray palaces and their aristocratic occupants, while the stone lintels were heavily decorated with mythical scenes and occasionally with depictions of court activities. At Hariharalaya, brick temples were decorated with images of deities as well as rich floral ornamentation rendered in painted stucco. The expansion of relief decoration, however, occurred with the increasing use of sandstone as a construction material. Panels bearing scenes from Hindu epics are a particular feature of the BAPHUON temple pyra-

mid, the mausoleum of UDAYADITYAVARMAN II (1050–66). The temples of ANGKOR WAT and the BAYON stand out on the basis of the quality and quantity of their relief decoration. The former contains the longest continuous bas-relief known, incorporating scenes from the court of King SURYAVARMAN II (r. 1113–50) and the king's army marching to battle. Individual commanders are named in small adjacent inscriptions. Battle scenes follow, including a dramatic rendition of the BATTLE OF KURUKSHETRA. There are also scenes of heaven and hell and an outstanding account of the mythical CHURNING OF THE OCEAN OF MILK to produce AMRITA, the elixir of immortality. A 17th-century Japanese visitor to ANGKOR drew a plan of the temple and observed that some of the reliefs retained traces of gilding.

The walls enclosing the Bayon temple pyramid of JAYAVARMAN VII (r. 1181–1219) are covered in reliefs. These, while of lesser quality than those of Angkor Wat, are particularly important in showing scenes drawn from everyday life, as well as battles against the Chams. The former include servants preparing food for a feast and serving it to the elite in an al fresco setting, a woman in labor attended by midwives, two men playing chess, hunting with a bow and arrow, net fishing, and construction work. One panel shows the interior of a Chinese merchant's house, another a Chinese trading junk. The battle scenes on land and water show vicious hand-to-hand fighting between the Khmer and the Chams. These must reflect the recent wars in which Jayavarman VII freed the kingdom from Cham invaders. Further scenes of warfare are seen at the remote temple of BANTEAY CHMAR, which was built by Jayavarman VII in honor of his son and four military heroes. BANTEAY SREI is one of the most attractive and famously decorated temples. Built in a hard pink sandstone, this miniature building incorporates many 14th-century reliefs that take inspiration from Hindu epics.

The same situation also applies to the CHAM CIVILIZATION centers in Vietnam. At DONG DUONG, there are many fine reliefs showing the Buddha, while dancers and ascetics are depicted on some of the reliefs from MY SON.

CHINA

Temple reliefs in stone have not survived to the same extent in China, but there is a large corpus of HAN DYNASTY carvings that portray aspects of everyday life. An example from Sichuan shows a group of people harvesting with hand-held sickles, another shows people husking rice with a tilt hammer. There are also clay reliefs that portray other industrial activities. One shows a winery, another depicts salt production in Sichuan. A market scene reveals a special walled precinct, within which people run their stalls, and purchasers, who have entered by the East Market Gate, as seen in an explanatory inscription, come to buy.

The region of Nanyang in southwestern Henan Province is noted for the stone slabs decorated in low relief or incised with images that illustrate the enjoyment of the table, of music, and entertainment. Several such mortuary reliefs contain scenes of men bull baiting.

Ba state The Chang (Yangtze) River Valley south to Lingnan in China followed a separate course of cultural development from that documented in the central plains of the Huang (Yellow) River, and it was long relegated to a supporting role in Chinese history. Recent excavations, however, have begun to redress this imbalance. Thus the origins of rice cultivation have now been sourced in the central Chang lakelands by 6500 B.C.E., followed by an expansionary series of movements up- and downstream and through the passes to the south. Early urbanization is seen at the site of Chengtoushan (4000 B.C.E.), and at SANXINGDUI (1400–1100 B.C.E.); bronzes even more remarkable than their contemporaries at ANYANG have been recovered from sacrificial pits. The southern populations in question almost certainly did not speak Chinese, but they were in exchange contact with the Shang and Zhou states, for it is recorded that turtleshells for divination, as well as kingfisher plumage, cowries, and rhinoceros horn, were southern products much in demand in the northern states. There was also a widespread bronze form not found in the central plains, the large ceremonial bronze drum.

The Ba were one of these southern groups. They occupied the land above the Chang gorges in eastern Sichuan and spread north into Shaanxi and south into Guizhou. To the east, they bordered the rising power of the Chu state, while their western margins coincided with the people of SHU. The earliest documentary reference to the Ba appeared in the Shang ORACLE BONES (1200–1045 B.C.E.), where the king divined on the prospects of a military campaign against the Ba. The Ba seem to have participated in the BATTLE OF MUYE that saw the Zhou triumph over Shang in 1045 B.C.E., and thereafter typically they are recorded as donating exotic birds to the Zhou king. The Ba survived in a competitive climate through military prowess. They cast fine bronze weapons, many decorated with their chosen icon, the tiger. Their large drums were also often surmounted by a cast tiger. These items were embellished with a rudimentary pictographic script unlike that of the central plains, which employed images of animals, plants, and humans, as well as some abstract signs. Some symbols incorporate a boat with masts and oars and a human arm linked with a flower bud. No long texts have survived, and it has so far proved impossible to decipher them.

The Ba people entered into military alliances with their powerful Chu neighbors during the Spring and Autumn period (770–476 B.C.E.), but there was always a tension fueled by the growing power and ambition of the Chu. In particular, the Ba people controlled important sources of salt, and as the Chu pressed westward, so the Ba impinged on the Shu.

See also ANGKOR.

Ba system The establishment of the WESTERN ZHOU DYNASTY of China in 1045 B.C.E. introduced a feudal system of government, in which members of the royal lineage were granted landed fiefs on the borders of the new kingdom to put alien land under central control. This was a logical and sensible step but had the inevitable consequence that over time the blood ties slackened with increasing genealogical distance between center and periphery. By the end of the Western Zhou, the kings who ruled with divine approval under the MANDATE OF HEAVEN had become so weakened relative to the powerful feudal states that they relied on the latter's support for their survival. While retaining the aura of sovereignty, they became increasingly enfeebled. Under these conditions, political leadership was taken by the rulers of the then BA STATE.

Ba means "the senior one." Zhuan Gong of the state of ZHENG was foremost in protecting Ping, the first ruler of the EASTERN ZHOU DYNASTY, after the king's move east at the end of the Western Zhou dynasty. However, his loyalty was tested under King Huan of Zhou (r. 719–697 B.C.E.), and in a confrontation the king was injured. This was an important turning point in the role of the king, and increasingly it was Zhuan Gong who took the political initiative, up to his death in 701 B.C.E. He could thus be seen as the first Ba. With the death of Zhuan Gong, the state of QI assumed dominance. Qi had several geographic advantages in terms of trade, the supply of salt, and potential for expansion to north and east. Moreover, under the lord Huan Gong, deep-seated changes were made to state administration whereby the splintering effect of a feudal system was replaced by the establishment of 15 divisions for administrative purposes, divided into groups of five. One division was controlled by the overlord, the others by senior ministers. The artisans and fieldworkers were also divided into groups under central administration. This had the effect of greatly increasing efficiency and the power of central mobilization of forces. Qi thus became the Ba state, with Huan Gong effectively the leader of a coalition. Resulting conflicts with the rising power of CHU to the south were successfully concluded, and the institution of interstate conferences led to the production of a uniform policy on such matters as the control of IRRIGATION water and the organization of trade. One provision was the exclusion of women from political affairs.

Huan Gong of Qi died in 643 B.C.E., and the renewed specter of feudalism was seen in a power struggle between his sons. The Qi state thus declined in power and influence, and under Jin Wen Gong (r. 636–628 B.C.E.), JIN became the Ba state. However, by the sixth century B.C.E., Jin, Chu, Qi, and QIN had all assumed dominance in their own territories, and the role of the Ba ceased to have relevance. As these states increased their power and ambition, the seeds were sown for the period of WARRING STATES.

battle scenes Commemorations of great battles fill many pages of the Indian epics the RAMAYANA and MAHAB-HARATA. These were subsequently depicted on the walls of both Hindu and Buddhist temples. Thus at SANCHI, located in Madhya Pradesh, India, the railings incorporating four *toranas* are decorated with narrative reliefs of scenes of war in which one can observe battle elephants, the walls of a besieged city, and groups of archers. Horse cavalry and chariots join the siege, while the defenders reply from battlements with bows and arrows or repel attackers with clubs. The Indian battles were also a fertile field of inspiration for the builders of ANGKOR in Cambodia. The reliefs on the BAPHUON of UDAYADITYAVAR-MAN II include images of war chariots, but full depictions of an army and battles are first seen on the bas-reliefs of ANGKOR WAT. The procession of the army of SURYAVARMAN II includes the king and his great generals, each riding a war elephant. Virendradhipativarman is seen surrounded by nine parasols. Ahead of him in the column is Jayayuddhavarman, with eight parasols. His troops wear distinctive helmets with deer-head images. Rajasinghavarman has 13 parasols and two banners, but pride of place goes to the king. He has 15 parasols, five fans, six fly whisks, four banners, and—in front of his elephant—a standard of Vishnu riding Garuda. Even his elephant wears a splendid jeweled headdress. His presence is signaled by the sacred fire being carried aloft and by an orchestra of trumpets, conches, drums, and a gong. There are ranks of foot soldiers and cavalry, including both Khmer and vassal troops.

The same men and arms are then portrayed in the mythical Battle of KURUKSHETRA. Leaders are seen on their elephants or on horse-drawn chariots. Most wield bows and arrows. The infantry carry spears and protect themselves with circular shields. Fighting appears to have included hand-to-hand encounters involving whole formations. The later reliefs of the BAYON and BANTEAY CHMAR include ballistae, for launching a large spear, mounted on elephants. These appear to have been an innovation in warfare that reached Angkor after the completion of Angkor Wat. The deadly effect of massed arrows was countered by the use of panels designed to withstand their impact without impeding the vision of the Khmer archers. There are also graphic scenes of naval encounters between the forces of JAYAVARMAN VII and the Chams (*see* CHAM CIVILIZATION), in which warships are used as floating fortresses from which soldiers fight with spears and bows and arrows. At the Bayon, two vessels seem to be in the act of ramming each other.

Battle scenes are also found in KUSHAN contexts. At KHALCHAYAN in Uzbekistan, a palace reception chamber dating from the first century B.C.E to the first century C.E. was decorated with images of warriors on horseback wearing leather armor and wielding bows and arrows as well as with deities that seem to have been modeled on Hellenistic gods, such as Athena and Apollo. PANJIKENT, a Sogdian center located about 40 (24 mi.) kilometers east of Samarqand, was occupied from the fifth to the eighth centuries C.E. The rich inhabitants decorated their homes with painted scenes, including archers on horseback leaping over dead bodies, a theme taken from their epic stories.

In China, battle scenes take the form of tomb models and decoration on ceramics or bronzes. The most notable battle scene comes from the funerary pits of the first emperor, QIN SHIHUANGDI (259–210 B.C.E.). These show units of archers, chariots drawn by four horses, and supporting infantry. Guards at the flanks and rear are located to withstand a surprise attack. Another pit contains a detachment of infantry, chariots, and cavalry. The archers carry crossbows. A third pit incorporated the command center, with some soldiers forming an honor guard.

A second set of terra-cotta soldiers comes from a pit associated with the tomb of a king of CHU at Shizishan in Jiangsu Province. Infantry and cavalry are represented, but there are no chariots. The same mix of foot soldiers and cavalry is seen at a rich WESTERN HAN royal tomb at Yangjiawan in Shaanxi. The 1,800 infantry soldiers and 580 members of the cavalry are modeled at about 50 percent full size, and each individual is completed in full battle dress. A third-century B.C.E. tomb of the WEI state known as the Jizhong tomb contains a remarkable battle scene cast into a bronze vessel. It shows archers, spearmen, and soldiers wielding halberds and fighting from boats. One can also see a wheeled scaling ladder to assault defensive walls. One panel depicts decapitated soldiers.

Bayon The Bayon temple, originally known as Madhyadri, lies in the center of the city of ANGKOR THOM in Cambodia. It began as the state temple mausoleum of King JAYAVARMAN VII (r. 1181–1219) and incorporates large carved stone heads, considered representations of the king as a BODHISATTVA, an enlightened one, on the temple towers. The outer walls are decorated with a series of reliefs, which provide an unparalleled glimpse of life during the reign of Jayavarman VII.

The Bayon was expanded and modified in at least three phases. Thus the central shrine began with a cruciform plan but was later given its unusual circular layout with an addition of radiating shrines. The outer enclosing wall contains eight cruciform entrance towers and is covered in reliefs depicting battle scenes and daily activities. The third level contains towers embellished with huge stone heads. The original dedicatory statue of the Buddha

The reliefs carved on the walls of the Bayon temple at Angkor reflect life there in the early 13th century. Here we see an oxcart like those still used in the area, followed by a family with their livestock. *(Charles Higham)*

that would have been housed in the main gilded chapel was smashed as a later religious reaction and cast into the deep shaft that underlies the central shrine. The scenes on the outer walls include battles on land and water, feasting, life in a rich person's house, hunting, playing of games, selling in the market, cooking, and building a palace. Military victories dominate many of the reliefs.

It is hard today to conceive of the monument's original brilliance; it was described by ZHOU DAGUAN as the golden tower. A contemporary inscription states that Queen Jayarajadevi, wife of Jayavarman VII, donated 100 banners of Chinese fabric to the god of Madhyadri, the Bayon.

be　A *be* was a group of craft specialists who, during the period of the YAMATO state in Japan, paid goods and services to the court. Such specialists are recorded in the Japanese history known as the NIHONGI, for example, as being established after the arrival of Korean artisans with specialist skills in weaving, writing, and the manufacture of iron goods. It is possible that the idea of tribute-producing specialists originated in Korea as well. An inscription on an iron sword from Okadayama employed the term *be*, suggesting that such occupational groups were established by the fifth century C.E. Their importance grew in tandem with the new demands placed on society as the Yamato state increased in complexity, highlighting the need for specialists in IRRIGATION technology, weaving, and the provision of iron items required in war and agriculture.

Bedsa　Bedsa, located in the western Deccan of India, is a notable example of an early rock-cut monastery. The inscriptions from this site date it to the middle of the first century B.C.E. There is a sanctuary of apsidal plan, and the front verandah was embellished with four decorated columns and a doorway giving access to the interior. The capitals of the columns were finely carved with sculptures of horses, elephants, and bulls and riders. Further columns are found in the interior, but these are plain except for the representations of pots at the top and bottom. Later in the monastery's history, with the spread of MAHAYANA BUDDHISM, the walls were decorated with images of BODHISATTVAS.

See also ROCK MONASTERIES; SATAVAHANA.

Begram Begram is located in ancient Kapisa, about 80 kilometers north of Kabul in Afghanistan. The second-century C.E. Greek historian Arrian, when describing the campaigns of ALEXANDER THE GREAT, mentioned two cities in Kapisa: Nikaia (City of Victory) and Hopain. The former has been identified as modern Begram. The most notable feature of the excavations at Begram, undertaken between 1936 and 1946 by J. Hackin, was the discovery of treasures in two storerooms. These goods may have been secreted for safekeeping during a period of trouble, for Begram suffered at least two episodes of destruction, first by the Sassanians in about 244 C.E. and then by the Huns in the fifth century C.E.

The city's walls enclose an area of 36 hectares (90 acres). Begram probably began as an outpost of the ACHAEMENID EMPIRE and was refounded as a city by the BACTRIAN GREEKS, with a regular street plan, public buildings, houses, and shops. It then became a summer capital of the KUSHAN king KANISHKA I, (r. 100–126 C.E.), and it may have been he who had a palace constructed and the fortifications strengthened.

Begram is located on a natural strongpoint above the Panjshir and Ghorband Rivers and was strategically placed to take advantage of the goods following the SILK ROAD linking China and Rome with India. The treasures hidden in Begram originated in China, India, and the Mediterranean world and provide a vivid glimpse of the opulence of a Kushan capital, as well as the variety of items obtained through trade. There was a fine bronze statue of Hercules cast in Alexandria, Egypt, dating to between the first and fourth centuries C.E., and a Greek vase decorated with scenes of Europa and the bull, likewise originating in Alexandria. The *PERIPLUS OF THE ERYTHRAEAN SEA* mentions the export of fine glassware from this city to the east, and the splendid glass goblets from Begram were probably among these exports. From Han China were outstanding LACQUER boxes and a lacquer cup. Perhaps the most impressive of all the finds in this hoard were the Indian ivories, including a statuette, openwork plaques, the back of a throne, and a panel that was probably part of a piece of opulent furniture. The ivories depict luxurious court scenes. In one example, a languid woman surrounded by luxuriant flowers reclines on a couch, holding aloft a cup into which a female servant pours liquid. Another scene shows the women's quarters of a court, with a decorated doorway on the right that would have led to an elegant chamber in which women play musical instruments.

See also HAN DYNASTY; SASSANIAN EMPIRE.

Beikthano Beikthano (City of Vishnu) is a walled city in the valley of the Yin River, a tributary of the Irrawaddy River, in the dry zone of central Myanmar (Burma). Janice Stargardt has suggested, on the basis of a layer of ceramics predating the early citadel walls, that the site originated as a late prehistoric village that grew rapidly into an urban form, perhaps through irrigated rice cultivation. It was occupied from at least the first or second century B.C.E. and continued to be a major center of the PYU CIVILIZATION for a thousand years. Curiously, few inscriptions or other written documents of any sort have survived, but it is known that the Pyu people spoke a Tibeto-Burman language and in all probability emerged locally in central Myanmar (Burma) from late prehistoric Iron Age ancestors. A small clay stud recovered during excavations by U Aung Thaw in 1959 to 1963 bore a brief set of written characters in the PALI language and BRAHMI script stylistically dated to the second century C.E. The text reads, *Samgha siri,* probably a person's name. Oral tradition has it that the city was founded by a princess Panhtwar in about 400 B.C.E. and that it finally succumbed to an attack by King Duttabaung of SRI KSETRA.

ARCHITECTURAL REMAINS

The city covers an area of 881 hectares (2,203 acres), demarcated on all but the western side by a massive brick wall in places 2.5-meters (8.25 ft.) thick. The bricks were liberally tempered with rice husks, indicating extensive rice cultivation in the surrounding area. These walls are punctured by 12 main gateways, in which the iron sockets and charred wooden pieces of the original doors survive. A canal issuing from the Sadoun River to the east carried water to the city. One branch of the canal entered the walled area and fed a large reservoir that made up the western edge of the city, while other branches directed water into the moats outside the walls. Excavations in 1959–63 concentrated on 25 sites in the city and immediately beyond its walls. The excavators recorded more than 100 brick structures in association with this site, and excavations revealed different plans that developed over 10 centuries. The city also had a citadel or royal palace near the center that was probably extended on several occasions and could have incorporated another royal palace. Unlike in other Pyu cities, however, no names of kings have survived.

Two early brick structures have furnished radiocarbon dates that suggest that the first monumental architecture dates in the period 200 B.C.E. to 200 C.E. The surviving structures belonging to this phase include two substantial brick buildings of rectangular plan, incorporating large wooden posts within. One contained 40 urn burials in the foundation layer; the mortuary vessels were of outstanding quality and held cremated human remains but no grave goods. A second such early building included 13 urn burials. These buildings are interpreted by Janice Stargardt of Cambridge University as mortuary chapels for highly ranked ancestors, built before the adoption of BUDDHISM and thus representing a magnification of prehistoric mortuary traditions involving a form of ancestor worship. Buddhism was adopted at Beikthano by at least by the mid-fourth century C.E. One of the many brick foundations took the form of a monastery building with eight individual cells for monks, following an Indian pattern. This building is also associated with a large cylindrical brick stupa associated with an outer circular pathway, the fill of which incorporated exotic stone beads. Structures in the citadel itself included what may have been a royal throne room and a thickly walled building for storing valuable or ritual objects. There are also many low mounds forming lines parallel with and beyond the outer walls. The excavation of one of these revealed a set of brick-lined vaults around a central cell, measuring about six by eight meters (20 by 26 ft.). The vaults contained cremation urns for receiving human ashes.

IRRIGATION AT BEIKTHANO

Beikthano is located in the dry interior zone of Myanmar (Burma), which receives an average of 870 millimeters (35 in.) of rainfall per annum. This is insufficient alone to sustain rice cultivation. The examination of air photographs, however, has revealed how the local rivers were diverted into canals that fed the city reservoirs, before the water was channeled into extensive irrigated rice fields to the west of the city. It is also possible that at least some of the area enclosed by the perimeter walls could have been cultivated with the benefit of IRRIGATION water.

FOREIGN CONTACTS

The material culture of Beikthano reveals an active interest in exchange. A corpus of silver coins has been assembled. They include specimens with the mother goddess, or *srivatsa*, motif associated with the Sun and the Moon. Bronzes include a small casting of a lion and bells recalling those of late prehistoric Thailand. Smiths made iron nails, clearly used in the construction of wooden buildings, knives, and arrowheads. There are exotic hard stone beads of agate, crystal, jasper, amethyst, and carnelian, and some of the pottery vessels found within the central citadel were probably imported from India. There was also a vigorous local industry for ceramics, which produced large and technically outstanding mortuary vessels in the form of drums. Sandstone molds have been recovered, indicating the casting of ornaments, and the presence of clay spindle whorls attests to a weaving industry.

Further reading: Aung Thaw. *Report on the Excavations at Beikthano*. Rangoon: Government of the Union of Myanmar, 1968; ———. *Historical Sites in Burma*. Rangoon: Sarpay Beikman Press, 1972.

Beng Mealea   In Cambodia, Beng Mealea, "lotus pool," is one of the most enigmatic of all Angkorian centers. It is located about 40 kilometers (24 mi.) east of ANGKOR and stylistically belongs to the middle of the 12th century C.E. However, no inscriptions have been found there, and nothing is known of its founder, its name, or its relation-ship to the rulers at Angkor itself. Its obvious wealth might be related to its location at the head of a canal linking the KULEN HILLS with the GREAT LAKE, a possible route for sandstone to reach Angkor. The temple lies within a moated enclosure almost one kilometer square, linked with a *baray* to the east. It includes a central sanctuary set within three galleries and incorporating cruciform structures as at ANGKOR WAT. A long causeway on the eastern side with a balustrade in the form of a *naga,* or snake, linked the temple with the *baray*. While there are no reliefs at this site, the temples are decorated with scenes drawn mainly from Hindu epics that feature Vishnu and SIVA.

Besnagar   Besnagar, formerly known as Vidisanagara, is located between the Betwa and Bes Rivers, in India. It is particularly notable in the history of Indian archaeology, because it was here in the 1840s that SIR ALEXANDER CUNNINGHAM undertook a pioneering study of the monuments and their associated material culture, later published in the monograph *The Bhilsa Topes*. Further investigations took place in 1910, when several mounds were opened by H. H. Lake, and more intensive excavations took place in 1913 by D. R. Bhandarkar.

The city covers an area of about 240 hectares (600 acres) and was probably the capital of the MAHAJANAPADA (state) of Avanti. The exposed western side is defended by a rampart and moat, the rampart having been constructed in the second century B.C.E. Although a site with a long period of occupation, it is best known for a stone pillar, inscribed by HELIODOROS, son of Diya, the Greek ambassador at the court of a local ruler, Kasiputra Bhagabhadra, on behalf of Antialcidas, king of TAXILA in modern Pakistan, during the late second century B.C.E. This column supported a statue of Garuda and was erected by Heliodoros. It is one of a row of eight associated with a religious shrine, the second to be built on this location. The text of the inscription reads: "This Garuda-pillar of Vasudeva, the god of gods, was constructed here by Heliodoros, the Bhagavata, son of Diya, of Taxila, the Greek ambassador who came from the Great King Antialcidas to King Kasiputra Bhagabhadra, the Savior, prospering in his fourteenth year. These three steps lead to immortality, when correctly followed, lead to heaven: control, generosity, and attention" (translated by R. Salomon, 1998).

The stump of a second inscribed column included a text recording the erection of a column with an image of GARUDA by Bhagavata, dedicated to the god Vasudeva in the 12th year since the consecration of Maharaja Bhagavata. Bhagavata is recorded in surviving texts as the penultimate king of the SUNGA dynasty, who ruled in the early first century B.C.E.

Bhandarkar's excavations produced a wide range of artifacts, including coins and sealings, figurines, wheels from toy carts, iron sickles, knives and nails, and cowry shells. Many punch-marked copper coins were recovered; the symbols included human figures, rivers with fish, a horse, elephants, and tortoises.

Bezeklik Bezeklik, "the place with paintings," was discovered during a German expedition to the TURPAN BASIN (Xinjiang province, China) in 1904 to 1905. Led by Albert van der Coq and Albert Grünwedel, the expedition explored a series of Buddhist temples cut into the rock. The two removed many of these and dispatched them to Berlin.

Bhadraniketana *See* SDOK KAK THOM.

Bhagavad Gita *Bhagavad Gita* (Song of the Lord) is a sacred SANSKRIT text that comprises the sixth book of the Hindu epic MAHABHARATA (500 B.C.E.–400 C.E.). The theme is a moral one, posed by the hero Arjuna when he is preparing for a battle that may lead to the deaths of his relatives. His charioteer is the god Krishna, and the issues covered in conversation between the two center on the relations between human and god and the nature of the deity.

Bhagwanpura Bhagwanpura is a site of the late INDUS VALLEY CIVILIZATION, (early second millennium B.C.E.), in the now-dry valley of the SARASVATI RIVER in northwestern India. Excavations have uncovered evidence for two periods of occupation in a cultural buildup 2.7 meters (9 ft.) thick. The earlier saw the construction of large, raised mud-brick platforms, the substructures of houses designed to alleviate possible flood damage. However, there is evidence of at least one major episode of flooding. The pottery and associated material culture belong to the late phase of the civilization. A SEAL with the Indus script, many terra-cotta figurines, and jewelry of carnelian and FAIENCE were discovered. The second phase saw a continuation of some Indus Valley traits together with PAINTED GREY WARE.

Bhaja The cave-temples at Bhaja in Maharashtra state, India, are probably the earliest such ROCK MONASTERIES in India. Dating to the late second century B.C.E., they incorporate some fine relief panels depicting Surya, the Hindu sun god, and Indra. The entrance to the most notable sanctuary cave takes the form of a large arch that shows clearly wooden prototypes in the design of its beams and balustrades. The monasteries are badly damaged, but in one a relief of Indra in his chariot, accompanied by a woman holding a fly whisk and parasol is preserved. The monks' cells were also embellished with fine reliefs.

Bharhut Bharhut is a major Buddhist center located in the state of Madhya Pradesh in India. The site was strategically placed between UJJAIN to the south and PATALIPU-TRA to the east and provided easy access to KOSAMBI. Now largely in ruins, the site dates to the third century B.C.E., when the original brick stupa was probably constructed under King ASOKA. The stupa is of great architectural importance given its date and style, the hemispherical form of which recalls the original purpose of the stupa as a burial mound.

Bharhut first drew the attention of scholars in 1873, after SIR ALEXANDER CUNNINGHAM had examined the stupa and identified the remains of a town, both published in the monograph *The Stupa of Bharhut*. The Bharhut style of sculpture, with narrative reliefs ornamenting temple structures, was widespread in northern India. The reliefs form a major corpus of material dating to the Sunga dynasty (185–73 B.C.E.). As at SANCHI, the favored motifs incorporated *yaksha*s and *yakshi*s, male and female fertility deities probably of great antiquity, which were adopted into early Buddhist art. The surviving stone railings also incorporate reliefs illustrating JATAKA TALES describing the previous lives of the Buddha and events in his life. The Buddha is not depicted but represented symbolically as a parasol, a wheel, or an empty throne. The brief inscriptions describe the events illustrated and thus provide a vital contribution to an understanding of Buddhist iconography. Some of the *jataka* stories differ from those current in texts written in the PALI language, suggesting that there were once several different versions. One of the most useful aspects of the decoration is the faithful manner in which it depicts scenes taken from life at the time. Thus the wooden houses had two or three stories and incorporated elegant balustrades. The four gateways were, according to an inscription, constructed during the reign of King Dhanabhuti in the early first century B.C.E.

Bharukaccha *See* BROACH.

Bhavavarman I (d. c. 600 C.E.) *Bhavavarman I, an early king of a Chenla polity in Cambodia, is referred to in an inscription as the son of a king Viravarman and grandson of Sarvabhauma.*
A further text from Roban Romas mentions him as the overlord of Narasimhagupta, the king of Indrapura. It appears likely that his court was located at or near ISHANAPURA. He was succeeded by his brother, Mahendravarman.

Bhir mound at Taxila The Bhir mound at TAXILA is the first of three major cities at this strategic site in northern Pakistan. It was a provincial center of the MAURYA EMPIRE and flourished from the fourth to the second centuries B.C.E.

Bhita Bhita is a fortified settlement with an area of 19 hectares (48 acres) located close to the Jamuna River near

Allahabad in central India. Originally named Vichigrama, it was initially used by railway contractors as a quarry for ballast. It was examined scientifically by SIR ALEXANDER CUNNINGHAM in 1872. He excavated two trenches, one of which sectioned the ramparts, where he found highly polished black ware and many bone arrowheads. It is best known as a result of excavations by SIR JOHN MARSHALL early in the 20th century. He opened a substantial area in the eastern part of the town against the defensive wall and smaller exposures in the center and the northwestern quarters. His examination of the town wall revealed a base 3.3 meters (11 ft.) thick incorporating a bastion, dating to the early Mauryan period or slightly earlier (fourth century B.C.E.). The excavation offered a rare opportunity to appreciate the planning of a Maurya and Gupta period settlement, while the many artifacts recovered open a window on the lives of the citizens during a period of more than six centuries. The excavations of Bhita provide a unique glimpse into the life of a city that flourished, albeit with periods of destruction, from pre-Mauryan times to the heyday of the GUPTA EMPIRE. Similar large-scale excavations employing modern techniques would add immeasurably to the understanding of early Indian history.

EXCAVATIONS OF THE CITY'S HOUSES

In the eastern area, Marshall excavated in a road down to the base of the site, reaching the earliest layer at a depth of 7.5 meters (25 ft.). There were sherds of what he described as fine black ware with a highly burnished surface, clearly the NORTHERN BLACK POLISHED WARE, which dates the initial occupation well back in the first millennium B.C.E. At the higher levels, he uncovered a series of streets and lanes. The main street was lined with rows of shops, behind which lay a series of large houses. The preferred plan involved rooms grouped around a paved courtyard. Walls were constructed of well-laid fired bricks, and some walls were thick enough to suggest that a second story was present. This idea has been supported by inspection of the stratigraphy of burning layers, which are compatible with material falling from the upper level.

Marshall was able to delineate and trace the history of a number of town houses, each of which he named on the basis of possible owners. The house of the guild is called after a Mauryan-period SEAL die bearing the text, *Shahijitiye Nigamasa*. The word *nigama* means "guild," and this house, interestingly adjacent to the city gate, might have been the office of a guild of merchants or the house of a guild member. The house itself has a square plan, 10.5 by 10.5 meters in extent. Twelve rooms are grouped around a courtyard, the largest measuring 4.2 by 3 meters. Two entrances give access to the courtyard, which is flanked on one side by a verandah. Excavations uncovered the wheels of a toy cart and three steatite caskets on the floor. The former were delicately ornamented with floral designs and included their spokes.

This MAURYA EMPIRE residence was leveled, and the area was incorporated as a courtyard of the new house built next door, which is known as the house of Navadeva because the name was found on an ivory seal; Navadeva may well have been the owner of the property. His house dates to the early second century C.E. on the basis of coins of the KUSHAN kings KANISHKA I and Huvishka found on the floor. Navadeva might have been a prosperous merchant, for many clay sealings were found in the house, and it was linked with a row of shops that lined the main street outside. It followed the preferred plan of the Mauryan houses, with rooms grouped around a courtyard. A small room on the northern side of the house contained an image of SIVA, his wife, and Nandi and a shrine containing seven seated female figures. These had been damaged, and a slingshot was lodged among the deities. Given the fact that many other missiles were found at this level, both in houses and in the streets, and that there is evidence for a major burning, Marshall suggested that the town was sacked, and the owners fled without taking the household gods or their copper tableware.

The house of Navadeva was separated from the adjacent house of Jayavasuda by a narrow lane. An ivory seal bearing the inscription, Sresthi Jayavasuda, "the banker, Jayavasuda," has given the house its name. The seal incorporated a tortoise, an avatar of Vishnu, perhaps indicating that the banker worshiped this god. The property was square, measuring 13.5 meters along each outer wall. Once again, rooms were grouped around a court, in this case equipped with a well. On the southwestern corner of the house, there is a small underground vault or strong room, almost four meters below the ground floor level. The building also yielded many clay sealings, indicating the opening of trade goods.

One probably imported item was a clay medallion of considerable sophistication, showing King Dashyanta on a four-horse chariot, with two antelopes in the foreground being hunted. Close inspection of the medallion reveals aspects of life in India during the Kushan and early Gupta periods, including a lake with a woman collecting lotus blossoms, a house from which a woman emerges holding a basket, and a bridge or walkway with travelers. A peacock with its tail feathers on display stands in front of the chariot, which has been stopped by a person probably pleading with the king to spare the antelopes. Marshall has suggested that this medallion was made with an ivory die, while the scene recalls those seen at SANCHI. This house, too, suffered burning and destruction, which fortuitously left a deposit of charred rice on the verandah, illuminating at least part of the agricultural round in the surrounding fields.

The house of Pushyavriddhi lies opposite the shops of Nagadeva, on the other side of the main street. Again it takes its name from an ivory seal found within. This property was begun in the Mauryan period and had additions during the first century B.C.E. It was abandoned and destroyed during Kushan times and then reoccupied in the early Gupta empire. Excavating north from this house, Marshall encountered a second road that he named Bastion Street, because it ran in an easterly direction toward the city wall, where a bastion was located. Beyond Bastion Street lay two further substantial town houses, then a lane, and finally part of another residence.

All these thoroughfares ran parallel with one another. Neither was fully excavated, and only their later history has been uncovered. One house fronting Bastion Street contained seals and sealings with the names Dharadasa, Guridasa, and Manoratha, probably successive owners of the property, and Marshall named it the house of Dharadasa.

About 150 meters to the northwest of this house, further excavations encountered a long building sequence beginning with the Mauryan occupation. The house in question had been abandoned, but the remains of wooden beams and roof tiles under the later reconstruction indicated the robust nature of Mauryan domestic buildings. The recovery of a crucible used by a goldsmith indicated the likely occupation of the owner. The next house probably belongs to the first century C.E. It included a deep well of ceramic rings and yielded a fine stone relief featuring a recumbent woman in front of a tray of fruit and a leaf, while a man holding a shield stands beside her with his left arm on her thigh. The woman has an elegant hairstyle and wears heavy earrings and an elaborate necklace. The third building level belongs to the Kushan period, on the basis of a sealing found just below the floor level.

SEALS AND SEALINGS

One of the most interesting aspects of the building phases at Bhita is the strong evidence for continuity of design and building techniques. This community seems to have continued through various changes in political dynasties and regimes, engaging in the trade encouraged by its strategic position on the Jamuna River. Such trade is best seen in the evidence of the 210 seals and sealings recovered. These are found in all the phases examined and represent 120 varieties. They were owned by individuals of high status or authority, and one of their uses was to authorize travel documents. This is clearly illustrated in a passage from the *Mahabharata,* which stated that nobody could enter or leave a besieged city without a stamped passport. The back of the clay sealings often incorporates an impression of the string that was passed around an object or letter. Others sealings have holes through the clay, indicating that clay was placed around the string before being impressed with the seal. The inscriptions on the Mauryan and Sungan seals are usually written in the PRAKRIT language, while the Gupta seals preferred SANSKRIT. The seals represent religious foundations, kings,

officials, districts, and guilds. One of the district seals refers to Vichhi and presumably represents Bhita itself. Five seals are from religious foundations or temples that worshiped Siva. Indeed, Sivaism was clearly favored, as religious symbols on seals included the linga, trident, and bull. Some of the seals provide the names and religious inclinations of the inhabitants of Bhita. One Dharadasa was the son of Samddhiyasas (Famous for peace), and the presence of a conch shell and a wheel on his seal proclaims him to have been a follower of Vishnu. On the other hand, a bronze signet ring carries the image of a bull and the caption, *Rudracharya.* Rudra is an alternative name for Siva, and the bull was his symbol.

The surviving sealings originated in letters or consignments from rulers, guilds, officials, and individuals. In some instances, they also provide evidence for offerings to gods and give an unusual insight into local affairs and government, particularly during the period of the Gupta empire. One example bears the text, *Kalesvarah priyatam,* "May *Kalesvarah* [a Siva lingam] be pleased." It was probably presented to a shrine to Siva in Bhita. Some particularly fine sealings include the names of rulers. One was referred to as the illustrious Maharaja Gautamiputra Vrishadhvaja. Another ruler is named as the illustrious Raja Vasishthiputra Bhimasena. Gupta period officials are well represented in the sealings, which indicate a wide range of titles and functions. One seal was from the office of Kumaramatya, the councillor of the heir apparent. There was a sealing of a *senapati,* a military general. Another mentions a man who was both a cavalry officer and chief of police. The minister Dharmadeva's sealing was recovered, as was that of a *mahadandanayaka,* the police chief. The word for "guild," *nigamasa,* is found on sealings dating to the Kushan and Gupta periods. Most sealings, however, were stamped by private individuals, many of whom were probably traders of the Gupta period. Their names emerge from anonymity: Bhutaka, Bhubhula, Gagasa, and Chuchaka. These personal seals usually include the image of an animal; the bull, lion, and peacock were popular.

It is also most useful that the expansive excavations at Bhita have yielded a large sample of coins, on which the Kushan kings Kadphises, Kanishka I, and Huvishka are well represented. Many terra-cotta figurines were found, and these illustrate the appearance of the populace at Bhita. Women had sophisticated hairstyles and wore a quantity of jewelry. The ornaments themselves include gold beads and amulets and copper bangles and rings. Beads were also fashioned from shell, glass, coral, crystal, LAPIS LAZULI, agate, carnelian, and topaz. The smiths forged iron arrowheads, axes, and chisels.

Further reading: Allchin, F. R., ed. *The Archaeology of Early Historic South Asia.* Cambridge: Cambridge University Press, 1995; Marshall, J. "Excavations at Bhita," *Annual Report of the Archaeological Survey of India 1911–1912* (1912): 29–94.

Bhumara Bhumara is a notable Hindu temple of the GUPTA EMPIRE located in northern Madhya Pradesh state, India. It was dedicated to SIVA and contained an *ekamukhalinga* (a lingam with a single face of Siva carved on it), which is widely regarded as one of the finest examples of Gupta art. Formerly the temple was embellished with other superb sculptures, including Ganesha, Indra, Surya, and other gods of the Hindu pantheon.

Bhumisambarabhudhara *See* BOROBUDUR.

Bianxianwang Bianxianwang is a major site of the LONGSHAN CULTURE, located behind the shore of Laichow Bay in Shandong province, central China. It is unusual among the early walled sites in having two enclosures, the inner one covering about one hectare, the outer one nearly six hectares (15 acres). It dates to the middle and late phases of the Longshan culture, between 2300 and 1900 B.C.E. The sacrificed remains of humans, pigs, and dogs were found in the wall foundations, which were made of stamped earth.

Bindusara (c. 297–292 B.C.E.) *Bindusara was the second king of the Maurya empire established by his father, Candragupta Maurya.*
Bindusara was entitled Amitraghata, "Slayer of Enemies." He maintained and probably enlarged the empire, which was prone to regional rebellions against central rule. He also engaged in a diplomatic correspondence with King Antiochus I of Syria.

birch bark scrolls Sacred Buddhist texts, written on birch bark and placed inside reliquary containers, have been recovered from a number of sites in Pakistan, Afghanistan (ancient GANDHARA), and Central Asia. These were written in the Gandhari PRAKRIT language and the KHAROSHTHI script and are thought to date from up to 2,000 years ago. They are, however, so fragile that few have survived sufficiently intact to be conserved and interpreted. Their potential importance in documenting the spread of early BUDDHISM into Gandhara and along the SILK ROAD to China cannot be overstated. Recently discovered texts provide new information on the relationships between the Indo-Scythian rulers of Gandhara during the first century C.E. and the role played by Indo-Scythian rulers in supporting and promulgating the early spread of Buddhism.

The HOTAN *Dharmapada* was the only such document to be published until recently. Discovered in 1892, it was five meters (16.5 ft.) long and comprised pieces of joined birch bark. Its original resting place is not known with certainty, but it may have been the Gosirsa monastery southwest of Hotan in China. Several other fragmentary texts have also been found in Central Asian sites. In

1833, John Honigberger discovered textual remains under the Shiwaki stupa in Kabul, and a year later, Charles Masson recovered scrolls in the Jalalabad region of Afghanistan about 100 kilometers (60 mi.) east of Kabul. One was found in the foundation deposit of valuables, under a stupa at Nandara. This was but one of several such discoveries of the period, whose script was noted to be similar to that on Bactrian coins. The scrolls have never been translated or commented on. In the 1930s J. Barthoux recovered a bark document from a stupa a Chakhil-I Gundi on the Hadda plain in Afghanistan and described it as a text of the Buddha's sermon at Benares (now Varanasi), but this has not been confirmed. Since the Second World War, excavations at Tapa Shutur on the Hadda plain have recovered bark manuscripts placed in clay or stucco images of BODHISATTVAS. Two such heads contained texts. Farther to the west, bark manuscripts have been found in a rock-cut chamber only 35 meters (116 ft.) from the great statue of the Buddha at BAMIYAN.

BRITISH MUSEUM SCROLLS

Given the almost complete lack of any translations or published reports on these documents, the British Museum's acquisition of a set of 29 birch bark scrolls bearing texts written in the Kharoshthi script has provided a major opportunity to learn more about the early spread of Buddhism. The scrolls were found with five inscribed pottery vessels, in one of which the scrolls were probably placed, but having been removed from the pots, the delicate scrolls had suffered serious damage. The provenance of these ancient texts is not known, as is always the case with looted antiquities, and this lack diminishes their scholarly value. However, it is considered likely that they were originally from the Hadda region of northeast Afghanistan. By identifying the pot that most probably housed the scrolls, it is possible to suggest that they were from the library of a monastery belonging to the Buddhist sect known as Dharmaguptaka. They almost certainly date to the first century C.E. The practice of depositing pottery vessels containing human ashes and texts in sacred places was widespread. One such pot was found in the monastery of Jaulian in TAXILA, Pakistan; others are from Tapa Kalan in eastern Afghanistan, where they were found forming a row.

The date of the 29 texts is not easy to define, given the lack of provenance, but it can be considered on the basis of the style of the writing and the references to historic figures. The manuscripts mention two people known from coins and inscriptions and thus provide historic information. The first person is Jihonika, who is described as a great satrap; the second is Aspavarman, who had the title *stratega*, or commander. Jihonika ruled during the period 30–40 C.E. and controlled the region of Taxila. Aspavarman is mentioned as a ruler who was asked to help provide shelter for monks during the rainy season. He is known from inscriptions on coins minted by Azes II and Gondophares to have been the son of Indravarman. He ruled a small area on the border of Pakistan and Afghanistan from 20 to 40 C.E. The new texts can thus be dated to the first half of the first century C.E., and the rulers named were almost certainly patrons and supporters of Buddhist foundations.

See also BACTRIA.

Further reading: Salomon, R. *Ancient Buddhist Scrolls from Gandhara.* Seattle: University of Washington Press, 1999; Salomon, R. *Indian Epigraphy: A Guide to the Study of Inscriptions in Sanskrit, Prakrit and the Other Indo-Aryan Languages.* New York: Oxford University Press, 1998.

bo   The Chinese conceived that a person was divided at death between the *hun* and the *bo.* The former may be translated as the "soul," which might migrate to the heavens or to the land of the yellow springs. The latter remained with the body. Particularly during the HAN DYNASTY (206 B.C.E.–220 C.E.), it was felt necessary to provide the *bo* with all the material goods required to satisfy the life to which the deceased had been accustomed to prevent him or her from returning as a spirit or ghost. Because of this belief, some Han tombs have revealed incredible grave gifts illustrating the sumptuous material goods the deceased had enjoyed in life—lifesize figures of warriors, jade suits to preserve the body, chariots and horses, and precious silks.

The quantity and the nature of these goods varied with the status of the dead. Some Han cemeteries have rows of graves containing the remains of slaves or prisoners who died on major construction works. They might include only a scratched text indicating the person's name and origin. On the other hand, the only imperial Han tomb to be investigated scientifically, that of the emperor Jingdi near Xi'an (d. 141 B.C.E.), included subterranean pits that contained thousands of lifesize ceramic warriors and animals and agricultural implements. His actual burial chamber remains to be opened, but historical records describe the interior of the tomb of Emperor QIN SHIHUANGDI (259–210 B.C.E.) in detail. They recount the lengths taken to provide the ruler with all that he might require, even down to a representation of his empire and lamps that would burn for a long time.

ELITE PRESERVATION OF THE BODY

The need to satisfy the *bo* with all its bodily needs has opened an extraordinary opportunity for archaeologists to document life during the period of Han rule. In the first instance, the body itself had to be protected from decay. For the elite, two principal techniques were developed. For members of the imperial family, the body was encased in a suit made of jade wafers linked by gold thread. The first two complete suits of jade were found at MANCHENG, where they encased the bodies of Prince Liu Sheng, the brother of the Han emperor WUDI (157–87 B.C.E.), and his wife. Jade was considered a source of life-giving properties that would preserve the body, but this of course was not the case. While the wearing of jade suits was reserved only for royalty, it was possible for the emperor to grant this privilege to his favorites. Thus the courtier Huo Guang was favored with a jade suit and a coffin of rare wood in 68 B.C.E. On such occasions, rank was determined by the nature of the thread that linked the jade wafers, ranging from gold to silver and bronze.

The second technique involved the interment of the body in nested wooden coffins covered first in a thick layer of charcoal, then in clay. Under favorable conditions, this coating excluded air and water from the tomb and led to the perfect preservation of bodily tissue. The most remarkable example is from Tomb 1 at MAWANGDUI. There the remains of the marchioness of Dai, interred in the mid-second century B.C.E., were so well preserved that even the arterial blood had not lost its red color, and the limbs could be moved as if the woman were still alive.

BURIAL OBJECTS

The artifacts interred with these aristocrats were listed in detail in the inventories of BAMBOO SLIPS, and those at Mawangdui were also sealed with the insignium of the marquis's household. At Mancheng the prince Liu Sheng was accompanied by his chariots and horses and the fine gold, silver, and bronze tableware he would have used in his household. One chamber was furnished with his bathroom, another with ceramic containers for food and wine. Food was also provided to the marquis of Dai, his wife, and his son, together with their fine LACQUER serving dishes and chopsticks. The marchioness was accompanied by an impressive wardrobe of silk garments and even rolls of silk for future tailoring. There were mittens, slippers, and robes. Musical instruments were neatly packed into the tomb, together with models of the musicians themselves. The marquis and his son were provided with silk manuscripts for them to consult, even including a military map.

The provision of everything needed by the *bo* was achieved across the Han empire by the provision of models and pictures, which give a rich insight into agriculture and entertainment. There are, for example, models of granaries and pigsties, of peasants working in their fields, watchtowers, and village ponds. The carved stone reliefs from many parts of China include scenes of bullfighting, acrobats and jugglers, music, and dancing. One set of painted wall scenes from Helingeer in Mongolia shows the principal events in the life of the deceased.

See also MINGDI.

Bodh Gaya   Bodh Gaya, ancient Uruvilva, India, is one of the most sacred Buddhist sites, for it was here, under a

The medieval temple dominates the site of Bodh Gaya, where the Buddha attained enlightenment. The *bodhi* tree that sheltered him survives there. *(© Philip Baird/www. anthroarcheart.org)*

bodhi (enlightenment) tree, that the Buddha gained enlightenment. The original tree, allegedly tended for more than 2,500 years, survives. A sapling taken from it was sent by the emperor ASOKA (r. 268–235 B.C.E.) to Sri Lanka to spread the DHARMA in that direction. The tree was surrounded by a railing during the SUNGA dynasty (first century B.C.E.), and part of the fence can still be seen. It is embellished with religious themes—the wheel of the law and some secular scenes, including musicians and people gathering flowers. The temple at this site, in the form of a narrow pyramid with a flat top, was added in the medieval period.

bodhisattva   A bodhisattva is one who, in the Buddhist religion, seeks enlightenment. The term comes from a combination of two PALI words—*bodhi,* "enlightenment," and *sattva,* "a being or one who is." In its original usage, the term *bodhisattva* applied to the Buddha before his enlightenment at the age of 35: The Buddha

referred to the days before his enlightenment as those when he was only a bodhisattva. In the Mayahana school of BUDDHISM, it refers to a person who renounces the path to nirvana to assist others in their search for salvation. It is important to note that the concept of the bodhisattva was linked with kingship. In Sri Lanka, for example, sovereigns from at least the fourth century C.E. were seen as bodhisattvas, and the term was included in their royal titles in a number of inscriptions. The practice also spread to Southeast Asia, particularly to ANGKOR, in Cambodia, during the reign of JAYAVARMAN VII (1181–1219 C.E.).

See also AVALOKITESVARA; BAYON.

A bodhisattva is a follower of the Buddha who renounces the path to nirvana in order to help others seek enlightenment. This wooden image of a bodhisattva is from Japan's Heian period. *(Art Resource, NY)*

Bohu Tong The *Bohu Tong* (*Discourses in the White Tiger Hall*) is a text compiled by the Chinese historian BAN GU. It records conversations involving the Han king ZHANGDI (r. 75–88 C.E.) on the subject of the Confucian theory of the complementary relationship between the ruler and his ministers and the good of the people ruled.

See also CONFUCIUS; HAN DYNASTY.

Borobudur Borobudur is the world's largest and most impressive Buddhist temple. It is located on the island of Java, in Indonesia, about 40 kilometers (24 miles) to the northwest of Jogjakarta, and was built between approximately 780–830 C.E. Its original name was probably Bhumisambarabhudhara, "the mountain of the accumulation of virtue on the 10 stages of the BHODHISATTVA." To a Buddhist pilgrim during the monument's heyday, the temple was a symbol for the attainment of enlightenment. To the modern visitor, the initial impression is of the immensity and magnificence of the stone reliefs, which line the four rectangular galleries at the base. It was covered by volcanic ash in about 1000 C.E. The earliest record of knowledge of this monument by a European is from 1814. Sir Stamford Raffles, then the lieutenant governor of Java during a brief period of British colonial rule, reported its existence as part of a program to record all the historic sites on the island and found it shrouded in vegetation. Intensive research during the next 100 years placed the monument into its historic and religious context. This has also involved two periods of restoration, the first in the early years of the 20th century, and the second during the 1970s and 1980s. It has now been fully stabilized under the *ANASTYLOSIS* technique, and provision has been made for the drainage of rainwater that had caused serious deterioration.

THE ARCHITECTURE

Borobudur, constructed on a natural hill, incorporates 56,000 cubic meters (2 million cubic feet) of the local volcanic stone. The summit stupa stands 31.5 (104 ft.) meters above the ground level. It was constructed during the rule of the SAILENDRA dynasty (c. 750 to 850 C.E.) in the agriculturally rich Kedu plain in central Java. The combination of esoteric Buddhist knowledge, labor, and skill of the masons that went into its construction is rivaled in Southeast Asia only by the Vishnuite shrine of ANGKOR WAT in Cambodia. Essentially Borobudur consists of a square platform surmounted by five square terraces comprising four galleries. Four sets of steps lead from one terrace to the next. Three circular terraces stand above these, leading up to the central, circular stupa. The basal terrace was built after the monument was completed, possibly to stabilize it and to contain the massive weight of the structure above. This addition had the effect of covering up the reliefs lining the original outer wall, and a few of these have been uncovered. Fragmentary inscriptions on the concealed base have assisted in the dating of Borobudur on the basis of the style of the script employed.

THE RELIEFS

The reliefs lining the galleries cover a linear distance of about five kilometers (3 miles) and are set in two rows within panels. The galleries are designed so that a visitor feels enclosed, for it is impossible to see any of the tiers above or below. The structure is designed to initiate the adherent into the path to nirvana. When following ascending terraces in a clockwise direction, the visitor first sees scenes from daily life illustrating human foibles, such as cruelty or idleness, and the retribution for sins in the next life. Then the themes on the reliefs begin to illustrate the true path of compassion and concern for fellow creatures. From the enclosed terraces, the visitor then ascends into open sunlit circular terraces again linked by four staircases on each side of the monument. Each terrace contains circular stupas, 32 on the lowest, 24 on the middle, and 16 on the uppermost. These are rendered in openwork stone in such a way that the statues of the Buddhas within can be discerned. These images symbolize increasing proximity to the ultimate spiritual state, or nirvana. The climax to the ascent is found in the huge central stupa, which contained an incomplete image of the Buddha completely hidden from view.

In addition to their religious significance, the reliefs provide information on the way of life in Java during the ninth century C.E. A particularly well-known relief shows an oceangoing vessel equipped with masts, multiple sails, a bowsprit, and outrigger. The passengers in the adjacent panel land are welcomed by the local inhabitants, who stand in front of a large house raised on stilts. People rest beneath the house, while two birds perch on the roof. Another scene shows a man plowing with the assistance of two oxen. Carousing dancers are seen in contrast to a serene family dinner. A sick person is being treated by concerned attendants who rub ointments onto his arms. The detailed knowledge of the life of the Buddha is also richly illustrated in panels showing, for example, Queen Maya sitting in a pavilion, having just been informed that she has been selected as the mother of the future Buddha. Her subsequent procession to the Lumbini Pleasure Garden in India includes a fine rendition of a horse-drawn coach richly furnished with a decorated throne. These reliefs are among the greatest achievements of Southeast Asian civilization.

Bouillevaux, Father Charles-Émile (1823–1913) *Father C.-E. Bouillevaux was a French missionary who visited Angkor in 1850 and published an account of his impressions eight years later.*

He described ANGKOR WAT and the BAYON, noting the giant statues then shrouded in vegetation at the southern entrance to ANGKOR THOM. HENRI MOUHOT is often referred to as the first Western visitor to discover Angkor, but Bouillevaux preceded him by nine years; Father Chevreuil, a French missionary, by 200 years; and the Portuguese by three centuries.

boundary markers   The INSCRIPTIONS covering the period from the seventh to the fourteenth centuries in Cambodia often refer to land divisions and private or corporate ownership of land. Ownership of land by the elite and by temple foundations provided considerable wealth, since the kingdoms of CHENLA and ANGKOR were essentially agrarian. At Angkor, from 800 C.E., inscriptions refer to an officeholder known as a *khlon visaya*, whose duties included the definition of land boundaries and the placement of stone boundary markers. During the civil war between Jayaviravarman and SURYAVARMAN I in the early 11th century, inscriptions describe boundary disputes that suggest conflict. In 1003 C.E., an order was issued to replace boundaries uprooted and destroyed at Prasat Trapan Sno; two years later at Prasat Dambok Khpo, someone incised on the doorjamb a demand to seize and impale those who had destroyed boundary markers.

Brahmi   Brahmi is the name given to a script that is ancestral to many of the modern scripts of India. The decipherment of Brahmi was achieved in 1837 by JAMES PRINSEP, on the basis of inscriptions from SANCHI. It is thought to have originated from an Aramaic writing system through maritime trade. Some of its letter forms are clearly related to Aramaic. The potsherds inscribed in Brahmi discovered at ANURADHAPURA, Sri Lanka, indicate that it was employed from at least the eighth or seventh century B.C.E. In the third century B.C.E. the Mauryan emperor ASOKA used Brahmi in most of his column inscriptions. Excavations at OC EO on the Mekong Delta in Vietnam have furnished a number of SEALS and rings inscribed in this script, the earliest-known writing in Southeast Asia. When compared with Indian styles, the inscriptions appear to date to the second to fifth century C.E. As it spread, so Brahmi may have generated most of the writing systems of East and Southeast Asia, including Khmer, Thai, and Burmese.

Brantas River   The Brantas River is a strategic waterway in east Java in Indonesia and was the focus of a major trading state from the early 10th century until 1222. The founder of this dynasty, a shadowy figure called Sindok, originated in central Java before moving to the Brantas River Delta. The first inscription to name him king is dated to 929 C.E., but he had been an official under previous rulers. Not only was the delta area suited to rice cultivation, but it also ultimately dominated the trade in spices. Inscriptions from this area include an important text from the site of KALADI, dated 909 C.E., which described the presence of foreigners and traders. Inscriptions dating to the reign of Sindok also mention the tax status of traders and the use of as many as seven types of ships in trading. Although it is highly likely that spices such as cloves, mace, and nutmeg were important exports, none is mentioned in the inscriptions.

brick, medium for building   Brick as a construction material was very much an Indian rather than a Chinese medium. In China construction of walls and building foundations followed the HANGTU technique, in which loess was compounded in wooden frames and surmounted by wooden buildings. The cities of the INDUS VALLEY CIVILIZATION, on the other hand, had structures built of mud brick or fired brick, a technique that continued in later Indian states and was transmitted to Southeast Asia.

INDIAN ARCHITECTURE

At Allahdino in India, third-millennium B.C.E. houses were laid out on an east-northeast to west-southwest orientation and were constructed of mud brick on stone foundations. They were equipped with stone-lined wells and drains. Many sites in India have been looted for their bricks, as seen at TAXILA and Charsada in modern Pakistan. At Arikamedu in southern India, SIR MORTIMER WHEELER was able to uncover the first-century B.C.E. foundations of what was probably a brick-built warehouse 45 meters (149 ft.) in length and the remains of two tanks or vats that had been used for dying cloth.

SOUTHEAST ASIAN ARCHITECTURE

Throughout the prehistoric period in Southeast Asia, buildings were made of wood or unfired clay. All that remains are postholes where the foundations formerly lay and occasionally the remains of clay wall foundations or floors. From at least the sixth century C.E., however, bricks were employed in the construction of religious buildings. Since the architects of ANGKOR had not developed techniques to span a large space in brick or stone, temple buildings were small and narrow, and the growth in their size was accomplished by adding similar cells or lengthening galleries. The use of bricks in increasing quantities must have had a serious effect on the environment, particularly through deforestation as a result of fueling brick kilns with wood or charcoal.

The earliest use of bricks is found in the Mekong Delta state of FUNAN in Cambodia, at such sites as NEN CHUA and OC EO (fourth–sixth centuries C.E.). At ANGKOR BOREI, brick temple foundations are numerous, and the city was protected by a substantial brick wall. Between 550 and 800, the period of the CHENLA kingdoms of central Cambodia, brick was widely used in the construction of temples and surrounding walls. There are numerous brick shrines at ISHANAPURA, many of which are decorated by molding or shaping the brick to form images of palaces and members of the court. The large brick sanctuaries at BANTEAY PREI NOKOR and Trapeang Phong reveal that brick was the preferred building medium in the late eighth century C.E., and it continued to be widely used at HARIHARALAYA, where the Preah Ko temple of INDRAVARMAN I (877–99 C.E.) was built in brick covered in ornamented stucco. The BAKSEI CHAMKRONG temple constructed at YASHODHARAPURA incorporates a brick shrine elevated on three tiers of laterite blocks. But the supreme example of brick construction is the contemporary temple known as Prasat Kravan that was dedicated in 921 C.E. It includes five brick towers in a linear arrangement, and the unique interior brick reliefs depict Vishnu. Brick remained in use during the reign of RAJENDRAVARMAN (r. 944–68 C.E.), but thereafter sandstone became increasingly popular, as at Ta Keo and ultimately at ANGKOR WAT and the BAYON. In Myanmar (Burma), VESALI on the Arakan (now Rakhine) coast was ringed with a substantial brick wall and moat, while many of the temples at PAGAN were built in brick.

CENTRAL ASIAN ARCHITECTURE

The technique of building in brick was also found widely in Central Asia, where Indian influence permeated the SILK ROAD. During the first millennium B.C.E., brick was used at the MERV Oasis (Mary in modern Turkmenistan); the fourth- to the seventh-century C.E. town houses of rich Sogdian merchants at AFRASIAB, ancient Samarqand in Uzbekistan, were constructed of compressed loess and mud brick, and the interior walls were coated with clay. A Greek-style temple at AIRTAM was also constructed of brick.

Broach Broach, formerly Bharukaccha or Barygaza, lies on the north bank of the lower Narmada River in Gujarat province, western India. After its initial occupation during the Chalcolithic period, a mud wall was constructed during the last few centuries B.C.E., and excavations have yielded a wide range of artifacts, including arrowheads and ornaments. The third period of occupation saw the defensive wall reinforced in brick, but virtually continuous settlement down to the present has prevented the intensive excavation that this strategic site deserves. The PERIPLUS OF THE ERYTHRAEAN SEA (first century C.E.) describes Barygaza as a major port handling imports of Italian wine, and Mediterranean amphorae, vessels for shipping wine in quantity, have been found over much of India in sites dating to the first and second centuries C.E.

See also NEVASA.

bronze casting

INDIA AND PAKISTAN

The properties of copper ore for the manufacture of metal artifacts was known at a very early date in India and Pakistan. At MEHRGARH, copper beads have been found in contexts dating as early as 6000 B.C.E. The metal workers of the INDUS CIVILIZATION were highly skilled. By the second half of the third millennium B.C.E., they were able to cast figurines by using the lost wax technique. This involved investing a clay core with wax in the form of the desired artifact and then covering the wax with an outer layer of clay, ensuring by the use of pins that the inner and outer clay bodies were separated at all times. Having melted the wax, molten bronze was then poured into the mold. The bronze smiths also used annealing, that is, heating and hammering an artifact to give it added strength, and were able to rivet castings into composite tools. Their output included vessels in a wide range of forms, spearheads, figurines, knives, and axes. During the second half of the second millennium B.C.E., a bronze industry was established in eastern India, in the context of small agricultural communities such as Navdatoli and Inamgaon. The range of artifacts included bangles, rings, axes, arrowheads, and chisels.

CHINA

Recent archaeological research has revealed that early knowledge of copper-based metallurgy reached western China from the West by means of the expansion of people and the spread of ideas along what later came to be known as the SILK ROAD. Settlements of the QIJIA CULTURE in Gansu Province have revealed the presence of copper or bronze implements by the mid- to late third millennium B.C.E. At Qinweijia, for example, pits have yielded copper or bronze implements, including an ax, an awl, discs, and rings. The ax was annealed to harden it. This is a technically sophisticated procedure. Dahezhuang and Huangniangniangtai have also yielded bronzes, 32 specimens from the latter site being found in occupation contexts and burials. Some of the knives, awls, and chisels were cast from copper, others from a tin bronze. This knowledge of the properties of bronze was assimilated in the LONGSHAN CULTURE of the Chinese central plains during the late third millennium B.C.E. Early urban centers there were associated with large cemeteries. At TAOSI, one rich grave included a copper bell. Bronze working took on a distinctive Chinese character with the development of the XIA DYNASTY. At ERLITOU, elite graves contained bronze grave goods, including vessels, bells, knives, and halberds (*ge*). There are also some unusual bronze plaques inlaid with turquoise. The vessel forms included a wine jug, which was cast in the piece mold technique. This technique stands at the threshold of the magnificent bronze ritual vessels cast during the ensuing SHANG DYNASTY. A series of clay molds, bearing a negative of desired decoration, was fitted together over a clay core prior to the pouring of the molten bronze into the intervening space. By this technique, the finest bronzes of the ancient world were produced in specialist workshops, and many found their way into imperial and aristocratic tombs. The richest Shang burial uncovered to date contained the remains of FU HAO, a consort of the emperor. Her bronzes provide a measure of her high status. Many vessels are of unusual form, and the two largest contribute 120 kilograms (264 lbs.) to the total weight of 1,600 kilograms (3,520 lbs.) of bronze in the tomb.

Further technical improvements and new designs mark the passage of the ensuing ZHOU DYNASTY, until arguably the summit of Chinese bronze working was reached in the vessels from the tomb of ZENG HOU YI, marquis of Zeng, dated to the late fifth century B.C.E. The tomb contained almost 10 tons of bronze, a figure not yet exceeded in the history of China. Two festive vessels, known as the *zun* and the *pan*, take pride of place. Minutely decorated, they were cast by the piece mold system, as well as the lost wax method. The latter allows for lifelike images to be formed, and hence the vessels incorporate dragons and serpents, each individually cast, before being soldered to the vessel.

SOUTHEAST ASIA

Since the Shang had established trade connections with the south, particularly for supplying turtle shells, it is highly likely that knowledge of alloying copper with tin reached Southeast Asia from Chinese sources, between 1500–1000 B.C.E. During the Bronze Age, most bronzes were cast in the form of personal ornaments, although one also encounters spears, arrowheads, and socketed axes. The Iron Age, which began about 500 B.C.E., saw a proliferation in both the quantity and the range of bronzes, including finger and toe rings, belts, and head ornaments. Early civilizations, therefore, had the opportunity to employ bronzes based on a millennium of expertise. At the FUNAN port city of OC EO, French archaeologist Louis Malleret found a gold workshop, including bronze awls and hammers, indicating an early industrial use of bronze. However, the principal developments were to be the casting of monumental statues of gods, the use of bronze for casting musical instruments, and the use of highly ornamented bronzes as components of vehicles, palanquins, and chariots. The excavators of the central temple of AK YUM, which was constructed before the foundation of the Kingdom of Angkor in about 800 C.E., found six bronze statues, two of a Hindu deity and four of the Buddha, varying between nine and 35 centimeters (9 and 14 in.) in height. A donation made to a temple in northeast Thailand during the reign of SURYAVARMAN I included rice, cloth, workers, a pair of buffaloes, four pairs of sacred cattle, and a bronze cymbal. An outstanding gilded bronze door guardian from the same region that was recently unearthed at Kamphaeng Yai stands 1.84 meters high. Perhaps the most impressive monumental bronze, however, is a part of a huge statue of Vishnu from the Western Mebon, an island temple in the middle of the WESTERN BARAY at Angkor. A cremation cemetery near the Sras Srang in Angkor was identified first with the recovery of pottery jars associated with bronze Buddha images. The French archaeologist B.-P. Groslier then excavated further the mortuary vessels containing human ashes, associated with Chinese ceramic vessels and figures, and bronze mirrors, iron weapons, ingots and pieces of lead. The mortuary jars were grouped with other vessels of local manufacture, a bronze pin 30 centimeters long, iron hooks, chains, axes, and knives. A tin vessel was associated with one cremation, along with animal teeth, stone mortars, and grinding stones. One pot contained seven lead ingots. In one instance, a pair of bronze mirrors was found, on a precise east-west orientation. The ivory handle survived on another mirror. Bronze palanquin rings and fittings and images of the Buddha and Vishnu riding the eagle GARUDA were also found. There must have been a considerable demand for copper during the Angkorian period, for we read that at PREAH VIHEAR, a leading dignitary had the floors of the towers faced with bronze plaques. The later foundation inscription of the PREAH KHAN temple lists 20,400 statues of gods in gold, silver, bronze, and stone in the government rest houses.

The establishment of such a vigorous bronze industry during the prehistoric period on the mainland of Southeast Asia was the springboard for the export of bronzes, and the ultimate establishment of a local industry, in the offshore islands. During the late first millennium B.C.E., DONG SON–style bronze drums were exported to island chiefdoms. These were soon copied in the form of the Pejeng drums, while stone mold fragments from Sembiran on the northern coast of Bali reflect local workshops on an island devoid of either copper or tin ore. Clearly, bronze working was a stimulus to trade in ingots. The products of this Balinese bronze industry included armlets, necklaces, belts, and ear- and finger rings that found their way into aristocratic burials dating to the first few centuries C.E.

Further reading: Gao Dalun. "Bronze Ritual Artefacts of the Shu Culture: A Preliminary Survey," *Orientations* 32 (2001): 45–51; Higham, C. F. W. *The Bronze Age of Southeast Asia*. Cambridge: Cambridge University Press, 1996; Kohl, P. L. *The Bronze Age Civilization of Central Asia: Recent Soviet Discoveries*. Armank: M. E. Sharpe, 1981; Masson, V. M., "The Bronze Age in Khorasan and Transoxania." In *History of the Civilizations of Central Asia,* Vol. 1, edited by A. H. Dani and V. M. Masson, 225–245. Paris: UNESCO, 1992; Shelach, G. "Early Bronze Age Cultures in North China," *Asian Perspectives* 33 (1994): 261–292.

Buddhism Buddhism is one of the oldest of the great world religions. It originated in the life and teachings of Sakyamuni, the son of royal parents, King Suddhodana and Queen Maya, and after it was established in India, it spread to Central Asia, Southeast Asia, China, Korea and Japan. Its teachings stress attaining enlightenment and escaping the cycle of life, death, and rebirth, which generate suffering.

EMERGENCE OF BUDDHISM

The date of the future Buddha's birth and events of his life are not firmly established. It is widely held that he was born in 543 B.C.E. Some sources, however, affirm that his birth was 218 years before the consecration of King ASOKA, others that it was only a century earlier than the consecration, respectively, either 486 or 368 B.C.E. He was born in Nepal, and his birthplace, LUMBINI, was the site of one of Asoka's columns. The future Buddha was a member of the Gautama clan of the Sakya tribe and had a rich and privileged upbringing, living in his father's palace and marrying Princess Yasodhara when he was aged 16. However, his appreciation of poverty and illness stimulated a concern for one of the central religious tenets of the day, the notion that all beings underwent a continuous cycle of life, death, and rebirth, which necessitated illness and suffering.

To break this cycle, he left home and traveled south, to the kingdom of Magadha in the Ganges (Ganga) Valley in India, and took up the life of a wandering mendicant, living under the harshest conditions of personal privation while meditating on the human condition. This way of life, which he endured for six years, he found debilitating and of little profit in his quest. He left his five fellow mendicants and, having bathed in the river of Nairanjana, sat near a fig tree. In the course of meditation, he attained complete and perfect enlightenment. At the age of 34, he thus became a Buddha, "enlightened one." After a further period of meditation lasting several weeks, he traveled to the Varanasi (formerly Benares) Deer Park and there expounded the DHARMA, the doctrine of deliverance from the cyclic pattern of life, death, and rebirth, to his former companions. This doctrine includes four basic truths concerning human sufferings: Suffering is found everywhere because of greed and desire, and the path toward an end to suffering, nirvana, is followed by the Buddha.

For the remainder of his life, until his death at the age of 80 years, he traveled widely, expounding the dharma, attracting followers, and founding a religious order of monks. He died just outside KUSINAGARA, in India, and after his cremation, his remains were distributed as holy relics and preserved under stupas. Even during his lifetime, the Sangha, or monastic orders of Buddhist monks, was established. This is a vital strand in the practice of Buddhism, which includes four entities—monks, nuns, laymen, and laywomen. The Buddha, having experienced six years of asceticism at the start of his quest, resolved to follow the middle path that eschewed extreme privation as contributing little to the attainment of enlightenment. Therefore, while the monks and their monastic foundations were maintained by meritorious gifts by the laity, the laity received in return the fundamental teachings of the Buddha. The Sangha entails the monks' renunciation of worldly possessions. Prescriptions govern the acquisition and nature of clothing: Monks can wear three garments given them by the laity. Their possessions include a begging bowl, belt, razor, strainer, needle, staff, and toothpick. A morning procession of monks with their food bowls can be seen today across much of East, South, and Southeast Asia. Monks are allowed to eat meat or fish only if the animal was not killed specifically for them. They have no fixed residence but often live in monasteries. Their daily round involves praying, meditating, perambulating to secure food from the laity, eating before noon, meditating, and receiving instruction.

SPREAD OF BUDDHISM IN SOUTHEAST ASIA

The Sangha was established by the time of the Buddha's death, after which a meeting of monks set about the task of formalizing his teachings and expanding his following through moving out from Bihar in India into the surrounding areas. The major triumph of early Buddhism was the conversion of the Mauryan emperor Asoka (r. 268–235 B.C.E.), who enthusiastically espoused the doctrine and sent missionaries throughout his kingdom and beyond. His son, Mahendra, established Buddhism in one of its greatest future centers, Sri Lanka. The KUSHAN king KANISHKA I (100–126) was another adherent, whose influence saw the Mahayana branch of Buddhism spread into Central Asia. One of Asoka's missions, led by his servants Gavampti, Sona, and Uttara, was dispatched to Southeast Asia in the mid-third century B.C.E.

The site of BAN DON TA PHET in central Thailand has provided the earliest archaeological evidence for knowledge of Buddhism in Southeast Asia, in the form of a small figurine of a carnelian lion, an animal employed to represent the Buddha. This site has been dated to the fourth century B.C.E. Buddhism was adopted by the PYU CIVILIZATION of inland Myanmar (Burma) and ultimately dominated the religious architecture of the DVARAVATI CIVILIZATION of the Chao Phraya Valley in central Thailand (500–900). There are numerous stupas, circular structures that house a relic of the Buddha, and *caityas,* buildings or temples that hold a sacred object, such as an image of the Buddha. Images of the Buddha show the adoption of this religion in the state of FUNAN (150–550), in the area of the Mekong Delta in Cambodia. Images of the Buddha have been found in the deep vault in the temple of AK YUM, which belongs to the period of CHENLA kingdoms (550–800). During the period of Angkor in Cambodia, Buddhism is often mentioned in the inscriptions; it became dominant during the reign of JAYAVARMAN VII (1181–1219). He had numerous images of the Buddha set up in his state temple, the BAYON, and in temples across the kingdom. However, a successor king, JAYAVARMAN VIII (r. 1243–96), reacted violently against Buddhism and had the images destroyed or modified in favor of Hindu gods. Buddhism was the religion of the SAILENDRA kings of the Kedu plain in central Java, in Indonesia, and they were responsible for the construction of the world's largest Buddhist monument, BOROBUDUR, between 780 and 830. In Vietnam, the huge temple complex of DONG DUONG was constructed in the late ninth century in the CHAM CIVILIZATION kingdom of Amaravati. Here MAHAYANA BUDDHISM was preferred, and numerous fine statues have survived.

BUDDHISM IN CHINA

Buddhism was introduced into China through two avenues. There was contact along the SILK ROAD, and from the second or third century C.E., from Southeast Asia, by what has come to be known as the southern or maritime Silk Road. The earliest evidence for Buddhism in China dates to the later HAN DYNASTY of the first two centuries C.E., and one of the earliest depictions of the Buddha in China has been found in a rock-cut tomb at MA HAO in Sichuan. The first historic record relates that in 65 C.E. Liu Ying, king of Chu and half-brother of Emperor MINGDI, followed certain Buddhist rituals. Buddhism initially made little headway in the face of the long-established and centralizing Confucian ethic, and it was only during the period of instability and lack of a firm central government, between the fourth and fifth centuries, that it secured a firm foothold. The basic problem faced by early Buddhism in China was that its doctrines of rebirth, enlightenment, and nirvana ran counter to the centralizing imperial administration. A strange sect whose adherents did not work, contributed no labor or taxes, and begged for their sustenance did not transplant readily into a society where agriculture, the soil, and hard work linked with ANCESTOR WORSHIP had predominated for millennia. Buddhism was officially tolerated under the later Han, but without any enthusiasm.

Having obtained a foothold, however, the faith did grow. There was a constant flow of new ideas and adherents along the Asiatic Silk Road. Thus in 148 C.E. An Shigao, a Buddhist missionary, from Parthia arrived at the court of LUOYANG in China. He was joined by other Parthians, as well as Sogdians and Indians, to form a small community whose members addressed the difficult task of translating specialized esoteric texts into an alien language without the necessary words to express their concepts. The Monastery of the White Horse at Chang'an was founded by at least the third century C.E. The name originated in an apocryphal story of the Han emperor Mingdi (58–75), who dreamed that he was visited by a god in the form of a golden man. His soothsayers said that this must have been the Buddha, and he sent envoys to India to learn more. The envoys returned with two Buddhist monks, a white horse, and Buddhist religious texts. During the political upheavals following the end of the Han dynasty, Buddhism strengthened its foothold. Dharmsaksa, a missionary from DUNHUANG, made many conversions in northern China, while the first of a number of Chinese monks, Chu Shixing, traveled on a pilgrimage to HOTAN in northwest China in about 260 C.E. to search for information and holy texts.

BUDDHISM IN JAPAN

In Japan the NIHONGI chronicle of 720 C.E. relates that King Syong Myong of PAEKCHE in Korea sent a gilded image of the Buddha along with sacred texts to the Japanese emperor Kinmei-Tenno in the hope of securing an alliance with him against his rivals. Consultations followed in the Japanese court, and the new image, against much local opposition, was tentatively accepted and placed in a temple. The temple and the image, however, were soon destroyed when a plague afflicted Japan and the new god was blamed for the misfortune. However, the emperor subsequently had new images made, and Buddhism secured a foothold. This adoption was part of a wider movement, favored by the influential Soga clan, of absorbing aspects of mainland culture, such as the Chinese writing system. It was from its acceptance by the court that this new religion spread more widely in Japan. Under PRINCE SHOTUKU (574–622), Buddhism became the official court religion. Shotuku allegedly founded the HORYUJI temple in Nara, thought to be the world's oldest surviving wooden building. This was not the only major Buddhist temple, for the popularity of this new religion at court led to rivalry among the elite families to construct religious foundations. It is recorded that at the prince's death, there were 46 Buddhist temples and 816 monks in Japan.

See also CONFUCIUS.

Further reading: Bechert, H., and Gombrich, R., eds. *The World of Buddhism.* London: Thames and Hudson, 1984; Bhikkhu Nanamoli. *The Life of the Buddha: According to the Pali Canon.* Seattle: BPS Pariyatti Editions, 2001; Hallade, M. *The Gandhara Style and the Evolution of Buddhist Art.* London: Thames and Hudson, 1968.

Bunjikat   *See* KALA-I KAHKAHA.

C

Calamadana *See* QIEMO.

canals The control of water through the construction of canals was a widespread, almost universal feature of early Asian civilizations. Canals were dug for many reasons. Foremost was the provision of water into irrigated fields to increase agricultural production. This was important in areas subject to the vagaries of the monsoon, as in southern China, Sri Lanka, and Myanmar (Burma). Canals were also built for drainage and for the movement of bulky and heavy commodities by water. In many instances, state intervention has been documented as the motivating force behind the execution of major IRRIGATION and infrastructure works, but this does not mean that it was through the control of water distribution that rulers maintained authority.

CHINA

Canal construction and the related digging of defensive moats often fed by rivers or canals began early in China and reached a high point under the QIN (221–206 B.C.E.) and Han dynasties (206 B.C.E.–220 C.E.). The Qin rulers conceived, or at least persisted with, the huge irrigation scheme based on the water of the Min River. Known as the Dujiangyan ("capital river dam") project, it was directed by Li Bing, the governor of SHU, appointed in 277 B.C.E. The Min River flows down from the mountains east of Chengdu and is prone to serious flooding. Li Bing, later deified locally for his efforts, divided the river into two channels. One continued on to its junction with the Chang (Yangtze), while the other or inner channel was directed along canals hacked through the surrounding upland and so onto the Chengdu Plain. There the water was reticulated to a vast area of rice fields.

The Han Chinese have left a large corpus of records that describe the widespread application of irrigation to agriculture. Essentially this had three objectives that varied with the local conditions. One was to introduce water into the fields and rice plots by means of canals, runnels, and dams. During the WARRING STATES PERIOD (475–221 B.C.E.) there had been some limited irrigation developments, but the expansion of irrigation networks during the HAN DYNASTY was dramatic. The Bureau of Command was responsible for organizing corvée or convict labor for government construction projects, such as the GREAT WALL, canals, dikes, and roads. In 130 B.C.E. a major canal was constructed to transport grain to the capital from the east, and this provided water to irrigate fields by means of small feeder channels. In 111 B.C.E. six canals were added to the Zheng Guo canal, which was fed by the Jing River, for irrigation. In this instance the heavy silt load carried by the water was deemed beneficial for millet production. The *Hou Han Shu* (*History of the Later Han*) also provides details of how irrigation facilities were put in place and the means whereby the equitable distribution of water was managed. In the second half of the first century B.C.E. Xin Zhen was appointed the grand administrator of the Commandery of Nan Yang. This was a large area located in southwest Henan province. He personally traveled over the region under his control, inspecting all possible areas that could be improved by irrigation facilities. He then ordered the construction of canals, dams, water gates, and dikes, which greatly improved agricultural production. He erected stone inscriptions to indicate how the water should be distributed for the benefit of all. When his works were called to the attention of the court, he was promoted and awarded gold for his encouragement of agriculture.

KOREA AND JAPAN

As in many other instances, the early states of Korea and Japan were familiarized with irrigation techniques through their contacts with the Chinese. In the early fifth century King Nintoku of Japan had the Ishiwara River diverted into a canal to bear water to thousands of hectares of formerly marginal land. On the Osaka Plain a 10-kilometer (6 mi.) canal between 8.5 and 9.5 meters (about 31 ft.) wide has been identified. The emperor's role in enhancing agriculture is amply demonstrated.

INDIA AND SRI LANKA

In India, the ideal of a city propounded by Kautilya (late fourth century B.C.E.) incorporated a royal palace in the center, surrounded by square precincts, each with its own function: an elephant park; areas for merchants, artisans, and entertainment; and residences. These were protected by a city wall with forts and moats. Religious sanctuaries could be built both within the walls and beyond them, and the dead were cremated in specified areas according to the class of the deceased. Given the monsoon climate and seasonal rainfall patterns, reservoirs were constructed, were linked to canals and often the surrounding moats, and were sources for irrigated fields.

In Sri Lanka the early irrigation system that developed in the dry zone is regarded as one of the most innovative and sophisticated in the preindustrial world. The earliest inscriptions, dating from the third century B.C.E., mention small-scale irrigation, and the enlargement of the system was facilitated by the invention of the cistern sluice, known as the *bisokotuva*, which regulated the flow of water from a large reservoir or tank without endangering weirs. One of the major early achievements was the diversion of the Ambanganga River, a tributary of the Mahavali, which originates in the wet central highlands south of ANURADHAPURA.

The Alisara canal, first mentioned during the reign of King Vasabha (65–109), flowed for about 50 kilometers (30 mi.) to the capital. This king is credited with a marked expansion of the system, including not only the canal but also 12 reservoirs. The Jayaganga canal, 80 kilometers (48 mi.) long, carried water to Anuradhapura as well as irrigated an area of 62,000 hectares (155,000 acres). The gradient for much of its length involved a fall of only 10 centimeters per kilometer.

SOUTHEAST ASIA

In 1931 ancient canals were detected crisscrossing the Mekong Delta landscape on the basis of aerial photography, linking the city of OC EO with another walled city known at ANGKOR BOREI. Canals have been prominent features of ANGKOR in Cambodia from the earliest European accounts. DIOGO DO COUTO, writing in the late 16th cen-

tury, noted that there was, at the city of ANGKOR THOM, "a causeway of the same width as the bridges, flanked by canals, fed by the great moat around the city. The water originates from the north and east, and leaves from the south and west. The system is fed by the river diverted there." A French aviator in the 1920s noted the lines of ancient canals crossing the Mekong Delta; these link centers of the early FUNAN state, such as OC EO and Ta Kev. The canal linking Oc Eo and Angkor Borei is 90 kilometers (54 mi.) long. At Angkor, canals were built to link the reservoirs with the rivers that fed them and the *baray*s, or reservoirs, they supplied. A text dating to the reign of RAJENDRAVARMAN of Angkor describes how a grandee named Mahendradhipativarman transformed forested land into a village, consecrated an image, and made a *baray*: "In a place of pasture where water was difficult to obtain, in a forested hollow, he made a reservoir fed by three rivers, as was the proper thing to do, for the benefit of others." The inscription proceeds with a description of the boundaries of rice fields, which include all the ponds to the east, to the south as far as the canal, and to the north to the canal at Panlin. GEORGES CŒDÈS has suggested that the word used for "canal" in this section implies use in irrigation. Moreover, many of the boundaries for rice fields are described as reservoirs. The canals, however, might not have been entirely or even partially concerned with agriculture. Those on the Mekong Delta might have assisted in drainage and transportation. The canals servicing the *baray*s of Angkor could have in effect been providing sacred water with no further reticulation to rice fields. One lengthy canal seems to have linked stone quarries with the GREAT LAKE and would have aided the transportation of building materials.

Farther west, in the dry zone of Myanmar (Burma), a series of large reservoirs are found to the east, west, and south of the city of Halin, the irrigation system of which incorporated the long Muhaung canal. This complex system of water distribution involved about 300 square kilometers (120 sq. mi.) of land.

CENTRAL ASIA

Central Asia is particularly arid but contains many large rivers that originate in the mountains and dissipate as they enter the deserts, or in the case of the Syr Dar'ya and Amu Dar'ya, the Aral Sea. Merv (Mary in Turkmenistan) was located to command its sector of the SILK ROAD but was also set in an arid environment. The economy of this nodal center on the Silk Road linking China with Rome and India depended not only on trade but also on agriculture. Many major irrigation canals are found in the area of the oasis.

Miran was a major SHAN-SHAN center. It was located in the bleak and arid Taklamakan Desert, but formerly the site lay between two rivers, long since dried up, and canals had transported water to the site.

The KUSHAN empire extended from Central Asia into India and was ruled by a dynasty of god-kings. It had relatively peaceful conditions, and trade linking China with the Mediterranean flourished. Also in that period agricultural production responded, in the dry conditions that prevailed over much of the territory, to the establishment of irrigation facilities. Major canals and the expansion of agriculture in the Amu Dar'ya Valley and the Tashkent and Samarqand oasis regions led to the foundation of new urban settlements. The Zang canal, originating in the Surkhan Dar'ya, led to increased prosperity for the inhabitants of Zar-tepe. Irrigation works in the Zerafshan Valley, according to A. R. Mukhamedianov, put 3,500 square kilometers (1,400 sq. mi.) under irrigation. A vast area was put under irrigation in Khwarizm, the region centered on the lower reaches of the Amu Dar'ya just south of the Aral Sea in Uzbekistan. Here a fully integrated system that involved major canals taking water from the river and feeding minor distributaries was established. One such canal was more than 90 kilometers in length and involved the removal of more than 222 million cubic meters (7.7 billion cu. ft.) of fill. Such agricultural improvements in the broad riverine floodplains were accompanied by parallel intensification in the piedmont areas. There small dams restrained the flow of mountain streams in the headwaters of the Zerafshan, and the water was fed into a series of terraced fields. Tunnels and aqueducts augmented such systems. Just to the east, the famous vineyards of FERGHANA relied on an extensive irrigation system involving the construction of a network of canals.

Further reading: De Silva, K. M. *A History of Sri Lanka.* London: Hurst, 1981; Hsu, Cho-yun. *Han Agriculture: The Formation of Early Chinese Agrarian Economy.* Seattle: University of Washington Press, 1980; Loewe, M., and E. L. Shaugnessy, eds. *The Cambridge History of Ancient China.* Cambridge: Cambridge University Press, 1999.

Canasapura A seventh-century inscription from MUANG SEMA in northeast Thailand, written in SANSKRIT and Khmer, records the donation of buffaloes, cattle, and slaves of both sexes to a Buddhist community by the king of Sri Canasapura. A second inscription, probably reused from elsewhere and found at Ayutthaya in central Thailand, dates to 937 C.E. Written by a ruler called Mangalavarman, it records that his ancestral line of kings ruled over Sri Canasapura. This inscription is also in Sanskrit and Khmer rather than the Mon language, which was used in most inscriptions of the Chao Phraya Valley. Both suggest that there was a small state in the upper Mun Valley over several generations during the period of the CHENLA kingdoms (550–802 C.E.).

Candragupta II (r. 380–413 C.E.) *Candragupta II, king of the Gupta empire in India, was, by common consensus, one of the greatest rulers of India.*
He was the son of a great military leader, SAMUDRAGUPTA (335–80), and was also known as Vikramaditya, a name indicating great prestige, power, and wealth. *Aditya* means "rising Sun," so his title can be roughly translated as the "Sun king." The considerable number of his gold coins that survive in hoards reflect a reign of widespread prosperity. This was noted by the Chinese Buddhist monk and pilgrim FAXIAN, who visited India during his reign and was struck by the opulent palaces and hospitals. As was his father, Candragupta was a potent military leader and won much renown with his victory over the Scythians, or SAKAS, earning the title Sakari, or destroyer of the Scythians.

Candragupta Maurya (r. c. 325–297 B.C.E.) *Traditionally, Candragupta Maurya was described as the son of the king of Magadha of the Nanda dynasty and is credited with the expulsion of the Greeks from that part of India and the establishment of the Maurya empire.*
After the short campaign of ALEXANDER THE GREAT in the Indus Valley in 326 B.C.E., the northwestern part of India was ruled by his appointees, who included the kings of TAXILA and Abhishara, as well as Porus, a follower of Alexander. This phase was short lived, however. When the Greek general SELEUCUS I NICATOR attempted to reestablish control over northwestern India, Candragupta entered into a diplomatic agreement whereby he maintained his hold over the disputed territory and gave Seleucus 500 elephants. At this point Candragupta took control of much new land in Gedrosia, the Paropamisadae (the area of Kabul), and Arachosia (Kandahar) in Afghanistan. This move meant that Greek colonies founded by Alexander the Great, such as Alexandria ad Caucasum (BEGRAM) and Alexandropolis (Kandahar), reverted to Indian control but maintained a strong Hellenistic presence. The establishment of official relations led Seleucus to send an ambassador, MEGASTHENES, to the court of Candragupta at PATALIPUTRA. Megasthenes' description of Pataliputra leaves no doubt as to the power of the king and the splendor of his capital. It is recorded that he possessed 8,000 chariots and 9,000 war elephants.

His principal achievements, however, were the defeat of the kingdom of Mahadhan in about 322 B.C.E. and the establishment of the Maurya empire. His death allegedly followed his becoming a Jain ascetic and starving himself.
See also JAINISM.

Canggal The shrine of Canggal is located 11 kilometers (6.6 mi.) east of BOROBUDUR, on the Kedu Plain of central Java in Indonesia. The site is notable for the discovery there of an inscription dated to 732 C.E., recording the erection of a lingam in this Sivaite monument by King Sanjaya of Mataram, in a land "rich in gold and grain." There are three principal shrines and three smaller ones.

Cera Cera, a kingdom in southern India, dominated the Malabar coast from approximately Calicut to Trivandrum, from the Mauryan period until at least the seventh century C.E. The narrow coastal strip that dominates Kerala state is well watered and today enjoys a dense population. The abundant forests in this area stimulated temple construction in wood, while the strategic location facing west allowed early contact with exotic influences from that direction. Its remoteness also provided an element of isolation from the rest of India. Cera rulers were independent of the MAURYA EMPIRE and were mentioned as such in the INSCRIPTIONS of ASOKA (r. 268–235 B.C.E.).

Chakranagar Chakranagar is a large city site adjacent to the Jamuna River in United Provinces, India. Under the name Ekachakra, it was mentioned as a major site in the Hindu epic the MAHABHARATA but has not been excavated. The outline of the city walls can be traced on the ground by the surface presence of broken bricks. In 1920, the inner citadel was destroyed through the erosion of the river. A coin of MENANDER (155–130 B.C.E.) from this site indicates at least part of its occupation period.

chakravartin In SANSKRIT, *chakra* means "wheel," and *vartin* "ruler." The title *chakravartin* has at least two meanings. One is "universal monarch" or "ruler of the world." The second is the "turner of the wheel," implying in this instance the wheel of the law, set in motion by the Buddha. The title can also be interpreted as "he who wields power." The term occurs in a number of early Hindu texts, such as the Maitrayana Upanishad and the MAHABHARATA. Fifteen *chakravartin*s were mentioned in the former work. The concept of a world ruler may have deep roots, going back as far as the early Vedas, and the wheel is metaphorically seen as the Sun. In this early context, the *chakravartin* is seen as a mighty and powerful ruler. In Buddhist usage, however, the wheel is seen as symbolic of the law and took on a more peaceful connotation, with the ruler enjoined to follow a righteous path.

The notion of the supreme ruler was adopted in Southeast Asia. In 802 C.E., JAYAVARMAN II was consecrated *chakravartin*, or supreme world emperor, king of kings. The kingdom of ANGKOR in Cambodia is often said to date from this ceremony, although it might well have been no more than an attempt to reinforce the royal claim at a time of continuing strife with rivals. The deity corresponding to the king of the Earth was the DEVARAJA (God who is king).

Chalukya dynasty The Chalukya dynasty, centered in the Deccan, in India, was a powerful force in this region from the mid-sixth century until the eighth century C.E. Its foremost rulers included Pulakesin I, who ruled from about 535 to 566. It is known that King Mangalesa founded the outstanding temples of Badami in the 12th year of his reign (579 C.E.), while King Pulakesin II conquered considerable areas, including the capital of the PALLAVA dynasty and much of Maharashtra. The Pallavas then defeated him and took his capital at Badami. The dynasty was restored to a position of power by Pulakesin's son, Vikramaditya, who ruled from 655 to 681. The Chalukyas are best known, however, for their temples, particularly those at BADAMI, AIHOLE, and MAHAKUTA, of the sixth and seventh centuries and the later buildings at Pattadakal.

Cham civilization The Cham civilization occupied the coastal plains of Vietnam from Saigon to the Hai Van Pass. The inhabitants spoke an Austronesian language most akin to the languages of Borneo, and their ancestors probably settled this coastal strip during the first millennium B.C.E. The Sa Huynh culture is seen by most as the ancestral Iron Age group that developed into the civilization of Champa. It is most unlikely that Champa was ever a unified state, but Chinese records contain many references to the Chams, who appear as a constant irritant to the maintenance of peace on the southern frontier. The territory of the Chams is divided into a series of restricted coastal enclaves, backed to the west by the Truong Son Cordillera. Cham centers are located at the estuaries of the major rivers that cross these coastal plains. The most southerly region of Champa lies from the eastern margins of the Mekong Delta to Cape Dinh, an inhospitable stretch of coastline with thin, sandy soils. Between Cape Dinh and Cape Nay, there are three well-watered valleys separated by low passes, an area known to the Chams as Panduranga. North of Cape Dinh, the coastal strip broadens into a plain about 70 by 70 kilometers (231 by 231 ft.) in extent. There are many sites here in a region known to the Chams as Vijaya. The region of AMARAVATI, which lies between the Hai Van Pass and Quy Nhon, was the dominant area of Cham political centrality. It has a reasonable area of land available for agriculture and several well-sheltered harbors. The last area lies north of the Hai Van Pass, with most archaeological sites being concentrated in the vicinity of Quang Tri. The relative importance and political reach of these polities named in the inscriptions almost certainly changed markedly over time.

It was Louis Finot who described the regions of Champa known from the inscriptions as "provinces." His suggestion was based on an inscription from Po Nagar, set up by King Jaya Harivarmadeva in 1160 C.E. This king claimed to have defeated Kambuja (the Khmer), Yavana (the Viet), Vijaya, Amaravati, and Panduranga. This is the earliest record of the location of Amaravati, while the first reference to Vijaya is of about the same date. Kauthara was first mentioned in an inscription from Po Nagar set up by King Satyavarman in 784 C.E. A kingdom known as Panduranga was recorded in an inscription from PO NAGAR, dated to 817 C.E., which describes the *senapati*, or commander in chief, of this kingdom.

RELATIONS WITH CHINA

Episodes of warfare and raiding were either repulsed by punitive expeditions or resolved through diplomacy. These episodes ceased during periods of central strength in China, which saw the restoration of tribute missions to the Chinese court. The Chinese histories recorded such missions as sent from the state of Lin-yi (effectively Champa, but after 757 C.E. known as Huanwang). Such Chinese histories also tell of the civil centers of Lin-yi, while the names of their overlords up to the early sixth century are known almost exclusively from Chinese sources. Toward the end of the third century C.E., a Chinese text recorded that the Lin-yi, the name by which the Chinese recognized the Chams, comprised numerous tribes who cooperated in resisting Chinese expansion. Border unrest was recorded in the *Hou Han Shu* (*History of the Later Han*) in 137 C.E. and again in 192 C.E. At this point the texts refer to the first dynasty of Lin-yi. Between 220 and 230, the Lin-yi sent the first of many tribute missions to the Chinese court.

In about 270 C.E., the grandson of the founder of the first dynasty was named as Fan-Hsiung. His son, called Fan-Yi, in 284 C.E. dispatched the first official embassy to the Chinese court. An interesting insight into the impact of China on the Lin-yi is provided by the activities of Fan-Yi's principal adviser, a man known as Wen, of Chinese origin, who advised the king on how to construct walled and moated defenses and to design and manufacture up-to-date weapons. He also helped design the palace. Wen, now titled Fan-Wen, was to seize power in 336 C.E. He imposed his authority on previously independent tribes and, while sending a tribute mission to China, continued a policy of border conflict. His embassy took a letter from him written in "barbarian," presumably Indian, script. It should not be overlooked that the expansion of trade to southern China from FUNAN occurred at this time and that Indian merchants and religious functionaries were regular callers at the ports that Fan-Wen would have controlled.

Fan-Wen was succeeded by his descendants Fan-Fo (from 349 C.E.) and Fan-Hua (399–413 C.E.). During the reign of the latter, SANSKRIT names were adopted, and the inscriptions refer to a king Bhadravarman. The establishment in his temple of a lingam called Bhadresvara confirms the development of the state cult of the named lingam, which has been seen as providing a unifying force in the CHENLA states of Cambodia. One of Fan-Hua's inscriptions contains a text written in Cham. This confirms that the Lin-yi were Cham speakers by the end of the fourth century C.E. Jia Dan (730–805), a Chinese traveler, described Champa as a series of kingdoms rather than a unified state. The archaeological record of Champa, from which most new information will come, has barely been tapped. The principal centers concentrate in riverine plains; MY SON, TRA KIEU, DONG DUONG, and Po Nagar are the best known.

Further reading: Guillon, E. *Cham Art*. London: Thames and Hudson, 2001; Higham, C. F. W. *Early Cultures of Mainland Southeast Asia*. Bangkok: River Books, 2002.

Champanagar Champanagar is a city site located in southern Bihar province, India, commanding traffic on the lower reaches of the Ganges (Ganga) River. One of the foremost cities during the period of MAHAJANAPADAS, or major states, it was the capital of Anga and was visited by the Buddha. In the sixth century B.C.E. Champanagara was conquered by Bimbisara of MAGADHA. Excavations have sectioned a large rampart, which was found to have had two periods of construction. The earlier was dated to the period of NORTHERN BLACK POLISHED WARE and the later to the late first millennium B.C.E. Artifacts dating to the former include soapstone molds for casting jewelry.

Chandraketugarh Chandraketugarh is a very large walled site located about 40 kilometers northwest of Calcutta in India. It might be the location of the trading port of Gange, mentioned in the PERIPLUS OF THE ERYTHRAEAN SEA (first century C.E.). Excavations undertaken in 1956–57 and 1967–68 have revealed evidence for a long period of occupation, beginning with the late prehistoric period and proceeding into the GUPTA kingdom and beyond. The second period belongs to the MAURYA EMPIRE and has yielded punch-marked coins, hard stone beads, and terra-cotta figurines. The SUNGA period III layers include shards inscribed in BRAHMI, and these underlie occupation dated to the KUSHAN period. A very large brick temple foundation has been ascribed either to the Gupta or to the Pala period.

Chang'an Chang'an was the capital of the Western HAN DYNASTY of China. It was chosen by the emperor GAOZU in 202 B.C.E., and construction was begun two years later. It is recorded that 20,000 convicts were set to work on the building program, augmented for a month at a time by corvée labor drawn from the local populace. When completed in 190 B.C.E., it covered 33.5 square kilometers (13.4 sq. mi.), with walls 25 kilometers (15 mi.) long, making it one of the largest cities in the world, with a population of between 80,000 and 160,000 households accounting for more than a quarter of a million people. The walls incorporated three huge gates on each side, so large that 12 chariots could enter simultaneously. The main roads within were 45 meters wide (148.5 ft.) and up to 5.5 kilometers (3.3 mi.) long. There were many royal precincts within, including the Weiyang, Changle, and Mingguang Palaces. These were associated with arsenals and official buildings of the administration. Officials were placed in charge of the nine markets and also each of the 160 wards. The city continued to be the capital under WANG MANG, who is usually described as a usurper, but he succumbed to external forces in 23 C.E., and after his death, the capital of the succeeding Eastern Han dynasty was moved to LUOYANG. At that juncture, Chang'an suffered extensive destruction.

Changjiang civilization

The Changjiang civilization are the states that developed in the valley of the Chang (Yangtze) River at the same time as the Shang civilization of the Huang (Yellow) River central plains. For decades since the recognition of Zhengzhou and Anyang as centers of the SHANG STATE, the origins of Chinese civilization have been firmly placed in the north. However, it is now known that rice cultivation began in the middle regions of the Chang, and at CHENGTOUSHAN one of the earliest urban sites has been found. Two discoveries provided stimulus to proposing the existence of a distinct southern civilization. One involved the city of SANXINGDUI in Sichuan, where two sacrificial pits have been excavated within a massive walled urban center. The bronzes, jades, and gold items from these two pits are larger than and quite distinct from those that define the contemporary Shang material to the north. The finds included masks, statues, and trees in bronze and one of the largest caches of jades known from this period in China. The second major discovery was made at WUCHENG and XIN'GAN in Jiangxi province. At the latter, the second richest intact tomb of the later second millennium B.C.E. has been excavated.

Undoubtedly, there were distinct states in the Changjiang tradition, but the many sites that can now be identified form a coherent and distinct grouping. In Sichuan, the SHU state dominated until it was conquered by the QIN in the fourth century C.E., and sites in the middle reaches of the Chang are probably ancestral to the historic Chu state. The accumulation of new information and reassessment of old finds now permit certain common features to be proposed. First and foremost, the southern civilization was based on the cultivation of rice; production was augmented by the early and vigorous application of IRRIGATION measures. Second, the form of the bronzes differed from those of Shang and the WESTERN ZHOU DYNASTY. The *zun* and *lei* ritual bronze vessels, for example, were favored in the south and appear over a wide area. A *zun* vessel was represented on the head of a bronze human figure seen in a ritual posture. A *lei* was represented on a SEAL from a burial at Majiaxiang in Xindu county, Sichuan, dating to the WARRING STATES PERIOD (465–221 B.C.E.). The seal's location underneath two figures with linked hands again suggests a ritual use. This SEAL also bore graphs of the Ba-Shu script, which

remains to be translated. *Nao* bronze bells were also typical of the Changjiang repertoire.

Further reading: Bagley, R. W. *Ancient Sichuan.* Seattle and Princeton: Seattle Art Museum, 2001; ———. "An Early Bronze Age Tomb in Jiangxi Province," *Orientations* 24 (1993): 20–36; ———. "A Shang City in Sichuan Province," *Orientations* 21 (1990): 52–67; He Jiejun. "Excavations at Chengtoushan in Li County, Hunan Province, China," *Bulletin of the Indo-Pacific Prehistory Association* 18 (1999): 101–103.

Chanh Lo

Chanh Lo is a site of the CHAM CIVILIZATION in Quang Ngai province, Vietnam, which has given its name to an art style dated from the end of the 10th to the middle of the 11th century C.E. The style is best represented at such sites as MY SON, where a lintel found on Temple E4 can be seen as representative. This example is particularly interesting, for it portrays a scene from a royal court in which the king, seated on a low throne and holding a sword, is flanked by two bearers holding parasols over him. Another courtier is holding a fly whisk. Both parasols and fly whisks are important accoutrements of the royal court at ANGKOR in Cambodia, as seen in the reliefs of SURYAVARMAN II (r. 1113–1150) at ANGKOR WAT, but in this Cham example there is a greater degree of informality evident. Music was also a vital part of the Cham court, as shown in the depiction of dancers and musicians on this same lintel. The dancers hold their arms over their heads, while the accompanying musicians play a drum, tambourine, and flute. A second group of two dancers and musicians counterbalances the scene at the other end of the lintel. Features of the group as a whole are the individuality of each person and the elegant costumes and jewelry.

A second lintel bearing scenes of a royal court has been discovered from Chanh Lo itself. Once again, the regal figure of the king holds center stage, sitting on a low throne and holding a sword in his right hand. He wears a fine high crown and is flanked by two courtiers holding parasols and offerings. It is notable that their hairstyle incorporates a bun on the left side of the head. The central figures are flanked by dancers and musicians, playing a drum and a flute.

Chanhu Daro

Chanhu daro, a settlement of the INDUS VALLEY CIVILIZATION, is located on the left bank of the Indus River in Pakistan, in such a position as to command not only good agricultural land, but also a major pass to the uplands of Baluchistan to the west. Excavations under the direction of Ernest Mackay commenced in November 1935 and continued until March the following year. The site includes three mounds in close proximity, with a combined area of 1.5 hectares (3.75 acres). Even if, as Mackay suggested, the three sites were once components of one settlement with the intervening spaces caused by erosion, the site would not have exceeded four hectares. This makes it intriguing in the sense that, in contrast to the large cities of MOHENJO DARO and HARAPPA, no small village community of this civilization has been extensively excavated. The fieldwork there makes it possible to examine the layout and activities removed from the main centers that have attracted most attention from archaeologists. Moreover, Mackay opened considerable areas, thus providing an impression of the site plan and the spatial distribution of various activities. One of the most impressive aspects of the Chanhu Daro excavation is the insight provided into intimate details of daily activities in this trading community.

STRATIGRAPHY OF THE SITE

The site is very deep, and the basal layers, as at Mohenjo Daro, lie beneath the water table, making it impossible to examine the original settlement. Three principal occupation phases were recognized. The lowest was described as the Harappa II period. It was separated from the later Harappa I occupation by a sterile layer, indicating a period of abandonment. Above this, there was evidence for settlement by a community whose ceramics and other aspects of material culture were distinct from those of Harappan phases. It belongs to the so-called JHUKAR culture.

The lower Harappan phase is the best preserved and most informative, since it has escaped the ravages of brick robbers and the forces of erosion. The streets were laid out in a relatively irregular plan; the main thoroughfare itself was of uneven width. However, the community placed considerable stress on the sewage and drainage system by providing well-planned brick-lined drains. One house incorporated a room 2.7 by 2.1 meters (9 by 7 ft.) wide, which contained the remains of an elaborate system of flues under a brick floor. There is no evidence for a high degree of heat in this hypocaust, but the presence of a mass of unfinished steatite beads on the floor above suggests that this area might have been a facility for bead finishing, since heat was part of the glazing process. Some white paste plaques used in the glazing process have been identified at Chanhu Daro. The floor also contained copper tools and knives, a flake drill, two large shells, and nodules of carnelian. The passage outside the room contained an unfinished seal in brown steatite, and a large ceramic vessel in the courtyard outside contained copper and bronze tools, bangles, razors, and a bronze ingot. Another room of this period on Mound II contained unfinished beads and a SEAL, in addition to a very well-preserved latrine connected to the sewage system in the street outside. Further evidence for local manufacture are blocks of carnelian, crystal, and amethyst and nodules of agate already subjected to heat as part of the early stages in the manufacture of ornaments, as well as many stone drill bits.

A possible house belonging to a seal maker, which yielded three unfinished steatite items in an early stage of manufacture, has been uncovered. The presence of metal workers is attested by the unfinished casting and hoards of items presumably stored for melting and recasting. Shell working took place, as seen in the unfinished bangles, ladles, and dishes, while other specialists made the weights, which are a widespread feature of the Indus civilization. Some of these weights were so polished and complete that they may have served as reference specimens in the manufacturing of new items. A complete elephant's tusk suggests that ivory was worked. The distribution of these various items of raw materials and craft tools suggests that certain quarters of the settlement were occupied by specialists in one or another activity. Seal making, for example, was carried on in the northern part of the excavated area.

The middle layer of later Indus civilization occupation was less well preserved. The layout of the buildings did not follow the preceding pattern, but manufacturing of ornaments and seals continued. The Jhukar phase represents a major change in the material culture. The occupants reused some of the bricks of their predecessors and seem to have used mats in the construction of their dwellings. Many bone awls were found, and a different form of seal was preferred.

MATERIAL CULTURE

The material remains of the people of Chanhu Daro clearly illuminate their activities. Steatite seals were made at the site. Of the 55 recovered, 44 carry the image of a one-horned bovid, often called a unicorn. The animal is usually seen in front of a stand that looks as if it might have been made, at least in part, of basketry, but its purpose is not known. Some say that it might have been a feeding tray, others an altar, and a third group a device for making soma, the ritual beverage described in the RIG-VEDA. The animal often wears a collar and a sort of saddle or ornamental cloth over the withers. The people of Chanhu Daro were literate, for the seals also incorporate a script. A few seals depict a tiger, which, in one case, is seen licking the face of a man who bends on one knee in front of the animal. Bulls and elephants are rarely depicted. These seals were used to indicate ownership, and at least two clay sealings, which survived through being accidentally burnt, have been found.

Many terra-cotta figurines were recovered. Hollow female figurines are thought by Mackay to represent a deity. The figurines are often pregnant and are heavily ornamented with necklaces and bangles. Some necklaces are embellished to resemble rows of beads, associated with a pendant. The women often wear a headdress in the form of braids worn on each side of the head, and where ears are shown, they are pierced to take a pendant. One figurine shows a woman kneeling in front of a quern, processing grain. Male figurines tend to be of solid terra-cotta and of so simple a form that Mackay has suggested that they were modeled by children or might have been made to take their place on the models of wheeled carts as children's toys. There are also many terra-cotta models of animals, with preference being given to the bull. The terra-cotta models of carts were in all probability made as children's toys, but their abundance and the preservation of at least two complete examples give insight into the form of a medium of transport that would have been vital to a trading community. The bases were framed in wood covered with a net of some sort, while the wheels were fashioned from three solid pieces of wood. Two bronze carts have survived, one including the driver wielding a stick. Idle moments at the site were passed by gambling with dice.

The metal industry at Chanhu Daro is well documented on the basis of many complete castings. The presence of unfinished castings and an ingot attests to local manufacture in one part of the settlement. Both copper and tin, however, had to be imported, perhaps in the form of bronze, rather than of copper and tin separately, for local alloying. Bronze was put to a wide range of uses. There are bowls and shallow dishes, weapons, and tools, including a large handled shovel. Weaponry included tanged leaf-shaped spears and arrowheads. Fishhooks were cast, and artisans used bronze awls, chisels, axes, and drills. A particularly fascinating bronze tool, found in a bead-making room, is a hollow tube ending in a point through which a fine abrasive paste could be squeezed into the stone being drilled.

None of the outstanding ornaments such as the carnelian belts from Mohenjo Daro and ALLAHADINO has been found at Chanhu Daro, but a range of jewelry was recovered beside the many beads found in the workshops. Bracelets were made of copper or bronze, FAIENCE, shell, and pottery. There were many varieties of beads made from a wide range of raw materials, including faience, onyx, quartz, shell, and hornblende. Some of the carnelian beads were etched, that is, painted with an alkali and fired to form a pattern against the background color of the stone. Some cowry shells had been converted into beads.

Many crafts and activities are represented by other categories of material culture. Whetstones were used to sharpen metal tools and implements, and saddle querns were used for grinding grain. The actual weights of the stone cubes thought to have been for weighing goods for exchange illustrate the care given to their manufacture. For example, the seven chert specimens in the intermediate category, some showing slight damage or chipping, weigh between 13.4074 and 14.0306 grams (about half an ounce).

These weights are a reminder that the excavations at Chanhu Daro have revealed the vitality of a small rural community of the Indus civilization engaged in manufacturing and exchange. Many raw materials were imported, converted into useful or decorative items, and then exported. The city was a center for the manufacture of seals, and the craftspeople responsible were clearly literate. There were streets, a communal sewage system, and

residential houses, but no sign of the major public buildings that characterize the cities of Mohenjo Daro and Harappa. Chanhu Daro, however, illustrates an equally significant component of the civilization as a whole.

Further reading: Kenoyer, J. M. *Ancient Cities of the Indus Civilization.* Oxford University Press, 1998; Mackay, E. J. H. *Chanhu Daro Excavations.* New Haven, Conn.: American Oriental Society, 1942.

Chansen Chansen is a moated urban site in central Thailand. It was defended by a substantial wall beyond which lay a reservoir. The first and second of six occupation phases have been dated to the late prehistoric period, ending in about 250 C.E. The later of these yielded an ivory comb, decorated on one side with horses and Buddhist symbols, and on the other side, a goose. Not dissimilar combs have been found at TAXILA in Pakistan. Phases 3 and 4 have been dated to between 250 and 650 and represent the establishment of the DVARAVATI CIVILIZATION. The material culture includes ceramic stamps, tin amulets, and bronze bells similar to finds from OC EO on the Mekong Delta. There are also eight bowls of a metallic black ware paralleled in Sri Lanka. A circular moat was dug around the site in the fifth phase, forming an urban area with a diameter of about 650 (2,145 ft.) meters. During this phase, the pottery became much more abundant and of the same tradition as that of other Dvaravati sites in central Thailand.

Chao Kuo (second century B.C.E.) *Chao Kuo, a statesman who served the Western Han emperor Wendi (r. 180–157 B.C.E.), submitted a memorandum to the emperor, known as the* Memorial on the Encouragement of Agriculture *in 178 B.C.E.*
This memorandum was composed not long after the unification of China in response to food shortages. It recalled the olden days, when wise kings stored supplies of grain against possible famine. Chao Kuo related vagrancy and banditry to humans not turning to productive agricultural pursuits, for poverty breeds crime. He argued strongly that the emperor should encourage agriculture and the storage of surpluses and remit taxation on the rural populace. On the other hand, he noted, merchants made fine profits and lived lives of ease and luxury. There is, he argued, a way to remedy this situation. Let producers purchase official ranks with grain, make grain a marketable commodity, and all will be well. This policy was followed with success.

See also HAN DYNASTY.

Chao Phraya Basin The Chao Phraya Basin controls a major communication route to India by means of the Three Pagodas Pass, which gives direct access to the sea and commands a rich hinterland. The DVARAVATI CIVILIZATION (SANSKRIT for "that which has gates") developed in this area at the same time as the states of FUNAN and CHENLA were forming in the valley of the Mekong River to the east. The Chao Phraya is the principal river that drains the broad, rich agricultural land behind the Gulf of Siam and that now produces most of the rice grown in the kingdom of Thailand. Three other main rivers also flow in a roughly north-south direction in the same area, the Mae Khlong, Ta Chin, and Bang Pakong. There are also many tributaries; the Pa Sak, which originates in the Petchabun Mountains, is one of the largest. During the late prehistoric and early historic periods (500 B.C.E.–900 C.E.), the sea level was probably rather higher than at present, and the extensive buildup of the Chao Phraya Delta occurred at an earlier stage. The major historic sites are now set back from the coast, but, when occupied, they were likely to have been on or near the shore.

The parallels between the Chao Phraya Basin and the Mekong Valley are further seen in the clear evidence for maritime trade, which is first evidenced at the Iron Age site of BAN DON TA PHET, where carnelian and agate jewelry and bronze bowls of Indian origin lay in the same cemetery as jade ornaments from coastal Vietnam. A coin of the Western Roman emperor Victorinus (r. 268–270), minted in Cologne, was found at the Dvaravati site of U-THONG. The Dvaravati civilization was strongly Buddhist, and the *Sasanvamsappadika* text records that the emperor ASOKA sent three missionaries, Gavampti, Sona, and Uttara, to Southeast Asia as early as the third century B.C.E.

Chardasila *See* KALAWAN.

chariots and chariot burials

The presence of a written symbol showing a wheeled vehicle on the ORACLE-BONE texts at ANYANG, together with the occasional recovery of bronze fittings for carts in royal graves, made it clear to early archaeologists that the rulers of the SHANG STATE of China had horse-drawn vehicles of some sort. Archaeologically, the use of chariots at Anyang was confirmed in dramatic fashion in 1936, when excavators at XIAOTUN encountered the red LACQUER outline of the pit of Burial M20, measuring 2.9 by 1.8 (about 10 by 6 ft.) meters. Further excavation exposed the remains of two chariots, four horses, and three human skeletons. Associated finds revealed that the chariots had been embellished with bronze terminals to the axles and shaft. The three sacrificed men interred with the chariot each retained his weaponry. The driver had a stone *ge* ax, whetstone, and jade whip haft. A second had a bronze *ge* ax and probably held a shield. The third member of the crew was buried with his bow and arrow, bronze knife, and whetstone. This was one of a group of five chariot burials, which are thought to have been a sacrificial offering in the vicinity of the royal palace area. The same part of the site also included pits containing one skeleton and 124 skulls of men who might also have been part of mortuary rituals. The sudden appearance of chariots at Anyang suggests an exotic source, perhaps the steppes of Near East.

TEXTUAL EVIDENCE OF CHARIOTS

The earliest written characters are from the group of bones ascribed to the diviner Bin, who was active during the reign of Wu Ding (c. 1200–1181 B.C.E.). There was no uniformity in the way of writing the word *che* (chariot), a finding that Edward Shaughnessy ascribes to the chariot's recent adoption in China. The available texts, dated to 1200–1045 B.C.E., describe various events linked with the use of a chariot. On one occasion while he was hunting rhinoceros, King Wu Ding's chariot tipped over, and Prince Yang fell out. It seems that he was severely injured, because further references to him immediately after this accident were involved with rituals to speed his recovery. Another text describes the king's servant Bi driving a horse-drawn chariot. A further divination predicted that the king, with a chariot, would catch deer. Evidently at least one initial use of chariots was in hunting. There are also texts, however, that involve warfare. In one battle against the state of Gongfang, which took place within the period 1180–1150 B.C.E., it seems that the Shang, fighting with chariots, were victorious. A second reference is from a bovid scapula and again records a great victory that took place during the late 12th century B.C.E. It describes how the Shang captured two chariots and horses, along with shields, arrows, quivers, four enemy generals, and 1,570 soldiers. The interesting point about this text is that it was the enemy who was using chariots. Indeed, chariots receive scant mention in the corpus of oracle inscriptions, again implying that they were a recent innovation at that juncture.

WESTERN SOURCES FOR CHARIOTS

The Chinese words used to describe the chariot, parts of the wheel, and the axle were borrowed from Indo-European sources. Even the word for "horse," a cognate in Mongolic, Korean, Japanese, and Chinese, suggests a single origin, possibly during one wave of contact across the steppes. Archaeologically, the evidence for Western sources is overwhelming, for it is now possible to compare dated chariots from China with those excavated in Western sites. Foremost among the latter is the site of Lchashen in Armenia, between the Caspian and Black Seas. Dated to about 1500 B.C.E., a burial at Lchashen hold the remains of two chariots. Their distinctive design features include wooden wheels one meter across, lined with two bent wooden felloes. Each wheel had 28 wooden spokes and turned on a fixed axle that supported the chariot box in the center. The wheels were 1.8 meters apart. The draught pole has not survived, but a bronze model of a chariot from the same site showed a pole with an upward curve at the end to accommodate the horse harnessing. Numerous rock engravings of chariots found across Central Asia depict a similar vehicle; while not precisely dated, they nevertheless illustrate the widespread presence of horse-drawn chariots. The similarity between the Chinese chariot and those seen in Armenia is so precise as to rule out any likelihood of an independent invention.

DISCOVERIES OF CHARIOTS IN CHINA

During the millennium when which chariots were favored in China, from the Shang to the QIN dynasties, there were minor changes and embellishments on a basic design. The form of the chariot began with two horses, attached to a yoke by two curved yoke saddles. The central pole had a curve at the terminus to allow proper harnessing to the horses and was about three meters (10 ft.) long. The axle was joined centrally under the box to the pole by means of leather straps flexible enough to allow rapid changes of course. Boxes were rectangular and made of wood, sometimes with a leather base to act as springs, and were large enough to take three people. Shang chariot wheels had 18 spokes, but this number increased over time. During the WESTERN ZHOU DYNASTY, there were between 18 and 26, rising to 28 in the Spring and Autumn period, and as many as 30 during the Qin unification. From the Spring and Autumn period (722–481 B.C.E.), there are also some chariots pulled by four horses.

The initial discovery of chariot burials at Anyang was but a prelude to the recovery of further examples. Fragments of a chariot were found in the entrance ramp to the massive royal grave numbered M1001. Three pits were examined in 1987 at Guojiazhuang, Anyang, and one contained the remains of a chariot associated with two horses and two men. This was a particularly well-preserved tomb, providing insight into the stages in the mortuary ritual of what must have been part of a sacrificial offering during the interment of a particularly eminent person. The horses and men had been killed and placed into the pit first. Both men were aged in their early 30s. One lay prone to the right of the horses, his hands tied behind his back. The other had been placed directly behind the chariot box. Cinnabar had been sprinkled over his body and beneath the horses, which had been neatly placed in their correct positions for pulling the chariot. One wore a bronze bell, and their heads had been embellished with cowry shells. Considerable attention had been given to decoration: The sides of the chariot box had been lacquered, and bronze had been used for the hubcaps and yoke saddles.

During the Shang dynasty, the evidence from the chariot burials and the oracle bones indicates that these sophisticated and complex vehicles had three main functions. They were used in war but sparingly, they were used by the king for hunting, and they were employed in mortuary sacrifices as an indication of the elite status of the deceased. Both the linguistic and the archaeological evidence concur that the chariot was of Western origin.

With the Western Zhou dynasty, there is considerably more evidence for the presence and function of chariots. The sources are both documentary and archaeological. Dedicatory inscriptions on bronze vessels are prominent among the contemporary written records, and the text of such a record on the Maogong *ding*, a form of large bronze ritual vessel, illustrates the gift of a richly caparisoned chariot to an aristocrat:

> The King said I confer upon you . . . a chariot with bronze fittings, with a decorated cover of the handrail; a front-rail and breast-trappings for the horses of soft leather, painted scarlet; a canopy of tiger skin, with a reddish-brown lining; yoke-bar bindings and axle couplings of painted leather; bronze jingle bells for the yoke bar; a mainshaft rear-end fitting and brake fittings, bound with leather and painted gilt; a gilt bow-press and fish-skin quiver; harness for a team of four horses; gild bridles and girth straps; a scarlet banner with two bells. I confer these gifts on you to be used in sacrifice and field service.

Chariots as Status Symbols

It is evident from this long list of embellishments that chariots were now regarded at least in part as significant symbols of status, for this is but one of many inscriptions that record the gifts of chariots by Zhou kings to the highly ranked. A second example recorded the gift of a chariot to a person called Baichen when he was given the title Duke Tan. The Dayu *ding* records a gift of chariots, horses, pennants, and slaves from the Zhou king to one of his senior courtiers. The king also took pains to ensure a supply of good horses, for inscriptions record the existence of stud farms. The custom of immolating chariots and charioteers with their horses also continued in the Eastern Zhou period. At Zhangjiapo near Chang'an, four pits containing chariot burials have been excavated. One contained the remains of two chariots, one pulled by two horses, the other by four. In virtually all respects, the chariots follow the Shang design. The hubs, however, were strengthened with bronze rings; in the case of the two-horse chariot, the right-hand end of the yoke was equipped with a bronze spear. A second pit at the same site contained three chariots, one of which involved four horses, the other two a pair.

Chariots in War and Peace

Further indications of the importance of chariots in combat are seen in a chariot from the tomb of the marquis Yi of Zeng at Songcun, Shaanxi province. The marquis died in about 433 B.C.E., and his chariot axles were fitted with sharp bronze points. It was during this period that four-horse chariots were preferred, and young aristocrats had special periods of training in chariotry. The numbers employed in battles also increased markedly; the

Zuozhuan (*Commentary of Mr. Zuo*) describes an occasion when the state of Jin put more than 700 chariots into battle against the CHU. The numbers of chariots and horses employed in mortuary rituals showed a corresponding increase. Three generations of the Jing clan, interred in the Middle Zhou cemetery of Fengxi near Chang'an, were all accompanied by chariots. There were only four in the earliest grave, but 15 in the latest. The ritual at this site involved dismantling the chariot and placing the components in the entrance ramp to the tomb, while horses, more than 40 in one pit, were buried separately. The horses were, it seems, killed by bow and arrow, for bronze arrows have survived with some of the skeletons. Even this number pales before later instances of horse immolation. One of the dukes of Qin during the Spring and Autumn period was buried at Fengxiang in Shaanxi alongside a pit more than 100 meters (33 ft.) long by 25

meters (82.5 ft.) wide, in which it is thought that more than 100 chariots rested. In Shandong the tomb of Jing Gong of QI (r. 547–490 B.C.E.) lay alongside pits containing neat double rows of more than 600 horses. This contrasts with a rare grave at Bianjiazhuang, which contained a chariot drawn by two small wooden statues of men.

The use of a chariot in peace during the WARRING STATES PERIOD is finely illustrated by a lacquer box from BAOSHAN, in Hubei. It was painted with a series of scenes demarcated by willow trees. An aristocrat is being driven on his chariot to a rendezvous. There are three persons in the box as the horses trot through the countryside, the driver holding a whip. Cranes fly overhead, and wild boar flee to the safety of the woods. The last scene shows the nobleman walking to meet three hosts, while the chariot remains, stationary, in front of a small dog. A second painted scene from the walls of a Qin palace at XIANYANG

Chariots were introduced into China across the steppes during the Shang dynasty. They were placed there in rich graves, complete with charioteers and horses. The use of chariots continued for more than 1,000 years, being used in warfare and ceremonies. This bronze model from Gansu in China dates to the Eastern Han dynasty and shows an aristocrat using his chariot for domestic travel. *(Erich Lessing/Art Resource, NY)*

shows a chariot drawn by four horses at full gallop. The earliest BAMBOO-SLIP tomb inventory is from the grave of the marquis of Zeng at LEIGUDUN and is dated to 433 B.C.E. The list includes a description of 43 chariots, but whether these were used only in the funerary procession or were actually buried adjacent to the tomb can only be determined by future excavations.

The use of chariots in warfare is best demonstrated by the Chu Tomb 1 at LIUCHENGQIAO. Excavated in 1971, this burial contained a seven-meter-deep shaft at the base of which lay three nested coffins and 270 objects of grave goods. These included bronze chariot fittings and a set of weapons—three types of arrowheads, the *ko,* or ax halberd, the *mao,* or thrusting spear, and the *ji,* which is a combination of both. The wooden hafts have survived, and these range up to 3.12 meters. According to the contemporary records, weapons of this great length were used when fighting from chariots.

All such depictions of or references to chariots must concede pride of place, however, to the half-scale bronze models of two four-horse chariots from the tomb complex of QIN SHIHUANGDI near modern Xi'an, the first emperor of China (r. 221–210 B.C.E.). The detail of this perfect specimen allows a full understanding of the complexities of harnessing four spirited horses to a light vehicle and provides much information that is unavailable on the basis of the remains that survive in the tombs. The pit containing the two models was located barely 20 meters from the main pyramid of the emperor. It measured 7 by 2.3 meters and reached a depth of 7.8 meters. The pit had been lined with timbers, and the two bronze chariots and their horses were placed in a line within. These bronzes represent the pinnacle of craftsmanship: The details and decoration are astonishing. When discovered in 1980, the roof had long since fallen into the chamber, damaging the two vehicles. However, careful restoration has returned them to their former perfect condition.

The foremost chariot was a war vehicle; the other represented the emperor's vehicle for travel. The war chariot followed the traditional design of a box placed over two wheels, each having 30 spokes. The charioteer stood holding the reins. A quiver containing 50 bronze arrows hung within the box; another quiver held 12 bolts for a crossbow. The shield also hung in the box, splendidly decorated with painted cloud designs. The horses were all painted white, with pink nostrils and mouths; the paint has preserved the bronze beneath from the effects of corrosion. The harnesses were represented in gold and silver components, and the bridle and headstall were intricately decorated and perfectly rendered. Even the tassels attached to the lead horse's head and the other horses' necks have survived. The charioteer stood beneath a large parasol, the staff of which was embellished with gold-inlaid decoration. He wore a double-tailed hat and a blue robe with white collar and cuffs. A long sword was slung from his belt behind him.

The emperor's chariot was even more beautifully decorated. It had a large two-roomed chamber with two sliding windows on each side and a further window at the front. The interior was sumptuously painted with blue, green, and yellow phoenix and dragon motifs on a white background. The wheels and the axle were covered in cinnabar.

The most impressive feature of these two vehicles is the detail provided for their construction; the leather strapping to join the component parts, the wooden structure of the boxes, and the details of the harnessing are clearly shown. At this stage of Chinese military history, however, the chariot was beginning to bow to the development of cavalry and infantry. During the Han dynasty, chariots were used less for war than for the display of status and rank by members of the ruling elite.

Further reading: Chang, K.-C. *The Shang Civilization.* New Haven; Conn.: Yale University Press, 1980; Shaughnessy, E. L. "Historical Perspectives on the Introduction of the Chariot into China," *Harvard Journal of Asiatic Studies* 48 (1988): 189–237.

Charklik Charklik was one of centers of the SHAN-SHAN kingdom of the southern TARIM BASIN in western China. It began as a military colony, founded during the Western Han Chinese domination of their "western regions" to ensure the free passage of trade along the SILK ROAD. It then developed into one of the oasis towns of Shan-shan during the second and third centuries C.E. SIR AUREL STEIN visited this area in 1901 and several times thereafter and noted the foundations of a Buddhist stupa and the old encircling walls.

Charsada Charsada, a village in northwestern Pakistan, has given its name to a series of mounds. These were recognized by SIR ALEXANDER CUNNINGHAM in 1863 as the ancient city of Pushkalavati, or the City of Lotuses. The location of this important city allowed access not only to extensive rich agricultural land, but also to strategic control of the trade route linking India via TAXILA to the Kabul Valley, BEGRAM, and so to the Mediterranean world. Pushkalavati lay next to the now-dry bed of the River Sambor and adjacent to the confluence of the Kabul and Swat Rivers. The site includes several discrete mounds. The tallest, which rises to a height of 20 meters (66 ft.) above the surrounding plain, is known as Bala Hisar. Barely a kilometer to the north lies Shaikhan, while Mirabad and Mirziarat are located east of the Swat River, between one and two kilometers east of Bala Hisar. In the second century C.E., the Greek historian Arrian, drawing on earlier resources, described how Hephaistion, a general of ALEXANDER THE GREAT, invested Pushkalavati in 327 B.C.E. during his march to the Indus. The city held out for a month and finally ceded control to Alexander in person.

WHEELER'S EXCAVATIONS

In 1903 SIR JOHN MARSHALL undertook a brief season of excavations there, but with no definitive findings. Knowledge of the site and its history relies on a seven-week season of excavations undertaken in 1958, under the direction of SIR MORTIMER WHEELER. He cut a section on the eroding edge of Bala Hisar and extended this opened area away from the main settlement in a series of squares in an attempt to identify the margins of the city. In particular, he sought evidence for defensive works that could have withstood a siege against the troops of Alexander the Great. At that juncture, it was not known whether the mass of Bala Hisar was a platform mound raised as the foundation of a city or whether the mound accumulated through a lengthy period of occupation. The excavation supported the latter alternative. The natural substrate was reached after removing 17 meters of cultural material comprising 51 successive layers. Wheeler suggested that the initial foundation dates back to the period when GANDHARA, the province of which Pushkalavati was a major center, was part of the ACHAEMENID EMPIRE. It flourished in one of the richest of the imperial provinces until it succumbed to Alexander the Great. The excavation, which extended out from the current eastern edge of the mound of Bala Hisar, encountered a deep defensive ditch, the foundations of a postern gateway, and a bridge. This ditch was then traced by further excavations north and south over a distance of 360 meters.

Artifacts from the Bala Hisar excavation included many human and animal terra-cotta figurines. The female figures wore multiple necklaces and had elaborate hairstyles. Two clay seal impressions were found, one of Achaemenid style, the other Greek. Both provide evidence for trade. A Greek coin of Menander (155–130 B.C.E.) was found in the fill of a well.

During the course of the excavations of 1958, air photographs were taken of the adjacent mound of Shaikhan. On the surface, the mound appeared as a confusing mass of robber trenches, where local villagers had removed bricks for their own purposes. The aerial photos, however, furnished a clear grid plan of streets interspersed with dwellings, as it were in negative form, the walls and roads indicated by the removal of the brick structures. A large circular Buddhist stupa also appeared in this city plan. Wheeler was able to contrast this sequence with that at Taxila, where the BHIR MOUND was succeeded first by the BACTRIAN GREEK and KUSHAN city of SIRKAP and then by the new Kushan foundation at SIRSUKH. Despite a lack of excavation at Shaikhan, it seems beyond reasonable doubt that the site represents a Bactrian Greek city foundation with later Kushan occupation. This is supported by the discovery of at least two hoards of Indo-Greek coins by the local villagers. It is possible that the mounds of Mirabad and Mirziarat repre-

sent a still later Kushan city, but this speculation requires archaeological verification.

Pushkalavati seems to have conceded its preeminent position to Peshawar, 32 kilometers (19 mi.) to the southwest. Peshawar was the capital of the Kushan king KANISHKA I from about 100 C.E. Visitors to the area in the seventh century C.E. found that Peshawar was twice the size of Pushkalavati.

See also SEALS.

Further reading: Wheeler, R. E. M. *Charsada, a Metropolis of the North-West Frontier.* London: British Academy, 1962.

Chau Say Tevoda   This small temple is located to the east of the later city of ANGKOR THOM in Cambodia and was probably built late in the reign of SURYAVARMAN II (r. 1113–50). The reliefs, in a ruined condition, include scenes from Hindu epics.

See also ANGKOR.

Chengtoushan   Chengtoushan is the oldest walled settlement in China, at least 1,000 years earlier than the LONGSHAN CULTURE sites of the central plains. This is best understood in the light of the evidence for early rice cultivation in the rich plain surrounding Lake Dongting. The city was founded more than two millennia after the establishment of early rice-farming villages in this part of China. Located northwest of Lake Dongting in Hupei province, central China, it occupies an elevated area, and the name means "hilltop walled city." Only two kilometers (1.2 mi.) distant lies the site of Pengtoushan, notable as one of the earliest sites to evidence the cultivation of domestic rice. Chengtoushan is roughly circular in plan and covers an area of about eight hectares (20 acres). It was extensively excavated by He Jiejun in the 1990s, with most surprising and important results providing social information. It was discovered that the earliest walled city was founded during the early Daxi culture, about 4000 B.C.E. There were then three further periods of wall construction or modification, dating to the middle Daxi, early Qujialing, and finally mid-Qujialing cultures. The site appears to have been abandoned during the Shijiahe culture in about 2000 B.C.E., after two millennia of continuous occupation. The excavation of the stamped-earth walls, which attained a width of 35 to 40 (115–132 ft.) meters and a height of at least six meters, revealed an early moat later covered by the expansion of the walls, which necessitated excavation of a further moat around the site.

Excavations have opened more than 4,000 square meters (4,800 sq. yds.) of the interior of Chengtoushan. Seven hundred burials have been unearthed, of which 200 date to the early Daxi culture, and the balance to the middle and late Daxi. While many of the inhumation burials were poor in terms of grave goods, a few were very rich. One person, for example, was interred with about 50 well-made pottery vessels and two jade pendants. Four individuals had been placed in a crouched position at the corners of the tomb. It is beyond doubt that this burial, as do other rich graves, reflects marked social divisions in society.

There is also abundant evidence for people's houses. Some had a living room and a kitchen; others had a corridor and several living rooms. Specialist manufacture is also seen in an extensive area given over to the manufacture and kiln firing of pottery. Moreover, the excavation of a 10-meter-wide moat dating to the Daxi culture revealed wooden agricultural tools, bamboo and reed basketry, linen cloth, and paddles and rudders for boats. There was also an abundance of rice remains and gourds. When the eastern wall was excavated, the physical remains of an actual rice field were found, complete with ridges around the plots and irrigation ditches.

Chengzi Chengzi is a site of the LONGSHAN CULTURE located in Shandong province, China. The site provides early evidence for the ancestor worship that was so evident in the ritual behavior of the early Shang state. The Longshan culture, dated to the third millennium B.C.E., occupies a key position in the development of early Chinese states in the Huang (Yellow) River Valley. Many settlements were walled and incorporated cemeteries that reveal the social divisions characteristic of societies close to statehood. Chengzi is no exception. Excavations there have uncovered 87 graves divided into four classes on the basis of wealth and energy expended in rituals. Fifty-four of the burials are classified as poor, with no grave goods. There are 17 Class 3 burials, among which only a few poorly constructed ceramic vessels were present. Class 2 burials incorporated a ledge for the placement of grave offerings that included fine pottery and pigs' mandibles, while the five rich graves equipped with wooden chambers included abundant eggshell-thin pottery vessels and pigs' jawbones.

While the sample is small, it was found that the two richer classes of burials contained male skeletons, while Classes 3 and 4 included the remains of men and WOMEN. Moreover, spatially there appear to have been two groups. The eastern group contained no rich graves and no pits associated with individual burials. The western, however, included all the rich burials as well as pits containing complete pottery vessels, artifacts of stone and bone, animal bones, and ash. These are located adjacent to specific burials and are interpreted as ritual pits to contain offerings to the ancestors.

See also TAOSI.

Chengziyai Chengziyai is a major walled settlement of the LONGSHAN CULTURE, located on the right bank of the lower Huang (Yellow) River in Shandong province, northeast China. It was occupied between about 2500

and 1900 B.C.E. The site covers about 17.5 hectares and was defended by a stout rampart of stamped-earth construction 10 meters (33 ft.) wide at the base and originally up to six meters (20 ft.) high. A particularly notable feature of this site is the recovery of 16 ORACLE BONES, and very early written symbols on ceramics, representing an early stage in the development of writing. The pottery vessels themselves are thin and elegant and suggest a local specialist industry.

See also SCAPULOMANCY.

Chenla Many observers have cited Indianization as the key to understanding the rise of Chenla state in Cambodia, which preceded the kingdom of ANGKOR; they claim that the inspiration to increasing social hierarchies was due to Indian visitors introducing new ideas. This view has been criticized for underestimating the strong and continuing contribution of indigenous Khmer culture. Thus Michael Vickery has summarized the many references in the inscriptions to local gods worshiped in Chenla temples. The local matrilineal descent system continued, and the Khmer language took its place alongside SANSKRIT in the inscriptions. Vickery prefers the notion of an Indic veneer, wherein the elites in society selectively adopted those Indian traits that suited their objectives. These included the SANSKRIT language for personal and place names, the Indian script, and architectural styles. These elements contributed to the increasingly strong divisions in society that signal the formation of states, but the essential characteristics of the Chenla kingdoms were Khmer.

Chinese histories record that a state called Chenla sent an embassy to China in 616 or 617 C.E. *The History of the Sui Dynasty (Sui-shu)* noted that Chenla was originally a vassal of FUNAN in Cambodia, but under its ruler Citrasena conquered Funan and gained independence. Subsequent references described further missions to the Chinese court; the descriptions give the impression that it was a unified state under a king, which had defeated and absorbed Funan. During the early eighth century, the histories record that Chenla was divided into two states, labeled Land Chenla and Water Chenla, respectively. These references have cast a long shadow on the interpretation of this vital period in the history of Cambodia, with much energy being expended on locating the two states.

INSCRIPTIONS AND HISTORICAL EVIDENCE

Many INSCRIPTIONS were erected during the period of Chenla (550–800), but none uses this or any other name for a unitary state or a division into Land and Water Chenla. Michael Vickery has stressed that the proper analysis of Chenla can be undertaken only on the basis of the original documents and their accurate analysis. A further source of information, still in its infancy, is archaeological investigation. Most inscriptions were erected to record the foundation of a temple or to note meritorious donations made by benefactors. The majority were written in Sanskrit, which a later section in Old Khmer. From the earliest days of research, the location of Chenla temples through fieldwork has provided much information on the distribution of sites and the evolution of art styles and architectural preferences. Some surviving inscriptions from these sites include references to kings, place names, the titles and status of temple patrons, the extent of temple property, and the names and duties of those assigned to maintain the foundation. Although these texts are heavily biased toward the religious side of Chenla, it remains possible to identify a wide range of social and economic information from their contents.

An inscription from the small sanctuary of Kdei Ang illustrates how original documents provide an insight into the actual transition from Funan to Chenla. Written in 667 C.E., the inscription names successive members of an elite family of court officials. It begins with Brahmadatta, a retainer of King RUDRAVARMAN of Funan (c. 514–50). His maternal nephews, Dharmadeva and Simhadeva, served the kings Bhavavarman and Mahendravarman. Simhavira, a maternal nephew of Dharmadeva, was an official under King Ishanavarman (r. c. 615–37). Finally, Simhadatta

served King JAYAVARMAN I (c. 635–80). This dynasty of rulers is the major, but not only, evidence for central royal authority. However, by following the rulers' history, it is possible to trace the development of increasingly centralized state authority. Mahendravarman claimed victories in a series of short Sanskrit inscriptions set up in the Mun Valley to the north, but these need not imply more than raiding expeditions with no long-term territorial gain. ISHANAVARMAN OF CHENLA seems to have exercised authority over a wide area, as many regional leaders acknowledged him as their overlord. One text from 250 kilometers (150 mi.) south of his capital records how the local magnate Ishanadatta referred to the heroic and illustrious Ishanavarman. An inscription from ISHANAPURA itself describes the valor and military prowess of Ishanavarman, a king "who extended the territory of his parents."

He was succeeded by his son, Bhavavarman II, about whom little is known except that from the region of Ishanapura he continued to maintain control over most if not all of his father's fiefs. It is intriguing that a series of inscriptions dating to his reign record foundations by local leaders without any reference to this king, a situation that might well indicate their independence. Jayavarman I

The Chenla period, from 550–800 C.E. in Cambodia, saw many royal centers being constructed. These, at Banteay Prei Nokor, incorporated brick-built temples in central positions. *(Charles Higham)*

was the great-grandson of Ishanavarman. His inscriptions indicate the tightening of central power and control over a considerable area, the creation of new titles and administrators, and the availability of an army, the means of defense and destruction. A text described how King Jayavarman's commands were obeyed by "innumerable vassal kings." Jayavarman also strengthened the legal code: "Those who levy an annual tax, those who seize carts, boats, slaves, cattle, buffaloes, those who contest the king's orders, will be punished." New titles were accorded highly ranked retainers who fulfilled important posts in government. One lineage held the priestly position of *hotar.* Another functionary was a *samantagajapadi,* chief of the royal elephants, and a military leader; the *dhanyakarapati* would have controlled the grain stores. The king also appointed officials known as a *mratan* and *pon* to a *sabha,* or council of state. Another inscription prescribes the quantities of salt to be distributed by barge to various foundations and prohibits any tax on the vessels going up- or downriver. Thus Jayavarman I intensified royal control over dependent fiefs begun by his great-grandfather, Ishanavarman. Thereafter this dynasty loses visibility, although the king's daughter, Jayadevi, ruled from a center in the vicinity of ANGKOR.

Some other ruling dynasties and their small states are also known, but not to the same extent as the line of Bhavarman. A succession of three queens ruled at Sambhupura, a center that controlled traffic up and down the Mekong River, and there was a line of kings with names ending in -*aditya,* or "rising Sun," who ruled during the eighth century. In the state of CANASAPURA in the upper Mun Valley, a local dynasty ruled—King Bhagadatta and his successors, Sundaraparakrama, Sundaravarman, Narapatisimhavarman, and Mangalavarman.

CHENLA ARCHITECTURE

The Chenla centers are recognized on the basis of brick temples, encircling walls, and associated BARAYS, or reservoirs. The best known is Ishanapura, dominated by three walled precincts containing single-chambered temples. The doorways incorporate sandstone lintels and columns decorated with a range of motifs drawing on India for inspiration. One lintel from Wat En Khna shows a king in his throne chamber, surrounded by members of his court. The facades of the temples are also decorated in shaped bricks that include representations of palaces. These reveal aspects of richly ornamented wooden structures that have not survived. Some idea of the wealth of such courts can be obtained from a Chinese account of the early seventh century, possibly describing Ishanapura. The king gave an audience every three days in a hall containing a wooden throne embellished with columns of inlaid wood and fine fabrics. He was protected by many guards and wore a crown of gold and precious stones and golden ear pendants. Courtiers and officials touched the ground three times with their head below the steps leading up to the throne. At the end of the audience, members of the court prostrated themselves.

ECONOMY

The Chenla states that rose and fell between 550 and 800 were essentially agrarian, and their economy revolved around the temple. Temples were more than centers for devotion and worship, for they played a vital economic role in the management and deployment of agricultural surpluses. Most inscriptions from this period are concerned with temples and the provision of resources to maintain the personnel. Men of high status with the title *pon* are often mentioned for their role in temple management. Inscriptions indicate that they could donate communal land to the temple and organize their kin to produce surpluses. This system involved the accumulation of wealth in the form of rice, cloth, and land. Donations to the temple, which housed ancestral spirits, resulted in the accumulation of the merit necessary for a harmonious reincarnation.

Stored assets were also a form of tradable wealth. Surviving texts suggest that rice, cloth, or ironware could be traded, thus allowing *pon* to indulge in trade not only for basic food and cloth, but also for bankable assets, such as gold and silver. Land could be mortgaged to a temple in return for silver or cloth, and the product of the land was assigned as a form of interest payment. A donor might give products to the temple but receive other goods in return, or deposit goods against which to make a later claim. The temple, then, performed a key role in the appropriation of a community asset into a medium for the creation and exchange of wealth items among the elite. The more successful could accumulate sufficient capital in this way to buy further land, or they could combine assets through marriage alliances and gain sufficient wealth to increase their power and status to such an extent as to control considerable areas. The established kings, therefore, were concerned with such wealth creation, for it might encourage rivals, and their permission was often described as being necessary in the amalgamation of temples and the rights to land ownership.

The inscriptions contain numerous references to the boundaries of rice fields. Many bordered reservoirs, roads, or forests. The temples name the duties of their officiants and servants. There were priests, musicians and dancers, and craft specialists. One text records the assignment to a temple of 17 dancers or singers, 23 or 24 record keepers, 19 leaf sewers, 37 artisans (including a potter), 11 weavers, 15 spinners, and 59 rice fieldworkers, 46 of whom were female. There was no system of coinage, but goods were valued by measures of silver by weight, quantities of rice, or length and quality of cloth. The list of workers set out in the corpus of Chenla texts covers a wide range of economic activities. Although rice cultivation is most prominent, weaving was also a central activity, and there were specialist potters, leaf sewers, smiths, cooks, producers of salt, perfume grinders, herdsmen, and basket makers.

During the eighth century, the number of inscriptions fell markedly, and the historic record became thin. This does not necessarily imply cultural decline. On the contrary, it was during this period that such large sites as BANTEAY CHOEU near ANGKOR and BANTEAY PREI NOKOR were occupied. These sites were probably the base of a ruler known as JAYAVARMAN II (c. 770–834 C.E.), and it was he who, through a series of military victories over rivals and a new ritual consecration, was crowned CHAKRAVARTIN, "supreme king of kings," on the KULEN HILLS and founded the kingdom of Angkor.

Further reading: Higham, C. F. W. *The Civilization of Angkor.* London: Weidenfeld and Nicholson, 2001; Vickery, M. *Society, Economics and Politics in Pre-Angkor Cambodia.* Tokyo: The Centre for East Asian Cultural Studies for UNESCO, 1998.

Chen She (third century B.C.E.) *Chen She was a Chinese peasant who toppled an empire.*
The establishment of the QIN empire, which concluded the WARRING STATES PERIOD in China, led to a complete transformation of governance and society and involved a harsh central dictatorial regime under the iron rule of the first emperor, QIN SHIHUANGDI, against whom Chen She led a revolt in 209 B.C.E. The SHIJI (*Records of the Grand Historian*, 145–86 C.E.) and HANSHU (*History of the Former Han*, 32–92 C.E.) both described the peasants' revolt against the second emperor of the Qin. Chen She, they record, was a peasant who, when plowing, stopped his work and said to his fellows that if he were ever to become rich and famous, he would not forget them. When they responded with derision, he asked: "How can sparrows understand the ambitions of a swan?" In due course, he and his fellows were ordered to a distant post to undertake garrison duties, but en route to their destination, they encountered heavy rain and were so delayed that there was no prospect of reaching the frontier by the appointed time. This was a crime punishable by beheading. One of Chen She's intimates, Wu Guang, courted immediate punishment by insolence, and the commanding officer, who was drunk, let his sword slip from his hand. Wu Guang seized the sword and killed the officer and his two colleagues. Rather than now face certain death, Chen She called on his men to follow him in revolt against the new emperor. Thus began the uprising that led, ultimately, to the rise of the HAN DYNASTY.
See also Liu Ji.

Cherchen *See* QIEMO.

Chok Gargyar *See* KOH KER.

Chongdi (143–145 C.E.) *Chongdi, "modest emperor," was the eighth emperor of the Eastern Han Dynasty of China.*
The son of Emperor Shundi of the Eastern HAN DYNASTY, he acceded to the throne in 144 C.E. at the age of only five months.

Choson In the northern Korean Peninsula, according to the *Shiji* (*Records of the Grand Historian*), the state of Choson was ruled by a king, aided by several ranks of ministers, and protected by an army under the command of military officers. The rulers instituted IRRIGATION measures to improve agriculture and promoted trade in horses, iron, and salt. However, in 109–108 B.C.E. a Han Chinese army invaded the region and after a long campaign took the walled capital of WANGXIAN from the third king of Choson, Youqu. The area taken was so large that it was carved up into four commanderies, the longest lived being known as LELANG.

The Korean state of Choson had lasted for three generations, from about 195 B.C.E. until its conquest by the Chinese HAN DYNASTY in 108 B.C.E. There are several myths as to its origins, the most probable one that a Chinese named Wiman moved into northern Korea with his followers, overcame the local leaders, and established a state with its capital in the vicinity of Pyongyang. For the three centuries preceding 108 B.C.E., the area centered on the Yalu River had lain to the east of the Chinese state of YAN, and there had been much influence and exchange between the two regions. Indeed, the name Choson in Chinese means "dawn fresh," pointing to its position to the east of Yan. However, in 221 B.C.E., the WARRING STATES PERIOD in China came to an end, leading first to the establishment of the QIN dynasty and then to the long rule of the Western HAN DYNASTY emperors. This more peaceful period in Chinese politics, allied to the unification of China, had profound effects on the polities lying on its south, east, and west margins. The Han emperor WUDI adopted an expansionist imperial policy, leading to the replacement of local leaders by provinces or commanderies ruled by centrally appointed bureaucrats.

Chu The state of Chu in China underwent many changes over the course of its history. Traditionally, this wealthy state with an opulent material culture was located to the south of the central plains, and Chinese historians such as SIMA QIAN and BAN GU compared the people with barbarians who practiced strange religious rituals and lived a life of easy affluence. This perception may well have been based on the mild climate enjoyed by the Chu and their concentration on rice cultivation rather than the millet that dominated in the cold north. Still far too little is known of the Chu people and their origins, but archaeological research in the Chang (Yangtze) Valley, notably the recovery of written records from Chu tombs, is beginning to redress this situation.

Thus it is now increasingly evident that early complex societies developed as early in the central Chang Valley as in the Huang (Yellow) River Basin, if not earlier. This is seen at such early town or city sites as CHENGTOUSHAN. The earliest historic records of a distinctive Chu culture date to the late SHANG STATE (1200–1045 B.C.E.), and there exists a graph showing a foot in brambles, which designates the Chu. During the WESTERN ZHOU DYNASTY (1045–771 B.C.E.), the Chu were described as southern barbarians, and military campaigns were mounted to secure booty and seek out sources of copper. One such inscription is from the *Ling* YI. This bronze vessel was looted by grave robbers from a site near LUOYANG in 1929 and states in its INSCRIPTION that "the king attacked the elder of Chu." This refers to King Zhao (r. c. 977/75–957 B.C.E.), who led a military campaign against the ruler of Chu. The upshot of this was the death of King Zhao in a failed campaign, allegedly by drowning when the bridge over the Han River collapsed, taking the king with it. This is confirmed by a second text on the Yiyu *gui*, which states that the Yiyu participated in the king's southern campaign.

EXPANSION OF CHU

The succeeding Spring and Autumn period (770–476 B.C.E.) saw the Chu fully enter the historic stage. This situation resulted largely from the increasingly ritual rather than politically powerful role of the Eastern Zhou court at Luoyang, which allowed regional states to compete for leadership. Chu was not slow to take up the challenge, and although it has not proved possible definitively to define the successive capitals of Danyang and Ying, they were almost certainly located well north of the Chang River in West Hubei and southwest Henan provinces. For example, in 703 B.C.E. Xiong Yi of Chu took for himself the title of king, while early Chu inscriptions make it evident that the kings regarded themselves as legitimized by divine authority, known as the MANDATE OF HEAVEN. From this base, with alternating periods of success and defeat, the Chu expanded their kingdom considerably. The wealth of Chu at this juncture can be seen in the rich tomb of Zeng Hou Yi at LEIGUDUN, Hubei province. Dating to 433 B.C.E., the mortuary offerings as listed on the BAMBOO-SLIP inventory run to 6,600 entries, including 43 CHARIOTS. The assemblage of bronzes from the four main chambers weighed 10 tons, but perhaps the most interest has been attached to the two magnificent nested coffins. The outer specimen was built of lacquered wood over a bronze framework and was embellished with many geometric designs. The innermost was also of lacquered wood, and some designs are thought to represent windows and doors. Despite such wealth, from about 400 B.C.E. Chu fell into a decline, largely due to the growing military power of the state of QIN, and finally collapsed at the end of the WARRING STATES PERIOD.

The material remains of Chu culture, like the historic record, had been fugitive until the beginning of the Spring and Autumn period (770–476 B.C.E.). During the ensuing three centuries, the bronzes placed in the graves developed from forms possibly inspired from the north into distinctive vessels incorporating lavish decorations of strange beasts, cloud patterns, coiled serpents, and phoenixes. The preference for bronze vessels as tomb furniture during this early period is best seen at the necropolis of Xichuan, the inscriptions ascribing them to members of the elite during the late seventh century B.C.E. Bronzes from this site and the slightly later cemetery of Xiasi provide a powerful indication of the quantity of bronze available and the audacious skill of the specialist workshops. Tomb 2, which contained the remains of an aristocrat named Wu, dates to 552 B.C.E. The grave goods included a richly decorated bronze altar more than a meter in length, weighing nearly 100 kilograms (220 lbs.).

Chu Bronzes

The Chu casters also adopted the lost-wax technique, which allowed greater freedom of expression in developing new designs compared with the traditional piece-mold technique. This reached its height of complexity in the *zun* and *pan* vessels recovered from the tomb of Zeng Hou Yi at the site of Leigudun. They also showed their innovative skill in the use of inlays to form decorative patterns of TURQUOISE, copper, and LACQUER. These developments are documented in a number of cemeteries, foremost being Zhaojiahu and Jiangling.

Chu Music

From all reports, the people of Chu enjoyed a distinctive musical genre. In 582 B.C.E., an imprisoned Chu musician in the state of Jin played southern music to the king. During the early Western Han period, Chu music, known as *chusheng*, was popular in the court of King Gaozu. The survival in tomb contexts of sets of bronze bells that can still be played makes it possible to appreciate part of the Chu repertoire. Likewise, wooden instruments, such as zithers from MAWANGDUI, can be copied for the same purpose. The earliest known bells with a possible Chu context fall in the period of Western Zhou and can be dated to the early ninth century on stylistic grounds. These were expertly cast so that by striking the bell in different areas two tones could be produced. Even the point on which to strike the bell to achieve this end was indicated with a decorative bird or elephant. Southern forms of bells seem to have been adopted into the Western Zhou repertoire and certainly became popular mortuary furniture as part of the changing Zhou metropolitan rituals. In Chu itself, a fine bell is known; to judge from its inscription, it probably dates to the reign of King Gong Wang of the early sixth century B.C.E. The wide distribution of similar bells in the Chu cultural sphere, allied with similar inscriptions, suggests the existence of a central specialized workshop, although no such site has yet been located. Royal gifts to client rulers constitute a likely context in which such bell sets were disseminated.

At a slightly later date, Tomb 1 at Xiasi (Henan province) included a set of nine bells. Tomb 2 at the same site yielded a remarkable set of 26 bells. The location of these bells in the tomb indicated that they were played when positioned in two rows, with the eight largest on the lower row, the balance on an upper tier. Even this number pales before the 65 bells found in the tomb of the marquis of Zeng at Leigudun. These were arranged in three rows. The largest was a gift to the marquis from King Hui of Chu (r. 488–532 B.C.E.) and stands almost a meter in height. The extraordinary skill of the musicians and casters, who must presumably have acted in concert, is reflected in the fact that the inscribed tone on each bell matches perfectly the sound ultimately produced. The tomb of Marquis Yi of Zeng also contained a virtually complete set of other instruments that would have made up a Chu orchestra of the period. There were seven large zithers, as well as drums, panpipes, flutes, mouth organs, and chime stones. These were from the central chamber of the tomb and contrast with a set of five large and two small zithers, two mouth organs, and a drum from another chamber. These probably represent chamber music, in contrast to the louder music produced by the full orchestra. The evidence for Chu music derives almost entirely from aristocratic tombs and indicates a widespread tradition closely related to that of the Zhou. The music of the lower classes remains unknown.

Development of Chu Tombs

The plan of Chu tombs also developed in complexity during the period of Eastern Zhou, from a vertical pit in the ground, containing a double wooden coffin, to more elaborate tombs for the elite. By the Warring States period, a rich burial included a covering mound and access ramps. Over time, the richer burials incorporated many chambers or compartments to receive the goods deemed necessary to maintain the same quality of life after death as that previously enjoyed. Such chambers, as at Suixian and Changtaiguan, were filled with musical instruments, drinking vessels, and weaponry and provided space for the consorts or servants of the tomb master. The former tomb contained 21 women, sacrificed and placed in one of the chambers of the tomb of Zeng Hou Yi. His private chambers would, if the tomb contents are a guide, have been filled with the scent of incense, while he dined from solid gold vessels. The range of grave goods also developed during this period, as lacquer ware and decorated silk were increasingly preferred to bronze. The lacquer was often finely decorated with humans, animals, and, as in a cup from BAOSHAN, a series of chariots. This material culture from the Chu tombs illustrates a powerful and sophisticated state society.

CHU TRADE

Trade was one factor underlying the wealth and opulence of the state of Chu. This has been amply documented on the basis of a unique set of *jie* (bronze tallies), in which the text is inlaid in gold, discovered in 1957 at Qiujiahuayuan. This site is located near the right bank of the Huai River in Anhui province. The tallies were issued in the year when Shao Yang defeated the forces of the state of Jin at Xiangling, 323 B.C.E. The texts stated that the tallies were issued to a high Chu administrator named Ejun Qi; they gave permission for merchants under his jurisdiction to travel by land and water over certain prescribed trade routes without payment of tolls or excise tax. However, they also make it clear that the merchants were not to be accommodated or fed at government expense. Since the names of certain towns and rivers can be matched today, it has proved possible to reconstruct the prescribed routes, but unfortunately not the goods traded, other than livestock, because of a ban on leather goods, metal, and bamboo for arrows, which might be useful to an enemy. This ban probably reflects the fact that some routes covered sensitive territory only recently captured from rival states. Boats followed the course of the Chang artery and moved north via the Han River. To the south, they followed the rivers flowing into Lakes Dongting and Poyang. Both river and land routes ended at Ying, the capital.

That metal was carried by land or river is seen in the tallies. The control of vital copper resources, such as the massive mine at Tonglushan, supplied the specialist workshops with the necessary raw materials. The Chang Valley was long renowned as the source of the finest lacquers. There was also a steady supply of gold, and golden vessels and gold inlay on bronzes were a particular feature of rich Chu tombs. Trade with the southern Yue people also carried tropical goods to Chu, including rhinoceros horn, ivory, and the kingfisher feathers cited in the CHUCI poems as being seeded with pearls and used in hangings and bedspreads. Cowry shells were also in demand.

THE CHU AND THE HAN DYNASTY

The climax of the Warring States period saw the victory of Qin over all its rivals, including the state of Chu, in 221 B.C.E. Unification of China under one rule generated the imposition of standardization in place of diversity. Roads were of uniform width; there was a common currency, legal system, and script; and former states were carved up into commanderies ruled by central appointees. In 207 B.C.E. the Chu, who harbored deep resentment against the Qin, were in the vanguard of the insurrections against the short-lived Qin rule, under the leadership of Xiang Yu and Liu Bang. It was said at the time that if only three families remained in Chu, Chu would see the downfall of Qin. Liu Bang, a Chu commoner, went on to found the HAN DYNASTY, when the close link between the new Han regime and Chu promoted a renaissance of the Chu culture in court circles. This did not spell the end of Chu as a historic entity. During the long period of Han dominance (206 B.C.E.–220

C.E.), a Chu kingdom was established under the Wu Jui family, centered at Changsha in the central Chang Basin, on the orders of the first Han emperor, Gaozu. This period saw the immense cultural output of the southern regions of Han, exemplified above all by the tombs of the marquis of Dai, his wife, and sons at Mawangdui.

Further reading: Cook, C. A., and J. S. Major, eds. *Defining Chu: Image and Reality in Ancient China.* Honolulu: University of Hawaii Press, 1999; Thote, A. "Continuities and Discontinuities: Chu Burials during the Eastern Zhou Period." In *Exploring China's Past,* edited by R. Whitfield and Wang Tao. London: Saffron Books, 1999, pp. 189–204.

Chuci The *Chuci* (*The Songs of the South*) is a collection of poems ascribed to Qu Yuan (c. 340–278 B.C.E.), a minister of the southern Chinese kingdom of CHU. The *Chuci* provide a vital source of information on the life and thought of Chu during the WARRING STATES PERIOD (475–221 B.C.E.). The rich lifestyle of the aristocracy, for example, is clearly reflected in the poem "Summoning the Soul," which describes "bedspreads of kingfisher feathers seeded with pearls, of dazzling brightness"; wall coverings of opulent silk fabric; and a diet of goose, chicken, turtle, and "jade-like wine." The verses of the *Chuci* also illustrate the extraordinary range of deities worshiped by the people of Chu. There was a particular emphasis on shamans, who in their trances are described holding snakes, tiger goddesses, and masked monsters, which anticipate the creatures depicted on the MAWANG-DUI tomb banners and the importance of snakes in the rituals of the southern chiefdom of Dian. Earlier but still in the Chang Basin, the bronze masks of the city of SANX-INGDUI in Sichuan are evoked by mention of gods with protruding eyes. The *Chuci* was to exercise an enduring influence on subsequent Chinese poetry.

See also DIAN CHIEFDOM.

Further reading: Cook, C. A., and J. S. Major, eds. *Defining Chu: Image and Reality in Ancient China.* Honolulu: University of Hawaii Press, 1999; Thote, A. "Continuities and Discontinuities: Chu Burials during the Eastern Zhou Period." In *Exploring China's Past,* edited by R. Whitfield and Wang Tao. London: Saffron Books, 1999, pp. 189–204.

Chunqiu Fanlu The *Chunqiu* (*Luxuriant Gems of the Spring and Autumn Annals*) is the historic record of the small kingdom of Lu in China, from 722 to 481 B.C.E. The *Chunqiu* has given its name to the first half of the EASTERN ZHOU DYNASTY, which is widely known as the Spring and Autumn period (770–476 B.C.E.). The work, held to have been inspired or edited by CONFUCIUS, a native of Lu in Shandong province, describes court rituals, religious practices, and the wars that involved Lu.

churning of the ocean of milk The myth of churning the ocean of milk originates in the Hindu Bhagavad Purana of India. It centers on the quest for AMRITA, the elixir of immortality. For a millennium the gods and the demons competed to produce *amrita*. After repeated failures, the god Vishnu advised them to cooperate rather than compete. This they did, the gods pulling on one end of the snake, which was coiled around Mount Mandara, the demons on the other. By spinning the mountain and churning the ocean of milk, it was hoped to produce *amrita*. However, the mountain began to sink into the ocean, and Vishnu, in the form of a turtle, descended to support the mountain. After another 1,000 years, the elixir was produced, and the gods and demons fought over ownership. Vishnu, on the side of the gods, obtained and stored it. A magnificent relief of the churning of the ocean of milk is seen at ANGKOR WAT. It has also been suggested that the symbolism of the city of ANGKOR THOM involves the same legend, in which the demons and gods pulling on the *naga* snake at the entrance gates are symbolically churning Mount Mandara, represented in the center of the city by the BAYON temple mausoleum.

cloves Cloves, with mace and nutmegs, are one of the triad of spices for which island Southeast Asia was renowned. Cloves are the flower buds of an evergreen tree, *Syzygium aromaticum*, which was in nature restricted to five small islands west of Halmahera in the Maluku Islands (the Moluccas). Cloves were in great demand in the West, and their distribution, which was based on the polities of the BRANTAS RIVER Valley in eastern Java, Indonesia, from at least the 10th century C.E., generated great wealth; access to the spice was jealously guarded by the rulers of that region. In 1982 cloves were found in a pottery vessel at the site of Terqa in the Euphrates Valley in modern Iraq. These are thought to date to about 1700–1600 B.C.E. If substantiated, this finding suggests a far earlier development of a maritime trade network than has hitherto been contemplated.

Cœdès, Georges (1886–1969) *Georges (G.) Cœdès, a Frenchman of Hungarian-Jewish origin, began his scholarly career as a member of the staff of the École Française d'Extrême Orient in Hanoi. His contribution to unraveling the history of early states in Southeast Asia is unrivaled.*
In 1918 he became the director of the National Library of Thailand, before returning to Hanoi 11 years later as director of the École. In 1946 he left Vietnam for Paris, where he was appointed professor of Southeast Asian History at L'École des Langues Orientales and curator of the Musée d'Ennery. For many decades he translated into French the corpus of SANSKRIT INSCRIPTIONS relating to the kingdom of ANGKOR and its predecessors; these were published with commentaries on the INSCRIPTIONS'

historic significance in seven volumes. He also synthesized the development of indigenous states in his major work, *The Indianised States of Southeast Asia.*

coinage   In any society, a system of currency is clear evidence for economic complexity, and coinage is often associated with the development of trade and acts as a stimulant to trade.

INDIA

The study of Indian coins began in the early years of the 19th century, when James Tod had local people collect them after the rains had caused erosion at MATHURA and other sites in the area. He reported coins of the Indo-Greek king Menander (r. 150–135 B.C.E.). Westerners in India were also interested in Roman coinage. A hoard of 522 coins of the Julio-Claudian dynasty was found at Vellaloor in 1842. A massive collection of gold coins from the Roman empire was discovered by chance in 1847 in a brass vessel near Calicut. They were in mint condition, and according to a contemporary report, they comprised "five coolly loads." From 1850 numismatists turned their attention to Indian coins, largely after the decipherment of the BRAHMI script, which made it possible to read the INSCRIPTIONS. JAMES PRINSEP made the early observation that the Indian issues were based on BACTRIAN GREEK models. This is only partially true. In India the earliest coins date to the end of the sixth century B.C.E. and took the form of rectangular pieces of silver on which a design was punched. Hence they are known as punch-marked coins, and the designs usually incorporated animals and plants, human figures, trees, and hills that follow a definite pattern. They were almost certainly issued by the rulers of *janapada*s, or early states, but some could have been made by craft or merchant guilds. The punch-marked coins found in central India, for example, bore specific designs that include a sphere in a pentagon specific to this area. Early examples of punch-marked silver coins are from a hoard found at Chaman Huzuri that contained 43 silver punch-marked coins together with coins minted in Athens and the Achaemenid empire. The Kalinga *janapada* issued a punch-marked coin almost square in form, but with one-quarter circular. An important hoard discovered in 1924 at the BHIR MOUND, TAXILA, modern Pakistan, contained more than 1,000 worn punch-marked coins in association with two coins of ALEXANDER THE GREAT in mint condition. Taxila was the center for the issue of a particular type of punch-marked coin known as the *satamana* (100 units) bent bar. These coins have a consistent weight of 100 *ratti*s of silver; a *ratti* weighs 0.11 gram. In due course early Indian coinage was denominated on the basis of one *karshapana*, or 32 *ratti*s. The unique shape and the regional forms of the silver punch-marked coins, together with their early date, make a local origin of coinage likely.

Mauryan Coins

The currency of the MAURYA EMPIRE (about 325–185 B.C.E.) included such silver and copper coins, particularly those bearing the symbols of three hills, a crescent, and a peacock. One issue showed three deities and a peacock, with a single peacock and a hill on the other side. These are widespread in India and reflect the establishment of central authority under the Mauryas. The political text known as the ARTHASASTRA of Kautilya, a minister to King CANDRAGUPTA MAURYA (about 325–297 B.C.E.), specified that coins be minted in silver and copper. The silver coinage began with the *pana*, then descended to a half, a quarter, and 1/16 of a *pana*. Copper coins were denominated in a unit of weight known as a *masaka*, one of which was the value of 1/16 of a *pana*. There were, in the ideal state, a minister in charge of mining and metalworking, a second for minting of coins, and a third for ensuring that the currency was sound and legal. The silver coins were punched with symbols that might have indicated the regnal period when they were minted; the copper coins were usually cast and bore symbols as well as images of the lion and elephant.

Indo-Greek Coinage

The earliest inscribed coins followed the establishment of the Bactrian Greek colonies and are an essential source of information on the many rulers of that period. Indeed, without the numismatic evidence, little would be known of the vast majority of Indo-Greek kings. The coins bear an image of the king and his name, first in Greek but increasingly in PRAKRIT (regional Indian languages descended from Sanskrit). The distribution of a given king's coinage provides historic evidence for the extent of his power. Some Greek issues, however, copied local punch-marked coinage. Apollodotus II (180–160 B.C.E.) was responsible for a square coin with an image of an elephant on one side and a bull on the other, associated with a KHAROSHTHI (a writing system of Northwest India) inscription in Prakrit that records the king's name. The coins of Menander are particularly widespread. An example minted at Taxila shows his portrait on one side with a Greek script reading, "King Menander," while the obverse has an image of Athena with the Kharoshthi legend "by King Menander, the savior." The coins of Strato showing him first as a youth and later as an old man attest to the longevity of his reign. Coins of Nicias (80–60 B.C.E.) are concentrated in the Jhelum Valley in Pakistan and reveal clearly the Indianization of the Greeks; the legend on the reverse of one of his coins reads, *Maharajasa tratarasa Nikiasa* (the great king, king of kings, Nicias) in Kharoshthi under an image of Athena, while the obverse shows the king with his name in Greek. Hermaeus (c. 40–1 B.C.E.) was the last Greek king before the SAKA invasions, and his coins show him riding a prancing horse and designated Maharaja on one side, and wearing a diadem with the Greek title *basileus* (king) on the other.

Saka Coins

Coins are also the source material for placing the Saka (Scythian) in their correct order, incorporating Vonones, Azes I, Asilises, Azes II, and Gondophares (about 75 B.C.E. to 46 C.E.). They copied the form of the Greek precedents, but their coinage also illustrates their methods of government. That they associated brothers or sons of the king in ruling their extensive territory is seen in the naming of more than one person on a coin, as in the association of Vonones with two brothers, Spalyris and Spalirises. Thus a silver coin of Azes shows the king holding a spear on the obverse and Zeus on the reverse holding a scepter. The inscription on the obverse is in Greek with the king's name and title *basileus;* the reverse bears the Kharoshthi inscription *Maharaja rajarajasa mahatasa Ayasa* (the great king, king of kings, Azes). Coins of Azilises also show the king on horseback with Zeus, but Indian influence is seen on some issues in the form of the Hindu goddess Lakshmi on a lotus flower, on the leaves of which stand elephants sprinkling water on her head. Another silver coin of this king reveals a male and a female god standing side by side, the former holding a long scepter, the latter a cornucopia.

Kushan Coins

The KUSHANS (78–200 C.E.) are also best documented on the basis of the coinage of their kings, which followed earlier forms by having an image of the king on one side and an inscription in Bactrian, employing the Greek script, on the other. KUJULA KADPHISES copied the coins of the areas he conquered, but in due course the Kushan currency was standardized across the empire. The Kushans issued the first gold coins in India, and their currency provides a unique opportunity to learn about the appearance of the kings and their adoption of Hindu deities. This applies in particular to Vima Kadphises, who ruled from about 90 to 100 C.E. In head and shoulder view is a powerful warrior king wearing a high helmet, while in full view he wears in addition a tunic, overcoat, and felt boots. The reverse of one of his gold coins shows SIVA and his sacred mount Nandi with a Sanskrit inscription that states, "emperor, king of kings, devotee of the great god Siva, the savior Vima Kadphises." His son, KANISHKA I, was responsible for a series of remarkable gold coins as well as copper issues. One of the latter shows him sacrificing at an altar, wearing the Saka peaked helmet, trousers, and a coat. He holds a spear in his left hand and has a halo. He is described on some of his inscriptions as *devaputra* (the son of god). A gold coin describes him as "king of kings, Kanishka the Kushan." Siva is often to be found on his coins, but Kanishka was renowned for his interest in BUDDHISM, and on very rare occasions, the Buddha appears on his coins, either standing or seated. His successor, Huvishka (126–64), issued outstanding gold coins over a long reign; the portraits of the king begin by showing him as a young bearded warrior with the typical Kushan dress, but they

end with a mature sovereign with a halo, crown, scepter, and jeweled tunic. On occasion he is seen riding a magnificent elephant, holding a spear and an elephant goad. On others, he is seen holding a scepter and seated cross-legged on a cushion. He also displayed a wide choice of Greek, Zoroastrian, and Hindu deities as associates on his coins—Hephaestus, Greek god of crafts and metals; Siva holding a trident and a gourd; Skanda, son of Siva and god of war; a male lunar deity, Mao, with the crescent moon behind his shoulders; the Sun god; and the wind god. By the reign of Vasudeva (164–200), the Kushan empire had lost much territory in BACTRIA and was becoming increasingly assimilated into Indian culture. This king's capital was probably in MATHURA, and the deities on his coins are entirely Indian, for example, Siva with a trident, accompanied by the bull Nandi, and Siva represented with five heads. The king himself is portrayed still with a peaked helmet, wearing chain-mail armor and undertaking a sacrifice before an altar. Kanishka II (200–222) ruled an empire further attenuated by Sassanian expansion and now governed only land east of the Indus, including mints at Taxila and Mathura. His coins show further Indian cultural penetration with inscriptions in the Brahmi script and Siva linked with Nandi the god most commonly represented.

Gupta Coins

Arguably, no event in Indian history is so elegantly portrayed on coinage as the advent of Candragupta I (r. c. 320–330), the first major king of the GUPTA EMPIRE. It is said that his rise to power was enhanced by his marriage to Kumaradevi, a princess of the powerful Licchavi lineage of Mithila. Although Candragupta himself probably did not issue his own coins, this union is illustrated in a gold coin initiated by his son, SAMUDRAGUPTA. On the obverse, Candragupta offers Kumaradevi a ring. Their names are inscribed in the Brahmi script. Samudragupta (335–380) minted many coins, and their designs clearly show a debt to Kushan rulers. His coins were the same weight, about eight grams, as those of the Kushan kings and are of seven principal types, each of which illustrates an aspect of his life and achievements, for example, the king playing the lyre, the depiction of a battle ax to stress his military successes, and a horse sacrifice to celebrate victory. The inscription on one of his gold coins reads, "the invincible king, victor of a hundred battles," while the lyre issue was inscribed, "Samudragupta, great king of kings," in Sanskrit. The king, an ardent Hindu, had Lakshmi, goddess of wealth, shown on the reverse.

His successor, CANDRAGUPTA II, or Vikramaditya (380–413), issued more gold coins than any other member of his dynasty. He expanded the Gupta empire by a famous victory over the WESTERN SATRAPS states in western India. Many of his coins show him holding a bow and arrow, with Lakshmi on the reverse, seated on a lotus. Kumargupta, also known as Mahendraditya (415–455), continued to rule a large and prosperous empire and had himself proclaimed *chakravartin,* or supreme king of kings. He minted 14 different types of gold coins, which included images of the king as a tiger slayer, holding a bow and arrow as he stood over the tiger, and as a rhinoceros slayer, as well as the king playing on the lyre. The reverse of the tiger slayer coin incorporated the goddess Ganga feeding a peacock. The same image of a goddess feeding a peacock is found on a fine coin showing the king on horseback. He also minted silver coins, imitating the style and metal of the recently defeated western satraps. One coin shows the king's face, while the reverse has an image of GARUDA, the eagle and symbol of the dynasty. Skandagupta (455–67) inherited a rich and stable empire but had to cope with the invasion of the Huns. At first he was successful, and his coins show him victorious in association with the goddess Lakshmi as his wife. However, the Huns continued to press down on the Gupta empire as it went into a decline.

Western Satraps Coins

The rulers of the WESTERN SATRAPS, who dominated much of Gujarat and adjoining parts of Rajasthan and Madhya Pradesh between the first and fourth centuries C.E., issued coins with the image of the ruler together with the name of his father and reign dates. These coins, which had a wide circulation, are an unequaled source of historic information. King Nahapana (119–124) pioneered the satrap practice of issuing coins bearing a portrait of the ruler. His coins show his image together with an arrow and a thunderbolt and the text "Satrap king Nahapanasa." Subsequent major satrap rulers were Chastana and Rudradaman (130–150). Their coins bore an inscription in Greek, but later ones preferred the Brahmi script.

Satavahana Coins

To the south, the SATAVAHANA rulers, who were rivals of the western satraps, copied Greek prototypes and were also familiar with the many Roman coins of the Julio-Claudian dynasty obtained through maritime trade. Most Satavahana coins were made of lead or copper, but certain alloys were also employed. *Potin,* for example, combines lead and copper, while *billon* is an alloy of copper and silver. The most common designs include an elephant, a lion, and a horse. One issue of King Satakarni is a circular coin with an elephant on the obverse along with the so-called UJJAIN symbol, a cross with four circles. The southern Indian Cola kingdom employed a coin with the king on one side and the king seated on the other, a type taken to Sri Lanka when the Cola conquered that island.

CHINA

The origins of Chinese coinage are to be found in the late Spring and Autumn period (770–476 B.C.E.). Before then strings of cowry shells were used as a form of currency, and WESTERN ZHOU DYNASTY bronze inscriptions record gifts of cowry shells from the emperor to faithful retainers. The tomb of Fu Hao at Anyang, dated to the late Shang dynasty, contained thousands of cowry shells. An important tomb of the Western Zhou dynasty at Fufeng Qiangjia, Shaanxi province, held a series of inscribed bronze vessels. The text of one inscription states that the owner had received a gift of cowry shells as part of an investiture ceremony. This form of wealth had permitted the casting of these ritual bronzes. The origin of the shells is not known with certainty, but they must have been from warm clean seas to the south of China or beyond into Southeast Asia. The DIAN chiefs at sites such as SHIZHAISHAN and Lijiashan during the Western HAN DYNASTY (second and first centuries B.C.E.) were interred with bronze cowry containers. These shells probably reached southern China from the Indian Ocean.

Early Chinese Coins

During the Spring and Autumn period there were basic changes to the Chinese economy. Iron began to be employed in agriculture and warfare, leading to a surge in productive capacity. There was sharp population growth, and the mercantile class rose. Many merchants are known to have grown very wealthy, and they played a prominent role in politics. This trend continued and greatly accelerated with the unification of China under the first emperor, QIN SHIHUANGDI (259–210 B.C.E.). He had roads and canals constructed, while peace encouraged trade after centuries of warfare. The emperor also standardized weights and measures and replaced regional scripts with that of QIN throughout the empire. It was also during this period and the ensuing rule of the Western Han dynasty emperors that the international trade across the SILK ROAD opened China to new commercial opportunities.

Before the Qin reforms, the first Chinese systems of currency had begun to replace cowry shells as media of exchange. The earliest minted form of currency was the *bu,* a coin cast of bronze in the form of a miniature double-pronged digging stick or hoe, complete with hollow socket. They are particularly densely concentrated in the vicinity of the Eastern Zhou capital of LUOYANG and in the states of HAN, ZHAO, and WEI. They were issued in considerable quantities, one hoard exceeding 1,000 items. A coin of the Zhao state is inscribed with the location of the mint, Songzi, and the coin's weight. Labeling of coins by the mint and weight was widespread. *Dao* coinage, which was identified with the state of QI, had the form of ring-handled miniature knives, each about 18 centimeters long. These also carry an inscription showing the mint where they were cast. The preferred form of currency in the state of CHU during the WARRING STATES PERIOD is known as a *bei.* Interestingly, these were cast in the form of a cowry shell and are often called ant-faced money because of their shape. The rulers of Chu also minted gold coins in the form of a flat semirectangular plate, inscribed with the weight and place of manufacture.

Qin, Han, and Xing Coins

All these issues were swept away with the unification of China under Qin Shihuangdi, the first emperor. In their place, he issued a gold coin, known as a *shangbi*, and a copper coin, the *xiabi*. These circular coins with a square hole in the center were cast in open copper molds, and their form was maintained in China for the ensuing two millennia. The central monopoly over coinage was maintained under the Western Han emperor WUDI, as three special officials were appointed to take charge of the imperial mint. Their duties were to oversee the casting of coins, check them for color to safeguard against using a debased metal, and supervise the production of the molds. One such copper mold has survived from this period, in which 12 coins could be cast simultaneously. They weighed five *zhu* (a *zhu* was a unit of weight).

WANG MANG of the Xin dynasty reformed the Western Han currency on four occasions, starting in 7 C.E. Six new coins were issued in the traditional circular form, known as *quan* coinage. Some of his new issues were in the form of a key with lettering inlaid with gold. Another, which has the usual circular shape joined to a square, is extremely rare.

JAPAN

The earliest coins from Japan date to the YAYOI period (300 B.C.E.–300 C.E.), but these were Chinese imports and were probably regarded as ornaments of no monetary value. By the late seventh century, a few silver coins were issued, but they did not have a large circulation. The construction of the FUJIWARA and HEIJO cities in rapid succession placed considerable demands on labor and resources during the early eighth century. To facilitate payments, which had hitherto been in the form of cloth or rice, the Japanese government initiated the minting of a large number of coins in 708, taking the Tang currency of China as the model. This move was related to the discovery of copper ore in Musashi province. The Tang coinage has been found in Japan in reasonable quantities, suggesting its use before the local discovery of copper and establishment of a mint for issuing local silver and copper currency. Copper cash was known as *Wado-kaichin*, and four were the equivalent of a silver coin. Several mints have been found. Later, gold coins were also minted in 760. The equivalent values saw copper coins being worth one *mon*, silver coins 10, and gold coins 100 *mon*. In 765, further minting of copper coins only was instituted at Nara.

SOUTHEAST ASIA

The minting of coins was not adopted by the civilization of ANGKOR in Cambodia. Measures of silver or gold, as well as animals, cloth, and slaves, however, were used in exchange transactions. This contrasts with the DVARAVATI CIVILIZATION of central Thailand, where currency involved circular silver coinage bearing symbols of wealth and royalty, as well as the occasional text. The symbols used reflect Indian practices of the first to fourth centuries C.E. The conch shell symbolized water and creation and was used in royal consecration ceremonies. The *srivatsa* motif was derived from Sri, the Hindu mother goddess representing fertility and kingship. The rising Sun was employed to indicate the origin of the royal line in the solar dynasty. The PYU CIVILIZATION minted silver coins. These too employed the *srivatsa* motif, as well as the rising Sun, the throne, a conch shell, and the *vajra*, or thunderbolt. A clay mold probably for casting coins has been recovered at Sri Ksetra. Excavations at the major cities on the Rakhine (formerly ARAKAN) coast of western Myanmar (Burma) have yielded locally minted coins. A sample from Vesali, which was occupied in the seventh and eighth centuries, shows the bull, symbol of the ruling Candra dynasty, on one side, and the *srivatsa*, symbolizing prosperity, on the other. The king's name was inscribed in Sanskrit.

See also PRINSEP, JAMES.

Further reading: Gupta, P. L. *Coins: India—the Land and the People.* New Delhi: National Book Trust, 1969; Gutman, P. "The Ancient Coinage of Southeast Asia," *Journal of the Siam Society* 66 (1978): 8–21; Wang Yuquan. *Early Chinese Coinage.* New York: Sanford Durst, 1980; Wicks, R. "The Ancient Coinage of Southeast Asia," *Journal of Southeast Asian Studies* XVI (1985): 2.

Colebrooke, Henry (1765–1837) *Henry Colebrooke was one of the principal pioneers in the translation of Sanskrit inscriptions in India.*

In 1801 he published an English version of a late text found on the Delhi Topra pillar erected by ASOKA (r. 268–235 B.C.E.). Although this inscription had been previously translated, Colebrooke was able to obtain the correct date (1164 C.E.) and publish the INSCRIPTION in facsimile form together with a transliteration of the text. He was also one of the first people to realize and begin to explore the vital importance of inscriptions for elucidating early Indian history. His contribution is seen in a series of articles published between 1823 and 1827 in the *Journal of the Royal Asiatic Society.*

See also JONES, SIR WILLIAM; WILKINS, SIR CHARLES.

Co Loa Co Loa is a very large walled and moated settlement located 15 kilometers (9 mi.) northwest of Hanoi, on the floodplain of the Hong (Red) River in Vietnam. This part of Vietnam was the preserve of the DONG SON culture during the second half of the first millennium B.C.E. There is a local tradition that the site was founded by a man called Thuc Phan after he defeated the last of the local Hung kings in 257 B.C.E. He went on to found the Hong River kingdom of Au Lac. The site is known for a wealth of metalwork discovered during limited excavations. There are three defensive ramparts of Co Loa up to 12 meters (40 ft.) high and 25 meters (82.5

ft.) wide. The outermost wall encloses an area of about 600 hectares (1,500 ft.) and was punctuated with guard towers. The local Hong River was diverted to fill a moat. Excavations of the ramparts have revealed that they were constructed some time after the third century B.C.E. While the interior has not been extensively opened, in 1982 a large bronze drum was uncovered. It was decorated with typical scenes of the Dong Son period (300 B.C.E.–50 C.E.), including musicians, plumed warriors, houses, and a platform over four drums. Drummers were beating a rhythm on these four instruments of descending size. The drum itself contained a hoard of about 200 bronzes, including 20 kilograms (44 lbs.) of scrap metal probably destined for recasting. There were also 96 socketed bronze plowshares of HAN DYNASTY affinities, six hoes, and a chisel. The 32 socketed ax heads were made in a variety of shapes, one of which matches in form that represented in a mold from the nearby site of Lang Ca. Other weaponry from this hoard includes a bimetallic spearhead, the hilt of bronze and the blade of iron; a dagger; and eight arrowheads.

Such an emphasis on weaponry reflects the troubled times of the later centuries B.C.E. in the Hong River Delta, a period when QIN and Han armies threatened to incorporate the area as a province of imperial China. A cache of crossbow bolts found at Co Loa are of Chinese form. Ultimately this region was taken into Chinese control when in 42 C.E. the great Chinese general Ma Yuan marched into the area and defeated the local rulers.

combs Combs for grooming the hair, usually made of ivory or bone, have been found regularly in India, in sites of the INDUS VALLEY CIVILIZATION and later. The specimens from MOHENJO DARO and HARAPPA in Pakistan are decorated with incised circles. Later examples were enhanced with scenes or geometric designs that often incorporated the same concentric circles. Some specimens from TAXILA in Pakistan include depictions of WOMEN with elaborate hairstyles on one side and a goose on the other; another shows two women, one bare breasted and wearing diaphanous clothing, while the other side has an elephant and a lion. The goose design is particularly interesting, since an ivory comb from the Thai site of CHANSEN, seen as a direct import from India, was also decorated with a goose.

Combs have a long history in Central Asia and China. A comb was found with a woman buried at LOULAN in the TARIM BASIN, in northwest China, a site dating to about 1800 B.C.E. Three combs were found in the Shang dynasty tomb of FU HAO. The Han emperor WENDI gave the XIONGNU leader MAODUN a comb, among other fine presents, in the early second century B.C.E. At the same period, wooden combs were found among the personal belongings of the marchioness of Dai at MAWANGDUI, a Chinese internment area near Changsha.

Confucius (551–479 B.C.E.) *Confucius was China's most famous and influential political philosopher and teacher. He taught the importance of behaving correctly to achieve moral power and believed that rulers should concern themselves with the well-being of their people.*

Confucius was called Kong Qiu in Chinese, but his students named him Kongzi, "Master Kong." As he grew in stature and reputation, he became known as Kong Fuzi, "Our Master Kong." This title was written in English as Confucius. He was born in the state of LU, in Shandong province of central China. His parents were impoverished, but of high status. Only three years old when his father died, he showed an interest in scholarship from an early age. He was first employed in minor government positions, but his passion for and skill in the six arts—calligraphy, history, poetry, archery, ritual, and music—soon equipped him to be a teacher and sage. His approach to teaching, to instill knowledge of and concern for public service, can be seen as a major turning point in Chinese education. He rose through increasingly important public positions in Lu, ultimately becoming the minister of justice. Disillusioned by the administration, he left Lu for 12 years of self-imposed exile, during which he visited the leaders of other states to outline his moral code, but he later returned to continue his teaching, editing of ancient texts, and writing on political philosophy.

Confucius's ideals are recorded in the *Analects*. In Chinese they are known as *Lunyu*, "Conversations." These were written over a period after his death, in which his followers recorded, in 20 chapters, their recollections of conversations with their master. Although he lived at a time of weakening central Zhou authority and constant friction between rival rulers, Confucius advocated the concept of *ru*, virtue or civility, leading a person to become *junzi*, that is, deserving of moral power through noble behavior rather than promoting militarism.

Confucius is credited with editing and commenting on a number of significant historical documents. He is said, for example, to have added commentaries on the *Yijing* (*Classic of Changes*), a notable text that explains the interpretation of divinations. He edited the *Shujing* (*Classic of History*), which includes statements made by early kings. The *Liji* (*Record of Rites*) and *Shijing* (*Classic of Poetry*) may also have been edited with commentaries by Confucius. Perhaps his most notable contribution to the literature, however, was the CHUNQIU FANLU, or *Spring and Autumn Annals*, which recorded the history of the state of Lu, his own birthplace, between 722 and 481 B.C.E. By compiling and safeguarding these texts, Confucius assured for himself an enduring place in the history of Chinese thought.

His influence was also felt well beyond his native China. With the Asuka enlightenment in Japan, for example, the YAMATO PRINCE SHOTOKU issued injunctions incorporating Confucian ideals for proper behavior. In 603 a system of court ranks was deployed in the

Yamato capital, and each of the 12 grades was accorded a name recalling Confucian virtues, beginning with the rank of greater virtue and ending with the rank of lesser knowledge.

Couto, Diogo do (1543–1616) *Diogo do Couto was the official historian of the Portuguese Indies.*

He recorded an account of ANGKOR in Cambodia in the second half of the 16th century. His is the most detailed summary on this subject of the period. He sent his text to Lisbon in 1599 but never visited Angkor, basing his writing on reports from a Capuchin friar, D. Antonio da Magdalena, who visited Angkor in 1585 or 1586. The friar died in a shipwreck off the coast of Natal in 1589 but gave do Couto his account in Goa that same year. This account was due to be published in 1614 but remained archived until it was identified and published in 1958. Do Couto wrote "of the grand and marvelous city which was discovered in the forests of the kingdom of Cambodia, on its construction and situation."

He further observed:

This city is square, with four principal gates, and a fifth which serves the royal palace. The city is surrounded by a moat, crossed by five bridges. These have on each side a cordon held by giants. Their ears are all pierced and are very long. The stone blocks of the bridges are of astonishing size. The stones of the walls are of an extraordinary size and so jointed together that they look as if they are made of just one stone. The gates of each entrance are magnificently sculpted, so perfect, so delicate that Antonio da Magdalena, who was in this city, said that . . . they looked as if they were made from one stone. And amazingly the source of the stone is over 20 leagues away, from which you can judge the labor and organization dedicated to the construction. And amazingly, there are written lines in the language of badaga, which say that this city, these temples, and other things were built by the order of 20 kings over a period of 700 years. On the sides of this city are monuments which must be royal palaces on account of their sumptuous decoration and grandeur. In the middle of the city is an extraordinary temple. From each of the gates, there is a causeway of the same width as the bridges, flanked by canals, fed by the great moat round the city. The water originates from the north and east, and leaves from the south and west. The system is fed by the river diverted there. Half a league from this city is a temple called Angar. It is of such extraordinary construction that it is not possible to describe it with a pen, particularly since it is like no other building in the world. It has towers and decoration and all the refinements which the human genius can conceive of. There are many smaller towers of similar style, in the same stone, which are gilded. The temple is sur-

rounded by a moat, and access is by a single bridge, protected by two stone tigers so grand and fearsome as to strike terror into the visitor.

There are many smaller temples there, of fine workmanship, which seem to be the tombs of the nobles of these kingdoms, like the great temple which seems to have been the tomb of the king who built it. Two leagues and a half from this temple, one finds a huge lake, thirty leagues long and 15 wide. This lake is 150 leagues from the sea in the interior of this country. The river Menam (Mekong) in June flows with so much water, that it cannot remain in its bed and floods the area. It changes its course, and water flows to the north west, one course flowing to the great lake, the other to the sea. This flood lasts for four months. Then the water returns to the river and the lake level falls. There is a rice which grows up with the water, and many boats venture out to harvest this rice, with dances and music. The king who discovered this city installed his palace there and peopled the city with inhabitants brought from other parts of the kingdom. He gave them land and distributed hereditary estates. The land is very rich, much rice is grown. There are many cattle, buffaloes, deer. In the forest there are numerous deer, boars, elephants.

(Translated from B.-P. Groslier; see Bibliography.)

See also MOUHOT, HENRI.

Ctesias of Cnidus (fifth century B.C.E.) *Ctesias was a Greek physician from Cnidus in modern Turkey, who served in the Achaemenid (Persian) court of King Artaxerxes Mnemon between 405 and 397 B.C.E.*

Parts of two books that he wrote, the *Persika* and the *Indika*, have survived in quotations in later writings. His books were the standard Western authority on India until the conquest of ALEXANDER THE GREAT and even later but contain little accurate information and many clearly fabulous descriptions.

See also ACHAEMENID EMPIRE.

Cunningham, Sir Alexander (1814–1893) *Sir Alexander Cunningham was a major pioneer of field archaeology in India. His many discoveries had used the works of ancient historians to locate actual sites.*

Cunningham arrived in India as an officer in the Bengal Engineers when aged 19 and was early influenced by JAMES PRINSEP's interest in inscriptions and numismatics. As a government surveyor and engineer, Cunningham followed up his interest in coins of the BACTRIAN GREEKS by developing a passion for identifying the sites mentioned by two Chinese Buddhist monks, FAXIAN, who visited India in the early fifth century C.E., and XUANZANG, who traveled there in the seventh century. Thus Cunningham sought the city of Sankisa by its stated relationship to the known center of MATHURA and identified Sankisa as a huge mound. With this discovery, he calculated that the Chinese unit of measurement was a little longer than 11 kilometers (6.6 mi.). His enthusiasm is expressed best in his own words: "With what joy and zeal would not one trace Faxian's route from Mathura." In 1847 to 1848 he worked in northern India and found the ancient capital of Kashmir at Pandritan. Still linking texts with fieldwork, he identified the citadel of Aornos, mentioned by historians describing the campaign of ALEXANDER THE GREAT, with the site of Rani-garh. He later excavated at SANCHI and found the remains of NORTHERN BLACK POLISHED WARE in the foundation deposit, the first time this important ceramic type was described. Further excavations in stupas allowed him to assemble the names of early Buddhist monks from their foundation inscriptions and match them with the surviving historic texts.

In 1861 he was appointed the archaeological surveyor to the government of India and embarked on a long period of virtually uninterrupted field research. His first year saw him at BODH GAYA, site of the Buddha's nirvana, where he traced 33 pillars and associated inscriptions. The next few years saw him active in the Punjab, following in the footsteps of Alexander the Great and the Chinese pilgrims. This took him to TAXILA in modern Pakistan, where he described the ramparts of "Kacha-kot" as more than 10 meters (33 ft.) in height. He traced the ruins in the city of Sirkap and described Bhir and Sirsukh. His initial appointment as surveyor came to an end in 1865, and Cunningham returned to England. In May 1870, however, the viceroy of India, Lord Mayo, approved the creation of the ARCHAEOLOGICAL SURVEY OF INDIA, with Cunningham as its first director-general.

With a permanent staff of two assistants, Cunningham was charged that "as far as possible intelligent natives should be employed in, and trained to, the task of photography, measuring and surveying buildings and the like, and deciphering inscriptions." One of his earliest tasks was to devise a scheme of different architectural styles, and then he turned his attention to the great site of Mathura to catalogue the inscriptions there. He visited and excavated at BHITA, a township on the Jamuna River. There he sectioned the ramparts and again encountered Northern Black Polished Ware. Over the ensuing years Cunningham visited and studied many of the key historic sites in India: BHARHUT, KAUSAMBI, BESNAGAR, and SRAVASTI. In 1875 he published the first description of an INDUS VALLEY CIVILIZATION seal, noting that above the image of a bull, there were six written characters: the seal, he concluded, was foreign to India. By the time of his retirement in 1886, Cunningham had established himself as the father of Indian archaeology.

Cyrus the Great (c. 585–c. 529 B.C.E.) *Cyrus the Great became the ruler of the Persians in 558 B.C.E. and ruled a rapidly expanding empire, extending from the Aegean to the Indies, from his capital of Pasargadae in modern Iran.*
An inscription from Bisutun in Iran, dated to about 518 B.C.E., claims that Margiana, BACTRIA, and GANDHARA had been conquered, implying that the valley of the Syr Dar'ya River and the upper Indus Valley were now part of the Persian Empire, a claim given substance in the writings of classical authors, such as Pliny (23 to 79 C.E.), Arrian (d. 180 C.E.), and Diodorus (first century B.C.E.). Pliny described how Cyrus laid waste the city of Capisa, north of Kabul in Afghanistan. Archaeological research in Turkmenistan has identified early oasis settlements with citadels, whose wealth was based on the application of IRRIGATION to agriculture. Their inhabitants would have been in a position to resist the eastward thrust from Persia. One of Cyrus's objectives was to secure his eastern frontiers against the steppe nomads, and his policy was to establish fortified settlements. One of these located in the upper reaches of the Syr Dar'ya was known as Cyropolis. Cyrus died while campaigning against the nomadic Massagetae between the Caspian and Aral Seas, in 530 B.C.E.

Further reading: Brosius, M., ed. *The Persian Empire from Cyrus II to Artaxerxes I.* London: Association of Classical Teachers, 2000; Lamb, H. *Cyrus the Great.* London: R. Hale, 1961.

D

Dabar Kot Dabar Kot is a site of the INDUS VALLEY CIVILIZATION, located in the valley of the Thal River in Baluchistan in Pakistan. With an area of 150 by 135 meters (495 by 445.5 ft.), it was a small settlement, but the mound rose to a height of 35 meters (115.5 ft.) above the surrounding plain. It was examined initially by SIR AUREL STEIN and later by Walter Fairservis, but the lowest layers have not yet been examined. The mature phase of the Indus civilization is represented by mud-brick structures, drains of fired brick, and SEALS and figurines. A unique carved stone head of a man was also recovered from this site.

Dadianzi Dadianzi is a settlement and cemetery of the lower Xiajiadian culture, located on the Mangniu River in Inner Mongolia. The importance of this site lies in the illustration of a culture in northeastern China and Mongolia, distinguished by social divisions and occupying defended sites contemporaneous with the development of equally complex LONGSHAN CULTURE communities in the Huang River Valley, Shandong Peninsula, and Chang (Yangtze) Valley in China to the south. This culture has been dated between 2300 and 1600 B.C.E. and includes more than 2,000 known sites, some of which were defended by stone walls and moats. Dadianzi is best known for its cemetery, which lay beyond the walls and covered an area of about 2,000 square meters (2,400 sq. yds.). Excavations have uncovered 800 burials whose grave gifts show that goods from the West passed through here. The soft loess soils of this area make it possible easily to excavate deep graves, and their depth has been found to correlate with the wealth of mortuary offerings. The interments were laid out in an orderly manner, and no grave was found to intercut another. The mortuary rit-

uals involved lining poorer graves with mud brick and burying the richer corpses in a large wooden coffin. The deepest grave was found 8.9 meters (29 ft.) below the present surface.

Men were found with their heads pointing toward the settlement, WOMEN in the opposite direction. Some women were found in the same grave as young males. A niche cut at the foot end of the burial was designed to take burial goods. Rich burials might have multiple niches, containing sets of pottery vessels, some of which were richly painted in designs that anticipate those found on Shang dynasty bronzes. Certain types of vessels, such as *gui* and *jue*, were restricted to rich graves. The former is a three-legged pitcher, the latter a tripod jug traditionally used for serving wine. There were also pig and dog bones and, in elaborate male graves, ceremonial battle axes. The elite were also distinguished by the presence of jade bangles and bronze earrings. Poorer graves might have one set of pottery vessels, few if any painted pots, but no jades. The skeletons of sacrificed dogs and pigs were often found in the grave fill.

A close study of the bronzes found in the cemetery reveals similarities with settlements to the west, along the steppes. Thus the earrings are similar to those of the Andronovo culture in Siberia, while the bronze finials attached to wooden hafts of weapons are matched as far west as BACTRIA. The communities of the lower Xiajiadian culture acted as a conduit along which knowledge of bronze working reached the central plains. Further parallels with the Huang (Yellow) River XIA DYNASTY of China are seen in ceramic forms and the animal-headed *TAOTIE* mask image, which is seen on Dadianzi ceramic vessels.

See also SHANG STATE.

Dai An   Dai An, in Quang Tri province, Vietnam, is a site of the CHAM CIVILIZATION. It is best known as the find location of a remarkable stone relief carving, showing what seem to be two polo players. The horses are animated, with tails held high, and have bells around their necks, while the riders wield what look like polo sticks and ride on saddles equipped with stirrups. Emmanuel Guillon has stressed that the horse trappings and stirrups are paralleled in Southeast Asia in BOROBUDUR, Java, in Indonesia, but otherwise they recall similar depictions of riders from Tang dynasty China. This particular example dates to the 10th century C.E.

Daibutsu   The Daibutsu was a massive gilded bronze statue of the Buddha, ordered by the Japanese emperor Shomu in 743 C.E. The statue stood in the largest wooden building in the world. Shomu adopted a policy of establishing BUDDHISM as the principal religion of Japan during the period of the NARA STATE, when the capital was at HEIJO-KYO. In 741 Shomu ordered that Buddhist temples be constructed in all provinces, with the finest and largest ones in the capital city. However, there was a rebellion against the emperor, who moved the court first to Kuni, then to Shigaraki. In 745 C.E. he returned to Heijo-kyo, and the task of casting the Buddha in the form of Vairocana, the source of creation including all other Buddhas, was begun. It was now located in the temple of TODAIJI on the eastern edge of Heijo-kyo. It finally stood 10.82 meters (about 36 ft.) high and required the pouring, over a period of at least two years, of 400 tons of copper. The hall was then built over the statue in 752 C.E., and the dedication took place. This hall was centrally placed in a large monastic complex that included two pagodas, each standing 100 meters (330 ft.) high.

Daimabad   Daimabad is a prehistoric settlement located in the Tapti Basin of the Godavari River catchment, in western India. It reached a maximal area of 30 hectares (75 acres) during the last of five phases of occupation that extended from about 2000 to 1200 B.C.E., representing the southernmost extension of the Indus civilization. The first phase belongs to the Savalda culture and covered only a tenth of the site's final size. It yielded evidence for mud-brick houses of modest proportions and an agricultural economy based on barley, lentils, and beans. The inhabitants had a knowledge of copper metallurgy and wore beads of carnelian and agate.

The second phase is notable for the evidence it has provided for an intrusion of the late INDUS VALLEY CIVILIZATION into this part of India. The houses were made of mud brick, and similar material was used to line a grave. House floors were covered with plaster. Undoubted evidence for the Indus civilization is seen in the recovery of two terra-cotta SEALS and three potsherds, all bearing the Indus script. Characteristic Indus pottery shards were found scattered over an area of 20 hectares (50 acres). The radiocarbon dates suggest that this occupation took place in about 1800 B.C.E.

Dalverzin Tepe   Dalverzin Tepe, an ancient city in southern Uzbekistan, flourished in the KUSHAN empire. The city was rectangular, covering an area of 32.5 hectares (81.25 acres), with an additional circular citadel on the southeastern corner. Like many other Kushan cities, it was originally a foundation of the BACTRIAN GREEKS during the third and second centuries B.C.E. but was embellished by the Kushans. Dalverzin was a center for the production of a wide range of artifacts, not least molded terra-cotta statuettes. These were devoted to a seated goddess probably deeply venerated at this site and the surrounding region. It occupies a naturally strong position on the bank of the Karmaki-say River, the dry bed of which is now seen to the south and west of the city walls. A canal ran the length of the eastern ramparts. These walls were strongly built and provided for defense. They were up to 12 meters (39 ft.) wide and 20 meters (66 ft.) high. There are many towers, and the interior incorporates passageways and commanding emplacements for archers. The top of the walls provided platforms for the mounting of ballistae. Beyond the city, there were fields, orchards, some residences, and temples. The lower city within the walls was divided by a street system and contained distinct areas of opulent homes, craft workshops, enclaves for merchants, the poorer part of the populace, and reservoirs. The burial ground lay outside the city walls.

The excavation of domestic dwellings revealed considerable sophistication in the size and decoration of the homes of the elite. Rooms were grouped around a courtyard or a hall and had splendidly painted walls. Each home contained a fire altar. A number of statues in clay and gypsum have been recovered, showing, for example, a high-status woman and a man dressed in a belted tunic, whose expression imparts an aura of serene confidence. The wealth of the leaders of this community can be judged from a hoard of gold found beneath the doorstep of a mansion, containing gold disks and bars whose weight was recorded on each with a KHAROSHTHI inscription, gold bracelets, earrings, and pectorals.

Archaeologists working here also examined Buddhist temples, one of which lies outside the city walls, the other located toward the center of the city itself. The former occupies a low hill about 400 meters (1,320 ft.) to the north of the city walls. It had a stupa and associated monastic buildings. One of the rooms in this monastery contained the modeled clay statue of a royal figure that encouraged the excavators to name the chamber "the king's hall." The serene figure wore a kaftan and trousers and a tall, conical hat embellished with disks and decorated at the base with a row of circular beads. A second clay statue from the same room shows a mustached man wearing a belted kaftan; there are also modeled clay heads of WOMEN, one of which still retains a hint of gold overlay. Coins of Vima Kadphises and Vima Tak [to] date this complex to the late first and early second centuries C.E. Statues of the Buddha, which seem to have been deliberately destroyed, littered the building's interior and probably reflect the Sassanian incursions into this region during the third century C.E.

The city declined toward the end of the Kushan period, and the defenses decayed. It was not abandoned at that juncture, however. The potters' quarter still functioned, and the temple was maintained.

Damb Sadaat   Damb Sadaat is a small but important archaeological settlement covering a little less than two hectares (5 acres) and located 14 kilometers (8.4 mi.) south of Quetta in Baluchistan in Pakistan. It has given its name to one of the four major regional groups of sites ascribed to the early Harappan culture. The site is strategically placed to control access to the Bolan Pass, which leads to the plains of the Indus. It had a long sequence of occupation, and the three areas excavated yielded many ceramic remains demonstrating continuity, including the so-called Quetta ware first described by Stuart Pigott.

The sites of the Damb Sadaat phase are nearly all of a similarly small size, but three stand out as being significantly larger. Quetta Miri covers 23 hectares, MUNDIGAK 19, and Kranai Hill nearly 11. The overall pattern obtained from investigating these settlements is that the Damb Sadaat economy was based on agriculture and the herding of domestic stock. The people were familiar with copper smelting and casting and made fine ceramics. The radiocarbon dates suggest that this phase belongs to the period between 2500 and 3500 B.C.E.

See also INDUS VALLEY CIVILIZATION.

danda   Literally a "staff," *danda* was the term used in the *Arthasastra* of KAUTILYA to describe the control of the means of power and destruction. A minister to King CANDRAGUPTA MAURYA (325–297 B.C.E.), Kautilya defined the nature of the state and its methods of governance in a document that was widely influential in India and Southeast Asia during the period of early states.

Dandan-Oilik   Dandan-Oilik is one of the sites in the area of the ancient state of HOTAN, in the southwestern corner of the TARIM BASIN, investigated by SIR AUREL STEIN in the early years of the 20th century. Stein found a number of administrative documents there, as well as painted wooden panels and fragments of painted stucco ornaments from a Buddhist shrine. The site dates in the eighth century C.E.

Daodejing (Tao Te Ching)   The *Daodejing* is the text that set out the basic tenets of TAOISM, ascribed to the Chinese philosopher LAOZI. It comprises 81 brief chapters and describes, largely in metaphorical terms, the philosophy underlying the Tao, the "way." Taoism recognizes that the world is subject to flux and change and stresses the need for people to mold their lives to external change in order to obtain a detached tranquility in the face of events beyond control. The text exercised a profound influence, particularly during the early HAN DYNASTY. In 1973 a remarkable discovery was made in the tomb at MAWANGDUI, dated to 168 B.C.E., where a version of the *Daodejing* was found written on silk. Its very presence in a tomb of this date stresses its importance among the early Han rulers.

Darius the Great   (550–486 B.C.E.) *Darius the Great was king of the Achaemenid empire of Persia.*
He attempted to extend the empire westward to Greece but met defeat in 490 B.C.E. at the Battle of Marathon. His earlier military campaigns included an unsuccessful drive against the Scythians north of the Black Sea in 519 B.C.E. In 521 B.C.E., he attacked the Punjab and Sind in modern Pakistan and incorporated them as the 20th satrapy, or province, of his empire.

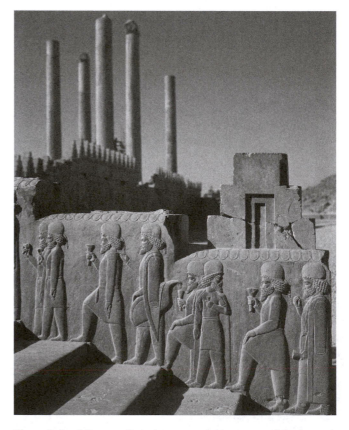

The reliefs of Persepolis in Iran reveal the power of the Achaemenid rulers. This stairway dates to the sixth–fifth centuries B.C.E. *(Giraudon/Art Resource, NY)*

Desalpur Desalpur is a site of the INDUS VALLEY CIVILIZATION, strategically located between the lower Indus Valley and the settlements of Gujarat. Two occupation phases were recognized during excavations undertaken in 1964. The site could have been a stepping stone in the trade and political links between the two regions. It was not large, covering only 100 by 130 meters 330 by 429 ft.), but it was still defended by a stout mud-brick wall four meters (13 ft.) wide at the base, reinforced with large stones. Houses within were constructed of mud brick on stone foundations, and the presence of typical Harappan weights in terra-cotta and jasper, as well as SEALS and sealings, indicates the importance of trade to the inhabitants.

Devanampiya Tissa (r. c. 247–207 B.C.E.) *Devanampiya Tissa was the king of Sri Lanka (Ceylon).*
It was under his reign that BUDDHISM is said to have been introduced into this kingdom. He was converted to Buddhism by the son of the emperor ASOKA and initiated the construction of Buddhist temples and monasteries.

Devanika A SANSKRIT inscription from Wat Luong Kao near WAT PHU in Laos names Devanika a *maharajadhiraja*, or great supreme king of kings. He is said to have traveled from a distant country and donated thousands of cattle to the temple when he was consecrated. The style of the INSCRIPTION suggests that it was erected in the second half of the fifth century C.E., making it one of the earliest in Southeast Asia to name a king. The site of the inscription lies within the walls of a city, suggesting the early inception of state formation away from the coast, but commanding the passage of the Mekong River.

devaraja The term *devaraja* is a SANSKRIT translation of the Khmer term KAMRATENG JAGAT TA RAJA. The rarity of the term in the epigraphic record probably indicates that the *kamrateng jagat ta raja* was a movable protective deity of no outstanding importance. Its first appearance in Angkorian epigraphy is in the SDOK KAK THOM inscription of 1052 C.E. in Cambodia. In this text, Sadasiva recounts the history of his family back to the late eighth century, when JAYAVARMAN II moved his court and followers from the region of BANTEAY PREI NOKOR to the land north of the Tonle Sap. His ancestors were given the exclusive right to maintain the cult of the *devaraja*. According to the INSCRIPTION, the *kamrateng jagat ta raja* moved from place to place, accompanying the king to respective capital cities. YASHOVARMAN I (r. 889–910 C.E.) moved the image to YASHODHARAPURA when he founded his capital there. It was moved to LINGAPURA under JAYAVARMAN IV (r. 928–942 C.E.) and was then returned by Rajendravarman to Yashodharapura. According to Hermann Kulke, the *kamrateng jagat ta raja* or *devaraja* was a movable object of veneration, a protective deity, the veneration of which was promulgated by JAYAVARMAN II (r. 834–77 C.E.) with his consecration as universal king on Mount Mahendraparvata.

An interpretative problem has arisen with the literal interpretation of the term as "the god who is king" or, more loosely, "the god king." This has encouraged the view that the king himself was worshiped as the *devaraja*. The only evidence for this supposition is the title Yasodharamaulidebaraja accorded King Srindrajayavarman (1307–27 C.E.), translated by Michael Vickery as "the *devaraja* at the pinnacle of Yashodharapura." As Vickery explains, however, the title *debaraja* or *devaraja* probably indicates no more than the royal title *deva*, followed by the term for king.

See also CHAKRAVARTIN.

Dhanyawadi The city site of Dhanyawadi is located on the ARAKAN (now Rakhine) coast of western Myanmar (Burma). It was here that a cast statue of the Buddha, held to be a precise image of the Buddha himself, was housed until Arakan was conquered by King Bodawpaya in 1784 and the statue was taken to Mandalay. The city includes an encircling brick wall and moat that encloses an area of 442 hectares (1,105 acres). The central part of the city covers 26 hectares (65 acres) and is dominated by a second walled and moated precinct that housed the palace. The site lies on the Tarechaung River, by which boats can reach the Kaladan River and thence the Bay of Bengal. The Rakhine coast is strategically located to take advantage of trade with India, including participation in the maritime exchange route that developed during the early centuries C.E. In addition, the city commanded good lowland rice land and had easy access to forest products in the hills to the east. Aerial photographs reveal canals and water tanks in the city, which might well have been used to irrigate rice fields. The entire area within the walls almost certainly included open areas for fields as well as settlements.

The early history of the site is recorded on the inscription of King Anandcandra of MRAUK-U, dated to 729 C.E. The text recorded the kings who preceded him, noting that it was King Dvan Candra who first defeated 101 rivals before founding the city in the mid-fourth century C.E. and who ruled from 370 to 425 C.E. His city, so the inscription records, "laughed with heavenly beauty." The PALI name Dhannavati means "grainblessed."

A hill adjacent to the royal palace houses the MAHAMUNI shrine, still one of the most venerated places in Burma, where the famous statue of Buddha once stood. The statue's original form cannot be determined because it is so covered in gold. The origin of this image is buried deep in a tradition that describes how the Buddha visited Arakan; it was at that time that the statue was cast. While this deeply venerated image is no longer located at Dhanyawadi, many sandstone images that once formed part of the original temple complex survive, albeit in a damaged or modified condition. These represent BOD-HISATTVAS, door guardians, and guardians of the four cardinal points. One such image still bears an inscription naming Yaksasenapati Panada, in the late Gupta style, while the statues themselves also reveal Gupta influence of the fifth century C.E.

dharma Dharma is a concept difficult to translate directly and simply into English. In certain contexts, it can mean the doctrine of righteousness, with implications for appropriate behavior for the followers of the Buddha. It can also be a phenomenon or fate, such as the dharma of growing old. In general Buddhist terms, it is best conceived of as the basic moral law of the universe.

dharmacakra The term *dharmacakra* means "wheel of the law" and represents the spreading of the Buddhist doctrine and was often seen carved in stone inscriptions. Several of these have been found in DVARAVATI CIVILIZATION sites in central Thailand, such as Lopburi. The *dharmacakra-mudra* is the Buddha's pose when he set the wheel in motion during his first sermon at SARNATH, thereby initiating the spread of his teachings.

Dharmarajika The Dharmarajika is the largest Buddhist stupa and associated monastery at TAXILA in modern Pakistan. In addition to the many structures, numerous rich finds came to light here, including an INSCRIPTION on

This stone *dharmacakra,* or "wheel of the law," represents the spreading of the Buddhist doctrine. This example comes from Phra Phatom in Thailand. *(Réunion des Musées Nationaux/ Art Resource, NY)*

a silver sheet in a silver vase. In 1913 excavations were begun by SIR JOHN MARSHALL, who considered it possible, given its size, that it was founded by ASOKA, king of the MAURYA EMPIRE from about 268 B.C.E. The principal stupa is 44 meters (145 ft.) in diameter and still stood to a height of 13.5 meters (30 ft.) when it was exposed. The complex includes living quarters for the monks and a large tank possibly for bathing. The great stupa is surrounded by a circle of smaller stupas, built probably about 200 years later. Eighteen reliquary vessels were found in the stupas. The votive deposit under one of these included a schist box containing a cylinder of gold, ashes of burnt bone, and a piece of carnelian. A second reliquary within the base of a stupa contained coins of the kings Maues and Azes I, a miniature gold casket, gold pins, and six beads of ruby, garnet, amethyst, and crystal. The tiny gold box itself was filled with fragments of bone, a piece of coral, and three pieces of silver. The foundation deposit of Stupa B6 is particularly opulent, and its contents indicate the far-flung exchange networks in which the people of Taxila participated. The jewelry included items of agate, amethyst, beryl, carnelian, garnet, jasper, LAPIS LAZULI, quartz, coral, pearls, and shell. Further stupas are found beyond this encircling set and date to the Scythian-Parthian period. The intact reliquary chamber in one of these contained a gold casket in which lay a coin of Azilises and another of the Roman emperor Augustus.

A chapel at the Dharmarajika contains a most unusual find, one that reveals what vital information can be lost to looters: a silver vase containing a rolled-up sheet of silver measuring 160 by 35 millimeters (6.4 by 1.4 in.). It contained a text in the KHAROSHTHI script, dated to 78 C.E., in which one Urusaka of Noacha placed holy relics in his chapel at the Dharmarajika temple of Taksasila (Taxila), in honor of his parents, relations, and friends. It expressed the wish that this would lead to nirvana.

Many more structures were added to this great religious complex, and by 1934 excavations made it possible to appreciate the complete plan. There were two courtyards, one to the north and the other to the east of a large stupa, each surrounded by individual cells for the monks. The northern court could have accommodated 19 monks, and it probably dates to the third century C.E. The eastern court is of poorer construction and would have housed no more than 13 monks. There is an open area south of the large stupa, which also contained a row of cells on its eastern wall. Perhaps the most poignant of all finds were skeletal remains, probably of the monks killed with the incursion of the White Huns between 390 and 460 C.E., thus effectively ending the occupation of Taxila.

Dharmasastra The Dharmasastra is the basic legal code that set down duties, rights, and laws for all people. It originated in northern India between about 300 B.C.E. and 500 C.E., and was widely known and followed in early states in Southeast Asia.

Dharmavansa (r. c. 985 to 1006) *Dharmavansa was king of an eastern Javanese state in Indonesia based in the Brantas River Valley.*
He organized a major attack on the Srivijayan capital of PALEMBANG, but he was ultimately defeated and lost his life. He was succeeded by AIRLANGGA.

See also SRIVIJAYA.

Dholavira Dholavira is a Harappan site in Gujarat, India. Dholavira stands out from virtually all other related sites of the Indus civilization because of the town plan, which has three distinct precincts. The site lies between two streams and was examined from 1990 by R. S. Bisht. The site was first occupied in the early period of the INDUS VALLEY CIVILIZATION, the early ceramics having AMRI-NAL–phase characteristics. Defense was clearly a key issue to the founders, because they constructed a wall up to 11 meters (36 ft.) thick, made of mud brick and stone. They were also familiar with copper technology, seen in the metal detritus, evidence for burning, and presence of ceramic crucibles. During the second occupation phase, the same but more developed material culture was encountered, while the third phase saw the introduction of typical Indus Valley items, in the form of SEALS, weights, and evidence for the script. The seals during this phase bore pictures of animals, but no writing. This style changed in Phase 4, when the seals included texts in the Indus civilization script. It was during Phases 3 and 4 that the site reached the height of its development, for in the succeeding Phase 5, there is less evidence for orderly town planning and some indications that it was briefly deserted. It was reoccupied with the sixth phase, again with typical Indus weights and seals, although now the latter bore no figures of animals, only the script. With the seventh and final phase, the site was again reoccupied, this time by a community who removed bricks from earlier buildings to construct round rather than rectangular houses.

The southern sector has a walled citadel. A walled middle town, which covered an area of 340 by 300 meters (1,122 by 990 ft.), flanks the citadel to the north. Both lie within an outer walled area measuring 615 by 770 meters (2,029 by 2,541 ft.). The southeastern part of the town has been lost to erosion from the Nullah Man-har stream. This layout belongs to the third phase of occupation. The walls were made of mud brick strengthened with stone at the corners, and there were gateways on the northern, western, and southern walls. During a late part of the sequence, the middle town was partitioned by a wall running laterally across its southern half.

The citadel was robustly constructed and presented a number of features unique in the Indus civilization. The northern entrance issuing onto the inner town was constructed of stone. It incorporated a large staircase leading up to the walls, off which lay a chamber containing the bases of stone columns. A remarkable INSCRIPTION was found in this feature: 10 large letters in the Indus script, each about 35 centimeters (14 in.) high and fashioned in stone. Again, the eastern gateway incorporated a chamber lined with polished stone columns. A broad roadway linked it with a third entrance on the western wall.

di In Shang oracle-bone texts, the term *di* means "god." It is occasionally employed in the word *Shangdi*, "high or supreme god." During the following WESTERN ZHOU DYNASTY, the concept of *tian*, or "heaven," came into vogue, as the Zhou ruler was known as *tian zi*, "son of heaven." The proliferation of kingdoms nominally subservient to Zhou but in fact independent during the Spring and Autumn period (770–476 B.C.E.) reduced the significance of this high title. From 770 until 31 B.C.E., the concept of *di* had a renaissance, but of a form different from that practiced under the SHANG STATE. There were now several *di*, named after the colors white, yellow, and blue-green, and fire. Under the Han, a fifth, black *di*, was added. The emperor WENDI attended the rituals for the five *di* at Yong in 165 B.C.E. After 31 B.C.E. the worship of *tian* again assumed a prominence that was to endure for the ensuing two millennia.

See also ORACLE BONES.

Dian chiefdom Chinese archival records compiled during the period of the HAN DYNASTY (206 B.C.E.–220 C.E.) describe groups of chiefdoms on the southern border, whom the Chinese progressively put under imperial control. The historian SIMA QIAN recorded that in 109 B.C.E. Emperor Han WUDI received homage from and granted to a southern chief a gold SEAL proclaiming him king of Dian. The actual seal was later excavated from a royal tomb in the cemetery of SHIZHAISHAN in Yunnan province, one of many rich royal graves. The records reveal that the chiefdom of Dian was incorporated then in the commandery or province of Yizhou. It comprised 81,946 households and 580,463 people. However, central control was marginal at best. The YANTIE LUN (Discourse on salt and iron) noted that there was incessant guerrilla activity in the south. The *Hou Han Shu* (*History of the Eastern Han*) records that the area, while rich in mineral and agricultural resources, was also given to war and head hunting.

Archaeological research in Yunnan province of southern China, with particular reference to the rich lacustrine plain surrounding Lake Dian, has identified the cemeteries of this southern chiefdom. At Shizhaishan and LIJI-ASHAN, royal graves of great wealth, in terms of grave goods and mortuary rituals, have been unearthed. It is clear that this society supported aristocratic leaders who controlled specialists in bronze, iron, and gold working and the manufacture of jewelry. However, its development toward an independent state was truncated by the expansionary imperial policies of the Han empire. In this, Dian was not alone. Similar expansionary forces also afflicted the many chiefdoms of Lingnan and Vietnam.

See also TIANZIMAO.

Dilberjin Dilberjin is a city on the northern slope of the Hindu Kush in Afghanistan. It began as a foundation of the BACTRIAN GREEKS but then became a major city of the KUSHANS. The outer walls have a square plan and enclose an area of 13 hectares (32 acres). The site is dominated by a central citadel on top of a circular mound, the defensive walls of which also follow a circular plan. There are many buildings beyond the walled area. Excavations of the interior have uncovered a number of large, opulent houses, one of which has corridors around a central court giving access to the rooms. Walls were embellished with paintings, one of which shows the Hindu god Siva and the bull Nandi.

Dinggong Dinggong, located on the right bank of the Huang (Yellow) River in Shandong province, northeast China, is a site of the LONGSHAN CULTURE, dated to the second half of the third millennium B.C.E. The walls and moat enclose an area of about 10 hectares (25 acres). The former were particularly impressive, being 20 meters (66 ft.) wide at the base. To the front, the wall was vertical, but the rear part was cambered. Sixty-two houses and many burials have been uncovered within the walls. The skeletons of adults and children, thought to have been sacrificial victims, were found in the foundations of buildings and in rubbish pits. One pit also contained a potsherd bearing very early Chinese writing. The eggshell-thin ceramic vessels from this site stand out as evidence of a specialized workshop.

Dipavamsa The *Dipavamsa* is the earliest surviving history of Sri Lanka and was compiled in the PALI language during the fourth and fifth centuries C.E. It describes the life of the Buddha, the history of BUDDHISM, and the arrival of the faith in Sri Lanka. King Devanampiya Tissa is mentioned, as well as the arrival on the island of a piece of the *bhodi* tree under which the Buddha found enlightenment.

Discourse on Salt and Iron See YANTIE LUN.

Doigahama Doigahama is a cemetery site of the early YAYOI culture. Located on the western shore of southern Honshu in Japan, it is notable for the extent of the area excavated, the quality of the surviving human bones, and the evidence for social organization. The Yayoi culture was seminal in the development of Japanese states. After the long period of hunter-gatherer occupation of the archipelago, known as the Jomon culture, which lasted until about 300 B.C.E., there was a sudden and major cultural change heralding the Yayoi in which many innovations were introduced from mainland societies in Korea and China. These included wet rice cultivation, weaving, metallurgy, and expanding trade networks.

The cemetery of Doigahama has been excavated on many occasions from 1953 on and has provided insight into the social changes that accompanied this transition. The dead were interred in extended positions, often with the legs flexed at the knees to fit within the four stones demarcating the edges of the grave. Some were placed in stone enclosures in association with others. Thus five men were found in one such ossuary. Others were interred singly, either with no evidence for stone markers or with stones simply beyond the shoulders and feet. The central graves were found to be the richest in terms of grave offerings, which included glass, jadeite, and jasper beads, shell bracelets, and finger rings. Moreover, there were many more men than WOMEN in the cemetery, although 15 percent of the individuals were infants or young children. Given the extent of the cemetery, it has been estimated that the total number of interments was close to 1,000, and the population of the settlement was around 400 people. The stone projectile points at this site were invariably found among the human bones, suggesting that by early Yayoi times friction and fighting occurred at the same time as social ranking, evidenced in the distribution and contents of the graves. Burial 124, for example, contained the skeleton of a young man who had been killed by an arrow.

Dong Duong The temple of Dong Duong is located in coastal Vietnam, in a region known to the Chams as AMARAVATI. It is a large complex, measuring 1.5 kilometers (.9 mi.) from east to west, and was probably built by King Bhadravarman in honor of his predecessor, King Jaya Indravarman, in the late ninth century C.E. The temple was designed for the worship of the Buddha in the MAHAYANA BUDDHISM practice of this religion. This adherence to BUDDHISM is clearly illustrated in the surviving statues and other works of art. Foremost is a huge statue of the seated Buddha, standing more than 1.5 (5 ft.) meters high, which was discovered in 1935 in the hall of the Dong Duong monastery. Another large statue, also from the monastic hall, depicts a monk holding a lotus with both hands. A third fine statue from this site shows a *dharmapala*, or guardian of the law. A *dvarapala* is a door guardian, and there were eight of these at Dong Duong. They are massive and forbidding, standing more than two meters in height. Each one tramples on an animal or person and flourishes a sword. The relief panels on the pedestal of the Dong Duong meeting hall rank among the outstanding examples of CHAM CIVILIZATION art.

The relief sculptures were assembled and studied from 1902, when excavations at this site commenced. Many scenes depict episodes in the life of the Buddha, but details also illustrate the dress and activities of the Chams. Thus a warrior is seen holding a long sword and riding a horse, while WOMEN wear elaborate headdresses and large ear ornaments. On another panel is a formation of Cham soldiers. There is also a court scene involving a king seated on a high throne, surrounded by courtiers, below which, on a second panel, a seated prince and princess converse. Episodes in the life of the Buddha include a relief showing his mother, Queen Maya, when pregnant and the Buddha leaving his father's palace on his quest for enlightenment. The art of the Dong Duong style is not restricted to stone reliefs or statues. The largest of all Cham cast bronzes represents a Tara goddess standing 1.2 meters in height. She wears an elegant double skirt and elaborate headdress.

Dong Si Mahosod The city site of Dong Si Mahosod in eastern Thailand belongs to the DVARAVATI CIVILIZATION. The moats enclose an area of 1,500 by 800 meters, and a rectangular reservoir covers two hectares (5 acres) at the northeast corner. Excavations have identified four phases of occupation. The first covers the late prehistoric Iron Age to the sixth century C.E. when a water tank was excavated and ringed by a laterite wall. The latter was decorated with *makaras* (a marine monster), lions, and elephants in the style of the sixth century. The second phase saw the construction of a series of monuments and belongs to the sixth to the eighth centuries. Occupation continued into the third phase, characterized by exchange in Chinese ceramics dating to the ninth and 10th centuries, while during Phase 4 the site was under strong influence, if not control, from ANGKOR in Cambodia. Monument 11 concealed a cache of inscribed bronzes, and one of these, in the Khmer language, recorded a gift by JAYAVARMAN VII (r. 1181–1219) of Angkor to a hospital at Avatayapura. This might have been the original name for the site during the Angkorian period. The name of a local ruler, Virendradhipativarman, was inscribed on a bronze bowl from the same hoard. A large ceremonial complex, which incorporates two Buddha footprints, lies at Sa Morakod, just three kilometers (1.8 mi.) to the southeast. It is in such proximity that it probably belonged to the same complex. The first phase there belongs to the Dvaravati civilization period; the second phase incorporated exotic ceramics imported from Persia and Tang China (11th–13th centuries).

Dong Son Dong Son is a settlement and cemetery site located on the southern bank of the Ma River in northern Vietnam. First excavated in 1924, the site has given its name to the culture that occupied the lower Hong (Red) River Valley between 500 and 1 B.C.E. that is famed for rich bronze objects, especially elaborately decorated drums. As did many other chiefdoms in Lingnan, southern China, the Dong Son people stood in the path of Han imperial expansion and were ultimately absorbed as the southernmost provinces of the HAN DYNASTY. However, the danger from without, linked with exchange ties with the Chinese, stimulated the development of a powerful and wealthy chiefly culture. This is documented by one large walled settlement at CO LOA, just north of Hanoi, on the Hong River floodplain, and several cemeteries. According to folklore, a leader known as Thuc Phan founded Co Loa in 257 B.C.E. and established a kingdom known as Au Lac in place of the previous rule of the "Hung Kings." The outer ramparts of Co Loa cover eight kilometers (4.8 mi.) and still stand up to 12 meters (39.6 ft.) high. The surrounding moats are fed by the Hong River. Excavations have uncovered a richly decorated drum weighing 72 kilograms (158.4 lbs.) and holding 96 socketed-bronze plowshares, six hoes, 16 spearheads, a dagger, and eight arrowheads. One of the spearheads had an iron blade and a bronze haft. The inclusion of 20 kilograms (44 lbs.) of scrap pieces of bronze suggests that this was a bronze worker's hoard.

Most information about the Dong Son culture has been found in burial sites. Several involved interring the dead in hollowed tree trunks. Those at VIET KHE include one interment in a boat-shaped coffin 4.76 meters long, containing many bronzes of local and Chinese origin. The favorable conditions for preservation at Chau Can, Xuan La, and Minh Duc have allowed a glimpse of less durable mortuary goods, such as the wooden hafts of spears and axes, wooden bowls and trays, a gourd in the form of a ladle, and fragments of woven material. The cemetery of Lang Vac has also furnished bronze daggers, axes, bells, and a crossbow trigger mechanism of Chinese form. One dagger has a hilt in the form of a man with an elaborate hairstyle, a hat, large bronze earrings in distended earlobes and bangles on each wrist. Drums are the tour de force of all Dong Son bronzes. They were elaborately decorated with scenes of ritual and war. The ritual scenes include platforms with four drums being played, musical ensembles, houses, and rice processing. The war themes portray large war canoes with plumed warriors, cabins, and a fighting platform over a chamber containing a drum.

When the Chinese finally incorporated the Hong River Valley into their empire under General Ma Yuan in 42 C.E., it was noted that the new masters confirmed the "Lac chieftains" in their traditional leadership. Apparently, the Dong Son people were able to augment rice production through the use of the plow and the application of tidal flows to draw water into their fields. The campaign of Ma Yuan effectively brought the period of Dong Son to a close in the mid-first century C.E., and there followed more than eight centuries of Chinese rule in the Hong River Valley.

Dong Zhongshu (Tung Chung-Shu) (c. 195–105 B.C.E.) *Dong Zhongshu, a philosopher and master of the Confucian canon, played a significant role in the administration of the Han Dynasty of China and was known for his withdrawal from court intrigue and devotion to scholarly meditation.*
The HAN DYNASTY inherited from the QIN emperor QIN SHIHUANGDI (259–210 B.C.E.) a recently unified empire

that had previously comprised a group of belligerent warring states. Controlling a new and vast empire presented new challenges, and the court contained many different schools of thought. Dong Zhongshu's writings were extremely critical of the autocratic excesses of the Qin emperors, and he was a strong advocate for the central role of Confucianism. Under Emperor WUDI (157–87 B.C.E.), he was instrumental in the foundation of a university for future administrators, where the teaching of Confucian principles was given practical expression. He was the principal author of the CHUNQIU FANLU (*Luxuriant Gems of the Spring and Autumn Annals*), a major work of political philosophy that incorporated the original views of CONFUCIUS with later ideas on appropriate government, such as TAOISM.

The *Hanshu* (*History of the former Han*) records the impetus given by Dong Zhongshu to the foundation of a state university in 124 B.C.E. for training imperial administrators. This had an enormous impact on the Han government, for bright young students were sent there from the provinces for a year's study before being posted to the civil service. Within two decades 3,000 students were enrolled, a number that had increased 10-fold by the end of the Han dynasty.

During the reign of Emperor JINGDI (188–141 B.C.E.), Dong Zhongshou was appointed an academician, and during the ensuing rule of Wudi, he became the chancellor to the king of Jiangdu. However, he returned to the central court soon afterward as a counsellor, but given the rivalries and jealousies, he was sent to trial when some of his writings were found to consider the question to arson in the royal shrine of Emperor GAOZU (247–195 B.C.E.). Only the personal pardon of the emperor saved him from execution. Despite his retiring ways, he was consulted on important matters of state, and his views on divine authority, the MANDATE OF HEAVEN, and the role of the ruler are recorded. He was particularly critical of the despotism of the brief Qin dynasty, declaring that changing from Qin to Han was similar to restringing a musical instrument. His views on the proper qualities of ministers and administrators identified intelligence and integrity as necessary attributes, again a sharp contrast with the Qin preference for LEGALISM. His foreign policy was in opposition to the expansionism of Wudi. He advocated a settlement with the XIONGNU, the northern nomadic adversaries of the Han, and antagonism toward imperial ambition. After his death, he continued to be revered by followers of Confucian ethics.

Dong Zuobin (Tung Tso-pin) (1895–1963) *Dong Zuobin, an employee of the Institute of History and Philology of the Chinese National Academy, led the first official excavation at Anyang between October 7 and 31, 1928.*
A native of Henan province, he was sent in 1928 to ANYANG to investigate the possibility of scientific research at the location of the archive of ORACLE BONES dating to the SHANG STATE, and he was fortunate to discover the oracle-bone archives of two Shang rulers in 1937. In 1928 it was widely thought that looters had removed all the oracle bones and that little was left to recover. His first objective, therefore, was to visit the find spot. He was taken to a mound in Xiaotun showing signs of recent looting, and in the spoil heaps he recovered several fragments of uninscribed tortoiseshell. This convinced him that more remained underground. Although he had no training in archaeology, the institute raised sufficient funds for him to return to Xiaotun. This epoch-making venture, which set in motion years of further excavations, resulted in the recovery of a treasury of new INSCRIPTIONS, 555 on tortoiseshell and 229 on cattle shoulder blades. He also showed that oracle bones were associated with other artifacts, including jades, bone tools, cowry shells, and ceramics. Dong Zuobin continued his interest in the oracle bones as part of the investigation team at Anyang through all seasons leading up to the cessation of research as a result of the Japanese invasion of north China in 1937. The most spectacular discovery was made in June 1937, with the opening of Pit H127. This underground chamber was found to contain the carefully stacked archives of two Shang kings. More than three tons of finds was removed, and when laboratory work was complete months later, 17,088 turtle carapace and eight cattle scapulae were available for detailed analysis. The Sino-Japanese War then made it necessary to move this precious archive to the safety of Kunming, in remote Yunnan, where Dong Zuobin pored over the texts with the aim of understanding the Shang calendar and relating it to the present system. His crowning achievement was to list 12 successive kings who ruled at Anyang for 273 years from 14 January 1384 B.C.E. He then worked out the individual reign dates and the intensive court round of sacrificial rituals to the ancestors.

dotaku A *dotaku* was a cast bronze bell typical of the later phases of the YAYOI culture of Japan. The distribution of the several hundred known examples concentrates on the eastern margins of the Inland Sea on the island of Honshu. The bells are found, singly or in groups, buried away from the Yayoi settlements, probably as part of ritual activity. The bells were cast with an exterior flange that rises above the body to form the hole through which a rope was placed for suspension. Some were decorated with geometric panels depicting scenes of Yayoi life. These include hunting deer with a bow and arrow and processing rice with a pestle and mortar. Knowledge of bronze casting reached Japan during the early Yayoi phase (from about 300 B.C.E.), probably from Korea and ultimately from China. The metal from which the bells were locally cast was almost certainly imported and recycled.

Dujiangyan   Dujiangyan, "Capital River dam," was a massive civil engineering work begun in China in the early third century B.C.E. by the QIN governor Li Bing, in Sichuan province. In 316 B.C.E. the powerful Qin state had sent a conquering army south into the rich Sichuan Basin to subdue the Shu people and to incorporate an area rich in agricultural and mineral resources into the Qin state. This took place against a background of the WARRING STATES PERIOD and was designed to ensure supplies of grain and minerals to sustain the Qin armies. One of the first tasks after defeating the Shu armies was to impose a new totalitarian regime, involving the subdivision of land into plots of fixed size on a grid network. There remained, on the rich Chengdu plain, the problem of the flood-prone Min River and the need to transport water to the expanding area under rice cultivation. In 277 B.C.E. the Qin governor Li Bing was put in charge of a project that has described as the most extensive engineering program up to that time in the eastern half of Eurasia. It involved dividing the Min River channel into two, the so-called out river continuing on its way to join the Chang (Yangtze), but the inner river being diverted through the intervening high country to enter the Chengdu plain, where it was progressively reticulated into the rice fields.

Duke Zhou   *See* ZHOU GONG.

Dunhuang   Dunhuang is located in a strategic position between the Gansu Corridor and the Taklamakan Desert. For 1,000 years from the fourth century C.E., it was a center of Buddhist culture, but even before then, it was an important strategic oasis on the ancient SILK ROAD that linked China with the West. The nearby caves of MOGAO are the focus of the Buddhist communities that absorbed a variety of influences to bequeath, through their decorative scenes on the walls, the sculpture, and the wealth of documents, one of the foremost assemblages of religious remains on the Silk Road. The site has also achieved a certain controversial status since the removal of the majority of the sacred texts to London and Paris by SIR AUREL STEIN and Paul Pelliot, respectively. The analysis of the art of Dunhuang has revealed that the caves were foci for the practice of esoteric BUDDHISM, a form of worship that involved a wide range of rituals designed to achieve both enlightenment and worldly ambitions. This tradition originated in the West and was introduced to Dunhuang by at least the fifth century, as is seen in the depiction of Hindu gods as protectors in a scene on the walls of Cave 285. There are also many depictions of the MANDALA, or cosmic diagram.

durga   In the ARTHASASTRA, a treatise on government written by KAUTILYA in the fourth century B.C.E.; a *durga* was a term referring to a fortified center. It was defended by walls and a moat and contained the treasury, administrators, and areas for specified economic activities.

dvarapala   A *dvarapala* was a door guardian or temple guard usually represented in stone, as part of a Hindu temple. A powerful statue of a *dvarapala* is seen at the early fifth-century C.E. temple at Udayagiri in India. Huge *dvarapala*s are seen in the SIVA cave at ELEPHANTA. The idea of guarding temples in this manner was adopted in Southeast Asia from Indian prototypes. A fine gilded bronze example was recently found at the temple of Kamphaeng Yai in Thailand.

Dvaravati civilization   The civilization of Dvaravati in Thailand flourished in the valley of the Chao Phraya River from about 400 to 900 C.E. It was then increasingly under the influence, and at times control, of the kingdom of ANGKOR in Cambodia. The people spoke the Mon language, which is closely related to Khmer. There are many Iron Age settlements in this area that reveal increasing cultural complexity between 400 B.C.E. and 300 C.E. These include BAN DON TA PHET, where rich burials contain a number of Indian imports. At Ban Tha Kae, the late prehistoric phase incorporates ceramics, gold beads, querns, and stamp SEALS similar to those from OC EO on the Mekong Delta. There is a continuous record for the transition from prehistory to the historic period of Dvaravati at the site of CHANSEN, where the second period of occupation included a notable ivory COMB decorated with a goose, two horses, and Buddhist symbols, probably dating to the first or second century C.E. Although these documentary sources for Dvaravati are few, it is known that the scribes employed SANSKRIT in their INSCRIPTIONS, and that BUDDHISM was particularly favored but not to the exclusion of major Hindu deities.

ARCHAEOLOGICAL REMAINS

The archaeology of Dvaravati is dominated by a series of large, moated city sites of irregular oval or subrectangular plan. The favored location involved a stream that fed the moats. Excavations have often revealed the foundations of religious buildings in laterite and brick. These were coated in decorated stucco with Buddhist figures or symbols. The buildings include stupas and temples for housing sacred relics (*caityas*). These were constructed to house relics or images of the Buddha. There are three geographic groups of centers, known as the eastern, central, and western. It is not known whether there was an overall integration into a single kingdom or a series of small, regional polities.

Major Sites

The major sites in the western group are strategically located on the floodplains of the Maeklong and Chao

Phraya Rivers. At that juncture, the sea level would have been slightly higher than at present, and there would have been less sedimentation. Large centers would then have been closer to the shore and able to participate in maritime trade. The principal sites in this group are PONG TUK, U-THONG, NAKHON PATHOM, and KU BUA. The central region is dominated by the sites of LOPBURI, Ban Khu Muang, and Sri Thep, while the eastern group incorporates Muang Phra Rot, DONG SI MAHOSOD, and Dong Lakhon.

INSCRIPTIONS

The few inscriptions of the Dvaravati civilization are important sources of information. Unlike in Cambodia, where the actual names of the FUNAN and CHENLA king-doms have not survived, it is known that the name of the Chao Phraya polity centered at Nakhon Pathom was Dvaravati, because two coins inscribed with the Sanskrit text *Sridvaravatisvarapunya* (Meritorious deeds of the king of Dvaravati) were found there. Six surface finds of coins from Muang Dongkorn also refer to the king of Dvaravati. The word *dvaravati* means "which has gates," perhaps referring to the gates giving access through the city walls. A mid-seventh-century inscription from the site of U-Thong reads, "Sri Harshavarman, grandson of ISHANAVARMAN, having expanded his sphere of glory, obtained the lion throne through regular succession." The king had given meritorious gifts to a lingam and described his exalted ancestry and military achievements. Two brief inscriptions from Lopburi were written in the Mon language, which indicates that Mon was the native language of the Dvaravati civilization. A further text from Lopburia names Arshva, son of the king of Sambuka. Finally, a seventh-century inscription from Sri Thep records, "In the year . . . a king who is nephew of the great king, who is the son of Pruthiveenadravarman, and who is as great as BHAVAVARMAN, who has renowned moral principles, who is powerful and the terror of his enemies, erects this inscription on ascending the throne."

See also CHAO PHRAYA BASIN.

Further reading: Brown, R. L. "The Dvaravati Wheels of the Law and Indianisation in Southeast Asia." In *Studies in Asian Art and Archaeology*, Vol. 18. Leiden: Brill, 1996; Higham, C. F. W. *Prehistoric Thailand*. Bangkok: River Books, 1998; Skilling, P. "Dvaravati: Recent Revelations and Research." In *Dedication to Her Royal Highness Princess Galyani Vadhana Krom Luang Naradhiwas Rajanagaraindra on Her 80th Birthday*. Bangkok, the Siam Society, 2003.

E

Eastern Baray King YASHOVARMAN I (r. 889–910 C.E.) of ANGKOR in Cambodia founded the city of YASHODHARA-PURA, now known as Angkor. As part of his new center, he ordered the creation of the massive YASHODHARATATAKA, or Eastern BARAY, or reservoir, the dykes of which are 7.5 by 1.8 meters (24.75 by 5.9 ft.) in extent. It has been estimated that more than 8 million cubic meters (280 million cu. ft.) of fill was moved to raise the dykes, which retained water canalized into the reservoir from the Siem Reap River. Inscriptions erected at each corner record this remarkable achievement; when full, the reservoir would have contained more than 50 million cubic meters of water. The purpose of this reservoir is controversial. Some consider that it formed the basis of a hydraulic system to irrigate rice fields; others view it as a symbolic ocean that surrounded the representation of MOUNT MERU, home of the gods, as seen in the BAKONG, King Yashovarman's state temple. The island in the center of the reservoir, which is now dry, is known as the EASTERN MEBON and was built during the reign of RAJENDRAVARMAN (r. 944–968 C.E.).

Eastern Mebon The Eastern Mebon is one of the few temples in Cambodia for which the name of the architect, called Kavindrarimathana, is known. The construction was widely appreciated, for an INSCRIPTION from Basak describes how King RAJENDRAVARMAN (r. 944–968 C.E.) constructed a temple Mebon on the Yashodhara Lake, with its five towers covered in stucco. The central tower held a lingam named Rajendresvara, and the four subsidiary temples on the uppermost platform housed images of the king's ancestors. Today the temple stands in the middle of rice fields where formerly the water of the BARAY lapped at its foundations.

Eastern Zhou dynasty The Eastern Zhou (Chou) dynasty was the direct descendant of the WESTERN ZHOU DYNASTY of China and lasted from 770 until 221 B.C.E. The Eastern Zhou dynasty led inexorably to the formation of a single political entity, the empire of QIN, and the beginning of traditions that have served China for more than two millennia. The inception of the Eastern Zhou followed the removal of the Zhou capital to LUOYANG, east of the WEI River heartland of Western Zhou, when the latter was finally overcome by military defeat. The four and a half centuries of Eastern Zhou are traditionally divided into two major periods. The first is known as the Chun Qiu, or the Spring and Autumn period. It is dated 770–476 B.C.E. and derives its name from a text of that name allegedly edited by CONFUCIUS and originating in the state of Lu. The second period is known as the Zhan Guo, or WARRING STATES PERIOD. The end of this second phase is sometimes given as the death of King Nanwang in 256 B.C.E., but most prefer the establishment of the Qin dynasty under QIN SHIHUANGDI in 221 B.C.E. as the terminal date. Any understanding of the political history of the Eastern Zhou dynasty must begin with the much earlier establishment of the Western Zhou after the overthrow of the SHANG STATE in 1045 B.C.E. The kings of Western Zhou claimed divine authority to rule, the MANDATE OF HEAVEN, to legitimize their hegemony of much of northern China and sent out leading members of the royal clan to form new border states in an essentially feudal system. This was an effective means of securing control over a far wider territory than had been claimed by the Shang kings and meant that the border states would act as a shield against attack, for there were many powerful and potentially dangerous groups beyond the area of Zhou control. However, with the passage of time, the bonds of kinship linking center and periphery loosened, and the dependent states began to exert their own authority by seeking a strong measure of autonomy.

BEGINNINGS OF EASTERN ZHOU

By the end of the Western Zhou, this situation reached a crisis point as the last king succumbed to external attack from the west, and the court moved to a new capital to the east, at Luoyang, hence the change of name to Eastern Zhou. By this juncture, while retaining the prestige and sanctity of the mandate of heaven, the kings at Luoyang were far too weak to control the power of the regional lords. In place of the central authority, large and potent regional states had become established, and these were known as the five hegemonies. Depending on their relative military prowess, the five were drawn from the states of Lu, QI, JIN, Qin, CHU, Song, ZHENG, WU, YUE, Cai, YAN, Wey, Chen, and Xu. Some of these, the Hua Xia states, controlled the old heartland of the central plains, and the center of gravity during the Spring and Autumn period was firmly placed there and east to Shandong. Other states were viewed from this center as barbarian. The states themselves were also subject to factionalism and splintering, depending on the strength of the ruler of the day. Indeed, the ZUOZHUAN (Commentary of Zuo) refers to 148 states during the Spring and Autumn period, many of which were absorbed by larger ones through force of arms. Friction and rivalry came to ahead during the aptly named Warring States period, when Qi, Chu, Yan, Han, Zhao, Wei, and Qin—the most powerful—were collectively known as the 10,000 chariot states.

LITERATURE

Whereas the Western Zhou dynasty is largely documented on the basis of inscriptions, literature during the Eastern Zhou flourished, and some texts survived the burning of the books by the first emperor of Qin. The Zuozhuan, for example, ascribed to Zuo Qiu Ming of the state of Lu, contains much historic detail later used by SIMA QIAN in his SHIJI, (Records of the Grand Historian). Most of this important source was written or assembled during the Warring States period. This was also the time of Confucius and MENCIUS, adding a philosophical flavor to the available documentary record. The burning of the books certainly had a serious effect on the survival of the textual record for Eastern Zhou, but nevertheless some documents did survive the holocaust. There is, for example, a romantic story that during the reign of the Western Han emperor JINGDI (188–141 B.C.E.), Prince Gongwang wished to extend his palace. This required the demolition of the house formerly occupied by no less a figure than Confucius himself. The prince found many important texts secreted within the walls of this residence, placed there, it is thought, by a descendant of Confucius to preserve them from burning. The texts included the important Xiaojing (Classic of Filiality), in which Confucius outlined the importance of obedience and respect for one's parents. Unfortunately, the archives or chronicles that recorded the events in the history of each state during the Warring States period were destroyed after wars of conquest. A few fragments of the chronicles of Qin survived the destruction of the capital Xianyang, and these were available to Sima Qian when he wrote his great history. There are also some texts on military tactics and strategy that have survived, such as the Sunzi, probably compiled between 350 and 300 B.C.E.

BAMBOO SLIPS

While these documents have been known and employed to assess Eastern Zhou history for centuries, archaeological research is now yielding many more vital documents that were placed in Eastern Zhou graves. These were written on jian (BAMBOO SLIPS)—slivers of wood. It is known from Shang graphs that such slips were employed at a very early date in Chinese history, but the earliest surviving examples belong to the Eastern Zhou and can add considerably to what is known about the period. Virtually all the bamboo documents have been recovered from the area of the Chu state, in all probability because of climatic conditions favoring their survival. They were strung together to form books, lengthy ritual texts, or records of invocations to the gods. Some contain hitherto unrecorded historic events, such as particular battles or deaths. Many provide lists of the contents of the tomb master's grave; others record how the illness of the dead person involved sacrifices of jade or animals to aid recovery. A large assemblage from the tomb of the marquis of Zeng at LEIGUDUN described the chariots and horses, weaponry, and armor that accompanied him in death. A text from Changtaiguan in Henan province referred to royal ancestors going back in time to the duke of Zhou (r. 1042–1036 B.C.E.). Slips from Wangshan Tomb 1 incorporated prayers given during the incumbent's illness, which, while interesting as an index of medical lore, also mention prayers offered to former kings of the state of Chu and jades and animals offered in sacrifice. Perhaps the most informative of all the assemblages of bamboo slips, however, is that from the tomb of Xi, an archivist and lawyer who lived at the very end of the Warring States period. His tomb at Shihuidi contained many sets of slips, which described battles and historic events, legal regulations, details of the unification of measurements, and accounts of legal decisions governing the establishment of Qin rule in the recently defeated state of Chu.

OTHER WRITINGS

In addition, two remarkable letters on wood from Heifu and Jing describe life as a soldier in this troubled region in the year 223 B.C.E. Further information on Qin law is from a source in Shandong province to the northeast, where at Haojiaping a text outlined the officially prescribed methods of land division and road maintenance during the reign of King Wuwang in 309 B.C.E. During the Eastern Zhou period, documents were also written on silk, but these are much rarer than those on bamboo or wood. The best-known example is from a looted Warring States tomb at Zidanku, Hunan province. Subsequent scientific excavations identified this tomb as belonging to a middle-aged man interred in two coffins. The extraordinary silk includes painted images of 12 deities corresponding to the months of the year and associated texts that detail the portents for each. Many more silk documents must await discovery through archaeology.

SEALS

SEALS are a further source of historic information, for many of those dating to the later Eastern Zhou dynasty were inscribed. It is particularly advantageous that the seals bear scripts typical of their state of origin. Some were used by local officials or military officers to seal letters, by using a special clay. Perhaps the most remarkable source of written evidence for Eastern Zhou history, however, is the former capital of the state of Jin. Both the *Zuozhuan* (dating to the Spring and Autumn period, 770 to 476 B.C.E.) and the *Zhouli* (*Rites of Zhou*, 1045–2563 C.E.) texts describe the practice of inscribing oaths of allegiance on jade and then burying them in pits, together with sacrificed animals. The complex of cities at Xintian in Shanxi province was the capital of Jin from 585 to 369 B.C.E. A remarkable group of pits, some up to six meters deep, has been unearthed and found to contain the remains of cattle, horses, sheep, and chickens, together with inscribed or painted texts on jade plaques. Some of these inscriptions can be related to specific historic events. For example, the *Zuozhuan* described how in 497 B.C.E. a dispute arose within the aristocratic Zhao family, leading to murder and deep dissension among its members. A set of oaths recovered by archaeologists records that individuals swore not to indulge in magic or communicate with the opposition party under a threat of punishment from the gods. The dispute ultimately led to exile and war between Jin and Qi. Thus an event recorded in historic documents has been confirmed through archaeology.

INSCRIBED VESSELS

Bronzes and pottery vessels were also inscribed on occasion. In the Wei state tomb of Guweicun, for example, a vessel bore the name of the potter. A hoard of bronze weaponry was unearthed in the Han state city of Zheng Han. Many were inscribed and dated with the name of the official in charge, indicating the importance of mass production of weaponry at the end of the Warring States period. Some of the items were damaged or broken, and their exotic inscriptions point to their being seized after a successful battle. Tomb 1052 from the SHANGCUNLING cemetery contained a bronze halberd inscribed with the name of Yuan, crown prince of the state of Guo. At Nan-

qiji just outside the city walls of Lingshou, capital of the state of Zhuoyang, a royal mausoleum has been investigated. The mid–Warring States Burial 1 of a king of Zhuoyang included 90 inscribed bronzes, the texts providing important information on the history and the genealogy of the rulers of this small but important Eastern Zhou state. One text describes a military campaign against the neighboring state of Yan. The late Yan capital of Xiadu has itself furnished an important set of inscriptions, found on most weapons in a hoard of 108 halberds (*ge*). Many of the kings of Yan named on these weapons are also known from historic texts. The Yan Hou Zai on one of the bronzes is the same person as the Yan Wengong mentioned in the *Shiji*, who reigned between 361 and 333 B.C.E. A halberd inscribed with the name Yan Wang Zhi has been found in Shandong province and may well have found its way there during a struggle with the state of QI between 284 and 279 B.C.E. Such evidence is basic to a realization of historic events during the period of Eastern Zhou.

HISTORY

The history of the Eastern Zhou dynasty provides a fascinating picture of the problems inherent in administering a territory of unprecedented extent and the means employed to resolve them. It must be recalled that the defeat of the Shang state by the Zhou led to a considerable increase in the area of the new state. The solution to maintaining central control was to award new states to trusted members of the royal clan. These men and their followers were sent into an alien countryside, and the nature of the new states was essentially the fortified city. Its occupants were known as the *guo ren* ("people of the state"), while the indigenous inhabitants, people often ethnically distinct from the ruling elite, were known as the *ye ren*. This feudal system worked well for a few generations, given that the Western Zhou kings not only were powerful, but they held the Mandate of Heaven to rule. However, the regional states became increasingly powerful in their own right, just as the bonds of kinship slackened with growing genealogical distance. By the beginning of the Eastern Zhou dynasty, the central court was virtually shorn of power and relied on the support of the major eastern states. Initially, the Zhou realm comprised many states, a few large and powerful and many small and weak. The bonds of feudalism broke down as the former swallowed the latter, and it became acceptable to base territorial expansion on naked power shorn of morality or the bonds of kinship. It was in this milieu that Confucius railed against such perceived immorality from his eastern base, the state of Lu.

It is possible to trace a series of strands in the history of this, the Spring and Autumn period. In the first instance, the takeover of a small state by another small one may hardly have caused a ripple on the political landscape. However, where two large and equally powerful rivals locked horns, major repercussions might well ensue. This problem was exacerbated as southern states beyond the pale of Eastern Zhou control rose in power, particularly the Chu of the middle Chang (Yangtze) Basin, the Wu and the Yue of the lower Chang, and the Shu of Sichuan. Adapting to this situation led to the development of the BA SYSTEM, in which it was acknowledged that the ruler of one major state would hold dominant political sway. The BA STATE was on occasion Zheng, Qi, Jin or, toward the end of the period, Yue. There was also a new or secondary trend toward a feudal system, for when a smaller state was subjugated, who was to be placed in control of the new territory? The answer was not appointing kinsmen, but men chosen on the basis of loyalty. Again, while this was a useful expedient, it held the seeds of future problems because it led to the formation of regional ministerial dynasties that could rise in due course against the center. In this manner, the great state of Jin was carved up into the new polities of HANN, Wei, and Zhao. Moreover, it was no longer easy to pick faithful male relatives to rule over newly won lands, because the succession in the major states was virtually always contested among rival claimants. For a century after 750 B.C.E., for example, there was a systematic extinction of all descendants of previous kings of Jin, a policy followed in other states, albeit with less zeal.

In the southern state of Chu, one that had not been part of the Zhou realm, an innovative system of government was developed in which territorial subdivisions, incorporating on occasion newly won land, were formed under the title of *xian*. These were ruled by a centrally appointed governor answerable to the Chu king. This system was copied in the major states to the north, leading to the foundation of powerful regional families. Again, the problem of controlling distant regions from the center arose. It was thus generally recognized that a change in social organization was needed, and over the generations there was a process of assimilation between the former *guo ren* and *ye ren*. Increasingly the latter entered the social scene not just as suppliers of tax revenue and corvée labor, but also as members of the army and specialists in the central workshops that turned out the weaponry and tools basic to the well-being of the state. Through these interrelated changes in the social structure, the stage was increasingly set for the development of a small number of powerful rival states whose internal organization favored the rapid deployment of well-equipped armies. This occurred at a time when the political philosophy of the day, despite the efforts of Confucius and his followers, followed the path of absolutism and self-interest.

The division between the Spring and Autumn and Warring States periods is set at 476 B.C.E. The latter period is aptly named, for it witnessed major advances in military strategy and wars of increasing intensity, leading to the annihilation of states and their ruling houses.

These events were fueled by rapid advances in agriculture, leading to the deployment of the surpluses necessary to maintain the armies and the rapid spread of iron technology. Successful states were led by kings with powerful ministers and well-organized social and economic systems, tending increasingly toward centralized absolutism. This process reached its apogee in the state of Qin under the first emperor, Qin Shihuangdi.

Rise of Qin

At the inception of the Warring States period, seven powerful states had emerged from the plethora of smaller entities formed under the Western Han feudal system of government. The most remote, and in a sense therefore the most secure from invasion, was the state of Yan in the northeast, which bordered the Gulf of Bohai to the south and east, and the states of Qi, Zhao, and Zhongshan to the south and west. Qi was located on the southwestern shore of the Gulf of Bohai and had only small rivals to the south. Its capital, Linzi, was reputedly the largest urban complex of the period. The formerly powerful Ba state of Jin had given rise to three new states in 403 B.C.E., the most powerful of which was Wei. It occupied the strategic middle reaches of the Huang (Yellow) River and had available a large amount of high-quality agricultural land. Its central position, however, meant that it was vulnerable to attack from all points of the compass, particularly from its immediate neighbors Qi, Zhao, Qin, and Chu. Zhao was also carved out of the state of Jin and lay to the north of Wei, while the third of this group, Hann, was both small and vulnerable from all sides. Qin lay to the west of the central plains, in the valley of the Wei River. It was naturally defended and had no serious threat from the west. It became even more potent after its seizure of the fertile Sichuan Basin in the fourth century B.C.E. The state of Chu differed from those to the north in being outside the Zhao realm and based on the cultivation of rice rather than millet and wheat. It grew considerably through conquest, and the advent of iron implements facilitated drainage and irrigation works to increase production.

The alliances and wars between the contending states form a tangled skein of events. Essentially, they began with severe internal friction in the state of Jin, with episodes of civil war leading in 403 B.C.E. to its disarticulation into three successor states. Meanwhile Qin, Chu, Yue, and Qi increased their respective territories through swallowing lesser polities on their margins. From 441 until about 360 B.C.E. the leaders of Qin eyed with envy the productive rice lands of the Sichuan Basin to their southwest and engaged in wars of conquest against Shu and Ba. They were therefore not to be seen in the struggles of the central area until the mid-fourth century B.C.E., when they could press from the west on the flanks of the state of Chu down the Chang River route. In the interim, both Chu and the successor states of Jin had been steadily increasing their respective territories. The former, for example, took advantage of new administrative reforms to increase efficiencies and move strongly to the south, where many Chu weapons and bronzes are to be found in the cemeteries of Lingnan.

With the newly conquered Sichuan Basin behind it to supply people and surplus rice, Qin was, from the mid-fourth century B.C.E., able to look east. In 366 B.C.E. the Qin army defeated Hann and Wei, which were in an alliance. Two years later, at the battle of Shimen, they again destroyed a Wei army. These portents of future Qin dominance were temporarily deferred by a reordering in the Wei territory and the movement of its capital away from the threat of further Qin attacks. At the same time, diplomacy involving conferences between leading ministers and alliances was employed to maintain the status quo. In the mid-fourth century B.C.E., Hui Hou, ruler of Wei, adopted the royal title of king, a move soon followed by other leaders of the major states.

Cooperation between states under the threat of attack, involving what were called vertical alliances, characterized the period from the second half of the fourth century B.C.E. While the state of Wei began this phase of the Warring States period in the ascendance, it soon suffered constant attacks from Qin. Qin had cemented its power by the seizure of the Sichuan Basin and had the advantage of a strong defensive heartland in the Wei Valley. Qin armies inflicted serious defeats on Wei at the Battles of Guiling and Maling (respectively, 353 and 341 B.C.E.), leading in 322 B.C.E to a virtual takeover when Zhang Yi, the chief minister of Qin, held the corresponding position in Wei. This situation encouraged the remaining states, now conscious of the increasing threat from Qin, to form what was known as a vertical alliance to counter it. There was now the dangerous situation of the expansive Qin state establishing a presence on the vital central plain of the Huang River. Initially, the resistance to the rising tide of Qin power was successful. In 298 B.C.E. Qi and its allies attacked Qin and regained some lost territory, but four years later Qin rebounded, and there was a marked increase in the intensity of warfare. In 288 B.C.E. the leaders of the two emerging powers, Qin and Qi, declared themselves, respectively, the eastern and western *di*, a divine title not hitherto accorded any leader in China. This presumption was short lived, however. Qin soon abandoned it, while an alliance of states crushed Qi and removed it from the political scene. This left the field to Qin and Zhao. In 269 B.C.E. the powerful Zhao army defeated Qin. Under the minister Fan Sui, King Zhao of Qin marshaled all his forces. A totalitarian policy involved not only a crushing defeat for the Zhao army, but also the immolation of the survivors of a long encirclement. No power could now resist Qin, which piecemeal mopped up any further resistance, and in 221 B.C.E., under Qin Shihuangdi, brought the Eastern Zhou dynasty and the period of Warring States to an end.

CULTURAL DEVELOPMENT

The competitive milieu of the period of Warring States encouraged major developments in art, architecture, industry, and warfare. The formation of so many states, the long presence of some but not others, and the propensity for display under competitive conditions led to the foundation of many cities and major changes in their layout and design. Even in the more durable states, new cities were founded after crises or strategic decisions. The Chu capital was moved five times to a new location in the last five decades of the Warring States period, while Zhang had three capitals between 425 and 386 B.C.E. The city also became an anchor for the social elite in times of stress, and the designs required considerable attentions to defense. Indeed the depiction of "cloud ladders," a Chinese term for the tall ladders used to scale walls, on some bronzes illustrates the techniques taken to capture enemy centers. The Warring States commentators themselves were aware that formerly, during the feudal heyday of the Western Zhou dynasty, the size of cities was rigidly scaled according to the rank of its leader in the social hierarchy. Again, the major technological advances, including iron foundries and bronze-casting techniques, the increases in trade, and the rise of the mercantile classes, all led to wholesale changes in the nature of the city, from the royal administrative center to the metropolis of many classes and occupations.

Cities

In the cities, the royal palace was the centerpiece, and the recommended location of the palace lay in the center of the city. In place of the enclosed system of courts at ground level, the palace took on a new form in which height and grandeur were employed to project the power and status of the ruler. Many historically documented and archaeologically verified palaces were raised high above their surrounds to create maximal visibility. At Linzi, for example, the foundations for the palace, known as the platform of Duke Huan, still stand up to 14 meters (46 ft.) in height. At Xiadu, capital of Yan in Hebei province, the palace stood on top of a mighty raised mound that is still 20 meters (66 ft.) high above the rest of the city. Handan in the state of Zhao also included platforms to raise the palace well above the surrounding cityscape. By building first an earth platform and then terraced pavilions against it, it also became feasible to make a palace appear much larger and more impressive than it actually was. Often the history of a city can be obtained from details of its internal layout and additions overtime.

Linzi of the state of Qi again stands as a clear example of a large Western Zhou foundation embellished with defensive walls and a moat, within which a grid of wide streets stretched for distances of up to four kilometers

(2.4 mi.). The northeastern part of the city has yielded many fine ritual bronze vessels that suggest that here lay a particularly rich suburb. The interior of such cities over the course of the Eastern Zhou period saw the establishment of specialized iron foundries to add to the areas long dedicated to the production of bronze, ceramic, and bone artifacts. During the troubled Warring States period, social upheavals provided a need for new defensive measures. At Linzi, a second city enceinte was added, probably after an internal coup against the ruling lineage. The new elite had a palace constructed within a strongly defended perimeter in which, paradoxically, the walls facing inward to their own city were twice as robust as those facing outward toward a potential alien enemy. The addition of a large additional wall at Xinzheng, capital of the state of Han, snaked around a huge bronze foundry that covered 10 hectares (25 acres). This new defensive system was added to the old city during the Warring States period, probably to protect the vital iron and bronze workshops that were established there.

Bronze Casting

The widespread presence of bronze and iron workshops in the major cities of the Eastern Zhou states reinforces the importance of their output and the concern to keep specialists within reach of the ruler and his ministers. BRONZE CASTING during the Eastern Zhou period underwent a series of highly significant changes. The development of powerful states with their in-house specialists encouraged regional styles, particularly those of the southern state of Chu, the western state of Qin, and the state of Jin. The rise of powerful ministerial families and layers of bureaucrats also spread the demand for fine bronzes over a wider segment of the social spectrum, leading to a hierarchical provision of bronzes in the tombs. The rise of warfare placed considerable demands on the technical skill of the casters to make weapons of unparalleled tensile strength, while ostentatious display led to the development of new techniques for decorating bronzes. The long tradition of casting bronze vessels saw established forms continue and new ones added. There was a trend toward increasing the degree of ornament on these bronzes, which included some exceptional vessels of which the *pan* and *zun* from Leigudun Tomb 1 represent the acme. These extraordinary vessels were cast using the lost-wax technique, a break with the long Chinese tradition of piece molding. Earlier examples of lost-wax castings are from Chu tombs, indicating the likelihood that this was a southern technological innovation. However, piece molding continued and reached new heights as multiple castings began to be soldered together to form a whole. The highly decorated bells and drum sets are just one example of new levels of expertise. This interest in highly decorated vessels may have stimulated a reaction in the later Warring States period, when plainer items were cast. However, decoration increasingly took the form of fine patterned inlays of gold or silver, on vessels as well as ornaments such as belt buckles and luxury items such as the mirrors that proliferated in this period.

Further innovations also characterized the Warring States period, such as beating copper vessels to less than one millimeter in thickness and decorating them with incised images of palaces and people. The Yue people in particular developed remarkable skill in the casting of decorated swords. Indeed, corrosion was identified and countered by the addition of a thin layer of chrome to the surface of weapons.

See also IRRIGATION; TONGLUSHAN; WU STATE; ZHOU GONG.

Further reading: Lawton, T., ed. *New Perspectives on Chu Culture in the Eastern Zhou Period.* Washington, D.C.: Smithsonian Institution, 1991; Li Xueqin. *Eastern Zhou and Qin Civilizations.* New Haven, Conn.: Yale University Press, 1985; Loewe M., and E. L. Shaugnessy, eds. *The Cambridge History of Ancient China.* Cambridge: Cambridge University Press, 1999; Mattos, G. L. "Eastern Zhou Bronze Inscriptions." In *New Sources of Early Chinese History: An Introduction to the Reading of Inscriptions and Manuscripts,* edited by E. L. Shaughnessy. Berkeley: Society for the Study of Early China and Institute of East Asian Studies, University of California, 1997.

École Française d'Extrême-Orient The École Française d'Extrême-Orient was founded in 1898 in Saigon, Vietnam, as the French institution responsible for research into the archaeology and early history of Southeast Asia. The headquarters were moved to Hanoi in 1901. In 1907 the École assumed responsibility for the conservation of ANGKOR in Cambodia and set in train the analysis and restoration of the major monuments there, a task still being pursued at the temple of BAPHUON. Political difficulties meant leaving Hanoi in 1957, and the advent of the Khmer Rouge involved the temporary abandonment of work at Angkor in 1975. However, the École has now been able to return to both countries and to expand its research to include Malaysia, Japan, China, and India.

Edafuna-Yama Edafuna-Yama is a keyhole-shaped *kofun,* or burial mound, located on Kyushu Island, western Japan. It is one of several such mounds that make up the necropolis of an elite group. In 1873 a local farmer excavated into it and encountered a stone sarcophagus with a lid in the form of a house. He extracted an extraordinary array of mortuary offerings, including an inscribed sword, which were sent to the capital and ultimately purchased by the government. Other finds included six bronze mirrors, at least five of which are probably imports from southern China. There were gold earrings, a necklace of jade beads, sets of gilt bronze diadems, a cap, and shoes. One of the people interred, for it is likely that this was a multiple grave, wore a belt incorporating ornamental gilt plaques. Twelve single-edged iron swords, spears, and arrowheads were recovered. Body armor had been placed in the tomb, and there was much fine horse gear. As a whole, the goods date to the late fifth or the early sixth century C.E.

One of the swords is particularly important, because it was embellished with a silver-inlaid inscription of 75 characters, some of which have proved difficult if not impossible to read. Controversy surrounded alternative translations, one of which was made by a Korean scholar who maintained that the text indicated that Kyushu was a vassal of King Kaero of PAEKCHE. However, the discovery of another text on a sword discovered at INARIYAMA in 1968 made possible a more accurate rendition of the regal name, and most scholars now agree that the sword was forged in the reign of Emperor Yuryaku, whose traditional reign lasted from 457 to 479. According to the historic records, his name when living had been Wakatake. The text on the Edafuna-Yama sword states that it was during his reign that one Murite served him as a civil administrator, or *tensojin*. It refers to Yuryaku as a great king and implies that by the late fifth century the YAMATO ruler was able to exercise authority as far west as Kyushu and, if the Inariyama sword is taken into account, as far east as the Kanto Plain.

Ekachakra   *See* CHAKRANAGAR.

Elephanta
Elephanta is an island in Mumbai (Bombay) Harbor, India. Its name derives from the discovery there by the Portuguese of a huge stone statue of an elephant. This carving, which was later removed to the mainland, was part of a large complex of cave temples, of which Cave 1 is the most imposing and best preserved. This temple was constructed by the Vakataka dynasty, whose control of the Deccan region was contemporary with the GUPTA EMPIRE. It probably dates from the mid-sixth century C.E., and was a center for the worship of SIVA. The magnificent stone depiction of the god in this cave, known as the Mahadeva, stands almost 5.5 meters (18 ft.) high and has three heads representing the god as destroyer, creator, and protector.

Elephant Terrace
Immediately to the east of the royal palace precinct at ANGKOR in Cambodia there is an open area flanked on one side by the Elephant Terrace and the TERRACE OF THE LEPER KING and on the other by the row of buildings known as the Prasat Suor Prat. A large gateway links the palace with the Elephant Terrace, which was probably once covered with gilded pavilions. Dating in its current form from the reign of JAYAVARMAN VII (r. 1181–1219 C.E.), the terrace provided a dais from which the court could view games and spectacles. These sports are depicted in the carvings that decorate the terrace walls. The elephants are seen participating in a tiger

The giant statue of the Hindu god Siva from Elephanta shows the deity with three heads. They represent him as destroyer, creator, and protector. *(Scala/Art Resource, NY)*

hunt, and there are chariot races, jousting with spears, and a game of polo.

Ellora
Like AJANTA, Ellora in India is the location of a series of cave temples hewn into the living rock. It is located 80 kilometers (48 mi.) southwest of Ajanta. There are 34 individual temples extending along a distance of two kilometers (1.2 mi.). Twelve of these are Buddhist, 17 are Hindu, and five are Jain. The Buddhist temples, which date between 200 B.C.E. and 600 C.E., include sancturaries and monasteries, with sleeping areas for monks cut into the rock. The most remarkable Hindu structure is the Kailasanatha temple. It is one of the world's largest statues, because by removing more than 200,000 tons of basaltic rock, the makers created a highly decorated free-standing monolith. Its inspiration lay in the recreation of Mount Kailasa, the home of SIVA. Its construction falls in the reign of King Krishna I (c. 756–773). It is 50 meters long by 33 wide, and it stands to a height of 30 meters (165 by 109 by 99). Remarkably, it is covered in carvings depicting scenes from Hindu epics, including the demon Ravana shaking Mount Kailasa. A contemporary copperplate INSCRIPTION described it as "compelling the admiration of even the celestials, who pause on their heavenly course to gaze at the beauty of so magnificent a monument, and wonder how anyone could create such an extraordinary structures."

See also BUDDHISM; JAINISM.

The Kailasanatha temple at Ellora in India was carved in the late eighth century. Created by the removal of about 200,000 tons of rock, it is one of the largest statues in the world and was dedicated to the god Siva. (© *Philip Baird/www.anthroarcheart.org*)

Further reading: Burgess, J. *Cave Temple of Ellora.* Columbia, Mo.: South Asia Books, 1999; Malandra, G. H. *Unfolding a Mandala: The Buddhist Cave Temples at Ellora.* SUNY Series in Buddhist Studies. New York: State University of New York, 1993; Pant, P. *Ajanta and Ellora: Cave Temples of Ancient India.* Columbia, Mo.: South Asia Books, 1998.

Endere Endere is a settlement of the SHAN-SHAN kingdom, located on the southern margin of the TARIM BASIN. Discovered by SIR AUREL STEIN in 1901 and examined then and in 1906, it was occupied during the first two or three centuries C.E. It was during this period that the SILK ROAD linking China with the West saw increasing traffic, allowing the Shan-shan kingdom to prosper. This kingdom was divided into a number of provinces administered by royal appointees, and Endere might well have been the center of one such unit, or *raja*. Stein found the remains of a stupa of sun-dried brick, raised on three square platforms. The dome still retained part of the original stucco facing. The site is well known for one of the five texts in KHAROSHTHI recovered by Stein, which names the great king of HOTAN, Vijida Simha. The date indicates that he was ruling in about 230 C.E.

epigraphic hybrid Sanskrit Epigraphic hybrid SANSKRIT, known as EHS, is the language found on most Indian inscriptions dating between the first and fourth centuries C.E. This language is a mixture of Sanskrit and PRAKRIT. Inscriptions in EHS are best known from MATHURA; other examples have been found at SANCHI and SARNATH in India.

Eran According to an inscription of the GUPTA king SAMUDRAGUPTA, modern Eran was formerly known as Airanika. It is a large urban site, located on the bank of the Bina River in Madhya Pradesh state, central India. Excavations in 1960–65 uncovered a long sequence of occupation in a nine-meter (30-ft.) stratigraphic deposit, beginning in the Chalcolithic period (about 1500 B.C.E.). There followed a long sequence of Iron Age occupation. The city was a major center of the Cedi Major state, or *MAHAJANAPADA*, and trade is reflected in the recovery of more than 3,000 punch-marked coins. Between the first and sixth centuries C.E. there were four structural phases seen in domestic-house construction in brick and stone and, again, widespread trade links seen in a wide range of coins. Coin molds also indicate the existence a local mint.

See also COINAGE.

Erligang Erligang is a site lying just southeast of the city walls of ZHENGZHOU in Henan province, China. It has given its name to the early Middle phase of the Shang dynasty (1766–1045 B.C.E.), during the course of which Zhengzhou was probably the royal capital.

Erlitou The SHIJI (*Records of the Grand Historian*), written by SIMA QIAN and completed in 100 B.C.E., described in considerable detail the XIA DYNASTY. This dynasty was said to have lasted for more than 400 years before being overturned by the SHANG STATE in the 16th century B.C.E. The discovery of the Shang city of ANYANG, with its large store of ORACLE-BONE texts, gave archaeological validation to the descriptions in the *Shiji* and provided the necessary impetus to seek the physical remains of Xia. It is clear from the place names mentioned by Sima Qian that the Xia rulers dominated the area now covered by western Henan and southern Shanxi provinces. Already in 1956, the site of Luodamiao near ZHENGZHOU had yielded promising material of the correct chronological context. Further fieldwork in 1959 revealed the remains of a large urban settlement covering at least 300 hectares (990 mi.), at a place named Erlitou on the south bank of the Luo River, south of the Huang (Yellow) River in western Henan province. The most intriguing material recovered from this early phase of research was pottery clearly related to that of the Henan LONGSHAN CULTURE, but earlier than the Shang dynasty, as well as a few bronze items and oracle bones that had been subjected to heat, but not inscribed. In a later phase it was a royal residence whose basic form and structure, linked with human sacrifice, set a precedent for later palaces for centuries to come. The cast bronzes discovered in graves represent both a marked innovation in skill and the point of departure for the extraordinary development of ritual bronzes that characterized the ensuing two millennia. The mortuary remains of Erlitou indicate the presence of a high-status rank in society, while the bronzes used to project such status were produced in specialist workshops. The site thus occupies a central position in tracing the origins and development of Chinese civilization.

EXCAVATIONS

Excavations have uncovered a deep stratigraphic sequence, in which four cultural phases have been identified. The available radiocarbon dates suggest initial settlement between about 2000 and 1700 B.C.E. The last two phases are radiocarbon dated to two or three centuries later. Such a span accords with a pre-Shang period of occupation. The first two phases are not well documented, as a result of later building activity and disturbance, but the material remains relate them to the Henan Longshan culture. There are remains of stamped earth structures and burials, some of which included ceramic vessels and the rare bronze as grave goods. Others, however, reveal less ceremony, as the dead were thrown into rubbish pits. There was a major cultural change with the third phase. A large enclosed area, measuring 108 by 100 (356 by 330 ft.) meters, was found elevated on a stamped-earth platform. The complex was demarcated by a columned portico, on the south side of which lay an entrance pavilion with three doors reached by the same number of steps. A large palace, no doubt a royal residence, lay within, looking south over the enclosed courtyard. It measured 30.5 by 11.4 meters, and the form of the columns suggests that it had a hipped roof. Several pits found in the vicinity of the building postdate its construction. These contained human sacrificial victims probably associated with later rituals.

Burial Finds

A rather smaller palace complex was unearthed about 150 meters away. A six-meter-deep tomb was found between the palace and the outer wall. In terms of form, it resembled rich burials found in late Neolithic sites and in the Shang cities, in having a shelf toward the base of the chamber. Unfortunately, this burial had been looted, but at least the skeleton of a dog with its own lacquered coffin remained from what must surely have been the tomb of a person of very high status. Other burials belonging to the later part of the occupation were, however, also recovered and while not as large as the tomb in the palace precinct, nevertheless provide much social and technological information. None was found to be completely unviolated, but the surviving remains of LACQUER coffins indicate the presence of the upper orders in Erlitou society. Some contain bronze grave goods, including vessels, bells, knives, and halberds (*ge*). There are also some unusual bronze plaques inlaid with TURQUOISE. Jades were relatively rare but occur in the form of *ge*, disk axes, and beautifully shaped YAZHANG, or arc-ended blades. These *yazhang* have a wide distribution, most of them from the sacrificial pits of SANXINGDUI in Sichuan to the south. There, a bronze model of a man on his knees holding such a blade suggests that it might well have had a ceremonial or ritual function. The burials have also yielded exotic cowry shells. This wide range of exotic goods, from tin and copper to turquoise, jade, and shell, is reminiscent of the items listed by Sima Qian in the *Shiji* as goods sent as tribute to the Xia court. These have been confirmed at Erlitou with a rich grave known as K3, which included a rectangular trench on a north-south axis in which lay an additional ledge. The base was liberally coated with cinnabar, and the offerings within included a bronze *jue*, or wine jug, a stone musical chime, bronze and jade weapons, cowry shells, and turquoise that had formerly been inlaid into a perishable artifact.

Bronze Casting

That the magnificent bronzes were locally cast is beyond reasonable doubt, for the remains of a large BRONZE CASTING workshop have been identified. The most significant among the bronzes is a series of three-legged handled wine vessels known as *jue*. A typical specimen stands about 14 centimeters (5.6 in.) in height and has a long spout. The technique used to produce such elegant vessels is known as piece-mold casting. This represents a Chinese innovation in bronze technology that was in due course to produce very large and intricately decorated vessels. It involved the manufacture of a clay core in the form of the intended casting. Three or more outer clay molds were then fashioned to envelop the core, leaving sufficient space within for the molten bronze to penetrate. The interior of each piece could be decorated by excising clay in the intended pattern; the pieces were then fitted over the core, and molten bronze was poured. The outer mold sections were then fractured to remove the vessel within. This is a highly demanding technique requiring skill of a high order, and it denotes the presence of full-time craft specialists. The casting of wine vessels also points to the presence of a ruling elite capable, through deploying surpluses, of sustaining specialists and seeking prestigious and rare items for ritual and feasting.

The other bronzes, and indeed the jades, also show an interest in improved weaponry. There are, for example, knives and dagger axes as well as horse frontlets. Small disks have been interpreted as mirrors. This bronze industry, when considered in relationship to such forms as the ring-handled knives at Erlitou, has suggested to some scholars an origin in the steppic cultures of Siberia, such as that of Afanasevo, which were familiar with the domestic horse and with metalworking at a far earlier date than in China. The interest in metal weaponry is also not surprising when the friction between the Xia rulers and their client rulers as described in the *Shiji* is taken into account. Indeed, the end of the dynasty occurred in the context of armed conflict.

EVIDENCE OF THE XIA DYNASTY

The excavations of Erlitou have successfully illuminated remains that beyond reasonable doubt represent the shadowy and once mythical Xia dynasty. They reveal a society able to organize a large labor force for monumental building activity and engage in long-distance exchange for high-prestige valuables. Investigations at the site of Huizui, located 15 kilometers (9 mi.) from Erlitou, have revealed a settlement involved in the specialized production of stone spades. Such spades have been found at Erlitou itself, suggesting that goods from subsidiary communities found their way to the center.

Further reading: Fitzgerald-Huber, L. G. "Qijia and Erlitou: The Question of Contacts with Distant Cultures," *Early China* 20 (1995): 17–68.

Er Shi *See* HUHAI.

F

face towers From about 1200 C.E., during the reign of JAYAVARMAN VII (r. 1181–1219 C.E.) of ANGKOR in Cambodia, many temples were embellished with gigantic human faces carved from blocks of sandstone. These can also be seen on the gate towers of the city of ANGKOR THOM. The greatest concentration, with more than 200 examples, is found in the BAYON, the temple mausoleum of Jayavarman VII, but they are also seen at BANTEAY CHMAR, PREAH KHAN, TA PROHM, and Banteay Kdei. ZHOU DAGUAN in 1296–97 described the heads over the entrances to Angkor Thom as being of the Buddha and said that one of them was covered in gold. Paul Mus also interpreted the towers as representing the Buddha. The original purpose might have been to depict the king as a BODHISATTVA looking out serenely over his kingdom.

faience Faience is a manufactured material used in the production of jewelry, pottery, and decorative attachments. The word derives from Faenza, a town in Italy where it was manufactured during the 16th to 18th centuries. Faience can be made by covering a clay core with a tin glaze or, as in the INDUS VALLEY CIVILIZATION, by firing powdered quartz and covering it with a glaze incorporating copper and silica to produce a shiny surface.

fan The title *fan* was recorded by Chinese visitors to the state of FUNAN in the Mekong Delta in Vietnam from at least the third century C.E. It is probably a rendition of the Khmer title PON, which was discovered on inscriptions dating to the period of the CHENLA kingdoms until 719 C.E. The latter title was restricted to highly ranked men with a SANSKRIT name and was inherited from the

holder by his sister's son. The most notable ruler holding the title *fan* was known to the Chinese as Fan Shih-man. He was recorded as a great military leader who defeated rivals and replaced then with his kinsmen to rule under him. He also led maritime expeditions against his enemies, but the extent of these campaigns is not known. *The History of the Liang Dynasty* describes how the ruler of Funan in the early third century C.E. "used troops to attack and subdue the neighboring kingdoms, which all acknowledged themselves his vassals. He himself adopted the style of Great King of Funan. Then he ordered the construction of great ships and, crossing right over the Gulf of Siam, attacked more than ten states."

Farhad-beg-yailaki The site of Farhad-beg-yailaki was among many centers of BUDDHISM investigated by SIR AUREL STEIN in the early years of the 20th century. This site lies about 100 kilometers (60 mi.) east of HOTAN, China, the kingdom with which it was affiliated. Excavations in 1907 revealed the foundations of a monastery dating to the eighth century C.E. Stein uncovered the remains of a stupa, records written in the BRAHMI script, and painted wooden panels.

Faxian (337–unknown) *Faxian was a Chinese Buddhist who traveled to the pilgrimage places of India in 402 C.E. and on his return translated many of the holy texts he had collected into Chinese.*
He was aged 65 when he embarked on his journey and 79 on his return to China. He wrote a book entitled the *Foguoji* (*Record of Buddhist Kingdoms*), which is an unparalleled source of information on the early history

of BUDDHISM in India. His journey began by following the SILK ROAD from Gansu to DUNHUANG, and across the oases of the TARIM BASIN to HOTAN and KAXGAR. The information he provided on his visit to the state of SHAN-SHAN is invaluable in indicating that Buddhism continued to flourish there in the early fifth century. He noted that the king of Shan-shan favored Buddhism and that 4,000 monks were to be seen. He chose a particularly dangerous route across the Tarim Basin, probably because of the abandonment of some of the major western centers of Buddhism in Shan-shan. He remarked that the desert was inhospitable, with only the bones of the dead to guide his path. He then crossed by snowy Pamir Mountains to GANDHARA.

The first stages of his travels saw him cross land controlled by the Kidarite Huns, and he noted many flourishing monasteries and large stupas. At TAXILA in modern Pakistan he described how the local rulers and nobility gave generously to Buddhist foundations, and at Peshawar he admired the great monastery and stupa of KANISHKA I (100–26 C.E.). This was the location of the Buddha's alms bowl, and 700 monks safeguarded it. At Hadda in Afghanistan he witnessed ceremonies revolving around the presence there of the Buddha's skull. It was placed on a high dais, was covered in glass, and was the object of worship. He then visited the holy places where the Buddha was born, attained enlightenment, and entered nirvana. His travels took him to MATHURA, KAUSAMBI, PATALIPUTRA, and NALANDA. He greatly admired India, then ruled by Candragupta II (376–413 C.E.), for its warm climate, genial people, and their custom of not eating onions or garlic. His return journey took him south along the western coast of India to Sri Lanka, where he spent two years, and then by the perilous sea route to Southeast Asia, where his ship was wrecked, probably on the island of Java. Thence, he returned to China, where he commenced with the translation of the manuscripts he had collected. His description of this epic journey became known in the West only with the publication of a French translation in 1836. This had a profound effect on the young ALEXANDER CUNNINGHAM, later director-general of the ARCHAEOLOGICAL SURVEY OF INDIA, who used the monk's account to trace the major centers of Buddhism. Thus Cunningham identified the site of SANKISA by following Faxian's description of his journey there from Mathura.

Fayaz Tepe Fayaz Tepe is located in northern BACTRIA, near the confluence of the Amu Dar'ya and the Surkhan Dar'ya. It was associated with TERMEZ, lying just outside the city walls and about a kilometer from KARA TEPE. The Buddhist monastery at Fayaz Tepe was discovered in 1968, when a shepherd found the head of a stone statue and drew the discovery to the attention of the director of the Termez Museum, a Mr. Fayazov. The site was named

after him. Extensive excavations have uncovered a complete Buddhist monastery covering an area of 117 by 34 meters (386 by 112 ft.) and embellished with wall paintings and exceptional sculptures.

Built in sun-dried brick, the monastery has three courts. The earliest and central court lies behind a brick stupa that has survived virtually in its entirety. Both are thought to date to the first century B.C.E. The court incorporates a colonnaded verandah in front of individual cells for the monks, while the surface of the stupa was painted with lotus flowers and images of the wheel of the law (the DHARMACAKRA). Four holes on its surface were found, to support flagpoles. Both the stupa and the central court were added to by the second century C.E. The stupa was embellished with four sets of steps to form a cruciform plan. The court had two further courts added. One contained rooms for prayers and meetings; the second included kitchens, a dining area, and facilities for weaving and making pottery vessels. Some shards in this area were inscribed in the BRAHMI and KHAROSHTHI scripts dating stylistically to the second century C.E.

One notable example of wall painting shows two haloed Buddhas with female adherents, standing on a bed of starflowers. The style of this painting resembles that of some of those at BAMIYAN. It is the sculptural remains, however, that stand out for their exceptional quality and completeness. Foremost is a third-century C.E. limestone carving of a seated Buddha with his halo represented by the branches of a pipal tree, in a niche 75 centimeters (30 in.) high. Two attendant monks stand, one on each side. The Corinthian-style columns that frame the niche indicate a strong Hellenistic influence. A stucco head of the Buddha still bearing much of the original paint was also found, its style suggesting that this site continued as an active monastery into the fourth century C.E.

Fengchu The site of Fengchu lies in the Zhouyuan, the Plain of Zhou, in the Wei River Valley, China. It is particularly notable as the site of a palace dating to the early period of the WESTERN ZHOU DYNASTY (1045–771 B.C.E.). The palace was constructed on a platform of stamped earth, and the design incorporated a central hall and two enclosed courtyards surrounded by colonnades and chambers. It differs from later palace structures in its air of secrecy and privacy, rather than an ostentatious location raised above its surroundings to ensure visibility. The roofs were probably made of thatch, and the plastered walls were decorated with mother-of-pearl. Perhaps the most significant find was a cache of ORACLE BONES. These are very rare in Western Zhou contexts, and the origin of this group is subject to debate, largely because it revealed the veneration of ancestors belonging to the SHANG STATE rather than the Western Zhou rulers. However, it is known that royal princesses were exchanged between the two dynasties before the conquest of Shang and that Zhou rulers did therefore have Shang ancestors. These divinatory texts reveal also the number of captives and cattle sacrificed during the relevant rituals.

feng shui   *See* GEOMANCY.

Ferghana   The region of Ferghana lies in the upper valley of the Syr Dar'ya River, north of the Pamir Range in Central Asia. It was strategically placed on the old SILK ROAD that linked China with India and the Mediterranean world. It lay too far east to be overtaken by the ACHAEMENID or Seleucid empires and was never controlled by the BACTRIAN GREEKS, although many of their coin issues have been found in Ferghanan territory. The dry climate linked with the presence of rivers flowing off the snows of the Tien Shan Range generated a great emphasis on IRRIGATION, even in the prehistoric period. The area first attracted the attention of the Chinese when it was visited by ZHANG QIAN in 121 B.C.E.; he reported that Ferghana was a place of vineyards and fortified towns, where fabulous horses sweated blood. In his own words: "The people are settled on the land, plowing the fields and growing rice and wheat. They also make wine out of grapes. The region has many fine horses. The people live in fortified cities, there being about seventy or more cities of varying sizes in the region. The people fight with bows and spears, and can shoot from horseback." Making fine wine was a major industry of Ferghana, but it was the superb horses that attracted most Chinese interest.

Five Classics   The Five Classics are a set of early historic tracts traditionally seen as the oldest and most revered sources of Chinese history. They are said to have been collected, edited, and enhanced by CONFUCIUS (551–479 B.C.E.), and they became the acknowledged source of knowledge on ancient wisdom and the moral behavior that was a central tenet of the Confucian school, particularly from the Western HAN DYNASTY on. The five texts cover a wide range of issues. Foremost is the *Spring and Autumn Annals,* which describe the history of the state of LU between 722 and 481 B.C.E., the period of the later Zhou dynasty, also widely known as the Spring and Autumn period. The *Classic of Changes* considers the nature of the universe and the procedure for interpreting divinations, and the *Classic of Documents* is a historic collection on the governance of early kings. The *Classic of Poetry* is a source for mainly early Zhou rituals, and, the *Record of Rites* sets out the norms for proper conduct.

Fu Hao   (r. c. 1200–1181 B.C.E.)   *Fu Hao was one of three principal consorts of the Shang emperor Wu Ding, although his recorded wives number more than 60. She was often mentioned in the texts of the oracle bones recovered from* ANYANG, *and it is possible to identify some of her responsibilities in the court.*

For example, she was a wealthy landowner in her own right. She undertook important court rituals to consult ancestors and commanded troops in a number of military campaigns against the Tu, Ba, Yi, and Qiang people. The king himself consulted the oracles to ensure her health and well-being during pregnancies.

Her tomb, discovered in 1975 at Xiaotun, Anyang, about 200 meters (660 ft.) from the walls of the royal palace, revealed during excavations the following year a complete, undisturbed Shang dynasty tomb dating to about 1200 C.E. and falling within the reign period of Wu Ding. This tomb is most renowned for the wealth of the mortuary offerings for Fu Hao. These include 468 bronzes, easily the most significant group of ritual wine and food vessels known from Shang contexts. A unique assemblage of jade provides remarkable insight into Fu Hao's interest in antiquities.

THE TOMB STRUCTURE

The tomb was no match for the massive cruciform royal graves in terms of size, but it uniquely had avoided the attentions of tomb robbers. In a rectangular pit 7.5 meters (about 25 ft.) deep and 5.6 by four meters in extent, at a depth of 6.2 meters, the builders had constructed a narrow ledge from which two niches were excavated into the walls of the pit. A further small pit was excavated into the ground at the very base of the tomb. On the surface, postholes suggested that a temple of some sort was constructed over the tomb, probably for holding ancestral mortuary rituals.

The excavators were able to reconstruct the internal ordering of the mortuary equipment. The base of the pit was lined with wood to form a chamber, within which lay nested and lacquered wooden coffins. Unfortunately, the base was so waterlogged that the human remains have not survived. The base of the pit had received a dog and a sacrificed human victim, one of 16 individuals accompanying the primary burial, a number that included men, WOMEN, and children. Some of these individuals were placed in the wall niches on each side of the tomb, and others in the grave fill of layers of stamped earth.

THE BRONZES

Some of the bronzes were inscribed with the name of Fu Hao, thereby, for the only time in the history of Shang studies, illuminating the burial of a person specifically named in the oracle bones. The grave also contained about 7,000 cowry shells, 755 items of jade, many hundreds of bone ornaments, and three rare ivory cups decorated with TURQUOISE inlay. The analysis of these unique assemblages has provided much crucial information. Thus the bronzes provide a measure for the high status of a royal consort. Many vessels are of unusual form, and others, while of established shape, are unusually large.

The two largest items are two *ding* vessels, each contributing 120 kilograms (264 lbs.) to the total weight of 1,600 kilograms (3,520 lbs.) of bronze in the tomb. Some bronzes seem to have been placed in dining sets; the numbers of wine vessels include 40 of a form known as a *jue* and 53 *gu*. Not all the bronzes were inscribed with the name Fu Hao. Two were inscribed with her posthumous name, Um Xin, and these are thought to have been cast by order of her sons when presenting sacrifices to her. It is also hard to avoid the conclusion that some of the bronzes were given to her by Wu Ding himself, a king who obviously held her in very high regard. Fu Hao had led Shang armies in a number of campaigns, and the bronzes in her burial also include 90 *ge*, or dagger blades, and several large axes. She owned bronze mirrors and bronze cheekpieces as part of a horse bridle. Fabric impressions that survive on the surface of many of the bronzes suggest that they were individually wrapped before being placed in the grave. An analysis of the composition of the bronzes reveals a mastery of alloying. Many of the vessels include between 15 and 20 percent of tin; others had up to 6 percent of lead added to ease the castability of the molten alloy.

THE JADES AND OTHER FINDS

Perhaps the most spectacular and unusual of all the mortuary offerings, however, were the three large ivory vessels inlaid with turquoise. Some of Fu Hao's jade ornaments were more than 1,000 years old and were derived from the LIANGZHU CULTURE in the lower Chang (Yangtze) Valley; others came from the HONGSHAN CULTURE in the far northeast of China. Most, however, were locally made. They included a rare jade bowl and carved animals—phoenix, tigers, elephants, fish, and dragons. The tiger might well have been the inspiration for the TAOTIE masks found so often on the bronzes. The dragon was reputed to have the ability to accompany the dead to heaven. At least some of the jades, according to their composition, were made of raw materials mined in Hotan, far to the west of Anyang. Further evidence for a trading relationship with steppe peoples is in the form of distinctive bronze knives and ornaments bearing horses' heads.

It is evident that bone hairpins were a treasured part of Fu Hao's ornaments, for 527 were found in her grave, each minutely carved at the head in a range of patterns. She also took with her three COMBS to accompany the bronze mirrors. Hitherto, only fragments of ivory vessels had been found in Shang contexts, but Fu Hao's tomb had three large examples.

For the social historian, the tomb of Fu Hao offers a unique opportunity to appreciate and evaluate the extremes of wealth associated with the royal members of Shang society. If such a relatively small tomb of a royal consort could contain such riches, the kings' deep cruciform burials most have included unimaginably wealthy offerings. For the student of Shang bronze technology,

the sophistication of Fu Hao's bronzes has required a reappraisal of the development of the casters' skills, for before the opening of the tomb, the style of bronzes like those of Fu Hao were thought to be much later in the sequence. Perhaps the most significant of all the findings from this grave, however, is the tangible link between a person previously known only from the oracle texts and her physical remains and possessions.

Further reading: Loewe, M., and E. L. Shaugnessy, eds. *The Cambridge History of Ancient China*. Cambridge: Cambridge University Press, 1999; Zheng Zhenxiang. "The Royal Consort Fu Hao and Her Tomb." In *Mysteries of Ancient China*, edited by J. Rawson. New York: Braziller, 1996.

Fujiwara Fujiwara was the new capital city of the YAMATO state and was occupied between 686 and 707 C.E. The importance of Fujiwara, however, may be judged from the fact that the streets of the new capital at Heijo-kyo were aligned precisely on those of its predecessor. At that period in Japanese history, the Korean Peninsula had just been unified under the SHILLA kings with the defeat of PAEKCHE and KOGURYO. This was accomplished through an alliance between Shilla and Tang China, and it posed an immediate threat to the independence of Yamato. It led to major changes in Japan. One change involved a much more rigorous system of taxation, another the exaltation of the imperial line, ushering in new legal codes according the emperor or empress autocratic power. One manifestation of such power, along the Chinese model, was investment in a capital city and palace so impressive as to leave no doubt as to the imperial authority. The architecture is known mainly from the NIHONGI, although the site has been somewhat explored. When Fujiwara was abandoned, a new capital was built at Nara.

The Fujiwara city was ordered by Empress JITO (r. 686–97 C.E.) and continued in occupation under her successor, Mommu (686–707). According to the *Nihongi*, Prince Takechi inspected the proposed site of the new palace on the 29th day of the 10th month, 690 C.E. The empress Jito herself, with a large entourage, was there on the 19th of the following month. The construction, which was under way by 694, was a colossal undertaking in a low-lying area prone to floods. The palace alone required an estimated 4,000 tree trunks seven meters (23 ft.) tall, to be carried over a distance of 54 kilometers (32 mi.). Many thousands of tons of stones were required for the massive wall around the palace precinct, which was almost a kilometer square, and many roof tiles were fired to cover the roofs of the palace and its subsidiary buildings. The palace lay in a central position in the city, but its precise location relative to the extent of the city has not been identified. It may have been in the center or to the north of center, but more extensive excavations are required to confirm either possibility. It is known, however, to have lain within a walled precinct defined by a large stone wall girdled both inside and out by a moat. The wall was three meters (9.9 ft.) wide; the moat was five. Beyond the outer moat lay a 40-meter-broad band of unoccupied land, giving way then to the city streets. The palace included three major structures. To the north lay the private quarters of the empress, covering an area of 305 by 350 meters (1,000 by 1,155); the interior details are not known because of later disturbance. An impressive audience hall was constructed south of the residence, designed to have the maximal impact of grandeur on those who visited from home or abroad. The buildings to house administrative departments completed the palace precinct.

The actual plan of the rest of the city has not been determined through excavation; one problem is the absence of an outer wall. If, as some authorities have suggested, it comprised 96 insulae divided on a street grid forming eight city blocks from east to west and 12 from north to south, then the city would have covered a rectangular area 3.2 by 2.1 kilometers (1.9 by 6.9 mi.) in extent. It is, however, also possible that it was square, with the palace in the center. This needs confirmation through further excavations. Each square block was divided by smaller streets, in which archaeologists have revealed the presence of homes, wells, and alleyways. With a population measured in tens of thousands, the issue of sanitation is raised. A privy excavated at Fujiwara in 1992 was a simple hole in the ground covered by two wooden boards. There was no apparent means of flushing it, so it must be presumed that waste remained in place or was physically removed and disposed of elsewhere. Such lack of hygiene is documented in the recovery of parasite eggs in this facility.

Estimating the population of an ancient city is not straightforward. In the case of Fujiwara, much information is from an entry dating to the year 704 C.E. in the *Nihongi* record, which describes how each household in the city was given rolls of cloth. There were evidently 1,505 households. A later tax register from HEIJO-KYO has provided an average figure of 16.4 people per household, leading to an population estimate of about 25,000 people.

The mausoleum of Jito and Emperor TEMMU (631?–686. C.E.) lies due south of the palace, beyond the city limit, but the city had a brief life. In 708 C.E. it was resolved to build a bigger and more magnificent capital on the lines of the Tang capital at Chang'an, 20 kilometers (14 mi.) to the north at Heijo (Nara).

See also NARA STATE.

Further reading: Aston, W. G. *Nihongi: Chronicles of Japan from the Earliest Times to A.D. 697.* Rutland, Vt., and Tokyo: Tuttle, 1995; Barnes, G. *Prehistoric Yamato: Archaeology of the First Japanese State.* Ann Arbor: University of Michigan, 1988; Brown, D. M. *The Cambridge History of Japan.* Cambridge: Cambridge University Press, 1993.

Funan Funan is the name given to one of the earliest states on the mainland of Southeast Asia. There is no certainty as to the origin of the name, which was given to the polity in question by the Chinese and may be a Chinese rendition of the Khmer name *phnom,* or "hill." It dates to about 100–550 C.E. and was located on the delta of the Mekong and Bassac Rivers in modern Cambodia and Vietnam. This is a strategic location, since it commands not only maritime routes leading from China to India, but also traffic up and down the Mekong River. The area was occupied in the prehistoric period, and the inhabitants prospered with the control of the international maritime trade to create a vigorous and powerful state. Funan was, however, equally vulnerable to any changes in the pattern of trade beyond its control. During the sixth century C.E., such a change occurred when the Chinese increasingly bypassed the delta. Funan then fell into a rapid decline, and the political center of gravity moved inland to emerging agrarian states known under the name of CHENLA.

EXPLORATIONS OF FUNAN

The first knowledge of this state was assembled and published by Paul Pelliot in 1903. A lengthy article was based on his translation of an archived Chinese report that resulted from a maritime mission to Southeast Asia by KANG DAI and Zhu Ying in the third century C.E. There were walled settlements and rulers who lived in a palace. A system of taxation involved dues on gold, silver, perfumes, and pearls, and there was a form of legal system that involved trial by ordeal. There were specialists in engraving and metalworking, and the ordinary people lived in houses raised on piles against the regular threat of flooding. The people kept written records, and a representative of the Indian Murunda king was present. The foundation of the state of Funan was, according to the Chinese visitors, the result of a union between an Indian named Kaundinya and a local princess.

It is not certain where the Chinese authors of the report employed by Pelliot made landfall in Southeast Asia. However, aerial reconnaissances by Paul Paris published in 1931 provide images of ancient canals crisscrossing the delta landscape and the outline of a large rectangular city now known as OC EO. On the northern margins of the delta, another walled city, known as ANGKOR BOREI, lay at the northern terminus of one such canal. The Chinese visitors noted that the capital of Funan had an inland location, and the size of Angkor Borei would qualify it at the very least as a major center.

Subsequent archaeological research, particularly by Louis Malleret and, more recently, by Vo Si Khai and Pierre-Yves Manguin, has confirmed much of what Kang Dai and Zhu Ying described. Oc Eo incorporated substantial brick temple foundations, workshops for the production of jewelry, evidence for casting metals, and wooden piles that would have supported houses. There are also

SEALS bearing brief texts in the Indian BRAHMI script and an abundance of evidence for trade involving Rome, India, and China. A series of sites has also been uncovered by Vietnamese scholars, again involving brick temples as well as brick vaults containing cremated human remains and rich artifacts. These include gold leaves bearing INSCRIPTIONS and images of WOMEN, gold disks, gold rings, a gold flower, and jewelry fashioned from precious stones and glass. The gold leaves were decorated with deities, turtles representing Vishnu and his mount the eagle GARUDA, water buffaloes, elephants, snakes, conch shells, the sun, a house on piles and plants; many of these symbols relate to Hindi gods.

RULERS OF FUNAN

The Chinese histories contain notes on the names of successive rulers and their predatory wars against their neighbors. One early ruler named Hun Panhuang conquered chiefs on the edge of his kingdom and installed his sons and grandsons to rule there under his command. His son, called Pan Pan, was followed by a ruler known as Fan Shiman. The title *pan* or FAN might well be a Chinese rendition of the Khmer title PON, widely documented in later inscriptions. Fan Shiman is said to have launched expeditions against his neighbors. The history of the Liang dynasty, compiled in the seventh century C.E., records that a second Kaundinya ruled Funan and "changed the rules according to the customs of India." The degree to which the indigenous peoples of Cambodia and southern Vietnam were subjected to Indianization has been critically examined, particularly by Michael Vickery. It is now considered probable that the local rulers selectively adopted certain Indian traits they saw as being advantageous. For example, a small corpus of inscriptions belonging to the Funan polity discloses the adoption of the SANSKRIT language and Indian royal titles toward the end of the fifth century C.E.

INSCRIPTIONS

Few inscriptions survive, but their Sanskrit texts provide important information. The mutilated first few lines of the inscription from GO THAP, for example, refer to a ruler whose name began with *Ja-*, probably JAYAVARMAN OF FUNAN (c. 480 C.E.), who had been victorious in battle against a king whose name began with *Vira*. VARMAN is a significant part of a royal name, for in Sanskrit it means "shield" or "protector." This ruler founded many sanctuaries dedicated to Vishnu and placed his son, Gunavarman, in charge of one, which had been "wrested from the mud." This might be an allusion to the drainage of the Plain of Reeds where the inscription was set up. The sanctuary in question was dedicated to Vishnu, and the consecration was undertaken by Brahmans. A second inscription from Nak Ta Dambang Dek was set up in honor of Buddha. It cites King Jayavarman and his son, Rudravarman ("protected by SIVA"), and describes how

the king named the son of a Brahman as his inspector of property. A third text again mentions King Jayavarman and his military victories. It also records the foundation of a hermitage, reservoir, and residence by his queen, Kulaprabhavati. *Kula* means "family;" *prabhavat* in Sanskrit may be translated as "majesty." Thus in the period 480–520 there were wars involving rival kings, the establishment of religious foundations in favor of exotic Indic gods, the presence of educated officiants, and a royal succession from father to son. Two inscriptions from the vicinity of Angkor Borei imply that this was the capital of Rudravarman, the last recorded king in this region. The inscription from Phnom Da mentions his name in several places.

Further reading: Higham, C. F. W. *The Civilization of Angkor.* London: Weidenfeld and Nicholson, 2001; Vickery, M. *Society, Economics and Politics in Pre-Angkor Cambodia.* Tokyo: The Centre for East Asian Cultural Studies for UNESCO, 1998; Vickery, M. "What and Where Was Chenla? "In *Recherches Nouvelles sur le Cambodge*, edited by F. Bizot. Paris: EFEO, 1994.

Fuquanshan Fuquanshan is a site of the Songze and LIANGZHU CULTUREs in China, located in the valley of the Suzhou River that links Lake Taihu with the estuary of the Chang (Yangtze) River. It is an artificially constructed mound measuring about 100 by 85 meters (330 by 280 ft.), in which 31 elite burials of the Liangzhu culture have been excavated. These are large graves including jades, ivories, and ceramics, each containing a coffin made by cutting and hollowing out a tree trunk. The primary interments are richly endowed with grave goods. Burial 139, for example, contained the remains of a young man, who was associated with 12 jade axes laid out in two rows from the waist to the ankles, a jade bracelet, a plaque, a bead, and a pendant in the form of a long awl. The cemetery appears to have been reserved for elite burials and was associated with much ritual activity. There is one part of the site where an area 20 by three meters (66 by 10 ft.) has been heavily burned and coated with shell fragments, while burnt clay was often placed over graves. Another larger pit had a depth of 1.5 meters. It contained a platform, surrounded by large quantities of ash, as if ceremonies linked with burning were undertaken. These probably involved sacrificial rituals in honor of the ancestors.

The awl-like ornament from Burial 139, to judge from its location in the grave, was probably worn in the hair. A globular jade bead had been placed in the mouth. Fourteen painted pottery vessels were found beyond the feet. The skeleton of a young woman in a flexed position was found in a corner of this grave. She was accompanied by seven jade ornaments. Burial 145 also included additional burials of an older woman and a young boy. The excavators noted that their position, with their hands behind their back and head outstretched, was compatible with sacrificial burial when still alive.

Fuquanshan provided a remarkable assemblage of jades and pottery vessels from mortuary contexts. A jade ax was found beside one of the elite skeletons. While finely finished, the blade was blunt and showed no sign of use. Its ceremonial nature is seen in two additional jade elements. It seems that the handle had a boat-shaped jade decoration on the far end and a curved and socketed jade terminus on the near end, with holes for securing it. The site has also furnished finely finished jade ceremonial tubes, or *cong*. One of these was decorated with four images of a god's face, with fine cloud patterns incised on the nose, above a second panel containing the image of an animal mask. There are also *bi* disks, with diameters of about 20 centimeters (8 in.), which were perforated with a central hole. These were often found under the body and are thought to have been placed there to drive off malevolent spirits. Crescentic jade ornaments, with holes bored for attachment, were often found near the waist, while a remarkable assemblage of long, thin pendants of jade was recovered from the elite graves from this site. One of these, 15 centimeters (6 in.) long, was decorated with the face of a god. Another long jade with a point at one end and a small handle at the other is 34 centimeters long and was ornamented with the eyelids of a god. It might well have been of ritual importance. Burial 74 includes a fine necklace of jade beads; another grave furnished a remarkable necklace of 32 jade beads, four of which had an elongated awl shape; others were tubular, and four were in the form of a *bi* disk. This unique assemblage of Liangzhu jades also included a fine belt hook, hat ornaments, and bracelets.

Other rare and beautiful offerings included an ivory-handled implement of an unknown but probably ceremonial function. A detailed animal mask had been carved on its surface. The ceramic vessels from the cemetery attest to highly skilled manufacture. Many of the forms suggest ritual or ceremonial feasting, such as a jar with a bulbous base, handles, and an elaborate lid. The body bore fine incised decoration of clouds, birds, and snakes. There are also several jugs that could have been used for serving wine. One tall example, 20 centimeters high, has a broad handle and fine lid.

G

Gandhara Gandhara, the region of northwestern Pakistan that centers on the city of Peshawar, in a general sense also incorporates the upper reaches of the Jhelum, Chenab, Indus, and Kabul Rivers, from Lahore in Pakistan in the east to Kabul and BAMIYAN in Afghanistan to the west. Lying just southeast of the Khyber Pass, it occupies a cultural crossroads that saw contact and numerous incursions over many centuries from north of the Hindu Kush range. Gandhara was a province of the ACHAEMENID EMPIRE of Persia until its conquest by ALEXANDER THE GREAT in 327 B.C.E. Thus began a period of Greek or Hellenistic influence in Gandhara, cemented by Alexander's settlement of veterans in new cities. However, the expansion of the MAURYA EMPIRE saw the foundation of the first city at TAXILA, and Gandhara received much Buddhist influence, notably during the reign of the Mauryan king ASOKA (268–235 B.C.E.). The DHARMARAJIKA stupa at TAXILA is a notable example of an early Buddhist foundation in this region. With the decline of the Maurya empire, Gandhara again came under strong Hellenistic influence when the BACTRIAN GREEKS established control over the province. There thus arose strong mutual influence between the Buddhist tradition of India and the art style of Greece, from which emerged the Gandhara school of art (from the early second century B.C.E.). Until this development, the Buddha was only portrayed symbolically, as a footprint, parasol, lion, or *bodhi* tree. But the Hellenistic contribution to Gandhara art saw the portrayal of the Buddha and other figures in Greek and Roman styles, as the Bactrian Greek rulers showed empathy with and interest in BUDDHISM. One of the most intriguing of Gandharan reliefs portrays the Trojan priest Laocoön and the Trojan horse before the gates of Troy, the entrance to which is dominated by Cassandra in Indian attire.

The Bactrian Greek dominance in Gandhara was relatively short lived, although the Greek architectural and artistic legacy was considerable. The Greeks were succeeded by the KUSHAN empire (70 B.C.E.–200 C.E.), which again patronized Buddhism. King KANISHKA I (100–26 C.E.), for example, had Buddhist monasteries built over a wide area from his capital at Purusupura (Peshawar). The Kushan empire was succeeded by numerous local kingdoms, and again Buddhism flourished and expanded north of the Himalayas and west into Afghanistan, where the mighty Buddhist images of Bamiyan, now destroyed by the Taliban, were created between the third and fifth centuries C.E. The end of the Gandhara school occurred in the second half of the fifth century C.E. with the invasions of the HEPHTHALITE, White, HUNS. Taxila was then abandoned.

GANDHARAN ART

The vigorous artistic tradition known as the Gandharan school was first recognized in 1852, when W. Jackson published a brief paper on two sculptured heads of BODHISATTVAS found near Peshawar. He noted with considerable prescience that the heads resembled those on Bactrian coins: "The expression of the face is somewhat of a Greek cast, but it is not a pure Greek countenance." E.-C. Bayler, writing at the same time, was at pains to stress the Greek stimulus and Buddhist character. The enormous output of the Gandhara sculptors between the first and fifth centuries can best be judged through the early excavations of Dr. D. B. Spooner (1906–7) and SIR AUREL STEIN at SAHRI-BAHLOL in 1912.

Sahri-Bahlol Sculptures

Already by that period, the Gandharan sculptures had been vigorously looted to satisfy British army collectors.

At this site, however, the owners had forbidden random digging to preserve the contents of the site for their own profit. Consequently much material survived at the time of Stein's archaeological research there. He collected more than 1,200 items of sculpture during a six-week campaign. At the site the surviving city walls were surrounded by mounds that, on excavation, revealed the foundations of Buddhist religious buildings. These furnished refreshingly complete stone statues of the Buddha and bodhisattvas, revealing strong Hellenistic influence in the facial features and dress. They are also highly informative in that the bases of the statues display miniature friezes of the donors of the image or of benefits to the foundation. One, for example, shows the donor and two male figures worshiping before an altar from which incense fumes rise; on the other side of the altar is a young man with a plow drawn by two oxen. There are also examples of a family seen worshiping a begging bowl, thus portrayed associated with an image of the Buddha. Another complete statue represents Hariti, the goddess of smallpox, holding a trident.

Stucco

Gandharan art from the first to the third century was dominated by stone sculpture, but thereafter images in stucco, painted and gilt, were also produced. This stucco is best known from the Jaulian and Mohra Moradu monasteries at Taxila, Hadda, Butkara, and Takht-i Bahi. The base foundations for religious buildings were embellished with fine stucco reliefs along their entire length, depicting bodhisattvas seated between columns. The classical element in Gandhara art is also seen in the representations of the Greek son of Poseidon, Triton, and centaurs.

Taxila

Examples of Gandharan stone art at Taxila itself are not as rich as those from Sahri-Bahlol, but many relevant sculptures have been uncovered by SIR JOHN MARSHALL at the Dharmarajika stupa and at the site of Kalawan. There are many fine examples of stucco art, and some architectural features, such as Corinthian column capitals, also show a strong Hellenistic influence. Miraculous and other scenes taken from the life of the Buddha have been found, including the first sermon and the visit of Indra.

Further reading: Geoffroy-Schneiter, Berenice. *Gandhara*. Paris: Assouline, 2001; Hallade, M. *The Gandhara Style and the Evolution of Buddhist Art*. London: Thames and Hudson, 1968; Marshall, J. *The Buddhist Art of Gandhara*. Philadelphia: Coronet Books, 1981; Tissot, F. *Gandhara*. Paris: J. Maisonneuve, 1985.

Ganesha Ganesha was the god of wisdom in the Hindu pantheon. He was depicted with an elephant's head, one tusk, and a large belly. In India the worship of Ganesha has been popular since the late GUPTA EMPIRE period. An inscription from Ghatiyala in Rajasthan, dated to 862 C.E., is regarded as one of the early references to this god. He was also depicted in the rock-cut temples of ELLORA (200 B.C.E.–600 C.E.). In Cambodia and Thailand, Ganesha was adopted as a popular god and is today the symbol and icon of the Royal Thai Fine Arts Department.

Gaozu (Liu Bang; Gaodi; High Emperor) (r. 206–195 B.C.E.) *Gaozu, High Emperor, the founder of the Han dynasty, acceded to the throne of China after participating in the widespread rebellion against the excesses of the second Qin emperor.*

Before becoming emperor, Gaodi was known as Liu Bang, from Pei, a district in central China. After several years of political chaos and conflict, he managed to defeat all rivals and became the sole ruler.

Later texts accord to Gaozu the MANDATE OF HEAVEN. From humble peasant origins, he became the founder of a great dynasty. While never losing his peasant manner and distrust of scholars, he showed a sharp insight into appropriate administrative reforms designed to secure support. However, his reign came to an end when a stray arrow killed him during a military engagement against the king of Huai-nan, and he was succeeded by his son, Huidi.

Three centuries later, during the Eastern Han dynasty, Gaozu was venerated still in the royal ancestral hall at LUOYANG, the capital. He was represented there by an empty seat placed under a richly embroidered canopy. Sacrificial vessels used in his honor had golden rims.

LIU BANG'S RISE TO POWER

Chafing under the extreme dictatorial regime of the Qin dynasty, Liu Bang had the local magistrate killed and took for himself the title lord of Pei. He then became one of several aspiring warlords intent on toppling the Qin dynasty and commanded a force that invaded the Qin heartland in December 207 B.C.E. while awaiting further orders from the king of CHU. *The History of the Former Han* (HANSHU) might have been extolling his magnanimity when it describes how, having received the surrender of King Zihing of Qin, he had the palace, armories, and mausolea sealed against looting and destruction and introduced new and less repressive laws. However, these acts of magnanimity were short lived, for two months later Liu Bang's superior and later rival, Xiang Yu, arrived and had the entire royal family slaughtered and the capital razed to the ground. This included the desecration of the mausoleum of QIN SHIHUANGDI (259–210 B.C.E.) and was probably the occasion when the emperor's underground terra-cotta army of lifesize figures was invaded and the weapons stolen.

By 206 Xiang Yu was in firm control of the situation and resolved to divide the empire into 18 separate kingdoms, each with a compliant ruler. This involved dividing the former kingdom of Qin, for example, into three separate realms. Liu Bang was lucky to escape with his life, for there were strong rumors of an assassination plot, and instead he was dispatched to rule the remote fief of Chang Han. This was a clear attempt to sideline him, but he was soon back in the Qin heartland, defeating the three new puppet rulers and challenging Xiang Yu himself. There followed a long and difficult civil war between the two rivals. On two occasions, the second in 204 B.C.E., Liu Bang was lucky to escape with his life and a few loyal followers. There was an uneasy truce in 203 B.C.E., during which China was divided between Liu Bang and Xiang Yu, but this was brief. Liu Bang broke the truce and in 202 B.C.E. triumphed at the Battle of Gai-xia in Anhui province, after which Xiang Yu committed suicide.

GAODI AS EMPEROR

Gaodi now controlled China without rival, and in the same year as the battle his followers persuaded him to assume the title *huangdi,* or emperor. He ordered a series of reforms designed to restore life to normal after a long period of civil war and to ensure widespread loyalty to the new dynasty of Han. These included a general amnesty and the restoration of law with less severe penalties. People were encouraged to return to their ancestral homes and reclaim their land and property, and the aristocracy again were granted titles and bounties on auspicious occasions.

On the wider scene, Gaodi faced a number of major organizational issues. The Qin dynasty had divided China into provinces, or commanderies, ruled by centrally appointed governors. During the civil war that brought down the Qin, Xiang Yu had returned to the earlier system of independent kingdoms, in which the rulers owed fealty to the central regime. Since Gaodi had approved and authorized his supporters to receive new kingdoms, maintaining the kingdoms and their rulers was a delicate issue. Gaodi resolved it by allowing the kingdoms to exist but, where practicable, replacing the kings over time with men of his own choice, particularly members of his own family. Some former kings were given lesser titles; others rebelled or deserted China. These kingdoms lay in the eastern half of the empire, while 16 commanderies, on the old Qin system, lay to the west. The commanderies were ruled by centrally appointed governors. These innovations were accompanied by a revival of Confucianism rather than the legalistic principles followed by the Qin.

The civil war had naturally weakened the concerted defense against the nomadic XIONGNU to the north, and in the year after his assumption of the throne, Gaodi had to lead an army against the northern invaders. In 209 the Xiongnu (a Chinese word meaning "fierce slave") had found in Mao-tun a new and dynamic leader who first defeated his own rival tribal leaders and then expanded his area of control to include the strategic Gansu Corridor in Northwest China. This direct threat to the Han capital could not be ignored, and in 200 C.E. Gaodi clashed with the Xiongnu at the Battle of Ping Cheng. The emperor was surrounded and extricated himself only with difficulty.

The Chinese then followed the path of diplomacy and in effect bought off the Xiongnu with gifts, including that of a Chinese royal princess in marriage. The border between the two states was fixed as the GREAT WALL of China. In the south, there was an independent ruler of Lingnan, an area over which the Qin had claimed sovereignty.

Garuda In Hindu mythology, Garuda was a being in the form of a bird who stole AMRITA, the elixir of immortality, from the gods. This impressed Vishnu, who asked Garuda to become his vehicle. Garuda is often represented in the sculptures of India and Southeast Asia, being particularly common in Khmer reliefs. There Garuda is often associated with its enemy, the *naga* serpent. Giant figures of Garuda are seen on the walls of Preah Khan, and Vishnu is depicted riding Garuda in the brick temple of PRASAT KRAVAN at ANGKOR in Cambodia.

geomancy Geomancy, or feng shui, is the Chinese method for ascertaining whether a particular location is auspicious or favorable for a specified purpose, such as for the foundation of a city, a memorial, or a temple. The practitioner takes into account the obvious features of the terrain, such as hills to protect the proposed site from injurious winds or the presence of flat, well-aspected land. But he or she also absorbs less tangible variables of the spirit world, when, for example, considering the location of a place for interring the dead. The origins of geomancy are not known, but the layout of the royal SHANG STATE tombs at ANYANG, aligned precisely to true north, may well be an early example. Shao Gong Shi is regarded as the patron saint of geomancy. He was instructed by KING WU, founder of the Zhou dynasty, to identify a suitable central location for a new capital later to be established at the junction of the Luo, Jian, and Chan Rivers at what became the city of LUOYANG. Several examples of early geomantic compasses, or divining boards, which combine a square disk representing the Earth under a movable circular disk depicting the heavens, have been found in tombs dated to the HAN DYNASTY.

Ghazi Shah Ghazi Shah, located on an alluvial plain of the Naing Nai River, west of the main Indus Valley, was occupied during the Amrian phase and the INDUS VALLEY CIVILIZATION. It covers only two hectares (5 acres), but rises 11 meters (36 ft.) above the surrounding plain in Sind province, Pakistan. The original area occupied was no doubt larger, but the outlying parts of the site have probably been covered in recent alluvium. It was first identified as an important site by N. G. Majumdar in 1930, and limited excavations revealed its cultural affiliations, but little else of note. In 1985 L. Flam began an intensive research program there and uncovered an area for making beads of agate and LAPIS LAZULI. The radiocarbon dates for this activity fall in the second half of the fourth millennium B.C.E.

Flam's excavations covered a far larger area than those directed by Majumdar, and in an area of six by 9.5 meters, Flam encountered the foundations of houses, associated with Harappan-style pottery shards, and lapis lazuli and STEATITE beads, associated with radiocarbon dates in the fourth millennium B.C.E. Mud-brick structural foundations were also identified in the third area excavated. Finds included bull figurines and much evidence for chert working, including drills. Beads were also abundant here and were manufactured from lapis lazuli, copper, and shell, as well as carnelian and agate.

See also AMRI.

Ghosh, Amalananda (1910–1981) *Amalananda Ghosh was one of India's most distinguished archaeologists.*
He was educated at Allahabad University in India and the University of London and in 1937 joined the staff of the ARCHAEOLOGICAL SURVEY OF INDIA. He later became the director of the survey (1953–68) and was responsible for many key excavations, particularly at KALIBANGAN in the SARASVATI RIVER Valley, India.

Go Thap
Formerly known as Prasat Pram Loven, Go Thap in Vietnam has yielded an important inscription dating to the FUNAN state, in which a prince Gunavarman was designated to reign over a kingdom wrested from the mud. More recently, a settlement site with a mound covering one hectare (2.5 acres) has been excavated and eight burials uncovered. Brick-lined pits were found within a brick surrounding wall measuring seven by 10 meters (33 ft.). These pits are square and varied from 1.27 to 3.5 meters in depth. Each had in the center a central block of BRICK with a hollow space in the middle, which contained human ashes and mortuary goods. The eight burials yielded 322 gold leaves, five gold coins, three gold rings, a gold flower, eight precious stones, and seven pieces of glass. Gold objects included decoration in the form of human (deity) figures, a turtle, GARUDA, a water buffalo, elephants, snakes, conch shells, the sun, a house on piles, and plants. Many of these symbols relate to Hindu gods. Two radiocarbon dates from the site fall in the period 400–600 C.E., matching the date of Gunavarman's inscription. The site provides important evidence for a Funan religious foundation, adoption of Hindu gods and their symbols, and conversion from inhumation to a cremation mortuary ritual.

Great Lake
The Great Lake, or Tonle Sap, dominates the geography of northwest Cambodia. It is fed by numerous rivers flowing south from the KULEN HILLS and the Dang Raek range and other tributaries originating to the west and south, and it empties via the Tonle Sap River into the Mekong at Phnom Penh. During the rainy season, when the Mekong River is swollen not only by the monsoon rains but also by the spring melt of snow in its headwaters, the Tonle Sap River reverses its flow. Instead of draining the Great Lake, it backs up with floodwaters to fill the lake. At its greatest extent, the lake is 160 kilometers long by 50 kilometers (96 by 30 mi.) wide. The rise and fall of the lake level provide opportunities for cultivating rice by retaining the floodwater behind long dikes for an early dry-season planting. The rising water level is also compatible with the cultivation of rapidly growing floating rice, which can be harvested into boats. The Great Lake is also one of the most productive inland fisheries in the world and provides links by boat with the sea via the Mekong River.

The lake has attracted settlement from early prehistory. During the period of CHENLA kings (550–800 C.E.), there were numerous settlements and temples along its margins. King JAYAVARMAN II (c. 770–834 C.E.) of Cambodia chose the northern margins for the earliest capitals and temple pyramids and imbued the area with sacred connotations in which the Kulen Hills supplied holy water to the region of ANGKOR via the Siem Reap River.

Great Wall
See WALL, THE GREAT.

Guang Wudi (Liu Xiu; Shining Martial Emperor) (5 B.C.E.–57 C.E.) *was the first emperor of the Eastern Han dynasty of China.*
When he proclaimed himself emperor on 5 August 25 C.E., Guang Wudi was one of many claimants. The ensuing decade was dominated by military campaigns in virtually every quarter of the compass. After long and bitter civil strife, Guang Wudi adopted a conservative foreign policy, preferring to strengthen the defensive walls against the XIONGNU to the north. He also had to grapple with the major problems posed by the court factions on whom he ultimately depended for support. His Confucian principles encouraged him to found new training establishments from which young men emerged to staff an apolitical civil service, and he attempted to keep his hand close to important governmental decisions by limiting the number of major ministerial appointments.

XIN DYNASTY

In 9 C.E. WANG MANG, a leading member of the court of the Western Han dynasty and former regent, had declared himself the emperor of the Xin (New) dynasty. The official history of the Han dynasty accorded him a very poor press, largely because in failing to maintain the throne and found a new dynasty, he was thought to lack the MANDATE OF HEAVEN. In fact, Wang Mang made a series of courageous attempts to remedy the effects of years of mismanagement by reforming land tenure, currency, and state ownership of key industries, such as salt and iron. He was, however, faced with dire difficulties when the Huang (Yellow) River broke its dykes, leading to catastrophic floods and the threat of famine in one of the most densely populated parts of the empire. In Shandong, peasants rose up against the central authority; to distinguish themselves from the government troops, they painted their foreheads red. Known therefore as the RED EYEBROWS, this motley army scored a number of significant successes and encouraged members of the old royal clans to join the insurrection. In 23 C.E. Chang'an, the capital, was invested and taken. Wang Mang was decapitated and the city sacked. It was abandoned as the capital, and in due course LUOYANG to the east was chosen to replace it.

EASTERN HAN

Guang Wudi entered Luoyang on 27 November 25 C.E. to claim the throne. The new dynasty is generally known as the Eastern Han, and Guang Wudi was but one of many claimants to the throne. Western Han emperors had many lesser wives, resulting in legions of men who could claim royal ancestry. These aspirants were divided among a number of lineages determined through the female who had borne the children of an emperor. Guang Wudi (shining martial emperor) was a descendant of JINGDI, who had ruled more than 150 years previously.

Guang Wudi had to cope first with the remnants of the Red Eyebrows in Chang'an (Xi'an), where they had busied themselves looting the royal tombs of the Western Han. Then he moved on the rival claimants, warlords in Shandong and Gansu. Only when he had settled most of the old empire could he turn his attention to remote but rich Sichuan, where Gungsun Shu had proclaimed himself king of Shu and emperor. With Chengdu as his capital and the rich rice lands of the upper Chang (Yangtze) Valley at his disposal, the king of Shu was a formidable rival, but after a long and difficult campaign, Guang Wudi's forces surrounded the capital and in late 36 C.E. mortally wounded Gungsun Shu.

Guang Wudi turned his attention to the restoration of finances by restoring the old state monopolies on salt and iron and to formalize the taxation base by instituting a census and encouraged agriculture. However, the system of maintaining a harem of aristocratic women proved a means for the major families to seek power, and their factional strife continued to weaken the authority of successive Eastern Han emperors. Guang Wudi sired 10 sons, five by each of his successive empresses. Thus the heir apparent to Guang Wudi was changed as a result of such palace intrigues on behalf of the empress Lin Yihua.

See also CONFUCIUS.

Gumla   Gumla is a small (0.7 hectare; 1.75 acre) settlement in the Gomal Valley of Pakistan. Its importance lies in the long sequence of occupation documented during excavations by A. H. Dani, which showed the early agriculture here and the later development of the INDUS VALLEY CIVILIZATION. Six distinct phases of occupation have been described, beginning with the remains of a community that probably undertook agriculture but did not make pottery vessels. The remains include small stone implements and grinding stones for processing grains. This undated initial phase of occupation resembles other early agricultural contexts at sites like Kili Gul Mohammed and MEHRGARH in Pakistan. At the former site, similar remains date to between 5000 and 4000 B.C.E. During the second phase, pottery making was undertaken, together with the production of a range of artifacts that include human and animal figurines, bone tools, and evidence for copper casting. The third phase saw the production of ceramics that conform with the KOT DIJI phase of the Early Harappan. The earliest evidence of construction in mud brick was also encountered, and further copper implements were found. A conflagration marked the transition from the early to the later Kot Diji occupation of the site. Further evidence for construction in mud brick was encountered, and new artifacts included carnelian beads, stone weights, STEATITE beads, and LAPIS LAZULI. This phase corresponds to the occupation of the major cities of the Indus Valley civilization. It was followed by further evidence for destruction through fire.

Gunavarman (c. 500 C.E.) *Gunavarman was a ruler mentioned on an* INSCRIPTION *from* GO THAP *on the plain of reeds in Vietnam, a flat expanse on the northern margin of the Mekong Delta.*
The inscription, dated toward the end of the fifth century C.E., states that a ruler, probably named Jayavarman, had been victorious in battle. It further describes how Jayavarman founded many sanctuaries dedicated to Vishnu and placed his son, Gunavarman, in charge of one, which had been "wrested from the mud." This might be an allusion to the drainage of the Plain of Reeds where the inscription was set up to foster rice production. The text is one of the few dating to the period of the early delta trading state known as FUNAN.

See also JAYAVARMAN OF FUNAN.

Guo Chin Lun   The *Guo Chin Lun* (The faults of QIN) was an influential tract written by JIA YI (201–168 B.C.E.) during the early years of the Western HAN DYNASTY of China. It explored the reasons underlying the collapse of the Qin dynasty and urged a more humane approach to rule by the Han emperors, instead of the autocratic repression practiced by the first emperor, QIN SHIHUANGDI (259–210 B.C.E.), and his successor.

Guojiacun   Guojiacun is a site located on the Liaodong Peninsula of northeastern China. It is important as a prehistoric jade manufactory. In the third millennium B.C.E., artifacts of jade assumed considerable importance in Chinese rituals. Sites of the LONGSHAN and LIANGZHU CULTURES have furnished consistent evidence for a relationship between elite individuals and the possession of ritually important jade objects such as *bi* disks, *cong* tubes, and *yazhang* blades. Guojiacun is a contemporary of these sites, and manufacturing tools and half-finished objects have been found there. Objects of a jade matching that of Liaodong have been found in Longshan sites in Shandong province.

Gupta empire

The Gupta empire had its genesis under King Srigupta I (270–290 C.E.), who ruled one of the many small kingdoms in the Ganga (Ganges) Valley in India from his capital at PATALIPUTRA. He was succeeded by his son Ghatotkacha and then by his son Candragupta I (305–325). The empire he founded lasted for about three centuries. Its hallmark was a series of kings who combined military success with an interest in culture, science, literature, arts, and architecture and the welfare of the people. In this wealthy and peaceful empire, the sovereigns took the title Maharajadhiraja, "great king of kings." An inscription from Allahabad composed by Harisena on an Asokan column describes the military successes of SAMUDRAGUPTA (335–380), successor to Candragupta I, who defeated many rival kings and took his army south to southern Andhra Pradesh to incorporate fresh areas into the empire but who still had himself depicted on his gold coinage playing the lyre. He was a Hindu who performed the ritually significant horse-sacrifice ceremony. A particular feature of the rule of his successor, CANDRAGUPTA II (r. 380–413), is that the empire was visited by the Chinese Buddhist pilgrim FAXIAN, who left a description of his visit. He commented on the peace and prosperity he witnessed. There was no capital punishment, but the legal code could order a series of fines. Public works were often evident, such as the endowment of the Buddhist university at Nalanda, despite the rulers' preference for Hinduism. Indeed, the kings were referred to as "equal to the gods," including Indra and Varuna. However, the reign of Skandagupta, who died in about 467 C.E., was disturbed by the first of several irruptions of the Huns in India, and in 530–540 C.E. a dissident leader named Yashodharman rose to beat not only the Huns, but the Guptas themselves. His inscription at Mandasor claimed his sovereignty over much of India.

WEALTH AND TRADE

The period of the Gupta empire appears to have been one of wealth and prosperity. The kings issued high-quality COINAGE in gold, silver, and copper, which is found widely over the realm. This wealth was based on international trade as well as productive agriculture. After the decline of the Roman Empire, the Guptas looked increasingly to Southeast Asia for trading opportunities, and the presence of Indian merchants is in evidence over much of that area. IRRIGATION was widespread in India, and there is evidence for state assistance in its provision. Industries were ordered on the basis of self-perpetuating guilds, who often owned their own assets in the form of trust funds. There were, for example, guilds of bankers, silk weavers, and oil pressers. State revenues were raised on the strength of a tax on agricultural and industrial production and on land. Salt, for example, was subject to a sales tax.

BUREAUCRACY

This system required a large bureaucracy. Civil departments were administered by *mantri*. Foreign affairs, including trade, were under the control of the *sandhivigrahika*. There were at least three ranks of military command, the *mahabaladhikrta, mahadandanayaka,* and *senapati*. The army itself was made up of cavalry, the elephant corps, and the infantry. There were also lesser officials, local boards, and a *nagarasresthin,* which assisted in governing rural communities.

ARCHITECTURE

In harmony with the civil order and wealth of the Guptas, their rule witnessed the initiation of major developments in Indian temple architecture. These took the form of a square or rectangular sacred chapel with a porch or covered walkway around it. Some forms have a low tower above the temple; others are circular. Notable examples are the Kapotesvara temple at Cezarla, dated to the fourth century C.E., and the Durga temple at Aihole. The Bhitargaon temple in Kanpur was constructed in brick. As befitted such temples, Gupta sculpture of deities also flourished, particularly in the SARNATH school. The gods were shown in various poses, such as the Buddha's attaining knowledge or imparting wisdom.

THE ARTS AND SCIENCES

Painting also flourished in the Gupta empire. This is clearly seen in the murals of the AJANTA caves in Maharashtra, with their landscapes, depictions of buildings, and splendidly attired people. Poetry was encouraged, and the works of Kalidasa, who lived during the reign of Vikramaditya, remain prominent in the SANSKRIT repertoire. The astronomer Aryabhatta in 499 C.E. calculated the value of pi and the length of the solar year as 365.358 days. More than a millennium before Galileo, he also proposed that the Earth rotated on its own axis and revolved around the Sun.

Further reading: Mookerji, R. K. *Gupta Empire.* Delhi: Motilal Banarsidass, 1995; Williams, J. G. *The Art of Gupta India: Empire and Province.* Princeton, N.J.: Princeton University Press, 1982.

H

Halin Halin is a city of the PYU CIVILIZATION of modern Myanmar (Burma). It is located in the valley of the Mu River, south of the modern town of Shwebo, an area that receives only about 750 millimeters (30 in.) of rainfall per year. The Mu River is a major tributary of the Irrawaddy. Tradition has it that the city was founded by an Indian prince. Of subrectangular form, the BRICK walls enclose an area of about 500 hectares (1,250 acres) and are surrounded by a moat. There are 12 gateways demarcated by inward-sloping walls. Radiocarbon dates for the charred gateposts suggest that they belong to the second or third century C.E. As at BEIKTHANO, there is an inner walled citadel. Excavations took place in 1904–5, in 1929–30, and again in 1962–67. Several square or rectangular brick structures were found to contain burial urns for the cremated dead. It was not, however, unusual to find extended inhumation burials as well, a survival from the prehistoric past. Site 9 included a brick hall incorporating 84 wooden columns to support the roof, perhaps an assembly or meeting hall. Unlike Beikthano, several INSCRIPTIONS have been found. One, inscribed in the Pyu language, records the burial of a high-status person called Ru-ba. A second contains eight lines of Pyu and mentions a queen Jatrajiku. Another text cannot be read, but it lies above a carved panel showing three rows of worshipers wearing elaborate headdresses, necklaces, and ear ornaments. A fourth inscription, also in the little-known Pyu language but employing an Indian script datable to the eighth or ninth century, mentions a person named Sri Trivigrama. A small agate SEAL also bore the name Dayadanam and employed a South Indian script dating to the fifth century C.E. Other finds showed skill in working iron and bronze. There was also a monumental aspect to the city architecture, for the *New History of the Tang Dynasty* describes a "great white image, over 30 meters (99 ft.) high, opposite the gate to the palace." A surviving base to a statue incorporates rows of worshipers, each wearing fine jewelry and a headdress.

Some of the artifacts found during the excavations reveal skill in iron forging and the role played by this metal: There are knives and arrowheads, as well as caltrops, spiked implements to counter enemy cavalry. These were concentrated outside the city gates. Gold working was obviously undertaken, and rings, pendants, and beads have been recovered. Bronze mirrors have also been found. The Halin coins bear an image of the sunburst or, rarely, the *srivatsa* a motif derived from the mother goddess.

The burial rituals at Halin involved cremation and the interment of the dead in ceramic jars placed in brick buildings beyond the city walls. Grave goods include gold rings, flowers, gold and silver leaves with writing, coins, and iron artifacts. One such offering was a six-sided plate of iron studded with rows of nails. A series of large reservoirs are found to the east, west, and south of the city, the IRRIGATION system of which incorporated the long Muhaung Canal. Janice Stargardt has reconstructed a complex system of water distribution involving about 300 square kilometers (120 sq. mi.) of land. The city was destroyed during the ninth century C.E.

See also COINAGE; SEALS.

Han dynasty The Han dynasty was founded in 206 B.C.E. and lasted until 220 C.E. It was a period of immense importance in the development of Chinese civilization and the Chinese empire, generating changes that are still an essential part of the fabric of China. The fact that the Han dynasty created relative peace and prosperity in

China for four centuries, after an equally long period of internecine strife, is a testament to the adroit manner in which the administration knitted together the fabric of the empire. Its rulers established many innovations that continued after the end of the Eastern Han rule. They established a central mint and the means to collect broadly based taxation. They invested in the infrastructure of agriculture and transport and organized the production of iron for a wide range of purposes. Their system of selection for the civil service has stood the test of time in many other states, and through aristocratic patronage the arts and literature flourished. The Han dynasty also saw China expand to frontiers still recognizable in the political map of East Asia.

GENESIS OF THE HAN DYNASTY

The genesis of the Han dynasty can be appreciated only in the context of events that took place during the preceding centuries. From 475 until 221 B.C.E., the country was split by deadly wars among seven great states. This took place at a time when iron was first available in quantity, which contributed to a marked acceleration in the power of the armies and the totalitarian nature of warfare. This period, which falls in the last few centuries of the EASTERN ZHOU DYNASTY, is known as the WARRING STATES PERIOD.

One by one, the states fell to the all-conquering state of QIN, which was centered in the Wei Valley. By 221 B.C.E., the king of Qin had defeated all his rivals and was proclaimed the emperor of China with the name QIN SHIHUANGDI (259–210 B.C.E.). Although he ruled for only 11 years, he instituted sweeping reforms. He was described by a member of his court as having "the proboscis of a hornet, the chest of a bird of prey, the voice of a jackal, and the heart of a tiger or a wolf." As King Zheng of Qin, he had acceded to the throne at the early age of 13. He was a rigorous and determined man, influenced toward legalist policies by his minister, Li Si. His first task was to convert a series of defeated rivals into a single empire, and this he achieved through ruthless centralization. Thus he built for himself a gigantic palace at his capital XIANYANG, but also had replicas of the palaces of his former rivals constructed there and required the defeated royal families to move to his capital so that he could keep them under surveillance. He had literature he regarded as being subversive burned, a list of texts that included some of the great classics by such authors as CONFUCIUS and MENCIUS. He standardized the script, currency, and weights and measures. Whole groups of people were moved from one part of the empire to another, and many conscripts ended up on the construction of the GREAT WALL in the north, to consolidate the frontier against the XIONGNU. Others were taken to Xianyang to work on the construction of his colossal tomb complex, now famous for its terra-cotta army of subterranean soldiers.

In 210 B.C.E., the first emperor of China was succeeded by his son, Prince Hu Hai. As Er Shi (230–207 B.C.E.), the second emperor, he lacked the resolve and energy of this father, and the empire was soon simmering with discontent. He was ultimately forced into suicide by his dominating minister, the eunuch ZHAO GAO. By now, the empire was daily disintegrating, as uprisings threatened the very existence of the Qin state itself.

One of the leaders of the various rebellions was a peasant known as Liu Bang. Another was Xiang Yu, an aristocrat from the former state of CHU. Liu Bang was the first to reach the capital, and King Ziying, who had been installed on the throne of Qin only 46 days previously by the manipulative Zhao Gao, capitulated. Unusually for the age, Liu Bang spared the Qin royal family and had the palace and royal tomb protected from looting and destruction. Xiang Yu, however, soon arrived on the scene and reversed this policy. The family was slaughtered and the great capital razed. Although the tomb of Qin Shihuangdi awaits excavation, it was probably at this juncture that it was opened and looted. Xiang Yu had Liu Bang rusticated to a remote kingdom of Han in the far west and set about restoring the old feudal system with its independent states. Liu Bang, however, was resolved to maintain the empire so recently created and led his army to the center. By 202 B.C.E., he had defeated the forces of Xiang Yu and, with the widely acknowledged MANDATE OF HEAVEN, was proclaimed Emperor GAOZU (247–195 B.C.E.), the first emperor of the Han dynasty. His new capital was at CHANG'AN.

FOUR CENTURIES OF HAN RULE

The Han dynasty was able to maintain central rule over China for the ensuing four centuries, and under some rulers, particularly WUDI (141–87 B.C.E.), it extended the frontiers to incorporate areas ruled by non-Chinese peoples. In the south, for example, Wudi incorporated forcibly the so-called Yue tribes. The Dian were a warlike tribe living in the vicinity of Lake Dian in Yunnan province. Given to frequent battles with their neighbors and relishing head-hunting, they were incorporated as a province or commandery. This policy also saw Han armies enter what is now Vietnam, as far as the Truong Son Cordillera. These mountains, known as the Fortress of the Sky to the Han, were the southern boundary of their empire. To the northwest, the Han expanded their hold on the Gansu Corridor to modern Dunhuang and periodically also controlled the small states that ringed the TARIM BASIN. By this means, they greatly expanded the lucrative trade along the SILK ROAD. Han watchtowers and agricultural settlements that had been peopled by veteran soldiers can still be seen in the remote northwest. The Han also expanded into the Korean Peninsula to the northeast and confirmed their hold over client rulers by giving them gold SEALS of authority. Some of these have been found through archaeological investigations.

There were also, ho wever, periods of chronic weakness that are best understood through the problems that beset the maintenance of a powerful central administration. Essentially, the Han dynasty falls into two approximate halves, with a so-called interregnum between 9 and 23 C.E. The earlier is known as the Western Han dynasty and the latter as the Eastern Han. These names reflect the location of the capital: After a long sojourn at Chang'an, the Eastern Han moved the capital eastward to LUOYANG. The period of the interregnum saw a ruler known as WANG MANG, the former regent, take power and establish his own, short-lived XIN, or new DYNASTY. Wang Mang's brief rule ended with a long and bitter civil war before Liu Xiu triumphed and founded the Eastern Han with the regnal name GUANG WUDI (shining martial emperor) in 25 C.E. This period of Han dominance lasted through the reigns of 12 emperors until 220 C.E., when a further period of civil strife saw the foundation of three kingdoms, known as Wei, Wu, and Shu Han.

The inheritance of an empire with an administration based on legalist principles posed a unique series of logistical challenges to the Han elite. It is self-evident that powerful former states, despite the upheavals under the Qin dynasty, would have harbored resentment and a desire for renewed independence. Under the Han, the notion of the commandery, or province, under central administration continued, but there were also some states ruled by centrally appointed kings, kings who usually belonged to the Han royal line.

Providing Administrators for the Empire

One of the first problems faced by the new imperial system was the supply of good and able administrators, men with loyalty to the crown rather than local interests. The HANSHU (*History of the Former Han*), is an essential source of information on the administrative procedures, although there may well have been gaps between theory and practice. The most important innovation of the Western Han was the establishment of a central training institution for promising candidates. Provincial governors were required to recommend able students, who were then sent to Chang'an for vetting through an examination on matters of topical importance, history, and philosophy. This system was the basis from which all future selection procedures in China developed. Officially it was open to all corners, but in practice merchants were excluded from consideration. The qualities of those selected were described in successive edicts and included men who were morally good and deemed to be capable, who spoke frankly and fearlessly, and who were sincere and talented. The selection for potential employment was made by a range of officials, from central bureaucrats down to officials in the commanderies and prefectures. The successful candidates were graded on the basis of their examination results into three groups and then underwent a training program under scholars versed in the Confucian ethic of

government before being given posts in the bureaucracy. Their work usually began with duties in the capital, but appointments to the commanderies then followed. In theory, promising young men, particularly those skilled in mathematics or industry, could progress from relatively humble beginnings to occupy the most powerful positions of state. Under the reign of Emperor Wudi (141–87 B.C.E.), an actual academy was founded with a staff of experienced mentors, known as the Tai Xue. The civil service incorporated between 18 and 20 grades, each receiving different amounts of grain as salary. In effect, payment was made in kind and cash, and on retirement those with a good record could expect a pension for life. The *Hanshu* recorded that toward the end of the Western Han dynasty there were 120,285 officials in the administration.

Naturally, very few appointees aspired to top positions in the hierarchy. Annual reports were required, and these determined progression through the ranks. However, the system was open to nepotism and cronyism despite the theoretically fair method of preferment. Again, it was toward the end of the long reign of Emperor Wudi that changes were made to develop the power of a so-called inner court, staffed by close associates of the emperor, who made the key decisions affecting the state. These were enacted by the secretariat, staffed largely by eunuchs who steadily grew in power and influence. In this lay the seeds of future problems. On the one hand, the eunuch administrators increased their hold on government, but on the other, there were numerous aristocratic families related to the empress or favorite concubines who vied for ascendance and opportunities for enrichment. For the aristocrats the chances of increasing their influence were greatly increased when a young emperor entailed a regency. There were, therefore, sequences of such child rulers that weakened both the Western and Eastern Han dynasties.

Government Bureaucracy

The governmental machine was headed by three senior statesmen, whose titles can be translated as chancellor, imperial counselor, and commander of the armed forces. The last post was rarely filled, because individual campaigns, as against the Xiongnu, were led by specific appointees. The first two posts were filled by those close to the emperor who could formulate policy at the highest level. Below them were nine ministries, each with its own extensive staff. One such ministry had the duty to record the emperor's actions and thus developed the role of official historian. Another was charged with control over divination and astrology, matters vital since the earliest Chinese dynasties of Shang and Zhou. There were ministries to oversee royal security and for the emperor's transportation. One minister was responsible for receiving and housing foreign delegations. This function was important particularly when the delegation involved powerful border peoples, such as the Xiongnu. The embassies often presented exotic gifts that had to be recorded and safeguarded, as when they included live animals, such as an exotic rhinoceros from the south. The provision of legal services was under the authority of one of the nine ministries, and this often entailed appeals from the provinces or visits from the capital to investigate unusual cases. Another ministry was in charge of recording the history and membership of the royal clan. This was a vital task that ordered precedence. As most adult emperors had several official consorts and many children, this ministry kept track of descendants and was called on when the succession was not clearly apparent. Thus during the last few reigns of the Eastern Han, the emperors ZHIDI (138–146) and HUANDI (132–168) were chosen in part because they were the great-great-grandsons of ZHANGDI, who had died in 88 C.E.

One of the most important ministries oversaw finance and the management of the economy. From 120 B.C.E., when it was resolved to nationalize key industries, this ministry also supervised the production and marketing of iron, salt, and alcohol products. Its officials collected tax revenues, often in kind, and paid the bureaucrats. The lower treasury worked in a supplementary role, collecting tax payments for less central industries, as well as controlling the royal workshops and the provision of music. Security in the capital beyond the immediate confines of the royal palace was the responsibility of a senior official, whose title translates as "bearer of the gilded mace." His officers, acting as policemen, were sent to patrol the city, and he also had charge of the arsenal.

The commandant of waters and parks was an office created in 115 B.C.E. His officials were numerous, and among other duties, he ensured the maintenance of royal parks, the provision of food for the royal table, and the building and maintenance of the pavilions that dotted the extensive pleasure gardens. The prefect of the stables ensured that the emperor's horses were well cared for. The host of orderlies employed in this office also manned the royal boats and cared for the water fountains and canals. In 115 B.C.E., the commandant of waters and parks was also placed in charge of the royal mint. With the Eastern Han dynasty and the move to Luoyang, this department was abolished. The Han center saw many major building projects, particularly palaces and royal parks and pavilions, and this program entailed a department of architects. This department was charged with many important duties. It was responsible for the design and building of palaces and the maintenance of the royal tombs. Its officials planted roadside trees and were active in repairing the dikes after serious flooding. Each of these ministries incorporated subsidiary offices. Thus the authorities in charge of the building program also had to identify and control sources of construction materials. There were prefects in charge of supplying large lengths of timber, and for quarrying stone.

The marked hierarchy in the administration, in which bureaucrats were ranked according to their salaries expressed as annual payment in bushels of grain, was also applied to that powerful institution the royal harem. WOMEN of high birth, unimpeachable personal life, and great beauty were carefully selected for admission. During the Western Han dynasty, the number of harem women rose to about 3,000, and the ranks increased progressively from six to as many as 14. Salaries matched each lady's rank, which began at the top with the so-called brilliant companion and ended at the bottom with six maids with such titles as "pleasing maid" and "night attendant." The most highly ranked ladies attracted salaries equivalent to those of the top bureaucrats. With the Eastern Han, only three grades were recognized, but the number of ladies doubled to about 6,000. The presence of so many attractive women in the household encouraged the employment of eunuchs.

Eunuchs also attended on the court of the empress. As many child or infant emperors were enthroned, the dowager empresses and their families wielded much power and in many cases, attracted such envy that they suffered virtual extinction. Each dowager empress had her own residence, known as the Palace of Prolonged Autumn, and a substantial staff. One was known as the prefect of the stables and would have been in charge of the chariots. Others supervised the provision of food, ran her treasury and accounts, and oversaw the pharmacy.

Provincial and Central Government

The interaction between the central administration and the provinces provides a fascinating insight into the means whereby a new imperial structure was devised and implemented. The reins of government, central and provincial, were also adjusted with time as problems, possibilities, or improvements arose. The land beyond the capital territory was divided into two forms of administrative units. The first was known as the *jun*, "commandery" or "province." The second was the *wang guo*, "kingdom." Commanderies were established under the Qin to replace the old warring states, but the institution of *jun* began under earlier kingdoms as a means of ruling outlying areas through trusted central appointees. The kingdoms under the Han were essentially a means of placing or rewarding members of the royal clan. However, they were not in any sense independent, since the client kings were required to present themselves at court annually to provide details of the previous year's administration and were forbidden to deploy armed forces without the express permission of Chang'an. Moreover, the emperor was empowered to determine the succession in the dependent kingdoms. Over time, the number and area under the control of commanderies increased at the expense of the kingdoms. There were, for example, 15 commanderies at the beginning of the Western Han dynasty, and 83 at the end.

The commanderies were administered by a *jun shou,* "governor." This title changed in 148 B.C.E. to *tai shou,* "grand administrator." He was ultimately responsible for the civil and military affairs of his commandery, and he directed a large bureaucracy whose duties varied with location. Thus, in areas threatened by exterior attack, there was a person in charge of horses and the supply of weapons. There were also bureaus that had specific duties. The *Hanshu* mentions a range of such institutions, whose functions included legal administration, suppression of banditry and maintenance of security, agriculture, and, in the remote northwestern new commanderies, responsibility for the self-sufficiency of agricultural colonies. There is mention of literary scholars and authorities on ancient matters, whose titles suggest that they were required to ensure the proper application of Confucian ethics. It is also recorded that the scholars ensured that proper legal proceedings were followed.

The central regulations on the monopolies on salt, iron, and liquor were under the control of a grand minister, but the implementation changed from one of central control under the Western Han to local direction with the Eastern Han. During the latter period, there were commandery officials in charge of iron and others for the office of salt. These well-staffed agencies oversaw the production and marketing of these commodities and the extraction of taxation revenue. The central court required a considerable income, and commanderies and kingdoms had agencies for the collection of dues from fishermen and the producers of gold and timber. Other agencies, for overseeing tax collection from workmen, orangeries, orchards, cloth manufacture, lakes, towered warships, and even the production of crossbows, are mentioned. The collection of revenue was a major preoccupation of the commandery administration.

The Bureau of Households was responsible for undertaking censuses. This provided essential information for taxation purposes, and the results offer a rare opportunity to appreciate the distribution of population in an early state and its changes over time. Thus there was a marked concentration of people in the Huang (Yellow) River Valley compared with the south, but over time this changed, perhaps as a result of flooding in the north and the danger of attack from the northwest.

The Bureau of Merit was the local channel for identifying promising candidates for preferment or sending them to the capital for examination and training before entry into the government service. The Bureau of Command was responsible for organizing corvée or convict labor for government construction projects, such as the Great Wall, canals, dikes, and roads. The Bureau of Markets oversaw the collection of revenue from traders. Not all commanderies had a complete set of bureaus, and some were formed to meet specific local conditions. Along the course of the Huang River, for example, it was essential to have a bureau in charge of dikes.

The important role of the administrator is well illustrated by the career of Xin Zhen, who was placed in charge of Nan Yang commandery in the second half of the first century B.C.E. This is a large commandery, located south of the capital in southwestern Henan province. According to contemporary accounts, he zealously toured his commandery, always seeking ways and means of improving agricultural production and creating wealth for rural communities. He had reservoirs, canals, dikes, and ditches dug to store and distribute water. Two of his major projects saw the completion of the Jian-li and Liu-men reservoirs. He then had stone inscriptions set up at key points in his IRRIGATION network to establish rules for the fair distribution of water. His success in improving the production and wealth of the farmers was recognized by an official inspector, and he was promoted to another commandery and given 40 catties (a weight) of gold. The degree of autonomy exercised by local grand commanders is well illustrated by the career of Ma Leng, who was placed in charge of Guang Ling commandery in 87 C.E. He found the people starving and suffering from high taxation. He initiated moves to have the local and onerous office of salt abolished and lowered taxes. Then he restored reservoirs and irrigation facilities, giving relief to the farmers. His staff erected a stone inscription recording his assistance.

The commanderies themselves were divided into prefectures (*XIAN*), districts, and communes. In 2 C.E., there were 1,577 prefectures in the empire, 6,622 districts, and 29,635 communes. The prefectures were administered by a prefect or a chief, depending on the size of the population. These were the lowest class of officials to be centrally appointed. They had their own bureaus and staff to handle local affairs, such as revenue collection and administration of markets, and there was also a commandant or chief of police. Contemporary documents also note that some prefects maintained schools. In 205 B.C.E., the emperor GAOZU, founder of the Western Han dynasty, decreed that the leaders of districts, titled the thrice venerable, should be aged older than 50 years. One of their tasks was to identify worthy or meritorious local people and have plaques commemorating their achievement placed on their residences. The communes were under the charge of a headman, or father of the commune, one of whose responsibilities was to oversee the local postal service. Prefectures could be assigned to the sisters of the daughters of emperors, while the daughters of kings were provided with communes or districts for their maintenance.

The Han administrative system also incorporated *wang guo,* "kingdom." Initially, these were ruled by the sons of the emperor and were granted a considerable measure of independence aside from the maintenance of an army. However, their very presence contained the seeds of possible dissension, and this became a reality with the rebellion of the seven kingdoms in 154 B.C.E.

Thereafter, the independence of the kings was severely curtailed. No longer able to raise their own revenue, the kings received a state salary, and the appointment of their staffs was also taken over by the court. In this way, the title became increasingly honorific, and kingdoms began to resemble commanderies in all but name. Specified lands were also provided to the nephews or grandsons of the emperor, who were given the title *lie hou,* "marquis." These aristocrats were awarded prefectures but had no effective power in their lands and received both retainers and an income from the court. The wealth of some marquises can be judged from their opulent burials.

THE HAN ARMY

The territorial expansion of the Western Han, notably under Emperor Wudi, placed considerable stress on the maintenance of the army. In the first place, military force was deployed to take new territory, particularly in the northwest, where huge tracts were occupied beyond the Jade Gates into the Tarim Basin. To the south, the Han empire was extended as far as the rich Hong (Red) River Basin in Vietnam, and colonization also extended into the Korean Peninsula. Thereafter, it was necessary to provide for frontier defense, particularly along the extended Great Wall, where the Xiongnu were a constant threat. There was also a problem of security within the empire itself, newly founded after the long Warring States period, for provincial discontent and uprisings, such as those of the Red Eyebrows and the YELLOW TURBANS, were always possible.

To provide for the army, military conscription was compulsory except for top aristocrats and, on occasion, those who could afford to buy exemption. At the age of 23, men underwent a year of military training in their home commandery, in the infantry, cavalry, or navy. Then they were posted for another year to active service, which could involve guard duties at the capital or frontier defense. Thereafter, they could return home but remained in a state of readiness for recall. Under the Western Han, they were required to return regularly for further training until they reached the age of 56. There was also the so-called Northern Army, a force of regulars under five commanders who served as guards of the capital and of the passes leading into the heartland of the empire, the Wei Valley. This force numbered about 3,500 men. If war threatened, as, for example, with Xiongnu incursions in the north, the militia reserve could be called up and deployed. Militia units were also assembled in the event of internal threats to security. With the Yellow Turban uprising of 184 C.E., there was a major mobilization appointment of a military commander with the title general of chariots and cavalry.

The growing administrative machine and maintenance of a standing army, not to mention the need to conscript young men into military training, placed major demands on agricultural production. An efficient rural sector and the ability to gather taxes were essential for the survival of the state.

HAN FOREIGN RELATIONS

The establishment of an empire, territorial expansion under Wudi, and the growth of long-distance trade relationships opened China to a new and wide range of contacts with foreigners. This even extended to Rome, whose empire was growing at the same time far to the west. It is recorded, for example, that a group of Romans claiming to be from the court of An-tun reached Luoyang in 166 C.E. This may well have been the Chinese transcription of the name of the Roman emperor Marcus Aurelius. The most immediate and persistent issue in Han foreign relations, however, centered on the Xiongnu, the confederation of tribes who occupied the steppes to the northwest of the Great Wall. The name *Xiongnu* is Chinese and means "fierce slave." The actual name used by the Xiongnu themselves is not known.

No sooner had he established himself on the throne as emperor than Gaodi faced a major challenge from the Xiongnu, for in 209 B.C.E., a new and dynamic leader, or *shanyu,* had emerged, named MAODUN (r. 209–174 B.C.E.). He won over rival tribal groups and expanded his territory to include the strategic Gansu Corridor that leads to the heart of China. His presence and his establishment of a capital at Lung Cheng in Outer Mongolia had the effect of attracting Chinese dissidents, particularly those who had suffered under the establishment of the Qin and Han empires. The list even included the king of the former state of Han. This Gaodi chose not to ignore, and in 200 B.C.E. he mounted a massive punitive expedition, which he led in person. At Pingcheng, his army was surrounded for a week by the Xiongnu cavalry, and only by good fortune did the emperor extricate himself. Clearly, the Xiongnu were not going to be easily defeated, and a diplomatic solution was sought. This involved a treaty, in which it was agreed to send a Chinese royal princess as a wife to the Xiongnu leader, provide gifts of silk and food, recognize the equality of the Han and the Xiongnu states, and agree on the frontier line of the Great Wall.

This treaty was renewed with each new emperor, at which point a further princess would be sent to the Xiongnu, with increasingly expensive gifts that included pieces of gold. The increasing quantity of gifts is a measure of the regard of the Han for the disruptive power of the Xiongnu. Indeed, before his death in 174 B.C.E., Maodun's demands steadily increased. He was succeeded by his son, Ji-zhu (r. 174–160 B.C.E.), who is named in the official histories as Lao-shang and then Jun-chen. Until 134 C.E., there was an uneasy relationship in which the Chinese adopted a policy of bribery and appeasement, while the Xiongnu mounted incursions beyond the frontier at will, even reaching close to the Han court. Under the emperor Wudi, however, there was a major change in policy. In 127 B.C.E., his general Wei Qing led a successful campaign against the Xiongnu, who were forced to retreat from the frontier. Six years later, the Han forces again defeated them. Despite almost insurmountable problems of food supply in these remote regions, a further campaign in 119 B.C.E. again scattered the Xiongnu, and the Han were able to establish themselves in new commanderies across the western regions.

The Han dominance thereafter had much to do with the fragmentation of the Xiongnu confederacy into factional kingdoms, whose rulers ceased to acknowledge the supremacy of the *shanyu*. There was also the problem so often faced by the Han themselves, that the Xiongnu succession was formally passed from father to son. This opened the possibility of succession of a very young ruler; the *shanyu* Hu Hanye (r. 58–31 B.C.E.) decree that the leader should be succeeded by his younger brother protected the succession. However, between the victories under Wudi and the end of the Western Han dynasty, repeated efforts by the fragmented Xiongnu to negotiate a renewal of the treaty on the basis of equality foundered, because the Han insisted on the formalization of a client relationship in which the Xiongnu acknowledged a vassal status.

In 52–51 B.C.E. Hu Hanye decided to acknowledge Han by sending his son as a hostage and settling on Han terms. He went to offer obeisance to the emperor. Treated with honor, he received five kilograms (11 lbs.) of gold, 200,000 cash, 77 suits of clothes, 8,000 bales of silk fabric, and 1,500 kilograms (3,300 lbs.) of silk floss. Further homage was offered in 49 and 36 B.C.E., accompanied by an increased quantity of gifts. Again, in 1 B.C.E. 30,000 bales of silk fabric was given. This acknowledged client status ended with the Wang Mang interregnum. During the civil wars that preceded the establishment of the Eastern Han, the Xiongnu leader Yu reasserted his independence, but this move was short lived because of internal divisions leading to the establishment of two groups of Xiongnu, the northern and the southern. By 50 C.E., the latter, now under Bi, again accepted client status in return for fine gifts and an official imperial golden seal. The Southern Xiongnu were now provided with annual gifts in return for peace and subservience. They were even encouraged to settle south of the wall and underwent a gradual process of assimilation into Chinese culture, accelerated by the regular rotation of Xiongnu princes for periods in the Han court. This vital buffer insulated China from the Northern Xiongnu, who lived beyond the pale of civilization.

Control over the Xiongnu was necessary not only to protect China from invasion, but also to provide access to the Silk Road. With a compliant Xiongnu and military successes over the semi-independent states of the TURPAN and Tarim Basins, trade burgeoned. In 60 B.C.E., the Han court created a new office, known as the protector-general of the western regions. The process of Han expansion involved the settlement of agricultural colonies, the construction of roads, and the extension of the Great Wall as far west as DUNHUANG. Again, Han weakness during the interregnum of Wang Mang and the tribulations that followed led to a slackening of control over the western regions; control was reasserted only in 73 C.E. and the following years with military intervention. The relations between the Han and the states of the Silk Road were cemented by the dispatch of gold and silk as gifts and the return of tribute missions bearing jade and wine and leading FERGHANA horses.

The Han were also actively engaged in imperial expansion to the south and southwest. While the local tribes never posed the same threat as the Xiongnu, they were fiercely independent, accustomed to fighting one another, and controlled by powerful chiefs. SIMA QIAN, the great Han historian, devoted a chapter to describing the Han conquest of these areas. He noted, for example, that the YELANG and DIAN people wore their hair in a bun, lived in fixed settlements, and cultivated fields, while the Kunming had plaited hair and adopted a pastoral life with no large settlements or chiefs. These descriptions have been confirmed by archaeological excavations at such Dian sites as SHIZHAISHAN and LIJIASHAN. Han policy was to appoint the local chiefs as rulers of newly formed Han commanderies, with gold seals of office for the leaders of Yelang and Dian. One such seal has been recovered from a royal grave at Shizhaishan in Yunnan. Persuasive gifts were offered, including silk and mirrors. Local rebellions were harshly punished, and Chinese officials were dispatched to assist in the administration of these newly won tribal areas.

In the northeast, the Han expanded into the Korean Peninsula. Already during the Warring States period in the late fourth century B.C.E., trade contacts with Korea grew, as is seen in the number of coins that found their way into the peninsula from the northeastern kingdom of Yen. During the Qin and early Western Han, it is said that a Chinese nobleman called Weiman founded a kingdom with a capital at Wangxian, near modern Pyongyang. In 109 B.C.E., under Emperor Wudi, it was claimed that the kingdom of Weiman was acting as a magnet for deserters from China, and this was used as an excuse for a military campaign into Chaoxian, the name given to the northern part of the Korean Peninsula. The grandson of Weiman was defeated, and five new commanderies were established. Two of these survived only until 82 B.C.E. Within the remaining three, known as LELANG, Liaodong, and Xuantu, the typical commandery structure was put in place. Archaeologically, this move can be documented by Han-style brick tombs with Chinese mortuary offerings, a trend that is precisely matched in the contemporary settlement of the Hong River Delta in northern Vietnam. With the Wang Mang interregnum and the civil wars leading to the establishment of the Eastern Han dynasty, Chinese control over the Korean commanderies slackened, and the populace suffered from attacks by the newly formed state of KOGURYO.

ADVANCES IN AGRICULTURE

The Han empire succeeded a long period of war between competing states, wars that absorbed much energy and population loss or movement. The dominant aspects of agriculture throughout Han rule were the growth in population and the pressures that this posed on the agricultural sector. Han administrators were well aware of the basic importance of agricultural production and took many steps to alleviate hardship and improve productivity. Fortunately, this interest in rural affairs involved censuses, so we have some detailed information on the population numbers over time in a number of marquisates. The population of China in 2 C.E. reveals a marked density in the Huang River Valley, the Wei Valley, and Sichuan. The Chang (Yangtze) River Basin was relatively thinly peopled, other than in the lower reaches. Yangdu marquisate was located in the lower valley of the Huang River. Between 201 and 155 B.C.E., the population rose from 7,800 to 17,000 households. The nearby marquisate of Zhuzhao in Guangbing commandery had one of the highest recorded population spurts in the same period, from 4,000 to 18,000 households. The pressure on good land under the stress of a rising population meant that land near the capital cost a hundred times more than that in remote border commanderies. Draught or flooding could exacerbate this growing problem and foster social unrest, with crowds of hungry peasants wandering the countryside, as seen in the rise of the Red Eyebrows movement in Shandong.

The government adopted several policies to cope with the growing number of people and the need to encourage agricultural production. In 163 B.C.E., Emperor Wendi issued an edict, On the Primacy of Agriculture. He noted the recent run of bad harvests and inquired about their causes. Was it that the ancestors were displeased, or was too much grain being fed to animals or used to make wine? Was it the flooding or pestilence? Are too many farmers turning to trade to make a living? He decided to authorize the sale of court ranks and to commute penalties on the payment of grain. This policy evidently met with considerable success.

Other policies were deeply embedded in foreign affairs, the organization of industry, and the administrative structure of the commanderies. In terms of foreign policy, the Han were constantly harassed by the problem of the Xiongnu, the warlike nomadic pastoralists of Mongolia, who, under their leader Maodun, achieved sufficient unity to invade China. As early as 178 B.C.E. the Han adviser Zhao Zuo identified a way of solving two problems by urging the settlement of farmers from the overpopulated center on the northern border regions as a bulwark against incursions. There were incentives for people to move. Land was provided, housing was constructed, and there were tax remissions and medical facilities. In 119 B.C.E. this policy was intensified after a serious flooding of the Huang River, when more than 700,000 people were moved to the northern frontier region. This move was made possible by the system of land tenure, whereby the emperor owned all land that was not demonstrably in private hands. This permitted land to be made available to indigent peasants at a time when large private estates were calling on serf or slave labor. Several land grants were made during the first century B.C.E., but this property was often let rather than given. The situation came to a head under the rule of Wang Mang, when he grasped the nettle and nationalized all land. This policy, however, lasted for only three years and created a chaotic situation. The population problem was also to a certain extent alleviated by a steady drift from the colder north to the south and into the area where rice replaced millet as the staple.

Any growth in rice cultivation entailed the issue of water supply. Whereas millet can flourish within the variations in natural rainfall, rice is a marsh grass that must be anchored in a wet field. Indeed, rice derives much of its energy from the nitrogen-fixing algae that proliferate in warm, gently flowing water. Any expansion of land under rice cultivation must therefore take into consideration the supply of water, and in China this situation was resolved by the provision of irrigation facilities. These included dams, canals, and runnels to carry water to the rice plots. During the period of Warring States, there had been some limited irrigation development, but the expansion of irrigation networks during the Han dynasty was dramatic. There were also large programs of water control in the Huang River Valley, seen in the provision of dikes to restrain flooding and canals to carry freshwater and silt to fields threatened by salinization. Canals served the double purpose of facilitating the transport of bulky goods to the most densely populated regions and taking water to an expanding network of fields.

The construction of canals and dikes and agriculture itself were facilitated by the increasing abundance of iron. The government attempted to secure a monopoly of iron and salt production, but according to Sima Qian, the historian of the Western Han dynasty, iron smelting was one of the principal avenues to amassing private wealth. A document of 81 B.C.E. described how aggressive and ambitious families smelted iron, employing in the process hundreds or thousands of laborers. The iron was turned into plows, sickles, scythes, spades, and hoes. Of these, the most important in terms of improving efficiency was undoubtedly the plowshare. Harnessing draft animals to the plow was a far more effective way of putting new land in production or tilling established fields than was human power alone. The establishment of large state-run iron foundries during the middle years of the Western Han contributed directly to agricultural improvement, as did refinements in iron technology, whereby tensile wrought iron replaced brittle cast iron. Moreover, the form of the Han plow was sufficiently sophisticated to allow the depth of the furrow to be determined. This is seen clearly in illustrations of plowing scenes, for example, from Sui-ning in Gansu province, dating to the reign of Wang Mang. The Han farmer also used a plow fitted with a moldboard to turn a furrow. The efficient Han plow with moldboard required no more than two animals, and this design in itself represented a considerable gain in efficiency and the amount of land that could be cultivated. The large plows themselves opened further innovations. They turned large clods of soil that then had to be comminuted into a fine tilth with a harrow that was also drawn by animal traction. The furrowed field lent itself to the seed drill in place of sowing by less efficient broadcasting. Zhao Guo was an official of the Western Han who introduced the seed drill into the region of the capital in 85 B.C.E. The plowshare was pierced by holes through which the drill was inserted, so that plowing and seeding were undertaken simultaneously. The Han dynasties witnessed other vital innovations in productivity, such as the water-powered bellows used in the production of iron and the application of water power to the milling of grain.

The Han empire was divided into two principal areas. Most of the population was concentrated in the Huang River Basin, and it was here that millet and wheat were the staples. This area comprises extensive loess plains, where the soil is relatively fertile and easily worked, and rainfall varies between about 400 (16 in.) and 800 millimeters per annum. It is cold in winter, with mean temperatures averaging just above freezing. The second area is the Chang River Basin and Sichuan, where the rainfall rises to 1,500 millimeters per annum, and the temperatures are much milder. Here rice was the mainstay.

In the northern area centered on the capital territory in the Wei River Valley, wheat, barley, hemp, and beans were cultivated in addition to millet. Wheat and barley are essentially winter crops, and millet is grown during the summer. In theory, therefore, the two could be rotated on the same land, and continuous cultivation practiced. Several contemporary tracts on agriculture have survived, and these display the common theme of increasing efficiency and productivity in the light of a growing population. The *Lüshi Zhunjiu*, which dates to the Qin dynasty, described the procedure whereby plowing was followed by the broadcasting of seed along the ridges created between furrows, each about 1.5 meters (4.9 ft.) wide. This system was superseded during the reign of the emperor Wudi by a system devised by the then superintendent of agriculture, Zhao Guo.

It is important to note that this was a period of agricultural experimentation to devise improvements. Guards in the capital were deployed to cultivate strips of land near the palace, in which the seeds were spaced in straight plowed furrows rather than on the intervening ridges. Weeding was then undertaken with long-handled hoes shod with iron, and as the season progressed, so the light soil gradually filled the furrows, sealing the roots

deeply and conserving moisture. By the end of the growing season, the fields were flat, and the returns greatly increased. The following season, the ridges and furrows were reversed, thereby allowing rotation of crops on the same plot and maintaining the fertility of soil already fed annually with manure. In this respect, the raising of pigs meshed with millet cultivation, because the pigpens were linked with the outflow from human latrines to furnish the necessary manure for mucking out into the fields. This so-called alternating field system was found to be such a marked improvement over any preceding method that it was widely advertised through the commandery officials. The state iron monopoly was deployed to produce the necessary iron plowshares, but the demand placed on the supply of draft animals was such that not all peasants had access to animal traction. Therefore, the new heavy iron plows were of little use to peasants called on to haul them themselves. Experimentation, however, continued, leading to the development of more efficient plows having two or three shares, seed drills, and a moldboard.

A manual on field techniques in agriculture, compiled by Fan Shengzhi in the reign of Zhengdi (33–7 B.C.E.), has survived in fragments and provides further information on the rapid advance of farming techniques under the Western Han. Fan Shengzhi covered the cultivation of a wide range of plants, including wheat, millet, soybeans, hemp, and mulberry trees, the last vital for sericulture. In addition to his work on the alternating fields, he described a further innovation, known as the pit field system. In the alternating fields, his figures reveal that 15,000 plants could be set out in a plowed field measuring only 42 by 11 meters (138 by 36 ft.). The pit field system involved the division of land into a grid of pits each measuring about 23 by 12 centimeters (9.2 by 4.8 in.). Twenty millet seeds were planted in each pit, after the provision of high-quality fertilizer. Thousands of such pits could be cultivated, and the returns were spectacular: 0.6 liters of grain per pit, or 2,000 liters (520 gal.) in barely 400 square meters (480 sq. yds.) of land. The principal problem with this technique, however, was its need for labor. Fields were not plowed, and the preparation of each pit and weeding relied on manual labor.

According to the official Han censuses, central China, the region centered on the Chang Valley west to Sichuan, was not as densely populated as the Huang River Valley, and only with large migrations during the later Eastern Han did the imbalance in favor of the north fall away. Consequently, there was not the same pressure for increasing agricultural efficiency, and there is less evidence for intensification. Central China also enjoys a warmer and wetter climate suited to rice cultivation, which created different demands on the irrigation system. Whereas major canals were dug in the north to transport water to the fields, in the south the system was based on dammed rivers and small reservoirs and a proliferation of

BRICK-lined wells and tanks cut below the water table. The availability of water resources in this manner made possible an extension of the system known as fire tilling and water weeding. Essentially, this involved the burning of the stubble and weeds in the rice fields after a period of fallow and planting of the rice seeds in the flooded field. After the rice and, inevitably, weeds had grown to a certain height, the grass was cut back, and water was allowed to rise higher than the unwanted weeds to drown and kill them. As the weeds decomposed, they fed the rice plants. This system relied on the control of water into and out of the rice plots, and surviving clay tomb models show bunded fields, with the peasants weeding or spreading manure. Such fields were also a source of fish. In the colder north, similar bunded fields were in use, but here the soil was plowed to a creamy consistency, and the reticulation of irrigation water through the field was carefully controlled to take account of temperature variations. Thus in the early and cooler part of the season, the water was allowed to flow slowly through the field to gather radiant heat, but during the hot summer months, its passage sped up to give it cooling properties. This was achieved by changing the course of access channels into the rice fields.

There are at least two methods of improving yields in the central region, and there is some evidence that these were put into practice during the later Eastern Han period. The first is to plow the soil to a good consistency. This turns over weeds and creates a hard pan under the level of the plow to help retain water in the field. The second is to grow rice seedlings in a nursery plot and later transplant them into the prepared fields. This reduces the competition between plants that occurs with broadcasting and allows other crops to mature during the period when the seedlings are growing in the nurseries.

The importance of domestic animals should not be overlooked. The most important were cattle, water buffaloes, and pigs. All produced the manure necessary to enrich fields that were under increasing strain as farming intensified. Thus the ridge and furrow and pit field systems are highly demanding of fertilizers. Again, the tomb models show how pigs were raised in small pens, with an attached structure to collect waste. These pens were linked with human latrines for the collection of night soil. The cattle and water buffalo were also highly in demand for meat, but particularly for their tractive power. The many improvements in iron technology, the form of the plow, and development of the seed drill all depended on the availability of tractive power.

HAN RELIGIOUS BELIEFS

Religious beliefs during the period of the Han dynasties were a mixture of old and new, exotic forms of worship. There was also a distinction between the court ceremonials and those of the countryside. The former began with the worship of DI, the supreme god with an ancestry going back to the period of the Shang dynasty and probably further. The concept di was enlarged during the Qin to four aspects, and under Emperor Guangdi to five, each determined by a different color. Emperor Wudi further expanded the official deities to include the Earth Queen and the Grand Unity. Rituals, on occasion attended by the emperor, involved animal sacrifices and burnt offerings. Mount Dai was regarded as a peak of great holiness, and it was scaled by Qin Shihuangdi, Wudi, and Guang Wudi. In 31 B.C.E. there was a change in favor of tian, "heaven," and new forms of worship were created to link the ruling dynasty with the heavenly mandate. The former ceremonies, which had become very expensive as the number of shrines to former emperors magnified across the empire, were discontinued. The emperors were often interred in large and grand tombs, not only to project their distinction, but also to impart an image of immortality through their size. The quest for immortality became a guiding passion of the emperor Wudi.

The Han rulers spent much energy in quelling the northern nomadic tribes known as the Xiongnu and establishing control over the western regions. This provided regular access to the so-called Silk Road and with it the introduction of BUDDHISM into China. This took place at least by the first century C.E., and there is a notable story of the emperor Mingdi's sending emissaries west to find out more about this mysterious religion after he had dreamed of seeing a god in the form of a golden man. The first historic record relates that in 65 C.E. Liu Ying, king of Chu and half-brother of Emperor Mingdi, followed certain Buddhist rituals.

The religious beliefs of the Han, in particular the quest for immortality, are closely linked with the development of mortuary rituals. Grandiose royal tombs had a long history in China before Qin Shihuangdi, the first emperor, took monumentality to new heights with his massive mausoleum at Mount Li and the associated subterranean mortuary pits filled with terra-cotta warriors. The major Han emperors, as well as the nobility who ruled the dependent kingdoms, invested much labor in creating their tombs and in ensuring that all their needs in the future life were met. They thus bequeathed to history remarkable assemblages of their possessions, from clothing to libraries, furniture, and retainers represented as clay or wooden models.

Such treatment of the dead under the Han was based on the notion that on death the body resolved into the soul, or HUN, which with proper assistance could enter paradise, and the BO, which remained behind on Earth. The hun required directions on its passage to paradise and had to pass through several strictly guarded gates before it could join di, the universal god, the Sun, the Moon, and other denizens there. The bo had to be accompanied below by the goods necessary to maintain the type of life to which the dead person was accustomed, and this was best achieved if the body could be preserved from corruption and decomposition. This latter notion contributes to an understanding of the extreme measures taken, for example, in the mortuary complex of the first emperor of China near Chang'an. There, his entire army was represented as life-sized terra-cotta warriors in subterranean pits, and his fine carriage was reproduced at half its actual size in bronze. It is reported in the *History of the Former Han* that the mausoleum itself was equipped with all the necessities of life.

Although there were occasional remonstrances against such lavish expenditure on royal burials during the Western Han period, the emperor's graves and associated temples and shrines continued to attract an enormous expenditure of effort. In the reign of Yuandi (49–33 B.C.E.), it was officially recorded that 45,129 guards were permanently employed to protect royal shrines, and that the rituals required a staff of 12,147 attendants who included cooks and musicians. Attempts were made to reduce the onerous burden on the court, but no serious changes were effected.

ARCHAEOLOGICAL INVESTIGATIONS OF HAN TOMBS

Until recently, the nature of imperial Han burials was not known through archaeological research. However, the tomb of Emperor Jingdi is currently under investigation, and it has been found that if anything it even exceeded that of the first emperor in size and splendor. Jingdi was born in 188 B.C.E. He was the fifth son of Emperor Wendi and ruled from 157 until 141 B.C.E. His tomb and that of the empress Wang are located near Xi'an, in a necropolis that includes the mausolea of 10 other Han emperors. Jingdi is regarded as a ruler who reduced taxation and did not live in an ostentatious style. His tomb lies under a steeply sided mound of earth and has not been opened by archaeologists. It is surrounded by a walled enclosure that formerly contained four entrance gateways. Excavations by the southern gate have uncovered a checkerboard game, perhaps used by guards during long shifts on duty. Between the wall and the mound, there were many subterranean pits, one of which was found accidentally in 1990. This led to major excavations that have opened a new perspective on the mortuary practices of the imperial line. The pits were laid out with mathematical precision, each one being long and narrow. So far, 86 have been identified and 11 opened by archaeologists. The contents of each are thought to represent specific departments of state. Thus one contains the models of about 400 dogs, 200 sheep, and many pigs laid out in neat rows. Two pits contain official seals, one from the kitchen. There are also 40,000 clay models of individuals, including foot soldiers and cavalry, court women, and eunuchs, all of whom once had wooden movable arms and fine silk clothing. The adjacent tomb of the empress has at least 31 pits of its own, and there is also a mound covering the tomb of a favorite concubine.

No royal Han tomb chamber has been opened under scientific conditions, and many, if not all, were looted in antiquity for their treasures. However, the wealth of goods placed in the tombs of high-status individuals during the Western Han dynasty can be seen in a handful of burials that have miraculously survived intact. Foremost is a group of three elite graves excavated at Mawangdui in a suburb of Changsha. These contained the remains of Li Cang, the marquis of Dai, his wife, and his son. The marquis, who died in 169 B.C.E., was an aristocrat who had been provided with a fief by the king of Changsha, a kingdom that survived under imperial authority in the old state of Chu in central China.

The tomb of the marchioness Xin Zhiu, like that of the emperor Jingdi, was covered by a mound. Just four kilometers (13.2 mi.) from Changsha city in central China, it was one of a group of three in which one of the three marquises of Dai who ruled this area between 193 and 141 B.C.E. was interred with two members of this family. This mound, Burial 1, which had a diameter of 60 meters (198 ft.), covered a deep rectangular shaft that reached a depth of almost 17 meters (56 ft.) below the present ground surface. The contents of the tomb represent with great clarity the distinction between the *bo* and the *hun*. In this tomb, the need to conserve the body free of decay was achieved by placing it in nested wooden coffins covered by layers of charcoal and clay to keep out air and moisture. The charcoal weighed about 5,000 kilograms (11,000 lbs.) and reached a thickness of 40 centimeters (36 in.). It was itself sealed by a layer of thick white clay. Excluding the air and damp perfectly preserved the body. The marchioness was found wrapped in 20 layers of silk and linen, kept in place by nine silk ribbons. She had died when aged about 50 years and had been about 155 centimeters (62 in.) tall. The pathologists who examined the body were amazed to find that the blood in the femoral arteries was of a color similar to that in the newly deceased.

The wooden burial chamber contained three lacquered coffins. The outermost was decorated with designs of white, red, yellow, and red clouds painted on a black background. Monsters are playing the zither, dancing, and hunting birds, deer, and cattle. A space between this and the middle coffin contained mortuary offerings. The middle coffin itself was painted a vermilion color with scenes of clouds and mountains, a battle between dragons and tigers, and deer, all within a border of geometric designs. Remarkably, the inner coffin was covered in silk that was embellished with colored feathers and embroidered patterns.

The items laid out neatly in the space between the second and third coffins included remains of food and chopsticks carefully placed on lacquerware platters. The marchioness could anticipate a fine diet: The plates and ceramic vessels contained lotus root, chicken, peaches and melons, dried ginger, and pickled vegetables. A complete wardrobe of fine silks accompanied the dead woman, neatly stored in bamboo boxes. More than 50 items of clothing were counted, of outstanding quality and retaining the original colors. One piece of silk was so fine that although it measured half a meter square (.6 sq. yds.), it weighed just less than three grams. A large gown with sleeves almost two meters (6.6 ft.) long weighed just 49 grams (1.7 oz.).

Her personal cosmetics were included, together with a hairpiece, mittens, and slippers. She was also destined to enjoy music, for a zither and a set of pipes accompanied her. The former was found in a brocade bag and had 25 strings still in place, while the latter were also found in their original bag.

The presence of 162 wooden figurines illustrates the courtly life of a Han aristocratic family. There is a musical ensemble, in which miniatures of the very instruments in their brocade bags are represented. Attendants dressed in silks would have waited on the noble family at a banquet, while dancers entertained them. All these offerings were neatly catalogued on 312 BAMBOO SLIPS.

Lady Dai was overweight when she died and had suffered from a cardiac disorder. The ingredients for treating heart problems then and now in China—magnolia bark, peppercorns, and cinnamon—were found in her tomb, and the autopsy confirmed her condition.

The passage of her soul to paradise is illustrated by a remarkable tomb banner that had, in all probability, been carried in her funerary procession and then placed over the coffin. Made of silk, it is one of very few to have survived from this period. The painted scenes, which have retained much of their original color, show her being laid out, surrounded by mortuary vessels and attendants, with the nether regions below her. Above, she is seen standing in an elegant robe accompanied by divine messengers, while the passage to paradise is seen above her, guarded by two leopards. Through this portal, we see heaven itself, with the Sun, Moon, and celestial beings.

Contemporary documents state that only emperors and very high-status aristocrats could be buried in suits of jade. Jade was held to preserve the body uncorrupted, to ensure the continuing life of the *bo* on Earth. The status of the deceased determined whether the wafers of jade were stitched together with gold, silver, or bronze thread. Given the incidence of tomb looting over the centuries, the chances of finding such a suit in an undisturbed burial are remote. Therefore, the opening of two rock-cut tombs at Lingshan Mountain near Mancheng, Hebei province, was a special event in the history of Chinese archaeology. In 1968, the tomb of Prince Liu Sheng, the older brother of Emperor Wudi, was opened. It had been cut into the living rock to a depth of 52 meters and incorporated a lateral chamber 37 meters wide. About 2,700 (94,500 cu. ft.) cubic meters of rock had been excavated to create this resting place for the prince; to guard against tomb robbers, the entrance had been sealed with a doorway created by pouring molten iron between two parallel walls. The second tomb, which housed his wife, was found 100 meters (330 ft.) distant, and it too was on a massive scale. The rock-cut chambers, up to seven meters in height, had been infilled with roofed rooms, each containing the items needed in the afterlife. Liu Sheng's tomb opened onto the long lateral corridor that housed his chariots and horses. One-half also included rows of ceramic containers for food and wine. The central hall was filled with his bronze vessels, lacquer bowls, and containers and fine ceramics. To the back of the complex lay the burial chamber itself, together with the most superbly crafted artifacts of gold, silver, and jade. The prince's bathroom was located beside the burial.

Both the prince and his wife were found interred in jade suits, confirmation for the first time that the Han documents accurately described such outstanding funerary wealth. That containing the remains of Liu Sheng was made of 2,690 finely shaped wafers of jade, held together with gold thread that weighed more than a kilogram (2.2 lbs.). His wife's suit took up 2,156 jade wafers. It has been estimated that one craftsperson would take 10 years to make such a suit.

Clearly, the majority of Han dynasty burials were far less opulent than those of the royal family and the leading aristocracy. Even relatively ordinary tombs, however, contained grave goods that reflect everyday life and the need to provide for the body after death. There are models of agricultural activities and also a number of illustrations showing festive scenes. The region of Nanyang in southwestern Henan province, for example, is noted for the stone slabs decorated in low relief or incised, with images that illustrate the enjoyment of the table, music, and entertainment. Several such mortuary reliefs contain scenes of men bull-baiting. These resemble the images of acrobats leaping over charging bulls seen on a seal from Mohenjo Daro, as well as the wall paintings of the palace of Knossos in Crete. The casting of three-legged bronze wine containers is documented since the Shang dynasty, but in the Nanyang scenes they are shown with their ladles being used, while musicians play bells, the zither, pipes, and drums and dancers entertain. There are also jugglers and acrobats. One of the former is seen wearing a mask while balancing a vessel on one arm and a ball on the other.

The Han tombs that have been excavated at Luoyang also throw light on religious beliefs and the energy that was expended on mortuary rituals. Bu Qianqui, for example, was buried with his wife between 87 and 49 B.C.E. The brick-lined chamber was decorated with mural paintings that portray the dead couple ascending to heaven as immortal beings. A second Western Han tomb from Luoyang of slightly later date incorporated paintings of a demon being consumed by tigers and a dragon, tiger, panther, toad, deer, and horse, divine creatures to escort the dead to heaven.

Further reading: Bielenstein, H. *The Bureaucracy of Han Times*. Cambridge: Cambridge University Press, 1980; ———. "The Restoration of the Han Dynasty," *Bulletin of the Museum of Far Eastern Antiquities* 26 (1954): 9–20; Twitchet, D., and M. Loewe, eds. *The Cambridge History of China*, vol. I. *The Ch'in and Han Empires, 221 B.C.–A.D. 220*. Cambridge: Cambridge University Press, 1986; Wang Zhongshu. *Han Civilization*. New Haven, Conn.: Yale University Press, 1982.

Hangsapurnagar   *See* RAJAGRIHA.

hangtu   *Hangtu* is a form of stamped-earth construction used in early Chinese defensive walls and the foundations of buildings. A foundation trench was first dug, and layers of earth 10- to 15-centimeters (4- to 6-in.) thick were stamped between constraining wooden boards. The earliest use of this technique has been found in sites of the LONGSHAN CULTURE of the third millennium B.C.E. The city walls of ZHENGZHOU have been excavated to reveal the details of this technique.

haniwa   A *haniwa* (clay ring) was a ceramic model that played a role in the mortuary rituals of the YAMATO state in Japan. According to the *NIHONGI*, they originated during the reign of King Sujin (r. 219–49 C.E.) as a substitute for human sacrifices. The first attested archaeologically are from the third century C.E. and took the form of simple clay cylinders in late YAYOI culture mounded tombs. Tombs, such as that at TATESUKI, contain broken ceramic vessels thought to have been used during mortuary feasting rituals. It is possible that these are ancestral to the *haniwa*. However, they developed into large human and animal figures, standing on occasion more than a meter high and laid out in concentric rows. During the fourth to seventh centuries C.E., Yamato aristocrats were interred in *kofun*, earth mounds covering tomb complexes. Some *kofun* reached enormous dimensions, the largest of all being almost half a kilometer long. *Haniwa* were placed not in the tomb chamber, but around the covering mounds. The earliest examples take the form of rings. They may have been symbolic food containers. With the passage of time, they depicted individuals, buildings, and scenes that clearly illustrate the aristocratic way of life of the Yamato elites. Figures of people include warriors, falconers, musicians, and farmers. The musicians are seen playing drums, mandolins, and harps. Warriors and their horses wear heavy iron armor. In one notable scene, the presumed tomb master is seen on a throne with his consort, accompanied by dancers, officials, soldiers, and horses with their grooms. Such assemblages recall the many instances of tomb models in China.

Hann   The state of Hann had no relationship to the later HAN DYNASTY. The Hann state was formed by the

Haniwa tomb figures were employed by Yamato aristocrats in Japan from the fourth to the seventh centuries C.E. This example depicts a warrior in full armor. *(Werner Forman/ Art Resource, NY)*

breakup of the powerful Spring and Autumn period (770–476 B.C.E.) state of JIN in 403 B.C.E. and was finally destroyed during the reign of King Wangan in 230 B.C.E. at the hands of QIN. It was the smallest and most vulnerable of the three states that emerged from Jin. In terms of administration, Hann is best known for its minister, Shen Buhai, who advocated a system of ministers who received a salary, SEALS, and insignia of office at the discretion of the ruler. Hann's territory almost encircled the small enclave left under the direct mandate of the EASTERN ZHOU DYNASTY to the south, east, and west. North and east, Hann bordered WEI. Qin lay to the west, and CHU to the south. These were all powerful states, and Hann had to arm itself to survive as long as it did. Hann was strategically placed, with the Huang (Yellow) River flowing through its territory, and its first capital was established under Marquis Jinghou at Yangzhai (Henan province). In 375 B.C.E., however, the forces of Hann defeated the army of ZHENG, and the capital was moved to Zheng Han. This site has been identified at the confluence of the Yushui and Huangshui Rivers. It is a massive site, comprising eastern and western walled sectors covering about 3,000 hectares (7,500 acres). There is a palace precinct that spreads over 18 hectares (20 acres) in the western sector, and many stamped-earth foundations together with water pipes and wells evidence the extent of this structural complex. Even the palace kitchens have been identified through excavations. The city had workshops for producing objects of iron and bronze.

As with most Chinese cities, starting from the Shang dynasty, Zheng Han incorporated many specialized workshops, and these were located in the eastern or outer part of the city. One bronze-working area was dedicated to the casting of production tools, such as sickles, spades, and picks. The clay molds for casting these bronzes have been found in abundance. Dating to the end of the Spring and Autumn and WARRING STATES PERIODS (475–221 B.C.E.), there was also a specialized iron workshop where further production tools as well as weapons, such as swords and halberds, were produced. A hoard of bronze weapons, many of which were inscribed with the name of the official in charge, indicate the importance of the mass production of weaponry at the end of the Warring States period. Some of the items were damaged or broken, and their exotic inscriptions point to their being taken after a successful battle, but the majority were locally cast as late as 231 B.C.E., the year before the Hann state was eliminated by Qin.

A second major city has been identified at Yangcheng in Henan province, where again there were extensive city walls and specialist workshops. At Fenshuiling in Shanxi province, a major Hann cemetery has been opened by excavation. Tombs took the form of rectangular pits, up to eight by six meters (26.4 by 19.8 ft.) in extent. A wooden chamber contained the coffin. Some of these were embellished with lacquered decoration and golf leaf, while the sumptuous bronzes were also decorated with inlaid gold designs.

Hanshu   The *Hanshu* (or *Han Shu; History of the Former Han*) was a history of the HAN DYNASTY covering the 250 years from the reign of Emperor Gaozu until the end of the rule of the usurper WANG MANG in 23 C.E. It was commenced by the historian BAN BIAO (3–54 C.E.) and continued to completion by his son, BAN GU. In the tradition of the SHIJI, or *Records of the Grand Historian*, by SIMA QIAN, it is a work of dense historic scholarship comprising 100 chapters. These include historic summaries, chronologies, and treatises. The *Hanshu* was a model dynastic history that set the standard for all later historic works in China. It provides a wide range of insights into Han policy making and the manner of thought that lay behind executive decisions. This is particularly well illustrated in an edict issued by the emperor WENDI (r. 180–157 B.C.E.)

on the importance of agriculture. The *Hanshu* stated that there had been a run of poor harvests and that grain was in short supply. The people were suffering, and the emperor was gravely concerned. No one could identify what was causing this agricultural failure. People wondered whether they had failed to follow the ways of heaven or, more practically, whether too much grain was being diverted to make wine. All the high officials were directed to seek the root cause. The solution was social rather than agronomic: It was decided that grain could be made into a negotiable commodity, and therefore of enhanced value, if it could be used to purchase honorary ranks or commute sentences. This solution had, again according to the *Hanshu*, already been suggested in 178 B.C.E. by Chao Cuo. He observed that the emperor could create titles at will and that if he did so in return for grain, there would be an abundant surplus for disposal.

However, the *Hanshu* also records the views of DONG ZHONGSHU (c. 195–105 B.C.E.), a well-known follower of the Confucian school, who described the high taxes and demands for labor imposed on the peasantry by the Qin and continued, he asserted, under the Han. In former times, peasants paid only 10 percent of their production and provided their labor for only three days of the year. But under the QIN, the impositions increased so savagely that the peasantry were reduced to penury and banditry while rich landlords prospered. Only a return to the old system of land tenure, when everyone had sufficient for his or her needs, would alleviate this social inequality.

Han state   *See* HANN.

Haojiatai   Haojiatai is a LONGSHAN CULTURE urban site located in central Henan province, China. Two radiocarbon determinations place its occupation in the mid-third millennium B.C.E. It was demarcated by HANGTU stamped-earth walls at least five meters (16.5 ft.) wide at the base, fronted by a moat. Stamped-earth platforms in the interior were raised to support elite buildings. However, the pit and urn burials contain very few mortuary offerings, and some skeletons were missing a skull or a hand. This might indicate warfare or sacrifice. The site has also provided evidence for a specialized ceramic industry.

Harappa   Harappa is one of the three great cities of the INDUS VALLEY CIVILIZATION. Located just south of a former bed of the Ravi River in the Punjab, Pakistan, it was the first such site to be discovered, in the early 19th century, and the first to yield evidence for a system of writing that bore no relationship to the BRAHMI or KHAROSHTHI scripts of later periods. Harappa has been more extensively excavated, and over a longer period, than any other site of the Indus civilization.

The history of Harappa can be divided into five successive phases, covering a period of 1,900 years. Period I, the Early Harappan, dates from 3400 to 2800 B.C.E. and is now known as the Ravi phase. This is followed by the transitional phase to the mature Harappan, which took place during the century from 2600 to 2500 B.C.E. The mature Harappan, which witnessed the full development of sophisticated urban life, lasted for five centuries until 2000 B.C.E. and was followed first by the posturban phase, lasting about a century, and then by the period during which Cemetery H was employed, which is dated 1900–1500 B.C.E.

Much remains to be learned about Harappa. The nature of the structures on the citadel requires attention, as does a detailed picture of the social organization, with particular reference to the status of the ruling elite and the means to attain social ascendancy. It is unknown whether rule was vested in a hereditary aristocracy or a royal lineage or was in the hands of a sacerdotal group of religious leaders. How trade was organized and who controlled the long-distance exchange so widely evidenced in the SEALS and sealings of this civilization also need investigation. However, the recent intensive excavations at this great city have already greatly expanded the range and detail of what is known about its internal history.

ARCHAEOLOGICAL REMAINS

A series of mounds covers an area of at least 150 hectares (375 acres), although the real area was probably considerably greater. As in other major cities, there was a separate citadel mound, known as Mound AB, located to the west of the lower city, known as Mound E. Two cemeteries have been identified to the southwest of the city, the earlier belonging to the classic period of occupation (Cemetery R37) and the later to the latest period (Cemetery H).

Excavations at Harappa began in 1872 under the direction of SIR ARTHUR CUNNINGHAM. Writing of his research in 1875, he described "a smooth black stone, without polish. On it is engraved very deeply a bull, without a hump, looking to the right, with two stars under its neck. Above the bull is an inscription in six characters, which are quite unknown to me. They are certainly not Indian letters; and as the bull which accompanies them is without a hump, I conclude that the seal is foreign to India." Much research has since been undertaken at Harappa to negate his suggestion of an exotic source for the script.

The major excavations began in 1920 and, under a succession of directors, lasted for 20 years. These seasons saw the opening of huge areas of the site. In 1920–21 a trench 152 meters (501.6 ft.) long and almost five meters (16.5 ft.) wide was excavated into the northern mound, known as Mound F. In 1926–27 M. S. Vats excavated almost 5,000 square meters and discovered about 350 items inscribed in a form of writing; most were seals. The following year, he worked in the late Cemetery H and

also found circular platforms near the supposed granary and workers' quarters. In 1937–38 K. N. Sastri revealed 50 burials dating to the main period of the occupation, in Cemetery R37 southwest of the main city walls; 11 more were found in 1966. The walls of the main citadel, Mound AB, were exposed by SIR MORTIMER WHEELER in 1946, during which campaign he identified deep pre-Harappan occupation remains. In 1986 a multidisciplinary project directed by George Dales commenced and, through the application of a wide range of techniques and approaches, cast much new light on the life of this great city. Excavations continue to this day as part of the Harappa Archaeological Research Project, under the direction of Richard Meadow and Mark Kenoyer.

Period I

Little is known of the Period I settlement, because it is so deep and is covered by later deposits. The cultural remains occupy a limited area in the northwestern corner of Mound E. It is evident that the community chose to live on a slight eminence commanding good agricultural land, near a major river, and giving access to important strategic exchange routes. The occupation took the form of mud-brick houses equipped with hearths. The people imported chert for making stone implements and fashioned polished stone adzes and stone beads. There was also much use of ceramics, and over time the deposits accumulated to form a low mound. A recent discovery of written characters belonging to the Ravi phase has pushed back the date of the first Indus script to 3300–2800 B.C.E. This makes it as early as the writing systems of Sumer and Egypt.

Transitional Phase—Period II

During the second, or transitional, phase, there was a series of important developments. The most recent excavations identified material of this period under Mound E, suggesting that the settlement now covered an area of at least 10 hectares (25 acres). Two successive mud-brick walls were constructed, the earlier two meters (6.6 ft.) wide, and the bricks still stood to a height of two meters. There was also evidence for a patterned layout of streets on a north-south axis, one of which still bore the rut marks of passing traffic. A kiln was found, with strong evidence for intensive use of this part of the site for ceramic production, while imports of chert, from a source 700 kilometers (420 mi.) to the south, and marine shell indicate long-distance trade. Some shards were found to have graffiti incisions, probably an early indication of the development of a script. The production of bricks and the construction of large perimeter walls strongly suggest the rise of an elite group in Harappan society.

Period III

Since intensive recent excavations, the mature Harappan can now be divided into three phases, all of which are represented on Mound E. During this long phase there was continuity in material culture and construction techniques with Period II, but with the addition of a range of new artifacts and developing preferences in the form and decoration on ceramic vessels. Pottery production continued, with the presence of firing kilns, and massive new walls were built on the Period II walls. The interior of the lower city incorporated mud-brick platforms, which were added to throughout the phase, together with streets and a drainage system. The walls at the southern periphery incorporated a large gateway 2.8 meters (9.2 ft.) wide, faced with fired bricks and giving access to a city street on a north-south axis. The full gamut of Indus Valley civilization artifacts was associated with this phase, including weights, figurines, STEATITE seals, terra-cotta sealings, and figurines, but there were also internal developments, wherein tiny steatite and FAIENCE tokens were introduced during Period IIIB. Since these tokens also recur on Mound F to the north, it is evident that the excavations there during the 1920s and 1930s had encountered an area belonging to the mature period of the city's history. The development of the city, however, was not without periods of urban decay. The division between Periods IIIA and IIIB, for example, saw clogged sewers and animal carcasses littering part of Mound E before a period of urban renewal began.

The earlier reports of prewar excavations, while representing less precise excavation techniques than those employed more recently, did have the one advantage of opening large areas to reveal the structures of the mature city. Excavations in 1931–32 on Mound F, for example, revealed a series of narrow lanes giving access to small, individual dwellings of identical plan. Small passages led off the lanes into rectangular houses, each with three rooms. Each house measured about 15 by six (50 by 20 ft.) meters. This same part of the city also included six granaries, disposed in rows, associated with circular brick working floors. The presence of chaff from wheat and barley on these floors leaves no room for doubt that they were for threshing grain. Significantly, these threshing floors were located near the ancient river bank, suggesting that the grain may have been shipped to the city by barge. This same period saw the construction of the elite structures on the citadel mound, though these are little known because of the activities of brick robbers.

Skeletal Studies

One of the advantages of Harappa, when compared with most sites of the Indus civilization, is the knowledge gained of the people themselves from the excavation of cemeteries. Cemetery R37b belongs to Period III and was first investigated in 1937. Subsequent excavations by archaeologists from the University of California have added to the number of individuals available for consideration. While many skeletons were fragmentary, enough were complete to permit some conclusions about the health and status of the inhabitants of Harappa. Among the first considerations of any such analysis are the ratio of men to WOMEN and the mortality figures expressed as

the approximate age of death. At Harappa, females outnumbered males in the samples from both major investigations of the cemetery, but many skeletons were too fragmentary for diagnosis. Of 90 individuals for whom the age at death could be identified, 13 survived beyond an age of about 55 years. Twenty-seven died when between about 35 and 55 years of age, but 35, more than a third of the sample, died between the ages of 17 and 34. Fifteen died before reaching 16 years. Compared with that of most prehistoric communities, there is a low incidence of infant and child mortality. This might well reflect the fragility of infant bones and therefore their smaller chance of survival, or perhaps infants were interred in another part of the cemetery. Teeth are a basic source of information on the health of a population, because diet, illness, and malnutrition are expressed in teeth in a number of ways. The Harappan population, for example, shows that 70 percent of individuals suffered from linear dental hypoplasia, which is a result of dietary deficiency or illness during the period of tooth formation. This figure is higher than those for the earlier population of MEHRGARH. The frequency of caries was also markedly higher at Harappa than at Mehrgarh, probably as a result of different methods of processing food and a greater reliance on cultivated cereals. Interestingly, girls revealed poorer dental health than boys, while even among adults, women exhibited more caries than men. This may be due to different eating habits, with women eating at shorter intervals. The investigators of the cemetery population have also suggested that boys may have been preferred to girls and that they received more attention as they developed.

Periods IV and V

Period IV is hardly known. It was probably of brief duration and is distinguished on the basis of differing styles of pottery when compared with the preceding Period III material. Again, knowledge of Period V is marred by the impact of brick robbing to create the foundations of the Lahore-Multan railway in the 19th century. Occupation continued, however, on Mounds AB, E, and F, and it was during this period that Cemetery H was in use. M. S. Vats has reported on the excavation of this cemetery, which lies to the south of Mound E. The area opened between November 1929 and February 1930 was substantial: One square measured 46 by 33 meters (151 by 109 ft.), and another 54 by 16 meters (178 by 53 ft.). He found two periods of burial. The earlier had inhumation graves, in which the dead were laid out with the head pointing to the northeast, in association with pottery vessels placed neatly beyond the head. Some individuals were also found in a crouched position, on their sides. The pottery was decorated with painted designs of peacocks, trees, leaves, and stars. The upper layer of burials involved interments in large ceramic vessels, again decorated with painted foliage and peacocks and incorporating tiny human images, but also including dogs and goats. The jars usually contained the remains of a single individual, in which adult bones were placed some time after death, while infants were interred fully articulated within a cloth shroud. The jars seem to be grouped, each possibly containing the remains of related individuals. The interpretation of the motifs on these burial jars is most intriguing. Vats has turned to the RIG-VEDA, the sacred hymns of early India, to interpret the peacocks as carrying the dead, as they must, across the river, while the dogs are those belonging to Yama, god of death. The bird is identified in the Rig-Veda with fire and the Sun. It is quite possible that in this cemetery there is a conjunction of later Indus mortuary practices with the origins of the Vedic hymns.

Animal and Plant Evidence

Another advantage of the recent research at Harappa has been the attention paid to biological remains as a means of illuminating subsistence activities. While it is well established that cattle, sheep, and goats played a central role in animal husbandry and that barley and wheat were the principal grains cultivated, little is known of the other plants propagated or the role of hunting and fishing. Recent excavations have redressed this situation through the careful collection of fragile microfaunal remains. It is evident that the Indus civilization sites were located close to major rivers or the sea, while decoration of fish and fishing nets or traps on pottery vessels and the recovery of copper fishhooks reflect the importance of riverine resources. Only with the study of material from Harappa, however, have even the major species of river fish been identified. It was found that catfish predominated; almost half the assemblage was one species, *Wallago attu*. The fact that these fish can grow to a length of two meters (6.6 ft.) indicates their potential as a food source. There were also carp remains and the bone from a marine fish, which must have been obtained through trade. Contexts that yielded fish bone were also closely scrutinized. In one room, for example, most fish bones were found in the vicinity of a hearth. In another room, fish bones were found in a pit. Turning to the mammalian remains, it is found that sheep are much more numerous than goats and may have been valued for their wool as much as for meat. Again, cattle played a central role in animal husbandry at the site.

Further reading: Kenoyer, J. M. *Ancient Cities of the Indus Civilization.* Oxford: Oxford University Press, 1998; Meadow, R. H. *Harappa Excavations 1986–1990.* Monographs in World Archaeology No. 3. Madison, Wis.: Prehistory Press, 1991; Ratnagar, S. *Understanding Harappa: Civilization in the Greater Indus Valley.* Chennai, India: Tulika Publishers, 2001; Vats, M. S. *Excavations at Harappa.* Columbia, Mo.: South Asia Books, 1997.

Harihara Harihara was a composite god combining aspects of Vishnu and SIVA. In India, there are several representations of him. Cave 1 at BADAMI, dated to the late sixth century C.E., has a fine example created during the CHALUKYA DYNASTY. The god reached his height of popularity in Southeast Asia during the period of CHENLA kingdoms but appeared rarely during the Angkorian period.

See also ANGKOR.

Hariharalaya Hariharalaya, also known as the Roluos Group, is a collection of temples and a reservoir located 15 kilometers (9 mi.) southeast of ANGKOR on the northern shore of the Tonle Sap, or GREAT LAKE, of Cambodia. It was probably founded by JAYAVARMAN II, first king of the state of Angkor, who was active in the region in the early ninth century C.E. Most of the buildings, however, were ordered by INDRAVARMAN I (877–899 C.E.), the third king of the dynasty founded by Jayavarman II. He was responsible for the temples of PREAH KO and the BAKONG and for the main dikes that constitute the INDRATATAKA, a reservoir of unprecedented size. It is likely that the royal palace, which is described in INSCRIPTIONS but has not survived because of its wooden construction, lay north of the Preah Ko temple. Several architectural innovations mark temple design, such as the use of a ceremonial portal (*gopura*), or snake (*naga*) balustrades, and large walled and moated boundaries.

YASHOVARMAN I, the son of Indravarman, completed the Indratataka and had the island temple known as LOLEI constructed, but he then diverted his attention to a new capital at Angkor, leaving Hariharalaya as a remarkably preserved reflection of an early Angkorian ceremonial and administrative center.

Hastinapura Hastinapura is a large site that spans the late prehistoric and early historic periods in northern India. Dated between 1100 and 800 B.C.E., it is one of the key sites in portraying the developments that took place during a vital period in the early development of civilization in the Ganges (Ganga)-Yamuna Valleys. It is also known from the Hindu epic the MAHABHARATA as the capital of the Kauravas. The site is substantial, measuring about 800 by 400 meters (2,640 by 1,320 ft.), and contains cultural layers to a depth of about 10 meters (33 ft.). Excavations undertaken in 1950–52 revealed that the site originated during the prehistoric period and was occupied through five phases into the medieval period. Period II belongs the PAINTED GREY WARE culture and has yielded the remains of rice, as well as domestic cattle, sheep, pigs, and horses. The inhabitants also forged iron arrowheads, spears, and sickles. Trade in exotic stone is reflected in the presence of carnelian, agate, jasper, and glass. Period III belongs to the NORTHERN BLACK POLISHED WARE culture, dated on the basis of radiocarbon determinations to the mid-fourth century B.C.E. It was a period of urbanization, in which mud-brick or fired-brick houses were laid out in orderly fashion, the streets were provided with a drainage system, and the application of iron tools greatly enhanced agricultural efficiency. The plow, for example, was now used. Punch-marked coins illustrate the rise of a mature trading system. The fourth phase dates to the second century C.E. on the basis of Kushan COINAGE. Few sites rival Hastinapura in illustrating the rise of urbanization in the Ganges Valley from prehistoric roots.

See also KUSHANS.

Heavenly Horse, Tomb of the The interment of the royal elite in the Korean kingdom of SHILLA (37 B.C.E.–918 C.E.) involved first the construction of a wooden tomb chamber containing the sarcophagus and a wooden chest for grave goods. This was then covered with tens of thousands of large boulders and capped with an earthen mound. Since there was no entrance passageway, this type of tomb proved difficult to loot, and many have survived intact to this day on the Kyongju Plain in southeast Korea. In 1973 one such mounded tomb was fully excavated. Forty-seven meters (155 ft.) across and nearly 13 meters (43 ft.) high, it has been named the Tomb of the Heavenly Horse, because one of the mortuary offerings consisted of birch-bark mudguards embellished with paintings of a galloping horse with wings on each foot. Among the spectacular mortuary offerings was a large gold crown.

One of the problems with such tomb construction is that the wooden chamber rotted with time, allowing the boulders to fall in on the contents. There were no human remains, but the dead king had been interred with the large gold crown, which bore symbolic deer antlers, with 58 jade pendants attached to these by gold wire. He also wore a gold and glass necklace, a gold girdle, and a gold ring on each finger. There were three layers of offerings in the wooden chest. The lowest contained iron kettles and ceramic vessels, and the next bronze and lacquerware. The uppermost included horse saddles and the painted horses on birch bark that gave the tomb its modern name. Many items are of absorbing interest, not least the 24 ox-horn items, for ox horn was known to symbolize supernatural powers in the Shilla kingdom, and ministers were accorded graded titles incorporating the name for ox horn. There were also seven lacquerware wine cups probably used in a ritual context and two glass cups.

The occupant of the tomb might have been King Chizung, who died in 513 C.E. This king was responsible for terminating the habit of human sacrifice as part of royal burial rituals, and the absence of such remains in this mortuary context is persuasive.

Hedi (Liu Zhao; Harmonious Emperor) (79–106 C.E.) *Hedi was the fourth emperor of the Eastern Han dynasty of China.*
The son of Emperor ZHANGDI (57–88 C.E.), he acceded to the throne in 88 C.E. Apart from various natural problems, such as floods and drought, Hedi also had to cope with the dominant influence of the dowager empress Dou, who died in 97 C.E. He enlisted the support of palace officials to reduce her power. There followed events similar to those that had plagued the last reigns of the Western Han: a succession of infant or child emperors manipulated by rival consort families. Thus Hedi was succeeded by Shangdi (106 C.E.), who died before he reached one year of age; another child, ANDI (106–125 C.E.), grandson of Zhangdi, ascended the throne at the age of 12 years.

Heijo-kyo Heijo-kyo, also known as Nara, was the capital of the NARA STATE of Japan from 710 until the city was abandoned in 784 C.E. There was, however, a five-year period during the reign of Emperor Shomu when Heijo-kyo was abandoned in favor of Kuni, near modern Kyoto, and Shigaraki, 40 kilometers (12 mi.) northeast of Heijo-kyo, as a result of an insurrection. Heiji-kyo was reoccupied in 745 C.E. Research at the site of the ancient city was initiated in the 19th century by Kitaura Sadamasa (1817–71). On the basis of field observations and relevant documents, he produced a site map. His work was a starting point for Sekino Tadashi (1867–1935) to undertake excavations of the palace area. Huge areas of the palace and, more recently, the suburbs of the ancient city have now been uncovered by archaeologists. The most significant find was made in January 1961, when the first of more than 135,000 MOKKAN, inscribed wooden records, was recovered. These have thrown much light on life in the city, making it one of the best understood of all urban sites in East Asia. Archaeological excavations have revealed that no more than 15 percent of the area was built on and that there were many gardens, broad roads, and temples.

In 708 C.E. the capital had been located at FUJIWARA, 20 kilometers (24 mi.) south on the Nara Plain. Fujiwara itself had set new standards in Japanese urban planning and size, but the empress Genmei resolved in 708 to move to a new site, on the basis, it is said, of propitious geomantic reports and a favorable response from the diviners, based on ORACLE BONES. A more mundane reason for the move probably lay in the fact that Heijo-kyo provided easy riverine passage to the Inland Sea, across the Osaka Plains to the west. At this period of Japanese history, the court was consciously following Chinese examples, and the layout of the new city was modeled on the great Tang dynasty capital at CHANG'AN. There have been various estimates as to the population of Heijo-kyo, ranging up to 200,000 people, but a population in the vicinity of 80,000 is more likely, a far cry from the 1 million inhabitants of Chang'an, but still a considerable number for the time.

CITY PLAN AND ROYAL PALACE

The city, which was surrounded by an earthen embankment and a moat, has been partially excavated. It covered an area of 4.3 by 4.8 kilometers (2.6 by 2.9 mi.), with an extension to the east measuring 2.1 by 1.6 kilometers (1.2 by .9 mi.). The entire area was thus 2,400 hectares (6,000 acres). The interior was divided into square blocks each measuring 1,500 *daishaku*, a unit of measurement equivalent to 35.4 centimeters (14 in.). The avenues were laid out on a grand scale, the broadest 37 meters (122 ft.) wide, and others five to 25 meters (16.5 to 82.5 ft.). Each city block was then further divided by lanes into 16 areas known as *cho*.

The city was dominated by a grand palace, covering an area just over one kilometer square. It lay behind a high wall that reached six meters (19.8 ft.) and contained two distinct precincts, an eastern and a western. These incorporated government buildings, stables, an audience hall, and quarters for the imperial family. Members of the court could enjoy access to private pleasure gardens: The garden in an extension to the eastern precinct of the palace has been revealed through excavation. It included a lake with a small island and a pillared pavilion. The foundations of an octagonal structure, resembling a gazebo, also over-looked the little lake.

PRIVATE HOUSES

Scarlet Phoenix Avenue ran due south from the palace, dividing the city into two halves. The residences of the populace varied markedly with status, as the most exalted had large allocations of land closest to the palace. Excavations have uncovered the private residence of PRINCE NAGAYA, a grandson of an emperor, and his principal consort, Princess Kibi, whose status was even higher than that of the prince. Nagaya was a senior minister between 724 and 729, and his compound covered four *cho*, an area approximately 300 meters (396 sq yds.) square. The layout recovered through excavations incorporated a series of walled areas. One was the residence of the prince, with an adjacent one for the princess. The prince's sleeping quarters alone measured 355 square meters (426 sq. yds.). The recovery of 35,000 *mokkan*, wooden slips containing Nagaya's administrative records, reveal that he owned estates distant from the capital and also received tribute from districts given to him and his wife because of their aristocratic status. Thus a further area of the compound incorporated the offices for the administration of their business affairs. A Buddhist chapel occupied a prominent place, next to a private garden with a pond. Divisions of the princely household were responsible for a variety of tasks, such as manufacturing weaponry, casting bronzes, working leather, weaving, building, and caring for horses and hunting falcons. Workshops therefore covered the northeastern past of the estate. The surrounding wall and the weapons factory, however, did not save the prince when he was accused of plotting against the emperor. In 729 he was surrounded by an armed faction of the Fujiwara family, and he committed suicide.

The estate for another high aristocrat, Fujiwara no Naka-maro, covered eight *cho* nearby, and 70,000 *mokkan* relating to his activities have been found.

Even the populace at large lived in relatively spacious surroundings. Excavations suggest that outlying blocks were divided into individual plots measuring 900 square meters (1,880 sq. yds.), within which lay two to five individual buildings, a garden, and a well. Disposal of human waste in such huge cities was a perennial health issue. A privy excavated at Heijo-kyo was connected with a ditch of running water. Sanitation might well have been facilitated by the fact that the East and West Horikawa Rivers and the Saho River ran through the capital. They were canalized to conform to the grid plan of the streets and would have been of use in transporting heavy goods.

BUDDHIST TEMPLES

The city also incorporated at least two major markets, the west and the east, and by 720 C.E., there were 48 Buddhist temples in the city, the largest covering an area of 27 hectares (67.5 acres). BUDDHISM played a central role in the city. There was a department for copying sacred texts in the palace, and numerous Buddhist monks lived in the city. Their services were called on when, in 735, Japan was hit by a smallpox epidemic that is said to have killed a third of the population. The most important of all the temples was undoubtedly the TODAIJI, located due east of the royal palace on the edge of the city. It housed a massive gilt bronze casting of the Buddha nearly 11 meters (36.3 ft.) in height. Completed in 749 C.E., it was associated with two pagodas about 100 meters (330 ft.) tall. At least 10 other major Buddhist temples graced the city, their pagodas rising above the surrounding houses. The Kofukuji lay immediately to the southwest of the Todaiji. It was constructed by the powerful aristocrat Fujiwara no Fuhito and occupied an area nearly 500 meters square (600 sq. yds.). The Gangoji lay just south. This temple was formerly the Asuka-dera. The palace was flanked to the east by the Kairyuoji and on the west by the Sairyuji and Saidaiji. The Kiko-ji was built southwest of the palace by the Haji clan. The Toshodaiji, YAKUSH-JI, and Dianji occupied prominent locations in the southern half of the city.

In 784 Nara ceased to be the capital, which was moved under Emperor Kammu to Nagaoka.

See also GEOMANCY; YAMATO.

Heliodoros *Heliodoros was the ambassador of Antialci-das, the Greek king of Taxila, in modern Pakistan, to the court of King Kasiputra Bhgabhadra of Besnagar in India.*
In the late second century B.C.E., Heliodoros had a column erected in Besnagar decorated with an image of GARUDA, accompanied by a dedicatory INSCRIPTION. This is a particularly clear example of the Greeks adopting an Indian religion.

Hephthalite Huns The Hephthalite Huns were a people of shadowy origins who ruled much of Central Asia and northern India from about 450 to 550 C.E. The word Hephthalite means "valiant" or "courageous," and the Sassanian rulers, who resisted the initial westward expansion of the Huns, rightly feared their prowess as mounted cavalry and archers. Their coins bore a Bactrian script, and they probably spoke an Iranian language. A description by the sixth-century historian Procopius of Caesarea noted that they were ruled by one king and resembled the Byzantine state in their legal system. There is also evidence in their conflict with the Sassanian kings Yazgird II and Peroz that they had a powerful army and observed sealed treaties over fixed frontiers. They were engaged in three campaigns against the King Peroz, captured him on at least two occasions, and finally defeated and killed him in battle. Thereafter, the Sassanians paid tribute in COINAGE to the Hephthalites, largely to keep the peace on their eastern frontier, until the reign of Khusrau I in the mid-sixth century C.E. The Huns territory at this juncture included Tokharistan and much of Afghanistan. They seized SOGDIANA in 509 and extended their authority as far east as Urumqi in northeast China. Although successful in India from 520 to the mid-seventh century, the Hephthalites in Central Asia had to withstand a new threat from the northeast in the form of the Turks. The Huns' king Gatfar was seriously defeated in 560 C.E. in the vicinity of Bukhara, and the Huns thereafter survived only in the form of small and remote principalities, whose leaders paid tribute to the Sassanians and the Turks.

EXPANSION OF THE HUNS

As had many groups before them, the Huns then turned their imperial thoughts south into GANDHARA. By 520 they controlled this area and came up against the western frontiers of the GUPTA EMPIRE under King Bhuhagupta. Under their own king, Toramana, they seized the Punjab, Kashmir, and Rajputana, a policy continued vigorously under their next king, Mihirakula, who established his capital at Sakala (modern Sialkot in the Punjab, Pakistan). He was a Sivaite, and this was a period of devastation for the venerable Buddhist monasteries, many of which were sacked and destroyed. Sakala was visited in the seventh century by XUANZANG, the Chinese monk, who noted that the walls were dilapidated but still had strong foundations. He described the presence of an inner citadel and learned that several hundred years earlier the city had been the capital of Mihirakula, who ruled over India. Pravarasena reigned from about 530 C.E. His capital, near Srinagar in Kashmir, was named Pravarasenapura after him. He issued coins inscribed with his name. We also know the names of his successors, who formed a Hun dynasty ruling over much of northwestern India and Afghanistan until the mid-seventh century C.E. Increasingly, these rulers absorbed Indian ways, particularly in respect to religion. Thus King

Gokarna founded and endowed a shrine to SIVA called Gokarnesvara. The last Hephthalite king, Yudhishthira, ruled until about 670, when he was replaced by the Turk Shahi dynasty. In Central Asia, one principality that persisted after the Turks overcame the Hephthalites was located in Chaganiyan, on the northern bank of the Surkhan Dar'ya River. Another was at Khuttal in the Vakhsh Valley. These places were described by Xuanzang, who noted the number of monasteries and monks, the system of writing, and the fact that people dressed in cotton and sometimes woolen clothing.

HISTORICAL AND ARCHAEOLOGICAL EVIDENCE

The historical sources for the Hephthalites are fragmentary and at times contradictory, but it seems that while some of the population continued the typically nomadic life on the steppes, the elite became increasingly sedentary and occupied permanent walled towns or cities. One report describes the king's gold throne and magnificent dress. Their coinage reveals kings, but there also appear to have been regional rulers. Little archaeological research has been undertaken on the major settlements of the Hephthalite empire. BALKH (Afghanistan) is known to have been one of their centers, and Xuanzang described it as their capital. It was, he said, defended with strong walls but was not densely populated. TERMEZ, on the Amu Dar'ya River, and Budrach were other cities of this period. The latter incorporated a citadel and covered an area of about 50 hectares (125 acres). KAFYR-KALA, in the Vakhsh Valley of Tajikistan was a walled regional capital with a citadel and a palace. The life led in such centers is illustrated by the painted feasting scene at Balalyk-tepe in the upper valley of the Amu Dar'ya River in Uzbekistan, which shows aristocratic men and WOMEN shielded by servants holding umbrellas. A second elite feasting scene is depicted on a silver dish from Chilek, in which female dancers are entertaining royalty. In Afghanistan, the massive rock-cut images of the Buddha at BAMIYAN in Afghanistan, the largest such statues known before their destruction by the Taliban in 2001, probably date within the period of the Hephthalite empire.

See also BACTRIA; SASSANIAN EMPIRE.

Herodotus of Halicarnassus (484–425 B.C.E.) *A Greek historian from Ionia on the coast of modern Turkey who wrote valuable texts about early India.*

His *Persian Wars* included early descriptions of India and its inhabitants. He described the variety of peoples and customs, although it is highly unlikely that he ever visited the subcontinent. He drew attention to the contrast between the Aryans and the Dravidian-speaking people, who lived in southern India and were not part of the empire of DARIUS THE GREAT (550–486 B.C.E.) of Persia, and noted groups who ate no meat. Herodotus described Indian clothing as made from wool that grew on trees, a clear reference to cotton.

Hiraide   Hiraide is a prehistoric village located in central Honshu Island, Japan. It was located adjacent to a series of springs overlooking a broad river plain and has seen continuous occupation from the middle Jomon period, with settlement phases ascribed to the YAYOI culture (300 B.C.E.–300 C.E.) and the period of the YAMATO state (300 C.E.–700 C.E.). A burned house of the Jomon occupation phase was found to contain numerous clay human figurines and may have been a house for WOMEN in childbirth, the figurines meant to ensure a successful outcome. While many rural Yayoi settlements, such as TORO, have been exposed by excavation, less is known of village life during the Yamato period (300–700 C.E.), because archaeologists have paid so much attention to the massive *kofun* burial mounds. Hence much is known about elite burials but less about the way of life in the vital villages that produced the rice surpluses to maintain the aristocracy.

Excavations have uncovered about 50 houses at Haraide. Their floor plans when considered in conjunction with the many house models from *kofun* tombs reveal square one-chambered dwellings sunk about half a meter into the ground. The roofs were supported by four large posts, and the area was around five meters (16.5 ft.) square. The largest measured eight meters (26.4 ft.) on each side. One door gave access to a room equipped with an enclosed ceramic or stone oven set against the wall, in contrast to the fires placed centrally in Yayoi houses. The disposition of some postholes suggests that there were village storehouses for grain surpluses, which, according to carbonized remains, included rice, millet, and barley. Taro and broad beans were also cultivated, and domestic horse, cattle, and chicken bones have been found.

By Yamato times, iron was widely smelted and forged into weapons and tools, and at Haraide it was used to tip wooden hoes and make sickles, knives, chisels, and needles. The needles, linked with the recovery of spindle whorls, also attest to a weaving industry. Domestic and fine ceramic vessels were regularly used.

Hmawza   *See* SRI KSETRA.

Hnaw Kan   Hnaw Kan is an Iron Age cemetery located 80 (48 mi.) kilometers east of PAGAN in the dry zone of central Myanmar (Burma). The late prehistoric period of this region, before the development of the PYU CIVILIZATION, is hardly known, and the excavations at Hnaw Kan in 2001 provided much new and important information after the discovery of the site when a farmer plowed there. The dead were interred in collective graves, each containing more than 12 individuals packed closely together. Mortuary goods were dominated by pottery vessels of many forms; one individual was found with more than 12. Iron grave goods included sword and dagger blades, axes, and spearheads. There were not many ornaments, but those recovered included blue-green glass beads, carnelian beads, and, in one case, a cowry shell held in a woman's hand. Although a considerable distance from the sea, many individuals had been interred with marine shells placed near the head. Seventy-two skeletons have been recovered, and these were reasonably well preserved. Of these, 16 percent were infants, and the sexes are equally represented among the adults. Unfortunately, the lack of surviving collagen in the bones ruled out radiocarbon dating, but the site probably dates to within the second half of the first millennium B.C.E.

Hongshan culture   The Hongshan culture of northeastern China is one of the prehistoric groups that reveal an early development of social complexity before the transition to the state. Located in Liaoning province and adjacent Inner Mongolia, the Hongshan culture is best known for its ritual sites associated with rich burials that date between about 4700 and 2900 B.C.E. NIUHELIANG is the best-documented site, notable for its spirit temple surrounded by mounded tombs that cover an extensive area. The temple itself covers 22 by nine meters (72.6 by 29.7 ft.) and was constructed of wooden-framed walls over stone foundations. The inner walls were plastered and painted. Several clay female figures were found within, as well as figures of dragons and birds. Burials clustering around the sacred structure included stone mounds raised over stone-lined graves. The presence of some particularly rich burials, measured by their jade grave goods, indicates an early development of social ranking. Furthermore, some of the jade figures, such as the coiled dragons, animal masks, and turtles, are matched by later developments in Shang and Zhou art. This suggests a long development of a ritual that was in train long before the establishment of early states. As also illustrated by the LIANGZHU CULTURE and YANGSHAO CULTURE, social complexity had early beginnings in several regions of China.

See also SHANG STATES; XIA DYNASTY.

Horyuji   The Horyuji is one of the earliest Buddhist temple-monasteries in Japan. It was established in 607 C.E. and was probably inspired by PRINCE SHOTUKU (d. 622 C.E.), an early supporter of this new religion in Japan. It is the oldest extant wooden building in the world and houses many fine statues of the period.

hospitals   The foundation inscription from the temple of TA PROHM at ANGKOR in Cambodia describes the foundation and administration of 102 hospitals during the reign of JAYAVARMAN VII (1181–1219). These were distributed across the kingdom and were identical in their basic design. They incorporated a chapel housing an image of Buddha the healer and an exterior water basin. Men and WOMEN, 81,640 in number, from 838 villages, were assigned to supply these hospitals with rice, clothing, honey, wax, and fruit. The doctors had two varieties of camphor, coriander, pepper, mustard, cardamom, molasses, cumin, pine resin, ginger, onions, and ointment made from 10 plants for the treatment of fevers. Almost 2,000 boxes of salve were also on hand to ease hemorrhoids. The staff of each institution included two doctors and their assistants, two dispensary workers, two cooks who also assisted in cleaning, water heaters, specialists in preparing the medicines, and various other attendants, including the servants who prepared the offerings to the Buddha. The stone ruins of many of these hospitals have been identified.

Hotan Hotan was one of the major states that straddled the SILK ROAD linking China with India and Rome. It is located in the southwestern corner of the TARIM BASIN, south of the Taklamakan Desert, in China. Here the rivers that flow north from the Kunlun Range form delta oases before their water dissipates in the desert sand. Hotan was known to the Chinese as Yutian and was renowned as a source of jade. Indeed, the river that flows south to the city is known as "the River of Precious Stones." The ancient capital of Hotan is located at the modern site of Yotkan. Formerly walled, it has been virtually destroyed by looting for gold, jade, and other precious artifacts there. During a visit to Hotan during his 1913 expedition. SIR AUREL STEIN found that many artifacts allegedly from Yotkan were available for sale. Most were terra-cotta figurines of men and WOMEN or animals, such as camels and horses. There are also figurines of monkeys. He collected some stone SEALS, agate and glass beads, and fragments of stucco ornamentation.

In terms of archaeological remains, several elaborate inhumation graves have been found at Shampula dating to the first and second centuries C.E., and these have yielded a remarkable assemblage of woolen, cotton, and silk fabrics. One of these, part of a pair of trousers, was probably taken to Hotan from the west, for it was decorated with a singular image of a man with Western features. Several expeditions have also left Hotan with clay and bronze Buddha images.

The description of Hotan by the Chinese monk XUANZANG, who passed through the kingdom on his journey to India in the seventh century C.E., provides a glimpse of the people and their industries. He noted, for example, that there was relatively little land under cultivation because of the aridity of the sandy desert, but that where there was sufficient water, people cultivated cereal crops and tended orchards. They were adept at making felt and carpets, for they maintained large herds of sheep, and they had an established silk industry. The people seemed content and welcoming, much enjoying music and dance. They read good literature and "showed a sense of propriety and justice." During his visit to Hotan in about 400 C.E., the Chinese monk FAXIAN noted the presence of many monks and monasteries. A recent royal foundation was magnificently decorated in gold and silver leaf, and the kingdom was dotted with large and impressive foundations. The pleasures of reaching Hotan, where space was available in monasteries for visiting monks, was all the greater for the privations suffered during the journey west.

In terms of documentary sources, the history of Hotan can be only partially reconstructed. The Hotanese spoke their own dialect of Saka, with close parallels to the southern Saka languages of MATHURA, SISTAN, and GANDHARA. This suggests strongly that the Saka Hotanese moved into the area probably by the second century B.C.E. Many of the shared words with southern Saka provide clues to the social order of the day, including expressions for "supervisor," "rich," "greatness," "ruler," "lord," and "official title." This language, linked with the BRAHMI script, was also the vehicle for written Buddhist texts, some of which were sought after and taken to China, for Hotan was an important stepping stone between east and west. The Tibetan document known as the *Li Yul* provides some indications of Hotanese history. It describes 56 kings and indicates that BUDDHISM was introduced 404 years after the nirvana, during the reign of King Vijaya Sambhava. The 14th king, called Vijaya Jaya, married the Chinese princess who took silk worms to Hotan to found the local silk industry. It was she who founded a Buddhist monastery known as Lu-she, south of the capital.

A brief period during the first and second centuries C.E. is also illuminated by the corpus of local bronze COINAGE. These have KHAROSHTHI and Chinese texts, the former naming a series of kings with the family name of Gurga and the titles *maharaja* (great king) and *yidaraja* (king of Hotan). Some also bore the symbol of a Bactrian camel. The presence of Chinese and Kushan coins also provides evidence for an extensive exchange system that incorporated Hotan.

Further reading: Bailey, H. "Saka-Studies: The Ancient Kingdom of Hotan," *Iran* 8 (1970): 65–72; Rhie, M. M. *Later Han, Three Kingdoms and Western Chin in China and Bactria to Shan-shan.* Leiden: Brill, 1999; Stein, A. *Ancient Khotan.* Oxford: Clarendon Press, 1907.

Hou Hanshu The *Hou Hanshu* (*History of the Later Han Dynasty*) is a work of historical scholarship that describes the period of Eastern Han rule between 25 and 220 C.E. Several authors were involved in compiling this text. The only contemporary commentary is from the *Dongguan Hanji* (*Biographies in the Eastern Lodge*); most commentaries were written by Fan Ye (398–446 C.E.), the balance by Sima Biao (240–306 C.E.).

See also HAN DYNASTY; *HANSHU*.

Hougang Hougang is a major walled site of the LONG-SHAN CULTURE, located barely 1.5 kilometers (.9 mi.) northwest of ANYANG, the later SHANG STATE capital, in Henan province, north China. It covered an area of about 10 hectares (25 acres) and was defended by stamped-earth walls. This site has revealed the practice of sacrificing children and burying them in the foundations of the walls and buildings. Traces of 37 circular houses with walls of mud and straw brick or wattle and daub have been encountered. These were circular, with a diameter of about five meters (16.5 ft.). They were also spaced with a distance of about five meters between houses and were rebuilt, over time, on the same sites. A kiln indicates local pottery production.

Huainanzi The *Huainanzi*, or 21 chapters on the art of government, were compiled in the court of the king of Huainan and presented to the Chinese Han emperor WUDI (157–87 B.C.E.) in 139 B.C.E. They were compiled under the rule of the king of Huainan, Liu An, by a group of scholars espousing the moral values of TAOISM. The *Huainanzi* can be seen as a late attempt to steer Han Wudi toward Taoist principles. Thus they encourage the ruler "to keep to endeavors that take no action" and note that "although [the emperor's] feet are able to walk, he permits his ministers to lead the way. Although his ears are able to hear, he permits his ministers to propose their own strategies." These proposals had little influence on Han Wudi, who proceeded to double the size of the empire by sending armies to conquer in the south, in Korea, and in the northwestern frontier region.

Wudi, the Martial Emperor, who ruled for 54 years, was one of the greatest Han emperors. His dynasty succeeded the centralized autocracy of the QIN. The latter were overthrown by the first Han emperor, GAOZU (247–195 B.C.E.), a man of humble origin, who was faced with the need to maintain an empire created out of the great warring states of the preceding two centuries. Many political philosophers offered their advice to successive emperors, and for the first six decades of the Western Han rule, Taoism dominated. This approach advocated an essentially detached and remote role for the ruler, whose tranquility and lack of action allowed him to react positively to any changing conditions. Under Han Wudi, however, there was a marked move to a Confucian model of government, in which the emperor adopted a proactive role toward policy.

Huanbei Huanbei, "north of the Huan River," is a city of the SHANG STATE, discovered in the autumn of 1999. It is about two kilometers (1.2 mi.) north of the later Shang capital of ANYANG, and its walls, 2,150 meters (7,095 ft.) long, enclosed an area of 470 hectares (1,175 acres). Very little is known about the site because of its recent discovery, but preliminary excavations have dated it to within the period

1400–1200 B.C.E., making it the likely Shang capital of Xiang, founded by King He Tan Jia, the 12th Shang king. Alternatively, it could have been the court center of King Pan Geng, the 19th king, and his two successors. This is a vital site and a remarkable discovery. A palace precinct has been found in the center of the walled area, covering more than 10 hectares and incorporating at least 25 individual buildings. Outside the eastern wall, a road has been identified, 10 meters (33 ft.) wide and 1.5 kilometers (.9 mi.) long, still retaining the rut marks of wheeled vehicles. Further excavations have the potential to illuminate the vital period of Shang history between the abandonment of ZHENGZHOU as the capital and the occupation of Anyang.

Huandi (Liu Zhi; Martial Emperor) (132–168 C.E.) *Huandi (Martial Emperor) was the 10th emperor of the Eastern Han dynasty of China.*
He was the great-grandson of Emperor ZHANGDI (57–88 C.E.) and acceded to the throne in 146 C.E.

Huang-lao boshu Huang-lao boshu, or Huang-lao silk texts, refer to a remarkable discovery made in 1973 in a rich tomb at MAWANGDUI in Hunan province, a tomb dated to 168 B.C.E. This was a set of documents written on silk, which included the *Daodejing* with four appendixes. The latter have proved controversial; some scholars identify them as the *Huangdi sijing* (Records of the yellow emperor), lost to historians for more than 2,000 years. Others, uncertain of their precise place in the documentary evolution of that text, refer to them simply as the *Huang-lao boshu* or *Huang-lao* silk texts. These four records are known as the *Jingfa, Shiliu, Cheng,* and *Daoyuan.* They have in common the advocacy of TAOISM, the constrained and detached relationship between the king and his subjects in accordance the Tao, the concordance between cosmic inevitability and human behavior.

Huang-lao was a philosophical approach to government that predominated during the first reigns of the HAN DYNASTY in the second century C.E. This approach was set out in the *Daodejing,* a set of 81 chapters ascribed to the sage LAOZI, who probably lived at the same time as CONFUCIUS during the late Spring and Autumn period (770–476 B.C.E.). Taoism was rooted in the notion that the world is subject to unpredictable but constant development and change and that the ruler should adopt a tranquil and detached acceptance of this fact, expressed in the concept *wuwei,* or avoidance of a personal policy. *Huang-lao,* the name given to this school of thought, is derived from Huang, the mythical yellow emperor, and Lao, or Laozi. However, their writings have survived only as brief allusions in later texts.

Huhai (Er Shi) (r. 210–207 B.C.E.) *Huhai was the second emperor of the Qin dynasty of China. He acceded to the imperial throne some time between the ages of 12 and 21.*

Huhai followed in the footsteps of one of the most charismatic and powerful rulers China has known, QIN SHI-HUANGDI (259–210 B.C.E.), and acceded through intrigues manipulated by the eunuch and minister ZHAO GAO. Fusu, the eldest of the first emperor's sons, was the legitimate heir, but Zhao Gao retained the emperor's instructions for Fusu to return from the northern frontier and substituted a requirement, allegedly from the emperor, that he commit suicide. Thus Huhai succeeded. He was evidently a weak and ineffectual leader, easily manipulated by his senior advisers.

The formation of the QIN empire followed the long and vicious WARRING STATES PERIOD, and while Qin Shihuangdi had been able to keep his state intact through his forceful measures, the former independent states began to assert their independence under the weaker hand of Huhai and his ministers. Thus Cheng Sheng in the former southern state of CHU declared himself king, while independence was also proclaimed by the state of WEI. Huhai then antagonized the powerful Zhao Gao, who coerced him to commit suicide. Under the HAN DYNASTY, which succeeded Qin, Huhai was cited as a weak and extravagant ruler who had lost the MANDATE OF HEAVEN and deserved to be ejected.

Huidi (Liu Ying; Beneficial Emperor) (210–188 B.C.E.) *Huidi was the second emperor of the Western Han dynasty.* GAOZU (247–195 B.C.E.), his father and founder of the dynasty, had married Lu Hou, a member of the Lu family of Shandong. They produced a son and a daughter. The emperor, however, also had other consorts and sired seven sons by them. Huidi was only 15 years of age when his father was killed by an arrow while on a military campaign, and for his entire reign Huidi was dominated by his mother, the dowager empress. She is reputed to have had several of his half-brothers and potential rivals murdered, while one of the lesser queens of Gaodi was put to death and so mutilated that Huidi was cowed for the rest of his brief reign. Huidi is best known for the establishment of shrines for the veneration of his late father. It was also during his reign that massive labor forces were galvanized for the construction of the walls around the capital, XIANYANG. This huge undertaking resulted in the enclosure of an area measuring 33.5 square kilometers (13.4 sq. mi.); the walls themselves were eight meters high and 12 meters wide (26.4 by 39.6 ft.) at the crest. Huidi died in 188 B.C.E., aged only 23 years. He was succeeded by Shaodi Gong, the infant son of a minor wife.

Hulaskhera Hulaskhera is a city in the Lucknow area of northern India, occupied during the KUSHAN and Gupta kingdoms, and dominated by a walled citadel built during the GUPTA EMPIRE. Excavations have revealed Kushan period brick houses and a road running through the city.

hun The Chinese believed that at death a person was divided between the *hun* and the *bo*. The former may be translated as the soul, which might migrate either to the heavens or to the land of the yellow springs. The latter remained with the body. Apparent death was followed by a ritual in which the robe of the deceased was taken to the roof of his or her house and pointed north in an attempt to tempt the *hun* back into the body. This was followed by the preparation of a talisman to place in the grave, which contained directions for the *hun* to reach either the Blessed Islands of DI to the east or the land of the Queen Mother of the West. The best-known such talisman is from Tomb 1 at MAWANGDUI, that of the marchioness of Dai, dated to 168 B.C.E. This was a painting on silk that had probably been carried aloft in the manner of a banner in her funeral procession before it was placed face down on her innermost coffin. The painting depicted a series of scenes that began with the corpse's being laid out, accompanied by items for interment. The lady is then seen with servants, before embarking on her soul journey, first to the island of Peng-lai, where she received an elixir before she passed through the gates of heaven, and then, in the uppermost scene, to paradise itself. A second such banner was found in the adjacent tomb of the marchioness's son.

From the mid-first century B.C.E., the talisman was often a fine bronze mirror decorated with a square within a circle, representing the Earth within the heavens. The symbolism on the mirrors also incorporated the green dragon, scarlet bird, white tiger and turtle, animals that represent four of the five phases that determined and explained the rhythms of the universe and of human destiny in Han thought.

See also HAN DYNASTY.

Hwangnam, great tomb of Burial 98 at the royal necropolis of Kyongju, also known as the great tomb of Hwangnam, belongs to the Old SHILLA kingdom of Korea, before Shilla unified the peninsula in 668 C.E. This is a double-mounded tomb attaining a length of 120 meters (396 ft.), and the higher mound rises to a height of 23 meters (75.9 ft.). The south mound is thought to have covered the tomb of King Nulchi, who died in 458 C.E., after a reign that lasted for 42 years. Excavations of the north mound, which is thought to have contained the burial of his queen, commenced in 1973; a year later, after the removal of 14,000 cubic meters (490,000 cu. ft.) of material, the main burial chamber was revealed. The ascription of this tomb to the queen is based on the lack of weaponry with the dead person, as well as a text on a garment that read, "Girdle for madame." While the remains of the queen have not survived, her tomb revealed the wealth of the Shilla aristocracy. She wore a gold crown and girdle, multiple gold bracelets, and two necklaces of gold and glass. Indeed the weight of gold exceeded four kilograms (8.8 lbs.). Such Shilla tombs had a mound of earth covering a tumulus of large stones raised over the wooden mortuary chambers. Both the mounds of Hwangnam, the name of the district of Kyongju where the mounds are located, contained horse harnesses in the topmost layer, while the king's burial mound, which also held rich grave goods, incorporated a small grave with the remains of a young woman thought to have been sacrificed during the mortuary rituals.

The queen's burial chamber covered an area of 6.8 by 4.6 meters (22.4 by 15.8 ft.) and was four meters (13.2 ft.) high. Timber lined, it lay under a mound of stones. A double lacquered coffin lay within, associated with a wooden chest to contain the mortuary offerings. A superb silver bowl of Sassanian style was found in the chest of mortuary offerings, as well as a rare imported Chinese ceramic vessel made in Nanjing and typologically belonging to the second half of the fifth century C.E.

The adjacent king's burial incorporated an additional chamber for grave offerings that included many ceramic vessels and armor. He was well equipped with nine swords, while his armor included silver leggings. The offerings chest included a silver crown, but the crown he wore, curiously, was made of gilt bronze rather than the anticipated solid gold. The king had a favorite glass wine flagon; made in the Levant and imported over a huge distance, it had a broken handle that had been repaired with gold wire.

I

I Ching (seventh century) *I Ching was a Chinese Buddhist who traveled to India in 671 C.E.*

On his way, he visited a walled center in the state of SRIVIJAYA on the island of Sumatra in Indonesia and there reported the presence of more than 1,000 Buddhist monks versed in the SANSKRIT texts. He then traveled to India, where he spent 10 years studying further Buddhist teachings before returning to Sumatra for four further years until 689 C.E. After returning to China, he worked again on texts in the state of Srivijaya, and his surviving writings are among the few documentary sources for this period.

Inariyama Inariyama is the location of a mounded tomb, known as a *kofun,* located in Sakitama prefecture, Japan. *Kofun* were the burial places of high elites during the YAMATO state, which was centered in western Honshu and lasted from the early fourth to the early eighth century. The Sakitima necropolis had nine large keyhole-shaped *kofun* and at least 36 circular ones, although most of the latter have now disappeared. In 1968–69, one of the keyhole tumuli, known as Sakitama-Inariyama, was excavated. Half the monument had been removed as a source of soil, but the rounded mound survived. The complex had been surrounded by a double moat, which was excavated and found to contain ceramic tomb models (HANIWA), some of the cylindrical form and others depicting human figures. These had tumbled into the moat from their original positions and had fragmented. Two tombs were found near the surface of the surviving half of the monument. One was complete; the other had been looted. The former held the remains of a large wooden coffin 3.7 meters (12.2 ft.) long and 0.8 wide (2.6 ft.), which lay an adult male skeleton. He was richly endowed with mortuary offerings. These included silver earrings, a jade bead, a bronze mirror, and a fine belt of silk from which gilt bronze pendants embellished with designs of dragons dangled. This warrior had also been interred with his iron armor and a large collection of weaponry, including knives, spears, arrowheads, and swords. His saddle, stirrups, and other horse accoutrements were found outside the coffin. Ten years after the excavations were completed, restoration of one of the double-edged swords revealed an inscription in gold inlay, with the oldest known genealogy in the history of Japan, describing how his ancestors had been in the service of a long line of kings.

The sword had been owned by Owake-no-Omi. Owake was his clan name, and Omi is thought to have been his *kabane,* or title conferred by royalty. The INSCRIPTION includes a number of passages that reflect on the expansion of Yamato during the vital fifth century. The sword, dated to 471 C.E., mentions *okimi,* a title meaning "great king," with the name Wakatakeru. This king has been identified as Yuryaku, whose traditional reign lasted from 457 to 479 C.E. According to the historic records, his name when living had been Wakatake. A member of a caste of sword bearers and palace guards had owned the sword. Such groups, known as *be,* were specialist unions that exemplified the rising power of the Yamato court in administering a growing kingdom at this period. Specialist examination of the metal revealed it to be steel wrought from iron ore mined in southern China.

India The name India derives from the SANSKRIT term *sindhu,* or river. First recorded in the west by HERODOTUS OF HALICARNASSUS in the fifth century B.C.E., the term originally referred to the Indus River and its environs. Knowledge about India spread westward as a result of the Achaemenid Persian conquest of GANDHARA, an area including much of modern Afghanistan, under King CYRUS THE GREAT (559–530 B.C.E.). In 521 B.C.E. DARIUS THE GREAT (550–486 B.C.E.) extended the Persian Empire into the Indus Valley. Indians were later to serve in the Achaemenid Persian army that invaded Greece in 480 B.C.E. The area now comprising India, Sri Lanka, Pakistan, and Afghanistan had sustained many civilizations. The earliest, known as the INDUS VALLEY CIVILIZATION, concentrated in the valley of Indus River and was at its height between 2600–1900 B.C.E. The major sites are MOHENJO-DARO and HARAPPA. The two powerful central states that followed were the MAURYA and GUPTA EMPIRES, but in the northwest of this region there were numerous states founded by the Greeks, Scythians, Parthians, and KUSHANS.

See also ACHAEMENID EMPIRE.

Indianization

From the last few centuries B.C.E., long-distance maritime trade linked Southeast Asia with the civilizations of China and India. This period saw a new range of exotic goods entering existing trade networks and the introduction of new ideas. Southeast Asian states adopted the SANSKRIT or PALI language, Hindu gods, BUDDHISM, and Indian writing systems and began minting their own COINAGE. Architectural forms, construction techniques, and symbols were also borrowed from India. In explaining the origins of Southeast Asian civilizations, therefore, many scholars identified Indian influence as a key contributor. This reached an extreme form in the description of early states as Indian colonies, but the role of India was almost certainly exaggerated.

Archaeological research has shown that local societies during the Iron Age that preceded the transition to states were much more complex and sophisticated than was previously imagined. The transition to statehood, under the new model, is now seen as being the result of local leaders' selectively adopting Indian traits if they suited their objectives. Thus adopting an esoteric language or the construction of impressive monuments can be seen as means of enhancing a leader's status. Although SIVA and Vishnu were worshiped in Southeast Asia, and Indian epics and religions contributed to the local culture, there remained powerful indigenous traditions, religions, kinship systems, and forms of social organization. Rather than stress Indian influence, therefore, it is more accurate to envisage indigenous change that incorporated an Indic veneer.

Further reading: Cœdès, G. *Angkor: An Introduction.* Hong Kong: Oxford University Press, 1966; ———. *The Indianized States of Southeast Asia.* Honolulu: University of Hawaii Press, 1968; Higham, C. F. W. *The Civilization of Angkor.* London: Weidenfeld and Nicolson, 2001; Vickery, M. *Society, Economics and Politics in Pre-Angkor Cambodia.* Tokyo: The Centre for East Asian Cultural Studies for UNESCO, 1998; Vickery, M. "What and Where Was Chenla?" In *Rechèrches Nouvèlles sur le Cambodge,* edited by F. Bizot. Paris: EFEO, 1994.

Indra

Indra was a major god of the Hindu Rig-Veda. Often depicted with a *vajra,* or thunderbolt, in one hand, he was the personified force of thunder. At the commencement of the monsoon season in India and Southeast Asia, so vital for the cultivation of cereal crops, the rains take the form of dramatic thunderstorms. It is a simple step to appreciate the importance of Indra, the giver of life. In Southeast Asia, the name *Indravarman* (Shield, or Protégé, of Indra) is found among the kings of ANGKOR in Cambodia. The Rig-Veda says of Indra that he was the one who wielded the *vajra,* which released water.

Indrapura

Indrapura was the name given to the sanctuary known today as DONG DUONG in Quang Nam province, coastal Vietnam. It was the capital of the dynasty of Indrapura, whose first king was named Indravarman. Given the title *maharajadhiraja,* "king of

Indra was a major Hindu god associated with thunder, rain, and fertility. This wall painting of him from Balawaste dates to the seventh or eighth century C.E. *(Art Resource, NY)*

kings," he ruled from 875 to 898 C.E. There is no firm evidence for the formation of a single CHAM CIVILIZATION state against the presence of several competing kingdoms. There can be no doubt, however, that Indrapura was a major center of Cham power as measured by the size and splendor of the Buddhist temple of Dong Duong. Nineteen available INSCRIPTIONS for the dynasty of Indrapura provide unmatched evidence for the history of a Cham royal dynasty. The evidence suggests an authority structure similar to that of contemporary ANGKOR in Cambodia, in which the king of kings was aided by a corps of aristocratic retainers, while local magnates continued to exercise their authority in the provinces. Even this situation, however, was fluid, as the demise of Indrapura after the 10th century indicates.

Indravarman was the son and grandson of men with the royal names of Rudravarman and Bhadravarman, but a text indicates that he took power not because he was high born but rather because the king chose him on the basis of his qualities. He was a Buddhist and was given the posthumous name of Paramabuddhaloka. His wife also bore the royal name of Rajakula-Haradevi. He was succeeded by his maternal nephew, Jaya Simhavarman (898–908 C.E.). This succession suggests a matrilineal succession as in the contemporary Angkorian kingdom. The third king was named Bhadravarman (908–16 C.E.). His relationship to his predecessor is not known, but he married Jaya Simhavarman's cousin, Ugradevi. After a short reign, he was succeeded by his son, Indravarman II.

The area under the control of INDRAVARMAN I of Champa can be perceived in the inscriptions. These concentrate in the province of Quang Nam and probably extend as far north as Bac Ha, where an inscription of the correct period but without mention of a royal name has been recovered. His successor, Jaya Simhavarman, extended the area under the center of Indrapura to cover more than 350 kilometers (210 mi.) of coastline from Chau Sa in the south to My Duc in the north. Anne-Valérie Schweyer has suggested that this expansion may have resulted from his marriage to a highly ranked princess. An inscription dated 965 at PO NAGAR described how Indravarman II rededicated an image after its predecessor was destroyed by a Khmer invasion. The precise relationship between Indrapura and Po Nagar is not clear, but their distance apart, more than 450 (270 mi.) kilometers, indicates the widespread influence at least of Indravarman II. A further text from Kon Klor in Kontum province mentions a local overlord, Mahindravarman, who acknowledged his dependence on Bhadravarman of Indrapura.

Indratataka The Indratataka reservoir at HARIHARALAYA was, for its time, by far the largest reservoir built in the Mekong Valley states; it measured 3,800 meters (12,540 ft.) long and 800 (2,640 ft.) wide. It was begun by King INDRAVARMAN I of ANGKOR, in Cambodia and completed by his son, YASHOVARMAN I (r. 889–910 C.E.). Despite many claims that it was designed to irrigate rice fields, there is no evidence for this, and the contemporary INSCRIPTIONS suggest that it had a symbolic purpose, as well as supplying water to the moats of Indravarman's temples of PREAH KO and the BAKONG. Moreover, there is very little land between the reservoir and the wet-season bank of the GREAT LAKE in which to cultivate irrigated rice.

Indravarman I (877–899 C.E.) *Indravarman I (Protégé of Indra) was the third king of Angkor in Cambodia.*
An INSCRIPTION describes him as an invincible warrior; he was also responsible for the construction of several impressive temples and a reservoir. His claim to the throne was marginal. He married a granddaughter of JAYAVARMAN II (r. 770–834 C.E.). Because Indravarman's mother's brother had married Jayavarman's daughter, Indravarman married his first cousin. His paternal grandmother was the younger sister of Jayavarman's wife, making him the great-nephew by marriage of Jayavarman II and step-first cousin once removed of his predecessor JAYAVARMAN III (r. 834–877 C.E.). In his official genealogy, Indravarman did not mention any relationship with Jayavarman II or III, and his accession was contested.

One of his inscriptions states that "the right hand of this prince, long and powerful, was terrible in combat when his sword fell on his enemies, scattering them to all points of the compass. Invincible, he was appeased only by his enemies who turned their backs in surrender, or who placed themselves under his protection." This claim was engraved on the foundation stela of the temple of PREAH KO in 879 C.E. Preah Ko is one of temples of the Roluos Group, also known as HARIHARALAYA, which lies southeast of Angkor near the wet-season shore of the GREAT LAKE. A second temple, the BAKONG, was also constructed there, and in its size, surrounding walls, entrance pavilions, and moat, it represents a major advance in the energy expended on such monuments. He also had a huge BARAY constructed, and it was recorded in another inscription that "he made the INDRATATAKA, mirror of his glory, like the ocean." This *baray* was of unprecedented size: 3,800 meters (12,540 ft.) in length and 800 (2,640 ft.) meters wide. He was succeeded by his son, YASHOVARMAN.

Indravarman III (r. 1296–1308) *Indravarman III (Protégé of Indra) was king of Angkor in Cambodia from 1296 to 1308 and is best known because he was ruling there during the visit of the Chinese traveler Zhou Daguan in 1296–97.*
Zhou Daguan provided a firsthand account of the capital and country; he described the city of ANGKOR THOM, a royal audience, and a royal procession. Although the kingdom had passed the zenith of its power, rich and splendid court rituals were still in evidence.

Indus Valley civilization The remains of one of the world's great early civilizations, the Indus Valley civilization, were first encountered in 1826, when James Lewis, a British army deserter, saw the mounds at HARAPPA. His description of this site was published 16 years later. The first serious excavations took place between 1856 and 1872 under the direction of SIR ALEXANDER CUNNINGHAM, then director of the ARCHAEOLOGICAL SURVEY OF INDIA. Among other finds, he recovered a SEAL containing writing in an unknown script, which remains undeciphered to this day. In 1920 SIR JOHN MARSHALL worked at Harappa, and a year later excavations began at a second center at MOHENJO DARO. The recovery of further seals, as well as brick foundations, a system of drains, and a range of exquisite ornaments in precious materials inspired an article published in 1924, claiming the discovery of a major early civilization. The Indus civilization was founded on the agricultural wealth of the Indus and Sarasvati floodplains. The latter river has now dried up, but formerly it ran parallel to and east of the Indus. The presence of many sites along its former course makes it clear that it flowed during the height of the Indus civilization. The extent of the alluvial plains of these rivers and the silt deposited during the floods provided a rich agricultural base for the rise of the state. The cultivation of barley and wheat on the floodplains can be accomplished with minimal effort: There is no need for fertilizers or plowing. Domestic sheep and goats, cattle, and pigs were also raised.

DATING THE INDUS CIVILIZATION

As a result of the intractable problems encountered by the many scholars who have sought to decipher and understand Indus Valley texts, less is known of the inner workings of this civilization than of any other, including the contemporary states in the Tigris and Euphrates Valley and in Egypt. There are two ways of dating the civilization. The first relies on the recovery of trade items from the Indus Valley found in well-dated contexts in Mesopotamia. The second lies in the radiocarbon dates taken from well-provenienced contexts. The latter have now refined the chronological span of the Indus civilization to the period between 2600 and 1900 B.C.E. There was, however, a long preceding period of increasing cultural complexity, and, equally, the end of the civilization was neither swift nor dramatic. These radiocarbon determinations, based on the sites of Sukotada, Mohenjo Daro, and KALIBANGAN, harmonize with the weight of archaeological evidence from the Middle East, allowing scholars to conclude that trade flourished in the period 2350–1770 B.C.E.

CULTURAL DEVELOPMENT PRECEDING THE INDUS CIVILIZATION

The Indus civilization developed on the basis of a long preceding cultural sequence, in which agriculture, craft skills, and widespread trade grew in complexity and range. This is nowhere better demonstrated than at the settlement of MEHRGARH, located so as to command the southern exit of the Bolan Pass onto the Indus floodplain, about 250 kilometers (150 mi.) north of Mohenjo Daro. Here excavations have revealed a long Neolithic occupation, which by 5000 B.C.E. already provided evidence for trade in copper and TURQUOISE, the construction of substantial mud-brick houses, and the burial of the dead with bitumen-coated baskets and exotic ornaments. The earliest clay figurines were also found in this early context. The second period saw a continuation of extensive trade networks, which now included the presence of exotic marine shell, lead, and LAPIS LAZULI. Pottery manufacture also began. By the period 4000–3500 B.C.E., pottery making flourished and trade continued to expand.

Even by the first period, there is some evidence for the cultivation of wheat and barley and the domestication of cattle. Agriculture expanded subsequently at this site, and it is important to note that the crops and domestic animals were those that later sustained the Indus civilization. The site continued through a further four occupation periods, beginning in about 3500 B.C.E. The seals that were to form such a central part of the Indus material record, the production of fine terra-cotta figurines of bejeweled WOMEN, and large structures built of mud brick all occur. One elaborate figurine of a woman, dated to about 3000 B.C.E., has an elaborate and sophisticated hairstyle and impressive jewelry. The sequence at Mehrgarh is vital in indicating a long, local development of many of the traits that were to characterize the Indus civilization. A similar sequence toward increasing complexity is seen at the trading center of Mundigak in Afghanistan, where the final phase saw the construction of walls and a palace equivalent in date to the foundation of the cities on the Indus floodplain.

DISTRIBUTION OF INDUS CIVILIZATION

The Indus civilization is best known on the basis of the major excavated cities, but there are also many smaller but no less significant sites. The area covered is considerable, from SUTKAGEN DOR on the coast of the Pakistan–Iran border to the port city of LOTHAL at the head of the Gulf of Khambhat in western India. Even farther to the east, Alamgirpur lies in the valley of the Jamuna River, while the trading post of SHORTUGHAI lies in northern Afghanistan and was positioned to command a source of lapis lazuli. Most sites, however, concentrate in the alluvial lowlands. The two outstanding sites on the basis of their size and structure are Mohenjo Daro, located near the Indus River in Sind and Harappa, commanding the plain of the Ravi River, between Lahore and Multan in the Punjab in Pakistan. Ganweriwala, which is unexcavated, covers 80 hectares (200 acres). Smaller sites that might qualify as regional centers for administration, trade, or manufacturing include BALAKOT, AMRI, KOT DIJI,

CHANHU-DARO and ALLAHDINO in Pakistan and, SURKHO-TADA, DHOLAVIRA, Lothal, and Kalibangan in India.

EARLY INDUS PHASES

The early and vital formative phases of this civilization are now recognized on the basis of four regional groupings that cover a substantial area, from Quetta in Baluchistan east into the valley of the now-extinct SARAS-VATI RIVER and south into Gujarat in India. These are known as the DAMB SADAAT, AMRI-NAL, Kot Diji, and SOTHI-SISWAL phases. All four have in common a large number of small settlements, less than about five hectares (12.5 acres), linked with a few four times or more that size, with the largest extending over 40 to 50 hectares (100 to 125 acres). The population of the majority of sites would therefore have been measured in the low hundreds of people. With the transition to the mature phase of the civilization, central sites grew much larger. These sites have hardly exhibited any communal effort in the provision of public works. A handful of the larger sites, such as Banawali and Kalibangan, were surrounded by walls, those at the latter site 250 meters (825 ft.) in one direction and 170 meters (561 ft.) in the other and reaching a thickness of almost two meters. Nor is there any evidence for the social stratification that characterized the mature tradition of the urban civilization. There is a marked uniformity among the sites, and while village crafts, such as ceramics and bead making, are evidenced, there is no sign of the craft specialization that was to follow.

MATURE PHASE

There appears to have been a swift and major change, and the excavation of the cities demonstrates the nature and complexity of this civilization. Two sites stand out on the basis of their size and complexity. Mohenjo Daro covers an area of about 130 hectares (325 acres), while Harappa covers about 150 hectares (375 acres), although these are minimal figures: More living areas may lie under river alluvium. These larger centers reveal a common spatial pattern: a large walled citadel to the west and a lower walled city to the east. The former area incorporates public buildings orientated to the cardinal points of the compass and built on a huge raised brick platform. These include the remains of a remarkable bath at Mohenjo Daro built of specially shaped bricks, with surrounding chambers and an elaborate system of drainage. SIR MORTIMER WHEELER also suggested that an adjacent monumental building might have been a granary and another structure a temple, although there is no general agreement on these interpretations. Whatever their precise function, there can be no doubt that the citadel area was employed by the ruling elite and that religious rituals were performed there.

The lower city had housing for the urban populace centered on a street system interspersed with narrow lanes. Houses were made of brick, and the more opulent buildings incorporated a series of rooms grouped around a central courtyard. Such houses included wells and bathrooms in which the drains were located in the walls and were directed to the main system in the street. Latrines were also provided, and the drainpipes for these fell vertically to the main sewer. There were also smaller and meaner houses, presumably for the less wealthy. There is no doubt that the cities were also manufacturing centers. There is evidence at Harappa and Mohenjo Daro for the firing of fine ceramic vessels. An unfinished steatite seal at Mohenjo Daro indicates their local manufacture. Dyers' vats reveal the manufacture of cloth, and there were specialized BRICK makers, coppersmiths, makers of jewelry from imported raw materials, and workshops for making decorative shell inlays. Cart ruts in the roads show not only that the carts were about the same size as those still to be seen in the area today, but also that the streets bustled with the carriage of goods.

Smaller centers in many cases followed the same urban planning of a walled citadel within a walled city. Excavations at LOTHAL, for example, have identified the former, which occupies the southeastern quarter of the city, and the lower area, in which a carnelian-bead factory has been uncovered. The fortified area was 330 by 180 meters (1,089 by 594 ft.) in extent and thus covered six hectares. A cemetery lies outside the city wall. Perhaps the most extraordinary feature of this city, however, is a huge brick-lined tank 219 by 37 (722 by 122 ft.) meters in extent lying alongside the eastern wall. This has been interpreted as a dock for oceangoing vessels, linked by a channel to the river that formerly flowed past the site. Others, however, see this basin as a possible freshwater reservoir.

Kalibangan is located adjacent to the ancient course of the Sarasvati River. The citadel on the western side of the site measures 220 by 125 (726 by 412.5 ft.) meters, while the lower city covers an area of 7.5 hectares (18.75 acres). Both are surrounded by large mud-brick walls. The citadel also has a central dividing wall and was entered by a recessed gateway on the northwest corner and another on the south wall. Two entrances have been found for the lower city, one again in the northwest corner, the other on the western wall. Both gave access to the river. There are towers at the corners of the walls and along the northwestern wall of the citadel. Some authorities maintain that the walls were to provide a barrier against floods, but the presence of complex entrances and bastions rather suggests a need for defense against attack. The first or early Indus phase of this site had an irregular street plan, later replaced by rows of more orderly streets on a north-south and east-west axis. Surkotada, located in the Rann of Kachch, is tiny, less than a hectare in extent. Yet it was heavily defended with a stone wall, bastions, and a gateway with guard chambers. Despite its size, it was still divided by an interior wall into a citadel and a residential area.

Dholavira is located between two streams, on an island in the Gulf of Kachch, just northeast of Jamnagar in India. This strategic location commanded the maritime trade route from the Indus Delta east to Gujarat. The building material included sandstone as well as mud brick, and the layout of the city differed from the norm, in the presence of three walled areas. The outermost covers an area of 33 hectares (82.5 acres) and is surrounded by a mud-brick wall. This enclosed a further rectangular wall of the middle town, which covered 7.5 hectares (18.75 acres). The walled citadel lay to the south of the middle town. A large inscription with characters 37 centimeters (14.8 in.) in height was found near the northern entrance to the citadel, which contained administrative and probably temple buildings. Industrial activity, such as bead making and shell working, took place in the lower city, which was divided into a grid pattern of streets on the cardinal directions. The dead were interred in a cemetery beyond the outer walls.

EVIDENCE OF CIVILIZATION

Such a settlement pattern, with a few dominant cities and regional centers on a descending scale of size, is widely seen as typical of civilizations. In view of the lack of any documentary evidence and the rarity of widely excavated cemeteries, it is not possible to identify all the details of the social organization of this civilization. There is no doubt that there were scribes, craft specialists, merchants, builders, and shopkeepers. But whether there was a ruling royal dynasty at Mohenjo Daro and a second at Harappa, or whether there was one centralized state or a series of independent polities based on the major centers, is unknown. In western Asia, Egypt, China, Cambodia, and Japan, the presence of complex architecture, royal graves, and a script that can be translated have enabled dynasties to be identified and the course of events appreciated. There can be no doubt that there was a ruling elite at sites such as Harappa and Mohenjo Daro, but at present little can be added to illuminate this important issue. This conclusion rests on a series of facts, largely involving material remains. Thus the Indus civilization engaged in widespread trading relationships that must have entailed careful central oversight. The provision of food for a population measured in the thousands, orderly layout of the street system, organization of a water supply, and proper sanitation would have required a bureaucracy and decision makers. Although some authorities are dubious about the presence of military or coercive force, the fact that centers were strongly walled with bastions and guard rooms and that the specialist metalworkers manufactured weaponry indicates the likelihood that friction was present and defensive measures were necessary.

There was also a system of standardized weights and measures. The former were expressed in the form of cubes of ascending size; the latter involved dimensions of 37.6 and 51.8 centimeters (15 and 20.7 in.), respectively. Perhaps the most compelling evidence for the organization of trade is to be seen in the surviving seals and sealings. Most seals were made of carved, then heat-hardened,

STEATITE, and a typical specimen would measure two to three centimeters square (.32 to .48 sq. in.). They bear a wide range of motifs. Most have an image of an animal, such as a bull, tiger, elephant, water buffalo, or unicorn. Some depict a god seated in a yogic position with a headdress of buffalo horns and foliage. In one instance, a seal from Mohenjo Daro shows a scene in which such a god figure stands within a pipal or fig tree, accompanied by a large ram and seven figures with plumed headdresses. In virtually all cases, the seals also incorporate a written text. The sealings are normally of clay and naturally bear the opposite image of the seal itself. On the reverse of the clay sealing is often the impression of fabric or cordage, suggesting that these seals were on occasion used to mark ownership of bales of goods destined for trade. By land, such trade would have involved wheeled carts, models of which have survived. By river or sea, it would have called on substantial vessels, some of which are depicted on the seals with large rudders and a cabin. Whether by land or sea, such trade required regulation and protection.

The trading system also involved raw materials from many sources. Shortughai appears to have been an Indus trading station in northeast Afghanistan, from which the local lapis lazuli sources could be exploited. Gold, silver, marine shell, copper, tin and lead, jade, carnelian, and amethyst were all obtained from far afield. Some of these items were transformed into high-quality ornaments and then exported. Indus carnelians, for example, have been found in Mesopotamia. Sumerian records describe a place called Meluhha, which is almost certainly the Sumerian name for the Indus Valley, from which the Sumerians obtained ebony wood, copper, gold, ivory, and exotic birds. Cotton cloth was also probably exported widely. A detailed examination of the products of the Indus workshops reveals a mastery of many media that would have called on a long period of specialization. The carnelian beads, for example, seen in the complex belt ornaments recovered from Mohenjo Daro and Allahdino would have taken months to complete. Ceramics were of a high quality and kiln fired. The steatite seals are miniature works of art. The copper and bronze workers made proficient axes, chisels, spearheads, fishhooks, and daggers, as well as lively models of people. The terra-cotta figurines show the sophisticated coiffures of men and women and their lavish use of personal ornaments. Surviving golden ornaments include beads, pendants, and brooches. Silver was beaten into elegant vessels. Rare stone carvings reveal men wearing a cloak and a headband. Similar headbands in gold have survived to this day. Some sites seem to have specialized in various aspects of craft production: Balakot for shell working, Chanhu-daro and Lothal for the manufacture of carnelian beads.

Excavations at the Mohenjo Daro and Harappa citadels uncovered substantial buildings thought to have been temples. The seals often depict a god wearing an elaborate head ornament of horns and foliage, seated on a throne. Some images show the god with three faces. Stone lingams, phallus-shaped objects of veneration common to the later Hindu religion and in particular the worship of SIVA, have also been recovered. The wide distribution of the horned god hints at a shared religion in the many Indus communities.

It is unfortunate that there is so little surviving evidence for elite mortuary practices. The presence of royal graves would, for example, enormously increase our appreciation of this civilization. However, some cemeteries have been uncovered, for example, at Harappa. The dead were inhumed with pottery vessels above the head, accompanied also by items of personal jewelry. Some graves contain the remains of a man and a woman. These cemeteries are normally found beyond the city walls.

The Indus civilization relied on the excellent agricultural soil of the riverine floodplains. It was enriched by an extensive trade network that involved access to widely dispersed sources of raw materials, an efficient transport system, and a high degree of craft skill. Trade with the civilizations of Mesopotamia also stimulated wealth and experience. The end of the civilization has on occasion been ascribed to the predatory attacks of intrusive Indo-Aryan speakers from the north. This hypothesis is no longer tenable. The decline, which was intense in the western Punjab and Sind, in Pakistan, but not apparent in Gujarat or the eastern Punjab in India, is more likely to have been caused by a series of interlinked changes in the very factors that encouraged its formation. Thus the drying up of the Sarasvati River would have been catastrophic for communities along its course. Subtle changes in international trade networks and loss of control over sources of vital raw materials might have been involved, no less than a growing threat to the food supply from serious flooding. Also, it is becoming increasingly evident that many aspects of the Indus civilization did not simply disappear, but, rather, continued in modified form and contributed to the subsequent rise of states, this time centered in the Ganges (Ganga) and Jamuna Valleys to the east.

Further reading: Kenoyer, J. M. *Ancient Cities of the Indus Civilization*. Oxford: Oxford University Press, 1998; Possehl, G. L. *Harappan Civilization: A Recent Perspective*. New Delhi: Oxford University Press, 1993; ———. *Indus Age: The Writing System*. Philadelphia: University of Pennsylvania Press, 1996; ———. "Revolution in the Urban Revolution: The Emergence of Indus Urbanisation," *Annual Review of Anthropology* 19 (1990): 261–282.

Indus Valley civilization script The SEALS recovered from excavations at MOHENJO DARO, HARAPPA, and other sites of the INDUS VALLEY CIVILIZATION bear brief written characters. Recent discoveries of written characters at Harappa, a major site of the Indus civilization, have been dated to the Ravi phase (3300–2800 B.C.E.). This script is thus as early as those of Egypt or Sumer. Wherever an

ancient script has been deciphered, information about the extinct society is enormously increased. Thus the translation of Egyptian hieroglyphics enabled by the Rosetta Stone made possible the reading of ancient Egyptian, and the oracle texts from ANYANG in China have permitted the names, dates, and thoughts of the Chinese SHANG STATE kings to be reconstructed. Because the Rosetta Stone was inscribed in three languages, one of which was Greek, it was possible to compare the names of kings written in both Greek and hieroglyphics. The ORACLE BONES can be read because the script employed is ancestral to modern Chinese. But the Indus script remains silent.

There have been many attempts to decipher it. These efforts, however, have been hampered by the brevity of the texts and the extinction of the writing system with the end of the Indus civilization. A further problem is that the script appears in the archaeological sequence as an established set of graphs, and there is no evidence of simpler forms or of a developmental sequence. The characters are found principally on small STEATITE seals no more than two to three centimeters square (.32 to .48 sq. in.), although there are examples of the writing on the surfaces of pottery vessels, copper tablets, and clay slabs. Examples are widely distributed over the Indus sites, even in such small provincial sites as CHANHU-DARO. Many seals are found in occupation deposits, as if they were in everyday use. Most space is taken up by an animal and people or scenes of a formal or ritual activity, associated with a line of symbols. There are just over 400 individual and distinct symbols. Some are very common, others rare. On some occasions, single symbols can be combined to form a composite. Most seals have about six of these signs in a line; the longest contains 21 symbols. The relative positioning of individual symbols forms a distinct pattern, in that when paired, one symbol invariably lies on the right-hand side of the other.

Walter Fairservis has approached the decipherment by assembling a corpus of all known texts and looking at any patterns or regularities in the order of the graphs one against the other. Although most appear to have been inscribed in a sequence from right to left, there are some in which the reverse order was followed. Having identified certain orders and frequencies, Fairservis then examined the individual graphs from the standpoint of archaeological knowledge about the Indus society and economy, to see whether it is possible to identify meanings. Many early scripts, such as that used in Shang China, employed a simple pictograph. In this system, a sketch of a chariot denoted a chariot, and a picture of a rice plant denoted rice. Often such graphs are combined with lines or strokes to denote numbers. The same approach to the Indus symbols suggested four major groups. Two of these are pictures of people or of artifacts that can easily be recognized. The third set incorporates two symbols combined into one; the fourth group involves signs that occur in conjunction with others, which might indicate a number. In identifying what these symbols actually meant, it is important that the object be represented in the Indus archaeological assemblage. Fairservis, for example, set out a series of graphs representing a bow and arrow, mortar and pestle, scales, a leaf from a pipal tree, and a house presumably raised on a mud-brick platform, all of which are known to have been part of Indus culture. Further examination of the corpus also reveals signs that probably represent a river, the Sun, a plow, and a wheat or barley plant. The underlying object represented can then be considered when a sequence of graphs is found. A simple example would involve a sequence showing symbols for a stick, followed by a house, cloth, and crucible. Using this very instance, Fairservis suggested that this meant a place where cloth and metal objects were counted and stored, or a central storehouse.

The next step was trying to detect regular patterning in the order of the symbols. One that regularly occurs first has been interpreted as meaning "the name of someone." Where this symbol is followed by a graph showing a man, it is assumed that the degree to which the man wore a distinctive headdress or was associated with a crucible or weaponry designated his status or specialization. In this manner, Fairservis has attempted to give some feeling for the meaning of the short inscriptions on seals. This procedure skates on thin ice when involving the hypothesis that the people of the Indus civilization spoke an early Dravidian language from which he derived possible individual names. Thus he has translated one seal, "The foremost merchant Irutol, son of the noble Iruvilan." Other translations are intriguing, such as "Collector of copper in the west, head chief in the south, the chief Iruvilaran." Another mentions a priest of the Sun, of the western storehouse, and a man who measured stored grain. There are a master of the mill, a person who constructed dams, a man in charge of a windmill, a chief priest, a maker of arrows, and a lord of herds and plowed fields. The graphs on a series of ivory sticks from Mohenjo Daro have also been interpreted as an Indus calendar of the phases of the Moon. It seems that the month was divided first into the cycle between crescent moons, that is 21.5 days, with an additional seven days for the dark period.

On the basis of this set of translations, Fairservis has proceeded to describe the principal characteristics of the Indus civilization, basing his conclusions on texts and supportive archaeological evidence. It is stressed that the translations must be seen as speculative, and it is hard to identify any means of rigorously testing them against independent data. However, his conclusions are interesting and at least place demands on more intensive research on the corpus of writing. He has suggested that the Indus civilization was made up of a series of what he calls chiefdoms, each with its paramount leader and subsidiary chiefs in dependent settlements. There were spe-cialized sites for making a variety of desirable goods, such as ceramics, bronzes, cloth, and shell jewelry. These goods were centrally stored and redistributed, requiring central administrators. Archaeologically, this can be seen in the walled precincts with public buildings at sites such as Harappa and KALIBANGAN and grain processing areas. Storage entailed the maintenance of records and a widely recognized system of weights.

The basic economy involved the cultivation of wheat, barley, and cotton and cattle herding. Prestigious positions appear to have been attached to the recorders of goods entering and leaving the warehouses and to traders who took exotic goods into the cities. There was also a hierarchy of priests, with special places set aside for rituals. Transport was by boat and by carts with solid wheels pulled by oxen.

It is interesting to note the rarity of artistic creations. The seals themselves were skillfully executed examples of miniaturist art, but there is little evidence for monumental statuary, wall decoration, or even attractive designs painted onto ceramics. The figurines are in general rather crudely manufactured. Yet the jewelers were able to create fine and complex ornaments. Some of these are seen on figurines of men and WOMEN wearing multiple bangles, necklaces, and belts. The visitor to a site like Mohenjo Daro would have found the occupants dressed in cotton clothing, the women with large headdresses.

In a final point, Fairservis has suggested that the little evidence so far adduced for warfare, defensive structures, royal dynasties, and a written literature sets the Indus civilization apart from the states of early China and the Near East. The writing system, he concludes, was restricted to the keeping of records and the naming of individuals on their personal seals.

See also LOTHAL; MARSHALL, SIR JOHN.

Further reading: Fairservis, W. A. *The Harappan Civilization and Its Writing: A Model for the Decipherment of the Indus Script.* Leiden: Brill, 1992; Possehl, G. L. *Indus Age: The Writing System.* Philadelphia: University of Pennsylvania Press, 1997.

inscriptions

INDIA

Inscriptions are a vital source of information for Indian history. Most were written on stone, but there are also examples on gold leaf, silver, copper, iron, ivory, terracotta, and shell. Much more will be known of the INDUS VALLEY CIVILIZATION if the decipherment of the INDUS VALLEY CIVILIZATION SCRIPT is ever accomplished, for there are thousands of brief written documents dating to the period 2500–2000 B.C.E. that remain silent. In an attempt at understanding what they might mean, Walter Fairservis has published a detailed analysis of the signs, their juxtapositions, and their possible meanings. The inscriptions are in the main found on small STEATITE SEALS, but a few can be read on clay and metal tablets. The small size of the seals restricts the length of the text, and few exceed 10 graphs, set out in a straight line above a scene that normally includes an animal and often a ritual event. Most symbols are easily recognized: There are men in various costumes that include a horned headdress, a crucible, a plow, a container, and a probable system of numbers. Fairservis has concluded that most seal inscriptions describe their owner and his place in society. Some are held to record the provisioning of storehouses with agricultural surpluses to be distributed by the leaders in society.

The earliest corpus of large inscriptions on stone belongs to the period of the MAURYA EMPIRE. The inscriptions of King ASOKA (about 268–235 B.C.E.) are one of the earliest and most important assemblages of Indian documents. Most were inscribed in a PRAKRIT language, using the BRAHMI script. Their decipherment owes much to the achievements of JAMES PRINSEP, who pioneered the translation of texts in the Brahmi script at SANCHI in 1837. However, in northeast India, the KHAROSHTHI script was used, and some inscriptions employed Aramaic or Greek. Thus the most northerly of the corpus of inscriptions from Pul-i Darunta is in Aramaic, a Semitic language spoken in the ACHAEMENID EMPIRE. The Greek language used in the Kandahar, Afghanistan, inscription reflects the continuing presence there of a Greek colony after the conquests of ALEXANDER THE GREAT. The distribution of the inscriptions provides compelling evidence for the extent of Asoka's empire. From Pul-i Darunta in the north, they extend more than 2,000 kilometers (1,200 mi.) to Brahmagiri in the south. The most westerly is from Kandahar, and the most easterly is found at Mahasthangarh, north of the Ganges (Ganga) Delta. The inscriptions themselves contained royal edicts and records of the king's religious devotion. At LUMBINI, for example, a text states that Asoka visited this, the birthplace of the Buddha, in the 20th year of his reign.

Thereafter, the number of texts multiplied, and the practice of erecting inscriptions spread to Myanmar (Burma), Thailand, Cambodia, and Vietnam, again using the Brahmi script. In India, the dynastic sequences of the SUNGA, SAKAS, SATAVAHANA, and many other minor dynasties have been reconstructed on the basis of the inscriptions. The WESTERN SATRAPS are also better known through inscriptions, such as those of RUDRAVARAMAN from Junagadh.

CHINA

Inscriptions in China have provided the basic documentary information for dynastic sequences, the activities and preoccupations of the central courts, and historic events not otherwise recorded in classical Chinese histories. Unlike those in India and Southeast Asia, Chinese scholars participated in a long tradition of historic scholarship, much of which has survived. Thus SIMA QIAN, writing in the second century B.C.E., could call on documents that have not survived to the present day in writing his monumental *shiji* (*Records of the Great Historian*). He described a long sequence of dynastic rulers of the XIA and Shang dynasties (c. 1700–1050 B.C.E.) who were unknown from relevant sources until the discovery through archaeological excavation of contemporary inscriptions on turtle shell and bronzes.

Oracle Bones

The turtle-shell records, known as ORACLE BONES, were first identified as very early written records in 1899, and many thousands have subsequently been unearthed, particularly at ANYANG, the capital of the late SHANG STATE. These result from divinations. The emperors consulted the bones to divine the most auspicious course of action to be pursued. The base of a flat turtle plastron, the lower part of the shell, first had pairs of holes bored so that when heat was applied to the depression, the thinness of the shell promoted cracking. On the basis of the form of the crack, the future was divined. In an early form of the Chinese script, the upper half of the shell was inscribed with the event of concern, the alternative courses of action, and the resulting event. Thus a text might ask whether the ancestors would be favorable to the emperor's attacking a particular enemy. Other common concerns were the weather and the likely success of the harvest. A third addressed the king's health and another, which ancestor to appease through sacrifice to cure an ailment. This method of divination had a long prehistoric ancestry, and oracle bones have been found distributed widely in northern China, particularly in the Huang (Yellow) River Valley. However, the method lost its appeal during the succeeding Zhou dynasty, although during the early reigns it was still followed, as seen in the discovery of Western Zhou oracle bones at Zhouyuan.

Bronze Vessels

The Shang also cast inscriptions into bronze vessels, and it is through this medium that it has been possible to identify the only intact royal tomb at Anyang as that belonging to FU HAO (r. 1200–1181 B.C.E.), a consort of Emperor Wu Ding often mentioned in the oracle-bone inscriptions. The practice of adding texts to the walls of large ceremonial bronze vessels was followed during the Zhou dynasty, and these have furnished much vital information. Before the growing corpus of bronze inscriptions attracted detailed study, the principal documentary sources of WESTERN ZHOU DYNASTY history were retrospective documents written long after the events. The degree to which such sources are reliable was the subject of controversy. However, the bronze texts have confirmed the general authenticity of the later documents and have added much new information.

The first part of the typical Western Zhou bronze inscription provides the date, expressed both as the year in which a great event took place, usually describing an occurrence such as a ritual offering to a royal ancestor, and then a more specific calendar reference. This is followed by a description of the incident that led to the commemorative bronze's casting. Such events are often of first-class importance, as it is desired to identify historic events, such as wars between Zhou rulers and their enemies. They also provide information on how battles were fought. Thus the Duo You cauldron describes a battle between the Zhou and the Xianyun, in which 23 manacled prisoners were herded for interrogation, and 117 enemy chariots were captured. The Ci *ding* records a second type of historic event, the loyal investiture of Ci, a high official, and mentions the emperor's taking his place at dawn for the proceedings. The description of the event is then followed by a recording of gifts usually provided by the king for the person who had the commemorative vessel cast. The inscriptions offer fresh and contemporary insight into the objects that were particularly valued. On one occasion, it was strings of cowry shells. The Maogong *ding* records donations of extreme opulence, including wine, a ladle with a jade handle, other jade ornaments, and a magnificent chariot with a canopy of tiger skin, bells, banners, and bronze fittings. Finally, the typical inscription dedicates the vessel to the ancestors and to future generations of the initiator's family.

Bamboo Strips

Bamboo strips are a source of documentary evidence of growing importance, since they are usually recovered from high-status dated tombs. The *Zushu Jinian* (BAMBOO ANNALS) were found in the tomb of King Xiang of WEI in 279 C.E. This king was interred in 296 B.C.E. The BAMBOO SLIPS in this case were tied together with silk cords, each containing 40 graphs. Although some doubt has been cast on their authenticity, there are solid grounds for believing that they are acceptable as valid historical documents. Another example of such inscriptions is from Yunmeng county in Hebei province. These documents are known as the *Records of Major Events*. Discovered in 1975, these 53 slips are each 23 to 28 centimeters (9.2 to 11.2 in.) long. They contain a description of the wars of conquest by the QIN and date from 306 to 217 B.C.E.

Stone Inscriptions

Stone inscriptions were also used in China. The most famous example is from the imperial college or university established under the HAN DYNASTY at LUOYANG in Henan province. During the reign of the Eastern Han emperor LINGDI in 175 C.E., a group of scholars were charged to write the Confucian classics. These were then carved on 46 stone inscriptions, a task that reputedly occupied the carvers for seven years. The inscriptions were then set up for all to admire and learn. It is recorded that these texts became such an attraction that they caused difficulties with visitors' transport. The first emperor, QIN SHIHUANGDI (259–210 B.C.E.), also set up inscriptions to record his achievements. One of his most famous texts was on Langya Mountain in Shandong province on the

occasion of his visit there in 219 B.C.E. SIMA QIAN recorded the message, but today only the first two lines remain in a very worn condition, and they list the officials who accompanied the emperor. There follow an edict issued by the second emperor in 209 B.C.E. and a list of his officials. The words recorded by Sima Qian a century after the event describe how the emperor was wise and righteous, giving peace and harmony to the world: "Weights and measures have a single standard, words are written in a uniform way . . . he rectifies diverse customs, crossing rivers, traversing the land."

The first emperor set up another inscription also in Shandong, at Mount Tai. On his way down the mountain, he sheltered under a tree from the rain and in gratitude for the shelter gave the tree the title of fifth-rank counselor. Sima Qian also recorded the text of this inscription: It begins by stating that the emperor after ascending the throne issued laws that all must obey. He united the world; all submitted to him. This wise and noble ruler produced universal peace, and his influence will last for succeeding generations.

In 215 B.C.E. Qin Shihuangdi traveled to the Gulf of Bohai, where he had an inscription placed on the gate of the city of Jieshi. This text also extolled his virtues, laying stress on how he "demolished walls and fortifications, opened up waterways, cut through embankments, and leveled the steep declivities." It ends with the statement that the officials sought permission to raise this inscription so that the emperor's achievements would be known to succeeding generations.

Tallies

During the WARRING STATES PERIOD (475–221 B.C.E.), tallies were used to provide permits for trade and the transport of goods. A particularly fine set was recovered from Qiujia, Anhui province, in 1957. The two halves were designed so that they were validated only when they fitted together. An example from the CHU state was made of bronze, inlaid with gold graphs. They state that King Huai gave the tallies to one Ejun Qi, with instructions as to his authorized route, what goods he was permitted to carry, and what taxes would be levied.

JAPAN

In Japan, inscriptions are known as *kinsekibun,* "writing on metal and stone." As Japan did not have a native script, the first inscriptions were on imported objects from China, such as bronze mirrors and swords. There is also a famous gold seal described in the *History of the Later Han Dynasty* (HOU HANSHU) as a gift to the ruler of Na, a small state located in Japan, by the Han emperor GUANG WUDI (5 B.C.E.–57 C.E.) in 57 C.E. In 1784, a golden seal was found at Fukuoka in Kyushu, inscribed, "The king of Na of Wa of Han." It measures 2.35 centimeters (.9 in.) across, and its knob was in the form of a snake. This is probably the same seal recorded in the history. The two earliest inscriptions of local origin were inlaid gold and silver texts on the blades of iron swords from INARIYAMA and Eta Funayama. These record the service of a palace guard and a civil bureaucrat to the emperor and date to the second half of the fifth century C.E. Later inscriptions of the YAMATO state recorded on bronze and stone the careers of the individual in a tomb, but these are very rare. With the late Yamato and Nara periods, written records survive on MOKKAN, wooden tablets that recorded tax receipts, requisition notes for supplies, and orders. These are found in their thousands, particularly at HEIJO-KYO, capital of the NARA STATE.

SOUTHEAST ASIA

The raising of inscriptions was adopted in Southeast Asia from at least the fifth century C.E. The language employed was SANSKRIT or PALI, both derived from India, and in Southeast Asia there are Mon texts in the CHAO PHRAYA BASIN and parts of northeast Thailand, Khmer in Cambodia and southern areas of northeast Thailand, Old Javanese on Java in Indonesia, and Cham on the coast of Vietnam. The locations of inscriptions in these indigenous languages are strong indicators of the ethnicity of people at the dawn of history. Many records must have existed on perishable materials, but only texts on stone or very occasionally on copper, gold, or semiprecious jewelry have survived. In Cambodia, the majority of these records are concerned with religious foundations and merit-making offerings. There is often a reference in Sanskrit to the ruling king, the donor, the god, and the date of the foundation or of a particular donation. The vernacular text follows and often incorporates a list of workers and their duties in maintaining and servicing the temple. The names of the temple servants are usually in the local language, whereas the names of the grandees or major donors are in Sanskrit. Many of the Angkorian period inscriptions were very long and assumed epic proportions both in their content and in the quality of the Sanskrit verses. They provide the genealogies of kings and noble families back through many generations and are thus vital sources for the reconstruction of dynastic histories. However, they must also be seen as advertisements and were often misleading.

JAVA

On Java, in Indonesia, the inscriptions were likewise concerned with land ownership, the organization of taxes, and donations to religious foundations. They were carved onto large stone stelae for permanent display or on copper for personal or corporate use. Most record the establishment of SIMA, defined villages, segments of villages, or rice fields whose tax status was redefined or permanently established. Thus, many texts take a part of a village and ascribe its tax revenue to be paid to a religious foundation through the request of the *rake* (lord) who owned the temple. The nature of the payment is occasionally specified. On the basis of the area of land in question, it would often be in the form of silver or gold. Corvée labor was another form of payment.

The texts were inscribed to record a permanent charter or relationship between the owners of land and the payment of tax revenue, but much of their contents gives insight into the organization of society. Thus, the formula begins with a royal order, often naming the king, to the beneficiary of a *sima*. It requires his officials to oversee the establishment of a charter and thus names the official titles in the court. This official then sets out the boundaries of the ascribed area. Some inscriptions indicate that a *sima* could be challenged, and the texts sometimes include curses against any future violators of the charter. A *sima* was also a means whereby the ruler could restrain the power and wealth of local lords, because it required much expenditure on celebratory feasting and also meant a reduction in the *rake's* income.

The detailed analysis of the texts illuminates aspects of the landscape, social order, trade, and subsistence in ninth- and 10th-century Java. The *rake* was an aristocratic title that could be held by both men and women, and a husband and wife often had the same honorific. It is not known with certainty how a person assumed this title, but it does not seem to have been inherited. WOMEN were given the same status as men. They received gifts during *sima* ceremonies and could own rice land.

The texts reveal a hierarchy in terms of status. A *rakryan hino* was the highest court official, who supervised administrators of lower rank, known as *parujar, citralekha,* and *pangurang.* On some occasions the *hino* succeeded to the throne, but at all times he was a person of very high status who received the greatest number of gifts. The next highest official was called a *rake halu,* followed by the *rakryan sirikan* and then the *rakryan wika.* A host of minor titles also appears.

The taxation system relied basically on rice production, and descriptions of land usually mention the term *sawah,* or wet rice field. There are also terms for dry rice field, implying lack of water control and lower rice production, and for garden land, housing land, and swamps. An inscription of King BALITUNG (r. c. 901–910) records how the owners of a rice field, because of low yields, were unable to meet their obligations and so asked the king to allow them to extend this holding and thus produce more rice for the same amount of tax. It indicates that the tax due was assessed on the basis of land area rather than actual production. An inscription from Rongkap describes an exemption from tax, for which a payment of silver was made to the official responsible. Labor for a certain proportion of a villager's time was another form of payment of dues. The texts often include people's occupations and give some idea of the activities in early Javanese villages. There are, for example, goldsmiths and jewelers, people who organized cockfights, traders, firemen, and cooks. Rarely there are officials in charge of prostitutes and Chinese traders.

The establishment of a *sima* required defining the boundaries of the land involved. This usually involved physical measurement, using the unit *tampah*. Alternatively, it could be defined by the amount of seed sown on a given plot. Land transactions were paid for in measures of gold.

See also CONFUCIUS.

Further reading: Barrett-Jones, A. M. *Early Tenth Century Inscriptions from Java.* Dordrecht: Foris Publications, 1984; Jacob, J. M. "Pre-Angkor Cambodia: Evidence from the Inscriptions in Khmer Concerning the Common People and Their Environment." In W. *Early South East Asia,* edited by R. Smith and W. Watson. Kuala Lumpur: Oxford University Press, 1978; Mattos, G. L. "Eastern Zhou Bronze Inscriptions." In *New Sources of Early Chinese History: An Introduction to the Reading of Inscriptions and Manuscripts,* edited by E. L. Shaughnessy. Berkeley: Society for the Study of Early China and Institute of East Asian Studies, University of California, 1997; Salomon, R. *Ancient Buddhist Scrolls from Gandhara.* Seattle: University of Washington Press, 1999; ———. *Indian Epigraphy: A Guide to the Study of Inscriptions in Sanskrit, Prakrit and the Other Indo-Aryan Languages.* New York: Oxford University Press, 1998; Shaughnessy, E. L. "Zhouyuan Oracle-Bone Inscriptions: Entering the Research Stage?" *Early China* 11–12 (1985–1987): 146–163; Vickery, M. *Society, Economics and Politics in Pre-Angkor Cambodia.* Tokyo: The Centre for East Asian Cultural Studies for UNESCO, 1998.

Iron Age   The Iron Age of the Ganges (Ganga)-Jumuna River system of northern India and Pakistan is synonymous with the PAINTED GREY WARE culture dated from the 11th to the sixth century B.C.E. This ceramic, which has a characteristic gray color embellished with black geometric designs, is found over a considerable area, from Lakhio Pir in Sind and HARAPPA in the west to KAUSAMBI in the east, from the foothills of the Himalayas in the north to UJJAIN in the south. The gray ware itself is relatively sparse at the various sites and probably represents a luxury item. Site surveys have identified more than 600 settlements, the vast majority of which are small agricultural villages rarely exceeding two hectares (5 acres) in area. However, there is also some evidence for the development of a two-tiered settlement structure, involving centers extending over an area of 10 to 15 hectares (25 to 37.5 acres), linked with the smaller villages. At the site of Jakhera, there are probably defenses in the form of a rampart around the settlement. Mud bricks were used for a multiroomed building at Bhagwanpura, and a blacksmith's forge has been excavated at ATRANJIKHERA. While some early sites have not revealed any trace of iron, this metal was of central importance because it facilitated the clearance of the thick forests covering the area. Iron was used for weaponry in the form of arrowheads and spears and also for sickles and hoes.

No plowshares have been found, but it is likely that plowing was used in an agricultural regime that was based on rice and that also had barley and wheat cultivation. This system, which continues in the area today, would have permitted double cropping. The subsistence regime also included the raising of domestic cattle, sheep, pigs, dogs, and horses. Fishing was also widely undertaken. Houses were made of timber and plastered wattle, as well as mud brick. Some houses were substantial and incorporated up to 13 rooms. Rice and animal bones have been found in the hearths. The material culture included highly proficient ceramics fired in kilns, a bone industry, and, rarely, glass bangle fragments and beads. A stone mold from Atranjikhera was probably used to cast jewelry. Gold, etched carnelian, and agate ornaments were used. There are some terra-cotta human and animal figurines, and dice indicate an enthusiasm for gambling.

This Iron Age culture of the Ganges (Ganga) Valley of northern India was a crucial period in the early formation of states. It is illuminated by the oral traditions known as the later Vedic hymns. When referring to this formative period, they mention the development of rulers termed the *ekaraj.* A prime role of the *ekaraj* was leadership in battle, but consecration ceremonies also hint at the presence of a court and functionaries, who include the military leader, a priest, court poet, and collector or distributor of revenue. Religious rituals were also an important feature of life in early centers by the sixth century B.C.E., with particular reference to sacrifices to the gods, for the king's role was to ensure prosperous agriculture.

CHINA

Iron, like bronze, almost certainly reached China from the West, along the course of the ancient SILK ROAD. It reached Xinjiang in far western China between the 10th and seventh centuries B.C.E., although the earliest artifacts there took the form of small tools and ornaments. There are some parallels between the iron objects in this part of China and those found in Ferghana. In due course, iron technology was adapted in the central plains and became increasingly important both for agriculture and warfare. Thus the period of WARRING STATES (475–221 B.C.E.) saw a proliferation in the use of iron. Armor, for example, was fashioned from iron plates, as seen in the surviving helmet from Xiadu, a capital of the state of YAN. This same city, like many others during the period of Warring States, incorporated areas where specialist smiths produced iron items. Chinese ironworking took on an impetus all of its own, particularly in the area of iron casting, rather than forging. The control over very high temperatures required in the production of molten iron was a hallmark of Chinese iron technology that long preceded the attainment of similar levels of skill in the West. It is manifested in the casting of an iron cauldron as early as 536 B.C.E. in the foundries of the state of JIN. This expertise, linked with the scale of production during the period of the HAN DYNASTY, led to a veritable economic revolution, as iron was applied to increasing agricultural production.

SOUTHEAST ASIA

How ironworking began in Southeast Asia is not known. It might well have been introduced through trade with southern Chinese states but could equally have been inspired through trade with India or through indigenous discovery. Whichever the case, iron was widely used in the manufacture of tools, weapons, and ornaments during the second half of the last millennium B.C.E. Iron ore is relatively widespread, and while there is some evidence for casting iron items in the DONG SON culture of northern Vietnam, the vast majority of Southeast Asian iron was worked through forging. The efficacy of the iron spades and hoes is seen in the construction of earthen banks to control water flow and create moats at such sites as NOEN U-LOKE in northeast Thailand. The same settlement has produced large socketed iron spears, while one young man was found with an iron arrowhead lodged in his spine, a sign of conflict during the late prehistoric period. At the site of BAN DON TA PHET, many iron billhooks and spears have emphasized this point.

irrigation

CHINA

With China's variable climate, relatively unpredictable rainfall, and growing population, irrigation played a crucial role in agriculture. Essentially, China was divided into two major regions, the northern half dominated by the cultivation of millet and the southern half of rice. Millet agriculture was concentrated in the vast plain of the Huang (Yellow) River. The loess soil deposited by the river from its passage across the plateau to the west provided rich and easily worked conditions, but floods from the river and its propensity to change its course were major problems. The monsoon region that had its most northerly extent in the Huai and Han River Basins and the land south to Lingnan was adapted to the cultivation of rice, a marsh grass. The monsoon, however, is unpredictable, and reticulating water from dams to the rice fields is an important means of ensuring a good harvest.

There is no compelling evidence for irrigation during the SHANG STATE (1766–1045 B.C.E.). The Shang were well able to drain wet or swampy areas with ditches or canals, as revealed through excavation at the site of Xiaotun. However, the available records indicate that it was wetter then than now, and the ORACLE BONES and other texts suggest that fields were drained and the Shang rulers had a consistent interest in opening new land to millet cultivation.

During the WESTERN ZHOU DYNASTY (1045–771 B.C.E.) inscriptions were commonly cast into bronze vessels. These form a vital contemporary source of historic information, a source that is constantly expanding with archaeological research. The bronze vessel known as the Qiu Wei *ding* was cast during the reign of King Gong (c. 917–900 B.C.E.). Its text incorporates one of the earliest Chinese references to a dispute over land and describes "King Gong's irrigation works at the two Rong rivers."

Further early records for irrigation are from the Spring and Autumn period (722–476 B.C.E.). These described the construction of the Shao reservoir in northern Anhui province under the rule of King Zhuang of CHU (r. c. 612–591 B.C.E.). This facility had five water gates to receive and distribute water from the tributaries of the Huai River, to maintain a steady supply to the rice fields. It was said that 1 million *mu* of land was irrigated from this reservoir. It is difficult to determine the precise area of a *mu*, but it is thought to have measured about 100 by 100 paces, or just less than one hectare. In a second system of extensive irrigation, water was taken from the Zhang River during the reign of Marquis Xiang of WEI (424–387 B.C.E.) to reduce salinization in the rice and millet fields.

In 316 B.C.E. the QIN state defeated the kingdom of SHU in Sichuan and set about improving its agricultural production. The first task was to redistribute land to new settlers on the basis of strictly ordered rectangular parcels within raised footpaths. The Min River flows southwest of Chengdu before its confluence with the Chang (Yangtze), and was prone to flooding. This problem, linked with the need to irrigate the new rice fields, led to the construction by Li Bing (306–251 B.C.E.) of the Dujiangyan dam on the Chengdu Plain, an irrigation project that exists to this day after a history of 2,300 years of continuous use. State intervention by the Qin in infrastructure projects such as major irrigation works continued to the end of the dynasty, and the massive Dujiangyan project has been described as the largest engineering work yet seen in the eastern half of Eurasia.

During the Han dynasty, China witnessed a massive increase in population and a period of relative peace after the drawn-out warfare that characterized the preceding WARRING STATES PERIOD (475–221 B.C.E.). Iron could now be applied to increasing agricultural production and providing the tools necessary to complete large engineering works. The Han Chinese have left a large corpus of records that describe the widespread application of irrigation to agriculture. Essentially, this had three objectives that varied with the local conditions. One was to introduce water into the fields by means of canals and dams, another was to drain swampy land to create fields, and the third was to reduce salinization. This knowledge is nowhere better illustrated than in a memorandum prepared by Jia Rang in 7 B.C.E. for the emperor Aidi (26–1 B.C.E.). He wrote that not digging canals had three detriments, and digging them had three benefits. Problems issuing from the lack of irrigation and flood-control measures meant that people suffered from the humidity as floodwater evaporated and the soil turned alkaline. This meant that grain did not flourish. The benefits of irrigation included the washing out of salts from the fields, the spreading of silt to increase soil fertility, and the increase in production fivefold on high ground and 10-fold in low-lying terrain. Finally, with canals, heavy goods could be more easily transported.

A memorandum of the second century C.E. named the principal components of an Eastern Han irrigation system. The *yanzhu* was the reservoir, and the *fang* the dike beside the reservoir. A *sui* was the channel at the top of the field that distributed water, and a *gui* drained water away from the field when necessary. The contemporary texts of the Han are virtually unanimous in describing the increased agricultural efficiency that resulted from irrigation works. The *History of the Later Han Dynasty* (HOU HANSHU) recorded that in 36 C.E. there had been little rain in Gansu, but officials repaired the irrigation works, and everyone prospered as a result. In 90 C.E. the grand administrator Lu Bei had canals dug in Dong commandery, and the people became very wealthy. Ma Yuan was a great military commander responsible for conquering the DONG SON people of the Hong (Red) River Delta in modern Vietnam in the mid-second century C.E. It is recorded that he also dug irrigation canals for the benefit of the people.

KOREA

Rice cultivation in Korea was beyond doubt introduced from China and was the mainstay of the SHILLA and PAEKCHE states in the south of the peninsula. By the fourth century, the agricultural system of China had developed considerable sophistication, involving the diversion of rivers into canals and reticulation into rice fields. Iron agricultural tools, such as the wooden spade and hoe tipped with iron, were also manufactured. This technology was applied to Korean agriculture where ponds developed for irrigation were linked with canal systems. Korea also became a conduit for the spread of this knowledge into Japan during the fifth century C.E.

Irrigation in Korea was instituted at least by the period of Chinese Han settlement, when reservoirs for feeding water to rice fields were constructed. During the subsequent period of Three Kingdoms, royal and aristocratic landowners sought to increase production. Extensive irrigation was undertaken, for example, during the reign of King Chijung of Shilla (r. 500–514 C.E.), together with the use of plow oxen. Slightly later, an inscription dating to 536 C.E., during the reign of King Pophung, described construction of the "luxuriant dike" as part of an irrigation facility. It had a long life, for in 798 C.E. another text described the undertaking of repairs. It must have been a major project, as it involved 136 ax men and 14,140 soldiers.

JAPAN

Rice cultivation began in Japan during the first millennium B.C.E, probably imported from established agricultural communities in Korea. The earliest agricultural villages, ascribed to the YAYOI culture (300 B.C.E.–300 C.E.), already practiced a developed form of rice cultivation involving the creation of small bunded fields. Many such fields were covered by flood deposits and have been investigated by archaeologists. It is clear that they involved irrigation and drainage ditches. With the application of iron technology, also obtained at about the same time from the mainland, agricultural tools were forged to facilitate earth moving. This made it possible, for example, not only to build massive mounded tombs, the largest of which covered 60 hectares (150 acres) and was ringed by three moats, but also to create irrigation facilities. Evidence for irrigation late in the Yayoi period has been discovered through excavations on the Nara Plain, where six-meter (19.8-ft.)-wide irrigation ditches up to 1.5 meters (4.95 ft.) deep have been identified. The YAMATO state, which lasted from about 300 to 700 C.E., was led by powerful military rulers whose courts relied ultimately on the production of rice surpluses. Kings therefore paid particular attention to agriculture, and the NIHONGI, an early eighth-century history text, records instances of royally inspired irrigation works, such as the diversion of the Ishiwara River into a canal to carry water to thousands of hectares of formerly marginal land. This was undertaken by King Nintoku in the early fifth century. Archaeological verification of such endeavors is also seen in the Furuichi Canal of the Osaka Plain, where a 10-kilometer (6 mi.) canal between 8.5 and 9.5 meters wide has been identified. King NINTOKU (313–99 C.E.), who was interred in the largest known *kofun*, or burial mound, also attracted Korean workers to help in the construction and maintenance of his projects. This system may well have been instrumental in the adoption of a range of iron agricultural tools to the construction of irrigation facilities, some of which were interred in rich tombs of the period.

The late Yamato state and the NARA STATE (710–794 C.E.) saw a marked intensification in central control over the populace at large. Legal codes prescribed the social position of every individual, from the highest minister to the lowest slave. Under the conditions of the Yoro Code of 718 C.E., the central ministries that operated under an autocratic imperial regime included one responsible for irrigation matters. The peasant farmers were allocated land, the amount varying with the composition of each household, in which people were counted from the age of six years. The allocation was reviewed every six years. These rice farmers paid a tax in kind to the state but otherwise enjoyed an element of personal freedom on their plots of land. Since the irrigation systems were state owned and controlled, however their freedom of action was strictly limited.

INDIA

That India has a long history of irrigation to improve agricultural production is evident from the description of canal excavation and bringing water to low-lying areas contained in the Vedas, the corpus of sacred hymns dating back into the second or even third millennia B.C.E. Identifying archaeological evidence for such irrigation works is not straightforward, although Gregory Possehl has suggested that irrigation may have been in place by the AMRI-NAL phase of the INDUS VALLEY CIVILIZATION (3200–2600 B.C.E.). In the case of Baluchistan, irrigation probably took the form of diverting mountain streams onto the extensive river terraces. On the Indus plains, however, it is more likely that river floods, reaching out over the extensive flood plains encouraged the sowing of wheat and barley, with the harvest proceeding as the waters receded. In southern India, tanks and canals were employed. KAUTILYA, who composed his *ARTHASASTRA* in the late fourth century B.C.E., was well aware of the importance of tracts with an assured water supply and the possibility of double cropping. He mentions the cultivation of rice, wheat, barley, millet, beans, and a wide range of other vegetables, herbs, and spices. Irrigation was also encouraged as a means to further reliable returns and increase the wealth of the state. One of the best examples of irrigation comes from the dam constructed during the Mauryan period on Lake Sudarsana near Junagadh during the reign of CANDRAGUPTA (325–297 B.C.E.). This was maintained over many centuries, for it was restored in the fifth century C.E. by the local governor during the reign of King Skandagupta. Indeed, irrigation works were widely applied during the Gupta empire as part of state concern for increasing production.

CENTRAL ASIA

The arid terrain that characterizes so much of the ancient SILK ROAD from the MERV (modern Mary) oasis to the TARIM BASIN is crossed by a series of rivers, of which the Amu Dar'ya and Syr Dar'ya are particularly notable. Irrigation there was a vital component to the development of states. Already by the fifth and early fourth millennia B.C.E., the oasis region that is now Turkmenistan had attracted agricultural settlements in which barley and wheat were cultivated on the basis of an irrigation system. Canals in the region of ALTYN TEPE reached many kilometers in length. Four thousand years passed before the BACTRIAN GREEK rulers instituted irrigation schemes. The Sogdians grew wealthy on their irrigation agriculture and control of trade along the Silk Road, while the KUSHAN kings expended much effort into the provision of irrigation works. Major canals and the expansion of agriculture in the Amu Dar'ya, the Tashkent, and Samarqand oasis regions led to the foundation of new urban settlements, while a vast area was brought under irrigation in KHWARIZM, the region centered on the lower reaches of the Amu Dar'ya. Here, a fully integrated system was established, with major canals taking water from the river and feeding minor distributaries. One such canal was more than 90 kilometers (54 mi.) long.

SRI LANKA

Although Sri Lanka enjoys a continually high temperature, there is considerable regional diversity in the amount and seasonal distribution of rainfall. Whereas the southern parts of the island receive up to 3,750 millimeters (150 in.) of rainfall per annum, the northern dry zone has only 750 to 1,750 millimeters (30 to 70 in.) a year, and the rain concentrates in the period of the northeast monsoon, from November to January. Droughts can then persist for more than three months. Under the development of an urban civilization, such as that of ANURADHAPURA, this rainfall pattern encourages systems of water control to ensure a predictable rice harvest. The early irrigation system that developed in the dry zone is regarded as one of the most innovative and sophisticated in the preindustrial world. The earliest inscriptions, dating from the third century B.C.E., mention small-scale irrigation, and the enlargement of the system was facilitated by the invention of the cistern sluice, known as the *bisokotuva*, which regulated the flow of water from a large reservoir or tank without endangering weirs. One of the major early achievements was the diversion of the Ambanganga River, a tributary of the Mahavali, which originates in the wet central highlands south of Anuradhapura.

The Alisara Canal, first mentioned during the reign of King Vasabha (65–109 C.E.), flowed for about 50 kilometers (30 mi.) to the capital. This king is credited with a marked expansion of the system, including not only the canal, but also 12 reservoirs. Between 164 and 192 C.E. two new sorts of reservoirs are named in the inscriptions: *mahavavi* (large) and *danavavi* (service) reservoirs. This period saw the development of interlinked irrigation systems. During the next century and under the reign of Mahasena (274–301 C.E.) the giant reservoir known as Minneriya was constructed. This, together with new canals and reservoirs representing a massive investment of labor, put much marginal land into production. King Dhatusena (455–73) further added to the infrastructure of irrigation. He had a dam constructed over the Mahavali River to harness a greater supply of water and further extended the irrigated area in the western part of the dry zone. An idea of the skill of the hydraulic engineers of this period is gained from the Kalavava reservoir. The dam across the Kala River was made of tightly fitting blocks of granite, the wall being more than five kilometers (3 mi.) long and standing to a height of 12 meters. The Jayaganga canal is 80 kilometers (48 mi.) long and carried water to Anuradhapura as well as irrigated an area of 62,000 hectares (155,000 acres). The gradient for much of its length involved a fall of only 10 centimeters (4 in.) per kilometer. The Manar region in northwestern Sri Lanka is particularly dry, and here Dhatusena had a further massive dam constructed, with a length of 11 kilometers (6.6 mi.). It was then linked with distribution canals that supplemented the water supply in numerous village tanks. Many further dams and canals were constructed so that, by the

10th century, the system covered most of the dry zone and the area of Rohana in the southeast of the island. In this last region, the initiative was taken more by local communities than by the king.

The Sri Lankan irrigation system supported the great urban center of Anuradhapura as well as the second center of Polonnaruva and myriad rural villages. The social correlates of this system are a vital issue in understanding the Sri Lankan civilization of the first millennium C.E. Was it, for example, under the central control of the court and thus an example of overarching central power and authority, or was it devolved to local administration and fragmented ownership of water rights?

Some reservoirs were owned privately, by *vapi-hamikas*. Others were communally owned, in some cases by monasteries. Thus, the Alahara Canal was granted to a monastic foundation shortly after its completion. The king was the principal owner and beneficiary of the canals, reservoirs, and tanks, but they could also be sponsored by or given to individuals. Water was subject to tax, and a *vapi-hamika* was one who owned and charged for the water passing through his facility. Owners also received a proportion of the production from irrigated land, known as the water share, or *dakabaka*. Entrepreneurs could take a share of profit without producers being alienated from their land. This made it possible to raise two to three crops a year in extensive tracts. Again, the control of land improved by major irrigation works gave rulers considerable economic and political power.

CAMBODIA

The manipulation of water has a long history in Southeast Asia. This reflects the monsoon climate, with its sharp contrast between the wet and the dry seasons. In the former, there is a superabundance of water in the lowlands, and flooding is widespread. During the latter, months can go by without any rainfall. This pattern encouraged communities, as they grew in size and population numbers, to control water flows, usually by building up earthen dikes to form reservoirs. These banks ring many large Iron Age sites, and where dated, fall within 1 to 400 C.E. During the life of the states of FUNAN and CHENLA, water was retained in rectangular reservoirs known as BARAYS. None was large enough to have any influence on rice production, but they could have satisfied domestic needs, as well as fulfilled a symbolic role as the oceans that surround the mythical home of the Hindu gods. With the foundation of the kingdom of ANGKOR in about 800 C.E., the size of the *barays* dramatically increased, culminating in the massive WESTERN BARAY of SURYAVARMAN I (r. c. 1002–1049 C.E.) at Angkor.

Were Reservoirs Used for Irrigation?

There are two opposing schools of thought on whether these reservoirs were constructed to irrigate rice fields. Bernard-Philippe Groslier and Jacques Dumarçay have described Angkor as a hydraulic city in which the reservoirs were the source of irrigation water. They believe that the very choice for the location of the successive cities of Angkor was determined by the availability of water that flowed south from the KULEN HILLS via the Puok, Siem Reap, and Roluos Rivers. The maintenance of a city with a population of a million or more, they claim, could have continued only with irrigation agriculture, and therefore its decline was at least in part due to the irrigation system's collapse. The opposing school, which includes Philip Stott, W. J. van Liere, and Robert Acker, argues against irrigation on technical and geographic grounds.

Despite their size and huge capacity, could the *barays* have held sufficient water to have a serious impact on rice production? And if so, how was the water reticulated, for there is no surviving evidence for irrigation canals or other distributaries, despite the abundant evidence that the engineers of Angkor were adept at controlling water flows? Moreover, is there actually sufficient land below the reservoirs for significant production, and are there any insuperable impediments to the provision of an overall irrigation system? Groslier has suggested that, in the absence of distribution canals, a channel was excavated outside and parallel with the southern dikes, which filled with water percolating through the bank of the reservoir. Van Liere has shown that this is technically impossible.

Acker has given detailed consideration to the area that could have been irrigated, the water requirement, likely yields, and the location of the *barays* relative to one another and the land below them. His calculations were based on Groslier's estimate of a population at Angkor in the vicinity of 1,900,000 people, of whom 600,000 were supported by 86,000 hectares (215,000 acres) of irrigated rice fields. In the dry season, a hectare would require 15,000 cubic meters (525,000 cu. ft.) of water. Assuming all the major *barays* at Angkor were full to a depth of three meters (9.9 ft.), they could have supplied 7,000 hectares (17,500 acres). If they yielded 1.46 tons of rice per hectare and annual consumption was 220 kilograms (484 lbs.) of rice per capita, the dry season yield would have maintained about 44,500 people, about 2.5 percent of the estimated population. This calculation is based only on the amount of water available when the *barays* were three meters deep. It does not take into account the possibility that the *barays* were constantly replenished with water from the Siem Reap River throughout the dry season. There is also the possibility that the reservoirs were used to supplement water supplies to the fields when there was insufficient rainfall during the wet season. If so, then a further 9,000 metric tons (9,900 tons) over and above anticipated wet-season production could have been obtained, making the total irrigated yield 19,200 tons, sufficient to feed nearly 100,000 people.

These figures assume that all the *barays* were being employed simultaneously, a situation possible only during the reign of JAYAVARMAN VII (r. 1181–1219 C.E.) and his successors. On the other hand, Acker has shown that the reservoirs mask one another from potentially irrigable rice fields. Again, the Yashodharatataka (EASTERN BARAY) could not have irrigated all the potential land below it, because the incised Siem Reap River would have made that system impossible.

No inscriptions that mention the reservoirs link them with irrigation. A description of an estate at HARIHARALAYA cites the Indratataka as a boundary marker but does not mention water. Another inscription describes YASHOVARMAN I (r. 889–910 C.E.) as the husband of the Earth, who filled it with virtue, pleasure, and fecundity, but the ensuing mention of his *baray* is too damaged to allow its full meaning to be obtained. His foundation inscriptions compare Yashodharatataka to the Moon, the source of life-sustaining ambrosia. RAJENDRAVARMAN (r. 944–68 C.E.), it is said, filled the water with his good works and made it a mirror to reflect his temple in the middle. The Jayatataka of Jayavarman VII contained a temple designed to wash away the sins of those who bathed in its pools.

ZHOU DAGUAN, who visited Angkor in 1296–97, reported that three or four crops a year could be obtained. This does not necessarily mean that irrigation was in place, because there are many ways of producing crops without it. The evidence available does not sustain the suggestion that irrigation was vital to the survival of Angkor. Even today, irrigation is not widely practiced in regions where wet-season rains are sufficient for rice cultivation. This removes the failure of the irrigation system as an explanation for the abandonment of Angkor and enhances the likelihood that the reservoirs were essentially symbolic.

MYANMAR (BURMA)

While the region of Angkor enjoyed sufficient annual rainfall for the cultivation of rice, the PYU CIVILIZATION (200 B.C.E.–900 C.E.) cities of Myanmar (Burma) are located in the dry zone of the interior, where the rain shadow means that at the sites of HALIN and BEIKTHANO precipitation falls to between 750 and 880 millimeters (35.2 in.) per annum. This is insufficient alone for the cultivation of rice. At the same time, the Irrawaddy River that links the Pyu cities is too prone to flooding to encourage cultivation along its floodplain. The Pyu cities of Beikthano, Halin, and SRI KSETRA share a preference for the tributary river valleys, where it was possible to divert water into canals and thence to large reservoirs. At Beikthano, for example, the main canal branches at an eastern city gate to feed the moat and also to fill the western reservoir in the city. There are many large reservoirs at Halin, all fed by a major canal system. In her study of aerial photographs of these cities, Janice Stargardt has recognized possible early field systems that could have received irrigation water from such reservoirs and has concluded that the urban population relied on rice grown in irrigated fields for survival.

Further reading: Bagley, R. W. *Ancient Sichuan.* Seattle and Princeton: Seattle Art Museum, 2001; De Silva, K. M. *A History of Sri Lanka.* London: Hurst, 1981; Hsu, Cho-yun. *Han Agriculture: The Formation of Early Chinese Agrarian Economy.* Seattle: University of Washington Press, 1980.

Ishanapura Known today as Sambor Prei Kuk, Ishanapura was a major royal center in Cambodia and capital of King ISHANAVARMAN OF CHENLA (r. c. 615–628 C.E.) during the early seventh century C.E. A 13th-century Chinese compilation incorporates a description of an early seventh-century ruler, probably King Ishanavarman. It describes how the king gave an audience every three days in a hall containing a wooden throne embellished with columns of inlaid wood and fine fabrics. He wore a gold crown and golden ear pendants. Courtiers and officials touched the ground three times with their head below the steps leading up to the throne. At the end of the audience, members of the court prostrated themselves. Ishanapura has yielded one of the outstanding examples of early Khmer art in the form of a statue of Durga 1.65 meters (5.4 ft.) in height, renowned for the natural representation of this goddess.

Ishanapura is located in the valley of the Sen River above the GREAT LAKE. It includes a series of three rectangular enclosures demarcated by decorated brick walls within which lie brick temple sanctuaries and ponds. It was recorded in detail by Henri Parmentier, but recent fieldwork has added to the number of temple foundations. The layout of the central area reveals the presence of three walled precincts, each dominated by a large sanctuary. These were designated the central, southern, and northern groups. The southern group includes one principal and five lesser sanctuaries, set within an inner wall that was in turn enclosed by an outer enceinte measuring 300 by 270 meters (990 by 891 ft.). A further row of six sanctuaries lies within this second enclosure, which gives access to a causeway. The four inscriptions that have been recovered reveal that this was a foundation of King Ishanavarman. The northern group is also surrounded by a double wall with a central shrine and numerous subsidiary sanctuaries. Outside the eastern gate on the outer wall, an avenue leads to a large reservoir demarcated by earthen banks.

No INSCRIPTIONS have been found with the central group. As do the other two, it has a central sanctuary that was raised on a platform reached by a flight of steps. Carved lions guard access to the immediate surrounds of the temple terrace, the sanctuary of which measures 14 by 14 meters (42 by 42 ft.), with walls 2.8 meters (9.2 ft.) thick. An aerial reconnaissance of Ishanapura has revealed that the sanctuaries are set within a double-walled enclosure measuring two by two kilometers. The

BARAY, or reservoir, was found outside the city walls. W. J. van Liere has considered the hydraulic system of Ishanapura, suggesting that it was probably designed more for supplying the moats, religious foundations, and urban populace than for irrigating rice fields.

Ishanavarman of Chenla (r. c. 615–637 C.E.) *Ishanavarman (protégé of Siva) was a son of King Mahendravarman and an important figure in the history of state formation in Cambodia. The available inscriptions reveal that he established central control over strategic areas.*

His capital at ISHANAPURA has been identified at Sambor Prei Kuk, and a contemporary eyewitness account indicates a rich royal center with a palace, armed retainers, and the presence of an aristocratic elite. In the far west, he appointed his son to rule over a place named Jyesthapura. An INSCRIPTION relates that Narasimhagupta, the ruler of Indrapura, was a vassal of Mahendravarman and Ishanavarman. A local leader called Bhadrayuddha acknowledged Ishanavarman's supremacy. The ruler of Tamrapura recorded the overlordship of Ishanavarman, in an inscription dated to 627 C.E. After defeating a rebellious prince, Ishanavarman also claimed authority over the settlements of Cakrankapura, Amoghapura, and a text from the capital describes him as a king "who extended the territory of his parents."

When he died shortly after 637 C.E., his state controlled access to the sea via the Mekong and Bang Pakong Rivers. He was succeeded by his son, Bhavavarman II.

Ishvarapura   *See* BANTEAY SREI.

Isong Sansong   Isong Sansong was a walled fortress located in the area of Seoul, Korea. The walls covered an area of 5.6 hectares (14 acres), and the hilltop location linked with the natural difficulty of access makes it highly likely that it was a strategic fortress. Its dates have not been fully determined, but it was occupied at least during the period of the PAEKCHE kingdom before it was absorbed by SHILLA in the seventh century C.E. It is possible that the walls relate to the Shilla occupation of the Han River Valley. Excavations have revealed very large rectangular buildings within the walls, one such structure attaining a length of 37 meters (122 ft.). There was also a remarkable nine-sided building that might have served a ritual function. Rituals of some sort are also suggested by the recovery of 27 images of horses in clay and iron.

Itazuke   Itazuke, a prehistoric settlement of the YAYOI culture, located in northern Kyushu, Japan, shows evidence for rice cultivation, pottery making, and weaving, as well as stone reaping knives of a form widespread in China. The Yayoi culture, dated from 300 B.C.E. to 300 C.E., was a vital period in the development of Japanese states. Hitherto the Japanese archipelago had been occupied by the so-called Jomon culture (10,000 B.C.E.–300 B.C.E.) of hunter-gatherers who had begun to be acquainted with the cultivation of rice and some local plants toward the end of this period. The Yayoi culture by contrast was characterized by the adoption of sophisticated methods of rice cultivation long since practiced in China, the forging and casting of iron and bronze artifacts, a weaving industry, and much evidence for increasing trade and social complexity. Itazuke is located in the direct and early path of any influence or immigrants from Korea. Korean societies had been cultivating rice and interacting with Chinese states for centuries before the development of the Yayoi culture, and it is to be expected that they would have had contact with the occupants of Kyushu. A long-standing question is whether Yayoi represents an actual immigration of Korean colonists or the local development of Jomon groups under Korean influence.

When Itazuke was discovered in 1918, mainland bronze swords and halberds were found there. Excavations since 1949 have uncovered the remains of an early Yayoi community with evidence for the cultivation and storage of rice and the manufacture of pottery vessels in the vicinity of rice husks, some of which adhered to the wet clay before firing to leave impressions. There were also spindle whorls, an innovation revealing a weaving industry. The site was ringed by a ditch up to 1.5 meters deep and 4.5 meters (4.9 by 14.85 ft.) across, associated with two other ditches that might have been designed for the control of water flows or for defense. Sharp cut marks on the side suggest that metal tools were used, though none have survived. The Yayoi ceramics and the stone projectile points are similar to those of the Jomon occupation phase, indicating that even if there were some immigrants from the mainland at the beginning of the Yayoi period, the area's preceding inhabitants remained.

J

Jainism Jainism is an Indian religion with about 3 million adherents. Followers observe five principles: celibacy, truthfulness, rejection of personal possessions, pacifism, and absence of theft. Jain temples are occasionally encountered in early historic cities, but this religion has never received the same world following as BUDDHISM, nor has it rivaled Hinduism at home in INDIA. Nevertheless, it has survived in India, and it is recorded that Mahatma Gandhi was much influenced by the ascetic qualities of Jainism. Believers look on Vardhamana Mahavira (sixth century B.C.E.), the great hero, as the most recent leader of their religion, which is at least as old as Buddhism. In fact, Mahavira was numbered the 24th leader, or Tirthankara, of the Jains. He was born in Vaisali, and in many respects his early life resembles that of his near contemporary, the Buddha, for he too left his home and spent several years wandering the Ganges (Ganga) Valley in search for salvation. He also found enlightenment when aged 42 and became what was known as a *jina*, or conqueror. This name was applied to the religion as a whole. After preaching his doctrine and founding an order of monks, he died at the age of 72 years at the village of Pava, near ancient PATALIPUTRA.

Jainism benefited greatly from royal patronage, specifically that of CANDRAGUPTA MAURYA (c. 325–297 B.C.E.), who reputedly became a Jain monk himself. During his reign, a schism divided the Jains into two sects. This followed a migration away from the Jain homeland by some monks who anticipated a famine. Others stayed behind, and when the migrants returned, they found that their coreligionists had adopted unacceptable customs, such as the wearing of white robes where the norm was nakedness. This schism endures to this day.

See also MAURYA EMPIRE.

Further reading: Dundas, P. *The Jains.* Library of Religious Beliefs and Practices. London: Routledge, 2002; Parikh, V. *Jainism and the New Spirituality.* Milan: Peace Publications, 2002; Tobias, M. *Life Force: The World of Jainism.* Paris: J'ai lu Editions, 2000.

Jalilpur Jalilpur is a site of the Early Harappan or INDUS VALLEY CIVILIZATION, located near the Ravi River in Pakistan. It covers an area of 13 hectares (32.5 acres). Excavations directed by M. R. Mughal in 1971 uncovered evidence for two phases of occupation. The earlier yielded many bone artifacts and ceramics, but no evidence for copper working. The later included pottery of the KOT DIJI phase of the Early Harappan, together with human figurines, shell and FAIENCE bangles, and beads of agate and carnelian. Cattle bones dominate in the faunal assemblage, followed by domestic sheep and goats.

janapada Janapada is an Indian term for a state with a capital, sustaining area, and political boundaries. It derives from the word *jana*, "tribe." *Janapada*s developed in the Ganges (Ganga) Valley during the sixth to fourth centuries B.C.E., and oral traditions record their names. However, endemic rivalries and conflict reduced their number by absorption, and by about 350 B.C.E. the state of MAGADHA ruled most of northern India. Much information on the *janapada*s and their participation in trade can be obtained from the silver punch-marked coins that were issued from at least 500 B.C.E.

Jandial temple The Jandial temple is situated on an eminence about 600 meters (1,980 ft.) to the north of the northern gate at Sirkap, the second city of TAXILA in Pakistan. Sirkap was built by BACTRIAN GREEKS and was a laid out on a precise grid plan. Excavations revealed a classical Greek temple. SIR JOHN MARSHALL excavated the temple between 1913 to 1934 after a preliminary examination by SIR ALEXANDER CUNNINGHAM in 1863–64 revealed wall foundations. This late structure was removed, and a further two meters down Marshall traced the plan of a Greek temple that incorporated sandstone Ionic columns. It is 47.5 meters (156.7 ft.) long and 25.5 meters (74.2 ft.) wide. Marshall compared its plan, which included a front porch (*pronaos*), a sanctuary (*naos*), and a back porch (*opisthodomos*), with the temple of Artemis at Ephesus and the Parthenon in Athens and concluded that the temple dates to the period of Greek dominance at Taxila. Even the methods of construction, seen in the joining of the parts of the Ionic columns, with a central dowel were typically Greek. Philostratus (c. 170–245 C.E.) may well have been describing this very temple in his *Life of Apollonius* when he wrote that waiting for admittance to the city, he saw a temple in shell-like stone, bearing bronze panels on the walls recording events in the conquests of ALEXANDER THE GREAT.

Jataka tales Jataka tales are a series of Indian stories that describe events in the lives of the Buddha before he attained enlightenment. The Jataka stories often contain a moral and are the inspiration behind themes depicted on Buddhist temples and monasteries. The reliefs at SANCHI and BHARUT and the frescoes in the AJANTA caves illustrate many Jataka stories. The popularity of the Jatakas is well illustrated at the MOGAO caves near DUNHUANG, where a famous incident is depicted: The future Buddha has the equivalent weight of his own flesh cut off to save the life of a dove. There are 547 Jataka stories, and it is thought that Prince Mahendra took them to Sri Lanka in the third century B.C.E. Each story has three parts. After an introduction, the Buddha describes his experiences in previous lives, when he was a BODHISATTVA. Sometimes he took the form of a king or a hermit, but on other occasions he was portrayed as a monkey, horse, or elephant. Finally, the story details the companions of the Buddha during his previous lives. On many occasions, the Jakata tales describe people and places that can be identified historically and throw light on life in India during the time of the JANAPADAS, or early states, in the Ganges (Ganga) Valley. The 256th story, known as the *Jarudapana Jataka*, saw the future Buddha as a caravan guide during the time of King Brahmadatta of Varanasi (formerly Benares). The caravan was made up of merchants with a variety of goods carried on carts. Being thirsty in their travels, they dug a well, but they found only jewels. The bodhisattva advised them to stop digging, but they greedily continued until they disturbed the king of the *naga*, or snakes. He blew poisonous air on them, and they all died, except the bodhisattva.

Jaugada Jaugada is a city located on the bank of the Rishikulya River in Orissa province, eastern INDIA. It is particularly well known as the location of a rock edict inscribed during the reign of ASOKA (268–235 B.C.E.), the Mauryan emperor, which was addressed to the people of Samapa, presumably the early name of the site. Excavations in 1956–57 revealed that the massive mud ramparts, which enclosed an area of about 65 hectares (162.5 ft.), were more than 20 meters (66 ft.) wide and still stood almost five meters (16.5 ft.) high. The interior incorporated structures made of stone and brick, and occupation, according to the recovery of coins, lasted into the KUSHAN period.

See also MAURYA EMPIRE.

Jayaksetrasiva *See* WAT BASET.

Jayatataka The Jayatataka was an immense BARAY, or reservoir, constructed at ANGKOR in Cambodia during the reign of JAYAVARMAN VII (r. 1181–1219 C.E.), but now dry. Its outline is easily seen from the air. There was an island temple at its center, known today as NEAK PEAN. According to the INSCRIPTIONS, the complex was a representation of the sacred LAKE ANAVATAPTA. This lake, located north of the Himalayas, was held in Buddhist writings and practice to have magical powers. It was the origin of four great rivers, the Amu Dar'ya, Tarim, Indus, and Ganges (Ganga), and its water, cooled by protective mountains that shielded it from sun and rain, was used in royal consecration ceremonies under Emperor ASOKA (268–235 B.C.E.) of the MAURYA EMPIRE dynasty in India. It was thought to bestow divinity on the sovereign. Queen Maya, mother of the Buddha, was bathed there to purify her before she was dressed in sacred clothes and flowers. Anavatapta water was taken daily to the court of Asoka for his own use and for that of his most holy followers. The Neak Pean temple in the center of the Jayatataka incorporates four stone images—a horse, a lion, an ox, and an elephant—on each side. The water in the central pool gushes through their mouths in a precise match for the way the Lake Anavatapta water emerges from the lake so that the temple was certainly a source for purification and ritual ablutions. Thus those traveling to the temple and bathing in its sacred water could wash away the slime of their sins. Such an interpretation for the purpose of the Angkorian *baray*s runs counter to the more mundane supposition that they were constructed to supply irrigation water to rice fields.

See also BUDDHISM.

Jayavarman I of Chenla (c. 635–680 C.E.) *Jayavarman I was a ruler whose royal ancestry can be traced back through his great-grandfather, Ishanavarman of Chenla (877–99 C.E.), to the earliest recorded kings of one of the major polities of Chenla.*

CHENLA is the name in Chinese texts of a state that controlled Cambodia between 550 and 800 C.E. A close analysis of the available INSCRIPTIONS, in conjunction with archaeological evidence, suggests that this was a period of state formation, in which there was a series of competing polities. There is a consistent thread of evidence for the formation of a centralized state in Cambodia well before the foundation of the kingdom of ANGKOR. Jayavarman's inscriptions, which are found over a relatively wide area including the lowlands bordering the Mekong River and the GREAT LAKE and thence west into Battambang, provide evidence for the tightening of central power and control through the appointment of ministers with a range of new titles. Through this administrative structure, the ruler issued edicts on land ownership and the collection of revenue in the form of goods and labor. One text also describes Jayavarman as the conqueror of the circle of his enemies, and another records his campaigning in autumn, when his enemy's moats were dry. "Innumerable vassal kings," he claimed, obeyed his commands. In combat, he was "a living incarnation of victory, the scourge of his enemies, lord of the land inherited from his ancestors, and conqueror of yet more lands." The king appointed the author of another inscription as his *rajasabhapadi,* or president of the royal court, and allowed him to use a white parasol and a golden vase. Jayavarman also issued a *rajna,* or legal edict, confirming the ownership of temple property, and warning "that those who contest the king's orders, will be punished."

New official titles are informative of the duties of the ruling aristocracy. One family held the priestly position of *hotar.* A member was made a *mahasvaphadi* and was given the governorship of a place called Sresthapura. His younger brother was successively officer of the royal guard, custodian of royal regalia, and chief of the rowers; finally, by order of the king, he was given a substantial military command. There were a *samantagajapadi,* chief of the royal elephants, and a *dhanyakarapadi,* chief of the royal grain stores. A further inscription, probably from this reign, specified the quantities of salt to be distributed by barge to various foundations and prohibited the imposition of tax on the ships that transported this vital commodity.

Jayavarman II (c. 770–834 C.E.) *Jayavarman II was revered as the sovereign who founded the kingdom of Angkor in the early ninth century C.E.*

INSCRIPTIONS show that he engaged in much warfare but also was responsible for founding several temples. Two sources of evidence illuminate his reign and achievements. The first involves the inscriptions set up when he was alive and those that describe him as a historic, founding figure. The second is the evidence of archaeology. Two contemporary inscriptions suggest that he was living at or near the huge walled city of BANTEAY PREI NOKOR, east of the Mekong River, ruling during the last two decades of the eighth century C.E. The next inscrip-

tion describes his dedicating a foundation to the north, in the region of the independent polity of Sambhupura. It describes Jayavarman as king of the Earth surrounded by the ocean. The inscription of SDOK KAK THOM, dated 260 years later than the event, describes how Jayavarman returned from Java to rule in the holy city of INDRAPURA. This is more likely to reflect a skirmish against the neighboring CHAM CIVILIZATION than a sojourn in distant Java in Indonesia. The inscription records that the king ordered Shivakaivalya, ancestor of the family of Sdok Kak Thom, to move himself, family, and followers to a place probably in the vicinity of Angkor.

According to a second inscription, these early years saw much warfare, for he evidently ordered Prthivinarendra, an official known as a *mratan,* to pacify all districts. Jayavarman rewarded his generals with land grants: An inscription from Thvar Kdei in Kompong Thom province, dated 150 years after these events, records how the king endowed land to *vap* Jataveda; *vap* was a new honorific title. He also granted land to one of his wives. Jayavarman established himself at HARIHARALAYA on the northern margin of the Great Lake. However, he moved his capital on several occasions, for we next find him at Amarendrapura, which was probably at the western end of the WESTERN BARAY of Angkor.

A later move took him to the KULEN HILLS, described in the inscriptions as Mahendraparvata, Mountain of the Great INDRA, where he had himself consecrated the supreme king of kings, in the presence of an image of SIVA that was named KAMRATENG JAGAT TA RAJA, or DEVARAJA, "the god who is king." There would henceforth be only one "lord of the lower Earth" who would be the CHAKRAVARTIN, or universal overlord. Finally, Jayavarman II returned to Hariharalaya, where he died in about 835 C.E. In terms of archaeology, it is likely that Banteay Prei Nokor, the temple of Trapheang Phong at Hariharalaya, AK YUM at BANTEAY CHOEU, and Rong Chen on the Kulen uplands date from his reign. Only archaeological excavations and the fortuitous discovery of more inscriptions can add further information about a king revered as the founder of the kingdom even 250 years after his death.

Jayavarman III (r. 834–877 C.E.) *Jayavarman III, son of Jayavarman II (c. 770–834 C.E.), was the second king of the first dynasty of Angkor in Cambodia. Little is known about his life and achievements.*

An INSCRIPTION from just north of Siem Reap ascribes the foundation of a temple to the year in which Jayavarman III ascended the throne. The text describes how, after the king failed to capture a wild elephant while hunting, a divinity promised to secure the animal if the king built a sanctuary there. Some other temples are known to date to the reign of Jayavarman III, indicating continuing interest in the region of Angkor. Due north of AK YUM, but on the opposite side of the WESTERN BARAY, lies the temple of Prasat Kok Po. An inscription records the erection of a statue of Vishnu here by Prithivindrapandita, a guru of the king, in 857. Jayavarman III may also have initiated the construction of the BAKONG at HARIHARALAYA. He was succeeded by INDRAVARMAN I (877–99 C.E.).

Jayavarman IV (r. 928–942 C.E.) *King Jayavarman IV of Angkor in Cambodia is often described as a usurper who established an alternative capital at Lingapura, now known as Koh Ker.*

In fact, he was the son of King INDRAVARMAN I's (877–899 C.E.) daughter, Mahendradevi, and was married to his aunt, who was a half-sister of King YASHOVARMAN I (r. 889–910 C.E.). According to the loose rules governing the succession, therefore, he had a legitimate claim through the proper female line, even if he seems to have claimed kingship while the sons of Yashovarman continued to rule from Angkor. Jayavarman IV must have been a very energetic, even charismatic, ruler, because he founded and had constructed a new capital center on a huge scale. Lingapura was a walled city 1,200 meters square (1,440 sq. yds.), enclosing an inner walled precinct containing the state temple complex, known as Prasat Thom. The sacred precinct within houses the principal temple pyramid, raised on seven tiers of descending size. He also constructed a BARAY that involved digging out the rocky substrate. Lingapura is surrounded by a series of subsidiary temples covering an area of 35 square kilometers (14 sq. mi.).

Some of the satellite temples at Lingapura contain exhaustive lists of the workers assigned to the construction of the capital. These inscriptions describe how construction was based on the mobilization of labor from many provinces, and taxation in kind, particularly rice, was levied to sustain workers. Provincial inscriptions also suggest that the king had a broad hold over the kingdom. One describes Jayavarman IV as a great warrior, who ruined his enemy on the field of battle; another called him king of Cambodia: "Fierce in battle, this King's arrows cloud the sky and fill the eyes of his arrogant enemies with the darkness of the night." Punishment awaited those who disobeyed a royal edict: They would be caged by the elders of the district and placed before the king for sentence.

Jayavarman V (r. 968–1001 C.E.) *Jayavarman V succeeded his father, Rajendravarman (r. 944–68 C.E.), as king of Angkor in Cambodia when only 10 years old.*

High court officials dominated his first years, but by the time he was 17 his state temple, known as Hemasringagiri, or the Mountain with Golden Summits, was under construction at ANGKOR. Now known as Ta Keo, it was never completed but is of grandiose size. One of the young king's advisers, Yajnavaraha, was responsible for the foundation of the temple of BANTEAY SREI northeast of the capital. Jayavarman's INSCRIPTIONS are concentrated in the good agricultural lands to the north and west of the

TONLE SAP, east to the Mekong River, and then south toward the upper delta. Unusually, his reign appears to have been relatively peaceful, and his inscriptions reveal the maintenance of large estates by the aristocracy and the meritorious donation of gifts to the gods. One text also describes how the king, when aged 16, founded two religious corporations with rights to land holding, inheritance, and exemption from taxes.

Jayavarman VI (r. 1080–1107 C.E.) *King Jayavarman VI of Angkor in Cambodia was a usurper who was a member of the aristocratic Mahidharapura lineage of the upper Mun Valley in Thailand.*

In about 1080, Divakarapandita, who had participated in the consecration of UDAYADITYAVARMAN II's (r. 1050–66 C.E.) golden LINGAM at the BAPHUON and who held a high court position during the next three reigns, crowned him. Jayavarman VI made no attempt to relate his ancestry to previous rulers at Angkor. His father was a local potentate in a border region to the northwest, beyond the Dang Raek range. A later INSCRIPTION from PHNOM RUNG names Hiranyavarman and Hiranyalakshmi as parents of Jayavarman VI.

See also BANTEAY SREI.

Jayavarman VII (r. 1181–1219 C.E.) *Jayavarman VII was one of the great kings of Angkor in Cambodia.*

After the kingdom was attacked and sacked by the Chams, he defeated the occupying enemy on land and on the GREAT LAKE and reestablished the rule of the Mahidharapura dynasty. Jayavarman had a new capital city constructed at ANGKOR, now known as ANGKOR THOM. Three kilometers square (1.2 sq. mi.), the city is surrounded by a high wall, five colossal gateways, and a wide moat. The BAYON, his temple mausoleum, lies at the center of the new city. The royal palace was located in a separate walled precinct north of the Bayon and gave access to the ELEPHANT TERRACE, a reviewing stand commanding a large open area. Jayavarman VII was a Buddhist king, and his temple mausoleum contained a large statue of the Buddha. The city gates, the Bayon, and his other major foundations incorporated large stone heads thought to represent the king merged with the Buddha. The Jayatataka BARAY, or reservoir, northwest of Angkor Thom was built in his reign; the island temple at the center, known as NEAK PEAN, was a holy place where pilgrims could bathe and wash away their earthly sins. Two very large temple complexes now known as TA PROHM and PREAH KHAN were built just beyond the city walls. They were dedicated to the king's parents. A third massive temple at the remote BANTEAY CHMAR was built to honor the king's son and four military heroes. The foundation inscriptions of Preah Khan and Ta Prohm set out the number of villages and thousands of workers assigned to provide goods, from rice to wax and clothing, to maintain

It is most unusual to encounter lifelike sculptures of Angkorian kings. This fine bust depicts Jayavarman VII, the great builder king who ruled Angkor from 1181 until 1219. *(Erich Lessing/ Art Resource, NY)*

the temples. Jayavarman had roads and bridges constructed across the kingdom. Rest houses were strategically placed to provide shelter for travelers, many of whom would have been pilgrims visiting the many holy places. There were also HOSPITALS that, like the temples, were ascribed villages and workers to supply them with all their needs.

The Bayon and Banteay Chmar temples contain reliefs that show the royal army in conflict, on land and water, with the Chams. They also depict many aspects of life in the city and countryside, including a woman in labor, a market scene, aristocratic feasting and servants preparing food, chess players, and fishermen. Several statues of the king survive; that from Preah Khan of Kompong Svay is the best known, revealing a serene and regal image.

See also BUDDHISM; CHAM CIVILIZATION.

Jayavarman VIII (r. 1243–1296) *Jayavarman VIII, king of Angkor in Cambodia, a dedicated adherent to Hinduism, ordered that all Buddhist statues at Angkor be destroyed or modified to accord with Hindu practice.*
The image of the Buddha, which had dominated the central shrine of the BAYON, was smashed and the pieces thrown

into the shaft beneath. It was restored and rededicated in 1935. It was during this reign that the last major religious building, the Mangalartha, was constructed; Jayavarman, however, actively remodeled several older buildings, including the reviewing terraces east of the palace.

Jayavarman of Funan (c. 480 C.E.) *Jayavarman of Funan was known as a victorious ruler and a founder of temples to Vishnu.*
Toward the end of the fifth century C.E. kings of the maritime state of FUNAN in Cambodia began to set up stone INSCRIPTIONS written in the exotic SANSKRIT language. The few that survive reveal that there was a line of kings in which the succession on at least one occasion passed from father to son; that they had adopted the honorific title *varman,* "shield" or "protector"; that WOMEN enjoyed high status; and that the elite founded temples. One of these texts mentions a person whose name began with *Ja-,* probably Jayavarman, who had been victorious in battle against a king whose name began with *Vira-.* He founded many sanctuaries dedicated to Vishnu and placed his son, GUNAVARMAN, in charge of one, which had been "wrested from the mud." A second inscription cites King Jayavarman and his son, RUDRAVARMAN (Protégé by SIVA), and describes how the former named the son of a Brahman as his inspector of property. A third text also mentions King Jayavarman and his victories won over rivals. It then records the foundation of a hermitage, reservoir, and residence by his queen, KULAPRABHAVATI.

Jhukar Jhukar is a site in the Indus Valley that has given its name to a culture that is known to have continued to occupy several sites of the INDUS VALLEY CIVILIZATION during the early second millennium B.C.E. The few exposures of JHUKAR material, which is best known on the basis of the excavations at CHANHU DARO in Pakistan, reveal elements of continuity and change. Thus while the writing system and distinctive SEALS of the earlier civilization were no longer found, circular seals bearing geometric designs were still employed. The pottery, revealing different designs, was derived from the preceding tradition. At Chanhu Daro, the people of the Jhukar phase continued to occupy the same mound and to reemploy bricks but did not invest the same energy in civic amenities, such as the drainage system. The Jhukar phase, which is dated 2000–1800 B.C.E., is important in the sense that it reveals continued occupation of some earlier urban sites, rather than the drastic and sudden demise of the civilization.

See also AMRI.

Jia Yi (201–168 B.C.E.) *Jia Yi, a statesman during the early Western Han dynasty, wrote a widely regarded study of the preceding Qin dynasty entitled* Guo Chin Lun (The Faults of Qin).

He lived in a period that followed the tumultuous end of the WARRING STATES PERIOD (475–221 B.C.E.), which culminated in the victory of Qin and the imposition of a brutal centralized autocracy under the first emperor, QIN SHIHUANGDI (259–210 B.C.E.). The early Han rulers and bureaucrats sought a means of ruling an immense empire other than through repressive coercion, and the period witnessed many philosophical tracts on governance centered on TAOISM but including elements of Confucianism. The work in particular focuses on the reasons underlying the successful peasant revolt against the second Qin emperor, which pitched poorly armed rustics against the largest and best-equipped army in the world. He pinpointed the difference between successfully defeating enemies and creating the empire on the one hand and maintaining peace on the other. For this, the ruler required empathy with his subjects, ensuring good agricultural practice, avoiding harsh taxation and repression. The opposite path toward autocratic repression was followed and led to the downfall of the dynasty in the face of desperate and determined peasants.

See also CHEN SHE; CONFUCIUS.

Jin   The state of Jin was located in the valley of the Fen River, in the modern Chinese province of Shanxi. It occupied a strategic location between the central plains and the heartland of the Western Zhou state and the western foothills of the Taihang mountain range. The state was responsible for guarding against any incursions or threats from the Zhou heartland. The history of the Jin state during the Spring and Autumn period (770–476 B.C.E.) was one of rivalry and conflict, particularly with the rising ascendancy of CHU in the south.

Archaeological excavations have greatly added to the knowledge of the Jin state, particularly the investigations at TIANMA-QUCUN. These have resulted in the uncovering of more than 600 burials. A group of 17 tombs excavated between 1992 and 1995 were equipped with access ramps together with pits containing the remains of chariots and horses, dating to the late Western Zhou and early EASTERN ZHOU DYNASTY periods. These graves contained bronzes inscribed with the names of the Jin elite, including sets of bells. Remarkably, some bronze vessels were never intended for use, because the lids and bodies were cast as one piece, and one specimen still had the central clay core in place. The Jin lords may also have been antique collectors, for a Neolithic jade *cong* and jades of SHANG STATE origin were recovered. Jade ornaments are a particular feature of these graves, and in the case of Burial 31, they were cut to cover the face of the deceased.

RISE OF JIN

Jin, like several other states that came to the fore politically during the Spring and Autumn period, had its origins in the wars of succession that followed the death of KING WU (d. c. 1043 B.C.E.), the first ruler of the WESTERN ZHOU DYNASTY. The succession should have passed to his oldest son, Song, who under the name Cheng was to rule from about 1042 until 1006 B.C.E. However, a younger brother of King Wu, Zhou Gong Dan, declared himself regent, on the grounds that Song was too young to rule alone. This fomented a civil war between the forces of Zhou Gong Dan and Cheng on the one hand and those of Dan's brothers on the other. Zhou Gong Dan fought successful campaigns to the east of the capital and greatly expanded the area under Zhou control. In a time-honored tradition, rulers of the new territories were found among the loyal members of the ruling lineage or high-ranking followers, and Tangshu Yu, one of the brothers of King Cheng, was granted the fief that was to develop into the state of Jin.

The initial threat from the north was met by the formation of the subsidiary state of Quwo in 746 B.C.E. This proved a Trojan horse, because in 678 Wu Gong of Quwo defeated the Jin and was recognized as the duke of Jin. His successor, Jin Xi'an Gong (r. 676–651 B.C.E.), expanded the power of Jin by absorbing 16 smaller states in its orbit. In an act typical of the power struggles that accompanied the death or murder of a Jin ruler, Jin Xi'an Gong had all the descendants of former Jin rulers put to death. After his own death there was a war over the succession involving his sons. One of these, Hui Gong, was captured by the Chu after a battle, and finally only one son, Jin Wen Gong (r. 636–628 B.C.E.), was still alive. He ruled that no member of the royal line was permitted to hold a court position. In 635 B.C.E. he further expanded Jin territory after a timely intervention to assist the king of Zhou. Three years later, in a temporary alliance with QI and QIN, Jin defeated the forces of the Chu in the Battle of Chengpu, but the Jin were defeated in 598 B.C.E. at the Battle of Mi. This led to a remarkable resolve among the states to engage in mutually agreed disarmament, but as are most such treaties, it was short lived, and Jin defeated Chu again at Yanling in 574. In the same year Jin Li Gong was murdered and succeeded by Jin Dao Gong (572–558 B.C.E.). In 546 B.C.E. there was a conference at Shangqui, leading to an agreement that there should be an agreed ceiling on the number of war chariots maintained by each state. Four decades of peace between Jin and Chu ensued. This period of external peace was not accompanied by internal harmony. By the end of the sixth century B.C.E., civil war in the state of Jin saw six factions reduced to four, and in 453 B.C.E. three houses remained: ZHAO, HANN, and WEI. In 403 B.C.E. each was officially recognized as a state in its own right, and Jin came to an end.

OTHER ARCHAEOLOGICAL DISCOVERIES

Archaeological research at XINTIAN in Shanxi province has revealed many features of the Jin capital from 585 B.C.E. The site included three walled cities, the smallest one by one kilometer in extent. It is thought that one of these was for the ruling lineage, and the others for lesser members of the elite. Each incorporates raised stamped-earth platform foundations for temple and residential buildings. Further walled precincts also lay beyond the central core. One of the most important aspects of the archaeological research has been the identification of specialist areas for casting bronzes, making bone artifacts, and manufacturing pottery. A number of cemeteries have been examined, some including large and richly endowed elite graves dating to the Spring and Autumn period, while another enclave held a concentration of pits containing the skeletons of sacrificed cattle, horses, sheep, and chickens. These were part of a ritual in which individuals took an oath of allegiance to their lineage head; the text was inscribed or painted onto jade tablets that were then placed over the sacrificed animals. The domestic quarters of the mass of the Jin population reveal the presence of house foundations, storage pits, wells, and drainage facilities. The site was abandoned in 369 B.C.E.

Jinancheng Jinancheng is a city occupied under the Chinese kingdom of CHU during the WARRING STATES PERIOD (475–221 B.C.E.). It is located about 17 kilometers (10.2 mi.) north of the Chang (Yangtze) River in Hubei province. Excavations there have revealed much vital information on the nature of a major urban center during this period, when the states of China were embroiled in a long struggle for supremacy. This ended in 221 B.C.E. with the victory of the QIN over all rivals, including the kingdom of Chu. As might be expected, Jinancheng was stoutly defended by a broad moat and wide stamped-earth walls up to 40 meters (132 ft.) thick. There were six main entrances into the city and two water gates to admit the course of the two rivers that flowed through the interior. Raised stamped-earth platforms that were concentrated in the northeastern sector of the interior supported the palaces of the elite together with their temples. The southwestern quarter included a number of ceramic-kiln sites for producing roof tiles and domestic pottery, while there was also a specialist bronze foundry. The city covered 1,600 hectares (4,000 acres) and would have supported a substantial population, to judge from the 400 or more wells that have been uncovered by archaeologists.

Jincun In 1928 heavy rain revealed the top of a tomb at Jincun, northwest of the EASTERN ZHOU DYNASTY capital at LUOYANG in China. Eight tombs were looted and the contents distributed to collectors. Fortunately, Bishop W. C. White was then resident at Jincun and described the necropolis. The tombs had octagonal wooden chambers joined by a doorway to long ramps, one of which reached 80 meters (264 ft.) in length. Three of the ramps were lined by long pits containing the remains of horses. The looted artifacts were outstandingly rich. Three giant *ding* tripods lined the doorway giving access to the tomb, each almost one meter in diameter. Within the chamber, the upper part of the wooden walls was decorated with a band of inlaid glass and bronze disks. Some of the bronze vessels and mirrors were inlaid with gold, silver, or glass, and there were silver vessels and a statuette. A jade and gold pectoral is now in the possession of a Washington, D.C. museum. The typology of these artifacts points to a date in the fourth century B.C.E., the WARRING STATES PERIOD (475–221 B.C.E.), and it is difficult not to ascribe such magnificent interments to the royal lineage of the EASTERN ZHOU DYNASTY.

Jingdi (Liu Qi; Admired Emperor) (188–141 B.C.E.) *Jingdi was the fourth major king of the Western Han dynasty in China.*
His father was the emperor WENDI (202–157 B.C.E.) and his mother the empress Dou. Jingdi's magnificent tomb was discovered in 1990. The terra-cotta army of the first emperor, QIN SHIHUANGDI (259–210 B.C.E.), is well known for its size and number of clay statues of soldiers. That of Han Jingdi covers five times the area of the famous terra-cotta army. There are 86 pits in association with his mausoleum, containing at least 40,000 clay figures. These were modeled at about a third of lifesize and were so constructed that their arms could be moved. Each was painted and clothed in silk. On the basis of the SEALS found, it is thought that each pit might represent a department of state. The one containing 400 dogs and 200 sheep, for example, would represent the kitchens. Unlike in the tomb pits of Qin Shihuangdi, there was less concentration on war and soldiery. The tomb also contained models of domestic animals, farm implements, tools, wheeled vehicles, and ceramic storage jars still brimming with grain. There are chisels, plowshares, model granaries, and chariots. Eunuchs and serving WOMEN were modeled in molds, and their faces retouched to take on an individual appearance. Adjacent to this main mound, there are subsidiary tombs for the empress and the favorite concubine. These too have many associated pits; at least 31 are already known for the empress herself.

Wendi had followed a policy of emasculating the power of dependent kingdoms by diminishing their size or replacing them where possible with commanderies (centrally controlled provinces). In 154 B.C.E., the third year of his reign, the king of Wu revolted against Jingdi, who, as heir apparent, had been responsible for the death of THE KING OF wu's son in an argument over a chess game. Wu was joined by other eastern-seaboard kingdoms, particularly CHU and ZHAO. The imperial army was too powerful, and government victory provided the opportunity to replace the kingdoms with provinces. A similar opportunity arose to the south when the king of Changsha, formerly the powerful state of Chu, died without an heir in 157 B.C.E. The new king was a member of Jingdi's own lineage. These changes had the effect of greatly expanding central control at the expense of distant but powerful semi-independent kingdoms. During the decade from 155 B.C.E., no fewer than 14 of Jingdi's sons were given their own kingdoms. The regional kings, however, had their powers severely reduced in that their advisers and ministers were increasingly appointed from the capital rather than through local favor.

Jingdi also reimposed a tax of 1/30th on production, which led to a considerable accumulation of central capital. While some of this wealth was stored against the possibility of adverse agricultural returns, it was also deployed to maintain central craft workshops. The models in Jingdi's tomb stress the importance attached to agriculture under Jingdi, and the infrastructure necessary for a prosperous economy, so vital to the maintenance of the state, was provided through a requirement for corvée labor by the peasantry. According to contemporary records, the vast majority of the population were agricultural peasants. In addition to serving two years of military conscription, they were required to work for the state for one month in 12. Thus a network of road, canals, and bridges was constructed. Jingdi was succeeded by one of his sons, WUDI (157–87 B.C.E.).

Jingyanggang Jingyanggang is a large urban site of the LONGSHAN CULTURE, located on the left bank of the Huang (Yellow) River in Shandong province, central China. Its stamped-earth walls enclosed an area of about 38 hectares (95 acres), making it one of the largest such sites of this period in China. Excavations within the walled enclosure have revealed substantial raised platforms of stamped earth, one of which is 520 by 175 meters (1,716 by 577.5 ft.) in extent. Early written graphs have been found on the surface of a pottery vessel there.

Jinshin disturbance The Jinshin disturbance refers to a civil war that broke out in Japan in 672 C.E. after the death of the emperor TENJI (626–672). At that juncture, there were no rules for the succession, and close kin of the emperor could claim equal rights irrespective of their sex. The Jinshin disturbance involved the son and the brother of Tenji. The deceased emperor had nominated his son, Prince Otomo, and bypassed Prince Oama, his uncle. The war was fought to a background of increasing centralization of power and authority in the YAMATO court at the expense of the provincial magnates. Under these circumstances, Prince Oama withdrew from the court with the broadcast intention of secluding himself in a monastery in the Yoshino Mountains. However, with the support of the provincial families, who had chafed under the centralizing regime of Tenji, he defeated Otomo. The latter committed suicide and was declared the emperor Kobun only posthumously in 1870. Paradoxically, having triumphed with provincial support, the new emperor TENMU (Oama) (631?–86) initiated even more intensive centralizing policies that ultimately led to the foundation of the NARA STATE.

Jinyang Jinyang in Shanxi province, China, was an early capital of the JIN state during the Spring and Autumn period (770–476 B.C.E.). Its cemetery lay beyond the northwestern wall, and more than 100 graves have been identified there. In 1987 the intact grave of Zhao Meng, a minister to the Jin court, was excavated and found to be intact. His three nested coffins were centrally placed in a rectangular chamber 14 meters (46.2 ft.) below the ground. Made of cedar, the chamber measured 11 by nine meters (36.3 by 29.7 ft.) and was encased in a layer of charcoal and stones. The primary burial lay in the center of this chamber and was accompanied by four coffins containing the remains of two male and two female attendants. The completeness of this burial permits the tracing of the mortuary rituals. Surviving documents of the Spring and Autumn mortuary practices reveal that first the corpse was washed, dressed, and laid out in state, for a period determined by the status of the deceased. The next stage in the mortuary ritual was to organize the funeral procession of carriages and chariots that wound their way to the cemetery to place the grave offerings around the central coffins.

In the case of emperors, the first stage would last for up to seven months. Zhao Meng had been treated thus, and while his actual clothing has not survived, the jade and gold ornaments found with the body reveal certain aspects of his dress. He wore a belt tied with a golden buckle from which two swords hung, each with a jade handle and pommel. Jade plaques used to cover his eyes were probably part of a cloth shroud. He wore two jade archer's thimbles, and the many plaques of jade on his skeleton had been attached to his robe. The body was then placed into the first of three lacquered coffins that were decorated with gold foil.

Zhao Meng was accompanied by a rich array of offerings that represented his social status and activities in life. One of the subsidiary coffins held a set of 19 bells and 12 stone chimes. The man within was probably the minister's music master. A second was linked with chariot fittings, surely the chief charioteer's. Seventy ritual bronze vessels were stacked in profusion beyond the head of the coffins. Some of these contained food remains that included grain and the bones of birds, cattle, pigs, and sheep. A pit adjacent to this tomb contained the remains of 44 horses and 15 chariots that would have been employed in the funerary procession.

Jito (645–703) *Jito was the 41st Tenno, or sovereign, of Japan.*
A daughter of the emperor TENJI (626–72), she married her uncle, Oama, who later became the emperor TEMMU (631?–686). She reigned from 686 to 697 C.E., when she abdicated in favor of her grandson, Emperor Mommu. A noted poet, she is particularly remembered for her decision to found the great city of FUJIWARA in the southern

Nara Basin. This move represented a departure from previous imperial residence patterns, whereby the emperor would move periodically from one palace to another. Fujiwara was a city built on Tang Chinese principles. It was dominated by a large palace compound containing the imperial residence, a reception hall, and government buildings. Beyond the palace walls, a grid system of streets was laid out, and the urban populace was allocated space according to rank. However, this city had a brief life before being abandoned in favor of an even larger center 20 kilometers (12 mi.) to the north at HEIJO-KYO.

Jones, Sir William (1746–1794) *Sir William Jones is best known for his study of Sanskrit and his recognition that this language was related to Latin, Greek, and all other languages of the Indo-European family.*
Educated at the University of Oxford, Jones was a gifted linguist who was to become proficient in as many as 28 languages. He also studied law, and it was as a prospective High Court judge that he sailed for Bengal in 1783. His proficiency in languages was already evident in his Persian grammar and his translation from Arabic of the Islamic law of property succession. In INDIA, he applied himself to the Sanskrit language largely to inform himself on traditional Indian law and furthered scholarly studies through founding the Asiatic Society of Bengal. As president of this society in 1786, he read a paper proposing that Greek and Sanskrit had a common origin. This was a pioneer study in comparative linguistics that has exercised a profound influence on all subsequent studies of the Indo-European language family.

Jori system The Jori system was a method of subdividing agricultural land, which was part of the TAIKA REFORM of 645 C.E. The YAMATO state at this period was experiencing a rapid development toward centralized power in the hands of the sovereign. This pattern involved the reduction in the role of local magnates but necessitated the foundation of a strong rural economy as a basis for taxation on production and people. The origins of the Jori system might be far older than the period of the Taiko edict, however, because some prehistoric rice plots uncovered through archaeological research, such as those at the YAYOI site of TORO, seem to conform to it. Basically, the agricultural land was divided into squares measuring six *cho* (109 meters) square (131 sq. yds.). This unit was further divided into 36 *tsubo*, each measuring one *cho* square and again into 10 equally sized strips called *tan*. Theoretically, a *tan* produced sufficient rice to feed one person for a year. The allocation of land by the court for individual use was facilitated by this method, by which even small units of land could be identified.

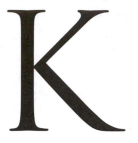

K

Kaberis Emporium   *See* KAVERIPUMPATTINAM.

Kafyr-kala   Kafyr-kala is one of the few sites providing evidence for the nature of a regional center of the HEPHTHALITE HUNS. The Hephthalites were a powerful Hun group who dominated Central Asia and northern India between about 450 and 550 C.E. While some segments of the community preserved their nomadic ways, the ruling elite adopted a sedentary urban life, minted coins, and administered a sophisticated system of justice. Kafyr-kala is located in the upper Vaksh Valley in Tajikistan and was surrounded by a wall incorporating defensive towers. A palace dominated the citadel, which is 360 meters square (432 sq. yds.), while the lower town included a central road flanked by residences, temples, and shops. The palace was strongly defended with two walls and towers at each corner. The Chinese pilgrim XUANZANG, who traveled through this area in the seventh century, observed monasteries and Buddhist monks in Hephthalite centers. At the palace of Kafyr-kala, a Buddhist sanctuary, the walls of which were embellished with paintings of the Buddha, has been revealed by excavation.

Kahaum   Kahaum is a site located in the lower Ghaghra Valley of Uttar Pradesh state, northern India. It is notable for the discovery there of an INSCRIPTION dating to 460 C.E. in which Madra, the donor, records the meritorious act of raising a stone pillar bearing the images of five Jain deities. It begins with a fulsome tribute to the reigning king, SKANDAGUPTA (455–467 C.E.), which dates the donation to the 141st year of the Gupta dynasty. The king is described as king of a hundred kings, and Madra set out his paternal ancestors' names and noted his benevo-lence toward Brahmans, gurus, and ascetics. He then expressed how his concerns for the transitory nature of the being had encouraged him to seek much merit by the erection of the stone pillar.

See also GUPTA EMPIRE; JAINISM.

Kailasa mountain   In Hindu mythology, Mount Kailasa was the home of SIVA. It was shaken by the giant Ravana, to attract the attention of Siva.

Kaladi   The Kaladi INSCRIPTION is a late copy on copper plates of an earlier text dated to 909 C.E. It is from the region of the lower Mas River in east Java in Indonesia and describes how King BALITUNG (r. c. 901–10) granted land to two officials. It also records the tax status of land dedicated to a temple. It is of considerable interest to note that land converted into rice fields was considered dangerous to traders and other travelers by day and night because of demons and robbers. There is also a long list of people not permitted to enter the land, which gives a good cross section of specializations, for it includes musicians, rice cooks, those in charge of orchestras and prostitutes, foreigners, spur makers, overseers of traders, traders of axes and rope, collectors of snails, umbrella makers, and mat makers. The presence in east Java of foreign merchants, presumably interested in the rich spice trade, is recorded in the list of those forbidden to enter the property: They were from India, Sri Lanka, Champa, Cambodia, and Myanmar (Burma). Clothing and gold were given to the witnesses of the *SIMA*, a resolution on tax status of land.

See also CHAM CIVILIZATION.

Kala-i Kahkaha Kala-i Kahkaha (Bunjikat) was a major city that flourished in Ustrushana during the seventh and eighth centuries C.E. It is located in the upper basin of the Syr Dar'ya River and was defended by a wall with regularly spaced bastions. The people of Ustrushana grew wealthy on the basis of irrigated agriculture, mining, and trade along the SILK ROAD. Kala-i Kahkaha incorporates a large storied palace richly decorated with wall paintings and wooden carvings, the houses of wealthy merchants, and a quarter for the specialist potters. Bronze coin issues were used in exchange.

Kalawan The Kalawan, originally known as Chadasila, is the second largest monastic establishment founded on the hills surrounding TAXILA in modern Pakistan. The complex covers an area of 135 by 80 meters (445.5 by 264 ft.) and includes a large court containing the main stupa with an unusually large relic chamber within and three courts lined with monks' cells to the south. The main stupa does not dominate in terms of size and is associated with several smaller stupas. By good fortune, the relic chamber in the stupa of Shrine A1 was found intact. It contained a small schist model of a stupa 16 centimeters (6.4 in.) high, covered in gold. The casket within, also covered in gold, contained 12 gold rosettes and 16 of silver and another gold casket, containing fragments of bone and beads of beryl, quartz, crystal, pearl, garnet, and glass. An associated INSCRIPTION in the KHAROSHTHI script recorded that in about 77 C.E., one Candrabhi and members of her family contributed offerings to the stupa shrine, for the attainment of nirvana.

Kalibangan Kalibangan, a city of the INDUS VALLEY CIVILIZATION, is located in Rajasthan, India, on the now-dry channel of the SARASVATI RIVER. The name means "black bangles," after the number found on the surface of the mound before excavations, which began in 1961 and lasted for nine seasons. Two major phases of occupation were identified. In the first, which is of the immediate pre-Harappan period, the site was a fortified area in the form of a parallelogram measuring 250 by 180 (825 by 594 ft.) meters.

After the first settlement was abandoned, a layer of sterile sand accumulated over the ruined walls, but the site was soon reoccupied during the period of the classic Indus civilization, which began about 2500 B.C.E. The importance of this second period of occupation lies in the clear evidence obtained for internal spatial organization of a small provincial center. There were, as at HARAPPA and MOHENJO DARO, two distinct walled areas. That to the west was built over the remains of the Period 1 occupation and was therefore elevated above the plain. It had a walled area divided in turn into two distinct sections, one of which seems to have been a ritual area. A gap of 40 meters (132 ft.) separates this elite and religious sector from the larger lower city, which is again located within a parallelogram form 360 by 240 (1,188 by 792 ft.) meters in extent.

EARLY PHASE

The mud-brick wall around the settlement varied in width from 1.9 to four meters (6.2 to 13.2 ft.). Houses within were also built of mud brick and had three or four rooms around a central courtyard. Cooking ovens and plastered pits, possibly for retaining drinking water, were found in the dwellings, which were equipped with fired-brick drains. Trade was actively pursued; finds include carnelian, STEATITE, copper, and marine shell. A unique discovery of the furrows of a plowed field was found outside the walled settlement. The furrows crisscrossed one another, two rows 30 centimeters (1 ft.) apart, the other rows separated by 1.9 meters. This arrangement was probably designed to grow two different crops simultaneously.

INDUS PHASE

One section of the western area contained five or six separate elevated platforms of mud brick, with access to the top by a flight of steps. Unfortunately, brick robbers had removed virtually all evidence for structural remains on the platforms, but at least one brick-lined pit, which contained the bones of a bovid and the antlers of a deer, was uncovered. There were also a number of fire altars, suggesting a religious use for these structures. This enclave was accessible to the northern half of the citadel by means of a gateway. It is thought that the other half was reserved for the residences of the elite, but unfortunately no complete domestic plans are available.

In the lower city the residential area had a grid pattern of streets, in which the widths varied from 1.8 to 7.2 meters (5.9 to 23.7 ft.). The houses in the city blocks were built around a courtyard and had six or seven rooms. Many houses had their own wells and cooking areas and drains of wood or fired brick issued from the houses into ceramic soak pits under the street level outside. Some houses also had their own fire altars. Wheeled carts would have carried goods through the northern entrance and down the main streets, where some corners were guarded against damage by posts. The western town gate led toward the citadel. A brick temple found 80 meters (264 ft.) to the east of the lower city held five altars, while the town cemetery lay to the southwest of the citadel about 300 meters (990 ft.) from the settlement. There was a series of inhumation graves, the dead laid out with their head to the north and accompanied by grave goods. These included ceramic vessels and items of personal jewelry. One or two of these graves were richer than the norm; one had a brick lining, and another had access steps. There were also oval graves containing large jars, but no human remains.

The fields surrounding Kalibangan must have been sown for barley, the remains of which predominated in the excavated areas, and wheat. No rice was encountered. A fine bronze statue of a bull recalls the widespread dominance of cattle as a form of wealth in other Indus cities.

Artifacts recovered included typical Indus SEALS, ceramics, weights, and an ivory COMB. The city was probably abandoned when the Sarasvati River dried up.

Further reading: Kenoyer, J. M. *Ancient Cities of the Indus Civilization.* Oxford: Oxford University Press, 1998; Thapar, B. K. "Kalibangan: A Harappan Metropolis Beyond the Indus Valley," *Expedition* 17 (1975): 19–32.

Kalinga Kalinga is a state centered in Orissa in India. It was conquered by ASOKA (r. 268–235 B.C.E.), third king of the MAURYA EMPIRE, but asserted its independence as Mauryan power waned. Most information about the subsequent history of Kalinga is from an important INSCRIPTION from Hathigumpha Cave near Bubaneshwar on the Mahanadi Delta in Orissa. It describes the exploits of the third king of the Cedi dynasty, Kharavela, who reigned in the early second or late first century B.C.E. He engaged in many successful military campaigns in the Ganges (Ganga) Valley and against the Greeks as well as in the south.

kami *Kami* are spirits and gods worshiped in Japan, which stand at the origin of the Shinto religion. They may include natural features with special powers, such as mountains, plants, trees, and animals, as well as dangerous spirits that require veneration. Thunder, lightning, and rain may host a *kami*, as can man-made objects such as boats or buildings. Both the KOJIKI and the NIHONGI, early eighth-century historical texts, contain sections on *kami*, the former in particular stressing their role in creation myths involving first the universe and then the imperial line. *Kami* can be identified in many aspects of Japanese life and thought, in the remote past as well as the present. They appear, for example, in rustic folklore concerning the powers of the spirit world as well as foundation sagas of the Japanese islands and the rituals to ensure a good harvest. *Kami* also are said to have guided Queen Jingu of YAMATO, who, in the fourth century C.E., led a military campaign against the Korean state of SHILLA. The myths contained in the *Kojiki* and *Nihongi* link *kami* with the beginnings of Japanese civilization. King Sujin, whose tomb lies near the foot of Mount Miwa bordering the Nara Plain, is said to have worshiped the *kami* of the mountain, thus linking his dynasty with the sacred world and giving it legitimacy.

Kampil Kampil is a site of the PAINTED GREY WARE (800–500 B.C.E.) culture in northern India, identified by SIR ARTHUR CUNNINGHAM with ancient Kampilya. It was mentioned in the Hindu epic the MAHABHARATA as the capital of the state of Pancala. Excavations have revealed traces of a mud rampart and a relatively thin occupation level.

kamrateng jagat ta raja *Kamrateng jagat ta raja* is the title given to a deity in the SDOK KAK THOM inscription of 1052 C.E. at ANGKOR in Cambodia. It translates into SANSKRIT as *DEVARAJA*, or the "god who is king." Many writers have mistakenly portrayed this as a reference to the deified king. In fact, it was probably a portable deity seen as the ruler of the heavens, in contrast to his equivalent, the king of the Earth.

Kandahar (Qandahar) Kandahar is the location of a major city in Afghanistan, excavated during the 1970s. The name derives from the region known as GANDHARA and is first recorded in a 13th-century Persian text. It includes a walled enclosure fortified with bastions and with gateways on the north, east, and south walls. Water tanks and a Buddhist monastery, as well as a cemetery, are located outside the confines of the city. The walls are massive, 10 meters (33 ft.) wide and up to 15 meters (49.5 ft.) high. The earliest layers probably date to the early first millennium B.C.E., making this one of the earliest city foundations after the end of the INDUS VALLEY CIVILIZATION. There followed an occupation during the period of Achaemenid dominance in Arachosia. It was later a major center under the MAURYA EMPIRE, the location of the most westerly Asokan inscription.

See also ACHAEMENID EMPIRE.

Kang Dai (third century C.E.) *In about 250 C.E., Kang Dai led an embassy southward to seek a maritime trade route to the west.*

Sent by the southern Chinese king of Wu, whose state was denied access to the SILK ROAD, the embassy probably made landfall on or near the Mekong Delta in Vietnam. There Kang Dai encountered what he called the state of FUNAN, a name of unknown origin or meaning. On his return to China, he submitted a report in which he described the Funan people as living in walled settlements that incorporated palaces. The kings imposed taxes on rare commodities and engraved semiprecious stones. There was a form of legal system involving trial by ordeal, and much rice was cultivated. Kang Dai reported the presence of a representative of the king of India and noted that the local writing system was derived from an Indian script. This report was later summarized in official Chinese histories and formed the basis of Paul Pelliot's seminal study of the culture of Funan. It was only in 1943 that excavations at OC EO in the Transbassac sector of the Mekong Delta provided archaeological proof of such a state. Louis Malleret found evidence for writing in the BRAHMI Indian script on SEALS and Indian imports within a large, walled city.

See also ANGKOR BOREI.

Kanishka I (100–126 C.E.) *Kanishka I was the ruler of the KUSHANS.*

His coins depict him with a halo, and he took the title *devaputra*, or son of god. One of his gold coins describes him as "king of kings, Kanishka the Kushan." An INSCRIPTION discovered in 1993 at RABATAK in Afghanistan describes the extent of his empire and lists the cities under his control. His empire covered a vast tract from Tajikistan to the Ganges (Ganga) Valley. He was a convert to BUDDHISM and called a notable council to consider Buddhist writings, and some rare issues of his coins show the Buddha in standing and seated positions. But he also was a devoté of Hinduism, and some coins show SIVA and the bull Nandi. His capital was located at Purusapura, modern Peshawar.

Kanoko Kanoko, a site in Hitachi province, Japan, had been an administrative center during the late eighth century. Excavations there in 1979–82 encountered almost 4,000 scraps of paper that had been impregnated with LACQUER. After they had ceased being of use to the administration, they had been recycled, probably as covers for lacquer pots. This preserved them, and under infrared light their texts can be read. One recorded the population of the province as 200,000. Such demographic data are of considerable value in the study of Japan during the late NARA STATE.

Kanva The Kanva dynasty of India was founded in about 73 B.C.E., when its first ruler, Vasudeva, killed the last Sunga king, Devabhumi. There were only four kings of this dynasty, who ruled in the Ganges (Ganga) Valley until about 30 B.C.E.

Kapisi Kapisi is a region that lies north of Kabul in Afghanistan, commanding the southern foothills of the Hindu Kush range. Kapisi in microcosm illustrates the long and complex history of the lands that saw the northwestern extension of BUDDHISM and the burgeoning of trade along the SILK ROAD. It is noted for its agricultural production and is first mentioned historically in the fifth century B.C.E. as one of the satrapies of the Achaemenid king DARIUS THE GREAT (550–486 B.C.E.). The second-century C.E. Greek historian Arrian, when describing the campaigns of ALEXANDER THE GREAT (356–323 B.C.E.), mentioned two cities in Kapisi, Nikaia and Hopian. The former has been identified as modern BEGRAM. It is described as Kapisa-Kani in the Bisitun INSCRIPTION of Darius the Great of the late sixth century B.C.E. in northwest Iran. The second-century B.C.E. BACTRIAN GREEK king Eucratides minted coins mentioning Kapisi, and it was referred to by the historians Ptolemy (second century C.E.) and Pliny (first century C.E.). The Chinese pilgrim XUANZANG (602–664 C.E.) visited Kapisi in the seventh century C.E. and described its capital.

The area occupies a highly strategic part of the ancient Silk Road. It is linked with GANDHARA to the east and probably saw the early arrival of BUDDHISM even by the reign of ASOKA (268–235 B.C.E.). It was then a major center of the Bactrian Greeks, but in the mid-first century C.E., with the declining power of the Bactrian Greeks, the area fell under the dominion of the Sakas. The Kushan

king, KUJULA KADPHISES (30–80 C.E.), then conquered much of northern Afghanistan, including Kapisi. Under the KUSHANS, Buddhism flourished, and trade drew much wealth to the region. This is seen in the finds from Begram, which include Han Chinese lacquerware, Indian ivories, and Roman glass.

See also ACHAEMENID EMPIRE; HAN DYNASTY; STEIN, SIR AUREL.

Kara-dong Kara-dong, a former oasis site on the ancient course of the Keriya River, lies about 130 kilometers (78 mi.) west of NIYA in western China. It has been known since at least 1896, when it was visited by Sven Hedin, and SIR AUREL STEIN undertook brief excavations there in 1901. He uncovered a rectangular mud wall that incorporated a series of rooms. In 1993, Kara-dong was excavated by a French team, who found the remains of a temple with the lower part of wall paintings intact. These depicted the Buddha in association with lotuses and garlands of a style paralleled at BAMIYAN to the west and DUNHUANG to the east. These date stylistically to the early fifth century C.E. Kara-dong was probably a way station on the SILK ROAD as it traversed the southern border of the TARIM BASIN from Niya to HOTAN.

Kara Tepe Kara Tepe (Black Hill) is a low hill within the walls of the city site of TERMEZ. It is located in the upper reaches of the Amu Dar'ya River in BACTRIA, just west of the confluence with the Surhkan Dar'ya in Uzbekistan. Excavations there began in 1926 and have continued intermittently ever since. The site includes a series of Buddhist monasteries and temples grouped around the hill. Kara Tepe was an active center of Buddhist worship during the Kushan period, between the first and third centuries C.E. The site has yielded a large assemblage of INSCRIPTIONS on pottery vessels. These were written in KHAROSHTHI, Bactrian, and BRAHMI scripts and recorded the names of visitors and donations made to the foundation. On several occasions, the text *Kadevaka Vihara*, "royal temple," appears. Other such inscriptions mention "the *vihara* of Gondofar's son" and "*vihara* refuge." A group of graves found at the entrance to one of the cave temples of Complex C included silver Sassanian coins, indicating that the site had ceased to be a Buddhist monastery by the late fourth century. Nevertheless, the site continued to be venerated, for excavations there have revealed an extraordinary complete SANSKRIT manuscript written on BIRCH BARK SCROLLS, containing Buddhist writings dated between the sixth and eighth centuries.

The typical form of monastic complex involved the construction of a square or rectangular court, which gave access to cave temples hollowed out of the adjacent hillside. Three of the more completely exposed complexes, known as A, B, and D, have a square columned courtyard incorporating cells for the monks and associated rooms for storage and wall niches to receive statues of the Buddha. There are also stupa foundations, while a drawing on a wall in a cave associated with Complex B provides an image of a stupa itself. It shows the dome under seven umbrellas, built over three square bases of descending size as one ascends. These courts provided access to the caves. The most common form involved a central shrine with a corridor or ambulatory around it. In the case of Complex C, however, the courtyard was rectangular and contained a stupa and a water tank. Four separate caves then penetrate the hillside.

The paintings and statues that have survived provide insight into the art of the period and the early spread of BUDDHISM into Central Asia. The torso of a Buddha from Complex B had a wood and straw core covered first with clay and then with stucco before it was painted. The style closely resembles that of another Buddha statue from TAXILA, and it is most probably dated to the late second or early third century C.E. Red images of the Buddha on a white background are also found on some of the courtyard corridors.

The layout of Kara Tepe reflects strong Indian influence as Buddhism grew in popularity in Bactria and indeed along the course of the SILK ROAD toward China. But there are also Hellenistic contributions in the layout of the courtyards, whereas the depiction of the Buddha with a halo was of local inspiration.

See also SASSANIAN EMPIRE.

Karli Karli, formerly known as Valuraka, is an important complex of four cave temples located in western Maharashtra province, India. Dating to about 70 C.E., they were constructed under the SATAVAHANA rule. Cave 1 has an entrance embellished with reliefs of the Buddha, BODHISATTVAS, and a couple who might represent the family responsible for endowing this sanctuary. The stonework of the interior, particularly the ceiling beams, was carved in imitation of wooden prototypes. The pillars of the sanctuary, or *caitya,* are powerful and imposing and bear inscriptions that record donors to the temple who traveled there from the city of Dhenukakata, as well as Greeks. Further inscriptions provide insight into the patronage of religion under the Satavahanas. Thus one mentions Ushavadata, son-in-law of the Kshaharata king Nahapana, who gave a village to the monastery here. Another records that the banker Bhutapala from Vaijavanti completed this rock mansion, described as "the most excellent in Jambudvipa" (India).

Kaundinya The founder myths of the early maritime state of FUNAN in Cambodia relate that Kaundinya traveled to the Mekong Delta from afar, married the local queen, and founded a ruling dynasty. Paul Pelliot has suggested that Kaundinya was from India. The Chinese sources for this myth describe successive members of the dynasty that, if it had any reality in history, would probably have existed during the first and second centuries C.E. Kaundinya conquered several rival cities and placed his son in charge as a minor king. Many later Angkorian kings claimed descent from these mythical ancestors. A second Indian Brahman called Kaundinya, according to the Chinese *History of the Liang Dynasty,* probably traveled to FUNAN in the fifth century C.E., became king, and introduced many Indian customs.

See also ANGKOR.

Kausambi Kausambi was a very large city located on the bank of the Jamuna River just west of its confluence with the Ganges (Ganga). It thus occupied a highly strategic location in northern India and enjoyed a long period of occupation before its destruction at the hands of the HUN. The site occupied a significant place in the history of the life of the Buddha. The capital of the Vatsa MAHAJANAPADA, according to an INSCRIPTION dated to the first century B.C.E. from the large monastery within the walls, names the location as Ghositarama. Here the Buddha resided while visiting Kausambi, then capital of King Udayana. This might have attracted ASOKA (268–235 B.C.E.), who later erected a pillar there. It also attracted the Chinese Buddhist monk and pilgrim XUANZANG in the early seventh century. He described the countryside as rich, producing much rice and sugarcane. He traced the bathhouse and well that had been used by the Buddha on his visits to Kausambi, finding the former in ruin but the latter still full of pure water.

The struggle for power leading to the formation of the MAURYA EMPIRE involved much warfare between the emerging states of the Ganges-Jamuna Valleys and this is reflected in the massive ramparts at Kausambi. Remarkably early dates for these defenses have been proposed, even back to the second millennium B.C.E., but the consensus is that they were constructed by about 400 B.C.E. Of mud brick revetted with fired bricks, the rampart was up to 40 meters (132 ft.) wide at the base and stood to a height of 15 meters (49.5 ft.). During the Mauryan period, the size of the city grew to cover about 280 hectares (700 acres), making it second only to the capital PATALIPUTRA in size. This period saw the maintenance of Ghosita's foundation, a monastery with a huge stupa and living quarters for monks. The houses had several rooms grouped around a courtyard and were provided with baths, latrines, and brick-lined drains. The city walls incorporated five major gates and six lesser entrances, guarded by substantial bastions overlooking a moat. A palace has been revealed by excavation. It experienced at least three building phases and itself was walled and provided with a moat. Measuring 315 by 150 meters (1,039 by 495 ft.), it included many rooms and a large audience hall.

Kautilya (c. 330–270 B.C.E.) *Kautilya was an Indian minister who wrote the* Arthasastra, *a Sanskrit treatise on* *statecraft, during the reign of the Mauryan king Candragupta Maurya (c. 325–297 B.C.E.).*

The treatise provides an appreciation of the philosophical and organizational basis for a state that enhances the understanding of the MAURYA EMPIRE. He identified seven vital elements: the king, the territorial boundaries, a fortified capital, taxation and the accumulation of surpluses, control of the means of defense and destruction, the maintenance of alliances, and bureaucracy. He recognized that the JANAPADA, or the territories of the kingdom, was vital for its provision of surplus production to maintain the court under the king, or *raja*. The court was located in a *durga*, a center fortified by moats and ramparts. The central *durga* housed the many classes of *amatya*, or administrators, necessary for running the state efficiently. It also contained the *kosa*, or the treasury. The *mitra*, or system of alliances, incorporates the foreign policy necessary for the survival of the state, and this required force of arms. A central theme, based on the foundation of the individual state itself, was expansion by the incorporation of rivals. This process involved the foundation of dependent centers in conquered territory and the encouragement of increased agricultural production and control over sources of minerals and metal ores.

It is possible to draw up a plan of his ideal defended fort. It has three gates on each side of a square, with streets linking each, except the main north-south thoroughfare, which circuits the central royal precinct. This incorporates a location set aside for chariots, workshops, councilors, and a stable for the elephants. Other blocks of the city are designated for foreign merchants, a hospital, jewelers, merchants, and entertainment, including a place for courtesans. Cremation of the dead took place beyond the walls, lower-class people to the south, the elite to the north. Kautilya was well aware of the importance of tracts with an assured water supply and the possibility of double cropping. He mentioned the cultivation of rice, wheat, barley, millet, beans, and a wide range of other vegetables, herbs, and spices. Irrigation was also encouraged to ensure reliable harvests and to increase the wealth of the state. Kautilya also gave detailed consideration to trade, the development of a currency through minting coins, the preferred trade routes, and trading partners, among whom he listed China, Burma, Afghanistan, and Sri Lanka.

Kaveripumpattinam   The port city of Kaveripumpattinam is located on the shore adjacent to the Kaveri River in Tamil Nadu province, southern India. It commanded the northern entry to the Palk Strait between India and Sri Lanka and was thus strategically placed to control a major maritime trade route. The *PERIPLUS OF THE ERYTHRAEAN SEA* of the first century C.E. describes it as a port on the bay, and the second-century C.E. geographer Ptolemy called it Kaberis Emporium. It was the major

port of the Cola kingdom. There are two major sources of information: contemporary records, including a description of the splendor of the city by the fifth-century Buddhist monk Bhuddadatta, and the results of archaeological excavations. Undertaken in 1962 to 1967, these revealed the remains of a BRICK wharf and wooden posts used to tie up ships. One such post was dated by radiocarbon to the third century B.C.E. The remains of a large reservoir were also found, together with the foundations of a Buddhist monastery. Artifactual remains included rouletted ware (a distinctive form of decorated ceramic vessel), a Roman coin, and COINAGE of the local Cola kings.

Kaxgar (Kashgar)   Kaxgar in northwest China occupies a strategic position on one of the routes on the ancient SILK ROAD linking China with the West and renowned as one of the rich oases flanking the western margins of the TARIM BASIN. The traveler heading east from Kaxgar could follow the northern route, skirting the Tarim Basin through Kuga and LOU-LAN en route to DUNHUANG, or the southern route. The latter, which passed south of the Taklamakan Desert, was dominated first by the state of HOTAN before passing through NIYA, QIEMO (Cherchen), and MIRAN to reach Dunhuang. The Chinese under the Han and succeeding dynasties were most interested in this region, and the degree of independence of Kaxgar fluctuated with the political situation in China. Under the powerful reign of the Han emperor WUDI (157–87 B.C.E.), Chinese authority extended progressively across western Gansu province. The imperial emissary Zhang Qian was dispatched to the western regions in about 121 B.C.E. and again six years later. On the latter occasion, his purpose was diplomatic, to open relations with the kingdoms of the Silk Road, and his travels took him beyond Kaxgar to FERGHANA, SOGDIANA, Hotan, and BACTRIA. The intelligence gained about the people who controlled trade must have been invaluable, and many missions to China followed. In 108 B.C.E., the emperor sent Zhao Po-nu to these western regions, and he conquered the state of LOU-LAN. At that juncture, the Yu-men Gate formed the frontier between Han China and the states of the Tarim Basin. Continuing Han interest and military presence in their new western commanderies expedited the flow of not only trade goods but also ideas. BUDDHISM spread to new adherents in the East, including China itself.

This expansion greatly affected Kaxgar and its people. The Western HAN DYNASTY archivists, who assiduously undertook censuses and recorded facts and figures for their empire and its peoples, recorded during the mid-first century C.E. that Kaxgar had a population of 8,674, including 1,510 families. This was during a period when it fell under the protection of China. It enjoyed relative independence during the interregnum of WANG MANG (45 B.C.E.–23 C.E.), but in the mid to late first century C.E. the Eastern Han reasserted control. There was also pressure from the west, seen in the invasion of Kaxgar by the KUSHANS in the early second century C.E.

The archaeology of this key region was the object of much fieldwork in the early years of the 20th century, particularly with the Central Asian expeditions of SIR AUREL STEIN of Great Britain and the French Sinologist Paul Pelliot.

Kaya Kaya, also known as Kara, was an agglomeration of city-states located in the southern tip of Korea, an area dominated by the Naktong River. This region is rich in agricultural soil but is also renowned for its deposits of high-quality iron ore. From the early centuries of the first millennium C.E. until its fall to the kingdom of SHILLA between 532 and 562, Kaya was heavily engaged in the smelting and export of iron utensils, armor, and ingots. Although a few fortresses are known in this region, most information on Kaya is from the burials. These are pit graves dug into hillsides, as well as mounds raised over stone-lined tomb chambers. A recurrent feature of the grave goods in these burials is the presence of iron armor, horse trappings, and quivers complete with iron arrowheads. The tradition of mortuary sacrifice evident in the graves underlines the authoritarian nature of a state constantly under threat until its final subjugation in the sixth century C.E. It is evident that Kaya's small size and vulnerability to its two powerful neighbors, Shilla to the east and PAEKCHE to the west, stressed the need for self-defense. At the site of Paekchonni, such armaments have also been recovered from graves. Near Pusan, the cemetery of Pokchondong has furnished iron armor, helmets, and horse masks, for the Kaya military was renowned for the strength of their cavalry. The presence of iron armor is particularly intriguing: Most such finds in Korea concentrate in this area, and the style is closely identified with those from fifth-century Japanese burials. Certainly there was much commerce and traffic with the growing states of Japan to the south.

A royal grave of the third century C.E. at Taesong-dong included rows of pottery vessels beyond the head and feet, while a Scythian bronze vessel reveals widespread trade contacts. Tomb 38 at this site included no fewer than 16 suits of armor, Han-style mirrors from China, quivers, swords, and shields. Bronze ornaments of Japanese origin were also recovered. The most remarkable graves was in the royal cemetery of Chisan-dong near KORYONG, capital of the Taekaya state. Two of these mounds opened in 1979 revealed not only the large central mortuary chambers for the royal dead, but also smaller stone-lined tombs for sacrificed victims immolated at the same time as their deceased ruler. These people ranged in age from girls barely seven years of age, to men and WOMEN in their 50s. Many other Kaya cemeteries have also been investigated. Okchon is thought to have been the royal cemetery of the Tara-

Kaya grouping and has yielded a series of tombs with helmets, neck armor, greaves, and cuirasses, one of the helmets gilded.

Further reading: Barnes, G. *State Formation in Korea.* London: Curzon Press, 2001; Nelson, S. M. *The Archaeology of Korea.* Cambridge: Cambridge University Press, 1993; Portal, J. *Korea: Art and Archaeology.* London: British Museum, 2000.

Kedu Plain The Kedu Plain is located in central Java in Indonesia. The terrain is dominated by a series of volcanoes, and the resultant volcanic soils provide a rich base for rice cultivation. The climate favors year-round agriculture, and the historic states that emerged to dominate the plain, particularly the SAILENDRA dynasty, were able to produce sufficient agricultural surpluses to sustain the workers necessary to construct huge temples. These temples, the physical manifestation of the rulers' spiritual power, are numerous; the two largest are BOROBUDUR and PRAMBANAN. The Borobudur temple is the largest Buddhist monument known; the other was dedicated to Hindu gods.

Kexingzhuang The Kexingzhuang culture of northern China played a prominent role in the transmission of knowledge of BRONZE CASTING to the people of the central plains. The site of Kexingzhuang itself is located near modern XIAN, but typical ceramics were widespread. They are found in the Wei River Valley and northward up the Fen and Huang (Yellow) Rivers, as far north as ZHUKAIGOU in Inner Mongolia. The latter site has produced an important sequence incorporating bronzes of steppe tradition, which are contemporary with ERLITOU and the early SHANG STATE (1766–1045 B.C.E.) in the central plains. However, many Kexingzhuang sites are earlier than Erlitou and the XIA DYNASTY (2100–1766 B.C.E.). This culture therefore is important in any understanding of how bronze technology reached China and probably beyond into Southeast Asia. It has for long been thought that the distinctiveness of the Chinese bronze-casting techniques implied a local origin for metallurgy. Now, however, with the important finds from Qijia and Kexingzhuang sites, it is considered highly probable that bronze casting reached China from the West, via intermediaries in the Asiatic steppes, such as the people of the Andronovo culture of Siberia.

Key-Kobad-Shakh Key-Kobad-Shakh is a town located on the Kafirnigan River just above its junction with the Amu Dar'ya River in Tajikistan. An area of 12 hectares (30 acres) was enclosed by a brick wall linked with defensive towers and gateways. Many of the bricks used in construction were incised with Greek characters, indicating a BACTRIAN GREEK foundation. The streets within were laid out on a geometric plan.

Khalchayan Khalchayan is a KUSHAN site located on the right bank of the Surkhan Dar'ya River, a major tributary of the Amu Dar'ya, in Uzbekistan. It was discovered in 1959, and excavations by Galina Pugachenkova took place from that year until 1963. The results indicated that the site was founded by the middle of the third century B.C.E. and flourished as a major walled city until the establishment of the SASSANIAN EMPIRE in the fourth century C.E. This led to troubled times, involving the failure of the IRRIGATION system that formed such a major part of the economic basis. Pugachenkova, on the basis of the remarkable similarity between Heraos, the Kushan king who united these people, and the sculptured head of a leader found at Khalchayan, has dated the Kushan occupation to the mid-first century B.C.E. The excavated remains of a palace building revealed an outstanding series of painted clay sculptures that formerly decorated its columned halls. These are foremost in a series of remarkable finds from this site. The excavator has suggested that this building began life as a reception chamber before taking on the role of a hall to commemorate the deified ancestors of the Kushan kings.

SCULPTURES IN THE PALACE

Dating from the first century B.C.E. to the first century C.E., these painted clay sculptures include warriors on horseback wearing leather armor and wielding bows and arrows, as well as deities that seem to have been modeled on Hellenistic gods, such as Athena and Apollo. The palace itself measures 35 by 26 meters (115.5 by 85.8 ft.) and was constructed of mud brick. The exterior elevation was dominated by a portico fronted by six columns; the interior incorporated a large reception hall and many other chambers, including a guardroom and a treasury. The sculptures, thought to date to the mid-first century C.E., were recovered in a very fragmentary condition. They were modeled of unfired clay over a reed base and painted. Some of the pieces can be identified.

For a visitor to this chamber, the most immediate impression would have been given by the three lifesize scenes of court life. The central frieze is dominated by a king holding a scepter and his queen, both sitting on thrones. Members of the court attend the royal couple to their left and right, all the men wearing headbands belted tunics, and trousers. They wore their hair long and had beards and mustaches. The WOMEN wore elegant togalike robes. The demeanor of the people beside the king and queen indicates their high status; none is in a servile position, and one is even seated on his own throne. The scene to the right reveals the king, again seated and attended by male court figures, one of whom is holding his armor. A goddess, probably Cybele, rides in a chariot, her head radiantly portrayed in a halo. Other deity figures in this part of the hall represent Herakles, Nike, and Athena. The left-hand scene shows four horsemen, the one in the center heavily armed, riding an armed horse, and wielding a spear. The other three are more lightly clad in tunics and trousers and fire arrows from the saddle. Their steeds all have elaborate trappings. Pugachenkova has suggested that the central scene represents the ancestors of the ruling family of Khalchayan, the Heraos clan, who were ancestral to the Kushans. The scene on the right might represent the present king, and the other scene shows the king or one of his sons with cavalrymen. The battle evidently involved the Heraos clan members on the one hand and a group of nomadic horsemen on the other. A frieze of garlands, satyrs, and musicians reflecting a Dionysian scene runs over these remarkable portraits of the ancestors. The representation of particular individuals in these sculptured reliefs has been seen as clear evidence for Hellenistic influence.

A silver medallion was also recovered. It shows a king seated on his throne and accompanied by a second figure, who may have been his heir. The throne is flanked by lions, and several commentators have noted its similarity with the full-sized statue, reputedly of King Wima I Tak [to], recovered from MAT.

See also SASSANIAN EMPIRE.

Kham Zargar Kham Zargar is a Buddhist monastery located 10 kilometers (6 mi.) north of BEGRAM in the city of KAPISI in modern Afghanistan. The monastery commands a panoramic view of the Kapisi Plain from its position on the southern foothills of the Hindu Kush range. Discovered accidentally by the local villagers and only briefly examined archaeologically in 1967, it includes a major stupa foundation, seven smaller stupas, and monastic buildings. The design of the main stupa indicated construction during the third century C.E. Excavations uncovered four statues of Buddhas and BODHISATTVAS and schist reliefs showing the worship of a bodhisattva and nirvana. Some fragments of schist also depicted the Dipamkara, a JATAKA TALE, a popular theme in the religious art of Kapisi also seen at the site of SHOTORAK in Afghanistan.

Khandgiri Udayagiri The cave temples of Khandgiri Udayagiri were inspired by King Kharavela, who ruled this part of Orissa in eastern India in the first century B.C.E. He and his consorts were followers of JAINISM, and the shrines were constructed for the Jain monks of this area. Many are single chambered; others have several cells with a verandah in front. Some of the rock surfaces were sculpted into impressive scenes. In one, a herd of elephants is seen in a lotus pool, while large and heavily armored guardians stand at the temple entrances.

See also KALINGA.

Khao Sam Kaeo Khao Sam Kaeo is an archaeological site in peninsular Thailand dating from the first to fifth centuries C.E. It is notable for the evidence it provides for the local manufacture of glass and etched carnelian and onyx beads, all of Indian inspiration. Some small items of jewelry were inscribed in the BRAHMI script, again indicating contact with India through trade. This same script was found on similar portable objects from OC EO in Thailand.

Kharoshthi Kharoshthi, a script with a wide but patchy distribution, was employed between the mid-third century B.C.E. and the sixth century C.E. The earliest-known examples of the script are the Shabazghari INSCRIPTION of ASOKA (268–235 B.C.E.), published in 1846 by E. Norris, and the Mansera rock edict of Asoka. It originated in GANDHARA, modern Pakistan, and Afghanistan, and was later employed from the third century C.E. in SOGDIANA and BACTRIA, in the Krorän (LOU-LAN) kingdom of the TARIM BASIN, and even as far east as LUOYANG in China. There a Kharoshthi text found on the wall surrounding a well describes the activities of a group of Buddhists who lived in Luoyang during the reign of Emperor LINGDI (r. 168–189 C.E.). Coins of northern

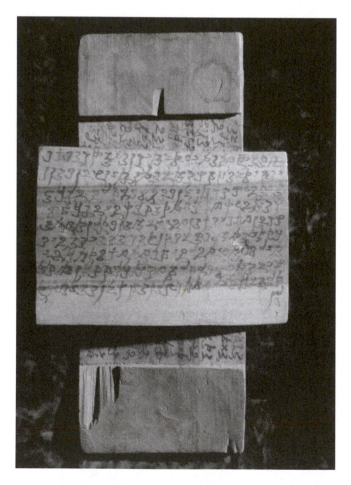

Texts in the Kharoshthi script from Hotan are vital sources of information on the operation of trade along the Silk Road. (©CORBIS SYGMA)

India and among the WESTERN SATRAPS also included Kharoshthi legends. Kharoshthi almost certainly originated in an Aramaic script at a time when Gandhara was under Achaemenid dominance in the fifth century B.C.E. In its area of origin and longest usage, the latest-known Kharoshthi text dates from the fourth to the sixth centuries C.E. The translation of Kharoshthi texts was facilitated by the fact that it was used in tandem with Greek names on COINAGE. Christian Lassen was able to decipher the Kharoshthi texts of the Greek kings Agathocles and Pantaleon.

In Gandhara, Kharoshthi survived principally as dedicatory stone inscriptions to mainly Buddhist foundations and as legends on Indo-Greek and Saka coins. The dry conditions in the Tarim Basin have led to the survival of Kharoshthi administrative documents on leather and wood. Most of these are from the site of NIYA and relate to the kingdom of SHAN-SHAN between about 250 and 340 C.E. These wedge-shaped slips of wood still bear their original and unbroken clay sealings and provide intimate insight into the minutiae of administration: An envoy who was going on a mission to HOTAN was to be provided by the state with an express horse for that purpose. However, such a horse was not supplied, and the envoy had to hire one. Inquiries were made on the cost of the hire, according to the laws of the kingdom. The king was even involved in an incident in which he instructed one of his staff, Tamjaka, to inquire into an alleged theft of two cows by soldiers. One was returned; the other they ate. The malefactors, if necessary, were to be returned in custody for trial.

Khmer language The Khmer language falls into the Mon-Khmer division of the Austro-Asiatic family. It is the principal language of Cambodia and some adjacent parts of Thailand, Laos, and Vietnam, and Old Khmer is the language used in CHENLA INSCRIPTIONS from the early seventh century. It probably has a deep antiquity in the Mekong Valley, of at least 4,000 years.

Khuan Lukpad Chinese histories contain references to a southern maritime trade route that passed through a series of port cities. These cities grew rich through their participation. Their location, however, is not easily resolved, but it is clear that many were situated on the shores of the Gulf of Siam. Identifying such entrepôts has not been easy, but some sites stand out on the basis of the quantity of exotic goods they contain. Khuan Lukpad on the western shore of isthmian Thailand contains quartz, chalcedony, and carnelian beads and bead blanks indicating local manufacture. Tin was smelted and cast into ingots. Some carnelian SEALS were found embellished with Greek and Roman motifs, including the goddess Tyche and Perseus. An inscription of PALLAVA script of the sixth to ninth centuries states: "Permission is granted;

those who dare can pass through." This might refer to merchants seeking to continue their dangerous journey east by sea. Glass was locally manufactured and turned into beads of numerous forms and colors.

Tun-sun is the best-known site, because it is described in *The History of the Liang Dynasty*. It was a center of intensive long-distance exchange in exotic goods. The history states: "More than 3,000 *li* from the southern frontier of FUNAN is the kingdom of Dunsun, which is situated on an ocean stepping stone. The land is 1,000 *li* in extent; the city is 10 *li* from the sea. There are five kings who all acknowledge themselves vassals of Funan. The eastern frontier of Dunsun is in communication with [Bac Bo], the western with India. All the countries beyond the frontier come and go in pursuit of trade. . . . At this mart East and West meet together so that daily there are innumerable people there. Precious goods and rare merchandise, there is nothing which is not there."

Khuong My Khuong My is a site of the CHAM CIVILIZATION in central Vietnam, which has yielded a notable relief sculpture of a man on horseback, associated with two chariot wheels. The wheels are large and heavy, with 16 spokes each, and resemble those seen on the reliefs of ANGKOR WAT in Cambodia. The pedestal dates to the 10th century C.E. and is in the style of MY SON.

Kidarite Huns There are few sources of historic information on the Kidarite Huns. Most is from Chinese historic texts, some Indian INSCRIPTIONS, and Kidarite COINAGE. The name derives from their early leader, Kidara, who was active during the latter half of the fourth century C.E. The Byzantine author Priscus called his followers the Kidarite Huns; Kidara himself, on his coins, styled himself the king of KUSHAN. The Chinese Annals of the Wei dynasty (220–264 C.E.) also describe the reign of Kidara. As far as these records go, it seems that the Kidarite Huns invaded Tokharistan, the region that is now the borderlands of Tajikistan, Uzbekistan, and Afghanistan, and established a capital called Yingjian Shi in the Chinese script. This was probably at or in the vicinity of BALKH. From this base, successive Kidarite leaders expanded east into GANDHARA and the Punjab and established a further center at or near Peshawar in Pakistan. The Indian epigraphic sources relate how successive GUPTA EMPIRE rulers engaged in war against the Mlecchas, almost certainly to be identified with the Kidarites. The Bhitari inscription describes war with the Gupta king KUMARAGUPTA (413–455 C.E.) in the Punjab, and the Jundagadh inscription of about 457 C.E. describes conflict between the Kidarites and SKANDAGUPTA. This series of wars on their northwestern frontier appears to have weakened the Gupta empire.

Archaeologically there is a consistent thread of evidence for the destruction or abandonment of towns in the Amu Dar'ya Valley in Uzbekistan toward the end of the fourth century C.E. The large city of Shahr-i Nau, defended by a wall and regularly spaced bastions, was abandoned during this period, as was DALVERZIN-TEPE in the Surkhan Dar'ya Valley. At TERMEZ, a group of skeletons have been found in a mass burial that might be the result of a massacre. The most likely cause of this disruption was the Kidarite Huns invasion.

Kim Pu-Sik *See* SAMGUK SAGI.

Kinewu Kinewu is a location mentioned in an INSCRIPTION dated to 909 C.E., found in the upper Brantas Valley of east Java in Indonesia. It is significant because its contents illuminate the system of land tenure and taxation in this region. The owners of a piece of wet rice land were unable to meet their tax obligations and therefore sought the king's permission to extend their holding and thereby produce sufficient rice to pay the tax owed. It indicates that land was measured and assessed on the basis of area rather than production. The agreement was followed by a feast that included two buffaloes.

Koganezuka The Koganezuka (gold hill) *kofun*, or burial mound, is located in the southern Osaka region of Japan. It is dated to the early *kofun* phase, during the initial development of the YAMATO state (300–552 C.E.). There are two structures, a main mound having a diameter of 57 meters (188 ft.), and a platform in front of it measuring 34 by 28 meters (112 by 92 ft.). Ceramic cylinders had been placed on the top of the mound and surrounding the platform. This is a particularly large mortuary complex for its period, and it survived intact. The mound contained three tombs; that occupying the central position was directly below a ceramic house model that had been placed on the top of the mound. This main burial vault, which reached a length of 10 meters (33 ft.), incorporated a wooden coffin within clay walls a meter thick. No human remains survived, but many mortuary offerings were recovered. The dead person, however, was accompanied by a bronze mirror, and wore fine bracelets of jasper and beads of jade, jasper, and alabaster. Outside the coffin, there were iron swords, tools, and sickles together with another mirror dated by a text to 239 C.E. The dated mirror has caused much speculation, which is due to an account in the WEIZHI text that describes how in 238 C.E. the Chinese emperor gave Princess Himiko, the shaman leader of the Wa people, 100 bronze mirrors. Could this possibly be her burial, described in the same text as measuring 100 paces? As romantic a possibility as this might be, the tumulus seems too late. However, the lack of iron weaponry in the coffin of the central burial has been held to indicate that it contained the remains of a woman, while the body armor and helmets of the two subsidiary graves strongly suggest that they contained male warriors of very high status.

The two other burials also contained many mortuary offerings, but the graves were smaller and lacked the thick clay walls. Iron swords were found within the coffin, together with iron body armor and a helmet. More iron weaponry had been placed outside the wooden coffin, together with a shield and 110 arrowheads. The same number of arrowheads were found with the third individual, again associated with armor and iron weaponry.

The size and splendor of the interments at Koganezuka provide compelling proof of the growing power of Yamato leaders and the rise of a warrior aristocracy.

See also YAYOI.

Koguryo The state of Koguryo, in northern Korea, was traditionally founded in 37 B.C.E., and it lasted until its defeat at the hands of SHILLA, allied with Tang China, in 668 C.E. During that period, it was the dominant force in northern Korean politics and economy. Although not blessed with the same extent of good agricultural land as in the south of the peninsula and experiencing a much harsher climate, it flourished in terms of both trade and agriculture. Indeed, its kings have bequeathed a rich archaeological legacy that includes the remains of large tombs, walled cities, palaces, temples, and defensive walls. This wealth grew markedly from 313 C.E., when Koguryo defeated the Chinese and ended the life of the LELANG commandery. It was recognized as an independent and powerful polity after 313 C.E., when its forces successfully defeated the Chinese province, or commandery, of Lelang, with its capital near Pyongyang. The rising chiefdoms of eastern Manchuria, the birthplace of Koguryo, had for centuries been in contact with the Chinese and adopted from them their writing system and political philosophies, such as Confucianism. Indeed, by the mid-fourth century, the rulers of Koguryo were the first in Korea to embrace BUDDHISM, and the KWANGGAET'O INSCRIPTION of 414 C.E. is the earliest such written text in Korea. Documentation of the genesis and development of Koguryo is in the main from the Chinese historical sources, with increasing supplementation from archaeology.

KINGSHIP AND CULTURE

As far as can be judged from the surviving documents, kingship was in a heredity line, and the rulers were assisted by a graded set of officials. The five highest grades were known as *hyong*, and the four lower grades were the *saja*. The upper classes were matched by the lower ranks in society, the farmers and the slaves, many of whom were won in war, but it is also recorded that poor families could sell their children into SLAVERY.

After the defeat of Lelang, the Koguryo leaders established a university in 372 to train their rising administrators with an understanding of Confucian ethics. Significantly, preferred imports from China included paper as well as silk clothing and weapons. In return, they exported furs, gold, and silver. Weaponry was important in the expansion of Koguryo to the south, as is recorded in an inscription in Chinese characters dated to the mid-fifth century from Ipsongni and recording a military victory.

CITIES AND TOMBS

The early Koguryo capital at Jian in the Yalu River Valley is impressively surrounded by stone walls and a moat. A reservoir lay within the walled precinct, together with a large royal palace. In 427 the capital was moved to Pyongyang, where again there are walled defenses, a palace, and the foundations of Buddhist temples. At Fushun, the walled city incorporated gateways, in which archaeologists have recovered plowshares, coins, and chariot fittings.

The tombs of Koguryo provide much evidence for the way of life of the elite. Large mounds were raised over stone chambers. While all the tombs have long since been looted, frescoes on the plastered walls have survived. The tombs at Jian include many vigorous scenes. Tomb 1, known as the tomb of the dancers, includes festive activities. The tomb master and his consort are depicted in Tomb 12, together with paintings of hunting scenes in which mounted noblemen hunt deer, tigers, and bears with bows and arrows. Mountains are figuratively depicted, and some paintings had been enhanced by the inclusion of gold inlay and jeweled ornaments. Armed soldiers in battle are also seen, their plumes of cockerel feathers figuring prominently. At Chinpari, 15 tombs have been counted, the fourth embellished with gold foil stars on the ceiling. Anak Tomb 3 in the lower reaches of the Taedeng River is particularly interesting, for the mound covered stone chambers in the form of a palace. The inscription records that this was the burial of Dong Shou, who was interred in 357 C.E. He was depicted in a carriage attended in a procession of 250 servants. Dong Shou himself had an interesting career: He began as an enemy of Koguryu, but in 356 he was given an administrative position by his former adversary.

One of the most important of the painted tombs was examined in 1976 at Tokhungni. Known as the painted tomb, it has a huge earthen mound over the burial chamber. The inscription within describes it as the tomb of one Zhen, though the rest of the name has been lost. It dates to 408 C.E. and describes how he fled from the region of Beijing in China to Koguryo; the reason is not given. The principal painting shows Zhen receiving 15 deferential county administrators.

Sadly, this and virtually all other mounded Koguryo elite tombs have been plundered, but some inkling of the wealth they once contained has been illustrated at Tomb 1 at Chinpari. Here a gilt bronze component of a funerary pillow has been found, decorated with two dragons and a phoenix around a central medallion ornamented with the image of a crow. The back of this plate was lined with *tamamushi* beetle wings embedded in birch bark. The grave must have been designated for a royal person of high status.

THE LAST YEARS

The Koguryo state, one of the THREE KINGDOMS, endured in northern Korea until 668 C.E. Its last seven years were dominated by a combined attack by the forces of Shilla allied with Tang China. In 661 C.E., a Tang naval force was defeated at the mouth of the Taedong River. However, disaffection with the rule of King Yon Kaesomun, followed by rivalry over the succession on his death, weakened Koguryo, which finally succumbed to Shilla. At this point a Koguryo general named Tae Cho-yong moved north into the valley of the Yalu River and there founded a new state, known as PARHAE. Unable to defeat Parhae, Shilla forces built a defensive wall from the Taedong River to the Gulf of Wonsan.

Further reading: Barnes, G. *State Formation in Korea.* London: Curzon Press, 2001; Nelson, S. M. *The Archaeology of Korea.* Cambridge: Cambridge University Press, 1993; Portal, J. *Korea: Art and Archaeology.* London: British Museum, 2000.

Koh Ker Koh Ker, also known as Chok Gargyar and formerly called Lingapura, was the royal capital of JAYAVARMAN IV (928–42 C.E.), a powerful ruler of Cambodia who chose to establish his center away from YASHODHARAPURA, ANGKOR. The layout of Lingapura followed in the tradition of the king's grandfather, INDRAVARMAN I (877–99 C.E.), at HARIHARALAYA. There was a walled city 1,200 meters square (1,440 sq. ft.), enclosing an inner walled precinct that contained the state temple complex, known as Prasat Thom. This incorporated two walled enclosures, to the east of which lie first a large cruciform entrance pavilion (*gopura*) and then two multiroomed structures sometimes referred to as palaces, but in truth of unknown function. The first major walled enclosure is entered by the Prasat Kraham and then by a bridge with a snake, or *naga*, balustrade over the moat. Beyond lie a series of libraries and brick sanctuaries that housed lingams. Across the moat once more and through a small *gopura* is the enormous principal temple pyramid, raised on seven tiers of descending size accessed by a single stairway. Beyond the wall of this second enclosure lies a tall mound of unknown function. The Rahal BARAY, or reservoir, is located immediately to the southeast. It measures 1,200 by 560 meters (3,960 by 1,848 ft.) and was partially hewn from living rock. Lingapura is surrounded by a series of subsidiary temples covering an area of 35 square kilometers (13.6 sq. mi.).

The many INSCRIPTIONS in the temples provide a glimpse of how labor was organized and maintained. An inscription also describes the erection of Tribhuvanesvara, a colossal lingam by Jayavarman IV in 921 C.E. Lingapura was built through the mobilization of labor from many provinces, and taxation in kind, particularly rice, was used to sustain the workers. RAJENDRAVARMAN (r.

944–968 C.E.) abandoned Koh Ker and returned to Yashodharapura.

Kojiki The *Kojiki* (*Record of Ancient Matters*) is one of the earliest histories of Japan, if not the earliest. It includes important aspects of the legitimacy of the imperial clan in an argument based on myths that link the creation of the universe seamlessly into the creation of the royal clan, which comes from KAMI, the charismatic spirit world that underlies Shintoism. The first section covers creation myths leading to the dynasty of Jimmu, the legendary first emperor of Japan. The second section enters a better documented period that ended with the rule of Ojin (r. 346–395 C.E.). In the third section, the history begins with the reign of Nintoku (385–427 C.E.) and ends with that of Empress Suiko (592–628 C.E. [defacto dates]). The grave of the author of the *Kojiki*, O-NO-YASUMARO, who died in 723 C.E., was discovered 10 kilometers southeast of the HEIJO-KYO palace in 1979.

In 682 C.E., the emperor TEMMU ordered high-ranking members of his court to compile "a history of the emperors and matters of high antiquity." This was to be based on two sources, the *Teiki* and the *Kyuji*. The former contained the ancestry of the royal family, and the latter comprised a collection of songs and legends concerning the major aristocratic lineages of Japan. It was presented to the empress Gemmei (661–722 C.E.) on 9 March 712 C.E. and is a major source of information on the Yamato state. Thus it describes the major centers of political power in northern Kyushu, the Tokyo region, and the strategic land on the shores of the inland sea. It is not as long as the NIHONGI and ended with the death of Empress Suiko in 628 C.E.

Kok Kho Khao Kok Kho Khao is an archaeological site on the west coast of peninsular Thailand. First examined in 1909 by the future king of Thailand, it is located on an island at the mouth of the Takuapa River. The site is significant for at least two reasons. It was clearly a center for the trans-Isthmian entrepôt trade, for a wide variety of Middle Eastern and Chinese ceramics have been found there. Second, an inscription in the Tamil language records that a reservoir was built there by a corporation of Indian merchants and that Indian guards were present. This is a very rare reference to the presence of a body of Indians in Southeast Asia. The reservoir, which measures 800 by 200 meters (2,640 by 660 ft.), has been identified. The site thus shows the establishment and maintenance of international trade links during the first millennium C.E.

Kondapur Kondapur is a large urban site located in Andhra Pradesh province, central India. It was excavated in 1941–42 and found to have been occupied between the first century B.C.E. and the second century C.E., the period when the SATAVAHANA dynasty was dominant in the region.

It was a center of BUDDHISM, evidenced by the foundations of a stupa and monks' cells in a monastery. The presence of molds for casting coins in the actual furnaces in the mint also reveals its commercial importance, a finding supported by the presence of medallions imitating those of the Roman emperor Tiberius and a gold coin of his predecessor, Augustus. There is also a wealth of jewelry, made from glass, FAIENCE, amethyst, carnelian, jasper, and beryl.

Koryong Koryong was the capital of the state of Taekaya, in southern Korea. Taekaya was part of the KAYA state, which flourished from the third century until it succumbed to its powerful neighbor, SHILLA, in 562 C.E. The site incorporates a set of very large mounds covering the burials of the kings of Taekaya. In 1977, two of these mounds were investigated. Tomb 44 measured 25 meters (82.5 ft.) in diameter and rose to a height of six meters (19.8 ft.). Tomb robbers had entered the three main chambers and ransacked their contents. The largest of these vaults was almost 9.5 meters long by 1.75 meters (31.3 by 5.7 ft.) wide and reached a depth of two meters (6.6 ft.). However, there were also a further 32 stone-lined graves under the mound. Ten of these were rather larger than the others and contained skeletons, some of which were accompanied by horse harness and weapons. The remainder were small and attracted no mortuary offerings. The excavators have reported that the 10 relatively wealthy tombs contained high-class individuals, while the poor burials were those of slaves or commoners. All were immolated at the same time, presumably to accompany their dead master. These sacrificial victims included adult men and WOMEN, some of whom had attained 50 years or more. But there were also the remains of young girls aged only seven or eight years at death. None showed signs of a violent death. The recovery of gold ornaments and ceramics in the central vaults date this grave to the fifth century C.E.

Burial 45 was rather smaller, with a diameter of 23 meters (76 ft.). It contained two central tombs, ringed by 10 smaller ones. The king lay in the center, accompanied by a female and a male dressed in armor. Smaller pits contained the remains of presumed sacrificial victims.

Kot Diji Kot Diji is a 12-meter (36.9-ft.) -high settlement mound located in the middle Indus Valley, on the opposite side of the river from MOHENJO DARO. The upper layers incorporate evidence for two major conflagrations; the latter is dated to about 2500 B.C.E. This chronological context thus places the earlier phases in the early third millennium B.C.E., which is therefore relevant to any consideration of the transition to the INDUS VALLEY CIVILIZATION. In addition to a vigorous ceramic industry, which

The mud-brick walls of Kot Diji in Pakistan lie over a deep and important cultural sequence that illustrates the rise of the Indus civilization. *(© David Cumming; Eye Ubiquitous/CORBIS)*

produced distinctive wares found in other sites of this phase, including early KALIBANGAN, there were terra-cotta human figurines with WOMEN depicted with sophisticated hairstyles and a model of a wheeled cart. Taken in conjunction with the presence of terra-cotta SEALS and script characters incised on potsherds, this finding underpins the hypothesis that increasing trade over a wide area contributed to the development of the state. Physical evidence for such trade is seen in the presence of copper artifacts, a marine-shell industry, exotic steatite, and LAPIS LAZULI. Kot Diji, which gives its name to a seminal stage in the development of the Indus civilization, has provided crucial evidence for state origins.

Kot Diji is not a large site, covering only 2.2 hectares, but stands out as a major feature over the surrounding plain. Excavations by F. A. Khan in 1955–57 revealed a deep cultural sequence with more than five meters (16.5 ft.) of accumulated material. The area opened was substantial, reaching from the center of the site to its margins, over a distance of 100 meters (33 ft.). The lowest layers were reached in one part of the excavated area, revealing the stone foundations for mud-brick walls. Radiocarbon determinations suggest that this initial occupation took place in about 3000 B.C.E., and the entire first phase lasted for five centuries. During the second stage of this early phase, a defensive wall was built around the site, again of mud brick on stone foundations. This wall was substantial, surviving to a height of 4.5 meters (14.8 ft.). It was built of stone foundations that rested on bedrock, the upper part made of mud brick. A strong emphasis on agriculture and cattle raising is evidenced by the biological remains as well as the pestles and mortars for processing grain.

The early phase of occupation is important in providing evidence for the culture of the area before the transition into the INDUS VALLEY CIVILIZATION. Kot Diji has given its name to one of the four Early Harappan regional groups. Relevant sites cluster first in the lower reaches of the now-extinct SARASVATI RIVER, then in the main floodplain of the Indus and west in the surrounding foothills. Sites are on average not large, with a mean size of about six hectares (15 acres). The majority of the 88 sites for which data are available are less than five hectares, and few extend beyond 10 hectares (25 acres). The largest are Gamanwala, Lathwala, and HARAPPA, with sizes ranging from 27.3 to more than 50 hectares (86 to more than 125 acres). Smaller sites probably reflect an element of pastoral mobility among the Kot Diji farmers.

Koy-Krylgan-Kala

Koy-Krylgan-Kala was occupied from the third or fourth century B.C.E. until the arrival of the KUSHANS and its abandonment in the first century C.E. It is located on the right bank of the Amu Dar'ya River in Uzbekistan, about 20 kilometers (12 mi.) southeast of TOPRAK-KALA. This site has a most unusual form, with two circular walled areas. The outer has a diameter of about 85 meters (280 ft.) and was entered by a gateway flanked by round bastions. The outer walls incorporated a total of nine such bastions that jut out to the exterior of the site. There is an intervening courtyard before the inner citadel, which is 40 meters (132 ft.) across. This building has 18 angles on the outer wall and rises two stories high to the crenellated top. The outer wall housed residential buildings, but the inner area was a mortuary and ritual area for the elite.

Excavations have uncovered a large quantity of artifacts as well as dating evidence, in the form of writing on potsherds in the Khwarizm language, employing the Aramaic script of the period 200 B.C.E.–150 C.E. Many terra-cotta figurines attest to the worship of Anahita, the local goddess of fertility. A complex mortuary tradition is attested by a lifesize ossuary in the form a man seated with crossed legs. He wears a helmet and sports a pointed beard and mustache. The remains of painted wall plaster also give some indication of the richly ornamented dwellings at this remarkable site.

kpon A *kpon*, in the INSCRIPTIONS of the kingdoms of CHENLA in Cambodia (550–800 C.E.), was a deity. Michael Vickery has suggested on the basis of all instances of its usage that *kpon* were essentially local lineage goddesses of considerable antiquity. The latest recorded use of the title dates to 713 C.E.

Krorän *See* LOU-LAN.

Ku Bua This site in west-central Thailand is a roughly rectangular moated enclosure of the DVARAVATI CIVILIZATION. Excavations have revealed 11 Buddhist structures within the moats and 33 beyond. The moats follow a roughly rectangular course over a distance of 2,000 by 800 meters (6,600 by 2,640 ft.). The central *caitya*, a building to house Buddhist images, is large and was formerly decorated in stucco. The site is best known for a series of stucco images, which reflect the class structure at the site and probably the presence of foreign merchants. There are a seated royal personage and a group of musicians playing stringed instruments and cymbals. A guard is seen chastising manacled prisoners, and another image shows a princess and her attendants. There are servants carrying goods, soldiers, and a group of foreign, probably Semitic, traders.

Kubukubu Kubukubu is the name of a village located in east Java in Indonesia. It has furnished a set of copper plates dated to 905 C.E., bearing an INSCRIPTION that describes the establishment of a SIMA, a legally binding charter setting out tax obligations or payments for religious foundations or local infrastructure. Although one of the plates is missing, it seems likely that King Balitung issued this *sima* to fund the construction of an aqueduct in gratitude to the local leaders who defeated his enemies in a place called Bantan. He also approved trading concessions. This may well refer to the neighboring island of Bali in Indonesia. The long text is most illuminating, in that it mentions six IRRIGATION pipes and the construction of an aqueduct. It describes the gift of men's clothing to various participants, including village elders, a supervisor of the woods, and a cook. A feast is indicated by the presence of not only the rice cook, but also a vegetable cook, a lead drummer, and providers of flowers. The establishment of the *sima* involved prohibitions on certain classes of people who could not enter the defined buildings or tract of land. These included people of ill repute, beggars, inspectors of gambling, tax collectors, and sailors. One of the officiants then broke an egg on the stone and cut off the head of a chicken, warning that all those who trespassed would suffer the same fate, and they and all their relatives would suffer hell. They would be bitten by a snake in the forest, seized by a tiger, struck by lightning, and, if going to sea, would be consumed by a whale.

Kubyaukkyi temple   The Kubyaukkyi temple at PAGAN in Myanmar (Burma) was built by Rajakumar after the death of his father, Kyanzittha, in 1113. It is particularly notable for its inscription, which is written in four languages: PALI, Mon, Pyu, and Burmese. This inscription has made it possible to clarify aspects of the Pyu language and establish the reign dates of preceding kings of Pagan.

Kujula Kadphises (30–80 C.E.)   *Kujula Kadphises was the founder of the Kushan dynasty and empire.*
Under his reign, the KUSHANS, who had settled modern Afghanistan and Tajikistan after their westward movement across the steppes from western China, expanded into Pakistan.

Kulaprabhavati   There are very few INSCRIPTIONS from the period of the kingdom of FUNAN. One in SANSKRIT mentions the principal queen of King JAYAVARMAN (c. 480 C.E.) and a queen in her own right, named Kulaprabhavati. *Kula* means "family," and *prabhavati* means "majesty." The high status of WOMEN in early Cambodian states is confirmed by this reference, which probably dates between 480 and 520 C.E.

Kulen Hills   The Kulen Hills lie to the north of ANGKOR and the GREAT LAKE, in Cambodia, and are the source of the Roluos, Puok, and Siem Reap Rivers, perennial watercourses flowing south to the Great Lake. The southwest monsoon winds between May and October water the Cardamom range but leave little rain for central Cambodia. However, they attract further moisture over the Great Lake, and this is beneficial for the Phnom Kulen, which rise up almost 500 meters (1,650 ft.) above the plain to the south. Symbolically, the Kulen Hills have been important since at least the reign of JAYAVARMAN II (c. 770–834 C.E.),

because they were seen to represent the Himalayas, while the Siem Reap River was the Ganges (Ganga). The Kulen Hills are described in the INSCRIPTIONS as Mahendraparvata, "Mountain of the Great INDRA." They have many temples, the most significant of which is RONG CHEN, one of the first raised temple mountains, with a central sanctuary on top of three terraces. It may have been the holy nature of Kulen Hills that attracted Jayavarman II to settle there and have himself consecrated the CHAKRAVARTIN, "supreme world emperor, king of kings."

Kumargupta I (415–455 C.E.)   *Kumargupta succeeded his father, Vikramaditya, as Gupta emperor.*
He was not only a great military leader who maintained his grip on the considerable extent of the GUPTA EMPIRE, but also an enthusiastic patron of culture, who founded an Institute of Fine Art at the University of NALANDA. He minted a wide series of gold coins, which survive most famously in the Bayana hoard, where almost 2,000 coins were discovered in 1946.

Kumsong   Kumsong was the later capital of the state of SHILLA in Korea. The *Somguk Sagi,* or *History of the Three Kingdoms,* is an 11th-century historical compilation that describes the development of the huge city of Kumsong. It was laid out on a grid system matching Tang Chinese models. Excavations have revealed that the grid layout of the city involved 36 precincts of 140 by 160 meters (462 by 528 ft.) each. In addition to the royal palace, there were several cemeteries of mounded tombs. One of the earliest constructions, under the reign of King Munmu (r. 661–681), was the Anapchi Lake, an ornamental masterpiece, part of the bank representing a map of Korea, Japan, and Taiwan, along with the coast of China. This was fed by a canal whose development reflects the drainage of surrounding low-lying terrain.

Shilla began as one of the Three Kingdoms but during the early seventh century overcame its rivals of KOGURYO and PAEKCHE to control the entire peninsula for about three centuries. Its heartland, the Kyongju Basin in southeastern Korea, incorporated rich iron ore deposits, and iron was one of the most important exports of the Shilla state. The extraordinary wealth of the royal graves, such as the TOMB OF THE HEAVENLY HORSE, attest to the power of the central elite. Shilla was widely known for the profusion of golden ornaments worn by its rulers.

Kuntasi   Kuntasi is a settlement of the INDUS VALLEY CIVILIZATION, located in the valley of the Phulki River in Gujarat state, India. It currently lies four kilometers (2.4 mi.) from the sea, and the discovery there of a stone anchor, linked with the salinity of the local water supplies, suggests that the settlement was placed there principally to take advantage of sea trade. It is clear that Kuntasi at this period was a manufacturing center and a port, with considerable store set on strong defenses. The second period of occupation was brief and represented a decline in population and activity level. This probably reflected a downturn in trade toward the end of the Indus civilization. It has been suggested that the occupation of this region was due to the rich local resources of clay for ceramic manufacture and of carnelian, agate, and shell for making ornaments, particularly beads.

The site covers only about two hectares (5 acres) and is divided into two sectors, a citadel and an occupation and industrial area. Excavations were mounted there in 1987–90 largely because the site was intact and could resolve issues regarding the expansion of the Indus civilization into this part of India from its heartland to the west. A large part of the site was revealed through excavation, and the sequence comprised two major periods divided into four building phases. The earlier period belongs to the mature phase of the Indus civilization; occupation commenced in about 2200 B.C.E. and lasted for three centuries. During this span, there were three major phases of construction. These included a citadel and a watchtower defended by a strong wall with bastions, spacious houses, and areas set aside for making ceramics and carnelian and agate beads and possibly for casting copper artifacts. Stone weights and terra-cotta models match those found in the major Indus sites to the northwest. A SEAL found in one of the houses, which had mud-brick walls on a stone base, is similar to one found at HARAPPA.

Kurukshetra, Battle of The Battle of Kurukshetra is a central story in the Hindo epic the MAHABHARATA and is notable for its depiction on the reliefs at ANGKOR WAT in Cambodia. It involved an 18-day struggle between the Kauravas and the Pandavas. King Bishma had no heirs, because he had taken an oath of celibacy, but through an arranged union between two WOMEN and the son of his stepmother each woman bore a son. One was King Dhiritarashtra; the other was called Pandu. Sons of the former were the Kauravas, the forces of darkness; sons of the latter were named the Pandavas, the forces of light. The Kauravas seized power, leading to the Battle of Kurukshetra. Numerous epic duels charged with chivalry as well as deceit followed until the forces of light triumphed. It is not difficult to trace parallels between this and other epic battles and those involving ANGKOR and the Chams. The realistic and vigorous depiction of the Battle of Kurukshetra at Angkor Wat incorporates many of the themes, such as the death of King Bishma on a bed of arrows.

See also CHAM CIVILIZATION.

Kushans The Kushan empire (c. 78–200 C.E.) extended from Central Asia into India and was ruled by a dynasty of god kings. It had relatively peaceful condi-

tions, and trade linking China with the Mediterranean flourished. It was also a period in which agricultural production responded, in the dry conditions that prevailed over much of the territory, to the establishment of IRRIGATION facilities. Major canals and the expansion of agriculture in the Amu Dar'ya, Tashkent, and Samarqand oasis regions led to the foundation of new urban settlements. One of the developments closely linked to, and in many respect dependent on improved agriculture was the expansion in the number and size of cities. Kushan cities were usually well fortified with surrounding walls and regularly spaced towers, and many also incorporated an inner defended citadel. They often succeeded BACTRIAN GREEK foundations and followed the existing regular street layout. Contemporary Indian texts illuminate the degree of craft and guild specialization during this period, and although no documentary evidence for guilds applies to the Kushan cities, it has been noted in excavations that specific manufacturing tasks were spatially limited. Some specialized output entered the widespread trade network.

This exchange was facilitated by the Kushan monetary system. The Kushan empire provided a stabilizing influence on the trade and politics of northern India, Pakistan, and TRANSOXIANA from the first to the third century C.E., but thereafter it rapidly declined. The rising powers included the SASSANIAN EMPIRE and the KIDARITE HUNs, the latter to succumb to the HEPHTHALITE HUNS.

KUSHAN HISTORY

The Kushans originated in western China and moved west with population pressure to settle south of the Aral Sea in northern Afghanistan and Tajikistan in the late second century B.C.E. They were known to the Chinese as the Yuechi and were united under the ruler KUJULA KADPHISES (30–80 C.E.). He expanded his dominion to the south, taking the region of Kabul south of the Hindu Kush, and established the Kushan dynasty in 78 C.E. His son, Vima I Tak [to] (r. 80–90 C.E.), and grandson, VIMA KADPHISES (r. 90–100 C.E.), continued this southward push, taking most of the Punjab and the upper Ganges (Ganga) Valley. This resulted in the formation of an empire from the Amu Dar'ya River to the Ganges. Much historical information is derived from the Kushans' introduction of gold COINAGE. Thus Vima Kadphises named himself *mahesvara*, or the lord SIVA. His successor and son was King KANISHKA I, who ruled from Purusapura (Peshawar in Pakistan) from about 100 to 126 C.E. His coins depict him with a halo as a divine figure, and he took the title *devaputra*, "son of god." Kanishka also instituted the so-called Saka era of dating, which originated in 78 C.E. An inscription from RABATAK in Afghanistan lists his main cities, including PATALIPUTRA, former capital of the MAURYA EMPIRE in the Ganges Valley. A devoted Buddhist who expanded the Kushan empire, he had a huge stupa constructed over sacred Buddhist relics at

Peshawar. At TAXILA, the Kushans founded the third city at SIRSUKH. Kanishka was succeeded by Huvishka (126–164 C.E.). He too was titled *devaputra,* and he supported the arts, particularly the Mathura school. He was followed by Vasudeva (164–200 C.E.), but by now the Kushan empire was in decline in the face of expansion from Sassanian Persia, losing control over BACTRIA and becoming increasingly assimilated.

IRRIGATION AND AGRICULTURE

The Zang canal, originating in the Surkhan Dar'ya, led to increased prosperity for the inhabitants of ZAR-TEPE. Irrigation works in the Zerafshan Valley, according to A. R. Mukhamedjanov, put 3,500 square kilometers (1,400 sq. mi.) under irrigation. A vast area was irrigated in Khwarizm, the region centered on the lower reaches of the Amu Dar'ya just south of the Aral Sea. Here a fully integrated system of major canals taking water from the river and feeding minor distributaries was established. One such canal was more than 90 kilometers (54 mi.) long and involved the removal of more than 222 million cubic meters (7.7 billion cu. ft.) of fill. Such agricultural improvements in the broad riverine floodplains were accompanied by parallel intensification in the piedmont areas. There small dams restrained the flow of mountain streams in the headwaters of the Zerafshan, and the water was fed into a series of terraced fields. Tunnels and aqueducts augmented such systems.

Agriculture was further intensified with the development of iron implements and the widespread use of the ox-drawn plow. A wide variety of crops has been identified on the evidence of archaeological remains. The principal grains were barley, millet, and wheat. Apricots, peaches, plums, and melons were also favored, and cotton supplied the local cloth industry. Viticulture, however, was one of the most intriguing developments. The terraced vineyards, grape pips, and Chinese records disclose the extent of wine production and trade in Khwarizm south to the FERGHANA Valley. The breeding of horses and raising of cattle, camels, sheep, and goats were integrated with the widespread agriculture.

KUSHAN CITIES

At Taxila, the Greek city of SIRKAP was taken over by the Kushans with its main street, lanes, homes, and shops intact, but they then founded a new city nearby at Sirsukh, about which little is known through a lack of excavation. BEGRAM (ancient Kapisa) is located north of Kabul in Afghanistan, and limited excavations there have revealed the walled city with its palaces, fortifications, and a notable treasury containing magnificent Indian ivories, Chinese lacquerware, and Roman glass and statuary. North of the Hindu Kush, there was a large network of cities, notably at DALVERZIN TEPE in south Uzbekistan, where the Bactrian Greek city was embellished with opu-

lent houses, Kushan statues, paintings, and craft workshops. A hoard of gold ornaments was found there beneath a doorstep of a fine city residence. TOPRAK-KALA in Khwarizm was laid out in symmetrical city precincts and incorporated a sumptuous palace for the ruler. The cities also included craft workshops or industrial facilities for the production of iron and bronze tools, weapons, and ornaments; manufacture of textiles; grinding of grain; and production of ceramics. Merchants often had a quarter of their own, as seen in the excavations of Begram.

KUSHAN COINAGE

The earliest Kushan coins copied issues of the later Bactrian Greek kings Eucratides and Heliocles and date to the period 125–50 B.C.E. More specifically, Kushan coins can be traced to the rule of King Vima Kadphises and show the king on one side and a god on the other, commonly the god SIVA. The text on the coins was usually in Bactrian, with the Kushan derivative of Greek script. Gold coins were used in major exchanges, bronze for day-to-day transactions. Outlying provinces of the Kushan empire appear, on the basis of their coinage, to have been semi-independent. Thus the coins issued in Khwarizm, dominating the lower Amu Dar'ya south of the Aral Sea, were of local inspiration. Bukhara and Margiana also had their own local mints.

KUSHAN RELIGIOUS PRACTICES

It is intriguing to note that in the religious sphere the Kushans encountered both an established Greek pantheon on reaching Bactria and increasing influence from India as they reached south of the Hindu Kush. Syncretism of Greek and Indian traditions is seen in the COINAGE of Kujula Kadphises. He described himself with the Indian term *maharaja rajatiraja,* the "great king, king of kings," but had a Greek god portrayed on the other side. A marked interest in Siva is to be seen in the coinage of Vima Kadphises. Kanishka I, on the other hand, showed a preference for Iranian gods, but this did not exclude the use of the Buddha by either Kanishka or his successors.

KUSHAN TRADE

The quickening of trade along the SILK ROAD, given impetus by the unification of China under the QIN and HAN dynasties, gave the Kushan rulers the opportunity to enrich themselves and support a flourishing period of artistic and architectural creativity. Trade also created contact with both East and West, and both influenced and were in turn influenced by Kushan artistic traditions. The sculptures of the King's Hall at Dalverzin-tepe are a good example of this trend, while the AIRTAM friezes fall within the period of Kushan dominance.

Some idea of the wealth that the trade along the Silk Road produced for the Kushans can be gained from the royal burials excavated at TILLYA-TEPE in northern Afghanistan. In 1978–79, excavations uncovered six graves, thought to represent a prince accompanied by five women aged between 18 and 30 years at death. The burials date, on the basis of associated coins, to the period 25–50 C.E., and were associated with more than 20,000 gold ornaments. These included headdresses, torques, plaques, and seals worn at the belt. There were also gold and silver scepters, and the heads of the dead lay in gold bowls. By minutely examining the location of these ornaments, it was possible to reconstruct the costumes in which the dead were buried. The wear on the gold ornaments showed that they had been worn over a lengthy period during life. The man wore a belted tunic and trousers. Women's wear included a variety of hats ornamented with gold, trousers, and a skirt or tunic. Some tunics opened at the front, others were enclosed, but all were heavily ornamented with golden plaques.

Further reading: Gupta, P. L. *Kusana Coins and History.* Columbia Mo.: South Asia Books, 1994; Litvinsky, B. A. "Cities and Urban Life in the Kushan Kingdom." In *History of the Civilizations of Central Asia,* Vol. 2, edited by J. Harmatta. Paris: UNESCO, 1994; Mani, B. R. *The Kushan Civilization: Studies in Urban Development and Material Culture.* Delhi, B. R. Publishing Corporation, 1987; Yatsenko, S. A. "The Costume of the Yuech-Chihs/Kushans and Its Analogies to the East and to the West," *Silk Road Archaeology* 7 (2001): 73–120.

Kusinagara Kusinagara is a central place in the history of BUDDHISM, because the Buddha died just outside the city. It is located on the northern margin of the Ganges (Ganga) Plain and was the center of a JANAPADA, or small polity, in pre-Mauryan times. The site has naturally attracted many pilgrims, and several large monasteries were built there. This most holy site was on the itinerary of XUANZANG, a Chinese Buddhist monk and pilgrim who traveled widely in India in the early seventh century C.E. To reach Kusinagara, he said, he had to pass through a dangerous forest full of wild cattle and elephants and robbers. He found on reaching the city that it lay in ruins, the streets and lanes deserted. He crossed the river to the grove of trees where the Buddha died and found there a temple with a statue of the Buddha lying down in the position of entering nirvana and an adjacent stupa standing 60 meters (198 ft.) high built, he said, by King ASOKA (268–235 B.C.E.).

These buildings, the Mahaparinirvana monastery, and associated nirvana stupa probably did originate with the reign of Asoka in the third century B.C.E. A relic casket retrieved from the stupa, dates from at least the reign of the Gupta king KUMARGUPTA I (415–55 C.E.). It contained one of his gold coins and a cowry shell, together with a dedicatory INSCRIPTION. Excavations undertaken at this temple in 1911 to 1912 uncovered sealings with the name Mahipari Nirvana, leaving little doubt as to the original name of this monastery.

See also GUPTA EMPIRE.

Kwanggaet'o The Kwanggaet'o is a stone INSCRIPTION standing six meters (19.8 ft.) high that was set up north of the Yalu River in China after the death of King Kwanggaet (r. 391–413 C.E.) of the same name in 414 C.E. He ruled the kingdom of KOGURYO, and the lengthy text in Chinese characters described his victorious campaigns that reached as far south as the state of KAYA in the southern tip of the Korean Peninsula. Kaya was particularly known for its rich iron ore resources.

Kyanzittha (r. 1084–1111) *Kyanzittha was king of pagan in Myanmar (Burma).*
He was responsible for some of the major middle-period temples at this royal capital in central Burma, including the huge ANANDA TEMPLE, the NAGAYAN, and the Patothamya.

L

lacquer Lacquer originates in the form of sap from the tree *Rhus verniciflua*. In China, this tree is native to the Chang (Yangtze) Valley, and it was here that the principal expertise developed. Lacquer has a long history in China. The earliest lacquered objects date to the Neolithic period of the Chang Valley. From the Spring and Autumn period (770–476 B.C.E.) to the HAN DYNASTY (206 B.C.E.–220 C.E.), the Chang region, particularly the state of CHU, produced the most and the best lacquers. One of the most impressive assemblages is from the three intact tombs of the marquis of Dai, his wife, and his son at MAWANGDUI in Changsha, Hunan province. A second remarkable collection of lacquered objects was recovered from the tomb of the marquis Yi of Zeng at LEIGUDUN.

MAKING AND DECORATING LACQUER

As with rubber, the sap is collected by placing a receptacle under slits cut into the bark. After the sap is passed through filters of decreasing mesh size for purification, it can be applied to the surface of an object of wood or, less frequently, of fabric, leather, pottery, or bronze. If the atmospheric conditions are humid and the temperature lies between 60°F and 85°F, the lacquer hardens and becomes both extremely durable and impervious to water. Lacquer contains a substance known as *urushiol*, a term taken from the Japanese *urushi*, "lacquer tree." This is caustic and difficult to mix with pigments to provide desirable colors. For reds, the Chinese lacquer worker mixed the sap with cinnabar; iron and arsenic were used for black, and orpiment for yellow. When still wet, lacquer can be applied to a surface and used as an adhesive to attach inlays or decorative materials such as TURQUOISE, shell, and glass. The lacquer surface can also be painted or incised to form decorative motifs or patterns.

Bronze Age coffins were often lined in red lacquer. Shang and Zhou craftspeople used lacquer as an adhesive for fixing gold, ivory, shell, and turquoise ornamentation. It was during the fourth century B.C.E. that innovative methods were used to produce ever finer lacquerware. The base was structured by taking strips of wood cut along the same grain, which could be steamed and bent to form curved surfaces in imitation of bronzes or ceramics. Some lacquerware of this period was inscribed with the manufacturer's name. It is evident that Sichuan was a major center of production at a time when it was recorded that a lacquer vessel was valued at 10 times the equivalent item in bronze.

LACQUER OBJECTS IN TOMBS

Tomb 1 at Mawangdui contained the remains of Lady Dai. Sealed in layers of charcoal and clay, the organic material has survived in virtually its original condition. The lady lay within three nested coffins each richly ornamented in painted lacquer images of good fortune, such as cloud designs and fabulous animals. Similar patterns were found on other items. There was a tray holding plates with food and chopsticks still in place. A wooden screen was richly ornamented in lacquer, and the lady's personal cosmetics, mittens, and wig were found in lacquered boxes. These were ornamented by incising designs with a sharp instrument through the outer surface.

A lacquered wooden box in the form of a duck was found in the antechamber of the Leigudun tomb reserved for the interment of the 13 concubines of the marquis Yi. The box was decorated with musical scenes in which a person strikes one of two bells supported by a stand in the form of two opposing birds. Two chime stones were suspended from a lower support. A second scene shows a

This lacquered basket from a Han dynasty tomb in North Korea bears images of model sons. The associated text describes the virtues of obedient children. Lacquer was imported into the Korean provinces from China. *(Werner Forman/Art Resource, NY)*

man playing a drum while a warrior dances. Two matching lidded cups from the burial chamber of the marquis himself were of far greater complexity. The handles were formed as dragons looking greedily at the contents of the containers, while the stems and sides of the cups were painted with geometric designs. A second lacquered item of remarkable elegance took the form of a deer at rest. It was carved from two pieces of wood and joined so that the head could rotate at the neck. The antlers are genuine.

See also SHANG STATE; WARRING STATES PERIOD.

Lakshmi In Hindu mythology, Lakshmi is the wife of Vishnu and goddess of good fortune. She was born as a result of the CHURNING OF THE OCEAN OF MILK, a popular theme on Angkorian reliefs in Cambodia.

Laozi (unknown) *Laozi, "old master," is a Chinese philosopher who is thought to have founded the school of Taoism and may have contributed to the* Daodejing *(The Way and its power).*
There is no firm evidence for the date of his life, a life that was in due course to assume mythical proportions. He may have been a contemporary of CONFUCIUS, and

Taoism and Confucianism represent the two major philosophical contributions to the philosophy of Chinese governance. Tao literally means "the way," and Laozi proposed that the universal forces of evolution and change encourage the wise to adapt and mold their lives to the power of external forces. Long after his death, Laozi became venerated as a god. In myths he was said to travel to the barbarian West, where he became either the Buddha or a BODHISATTVA. While this is historically impossible, the translation of Buddhist texts into Chinese employed many of the words and thoughts contained in the *Daodejing*.

Historical texts record that in 165 C.E. the Eastern Han emperor Huan (r. 147–67 C.E.) dispatched two of his courtiers to sacrifice at the shrine at the sage's birthplace, Kuxian in Henan province. He also required the local governor to inscribe a stone dedication to Laozi to be placed next to his shrine. In it, Laozi was described as the creator of the universe. Subsequently, the worship of Laozi was undertaken in the Hall of Washing the Dragon, in the capital, LUOYANG. Under the Tang dynasty (618–907 C.E.), Laozi's divine status was confirmed, and the emperors claimed him as their ancestor.

See also BUDDHISM.

Further reading: Csikszentmihalyi, M., and P. J. Ivanhoe, eds. *Religious and Philosophical Aspects of the Laozi.* SUNY Series in Chinese Philosophy and Culture. New York: State University of New York, 1999; Ivanhoe, P. J. *The Daodejing of Laozi.* New York: Seven Bridges Press, 2002.

lapis lazuli   Lapiz lazuli is a deep blue stone valued as a source of raw material for manufacturing jewelry. The world's best source is in Badakhshan in Afghanistan, where four mines have been discovered at an altitude of between 2,000 to 5,500 meters (6,600 to 18,150 ft.). One at Sar-i-Sang is still being exploited. The output was so valued by the people of the INDUS VALLEY CIVILIZATION that Shortugai, a trading outpost, was established in this region. According to Sumerian texts, lapis lazuli was obtained by trade with the people of Meluhha, indicating that the Indus civilization was a source for a material that was used in Sumer not only for jewelry, but also for decoration of temples. Lapis lazuli beads have been found in many pre-, early, and mature Harappan sites, including JHUKAR, KALIBANGAN, CHANHU-DARO, and AMRI.

See also HARAPPA.

Lauriya-Nandangarh   Lauriya-Nandangarh takes its name from the word *laur,* "pillar," for it is the location of one of Emperor ASOKA's (268–235 B.C.E.) columns. It is located in northern Bihar province, India. The column itself is one of only two that survive undamaged and in their original position (the other is that at Basarh). Inscriptions on the column record six of Asoka's edicts dating to the 27th year of his reign. The lion at the top is one of the best of all those surviving and was carved in the act of roaring. Three rows of stupas associated with the column, one stupa among the largest known, are a dominant feature of this site. Some were examined by SIR ARTHUR CUNNINGHAM and others during the late 19th century.

One stupa yielded a votive deposit of gold leaf and a female figurine in association with cremated bone. These are paralleled in similar stupas at Piprawa and probably date to the last centuries B.C.E. Excavations at the mound of Nandangarh, which commenced in 1935, revealed that it had been a colossal stupa still standing to a height of 25 meters (82.5 ft.). It would have been one of the largest known in India. The core of the stupa contained coins and sealings of first- or second-century B.C.E. date, so the stupa itself must be later than these items. Explorations of the inner core revealed a miniature stupa, beside which lay a copper vessel containing a BIRCH BARK SCROLL dated stylistically to the fourth century C.E.

Legalism   *Legalism* refers to the school of thought in China that developed during the WARRING STATES PERIOD (480–221 B.C.E.). During this period, endemic warfare between a diminishing number of independent states resulted in the ultimate victory of the state of QIN. It was in this atmosphere of increasing militarism and competition that the policy of centralized bureaucratic power over the individual was promulgated, a policy that ran counter to the influential teachings of CONFUCIUS and MENCIUS. SHANG YANG (d. 338 B.C.E.) was one of the proponents of Fajia, as Legalism was known at the time. He was the principal minister in the state of Qin during the fourth century B.C.E. His thoughts are well represented in the *Shangjun shu (The Book of Lord Shang).* He advocated a single-minded autocracy with all power vested in the king. All policies would be based on an impartial legal code determined on the basis of ensuring the strength and survival of the state. Agriculture was to be fostered, but academic pursuits would wither as an act of policy. This policy reached its nadir with the burning of the books and the execution of scholars under the Qin, the dynasty that put legalism into practice with most rigor and enthusiasm. The *Shangjun shu* set out the vital importance of intelligence under 13 headings. These particularly stressed figures on the stores of grain, numbers of men able to fight, number of horses, and availability of fodder. The text continues in a mode of state totalitarianism. Music, history, goodness, and righteousness are described as parasites on the state. What matters above all is knowledge of statistics. What is available to support the army? How can taxes most benefit the central authority?

Until the triumph of Qin, Legalism had been more a theoretical than a practical construct. However, the unification of China under the first emperor, QIN SHIHUANGDI, in 221 B.C.E. led to the appointment of Li Si as the first minister of the new state. He was then able to put the totalitarian theory into practice across the entire country. Old frontiers were dismantled, and former states were replaced by new provinces, or commanderies. Uniform weights, measures, and writing were imposed, and large groups of workers were deployed on massive building projects, not least the first major construction of the GREAT WALL of China. The seeds of destruction of Legalist principles, however, lay in the very centrality of the exercise of power. When the first emperor died, a Byzantine series of secret palace intrigues by top officials, including Li Si, led to the end of the Qin dynasty.

Leigudun   The tomb of ZENG HOU YI (d. c. 433 B.C.E.), marquis of Zeng, was opened in 1978. The site is located in Hubei province and is dated to the late fifth century B.C.E. The marquis ruled Zeng, a small client state of the mighty CHU kingdom. For the first time in Chinese history, the tomb was divided into chambers to represent a palace. Small portals in the double coffin and the walls were put in place to allow the marquis's soul to roam at will through his subterranean realm. The central chamber was designed as the ceremonial palace hall. It contained bronze vessels and musical instruments for state occasions. The magnificence of the bronze grave goods can be judged by their total weight—almost 10 tons of metal—and their individual size. No tomb anywhere matches this quantity. The most remarkable of all the finds are the two complete coffins, one nested within the other, both intricately painted. One of the mortuary offerings in the tomb was a bell cast, according to its inscription, in the 56th year of the reign of King Xiong Zhang of CHU (r. 488–432 B.C.E.). It has been suggested that it was cast in 433 B.C.E. to record the marquis's death, but this is not established.

Pride of place among the bronzes must be accorded the *zun* and the *pan*. The former has been described as "unrivaled by any metalwork from the ancient world." Both were made first by the traditional piece-mold system, incorporating a newly developed modification known as the pattern-block technique. Other parts of the vessels were cast by means of the lost-wax method. Decorative embellishments, most in the form of dragons and mythical serpents, were individually cast and then attached to the vessel with solder of tin and lead with a small admixture of copper. The inscription on the *pan* records that it was cast for Marquis Yu, probably the father of Marquis Yi. These items are outrageously complex and innovative and reveal the inventive expertise of the Chu bronze specialists.

The tomb was contained in a pit 13 meters deep (43 ft.). A wooden structure of massive timbers measuring 19.7 by 15.7 meters (65 by 51.81 ft.) and with a ceiling height of 3.3 meters was encased in layers of charcoal and wet clay below a layer of stones. This design led to the survival of a wide range of organic grave goods that would not survive under normal conditions. Among the metalwork are, for example, 65 bells and hundreds of vessels. The bells were cast with inscriptions indicating their tone, which in one of the sets covered more than two octaves. The marquis clearly enjoyed music, because his tomb has furnished a veritable treasure trove of instruments representing a full orchestra: seven zithers, chime stones, mouth organs, flutes, drums, and panpipes. A bronze crane with antlers standing nearly 1.5 meters (about 5 ft.) high was used to support a drum. It is most unfortunate that no musical scores have survived to allow scholars to appreciate the full nature of music of the period. There was, however, a distinction between the court music produced by the full orchestra represented by this assemblage and that preferred in the marquis's private quarters, for a further chamber in the tomb contained another assemblage of five large and two small zithers, a drum, and two mouth organs.

BURIAL CHAMBER

A smaller compartment contained his weapons, chariot, and the marquis himself, together with eight of his servants. Largely because of the covering coat of LACQUER, the coffins have survived with little deterioration over 2,500 years. The outer coffin is unique in being built of wood with a bronze framework. It is in the form of a box, 3.2 meters (10.5 ft.) long and just over two meters high and wide. The bronze frame took the form of 10 upright sections cast with a rectangular support, over the top of which a second frame was attached. The inner coffin was 2.5 meters (8.2 ft.) long and 1.32 meters (4.3 ft.) high. The outer walls are curved outward to form a convex cross section. Both coffins were covered with intricate painted designs. One finds a complex series of animal motifs on the innermost, incorporating dragons, birds, hybrid half-human–half-animal creations, and snakes. One of the most intriguing of the geometric designs was found on the ends and the sides: a rectangular form thought to represent doors and windows. The outermost was ornamented with a series of geometric motifs and lacks the animal or human figures. The marquis himself lay within the inner coffin. A man who died in his early 40s, he wore silk clothing and jade and gold ornaments, including four gold belt hooks. A jade pendant in the form of a dagger lay at his waist. It was made of five tabs linked by metal clips and had formerly been covered in silk, for impressions of silken fabric remained on the metal components. A lidded gold bowl and spoon had been placed under the coffin and would surely have been for the marquis's personal use. The spoon had perforations, suggesting that it was used to drain fluid from a meat or grain dish. The bowl was cast by the same technique as bronze production and was decorated with dragons and spiral designs.

SUBSIDIARY BURIALS

The eight other coffins in this area held his concubines, aged from about 13 to 24 years when they accompanied their master into the grave. There were also clothes chests, gold vessels, lacquerware, and a table laid out with spindle whorls still wrapped around with silk threads.

The northern room of the palace contained the marquis's weaponry, including lacquered leather armor, halberds, spears, and bows and arrows. One remarkable weapon was made of three halberds and a spear that with the wooden haft was 3.25 meters (10.7 ft.) long. It would have been used from a chariot. The recovery of 12 suits of armor greatly increased the appreciation of its form and manufacture. It was made of leather plates reinforced with lacquer, reaching to the midthigh region. A broad flaring collar protected the neck, and the sleeves were made flexible by joining thin lengths of horizontally oriented leather strips. The helmets were made of similar lacquered leather, the top piece in the form of a crest.

The BAMBOO SLIPS in this chamber listed the mourners at the funeral and the inventory of grave contents. The former was dominated by members of the Chu elite. In the western chamber, the excavators found the remains of 13 WOMEN, presumed to have been servants in the court, together with some of their personal possessions. In no way rivaling the items associated with the marquis, there were some fine objects, such as a lacquered box in the form of a duck with a movable head. This piece is particularly interesting because decorative panels on the side show musicians. One person is seen striking a chime bell. The details reveal that the two bells were suspended from a pole held by birds confronting each other, while the musician holds a long mallet to one side. A second lateral pole under the bells supported a pair of chime stones. A second panel depicts a person beating a drum with a drumstick in each hand. The drum is supported on a stand matching those found in the tomb, while a warrior is dancing to the rhythm.

COURT FEASTING

The intact tomb allowed a penetrating insight into the etiquette of court feasting. One large *ding,* a tripod vessel 57 centimeters (22.8 in.) high, was found with the two hooks used to hoist it over the heat and the ladle that dispensed the cooked meat or fish. The set of eight *gui* vessels indicates that the marquis had very high status, for this number was traditionally the prerogative of the Zhou emperor himself. They are fine bronzes inlaid with TURQUOISE.

Further reading: Thote, A. "The Double Coffin of Leigudun Tomb No. 1: Iconographic Sources and Related Problems." In *New Perspectives on Chu Culture during the Eastern Zhou Period,* edited by T. Lawton. Washington, D.C.: Smithsonian Institution, 1991.

Leitai Leitai is a site located just south of the GREAT WALL of China in Wuwei county, Gansu. Discovered in 1969, it is a tomb dating to the Eastern HAN DYNASTY (25–220 C.E.). The burial is most famous for a bronze

This bronze horse comes from the tomb of a high-ranking official at Leitai in western China. Dating to the Eastern Han dynasty (25–220 C.E.), the galloping horse has one hoof on a flying swallow. *(Erich Lessing/Art Resource, NY)*

model of a galloping horse supported by only its rear hind leg with its tail trailing behind, atop a swallow in full flight. The tomb contained the remains of a very high-ranking mandarin in this strategic border area. Inscriptions on some of the bronzes, which included 14 bronze chariots, 17 horses, and 45 bronze statuettes of chariot drivers and retainers, describe him as a governor. His seals in the tomb name him a general. The 17 horses formed a procession, with the famous flying horse representing the dead general's mount prominently placed. One horse wore a saddlecloth of two pieces of sheet bronze in which were engraved images of the horse itself. One particularly fine item is a single bronze horse harnessed to a two-wheeled carriage, each wheel having 10 spokes. The driver is shaded by a parasol. The emphasis on horses in the elite tomb is a reflection of their importance in the military affairs of the northern border. Ma Yuan, a renowned general, noted that "horses are the foundation of military might, the great resource of the state."

The tomb has three chambers, each with a ceiling in the form of lotus flowers. It is thought that lotuses were an auspicious symbol for protection against fire.

Lelang Lelang was a major Chinese commandery, or province, in northern Korea, founded after the Han Chinese subjugation of the preceding state of CHOSON in 108 B.C.E. Excavations at one site revealed a fortress of the governor, an official mint, and many Han objects, as well as a cemetery with more than 2,000 burials. At another site was a unique and wealthy burial of a local Han dignitary. Trade linked Lelang to China and Japan.

HAN SUBJUGATION

After the WARRING STATES PERIOD (475–221 B.C.E.) in China and the establishment of the long HAN DYNASTY, the Han court adopted a policy of expansion whereby border chiefdoms and small states were defeated and converted into provinces of the empire. To the south, DIAN and DONG SON chiefs were thus incorporated as commanderies with centrally appointed governors answerable to the emperor. To the northeast, the sprawling state of Choson was divided into four provinces. The Chinese occupation of the Korean peninsula endured for approximately four centuries, during which the local elites were accorded Chinese titles and administrative functions. The *HANSHU* history recorded that the Lelang commandery had 25 counties, with a combined population of slightly more than 400,000 people.

T'OSONG-NI SITE

In 1934 three seasons of excavations commenced at the site of T'OSONG-NI, a defended site on the southern bank of the Taedong River opposite Pyongyang. This walled fortress covers an area of 31 hectares (77.5 acres), and excavations have uncovered a wide range of artifacts that relate to the Han occupation of this region and the establishment of the Lelang commandery. Foremost are the SEALS and sealings that reveal the presence of the actual governor of Lelang at this site. There are also ceramic eave tiles, inscribed with the title *liguan*, a Chinese official responsible for rituals, education, divination, and music. There are not only Chinese Han coins, but also coin molds, indicating the presence of an official mint. Other Han artifacts include bronze mirrors, belt buckles, and arrowheads. More than 2,000 burials have been found beyond the walled precinct of this site. About a third were wooden chambers that contained the coffin with a compartment for mortuary offerings. The balance were constructed of BRICK, although there were one or two unique interments. Chestnut trees were employed in the wooden tomb structures to line the sides and roof of the chamber, and on numerous occasions, men and WOMEN, presumably affinally related, were buried together.

SOKKAM-NI SITE

The unique Burial 9 from the site of Sokkam-ni, 25 kilometers (15 mi.) south of the Taedong River, was investigated after its discovery in 1916. The floor of the mortuary chamber and the walls enclosing the chestnut-wood coffin were constructed of stones, including pieces of jade. After the wooden ceiling was put in place, the tomb was sealed with a layer of coal. This burial was found intact, and the grave goods reflect the wealth of the local Han magnates. Eleven ceramic vessels were included, each containing food: shellfish, meat, fish, and sauces. He was accompanied by a range of iron weaponry: a crossbow, dagger, swords, spearheads, and halberds. The presence of iron sickles reveals a local interest in agriculture. This person's chariot was represented in the grave by decorated axle components, while gilt bronze frontlets for horses and two bridles were also found. Fine LACQUER tables, trays, and food vessels had been placed for the use of the dead, as well as bronze vessels, mirrors, and jades, including a seal and a *bi* disk. There is no doubting the wealth of the Han elite of Lelang. The disposition of the ornaments in a black lacquer coffin indicates that the tomb master was buried with his eyes, ears, and mouth filled with jade stoppers, and a jade rod had been placed in his anus. This was a Han practice also seen in the burial of Liu Sheng at Mancheng. His clothes were held in place with a gold belt buckle, and he had a jade ring in his hands. Brick tombs were found with between one and three chambers. They were built above ground, sealed after burial was complete, and covered with an earthen mound. A compartment within was reserved for placement of mortuary offerings.

TRADE

One of the recurrent aspects of the Lelang politics was trade with China. Luxury goods, jades, seals of office, and fine fabrics found their way to Lelang, and some ended up in elite tombs of the period. One fine lacquer bowl manufactured in 69 C.E. reached Lelang from the distant southwest Chinese province of Sichuan. In return, timber, iron, fish, and salt were sent to China. Lelang was also an important node in an exchange network that linked China through Korea to Japan. However, the vitality of trade depended on political stability in China, and during the WANG MANG (45 B.C.E.–23 C.E.) interregnum and the troubles that followed the end of the Eastern Han dynasty and formation of the three kingdoms, Lelang suffered instability. It finally came to an end with defeat by the rising power of KOGURYU in 313 C.E. The Chinese then left their Korean colonies, just as they were later to leave northern Vietnam.

Further reading: Barnes, G. *State Formation in Korea.* London: Curzon Press, 2001; Nelson, S. M. *The Archaeology of Korea.* Cambridge: Cambridge University Press, 1993; Portal, J. *Korea: Art and Archaeology.* London: British Museum, 2000.

Leshan Leshan is located on the eastern side of the Min River in Sichuan province, China. The Min flows south to join the Chang (Yangtze) River. More than 1,000 cliff tombs have been identified there, dating to the Eastern HAN DYNASTY (25–220 C.E.). Many of them were ornamented with carvings on stone, as well as INSCRIPTIONS. These have been divided into early (76–146 C.E.), middle (147–189 C.E.), and late periods (190–240 C.E.). The corpus of carvings covers a wide range of themes centering on the notion of loyalty and filial piety. This finding confirms the deep-seated adoption of Confucian ethics among the SHU and BA people during this period. These tombs, which penetrate far into the cliffs, must once have contained a vast number of other items. In 1990, for example, a series of stone statues was found in one cave, including a horse, dog, hen, and human figures. One attendant in this group stands more than a meter high.

See also CONFUCIUS.

Lewan Lewan is a prehistoric site located in the Bannu Basin of northwestern Pakistan. It had an area of 14.5 hectares (36.2 acres) and formerly lay adjacent to the River Tochi, which has since changed its course.

Lewan, and many sites on the same plain that superficially resemble it, is important in linking the developing Indus civilization with the communities on its piedmont margins that supplied regional products for exchange. Lewan was clearly a manufacturing site for a range of stone artifacts, but bead manufacture also took place there, and a sealing on clay from the latest phase of occupation is probably the remains of a SEAL on a storeroom or a consignment of goods.

Deflation had removed some of the uppermost deposits at Lewan, leaving a thick layer of stone artifacts lying on the surface. Excavations in 1978–79 were on a small scale. They encountered the remains of hut foundations, together with a large sample of pottery remains, ceramic figurines of humans and animals, and stone beads. The pottery included vessels decorated with fish painted in white on a red background, goats, and buffalo horns linked with sets of three pipal leaves. These allow the sequence at the settlement to be related to the better known site of Rehman Dheri and date its occupation from about 3500 until 1900 B.C.E. The buffalo with pipal-leaf motif, which resembles designs found on INDUS VALLEY CIVILIZATION seals, places the site in the orbit of the lowland Indus sites.

Liang Dynasty, History of the   The *History of the Liang Dynasty* of China (502–556 C.E.) is a major documentary source for information on Southeast Asia during the early centuries of the Common Era.

Liangzhu culture   For many years, research on the origins of Chinese civilization has concentrated in the central plains of the Huang (Yellow) River Valley, where the LONGSHAN CULTURE was seen as the progenitor of the state. Since the first discovery of relevant sites in 1936, it has become clear that the Chang (Yangtze) Valley was equally important to growing cultural complexity in China. The Liangzhu culture sites, of which more than 300 are known, are located in the marshy, lacustrine lowlands flanking the lower valley of the Chang River. Already by 5000 B.C.E., rice-farming communities were widely established around Lake Taihu, and the people of the Majiabang culture were making jewelry items of jade. Their successor was the Liangzhu culture, which flourished from about 3200 to 2000 B.C.E. It was an extremely complex and rich society, based on irrigated rice agriculture linked with the raising of domestic stock, hunting, and fishing. Agricultural tools were made of stone, for no knowledge of metal had yet reached this part of China. Other craft industries included jade working, basketry, silk weaving, and the manufacture of fine ceramics. From the mid-third millennium B.C.E., craft workers lacquered wood to produce lacquerware. While many Liangzhu graves are relatively poor in terms of grave offerings, a few special sites incorporate tombs of considerable wealth and distinction. The Liangzhu culture thus takes its place, along with the HONGSHAN CULTURE of Liaoning province and Longshan groups of the central plains, as a forerunner of early Chinese civilization.

TYPICAL SITES

The typical Liangzhu community chose to live beside rivers, and the recovery of the remains of wooden boats and oars indicates proficiency with watercraft. The site of Longnan has provided the remains of a wooden pier and an embankment for flood protection along the river margin. At Qianshanyang, houses were raised on wooden piles against possible flooding, but sites on higher ground included semisubterranean houses roofed with thatch.

SOCIAL COMPLEXITY

This economy underwrote an increasingly complex and ranked social system. Some sites grew to a considerable size. Mojiashan, for example, covered about 30 hectares (75 acres) and incorporated stamped-earth platforms and storage pits. At SIDUN, Liangzhu remains spread over an area of 90 hectares (225 acres) ringed by a broad series of moats. This site included a number of rich inhumation graves associated with fine jades and pottery vessels. One of the best examples of elite burials is the site of Fuquanshan, an artificial mound of just less than one hectare, which was reserved for rich interments. The dead were inhumed in hollowed tree-trunk coffins, associated with numerous jade artifacts, which included ceremonial axes, hairpins, bead necklaces, and belt hooks. Some burials also held the skeletons of what seem to have been sacrificial victims. The mortuary rituals included the use of altars as foci for burning, and burnt slabs of clay were placed over the graves.

GRAVE DISCOVERIES

At Fanshan, 11 tombs have been investigated in a raised mound of earth 3.5 meters (11.5 ft.) high and covering an area 88 by 28 meters (290 by 92.4 ft.). A similar raised necropolis at YAOSHAN was encircled by a two-meter-wide moat and a U-shaped platform. Twelve tombs in this mound held double wooden coffins and many offerings. Jade was of particular importance to the Liangzhu elite and was made into a range of ritual and ceremonial items that persisted in subsequent Chinese cultures. They include *bi* disks, *cong* cylinders, decorated plaques, bracelets, and beads. The discovery of a jade workshop at Mopandun reveals that the jades were locally manufactured by sophisticated techniques, including use of drill bits, rotating wheel saws, and fine quartz sand for final polishing. The source of Liangzhu jade has not been identified.

Li *gui*   The Li *gui* is a bronze vessel cast by a person named Li after the defeat of the last king of China's Shang dynasty (1766–1045 B.C.E.) by the Zhou. It was discovered at Lintong in Shaanxi province in 1976 and is one of the most important of the growing corpus of WESTERN ZHOU DYNASTY bronze texts cast into ceremonial vessels. The documentary evidence confirms and expands on surviving literary texts describing the BATTLE OF MUYE, which is thought to have taken place in 1045 B.C.E. It describes a divination ceremony on the morning of the battle and the victory of Zhou forces under KING WU on the evening of the same day. A week later, the king congratulated and blessed Li, who it seems was the person who made the divination predicting a victory.

Li Ji (1896–1979) *Li Ji was the archaeologist in charge of excavations at Anyang after the initial season of work under Dong Zuobin.*

In 1929 he planned to undertake trial excavations to test the size of the site at Xiaotun and investigate its potential. He found two major early layers, one dating to the late Shang period (1766–1045 B.C.E.), which yielded 685 pieces of inscribed ORACLE BONES, the divinatory records of the Shang kings. This level lay under graves of the Sui (581–618 C.E.) and Tang (618–917 C.E.) dynasties. Arguably the crowning achievement occurred in the last season before the outbreak of the war in 1937, when his team found a complete archive of royal divinations in the royal palace area together with a group of chariot burials.

Having completed a detailed contour plan of the area between the village at Xiaotun and the Huan River, he identified two raised mounds, and in November 1929 he proceeded to carry out extensive excavations to identify the nature of the deposits. The results defied the most optimistic hopes. His excavation proceeded through 11 layers to a depth of 3.3 meters (10.98 ft.), where he discovered a circular pit adjacent to a second pit of rectangular form. The former was two meters across and three meters deep. At the base, Li Ji found a cache of inscribed bones and tortoiseshells. Again, the associated finds were of profound interest, for he collected molds for casting bronzes, carved ivories, and a rich collection of glazed ceramics.

In 1930 Li Ji was appointed a professor in the Institute of History and Philology at the Academia Sinica. In his next season at Xiaotun the site was divided into five areas for intensive large-scale excavation. Further oracle bones were recovered, as was a store of animal bones, including the remains of whales and elephants. He also recovered more molds for bronze casting. At the same time, surveys were undertaken in the adjacent areas bordering the Huan River to seek further sites. One result was the discovery that Xiaotun was not the only site to yield oracle texts. Under Li Ji's overall direction, excavations continued until the outbreak of the Sino-Japanese war in 1937. He was responsible for the opening of the royal Shang graves at Anyang. Although they had been robbed in antiquity of their treasures, he was able to identify their enormous size, method of construction, and form and, in certain cases, to find bronzes and jades left behind or overlooked by tomb robbers. He then moved the surviving members of his team and the precious finds to remote Kunming in Yunnan, to begin the task of analysis and publication. This resulted in the establishment of the dynastic succession of kings at Anyang, together with their reign dates. After the Second World War, the Academia Sinica moved to Taiwan, where major reports on the excavations of Anyang, under the aegis of Li Ji, were published.

Lijiashan Lijiashan is a royal necropolis of the Dian people, located on a hill that dominates Lake Xingyunhu in Yunnan province, China. Excavations in 1972 uncovered 27 graves of great wealth, dating to the last two centuries B.C.E. The DIAN CHIEFDOM grew in power in the face of HAN DYNASTY imperial expansion but was finally absorbed in the Chinese empire. At Lijiashan, it is possible to measure the growing wealth of the ruling elite. A row of seven graves stands out on the basis of mortuary wealth. The grave goods found in a wooden coffin in Burial 24 include a ceremonial bronze staff and a mass of bronze weaponry—a sword, spears, arrowheads, a mace, and a battle ax. There is also decorated bronze armor. Feasting is represented by bronze wine containers and a ladle; two drums contained cowry shells, symbols of wealth. No bones survive, but a bronze headrest and rows of jade and agate beads make it clear where the body would have lain. Perhaps the most spectacular of the items in this grave is a sacrificial table or altar in the form of two cattle and a leaping tiger, which is 76 centimeters (30.4 in.) in length. Burial 17 contrasts with this warrior's grave. It also contains a bronze headrest, but the place of weaponry is taken by decorated bronze weaving implements. Such tools in this and other graves suggest that the wealthy interments contained aristocratic men and WOMEN. The drums of the Dian chiefdom were highly decorated and reveal the presence of war vessels that would have plied the lake and facilitated central control over the rich lacustrine rice soils. Scenes of the storage and distribution of rice likewise stress the importance of agricultural surpluses in the maintenance of the ruling elite.

Lijiazui *See* PANLONGCHENG.

lingam A lingam is a phallic symbol associated with the Hindu god SIVA in his guise as the god of fertility. The lingam assumed great significance in Cambodia, where stone lingams, some of which would have been gilded, were placed in temples as objects of veneration and ritual worship. In due course, a lingam also represented the essence of the king and took a central place in the royal temple mausolea. Lingams are found as offerings in cremation burials at NEN CHUA, dated to 400–600 C.E. In association with the yoni, representing female genitalia, they were placed in CHENLA temples. According to GEORGES CŒDÈS, the essence of the king was contained in a lingam on a temple mountain, which was located in center of the realm and therefore of the cosmos. This supernatural lingam, the phallic symbol of Siva, was passed via a Brahman to JAYAVARMAN II (c. 770–834 C.E.) on Mount Mahendraparvata. INDRAVARMAN I (877–899 C.E.) established the lingam Indresvara on the BAKONG, and YASHOVARMAN I (r. 889–910 C.E.) established YASODHARESVARA on the BAKHENG temple. An inscription from Lovek dating to the reign of Harshavarman III described how UDAYADITYAVARMAN II (r. 1050–66 C.E.) erected a gold mountain, vying with the abode of the gods. On the summit he consecrated a golden lingam. In the Prah Nok inscription, General Sangrama endowed this lingam, which incorporated the essence of the king, with the spoils of war. The temple of Prasat Damrei at KOH KER mentions the erection of an enormous lingam by JAYAVARMAN IV (r. 928–942 C.E.). On his return to Yashodharapura, RAJENDRAVARMAN (r. 944–968 C.E.) had the temple of PRE RUP constructed. The foundation inscription described the image as Isvara Rajendravarmesvara, a lingam combining the names of the king and SIVA.

Lingapura   *See* KOH KER.

Lingdi (156–189 C.E.) *Lingdi (clever emperor) was the 11th emperor of the Eastern Han dynasty of China.*
He was the great-great-grandson of Emperor ZHANGDI and acceded to the throne in 168 C.E. Lingdi was one of the few later Eastern Han emperors to live long enough to achieve a reign of any sort. The death of his predecessor, HUANDI (132–168), had left the empire without a clear path to the succession, and the dowager empress was enjoined to identify a person who would fulfill the necessary genealogical requirements. She called together a conclave of influential people representing the major factions to consider the alternatives. The final choice fell upon an 11-year-old boy called Liu Hong, the marquis of a fief, who had no prior experience of the court or life in the capital but whose great-great-grandfather had been the emperor Zhangdi. There followed the customary bid for titles, status, and ultimately power by the various families representing the former court of Huandi and Lingdi's own followers, as well as the corps of eunuchs in the palace. This resulted in the hatching of a plot to murder the eunuchs, led by a minister named Dao Wu. The plot was discovered, and the eunuchs took the royal SEALS from the dowager empress and sequestered her without influence, for they did not trust her to protect them. Then they marshaled their forces against those of Dao Wu and were able to persuade sufficient soldiers to follow their party; the death of Dao Wu and the reaffirmation of the eunuchs' power in LUOYANG followed. There resulted the beginning of the end for the Eastern Han dynasty.

REBELLIONS AND CORRUPTION

The now all-powerful eunuchs gave their relatives and supporters positions of status and authority. Despite attempts to reduce their power, they continued to dominate the court. However, the overall administrative machine began to break down as the sale of offices and corruption took increasing hold, and without sufficient revenue the central relief agencies could not assist the provinces affected by agricultural failures. This led to disturbances, most clearly seen in the "magic rebellion" of 172 C.E. and the uprising of the so-called YELLOW TUR-

BANS in 184 C.E. The rebellion raged in southern China. The Yellow Turbans formed as a result of the teachings of Zhang Jue. He organized cells of followers with his prediction that the time was nigh for the replacement of the dynasty. This was predicted on the basis of a 60-year cycle with the next year of the cycle commencing in 184 C.E. The uprising began across 16 commanderies, timed to begin simultaneously. With limited success, the central army was deployed to counter this threat, but, as a brushfire, the uprising recurred in different forms. Some historians maintain that the Yellow Turban movement was responsible for the ultimate fall of the dynasty, but the role of peasant revolts, fashionable in modern Communist historic writings, could well have been overemphasized.

Despite such insurrections, the corruption and open sale of government posts continued. In the office known as the Western Quarters, the rich could purchase ministerial posts and the governorships of commanderies. Naturally, these people sought a return on their investment, and this practice resulted in further corruption and extortion. When Lingdi died in 189 C.E. the effective rule of the Han dynasty also came to an end, although the dynasty itself survived until 220 C.E.

Ling yi   During the WESTERN ZHOU DYNASTY (1045–771 B.C.E.) in China, ritual bronze vessels were cast in a wide variety of forms. Many bore INSCRIPTIONS recording the circumstances under which they were cast. Often the vessels were given by the king to a high official in recognition of services rendered to the court. The corpus of inscriptions is one of the key sources for reconstructing Western Zhou history. In 1929 a large number of such vessels were robbed from a Western Zhou grave outside LUOYANG, among which was the Ling yi. This bronze has one of the longest inscriptions dating to the period of the early Western Zhou dynasty. In respect to historic content, it describes in general terms the appointment of administrative officials and proceeds to describe how one Ling was given wine, metal, and a small ox. He then had the yi cast. The balance of evidence points to a date in the reign of King Zhou (977–957 B.C.E.).

Linjia   Linjia is a site in Gansu province, northwest China, belonging to the Majiayao phase of the late YANGSHAO CULTURE. It dates to about 3000 B.C.E. Its significance lies in the fact that a bronze knife found there in one of many underground storage pits is the earliest cast-bronze artifact discovered in China. This presents an anomaly, because its skillful casting in a double mold, involving alloying of copper and tin, is almost 1,000 years earlier than the next dated bronzes in this region. The origins of the Gansu and the Chinese bronze-working tradition are thought to lie in the West. The expansion of people and the spread of ideas along the course of the

future SILK ROAD would have introduced the knowledge of alloying and casting.

Lin-yi Lin-yi is the name given in Chinese records of the second to mid-fifth centuries C.E. to a polity lying to the south of Chinese provinces in the Hong (Red) River delta of Vietnam. The records describe a pattern of border conflict and friction that culminated in 446 C.E. with a major punitive raid. The people of Lin-yi were Cham speakers centered on the fertile river plain of the region of Hue.

See also CHAM CIVILIZATION.

Linzi The city of Linzi in Shandong province, China, was the capital of the state of QI, one of the major states that emerged during the Western and EASTERN ZHOU DYNASTIES. Many seasons of archaeological research make Linzi one of the best-known cities occupied at a time when urban life was in a period of rapid development. In essence, this period witnessed the rise of an urban society involving artisans and merchants, as well as a considerable expansion in the size of the enclosed area at Linzi. The earlier of the two walled cities, founded during the WESTERN ZHOU DYNASTY (1045–771 B.C.E.), covered an area of approximately 1,720 hectares (4,300 acres). Its interior was dominated by a series of broad streets, up to 20 meters (66 ft.) wide, laid out on a grid pattern. The richest part of the interior was probably the northeastern sector, where a number of fine ritual bronze vessels have been recovered. There was also a cemetery containing tombs dating from the Spring and Autumn period (770–476 B.C.E.) to the WARRING STATES PERIOD (475–221 B.C.E.). One of the tombs in this area, while looted, displayed considerable wealth; the surrounding pits contained the remains of 600 horses. It is thought to have been constructed for Qi Jing Gong, who ruled Qi from 547 to 490 B.C.E.

The smaller city, constructed during the Warring States period, covered an area of about 300 hectares (750 acres). It was adjacent to the southwestern corner of the old city and may well have been constructed after the replacement of the old ruling family of Jiang by the usurping ministerial lineage of Tian. Its defenses are most solid on that part of the enclosure facing inward to the old city rather than to the outside, which suggests internal discord. There are palace foundations in the northern part of the new city as well as bronze and iron workshops and a mint. About 500 meters (1,650 ft.) south of Linzi, a very large tomb has been examined, under a mound 10 meters (33 ft.) in height. Although looted, it still contained individual chambered pits for 17 young WOMEN and nine further sacrificial victims who had been decapitated or otherwise mutilated.

Liuchengqiao Tomb 1 at Liuchengqiao in China is a particularly notable CHU grave dating to the late Spring and Autumn (770–476 B.C.E.) or early WARRING STATES PERIOD (475 to 221 B.C.E.). It was discovered in 1971 and contained the remains of a military leader, if the number of weapons found within is any guide. The tomb had a vertical shaft seven meters (23 ft.) in depth, at the base of which were two double chambers and three nested wooden coffins. The coffins were covered in a layer of white clay to keep out air and moisture, and this arrangement led to the preservation of wood, LACQUER, and silk grave goods. The outermost coffin was fashioned from cypress planks held together with bronze nails in a zigzag pattern. The middle coffin was also made of wood neatly linked by mortise and tenon joints and secured with bronze nails, while the innermost coffin was painted black on the exterior and red within. A smaller coffin, possibly containing a sacrificial victim, was found in the corner of one chamber. The lacquerware includes a fine quiver still holding arrows, a drum, a table, and tomb guardians. Arguably the earliest example of a zither was also found. There are many ceramic vessels, jades, and fragments of silk, including one of the oldest examples known. The tomb master was interred with chariot trappings, and his weapons are of particular interest, because they seem to include a set used in chariot warfare. There are 93 weapons in all, including bronze swords, examples of the *ko*, or ax halberd; the *mao*, or thrusting spear, and the *ji*, which is a combination of both. The wooden hafts have survived, and these range up to 3.12 meters (10.2 ft.) in length. Such extremely long weapons are documented as being specific to chariot warfare. There is also a collection of three different types of arrows, some for long-distance shooting; other, heavier examples for piercing leather armor. The surviving bows were made of bamboo.

Liu Ji *See* GAOZU.

Liujiahe Liujiahe, an archaeological site just to the east of Beijing in China, is notable as one of the most northerly sites to yield material remains that can be referred to the SHANG STATE (1766–1045 B.C.E.). A burial was excavated and found to contain bronze vessels and a bronze ax with a blade fashioned from meteoric, or natural, iron. The remains of bronze horse trappings and chariot components are particularly interesting, as they represent one of the earliest such finds in China. Jade, gold, and TURQUOISE ornaments complete the rich mortuary offerings from this tomb.

Liu Sheng (d. c. 113 B.C.E.) *Liu Sheng was the brother of the Western Han emperor Wudi (157–87 B.C.E.).*
Liu Sheng's tomb at MANCHENG was discovered and excavated in 1968 and revealed for the first time two complete mortuary suits of jade wafers joined by gold thread, hitherto known only from documentary references. Such suits

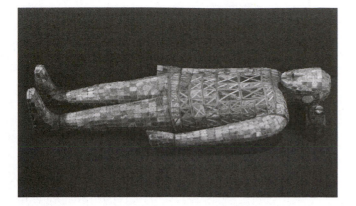

The jade suit of Princess Dou Wan, wife of Prince Liu Sheng of the Western Han royal family. It was discovered at Mancheng, China, in 1968. Jade was used to encase the royal dead, anticipating that it would preserve the body. *(© Asian Art & Archaeology, Inc./CORBIS)*

were reserved for the highest members of the royal family and were held to suppress the decomposition of the body.

See also HAN DYNASTY.

Liu Taiyun　*Liu Taiyun was one of the pioneers in the collection and study of the ancient Chinese texts on oracle bones from Anyang in China.*
During the early years of the 20th century, he collaborated with Wang Yiyong in saving these priceless records from drug dealers who powdered and used ORACLE BONES as medicine. He inherited Wang Yiyong's collection when the latter committed suicide in 1900, and he proceeded to assemble at least 5,588 records. In 1903 he published 1,058 fragments in the first scholarly study of the records of the Shang kings of ANYANG.

See also SHANG STATE.

Liu Xiu　(d. 55 B.C.E) *Liu Xiu, Prince Huai of Zhongshan, was an aristocrat of the Chinese Western Han dynasty.*
He was interred in a tomb at Bajiaolang, Hebei province. Although his tomb was looted, his jade suit has survived, despite being burned. It was made of 1,203 wafers of jade, sewn together with gold thread that weighs 2.56 kilograms (5.6 lbs.). This is one of the rare surviving suits. Jade was held to provide immortality. Others are known from MANCHENG and the tomb of Zhao Mo, also known as Wen Di (r. 137–122 B.C.E.), whose intact tomb has been found at Xianggang in Guangzhou (Canton).

See also YUE.

Lolei　The temple of Lolei is located on what was an island in the Jayatataka reservoir at HARIHARALAYA, Cambodia. This center was a major capital of the dynasty of JAYAVARMAN II (c. 770–834 C.E.) from the late eighth cen-

tury C.E. until the foundation of YASHODHARAPURA. King YASHOVARMAN I (r. 889–910 C.E.) had the shrines constructed to commemorate his parents, and it was consecrated on 8 July 893 C.E.

Lomasa Rishi　Lomasa Rishi, one of the earliest ROCK MONASTERIES of India, is located in the Barabar Hills of Bihar. These were built for Buddhist worship from the third century B.C.E., and most are concentrated in the western Deccan. The sanctuary of Lomasa Rishi has a narrow entrance, and the *caitya* shrine within runs parallel with the rock face. This portal was decorated with a frieze of carved elephants and *makaras*, mythical sea monsters. It probably dates to about 250 B.C.E.

See also BUDDHISM.

Longshan culture　The Longshan culture of the Huang (Yellow) River Valley in China has local roots in the Dawenkou and the YANGSHAO CULTURES. It dates between about 2500 and 1800 B.C.E. and is a crucial period because many of the Longshan sites reveal trends that anticipate the development of the first civilizations in the area. The Longshan communities that commanded the Huang River Valley and Shandong Peninsula reveal a quickening of social complexity. Archaeologically, this is manifested in defensive walls, rich burial assemblages, the adoption of metallurgy, and an increase in artifacts associated with armed conflict. Jades and bronzes, which were to reflect high social distinction for millennia to come, made their first appearance. The quality of the jades and ceramics is consistent with the establishment of craft specialization.

This development of defended settlements and craft specialization was rooted in a long preceding Neolithic period in which stamped-earth enclosures and growing settlement sizes were already beginning to appear by the end of the fourth millennium B.C.E. During the Longshan culture, certain well-placed communities grew further in size and commanded sufficient resources to construct large walls and platforms for elite buildings. Extensively excavated cemeteries, such as TAOSI, provide evidence for sharp social distinctions. This trend was accompanied by a growing density of sites and a sharp rise in population. Growth took place at a time of increasing evidence for violence and warfare. More weapons were manufactured, and some sites reveal evidence for the disposal of men who had been severely handled. Long-distance trade in exotic valuables was a further major development. There are four distinct regional foci for Longshan, extending from Shaanxi province in the west through Shanxi and Henan to Shandong in the east. Associated trends toward social stratification and the development of states, although not named Longshan, have been identified during the third millennium B.C.E. in the Chang (Yangtze) Valley from Sichuan to Hunan of Jiangsu and Zhejiang provinces.

LONGSHAN SITES

The site of CHENGZI is located in the southern part of the Shandong Peninsula; excavations have revealed a cemetery in which graves were now increasingly distinguished on the basis of mortuary wealth and spatial differentiation between rich and poor. Five rich interments of a sample of 87 graves were equipped with a ledge to display lavish offerings, including elegant tall-stemmed cups and the jaw-bones of pigs, presumably sacrificed as part of the mortuary ritual. The poorest graves, which were in the majority, however, had no ledges and fewer mortuary offerings.

CHENGZIYAI is situated on the right bank of the lower Huang River in Shandong province. It is particularly important because of the discovery there of 16 fragments of inscribed ORACLE BONES, dating to 2500–1900 B.C.E. These provide evidence for divination and an early system of writing in Longshan contexts. At DINGGONG, another site of the Longshan culture in Shandong province, there is early evidence for writing in the form of graphs on pottery vessels. It also provides evidence for domestic structures and the sacrifice of adults and children, whose remains have been found in the foundations of buildings. BIANXIANWANG has two stamped-earth enclosures and again has yielded the remains of sacrificial victims in the wall foundations. JINGYANGGANG is one of the largest Longshan centers in Dawenkou, with an area of about 38 hectares (95 acres). Early graphs have also been found on potsherds at this site.

Pingliangtai, located south of the Huang River in Henan province, offers a further and highly significant innovation in the middle reaches of the Huang River, in the provision of defensive stamped-earth walls. These enclosed a relatively small area of five hectares (12.5 acres), but inner walls were located around a citadel 185 meters square (222 sq. yds.). The outer walls were equipped with gateways; the interior contained house foundations and a drainage system. One of the pits in the site contained a trace of copper residue, and a piece of bronze was recovered. As in Shandong, some of the pottery shards had scratched written graphs. Hougang and Wangchenggang, in the same province, also incorporate walls, those at the latter site enclosing an area of rather less than a hectare. Stamped-earth foundations in the defended area were probably the residences of the elite. Part of a bronze bowl again indicates that copper was now being alloyed with tin and lead and locally cast. The date for this site lies toward the end of the third millennium B.C.E.

Taosi, in Shanxi province, is one of the most significant sites of this period, because it grew to cover more than 300 hectares (750 acres), and extensive excavations in the cemetery have involved opening more than 1,000 graves. This huge sample has allowed an appreciation of growing social differentiation, because nine contained considerable mortuary wealth. Up to 200 offerings were found in such wealthy interments, and the range included fine jade rings and axes and the remains of two remarkable wooden drums, each with a striking surface of crocodile skin. Crocodile scutes from a rich grave at YINJIACHENG in Shandong were also probably part of a drum. Historical texts refer to drums as being associated with royalty. The personal ornaments in these rich graves are of outstanding refinement. A hairpin from Tomb 2023, for example, had a bone stem enhanced with a sphere inlaid with TURQUOISE and jade inserts with a perforated terminal. This held in place a further thin slat of jade that would have rung when striking the adjacent sphere. A middle group of about 80 graves included jade axes, tubes, and rings, as well as pigs' jawbones, but the vast majority of poor graves had few, if any, offerings. In this huge assemblage, only one bronze was found, a bell of a copper-lead alloy. At the contemporary site of Meishan, however, dated to 2300–2000 B.C.E., two pieces of bronze crucibles made of clay have been found.

A jade pin from ZHUFENG in Shandong province had two sections: The pin itself, about 21 centimeters (8.4 in.) long, slotted into a decorated plaque inlaid with turquoise. Its location beside the skulls suggested that it was a hairpin. Other jade items from this grave, which held a wooden coffin nested within another, included a second pin, a blade, and two axes. There were also fine ceramic vessels and 980 turquoise plaques. Some jade items in the central plains and Shandong were being of Liangzhu origin. Alligator skin has been found on a drum from Taosi and probably originated in the south, which was also a source of exotic feathers and turtle shell. The nascent bronze industry would also have encouraged prospecting and exchange of copper and tin. The organization of such trade and ownership of rare prestigious goods have been widely observed in association with the rise of social elites.

It is also notable, however, that the areas within the Longshan walled sites are not large. Indeed, at Wangchenggang, only one hectare was defended. Other sites rarely exceed 20 hectares (50 acres) and would hardly have housed a population of 1,000 people. This small size scarcely qualifies for the term *city* as a characterization of Longshan centers, but it must be recalled that there might have been substantial settled areas outside the walls. In this situation, the defended sites could be seen as special areas fortified for the elite residences and communal structures, such as cult temples. This and other possibilities, however, must await specifically directed excavations.

EVIDENCE OF TRADE AND SOCIAL COMPLEXITY

The examination of cemeteries such as Taosi and Zhufeng has revealed a number of important common features. A small number of elite graves were included in clusters that also had much poorer interments. The largest and most lavishly equipped burials nearly always contained males.

They were associated spatially with pits containing complete pottery vessels and on occasion animal skeletons that suggest the practice of making ritual offerings to the dead. These elite burials are also distinguished by the presence of special grave goods, such as jade disks, *yazhang* blades, *yue* axes, and *cong* tubes. Jade is a very hard medium to work, and its presence in Longshan graves is a sure sign of elevated social rank. The sources of the Longshan jades included the Liaodong Peninsula across the Gulf of Bohai, where several sites, including Guojiacun and Wenjiatun, have yielded manufacturing tools for jade and contain finished jade artifacts. Control of long-distance trade in such precious substances would have been one route to elevated social status.

Pig skeletons were offered within the context of mortuary rituals, and later oracle texts from the SHANG STATE are known to indicate the age and sex of the animals required for sacrificial purposes. Superb eggshell-thin ceramic goblets were found in elite burials, and these are thought to have originated in specialized workshops rather than being made at the site where they rest. Several sites have also yielded the crocodile scutes that would once have formed the striking surfaces of drums. There is thus a consistent pattern informing us that the Longshan societies were forming a hierarchical social structure on the brink of state formation.

Early Chinese histories, such as the *SHIJI*, refer to a distant period of Five Emperors. They name kings and cities and many battles between innumerable rival kingdoms. The *HANSHU*, in referring to this remote predynastic period, also cites the existence of walled cities. It is an intriguing possibility that the much later Chinese historians were still in touch with the very origins of their civilization.

Further reading: Dematte, P. "Longshan-Era Urbanism: The Role of Cities in Predynastic China," *Asian Perspectives* 38 (1999): 119–153; Underhill, A. "Variation in Settlements During the Longshan Period of Northern China," *Asian Perspectives* 33 (1994): 197–228.

Lopburi   Lopburi is a major center of the DVARAVATI CIVILIZATION in central Thailand. It is difficult to excavate because it is covered by a modern town. Two Buddhist images have been found there, one inscribed in SANSKRIT dating to the eighth century. A stone "wheel of the law" (DHARMACAKRA), inscribed in Pali, has also been found. A mid-eighth-century Mon INSCRIPTION recorded the gift of slaves and cattle to a monastery. Lopburi was later taken by the kingdom of ANGKOR in Cambodia and was one of the centers mentioned in the reign of JAYAVARMAN VII (r. 1181–1219 C.E.).

Lothal   Lothal is a small settlement of the INDUS VALLEY CIVILIZATION, located at the head of the Gulf of Khambhat in Gujarat, India. The name derives from the Gujerati word *loth*, "dead." Lothal is an unusual Indus civilization settlement. It is not large, it lies at the southeastern edge of the known distribution of Indus sites, and it was a center for a wide range of manufacturing activities. The raw materials, such as carnelian and copper, were imported from beyond the borders of the civilization. The site can thus be seen as a trading and manufacturing center, drawing on foreign resources and sending finished goods to the cities of the Indus Valley and possibly beyond to the Persian Gulf. The settlement covers an area of 330 by 180 meters (1,089 by 594 ft.) and, as in larger contemporary sites in the Indus Valley, has a separate walled citadel. One probably held temples and elite residences, and the other, which was also walled, incorporated the houses of the majority of the occupants.

The excavations of S. R. Rao between 1954 and 1962 disclosed five building levels dating between about 2550 and 2150 B.C.E. During the height of the town's history, Periods II–IV, the citadel enclosed a series of mud-BRICK structures divided by streets. One such structure revealed a row of 12 bathrooms, but the function of other foundations is not clearly apparent. The lower area was given over not only to residences, but also to a wide range of craft activities. These included ivory working, for whole elephant tusks were uncovered, as well as ivory prepared for further attention, but not yet in the form of completed artifacts. There were also a furnace for heating carnelian, as part of the process involved in the production of beads. Other raw materials for manufacturing jewelry included jasper, opal, and crystal. Ingots of copper and metal slag make it clear that BRONZE CASTING was undertaken, while marine-shell bangles were also fashioned.

Excavations also uncovered a large brick-lined basin, 219 meters (722 ft.) long and 37 meters wide (122 ft.), still standing to a height of 4.5 meters. There are no steps leading down into it, and there is an inlet or outlet at the southern end. Rao forcefully interpreted this as a dock, which he argued was linked by a canal to the river and on to the open sea. This line of reasoning then saw the site as an important port, engaged in trade with the cities of Mesopotamia. The evidence for such trade is minimal: The excavations furnished a Persian Gulf type SEAL and a seal impression, but little else to sustain the notion of a busy port city. A series of technical reasons that have also been advanced do not sustain the interpretation of the basin as a dock. An alternative that has gained widespread support is that the basin served as a source of freshwater for the city population in an area where much water is saline.

Further reading: Kenoyer, J. M. *Ancient Cities of the Indus Civilization.* Oxford: Oxford University Press, 1998; Leshnik, L. S. "The Harappan 'Port' at Lothal: Another View," *American Anthropologist* 70: (1968): 911–922; Possehl, G. L. *Harappan Civilization: A Recent Perspective.* New Delhi: Oxford University Press, 1993.

Lou-lan Lou-lan is the name of a state located in the vicinity of Lop Nor Lake on the eastern margin of the TARIM BASIN. This area had a long period of occupation before the establishment of an early state on the SILK ROAD. Excavations in the area have uncovered remarkably complete graves with well-preserved human remains. The cemetery of Qäwrighul, in the center of the later Lou-lan state, dates back to at least 1800 B.C.E. Several burials have been uncovered, the most famous that of a well-preserved woman labeled the beauty of Lou-lan. She was warmly dressed in a leather skirt and woolen wrap, short leather boots, and wool cap with a feather in it. She was accompanied by a COMB, a basket still containing wheat, and a winnowing tray. Her features were Western, and her hair auburn. The graves at this cemetery were laid out in wooden boards, with the head pointing to the east. Grave goods often included a bunch of ephedra twigs. A ring of wooden stakes was then placed around the interments. The availability of sufficient trees and the presence of flocks of sheep indicate that the area must have been much wetter and more amenable to agriculture.

Surviving documents record that Lou-lan's original name was Krorän. After 77 B.C.E., it formed part of the kingdom of SHAN-SHAN. For the traveler heading westward from China to take the Silk Road in the first century B.C.E., Dunhuang was one of the last stopping places before passing through the Jade Gate and confronting the arid Tarim Basin. The route would then inevitably lead to the Lop Nor Lake and divide into a northern or a southern passage to avoid the arid Taklamakan Desert. The area around the lake, therefore, was inevitably strategic, particularly when it was better watered than at present.

EARLY EXCAVATIONS

Both the *SHIJI* and the *HANSHU* (*History of the Former Han*) describe how the Han official ZHANG QIAN visited this area in the late second century B.C.E. and gave accounts of walled cities. He described the state of Lou-lan as having 1,570 households with 14,100 people, located 1,600 *li* from the Jade Gate. Two thousand years later, when Sven Hedin was seeking the lake during his expedition of 1900, he encountered by chance an early settlement. Digging turned up a piece of shaped wood bearing writing in a script he could not decipher and several pieces of wood carving. When news spread of this discovery, interest was aroused in this site and the general area, and in 1906 SIR AUREL STEIN undertook further surveys and excavations. Stein identified many sites to the north and west of the old lake and gave each the name Lou-lan followed by a letter of the alphabet.

STEIN'S EXCAVATIONS

Lou-lan A lies north of the lake and is a walled settlement covering an area of nine hectares (29.7 acres). The thick walls were made of stamped earth interleaved with layers of branches to provide resistance to the strong wind that prevails in this desolate region. The early Chinese accounts noted the scarcity of good agricultural land in the Lou-lan area. Nevertheless, Lou-lan A incorporated a large stupa and administrative buildings and had a lengthy period of occupancy. Further stupas were noted at Lou-lan B, lying about 13 kilometers (7.8 mi.) northwest of the town site; 10 kilometers (6 mi.) to the northwest Stein found a bluff on top of which were building foundations and a cemetery known as Lou-lan F. His investigations in the latter are graphically described in his report, which is accompanied by a photograph of the body of a young man in a wooden coffin. He wore a felt hat and leather boots and was interred under a woolen blanket. Three baskets accompanied him, but their contents had not survived. However, a bunch of ephedra twigs lay beside the body, reminiscent of the consistent association between burials and ephedra in the much earlier prehistoric graves of the Tarim Basin. This plant has medicinal properties and might well have been the constituent of soma, a beverage often described in the RIGVEDA. The body was very well preserved and revealed a face with clear Western features. It is important to note that the mortuary traditions at this cemetery match closely those observed in the area almost 2,000 years previously: the same felt caps embellished with feathers; the same woolen wraps, baskets for grain, wooden posts surrounding the graves, and Western features of the dead.

Lou-lan E is another fortified town lying 30 kilometers (18 mi.) northeast of Lou-lan A. It covers only 1.6 hectares (4 acres) but was nevertheless defended by stout earthen walls three meters wide at the base. Surviving documents from this site suggest that it was occupied from the late first century B.C.E. until the late third century C.E. It may also have been the capital of the Lou-lan kingdom before the imposition of Chinese domination after 77 B.C.E. Lou-lan K is also walled and covers 1.8 hectares. It is located on the western margin of the old lake and was entered by a single gateway, the wooden posts and gates of which survived, to be described by Stein. The same area included at Lou-lan K a small fort from which a document in the KHAROSHTHI script, and silk, wool, and paper remains have been recovered.

The Lou-lan sites contain much evidence for the establishment of BUDDHISM in the area. Stupas were constructed of mud BRICK and were probably covered in stucco. The typical form saw the oval stupa proper raised on top of three square platforms. A wooden flagpole issued from the top. Wood has been preserved in the dry desert conditions and provides a glimpse of the fine architectural details seen, for example, in a lintel from Lou-lan A embellished with images of the Buddha in carved niches. Although severely worn, a wooden doorjamb from Lou-lan B was carved to include the image of a BODHISATTVA. A meter-high wooden statue is from the same site. While Buddhism expresses strong cultural influences from the West, the excavations of burials in the vicinity of Lou-lan A undertaken first by Stein and in 1980 by a Chinese team have also uncovered many Chinese imports. As might be expected, these include fine silk clothing in which the dead were buried, lacquerware, Chinese coins, and a bronze mirror.

Lou-lan depended for its existence on the Könchi Dar'ya and its replenishing Lop Nor Lake. This river is prone to change its course as it traverses the flat terrain north of the lake with major consequences for those who live along its banks. Just such a movement in the fourth century could well have led to the abandonment of the many sites of Lou-lan.

Lovea   Lovea is a village located northwest of ANGKOR in Cambodia. Viewed from the air, it appears to be surrounded by an earthwork and a moat similar in form to those in many Iron Age sites in northeast Thailand. It is reported that human remains with bronze and iron artifacts were unearthed there when the present temple was under construction. The nature of prehistoric occupation before the foundation of Angkor is hardly known, and Lovea is one of a series of similar sites that have the potential to illuminate this problem.

Lower Xiajiadian culture   The Lower Xiajiadian culture has been recognized for many years; the first major excavations were at Dongbaijia in 1943 and at Xiajiadian in 1962. Both sites lie in the outskirts of Chifeng in Inner Mongolia. More than 2,000 sites are now known, distributed in Inner Mongolia, Liaoning, and Hebei provinces. It is a Bronze Age culture, dating between about 2300 and 1600 B.C.E., and thus contemporary with the LONGSHAN CULTURE sites in the Huang (Yellow) River Valley and Shandong province to the south. On the basis of excavations of Fengxia, three developmental phases can be recognized in changing pottery forms through the layers of the site.

The importance of the Lower Xiajiadian culture lies in the evidence it provides for an extension of the area of increasing social distinctions into a region relatively remote from the central plains. Moreover, the bronzes found as grave offerings have Western parallels, suggesting they provided a conduit for the introduction of bronze working into China from the West. The origins are controversial, for the material culture differs markedly from the preceding HONGSHAN CULTURE, and the ceremonialism of the latter is no longer in evidence. Moreover, it ceased in about 1700 B.C.E., followed by 500 years when little or no settlement of the area has been identified. Some Chinese archaeologists find in the Lower Xiajiadian culture elements that anticipate and might well be ancestral to the SHANG STATE of the central plains.

ARCHAEOLOGICAL REMAINS

Settlements fall into three categories: large defended sites, the largest covering more than 10 hectares (25 acres); smaller defended sites, and settlement with no defenses. There appear to be clusters of sites, each containing one distinctively large central place, such as Chijiayingzi. The defensive walls were constructed of stone, often in the form of an inner and an outer skin containing stamped earth within. Many were punctuated with bastions. The houses were usually at least partially underground, also constructed of stone where available or stamped earth, with plastered walls and floors. At the site of Sifendi, houses were circular, with a diameter rarely exceeding four meters. They were reached by a set of steps, and the single room within was dominated by a hearth. On many occasions, the hearth was accompanied by a pottery vessel that might have contained tinder. There is some evidence that larger square houses occupied elevated ground in the settlements. At Fengxia, a rectangular house with two rooms, measuring nine by 8.5 meters (about 900 sq. ft.), was uncovered. Houses from a variety of settlements had plastered floors that were renewed on at least six occasions, indicating long-term occupation. The houses at Dongbaijia were so strongly constructed that 57 survive to this day on the present surface of the site.

The economy was based on grain cultivation, with an emphasis on millet, two varieties of which have been found at Fengxia. Agricultural implements included stone hoes and sickles, as well as spades fashioned from animal shoulder blades. Many storage pits were dug, probably to safeguard the millet harvest for winter consumption. Domestic pigs, dogs, cattle, goat, and sheep bones indicate the raising of livestock, and deer were hunted. Large domestic pig skeletons have often been found as ritual offerings in graves.

SOCIAL ORDER AND MATERIAL CULTURE

A substantial exposure of graves at Dadianzi has greatly illuminated the social order. Here 800 burials have been excavated. The ritual involved single inhumation burial, and interestingly some interments are relatively large and richly endowed with grave goods. These richer individuals, whose graves could be up to 8.9 meters deep, were interred in wooden coffins. The graves contained niches for receiving fine painted ceramic vessels and the limbs of domestic pigs. Polished stone battle axes, lacquerware, rare jades, bronze ornaments, and up to six complete skeletons of dogs and pigs were also found. Other graves had fewer offerings and lacked some of the sumptuary ceramic vessels such as wine jugs, but the heads of pigs and dogs often accompanied the dead.

There is some evidence for craft specialization, in the form of fine ceramic vessels and stone and ceramic molds for BRONZE CASTING. The actual bronzes recovered include earrings, knives, and rings. Their parallels lie to the west, in the Andronovo culture of the Siberian steppes, and in the case of decorative finials, in BACTRIA. Long-distance trade would have carried jade and marine shells to these communities, in which the drilling and heating of animal scapulae for divination purposes were widespread.

See also ORACLE BONES; XIA DYNASTY.

Lu Lu was a Chinese state dating to the Western and EASTERN ZHOU DYNASTIES (1045–221 B.C.E.). It was located in the lower Huang (Yellow) River Valley, in the present province of Shandong. After the defeat of the Shang dynasty, the new Zhou court assigned leading members of the royal lineage to rule over peripheral territory by founding new states. The duke of Zhou was given Lu, and he sent his eldest son, Bo Qin, to take control of this region, which had included the former state of Pugu, an enemy of the Zhou. The descendants of Bo Qin then ruled Lu under the royal Ji clan for many generations. The state of Lu is best known as the home of CONFUCIUS (551–479 B.C.E.), China's most famous and influential political philosopher and teacher. His temple survives at QUFU, the capital city of Lu. With the demise of the WESTERN ZHOU DYNASTY and the move to Luoyang by King Ping, Lu was one of the states that supported the continuation of the Zhou royal house under the MANDATE OF HEAVEN.

Qufu is the city that most closely conforms to the model Zhou city, with a rectangular walled precinct, 12 gates, and interior roads forming a grid pattern. However, archaeological research has identified only 11 gates, and the interior roads are not on a grid plan. The royal palace stood in the center of the city, and areas were devoted to BRONZE CASTING, bone-artifact manufacture, and ceramics. Several lineage cemeteries have been found within the city walls, and some of the wealthier graves included chariots, horses, and bronze vessels. The state endured until its defeat at the hands of CHU in 256 B.C.E., but the city continued in occupation during the HAN DYNASTY.

Lü Buwei (d. 235 B.C.E.) *Lü Buwei gave his name to an important Chinese text on political philosophy known as the* Lüshi Chunqiu, *or* The Springs and Autumns of Mr. Lü, *published in 241 B.C.E.*
He was a high official in the state of QIN after he had become wealthy as a merchant. Some rumors assert that he was actually the father of QIN SHIHUANGDI (259–210 B.C.E.), the first emperor of China and founder of the short-lived Qin dynasty. The state of Qin rose to become the most powerful and widely feared of the Warring States, and the *Lüshi Chunqiu*, which was written by Lü Buwei's protégés, was a manual of statecraft offered to the king. The basic philosophical reasoning advocates that proper order in the state relied on both the king and his ministers. The former, through self-discipline and reflection, projected the moral order of the universe and state

but remained distant from the day-to-day administration of the bureaucrats. Although Lü Buwei may have hoped to influence the future emperor, this was not to be. Qin Shihuangdi ignored all the advice offered except for the moral justification for armed aggression and, in due course, sent Lü Buwei into exile. However, the *Lüshi Chunqui* enjoyed a more tangible influence on the subsequent rulers of the HAN DYNASTY.

Lu Hao (d. 180 B.C.E.) *Lu Hao was the senior wife of Gaozu, the founder of the Western Han dynasty of China.*
On the death of the emperor GAOZU in 195 B.C.E., she first dominated her son, HUIDI, and then ruled as regent while two infants were nominally on the throne until her own death in 180 B.C.E. She consolidated her position of power by appointing members of her own clan to positions of authority at court and authorizing them to rule over subsidiary kingdoms. This policy failed with her death, when members of the Lu clan were massacred and the Liu family of Gaozu reasserted itself with the appointment of WENDI as the new emperor.

Lumbini Lumbini, modern Rummindei, was the birthplace of the Buddha. It is located just north of the border between India and Nepal. In about 252 B.C.E. it was visited by King ASOKA, third ruler of the MAURYA EMPIRE and an enthusiastic convert to BUDDHISM. He had one of his columns erected there, with a brief INSCRIPTION. The text described how the king visited in the 20th year of his reign to worship at the birthplace of the Buddha Sakyamuni. He had a stone building constructed and granted the community a tax concession whereby their payments were reduced from one-sixth of production to one-eighth.

Luoyang Luoyang was the capital of the EASTERN ZHOU DYNASTY from 771 B.C.E., after the sacking of the former royal center near Xi'an to the west. It lies at the junction of the Jian and Luo Rivers, south of the Huang (Yellow) River in the central plains of China. Little is known of the capital, whose first ruler was King Ping, because of later building. By the early WARRING STATES PERIOD, however, a walled city covering an area of about 900 hectares (2,250 acres) had been constructed. In 25 C.E., Luoyang again became the capital under the Eastern HAN DYNASTY, and a new city was built between the Lo and Ku Rivers, the latter feeding the moat that lay in front of massive walls. Excavations beyond the walls of the early capital have revealed an extensive series of burials, at least 1,000 of which have been opened. They date to the Warring States period (475–221 B.C.E.) and appear to contain the remains of middle-class occupants of the city. These contrast with the outstandingly rich and probably royal graves unearthed at Jincun. Despite looting, they still contained fine mortuary offerings. The tombs were octagonal wooden chambers, joined by a doorway to long ramps, one of which reached 80 meters (264 ft.) in length. Three of the ramps were lined by long pits containing the remains of horses. The looted artifacts were outstandingly rich. Three giant *ding* tripods lined the doorway giving access to the tomb, each almost a meter in diameter. Within the chamber, the upper part of the wooden walls was decorated with a band of inlaid glass and bronze disks. Some of the bronze vessels and mirrors were inlaid with gold, silver, or glass, and there were silver vessels, a statuette, and a jade and gold pectoral.

Still surviving to a height of 10 meters (33 ft.), the walls of the later capital were constructed of stamped earth and enclosed an area of 10 square kilometers (4 sq. mi.). Two palaces lay within the north and south, connected by a causeway. The city, as was its immediate predecessor at Chang'an to the west, was divided into walled precincts and incorporated workshops and markets. Outside there was a substantial urban sprawl that included temples, a university, and the royal observa-tory. The population was probably in the region of 500,000 people. The city, however, was razed to the ground in 189 C.E.

See also WANGCHENG.

Luo Zhenyu (1866–1940) *Luo Zhenyu was an early scholar of the texts of the Anyang oracle bones.*
Until his research, the source of these records was kept a secret by the dealers. However, Luo Zhenyu tracked down their origin in the village of Xiaotun. He also minutely examined the texts to distinguish the genuine articles from fakes and then proceeded to identify the names of the Shang kings of Anyang, date the bones to their historic context, and illuminate their purpose as divination. He wrote on the identity of the capital city of the SHANG STATE (1766–1045 B.C.E.), the names of the kings, the translation of the ancient characters, and the methods of divination. He published several volumes, entitled "The *Yin-hsü* Oracle Bone Inscriptions," between 1913 and 1915; in them he discussed the capital cities, kings, geographical terms, ritual systems, and methods of divination.

M

Madhyadri *See* BAYON.

Magadha Magadha was one of the 16 MAHAJANAPADAS, or great states, and was flourishing during the life of the Buddha. It was located in the vicinity of Patna, India, and comprised the kernel of the MAURYA and GUPTA EMPIRES.

Mahabharata The *Mahabharata* is an enormous compendium of myths, legends, and epic sagas compiled in India between approximately 500 B.C.E. and 400 C.E. It incorporates the legends surrounding the activities of SIVA and Vishnu and describes the mighty BATTLE OF KURUK-SHETRA between the forces of good and evil. It was employed as a rich source of themes depicted on the temple reliefs of the kingdom of ANGKOR.

mahajanapada The term *mahajanapada* is central to an understanding of the formation of states in northern India during the period 600–350 B.C.E.

The development of states in the Ganges (Ganga) Valley took place over a relatively short time span of about three centuries. It was based on the successful prosecution of agriculture and trade in association with intensive competition and warfare reflected in the presence of mud-BRICK or, occasionally, fired-brick or stone defenses. The process culminated in the late fourth century B.C.E. with the emergence of the state of MAGADHA, precursor to the MAURYA EMPIRE.

Before the establishment of the MAURYA EMPIRE in the fourth century B.C.E., northern India was divided into many small states, of which 16 were described as *mahajanapadas*. The four major states were Magadha, the ultimate victor in predatory wars; Kosala; Vatsa,

under the Paurava dynasty; and Avanti, based at UJJAIN. Much of the information on the names and events concerning these kingdoms is from the Buddhist scriptures, which mention two *mahajanapadas* in the northwest of the Ganges Valley known as Kamboja and GANDHARA. Other *mahajanapadas* were Pancala, in the Ganges Valley; Vriji; Malla; Kasi; Kuru; Cedi; Surasena (with its capital at MATHURA) Matsya (southwest of Delhi); Asmaki (on the Godavari River); and Anga north of the Ganges Delta.

ARCHAEOLOGICAL INFORMATION

There are two main sources of information: archaeological finds and the record contained in oral traditions when they were finally recorded in written form. Archaeologically, the most informative program of research has concentrated on the settlement patterns of the Allahabad district, just above the confluence of the Yamuna and Ganges Rivers. During the sixth and fifth centuries B.C.E. one site, KAUSAMBI, grew to cover an area of about 50 hectares (125 acres); other settlements fall into two groups by size: The secondary centers covered about six hectares (15 acres), and the small villages covered less than two hectares (5 acres). Large centers in this district and beyond were now equipped with large mud-brick fortifications, reflecting increased competition and warfare. From about 400 B.C.E. there were further fundamental changes, in which the population grew, and secondary centers expanded up to 30 hectares (66 acres). This was a period of agricultural expansion, involving forest clearance, marsh drainage, and the application of iron technology to increase production, particularly through the use of iron plowshares and animal traction. Rice grew in importance, but wheat, millet, and barley were also cultivated, while pigs, cattle, and horses were raised. Little is known of the internal layout of the early cities, because the relevant layers are usually stratified deep below historic remains. Early excavations at the site of BHITA by SIR JOHN MARSHALL, however, suggest that there were city gates, orderly streets lined with shops and houses, and a drainage system. This period is characterized by a style of pottery known as NORTHERN BLACK POLISHED WARE. It is widely distributed in the valley of the Ganges River, and relevant sites reveal widespread iron smelting, specialized copper and bead production, and bronze working.

ORAL TRADITIONS

The late Vedic and Buddhist oral traditions greatly expand on the rather thin archaeological record. Initially, there were many competing states (JANAPADAS). These were reduced through war and absorption into 16 maha-janapadas, then to four, and finally by 321 B.C.E. to the supreme state of Magadha. There are hereditary rulers known as rajyas, whose duties included the successful prosecution of warfare, protection of the populace, and adherence to moral law, the DHARMA. There was a growing bureaucracy within the court centers, including a chief minister, a purohita, or religious leader, and ministers. These states were sustained on the basis of a taxation system that involved levies on production, commercial transactions, and sales, while silver and copper COINAGE facilitated trade. The records also describe the cities as being populous, incorporating merchants and craft workshops. Descriptive terms like pura (city) and nagara (holy city) also enter the literature for the various types of major settlements.

Mahamuni　The Mahamuni shrine is located in the Arakanese (now Rakhire) city of DHANYAWADI in western Myanmar (Burma). It is one of the most revered holy places in Myanmar, because it was here that the statue of the Buddha, known as the Mahamuni (great sage), was located until the region was conquered and the image removed to Mandalay in 1784. According to tradition, the Buddha visited this region, and an image was cast in his likeness, the only such image known. Today it is impossible to identify the original form because devotees have covered it in so much gold. The shrine itself survives but has been the subject of much reconstruction. Some of the original sandstone guardian figures and BODHISATTVAS, dating to the fifth century C.E., have been restored there.

See also ARAKAN.

Ma Hao　Ma Hao is one of the earliest sites in China to provide evidence for the adoption of BUDDHISM. It is located in Sichuan province, on the Min River, a tributary of the Chang (Yangtze). The Cave 9 tomb had a series of shafts cut into the hillside, decorated with carved panels. Many of these illustrate scenes from Chinese history, even

dating back to the overthrow of the SHANG STATE (1766–1045 B.C.E.). One, placed in a prominent position, shows the Buddha in a seated position with a halo. This form of representation has its closest parallels, and in all probability its origin, in the depictions of the Buddha seen along the eastern sections of the SILK ROAD to the north.

Mahasena (274–301 C.E.)　*King Mahasena of Sri Lanka was responsible for the massive reservoir known as the Minneriya.*
He was antagonistic to the monks of the Mahavihara Monastery, who dispersed under his reign.

Mahasthana　Mahasthana is a city site in Bangladesh, which, according to a local INSCRIPTION, was formerly known as Pundranagara. The text of the inscription refers to a storehouse for grain. The city was occupied during the period of the GUPTA EMPIRE (320–c. 500 C.E.) and held a temple to Vishnu and another to the Buddha.

Mahavira　*See* NALANDA.

Mahayana Buddhism　The centuries following the attainment of nirvana by the Buddha saw the development of different schools of thought in the Buddhist congregation. One of the problems of early Buddhist doctrine, at least for the masses, was the strictly separate nature of the individual quest for nirvana. This did not readily attract a large following. As a consequence the Mahayanist school developed around the notion that the BODHISATTVA, the person on the path to nirvana, would forgo the final transition to help others in their quest. This had the effect of popularizing and secularizing BUDDHISM so that followers could take the bodhisattva vow, which specified the aim of living a holy life and helping others. In this way, fulfillment of the vow replaced nirvana as the objective of the Mahayanist. Bodhisattvas themselves became objects of veneration and worship and were depicted as celestial beings. The Bodhisattva Avalokitesvara was, for example, the exemplar of compassion, and Manjusri of wisdom.

This contrasts with the school of THERAVADA BUDDHISM, in which death for the enlightened automatically produces nirvana, and the god in the form of a bodhisattva no longer has an existence. Consequently, in this school there were no benevolent bodhisattvas. This development provided for tricky theological dilemmas for Theravada Buddhists, because it meant that the Buddha himself attained nirvana while there were still countless creatures requiring the guidance of bodhisattvas. This was resolved by progressively identifying the truth, DHARMA, rather than nirvana, as the true goal. By a further philosophical avenue, the Buddha in the Mahayana school began to symbolize universal truth, whereas in the

Theravada school the Buddha remained the physical being who attained nirvana. Nagarjuna, who was active during the KUSHAN period (78–200 C.E.), was one of the great early philosophers of Mahayana Buddhism. He is widely associated with the Buddhist center of learning at NALANDA and was responsible for the early formulation of the philosophical basis of the school; his most famous work is the *Madhyamaka Karika*.

Mahidharapura dynasty The founding dynasty of ANGKOR in Cambodia can be traced back to JAYAVARMAN II, who established the kingdom when he was consecrated king of kings in 802 C.E. With the possible exception of the accession of SURYAVARMAN I in the early 11th century, this dynasty proved durable. In about 1080 C.E., however, there was a major dynastic change when JAYAVARMAN VI seized power. He was a member of the powerful regional family of Mahidharapura, whose base lay in the Mun Valley of Thailand. His father had a royal title, and it is likely that the Mahidharapura dynasty had long exercised a form of local rule in the kingdom of Angkor. The dynasty provided two of the great kings of Angkor, SURYAVARMAN II (r. c. 1002–49 C.E.), a warrior responsible for the construction of ANGKOR WAT, and JAYAVARMAN VII (r. 1181–1219 C.E.), who was by far the most energetic founder of temples, rest houses, hospitals, and roads in the history of the kingdom.

Mai *zun* The Mai *zun* is a bronze vessel dating to the reign of King Cheng (r. c. 1042–1006 B.C.E.) of the WESTERN ZHOU DYNASTY. A person called Mai, a retainer of the lord Xinghou Zhi, cast it. As do many other Western Zhou vessels, it incorporates a text explaining its origin. Such texts often provide important insights into the history of the period. The INSCRIPTION on this *zun* describes how the king appointed Xinghou Zhi to proceed to Xing, located north of the old Shang capital of ANYANG, to found a new colony. In this manner the early Western Zhou rulers enfeoffed relatives or loyal followers with land to form dependable provincial government. The text of the Mai *zun* describes the rituals attendant on this appointment and the lavish gifts bestowed on the appointee, including a horse harness, a robe, a dagger, ax, and even a pair of slippers. He was also accompanied by soldiers and 200 families to settle the new territory. This feudal system, however, ultimately held the seeds of the downfall of the Zhou, because with time the new provinces grew powerful in their own right and began to form independent states.

Majiayuan Majiayuan is a large urban center located near the confluence of the Chang (Yangtze) and Zhang Rivers in Hubei province, central China. It comprises a roughly rectangular walled enclosure covering about 20 hectares (50 acres). The walls are up to eight meters (26.4 ft.) wide at the base, and the moat, which lies beyond the stamped-earth walls, is 50 meters (165 ft.) wide in places. The site dates to the Qujialing and Shijiahe periods and is one of several that show an early development of complex urban societies in the middle Chang Valley during the third millennium B.C.E.

Majumdar, R. C. (1888–1980) *Ramesh C. Majumdar was a prominent Indian historian who traveled widely in Southeast Asia.*
His visits to the major cities there convinced him of their pervasive Indian influence, and he wrote several works, including *Indian Colonies in the Far East,* which proposed a large-scale movement of Indian people involved in the formation of Southeast Asian civilization. This idea has now largely been discredited.
See also INDIANIZATION.

Mancheng Mancheng, a city in Hebei province, northern China, has given its name to one of the most extraordinary finds in the history of Chinese archaeological exploration. In 1968, two rock-cut tombs were discovered intact. Excavations revealed that they contained the remains of Prince LIU SHENG, son of Emperor JINGDI (188–141 B.C.E.) and brother of the Han emperor WUDI (157–87 B.C.E.), and his wife, Dou Wan. This is the first and only burial of a Western HAN DYNASTY prince to be found intact. His tomb reached 52 meters (172 ft.) into the hillside and had a series of chambers up to 37 meters (122 ft.) wide, while that of his wife was of similar form but slightly larger in terms of volume of rock removed. The interior vaults, which reached up to seven meters in height, contained roofed chambers filled with the requirements of both aristocrats in the life after death. The most remarkable discovery in an excavation renowned as one of the richest recorded in China were the jade suits that contained the two bodies. Jade was held to be an auspicious material to cover the body, because of the belief that it stopped decomposition. At a time when *bo*, that part of the dead person that remained on Earth, required an uncorrupted body in which to reside, it was considered vital to encase the body in jade. However, this was so demanding of labor that only the emperor and the highest echelon in the royal family were permitted such suits, their relative status displayed by the use of gold, silver, or bronze thread to stitch the jade wafers together. It has been estimated that the 2,690 pieces of jade and one kilogram (2.2 lbs.) of gold thread in Liu Sheng's suit would have required 10 years for a skilled craftsperson to complete. There is a record of this mortuary custom in the text known as the *Han jiuyi buyi*, dating to the first century C.E., which states: "When the emperor died, a pearl was placed in his mouth; his body was wrapped around with twelve layers of reddish yellow silk. Jade was used to make the garment. It had the shape of armor and the jade pieces were stitched together with gold threads." In an additional refinement, a much earlier jade *cong,* a sacred tube typical of the

LIANGZHU CULTURE, was reemployed to hold the prince's genitals. Each bodily orifice was plugged with jade, and the royal head lay on a headrest of gilded bronze and jade, ornamented with dragons and feline, tigerlike creatures.

LIU SHENG'S TOMB

The tomb of LIU SHENG, who died in about 113 B.C.E., was divided into chambers to contain the worldly belongings that befitted the life of a senior prince of the royal family. One chamber stabled his horses and contained his chariots. Another was set aside for the sealed containers for his food and wine. His fine bronze and LACQUER serving dishes occupied a central hall, but his finest gold, silver, and jade vessels and ornaments were found in the rear mortuary room that included his body. An exceptional pair of wine vessels was present, inlaid with gold figures incorporating written texts. These reflect the anticipation of a long and enjoyable life in eternity: "We desire longevity and the dispelling of disease. Even 10,000 years would not be too much."

Liu Sheng had the reputation of enjoying life, as befitting one whose wine vessels note that "fine food fills the gates to the bursting point. The more sustenance, the more we become fat and healthy." His jade suit reveals a corpulent frame, when compared with that of his wife.

DOU WAN'S TOMB

The tomb of his wife, Princess Dou Wan, also contained some of the finest artifacts to survive from the Western Han dynasty. Perhaps best known is a gilt lamp in the form of a palace maid. She holds the base of the lamp in her left hand, and her right hand acts as a conduit to take away the smoke from the flame. The light can be directed by a revolving mechanism. The texts on this lamp tell of its history: It probably once belonged to the dowager empress Dou, who resided in the Changxin palace. She may well have given it to the princess Dou Wan, a member of her own family. It thus entered the Mancheng tomb as a treasured family heirloom.

Manda   Manda is one of the most northerly of INDUS VALLEY CIVILIZATION sites in India. It is located on the right bank of the Chenab River. Excavations in 1977 revealed three cultural phases encompassing pre-Indus and Indus civilization material culture, dating between about 2350 and 1750 B.C.E., beneath a second occupation belonging to the period of the KUSHAN empire (78–200 C.E.). Period 1 at the base of the site yielded pottery similar to that from early KALIBANGAN, as well as an unfinished SEAL, bone arrowheads, and a copper pin.

mandala   *Mandala* is a word with several meanings. It is a magic or symbolic diagram used in Tantric BUDDHISM, held to represent the universe and inspire meditation. It is also a division in the RIG-VEDA, which contains 10 mandalas. Its most widespread meaning refers to a group

of kings and their relationships, whether hostile, friendly, or neutral. The term has more recently been used, not without controversy, to describe ephemeral early states in Southeast Asia.

See also CHENLA.

Mandate of Heaven   The Mandate of Heaven, or *tian-ming*, was a concept advanced to provide legitimization to the overthrow of the SHANG STATE by the Zhou in 1045 B.C.E. The Mandate of Heaven was given considerable weight in the writings of CONFUCIUS and MENCIUS, and this assisted in its long dominance of royal legitimization. According to SIMA QIAN, writing in the second century B.C.E., the last Shang king at Yin (ANYANG) followed a path of depravity and oppression. The ruler of Zhou led a successful revolt and assumed power. After centuries of Shang authority, it was necessary to provide a charter to legitimize the new Zhou kings. Several later texts referring to this period described the principles of the Mandate of Heaven as articulated through the deeds and sayings of the early Zhou nobility. The *Classic of Documents* (from the Western Zhou period, 1045–771 B.C.E.), for example, records that the Mandate of Heaven gave kings the authority to rule provided that they did so with regard for their people, showing concern, wisdom, and respect for the ancestors. If a ruler ignored these principles, then the mandate could be withdrawn and given to a more righteous lineage. It cites the precedent of King Tang of Shang, who overthrew the last XIA king when the latter lost the moral approval to govern. The text known as the METAL-BOUND COFFER (late fifth century B.C.E.) describes how Duke Zhou offered his own life to save that of the ailing king WU, the person who had received the Mandate of Heaven. This same duke in the *Shaogao* (*Shao Announcement*) declared during the foundation ceremonies for the new Zhao capital how vital it was for the young king to follow a righteous path to ensure that he and his descendants retained the mandate. The *Classic of Odes* likewise encourages the proper moral path for the ruler, but it warns also that "the Mandate is not easy to keep."

Under the legalists and the centralizing power of the QIN dynasty, however, the mandate was ignored. With the Confucian revival under the HAN DYNASTY, the concept enjoyed a renaissance, particularly after 31 B.C.E. when *tian,* "heaven," superseded DI, "god," as the preferred object of devotion. This brought into focus the fact that emperors were the instruments of heaven and ruled under its mandate. Wang Mang adhered to the belief in holding the Mandate during his period of rule. The *Book of Documents* states that the emperor was the father and the mother of his people and king of all under heaven. The historian BAN BIAO (3–54 C.E.) set out his view of the concept during the early years of the Eastern Han dynasty, noting that it harmonized with the five phases that were thought to determine the rhythms of the universe and was conferred only on those fit to conform to its requirements of humane and caring government. Thus the Eastern Han, in harmony with the five phases, claimed to rule under the aegis of fire, while their predecessors ruled under the phase of water until 104 B.C.E. and then under that of earth. The last emperor of the Han dynasty was observing the full force of the Mandate of Heaven when he sent the imperial SEALS to his successor, the first king of the new WEI dynasty, in 220 C.E.

Further reading: De Bary, W. T., and I. Bloom, eds. *Sources of Chinese Tradition*. New York: Columbia University Press, 1999; Loewe, M. *Divination, Mythology and Monarchy in Han China*. Cambridge: Cambridge University Press, 1994; Loewe, M., and E. L. Shaugnessy, eds. *The Cambridge History of Ancient China*. Cambridge: Cambridge University Press, 1999; Marshall, S. J. *The Mandate of Heaven*. New York: Columbia University Press, 2001.

Manikiyala   Manikiyala is a Buddhist site in the Punjab which was one of the first sites to be explored archaeologically in India. The stupa was opened in 1830 by the Chevalier Ventura. At a depth of about one meter (3.3 ft.), he encountered a collection of coins. Further coins were found at depths of three and six meters. As they dug deeper, the workers found a box of gold and a second box of copper under a stone slab 13 meters down. This was interpreted at the time as a royal tomb. JAMES PRINSEP, however, who wrote on this digging, correctly identified the stupa as a Buddhist monument.

See also COINAGE.

Mantai   Formerly known as Mahatittha, Mantai is a large mound located on the northwestern coast of Sri Lanka. Its location is pivotal in the great maritime exchange route that linked the Mediterranean world with China and the countries between. Excavation, aborted before completion by civil war, revealed much exotic pottery and the remains of BRICK structures.

Maodun   (r. 209–174 B.C.E.) *Maodun was the greatest shanyu (great leader) of the Xiongnu, a nomadic people who occupied the Mongolian steppes.*
Traditionally the Xiongnu were divided into 24 tribes, but under Maodun they were united and presented an immediate threat to Han China. To keep peace on the northern border, the Chinese emperors negotiated treaties with Maodun and gave him lavish presents. Maodun was the senior son of the Shanyu Touman. The latter preferred a younger son and sent Maodun as a hostage to his enemy, the nomadic Yuezhi, before promptly attacking them. This would traditionally have led to the death of Maodun, but he managed to escape. Impressed by his bravery, Touman gave him his own command. Maodun then trained his men to fire their arrows at any target he chose with his own bow, on pain of death. When the opportu-

nity arose, he fired at his own father and killed him. Maodun then seized overall power at the same time as GAOZU (247–195 B.C.E.) was consolidating his position as the first emperor of the Western HAN DYNASTY.

MAODUN'S VICTORIES

A clash was precipitated by Maodun, who moved his forces into China, capturing the king of Dai. It was winter, and Gaodi personally led his troops north. SIMA QIAN described how three out of 10 soldiers suffered from frostbite. It was now that Maodun revealed his wily military brain. He placed only his weakest troops in view of the Han and tempted them forward to attack. With an army estimated at 320,000 men, Gaodi advanced as far as the city of Pingcheng. Maodun's cavalry then surrounded the Chinese host, and there was no escape. For a week, they remained immobile. At the behest of his wife, Maodun left open a sector of the encirclement and allowed the emperor to escape. His wife argued that there was no possibility that the XIONGNU would ever occupy all China and that the emperor was protected by his gods. Maodun then withdrew north but continued to support disruptive border raids into China.

TREATIES WITH MAODUN

The next step in diplomatic relations was a treaty in which Gaodi sent a Han princess to be a consort of Maodun, together with gifts of silk and grain. This move, in effect, was an act of appeasement to restrain the Xiongnu from further attack and set a precedent only to be reversed under the reign of Emperor WUDI (157–87 B.C.E.). Maodun, however, became more truculent, even proposing marriage to the dowager empress Lu.

In 180 B.C.E., Emperor WENDI was consecrated and renewed the treaty with the Xiongnu. Three years later, however, one of Maodun's subsidiary leaders, known as "the wise king of the right," invaded China, and Wendi led a punitive expedition. The king of the right withdrew north, but Maodun decided to consolidate the treaty relationship. In a carefully worded letter to the Han emperor, he described how he had dispatched the king of the right against the Yuezhi people and annihilated them. Now the Xiongnu were united and controlled vast tracts of Mongolia and the TARIM BASIN. The message was clear: He was negotiating from a position of strength. This peace proposal was accepted, and the Han gave Maodun, in the words of the emperor as recorded by Sima Qian, "from [their] own wardrobe an embroidered robe lined with patterned damask, an embroidered and lined underrobe, and a brocaded coat, one each; one COMB; one sash with gold ornaments; one gold-ornamented leather belt; ten rolls of embroidery; thirty rolls of brocade; and forty rolls each of heavy red silk and light green silk."

Maodun died in 174 B.C.E., the most powerful and successful of the leaders of the Xiongnu, and was interred in the remote cemetery of Khunui-göl.

Marshall, Sir John (1876–1958) *Sir John Marshall was the director-general of the Archaeological Survey of India from 1902 until 1931.*

He was aged only 26 when he took up his duties. He went to India with previous experience in the eastern Mediterranean, particularly Greece and Crete. At a time when laws were enacted to prohibit the removal and sale of antiquities and to safeguard ancient monuments, the period of Marshall's directorship saw a major increase in archaeological activity, and he excavated at many major Indian sites. His early fieldwork took him to CHARSADA in Pakistan, where he began excavations on the Bala Hisar mound, while his colleagues worked at SAHRI-BAHLOL and Takht-i-Bahi. In 1913 he commenced a program of research at TAXILA, in modern Pakistan, which to this day represents one of the most important excavations on any urban complex in India. From the outset, he resolved to uncover as much as possible of the layout and history of the three cities there. Moreover, the Greek inspiration of the second city on this site recalled his earlier experiences in Greece; he himself expressed his sentiments almost half a century later when he wrote: "I still remember the thrill I got from the first sight of the buried cities." Few archaeologists today could envisage cutting an excavation 150 (495 ft.) meters long into an early city site.

Similar large-scale excavations were also undertaken at BHITA, where he revealed the plan of a Mauryan and Gupta town that remains unparalleled to this day. From 1921, the Archaeological Survey of India was responsible for the excavations at MOHENJO DARO and HARAPPA that revealed one of the world's few civilizations that originated with no influence or contact with any other state. The early results, incorporating the recovery of SEALS inscribed in an unknown script, encouraged Marshall to state in the *Illustrated London News*, an English weekly, that a new civilization had been discovered, a civilization roughly contemporary with those of Sumer and Egypt. Nor did he delay in publishing a three-volume report on Mohenjo Daro, *Mohenjo-daro and the Indus Civilization* (1931). He ceased being the director-general in 1928 and left a legacy of fundamental research and tradition of site conservation in the history of Indian archaeology that can be called the Sir John Marshall period.

See also INDUS VALLEY CIVILIZATION; MAURYA EMPIRE.

Mashan Mashan is a cemetery of the CHU state near the capital, Ying. It is best known because of a remarkable find, that of a middle-ranking aristocratic woman who was buried between 340 and 278 B.C.E., toward the end of the period when Ying was the Chu center. The grave contained two coffins nested one within the other, and the good state of preservation was largely due to the very thick wood employed and a sealing of lime mortar that arrested the forces of decay. The outer coffin contained two compartments other than that containing the woman's corpse. These were filled with bamboo baskets containing offerings, a small dog skeleton, and figurines 60 centimeters (24 in.) high wearing silk clothing. The skeleton of the woman, who died when aged in her early 40s, was wrapped in successive layers of fabric tied into a tight bundle with nine brocade bands. Her hair and wig survived, and she had been interred fully dressed in a skirt, robe, and gown over the earliest-known underwear in China. Her thumbs and toes had been tied together with cords, and she held in her hands small rolls of silk. The most important items recovered, however, were the many varieties of woven and embroidered fabric, including designs of dragons, phoenixes, and tigers.

Mat Mat is the name of a village located on the Jumuna River, 14 kilometers (8.4 mi.) north of the great center of MATHURA in India. A substantial excavation of a mound called Tokri Tila, which lies northeast of the village, was undertaken in the early years of the 20th century. Despite much brick robbing from the site, the foundation plan of a rectangular temple measuring 48 by 32 meters (158.4 by 105.6 ft.) was reconstructed, confirming the text of two inscriptions that record the presence of a *devakula*, or temple, at this location. The building incorporates a circular chamber at the eastern end and a series of rooms around a court. A large water tank, lined with brick, was associated with the temple, and excavations there recovered the sculpture of a *naga*, a mythical snake, holding a plow. The site is best known for the recovery of a series of large stone statues of KUSHAN kings, including a nearly complete life-size statue of King KANISHKA I (100–26 C.E.).

The image of the standing king includes an inscription in the BRAHMI script that states: "The king, king of kings, his majesty Kanishka." Although lacking the head and arms, it projects an image of robust power. He holds a mace in his right hand and a huge sword in his left. He wears a knee-length tunic and a pair of heavy boots. His ornamented belt incorporated two plaques at the front. A second statue was reconstructed from several fractured pieces and, although still lacking the head, reveals a king seated on a throne flanked by lions. It stands just over two meters (6.6 ft.) in height. He seems to have been portrayed holding a sword over his right shoulder. The king had been identified as Wima I Tak [to], father of Wima Kadphises. He wore an embroidered tunic with long sleeves decorated all over with rosettes, a torque, or neck ring, and a bracelet. His boots had spurs and supporting straps. This fine statue is associated with an inscription that records the foundation of the temple, together with the water tank, a garden, and a well. The name of the king who endowed this foundation cannot be determined, but the full royal titles are included. A third statue, again missing the head and arms, depicts a prince wearing a knee-length tunic held in place by a belt with a series of interconnected plaques. Each of these is ornamented with a fish god or a man riding a horse, wearing a typical high Kushan hat, as seen on coins, and carrying a spear over his shoulder.

These statues provide an image of the power and majesty of the Kushan royal line, and the quality of the craftsmanship emphasizes the skill of the Mathura school of sculpture.

See also KHALCHAYAN.

Mathura   Mathura is a major urban center located on the western bank of the Jamuna River in Uttar Pradesh state, India. There are three sources of information on this important site. The first is from the continual and widespread looting of works of art commencing in 1836, and the second involves the scientific archaeological examination of the site and its history. Finally, there is the eyewitness account of Mathura written by the Buddhist monk XUANZANG in the early seventh century. He noted the fertility of the land and excellent agriculture. There were many mango trees, and kapok was extensively grown. The climate was hot, the people virtuous. They honored the dead and encouraged learning. The city included 20 monasteries and more than 2,000 monks, but also five Hindu temples. Three stupas at Mathura, he said, were built by King ASOKA (268–235 B.C.E.). He named the monks whose remains lay beneath stupas in the city: Sariputra, Maudgalyayana, and Purnamaitraniputra.

ARCHAEOLOGICAL EVIDENCE

Scientific archaeology, initiated in 1954 and continuing in the 1970s, has revealed five major phases of occupation, beginning in the late prehistoric Iron Age with a small settlement beside the river, a situation offering the advantages of river trade and access to good agricultural land. This first phase, which began in about 600 B.C.E., was followed in Period II with the construction of an extensive mud rampart that stood at least 6.5 meters (21.4 ft.) in height and enclosed an area of 350 hectares (875 acres). This period dates from the end of the fourth century until about 200 B.C.E. Interior structures have been uncovered, built in mud or, on occasion, burnt mud BRICK. There were bone arrowheads in the occupation layers and beads of exotic amethyst and topaz. The third period covers the last two centuries C.E. and saw further domestic constructions in baked brick, the construction of mud platforms, and the presence of roof tiles. It was, however, during Period IV, ascribed to the KUSHAN empire (78–200 C.E.), that Mathura was at the height of its cultural powers. An inner enclosure was demarcated by a rampart wall, reservoirs and temples were constructed, and inscriptions recorded donations to religious foundations, including the names of the Kushan kings KANISHKA I and Huviska. Kushan coins of this phase date to the first to the third centuries C.E., the period when the Mathura school of sculpture was active. Excavations have yielded sculptures of the Buddha, scenes from his life, a lion, and

the head of a king with Buddha figures on the crown. Further examples of Mathura sculptures are found in Period V, which has been dated to the period of GUPTA EMPIRE dominance from the fourth to sixth century.

WORKS OF ART

Another source of information on Mathura derives from the examination of works of art that do not have a known provenience. The source of red sandstone, the nearby Sikri quarry, was used by sculptors of the Mathura school, and their products are widely distributed in north and central India. The Mathura tradition developed in tandem with the other great artistic center of GANDHARA, both encouraged by the Kushan rulers, but with a clear debt to Greek inspiration. Beginning in the first century C.E., the Mathura workshops paid particular attention to the production of large and robust images of the Buddha with his arm held up in the position of offering reassurance. They also produced statues of Kushan kings, in which the ruler was depicted wearing traditional Central Asian clothing: a tunic, boots, and a distinctive conical cap. It is interesting to detect, in the depiction of female figures, the continuation of a preference for the traditional *yakshi,* or female fertility figure. These are usually seen associated with a tree.

The stone monuments that survive give no impression of the splendor that was witnessed by Xuanzang. In his own words: "On such a day offerings are made in competition to the various stupas, and pearled banners are displayed and gemmed canopies arranged in rows; the smoke of incense pervades the air like clouds, and flowers are scattered in showers that obscure the Sun and the Moon and cause great tumult in the valleys."

Maurya empire   The Maurya empire of India was established as the rulers of the state of MAGADHA defeated rivals and incorporated them in the dominant polity of the Ganges (Ganga) Valley in about 325 B.C.E. From a base in the north, these rulers, particularly ASOKA, the third king, expanded their control over much of India. The Mauryan period saw the reestablishment of urban life and widespread state control under a royal dynasty based at the capital, PATALIPUTRA. Agriculture, the mainstay of the state, was encouraged through large IRRIGATION works, and India entered an expanding sphere of trade and industry in which iron smelting played a key role. Both BUDDHISM and Hinduism grew in importance, particularly the latter under Asoka. It was he who sent Buddhist missionaries to Southeast Asia. Many of the later Indian institutions, architectural styles, religious foundations, forms of governance, and writing had their origins in the Maurya empire. There were five kings: CANDRAGUPTA MAURYA, who ruled from about 325 until 297 B.C.E.; followed by Bindusara (297–292 B.C.E.); Asoka (268–235 B.C.E.); Dasaratha (235–221 B.C.E.); and, finally,

Brihadratha. The last king was murdered by a rival ruler, Pushymitra Sunga.

LITERARY SOURCES

Any consideration of the Maurya empire is based on two major sources: literary and archaeological. The ARTHASAS-TRA of KAUTILYA (c. 330–270 B.C.E.), a minister to Candragupta Maurya, is a treatise on the management of a state and includes the gamut of activity, from the proper form of the capital city to the layout of a fort, the means of governance through ministers, foreign policy, trade, industry, and infrastructure. This is an idealistic document, and it is the role of archaeology to test the degree to which it was realized. Excavations, however, have so far only scratched the surface of the potential, particularly in the area of urban planning and city layouts.

Other literary sources include the first corpus of inscriptions, set up to proclaim the virtuous foundations and activities of Asoka, who was an enthusiastic devoté of Buddhism. His conversion, which took place about 10 years into his reign, was a vital event in the history of Buddhism and also brought about enlightened changes in the harsh and repressive Mauryan rule. These inscriptions not only describe the royal policies, but through their wide distribution provide an understanding of the extent of his kingdom. The Maurya empire also arose in the aftermath of the invasion by ALEXANDER THE GREAT (356–323 B.C.E.) of northeastern India and Pakistan. There was direct contact with the Greek empire in the east, and it is highly likely that aspects of Mauryan architecture, COINAGE, and art were influenced by the Greeks. Certainly, many Greeks visited Pataliputra, the Mauryan capital, and one, MEGAS-THENES, wrote down his impressions.

The Maurya empire forcibly absorbed other developing states. To the northeast, in modern Pakistan and Afghanistan, the BHIR MOUND at TAXILA, CHARSADA, and Nagarahara were provincial centers in the Mauryan sphere. Many formerly independent cities in the Ganges (Ganga) Valley became Mauryan dependents. The Kunwari and Pahuj Rivers link the Ganges and Jamuna Plains with Madhya Pradesh, and here are the Mauryan cities of UJJAIN, Eran, Vidisha, and Tripuri. Farther south still, the Krishna River and the valleys of its major tributaries, the Hagari and Tungabhadra, sustained a group of impressive cities, including Madhavpura and SANNATHI, both of which covered more than 40 hectares (100 acres); Brahmagiri, and BANAVISI. On the west coast of India, the potential of maritime trade was realized with the development of port cities, as it was with the long coastal tract on the east coast from Dhanyakataka to Candraketugarh on the Ganges Delta.

ARCHAEOLOGICAL SOURCES

The Kautilyan ideal of a city incorporated a royal palace in the center, surrounded by square precincts each with its own function: an elephant park, areas for merchants, artisans, and entertainment, and residences. These were protected by a city wall with forts and moats. Religious sanctuaries could be built both within the walls and beyond them, and the dead were cremated in a specified area depending on the class of the deceased. Given the monsoon climate and seasonal rainfall patterns, reservoirs were constructed, were linked to canals and often surrounding moats, and were sources for irrigated fields. The archaeological verification of the ideal has been realized only in the most limited manner, through early excavations by SIR JOHN MARSHALL at BHITA and the Bhir Mound of Taxila. At Bhita, some evidence was found in favor of a regular street plan flanked by domestic houses. A gate on the eastern wall led directly into a street on an east-west axis along which shops were located. Narrow lanes led off to north and south, each flanking a residence with rooms around a central court. The walls were constructed of fired brick, and the residents enjoyed drainage and obtained their water from deep wells. Marshall's excavations at the Bhir Mound at Taxila found a less orderly street plan, but the houses, with walls of stone, conformed to a plan of a series of rooms around a court. Excavations at Bhita concentrated on the eastern margin of the ancient city, and no sign of monumental architecture was encountered. An unpublished excavation at Taxila by SIR MORTIMER WHEELER uncovered a large apsidal structure, which might have been some form of religious building. At the imperial capital, Patilaputra, a huge pillared hall has been discovered, confirming Megasthenes' description of monumental buildings there. Little else is known of this dominant city, other than its elongated form along the southern bank of the Ganges River and the survival of the wooden components of the defensive wall. If the splendid headdresses, costumes, and jewelry of the Mauryan terra-cotta models of dancers and goddesses are a guide, the inhabitants of these cities would have been most elegant.

Further evidence for monumental architecture is gained from the Mauryan columns and surviving religious buildings. The columns were in all known cases obtained from the sandstone quarries of Chunar, west of Varanasi (Benares). They stand between 12 and 14 meters (39.6 and 46.2 ft.) high and bear a capital of carved Buddhist symbols and usually the carved figure of a lion. Their ascription to the reign of Asoka is based on the presence of his inscriptions on at least 10 examples. At both SANCHI and SARNATH, a column is associated with a Buddhist foundation. Another was transported to LUMBINI, birthplace of the Buddha, a major task, as with other remote sites, given their enormous size. The brief inscription associated with this column is interesting, because it records how Asoka visited Lumbini, worshiped there, and gave the community the advantage of paying only one-eighth of its production to the state, rather than the regulation one-sixth.

The association of Asokan columns with Buddhist sanctuaries clarifies their purpose and confirms the development of religious architecture in permanent materials. The Buddhist foundation at Sarnath has a stupa, a shrine, and a *caitya*, or hall, in addition to its column. The stupa is a widespread Buddhist form of monument, which, over the centuries, grew greatly in size and monumentality. In origin, it was a mound of earth placed over a cremation, but its significance increased as it was seen as a monument over a relic of the Buddha. The DHARMARAJIKA stupa of Sarnath was made of brick. There is also evidence for the construction of temples to the Hindu gods at Vidisa and Nagari, the former in honor of Vishnu and the latter dedicated to Krishna. Rock-cut temple shrines also date back to the Mauryan period. In Bihar, just south of Patna, the Lomas Rishi cave in the Barabar Hills has an ornate portal cut into a rectangular rock-cut chamber that in turn gives access to a circular, domed shrine room.

WRITING

The origins of writing after the demise of the INDUS VALLEY CIVILIZATION SCRIPT are not clearly defined, but the recent recovery of inscribed potsherds at ANURADHAPURA in Sri Lanka reveals that the BRAHMI script was possibly used there by 600–450 B.C.E. There are two scripts: In the northwest, the KHAROSHTHI originated in Aramaic; it is likely that the Brahmi script used over the rest of the subcontinent was adapted from an Aramaic script encountered through mercantile contact with the West. The largest corpus of inscriptions are the edicts of Asoka, but there are also texts on copper and SEALS containing the names of the owners. According to the *Arthasastra*, state records were maintained and stored, but they were presumably written on perishable materials and have not survived, Mauryan coinage was also probably inspired through direct contact with the Achaemenid provinces and through the irruption of Alexander the Great into the northwest. The coins were made of silver and copper and had fixed sizes and values.

See also ACHAEMENID EMPIRE.

Further reading: Chopra, P. N., ed. *The Gazeteer of India.* Vol. 2, *History and Culture.* New Delhi: Department of Culture, Ministry of Education and Social Welfare, 1973; Harle, J. C. *The Art and Architecture of the Indian Subcontinent.* London: Penguin Books, 1986; Mani, V. R., and R. Chakravarti. *A Sourcebook of Indian Civilization.* Hyderabad: Orient Longman, 2000; Sivaramamurti, C. *The Art of India.* New York: Harry N. Abrams, 1977.

Mawangdui Mawangdui is best known for three tombs that date to the Western HAN DYNASTY (206 B.C.E.–c. 9 C.E.) and contained the remains of a high but not supreme family in the former state of CHU. Tomb 2 contains the remains of Li Cang, the marquis of Dai and chancellor to the king of CHU; Tomb 3 was that of his son, who died when aged about 30 years. The marquis died in 168 B.C.E., and since the third tomb cuts into the earlier burials, it dates to at least 168 B.C.E. and possibly later. The contents of Tomb 1 were extraordinarily well preserved, including the body of the marchioness of Dai. No fewer than four coffins were found placed one within the next, descending in size until the innermost measured two by 0.7 meter (6 by 2.3 ft.). Each was finely constructed, covered in LACQUER, and painted with scenes that included auspicious animals and symbols. The coffin containing the corpse was covered in silk fabric, and a silk tomb banner lay on the top. This banner, preserved in its entirety and still retaining its original colors, would have been carried in front of the coffin during the funeral rituals. It is not uncommon to find the dead person portrayed on such mortuary banners in conjunction with the necessary symbols for the passage of the spirit to the heavenly world. That from Tomb 1 of Mawangdui is the best yet recovered. But perhaps even more impressive were the silk manuscripts in Tomb 3.

Not long after the establishment of the Han dynasty in 206 B.C.E., the traditions of the old kingdom of Chu remained a powerful influence. Li Cang had been given his fiefdom by the king of Changsha, a dynasty that survived in local authority but was not related to the imperial Han. Mawangdui lies in a suburb of Changsha in Hunan province of China, which under the name Linxiang was the capital of the kingdom.

TOMB 1 STRUCTURE

Tomb 1 incorporated a mound raised above the ground and measuring about 60 meters (198 ft.) in diameter. A rectangular pit lay in the center of the mound, measuring 19.5 by 18 meters (64.3 by 59.4 ft.), below which a deep shaft had been excavated to contain the remains of Xin Zhui, the marchioness. This shaft began in a rectangular form of decreasing steps, but below a depth of four meters (13.2 ft.) it assumed a funnel shape. It attained a depth of nearly 17 meters below the present ground surface and was formerly reached by a long access ramp. The coffin chamber at the base was encased in protective layers of charcoal and clay. The former was nearly a half-meter thick, the latter up to 1.3 meters deep. These had the effect of shutting out air and moisture, thereby preserving the contents in a remarkable condition. After the interment, the shaft was filled with stamped earth, following the same technique that had been used at ANYANG a millennium earlier.

The wooden mortuary structure at the base was fashioned from cypress wood; and with a length of almost seven meters and a width of five meters, it was large enough to contain a series of chambers. One of these incorporated four nested lacquered coffins that required an estimated 1 million hours to complete. The other chambers were designated for the goods necessary to sustain Xin Zhui in the afterlife.

TOMB 1 SILK BANNER

Xin Zhui is seen twice on the silk banner, once on a dais laid out before interment, surrounded by retainers and ritual offering vessels. On the second occasion, she stands in front of two figures, possibly divine messengers, supporting herself with a stick. This very stick has been found in the tomb. Three waiting maids are grouped behind her. She wears an elegant robe decorated with cloud patterns. Below both these scenes are the nether regions, represented by fish. Out of the depths rise two dragons, whose bodies pass through a jade ring as they ascend toward the heavens. The celestial world, to which the woman's soul is destined to journey, is seen on the top crosspiece. The Sun and crescent Moon are seen to right and left there, with two further dragons and goddesses. The portal through which the woman must pass is guarded by two leopards and two male figures representing the lords of fate who guarded the gate into heaven.

THE BODY IN TOMB 1

This silk banner alone would have satisfied the ambitions of most archaeologists investigating such a tomb, but there was much more to follow. The woman's body lay within, under 20 quilts and many silk garments tied with ribbons. These included a complete silk gauze robe with broad sleeves trimmed with silk braid. The corpse was so well preserved that the flesh survived, and the limbs could still be moved. Even her long black hair remained neatly coiffured, and blood remained in her veins. Indeed, it was possible to undertake an autopsy. She had stood to a height of about 1.54 meters (5 ft.) and was overweight. This might have induced her fatal heart attack, and she suffered from a compressed spinal disk and an infestation of intestinal whipworms. Other ailments included lumbago, gallstones, and tuberculosis. Her last meal had included melon, for 138 melon seeds were found in her digestive tract. The tomb contents included the ingredients for treating cardiac disorders then and now in China: magnolia bark, peppercorns, and cinnamon.

TOMB 1 OFFERINGS

The offerings to provide for the marchioness's afterlife number more than 1,000 and are among the most complete and important sets from early China. In Chu tradition, the personal articles needed for the deceased in her afterlife were placed into the tomb either as the original items she had owned or used or as replicas, such as clay coins. The marchioness of Dai's wardrobe was found, for example, sealed in bamboo cases. The quality of the silks was of the highest order, with richly embroidered gauzes and painted or printed garments. Dyeing had reached remarkable standards with a range of colors, including reds, purple, silver, gray, brown, and blue, used to depict elegant cloud designs, meanders, and scroll motifs. The clothes themselves included a fine silk dress with broad sleeves, shoes and socks, skirts, gloves, and a sachet for perfumes.

The compartment to the north of the main coffin chamber is most informative, for it contains a seat as part of a stage for a performance. There was a bamboo mat on the floor, and silk curtains hung from the walls. The couch was covered in cushions, and a painted screen had been placed behind it. It must have been intended for the lady herself, for a pair of her silk shoes was in place in front of the couch, and her cane, presumably the same as that which she holds on the tomb banner, lay beside it. There were also boxes containing her wig and cosmetics. A musical performance had been prepared for the dead woman. Wooden figurines of five musicians playing their panpipes and zithers and eight dancers were arranged in front of her place on the couch.

Intimate details of the lady's personal appearance are discovered by opening her lacquered toilet boxes. These contained compartments and little boxes. She had used these to store her hairpiece and wooden COMBS, cosmetics, a towel and belt, and silk mittens. Food to sustain the woman on her ascent to heaven was laid out on lacquered plates with the chopsticks neatly arrayed. Forty-eight baskets of food and 51 pottery vessels contained rice and wheat, beans, and lotus roots. There was a wide variety of fruits, including melons, pears, and peaches. Much meat was consumed: mutton, venison, hare, and duck. Even sparrows' eggs were neatly stored. Carp, bream, and perch were part of her table, and the cooks used soya sauce, salt, ginger, and cinnamon for seasoning. The BAMBOO SLIPS describe some of her favorite dishes, such as a stew of venison and taro as well as sturgeon.

Music was obviously enjoyed in the court of the marquis. A sophisticated 25-string zither was found in the woman's tomb, as well as mouth organ with a note on each of the 12 pipes to indicate the individual pitches. Her son's tomb also included a seven-stringed zither. Five figurines from Tomb 1 represent a musical ensemble, three kneeling musicians playing the zither and two still holding their pipes.

TOMB 3 FINDS

The tomb containing the remains of her son had suffered water damage, but much remained within. A second complete silk banner had been placed over the inner coffin, and the bamboo slips containing an inventory of the grave offerings survived. The tomb banner, slightly longer than that in Tomb 1, contained essentially the same format. Sun and Moon are depicted in the upper register, with a goddess whose lower limbs are in the form of a snake holding out a hand. The dead man is depicted walking, in the upper part of the central register. He wears a red robe and hat. Scenes presumably drawn from his life are also painted. He has six servants and is seen being welcomed by three men. There is a feasting scene and a sacrifice is being undertaken. As with the Tomb 1 banner, these scenes involved the appropriate passage to heaven. There are three other notable paintings on silk. One shows a procession incorporating hundreds of people, chariots, and horses. Another includes women in boats and houses. The last silk had been stored in a LACQUER box and showed rows of people in various postures. The bamboo slip associated with it reveals that they were engaged in deep-breathing exercises, and it is thought that it was a means of maintaining fitness. Similar activities can be seen in China to this day.

TOMB 3 SILK MANUSCRIPTS

Perhaps the most significant of the finds represent the aristocrat's library of silk manuscripts. About 120,000 characters are included, making up parts of 20 books hitherto known only from later references. This represents one of the most significant archaeological and literary finds from early China, and they reveal a man interested in philosophical writings, divination, history, and medicine. Foremost among this extraordinary collection is the oldest surviving text of the *Yijing (Classic of Changes)*. There are also two astrological almanacs known as the *Prognostications of the Five Planets* and the *Miscellaneous Prognostications of Astronomy and Meteorology*. They illustrate a detailed knowledge of the movements of the visible planets and record the passage of comets. The manuscript known as *Zhan Gue Ce* has 28 chapters that detail diplomatic activity during the WARRING STATES PERIOD (475–221 B.C.E.). There was also a practical side. One of his manuscripts provides a detailed map of the Xiang River Valley toward the south of the kingdom facing the warlike YUE tribes; another shows the principal fortified centers and can be seen as a map central to military intelligence. Leisure time was also represented, in the form of a *liubo* set, a form of board game, but one of the most arresting documents from this tomb is known as the *Zaliao fang* (Prescriptions for miscellaneous cures). It is a detailed description of the arts of sexual intercourse, including treatments for impotency and elixirs to improve performance. These are the earliest detailed and complete texts on sexual intercourse known.

See also SILK TOMB OFFERINGS.

Further reading: Chang, L. S., Yu Feng, and Ch'un Chang. *The Four Political Treatises of the Yellow Emperor: Origin Mawangdui Texts with Complete English Translations and an Introduction.* Honolulu: University of Hawaii Press, 1998; Loewe, M. *Chinese Ideas of Life and Death.* London: Allen and Unwin, 1982; Twitchet, D., and M. Loewe, eds. *The Cambridge History of China.* Vol. I, *The Ch'in and Han Empires, 221 B.C.–A.D. 220.* Cambridge: Cambridge University Press, 1986; Wang Zhongshu. *Han Civilization.* New Haven, Conn.: Yale University Press, 1982; Wu Hung. "Art in Its Ritual Context: Rethinking Mawangdui," *Early China* 17 (1992): 111–145.

Megasthenes (c. 350–290 B.C.E.) *Megasthenes was the ambassador of King Seleucus I Nicator (356–281 B.C.E.) to the court of Candragupta Maurya (325–297 B.C.E.) at Pataliputra in India.*
His observations of India were later summarized in his book *Indika*. Although the text has not survived, passages quoted by later authors provide a rare opportunity to read an eyewitness account of the country, settlements, and people. Megasthenes was much impressed by the splendor of Pataliputra and the fertility of a land that produced two crops a year. He also mentioned that peace reigned and that society was divided into castes that included philosophers, farmers, merchants, soldiers, and councilors. There was an army of informants who reported to the king.

Mehrgarh Few archaeological sites have opened such a major new vista on the past in South Asia as Mehrgarh. It is situated on the Kachi Plain of Baluchistan between Iran and India, in a position to command the Bolan Pass and therefore trade with the Iranian uplands to the west. The investigations, beginning in 1974, revealed a series of successive settlements, which cover an area of about 200 hectares (500 acres). The excavations of Mehrgarh are vital in any consideration of the origins of the INDUS VALLEY CIVILIZATION, for they reveal a very long sequence of increasing cultural complexity where previously there had been a void in the knowledge of early agriculture, pottery making, and trade.

FIRST SETTLEMENT

The earliest settlement, known as M3, incorporates 10 meters (33 ft.) of stratified deposits, known as Mehrgarh Period 1. Dating from about 7000–6000 B.C.E., this site belongs to what is known as an aceramic Neolithic, in which there is a farming economy but the inhabitants did not make fired pottery vessels. The remains of barley and wheat indicate cultivation. While the earliest faunal remains show a predominance of gazelles and other hunted animals, including elephants and water buffaloes, cattle were domesticated and began to dominate numerically as the proportion of wild animals declined. The remains of mud-BRICK houses and storerooms lay between areas in which the dead were interred. Bodies were buried, liberally covered in red ocher, in flexed position and in association with a range of grave goods. These included polished stone adzes, stone vessels, and personal ornaments that include beads of LAPIS LAZULI and TURQUOISE and, in one instance, a bead of copper. One person was accompanied by the skeletons of five young goats. The place of pottery seems to have been taken by bitumen-coated basketry, and although no fired pottery vessels were found, the inhabitants were familiar with the plastic qualities of clay in forming human and animal figurines and containers. Flint blades were the most abundant artifacts found in this early settlement. They would have been used with wood or bone to form composite artifacts.

SECOND SETTLEMENT

MR4 is a second occupation area that lies just to the south of the aceramic Neolithic mound, dated to the fifth millennium B.C.E. One of the uses of the flint blades, which were so prolific in the earliest phase of the site, was immediately indicated, since several were found still inserted in bitumen, which would in turn have been inset into a wooden handle to form a knife or sickle. Two such sickles were in fact recovered from a structure with a series of small compartments that still contained the imprints in the clay of barley and wheat grains. These structures are most logically interpreted as granaries. There are also some cottonseeds, which might well indicate interest in weaving. Craft activities included the manufacture of shell and soapstone beads and the firing of pottery vessels. Cattle ultimately dominated the faunal assemblage. Copper was still very rare.

4000 B.C.E. SETTLEMENT

By about 4000 B.C.E. the settlement focus moved to the south. There were further innovations: Houses became larger, the ceramic industry flourished, and wheelmade vessels, decorated with images of birds and goats, were created in considerable numbers. Beads were fashioned on the site from imported lapis lazuli, turquoise, and carnelian, the holes drilled with a jasper bit. The copper industry became locally established, and crucibles still containing metal were found. The subsistence base now supported a sizable population in a settlement that grew to cover an area of about 50 hectares (125 acres).

3500 B.C.E. SETTLEMENT

A further move to the south in about 3500 B.C.E. saw the foundation of Mehrgarh Site I. The domestic dwellings of mud brick, with plastered clay floors, grew in size, and some rooms contained large storage jars. The ceramic industry further strengthened with an increased output, and the earliest bone and terra-cotta SEALS, which were probably used to indicate personal ownership, occur.

3000–2700 B.C.E. SETTLEMENT

The period from 3000 until about 2700 B.C.E. has provided further evidence, in the form of an abandoned kiln, for the mass production of pottery vessels. Two hundred pots were rejected because of unsuccessful firing; they were probably intended for trade purposes. The clay figurines also provide a glimpse of the appearance of the WOMEN of Mehrgarh at this period. They wore multiple strands of necklaces and elaborate hairstyles. The final phase lasted for a century until about 2600 B.C.E. This is the period when the Indus Valley civilization of the river plains to the east of Mehrgarh was beginning to develop. The houses were now raised over a set of low storage rooms, one of which contained many pottery vessels. There was a specialized area of kilns for ceramic firing, and pots of outstanding merit were produced. Figurines now included men as well as women, once again with a variety of hairstyles and ornaments, which were painted black and yellow, respectively, on the females; men wore turbanlike headdresses and pendants around the neck. The proliferation of terra-cotta seals almost certainly reflects a further growth in trade and exchange; one of

the designs was a bull, and another was a geometric design.

Meluhha   Meluhha is the name given to one of the trading partners of the Mesopotamian kingdoms in the Tigris and Euphrates Valleys. Along with Magan and Dilmun, Meluhha is cited by Sargon of Akkad (2334–2279 B.C.E.) as the land from which ships anchored at his port. Dilmun has been identified with the land bordering the western shore of the Arabian Gulf. Magan, supplier of copper, probably lay on the shore of the Gulf of Oman. Meluhha almost certainly referred to the INDUS VALLEY CIVILIZATION, dated between 2500 and 2000 B.C.E. The Mesopotamian documentary sources make it possible to list the products imported from the Indus Valley. Carnelian is mentioned most often. The production of high-quality carnelian beads in the Indus cities is well documented archaeologically. Allahdino in Pakistan, for example, is a site that has produced outstanding carnelian ornaments. LAPIS LAZULI and pearls are also mentioned, as are bird figurines, wood, dates, copper, and gold. The texts also describe ships of Meluhhan form. SEALS and sealings of Indus type, bearing characters in the INDUS VALLEY CIVILIZATION SCRIPT, confirm an ocean trade between the Indus and the Near East. An Indus unicorn seal impression has been found at Umma. A seal with Indus script has been found at Ur, as well as others from Tell Asmar and Kish, all in Mesopotamia. The technique of etching carnelian beads was mastered in the Indus civilization, and there is clear evidence for decorating beads in this manner at CHANHU-DARO. Many etched carnelians have been found in the Near East, including the royal graves at Ur and at Kish and Nippur in Mesopotamia.

Segmented faience beads are another possible export. These are found at HARAPPA, MOHENJO DARO, and Chanhu-daro and also recur in the Mediterranean and Near East. Two specimens, one from Knossos on Crete and the other from Harappa, are chemically identical. A particular type of long bead in the form of a cylinder, made of carnelian, lapis lazuli, or terra-cotta, is most commonly found in the Indus Valley sites. At Chanhu-daro, they have been found in various stages of manufacture. Specimens have also been recovered in the Tigris–Euphrates sites, within the appropriate period.

There are many more compelling parallels between the two great civilizations. Dice, for example, were commonly found in the sites of the Indus civilization, and the RIG-VEDA describes a passion for gambling and the use of dice. These are also found, with the same pattern of numeration, at Ur and Tepe Gawra. Gold-capped stone beads have been found at Mohenjo Daro, LOTHAL, and Ur. Ceramic human figurines with movable arms link the two areas. There are shell and ivory inlays with identical heart-shaped patterns, and even the stone weights of the Indus civilization have been found in the Near East.

There is literary evidence, too, for the presence of a translator of the Indus language resident in the Near East.

Gregory Possehl has not only described these links in detail, but he has also suggested that the surge in trade and the demands for exotic jewelry and metals by the rich and powerful Tigris–Euphrates civilization contributed to the swift rise to dominance of the elite groups who developed in the Indus Valley during the first part of the third millennium B.C.E. Likewise, a later decline in demand and a slackening in the intensity of this exchange would have lessened the central role of the urban centers in the Indus civilization and hastened their demise.

Further reading: Possehl, G. L. *Harappan Civilization: A Recent Perspective.* New Delhi: Oxford University Press, 1993; ———. "Meluhha." In *The Indian Ocean in Antiquity,* edited by J. Reade. London: Kegan Paul, 1996, pp. 133–208.

Menandros (r. 155–130 B.C.E.) *Menandros, or Menander, was a* BACTRIAN GREEK *who ruled a Hellenistic kingdom with its capital at Sakala (probably Sialkot), in the modern Punjab in Pakistan.*
He exemplified the mixing of Greek and Indian customs by issuing COINAGE declaring himself a *chakravartin,* or supreme king. He is also the subject of a notable treatise known as the *Milindapanha,* dating to 150–100 B.C.E., in which the king debated BUDDHISM with the monk Nagasena, ultimately to become one of his followers.

Mencius (Mengzi) (372–c. 289 B.C.E.) *Mencius was a Chinese philosopher who followed many of the precepts of Confucianism and traveled widely to discourse with rulers and ministers about proper conduct following the course of yi "rightness," and ren, "humanity."*
The fourth century B.C.E. was part of the WARRING STATES PERIOD. Some of Mencius's conversations have survived in written form and provide a fascinating source on both his thoughts and those of various rulers of the Warring States. His philosophy centered on the basic requirements for a happy and prosperous society and the need for good agricultural practice. In a conversation with Duke Wen of the state of Teng, Mencius stressed this point. He discussed the importance of proper field boundaries. If there were corrupt officials and unfair boundaries, there would be serious problems. He then pointed out the basic truth of the relationship between the ruler and the countryside: "[W]ithout the country people, there would be no one to feed the noblemen." Land should be apportioned between the public area, tilled for payment to the central authority, and the private plots to satisfy the peasants. This notion underlines many of Mencius's basic thoughts. He declared that the people were of the greatest importance, then the soil, and the ruler was least important. Therefore, he argued, if the ruler did not behave prop-

Mencius (Mengzi) lived during the Warring States period in the fourth century B.C.E., and some of his conversations provide a glimpse into the thoughts of a one of the great Chinese philosophers. He is seen here in an 18th-century C.E. portrait. *(© Archivo Iconografico, S.A./CORBIS)*

erly toward the people, they had the right to rescind the MANDATE OF HEAVEN and overthrow him.

See also CONFUCIUS.

Further reading: Cao Raode, and Cao Xiaomei. *The Story of Mencius.* San Francisco: Foreign Language Press, 2001; Hinton, D. *Mencius.* Boulder, Colo.: Counterpoint Press, 1999; Lau, D. C., trans. *Mencius.* London: Penguin, 1970.

Meng Tian (third century B.C.E.) *Meng Tian was a general in the Qin army that defeated Qi in 221 B.C.E.*
His father and grandfather were high officials in the state of Qin during the WARRING STATES PERIOD (475–221 B.C.E.), the former leading Qin forces against the state of CHU. The defeat of Qi led to the foundation of the first Chinese empire under QIN SHIHUANGDI (259–210 B.C.E.). Six years later the emperor ordered Meng Tian to move north with a large force to counter the threat of the XIONGNU. As part of his duties to secure the borders of the empire, he was responsible for the initial construction of what was to become the GREAT WALL OF CHINA. The Qin empire saw the standardization of weights, measures, script, currency, and even the widths of roads, and it was Meng Tian who was placed in charge of constructing the great road that was intended to link the northern and southern parts of the state. However, it was never completed. With the intrigues that attended the accession of

HUHAI as second emperor, the cabal of conspirators required Meng Tian to commit suicide. This he at first refused to do, but ultimately he poisoned himself.

Mengzhuang Mengzhuang is one of the largest of the LONGSHAN CULTURE sites in the middle Huang (Yellow) River Valley. It is situated north of the Huang River in Henan province and was occupied over four periods. The first corresponds to the middle and late phases of the Longshan culture and dates from 2300 to 2000 B.C.E. The stamped-earth walls and encircling moat covered an area of about 16 hectares (40 acres), and the walls were 8.5 meters (28 ft.) thick at the base. The site was occupied during the XIA, Middle Shang, and WESTERN ZHOU dynasties.

See also SHANG STATE.

Merv Merv (now called Mary), once known as Antiochia Margiana, an oasis in southern Turkmenistan that attracted settlement from the Bronze Age to the Middle Ages, was the seat of several ancient kingdoms and the legendary home of the Aryans. The water of the oasis was a clear attraction, located as it is in the Kara-Kum Desert. Merv was strategically placed on the ancient SILK ROAD and was for centuries an important capital and military center. There are at least three successive cities at Merv. The first is known as Gyaur Kala, the walls of which enclose an area of about 400 hectares (1,000 acres). This was occupied from the sixth century B.C.E. until the 10th century C.E., when it was superceded by Sultan Kala, an Islamic Seljuk foundation. The latter was built next to its predecessor and covered an area of 650 hectares (1,625 acres). A still later city, known as Abdullah Khan Kala, was founded in 1409 C.E., more than a century after the Mongols sacked the Seljuk city.

ACHAEMENID CITY

There have been many excavations at Merv, beginning with the expedition of Raphael Pumpelly early in the 20th century. A long program of research began in the 1950s, and renewed interest and fieldwork began in 1992. These have shown that the sequence at Gyaur Kala, with its citadel of Erk Kala, began during the period of the late ACHAEMENID EMPIRE (fifth–fourth centuries B.C.E.). At that juncture, Margiana was part of a great empire that stretched from northern India to Egypt. The earliest reference to Margiana is to be found in the Bisitun, Iran INSCRIPTION of the Achaemenid Persian DARIUS THE GREAT (522–486 B.C.E.), a word meaning "grassland" or "lowland."

SELEUCID AND PARTHIAN CITY

The collapse of the Persian empire at the hands of ALEXANDER THE GREAT (356–323 B.C.E.) led to the foundation of a Hellenistic city on the site. The Seleucid king Antiochus Soter (r. 281–261 B.C.E.) had a defensive wall built round the city. The roughly square walls were two kilometers square, and each contained a city gate. Within, along Seleucid forms of town planning, the roads formed a grid pattern. The Seleucid kingdom was relatively short lived, and Merv was to fall to the Parthians. They had their own mint in the city and defended it with a line of forts along the northern edge of the oasis. This third phase belongs to the first to second centuries B.C.E., and it is possible that some of the prisoners taken at the Parthian defeat of the Roman forces at Carrhae (53 B.C.E.) were settled in Merv.

SASSANIAN CITY

The decline of Parthian power saw Merv change hands yet again, this time to the SASSANIAN EMPIRE, whose occupation lasted until the fifth century C.E. Under the Sassanian kings Shapur I (r. 241–272 C.E.) and Shapur II (r. 309–379), the oasis city was placed in the hands of a military governor, or *marzban*. It was during this phase that the Durnaly fortress in the northern outskirts of Merv was constructed. Christianity flourished there, and by the fifth century there was a metropolitan bishop in residence. BUDDHISM also penetrated as far west as Merv, but no farther. The fourth-century stupa and associated monastery there constitute the westernmost such foundation known.

ARAB CONQUEST

Late Sassanian occupation took the history of Merv to the seventh century, a difficult time because of the appearance of the HEPHTHALITE HUNS. Merv was in the eye of this storm, and it is highly likely that it was from this base that the Sassanian emperor Peroz (459–84) marched to his catastrophic defeat at the hands of the Huns. However, Sassanian power was restored by Khusrau I (531–79), and Merv continued in its traditional role as a military and trading city until 651, when the expanding power of the Arabs led to the death, near Merv, of the last Sassanian king, Yazdigird III. Under new Arab rule, Gyaur Kala continued as the capital of the region until the 10th century.

The economy of this nodal center on the Silk Road linking China with Rome and India depended not only on trade but also on agriculture. Many major irrigation canals are found in the area of the oasis. Merv was also the location of a mint. Coins covering many centuries of its history have been recovered during excavations.

Further reading: Bader, A., V. Gaibov, and G. Koshelenko. "The Northern Periphery of the Merv Oasis," *Silk Road Art and Archaeology* III (1993/1994): 51–70; Herrmann, G. *Monuments of Merv: Traditional Building of the Karakum.* London: Society of Antiquaries of London, 1999.

Metal-Bound Coffer The *Metal-Bound Coffer* is a text in the *Classic of Documents* and was probably written in the fifth or fourth century B.C.E. It describes an incident that clearly illustrates the attitudes of the early Zhou dynasty nobles about their recent overthrow of the SHANG STATE. In 1045, the Zhou defeated the last Shang king, who had a well-deserved reputation for cruelty and depravity. Legitimization of the new dynasty was provided by the MANDATE OF HEAVEN, whereby heaven decreed that any ruler who failed to observe righteous and caring benevolence toward his people would be replaced by a new lineage imbued with higher moral force. The duke Zhou, the text states, offered his own life in return for the recovery of the ailing king who had been given the Mandate of Heaven. He took soundings of the ORACLE BONES that returned a unanimously favorable prognostication and so lived, while the king himself recovered on the following day.

Mikumo Mikumo is a settlement and cemetery site of the middle to late YAYOI culture (300 B.C.E.–300 C.E.) of Japan, with evidence for continued occupation into the Kofun period (300–710 C.E.). It is located in northern Kyushu, on a ridge flanked by two streams that cross a rich area of rice fields. This is the area geographically most exposed to influence from the mainland, particularly the PAEKCHE and SHILLA states of Korea and the preceding Chinese LELANG commandery. In the 1820s, a jar containing 35 mirrors of Chinese HAN DYNASTY manufacture was found, together with a bronze spear and sword. This was some of the first evidence for a major cultural transformation in Japan, wherein intensive rice farming, metallurgy, and increasing trade contributed to the development of states. Excavations at Mikumo from 1975 have recovered more Chinese Han mirrors, artifacts that later Japanese accounts suggest gave the owner special magical status. House plans, either circular or rectangular, were also traced, along with burials dug in their vicinity. The dead were placed inside either two ceramic vessels or stone-lined pits. The richer graves contained glass beads, iron arrowheads, gilt bronzes, and mirrors as mortuary offerings, but the presence of many poor graves suggests that social differentiation was already well developed by middle Yayoi times.

milfoil Milfoil stalks were used in China as a means of divination from at least the beginning of the Zhou dynasty (1045–256 B.C.E.) and quite possibly earlier. This school of divination, which was employed alongside the well-known use of turtle ORACLE BONES, used stalks of the yarrow, a plant with magical properties. The plant is long lived, and the stalks grow to a great length. It was said that when there were peace and harmony and the king was ruling under the MANDATE OF HEAVEN, the yarrow plant would grow to a great height and produce many stalks.

Specialists in milfoil divination would take 50 stalks and remove one. Then they divided the remainder into two groups and reduced each group by four stalks at a time until between zero and four remained. They would form a line with the residue. Repeating this procedure six times allowed the formation of a hexagram to provide the basis for answering questions and divining the future. The philosophical basis for milfoil divination changed markedly over time. An example of the application of milfoil divination is in a tomb text from BAOSHAN, dated to the WARRING STATES PERIOD (475–221 B.C.E.). In 316 B.C.E., the diviner Wu Sheng pronounced on the illness of the tomb master, Shao Tuo, who had difficulty in eating and a heart ailment. The finding of the milfoils was that the illness could be cured by prayers and sacrifice of five cattle and five pigs. His prediction of the likelihood of a cure was auspicious.

Mingalazedi stupa The Mingalazedi stupa at PAGAN in Myanmar (Burma) was built in 1284 by King Narathihapati. It is raised on four rectangular terraces, each with a supplementary stupa at the corners. The walls of the terraces are decorated with plaques depicting JATAKA stories.

Mingdi (Liu Xang; Brilliant Emperor) (28–75 C.E.) *Mingdi was the second emperor of the Eastern Han dynasty of China.*
He was the son of GUANG WUDI, the founder of the dynasty, and his second empress, Yin Lihua. He acceded to the throne in 57 C.E. In general, Mingdi received a poor press from early historians. He was accused of being narrow minded, and his court was filled with fear and repression. Many were punished on specious grounds, and there are reports of considerable extravagance in the construction of new palaces. It was, however, also the case that major public works of considerable benefit were initiated, not least the restoration of the dikes that restrained the flow of the Huang (Yellow) River. It was also under the reign of Mingdi that the Chinese empire began a further period of expansion that was to involve more occupied territory than ever before. Under the great general Bao Chao, the TARIM BASIN west of the Jade Gate was taken and absorbed. This gave China increased control over and access to the SILK ROAD and its trade links with the West.

mingqi Mingqi is a Chinese term that came into vogue during the WARRING STATES PERIOD (475–221 B.C.E.) to describe a spirit object placed into a grave of a person of high status. It contrasts with a *shenqi*, which was an item used during the lifetime of the deceased, and a *jiqi*, a piece of sacrificial equipment. It was customary to display mortuary goods before the funeral and to list them, often on BAMBOO SLIPS that were then positioned inside the tomb. *Mingqi* had many forms. Bronze vessels, for example, could be represented in clay. Ceramic vessels would be copied but would not be functional. They were often fired at a low temperature so that the vessels could not contain water or jugs could not pour. This was deliberate, as has been described in the *Li ji*. Musical instruments could be stringed, but not in tune. Chime stones or bells could be used, but without a stand. Tomb 13 at the Yan state cemetery of Wuyang illustrates this clearly, for 135 pottery imitations of bronze vessels were included as offerings, and pottery vessels were fired at too low a temperature to be useful. The Guo lineage cemetery of Shangcunling in Henan province, dated to the early EASTERN ZHOU DYNASTY (770–221 B.C.E.), shows that some of the miniature bronzes in elite graves represented earlier ritual practices. Poorer graves contained *mingqi* ceramic vessels.

HUMAN BEINGS

The concept of *mingqi* also applied to human beings. Whereas formerly people were sacrificed and interred with the high-status tomb master, figurines began to represent the servants and followers required in the afterlife. Their purpose is seen in a grave inventory from Wangshan, where they were described as dead servants. The replacement of real people by spiritual representations, however, was gradual. At Langjiahung, for example, 26 people were included in the grave, 17 of whom were young WOMEN in their own individual coffins. The remainder had been butchered or immolated while still alive. This suggests a contrast between those chosen to accompany the master in the next world and others who were sacrificial victims. At the CHU tomb of Changtaiguan, however, figurines were found in a series of rooms around the main tomb chamber. Wooden models of drivers were found in the stable and cooks in the kitchen. Richly dressed clerks or scribes had been placed in the master's study and a guard in the storeroom.

CLOTHING

Mingqi also applied to clothing. Where organic material has survived, as at Mazhuan, the corpse was dressed in specially made spirit clothes including embroidered silks. *Mingqi* can also be a profitable source of information on changing ritual practices. For example, the change during the period of the Zhou dynasty from ritual use of music to music as entertainment can be seen in the inclusion of *mingqi* musical instruments in mortuary contexts. Thus small representations of bells and chime stones were placed in burials, in many cases of inferior materials.

See also TOMB MODELS AND RELIEFS.

Miran Miran is one of the major sites of the kingdom of SHAN-SHAN, which controlled the cities of the oases of the eastern TARIM BASIN between the first century B.C.E. and the mid-fifth century C.E. The kingdom was always under threat of coercion from the Chinese on the one hand and the nomadic XIONGNU on the other. Particularly during periods of Chinese power, trade along the SILK ROAD flourished, carrying both goods and ideas to Shan-shan from east and west. In 1906 SIR AUREL STEIN came across the site of Miran whose ancient name under the Shan-shan kings is not known, while seeking the location of a site known from Chinese records to have been a major Shan-

shan center. It was located in a bleak and arid desert, but his research that began the following year revealed that formerly the site lay between two rivers, long since dried up, and that canals had moved water to the site. Miran had about 15 Buddhist structures, including small stupas set within walled enclosures, and monasteries. Virtually all that is known of the site depends on Sir Aurel Stein's fieldwork of 1907 and 1914. On clearing the interior of two of the stupa shrines, known as Miran Structures III and V, he uncovered some remarkable paintings. These depicted winged men of distinctly Western appearance; the image of a prince leaving his palace gates on horseback, watched from a window by his wife and children; and a man fighting with a centaur. There is also a rendition of the Buddha, again of distinctly Western appearance, with dark hair and a small mustache, accompanied by six disciples. A text in the KHAROSHTHI script identifies the artist of one of these sets of paintings as Tita, who was paid for his efforts. The style of the paintings indicates a date in the third century C.E., when Shan-shan prospered under peaceful conditions; the paintings show strong influence from eastern Roman and Gandharan schools. A monastery wall that was part of Structure II incorporated a row of massive seated Buddha figures, which, together with some detached modeled heads, belong to a rather later date in the fourth century C.E. This confirms what was known from the reports of the monk FAXIAN, visiting Shan-shan on his passage to India in 399 C.E.: BUDDHISM flourished still under royal patronage.

See also GANDHARA.

Mogao Mogao is located about 25 kilometers (15 mi.) from DUNHUANG on the eastern margin of the TARIM BASIN in western China.

A center of Buddhist monastic life, Mogao has about 1,000 caves cut into the rock, some embellished with sculptures and mural paintings and used for Buddhist worship. The painted caves bear scenes of the Buddha's life, JATAKA TALES depicting his previous existences, and illustrations of aspects of life over the period of a millennium. There are also Buddha images that follow the varying artistic styles as they developed over the centuries, for these caves were often sponsored by noble families, groups of merchants, and, on occasion, members of the royal family of China. While the wall paintings and sculptures alone make Mogao one of the supreme sanctuaries of Buddhist art, the documents hidden around 1000 C.E. in the face of Arab expansion add a unique new dimension to the historic record. They not only represent many centuries in the development of BUDDHISM, but they also include letters, poems, paintings on silk, banners, and other memorabilia. Mogao was a strategic location during the course of the first millennium C.E., because it commanded a vital staging post on the SILK ROAD, the great trading route that linked the empires of East and West. At Dunhuang, the traveler heading to the west had the choice of following the route to the north of the Tak-lamakan Desert via BEZEKLIK and Kuqa or KAXGAR or the southern route through MIRAN, NIYA, and HOTAN. In the opposite direction, any merchant caravan on reaching Dunhuang would have successfully traversed the most arduous and difficult sector of the Silk Road. This region was also the westernmost extremity of the GREAT WALL of China, while the Jade Gate was seen as the symbolic and physical entry into China itself.

THE CAVES

Mogao is a long cliff facing a perennial stream that encourages a luxuriant vegetation on the very edge of the desert. Mogaoku, "peerless caves," is the most fabulous of all the Buddhist monastic sanctuaries on the ancient Silk Road. It is said to have been founded by the monk Yuezun, who in 366 C.E. was attracted to its solitude compared with the bustling border post of Dunhuang, and he cut out a cell in the rock as a location of meditation. Other monks soon followed him, and for a 1,000 years Mogao was a center of Buddhist monastic life. For those who had survived the harsh conditions and banditry of the journey around the desert, here was an opportunity to give thanks and make offerings. Those traveling in the opposite direction could pray and give donations to ensure safety in the journey that lay ahead.

Ultimately, about 1,000 caves were cut into the rock, some large enough only for a single cell for meditation, others of sufficient size for large congregations. Two groups are recognized: the northern and the southern. The latter, numbering almost 500, have painted decoration and are distributed over a distance of more than a kilometer. The 248 caves in the northern sector are not painted and were largely ignored until excavations were undertaken between 1988 and 1995. The caves can be divided into four groups. A few were used for storage. Meditation caves included an antechamber and individual cells equipped with a couch and often a platform. The residential caves were relatively spacious, with high ceilings, a stone fireplace and flue, and a bed. Wall niches were cut to receive lamps to illuminate the interior. There were also burial caves, typically low and small, containing cremated ashes. Rarely, a residential cave was converted for mortuary use, with the flue blocked.

THE PAINTINGS

The caves lie in serried rows and tiers one above the other, overlooking the stream valley below. Despite the ravages of this harsh desert environment, many paintings have survived in remarkably good condition. One, for example, shows a caravan crossing the desert and being attacked by brigands. Another specifically identifies the famous seventh-century monk XUANZANG on his return journey to China, accompanied by an auspicious white elephant. Another shows a tranquil domestic building in a courtyard. Horses are being stabled in the foreground,

while two oxen haul a plow in the distance. The caves of Mogao thus are a pictorial guide through a millennium of Silk Road history. Some paintings date to the Northern Liang dynasty that controlled the area in the early fifth century C.E. It was during this period that the painting depicting the future Buddha having his own flesh cut away to save the life of a dove, one of the most notable of the *jataka* stories, was created.

Many caves were founded during the life of the Northern Wei dynasty of China (386–535 C.E.). There were vicissitudes as well as periods of tranquility. During the late sixth century, there was a reaction against Buddhism under the Northern Zhou dynasty, and it is reported that some monasteries that were located in front of the cliff face were destroyed. However, the accession of the Sui dynasty in 589 brought this period of difficulty to an end. What could be described as the golden age of Mogao followed during the Tang dynasty (618–907 C.E.), and during this period the famous monk Xuanzang embarked on his epic journey to India and returned to be welcomed at Dunhuang. In 695 the empress Wu ordered the construction of a giant statue of the Buddha 33 meters (109 ft.) high at Mogao. In the late eighth century, with Yang power on the wane, Mogao came under the control of the empire of Tibet, a dominance that lasted until 848 C.E. Thereafter, under a series of local rulers, caves continued to be commissioned or restored until about 1000 C.E., when the Arabs seized Hotan and threatened further expansion to the east. Their aversion to images and representations of deities was probably responsible for the precautionary secreting of precious documents and paintings behind a sealed door in Cave 16.

WESTERNERS AT MOGAO

During the course of the late 19th century, the existence of the painted shrines of Mogao drew the attention of Western explorers. In 1879, the Russian Nikolay Przhevalisky visited Dunhuang and admired the paintings. It was not, however, until 1900 that the local abbot Wang Yuanlu noticed the concealed entrance to the chamber where the documents had been secreted away 1,000 years earlier. Wang Yuanlu was aware of the significance of his discovery and recommended that the cache be taken to Lanzhou for safekeeping. This was not to be, and in 1907 SIR AUREL STEIN, already well aware of their existence but not knowing of the quantity or their historic significance, arrived at Mogao. In the words of Sir Leonard Woolley, his arrival heralded "the most daring and adventurous raid upon the ancient world that any archaeologist has attempted." Stein could not read Chinese, but his secretary was able to examine some of the documents and discovered that some were of inestimable historic importance, being Buddhist texts translated into Chinese 1,200 years previously by the famous monk Xuanzang. Stein then played on the credulity of his host and persuaded him that such texts should be returned to India, their original home. For an outlay of 130 pounds he obtained 13,000 complete or partial manuscripts as well as paintings and embroidered fabrics of outstanding quality. Presently in the British Museum, in London, England, this assemblage threw a new light on Chinese history and the practice of Buddhism from the early fifth to 10th century.

Sir Aurel Stein's inability to read Chinese was, however, a major impediment to appreciating the significance of individual items. Paul Pelliot, however, the next Western scholar to visit Dunhuang, was the most brilliant Sinologist of his day, and in 1908 he pored over the large collection of manuscripts still at Mogao before selecting the choicest and most important for removal to the Musée Guimet and the National Library of France in Paris. The remainder were ultimately to be housed away from predatory foreigners in Beijing.

This was not, however, the end of these cultural raids. The American art historian Langdon Warner visited Mogao in the 1920s and hacked a number of wall paintings from the caves and took them back to the Fogg Museum of Harvard University in the United States. Today, despite the loss of so much, the Chinese authorities have established a research center at the site of the Buddhist shrines, and visitors are permitted to visit a selection of the many caves that can veritably be described as the Sistine Chapel of early Buddhist art.

See also HAN DYNASTY.

Further reading: Peng Jinzhang. "New Archaeological Discoveries in the Northern Area of the Mogao Caves at Dunhuang," *Orientations* 32 (2001): 72–75; Rhie, M. M. *Later Han, Three Kingdoms and Western Chin in China and Bactria to Shan-shan.* Leiden: Brill, 1999; Whitfield, R., S. Whitfield, and N. Agnew *Cave Temples of Mogao: Art and History on the Silk Road.* Los Angeles: Getty Conservation Institute and the J. Getty Museum, 2000.

Mohenjo Daro   Mohenjo Daro, one of the great cities of the INDUS VALLEY CIVILIZATION, is located west of the Indus River in the Sind province of Pakistan. Sir John Marshall's excavations, directed in the field by R. D. Banerji, revealed brick structures, stone SEALS with an undeciphered script, stone cubes that he thought were a series of weights, and terra-cotta toys. His publication of the seals and the announcement of the discovery of a major new world civilization in 1924 inspired comment among scholars who worked in the Tigris and Euphrates sites that similar seals had been unearthed there. This find provided an indication that the civilization belonged in the third millennium B.C.E. Further parallels, together with radiocarbon dates, now place the occupation of Mohenjo Daro within the period 2500–2000 B.C.E. The name Mohenjo Daro means "mound of the dead men," and the area and its archaeological potential had been recognized by Henry Cousens

Mohenjo Daro, "mound of the dead men," was one of the major cities of the Indus Valley civilization. There are two mounds, one of which contains elite buildings. Houses were equipped with a sophisticated drainage system. *(Borromeo/Art Resource, NY)*

in 1897. In 1911 D. R. Bhandakar had visited the site and found it most disappointing. He concluded that it was no more than 200 years old. In 1920 R. D. Banerji took a more sanguine view of the site, noting the huge extent and height of the mound and the fact that it had been quarried for BRICKS over many generations. The villagers described how the mound had formerly been capped by a huge brick platform bearing the foundations of circular buildings. Banerji suggested that the site had lain on both banks of the Indus River, and his fieldwork there in 1921–22 began a series of excavations there that continued under the aegis of SIR JOHN MARSHALL and the ARCHAEOLOGICAL SURVEY OF INDIA until 1931. SIR MORTIMER WHEELER worked there briefly in 1950, and George Dales likewise 14 years later. Further research was initiated in 1979, and currently nearly a third of the site has been examined in one way or another.

EXCAVATIONS

There are two separate mounds at Mohenjo Daro. The smaller, to the west, is sometimes known as the stupa mound or the mound of the great bath. A Buddhist monument was placed there long after the site was abandoned; the bath was one of several large ceremonial structures that capped this part of the site. The eastern, larger mound was largely a residential and industrial area. Both mounds appear to have been surrounded by massive mud-brick walls.

Deep soundings undertaken in 1964 revealed that cultural layers lie up to 11.7 meters (38.6 ft.) below the present surface of the Indus floodplain. Because the water table has risen with the accumulation of riverine alluvia, the lowest layers are very difficult to expose as a result of the inflow of water, nor is the full extent of the city known: Visible remains cover about 100 hectares (250 acres), but further occupation areas are known to lie under the alluvium beyond the raised mounds. The height of cultural material above the plain, when added to that below, means that the stratigraphic sequence is more than 22 meters (72.6 ft.) deep. This extreme depth is largely due to the choice of building material. Houses were constructed of brick and timber, and when these collapsed or needed replacement, the simplest procedure was to level the structure and build on top of it. Moreover, the people of Mohenjo Daro also constructed huge mud-brick platforms on which were located public buildings, and this is particularly apparent on the western mound, where many such structures have been uncovered. The bathhouse is the easiest to interpret. The pool itself is 12 by seven meters (39.6 ft.) in extent and was lined with a layer of bitumen to ensure against leaks. A deep well in an adjacent chamber probably supplied the water.

Acropolis

A series of colonnaded rooms lies alongside the bath, which was probably used for ritual cleansing rather than for recreation. Immediately to the west is a further large civic building, which Wheeler labeled a granary. There is no supporting evidence for this conclusion in the form of cereal remains or storage facilities, and in fact the structure could just as well have been a columned hall or a temple. There are other large buildings on this acropolis, all laid out on a north-south axis, and they contrast markedly with the domestic quarters seen in the lower city. The size and quality of these buildings point strongly in the direction of there being a special area that served the elite, but the nature of the higher echelons of Mohenjo Daro society remains speculative in the absence of translated historic records, royal graves, or even evidence of later folklore. It is not known whether there was a royal dynasty, an oligarchy, or a town council. However, some surviving statues do show what seem to be high-status men wearing hair fillets and cloaks, while the seals also depict gods and worshipers. The INSCRIPTIONS on the seals are thought most probably to be personal names of the highly ranked, but this interpretation is speculative.

Lower City

That the community of Mohenjo Daro, which might have included between 20,000 and 40,000 people during the height of its prosperity, was divided into social classes is supported by an examination of the houses in the lower city. The scale of the excavations at this site is well illustrated in the work undertaken during the 1926–27 season under the direction of Rai Bahadur Daya Ram Sahni. An area of 150 by 133 meters (495 by 439 ft.) was exposed to a depth of seven meters, incorporating three building phases. As the city plan emerged from the excavation, it became apparent that the area incorporated a main street running on a north-south axis. It extended for at least 300 meters (990 ft.), and various artifacts lay on its surface, including copper amulets, beads, and spear- and arrowheads. To the west lay a series of 66 buildings, divided by narrow lanes in an orderly, but not precise, geometric grid. The houses of the earliest of the three phases were well constructed, with large rooms and high ceilings. One particularly fine building had as many as 35 rooms around a court 19 by 16 meters (62.7 by 52.9 ft.) in extent. It was possible to ascertain the ceiling height as being 3.15 meters (10.3 ft.) in one room by the presence of the holes to take the wooden beams. The walls above this height were part of an upper story. It was found to contain 18 well-cut stone rings with a hole in the middle and two stone plugs with rounded heads that would have fit in the holes in the rings. Their function is unknown, but they may have been LINGAMS and yonis, so familiar in much later Indian and Southeast Asian contexts as representing the male and female genitalia. Two steatite seals were also found in this large house, which must have been occupied by an affluent member of the community.

Immediately to the north, another house lay on the corner of the main street and a narrow lane. A visitor entering the front door from the street would have found herself or himself in a small lobby with a well in one corner. A set of stairs went up to the first floor, and under the stairs there was a small room about one meter square equipped with a drain. This was probably the latrine. A passage divided the rest of the house into two parts and led directly to the bath. Sahni suggested that two living rooms were located on the northern side of the corridor, and a kitchen lay to the south. A seal was found in the debris in the house. By leaving through the front door and turning left into a narrow lane, the occupants could visit a street lined with shops.

Drainage

Many houses had their own wells, lined with bricks of a special wedge shape to add strength. Some were as deep as 10 to 15 meters, and grooves on the surface of the bricks lining the top layer reveal where the rope pulled up a bucket. Access from the street often involved a step to gain access through the front door. More opulent homes were also equipped with baths lined with specially shaped bricks and plaster. Water was flushed through drains set in the thickness of the walls to connect with the municipal drainage system. Latrines took the form of large ceramic vessels with a hole in the base, and wastes were removed through an internal drainage system. The visitor to the city could take advantage of strategically placed public wells.

Evidence of Crafts and Trade

The drainage system is a well-known feature of Mohenjo Daro, but the city was also a manufacturing center, incorporating workshops for making STEATITE seals, beads, marine-shell inlays, ceramics, cloth, and copper and bronze artifacts. There must also have been markets for the sale of produce from the surrounding countryside, where wheat and barley would have grown on the alluvial soils enriched by the silt deposited annually by floodwater. Cattle predominate in faunal collections and were popular motifs on the steatite seals and in models, virtually all of which depict bulls rather than cows. The widely adopted system of weights and measures would have ensured fair trading, except that at least one weight in a series of stone cubes of ascending size appeared too light. The steatite seals added security to trade; the clay sealings themselves were backed by impressions of fabric or cordage.

Evidence of Daily Life

As the major excavations of the 1920s proceeded, so were many aspects of life in the city and the appearance of its inhabitants illuminated. Marshall made the point that two major rivers then flowed where now there is only the Indus and that the area was therefore better watered. He noted that the wheat remains were similar to that grown in the region today and that the inhabitants ate bread and the meat of cattle, pigs, and sheep, and a large quantity of freshwater fish and dried sea fish. There were two varieties of dog, one of which was

very large and probably used in hunting tiger, rhinoceros, and elephant. The horses were relatively small. The excavation of individual houses provided glimpses of domestic life. Many spindle whorls, for example, were encountered. These were attached to a spindle to facilitate drawing out a thread from a mass of cotton and together with surviving fragments of cotton cloth show that spinning and weaving were undertaken in the home. The Greek and Babylonian words for cotton, *sindon* and *sindhu*, could indicate that cotton fabrics were also exported. The human figurines show that men wore a kilt and a shawl that covered the left shoulder but passed under the right armpit. They were bearded but did not have mustaches. Ornaments were very popular, particularly necklaces, earrings, bangles, and anklets. Gold, silver, ivory, faience, steatite, carnelian, and jadeite were used, and composite belts of gold and carnelian are the most impressive of all jewelry. Two silver vessels wrapped in cotton cloth and a copper vase were found in one of the domestic rooms. The former contained jewelry, the latter a copper ax and chisels. The jewelry included gold earrings, gold disks for placing in the ear lobes, three gold diadems, nearly 300 gold beads, beads of faience and silver, and many other gold components of hair ornaments and necklaces.

END OF THE CITY

Little is known of the reasons for the abandonment of this great city in about 2000 B.C.E. Many other cities in Sind and the western Punjab, including HARAPPA, were also deserted at about the same time, although the Indus civilization settlements continued unabated to the east. In the uppermost layer of the site, Dales encountered clear evidence for the burning of a house. The wooden doorjambs had suffered a conflagration, pottery vessels littered the floor, and in a narrow lane five skeletons lay among the burnt debris of houses. Fourteen skeletons were found in a room in one of the houses of the lower city. Yet there is no evidence to date these remains, and they could well represent late burials with no reference to massacre in any shape or form. In the past, such evidence has been linked with the invasion of Indo-Aryan warriors who allegedly wrought the destruction of the cities of the Indus civilization, but this theory is no longer tenable because of a complete lack of evidence. Other theories to explain abandonment include an accumulation of river water due to tectonic movements, followed by a massive flood, but this interpretation has not stood the test of time either. It is, however, possible that salinization and overexploitation of the agricultural soil might have been a contributory factors.

Further reading: Dales, G. F. "The Mythical Massacre at Mohenjo Daro," *Expedition* 6 (1964): 36–43; Kenoyer, J. M. *Ancient Cities of the Indus Civilization.* Oxford: Oxford University Press, 1998; Marshall, J. *Mohenjo-Daro and the Indus Civilization.* Ottawa: Asian Educational Ser-

---

vices, 1996; Wheeler, R. E. M. *Early India and Pakistan.* London: Thames and Hudson, 1959.

Mojiaoshan Mojiaoshan is a large site of the LIANGZHU CULTURE, located on the northern margin of Hangchow Bay, central China. Excavations there in 1991–92 revealed a major center covering an area of more than 30 hectares (75 acres). It was founded in the early fourth century B.C.E. and was probably defended by a moat rather than walls. The Liangzhu culture of the lower Chang (Yangtze) Valley has many settlements that indicate a marked development of social ranking. Some graves were very richly endowed with jade offerings, and the size and presence of stamped-earth building foundations at Mojiaoshan are important indications of this trend.

mokkan A *mokkan* is a wooden tablet bearing a written statement, found in the Japanese state of YAMATO by the second half of the seventh century C.E. and in considerable quantities during the period when HEIJO-KYO was the capital (710–84 C.E.). First recognized at Yui in 1928, *mokkan* were found in quantity at the Heijo palace at NARA (710–794 C.E.) in 1961. One of the first to be discovered was a request for supplies by a court lady. *Mokkan* have opened a new and exciting chapter in the study of documentary sources that illuminate early Japanese civilization. The vast majority are from Nara, but hundreds of other sites have also yielded them. Before their discovery, the study of documents relating to the Yamato state had been based largely on the NIHONGI, a historic tract completed in 720 C.E., which drew on earlier sources long since lost. The minute study of this text by historians had reached its effective limit, but many areas of disagreement remained. The *mokkan* records have contributed fresh information of considerable importance. One such contentious area, for example, is the nature of the so-called TAIKA REFORM. These edicts, which were said to have been issued in 646 C.E., had the effect of putting the Yamato administration in line with that in Tang China, with particular attention paid to the taxation system and the organization of rural communities. Some historians found the relevant passages in the *Nihongi* inconsistent with this date. However, the discovery of contemporary records on the wooden tablets confirms the mid-seventh century date.

MOKKAN TYPES

Mokkan were fashioned from cedar or cypress wood to a length of between five and 20 centimeters (8 in.). The longest reach about one meter in length. One of these, sharpened at one end, announced the disappearance of a horse and may have been stuck in the ground so that passersby could learn of the loss and look out for the stray animal. The *mokkan* were recycled, sometimes on many occasions, by shaving off the existing text to make way for a new one. Thus they were shortened or became wafer thin. The texts vary. Some are official documents. Many are labels attached to cloth, shellfish, seaweed, rice, or iron delivered as tax goods to the court. There were passports to permit travel and orders issued from the court. They open the fine details of the administration and tax system to analysis. The capital at Nara employed an army of bureaucrats to follow the emperor's administrative demands, as promulgated in the Taiho code of 702 and the longer Yoro code of 720 C.E. How these were implemented and the mechanics of this administrative machine were little known until a hoard of more than 12,000 *mokkan* were discovered just outside the Nara palace.

Employee Records

The Taiho Code announced 30 grades and nine ranks of bureaucrats. Records of individuals included their name, present rank, length of service, number of days worked, age, and an assessment of performance. One employee named Takaya no Muraji Yakamaro, for example, was aged 50 at the time of his annual assessment, which graded his performance as average. He had worked for 1,099 days over the previous six years, meaning that he was a part-time worker as described in the Taiho code. His performance would have earned him a one-step promotion. Other individual records show that the sons or grandsons of the nobility could enjoy a higher entry level and accelerated promotion prospects when compared with Takaya. This system tended to perpetuate rule by an elite aristocratic group, while allowing people of the lower class the opportunity to pursue a career in government.

Shipping Records

Wooden tags were attached to goods shipped to the capital in payment of tax dues. The tags noted the origin of the goods, normally in terms of a village or district rather than an individual. Rice was clearly important, and the bales sent to the center would have fed not only the court and administration, but also the people deployed there as corvée workers. Other labels mention a wide range of payments in kind. Abalone shellfish, jellyfish, seaweed, and bonito were from coastal groups, and iron, hoes, salt, and bean paste are mentioned.

Domestic Records

A highly significant cache of about 35,000 *mokkan* was discovered in August 1988, when the foundations for a new department store were being excavated. This was located in the aristocratic center of Nara city, just southeast of the royal palace precinct. Someone seems to have dumped them by the eastern gate to a large and opulent private residence. They cover the activities of the household of a royal prince named Nagaya (684–729 C.E.) and his wife, Princess Kibi, during the years 711–716 C.E. He was a grandson of Emperor TEMMU (631?–86 C.E.) and a high minister in the court of Emperor Shomu (r. 742–749 C.E.)

and thus entitled to a household maintained at state expense. His principal wife, Kibi, was a granddaughter of Emperor Temmu but by a different son than her husband and a sister of Emperor Mommu. She was of higher rank than her husband. The records should be read in conjunction with the excavation of his compound, which incorporated at least 30 buildings. This household was sustained by dedicated tax payments from more than 200 ascribed rural estates, where peasant and slave workers produced the rice and other goods required. The prince also owned timber and salt-making enterprises. Some of his land appears to have been inherited, but other estates were probably ascribed him by the state because of his rank. We learn that he maintained at the capital specialists in the production of leather goods, BRONZE CASTINGS, dyers, cooks, makers of arms and musical instruments, and sculptors. There were also grooms, falconers, and dog handlers.

More than 70,000 *mokkan* dating to 732–739 C.E. have been found in a second aristocratic household at Nara, this one probably belonging to Fujiwara no Maro. He was a minister of war, and his records include the provision of many services, from guards for the royal palace to rats to feed his falcons.

A small number of *mokkan* were used for practicing calligraphy and even for drafting images. One of the latter, dated to 738 C.E., is the earliest-known Japanese landscape. It shows a compound incorporating three walls, a lily pond, and elegant halls in front of a rugged mountain from which a waterfall tumbles. Another painting shows a horse and would have been presented to a shrine. It had been painted and gilded.

The deep insight into the administrative minutiae of the late Yamato and Nara periods of Japanese history has already greatly enlarged the understanding of this period, but it is stressed that many more such records are likely to be found and their analysis is in its infancy.

Further reading: Brown, D. M. *The Cambridge History of Japan.* Cambridge: Cambridge University Press, 1993; Kiyotari, T., ed. *Recent Archaeological Discoveries in Japan.* Tokyo: The Centre for East Asian Cultural Studies, 1987; Totman, C. *A History of Japan.* Oxford: Blackwell, 2000.

money tree A money tree is a distinctive type of mortuary offering that was particularly prevalent in the Chinese province of Sichuan during the HAN DYNASTY (206 B.C.E.–220 C.E.). The ritual pits of SANXINGDUI have revealed several examples of bronze trees dating to the second half of the second millennium B.C.E. The most complete had three sets of branches embellished with birds and fruit and holes for the suspension of precious items of jade, gold, and bronze. The top of this tree was designed to receive a further BRONZE CASTING that might well have been one of the bronze birds found in the same pits.

These money trees are not in fact related to money per se, but rather are symbols of the ascent to heaven. A similar iconography is seen in the contemporary tomb banners of MAWANGDUI, where a crow is perched in a tree in heaven.

This tree, of ritual and symbolic importance, is probably the predecessor of a mortuary offering that continued in favor for more than a millennium among the SHU people of Sichuan. The Han examples stand between 1.0 and 1.8 meters (3.3 and 5.9 ft.) tall and include a ceramic base, a long bronze tree trunk, and attached branches. A rose finch or golden crow, symbols of the Sun, perched on the top of the trunk. Each branch was cast integrally with Han coins, but the coins were embellished with rays and thus represent the Sun. Other celestial images include the queen mother of the West and mythical beasts, such as the toad and the hare. The toad is relevant because after the legendary chieftain Hou Yi obtained the elixir of immortality from Xiwangmu, the queen mother, it was stolen by his wife, who fled to the Moon. There she was turned into a toad. The hare is seen on the trees with a pestle, pounding the herb that conferred immortality in his mortar.

Mongchon Mongchon was a city of the PAEKCHE state, one of the states existing in the period of THREE KINGDOMS in Korea. It is located in the area of Seoul near a tributary of the Han River. The site is demarcated by a moat and walls of stamped earth, following the Chinese model. The walls rise to a height of 17 meters (56.1 ft.) and incorporate high watchtowers. Paekche was under threat from the rival kingdom of KOGURYO, and excavations in 1987 uncovered much evidence for warfare in the form of bone-plate armor, horse equipment, such as stirrups and bits, and weaponry. The bone plates had been drilled for joining with other pieces and many well have been used to protect horses from injury in battle. There was also a domestic element to the site, revealed by the presence of storage pits, possible pit houses, and roof tiles. The imported Chinese pottery dates to the third and fourth centuries C.E., confirming occupation before the conquest of the area and the relocation of the Paekche capital to the south that occurred in 475 C.E.

Mouhot, Henri (1826–1861) *Henri Mouhot is often credited as the first Westerner to "discover" Angkor in Cambodia.*
In fact, his posthumously published journals contained early engravings of Angkor, which revealed the size and majesty of the temples to a wide Western audience. Many Westerners had visited and described Angkor before Mouhot's visit, however, beginning with Portuguese missionaries in the second half of the 16th century. For three years from 1858, Mouhot traveled extensively in Southeast Asia, following his interest in biology. His observant eye and drafting skill are seen in his plan of Angkor and engravings of the principal monuments, some of which were published with his journals in 1864.

Mount Meru Hindu sacred texts describe Mount Meru as the center of the universe. It was ringed by a series of concentric circles. The first is known as *jambudvipa*, the land of the rose apple tree, beyond which lies the saltwater ocean, and so through various realms until outer darkness. There are also seven layers below the surface, under which lie the realms of hell. The cosmos is inhabited by many kinds of beings, including celestial nymphs, the APSARAS, and snakes, the *naga*s. The temple mausolea of the kings of ANGKOR in Cambodia were built to represent the sacred mountain. Ta Keo, the mausoleum built for JAYAVARMAN V (r. 968–1001 C.E.), was known as Hemasringagiri, Mountain with the Golden Summits. The BAPHUON, mausoleum of UDAYADITYAVARMAN II (r. 1050–66 C.E.), was described as an imitation of Mount Meru in an INSCRIPTION from Lonvek. A later inscription from Ban That describes how SURYAVARMAN II (r. 1113–50 C.E.) built three stone towers like the summits of Mount Meru with surrounding walls, a series of shrines, and great BARAYS, or reservoirs, surrounded by groves of flowering plants, populated by celestial beings and holy men. This temple was said to resemble the paradise of INDRA.

Mount Tai Mount Tai is a mountain that was sacred to the Chinese over many centuries. It is located in Shandong province. Ascent of the mountain to conduct religious rituals by an emperor was rare. It is, however, recorded that in 219 B.C.E., an ascent was made by QIN SHIHUANGDI, and an INSCRIPTION was set up to proclaim his sovereignty over a united empire. The mountain achieved particular prominence under Emperor WUDI of the Western HAN DYNASTY, who conducted ceremonials on the summit in 110 B.C.E. This was a period of Chinese imperial expansion and projection of national unity and pride, but the principal motivation to ascend the mountain followed the discovery of an ancient tripod said to have been associated with the yellow manifestation of DI. Since the physical manifestation of the yellow DI, the yellow emperor Huangdi, had achieved immortality, Wudi was persuaded that by participating in ancient ceremonials at Mount Tai, he too could fulfill his desire to become immortal.

mratan The inscriptions dating to the CHENLA kingdoms in Cambodia (550–800 C.E.) refer to certain men by

The huge stone pyramid of Ta Keo at Angkor was built as the temple mausoleum of King Jayavarman V (r. 968–1001 C.E.). It was struck by lightning, an evil omen, and never completed. *(Charles Higham)*

the title *mratan*. Unlike the contemporary title of PON for highly ranked men, this title seems to have been accorded to individuals irrespective of their ancestry. It thus provides evidence that kings could recognize their followers with distinguished titles, a feature that continued in a greatly magnified form during the ensuing kingdom of ANGKOR.

Mrauk-U

Mrauk-U is one of the major royal capitals of the ARAKAN (Rakhine) region of western Myanmar (Burma). Its present form dates from the 15th century, and its multitude of temples, monasteries, and parks and the royal palace made it at the time one of the great centers of Southeast Asia. A number of finds reveal settlement that was contemporary with the occupation of the capital city of VESALI, 10 kilometers (6 mi.) to the north. These include two decorated stone lintels bearing *makara*s, "monsters," disgorging garlands. Such motifs are matched in the lintels of early seventh-century date from ISANAPURA in Cambodia. The Nibuza temple at Mrauk-U has also yielded part of a lintel decorated with the sun god Surya, which has been dated to the eighth century on stylistic grounds.

Muang Dongkorn

The city site of Muang Dongkorn in central Thailand was occupied during the period of the DVARAVATI CIVILIZATION (c. 400–c. 900 C.E.). Never excavated, it reveals surface remains of brick temple foundations inside and outside the large moated enclosure. It is also well known for the number of Dvaravati coins found, including those with the conch shell, rising Sun, cow with calf, and mother goddess, or *srivatsa*, motifs. Six coins bear a text describing the king of Dvaravati, and one mentions a royal consort. There are also a stone ritual tray fragment from this site, a relief image of Buddha, and bivalve stone molds for casting earrings and finger rings of bronze.

Muang Fa Daet

Muang Fa Daet is a large settlement located north of the Chi River in northeast Thailand. It has three moated enclosures with a fourth feature thought to have been a reservoir to the northeast. The reservoir covers an area of 15 hectares (37.5 acres), while the settlement proper appears to have been enlarged on three occasions, ultimately to cover 171 hectares (427.5 acres). Its location commands traffic up and down the Chi Valley and north via the Pao River Valley to the Sakon Nakhon Basin. A mound in the northwestern corner of the site was occupied during the Iron Age (500 B.C.E.–200 C.E.) and has yielded inhumation graves associated with red painted pottery vessels. Erik Seidenfaden (1954) reported the presence there of many Buddhist sacred boundary marker (*sema*) stones. The location of the actual precincts is now lost as a result of the relocation of the stones to the principal modern village in the ancient site. They still provide much information because

they are carved to depict Buddhist scenes. One shows the Buddha in association with Indra and Brahma. A second shows Buddha with his wife and son after his enlightenment, seated in front of a *sala*, or wooden hall, which provides a glimpse of the nature of secular architecture at that period. A wall and gateway defended by soldiers at the base of this *sema* stone give an idea of the former defenses. This site provides evidence for the development of small states in northeast Thailand in 500–800 C.E.

See also DVARAVATI CIVILIZATION.

Muang Phra Rot

The moated DVARAVATI CIVILIZATION center of Muang Phra Rot, in the Bang Pakong Valley east of the CHAO PHRAYA RIVER in Thailand, encloses an area of 1,350 by 700 meters (4,455 by 2,310 ft.). It is interesting to note that a stone mold for casting tin amulets, identical to those from OC EO, has been found there, indicating occupation in the early centuries C.E. Statuary representing the Buddha as well as Brahma and INDRA has also been found, and excavations have yielded an occupation layer of Dvaravati-style pottery dated from the sixth to the 11th century C.E. This site was included in an area subjected to an intensive survey for archaeological remains in 1984. The pottery found on the surface was matched at several small, unmoated settlements in the surveyed area. This suggests that the moated city was contemporary with dependent agricultural villages in its hinterland. Furthermore, the presence of marine shells at Muang Phra Rot suggests that it was located much closer to the sea than it is at present (c. 26 kilometers; 15.6 mi.) and could have been a port city.

Muang Sema

Located just north of the modern city of Nakhon Ratchasima in northeast Thailand, Muang Sema is a large historic town covering an area of 1,845 by 755 meters. It has two walled enclosures and a moat. Excavations have revealed deep prehistoric layers with inhumation graves dating to the region's Iron Age (500 B.C.E.–200 C.E.). This was followed by two periods of occupation. The earlier held ceramics similar to those of the DVARAVATI CIVILIZATION sites of the central plain of Thailand; the later saw strong Angkorian influence in material culture. During the period of Dvaravati dominance, there is abundant evidence for the practice of BUDDHISM, indicated by the presence of statues, a "wheel of the law" (DHARMACAKRA), and a large representation of a reclining Buddha. The central part of the site incorporates the Bor E-ka temple sanctuary from which a SANSKRIT and Khmer inscription, dated stylistically to the ninth century C.E., records the meritorious gift of water buffaloes, cattle, and slaves by the overlord of a polity named as Sri Canasa. This polity is also recorded in an INSCRIPTION from Ayutthaya that names a king, Mangalavarman, as the ruler. It is considered likely that Muang Sema was the capital center of the small, independent state in the upper Mun Valley contemporary with late CHENLA and early ANGKOR.

Muang Tam This temple complex lies about eight kilometers south of the hilltop sanctuary of PHNOM RUNG in the Mun Valley of northeast Thailand. It dates to the 11th century on stylistic grounds and was dedicated to SIVA. No INSCRIPTIONS survive, and little is known of the site's history. It is notable for the five central brick towers built in imitation of MOUNT MERU, home of the gods, and the four sacred pools. *Naga*, or snakes, are found in profusion. Outside the precinct lies a very large BARAY, or reservoir, more than a kilometer long and 400 meters wide. Elizabeth Moore and Smitthi Siribhadra have also noted that Muang Tam and Phnom Rung lie in an area crossed by canals, one of which is more than 20 kilometers long. They suggest that the canals assisted drainage and the carrying of water to rice fields in times of unseasonable draught.

Mundigak Mundigak is a settlement site in the Kushk-i Nakhod Valley of central Afghanistan. Its importance lies in its documentation of cultural elaboration in the uplands to the west of the Indus Valley between the early fourth and the second millennia B.C.E. It was during this period that the INDUS VALLEY CIVILIZATION arose, and the impact of new and extensive exchange relationships in, for example, TURQUOISE beads, can be seen in the sequence at Mundigak. Thus, during the early occupation of Period I, there was an initial absence of any permanent structures, implying occasional visits to the site, but this was in due course succeeded by the construction of buildings of unfired clay BRICK, associated with bread ovens. Wells were excavated for the domestic water supply. During the second phase, it is possible to trace the first presence of stone SEALs, the development of copper and bronze technology, and a proliferation of human and animal terra-cotta figurines. By this juncture, in tandem with urbanization in the Indus Valley, Mundigak was expanding in size and complexity with the construction of a massive defensive wall, and a palace building and temple were found within.

Muro Miyayama Muro Miyayama is a massive *kofun*, or burial mound, located on a ridge overlooking the YAMATO Plain in Japan. It has a typical keyhole form, comprising linked circular and rectangular mounds. The former has a diameter of 105 meters; the latter measures 110 by 110 meters. The total length is 285 meters. The mortuary rituals of this period involved the placement of ceramic figures, known as HANIWA, around the tombs, and at Muro Miyayama these took the form of house models, shields, and armor.

The soil used to raise these mounds to a height of 25 meters has left a form of moat around the complex, which on typological grounds of form and associated artifacts dates to the early fifth century C.E. It is thought that there were formerly three major tombs in the main mound, but two had been so badly looted that little remained. The third, although entered and robbed, was still in part intact. It had a stone chamber 5.5 by 1.9 meters in extent, surrounding a grave of stone walls and ceiling. The burial offerings included iron swords, armor, and bronze mirrors, together with hundred of talc beads.

Muryong, King (r. 501–523) *King Muryong was the 25th king of the Korean state of Paekche.*
The recovery of nearly 5,000 objects of gold from the tomb of the king and his consort serves to emphasize the wealth of the Paekche kingdom and the splendor that has been lost to looting. It was a miracle that this great burial, discovered in 1971, has survived intact to reveal to generations of Koreans the splendor of their cultural heritage.

When Muryong was only 14, the rival army of KOGURYO defeated the forces of Paekche at Seoul, and the king was executed. With other members of the royal family, Prince Sama, as Muryong was then known, fled to the safety of Kongju in the south. The SAMGUK SAGI, a vital source of information on early Korea written in the 12th century C.E. from earlier documents that have not survived, described King Muryong as a prominent ruler whose posthumous name, Muryong, means "brave and peaceful." However, the earlier years of his reign were marked by the provision of a defensive line punctuated by forts as a measure against further Koguryo attack and the cementing of an alliance with the southern Chinese dynasty of Liang. He is also known for devoting much effort to the improvement of agriculture.

THE ROYAL TOMB

In 1971, a fortuitous discovery of a brick façade behind a looted tomb at Kongju, about 90 kilometers south of Seoul, resulted in the recognition of the intact tomb of Muryong. In accordance with the strong Chinese influence that characterized his reign, the tomb was cut into a hillside linked to the outside by a passageway that incorporated a drain about 17 meters long. The bricks, another element of Chinese inspiration, are finely molded with lotus designs and line the main chamber. Wall niches still contained the porcelain lamps and wicks that had illuminated the burial chamber. Two diorite INSCRIPTIONS faced the entrance passageway, one for the king, the other for his consort. They describe the purchase of the land from the Earth god by means of a payment of 10,000 coins. The text of this inscription reads: "The great general and pacifier of the East, King Muryong of Paekche, died at the age of 62 on 5 June 523. On 14 September 525 he was interred in a great tomb with due ceremony. We have recorded that the plot was purchased from the Earth god." The Chinese *wushu* coins used in the purchase were still present on top of the stela. The entrance also included a tomb guardian in the form of a stone animal statue standing to a height of 40 centimeters.

Grave Gifts

Both the king and his consort were interred with outstanding offerings. They lay with their heads directed to the south, resting on lacquered wooden pillows ornamented with gold. A large bronze mirror and a gold hairpin in the form of a bird lay under the upper part of the king's body, and he also wore golden earrings and a gold crown that would have been attached to a silk cap. A lacquered wooden footrest was decorated with strips of gold adorned with golden flowers. The coffins were of lacquered wood ornamented with gilt bronze rivets. Other grave goods included a lute, bronze wine cup, and sword of Chinese type almost a meter in length. A silver wine cup on a bronze stand had been decorated with scenes of mountains, flowers, and dragons.

The queen's pillow was painted with animal designs and lotuses. Two carved phoenixes found lying adjacent to the pillow were probably once positioned at each side of the head, looking inward. Her clothes were evidently covered in tiny gold beads and flowers, and she wore silver and gold bracelets. A glass pendant of a young boy hung from her waist. The royal shoes were made of gilt bronze over soles bearing spikes, thought to have been designed to trample demons on their way to paradise.

Muye, Battle of The Battle of Muye, "shepherd's field," was the decisive trial of strength between the emergent Zhou of the Wei Valley and the SHANG STATE, the dominant dynasty of northern China that controlled the central Huang (Yellow) River Valley. The Battle of Muye has been described as one of the major events in East Asian history, for it ushered in the longest dynastic rule in the history of China. The battle was fought in 1045 B.C.E., and a poem incorporated in the *Classic of Odes* (early Western Zhou dynasty) described the battle in dramatic fashion, giving a graphic account of the massive Shang army with its battle standards thick as a forest and the gleaming power of the Zhou chariots as they put the Shang to the sword. It was a seminal victory, leading to the establishment of the WESTERN ZHOU DYNASTY, although the leader, KING WU, survived only two years. In 1976, the LI GUI, a ceremonial bronze vessel, was excavated. It contains an important text describing the battle and confirming descriptions contained in other documentary sources.

My Son My Son is a great ceremonial center in the CHAM CIVILIZATION kingdom in Vietnam, known as Amaravati. It is located in a small valley and has a series of brick shrines set out in seven walled groups with many outliers. It was founded at least as early as the fifth century C.E. under a ruler known by the SANSKRIT title of Bhadravarman. An inscription in Sanskrit records the gift of land to a temple dedicated to SIVA by this king. King Vikrantavarman initiated a major building program at My Son in the seventh century C.E. As do most temples of Champa and ANGKOR, it has an exterior wall enclosing a single-chambered sanctuary. The temples were built of brick, and the exterior surfaces bore strip pilasters, false doors, and window niches. Further temples were erected at least until the reign of Jayaindravarman toward the end of the 11th century. Temple E1 is particularly notable for the presence of fine Cham relief sculptures that belong to the early seventh century. Freestanding sculptures were also recovered from My Son, the earliest from Temple E5 and dating to the late seventh century. It portrays GANESHA, the elephant god of wisdom. Indian inspiration is apparent in this fine statue, which stands almost a meter high. Ganesha is portrayed with four arms, and he holds a rosary, an ax, a bowl of sweets, and the root of a plant elephants are known to appreciate. He wears a complex decorated belt and a tiger skin.

INDIAN AND CAMBODIAN INFLUENCE

It was during this period that influence from the court of ISHANAVARMAN (r. c. 615–28 C.E.) in Cambodia at ISHANAPURA was evident. The inspiration of Indian art and religion is also seen, for example, in a carved sandstone pediment more than two meters wide, illustrating Vishnu recumbent on the ocean of eternity, represented by a seven-headed serpent. A bearded ascetic watches the god from his side, and two figures grasp snakes in birds' talons beyond his head and feet. The temple within was dominated by a large LINGAM representing Siva, which stood on a richly ornamented pedestal. Access to the top of this platform, which represents Mount Kailasa, the home of Siva, was by three steps. The outer walls of the pedestal incorporate a series of carved reliefs. One of these is regarded by Emmanuel Guillon as a masterpiece of Cham civilization art, showing three dancers wearing rich ornaments and holding scarves. Their jewelry includes multiple necklaces, belts, armlets, and heavy ear disks. Another scene shows an ascetic, seated between two columns, and playing a flute. In a third panel, an ascetic lies down while a novice massages his right leg.

Perhaps the same pair are seen elsewhere on the pediment, but this time the ascetic is lecturing while holding a fly whisk, and the pupil kneels in front of him, listening attentively. Another ascetic has a different audience: He is out in the countryside, talking to animals. On the one hand, he turns and talks to a parrot, while a squirrel leans against a tree in front of him. A second statue of GANESHA from Temple B3 again stresses the local attachment to this god. In this case, the elephant is portrayed seated. The complex was severely damaged during the Vietnam War by bombing, but many of the sculptures survive in the Da Nang Museum, formerly the Musée Henri Parmentier.

N

Nagara Jayasri *See* PREAH KHAN.

Nagarjunakonda Nagarjunakonda, also known as Vijayapura, India, was a major center of Buddhist learning named after Nagarjuna, a leading philosopher of MAHAYANA BUDDHISM, and attracted pilgrims from India and beyond to its university. The site was discovered in 1926 and excavated over the following two years and again in 1954. It was located on the bank of the Krishna River and flourished during the second to fourth centuries C.E. The brick defensive walls enclose an area of about 50 hectares (125 acres), but many monasteries and temples as well as bathing areas lie outside the walls. The interior is reached through two major gateways to the eastern and western sides, and it incorporates a citadel, residential areas equipped with a drainage system, and barracks. The Buddhist monuments are well known for the quality of their sculptures, but the site itself has now been drowned with the construction of the Nagarjunasagar Dam, and some monuments have been relocated to higher ground.

Nagayan temple The Nagayan temple at PAGAN in Myanmar (Burma) was built by King KYANZITTHA (r. 1084–1111) and is located where legend describes that a *naga*, or snake, gave him protection when he was in danger. In traditional fashion, it has a central temple and adjoining hall. The latter contains statues relating to the life of the Buddha, while corridor walls were painted with similar themes. A large image of the Buddha occupies the central shrine, associated with the *naga*.

Nagaya, Prince (684–729 C.E.) *Prince Nagaya was a grandson of the Japanese emperor Temmu and a high-ranking minister in the court of Emperor Shomu (r. 724–749 C.E.).*
His career has been documented on the basis of historic accounts and the evidence from MOKKAN, the wooden slips used to record transactions and orders. In 709 C.E. he was appointed to the royal council and a year later became the minister of ceremonies, thereby occupying a central role in court appointments. In 718 he was a counselor and in 724 assumed the powerful and elite role of minister of the Left. His wife, Princess Kibi, was a granddaughter of the emperor TEMMU, and her father was Crown Prince Kusakabe. The crown prince died before enthronement but was posthumously given the imperial title, thus making his daughter a *naishinno*, or female imperial offspring. Officially, she was of even higher status than her husband, the prince, who later in his career became embroiled in an intense court rivalry with the rival FUJIWARA clan. It was alleged that he had laid a fatal curse on the infant crown prince, and in February 729 he was ordered to commit suicide.

EVIDENCE OF *MOKKAN*

In August 1988 a huge find of *mokkan* was discovered during the digging of the foundations of a new construction in NARA. About 35,000 of these inscribed wooden slips had been dumped beside the eastern entrance to an elite residential compound shortly after 716 C.E. They revealed that this had been the home of Prince Nagaya and Princess Kibi. The translation of this archive has illuminated not only the organization of this princely household, but also the possible circumstances leading to his suicide. Along with complete excavation of this quarter of HEIJO-KYO, a new chapter has been opened on the early Japanese history during the Nara period (710–94 C.E.).

The prince's establishment was located just over the road from the southeastern corner of the royal palace. It covered four of the 16 *cho*, or subdivisions in a city block, an area of nine hectares (22.5 acres). A series of compounds lay within the encircling walls. One was for the prince's residence, another for Princess Kibi's. The *mokkan* texts reflect the various duties of the servants and clerks, who numbered 130 people. There were smelters of metal, saddlers, and armorers. Some worked in the pottery workshop; there were a blacksmith and painters, falconers, and dog handlers. Each of these occupations required workshops and facilities. One group of scribes was kept busy copying holy Buddhist texts. Others naturally wrote the *mokkan* records that have survived. Accountants were needed, because goods from 19 provinces were taken as tax payments to this household, some of which were retained and others exchanged in the market for the coins that were by now being minted since the discovery of copper ore. Food for the table included rice, shellfish, fish, and vegetables carried in by packhorse. Ice was supplied by a special ice house. The status of the prince meant that the retainers were paid from the imperial palace, but still 500 sustenance households were required to supply his establishment, and in addition he was in his own right a major landowner with lumber interests and salt works. Some servants worked in the garden, where cranes paraded beside ornamental ponds.

One *mokkan* provides new insight into the prince's suicide. It reads, "For imperial offspring Nagaya, ten abalone as imperial tribute." The title *shinno* used in this record indicates that the prince was of higher status than the historical text *Shoku Nihongi* indicates. It implies that Nagaya was crown prince, a compelling reason for his Fujiwara rivals to plot and engineer his downfall.

Nakhon Pathom   Nakhon Pathom is the largest-known moated city of the DVARAVATI CIVILIZATION (c. 400–c. 900 C.E.) of central Thailand. It follows a roughly rectangular plan measuring 3,700 by 2,000 meters (12,210 by 6,600 ft.). Two silver medallions bearing the INSCRIPTION "Meritorious deeds of the king of Dvaravati" were found beneath a sanctuary in the moated area. GEORGES CŒDÈS has dated the foundation on the basis of the script to the seventh century C.E., and the sanctuary in question may have been associated with the Pra Paton shrine, a large and impressive structure in the center of the city. This building was of considerable importance and was altered on three occasions. It was designed as a rectangular building, with access by flights of steps at each end. It was decorated with alternating eagles (*garuda*s) and elephants, and carved lions guarded the steps. Excavations in an occupation area have revealed a relatively thin layer. Artifacts include several that recall prehistoric forms,

including spindle whorls, bronze ornaments, and iron spears. There are many smaller artifacts from Nakhon Pathom dating from the Dvaravati period, including statues of the Buddha and stucco or moldings used in the decoration of the religious buildings. The site has also yielded two terra-cotta *abhisekas*, "trays," decorated with the symbols of royalty. These were probably used in the investiture of a ruler and are closely paralleled in a steatite example from near VESALI in ARAKAN (Rakhine), western Myanmar (Burma).

Nalanda   According to SEALS discovered at Nalanda, the site was called Mahavihara, or Great Monastery. It is located southeast of Patna, India, and is often referred to as a university. During the visit of XUANZANG (602–664), the famous Chinese pilgrim, it was a flourishing center of Buddhist learning, with thousands of monks and students and many monastic foundations. Xuanzang and other pilgrims described the many temples, hostels, libraries, and observatories. The name derives from that of the local king, BODHISATTVA Nalanda. ASOKA (268–235 B.C.E.) is believed to have had temples constructed there. It also flourished under royal endowment during the GUPTA dynasty (c. 320–c. 500 C.E.): King Harshavardhana endowed a monastery and called himself the servant of the Nalanda monks.

SIR ALEXANDER CUNNINGHAM explored the site in his first year as surveyor to the government of India in 1861. By following the descriptions of the Chinese monk Xuanzang in the seventh century, Cunningham was able to identify various foundations. Excavations have uncovered the monks' cells, and monasteries still preserve images of Buddhas and bodhisattvas in wall niches. The monastery's foundation precedes by several centuries the surviving brick buildings, which cover an area of about 14 hectares (35 acres) and date between the fifth century C.E. and the destruction at the hands of the Turks in the 12th century.

Nanaghat   Nanaghat is a cave located in the western Deccan of India, notable because it was chosen as the location for depictions and INSCRIPTIONS of the kings of the SATAVAHANA dynasty that date to the period 60–70 B.C.E. The site commands a vital pass from the Satavahana capital to the coast, a pass involved in trade as commerce with the Mediterranean increased during the late second century B.C.E. The lengthy inscribed texts on the cave walls were initiated by the consort of King Satakarni and record rich sacrificial offerings of thousands of cattle in Brahmanic rituals. Although the reliefs of the rulers have not survived, the texts are a vital source of evidence for their names and the duration of their reigns. The statues, of which only the feet of three figures survive, depicted the founder of the Satavahana dynasty, Simuka, with King Satakarni and his consort, together with a general and three princes. A number of water cisterns lie alongside the cave, perhaps to sustain merchants as they traveled from the coastal ports to the cities of the interior.

See also ROCK MONASTERIES.

Nara state

Nara state The Nara Plain on the western end of the Japanese island of Honshu was the center of political power during the seventh and eighth centuries C.E. It saw the foundation of the Nara state, which can be dated from the foundation of the capital city of HEIJO-KYO in 710 to its abandonment in 784 C.E. This period witnessed the establishment of a dominant state in Japan and the development of a typically Japanese culture from foundations laid during the preceding YAMATO period (300–552 C.E.). The policy behind the new capital city was rooted in an absolute monarch with a divine ancestry. Empress JITO assumed the title TENNO, "heavenly sovereign." The essential feature of the Nara state was a rigid social hierarchy, linked through the bureaucracy with the provinces. The *tenno,* the title accorded the sovereign, male or female, stood at the apex of society, a person of godly ancestry charted by the NIHONGI and KOJIKI texts back to the mythical ancestors. In theory they ruled with absolute power, and no code put impediments or restrictions on them. In practice there was more than one rebellion by leaders of high-ranking families. The central administration had two divisions, the *jingikan,* which oversaw the appropriate Shinto religious rituals, and the *daijokan,* which was composed of eight ministries, linked to the *tenno* by members of the Council of State. Four of these ministries were under the direction of the minister of the Left. These covered civil and personnel issues. The most important of his ministries, known as Ministry of Central Affairs, linked the emperor with the Council of State. The Ministry of Popular Affairs had responsibility for agriculture, including irrigation facilities. The minister of the Right had control of war, justice, taxation, and the royal household. An independent unit outside these two groups of ministries rooted out corruption.

YAMATO PERIOD CHANGES

Toward the end of the seventh century the royal dynasty was faced with a series of issues that generated a sharp move toward this fully fledged bureaucratic state along the lines of Tang China. The first concerned political developments in Korea, only a short distance across the Tsushima Strait. There the forces of the state of SHILLA, in alliance with the powerful Tang empire of China, defeated PAEKCHE and KOGURYO, its rivals to the west and north. A single and possibly predatory kingdom in Korea placed Yamato Japan in a hazardous condition, since Japan had traditionally been the ally of Paekche against Shilla. The second threat arose from Tang China itself. Yamato rulers were familiar with the Tang dynasty, having sent embassies to them at regular intervals.

To counter these threats, Yamato became increasingly centralized and bureaucratic in its organization. A series of legal edicts along Chinese models was issued, such as

the Taiho Code of 702 C.E. These edicts formalized the status of the royal dynasty and set down in written form the grades of the aristocracy, their rights and duties, and the role of the supporting peasantry in sustaining the court. BUDDHISM was adapted to Japanese needs and was incorporated as a state religion. Those Buddhist sutras that supported the idea of a supreme royal line were favored, and magnificent new Buddhist temples were constructed. Another policy decision was to order the preparation of a history that traced the royal dynasty back to mythical godly origins. These histories, the *Nihongi* and *Kojiki,* appeared in the first two decades of the eighth century, using the writing system taken from China. In theory land was owned by the emperor or empress, and the tax system allocated a proportion of production to the ruling aristocracy. This involved a wide range of agricultural, industrial, and marine products. Finally, it was decided to pour resources into the construction of a magnificent new capital to show the world the power of the imperial line. The first capital, modeled on the Tang capital at CHANG'AN, was constructed at FUJI-WARA under Empress Jito (645–702 C.E.), who took up residence in a huge new palace complex in 694 C.E. This palace dominated a city laid out on a rigid geometric plan, in which people were granted land according to their status. With the accession of Jito's sister, Genmei (661–721 C.E.), a decision was taken to move the palace and capital 20 kilometers (12 mi.) north of Fujiwara, to Heijo-kyo, where a far larger city was built, again centered on a walled royal palace. The city itself was not defended and was again laid out on a grid plan that was aligned with the streets of Fujiwara to the south.

THE NEW NARA CAPITAL

Knowledge of this capital is gained not only from the official history of the day, but from a growing collection of MOKKAN, wooden slips that were used to record in writing tax receipts, requisitions, and even assessments of the performance of individual civil servants. These are now numbered in the tens of thousands and permit a far more detailed image of life in the Nara capital of Heijo-kyo than was available before they were first encountered in 1961. Heijo-kyo has also been examined by excavation, and even if much of this fieldwork has responded on an ad hoc basis to industrial developments in Nara city, much new information has been gained. Thus the accounts and receipt of goods into the elite household of PRINCE NAGAYA (684–729 C.E.) show the reach of a high official in the provision of necessities for his household. His house lay at the southeastern corner of the walled royal precinct, as did several other elite residence compounds. The farther south, the smaller the allotments for the minor bureaucrats and lesser members of the community.

There were two large markets in the city, each under state control. Goods from the countryside or from abroad were exchanged there; the medium of trade was rice and, from 708 C.E., the issues of copper COINAGE. The building program included Buddhist temples, the largest of which was known as the TODAIJI. This housed a massive bronze statue of the Buddha in a hall that remains the largest wooden hall in the world. The complex included two pagodas standing about 100 meters (330 ft.) high, a royal treasure house, a monastery headquarters, and its associated buildings.

The title of *tenno* did not connote the ruler's gender, and Jito was succeeded by her sister, Genmei, the empress who ordered the construction of Heijo-kyo. She was followed by her daughter, Gensho (680–748 C.E.), and on Gensho's abdication in 724 C.E., by her nephew, Shomu (701–756 C.E.). He was succeeded by his daughter, Koken (718–770 C.E.), who ruled until the ascent of Kanmu (737–806) in 781 C.E. He abandoned Heijo-kyo in favor of new capitals, first at Nagaoka, then at Heian.

INFORMATION FROM *MOKKAN*

The mokkan, wooden administrative records, provide a clear picture of the lives of the thousands of bureaucrats who made up the administrative heart of the Nara state. The records reveal how they were assessed for promotion, in a hierarchy that gave special preference to the members of aristocratic families. For these favored individuals, there were 30 ranks. Under the provisions of the Taiho Code, rank determined their allowances of rice land and ascribed households to provide for their needs and their number of retainers. Thus a person of the 14th rank was given eight *cho* of rice fields, 20 retainers, but no sustaining households. By contrast, a minister of the Right was given 30 *cho* of rice fields, 2,000 sustaining households, and 300 retainers. Some worked full time, others on a half-time basis. Many lived in Heijo-kyo itself, but others commuted to the center from outlying villages. The total size of the administration probably reached about 10,000 individuals.

Grades of the Elite and Rural Bureaucracy

The top 14 of the 30 grades of officials were reserved for the elite aristocracy, members of powerful *uji*, or clans. It was virtually impossible for the less exalted in status to break into this group, which was privileged by much higher rewards, land grants, and power. Responsibilities were also inherited to the second or third generation, again ensuring continuity within the *uji*. These elite individuals had large and opulent compounds located near the royal palace at Heijo-kyo. They were provided with substantial incomes in kind, sustaining land and villages, and were exempt from most tax imposts. There were probably no more than 250 such privileged aristocrats at any given time. Below them lay 16 further grades occupied by those who held lower court ranks. Some of these had important regional administrative posts that joined the center with the provinces. They received far less in terms of goods and services.

The supporting rural population was also rigidly ordered in about 60 provinces, each controlled by a governor appointed for a period of six years. He had his own administrative staff and was responsible for maintaining a census, encouraging production, and resolving disputes. An excerpt from the YORO CODE of 718 C.E. decreed that the governor should have responsibility for the supply of labor, oversee tax collection, and maintain storehouses. He was in charge of troops in his province and their necessary supplies. An idea of rural Japan during this period can be gained from references in the same code to beacons for signaling, forts, Buddhist monasteries, and rice fields. Provinces were further divided into about 600 districts that were usually administered by a local leader, responsible for ensuring production and collection of taxes.

Commoners and Slaves

Beyond the court aristocracy, the state classified individuals as commoners or slaves. The commoners were the backbone of the Nara state, producing the necessary goods and services for its maintenance. Most were rice farmers, but there were also fishing communities and regional specialists in mining, salt production, and transportation. Under the strict conditions of the Taiho and Yoro Codes, the number of households in a village was defined as 50, each household having between 10 and 25 people related by blood or through marriage. The lowest stratum of this rigid social spectrum was composed of five classes of slaves. One group was assigned to the maintenance of the royal mausolea. The state as well as wealthy commoners could own slaves. Others were kept to work in temples. It was possible to buy and sell the state-owned or privately owned chattel slaves.

The commoners were required to pay a proportion of their rice production to the state. This was not onerous in itself, amounting to about 5 percent of their crop, but they were also required to transport it to the provincial collection point or to the capital. However, the taxation system became onerous when it is considered that commoners also had to supply labor for construction projects, such as roads or bridges, or for work in the capital. This requirement applied to men aged between 17 and 65 and could be remitted by the payment of additional rice. The amount required to buy out such a demand was related to the age of the individual in question. Further payments were required on the production of other necessities, such as fabric, particularly silk. LACQUER, paper, and salt likewise fell into this category. That such a system worked can be seen in the surviving *mokkan* from the elite households in the capital. These record the inflow of goods from these rural communities. One of the most onerous and unwelcome of all demands was conscription for military service. This could take a man away from his home for lengthy periods to garrison the northern frontier in Kyushu or guard the palace. Although the length of service was specified, this limited period was often ignored by the authorities.

Markets and Trade

The bureaucratic stranglehold on the Nara state also applied to the marketplace. Two large markets were located in the eastern and western parts of the capital, and each provincial center likewise had a market linked with the ports and production points. But the state prescribed the amount that could be paid and provided a system of weights and measures. Following the Tang dynasty system, the state also issued coinage to facilitate transactions. This received considerable impetus from the discovery of copper ore in Japan in 708 C.E. Little is known regarding the presence or emergence of a merchant class during the move toward a copper currency system. However, it is known that temple authorities would loan copper cash to individuals to assist in trading ventures in anticipation of profit and that ships were used to transport a range of goods. A copper currency also assisted in land development through the foundation of *shoen,* estates that could be owned by private individuals, or temples, where laborers were often remunerated by cash wages.

INFLUENCE FROM CHINA AND KOREA

The importance of continental influence on the Nara state was profound. The capitals, for example, were modeled on Chinese cities, such as Chang'an. The writing system of Japan was introduced from China and Korea, while Buddhism reached Japan through the aegis of Korean monks in the middle of the sixth century C.E. The adoption of an alien writing system led directly to the publication of the two early histories of Japan, the *Kojiki* and the *Nihongi.* Both resulted from royal orders, and they appeared within eight years of each other in the early eighth century. Buddhism was also a key factor in the early development of literacy. PRINCE SHOTOKU and Soga no Imako, for example, founded Buddhist temples. Each was equipped with a building for storing sacred manuscripts.

In 713 C.E., the *tenno* (reigning emperor) Gemmei commissioned the compilation of documents recording the traditions, geography, and natural resources of the provinces that made up the Nara state. The fragments that survive reveal a lively interest in antiquarian matters as well as folklore and facts. The origin of place names, for example, was obviously of interest at the time. It is evident too that poetry was part of the Japanese oral tradition, and with the development of a writing system, poems were set down initially in the *Kaifusu* of 751 C.E. This compilation of 120 poems was the product of several hands, including those of the emperor Mommu. The second compilation, dating after 759 C.E., is the massive *Man'yoshu,* which had just over 4,500 poems, some of considerable but unknown antiquity. Poetry also went

hand in hand with music. It is known that court dance and musical performances drew on a wide range of stringed instruments, including zithers, lutes, and harps. There were also mouth organs, panpipes, sets of bells, drums, and flutes.

In 781 C.E. after a period of intense intrigue over the succession, Prince Yamabe became the *tenno* Kammu. Three years later, a decision was taken to abandon Heiko-kyo for a new capital at Nagaoka, bringing to an end the period of the Nara state—the seminal phase in the development of a distinctly Japanese civilization.

See also CONFUCIUS; NINTOKU.

Further reading: Brown, D. M. *The Cambridge History of Japan.* Cambridge: Cambridge University Press, 1993; Kiyotari, T. ed. *Recent Archaeological Discoveries in Japan.* Tokyo: The Centre for East Asian Cultural Studies, 1987; Totman, C. *A History of Japan.* Oxford: Blackwell, 2000.

Nasik   Nasik is located northeast of Mumbai (Bombay) in western Maharashtra state, India. The site is a series of Buddhist sanctuaries, of which the earliest is probably the Pandulena *vihara,* or meeting hall, dating to the second or first century B.C.E. An inscription at the entrance declares that the sculptures over the doorway were paid for by the villagers of Dhambika. Within the hall takes the form of a long rectangle flanked by octagonal columns, with a stupa at the far end. Ceiling beams carved in stone take the form of wooden prototypes. The Gautamiputra *vihara* is so called because of an INSCRIPTION recording that it was dedicated to the monks by Balasiri, the mother of the SATAVAHANA king Gautamiputra Satakarni. The lintel contains fine Buddhist scenes, including the *bodhi* tree under with the Buddha found enlightenment, the "wheel of the law" (DHARMACAKRA), and stupas. Within there are monks' cells.

The Nahapana cave temple includes an important historical inscription that records how Ushavadata, the son-in-law of King Nahapana, founded not only this temple but provided for the establishment of rest houses and river ferries in the area. He also engaged the local guild of weavers to make garments for the monks.

Nausharo   Nausharo is a settlement of the INDUS VALLEY CIVILIZATION, located on the Kachi Plain of Baluchistan between Iran and India. It is only six kilometers (3.6 mi.) south of the important site of MEHRGARH. Excavations by Jean-Francois Jarrige have revealed a long sequence in which the early settlement corresponds to Mehrgarh Period VII. Radiocarbon dates place this Period 1A–C occupation in the first half of the third millennium B.C.E. The excavators uncovered the remains of mud-BRICK houses and storerooms grouped around courtyards embellished with pillars of mud brick. The occupants were already familiar with copper metallurgy; finds included a large bronze spear and a SEAL. During Period 1D, there are signals that the culture was developing into the mature phase of the Indus civilization. Houses were now raised on mud-brick platforms, while the ceramics were decorated with typical designs of the large Indus sites, such as fish and pipal trees. There was a severe episode of burning at the end of Period 1. Periods 2 and 3 belong to the mature period of the Indus civilization, dating from about 2300 until 2000 B.C.E.

Settlement commenced with the construction of a substantial mud-brick wall faced with plaster, which was up to seven meters (23 ft.) broad at the base and stood at least four meters (13 ft.) high. Within, the site was laid out on a grid plan, with roads up to five meters wide and intersecting lanes 1.5 meters in width. A large platform of mud brick at least 13 meters long and 4.5 meters wide was uncovered. Houses were multiroomed and grouped around courtyards. Some rooms contained large hearths and kilns. As on the Indus Plain itself, dwellings were equipped with ceramic drains and jars into which the water soaked away. The excavator also identified a large canal-like structure or water reservoir. Artifacts include bull figurines, terra-cotta figurines of WOMEN, and a copper knife.

Period IV is radiocarbon dated to around 2000 B.C.E. The pottery, while still belonging to the Indus tradition, now showed a trend to regional preferences, as is found in other parts of the late Indus world.

See also AMRI; KOT DIJI.

Neak Pean   The island in the middle of the Northern BARAY at ANGKOR (the Jayatataka) in Cambodia housed Neak Pean, formerly known as Rajasri, one of the most beautiful Angkorian temples. It was constructed as part of the rebuilding of Angkor during the reign of King JAYAVARMAN VII (1181–1219 C.E.). The principal features of the temple are a water basin, 70 meters square (84 sq yds.), in which a circular island supports a temple shrine ringed by two *naga*, "snakes," with tales entwined. This gives the temple its modern name, which means "entwined snakes." The water from the basin gushed through the mouths of four figures into a smaller pond. In one chapel water spurted through the mouth of an elephant; in the others there were a horse, a lion, and a human. The contemporary inscriptions state that the complex is a replica of LAKE ANAVATAPTA, a sacred Himalayan lake imbued with miraculous curative powers to remove human sins, and pilgrims could cross the reservoir to this temple to pray and use the water to wash away the slime of their sins.

Nen Chua   The site of Nen Chua is located on the Mekong Delta in Vietnam. It dates to the period when the maritime state of FUNAN flourished on the basis of widespread trade relations linking China with Rome.

Excavations by Vietnamese archaeologists have revealed a rectangular structure in stone and brick 25.7 by 16.3 meters (84.8 by 53.7 ft.) in extent with what appear to be two internal chambers. The presence of a LINGAM and gold ornaments suggests that it had a religious function. There is also evidence for a complex mortuary ritual involving small BRICK-lined chambers dug up to 2.5 meters into the ground. These held cremated remains associated with spectacular gold grave offerings. There are, for example, rectangular or oval gold leaves decorated with human forms. One person appears to have four arms and might represent HARIHARA, the combined image of SIVA and Vishnu. The radiocarbon dates from this site suggest occupation in the period 450–650 C.E.

See also ANGKOR BOREI; OC EO.

Nevasa   Nevasa is an important prehistoric and historic site located on the bank of the Pravara River in the state of Maharashtra, western India. It was excavated by H. D. Sankalia between 1954–56 and 1959–61. The site covers an area of 350 by 100 meters (1,155 by 330 ft.) and has revealed a long sequence, from the Paleolithic to the Muslim period, with layers belonging to the Chalcolithic, early historic, and historic, from 50 B.C.E. until about 200 C.E., when trade with Rome flourished. During this last period, Nevasa was significantly located on a major exchange route that linked the SATAVAHANA capital at Paithan with the coastal ports of Kalyana and Soppara. Shards of Roman amphorae, glassware, and beads were discovered at the site. Some of the amphorae have a distinctive fabric of black sand characteristic of ceramic production centers in the Bay of Naples area and probably predate the eruption of Mount Vesuvius in 79 C.E., which severely disrupted manufacture there.

Nihongi   The *Nihongi* is a history of Japan up to the year 697 C.E., which originated through an imperial decree to gather historical records. It has been the most influential of such Japanese histories, often recited, quoted, or commented on since its completion in 720 C.E. It describes the history of Japan in terms of myths, legends, and oral tradition and at the same time incorporates information from earlier histories that have not survived. One source was the *Katari Be*, the traditional corporation of reciters who performed at the imperial court. While the earlier periods of Japanese culture are understandably based only on myth or fiction, the *Nihongi* is a more reliable historical source for the period after about 500 C.E., and its contents provide many insights into the activities of the court. This was the formative period when Chinese and Korean influence in the forms of BUDDHISM, writing, the arts, and medicine took deep root in the archipelago. The word *Nihon* in Chinese characters means "rising Sun," giving recognition to Japan's location east of the Asian mainland.

Among courtly activities the *Nihongi* describes is the emperor's passion for hunting with chariots. A passage tells of a gift of iron shields to the court and a test that followed, in which the greatest archers of the day were invited to try to pierce them. The emperor's role in enhancing agriculture is amply demonstrated. In 446 C.E., a bridge was constructed at Wo-bashi, and a road was built in a straight line from the south gate of the capital. A great canal was excavated to take the water of the Ishikaha River to the plains of Suzuka and Toyora. This opened a huge new area to rice cultivation and ensured that the peasants no longer had to suffer periodic crop failures. A few years later, it was recorded that the people of SHILLA had not sent tributes. Inquiries were made as to the reason; afraid of retribution, Shilla sent 80 shiploads of offerings, including fine silks. The later the entry, the more historic validity can be credited to the words of the *Nihongi*.

The entries for the seventh century provide details of the series of legal reforms that moved Japan closer to the Chinese Tang form of government. Laws, for example, confirmed the emperor in autocratic government at a time when Tang expansion into Korea carried military threats to the doorstep of Japan. Court officials were given one of a series of grades, each conferring the right to wear a particular style of deep purple cap. With the adoption of Chinese precedents, successive rulers of YAMATO constructed increasingly grandiose palaces to exhibit their exalted status and power, and the text describes how they were conceived and built. The historic validity has been in many respects confirmed not only by the results of archaeological excavations at the sites it described, but also by the recovery of the MOKKAN, contemporary court records of the actual implementation of the reforms it outlined.

Further reading: Aston, W. G. Nihongi: *Chronicles of Japan from the Earliest Times to A.D. 697*. Rutland, Vt., and Tokyo: Tuttle, 1995; Totman, C. *A History of Japan*. Oxford: Blackwell, 2000.

Nintoku (r. 313–399 C.E. [traditional dates]) *According to traditional Japanese sources, Nintoku was the fourth son of Ojin and second king of the Ojin dynasty of the Yamato state.* This span is almost certainly in error, and it is more likely that he ruled during the fifth century C.E. The NIHONGI records that he was a victorious warrior, who also initiated major IRRIGATION works to encourage the production of rice. In the 14th year of his reign, he inaugurated the massive Ishikawa River irrigation project that transported water via a canal to thousands of hectares of formerly marginal land. He also recruited Korean specialists to work on irrigation projects and repair dykes. His *kofun*, or mounded tomb, is located in the city of Sakai in Osaka prefecture and has the distinction of being the largest known, with a length of 486 meters (1,604 ft.). It covers

32 hectares (80 acres) and rose to a height of 30 meters (99 ft.). Since it was built on a plain and all the earth had to be moved by hand, some of it created three surrounding moats. Such imperial tombs are not open to archaeological inspection, but the wealth of goods associated with the interment must have been very great. In 1872 a natural collapse of part of the mound revealed a stone chamber containing a coffin. It would not have been the main interment of the emperor, but it contained a Persian glass vessel and iron armor.

Nisa   Nisa is a Hellenistic city foundation (second century B.C.E.) 12 kilometers (7.2 mi.) west of Ashkhabad in southern Turkmenistan that continued to be occupied during the succeeding Parthian period (up to 100 C.E.). The walls were up to 10 meters (33 ft.) wide and made of clay with a brick veneer at the front. There is a separate precinct for the royal palace. Nisa is known for the cellars of domestic buildings that were used to store wine, as well as for the large clay statues recovered during the excavations. Foremost among the works of art, however, are a set of ivory rhytons, horn-shaped drinking vessels elegantly carved at the tip with figures of centaurs, horses, and lions. The upper ends bear relief depictions of Greek gods. A unique assemblage of Parthian INSCRIPTIONS, written in the Aramaic alphabet, has also been found, recording the origin and receipt of wine for the royal cellars. Excavations there in 1950–51 uncovered a large number of clay sealings bearing texts in the Parthian script, dating to the period 50 B.C.E.–100 C.E. It is thought that the sealings must have accumulated after the opening and closing of a treasury door by Parthian officials.

Niuheliang   Niuheliang is a site of the HONGSHAN CULTURE in northeastern China and Inner Mongolia. The Hongshan culture is dated to 4700–2900 B.C.E. and is notable for the ritual nature of its surviving monuments. Sixteen so-called localities have been mapped at Niuheliang, 13 of which are groups of mounded burials. There are also a large mound shaped as a pyramid that covers one hectare in area, a female spirit temple, and a building of which only the stone foundations survive. Niuheliang is one of more than 500 known Hongshan sites and joins the LIANGZHU AND YANGSHAO CULTURES in documenting an early development of rituals and mortuary wealth well before the transition to the first states.

The spirit temple has a stone foundation covering an area of 22 by nine meters (72.6 by 29.7 ft.), with internal walls of clay-plastered wood decorated with red-painted designs. Within were clay representations of female forms associated with dragons and birds. The clay was unfired, and the figures are difficult to interpret, but some of the representations were up to three times life-size. This temple and the pyramid were the focus of many large and richly endowed mounded tombs in which the dead per-

Nisa, in southern Turkmenistan, was founded as a Hellenistic city before being occupied under Parthian rule between 50 B.C.E. and about 100 C.E. *(© David Samuel Robbins/CORBIS)*

son was interred in a stone-lined grave. Variations in grave goods are seen to indicate social ranking in the Hongshan communities, some of which may have led a relatively mobile herding lifestyle. The rich graves are denoted on the basis of the jades that accompanied the corpse. Thus two coiled dragons, found in Tomb 4 in Locality 2, excavated in 1984, had evidently been suspended as ornaments on the chest. This person also wore a cylindrical jade so positioned as to suggest a hair ornament. Other jades from the Niuheliang tombs include a finely carved turtle, *bi* disks, and plaques bearing animal masks. As with the coiled dragon image, these images and designs continued to be used in much later ornaments. Thus a coiled dragon was found in the tomb of FU HAO (r. c. 1200–1181 B.C.E.) at ANYANG, and the tortoise or turtle, symbolizing longevity, continues to be seen in Chinese art. Ceramic vessels were also included in burials but seem to have been less prestigious. Some were very finely painted with red designs.

Niya   The site of Niya, on the southern margin of the TARIM BASIN in western China, was discovered by SIR AUREL STEIN in 1901 during his first major expedition to this area. Niya was one of the oasis cities that formed part of the state of SHAN-SHAN during the first centuries C.E. For the merchant traveling along the SILK ROAD linking China with India and Rome, it was possible on reaching DUNHUANG to set out for KAXGAR by going north to avoid the Taklamakan Desert or south through Shan-shan. The latter route would have involved passing through Niya. The Silk Road saw not only the passage of goods, but also the spread of ideas as merchants moved and settled along its many transit points. By this means, BUDDHISM became established in Shan-shan and beyond, to the great center of Dunhuang and into China itself. Niya is a vital site in documenting this phenomenon, because of the survival there of religious and domestic structures and an archive of documents, mainly on wood, dated to the third and fourth centuries C.E. These illustrate the administrative machinery of the Shan-shan state. They also help to date the period when Niya flourished, for the documents, written in KHAROSHTHI and less often in Chinese, include the name of the king and his reign date. A document describing King Sulica indicates that the site was still occupied in the fourth century C.E., but its survival, as did that of all the oases cities, depended on river water. Only one river serves Niya, and its drying up would have rendered life there untenable.

Stein suggested that it was visited in the seventh century by the Chinese monk XUANZANG, who named it Nijang, but it could also have been the location of his city of Nei-nang. Contemporary documents from LOU-LAN to the east refer to Niya as Cadota.

The prosperity of trade on the Silk Road relied very much on the maintenance of peaceful conditions, and during periods when the Chinese exercised military control this was assured. However, at times of Chinese weakness, such as the period that followed the downfall of the Eastern HAN DYNASTY (c. 25–220 C.E.), the XIONGNU, or steppe horsemen, made travel hazardous. Niya and the Shan-shan state exercised a limited sovereignty over the southern route in the sense that they were either Chinese clients or subjected to Xiongnu pressure.

TEXTS FROM SHAN-SHAN SITES

Almost 800 texts have been found in the Shan-shan sites, the largest assemblage, 186 documents, from Site V.xv at Niya. They were written in the Kharoshthi script on slips of wood. Often these documents were two pieces of wood placed together face to face, wrapped with cordage, and sealed. Since some contain the names and reign years of kings of Shan-shan and were found associated with datable Chinese texts, it has been possible to trace the dynasty and learn that the rulers were on the throne from the early third to the middle of the fourth century. The documents also illuminate the organizational structure of the kingdom, which included districts known as *rajas*, under royally appointed governors, subdistricts called *nagaras* or *avanas*, and still smaller groupings called *satas*. Officeholders known as *sothamgas* were in charge of a system of taxation of payment in kind of agricultural surpluses, such as cereal crops, wine, butter, wool, carpets, and sheep. The list provides a good indication of the economy of oasis settlements such as Niya.

VINEYARD AT NIYA

The listing of wine among the taxable items in the documents received a most unusual archaeological confirmation when Sir Aurel Stein identified an ancient vineyard while exploring the ruins of Niya. It was enclosed by a fence 230 by 135 meters (759 by 445.5 ft.), within which the posts that would have supported the trellises remained in serried rows about five or six meters (16.5 to 19.8 ft.) apart. Even the vine stems survived against supporting posts. Fruit trees also grew there: apricots, peaches, apples, and walnuts. The aridity of the region and the long period of undisturbed abandonment also ensured the survival of domestic residences. Stein found, for example, that the wooden house posts were still in place, supporting wattle and daub walls. Fireplaces were intact, and the mud floors of the homes had been mixed with wheat straw and cow dung for added strength. He found much evidence for local iron smithing, and textile remains in wool, linen, and cotton revealed a long tradition of outstanding craft skill that stretched back in this region over at least 2,000 years. Even the remains of a wooden bridge still crossed the dried-out river bed. The settlement must have been very extensive, for as Stein traced the ruins along the line of the river, he found that they stretched over a distance of 25 by 10 kilometers (15 by 6 mi.).

BUDDHISM AT NIYA

The Buddhist community at Niya, according to the surviving documents, was under the wing of the main monastery at Lou-lan, for one text complained that the monks of Niya showed insufficient respect to their superiors. A second Kharoshthi text from the Shan-shan kingdom provides further insight into the day-to-day events in the life of a Buddhist community at Niya. In Cadota, the text declares, a monk named Anamdasena received a loan of corn and wine from a certain Cugopa. The slave of this monk evidently stole from the author of the text, Larsua, and Cugopa, 12 lengths of silk, two ropes, three felt garments, and four sheep. The monk was required to repay the value of the stolen goods and pay a fine designated as one cow. The whole affair was finally settled out of court when the monk gave the thief to Larsu as the equivalent of the value of the stolen items.

Stein investigated one BRICK stupa at Niya, finding that it was fashioned of mud brick, the dome raised on a series of square bases as in other Shan-shan stupas. It dates earlier than 300 C.E. Just as the religion and language of Niya were inspired by the West, so too were the motifs that survive on wooden furniture and architectural details. Thus a carved wooden lintel includes an image of a vase overflowing with pomegranates, a scene of Indian origin, flanked by fantastic animals. A wooden table standing 60 centimeters (2 ft.) in height and completely preserved was carved with a similar overflowing vase. The Niya wooden documents were often found bearing their original sealings, and these too show strong Western influence, not least a SEAL with the image of the Greek goddess Athena.

BURIALS AT NIYA

While the domestic and religious remains provide a vibrant image of life in a desert oasis in the third century C.E., much information is derived also from the mortuary remains of Niya. One burial yielded a wide range of grave goods. The double grave of a man and woman, it contained a complete silk coat of outstanding craftsmanship and woolen garments embellished with motifs matching those found on the wooden furniture. It incorporates a woven text that states: "The appearance of the five stars is favorable to China." This text is found in late Han and Jin dynasty texts and helps to date the tomb. There were also a bronze mirror, a bow and arrow, COMBS, and even fragments of paper. Of particular interest in this unique assemblage is a large section of patterned cotton cloth decorated with a series of designs of Indian inspiration. These include a garland sprouting from the mouth of a mysterious beast. The most intriguing part of the decoration is the depiction of a goddess holding a cornucopium. She has been identified by several authorities as Tyche, the Greek goddess of prosperity. If this item has Western parallels, the silk coat, lacquerware, and bronze mirror in this burial were from China and date to the third century C.E.

An important new research program at Niya began in 1995. It mapped the extent of the site and investigated further tombs and houses. Eight burials were uncovered; the dead were laid out in hollowed tree trunks attired in splendid garments. Tomb 3 contained the bodies of a man and a woman. Just as in the prehistoric period in this area, the grave goods included the woman's toilet articles, on this occasion a comb, sewing kit, and cosmetics. The man was accompanied by a bow, quiver, and metal-tipped arrows. They wore silk trousers, shirts, a hood, and embroidered leather shoes, while the woman's jewelry was of gold and glass. The dead were also accompanied by food, including pears, grapes, and mutton.

Further reading: Burrow, T. *A Translation of the Kharosti Documents from Chinese Turkestan.* London: The Royal Asiatic Society 1940; Rhie, M. M. *Later Han, Three Kingdoms and Western Chin in China and Bactria to Shan-shan.* Leiden: Brill, 1999.

Noen U-Loke   Noen U-Loke is an Iron Age site in the Mun Valley of northeast Thailand. Noen U-Loke is one of many similar moated sites in the Mun Valley, which would have participated in the exchange networks that increasingly centered on the river systems of Southeast Asia. Extensive excavations in 1997–98 revealed unprecedented evidence for the social development of an Iron Age society just before the transition to statehood. The five-meter (16.5-ft.)-deep stratigraphic sequence began in the eighth century B.C.E., and the site was abandoned in about 400 C.E. Five mortuary phases have been recognized. The first belongs to the early Iron Age, when iron was already in use for spears, jewelry, and hoes. Other mortuary offerings, which include shell and bronze ornaments, pottery vessels filled with fish, a tiger's tooth necklace, and pigs' limbs, indicate a considerable social investment in mortuary ritual. This grew over time, as agate, carnelian, and glass were added to the range of ornaments, and bronzes became more varied and abundant.

The peak of mortuary elaboration was reached during the fourth phase, when people were interred in graves filled with burnt rice, lined and capped with clay. Certain individuals stood out for the wealth of their grave goods. One man wore 75 bronze bangles on each arm, three bronze belts, bronze finger and toe rings, silver ear coils covered in gold, and an agate neck pendant and had an iron knife, many pottery vessels, and glass beads. A woman of the same phase wore a necklace of gold and agate beads and silver and bronze bangles. During the fifth phase, mortuary wealth declined. It is possible that by this juncture wealth and social status were concentrated in an elite group buried elsewhere on the site.

The rise of social complexity took place at a time when conflict was also increasing: One man of the final phase had been killed by an iron arrow, which was found lodged in his spine. There was also a proliferation of iron points at this juncture and a major investment in water-control measures. In the latter a series of banks constructed around the site probably acted as retaining walls for the streams flowing nearby. There was also a marked increase in exchange for exotic valuables, such as gold, silver, agate, and carnelian, which would have encouraged the development of a ruling group.

Noh   The site of Noh is located southeast of MATHURA in the middle reaches of the Jamuna Valley in India. It was excavated in 1963–67 and revealed a long prehistoric period of occupation that terminated with the Iron Age (about 700 B.C.E.). The remains of carbonized rice and iron artifacts have been recovered. The historical period followed, with evidence for occupation during the SUNGA (185–73 B.C.E.) and KUSHAN periods (78–200 C.E.). There were eight successive phases determined by the rebuilding of domestic structures in fired BRICK. These were associated with a drainage system and a material culture typical of the period, including toy carts, shell and glass beads, and animal and human figurines.

Northern Black Polished Ware   In northern India, a distinctive variety of pottery known as Northern Black Polished Ware (NBPW) appeared in many sites over a wide area. It was first recognized and described by SIR ALEXANDER CUNNINGHAM during the examination of a stupa at Andher near SANCHI. At the base of the stupa, he found a pottery vessel "beautifully smooth . . . of bright metallic lustre." This ceramic horizon was contemporaneous with a series of cultural changes characterized by a rapid development of urbanization, the expansion of agriculture as iron implements proliferated, and a sharp population increase. The distinctive polished ware itself represents a technical advance involving firing at a high temperature under carefully controlled conditions. Given its widespread occurrence and typological changes over time, dating this type of pottery is important in relating events at different sites. Unfortunately, it is difficult to calibrate radiocarbon dates that fall within the span of NBPW, but the consensus is that it first appeared between 550 and 500 B.C.E. Early contexts to have yielded NBPW include AHICCHATRA, UJJAIN, and KAUSAMBI. Three phases in the typological development of this ware have been proposed; the middle phase lasted from 400 to 250 B.C.E., and the third ended in about 100 B.C.E.

Nulchi, King　*See* HWANGNAM, GREAT TOMB OF.

nutmeg　Nutmeg is the seed of the evergreen tree *Myristica fragrans*. It is a native of the Malukas (Moluccas) in Indonesia and was greatly in demand as one of the spices for which island Southeast Asia is famous. The same tree also supplies mace, part of the outer rind of the nut.

　　See also CLOVES; SPICE ISLANDS.

O

Oc Eo Oc Eo is a rectangular city, demarcated by five moats and banks, that lies on the flat delta terrain of the Transbassac region of the Mekong Delta in Vietnam. Two Chinese emissaries, KANG DAI and Zhu Ying, visited this region in the mid-third century C.E. and reported on the presence of walled cities, kings, a system of taxation, rice cultivation, and extensive maritime trade with India. Excavations at Oc Eo have verified these reports. Oc Eo was a maritime port where trade goods from far afield reached Southeast Asia. Air photographs taken during the 1920s led to the discovery of the city, which lies at the hub of a series of canals. Aerial views also indicate that the city was divided into wards or sections by further regularly placed canals. Beginning in February 1944, Louis Malleret uncovered a series of brick structures. The presence of a stone LINGAM, or phallus, together with ceramic figures of a lion, indicates that these were probably early temple foundations. He also encountered the remains of jewelry workshops where ornaments of gold, tin, copper, and glass were manufactured with the aid of bronze awls and hammers. One area contained a mass of gold leaf; finished golden plaques incorporated images of a woman sitting cross-legged and playing on a harp, while another woman stood in an elegant posture with a lotus flower beside her head. Two Roman medallions of the Emperors Marcus Aurelius (121–180 C.E.) and Antoninus Pius (86–161 C.E.), together with carnelian ornaments, evidence trade involving the Roman Empire. There are also Iranian COINAGE and a Chinese mirror. The range of locally manufactured jewelry covers virtually all possible raw materials, including diamonds, gold, carnelians, amethysts, beryls, zircons, quartz, rubies, olivine, jade, malachite, and magnetite. The Chinese visitors described a local tradition of engraving jewelry, and carved carnelians have been recovered. Some bear writing in the Indian BRAHMI script translated as *jaya* (from the SANSKRIT word for "victory"), as well as personal names. The wet substrate has preserved wooden posts that would have raised domestic structures above the floods that cross the delta during the rainy season, and an abundance of biological finds indicates the raising of domestic stock as well as hunting and fishing.

Excavations in the vicinity of Oc Eo have now recommenced. Pierre-Yves Manguin and Vo Si Khai have investigated sites scattered at the foot of Ba The hill nearby. Their research program is designed to investigate the wide range of sites on the plain below Ba The; to obtain a solid dating framework for the critical centuries during which the sites were occupied, including the moats, canals, and walls; and to illuminate the major stages of cultural development there. Early results at Linh Son and Go Cay Thi indicate that settlement involving houses raised on piles occurred during the first century or two of the Common Era, representing essentially the late prehistoric occupation of the delta. There followed a period dated to the fifth through the seventh centuries, when brick structures were erected. The moats, canals, and walls might belong to this period but remain to be dated.

See also FUNAN.

Ojin (r. 270–310 C.E.) *Ojin was the 15th sovereign of Japan and probably ruled in the late fourth to the early fifth century C.E., according to the Nihongi.*
The reign dates given in the *Nihongi* are almost certainly inaccurate. During his reign there were strong contacts with the Korean states, and he was sufficiently powerful to send armed forces into Kyushu. Ojin's reign saw a

number of major cultural changes as a result of contact with the emerging states of Korea. The *Nihongi*, for example, records that the men of PAEKCHE and SHILLA, two Korean kingdoms, traveled to his court, and he ordered that they dig an IRRIGATION pond. There are many other references to contact with Paekche. One described the arrival of a seamstress, another a gift of two horses. Perhaps the most significant entry, however, refers to the arrival of a scribe, who had books that included the *Analects* of CONFUCIUS and who tutored the crown prince in literacy. These immigrant groups, according to the *Nihongi*, formed the *be*—a regional group specializing in an aspect of manufacture, or a craft corporation, which paid tribute to the YAMATO court (300–552 C.E.).

Ojin's tomb at Habikino ranks second only to that of NINTOKU in terms of size. It is a keyhole *kofun* (burial mound) 415 meters (1,369.5 ft.) long, surrounded by two moats. The interior has not been examined, but HANIWA (tomb models) figures in the form of houses and water-birds have been found there.

O-no-Yasumaro (d. 723 C.E.) *O-no-Yasumaro was the compiler of the* Kojiki, *by order of the emperor of Japan.*
The KOJIKI gave the ancestry of the royal family back to its mythical origins. It was completed in 712 C.E. At his death, O-no-Yasumaro was a lower junior fourth-rank official and head of the Ministry of Civil Affairs, with responsibility for the census and taxation. His cremated remains, together with an inscription on bronze, were discovered in 1979, about 10 kilometers (6 mi.) southeast of the royal capital of HEIJO-KYO. The text gave his residence in that city, which can be identified on the reconstructed street plan.

oracle bones Oracle bones refer to the animal bones and shells used over a lengthy period in ancient China for divining the future.

These bones first came to scholarly attention in the late 19th century in Beijing, when Wang Yiong (1845–1900), a scholar and Qing dynasty official, noticed archaic writing on tortoise shell that had been prescribed as medicine to treat malaria. He forthwith purchased all the specimens available in pharmacies in the city and assembled the first collection. On his death in 1900, his collection passed into the hands of a colleague, LIU TAIYUN (1857–1909), who continued to save as many specimens as possible from pharmacists, and published 1,058 texts. Further impetus to the collection and study of the oracle bones was provided by the 1917 publication of SONG YIRANG's book *Chiwen Juli* (Examples of oracle bone Inscriptions).

Given the new scholarly interest in the oracle bones, the first three decades of the 20th century saw systematic looting of key sites and the sale of an unknown number of treasures to Chinese and Western collectors, including James Menzies, a missionary. Some of these collections were later sold to the British Museum in London, the Carnegie Museum in Pittsburgh, and the Scottish National Museum in Edinburgh. Thousands of items were also bought by Japanese collectors. A flourishing counterfeit industry sprang up, and many fakes entered the market. Luo Zhenyu was a scholar who set himself the task of distinguishing between the original and fake specimens and then seeking their actual place of origin, a secret closely guarded by the dealers. He wrote a key article, published in 1910, in which he listed the names of the kings of ANYANG, the location of their capital, and the process of divination in which the oracle bones played a key role. This work proceeded with a series of volumes that expanded on the kings, the role of divination, and geographic terms. His research also concentrated on the meaning of the individual characters. This was facilitated by the fact that they are the script from which later developments derived. The words for "hunting," "animals," "directions," "numbers," and "fishing" provided a basic lexicon for identifying the questions posed by the diviners in the procedure of providing a question with two potential answers and then heating the bone so that the resultant cracks provided the reply. Of 1,207 items, it was found that almost half the questions concerned making sacrifices to the ancestral spirits. The next most frequent questions related to hunting and fishing, followed by questions concerning the king's travel. Other important issues included war, the weather, and the harvest. Between 1915 and 1926, Wang Gouwei (1877–1927) contributed significantly to the early analysis of the inscriptions by piecing together texts on sacrifice to the ancestors. This allowed him to reconstruct the names of 31 Shang kings over a period of 17 generations.

Until 1928, all the studies of the oracle bones were based on looted finds purchased from dealers or pharmacies. In October 1928, however, Dong Zuobin of the Institute of History and Philology of the Chinese National Academy began excavations in a mound near Xiaotun and recovered not only 784 new texts, but also the remains of pottery, jade, and bone artifacts. This discovery initiated many more years of excavations. LI JI (1896–1979) took charge of the Xiaotun excavations, and working in conjunction with Dong Zuobin, he opened a large area north of the village in November 1929. Any doubt as to the presence of further records was dispelled when he came across a deep circular pit filled with inscribed bones and tortoise shells. Even this, however, paled before the spectacular discovery, in 1936, of another underground storage pit. On the last day of the season, late in the afternoon, Pit H127 was opened to reveal a mass of oracle bones together with a human skeleton. They were so densely packed that it appeared likely that this was a deliberately placed archive. It proved impossible to do justice to this cache in the field, so it was decided to lift the entire contents of the pit in one block and dissect it in the laboratory. This block weighed more than three tons, and with great difficulty given the hazardous state of local transport, it was shipped to the Institute of History and Philology in Nanjing. After months of careful excavation, 17,096 individual pieces were assembled, and it was possible to analyze the group as a whole. It was found that they were from the reigns of Pan Geng and Wu Ding and that they were placed underground during the reign of the latter. Their condition was so good that even the vermilion writing on the carapaces was visible before the characters were traced over with incisions. Notes on some specimens also indicated the source of the turtle shell. With this outstanding discovery, research on the oracle bones in the field ceased, because Japanese forces invaded northern China, and the precious finds were removed for safety to the remote southwestern province of Yunnan.

THE ORIGINS OF ORACLE BONES

The origin of divination employing bones in this manner has deep prehistoric roots in China. The bones of sheep,

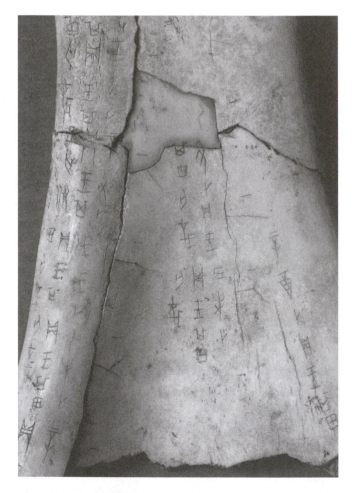

The court records of the Shang emperors were carved on the surface of bones. They were concerned with divining future events on the basis of the form of cracks resulting from applying heat to the underside. This bone is a cow's scapula, but most records were carved into turtle shells. (© LowellGeorgia/ CORBIS)

pigs, and deer as well as cattle were heated and interpreted as early as the fourth millennium B.C.E., probably as part of a religion based on ANCESTOR WORSHIP. Most divinations were made on turtle plastrons, but cattle ribs and scapulae, being thin and flat, were also used. The earliest evidence for oracle bones comes from the late Neolithic sites of the Fuhe culture in Liaoning province in the far northeast of China. Here sheep and deer scapulae had holes bored in them before being cracked through the application of heat. Most sites of the LOWER XIAJIADIAN CULTURE of Inner Mongolia have also yielded early oracle bones dating to the end of the third millennium B.C.E. Oracle bones are present at the Shandong LONGSHAN CULTURE site of Chengziyai (2500–1900 B.C.E.), where 16 fragments have been recovered. The site of Zhukaigou in western Inner Mongolia has yielded oracle bones that were carefully polished, bored, and subjected to heat several hundred years before the SHANG STATE. A few oracle bones have been found at the earlier Shang capital of ZHENGZHOU and in Western Zhou contexts at Fengchu, Zhangjiapo, Changping, and Qijia, and their use was probably more widespread than the present distribution implies.

ORACLE BONES AND THE SHANG DYNASTY

With the Shang dynasty (1766–1045 B.C.E.), the bones were inscribed and therefore provide a vital source of historic information matched only by inscriptions cast onto the surface of bronzes. The basic procedure of Shang oracle-bone divination involved two complementary outcomes on an issue that concerned the king. On the right-hand side of the plastron was the positive outcome: "The king should hunt today." Opposing it on the left-hand side was the alternative: "The king should not hunt today." The applied heat in a depression on the right-hand side would lead to a sharp report and a crack in the bone. The shape of the crack might be a positive signal, that the king should hunt. Then the negative side would be similarly treated and the resultant crack interpreted. A postscript was added on occasion: "the king hunted."

Currently, more than 100,000 such bones have been recovered, but many more have been looted or powdered for Chinese medicinal purposes. Turtles were imported from considerable distances; some of the species of turtle represented at Anyang were of south Chinese distribution. On arrival at Anyang, the carapace was usually labeled as to its origin in archaic Chinese script and then prepared for use by smoothing and polishing the surface. Female plastrons were preferred because they are flatter and thinner and have a smoother surface than male specimens. Careful analysis has revealed that the plastron or bone was bored with regularly spaced holes as a preliminary to the application of heat. These holes were bored in pairs on the underside of the bone, probably because it was easier to obtain cracks on a thin surface. The two holes were carefully shaped in contrasting forms. One was circular, the other lentoid. When cracks were achieved, they followed a certain pattern that aided interpretation. This was often undertaken by the Shang king himself to divine future events, and the bone was then incised with the king's pronouncements, which provide a clear insight into his concerns. They cover, for example, the most propitious time to make sacrifices to the ancestors, whether to go to war, whether a royal consort will have a successful delivery, whether it will rain, the degree to which there will be a good harvest, or even which ancestor is afflicting the king with a toothache. Sometimes there is a postscript, saying whether there was indeed rain or whether a disaster or military success did occur.

The script employed was ancestral to modern Chinese writing, making some of texts decipherable. Since the texts often refer to ancestors and provide dates, it has been possible to identify the names of the Shang kings and the dynastic succession well before the foundation of the royal capital at Anyang.

THE MESSAGE IN THE EARLY WRITING

The symbols found on the oracle bones provide evidence for craft activities representing the majority of the populace beyond the court and its functionaries. A human figure seen holding baskets probably represents a merchant or trader, while the texts themselves describe the importation of carapaces and horses. A person holding a brush has been interpreted as a painter, and other symbols depict a butcher and hunter. In these cases, the symbols are very clear, as the butcher has a knife hovering over an animal lying on its back. There can be no doubt of the presence of the executioner, seen as a person wielding an axe over a decapitated victim. This symbol is strongly reminiscent of the presence of headless skeletons in the sacrificial pits near the royal Shang tombs. Other symbols are less obvious in their implications. A complete chariot might represent a maker of chariots or might simply be the word for the vehicle itself. The graph showing a house or gate tower could be the word for a builder, while a man seen holding a pennant might have been a flag maker or have a rank of soldier. Many symbols show different forms of bronze vessels and possible manufacturers of arrows, halberds, knives, and quivers, the last symbolized by two arrows in a container.

IDENTIFYING THE SHANG KINGS

Dong Zuobin's analysis of the H127 archive led to the discovery of the Shang calendrical system and, thus, reign dates and other major events. He found that many of the texts included the name of the reigning king, as well as the day, month, and even, on occasion, year of a particular divination. As a result, he was able to name and order the reigns of 12 Shang kings. This added up to a total of 287 years, but the first 14 of these belonged in the period before the establishment of the royal capital of Anyang by Pen Geng. Dong Zuobin's calculations were so precise that he was able to pinpoint the 15th year of Pan Geng's rule and, therefore, the date of the move to Anyang. From this basic chronological foundation, Dong Zuobin began to explore the nature of the rituals associated with divinations that marked the Shang court's annual round of activities. The vital importance of ancestor worship and the offering of sacrifices to the named ancestors on certain days were soon realized. Specific military campaigns led by various Shang kings were also identified.

MODERN INTERPRETATIONS

The analysis of the increasing number of specimens that have accumulated since the early days of discovery has now become highly specialized, and earlier interpretations have been modified and expanded. In the first instance, proper historic interpretation of the texts requires that they be dated. This can be determined on the basis of several criteria. Foremost, if known, is the location of the specimen. Where 17,000 come from the same pit, for example, it can be assured that an element of contemporaneity exists. Detailed reading of the texts also makes it possible to list the actual names of the diviners. These include Bin and Zheng, who collaborated on a divination and were therefore contemporaries. They were active during the reign of King Wu Ding. Their contemporaries can also be named, and their successors can be assigned to one of the five periods into which the oracle bones are now divided. Thus Shao was active in Period II, and Peng in the third period. References to the titles of members of the royal dynasty can also provide essential dating information. When, for example, a script refers to a father whose place is known in the genealogy, then the bone must date to within the lives of his sons. Similarly where it refers to an older brother, then it must belong to the same generation as the younger brother who performed the divination. There are, however, pitfalls in following this line of inquiry too literally, because, for example, the term zu means "grandfather" but can also refer to a male ancestor going back more than two generations. Supporting information for dating can also be obtained from the writing style, which began large and bold and became smaller. It is likely that the scribe-engravers were specialists distinct from the school of diviners, and, therefore, it should be possible to recognize individual handwriting. There were also changes over time in the way in which the inscriptions were set out on the bone and the method of recording the origin. On the basis of these approaches to the analysis of the texts, a list of Shang kings has been produced that covers much of the occupation of Anyang, the late royal capital.

KING WU DING

What was the underlying motivation behind the intense and continuing devotion to divination, and what topics concerned the king? One of the foremost issues was the making of sacrifices to appease the ancestors, sacrifices often taking the form of killing an animal in the ancestral temple. Another revolved around military campaigns against rival polities on the border of the Shang realm. A charge might read: "This season, the king should attack the [named] enemy, because he will gain assistance on this occasion." This is the positive outcome. The opposing negative would read: "This season, the king should not attack the enemy, because if he does, he might not receive assistance." The resulting cracks would determine whether to attack or not. This is best illustrated in a particular set of five plastrons considered in detail in an exercise by David Keightley. They greatly exercised the mind of King Wu Ding on November 24, 1311 B.C.E. At least two of the original plastrons came from a garrison settlement called Tuan. Three issues were being divined. Should the king follow General Wang Cheng and attack the state of Xia Wei, or should he follow General Zhi Guo and attack Bafang? Positive and negative charges were set out on the plastrons couched as the question: "If the king followed this course, would he receive divine assistance?" Multiple cracking on the five plastrons was undertaken, but the outcome is uncertain. Another issue was treated by using other holes on the same set. This time it concerned the king's toothache. Which ancestor was responsible for this affliction, and what sacrifice would appease the ancestral spirit? Four possible royal ancestors were named, in the order in which they ascended the throne. Pan Geng was identified as the one responsible, leading to the question of whether the sacrifice of a dog or a sheep would alleviate the pain. The answering crack was recorded as being slightly auspicious.

The range of subjects requiring divination during the reign of Wu Ding provides a unique glimpse into issues of royal concern in any early state. The king, for example, required information on the childbearing of his consorts. He was concerned to have his dreams interpreted. Would it rain, and how good would the harvest be this year? He sought to understand the portents of celestial phenomena and whether it was auspicious to hunt, go to war, or found a settlement. Sometimes he wished to seek guidance on a future plan, at other times he set out his wishes and sought reassurance that they were the correct course. If there was a crop failure, the king would try to find out the reasons. Was a particular ancestor wreaking vengeance and requiring sacrifices to be made? He was, in sum, attempting to meet and negotiate with the divine powers that molded the world.

THE NATURE AND ROLE OF KINGSHIP

The oracle-bone texts thus permit a penetration of the nature and role of kingship in the Shang state. In the first instance, the royal ancestors remained a vital part of the day-to-day lives of their descendants. On one divination we read: "Crack making on guiyou day: To father Jia, we pray for good hunting." Jia was the 17th king in the dynastic sequence. On another occasion the text reads:

"[W]e pray for Lady Hao to Father Yi." FU HAO was a consort of King Wu Ding, and Father Yi was the 20th king and Fu-Hao's father-in-law.

Second, the power to communicate with the god-ancestors to secure good fortune or successful outcomes can be seen as a powerful means of legitimizing the king's position of authority. Where agricultural surpluses maintained the court, rain was a consuming issue. Thus the king is often portrayed through divination as a rain-maker. A relevant text reads: "Crack making on jimao day. Que divined 'It will rain.' The king read the cracks and said: 'If it rains, it will be on a ren day.'" Later came the verification statement: "On renwu day, it rained."

The role of the king can also be seen in anticipating problems. One text reveals not only the Shang conception of the state's borders but also the problems posed by enemy action. King Wu Ding said on one oracle bone: "The king read the cracks and said, 'there will be calamities, there will be alarming news.'" There followed the record that enemies attacked his kingdom from east and west. Keightley, in commenting on this plastron, noted that the letters were large and highlighted in red as if displayed publicly to reinforce the king's divinatory powers.

Toward the end of the Shang dynasty, the use of oracle bones underwent several changes. The size of the script became smaller; the divined topics were reduced to hunting, the weather and avoiding calamities; and there were no longer paired positive and negative forecasts. It is probable that other methods of divining the future grew in popularity.

THE SHANG ENVIRONMENT AND ECONOMY

Apart from the divinations themselves, incidental information provides an unparalleled documentary source for many aspects of the Shang culture and environment. There is botanical and faunal evidence that the Shang people enjoyed a milder winter climate than at present, with some influence of the monsoon reaching much further north. Since the kings were concerned with rainfall, and the oracle bones can often be dated to the month of the divination, it is possible to assess the climate. Today there is regular snowfall in the Anyang area from January to March, but the oracle texts rarely mention snow, and when they do, it took the form of sleet. There are also records for rains falling throughout a 10-day period, a pattern that is rare today and more akin to the monsoon climate of the Chang (Yangtze Valley). The animals mentioned, in particular the rhinoceros, elephant, tiger, and pheasant, are also more compatible with a warmer climate than is found today.

The subsistence economy was based on agriculture and domestic stock. Animals were used in considerable numbers in sacrificial rituals, and cattle, sheep, horses, pigs, and chickens are all mentioned. Many animals were involved. The highest recorded number of cattle sacrificed in one event exceeded 1,000, and about 100 human victims were mentioned at least nine times. Horses were sacrificed, but usually only when interred with the chariots they pulled. Since the kings were passionate about hunting, the animals they sought provide environmental information. The most common prey were elaphures, a species of deer, and foxes. Next were wild boars and wild cattle. Tigers were relatively rarely killed in hunts, but the faunal assemblage taken as a whole implies a low-lying, forested, and swampy environment. This is confirmed by a study of references in old poems describing the area only a few centuries after the fall of the Shang dynasty.

There are many references to agriculture and crops. The oracle bones include a symbol for the creation of new fields, in the form of two arms reaching down to the soil. The most common is the word *shu*, which almost certainly refers to millet. Another word, *ji*, is also regularly encountered and is probably a second species of millet. *Dao*, a third word for a grain, is thought to refer to rice, while *mai* is the word for "wheat." It is unlikely that the Shang cultivated wheat, because it is not referred to as being harvested. There are also words for all aspects of silk weaving, from mulberry trees to the silkworm, and the presence of silk fabric is confirmed on the basis of impressions and even jade carvings of silkworms.

THE SHANG COURT

One of the most telling features of a developing state is the central administration. Once again, the oracle bones are a vital source of information, in that they include many references to the bureaucracy that surrounded the king and made up so much of his court. The title *fu* was given to the king's consorts, the most famous of whom was Fu Hao, because of the discovery of her intact tomb. She was a consort to King Wu Ding, and the number of references to her in the oracle texts makes it possible to appreciate some of her responsibilities. These included leading military expeditions and taking part in court rituals. She was also a rich landowner, and her wealth is manifest in the number and quality of the bronzes and jades in her tomb, not to mention the sacrificial victims.

The word *zi* refers to a prince and is also the name of the Shang king's clan. As with the consorts, we find *zi* taking part in rituals, accompanying the king on his hunting ventures, and leading war parties. There were numerous court officials. Diviners and interpreters were prominent, and given the intensity their results inspired, they must also be numbered among the most important. They also had specific titles: Diviners were known as *pu*, interpreters had the title *chen*. *Wu* was the title given to a priest. There were also highly ranked lords who were granted settlements and estates beyond the capital. Some were often referred to in the oracle records. War was a common theme. There appears to have been a permanent army, known as a *lü*, while the lords with landed estates were required to contribute forces when required. The list of military personnel is also of considerable interest in any consideration of Shang warfare. It includes the titles for those responsible for frontier defense; the command of archers, horses, and dogs; and for those in command of strongpoints. One purpose of war may well have been to secure sacrificial victims, and the numbers of individuals who met this fate are very high. In one case, 600 died with the construction of one building.

THE WESTERN ZHOU DYNASTY

Divination continued under the WESTERN ZHOU DYNASTY (1045–771 B.C.E.). A passage in a fifth-century text known as the METAL-BOUND COFFER referred to a notable event shortly after the Zhou defeat of Shang. KING WU fell ill, and ZHOU GONG, his brother, decided to consult the turtles concerning the king. The procedure reveals the importance attached to the prognostications. First the duke had four altars constructed, on three of which he placed jade disks. He held his own jade mace, his symbol of high status, and prayed to the ancestors that by the substitution of his own life, the king would recover. He then divined of the turtle that if his death would save the king's life, he would gather up the jades and await his end. But the divinations were favorable. The duke was permitted to live, and the king recovered on the next day. Archaeological documentation of the continuation of oracle-bone divination during the Western Zhou dynasty is derived from the site of Fengchu in the Zhouyuan, the Plain of Zhou, in the Wei Valley. A cache of oracle bones was found there under a large palace structure, and this makes up the vast majority of specimens of this date. There has been an element of controversy over their origin, because some refer to Shang ancestors. This can, however, be explained by the fact that the exchange of high-ranking princesses between the Zhou and the Shang led to the Zhou kings' having Shang ancestors. Thus two Zhou kings at least, Wang Ji and Wen, were married to Shang princesses, and their offspring had legitimate Shang ancestors. An important point about the Fengchu inscriptions is that they present a number of consistent differences from their Shang counterparts in the way in which the text was organized. Nevertheless, the texts themselves make it clear that divination of future events through the cracks produced by heat was their prime purpose. Sacrifice to the ancestors played a key role in these rituals. For example, 30 penned cows were killed and 30 people beheaded, and captives were sacrificed. On one occasion, 100 cows were sacrificed.

DIVINATION IN THE STATE OF CHU

Elite burials of the CHU state that centered on the middle Chang (Yangtze) Valley until the late third century B.C.E. often contained BAMBOO SLIPS that recorded the divination records of the person interred. Thus Tomb 1 at Tianxingguan in Hubei province holds the records of divinations using turtle bones undertaken on behalf of Pan Cheng, lord of Diyang in the mid-fourth century B.C.E. In the year that a guest from QIN inquired after the king at Ying, a person called Gu Ding asked the bones whether Pan Cheng would gain benefit from serving the king during the forthcoming year. The answer from the oracle divined an auspicious outcome. These slips show that some diviners worked for several clients. Fan Huozhi divined for Pan Cheng as well as the person interred in a tomb at nearby Wangshan. The daily reference to the oracles emphasizes how the spirits continued to exercise a vital role in the life of high-ranking leaders of Chu society.

The ancient practice of divination by turtle shells and MILFOIL stalks was well known to the historian SIMA QIAN, and a chapter of his history describes how the rulers of old would consult diviners to ascertain the will of heaven. It was also, he said, much employed during the Zhou and Qin dynasties. One of his chapters describes the presence of diviners in the market of the Western Zhou capital of CHANG'AN. Another details the procedures for divination from shells. Although no stores of oracle texts come from HAN DYNASTY sources, it is clear that their use continued into the early first millennium C.E. That they were preserved is not in doubt; there is a reference in the SHIJI to the shells used in divination being preserved in the imperial shrines of the early Han emperors.

DIVINATION IN JAPAN

Chinese histories also described the practice of divination by burning bones when referring to Japan during the late YAYOI period (third and fourth centuries C.E.). This has been archaeologically verified by the discovery of bones with burning pits in the relevant Yayoi sites. The use of oracle bones continued into the YAMATO period (300–552). When, in 708 C.E., consideration was given to the construction of a magnificent new capital at HEIJO-KYO (NARA) to replace FUJIWARA, GEOMANCY and divination played their part in selecting the site. As was said at the time, "Three mountains establish a bastion and the divining rod and tortoise shells both follow."

Further reading: Keightley, D. N. *Sources of Shang History: The Oracle Bones of Bronze Age China.* Berkeley: University of California Press, 1978; Shaughnessy, E. L. "Zhouyuan Oracle-Bone Inscriptions: Entering the Research Stage?" *Early China* 11–12 (1985–1987): 146–163.

Otsuka Otsuka is a village of the late Middle YAYOI period, located on an eminence near the western shore of Yokohama Bay, Honshu Island, Japan. It is notable for the fact that it has been completely excavated. The Yayoi culture (300 B.C.E.–300 C.E.) was seminal in the development of early Japanese states. It began about 300 B.C.E. with the movement of immigrants from southern Korea into an archipelago in which hunting and gathering still dominated in the Jomon culture (10,000–300 B.C.E.). However, the Yayoi culture saw the serious beginnings of wet-rice cultivation and metallurgy of both bronze and iron as well

as an increase in maritime trade. It rapidly spread northeast from its homeland in Kyushu into Honshu. Otsuka represents this expansionary movement, and its complete excavation demonstrates its size and likely population. The site itself covers a kidney-shaped area measuring 200 by 130 meters (66 by 429 ft.), bounded by a defensive ditch two meters (6.6 ft.) deep and up to four meters (13.2 ft.) wide. There are hints of an earth bank as a further defensive measure, for it is known that intersettlement fighting was endemic at this period. Ninety house foundations have been identified, but overlapping and rebuilding imply that no more than 30, each large enough to house a single family, were occupied simultaneously. Hence the population is unlikely to have exceeded 250 to 300 people. The houses were subrectangular with roofs supported by large wooden posts. There were also raised storehouses for the community's vital rice. A cemetery lay 100 meters (330 ft.) southeast of the perimeter ditch. It held mounded tombs ringed by a ditch, but since there are relatively few for a settlement of this size, it is thought that only the village elite were interred there, and that there must be another cemetery attached to the village.

Otsukayama Tsubai Otsukayama is a *kofun,* or burial mound, of the early phase of the YAMATO kingdom of Japan (300–552 C.E.). The Otsukayama *kofun* is typologically early, but its enormous size—185 meters (610 ft.) long and 75 (247 ft.) wide—dwarfs the antecedent mounded tombs of the YAYOI culture (300 B.C.E.–300 C.E.) and exemplifies the rise of powerful Yamato rulers. Otsukayama is located near the Yamato center of NARA on the island of Honshu. Natural contours at the edge of a hill were modified to form two mounds, one square and the other round, to form a keyhole shape that gives such monuments their name. The site was severely damaged in 1894 when a railway track was cut through it, but excavations in 1953 revealed an intact tomb below the circular mound. This measured 4.9 by 1.1 meters (16.1 by 3.6 ft.) and was sunk four meters into the ground. It was lined and capped with stone slabs and rested on a clay floor. Clay had also been used to seal the tomb. A wooden coffin had lain within, and no grave offerings were found. However, the mortuary offerings in the chamber were rich and numerous. Thirty bronze mirrors had been placed on end leaning against the stone walls, some from the same workshops, dating to the mid-third century C.E. There were also iron swords, arrowheads, and spears and slats of iron from body armor. Iron tools include sickles, axes, adzes, knives, harpoons, and one fishhook.

Oxus treasure The Oxus treasure was brought to light in 1877 in Afghanistan, when items of gold and silver were found, probably in the vicinity of the ancient city of Khandian (Kabadian) on the Amu Dar'ya River, formerly known as the Oxus. However vague the original find spot of the Oxus treasure might be, its fortuitous survival has proved an extraordinary source of information on the technical skill of the Achaemenid gold-working tradition and the wealth and splendor of their eastern province of BACTRIA. It has been suggested that the treasure represents offerings at a shrine, which were buried for safety, perhaps in the face of ALEXANDER THE GREAT'S army (356–323 B.C.E.). The outstanding gold and silver objects date to the fifth and fourth centuries B.C.E.; culturally, most belong to the ACHAEMENID EMPIRE. Some items show Greek influence, however, and others seem to have been inspired by Scythian motifs. The hoard provides a clear insight into the quality and wealth of Achaemenid Bactria. The treasure might have been washed out from its original location by floodwaters and redeposited, for it is alleged that it was found scattered in the sandy bed of the river. The treasure had a checkered history.

It was bought by three traveling merchants who took it to Kabul, in Afghanistan, but they were waylaid by brigands en route. The local British administrator, Captain F. C. Burton, tracked down the thieves and recovered part of the treasure, which was then returned to its original owners. They took it to Peshawar in Pakistan and sold it. It was purchased by SIR ALEXANDER CUNNINGHAM and then by Sir Augustus Franks. A large number of coins were bought at the same time, but it is not certain whether they were from the same source. Many were minted during the reign of Alexander the Great and SELEUCUS I NICATOR (356–281 B.C.E.). The latest coin belongs to Euthydemus and dates to the end of the third century B.C.E. The Oxus treasure is now housed in the British Museum.

Some fine silver and gold statuettes of men show their elaborate aristocratic clothing. Miniature golden chariots, one of which is only 19 centimeters (7.6 in.) long, were pulled by four horses. They had spoked wheels, a charioteer, and a passenger. One superb horse's head, fashioned in hammered gold with wire for reins, was only four centimeters (1.6 in.) long. Another was even smaller. The interest in depicting animals is also seen in the silver rendition of a rampant goat that once embellished a gilt ewer, bowl, or plate. The goat's features, such as the horns and beard, were gilt. The cast figurine of a deer was rendered in gold, while the antlers and ears were soldered onto the body after being separately cast. It is an exquisite miniature, only 5.5 centimeters (2.2 in.) in length. There are also a figure of a goose in silver with gold inlay for the eyes, and a large hollow gold fish, 24 centimeters (9.6 in.) long, which might have been used as some form of serving vessel with fluid being poured through the mouth. Many of the gold vessels were also embellished with images of animals. A gold jug, for example, had a handle that terminated in a lion's head. A gold bowl is decorated with rampant lions that resemble those seen on Persian hunting scenes.

The Achaemenid interest in the chase is vividly seen in a silver disk decorated with hunters on horseback spearing deer, goats, and hares. The horses in this scene had the tail tied in ribbons, while the men rode with no stirrups. Hunting scenes also decorate the gold covering for a sword scabbard. There are many images of men depicted on gold plaques, perhaps offerings given by worshipers at a temple. They wear tunics and trousers and peaked caps that cover the ears, and many have a dagger at the waist.

Personal jewelry had many forms. The signet rings were variously decorated with images on a flat plate. One shows strong Greek influence or origin, with two female figures. Another bears an image of Herakles, while a third has a winged bull and a short inscription in Aramaic. There are also several gold armlets decorated with animal heads at each end and spiraliform torques originally worn around the neck.

P

Paekche Paekche (18 B.C.E.–663 C.E.) was one of the states of the period of the THREE KINGDOMS in Korea; the others were KOGYURO and SHILLA. It was located in the southwestern part of the Korean Peninsula. The three kingdoms coexisted, often at war with one another, in the first to seventh centuries C.E. Documentary sources give the date 18 B.C.E. for the foundation of Paekche, but the origins are not well known. Twenty-two administrative districts have been described, each governed by a member of the ruling family. There were also high ministers distinguished by their dress and headgear. Paekche was blessed with rich rice lands, and the economy was basically agrarian, although having a long coastline; it was in contact with China and Japan and possessed a naval force. The court was literate in Chinese by the fourth century B.C.E. and adopted BUDDHISM in 384 B.C.E. Wars with Koguryo and Shilla generated at least two moves of the capital, and Paekche was finally confronted by an alliance between the Chinese Tang and Shilla in 660 C.E. A large force of combined Korean and Chinese troops landed in Paekche from the Liaotung Peninsula. Caught in a pincer move involving a further army sent from the east by King Muyol of Shilla, Paekche was defeated at the Battle of Yonsun. Attempts at a restoration now hinged on the support of the Yamato kingdom in Japan, which had, since 631, held Prince P'ung as a hostage. Support was forthcoming, and the restoration movement seemed to have succeeded, but Tang forces again returned and this time won a decisive naval victory at the mouth of the Kum River. China's hold on the Korean Peninsula was strengthened, as Paekche was now eliminated.

ARCHAEOLOGICAL REMAINS

This defeat was accompanied by widespread destruction and looting, so few structures survive intact. However, archaeological research has produced much information about this state. Thus many forts have been examined. At MONGCHON, the walls and moat enclosed an area of nearly 23 hectares (57.5 acres), within which lay a palace and a reservoir. Imported Chinese ceramics attest to occupation during the late third and early fourth centuries C.E., but it was finally taken by Kogyuro forces. A small gilt bronze statue of the Buddha was found in the vicinity of this site. Another fort at ISONG SANSONG was defended by an extensive stone wall and again contained a palace structure. A large urban site has been identified at Pungnamni, with walls at least five meters (16.5 ft.) in height and covering an area of 1,500 by 300 meters (4,950 by 990 ft.) at a minimum, although river erosion has taken away part of the complex.

Tombs

Paekche mounded tombs were usually designed with a reentry passage, which facilitated later looting. Tomb 3 at Sokchondong, however, which reaches a width of 30 meters (99 ft.), still contained two gold earrings and part of a gold crown that the looters had missed. It also contained Chinese pottery of the fourth century C.E. Wooden coffins were present at the Karakdong cemetery; to the south at Naju, mounds covered jar burials in which two vessels were placed mouth to mouth. One contained part of a gilt bronze crown. At Kongju, however, extraordinary intact royal burials were found. The foundation inscription recorded this as the burial of KING MURYONG, who died in 523 C.E. He and his queen were interred with great pomp and ceremony. The land was purchased from the Earth god; the price was recorded on an INSCRIPTION that still bore the coins used in payment. Within, the two royal corpses had been interred with a wealth of superb grave goods, including typically shaped gold crowns that would have been joined to silk caps.

HISTORY OF PAEKCHE

The kingdom of Paekche was arguably the most cultured of the three kingdoms of Korea and exercised considerable influence over Japan, sending the first Buddha images there in 552 C.E. However, it was always under threat from Kogyuro and at war with Shilla. In 641, ill advisedly, King Uija (r. 641–660) attacked the western border of Shilla, successfully taking 40 strongholds. The reaction of King Muyong of Shilla was to seek an alliance with Koguryo. When this was not forthcoming, he turned to the Chinese Tang emperor for support. In 660 C.E., Paekche was subjected to a naval attack on the west from China and an armed incursion from Shilla in the east. Unable to resist such force, the Paekche kingdom was absorbed into the Shilla state after the capital of Sabi was taken. This was not the end of resistance. For the next three years, there was a spirited attempt to regain independence by Poksin, a member of the royal line, and a Buddhist monk named Toch'im. They secured several victories and reclaimed some strongpoints but were finally defeated.

Further reading: Barnes, G. *State Formation in Korea*. London: Curzon Press, 2001; Hong, W. *Paekche of Korea and the Origin of Yamato Japan*. Seoul, Korea: Kudara International, 1994; Nelson, S. M. *The Archaeology of Korea*. Cambridge: Cambridge University Press, 1993; Portal, J. *Korea: Art and Archaeology*. London: British Museum, 2000.

Pagan   Pagan, originally Arimaddanapura, was the capital of the Myanmar (Burma) state from the mid-ninth century until it was destroyed by a Mongol invasion in 1287 C.E. The sandstone ANANDA temple is the most famous structure at Pagan. It was built by King Kyanzittha in 1091 C.E. and is prominent for the tall central spire of its stupa. The power of the Buddha is represented in the form of lions on the roofs. An inscription in Mon by King Kyanzittha (r. 1084–1111) mentions a large palace incorporating a throne room and an audience hall. The foundations of a palace in the old walled area were excavated in the early 1990s, and the excavators proposed that it could well represent that built by King Kyanzittha. The BRICK foundation walls of this building covered an area of at least 75 by 75 meters (247 by 245 ft.), and the excavation represents one of the very rare examples of a secular structure from an early Southeast Asian city. There are

many circular pits, lined with brick, that are thought to have supported massive wooden columns, but the palace was destroyed by a fire that razed it to the ground. The radiocarbon determinations suggest that the palace was built after the reign period of Kyanzittha. The analysis of this site suggests that Pagan may have begun as a series of specialist village communities. At nearby Otein Taung, ceramic production continued for several centuries, and toward the later stages of its occupation the craft specialists may have founded or patronized their own religious foundation, since temples were built in the vicinity of the mounds.

The core of the site is a moated and walled city located on the eastern bank of the Irrawaddy River in the dry zone of central Myanmar (Burma), but many temples lie beyond this precinct, which covers at least 80 square kilometers (32 sq. mi.). The intensity of construction activity can be measured by the publication of findings of at least 2,250 temples or monasteries to date, with many more known to await future surveys. There are several suggested dates for the foundation of Pagan, based on folklore or less than satisfactory historic evidence. The *Glass Palace Chronicle*, for example, cites 107 C.E. as the founding date, but this has no substance in fact. Traditional histories have it that the walled city was built in 849 by King Pyinbya after the sack of the previous PYU capital by the Chinese. Archaeological research does not support this early context, but rather it points to the construction of the walls between 1000 and 1230 C.E.

CHRONOLOGY OF SITE

On the basis of the dated inscriptions, Robert Hudson has identified the main phases of temple construction. There are two main concentrations of effort. The first took place between 1050 and 1100 C.E. under the reign of King Anawratha (1044–77). He also is reputed to have initiated an efficient system of rice IRRIGATION facilities. There was a second major building phase during the 13th century, by which time the central area was so densely built over that the city expanded to the east. Further attempts to obtain a valid chronology for the history of this city have turned to radiocarbon dates. In 1990, when the walls were being cleared and restored, exposed sections made it possible to obtain radiocarbon samples. One is from a ceramic pipe, thought to have been part of a latrine system, filled with a yellow deposit rich in rice phytoliths. The pipe was from a location between the city wall and the moat and dated to the 11th and 12th centuries C.E. Two further samples from under the wall provided dates that range within the period from the 11th to the mid-13th century.

BRICK ARCHITECTURE

The Irrawaddy presented many opportunities for trade, and as the power of Pagan extended over much of

Myanmar the Mon and Pyu people were absorbed and contributed to the artistic heritage of the city. It was, however, first and foremost occupied by Burmese-speaking people, who constructed many shrines dedicated to the *nat*s, their local deities, and to the Buddha. Two early examples of the former, the oldest surviving *nat* shrines in Burma, are located beside the Sarabha Gate into the city. The construction of Buddhist monuments both inside and beyond the city walls makes this one of the greatest of Buddhist centers, although many of the buildings were damaged or destroyed in an earthquake in 1975. It is recorded that King Anawrahta overcame the Mon capital of Thaton and relocated the craftsmen and artisans to Pagan to work on his ambitious building program in the cause of THERAVADA BUDDHISM. About 5,000 temples survive from an estimated earlier number of 13,000, many of which were linked with monasteries. Most of the temples were built of brick decorated with stucco and terra-cotta. Individual markings on some of the bricks reveal that they originated in villages located in the sustaining countryside. The brick was usually covered in stucco and ornamented with images and decorative motifs.

SANDSTONE ARCHITECTURE

A few buildings, such as the Nanpaya temple, were constructed in sandstone. Wall paintings on the interior walls reveal that wooden structures were also both abundant and elaborate. The Bupaya stupa is one of the earliest and is found adjacent to the city wall. Both are dated to the ninth century C.E. Foremost is the Shwe Zigon stupa, begun by King Anawrahta and completed by Kyanzittha. It is said to house the clavicle, a tooth, and part of the skull of the Buddha. Anawrahta was also responsible for the Shwe Sandaw stupa, raised on a series of rectangular terraces with steep steps, representing a temple mountain, and the Myinkaba temple, built as penance for killing his predecessor in a struggle for the throne. The later 12th-century Dhammayangyi temple has a cruciform ground plan and has massive dimensions but was never completed. The Gawdawpalin temple was built in the 13th century, just before the city was sacked by the Mongols. A further important late stupa, the Mingalazedi pagoda, was built in 1284 by King Narathihapati and is notable for its decorative plaques illustrating scenes from the life of the Buddha found on the terrace walls. Although the temples, built of permanent materi-

The skyline at Pagan in Myanmar (Burma) is dominated by numerous Buddhist temples. The Shwe Sandaw was built by King Anawrahta, who ruled from 1044 to 1077 C.E. *(© Tibor Bognár/CORBIS)*

als, have largely survived, their foundation inscriptions describe ordination halls, libraries, and monasteries. These were constructed of wood and have disappeared.

CRAFT WORKERS

Pagan was home to specialist craft workers. The temples were ornamented with proficient images of the Buddha, including many fresco paintings. Bronze casters used the lost-wax technique to produce complex bronzes, such as a lotus with petals bearing Buddhist scenes. On a larger scale, there are many bronze images of the Buddha, which would have required all the skills of a master metalworker. There was also regular trade contact with India; the Nathlaunggyaung temple was built to honor Vishnu by a resident group of Indians. Ceramic vessels were also manufactured at Pagan, and two mounds covered in broken potsherds at Otein Taung, two kilometers to the southeast of the Ananda temple, have been examined archaeologically. These rise between six and 7.5 meters (20 and 25 ft.) high. Small test squares have revealed bamboo ash that might have been used as a fuel for firing vessels, clay anvils for shaping the clay, and a stamp that might have been used to decorate vessels. Moreover, the area is well known as a source of good potting clay, and several depressions in the vicinity could well represent clay pits. Apart from pottery vessels, the excavations also yielded roof tiles and large cylinders up to 40 centimeters (16 in.) in diameter that might have been latrine or drainage tubes. The radiocarbon dates from Otein Taung suggest initial use of the site in the late first millennium C.E. A determination from a depth of five meters gave a date range of 880–1030, while a second date from the western of the two mounds provided a date of 650–830 from a depth of 1.5 meters.

See also BRONZE CASTING.

Further reading: Aung-Thwin, M. *Pagan: The Origins of Modern Burma.* Honolulu: University of Hawaii Press, 1985; Luce, G. H. *Old Burma: Early Pagan.* New York: Augustin, 1970; Strachan, P. *Imperial Pagan: Art and Architecture of Old Burma.* Honolulu: University of Hawaii Press, 1990.

Painted Grey Ware Painted Grey Ware is a distinctive style of pottery vessel found in late prehistoric sites in the Ganges (Ganga) Valley dating between 800 and 500 B.C.E. The surface of the pots was embellished with painted designs in black, forming bands, dots, loops, and, occasionally, more complex flower designs, leaves, and the Sun.

Paithan *See* PRATISTHANA.

Palembang Palembang is a city in southeast Sumatra, Indonesia, which has long been cited as the capital of the powerful state of SRIVIJAYA (seventh–14th centuries C.E.). It lies at the junction of the Musi and Ogan Rivers above an extensive low-lying coastal plain. An intensive survey and excavation program began there in 1979 to identify archaeological evidence for this supposition. The results of this research suggest that Palembang extended more than 12 kilometers (7 mi.) beside the Musi River. Many earlier authorities have referred to it as the capital of a huge empire based on its control of trade. In reality it was more likely to have been a powerful trading center that probably exercised a form of dominance over the several settlements in its immediate riverine hinterland.

The survey incorporated the hill of Bukit Seguntang, the location of INSCRIPTIONS dated to the seventh century. Excavations uncovered the brick foundations of a probable stupa, a structure designed to hold a relic of the Buddha. Excavations in the middle of the present city revealed a three-meter-deep (10 ft.) stratigraphic sequence beginning in the eighth century C.E. Just above the main city, where a small stream enters the Musi River, archaeologists have identified glass for bead manufacture, iron, and a considerable concentration of Chinese Tang dynasty green-glazed ceramics in many forms of storage jars. Excavations recovered iron slag and much glazed pottery, and material that yielded a radiocarbon date of 600–900 C.E. A third location demonstrated the presence of a glass industry in the form of glass waste from bead manufacture. A waterlogged site near the base of the hill also contained the remains of a large wooden ship, radiocarbon dated to between the fifth and seventh centuries C.E. This is not the only ship recovered from the site of Palembang, for other vessels of roughly similar age have been found downstream. The discovery of such vessels emphasizes the importance of Palembang in oceanic trade.

Pali Pali is the language used in the literature of THERAVADA BUDDHISM. It is an Indo-Aryan language of North Indian origin and was preferred by the Buddha to the priestly language of SANSKRIT. Shortly after the Buddha's death, his followers convened to establish the Pali canon—the contents of his sermons as they were recalled and then recorded in oral tradition passed down through generations of monks in their monasteries. Pali was the language employed in the earliest sacred writings of the Theravada canon at Aluvihara, Sri Lanka, in the first century B.C.E. This is widely seen as the seminal and most vital contribution of Sri Lankan literature, to be followed by other major works, including religious texts compiled in the Mahavihara temple of ANURADHAPURA. Commentaries on sacred texts by the monk Buddhaghosa, including the *Visuddhimagga,* were employed by Buddhist missionaries active in Southeast Asia. Pali texts and INSCRIPTIONS were employed in the DVARAVATI CIVILIZATION of Thailand, to a lesser extent in Cambodia, and in Vietnam and Laos. The language died out in India in the 14th century but survived in parts of Southeast Asia until the 18th century. It was observed and commented on by Simon de la Loubère, a member of a French embassy to the Thai king in the late 17th century.

Pallava The Pallava dynasty began to rule in east-central India, in the vicinity of Madras, toward the end of the third century C.E. Its kings were the military rivals of the rulers of the Western Chalukya dynasty, and their rulers' names ended in –*varman*, "shield" or "protégé of." The earliest prominent king was Mahendravarman, who ruled from 600 to 630 C.E. It is highly likely that the Pallavas, given their geographic position, engaged in trade with Southeast Asia, for this regal terminology was adopted in the emerging states of FUNAN and CHENLA in the lower Mekong Valley in Cambodia. There are several impressive religious complexes at Kanci (Southeast India), including the early eighth-century Kailasanatha shrine. This temple includes a shrine containing a LINGAM named Mahendravarmesvara. Again, the placement of a lingam named after the sovereign was adopted widely in mainland Southeast Asia, particularly in the Chenla and ANGKOR states in Cambodia.

Southern India has little early stone architecture, possibly because the principal local source material, granite, is so hard. However, the Dharmaraja temple at Mamallapuram in India was constructed in this stone during the seventh and eighth centuries, and there are also some impressive cave temples of this state. Mamallapuram, named after Mamalla, King Narasimhavarman (r. 630–638) was the principal port of Pallava, while Kanci was the holy city and capital. The temples were dedicated to the principal Hindu gods SIVA and Vishnu.

Pandya Pandya was a kingdom located in the far south of India in Tamil Nadu province. It was independent of the MAURYA EMPIRE in the third century B.C.E. and was mentioned in ASOKA'S INSCRIPTIONS. It entered history again in the late sixth century under a powerful king, Kadungon; King Arikesari Maravarman (670–700 C.E.) led a successful campaign against the rival CERA state.

Panini (sixth or fifth century B.C.E.) *Panini is renowned for his grammatical work on the Sanskrit language.*
An Indian, he was the author of what is probably the oldest known grammar in the world (the *Astadhyayi*).

Panjikent Panjikent was a major city of SOGDIANA, located on the Zerafshan River in Uzbekistan, about 40 kilometers (27 mi.) east of Samarqand. It was occupied from the fifth to the eighth century C.E. The Sogdians occupied a strategic territory between the Syr Dar'ya and Amu Dar'ya Rivers, which controlled the east–west flow of trade goods along the SILK ROAD in modern Uzbekistan. They traveled widely and grew wealthy. Living farther east

than Khwarizm, the Sogdians retained a greater degree of political independence, particularly from the KUSHANS. Excavations began in 1946 under the direction of A. Y. Yakubovky. He found four distinct parts of the city in an area exceeding 14 hectares (35 acres): a royal palace and citadel, the main occupation area, a suburban adjunct, and the cemetery. The palace and domestic structures reflect the taste and cosmopolitan contacts of rich Sogdian merchants, particularly during the city's heyday during the sixth and seventh centuries C.E. The house walls were built of compressed loess and mud BRICK, with brick vaulted roofs. There is some evidence that clay tiles were used in the opulent residences, some of which were two or even three stories in height. A particular feature of the domestic structures was the predilection of the owners to decorate the walls with paintings of events of everyday life, such as feasting, hunting, ritual bathing, scenes from mythology, and even scenes from Aesop's fables. The rooms of the well-to-do were decorated from ceiling to floor with richly colored images.

In the paintings the WOMEN wore elegant costumes and ornate jewelry, while battle scenes show archers on horseback, leaping over dead bodies, a theme taken from favored epic stories. One theme derived from India shows a hare inducing a lion to jump into a lake, thereby obtaining freedom from fear. In vivid hunting scenes, aristocrats riding on elephants spear rampant tigers. Where charred by fire, some of the surviving wooden fittings reveal elaborate carving. Access to the upper floor involved spiral ramps, and although the upper rooms have not survived, it is evident that they were used for domestic purposes. Some of these rich houses also incorporated private shrines and altars sunk into the walls. The decoration included religious imagery, scenes of daily life, and folk tales. The far reach of the Sogdians is well illustrated by the incorporation of some of Aesop's fables in these decorative scenes. The houses of the less wealthy inhabitants also contained two stories but were smaller and lacked the richly decorated wall paintings. Shops and artisans' quarters had only a single story.

The material culture was rich and varied. Ceramics were made in many forms, and jewelry of exotic carnelian, TURQUOISE, agate, and LAPIS LAZULI was favored. The inhabitants also wore bronze ornaments, such as earrings, bracelets, and belt fittings, and blacksmiths forged iron into a wide variety of tools and weapons.

From about 700 C.E., the local ruler of Panjikent was named Divashtich, and his archives were first identified at the fortress site of Kala-i-Mug located in the upper Zerafshan Valley. These include legal documents regarding marriage contracts and land leases, letters sent from a Sogdian colony far to the east at the Buddhist oasis of Dunhuang, and financial records. Sogdians also resided in China, and the Sogdian language was widely spoken along the Silk Road. Panjikent was abandoned between 730 and 770 after the Arab conquest of the area.

Panlongcheng Panlongcheng is a city site located in the middle Chang (Yangtze) Valley, just to the north of the modern city of Wuhan in China. The Fu River, a tributary of the Chang, flows south of the site. The occupation dates to the Erligang phase of the Middle Shang dynasty, or about 1500–1200 B.C.E. In many respects, Panlongcheng is a smaller version of ZHENGZHOU, having a similar set of stamped-earth walls and much evidence of individual activity beyond this defended area. The ORACLE BONES of the late Shang capital at ANYANG often mention small states on their borders, and the site of Panlongcheng is precisely the sort of archaeological assemblage that could represent local principalities of the period. It lies, however, at the southern periphery of the area that has yielded the Shang bronze industry and might have local roots rather than show evidence of an intrusive movement from the north. Such sites might well have grown wealthy on the basis of trade with the SHANG STATE, for the Shang records make it clear that they sought southern products, not least the turtle carapaces for their divination ceremonies.

The walls of Palongcheng enclose an area of only 7.5 hectares (19 acres) but were clearly constructed to house the elite in society, for a substantial raised rectangular platform in the northern sector bore a colonnaded building that may well have been a palace. The platform is at least 60 meters (198 ft.) long and more than 10 meters (33 ft.) wide. Beyond the walls and moat, excavations have revealed a BRONZE-CASTING area, complete with the remains of copper slag and broken crucible fragments. Many of the bronzes were placed in the cemetery that was evidently restricted to the elite members of the community; one such grave contained 63 bronzes, including ritual vessels, weapons, and tools. There were also many items of jade and the skeletons of three sacrificial victims. These rich graves were set apart also on the basis of elaborate wooden coffins and linings in the tomb. The bronze vessels in one elite burial were placed around the principal interment. The assemblage included vessels for serving food and wine, heating, and offering ritual items. A common characteristic of such tombs is the provision of a *yaokeng,* or waist pit. These were found under the waist of the dead, and one at Panlongcheng contained the remains of a sacrificed animal and a broken blade. Other bronzes included daggers and a finely decorated ceremonial ax. The ornaments on these bronze vessels and weapons are closely paralleled at Zhengzhou to the north, and it must be concluded that they represent a shared ritual culture.

Two other cemeteries at this site contain poorer graves. In one, the grave goods were only ceramic vessels and the rare bronze. A group of moderately wealthy tombs in a second group included bronzes, pottery vessels, and jades but not in the same quantity as in the richest group.

Panwol-Song Panwol-Song is a mounded defended settlement in the Kyongju Basin of southeast Korea. It lies within the area of the future city of KUMSONG, capital of the unified SHILLA state. This smaller enclosure was probably an earlier Shilla capital, belonging to the fourth and fifth centuries C.E.

Parhae Parhae is a state that flourished in northern Korea and south-central Manchuria from its foundation in 698 to its fall in 926 C.E. It was founded by Tao Cho-yong, a general of the former state of KOGURYO, after its fall to SHILLA. The kings of Shilla were unable to extend their authority north of the Taedong River, and thus the kings of Parhae held sway over a vast part of Manchuria. Indeed, Shilla forces constructed a defensive wall along the line of the Taedong River to the Bay of Wonsan. Much of this territory, which was bisected by the Yalu and Tumen Rivers, was occupied by Tungus, semino-madic herders, who formed an underclass to the Parhae elite. The early rulers were antagonistic toward Tang China. Under King Mu (r. 719–737), a Parhae fleet attacked the Shandong Peninsula. Parhae further expanded its territory under King Mun (r. 737–793) and King Son (r. 818–830). Administration was centered in the capital, Sanggyong, located near Mudanjiang. This walled city was laid out on the same geometric principles as the Tang capital of CHANG'AN. A walled precinct within contained the royal palace and the administrative offices. Excavations of the palace have revealed a system of under-floor heating by means of flues. The culture and administration of Parhae were heavily influenced by those of Tang China, to which Buddhist monks traveled for education. There was also a vigorous trade relationship with both China and Japan.

Under the king, the government of Parhae was divided into three chancelleries; the principal minister was known as the *taenaesang.* These were further divided into ministries in charge of finance, ritual, war, the law, and public works. There were also four regional capitals linked by a series of roads. Parhae, however, succumbed to invasion in 926, and the leaders moved south to live in the southern Korean kingdom of Koryo.

Parthia Parthia is traditionally located just southeast of the Caspian Sea. It was a part of the Seleucid empire, the eastern Greek realm founded by SELEUCUS I NICATOR (356–281 B.C.E.), a former general of ALEXANDER THE GREAT (356–323 B.C.E.). As Seleucid power waned in the mid-third century B.C.E., Parthia declared independence. A century later, the Parthian king Mithradates I invaded Sind in modern Pakistan. Parthia grew wealthy through its control of the goods crossing the SILK ROAD from China to Rome, and its COINAGE was minted in many centers, such as MERV (modern Mary) on the Mehrgarh River in southern Turkmenistan. Here the Seleucid city of Alexandria in Margiana was greatly expanded under Parthian rule. On the eastern edges of the Parthian empire, small states began to develop as central control slackened.

Pataliputra   Pataliputra, modern Patna in India, was the capital of the MAURYA EMPIRE (c. 325–c. 185 B.C.E.). It is of elongated form, lying on the southern bank of the Ganges (Ganga) River, and was defended by a wooden palisade and a moat that linked with the river. Its precise area, which has not been defined, probably exceeded 1,350 hectares (3375 acres). MEGASTHENES, ambassador of the Greek king SELEUCUS I NICATOR, visited the city during the reign of CANDRAGUPTA MAURYA (325–297 B.C.E.) and described the broad moat and palaces within. He admired the palace as one of the finest in the world and noted its gilt pillars decorated with gold and silver vines and birds. One such palace structure, a hall with pillars to support the superstructure, was identified in 1913. It was of complex design and construction, the stone columns resting on clay and timber footings buried nearly two meters deep into the substrate. Each column would have been nearly 10 meters (33 ft.) high, although some of its length would have been buried in the foundations. It was destroyed by a fire in the mid-second century B.C.E.

Pataliputra was still renowned in tradition when XUANZANG, a Chinese Buddhist monk, visited the site in the early seventh century C.E. He described it as ruined but still noted the foundations of buildings there.

Patothamya temple   In contrast to the predilection for stupa, shown by his predecessor, Anawrahta, King Kyanzitta (r. 1084–1111) of PAGAN in Myanmar (Burma) founded a rich tradition of temple building. The Patothamya temple is an example that probably dates to his reign. It has a square central shrine under a bulbous tower, adjoining a rectangular hall on the eastern side. Stone Buddha images were placed within, and the walls bear painted scenes from JATAKA TALES.

Pattadakal   Pattadakal is, with AIHOLE and BADAMI, one of the major religious centers of the CHALUKYA DYNASTY (sixth–eighth centuries C.E.) of the Deccan in India. They date in the main to the reign of King Vikramaditya II and are particularly notable for the corpus of INSCRIPTIONS that record the founders and even the names of the architects and sculptors. Thus the magnificent Virupaksha temple was constructed by the architect Sutradhari Gunda to celebrate the king's victory over Kanchi in the mid-eighth century C.E. It is said that this temple was the finest of its time in India. Its embellishments include a special pavilion to house Nandi, SIVA'S bull, and reliefs showing scenes from the Hindu epics the RAMAYANA and MAHABHARATA on the columns. One of these depicts the CHURNING OF THE OCEAN OF MILK to obtain the elixir of immortality (AMRITA). This theme became particularly popular at ANGKOR in Cambodia. The adjacent Mallikarjuna temple is similar in design and style and was also built to commemorate the victory of King Vikramaditya over Kanchi. It was dedicated to the worship of Siva.

Periplus of the Erythraean Sea   *Periplus* means "circumnavigation," and the Erythraean Sea refers to the area of the Red Sea, the Persian Gulf, and the Indian Ocean. The document with this name probably dates to the late first century C.E. The dating has been controversial, but the identification of the Indian king named as Manbanos in the *Periplus* with the Kshaharata king Nahapana and the dating of the latter's reign make a late first-century C.E. date likely. The author is unknown, but he was probably a Greek merchant. His work is a vital source of information on trade between the Roman Empire and India, trading ports in the area. Barbarikon was a port near the Indus Delta, and there the Greeks took linen, coral, glass, and silver and gold vessels. These they exchanged for perfumes, jewelry, cotton, and silk cloth. The port of Barygaza on the Narmada River is cited for its trade in Mediterranean wine, gold COINAGE, copper, tin, and lead; Indian exports included agate, carnelian, and cotton and muslin cloth. The Greeks were also interested in pepper, pearls, ivory, silk, and tortoise shell.

Although the Western traders at this juncture did not regularly visit the ports of eastern India, they were familiar with Southeast Asia and China. They thus participated in trade along the southern or maritime SILK ROAD, linking Rome with the ports of Southeast Asia, India, and China and generating much wealth for those who controlled the ports. There was the imposition of customs dues by local rulers, but also considerable encouragement to piracy. Silk was in much demand in the West, and the *Periplus* mentions that silk traveling overland from China had to be diverted south from BACTRIA to India because the Parthians at that juncture barred land access to the eastern Roman Empire. The Greeks borrowed Indian names for the products obtained by trade, such as the words for "cinnamon," "CLOVE," "ginger," and "rice." There is also reference to the trade relationship in Indian literature. The *Shilappadikaram* Tamil epic refers to Greek ships' bearing gold in exchange for pepper. Early Tamil poems describe the arrival of Mediterranean wine in Indian ports. This has been confirmed archaeologically by the recovery first at Arikamedu and subsequently at many other Indian sites of Roman amphorae, large handled vessels used to ship wine.

See also PARTHIA.

Phimai   The Mun Valley in northeast Thailand was part of the kingdom of ANGKOR in Thailand, and Phimai is its largest and most impressive Angkorian city. The site has prehistoric origins. Just to the southeast of the outer walls lies Ban Suai, where excavations have uncovered an Iron Age settlement at least five meters (16.5 ft.) deep. It has yielded black burnished pottery known as Phimai black, which dates between about 200 B.C.E. and 400 C.E. Inhumation burials and the remains of industrial activity have been encountered, including local BRONZE CASTING

The sanctuary of Phimai, ancient Vimayapura, lies in the Mun Valley of northeast Thailand. It was the home of the major dynasty of Mahidharapura. *(Charles Higham)*

and iron forging. Burnishing stones and anvils for shaping pottery vessels show that the site was also a center for ceramic industry. Phimai black pottery was found below the main sanctuary of the Phimai temple complex during excavations in 1998, and these lay under a layer of BRICKS that represent an early building that probably dates within the period 600–800 C.E. Phimai is renowned for the range and quality of its stone decoration. Scenes of a dancing SIVA, narrative reliefs inspired by the RAMAYANA, and Vishnu riding the eagle GARUDA are particularly notable, while the floral motifs recall the BAPHUON style (11th century C.E.).

ÉTIENNE AYMONIER visited Phimai in the late 19th century and recorded the presence of several INSCRIPTIONS, together with ruined temple foundations and lintels indicating adherence to MAHAYANA BUDDHISM as well as to gods of the Hindu pantheon. Subsequently, the temples have been reconstructed by using the ANASTYLOSIS method in a joint program of the Fine Arts Department of Thailand and the ÉCOLE FRANÇAISE D'EXTRÊME ORIENT,

and the central part of the city now lies within a historic park.

The upper Mun Valley contains several major Khmer centers apart from Phimai, and the available inscriptions indicate that the line of King JAYAVARMAN VI (1080–1107 C.E.) originated in this area and founded a new Angkorian dynasty, MAHIDHARAPURA DYNASTY. The principal shrine of Phimai, ancient Vimayapura, belongs to his reign and in terms of its architectural design anticipates several of the features later to be seen at ANGKOR WAT, the temple mausoleum of SURYAVARMAN II (1134–50 C.E.), a later ruler of the Mahidharapura dynasty. Much of the present layout of Vimayapura, however, is from the reign of JAYAVARMAN VII (1181–1219 C.E.). This includes the city walls, which measure one kilometer by 500 meters (1,650 ft.). The southern entrance, known as the *pratu chai*, or victory gate, opens to the southeast, from which a road connected the city with a landing stage on the Khem Stream, one of the rivers that converge at Phimai. This road is flanked on the east by the Kuti Rishi, one of the many HOSPITALS built during the rule of Jayavarman VII.

Little is known of the domestic buildings of the city itself, because it remains densely occupied, and no excavations have been undertaken. The center of the city is dominated by an inner wall that encloses the sacred space of the temple grounds. These are reached by a raised causeway flanked by sacred *naga* (snakes), which leads to an entrance gateway, or *gopura*. The maintenance of Vimayapura as a special location to members of the Mahidharapura dynasty is seen in the addition of two further temples, the Prang Hin Daeng and Prang Bhromathat, in the shadow of the main sanctuary. Two statues were found in the latter, one representing Jayavarman VII and the other probably his wife, Jayarajadevi. The central shrine, which rises to a height of 28 meters (92 ft.), has a stone foundation resting on a sand platform. It is integrally linked with three chambers. The principal chamber, or *garbhagrha*, houses an image of the Buddha. The tower above rises in five tiers in the form of a lotus.

Phimeanakas The Phimeanakas, or aerial palace, was the temple built by King SURYAVARMAN I (r. 1002–49 C.E.) at ANGKOR in Cambodia after he assumed overall control of the kingdom. It is a relatively small, steep-sided structure with a single sanctuary on the summit terrace, located in the walled palace precinct of ANGKOR THOM. A later inscription, known as the great stela of the Phimeanakas, was discovered smashed to several pieces and deeply buried. It was set up by Indradevi to honor her sister, Jayarajadevi, queen of JAYAVARMAN VII (1181–1219 C.E.), and provides insight into the meritorious donations made by a highly ranked member of the royal family. It mentions both TA PROHM and PREAH KHAN, to which Jayarajadevi had offered ritual objects and placed her riches at the disposal of the gods and the poor.

Thus she donated two gold statues of the sacred ox Nandi, four gold eagles, and an eternally burning lamp to the shrine of her mother-in-law. She donated lions, a mirror, and a magnificent fly whisk of gold, a golden stool of great beauty, a gold box, a crown of gold, and two villages to the temple of Preah Khan. To the god of Madhyadri (the BAYON) she donated 100 banners of Chinese fabric, and she gilded Vasudhatilaka (probably the Phimeanakas), which had been damaged by the CHAMS.

Phnom Chisor The hilltop temple of Phnom Chisor in southern Cambodia was formerly known as Suryaparvata (the mountain of Surya). One of four inscriptions set up by SURYAVARMAN I (r. 1002–49 C.E.) to mark the boundaries of his kingdom was located there. Its foundation probably dates to the reign of Suryavarman. While the temple is located on the shoulder of the hill, a large reservoir was built on the plain to the south, linked to the shrine by a steep flight of steps. Most of the temple was built of BRICK, but the lintels and other stone features include reliefs of Hindu deities, for the temple was dedicated to SIVA and Vishnu. There are scenes showing the mythical CHURNING OF THE OCEAN OF MILK and the birth of Rama.

Phnom Da This hill is located three kilometers (1.8 mi.) from ANGKOR BOREI in southern Cambodia. It is notable for the number of outstanding stone statues dated to the sixth century C.E. These belong to the period of transition from the maritime state of FUNAN to the inland agrarian states of CHENLA. The statues reflect the Hindu religion, with a particular preference for Vishnu. There is also a striking image of HARIHARA, Vishnu and SIVA combined in one figure. This hill has also furnished an INSCRIPTION naming King RUDRAVARMAN (c. 514–50 C.E.), the last recorded king of Funan.

Phnom Rung The choice of a hilltop for an Angkorian sanctuary reflects the desire to replicate the setting of MOUNT MERU, the home of the Hindu gods. Phnom Rung, "broad mountain," is the original name of the temple that was constructed on top of a volcanic hill in northeast Thailand. An early INSCRIPTION, dated to the seventh or eighth century, together with a statue of GANESHA in

Phnom Rung is set high on a hill in northeast Thailand. It is one of the finest examples of a provincial Angorian center. *(Charles Higham)*

eighth-century style, indicates that Phnom Rung was an early temple foundation dating to the period of CHENLA. However, its main construction dates to the 12th century and in particular to the reign of SURYAVARMAN II (r. 1113–50 C.E.). As at other hilltop temples, such as PREAH VIHEAR and PHNOM CHISOR, the layout of Phnom Rung has been tailored to the natural conditions. A long access stairway leads up to the main precinct. The approach to the temple proper is dominated by a long (160-meter) causeway flanked by columns leading to a sacred *naga*, "snake," bridge. Such bridges indicate the passage from the profane to the sacred world. A further staircase leads to a terrace embellished with four water basins and across a second *naga* bridge to the enceinte of the temple itself. Phnom Rung is particularly noted for the quality of its stone carvings, one of which depicts a war elephant trampling an enemy. This may be one of the earliest specific historic scenes depicted in Angkorian art. Most of the decoration, however, reflects the role of ascetics in the worship of SIVA. A particularly famous lintel bearing a carving of Vishnu was stolen and sold to the Art Institute of Chicago. Protracted negotiations finally secured its return.

The 11 inscriptions from Phnom Rung are particularly notable for the information that they provide for regional organization. The local ruling family, the MAHIDHARAPURA DYNASTY (c. 802–1219), exercised considerable autonomy while still acknowledging their relative Suryavarman II at ANGKOR. There was a king called Hiranyavarman, the father of JAYAVARMAN VI and Dharanindravarman. King Ksitindraditya, grandson of Hiranyavarman, was the father of Suryavarman. Narendraditya, a cousin of the king, was responsible for the monument of Phnom Rung. His son, Hiranya, erected a gold image to him there.

Phnom Wan Phnom Wan is one of the three large Angkorian temples found in the upper Mun Valley in Thailand. It has a long history. Excavations in 1997–98 by the Fine Arts Department of Thailand uncovered an Iron Age inhumation cemetery. One prehistoric grave only a meter from the foundations of the main sanctuary lay on exactly the same orientation as the temple. There are also the BRICK foundations of a temple that probably dates to the kingdoms of CHENLA (550–800). It was added to until at least the early 12th century. It has a central walled temple and two large BARAYS, or reservoirs. An inscription mentions how a soldier named Viravarman was given property and symbols of status, including a golden palanquin and an ivory parasol with peacock plumes, by King UDAYADITAVARMAN II (1050–66 C.E.). He erected a sanctuary in the settlement of Sukhalaya and endowed it with 200 slaves, land, a herd of buffaloes, and other animals. He restored 23 villages and built a large reservoir, perhaps that seen today beside the sanctuary. The MAHIDHARAPURA DYNASTY of King JAYAVARMAN VI (r. 1080–1107 C.E.) originated from the region of Phnom Wan. An inscription from his reign describes the career of a certain Subhadra, also known as Murdhasiva. This ascetic man, who "shone like a newly lit fire," was appointed inspector of sacred property and religious foundations with the title *bhupendrapandita*. Among his responsibilities was the sanctuary of Phnom Wan. It later became a center for BUDDHISM, to judge from the number of statues to the Buddha found in the precinct.

Pingcheng The Battle of Pingcheng took place in 200 B.C.E., between the XIONGNU under the Shanyu MAODUN and the Chinese Han emperor GAOZU. Maodun was the greatest leader of the Xiongnu, a nomadic pastoralist people of Mongolia, whom he united into a formidable state in the late third century B.C.E. Gaozu was the founding emperor of the Western HAN DYNASTY. For years northwestern China had been exposed to raids from the steppe nomads, and the first emperor, QIN SHIHUANGDI, had countered this threat by beginning the construction of the GREAT WALL. When Maodun advanced at the head of an armed host south of the wall and captured one of Gaozu's client kings, the emperor led an army in person through bitter winter weather to engage the Xiongnu. Maodun, a brilliant tactician, placed only his weakest troops in view of Chinese. Gaozu advanced to Pingcheng in China and was rapidly surrounded by Maodun's cavalry and cut off from support. For a week the Chinese were trapped. Then according to the Chinese historian SIMA QIAN, Maodun's wife argued that the Xiongnu could never rule China and that the emperor had a powerful force of guardian spirits. Maodun allowed the emperor to escape through a gap in the investing force. There followed a treaty of appeasement in which the Han bought off any future threat through handsome payments of gold, silk, and food.

Pingliangtai Pingliangtai is a walled settlement of the LONGSHAN CULTURE, located in eastern Henan province, northern China, dated to 2500–2000 B.C.E. The stamped-earth walls enclose an area of 3.4 hectares (8.5 acres) and were fronted by a 30-meter (100-ft.)-wide moat. The northern and southern walls, between eight and 13 meters wide, contained gateways complete with two guardhouses. Within the settlement, there were raised platforms for major buildings and a subterranean system of drains made of terra-cotta. A piece of bronze was found in the third period of occupation, and some ceramic shards bear written graphs. Kilns in the walled area indicate a local ceramic industry; one such kiln was attached to a large house.

Piprahwa Piprahwa is located on the northern margins of the Ganges (Ganga) Plain in northern India. It is only 15 kilometers (9 mi.) from LUMBINI, the birthplace of the Buddha, and several claims have been made that it is located at the site, or at least near the site, of Kapilavastu, the capital of the clan to which the Buddha belonged. There is a large stupa at Piprahwa, surrounded by monastic buildings, which was examined in the late 19th century. A shaft bored into its center, at a depth of more than five meters, yielded a sandstone box containing four STEATITE beads and a crystal relic casket. Claims were made that this stupa covered those parts of the Buddha sent to his birthplace after his cremation. Further excavations at the stupa and associated monastic buildings, beginning in 1971, yielded not only further relic caskets contained in BRICK cells at a greater depth than the earlier set, but also sealings carrying the name Kapilavastu. The newly discovered caskets contained cremated bone and date to within the late first millennium B.C.E. Piprawha is thus a site of immense significance to BUDDHISM, with a long history of monasticism until the site suffered from a conflagration in the third century C.E.

plastromancy   Plastromancy is the process of divination by applying heat to the lower half of the carapace of a turtle to predict future events. Kings of the SHANG STATE and WESTERN ZHOU DYNASTY in China from about 1200 B.C.E. retained court diviners. Carapaces were imported to the Shang capital, and their origin was recorded on their surface. Female specimens were preferred because they were thinner and flatter than their male counterparts. Holes were excised, and heat was applied. The resultant cracks were then interpreted by the king, and his prophecies were inscribed on the bone in archaic Chinese characters. These covered such subjects as war, the harvest, the weather, when to make sacrifices to the ancestors, and whether royal consorts would enjoy a safe childbirth. The records were then stored in state archives. Many have been recovered through archaeological excavations and provide the basis for understanding later Shang dynastic history.

   See also LI JI; LIU TAIYUN; ORACLE BONES; SCAPULO-MANCY; SONG YIRANG.

pon   The social history of the CHENLA period in Cambodia saw the rise of states under the rule of kings (550–800 C.E.). Several dynasties have been identified through an examination of the surviving INSCRIPTIONS. These were usually set up to record temple foundations, aspects of their organization, and the donation of meritorious offerings. They employ the SANSKRIT language for the main part of the text, but many also incorporate Old Khmer to record such details as the number of slaves who supported the foundation through their labor and their names and duties. The title *pon*, probably the same title as *fan* mentioned by the Chinese, occurs in the KHMER LANGUAGE inscriptions from the earliest period until 719 C.E. The status of a *pon* appears to have been inherited, the *pon* themselves occupying a broad band in the social

spectrum depending on their rank and wealth. The inscriptions reveal how *pon* assumed political and religious leadership in local affairs.

   Sivadatta, the son of King ISHANAVARMAN OF CHENLA, who ruled in the early seventh century, bore this title. Some *pon* acted on behalf of the king in the foundation of a temple, but others did so on their own initiative. They controlled the organization of rice production and the deployment of surpluses, took a keen interest in land titles and boundaries, and oversaw the provision of labor in servicing the physical and ritual needs of their temples. *Pon* are often cited as controlling ponds and swamps, both important in the maintenance of communities during the long dry season. The title was inherited through the female line, as a *pon* was succeeded by his sister's son. The title became rare as inscriptions began to describe the new titles and bureaucratic positions established under the reign of King JAYAVARMAN I (c. 655–700 C.E.). No *pon* are recorded in the inscriptions after 719 C.E.

Po Nagar   Po Nagar is the major center of Kauthara in Vietnam, the most southerly polity of the CHAM CIVILIZATION. Six BRICK sanctuaries are built on an eminence that commands a major estuary. There is a lengthy history of construction, commencing in at least the seventh century C.E. with a wooden temple that was destroyed by fire in 774 C.E. The northwestern tower was built in 813, and further sanctuaries were added until 1256. King Jaya Harivarmadeva set up an inscription in 1160, claiming victory over the Khmer and Vietnamese, as well as the Cham kingdoms of Vijaya, AMARAVATI, and Panduranga. The site was located so that it could control sea traffic from China south to the states of mainland and island Southeast Asia.

Pong Tuk   The relatively small and unmoated site of Pong Tuk in western Thailand was among the first DVARAVATI CIVILIZATION sites to be excavated. It has yielded the remains of Buddhist structures and an exotic bronze Byzantine lamp dating to the fifth or sixth century C.E. A circular foundation is thought to have been part of a stupa, and a square building may have been a *caitya*, or shrine. A third is a rectangular structure to which access was gained by a flight of steps. Bases for columns were noted, and it is probable that they represent the remains of a *vihara*, or meeting hall. These discoveries were the first archaeological evidence in central Thailand for a state that had adopted BUDDHISM and could build large monuments in stone and brick.

Prakash   Prakash is a deep archaeological site located in the Tapi Valley of India, where the Tapi and Gomai Rivers converge. It was excavated by B. K. Thapar in 1955, and a stratigraphic sequence 17 meters (56 ft.) deep was exposed. There was a long prehistoric period of occupation dating back to the early second millennium B.C.E. and running through the Iron Age. From the second century B.C.E. until about 500 C.E., the settlement continued in occupation; finds included shell and glass jewelry and coins typical of the center of UJJAIN.

Prakrit Prakrit is a Middle Indo-Aryan language that originated from SANSKRIT but evolved into about 16 dialects with regional distinctiveness. It is the language employed in Indian INSCRIPTIONS from the third century B.C.E. until the early centuries C.E., but in time it was replaced by Sanskrit. By the fourth century C.E., it ceased to be employed. There are several regional dialects. In the Asokan inscriptions, eastern Prakrit, spoken in the capital PATALIPUTRA, was used, but this practice changed in the west and northwest of the MAURYA EMPIRE (324–c. 200 B.C.E.). In the latter area, for example, a northwestern Prakrit known as Gandhari was used in conjunction with the KHAROSHTHI script. Gandhari had a wide currency, extending as far east as the LOU-LAN kingdom of the TARIM BASIN.

See also ASOKA.

Prambanan Prambanan is the name of a village in central Java in Indonesia that is often used when referring to a complex of nearby Hindu temples known as Candi Loro Jonggrang. It is ascribed to King Dhaksa of Mataram, who succeeded King Balitung in about 913 C.E. The three largest shrines in a group of eight were dedicated to SIVA. Vishnu, and Brahma; a further shrine was for the worship of Nandi, Siva's sacred ox, but the dedication of the remainder is not clearly understood. The temples are particularly notable for their reliefs, which depict scenes from the *RAMAYANA*.

Prasat Kravan Prasat Kravan is a temple located at ANGKOR in Cambodia. It was dedicated, according to its foundation INSCRIPTION, in 921 C.E., and has an unusual linear arrangement of five brick sanctuaries. Notable reliefs in BRICK of Vishnu are found within.

Pratisthana Pratisthana, now known as Paithan, is a series of mounds covering an area of more than four square kilometers (1.6 sq. mi.), on the Godavari River in Maharasthtra province, central India. It was the capital city of the *MAHAJANAPADA* of Asmaka. The *PERIPLUS OF THE ERYTHRAEAN SEA*, composed in the first century C.E., knew of this center and named it Paethana. Evidently it was renowned as a source of onyx. That its inhabitants were involved in long-distance trade is evidenced by the presence of coins of the Roman emperors Augustus and Tiberius. It also had a mint for the issuing of Satavahanan coins. Small excavations have revealed evidence for SATAVAHANA occupation above prehistoric remains, but little is known of the site's history.

Preah Khan Preah Khan, originally known as Nagara Jayasri, "holy city of victory," is a temple complex built by royal order of JAYAVARMAN VII (1181–1219 C.E.) just outside the northeastern corner of ANGKOR THOM in northwest Cambodia. The foundation stela was written by Virakumara, one of the king's sons, who stated that it was built where his father had defeated the CHAMS. The temple was constructed to make merit for the king's father, whose image was consecrated in 1191 C.E. His statue was located in the central shrine and was accompanied by 283 other images. The foundation eulogizes the king and contains a description of his ancestry. The number and placement of images to a pantheon of gods are then set out. One was in the rice warehouse, four in the pilgrims' rest house, and three in the HOSPITAL. Twenty-four were placed in the four entrances to the temple. The text lists the food dedicated to the gods, other offerings, villages needed to support the sanctuary, and an inventory of the temple property.

The buildings of Preah Khan are on the same level, surrounded by a moat and wall 800 by 700 meters in extent. Access is by four causeways flanked by gods and giants who hold sacred *naga*, or snakes. The interior incorporates two enclosures with numerous shrines and intervening courts. Brief INSCRIPTIONS associated with the shrines detail the name of the images within and their initiator. Some temples were established by aristocrats to honor the images of their ancestors.

The text also enumerates the food needed to sustain the gods, listing rice, sesame, peas, butter, fresh milk, honey, and molasses. There follows a list of 645 lengths of white and red cloth to clothe the gods as well as to use for bedding and seating. Silk mosquito nets were required to protect the deities. Food for the temple officials, with special reference to the New Year and feast days, is then set out in a list that includes oil, possibly used as a cosmetic after ritual ablutions. The grand total of offerings included pine resin, presumably for lighting and tapers, 423 goats, 360 pigeons, and peacocks. The king ascribed 5,324 villages housing 97,840 people to the service of this temple, including cooks and 1,000 dancers. The inventory of temple property includes large quantities of gold and silver vessels, precious stones, 112,300 pearls, and a brown cow with gilt horns and hooves.

Preah Khan of Kompong Svay Preah Khan of Kompong Svay is one of the largest Angkorian centers, if not the largest one. It lies east of ANGKOR in Cambodia and was first recorded by Louis Delaporte in 1873. Air photographs taken in 1937 revealed that the outer walls enclose an area of 25 square kilometers (10 sq. mi.). The interior contains a further two-walled enclosure culminating in the central shrine. An inscription from the second enclosure records the presence of SURAVARMAN I (r. 1002–49 C.E.), and some architectural features belong to his reign. However, it was also a major center during the reign of JAYAVARMAN VII (r. 1181–1218 C.E.) and has furnished arguably the most famous of Angkorian portrait busts, that of Jayavarman himself. Further archaeological research is needed to unravel the history of this site, for some of the buildings are from later periods. Unfortunately, as a result of its remoteness and civil disorder, this site has been severely damaged by vandals and looting.

Preah Ko   Preah Ko is one of the major temples built by INDRAVARMAN I, king of ANGKOR, at HARIHARALAYA in northwest Cambodia. It is a recent name meaning "sacred ox," after the statues of the bull Nandi, SIVA's sacred mount, which guard the entrance. It was dedicated in January 880 C.E. The complex is surrounded by a 50-meter (165.5-ft.) -wide moat measuring 600 by 550 meters on each side and incorporates six major shrines. The three towers of the front row were dedicated to RUDRAVARMAN and Prithivindravarman, the king's maternal grandfather and father, and the central tower was dedicated to King JAYAVARMAN II. The three rear temples were dedicated to their wives. This was thus a temple for the worship of deified ancestors whose presence would have advertised the king's credentials.

Preah Vihear   This temple was built in the most spectacular of all locations, on the crest of the Dang Raek range, so as to command a view to the south across the plain of northern Cambodia. Preah Vihear was associated with miracles, and an official named Sukavarman maintained a record of all the offerings made as a consequence. A reference to these miracles dates to 1038 C.E. and to the reincarnation of the god Bhadresvara as Sikharesvara at Preah Vihear, as a result of the king's ascetic devotion. Preah Vihear functioned as a retreat for ascetics and a center for pilgrimages. Its mountaintop setting afforded it particular sanctity. The date of the initial foundation is not known, but many Khmer kings contributed to its maintenance and embellishments, from YASHOVARMAN I (r. 889–910) to SURYAVARMAN II (r. 1113–50). SURYAVARMAN I (r. 1002–49) was particularly interested in this foundation. It was approached by a series of causeways lined by boundary pillars and punctuated by entrance pavilions (gopuras) flanked by water basins. The temple decoration is renowned for its scenes from Hindu legends, such as the CHURNING OF THE OCEAN OF MILK to obtain the elixir of immortality (AMRITA). Many of the surfaces still bear a red pigment, made from hematite, which was probably a base to receive gold leaf.

The INSCRIPTIONS on the walls of the second gopura indicate a foundation by Suryavarman I, because the earliest, dating to 1018 C.E., describes the establishment of a LINGAM bearing the name Suryavarmesvara. A further text provides the name of this temple, Sikharesvara, and mentions Sukavarman, the keeper of state archives who maintained the records of the kings going back to mythical ancestors.

Prei Monti   There are several temple enclosures at the Roluos Group (HARIHARALAYA), southeast of ANGKOR in Cambodia. While the complex as a whole owes much to King INDRAVARMAN I (r. 877–889 C.E.), the temple of Prei Monti could on stylistic grounds belong either to his immediate predecessor, JAYAVARMAN III (834–877 C.E.), about whom virtually nothing is known, or to the founder of the kingdom of Angkor, JAYAVARMAN II (c. 770–834).

Pre Rup   When King RAJENDRAVARMAN of ANGKOR in Cambodia reestablished the capital at ANGKOR in 944 C.E. after his brother, JAYAVARMAN IV (r. 928–42 C.E.), had built the new center of KOH KER (Lingapura), he ordered the construction of a large temple pyramid in a location south of the YASHODHARATATAKA, the EASTERN BARAY. It is known today as PRE RUP, the "turning of the body," as in the cremation ceremony, but this cannot have been its original title. It was designed to honor the king and his ancestors in the context of the god SIVA. Its five major towers rise on two laterite tiers and were originally covered in stucco. The central sanctuary on the uppermost tier housed Rajendrabhadresvara, the royal LINGAM. The four subsidiary towers were dedicated to Isvara Rajendravarmesvara, representing the king; Rajendravesvarupa, in favor of the Brahman Vishvarupa, a distant ancestor of the king; the king's aunt, Jayadevi; and his predecessor; Harshavarman. The temple also housed numerous subsidiary shrines, libraries, and entrance pavilions in two walled precincts.

Prinsep, James (1799–1840) *James Prinsep was the master of assays at the British mint in Calcutta, India.*
In 1837 he made what has been described a "the single most important discovery in the unraveling of India's ancient history" by identifying the letters *d* and *n* on an inscription at the Buddhist stupa at SANCHI. He found that the language in question was PALI and was able to translate the INSCRIPTION as a record of a donation of stones to the building of the temple. This opened the door to further translations, and explorations into early history proceeded. Foremost among these was his work on the meaning of the Asokan column inscriptions and a Buddhist inscription from SARNATH. Through his intensive efforts, historic figures began to emerge from oblivion. In 1838 he published a paper on the name of Antiochus the Great, named in two of ASOKA's (268–235 B.C.E.) edicts.

Puranas   The Puranas are a group of Indian religious works of great antiquity, although there is no certainty as to the date of their origin. There are traditionally 18, each dedicated to a particular god. They record in SANSKRIT religious doctrine, law, legends, and dynastic histories.

Pre Rup rises aloft just south of the Eastern Baray at Angkor. It was the temple mausoleum of King Rajendravarman, a king "who could cut an iron bar as if it were a banana stalk." *(Charles Higham)*

The gods to whom the Puranas are dedicated include SIVA, Vishnu, Skanda, and GARUDA. The Puranas thus form the basic creed for the Hindu religion.

Purandarapura The cave of Prah Kuha Luon in Cambodia has furnished an INSCRIPTION dated to 674 C.E., which contains a *rajna* (edict) of King JAYAVARMAN I (c. 635–80) from the palace at Purandarapura, confirming the ownership of fields, cattle, buffaloes, servants, and gardens by ascetics and not by any private person. Unlike ISHANAPURA, the former capital, which has an undoubted identification with modern SAMBOR PREI KUK, Purandarapura has not been positively identified. This is a matter of regret, because Jayavarman I was responsible for the centralization of authority that indicates state formation. Michael Vickery has assembled all the relevant information, and on balance a location in or near the large center of BANTEAY PREI NOKOR seems the most probable.

Purnavarman (fifth century C.E.) *A king named Purnavarman is known through four inscriptions located on the western coast of Java in Indonesia.* Dated to the fifth century C.E., they describe how the king had a canal built for IRRIGATION, about 15 kilometers (9 mi.) in length. Two of the inscriptions also contained a representation of his footprint. Purnavarman evidently ruled a state called Taruma and worshiped Hindu deities.

Pushkalavati *See* CHARSADA.

Puso Sansong Puso Sansong, also known as Sabisong, is part of the capital of the PAEKCHE state (18 B.C.E.–663 C.E.). Paekche was one of the three kingdoms of Korea, occupying the southwestern part of the peninsula. It suffered constant threats from its northern rival, KOGURYO, and finally yielded to the SHILLA state in the seventh century C.E. From 538 C.E. Sabi was the Paekche capital, and Puso Sansong seemed to have fulfilled a military and defensive function as part of the capital complex. Its walls cover an area of 237 hectares (592 acres), and three further walled precincts lie within them. One of these incorporated granaries and a lookout tower; the others also had watchtowers in the citadel area. The walls linked with further long defensive walls on the exterior, designed to protect the palace and residential area, which, from the sixth and seventh centuries, was laid out on a grid plan akin to those of Tang China.

Pyu civilization   The Pyu civilization was developed in the dry zone of central Myanmar (Burma) between about 200 B.C.E. and 900 C.E. It is best known on the basis of three large walled cities, BEIKTHANO, SRI KSETRA, and HALIN. All were located in tributary valleys of the Irrawaddy River, where it was possible to harness the local rivers and streams for IRRIGATION purposes. There is compelling evidence at Beikthano for a pre-Buddhist mortuary tradition involving large brick and timber halls containing the cremated remains of high-status individuals. By the fourth or fifth centuries C.E., however, BUD-DHISM had taken root; many large public buildings included stupas, and monasteries were constructed. Meanwhile, the cremated dead were interred in large ceramic mortuary jars set in brick structures outside the city walls. The Pyu spoke a Sino-Tibetan language and employed Indian scripts in their INSCRIPTIONS. They were proficient bronze casters; one set of figurines from Sri Ksetra shows dancers and musicians richly appareled and ornamented. Skilled artisans also made silver Bud-dhas, images of great beauty. They took part in a widespread trading network that included India. The civilization was ultimately to be succeeded by the state of PAGAN. There is a major destruction layer at Halin. However, many of the Pyu arts, crafts, and ideas were incorporated into the Pagan civilization. It is recorded that King Anawratha of Pagan removed votive tablets and offerings from Sri Ksetra and placed them in his Shwesandaw temple at Pagan.

The Pyu or Tircul people of Myanmar (Burma) were first mentioned in a mid-fourth-century C.E. Chinese text listing the tribes on the frontier of southwestern China. The author, Chang Chu, described them as the Piao. Other early Chinese records that survived in later editions describe the Piao as civilized, "where prince and minister, father and son, elder and younger, have each their order of precedence." The Chinese called them the Pyu, but the Mon people knew of them as the Tircul.

Further reading: Donovan, D. G., H. Kukui, and T. Itoh. "Perspective on the Pyu Landscape," *Southeast Asian Studies* 36 (1998): 19–126; Stargardt, J. *The Ancient Pyu of Burma.* Vol. 1, *Early Pyu Cities in a Man-Made Landscape.* Cambridge: PACSEA Cambridge and ISEAS Singapore, 1990.

Q

Qandahar *See* KANDAHAR.

Qi The state of Qi was located in northeastern China, centered on the modern provinces of Shandong and Hebei. The Ji River flowed through this region, and it was one of the richest of the Warring States of China, in terms of both agriculture and marine and mineral resources. Qi, as had several other states that came to the fore politically during the Spring and Autumn period (770–476 B.C.E.), had its origins in the wars of succession that followed the death of KING WU (d. c. 1043 B.C.E.), the first ruler of the WESTERN ZHOU DYNASTY. The succession should have passed to his oldest son, Song, who under the name Cheng was to rule from about 1042 until 1006 B.C.E. However, a younger brother of King Wu, Zhou Gong Dan, declared himself regent instead, on the grounds that Song was too young to rule alone. This fomented a civil war between the forces of Zhou Gong Dan and Cheng on the one hand and those of Dan's brothers on the other. Zhou Gong Dan fought successful campaigns to the east of the capital and greatly expanded the area under Zhou control. In time-honored tradition, rulers of the new territories were found among the loyal members of the ruling lineage or powerful supporters, and Tai Gong Wang, a leading military commander, was granted the fief that was to develop into the state of Qi, with LINZI as its capital. While under the Western Zhou such fiefs owed fealty to the emperor; they assumed independence with the end of the Western Zhou dynasty in 771 B.C.E. Qi thus became an independent state during the period of the EASTERN ZHOU DYNASTY (770–221 B.C.E.).

Qiemo (Cherchen) Qiemo was one of the major sites of the SHAN-SHAN kingdom in northwest China, which controlled the SILK ROAD as it traversed the southern margin of the TARIM BASIN. The cemetery of Zaghunluq lies in the area of Qiemo, and excavations there in 1985 uncovered burials in which textiles had been exceptionally well preserved. The bodies themselves were amazingly intact. The grave of a man interred about 1000 B.C.E. is particularly important, for it provides evidence of the ethnic group that contributed to the development of the first oasis states of the Tarim Basin a millennium later. The body lay in a pit almost 3.5 meters (12 ft.) deep, cut into salty soil that through desiccation would have contributed to the preservation of organic remains. The mouth of the grave contained a woolen blanket, the man's saddle, as well as a felt blanket, layers of reeds and tree branches, and tanned horse hides. The man himself had been laid out on top of mats woven from willow branches. He wore a short beard, and his hair was braided. His clothing was woven from sheep's wool and was dyed in a wide variety of colors. He wore woven trousers and a shirt made of lengths of cloth stitched together, while his leggings were brightly colored strips of wool wrapped around his lower legs. His boots were of deer leather, and he held an enigmatic strip of leather in his left hand. Ten hats were found in the grave, one in the form of a beret, another with a peak similar to those worn by the Phrygian people who had settled in northern Turkey at about the same time as the Qiemo burials. One of the WOMEN found in the same grave also wore white deerskin boots and a large woolen shawl; another had yellow leggings with red spiral decoration. This tomb seems to have contained the members of a family, for their clothing shows many similarities in manufacture and color. It is notable that the man wore trousers and was interred with his saddle, two vital constituents to life in this open region, while his ancestors are most logically sought in the expansion of agriculturalists from the west into the Tarim oases.

Qiemo was to become the major center of the state of Shan-shan. It was particularly prosperous during the second and third centuries C.E., when Chinese power in the area encouraged peaceful conditions and favored trade. Indeed, Qiemo was the base for the Chinese administration in their western regions during the Western HAN DYNASTY. Exposure to new ideas also saw the establishment of BUDDHISM. Qiemo was, according to the surviving documents of Shan-shan, formerly known as Calamadana. Because the ancient site is occupied today, little is known of the layout of Shan-shan Qiemo, but one stupa foundation was noted by SIR AUREL STEIN. The surviving documents in the KHAROSHTHI script of Shan-shan, however, do illuminate aspects of life in ancient Qiemo. One text relates how wine must be packed, sufficient to be carried by five camels and transported to Calamadana on the fifth day of the fourth month. SLAVERY was also part of life in this site. Thus on the fourth year of the reign of the great King Mairi, the son of heaven, it is recorded that foreigners named Supis entered Calamadana, plundered the country, and seized the inhabitants. One of the captives is named as the slave Samprina.

Qijia culture

The Qijia culture is a regional variant of the LONGSHAN CULTURE, which succeeded the Machang phase of the YANGSHAO CULTURE in Gansu province, northeast China. The sites have been dated between 2300 and 1700 B.C.E. Their interest lies in the fact that although located in the remote northwest, they have furnished the earliest group of bronze artifacts in China. It might at first seem surprising to find the earliest evidence for bronze in remote Gansu rather than the home of the SHANG civilization on the central plains. However, the Gansu corridor is China's natural route to the steppes of Central Asia and beyond, to India, the Near East, and Rome. In later years, this was named the SILK ROAD, but recent archaeological research has stressed its early beginnings. The movement of people and spread of ideas most probably introduced to western China a knowledge of copper-based metallurgy, which is manifested in the finds from the settlements and associated cemeteries of the Qijia culture. The Qijia sites are of central importance in any consideration of the origins of the Chinese Bronze Age; the weight of evidence now points to the transmission of knowledge across the steppes ultimately from the Near East.

At Qinweijia, rows of graves have been unearthed, together with a series of pits. The dead were interred with pottery vessels, pigs' jaws, and bone artifacts. The pits have yielded copper or bronze implements, including an ax, awl, disks, and rings. The ax, after being cast in a stone mold, was heated and hammered repeatedly, a process known as annealing, to harden it. This is a techni-

cally sophisticated procedure. Dahezhuang is a second site to reveal the presence of bronze and copper artifacts. One knife was recovered from near the foundations of a house, with millet still adhering to it. There were also knives, chisels, awls, and rings, in contexts radiocarbon dated to about 2000 B.C.E. Excavations at Huangniangniangtai have uncovered the remains of houses, pits, and burials, as well as 32 bronzes from occupation contexts and burials. Some were cast from copper, others from a tin bronze, and the preferred artifacts were knives, awls, chisels, and a ring.

Qin

The state of Qin in central China was the ultimate victor during the WARRING STATES PERIOD (475–221 B.C.E.). The political situation in 361 B.C.E. included seven major states; Qin ranked equally with the others, but also with many smaller states. SIMA QIAN describes how the feudal lords were ruling by force and attempting to subdue and annex one another. In these conflicts, Qin consistently showed itself superior to the state of WEI, defeating it in 354 B.C.E. and taking its former capital, Anyi, two years later. These two victories were instigated by SHANG YANG, who persuaded the duke Xiao of the dangers presented by the state of Wei. His Machiavellian approach to diplomacy and war is well illustrated in the deceitful methods he employed. After inviting the general of the Wei forces to parley and agree to a truce, he had the general arrested and then destroyed the Wei army. After victory the Qin rulers had to devise some means of ruling a huge area of former rivals, populated by subjugated and disaffected populations. The king of Qin first chose a new name, QIN SHIHUANGDI (259–210 B.C.E.). This is a highly symbolic title, meaning "august emperor." Administratively, the Qin authorities devised a series of policies to unify the newly created empire, one that the emperor planned should last for limitless generations. The legal system, based on the tenet of mutual responsibility, was applied uniformly. This meant that a misdemeanor by an individual would involve punishment for his extended family. The sentences were also designed to ensure that there would be no repeat offense. Some were draconian: being boiled alive, cut in two, torn apart by chariots, or castrated as a commutation for the death sentence. The burning of the books was the most notorious of the policies promulgated under the Qin dynasty. After a court intrigue, the legitimate successor to the first emperor was ordered to commit suicide on the basis of a forged directive, and the throne passed to the second emperor HUANDI, who was then aged 21. His reign was brief. Rebellions broke out in 209 B.C.E., and the second emperor committed suicide two years later, bringing the Qin dynasty to an early end.

Qin was located in the valley of the Wei River, known as the Guanzhong, "land within the passes." This name recognized its ideal defensive position, with access restricted to the Wu Pass to the southeast and the Hangu

Pass on the eastern border. Qin came to prominence at the beginning of the Spring and Autumn period (770–476 B.C.E.) of the EASTERN ZHOU DYNASTY, after the capital was moved to LUOYANG. Over a period of four centuries, its capital was moved on at least seven occasions, and archaeological investigations have traced the remains of at least three centers. They were invariably large and imposing, containing palaces and large domestic residences, as well as manufacturing facilities, within walls of stamped-earth construction. Yong, the capital founded in 677 by Duke Degong, covered an area of 4.5 by two kilometers (2.7 by 1.2 mi.). Under Duke Xiangong in 383 B.C.E., the capital was located at Yueyang. It covered 1.8 by 2.2 kilometers, and, according to the excavations, six gates severed its walls. The final capital at XIANYANG was the biggest of all, and its foundation reflects a major political move. Not only was Xianyang strategically placed for trade, but it was also closer to the rival states that were to assume such a prominent position during the Warring States period. It provided a clean slate to work out new social and political agendas, free of the dynastic and lineage loyalties that encumbered the previous capitals, particularly Yong.

CHANGES OF SHANG YANG

These basic social changes were in many respects inspired by the reformer Shang Yang. He hailed from the state of Wey and after traveling to Qin gained the ear of Duke Xiao Gong. He set aside the old feudal order and its serf labor, freeing farmers to become tax-yielding citizens. Shang Yang further instituted changes vital to securing the power of Qin. His policies enforced military conscription and, through changes in the administration of the kingdom, called on people of talent rather than those owing their position to hereditary titles and place in the hierarchy. His new laws were dedicated to cementing the king as the unrivaled head of state. Hints as to the importance of the new laws are found in the documents recovered from a tomb at Yunmeng, dated to 217 B.C.E. The statutes set out the proper duties and behavior of state officials and the way in which they communicated information from the outlying districts to the capital. The social changes of Shang Yang were accompanied by a policy of centralized organization of arms production so that the most up-to-date weaponry was available for the army. With such backing, the Qin became a formidable and powerful state that was ultimately to forge rivals into a unified empire.

The capital was not walled, but stretched along the bank of the Wei River. The historian Sima Qian states that it was decided not to build, according to tradition, an ancestral temple as the first construction in the new capital, but rather two imposing halls called the Ji wue. This probably reflected the practice of posting imperial edicts on palace gate towers. The Jique palace followed. Excavations have revealed a massive structure raised high on stamped-earth foundations. It stood three stories high, the lower story dominated by a long colonnaded hall. The interior chambers, covered in plaster, were decorated with painted scenes that included a four-horse chariot and elegant WOMEN. Roof and floor tiles were embellished with geometric images and pictures of exotic birds. The Jique palace was but one of up to 300 palaces that describe in microcosm the successful military campaigns waged by successive Qin rulers.

QIN EXPANSION

The pattern of expansion of the Qin state from its Wei Valley heartland began in the mid-fifth century, when it moved southwest against the smaller states of BA and SHU in Sichuan. This was a vital strategic move, because the Shu, who had long since been established in the vicinity of Chengdu, controlled the rich rice-growing land of this region. Swallowing the Shu state, however, was a long and difficult task, and only after a century did the Qin reenter the struggle for power in the central plains. The takeover of Sichuan was a seminal move for Qin, because it made available a vast area of rich agricultural land as well as mineral resources. It also outflanked the mighty state of CHU on its western boundary. From 316 B.C.E. when the decisive move south commenced, there developed a most intriguing political situation in which one of the world's earliest totalitarian states was faced with the task of imposing its governance on a large, sophisticated, powerful, but alien society. At first, administration was imposed through the appointment of the son of the former king as a marquis subservient to the Qin court. But real power in Sichuan lay in the hands of the appointed administrator and military commander, both of whom moved from Xianyang to take up their posts.

This device was a failure, because not only the new line of marquises, but also the first administrator rebelled against the Qin authority. In due course, many new bureaucrats were appointed, and major centers were fortified. The walls of Chengdu, the capital of the now dependent commandery, were raised to a height of 23 meters (76 ft.), around a city extending more than 250 hectares (625 acres). A mint was established to expedite commercial development, and according to a series of important BAMBOO SLIPS or tomb texts, thousands of new settlers were dispatched south, and the rigorous Qin system of land tenure was established. Some of the immigrants are recorded to have branched out successfully into salt production, iron smelting, and mining of cinnabar. Absorption took several generations, but the grain and other goods, not to mention the increased population that became available to the rulers of Qin, played a major, perhaps decisive, part in the wars that lay ahead.

In 364 B.C.E. Qin defeated the forces of Wei at the battle of Shimen. This was described by Sima Qian in his history: "Qin fought with Jin at Shimen and cut off sixty thousand heads. The Son of Heaven congratulated Qin with an embroidered sacrificial garment." On this occasion, Sima Qian still described Wei as Jin despite the fact that Jin had by then split into three states. Four years later, Qin again defeated Wei at the Battle of Shao Liang and took its general captive.

The new era of struggle between the contending states saw further rapid changes in military organization and tactics. There were now universal military conscription and an increasing reliance on large bodies of well-trained and equipped infantry, in place of the former dominance of chariots. New weaponry included the replacement of the old traditional longbow with the powerful crossbow, which fired a triangular-headed bolt. There were also bronze swords and iron swords. With the proliferation of defensive walls and walled cities scaling ladders and tunneling to take enemy strongholds were developed. The Qin leaders were foremost in developing such new techniques for total warfare. As the fourth century B.C.E. progressed, they consolidated their hold over the Shu in the Sichuan Basin and began to develop major irrigation schemes there. Another major rival to the south was the state of Chu, which commanded rich agricultural land and mineral resources. In 312 B.C.E. General Zhang defeated the Chu at the Battle of Danyang on the Chang (Yangtze) River, captured his opposing leader Chu Gai, and allegedly cut off 80,000 heads. This effectively ruled Chu out of further serious contention for supremacy.

The next phase of warfare saw the dominance of a QI-led alliance, but by 294 B.C.E. Qin armies were again on the move. By 288 B.C.E. the dominance of Qin to the west and Qi in the east encouraged a pact whereby the two rulers assumed the divine title of DI. This truce was of brief duration. The power of Qi was virtually extinguished by alliances of rival states, leaving Qin free to overwhelm Chu. The general Bo Qi attacked and occupied its capital, Ying, and converted the area into a Qin province. With Qi and Chu defeated, only ZHAO and HANN stood between Qin and total dominance. In this period the rise to prominence of Fan Sui (d. 255 B.C.E.) occurred. He became the chief minister of Qin and established a policy of total wars of annihilation. In the final locking of horns, a three-year struggle between Qin, led by Bo Qi, and the combined forces of Hann and Zhao occurred. It ended with the Zhao army encircled, then starved into submission, and finally, its soldiers buried alive.

THE FIRST EMPEROR'S REFORMS

The first king of Qin resolved not to follow the Zhou precedent of providing kingdoms within the empire for relatives, because this system historically had held the seeds of disaffection and rivalry. Rather, he created 36 provinces, or commanderies, each subdivided into counties. These provinces were placed under the rule of three centrally appointed and salaried bureaucrats. There was a *shou*, or governor; a *wei*, or military commander; and an inspector, who ensured that the central directives were enforced, known as a *jian yushi*. With additions and minor modifications, this provincial system has continued to the present. There was, however, the problem of dealing with the leaders of the former rival kingdoms. This was resolved by moving them and their entourages to the Qin capital, where a series of replicas of their palaces were constructed to house them. In the meantime, their former capitals had their defenses razed to the ground to remove any likelihood of local rebellions.

The emperor's ambition proved unsuccessful, although the Qin dynasty lasted about 15 years. The reforms involved first the script. For a millennium, the Chinese script had developed strong regional characteristics. Under the Zhou, it was known as the large SEAL script, and the Qin reformers found that many of the graphs had grown obsolete as objects or ideas were consigned to history. These were removed from the lexicon, and uniformity was then applied to the remaining variants under the new small seal script. This was a vital step in consolidating hold over a unified state. The same policy was applied to weights and measures and sensibly even to the gauge of wheeled vehicles. Many different forms of currency had existed during the Warring States period, but these were set aside in favor of COINAGE in gold and bronze. The coins themselves, of circular form with a central square hole, set the style of Chinese currency for the next 20 centuries.

The burning of the books involved specifically the destruction of historical texts, which could be employed by academics to criticize the Qin legalist regime, such as the *Book of Documents* and the *Book of Songs*. It also extended to any historic tract describing former rival states. The order to destroy these historic documents was sent out to all the commanderies, linked with the command to punish severely those who ignored it or connived at the retention of the proscribed texts.

STATE LABOR PROJECTS

Under strong encouragement of agriculture at the expense of trade, the state disposed of sufficient surpluses to maintain huge resources of labor. These were deployed on massive construction projects designed to knit together the regions and defend the state against external threats. The road system, for example, radiated out from the capital, with a standard form in which the thoroughfares were lined with trees. A force estimated at 300,000 was set to work on the construction of the GREAT WALL, which stretched like a shield along the northern frontier, while more than twice that number were, by 212 B.C.E., engaged on building the great tomb of the first emperor. As part of his military expansion, transport also involved the cutting of canals to permit the passage of bulky goods. This move involved a canal across the watershed that had separated the Chang River catchment from the rivers flowing south to Lingnan.

THE ROYAL TOMB

Qin Shihuangdi made many progresses through the empire on what today are termed fact-finding missions. These led to new policies, not least the resettlement of his subjects in thinly populated regions to strengthen defense and increase agricultural production. It was on one such progress that he died when aged only 49. In 11 years he had transformed China from a series of powerful rival states into a unified empire, but it was the Han emperors rather than his own dynasty that reaped the rewards of this achievement. His body was returned to the capital, where it was interred at Mount Li. His mortuary complex is the largest known. Early Chinese records describe its extent, and it is known from archaeological excavations. The records describe the layout and contents of the interior of the great pyramid that dominates the above-ground portion of the site. Evidently—for it has never been examined scientifically—the interior held a tomb chamber filled with the emperor's personal belongings. The roof displayed the heavens, while the ground displayed the extent of the empire and was ringed by rivers of flowing mercury. Great lamps with walrus oil were lit to burn for a very long time. For the last known time in Chinese history, members of his harem were immolated within the tomb, while the construction workers who would know the internal layout and contents were butchered. Crossbows were placed with tripwires to kill unwanted intruders. Whether this tomb survived the destruction of the capital that accompanied the wars that followed the collapse of his dynasty is not known, but it is extremely unlikely. However, the subterranean chambers that surrounded the pyramid, although damaged during those wars, have survived sufficiently to allow reconstruction. Some of these were filled with terra-cotta replicas, cast at life-size, of the emperor's armies, including the infantry, chariots, cavalry, and a command center. Each soldier, individually modeled, was painted and armed. There were also the imperial zoological garden and a half-sized replica in bronze of the royal chariot resplendent with four horses and charioteer.

Further reading: Li Xueqin. *Eastern Zhou and Qin Civilizations.* New Haven, Conn.: Yale University Press, 1985; Loewe M. *A Biographical Dictionary of the Qin, Former Han and Xin Periods (221 BC–AD 24).* Leiden: Brill, 2000; Loewe, M., and E. L. Shaugnessy, eds. *The Cambridge History of Ancient China.* Cambridge: Cambridge University Press, 1999.

Qin Shihuangdi (259–210 B.C.E.) *Qin Shihuangdi is renowned as the first emperor of China, responsible for the largest mortuary complex known.*

He was born with the name Zheng toward the end of the WARRING STATES PERIOD (475–221 B.C.E.). The circumstances of his birth are rather mysterious. His father was King Zhuang Xiang of QIN, and when still a prince, Zhuang Xiang was sent as a hostage to the court of the state of Zhao. While restricted there, the prince had a relationship with a concubine, and it was uncertain whether the father of the future emperor was Zhuang Xiang or one LÜ BUWEI, who supplied the concubine, possibly already pregnant. Zhang Xiang in due course ruled Qin, and Zheng succeeded him in 246 B.C.E., at the early age of 13. He followed the legalist doctrine of centralized autocratic authority, increasing the efficiency of agriculture and training his troops to be brutally efficient in war. They never took prisoners. By 221 B.C.E., Qin finally triumphed over its rival states, and King Zheng took the new title of Shihuangdi, "august emperor." The irony of the career of Qin Shihuangdi is that with furious energy he forged an empire from previously warring states, but his career as emperor spanned only 11 years, and his dynasty barely outlived his death. But it is in death that he is now best known, through the incredible remains of his tomb.

QIN SHIHUANGDI'S REFORMS

His brief period of imperial rule, which lasted 11 years, produced the most rapid and drastic reforms in the history of China. He standardized the script, which had developed along several distinct paths over the preceding millennium, and ordered that there be only one official currency. The legal system was systematized, and he decreed savage punishments for transgressors on the principle of joint responsibility. This meant that the relatives of a criminal were deemed equally guilty. Axle widths were set at the same gauge throughout the empire, and new roads and canals ensured rapid and efficient transport.

There was also a massive building program at the capital, Xianyang, where his own palaces and those of conquered rulers spread along the margins of the Wei River. The latter were constructed to house former sovereigns and their families were moved to Xianyang to reduce the risk of provincial insurrections. The GREAT WALL of China was begun with a force of conscripted labor, and it is recorded that nearly 750,000 workers were eventually deployed in the construction of the royal tomb. When certain scholars used ancient texts to criticize the legalist regime, the emperor ordered that they be branded and dispatched to help build the Great Wall and that the books they quoted be burned. Some scholars were also put to death.

We know little of the emperor's personal life, except that he engaged soothsayers and medical specialists in an attempt to secure immortality. It was, however, on one of his imperial progresses that he died and was returned to Xianyang for burial. By the time of his death, he had transformed China from seven major competing states to a unified empire divided into 36 commanderies, or provinces, each governed by central appointees. The succeeding Western HAN DYNASTY inherited this unified state, which was to endure for more than four centuries.

THE TOMB

Today Qin Shihuangdi is more widely known for his tomb than for his reforms. In spring 1974, peasants excavating a well more than a mile from his mausoleum at Mount Li encountered life-size terra-cotta figures and bronze weapons. The early historical records of the tomb itself described a magnificent chamber with a bronze roof, in which the constellations were set in pearls. The reconstruction of the empire was surrounded by the oceans filled with flowing mercury, and there were lamps filled with "man-fish" oil, set to burn for a very long time. The term *man-fish* might refer to a walrus or a marine mammal such as a whale. The historians SIMA QIAN and BAN GU concur that vast riches were accumulated in the tomb, which was not quite completed at the time of the emperor's death, even after being under construction for more than 30 years. Sima Qian described how work on the tomb began as soon as the emperor took power as king of Qin. Workers excavated deep into the ground and poured molten bronze to form the outermost coffin. The tomb chambers incorporated replicas of the palaces and towers, and there were countless rare and beautiful offerings. Protection against tomb robbers involved the placement of armed crossbows, while those involved in the construction of the interior, with knowledge of its contents and layout, were exterminated.

Underground Chambers

The discovery of the first terra-cotta figures set in train a series of major excavations, which have revealed the presence of many subterranean chambers filled with representations of the emperor's armies, retainers, chariots, and possessions. The entire complex included two walled enclosures covering an area of 5,600 hectares (14,000 acres). The central pyramid once reached a height of about 115 meters (380 ft.), though erosion has now reduced the height to about 70 meters. While no formal excavations of the tomb pyramid itself have been undertaken, borings have revealed unusually high readings of mercury in the central part of the pyramid, thus confirming the historic accounts of rivers and oceans filled with quicksilver that constantly flowed by means of an ingenious mechanical device. Soundings in the periphery of the pyramid have also uncovered magnificently finished bronze bells inlaid with gold and silver, huge eave tiles, sewer pipes, bricks, and burial pits. The pits containing the remains of the terra-cotta divisions of the Qin army

The terra-cotta army of Emperor Qin Shihuangdi is one of the most remarkable archaeological monuments in the world. (© Keren Su/CORBIS)

have been excavated in part. These have provided a glimpse of not only the energy devoted to equipping the emperor's tomb, but also the nature of the structure and arms of the all-conquering Qin military machine.

Largest Chamber

The largest of the pits contains a formation, probably in excess of 6,000 individual soldiers, each life-size and individually modeled. They were originally painted and bore real armaments: halberds, crossbows, and spears of bronze, with a few weapons of iron. These weapons are particularly interesting, for they reveal not only the skill of the manufacturers, but also the degree to which even their form and size were standardized. The alloy mix varied in each type of weapon to suit the stresses it would have been exposed to in battle. Many, particularly the swords, bear small inscriptions in the standardized Qin small SEAL script, denoting the workshop in which they were produced or their date of manufacture and the craftsperson who made them. The bronze swords have retained their finely honed surface even after two millennia underground, and detailed metallographic analyses have revealed that they were coated in a layer of chromium that was only 10 to 15 micrometers (400 to 600 μin.) thick. Apart from the abundant spears, halberds, and arrows, there are a few unusual double-edged long knives in the form of a hook, known as the *wu* hook, because they originated in the state of the same name. A weapon known as a *pi*, or short dagger, was also found for the first time.

The battle formation began at the front, with a vanguard of crack archers, divided into three units of 68 men. Behind them were 11 long corridors that had originally been roofed with timber beams, in which the main force was arrayed. This included chariots drawn by four horses and supporting infantry. The flanks and rear were made up of guards against surprise attack, each group looking in a different direction.

Second Chamber

A second pit lies adjacent to the first and is smaller, measuring 124 by 98 meters (410 by 323 ft.), and reaching a depth of five meters. It has not been exposed to the same extent as the first, from which more than 1,000 warriors have been uncovered. However, it is known that the second pit contains another detachment of infantry, chariots, and cavalry, the chariots made of wood. The archers with their powerful crossbows are situated so that as one line has finished firing, the second is ready to take its place in the line to fire in turn. A force of 64 four-horse chariots each carrying three men, follows behind the archers. The third section is made up of further chariots, associated with infantry and cavalry, while the last group is a wing of cavalry. This must have been a highly mobile and flexible division of the Qin army.

Third Chamber

A third pit was opened in 1979 and found to be much smaller than the other two, measuring only 520 meters square. The method of construction was clearly apparent, because it had not been damaged by fire. It was U-shaped and opened to the east by means of a ramp. Descending the ramp led to a chariot with four horses. High-status warriors stood behind it. Sixty-four figures of soldiers stood in the two corridors thus created by the U-shape of the structure. Those in the northern sector face inward, looking at one another across a gap. The figures in the southern part stand in two detachments of 12 or with their backs to the corridor walls. The presence of a large collection of animal bones, along with the shape of the pit and disposition of the soldiers and the chariot, suggests that this pit was the command center, and the soldiers formed an honor guard. The presence of the animal bones is a reminder that sacrifices were made as good omens for an impending battle.

Other Discoveries

The pits so far identified and uncovered are likely to form but a small fraction of the subterranean feature that made up the mortuary complex. One pit to contain further echelons of the imperial army lies unfinished. In 1980 archaeologists investigated a rectangular pit seven meters (23 ft.) long by 2.3 wide (7.6 ft.), which reached a depth of nearly eight meters. This pit was located only 20 meters west of the actual mausoleum pyramid and was found to contain a wooden chamber, in which were the remains of two stunning bronze conveyances and of hay to feed the horses. One was a chariot drawn by four horses; the other was a sumptuous decorated carriage. They were found in a collapsed and ruined condition, but a lengthy and arduous restoration now conveys not only the outstanding skill of the Qin bronze specialists, but also the manner in which the emperor traveled on his progresses. The horses drawing the chariot were bedecked with plumes and fine decorated harnesses. Even the bridles were made of gold and silver. The charioteer stands under a raised parasol. He wears a long tunic and double swallowtailed hat, while his long sword hangs behind him from his belt. The shaft of the parasol was inlaid with golden designs. The second carriage was also drawn by four horses, the driver seated in front of a closed compartment. The doors and interior were decorated with painted designs. The predominant color employed for the horses and chariots was white, traditionally the color of the west, from whence the Qin originated. The other four colors employed—red, blue, black, and yellow—represent, respectively, the south, east, north, and center. Motifs included cloud patterns and geometric designs.

There are 19 tombs near the central pyramid that probably contained the remains of the emperor's retainers, and his stables are represented by nearly 100 pits with hundreds of horse skeletons and their grooms rendered in terra-cotta. The emperor's menagerie is represented by pits containing models of birds and animals.

Further reading: Li Xueqin. *Eastern Zhou and Qin Civilizations.* New Haven, Conn.: Yale University Press,

1985; Loewe, M. *A Biographical Dictionary of the Qin, Former Han and Xin Periods (221 BC–AD 24)*. Leiden: Brill, 2000; Loewe, M., and E. L. Shaugnessy, eds. *The Cambridge History of Ancient China*. Cambridge: Cambridge University Press, 1999.

Qiuwan Qiuwan is a remarkable site of the late SHANG STATE period (1766–1045 B.C.E.) located in the Huai River Valley of Jiangsu province in China. It was probably a major center of the Dapeng state, which was mentioned in the Shang ORACLE BONES as being at times an ally, at others an enemy. The oracle bones also describe ritual sacrifices to the ancestors, and at Qiuwan the site of one such sacrificial area has been excavated. Around four upright stones, 32 skeletons were found, of which 22 were human, the remainder dogs. The human victims were found in a crouching position, heads to the ground, with their hands behind their backs. Two people were represented only by skulls.

quarry sites Temples at ANGKOR in Cambodia were made of BRICK, sandstone, and laterite. Often the sandstone had to be quarried at some distance from a temple. That for Angkor, for example, was from sources in the KULEN HILLS 30 kilometers to the north and may have been transported to the temple site by canal. Two large sandstone sources have been identified in Thailand. At Si Khiu, the cut marks for stone that was never removed are visible over a considerable area. Similarly, the Ban Kruat quarry, which lies about 20 kilometers south of PHNOM RUNG and Muang Tam, was intensely exploited. Laterite is an iron ore that can be cut out of the ground when soft to the form required. It then hardens on exposure to air. It has been suggested that the excavation of the WESTERN BARAY, the only reservoir at Angkor created by digging rather then raising of dykes, provided laterite for the nearby temple of BAPHUON.

See also PHNOM WAN.

Qufu Qufu, a town in Shandong province, China, was formerly the capital of the state of LU during the Western and Eastern Han dynasties. It is notable in Chinese history as the birthplace of CONFUCIUS (551–479 B.C.E.), China's most famous and influential political philosopher and teacher. The earliest known temple to Confucius at Qufu was built a year after the sage's death. During the WARRING STATES PERIOD (475–221 B.C.E.) and the QIN dynasty (221–206 B.C.E.), LEGALISM was favored, giving rulers the right to autocratic rule. Under QIN SHIHUANGDI, philosophical books were ordered burned, and scholars were immolated alive. However, Confucianism returned to favor under the Han, and in 195 B.C.E. under the rule of Emperor GAOZU, sacrifices were made at the tomb of Confucius. From the first century B.C.E., the family of Confucius was ennobled and granted land. The family home was built adjacent to the temple. A temple to Confucius remains at Qufu to this day. Qufu is important not only because it was the home of Confucius, but also because it was continuously occupied from the early WESTERN ZHOU DYNASTY (1045–771 B.C.E.) to the HAN DYNASTY (206 B.C.E.–220 C.E.). The intensive archaeological investigations there have provided details of Western Zhou city planning hitherto hardly known. Thus the concentration of workshops and habitations in the northern part of the city was matched by the proximity of the gates to one another to facilitate the passage of goods and people.

LITERARY REFERENCES TO CITY

The association with Confucius, linked with the exemplary ritual conservatism of the rulers of Lu, has stimulated many literary references to the city. BAN GU in the HANSHU (*History of the Former Han Dynasty*), for example, covers the association of Lu with the duke of Zhou and Confucius. The *Guoyu* (*Discourses of the States*) dedicates one of its eight parts to the state of Lu between the 10th and sixth centuries B.C.E. The most notable literary text, however, is the CHUNQIU (*Spring and Autumn Annals*), which describe the period from 722 to 481 B.C.E., which followed the reigns of the 12 dukes of Lu. The editing of this text is traditionally ascribed to Confucius himself.

HISTORY AND ARCHAEOLOGY

The state of Lu was enfeoffed to the duke of Zhou early in the Western Zhou dynasty, and the duke sent his son there to rule. The royal Ji clan continued to control Lu for much of the remainder of the Zhou dynasty. The city name means "curved hillock" after a raised feature that lies within its walls, and as were many other Chinese cities, it was situated between two rivers. Archaeological investigations in the ancient city have revealed its walled defenses that enclose an area of 1,200 hectares (3,000 acres). The research began in 1977 and was systematically applied to most of the enclosed area. Particular attention was paid to the walls, burials, raised platforms, and rubbish pits. This revealed that the city was founded at least by the Western Zhou period and that it was probably constructed over an even earlier urban complex dating to the late Shang dynasty called Shao. The walls had 11 gates linked with the roads that ran across the city interior. A large palace precinct was found in the center of the city, and as is almost invariably the case with such cities, there were precincts set aside for the specialist manufacture of bronzes and bone and ceramic products. Several cemeteries have been found, and their interpretation has proved controversial. One school of thought identified two groups, one representing the local pre-Zhou population and a second group of burials belonging to the ruling Ji clan and its newcomers from Shaanxi province, based on distinctions in wealth, tomb structure, and the orientation of the body. On the other hand, survival of two such distinct groups in parallel for so many centuries is inherently unlikely, and the alternative interpretation—that the cemeteries reflect lineage groups with differing wealth—is more likely.

The axial distribution of the central palace, the raised ceremonial and ritual platform, and the Pheasant Gate into the city indicates careful central planning. The roads are wide and impressive. The grid layout includes main routes up to 17 meters (56 ft.) wide linking the center with the gates. There are Western Zhou bronze foundries in the city walls; during the Warring States period, iron-working facilities were established.

In 249 B.C.E., the widely admired state of Lu, respected for its adherence to traditional rituals during the period of the EASTERN ZHOU DYNASTY (770–221 B.C.E.), fell to the forces of Chu. The latter established a *XIAN,* or local administrative unit there, an administrative system also used by the Qin and Han emperors. In 154 B.C.E. Emperor JINGDI enfeoffed his son, Liu Yu, as prince of Lu, and the latter built the notable Spirit Light temple. It was during this Western Han dynasty that the third major city wall was constructed. Smaller than its predecessors, it still incorporated Han workshops and residences.

Qu Yuan (c. 340–278 B.C.E.) *Qu Yuan was a minister of the Chu kingdom of China, who is thought to have written the* Chuci, *or Songs of the South.*
This collection of poems provides a vital source of information on the nature of Chu society during the WARRING STATES PERIOD (475–221 B.C.E.). Qu Yuan committed suicide by drowning, but his poems survive as a romantic reflection of life in the warm southern regions.

R

Rabatak   In March 1993 fragments of a stone INSCRIPTION were found at Kafir's Castle, a hill in the Rabatak region of Afghanistan. It has 23 lines of Greek text and decoration of lion paws and lotuses. The text began by naming King KAN-ISHKA I, the KUSHAN, the righteous, the just, the autocrat, and the god, worthy of worship, who obtained kingship from Nana and all the gods. It listed the cities in India that acknowledged his overlordship, a list that includes PATAL-IPUTRA and KAUSAMBI. The king then recorded his foundation of a sanctuary to a series of deities, including Umma, Nana, Sroshard, Narasa, and Mihr, together with their statues, in honor of his ancestors. Vitally, the inscription then lists Kanishka I's royal line, beginning with his great-grandfather, KUJULA KADPHISES, followed by his grandfather, Vima Taktu, then by his father, Vima Kadphises. As a consequence, it is now known that a Kujula Kadphises was the father of a king called Wima Tak [to] . . . (the rest of his name remains unknown as a result of the fragmentary nature of the inscription). He, in turn, was the father of Vima Kadphises and grandfather of Kanishka. The approximate dates of these rulers have also clarified: Kujula Kadphises reigned from 30 to 80 C.E., Wima Tak [to] from 80 to 90 C.E., Wima Kadphises from 90 to 100, and Kaniska from 100 to 126.

Rahal Baray   The Rahal BARAY is the reservoir constructed under the king JAYAVARMAN IV (r. 928–42 C.E.) of ANGKOR in Cambodia at KOH KER (Lingapura). It measures 1200 by 560 meters (3,960 by 1,850 ft.); less massive than those at Angkor, it is still notable, because it was partially hewn from living rock.

Rajagriha   Rajagriha, modern Rajgir, was the capital of the kingdom of MAGADHA before the establishment of the capital of the MAURYA EMPIRE at PATALIPUTRA in India. Its name means the "seat of royalty," and it is located in a position of natural strength on the southern margin of the Ganges (Ganga) Valley. The site has strong associations with the Buddha, who is said to have visited and stayed there often. A series of six caves in the vicinity of the city may be the Saptaparni site, the location of the first Buddhist council held shortly after the death of the Buddha, and the remains of a monastery might be that given to the Buddha by a person named Jivaka.

Archaeological excavations have now shown that the site was first occupied during the late Iron Age at about 500 B.C.E., but that the mud ramparts were built over a deposit radiocarbon dated to the mid-third century B.C.E. The walls of the second city, which have been sectioned, stood at least 7.5 meters (25 ft.) high and were very broad at the base. They were later embellished with brick support. However, despite its naturally defensive position, religious associations, and presence of hot springs, Rajgir was abandoned as a royal capital with the establishment of Pataliputra as the capital of the Maurya empire.

When the Chinese Buddhist monk FAXIAN visited Rajagriha in the early fifth century C.E., he found the city deserted. Nevertheless, he wrote that the city had once been the capital of King Bimbisara and that there were four stupas, including "at a bend of the mountain city wall," the remains of the Jivaka monastery, and the hollow in the ground where an old well was still visible. When a Dr. Buchanan visited the site in 1812, the local people told him that the site was known as Hangsapurnagar, an ancient city.

INVESTIGATION AT THE SITE

The site itself has a massive stone wall that encircles a series of hills and incorporates further walled divisions within. A second walled complex, known as New Rajgir, is located beyond the north gate of the old city. The association with the Buddha encouraged a series of explorations that began in the 19th century under SIR ARTHUR CUNNINGHAM. Early efforts were directed at finding structures with historical associations, and these are always difficult to relate to the actual events or foundations recorded in the literature. In 1905, SIR JOHN MARSHALL and D. R. Sahni undertook extensive excavations and surveys of the walls. The excavations revealed three major levels, the lowest containing SEALS dated to the second or first century B.C.E.

Between 1912 and 1914, V. H. Jackson prepared a detailed plan of the city, despite the difficulties posed by dense jungle cover. The ramparts still survived, particularly along the southern edge, where the walls stood more than 10 meters (33 ft.) in height. On the eastern side, the walls were fronted by a moat partially cut from rock, and the city gate at this point crossed the moat by a bridge whose foundations were still visible. The interior contains a number of elevated areas that supported building foundations. One of these, which Jackson called a fort, has thick stone walls with bastions. It is also most intriguing because it is one of the few parts of the city commanding a view of a hill that formerly held a Buddha statue. There is a tradition that when King Bimbisara was imprisoned by his son, he could see that statue of Buddha from his cell. A second fort or citadel, represented by solid stone foundations, was found beside the western wall. This survey also traced the course of some of the main city streets and encountered many wells, some cut into the living rock and still containing water. Several rectangular water tanks were also found.

rajakulamahamantrin During the course of the history of ANGKOR in Cambodia, there was a steady accretion of titles and associated duties given to high state officials. The title *rajakulamahamantrin* appears first in a text dating to the reign of Harshavarman I (910–22 C.E.). Several INSCRIPTIONS show this ruler's involvement in considering tax immunity for religious institutions and permission for the joining of foundations. He also exercised authority in the sacred court, with powers to punish those who transgressed a royal edict. Thus the Tuol Pei inscription dating to 922 C.E. describes an order from of Harshavarman I to the *rajakulamahamantrin* exempting the foundation from the tax on rice.

Rajasri *See* NEAK PEAN.

Rajavihara *See* TA PROHM.

Rajendravarman (r. 944–968 C.E.) *Rajendravarman was king of Angkor in Cambodia and returned the court to Yashodharapura after the interval at Lingapura under his younger brother, Jayavarman IV.*

Rajendravarman's inscriptions claim that he had superior qualities as a king compared with his predecessor, Harshavarman II, who was both his cousin and his nephew. Rajendravarman restored the temple of BAKSEI CHAMKRONG in 948, dedicating it to the previous kings. His two major temple pyramids are located east of the city of YASHOVARMAN. The EASTERN MEBON was placed on an island in the middle of YASHODHARATATAKA, while PRE RUP lies to the south. His accession was not peaceful, according to an inscription at Pre Rup. The inscription includes a eulogy to the king, setting out his illustrious royal ancestry traced to the mythical founders of Cambodia.

It is evident from his inscriptions that Rajendravarman had to fight for the succession and then maintain himself as king of kings through military means. His inscriptions contain many vivid descriptions of the king in battle, his sword red with the blood of his enemies. There is some evidence, however, that former semi-independent regions became increasingly under central control as provinces during his reign, and he was also sufficiently powerful to mount a military campaign against the neighboring Chams.

See also CHAM CIVILIZATION.

Rakhigarhi Rakhigarhi is one of the most easterly sites in India with remains of the pre-INDUS VALLEY CIVILIZATION. The site, as do many of the Indus Valley civilization, has two mounds, a small citadel to the west, and a larger mound also to the west. It lies on the now-dry bank of the Chautang River about 90 kilometers northwest of Delhi. In due course, this site grew into one of the largest of the Indus cities, covering an area in excess of 80 hectares (200 acres).

Ramannadesa The Mon people were responsible for the DVARAVATI CIVILIZATION (400–900 C.E.) of the CHAO PHRAYA BASIN in Thailand and also for a state that developed in the lower reaches of the Salween and Sittang Rivers in southeastern Myanmar (Burma). This kingdom was known as Ramannadesa and also on occasion as Suwannabhumi, the "land of gold." Little is known of this kingdom, although it occupied a strategic position commanding the Three Pagodas Pass that links India with Southeast Asia. The area received Buddhist influence in the form of missionaries during the third century B.C.E., and BUDDHISM flourished from early beginnings. The capital city is known as THATON. It is of rectangular plan, demarcated by two laterite walls and a moat, and it covers an area of about 275 hectares (690 acres). A palace precinct occupies the area just north of the center of the enclosure. There are several impressive Buddhist temples. The present Shwezayan temple is thought to overlie a fifth-century foundation housing four teeth of the Buddha. Five 11th-century INSCRIPTIONS in the Mon language have been found on the temple grounds. A few of the surviving terra-cotta plaques that embellished the Myatheindan temple survive and illustrate 11th-century images of passages in the life of the Buddha. Hinduism at Thaton is seen in ninth- and 10th-century reliefs of Vishnu, SIVA, and Brahma. Other major settlements of this state have been identified at the walled center of Taikkala, probably originally known as Suwannabhumi, and the decorated wall at Ksindat Myindat.

Ramayana With the MAHABHARATA, the *Ramayana* is one of the epic histories of India. In seven books, it is reputedly the work of Valmiki. It was probably completed by the first century B.C.E. The saga centers on the person of Rama, the god Vishnu in human form, who descended to Earth at the behest of the gods to end the dominance and churlish behavior of the giant Ravana. Born as the son of the king of Ayodhya, Rama developed heroic proportions and won the hand of Princess Sita in an archery competition. By now the crown prince, he was exiled by his father and spent 14 years in the wilderness, accompanied by his wife, Sita, and his faithful brother. When Sita was seized by the giant Ravana, Rama resolved to find and free her. He formed an alliance with Sugriva, a prince of the monkeys, and Hanuman, a monkey general. Hanu-

man learned that Sita was a prisoner in the palace of Ravana, and the mighty Battle of Lanka between Rama and his monkey allies and the forces of Ravana ensued. In single combat, Rama killed Ravana and regained Sita. Having been abducted and taken to the Lankan palace, however, Sita was required by Rama to undergo an ordeal of fire to test her purity. After she survived the test, Sita and Rama returned in triumph to Ayodhya for their coronation. There are numerous twists and turns and many subplots in the seven chapters of the saga, which is widely perceived as a triumph of good over evil. Various allusions to places and events render it at least partly useful to historians.

The *Ramayana* was adopted and modified in the early Southeast Asian states. Known as the *Rieamker* in Cambodia and the *Ramakien* in Thailand, it was a rich source of the legends depicted on the temple reliefs. Many notable scenes from the *Ramayana* may be seen on the Angkorian temples. At BANTEAY SREI and ANGKOR WAT in Cambodia, Ravana is depicted shaking Mount Kailasa. Angkor Wat also includes the archery contest in which Rama won the hand of Sita. The abduction of Sita by Ravana appears at Banteay Srei, but probably the most popular theme is the Battle of Lanka.

Scene from the *Ramayana* depicted on a stone lintel in Thailand *(© Wolfgang Kaehler/CORBIS)*

Rang Mahal Rang Mahal is a site on the former course of the SARASVATI RIVER in Rajastan province, northwest India, which has given its name to a distinctive culture dated about 250–550 C.E. More than 20 other sites with the distinctive pottery styles of Rang Mahal are known from this region. The coins recovered from excavations undertaken in 1952–54 show that the most intensive occupation of the site occurred during the reign of the KUSHAN king Kaniska III. Eight periods of construction have been identified, in which the houses were built of mud BRICK. Gandharan influence has been suggested in a number of terra-cotta plaques belonging to the period of the early GUPTA EMPIRE.

See also GHANDARA.

Rangpur Rangpur is a settlement located on the Bhadar River in the Kathiawar Peninsula, western India. It was first investigated in 1935, but the major excavations took place between 1953 and 1956. There is an early prehistoric phase, but the principal interest in this site lies in the Period IIA occupation in 2000–1500 B.C.E. of the INDUS VALLEY CIVILIZATION. The typical mud-BRICK houses had baths, and there was a public drainage system. STEATITE, carnelian, and agate beads and ceramics were found. No SEALS or sealings, however, were recovered. Further interest lies in the continuity of occupation during the course of the second millennium B.C.E., properly defined as a post-Indus civilization. Phase IIB did not reveal evidence for mud-brick structures, baths, or drains, but brick structures were again encountered in the layers dated 1100–800 B.C.E. Unlike many Indus sites, Rangpur was not abandoned, although the relationship between the earlier and later occupants remains conjectural.

Rawak Rawak, "high palace" or "mansion," is a major site of the HOTAN state located northwest of the capital, Yotkan, on the road to NIYA in western China. It was discovered by SIR AUREL STEIN in 1901, when it was a tall mound virtually covered in sand, rising to a height of nine meters (30 ft.). His excavations uncovered the foundations of a stupa raised on square platforms whose size decreased upward toward the dome. It was surrounded by an enclosing wall measuring 49 by 42 meters. This exterior wall was embellished by a remarkable series of clay and stucco statues of the Buddha, outstanding examples of early Buddhist sculpture in Central Asia. Stein suggested, on the evidence of Chinese coins, that the site dated to the fourth to seventh centuries C.E. In 1928 a further excavation took place under German direction, and more statues were uncovered. The complete assemblage known through the surviving statues or photographs now includes about 116 individuals items, most life-size but some larger than life. The sculptures fall into two main chronological groups. The earlier, dated to the late third or early fourth century C.E., show marked parallels with sculptures from the west, including MATHURA, TAXILA, DALVERZIN TEPE, and TOPRAK KALA. This group does not include any BODHISATTVAS and might belong to a period in Hotan when Hinayana, or Low, BUDDHISM predominated. The second group has been dated to the first half of the fifth century C.E. and includes bodhisattvas and door guardians. By this juncture, MAHAYANA BUDDHISM seemed to have achieved dominance in the region.

Red Eyebrows The name Red Eyebrows refers to an army of rebellious peasants from Shandong province, China, who rose up against the emperor WANG MANG in 22 C.E. This uprising followed a series of disastrous floods as the Huang (Yellow) River burst its banks and followed new channels. Such flooding led to crop failure and the threat of starvation. Peasants painted their foreheads red for easy identification on the battlefield, and their revolt led members of the old Western Han royal line to rise up in concert, leading to the death of Wang Mang and the establishment of the Eastern HAN DYNASTY. *The History of the Later Han* (HOU HANSHU) contains an intriguing reference to the means taken in the countryside to counter the threat of the Red Eyebrows. It describes how, at the end of the reign of Wang Mang, there was a plague of bandits and outlaws. A local leader called Diwu Lun attracted many kinsmen and other followers, and he organized the construction of a walled fortress. He then armed his men with bows and arrows; despite attacks by the Red Eyebrows on several occasions, this group was never defeated in its stronghold.

Rehman Dheri Rehman Dheri is a site of the INDUS VALLEY CIVILIZATION, located in the Gomal Valley to the west of the Indus River. It was occupied from about 3000–2000 B.C.E. It is considered likely that the Indus River was once closer to the site, to judge from an ancient course just five kilometers away. The site covers 19 hectares (47.5 acres) and rises to a height of six meters (20 ft.) above the surrounding plain. It was excavated by F. A. Durrani in the late 1970s and again in 1991. Four areas were opened, ranging from the center of the mound to its periphery, and three occupation phases were discovered. The initial settlement took place during the KOT DIJI phase of the Early Harappan, and a series of mud-slab walls were exposed. A large wall of similar materials surrounded the site. The radiocarbon dates for this early phase place initial settlement in the vicinity of 3000 B.C.E., a date of considerable interest, for it is associated with an ivory SEAL bearing three possible antecedents of the INDUS VALLEY CIVILIZATION SCRIPT. The seal was also embellished with images of mountain goats, scorpions, and a frog. The second period has furnished pottery of the Kot Diji style decorated with peacocks and pipal leaves. Artifacts representative of the mature Harappan civilization of the Indus Valley have been recovered from the upper deposits. These include carnelian, LAPIS LAZULI, and TURQUOISE beads, many in an unfinished state, indicating local manufacture. There is also some evidence for a formal layout, for a street divides the site into two parts. The inhabitants cultivated wheat and barley, maintained domestic cattle, sheep, and goats, and also fished and hunted the local wild fauna.

The Rig-Veda asserts: "If we have deceived, like gamblers in a game of dice," a passage that recalls the common discovery of gambling dice in sites of the Indus Valley civilization.

Ribadeneyra, F. Marcello de (16th century) *F. de Ribadeneyra published* Historia de las Islas del Archipelago y Reinos della gran China, Tartaria, Cochinchina, Malaca, Siam, Camboxa, y Japan . . . *in 1601, the first account of Angkor in Cambodia in a European language.*
He wrote:

> We suppose that the founders of the kingdom of Siam came from the great city which is situated in the middle of a desert in the kingdom of Cambodia. There are the ruins of an ancient city which some say was built by Alexander the Great or the Romans, it is amazing that no one lives there now, it is inhabited by ferocious animals, and the local people say it was built by foreigners.

Rig-Veda Vedas are sacred ritual hymns that survived through oral tradition in India until first transcribed in the 14th century C.E. They have been intoned by Hindu priests during religious ceremonies for millennia, especially during ceremonies incorporating sacrifice and the soma ritual. The gods worshiped include the principal deities of Hinduism in their early manifestations: Foremost is Agni, the god of fire; Surya, the Sun god; Rudra, god of storms; and INDRA and Vishnu, the gods of war. The Rig-Veda is the principal and earliest such collection of hymns. These contributed to the later Yajur Veda and the Sama Veda. The vedas continue to be recited to this day.

WHEELER'S VIEW EQUATING PEOPLE OF RIG-VEDA WITH END OF INDUS CIVILIZATION

SANSKRIT, the language of the Rig-Veda, belongs to the Indo-European family. Dating the hymns takes on profound significance, for it would indicate not only the presence of Indo-European languages in India, but also the nature of the societies at that time. There is no agreement on the chronological context or even the archaeological correlates of the activities and places described in the Rig-Veda. Indeed, there are at least two diametrically opposing schools of thought and groups that occupy the middle ground.

First, a widely repeated view is that the Indo-European peoples of the Rig-Veda swept into northwestern India and Pakistan in the early second millennium B.C.E.

and were responsible for destroying the cities of the INDUS VALLEY CIVILIZATION. This view has its clearest expression in the writings of SIR MORTIMER WHEELER, who was the director-general of archaeology in India during the 1940s and adviser to the Pakistan government after partition in 1947. He excavated at MOHENJO DARO and HARAPPA, the two major Indus cities, and at the former, he found a number of skeletons and evidence for burning: "Men, women and children, some bearing ax or sword cuts, found lying on the topmost level in the sprawled or contorted positions in which they fell." Wheeler then proceeded, in his own words, with a "guess." He proposed that the Indus cities fell to the invading Aryans, whose sacred chants incorporated in the Rig-Veda constantly refer to an onslaught on walled cities. The barbarians responsible, he noted, were not accustomed to city life, but were nomadic people from the steppes. These, Wheeler noted, were nothing more than conjectures, but the linking of the Mohenjo Daro "massacre" with the Aryan invasion was a tempting path to follow.

FRAWLEY'S VIEW THAT RIG-VEDA PEOPLE WERE THE INDUS CIVILIZATION

However, his conjecture has drawn considerable criticism from many quarters, and David Frawley has countered it on every front in a lengthy essay. In the first case, were there nomadic warriors and the destroyers of cities? There is no doubt that the Vedics mention their gods as the conquerors of cities, but they themselves were also city dwellers. The cities destroyed were also evidently occupied by other Vedic people. One reason for war, it is said, was that one group destroyed the dam belonging to another. The alleged barbarian nomads also cultivated barley and maintained herds of cattle. They dug wells, used buckets to remove the water, and employed IRRIGATION channels to sustain their crops in fields that were plowed for planting. Details of houses can be culled from a reading of the sacred hymns. It is possible to reconstruct aspects of urban life from the Rig-Veda. There was always a sacred fire burning in a room "where Agni, the fire god, rests at ease." There was a room set aside for WOMEN; there were couches with pillows. The life described is one of opulence in spacious homes. The people held wealth and generosity in sacrificial rituals in high esteem. There was mention of traveling merchants, and the accumulation of riches; words for price, value, costly, and debt are found. There was a standard for exchange. Wealth was measured in gems, gold, silver, land, horses, and cattle. Ships with 100 oars were mentioned, and the sea with billowing waves was described. The city dwellers consumed beans, grain, and sesame cooked with milk. They were fond of gambling: The Rig-Veda asserts, "If we have deceived, like gamblers in a game of dice," a passage that recalls the common discovery of gambling dice in sites of the Indus Valley civilization. There were numerous references to weavers, the art of weaving, and shuttles, and many spindle whorls and remnants of cloth were found at Mohenjo Daro. However, early vedas mention wool and silk rather than cotton.

Where were these cities located? The river most often described is the sacred Sarasvati, the gold-streamed course of which flowed to the sea past green fields. The rulers of these cities possessed horse-drawn chariots, and their prestige increased with their sacrifices of horses and cattle, particularly to the god of fire. Frawley, noting the vital importance of the SARASVATI RIVER to the Vedic people, asks how they could have known about it if it had dried up before the proposed second millennium B.C.E. date of their arrival. Again, the Vedas reveal familiarity with the entire course of the Sarasvati and of much of northern India and Pakistan.

Archaeological Evidence Confirming Frawley's View

What, then, is the archaeological legacy of the society so richly documented in the Rig-Veda? There should be evidence of an urban society with religious leaders and evidence for a sacrificial bull cult and a god of fire. There should be evidence for trade by river and sea, large houses for an elite, plows and irrigation employed in the cultivation of barley and wheat, dairy cows, metal, and horse-drawn chariots. Finally, there should be the cities themselves. Given that there is no conclusive evidence for the date of the original Vedas, Frawley finds no reason to ignore as the prime candidate the civilization of the Indus Valley itself. The archaeological evidence is indeed convincing. Sites such as Kalibangan have furnished fire altars and sacrificial pits containing cattle bones on the BRICK temples. SEALS show horned gods and animal sacrifice. There were opulent houses, and the elite wore gold ornaments. Some seals bear images of large boats. Indus seals in Mesopotamia and Mesopotamian seals in India indicate sea trade. The remains of a plowed field have been uncovered at Kalibangan. Terra-cotta figurines of horses survive, as do models of wheeled vehicles. The Indus civilization relied on the cultivation of barley and wheat. Harappa has a large series of threshing floors beside a granary. Many dice reflect a passion for gambling.

It would indeed be fascinating if the great body of religious lore contained in the Rig-Veda did in fact describe the cities of the Indus civilization, for the script remains undeciphered, and knowledge of the social organization is hazy at best. Further implications have the potential to alter profoundly the appreciation of the course of Indian civilization. Thus, are the gods seen on the Indus seals and the stone LINGAMS recovered from such sites as Mohenjo Daro representatives of early Hindu deities? If the people of the Indus civilization spoke an Indo-European language, for how long had their ancestors been present in this region, and how did a branch of this language family reach South Asia? Many authorities consider it likely that the early Vedas date between 1800 and 1000 B.C.E. However, there remains the possibility that some are considerably earlier and would thus fall within the compass of the Indus civilization. Indo-European speakers were also early farmers who expanded from the Near East and took with them knowledge of agriculture.

THE MIDDLE GROUND

The equation of the Rig-Veda with the Indus civilization, however, has not received widespread acceptance. There remains a substantial middle ground of scholars with a third view, who accept neither this straightforward linkage nor the notion of an invading horde of nomadic barbarians. Raymond Allchin, for example, has suggested that far from being an invading force, the Indo-Aryan people infiltrated Pakistan over many centuries.

ritsuryo   A *ritsuryo* is a civil and penal code. Several were issued by Japanese emperors in the late seventh and early eighth centuries to establish the legal basis of the imperial late YAMATO and NARA STATE. They were modeled on the Chinese system and provided the framework for a tightly structured aristocratic regime in which the state owned all the land and people. The emperor Tenchi issued an early set of laws when ruling from Omi in 662 C.E. Revised in 689 C.E. these formed the basis for the minute regulation of society embodied in the Taiho Code of 701 C.E. and the YORO CODE of 718 C.E. No copy of the former survives, but the latter is embodied in later commentaries. The purpose of the codes was to provide for social stability and establish the status of the ruling family and aristocracy. In the same context, the NIHONGI was ordered at the same time as the Yoro Code to confirm the antiquity and legitimacy of the royal lineage.

ritual bronze vessels   In the Chinese ritual tradition bronze vessels played a key role. Many thousands have been recovered under controlled conditions from tombs, particular those dating to the SHANG STATE (1766–1045 B.C.E.) and WESTERN ZHOU DYNASTY (1045–771 B.C.E.); more have been looted and sold to collectors. One of the most important aspects of the study of these bronzes is that many, particularly during the Western Zhou dynasty, were embellished with INSCRIPTIONS of inestimable historical value. The bronzes also changed over time in both form and decoration, and the quality and quantity of vessels can be used to identify both the tomb occupant and the person's status.

The vessels were cast by using the complex piece-mold system, in which a ceramic negative in separate pieces was assembled over a corresponding clay core before the casting procedure. This was a distinctive Chinese technological accomplishment that demanded high skill of specialists. Their accomplishments are nowhere more clearly reflected than in the tomb contents of FU HAO (c. 1200 B.C.E.), royal consort to King Wu Ding, at ANYANG. More than 200 bronzes were found, totaling

1,600 kilograms (3,520 lbs.) of bronze, some weighing up to 70 kilograms (154 lbs.) each. These were Fu Hao's ritual and banqueting ware, one feature of which was an assemblage of more than 50 wine vessels, or *gu*. Other major forms were used for serving food and drink.

During the period of Eastern Zhou, ritual bronzes continued to be cast in considerable quantities, and the inscriptions that recorded their owners and the circumstances of casting provide a vital source of historical information. Often bronzes along with chariots were given by the king, and the services that attracted such rewards are recorded. Indeed, the first historic document describing the successive rulers of the Western Zhou dynasty and their achievements is found on the SHI QIANG *pan,* a vessel from the ZHUANGBAI hoard (c. 771 B.C.E.) of 103 items belonging to five generations of an aristocratic family.

rock monasteries   More than 1,000 rock monasteries have been identified in central and southern India. They were built between the second century B.C.E. and the ninth century C.E. as centers of Buddhist life and learning. They typically have rooms for the monks, with stone beds and pillows, a *mandapa,* or hall for meetings and religious ceremonies, and a sanctuary, or *caitya,* incorporating a stupa. A stupa is a mounded structure that in the early days of the rock monasteries represented the Buddha and would be deemed to contain a relic of the Buddha or one of his followers. Early examples in the Deccan are seen at Lomasa Rishi and Sudama. Their architecture clearly reveals that they were built in imitation of wooden structures with a thatched roof. As at Lomasa Rishi, which has a simple *caitya* and apsidal-end chamber, the early rock monasteries of the Decan began with a small and spare plan, extending only about 10 meters (33 ft.) in the rock face and terminating with a circular chamber containing the stupa. Over the course of time, these temples became larger and of more complex design. At Bhaja, for example, the interior had a series of columns, and similar trends are seen among the earliest *caityas* at AJANTA, dated to about 70 B.C.E., and soon to be embellished with the first paintings. The most famous at ELLORA and Ajanta are major architectural achievements, incorporating fine sculptures and paintings. All are now deserted.

Rojdi   Rojdi is a settlement site that falls broadly in the tradition of the INDUS VALLEY CIVILIZATION but also reveals a number of distinctive local characteristics. It is located on the Saurasthra Plateau in Gujarat state, India. Its location beside the Bhadar River might explain its long but narrow form, 500 meters (1,650 ft.) in length but only 150 wide (495 ft.). Excavations in 1982–86 and again in 1992–95 showed that a threefold sequence, dating within the outer limits of the Indus Valley civilization (2500–1700 B.C.E.). The ceramics show only a few parallels with those of sites to the west, while there is a notable absence from the site of the weights and SEALS so characteristic of this civilization. Again, the typical food plants, wheat and barley, gave way at Rojdi to the harder millet. The site was ringed by a stone defensive wall that began two meters wide, but was later strengthened; while the houses were typically built of mud over a stone base, there is no evidence for a drainage system. Rojdi thus represents a singular Harappan adaptation of considerable durability in this inland region of Gujarat.

Rong Chen   The temple pyramid of Rong Chen is located on the KULEN HILLS north of ANGKOR in Cambodia. It is widely considered to be the most likely location for the consecration of JAYAVARMAN II as *CHAKRAVARTIN,* supreme king of kings, in 802 C.E., thus initiating the kingdom of Angkor.

Rongkab   Rongkab is the name of a village mentioned in a copper plate INSCRIPTION dating to 901 C.E. from central Java in Indonesia. The actual find spot of this inscription is not known. It records how the villagers were granted exemption from paying a certain form of tax. The minor officials involved were paid measures of silver in return. It also mentions the names of village elders, one of whom held the office of chief of the rice supply.

Ropar   Ropar, also known as Rupnagar, is a settlement and cemetery of the INDUS VALLEY CIVILIZATION (2500–1700 B.C.E.) located on the south bank of the Sutlej River in northwestern India. It was excavated in 1950 and again in 1982. There are three distinct mounds, the northern 21 meters (70 ft.) high and revealing evidence for settlement from the early and mature Indus civilization through the period of PAINTED GREY WARE (800–500 B.C.E.) and into the Indian medieval period. The western mound covers an inhumation cemetery in which the dead were interred with the head to the northwest and associated with pottery vessels, personal ornaments, and, in one case, the skeleton of a dog. Deep soundings in the northern mound have revealed the remains of mud-BRICK houses on stone foundations, together with a typical Indus material culture that includes stone weights, a STEATITE SEAL, the remains of clay bearing three separate sealings, and terra-cotta carts. Copper arrowheads and spears are also characteristic of the Indus civilization.

royal palaces

SOUTHEAST ASIA

The presence of a royal palace is widely seen as one of the indications of civilization. In Southeast Asia, palaces were built principally of wood and therefore have not survived. However, there is a continuous thread of evidence for their existence from the earliest state of FUNAN (150–550 C.E.) to the duration of the kingdom of ANGKOR. Two

Chinese emissaries who visited Southeast Asia during the third century C.E. described walled settlements and a palace. Some temples of the CHENLA period (550–800 C.E.) were decorated with what have been termed flying palaces. An example from ISHANAPURA shows elevated and richly decorated pavilions with windows separated by columns. Figures can be seen within, presumably members of the aristocracy. The lintel of Wat En-Khna of the same period shows the enthroned king in his palace, surrounded by retainers. The description of a Chenla palace has survived in the writings of Ma Duanlin. The king gave an audience in a hall containing a wooden throne embellished with columns of inlaid wood and fine fabrics. At the Roluos Group (HARIHARALYA) of INDRAVARMAN I at Angkor, there is a raised rectangular area between the moat and the wall of the second enclosure at PREAH KO that might well be the foundation for the royal palace. Indravarman's own inscription mentions his "lion throne, a vehicle, the palace Indravimanaka and a golden pavilion."

Namasivaya was a royal herdsman with responsibility for the sacred cattle. It is recorded on an inscription that under JAYAVARMAN VI (r. 1080–1107 C.E.) he led the cattle in a procession around the royal palace. During the reign of JAYAVARMAN VII (1181–1219 C.E.), the royal palace lay north of the BAYON, where today there is a walled precinct dominated by the temple of the PHIMEANAKAS. Tranquil basins lie between this temple and the northern enclosing wall. This area has recently been excavated, and huge wooden post foundations were encountered, presumably the foundations for the palace.

ZHOU DAGUAN in 1296–97 visited Angkor and described this palace as being set apart by its own walls and guards: "The Royal Palace lies to the north of the Golden Tower and east of the bridge of gold; its circumference is nearly 2.5 kilometers (1.5 mi.). The tiles of the central dwelling are of lead, other parts of the palace are covered in yellow pottery tiles. Lintels and columns, all decorated with carved or painted Buddhas, are immense. The roofs too, are impressive. Long colonnades and open corridors stretch away, interlaced in harmonious relation. In the chamber where the sovereign attends to affairs of state, there is a golden window. . . . I have heard it said that within the palace are many marvelous sights." Similar walled precincts around the royal palace may be seen today in Phnom Penh and Bangkok.

CHINA

Royal palaces form a central part of the architectural tradition of China from the XIA DYNASTY to the early 20th century, as can be seen in the Forbidden City and the Summer Palace in Beijing. The earliest evidence for a palace structure is from Phases 3 and 4 at the site of ERLITOU in the Huang (Yellow) River Valley, dated to the first half of the second millennium B.C.E. It included an enclosed court measuring 108 by 100 meters (356 by 330 ft.); the palace itself was located facing south. The complex was raised on a stamped-earth platform. A second, slightly smaller palace was also uncovered during the excavations; a large but unfortunately looted grave lay within the enclosed precinct. The early Shang capital of ZHENGZHOU was a large walled city. Here again the foundations for a large columned building were found, and these are thought to be the remains of a palace that was surrounded by a moat.

Shang Palaces

Excavations at Xiaotun, the core of the Late Shang capital known as ANYANG, have uncovered the foundations for a large series of buildings raised on stamped-earth foundations. These cluster in three groups, known as the northern, central, and southern. The northern group, which includes the foundations for 15 buildings, is thought to be the earliest. The expansion of this royal area then saw the 21 buildings of the central group constructed, and, finally, the southern group completed the complex. The buildings of the last group were associated with many human and animal sacrificial burials. As it grew, the palace incorporated earlier royal tombs, including that of FU HAO, a principal consort to King Wu Ding. An overall interpretation of this complex leads to the conclusion that the northern group was the royal residential area, while the ancestral temples are found in the middle group. The southern buildings held ritual ceremonials.

One of the palace buildings measures 85 by 15 meters (280 by 50 ft.); another covers an area of 70 by 40 meters. They were raised above the ground on stamped-earth foundations and built on a north-south axis. Access to a broad verandah was gained by ascending broad staircases. The principal structure was a long building with a columned front, and the roof was made of thatch. The central area included many sacrificial burials, chariot burials, and subterranean pits for storing grain. Such pits were also used to house ORACLE-BONE archives.

Western Zhou Palaces

The construction of substantial palaces continued during the WESTERN ZHOU DYNASTY (1045–771 B.C.E.). Excavations at Fengchu and Zhaochen in Shanxi province have uncovered the foundations of substantial buildings. At Fengchu there was an area of nearly 1,500 square meters (1,800 sq. yds.), enclosed on all sides with three courtyards within. The recovery of oracle bones during the excavations indicates that this building would have been occupied by royalty. The entrance pavilion gave access to a large court, while the flanking buildings were broad columned passageways linked to eight rooms on each side, each room three meters (10 ft.) wide and up to seven meters long. The court was the location for the investiture ceremonies described in detail in the inscriptions on bronze vessels. The central hall, reached by a series of steps, was 17 meters wide and six meters deep and bisected the complex. Beyond lay two smaller courts, divided by a covered passageway leading to the rear external corridor. The walls and floor were plastered and then decorated with patterns formed by inserting mother of pearl. A system of subterranean pipes facilitated drainage.

Excavations at Zhaochen, only 2.5 kilometers from Fengchu, yielded the remains of a later palace. It also had a large central hall, demarcated today by the large holes designed to receive the supporting pillars. One of these had a diameter of almost two meters; the others were half this size. Columns of such size could have spanned a considerable space, compatible with the descriptions of grand halls in the Western Zhou palaces contained in the contemporary inscriptions. By this period, the thatched and plastered roof was replaced by interlocking tiles. These Western Zhou palaces were screened from the outside and had enclosed courts bordered by colonnaded walkways and residential chambers. This pattern was continued, but on a grander scale, in the EASTERN ZHOU DYNASTY (770–221 B.C.E.) and Spring and Autumn period (770–476 B.C.E.) at Yong. This was the capital of the state of QIN, and the palace now incorporated five linked courtyards with a total length of more than 300 meters. According to a section from the *Shijing,* or *Book of Odes,* this enclosed set of courtyards was designed to impart the feeling of mystery.

Warring States Palaces

With the progress of the WARRING STATES PERIOD (475–221 B.C.E.) and the unification of China under the first emperor, QIN SHIHUANGDI (259–210 B.C.E.), the nature of the palace changed from indicating mystery to projecting might. The establishment of large and powerful states created a demand for monumentality, and the new cities that sprang up during the Warring States period had their own precinct to house the royal palace and associated buildings. These new palaces were raised on a structure known as a *tai,* a high earth platform the size of which projected the image of royal power. Xu Wan, the minister of the king of WEI, found it necessary to remind his sovereign, who nurtured the ambition to build a *tai* halfway to heaven, that this would require his conquering all the neighboring states simply to obtain a sufficient area of land for the foundations.

LINZI was the capital of the state of QI, which dominated Shandong province during the Warring States period. The palace there was raised up on a high mound that still stands 14 meters above its surroundings. This building and its associated temples occupied a special walled enclave in the southwestern part of the city. The palace platform was known as the platform of the duke Huan. At Xiadu, capital of the remote northwestern state of YAN in Hebei province, the palace stood atop a mighty raised mound that is still 20 meters high above the rest of the city. HANDAN in the state of Zhao also included raised platforms to elevate the palace well above the surrounding cityscape. By building an earth platform and constructing terraced pavilions against it, it also became feasible to make a palace appear much larger and more impressive than it actually was.

Indeed, the labor required to construct such vast platforms engendered a critical literature. One such platform in the state of Wei was called the platform that reaches half way to heaven, and there are numerous references in historical sources to rulers using the magnitude of their palaces to symbolize and project their power. This is seen in the creation of a new capital at XIANYANG by SHANG YANG (d. 338 B.C.E.), the great reformer of the state of Qin. He set aside the traditional task in construction of a new foundation—building the ancestral temple—and rather had a new palace, known as the Jique, built. This was a major innovation: The name translates as posting a royal order on the gate tower, and it emphasizes the new administrative and legal reforms that Shang Yang was to promulgate. The Jique palace is a monumental structure built around its earthen core. There are three stories, the lowest fronted by a long verandah supported by a row of 38 columns. Above the verandah rise two sets of chambers that in section are a mirror image of each other. Excavations there have uncovered a rich assemblage of decorated floor tiles bearing geometric motifs and painted plastered walls. These include images of elegant court women and a chariot drawn by four horses. This was but the first of many palaces built at Xianyang over the ensuing century, culminating in the victory of Qin over its rivals and the creation of the first Chinese empire under Qin Shihuangdi.

Qin Palaces

The vital symbolic role of the palace during this period of Warring States is clearly reflected in the writings of SIMA QIAN in the *SHIJI:* "Each time the Qin had conquered a state, a replica of its palace was built on the northern bank of the Wei River." Thus not only was the defeated king's palace destroyed, but its image was removed to the Qin capital at Xianyang. The noble families, those who survived each conquest, were likewise removed to Qin. The first emperor, again in the words of Sima Qian, found his predecessors' palaces too small. He therefore ordered the construction of his Efang Palace south of the Wei River. The historian described it as being 500 paces wide with a terrace large enough to accommodate 10,000 people, and from which huge banners could be suspended. However, this splendid edifice and the myriad other palaces barely outlived the life of the first emperor. In 206 B.C.E., the buildings were sealed and retained under the orders of the first ruler of the new HAN DYNASTY, GAOZU.

Han Palaces

Four years later, when he returned there, the entire complex had been razed to the ground. An orgy of looting continued for months under General Xiang Yu (232–202 B.C.E.), and there was nothing left. Only the Xingle Palace remained habitable, and this was restored for the new ruler. The restoration and extensions took 18 months to complete, and when it was fit again for use, it was renamed the Changle Palace. The compound measured 2.6 by 2.6

kilometers, covering 676 hectares (1,690 acres), and contained 14 halls, two lakes, and the massive bronze statues that the Qin emperor had cast from the melted-down weapons of his adversaries. The *Li Ji* (*Book of Rites*) provides a compelling view of the first major ceremony of the new dynasty that was held in the Changle Palace: "Before dawn, the master of guests, who was in charge of the ritual, led the participants in order of rank through the gate leading to the hall. Within the courtyard, chariots and cavalry were drawn up. . . . At this point the emperor, borne on a litter, appeared from the inner rooms, the hundred officials holding banners and announcing his arrival." Every official or noble present then came forward to swear allegiance, trembling according to the *Li Ji,* with awe and reverence. The emperor concluded: "Today, for the first time, I realize how exalted a thing it is to be an emperor."

Gaozu rarely used this palace but had a new compound built just to the southwest, called the Weiyang Palace. The choice of site was highly symbolic, for here rose a hill in gradual stages, the summit of which commanded a view over CHANG'AN and the surrounding landscape. Moreover, it was visible for miles in every direction. The hill also had a mythological and auspicious aspect, for it was reputed that a black dragon had gone to the Wei River to drink and that the top of the hill represented the dragon's head. Black was also the preferred color of the new dynasty. The Changle Palace represented continuity with the previous and hated Qin dynasty, but it was designed to symbolize the new grandeur of Han. The hill was converted into a series of ascending terraces with the main hall on the peak. The distance from the entrance to the summit, which involved passing through three successive courts, was more than 350 meters (1,155 ft.). Indeed, such was the scale of the complex, which is now quite destroyed, that the emperor remonstrated with the head architect and in words recorded by Sima Qian, the grand historian, complained: "The empire is still in turmoil. . . . We cannot tell whether we will have final success. What do you mean by constructing palaces like this on such an extravagant scale?" The answer from Xiao He reveals the ultimate purpose: "If the Son of Heaven does not dwell in magnificence and beauty, he will have no way to manifest his authority, nor will he leave any foundation for his heirs to build upon."

The Weiyang Palace was embellished and expanded over the course of the ensuing reigns, but during the rule of Gaozu, according to the surviving texts, it included the central hall and two pillar-gates. Much new building at Chang'an also took place during the 54-year reign of Emperor Han WUDI (157–87 B.C.E.) After a period of peace and prosperity, this ruler set in train an expansionary policy of imperial conquest and at home authorized a huge building program. Within the city walls of Chang'an, three new palaces emerged: the Mingguang Palace (palace of brilliant light), the Bei, or Northern, Palace, and the Gui, or Cassia, Palace. Beyond the walls and to the southwest, he ordered the construction of Shanglin Park, which incorporated palatial buildings around Kunming Lake.

Shanglin Park
Contemporary records provide an image of this remarkable complex. It housed animals from every point of the compass, including a rhinoceros from Thailand, white elephants, and albino deer, each accompanied by a viewing pavilion. It was studded with more than 70 pleasure palaces large enough to house thousands. The extensive Kunming Lake was embellished with three large stone statutes, one of a whale to indicate that it represented the sea. All three have been recovered through archaeological research.

Ganquan Palace
The most extraordinary construction of all, however, was the Ganquan Palace, located 60 kilometers to the northwest of the capital. Han Wudi was an enthusiastic follower of soothsayers and astrologers, one of whom, Shao Weng, found that the emperor had suffered the bereavement of one his favorite consorts. Shao Weng promised that the ruler would see her again and ensured that he did through the medium of a shadow play. Delighted, Wudi favored him and responded when Shao Weng recommended the construction of a palace "patterned after the shapes of the spirits." There, he declared, the emperor would be able to communicate with the spirit world. Thus was constructed the Ganquan Palace, the palace of sweet springs. Huge towers were built and a terrace that was said to pierce the clouds. Another soothsayer, Gongsun Qin, recommended that the emperor lay out jujubes and dried meat to attract the immortals, who liked to live in such high pavilions.

Wudi's Last Palace
The final edifice raised by Han Wudi at Chang'an was known as the Jianzhang Palace. Contemporary accounts describe its appearance. The central Jade Hall, for example, was built of white marble. The entrance portal stood 60 meters (198 ft.) high. A bronze pillar supported an immortal holding aloft a bowl to collect dew, which, mixed with powdered jade, was given to the emperor. The complex was conceived as a paradisiacal realm for Wudi to inhabit.

Wang Mang's Palaces
WANG MANG (45 B.C.E.–23 C.E.) was the nephew of the dowager empress Wang and thus a highly ranked member of the imperial court. He seized the throne in 9 C.E. and founded his own XIN (New) DYNASTY. He swept away the buildings of Han Wudi and recycled the materials in advancing his own plans. These involved the construction of the Mingtang (bright) hall to the south of the city walls, a monument based on Confucian ideals for the worship of the ancestors.

With the death of Wang Mang and after a long and bitter civil war, Guang Wudi (5 B.C.E.–57 C.E.) emerged as the new emperor. Chang'an had been destroyed and the imperial tombs looted. Guang Wudi moved the capital downstream to LUOYANG. The walled city accommodated two palaces at the northern and southern borders, each covering an area of 1,300 by 700 meters (1,430 by 770 yds.). They were linked by a straight, elevated corridor four kilometers long. This complex lacked the magnificence and spiritual aura of Chang'an and did not survive beyond 190 C.E., when the whole city was razed to the ground.

JAPAN

The earliest excavated palaces in Japan belong to the seventh-century YAMATO state, but an important inscription on the Imariyama sword attests to their presence at an earlier date. The text says that the owner of the sword was head of the sword bearers when the court of the great king Wakatakeru was in the palace of Shiki. This sword, which was from Tomb 1 on a keyhole *kofun*, or burial mound, is dated to 471 C.E.

Palaces in Nara Basin

Palaces reflected the social relations in the ruling elite. Emperors tended to have multiple consorts, who would live in their natal region for some years after a relationship was formalized, so the emperor would move his residence from time to time, living in one of several relatively modest palaces. Investigations at Asuka in the southern Nara Basin, which begin in 1951, uncovered foundations of what may have been the Itabuki Palace, occupied in 643 C.E. It is difficult without the precise dating evidence supplied by the MOKKAN, wooden slips containing dated records, to be sure which of many palaces mentioned in the NIHONGI correspond to foundations revealed through archaeology. The same problem of ascription applies to the Naniwa site, where two layers have been found. It has been suggested that the earlier represents the remains of the Nagara Toyosaki Palace of Kotoku, who reigned 645–654 C.E. The *Nihongi* recorded that on the ninth day of December 645 C.E., the emperor "removed the capital to Toyosaki in Nagara at Naniwa." By autumn 652, the palace was complete. It was clearly an impressive structure, for the *Nihongi* noted: "The building of the palace was completed. It is impossible to describe the appearance of the palace halls." Excavations have revealed the layout of this complex. The royal residence, two structures joined by a passageway, the whole covering an area of 113 by 123 meters (373 by 406 ft.), lay at the north. To the south a massive gate opened onto a courtyard containing official administrative buildings, On each side of the gate there stood octagonal towers. This court was walled and could be entered by a further gate on the southern wall. The records note that the palace was destroyed by fire, and this has been confirmed by the quantities of ash encountered during the excavations. With the death of Kotoku, the palace was abandoned and moved, under the

emperor TENJI (r. 668–671 C.E.), to Otsu north of Nara city. It was occupied for only a few years until the emperor's death; its location was identified in 1993.

Palaces in Capital Cities

Toward the end of the seventh century a major policy change saw the construction of large and visually impressive capital cities, first at FUJIWARA and in 710 C.E. at HEIJO-KYO. Each had at its center a palace compound that combined living quarters for the ruler, an audience hall, and administrative offices for the bureaucracy. There can, therefore, be no doubt as to the authenticity of the palace at Fujiwara, the capital between 686 and 707 C.E. built under the orders of the empress JITO (r. 686–97 C.E.). Measuring nearly a kilometer square and located centrally in the new city, it was surrounded by a large stone wall flanked on the inside and on the exterior by moats. The royal residence was placed in the northern part of this precinct, and although largely destroyed, it is known to have covered an area of 305 by 350 meters (1007 by 1155 ft.). To the south lay an impressive audience hall and beyond it the buildings of the state administration. Much energy was expended in the construction of this palace, including the moving of 4,000 wooden posts seven meters high from a distance of 54 kilometers. However, with the death of Emperor Mommu in 707 C.E., this city was abandoned in favor of a new capital at Nara. The choice of the new capital and palace was determined by several factors. First, GEOMANCY and divination decreed the most auspicious site. This happened to be precisely to the north of Fujiwara, the existing capital, and 20 kilometers distant. In more mundane terms, the site provided easy and direct riverine access to the Inland Sea to the west.

The capital at Nara was longer lived than its predecessors, and the energy expended in its construction exceeded that at Fujiwara. Massive tree trunks had to be rafted to the site, stone quarried, and thousands of ceramic tiles fired. Modeled on the Tang capital of Chang'an, then the largest city in the world, the walled palace at Nara covered an area of 1.3 by 1.0 kilometers and was entered by 12 gateways. Archaeologists have identified through the recovery of *mokkan* the foundations of the war ministry at the southwest corner of the complex and the imperial stables, including barns for the storage of hay. The kitchens were associated with huge wells, and the status of the palace as a virtual city within a city is further to be seen in the presence of processing plants, such as that for the preparation of rice wine. Pleasure gardens were laid out on a grand scale. There were two distinct parts of the royal palace complex, the western and the eastern. These were constructed over a large *kofun*, or keyhole tomb, that had to be removed. Both parts of the palace were modified over the course of time, leading to the presence of two construction layers. During the earlier phase, the western palace had two compounds. One contained four long halls of unknown function. The northern section probably contained an audience hall. The eastern part was more complex with three precincts, the northern one the living quarters of the emperor. A more complex series of buildings was constructed during the second phase, including an additional compound on the eastern section. The two new halls and those in the compound to the north were designated for administrative officials' use. These in turn gave way to the audience hall, with the imperial residence beyond that. It has been suggested that the construction of two separate palaces was a deliberate attempt to copy the layout of the Tang palaces of Chang'an in China.

See also CONFUCIUS.

Rudravarman (c. 514–550 C.E.) *Rudravarman (Protégé of Siva) is mentioned in Chinese records as being the king of Funan who sent a tribute mission to China in 519 C.E.* He was the younger son of JAYAVARMAN OF FUNAN and overthrew his older brother to claim the throne. Michael Vickery has noted that succession of the younger son is not unusual in Angkorian politics. An INSCRIPTION from Kdei Ang dated 667 C.E. gives the names of successive members of an elite family and the kings they served. It begins with Brahmadatta, a retainer of King Rudravarman of Funan, and then proceeds to list those who served early rulers of a CHENLA kingdom. Not only does this text confirm the existence of a king Rudravarman detailed in the Chinese records, but it also reveals a thread of political continuity between Funan and Chenla.

Rummindei *See* LUMBINI.

Rupnagar *See* ROPAR.

S

Sahri-Bahlol Sahri-Bahlol is a walled city associated with a number of extramural temple mounds located in the Peshawar district of northwest Pakistan. It was first examined in the 1860s, at a time when the looting of such sites for collectible items of sculpture for sale to members of the occupying British army was a popular pastime. It was excavated again between 1906 and 1910 and the foundations of two Buddhist temples were uncovered. The most fruitful period of research, however, took place under the direction of SIR AUREL STEIN in 1911–12. He excavated a series of monasteries and Buddhist shrines, the latter the source of more than 1,000 stone sculptures of the Gandharan school (first to fifth century C.E.). The solid stone foundations of Buddhist halls and temples were accompanied by stucco ornaments around the bases and by many stone statues. The latter included images of the Buddha and of BODHISATTVAS with clear Hellenistic influence, for until the establishment of the Gandharan school of art in this region, the Buddha was depicted symbolically, not as a person. At Sahri-Bahlol, the Buddha takes on a clearly Western image. Such statues also incorporate miniature representations of the benefactors, who are often seen worshiping. The Gandharan tradition was extinguished with the invasion of this area by the White Huns in the fifth century C.E. It is said that the Hun king Mihirakula destroyed 1,600 Buddhist foundations in this area in the sixth century, even though the foundations of Sahri-Bahlol were among the architectural wonders of Asia.

See also GANDHARA.

Sa Huynh culture The Sa Huynh culture encompasses a series of occupation and cemetery sites located along the coast of Vietnam from the Hai Van Pass to Saigon. The Sa Huynh groups occupied the same territory as the later Cham states. The Cham language is Austronesian, with its closest parallels in Borneo. All available evidence points to a relatively late intrusive settlement of this region by sea from Borneo, a move that resulted first in the culture of Sa Huynh, then in the development of the CHAM CIVILIZATION. This culture dates to c. 300 B.C.E.–200 C.E. and is particularly distinguished by the cremation burial rite involving the interment of human ashes in large lidded vessels, accompanied by a range of offerings. This contrasts with a preference for inhumation burial in other Iron Age societies of mainland Southeast Asia. Over time, cemeteries grew to include many hundreds of mortuary jars. The urnfield at Hang Gon near Saigon covered an area of about 100 by 50 meters (330 by 165 ft.), and many burial offerings were ritually broken. Smashed pottery vessels were placed inside the large urns. Polished stone adzes were damaged, bowls deformed, and even the sockets of iron axes broken. Ear pendants and beads of imported carnelian, agate, olivine, and zircon were found at Hang Gon, as well as blue and red glass beads and a solitary bead of gold. There was also a distinctive nephrite ear pendant representing a double-headed animal. Iron working is documented in the form of slag, as well in axes and swords.

A major excavation at Giong Co Va near Saigon has uncovered 339 jar burials and 10 inhumation graves. The dead were interred in vertically placed jars often in a seated position and were accompanied by a wide variety of grave goods, foremost being 21 double-animal-headed ear ornaments in glass and jade. There were also beads and bangles of shell, exotic stone, and glass, and some ornaments were fashioned of gold. Another cemetery of

Giong Phet furnished many carnelian, jade, and agate beads, indicating late prehistoric maritime trade. The strategic location of these sites near the Mekong Delta and the wealth of exotic ornaments represent a critical late prehistoric stage in the subsequent formation of the FUNAN state (c. 100–550 C.E.). The distribution of distinctive double-headed ear ornaments, for example, reveals wide maritime exchange links including with Taiwan, central Thailand, and the Philippines.

See also CHENLA.

Sailendra   The Sailendra (Kings of the Mountain) dynasty ruled the KEDU PLAIN of central Java from the middle of the eighth century C.E. for at least a hundred years. The rulers followed MAHAYANA (or High) BUDDHISM and were responsible for a group of extraordinary monuments that still defy full understanding. Foremost among these is BOROBUDUR, a temple on 10 levels, which prescribes the path to enlightenment on its successive stages. The success of the Sailendras may well have been related to their control over irrigated rice fields of the rich Kedu Plain and their attachment to BUDDHISM as a means of legitimizing their power. They styled themselves MAHARAJAS great kings, in INSCRIPTIONS.

Saimei (594–661 C.E.)   *Saimei was the* tenno, *or sovereign, of the* YAMATO *state in Japan.*
She is counted as the 35th and 37th *tenno* because she ruled first under the name Kogyoku from 642 to 645 and subsequently as Saimei from 655 C.E. until her death six years later. She was the mother of the later emperors TENJI and TEMMU, and during her reign she organized military expeditions to extend her kingdom or to assist her Korean ally, the state of PAEKCHE. She died while in Kyushu during the preparation for an expedition to Korea that led to the naval disaster for Yamato at the Battle of Hakusukinoe.

Saivism   Saivism is the cult of SIVA who, with Vishnu, is one of the major gods of the Hindu religion. He is often associated with power and may have been a god of the INDUS VALLEY CIVILIZATION, in which SEALS bearing a god sitting in Siva's accustomed yogic position have been identified. His symbol, the phallus, or LINGAM, has been found at sites such as MOHENJO DARO in Pakistan. He later was combined with the god Rudra, who symbolized the forces of destruction. Thus Siva ultimately represented both destructive power and regeneration. He was married to Devi, and Skanda and GANESA were his sons. The worship of Siva is widespread in India, and he also became very popular in the ANGKOR civilization of Cambodia. There, the king and Siva were often linked by name and symbolized in the state lingam. RUDRAVARMAN, for example, was an early king of the state of FUNAN.

Sakas   The Sakas or Scythians originated as nomadic groups on the Eurasian steppes who, pressed from the east, moved to the west during the third and second centuries B.C.E. until they reached a solid wall of Parthian resistance in the region of the Caspian Sea. They then moved south into northwestern Pakistan and established there a state in the early first century B.C.E. The principal evidence for the names of the Saka kings is derived from their coins, which were minted at TAXILA in Pakistan and Puskalavati. The earliest, named Maues, styled himself Maharaja (great king) Moasa on his coins. Some of his early issues had his image overstruck on coins of his BACTRIAN GREEK predecessor Apollodotus II. He was followed by Azes I, Azilises, and Azes II. The Sakas were tolerant of the religious beliefs of others and showed considerable enthusiasm for BUDDHISM. They also followed many of the customs of the Bactrian Greeks, particularly in their COINAGE, architecture, art, and town planning. At the city of SIRKAP, Taxila, they continued to follow the Greek city layout. However, it is also possible to detect Indian influence in some of their styles and motifs. The Saka rule of this area, centered on Taxila, has been dated between 50 B.C.E. and 30 C.E., after which the area was taken by the Indo-Parthian king Gondophares. The Saka dating system began in 78 C.E. and was widely used in India, as well as in Angkorian and CHENLA INSCRIPTIONS.

Sambor Prei Kuk   *See* ISHANAPURA.

Samguk Sagi   The *Samguk Sagi* (*History of the* THREE KINGDOMS) was compiled by Kim Pu-Sik (1075–1151 C.E.) during the reign of King Injong (1122–46 C.E.) and is the principal historic source for the development of early Korean states. Based on earlier documents that have not survived, it provides the foundation date for each of the three kingdoms of KOGURYO, PAEKCHE, and SHILLA and then lists the respective kings. It is also an invaluable source of information on battles, regulations for agriculture and IRRIGATION, and trade relations with China. However, the author had the objective of providing legitimacy for the Koryu dynasty of Korea, and his dates cannot be relied on other than in the most general sense.

When presenting his work to the king, Kim PUSIK recorded how the Chinese had consistently produced histories of their dynasties, referring in particular to the *Spring and Autumn Annals* (CHUNQIU FANLU) of Lu written by CONFUCIUS. He acknowledged royal patronage in the preparation of his lengthy work and the need to match Chinese models.

Samguk Yusa   The *Samguk Yusa* (*Memorabilia of the Three Kingdoms*) is a historic work on the history of Korea that was compiled by the monk Iryon (1206–89 C.E.) and added to by the Confucian scholar Paek Munbo, who died in 1374. It contains information not referred to in the *SAMGUK SAGI*, with a strong Buddhist emphasis. For example, it is the first document of Korea to mention the mythical founder of the state, Tangun. The Confucian ethic is clearly seen in the introduction to this work, where Iryon wrote: "Sages of the past enabled states to flourish through propriety and music and fostered learning through humaneness and righteousness."

See also CONFUCIUS; SHILLA.

Samhitas   The Samhitas include the four sacred Hindu hymnals known as the RIG-VEDA, Yajur Veda, Sama Veda, and Atharva Veda. These are essentially religious hymns or chants, the oldest of which, the Rig-Veda, has considerable antiquity. It is often placed in the second millennium B.C.E., and some authorities maintain that it entered India with Aryan invaders, who destroyed the INDUS VALLEY CIVILIZATION. This would have occurred in the early to mid-second millennium B.C.E. However, other authorities place the Rig-Veda within the Indus civilization itself, giving it an antiquity as early as the mid-third millennium B.C.E. This dating dilemma has not been solved but is of considerable interest. The Rig-Veda often mentions fire worship and a stimulating drink known as soma. Fire altars have been documented archaeologically in Indus sites, such as KALIBANGAN. The curious receptacles often represented on Indus SEALS have been interpreted as containers for soma. Again, the Indus civilization sites provide evidence for a bull cult and the manufacture of stone phalluses (LINGAMS), both of which continue to be associated with the Hindu god SIVA. With time, the Samhitas assumed a central position in Indian religious development and were the subject of lengthy interpretation works, known as Brahmanas, and the philosophical implications were explored in a series of works called Upanishads.

The Rig-Veda described many gods based on natural forces, but INDRA was preeminent. He was responsible for the creation of the human race when he killed the demon serpent Vritra and released the elements vital for existence: heat, light, and water. Worship and sacrifice to the gods required the chanting of sacred hymns, undertaken by a person known as a Brahman. The Brahmans, those who had the knowledge and power to fulfill rituals, ultimately occupied a central position in society.

Samudragupta (335–380 C.E.)   *Samudragupta was by common consent one of the greatest kings of the Gupta dynasty, if not the greatest.*
His military successes expanded the GUPTA EMPIRE to cover much of modern India, victories recorded in an INSCRIPTION at Allahabad. One of his coins has a text in SANSKRIT, written in the BRAHMI script, which describes him as "the invincible king, victor of a hundred battles." A confirmed Hindu, he performed the rite of horse sacrifice and was entitled *maharajadhiraja*, or great king of

kings. Another coin issue shows him performing this ritual. Indeed, one of his enduring achievements was the establishment of the monetary system of the Gupta empire. Stimulated by the Kushan COINAGE of northwest India, which in turn was based on the Roman system, Samudragupta issued coins known as *dinara*, after the Roman *dinarius*. While clearly a most successful leader in warfare, he also had a musical talent, seen in his rare coins portraying him playing the lyre, accompanied by the text "Maharajadhiraja Sri Samudragupta."

Sanchi   Sanchi, in Madhya Pradesh near the city of Bhopal, is one of the most important and impressive Buddhist centers in India. It was discovered in 1818 by of the Bengal Cavalry and was soon despoiled by treasure hunters, looters, collectors, and vandals who, among other acts, destroyed an Asokan column to make a sugarcane press. Four years after its discovery, Sir Herbert Maddock drove a shaft to the center of Stupas 1 and 2 without finding anything of importance, instead causing great damage. In the 1840s, however, Lieutenant F. Maisey initiated the recording of the temples and sculptures. The great stupa of Sanchi, decorated with reliefs depicting the life of the Buddha, commands a hill near the Betwa River. It is associated with an Asokan column and a monastery, and the original third century B.C.E. foundation clearly owes much to the zeal of the MAURYA EMPIRE king ASOKA. It was one of the many hundreds of INSCRIPTIONS at this site that provided the key to the translation of the Asokan columns in 1837 by JAMES PRINSEP.

MARSHALL'S EXCAVATIONS, RELIEFS, AND SCULPTURE

Major excavations were undertaken on the Sanchi Hill by SIR JOHN MARSHALL in 1912. At that stage, only the Great Stupa and one or two walls were visible; the remainder of the site was covered by debris and concealed by thick vegetation. Marshall's excavation of the foundations of the Asokan column, together with the earlier discovery of a brick core to the stupa, convinced him that the brick represented the original structure, probably begun in the third century B.C.E. under Asoka, but that the facing stone represented a later enlargement. The encircling wall of massive stones and the four *torana*s (gateways) were added during the first century B.C.E. Two further stupas were built later, one during the first century B.C.E. and a third during the early first century C.E. The Great Stupa is surrounded by a railing incorporating four *torana*s that stand at the pinnacle of the art of this period. They are decorated with narrative reliefs depicting events in the life of the Buddha and JATAKA TALES or legends of his previous lives. The Buddha himself is never depicted as a person but is represented in the form of footprints, an empty throne, or the "wheel of the law" (DHARMACAKRA). Others provide illuminating scenes of war, with battle elephants, the walls of a besieged city, and groups of

The four gateways at the Great Stupa of Sanchi were decorated with scenes taken from the life of the Buddha. This was one of the major Buddhist centers in India, patronized by Emperor Asoka. *(© Archivo Iconografico, S.A./CORBIS)*

archers. Horse cavalry and chariots join the siege, while the defenders reply from the battlements with bows and arrows or repel attackers with clubs. These gateways also incorporate *yaksha* figures, female symbols of fertility that are entwined in a tree and again represent the pinnacle of early Buddhist sculpture. More than 400 inscriptions give details of the history of the site. One, for example, records the donation of one of the reliefs by a guild of ivory workers. Others, found on reliquaries, record the names of the monks who led missionary journeys at the behest of Asoka. Another text of Asoka forbade the development of schisms in the Buddhist congregation.

Two smaller stupas are also found on the hilltop. One of these, Stupa 3, was examined earlier by SIR ALEXANDER CUNNINGHAM, who identified STEATITE caskets containing the relics of two of Buddha's disciples, Sariputra and Mahamogalana, together with the foundation offerings. These sacred stupas were located among a cluster of temples and monasteries. The latter form a square courtyard around which are rows of monks' cells. The center of Sanchi had a long history. A Gupta period temple was con-

structed in the early fifth century, and the complex as a whole remained active until at least the 11th century, giving the complex a history well in excess of a millennium.

Sankisa   Sankisa is a large city site located in the Ganges (Ganga) Valley of northern India. JAMES PRINSEP sought the city of Sankisa by its stated relationship to the known center of MATHURA and identified it as a huge mound that was subsequently examined by SIR ALEXANDER CUNNINGHAM and K. N. Sastri. This site is known as Sankasya in the *RAMAYANA* and is venerated by Buddhists, because it was here that the Buddha descended from heaven by means of a gold ladder. Hence, it became a pilgrimage site. The Chinese traveler XUANZANG described an Asokan pillar and several stupas there. The capital of this pillar survives to this day, and Cunningham identified one of the mounds at the site as a monastery. The city itself was enclosed by a wall with three entrances, while the excavations have revealed prehistoric foundations to the site, followed by layers dated to the period of *MAHAJANAPADAS* (600–350 B.C.E.) and the SAKAS (50 B.C.E.–30 C.E.).

Sannathi Sannathi is a fortified city covering about 40 hectares (100 acres) in Karnataka state, southern India. It is located in the valley of the Bhima River, and despite a lack of excavations, surface finds of coins reveal it to have been a center during the SATAVAHANA dynasty (late first century B.C.E.–third century C.E.). Other finds include carnelian beads, shell bangles, and the foundations of a stupa dating to the first two centuries C.E.

Sanskrit Sanskrit is an Indo-European language belonging to the Indic branch of the Indo-Aryan subgroup of this family. The pioneering work of Indologists, such as SIR WILLIAM JONES (1746–94) and SIR CHARLES WILKINS (1749–1836), led to the realization that Sanskrit has close genetic links with Latin and Greek, leading scholars to identify the Indo-European language family. Some have suggested that Sanskrit was introduced into India during the mid-second millennium B.C.E., for it is the language of the RIG-VEDA. In the fourth century B.C.E., a grammarian called Panini worked to perfect and refine the language, and he gave it its name, which means "cultivated" or "perfected." Classical Sanskrit, as opposed to the earlier Vedic version, remains to this day the literary and priestly language of Hinduism and is traditionally written in the Devanagari alphabet, which originated ultimately in the BRAHMI script.

Sanskrit as a priestly and refined language existed alongside related vernacular languages, known as PRAKRITS. The best known of the latter is PALI. Curiously, the early INSCRIPTIONS of India, particularly those of the Mauryan emperor ASOKA (268–235 B.C.E.), were written in regional Prakrits, whereas Sanskrit texts appeared later. The earliest Sanskrit inscriptions in India date to the first century B.C.E. and are from Ayodhya, Ghosundi, and Hathibada. These record temple foundations. The Sanskrit inscriptions from MATHURA belong to the first and second centuries C.E. The earliest of these, inscribed early in the first century C.E., again records a temple dedication. The Junagadh inscription of the WESTERN SATRAP King Rudradaman, dated to 150 C.E., is widely seen as an important text because of the standard Sanskrit employed and its poetic meter. Sanskrit was first employed in inscriptions rather later in southern India than in the north; the earliest examples are from NAGARJUNAKONDA and date to the late third century C.E. Sanskrit was preferred when the text used poetic rhythms rather than a prose style. After the fourth century C.E. in southern India, Prakrit inscriptions ceased, and Sanskrit dominated. This trend was expedited from the same century under the GUPTA EMPIRE, when Sanskrit became the preferred language of virtually all the inscriptions in their extensive domains.

This ascendance has important implications when considering the inscriptions of Southeast Asia. The earliest of these, from VO CANH in southern coastal Vietnam, was written in Sanskrit, as were those of the coastal state of FUNAN. Indeed, Sanskrit was the preferred language of all the major inscriptions of CHENLA and the kingdom of ANGKOR, in Cambodia, although Old KHMER was also used in subsidiary texts on many occasions. The quality of the Sanskrit employed was admirable, as seen in the long dedicatory inscriptions of the temples of the PRE RUP, PREAH KHAN, and TA PROHM at Angkor.

See also MAURYA EMPIRE.

Sanxingdui Sanxingdui is a huge walled city of the SHU kingdom in China. In its own right, Sanxingdui stands out as a massive early urban center and capital of the long-lived Shu state. The site, however, is best known for two remarkable discoveries made quite by accident in July and August 1986 by local workers excavating for clay to make bricks. On July 18, they encountered ancient jades and bronzes. Archaeologists were called to the site, and excavations proceeded at once. The artifacts were contained in a pit about 4.5 by 3.5 meters (15 by 12 ft.) in extent and 1.6 meters deep. The uppermost layer in the pit contained about three cubic meters (10.5 cu. ft.) of burnt bones from cattle, pigs, sheep, and goats together with 13 elephant tusks. The excavators then encountered jades in the form of *yazhang* blades and *ge* daggers before reaching the basal contents. These were objects of bronze, gold, and jade. The sheer quantity of the finds, all of which had been burned before deposition, was stunning. There were 178 items of bronze, four gold artifacts, 129 jades, and other objects of stone and pottery. Exotic cowry shells were also present. Radiocarbon dates indicated that this pit dates to the 13th or 12th century B.C.E.

A few days later, again by chance when digging for BRICK earth, a second pit was discovered about 40 meters from the first. It measured 5.3. by 2.3 meters and was as deep as the first. This pit was slightly later in date, perhaps belonging to the 12th or the 11th century B.C.E., and it was also markedly richer in terms of the burnt offerings. The bottom layer included relatively small items of bronze, jade, gold, and stone, including BRONZE CASTINGS of trees and diamond-shaped fittings. The next layer had the most extraordinary range of finds among a unique assemblage. There were a gigantic bronze statue, 44 bronze heads, bronze masks, a large bronze tree complete with birds perched on the branches, and bronze vessels containing jade and cowry shells. This layer was capped by 60 elephant tusks, but, on this occasion, no burnt bone. The final count revealed 735 bronze items, 61 gold, 486 jade, and several items of TURQUOISE. There were also tigers' teeth and ivory. The name Sanxingdui means "three star mounds," so-called because three mounds in the city resemble a stellar constellation. It is located 40 kilometers north of Chengdu in Sichuan province, southwest

China. The Chengdu Plain is renowned for the cultivation of rice, and the presence of LONGSHAN CULTURE walled settlements that anticipate the local development of a powerful state is now well attested at Baodun, Mangcheng, and Yufu. The walls of Sanxingdui enclose an area of about 450 hectares (1125 acres) and lie adjacent to the southern bank of the Yazi River. The Mamu River flows through the site.

EARLY DISCOVERY OF JADES

In 1929, a pit containing a large number of jades was discovered within the city precincts by the members of the Yan family. They kept the discovery secret for several years and then sold them to the Chendu antiques market. An English priest, V. H. Donnithorne, managed to persuade local authorities to get at least some of them into their possession and place them in the museum of Huaxi University. In 1964 and 1974, further jades were discovered, leading local archaeologists to conclude that this site had been a jade manufacturing center, for some were unfinished.

EXCAVATIONS OF CITY

In 1980, excavations of the three star mounds revealed that they were part of the city walls, made by following the same technique of stamped earth known from the well-documented Shang cities to the northeast. These walls were massive, up to 47 meters (155 ft.) wide at the base, and probably up to 10 meters high, fronted by a deep moat. The walls are dated to about 1400–1300 B.C.E. Archaeological inquiries have revealed that the city had a long history, beginning 6,000 years ago with a Neolithic settlement. This was followed by occupation dating to the same period as the XIA and early SHANG dynasties as seen at ERLITOU in the central plains. The third and fourth phases were contemporary, respectively, with the Middle and Late Shang dynasties. Shang dynasty ORACLE BONES refer to a state called Shu, and at least one Shang ruler, King Wu Ding, campaigned against them, although the capitals are more than 1,000 kilometers apart. The wall was constructed during the period of the early Shang state, and the site was apparently deserted by the early Zhou period. There were domestic dwellings in the city and large halls. But the city also spread beyond the walls, to cover an area of at least 15 square kilometers (6 sq. mi.).

Excavations in 1980, 1982, and 1986 over an area of 1,325 meters uncovered many items of jade, ceramics, lacquer, and bronze, allowing activities within the walls and beyond them to be assessed. Specialized craft activities were located in the vicinity of the city, including ceramic production. The discovery of many unfinished jades also indicates specialist lapidaries. By contrast, the bronze-casting workshops were located inside the city, where fragments of clay molds and bronze residues have been recovered.

THE PITS' CONTENTS

The purpose of the pits has been the subject of considerable speculation and has stimulated further archaeological inquiries. The most exciting possibility is that they were associated in some way with the royal burials of the kings of Shu, but as yet no such tombs have been uncovered. The burning of the contents of the pits, despite their intrinsic value, rarity, and beauty, strongly suggests a sacrificial or ritual purpose. Many of the items were deliberately damaged before being buried. There are, for example, bronzes that have lost their form entirely through extreme heat. Other items were probably components of artifacts made of different materials, some of which have perished. This makes it unlikely that the pits were intended for storing precious items, despite the fact that the pit discovered in 1929 and another deposit investigated in 1988 contained jade *cong* tubes and *bi* disks neatly stacked one on another. The majority opinion among specialists now is that they were probably pits associated with sacrificial ceremonies connected with royally inspired rituals. The quality of the offerings is only compatible with extreme wealth, and some of the smaller objects themselves provide clues. There are for example, many *yazhang* jade blades. One of these is represented on a small bronze figure seen in a kneeling posture from Pit 2. In the same pit was another kneeling figure supporting a *zun* bronze vessel on his head. Both seem to indicate a form of worship or sacrifice. Shang oracle-bone texts and later Zhou records provide supporting evidence, for they describe the burning of sacrificial items and their burial. This interpretation, however, is not a final one. There are also records that a violent change of dynasty could be accompanied by the destruction of the sacred symbols of the previous rulers. In this context, it is possible that the pits represent the seizure of power in the Shu state by Duyu, who established the fourth dynasty when he defeated his predecessor, Yufu. This interpretation does not explain the probable gap in time between the two pits, however. Whatever the explanation, the contents of the pits provide an unrivaled opportunity to examine the beliefs and technical expertise of a major but little known contemporary of the Shang state.

Unique Bronze Figure

The most extraordinary of all bronzes is from Pit 2. It is a complete statue of a man 2.61 meters (8.6 ft.) high and weighing 180 kilograms (396 lbs.). The figure stands on top of a four-legged stool, the legs of which are four stylized animal heads, and this, in turn, stands on a bronze support. The human figure is 1.8 meters (5.9 ft.) high and is the only bronze casting of a person known from this period of Chinese history. The face resembles many others from the pit, which might themselves have belonged to complete statues before they were broken up and damaged by intense heat. It has a disturbing, mask-like face. The man wears a circular crown under an elaborate headdress, anklets, and three bangles. His outer tunic is richly decorated with dragons, animal heads, and crowns. It lies over another tunic that ends in pointed swallowlike tails and is again enriched with dragon and animal-head designs. A band runs across his chest and is tied at the back. But it is the arms and hands that attract immediate attention, for they are larger than life-size and are so positioned that they must have formerly held something large and heavy. The curvature between the two hands and the size of the intended grip make it likely that he held an elephant's tusk. Sixty-seven tusks had been placed in the same pit. The motifs cast into the clothing and stool strongly recall those found on Shang RITUAL BRONZE VESSELS, and the casting technique was also similar, for the different parts of the statue were cast separately in piece molds over a clay core before being joined together.

There are other human figures in bronze, but none so complete as this specimen. One has survived only from the waist up, but it still stands to a height of almost half a meter (1.6 ft.). It too has hands outstretched as if to hold something impressively large, and its tunic is finely decorated with a pattern of dragons and meanders. There is an impressive animal headdress with a huge mouth, eyes, and ears standing out prominently. A third figure is a man with a bird's feet, standing atop two highly stylized bird figures. The human, of which only the body from the waist down has survived, wears a fringed kilt or skirt covered in a geometric set of bands infilled with spirals. Instead of human feet, the person has robust bird talons, each of which grasps a bird head on top of a long and decorated body.

Unique Bronze Trees

A second unique type of bronze takes the form of a tree, standing on a circular base and reaching a height of nearly four meters (13.2 ft.). Birds perch in the branches, which bear leaves, fruit, and buds. Although reassembled from many pieces as far as possible, it remains incomplete. A dragon entwines itself around the trunk, descending from the heavens. There are many holes for suspension of dangling objects, and some fragments from other trees still retain such jade or bronze disks. There is also provision at the top of the trunk for the placement of a further embellishment that might well have been one of the bronze bird images recovered from the same pit. This would almost certainly have been a representation of a crow, which in Chinese legends lives in the Sun. Such a crow linked with the Sun is seen much later in the tomb banner from MAWANGDUI. Two other incomplete trees were also found. These must have held considerable ritual importance. The traces of gold are still found on some of the fruit. One tree had trunks that terminate in a hybrid human–bird figure wearing a crown.

Human Heads and Masks

A similar figure is found on part of a bronze altar half a meter high, made up of a dragon, human figures wearing crowns, masks, and birds. The human heads cast in bronze are also unique to this period in China. They are about 40 to 50 centimeters (16 to 20 in.) high, and many would have worn a headdress or crown. Others wear a flat cap cast first and then later cast on to the face. One of these heads contained jades, cowry shells, bronze daggers, and a gold ornament in the form of a tiger. Four of the bronze heads in the second pit wore gold masks secured to the face by a resin. Only the eyes and holes for the attachment of ear ornaments are not covered. Other gold masks were found in Pit 2, but they have not been matched with individual heads. A large human head, half a meter high, wore an elaborate headdress in the form of two *yazhang* blades; another wore a turban, and his ears were pierced three times, probably to retain ornaments.

The human heads are thought to have worn masks. In other bronzes, the masks themselves are complete and separate. Some are massive. One example is 60 centimeters (2 ft.) wide and weighs 13.5 kilograms (29.7 lbs.). This bronze was apparently cast in one pour, a testament to the skill of the specialists who worked at Sanxingdui. Holes left at strategic places suggest that it was once attached to a face sculpted in another medium, such as wood. In a second type of mask, which is bigger than the previous group, the masks combine human and animal faces and have grotesquely prominent eyes on protruding stalks. One of these is almost 1.4 meters wide, with pointed ears, tight lips with a slightly protruding tongue, and jutting chin. There is a rectangular hole on the forehead that was cut out after the mask had been cast. This might well have held in place a tall bronze projection with curved ends and an ornamental forepiece like that seen on a second giant animal mask. This projection is known as a *kuilong*, or dragon image without horns. The mask also has broad lips and pointed ears, but the eyeballs are rounded and projected in front of the face in tall, slanted eyes. Again, it has square holes under the ears probably to attach the mask to a body. Purely animal masks were also cast. Their schematized but forbidding features are matched on the designs cast into the ritual vessels of the period, but these masks are large, measuring up to 30 centimeters wide. Some of the ritual bronze vessels from Sanxingdui show marked similarities to those from the late Shang capital at ANYANG. A large *lei* vessel, for example, a little more than a half-meter in height, matches the shape and decoration of analogous vessels at Anyang. On the other hand, details of the casting techniques employed at Sanxingdui reveal local preferences. In casting a *lei* the Shu casters used four-piece molds, against the three preferred at Anyang.

The massive bronzes were probably decorations for one or more large ritual structures. Their placement may be reconstructed on the basis of a bronze model of an altar, a little more than a half-meter in height, that has been reconstructed from fragmentary remains from Pit 2. It has a series of tiers separated by platforms, supported by a four-legged animal. The first tier incorporates bronze figures closely resembling the large face masks, each holding in outstretched hands a curved offering of some sort. These match the small model of a kneeling man holding a *yazhang* blade in the same posture. The uppermost tier of the altar includes rows of kneeling figures in half-relief, with their arms again in a position of holding a ceremonial offering of some sort.

Animal Figures

Animal castings were abundant at Sanxingdui. Apart from the birds, there is a unique complete snake resembling a python, about 1.1 meters long. The body is richly ornamented with geometric designs. Two lugs beside the head were probably intended to suspend or hold it against another object.

JADES FROM PITS

Jade was one of the most prestigious materials found in Shang period burials and had a long period of use preceding the first states. At Sanxingdui, many jades of the highest quality were recovered. The *ge* is a dagger with a broad blade and a hilt. Eighteen such daggers in jade were found in Pit 1, and 21 were taken from Pit 2. A *yazhang* is a long-handled blade or knife, characteristic of the period beginning with the Xia dynasty (2100–1766 B.C.E.) and ending with the early WESTERN ZHOU DYNASTY (1045–771 B.C.E.). They are widely distributed in China, including Hong Kong, and even extend into northern Vietnam. However, only about 200 specimens are known. The importance of the two pits at Sanxingdui can, therefore, be appreciated when it is considered that 57 *yazhang* were recovered. Some show local design preferences. There is, for example, a blade with a forked end and hooks close to the handle. It is very long and weighs almost a kilogram. Even this specimen, however, pales before a broken blade from Pit 1, which would have been more than a meter and a half long. The recovery of a small bronze figure of a kneeling man holding just such a forked blade in front of him emphasizes their probably ritual function.

Other jades include axes, rings, and the *cong*, a ritual object of considerable longevity, and all these forms are widespread. Two types of jades, however, are unparalleled: There are a jade pendant, and a long chisel, of which 43 were found in a bronze vessel. Another unique object recovered from the first pit is the gold sheath for a staff of some sort, decorated with fish and human faces wearing earrings and a crown.

RESULTS OF EXCAVATIONS

The site of Sanxingdui has reoriented the appreciation of early civilization in China. Hitherto, virtually all atten-

tion had been paid to the central plains and the Shang state, with its huge royal graves, oracle bones, palaces, and rich culture of ritual bronzes, but there was another early state in Sichuan, the state of Shu. While adhering to the same ritual traditions and following the same symbolic designs, such as the TAOTIE (animal's head) mask so familiar at Anyang, the rulers of Sanxingdui encouraged a remarkable local school of bronze casting that delighted in the gigantic. There are few, if any, parallels in the ancient world for the size of the freestanding statue of a man, the trees, or the huge masks with animal features and eyes on stalks. The trees reveal remarkable and innovative skill, and even the jades show a taste for the spectacular and novel. One bronze of a woman holding above her head the model of a bronze *zun* container indicates how ritual offerings were probably made. Further excavations at this great city and its environs can only produce more remarkable discoveries.

Sanxingdui was almost certainly the seat of a powerful Shu kingdom, for ceramics similar to those recovered there have also been found over large parts of Sichuan province, including Yaan to the south and Yangzishan in Chengdu city. The latter site has revealed a large earthen platform, probably designed to perform rituals. It stood at least 10 meters (33 ft.) high, and its base was a little more than 100 meters square (120 sq. yds.). A further important site has been examined at Chengdu. It was a long wooden structure; one significant find there was a clay spindle incised with a written character.

Sapallitepa   Sapallitepa is a prehistoric settlement located on the delta of the Ulanbulaksai River, a tributary of the Amu Dar'ya, in northern BACTRIA (now Afghanistan). It was excavated in the early 1970s, and although estimating its area has proved difficult, it is thought to have covered at least four hectares (10 acres). It was occupied during the Bronze Age between 2200 and 2000 B.C.E. and aids an understanding of growing social complexity in this strategic region. A large palace complex covers about a hectare of the site and includes separate occupation areas, revealing the presence of specialists in the manufacture of bone, horn, and bronze artifacts. Late in the occupation period, the palace area was used as a cemetery, and 138 inhumation graves have been uncovered. Female graves in this cemetery not only contained more wealth measured in terms of ceramic and bronze artifacts, but they also were the only burials to contain certain high-prestige items, such as SEALS. The male graves are outnumbered by a ratio of 2:3 by the female and contained far fewer bronzes.

Sarasvati River   The Sarasvati River was formerly a sacred river originating in the Himalayas and entering the sea at the Rann of Katchchh. It is now extinct, although its course, roughly parallel to and east of the Indus River, can still be traced. It was mentioned as a living river in the RIG-VEDA. Archaeological surveys along its course have yielded many sites, including those occupied during the period of the INDUS VALLEY CIVILIZATION (c. 2500–c. 1770 B.C.E.). Of these, KALIBANGAN is probably the best known. In about 1750 B.C.E. the water that had fed the Sarasvati appears to have been diverted east into the Ganges (Ganga) system, leading to a major abandonment of settlements along its course.

Sarnath   Sarnath, near Varanasi (Benares), in India, is the location of the Buddha's first sermon and thus holds a special place in the history of this religion. Now ruined, the earliest monasteries at Sarnath are thought to have been constructed during the Buddha's own lifetime but attracted much further building under the Mauryan king ASOKA. The Great Stupa, thought to date to the fifth century C.E., survives despite the removal of the outer dome. The substructure contains wall niches and relief carvings. Between 1834 and 1836, SIR ALEXANDER CUNNINGHAM opened the monument, a monumental task that required scaffolding and the employment of quarrymen from the Chunar sandstone quarries. The stupa had large stone blocks secured in place by iron cramps, and removing them over a depth of 33 meters from the top revealed a layer of bricks. The basal soil was reached after continuing down for a further 8.5 meters, and then galleries were run out at the level of the bricks, but no foundation deposit was encountered. Apart from stupas and monasteries, Asoka had the most famous and elegant of his columns erected there; one has as its capital four lions facing the cardinal points of the compass. Many religious buildings were constructed over the centuries, including the Dhamekha stupa, and the Dharmacakrajinavihara has the distinction of being among the latest monasteries built there before the slaughter of the monks at the hands of Muhammed Ghori in 1194 C.E. Sarnath was also a major center of Buddhist art, based on the locally available Chunar sandstone. This art style had its origins in the fifth century C.E., and its justifiably most famous work represents a seated Buddha.

See also MAURYA EMPIRE.

Sassanian empire   The Sassanian empire of Persia was founded by Ardashir I in about 216 C.E., when he defeated the last Parthian king, Artabanus V. One of Ardashir's ancestors, Sasan, gave his name to this new dynasty. Ardashir's early eastern conquests included the strategic MERV (now Mary) oasis in Margiana. His son, Shapur, continued the expansion of the Sassanian empire, most notably by defeating and capturing the Roman emperor Valerian at the Battle of Edessa in 260 C.E. He also consolidated and expanded the eastern provinces, claiming success over the western KUSHANS by taking

Purusapura, modern Peshawar in Pakistan, as well as BACTRIA, and extracting tribute. He had fortresses constructed on the eastern frontiers and greatly expanded Mary (Merv). This vital oasis center was formerly under semi-independent rulers, who were replaced by Sassanian appointees. Already by the third century C.E., Mary boasted a Christian monastery as well as Buddhist foundations. It was also a trading and manufacturing center for armaments, and a quarter of the city was given over to the production of ceramics. The stability provided under Sassanian rule stimulated trade across the SILK ROAD at least until the demise of the empire in the mid-seventh century C.E.

The archaeological evidence of trade is abundant. Chinese silks have been recovered from Palmyra, and Sassanian glass reached China and even farther east in Korea and Japan. The Sassanians also showed considerable interest in maritime trade that incorporated India, Sri Lanka, and beyond. The principal source of evidence for this trade network is the *Topographia Christiana (Christian Topography)* of Cosmas Indicopleustes of Alexandria in Egypt, which dates to about 550 C.E. This text emphasizes Sri Lanka as a key player in Sassanian eastern trade. Cosmas describes how Chinese and Southeast Asian goods reached Sri Lanka, including silk, CLOVES, and sandalwood, and were then taken west by Sassanian merchants. Further items of Indian origin, obtained by the same means, were elephants, copper, and pepper. Such was the Western demand for silk via this route that the Byzantine historian Procopius (born between 490 and 507 C.E.) indicated that it was impossible to buy in Indian ports because the market was dominated by Persians. It is even possible that the Sassanians traveled beyond Sri Lanka. The *Nestorian Annals* note that one of the bishops attending a synod in 410 C.E. was entitled, Metropolitan of the Islands, Seas and Interior, of Dabang, Chin, and Macin. Dabang was probably Java; the other two locations were in China. By the end of the Sassanian empire between 637 and 651 C.E., dominance of the Eastern maritime trade was complete.

Satanikota   Satanikota is a walled SATAVAHANA city site, located on the Tungabhadra River in central India. It is particularly notable for the work put into its surrounding moat, which was chiseled from rock to a depth of up to three meters. The principal phase of occupation falls between 50 B.C.E. and 250 C.E., when the walls and moat were constructed; the former was equipped with gateways and probably a drawbridge. There were once many BRICK structures in the defended area, but brick robbing has destroyed most of the evidence. However, an impressive assemblage of material cultural remains were found, in particular a wide range of beads in glass and semiprecious stones, including carenelian, opal, jasper, and agate.

Satavahana The Satavahana dynasty dominated the Deccan in India from the late first century B.C.E. to the third century C.E. and resisted invading elements from the northwest. The people are known as the Andhras, Dravidians who spoke Telugu. Their state had two great rivers, the Krishna and the Godavari, and commanded a long tract of coast looking east across the Bay of Bengal. By this location, the kingdom was able to dominate the growing trade between the East and the Roman Empire, and the *PERIPLUS OF THE ERYTHRAEAN SEA* mentions two sites that participated, Pratisthana and Tagara. Finds of COINAGE and INSCRIPTIONS also indicate the importance under the Satavahanas of SANNATHI, which grew to cover an area of 40 hectares (100 acres) in the defensive walls. Other important urban centers were Kondapur, Banavasi, and Madhavpur. The success of the Satavahanas has been ascribed to their dominance of a growing trade with the West, in which command of these passes linking the western coast of India with the cities of the interior was a paramount consideration.

NANAGHAT, commands a vital pass linking the capital Paithan with the sea, and there the Satavahana consorts of King Satakarni set up images of themselves and inscriptions describing their sacrificial donations. These date 60–70 B.C.E., but according to reports from Agatharchides of Alexandria, the Indian trade had been dominated by Arabs already half a century earlier.

HISTORY OF THE SATAVAHANAS

The date of the first Satavahana king, Simuka Satavahana, is not known with certainty. Some claim that he ruled during the third century B.C.E., just after the Greek envoy MEGASTHENES described the Andhras as a powerful people. However, evidence from coins suggests a slightly later end to his reign but certainly by 120 B.C.E. He was followed by two other powerful leaders, Kanha and Satakarni, the latter ruling until about 60 B.C.E. At its zenith, under a succession of charismatic leaders, the Satavahana empire covered much of central and southern India. An image of Simuka was formerly in the Nanaghat cave, along with representations of later Satavahana rulers. This bright beginning was followed by fragmentation and defeat at the hands of the Kshaharata satraps under Nahapana, who ruled the area for almost 50 years. Gautamiputra Satakarni (c. 103–127 C.E.) is usually regarded as the greatest Satavahana king, and his military prowess resulted in the incorporation of territory from Rajasthan to Andhra and from Gujarat east to Kalinga. He was described as the restorer of Satavahana glory, the king who defeated Nahapana. He was followed by Pulumavi in 110 C.E. and then by Vasishtiputra Siri Satakarni in 138 C.E. The latter consolidated his position through a strategic marriage with the daughter of the powerful WESTERN SATRAP leader Rudradaman. When his reign ended in 145 C.E., his successor, Shivaskanda, was twice defeated in battles by Rudradaman, and the main line of kings ended in 181 C.E. with the death of Yajnasri Satakarni.

The later history of the dynasty is best traced through the coin issues. The coins of Yajnasri Satakarni bear images of ships, which might represent naval and trading success. The last king, Pulumavi IV, ruled until about 225 C.E., and during this period many major Buddhist monuments were constructed at Nagajunakonda and Amaravati. After his reign, the power of the empire declined, as it fragmented into smaller regional entities, and the Satavahanas pass from view by the early fourth century.

Satingpra Satingpra is a city site on the east coast of isthmian Thailand, one of the early sites that grew rich on the basis of the southern maritime SILK ROAD. It is a moated site covering an area of 1,600 by 900 meters (5,280 by 2,970 ft.), and excavations by Janice Stargardt have revealed that settlement began between about 300 B.C.E. and 200 C.E. From the sixth century, the site assumed an urban form, linked with the development of hydraulic engineering works that encompassed canals and storage tanks. These were probably employed to increase rice production on the alluvial soils north of the center. A sixth-century temple was dedicated to Vishnu, and the ceramics are clearly very similar to those from OC EO, the trading port of the state of FUNAN.

scapulomancy Scapulomancy is the process of divination by applying heat to scapulae or shoulder blades to produce cracks used to predict future events. The earliest record of this procedure is from the Shandong LONGSHAN CULTURE site of Chengziyai (2500–1900 B.C.E.), in China, where 16 specimens have been recovered. Kings of the SHANG STATE and WESTERN ZHOU DYNASTY in China from about 1200 B.C.E. retained court diviners. Cattle scapulae had holes excised, and heat was applied. The king then interpreted the meaning of the resultant cracks, and his prophecies were inscribed on the bone in archaic Chinese characters. These covered such subjects as war, the harvest, the weather, when to make sacrifices to the ancestors, and whether royal consorts would enjoy a safe childbirth. The records were then stored in state archives. Many have been recovered through archaeological excavations and provide the basis for understanding later Shang dynastic history.

See also LI JI; LIU TAIYUN; ORACLE BONES; PLASTROMANCY; SONG YIRANG.

Sdok Kak Thom Sdok Kak Thom is a small temple located just inside Thailand. Its original name was Bhadraniketana. It has an outer laterite wall that encloses a moat and an inner set of walls. Three temple sanctuaries lie within. The site is particularly well known because of a lengthy INSCRIPTION that was set in place by Sadasiva, a member of an aristocratic priestly family, who traced his ancestors back to the time of JAYAVARMAN II (c. 770–834 C.E.) of ANGKOR in Cambodia. Although its prime purpose was to record the erection of a LINGAM and gifts from the king, it also describes the history of the Shivakaivalya family. Interwoven with this dynastic record are vital clues to the establishment of the state of Angkor by Jayavarman II. It describes, for example, how Jayavarman returned from Java to rule in the holy city of INDRAPURA. The king then moved with his followers to the vicinity of modern Angkor. The inscription records the establishment by Jayavarman more than 250 years before the text was inscribed of a cult honoring the KAMRATENG JAGAT TA RAJA. This title, which translates into SANSKRIT as DEVARAJA, means "the god who is king." Shivakaivalya and his descendants were given the exclusive right to undertake the rituals associated with this god.

seals

INDIA

Seals are one of the most significant and productive artifacts recovered from excavations in the sites from the INDUS VALLEY CIVILIZATION (c. 2500–1700 B.C.E.) to the GUPTA EMPIRE (c. 320–c. 500 C.E.). In 1872, SIR ALEXANDER CUNNINGHAM discovered a seal at HARAPPA decorated with the image of a unicorn and a text in a still undeciphered script. This indicated the possibility of a civilization in the Indus Valley earlier than any then known on the subcontinent. Subsequently, hundreds of seals have been recovered, and the images have provided much information on the life and thoughts of the people of the Indus civilization. An unfinished specimen from MOHENJO DARO shows the outline of a unicorn on the surface of a piece of STEATITE nearly three centimeters square (0.48 sq. in.) as

Steatite seals are a vital source of information on the Indus civilization. They incorporate texts in the undeciphered Indus script, ritual scenes, and the images of animals. *(Borromeo/Art Resource, NY)*

well as faint outlines of a text. This shows beyond doubt that manufactories were established in major sites.

Most seals were made of steatite, which was first incised with the appropriate text and motif that stand out from the background, then polished and fired to harden the surface. Rarely were seals made of silver and copper. They were used to make an impression on a clay sealing affixed, it is assumed, to merchandise destined for trade. Where the actual clay seal impressions are found, they have on occasion the impressions on fabric or string on the reverse side. Few seals exceed five by five centimeters (2 by 2 in.) in size, and most were equipped with a perforated boss or a hole through them for suspension by the owner. Broken seals are not uncommon and have been recovered from houses and the streets of the major sites.

Motifs

The motifs employed include in the main a male animal, often associated with a vessel raised on legs under the head, which might be an altar or a feeding stand. Bulls are commonly depicted; a fine example from Mohenho Daro was found without a feeding stand, but with a clear text of six pictographic characters. Unicorns are regularly encountered. Other animals include antelopes, elephants, tigers, water buffaloes, gharials, crocodiles, and rhinoceroses. A second specimen from Mohenjo Daro has a bull on one side and a swastika motif on the other and is pierced through the center. Script alone is seen on a third example from this site. The depiction of boats emphasizes the importance of river and maritime trade. One such specimen shows a boat with a cabin and rudder, with both stern and prow raised up from the level of the deck. Perhaps the most revealing, however, are those seals that depict a deity. Although a seal with a god figure from Mohenjo Daro is only 2.7 centimeters (1 in.) in height, it shows a remarkably detailed image of a male god seated on a throne with legs in a yogic position. His arms are covered in bangles, and he wears an elaborate horned headdress with three branches of a pipal tree. The throne, presumably of wood, has feet carved in the form of bovine hoofs. An even more complex scene of a deity incorporates a god standing within a sacred fig or pipal tree, again with a horned headdress and many bangles on each arm. A figure kneels before the god, associated with a ram. Below, seven people are seen in a row. All this imagery, with script, is set out in a seal barely exceeding four by four centimeters (1.6 by 1.6 in.).

The possible ritual importance of animals, perhaps in sacrifice to the deities as in the case of the ram, is seen in an extraordinary seal from Mohenjo Daro with an animal with a human face, elephant's trunk, bull's hooves, buttocks of a tiger, and a cobra as a tail. Gods are also seen battling with animals: A terra-cotta tablet that might have served as a seal from Harappa has a goddess on top of an elephant, holding off two tigers on one side, and the killing of a water buffalo in front of the horned, seated

god on the other. Many seals show a unicorn in front of a bowl-shaped receptacle raised on a pedestal, which itself supports a mushroom-shaped object with three disks above it. The purpose of this enigmatic but commonly depicted artifact remains controversial; none has survived, but an ivory miniature has been recovered from Harappa. It is also seen in a ritual procession scene. It has been suggested that it was a filter to make the intoxicating ritual drink soma, which is described in Vedic texts. There are also some seals or sealings from Mohenjo Daro that depict a remarkable scene of acrobats vaulting over the horns of a bull. Others show a bull being sacrificed by a man with a foot on the bull's horns and reaching over to spear the animal in the neck, as a modern matador would. This scene and details of associated figures such as a tree and a dove are matched in similar scenes from Minoan Crete.

These seals probably hold the key to any future decipherment of the INDUS VALLEY CIVILIZATION SCRIPT. They were probably in personal, corporate, or temple ownership, and the texts might well be royal titles, personal names, or other names or attributes of a temple. The symbol for a structure, which might be a temple, is often associated with a seal depicting the horned god. Their distribution is widespread, and the location of specific varieties again holds a key to reconstructing trade relationships. This is seen clearly in the remains of sealings from a burned warehouse at the site of LOTHAL, which bore images of a unicorn, an elephant, and a swastika, although the seal in question has not been found. The presence of Indus seals in Mesopotamia provides compelling evidence for long-distance trade.

Later Seals

Seals continued to be used in the Maurya and Gupta empires. They were made of ivory, bone, various varieties of stone, and terra-cotta and normally contain the name of the owner in the BRAHMI script. The excavations of BHITA yielded a large sample of both seals and sealings dating from the MAURYA EMPIRE to the Gupta empire. Some ivory seals, with the names of individuals or in one instance a corporation or guild, were found in houses, and the excavator, SIR JOHN MARSHALL, gave their names to the residences they may once have occupied. Unlike the Indus seals, those of Bhita can be translated and thus provide much more information. There are seals issued by kings. Those of the Gupta empire also include the titles of officials, naming military leaders, police, chiefs of police, and administrators assigned to the office of a crown prince. Individuals, probably merchants, had their own seals, and the motifs employed, such as bulls, peacocks, or LINGAMS, provide insight into their religious preferences.

SOUTHEAST ASIA

Seals inscribed in the Brahmi script have been recovered from the site of OC EO on the Mekong Delta and provide compelling evidence for the presence of Indian traders in Southeast Asia between 200 and 500 C.E.

CHINA

Although two bronze seals are thought to date to the Shang dynasty, seals in China only became widely used during the period of EASTERN ZHOU DYNASTY (770–221 B.C.E.). They were made of a variety of materials, including jade, bronze, silver, opal, antler, and bone. The seals employed in the various Warring States were of distinctive regional shapes and forms of script. A particularly well-known example probably from Shandong province was used to brand horses. Others were used by local officials or army officers. During the HAN DYNASTY (206 B.C.E.–220 C.E.), there were seals of gold.

Early Seals

The seals were usually square with a pierced knob. Until the QIN unification of China, they were known as *xi,* but thereafter, this term was used only for official government seals, and others were known as *yin.* Throughout the WARRING STATES PERIOD (475–221 B.C.E.), seals were given to officials to reflect their status. They were normally worn at the waist and indicated the rank of the owner. They could also easily be removed. The Warring States had their own distinctive form of seals, which usually bore the name of the office held by the owner and the place where he undertook his duties. One seal of the state of YAN, for example, mentions an official in charge of a market at Danyou. Some of the state of QI seals are distinctive for their large size. A Zhou seal was evidently used for branding horses. Seals were also used to stamp manufacturers' or owners' marks on fabric: Burial 44 at Zuojiatang, a tomb of the CHU state, bore the imprint of a red seal mark. A looted grave found at Majiaxiang in Sichuan province, dating to the Warring States period, yielded a seal that probably belonged to the dead individual interred there. It has on the reverse animal face (*TAOTIE*) mask designs, while the surface was inscribed with emblems of the undeciphered Ba-Shu script.

Later Seals

With the expansion of the empire under the Han dynasty, emperors gave seals to client rulers to confirm them in office. These hold a particular attraction, because the form of the knob seems to reflect local traditions or interests. Thus a gold seal described in the *Records of the Grand Historian* (SHIJI) as being conferred on the king of Dian in 109 B.C.E. had a knob in the form of a snake. The snake was a symbol of prosperity among this tribe in Yunnan province far to the south, and the seal text reads, "Seal of the King of Dian." It was found in a royal grave at the necropolis of SHIZHAISHAN during the excavations there. Nine seals were found in the tomb of the second king of Yue (r. 137–122 B.C.E.), all placed close to his body, which had been interred in a jade suit. The largest

is inscribed, "Administrative seal of the Emperor Wen," and the handle is in the form of a coiled dragon. This seal is the largest of its type found, measuring 3.1 centimeters (1.2 in.) square. A seal in bronze from Yushigeti in remote western Xinjiang had a knob in form of a sheep. The local tribes people were sheep pastoralists, and their ruler was given the official title *gui yi* to confirm his official status. In 1979 a bronze seal was found at Sunjiazhai in Qinhai province. It conferred the right to rule there on the chief of the Xiongnu, and the knob in this case was in the form of a camel. The *History of the Later Han Dynasty* (HOU HANSHU), compiled in 445 C.E., recorded the gift of a gold seal and ribbon to a delegation representing the ruler of Na, a small state in Japan, by the Han emperor GUANG WUDI in 57 C.E. In 1784, a golden seal was found at Fukuoka in Kyushu, inscribed, "The king of Na of Wa of Han." It measures 2.35 centimeters (0.94 in.) across, and its knob was in the form of a snake. This is quite probably the same seal recorded in the history.

The Han people themselves could own their own seals for closing documents or letters, and these often had an auspicious saying or the figure of a human, animal, or bird. A rare example of the use of sealings was found in the tombs of the marquis of Dai, his wife, and son, from MAWANGDUI. Dated to 168 B.C.E. in the case of the marquis and a few years later for his wife, these graves were found in a remarkably well-preserved condition. Tomb 1, for example, was covered by layers of charcoal and clay to exclude air and damp. Within lay bamboo cases containing a wide range of mortuary offerings, and these were sealed with the words "Steward of the house of the Marquis of Dai."

See also FUNAN; RIG-VEDA; SILK BURIAL OFFERINGS.

seismograph The world's earliest known seismograph was manufactured by Zhang Heng during the reign of the Chinese emperor SHUNDI in 132 C.E. It is a large cylindrical bronze vessel with a diameter of almost two meters (6.6 ft.). The center of the vessel contains a long, vertical bronze rod that could move laterally as a pendulum when the vessel was rocked or moved, as in an earthquake. The edges of the vessel had eight levers that would be depressed downward when touched by the central rod. On being touched and moved, the corresponding eight cast dragons on the exterior of the vessel would rotate with the mouth downward, thereby releasing a bronze ball held in the mouth. The bronze ball would then fall into the waiting mouth of a toad, positioned on the base of the seismograph under each dragon. It is said that this instrument was so delicate that it could record a tremor imperceptible to human senses and point to its direction.

Selagiri Hill Selagiri Hill is located near Kyauktaw, in the upper reaches of the Kaladan River in ARAKAN (Rakhine) province, western Myanmar (Burma). It is a location of the greatest sanctity, because according to legend the Buddha and some followers flew here from India. This led to the casting of the MAHAMUNI (Great Sage) image of the Buddha, said to be the only such representation cast in his likeness during his lifetime. After being revered at the Mahamuni shine at DHANYAWADI for more than a millennium, the image was moved to Mandalay in northern Myanmar in the late 18th century. There it continues to attract the deepest possible veneration and is so covered in gold that its original form cannot be discerned. Investigations on Selagiri Hill have identified a brick stupa, associated with a series of magnificent sandstone reliefs depicting events in the life of the Buddha. While clearly showing Indian inspiration, the local school of sculptors created some innovations. One shows the Buddha's enlightenment as he sits on a throne under a stylized *bodhi* tree, surrounded by a scalloped backdrop representing radiant light. The style of this and the other reliefs indicates an origin in the period when Vesali was the capital of this region in the sixth and seventh centuries C.E. A second sculpture, found complete and undamaged, shows the Buddha delivering his first sermon in the Varanasi (Benares) Deer Park. Again he sits on a throne, his feet resting on a stool. Two ascetics kneel beside him, and a deer lies in the foreground. A third example shows the Parinirvana, the death of the Buddha. He is seen lying under three trees, while mourners kneel beside him. A fine example of a BODHISATTVA was also found in this group, its presence indicating that MAHAYANA BUDDHISM had a strong hold in this region.

Seleucus I Nicator (356–281 B.C.E.) *Seleucus I Nicator was a prominent general of Alexander the Great.*

He was born in Macedonia and died in Thrace. He took part in Alexander's eastern campaigns, and after the death of ALEXANDER THE GREAT (356–323 B.C.E.) and the division of his empire, Seleucus took control of Babylon and Persia. In 305 B.C.E. he took the title of *basileus*, or king, and set in train a campaign to recover the ground lost in northwestern India. This campaign, however, failed in the face of opposition from CANDRAGUPTA MAURYA (r. c. 325–297 B.C.E.). He is renowned for having founded the Seleucid empire.

Shangcunling Shangcunling is a cemetery located in Henan province, China. It was in use for about 120 years until the defeat of the small state of Guo by the JIN in 655 B.C.E. Two hundred forty-three burials have been excavated there, and they have provided unusually clear evidence for the status differences within a senior line of the Guo lineage. Texts of the later WARRING STATES PERIOD (475–221 B.C.E.) stated that status distinctions were reflected in mortuary rituals by the presence or absence of tomb chambers and multiple wooden coffins. This cemetery also provides compelling evidence that even within related members of the same lineage, distinctions

were made in the number of *ding* tripod bronze vessels, the presence of bell sets, and the provision of chariots and horses. The excavations at Shangcunling illustrate the importance of large-scale excavations in cemeteries that concentrate on the total assemblage of burials, be they rich or poor. In this way, vital social information confirming what is known from textual records can be obtained through archaeological research.

Information is available on the cemetery's spatial layout. Small graves tended to cluster around two large and rich tombs, which probably contained the remains of the lineage heads of the time. The largest burial, Tomb 2009, included multiple sets of bronze *ding* tripods, bells, and ritual bronzes as well as a large assemblage of jade ornaments. Some jades were placed over the head and body. Large chariot and horse pits were associated with this burial, which held two coffins, one placed within the other. An inscription reveals that the dead person had been the head of a younger branch of the lineage. The inscription on the halberd from Tomb 2001, which also had sets of *ding* tripods, ritual vessels, and jades, states that the dead person was a senior member of a junior Guo lineage. Tomb 1052 is also a large and opulent interment. The text on the halberd states that it belonged to Yuan, the heir apparent to Guo. It has two wooden chambers and a coffin. Bells and bronze vessels were found in the northeastern corner of the tomb, while a chariot and its fitting lay in the northeast. Weapons had been placed east and west of the coffin. The prince had worn jade earrings, and other jade ornaments lay on his chest. Ten chariots and twenty horses lay in the associated pits. High-status burials also contained MINGQI, miniature bronze wine vessels of a form that had not been used since the ritual reforms of the preceding WESTERN ZHOU DYNASTY (1045–771 B.C.E.). Rare cast-iron artifacts, including a dagger with jade handle and TURQUOISE inlay on the blade, were found in silk-lined leather sheaths.

One grade of burials was associated with three *ding* tripods. Those without weapons are particularly interesting, because they contained the remains of high-status princesses from the state of Su, a polity that had marriage relations with Guo. Lower-ranked members were buried with one or two *ding*, but the majority of the tombs had only ceramic *mingqi* vessels and jades, and some had no grave goods at all.

See also EASTERN ZHOU DYNASTY.

Shangjun Shu The *Shangjun Shu* (*Book of the Lord Shang*) is a text that reflects the policy of SHANG YANG (d. 338 B.C.E.), the first minister of the state of QIN in China during the WARRING STATES PERIOD (475–221 B.C.E.). He advocated a totalitarian regime in which an autocratic king ruled through a rigorous and impartial legal system designed to strengthen agriculture and the military. This school of thought, known as LEGALISM, was generated in

an atmosphere of endemic and merciless warfare that resulted in the final triumph of the state of Qin. It was diametrically opposed to the philosophy of CONFUCIUS and MENCIUS and had its fulfillment in the burning of books and execution of scholars under the regime of QIN SHIHUANGDI (259–210 B.C.E.), the first emperor of China.

Shangqiu, Treaty of The Treaty of Shangqiu, signed in 546 B.C.E., is probably the earliest arms-limitation pact known. The Spring and Autumn period of China (c. 772–c. 481 B.C.E.) saw rapid political developments that transformed the earlier Western Zhou feudal system. In place of loyalty by the lords of feudal states to the Zhou king, there was a major move toward independence. At first rivalries were contained under the BA SYSTEM, whereby one state would be accorded a leadership role. This was first held by the state of ZHENG, then QI, and finally JIN. However by the sixth century B.C.E., lesser states had been increasingly absorbed by larger and more powerful ones, and four stood supreme: Qi in Shandong, QIN in the west, Jin in the center, and CHU in the Chang (Yangtze) Valley. The smaller surviving rulers were subjected to increasing threats to their security and warfare. The meeting at Shangqiu was designed to reach agreements between the big players and resulted in the limitation of the number of chariots that each could maintain and deploy. Four decades of relative peace ensured.

See also EASTERN ZHOU DYNASTY; WESTERN ZHOU DYNASTY.

Shang state Shang is the name given to the second historically documented state of China. Although Shang was a literate civilization, virtually no texts survived for modern analysis until the discovery of the ORACLE BONES. Most oracle-bone archives have been recovered through excavations. Many graves, from that of the meanest commoner to those of members of the royal family, have been opened, and Shang cities have been examined. Fieldwork has expanded beyond the Shang heartland in the central plains of the Huang (Yellow) River, and the extent of Shang influence has been recognized. Such work has also emphasized that the Shang were not alone in the formation of Chinese civilization. In Sichuan, for example, the separate and independent state of SHU has been identified as being a contemporary of late Shang society, with its capital at the city of SANXINGDUI.

The documentary and archaeological evidence for Shang reveals that it was a markedly stratified society, ruled by a royal clan in which the succession followed in the male line, either from father to son or from brother to brother. The ruling elite controlled widespread trade networks that carried necessary goods to the capital, including the vital turtle bones from the south, copper and tin from the mines, salt from coastal sources, and surplus agricultural products from the sustaining countryside.

Specialist manufacturing complexes were established for the casting of the large RITUAL BRONZE VESSELS and metal armaments. One of the features of late Shang military equipment, the chariot, would have demanded considerable expertise. Specialization was an important aspect of the Shang centers. There were outstanding ceramics, bone workshops, and the manufacture of a wide range of ornaments, weapons, and ritual objects from jade, TURQUOISE, shell, and ivory. Silk was being woven into fine fabrics.

The name Shang derives from that used for the first capital. Traditionally, the Shang state dates from 1766 B.C.E. and ended with its defeat at the hands of the Zhou at the BATTLE OF MUYE in 1045 B.C.E. However, the unusual field of archaeoastronomy has afforded a more precise date. A conjunction of five planets that occurred in 1576 B.C.E., described in later Zhou records, has pinpointed the year 1554 B.C.E. as that in which Cheng Tang, the founder of the Shang dynasty, began his reign. Until the late 19th century, knowledge of the Shang was confined to Chinese histories, particularly the *SHIJI* of SIMA QIAN. These texts listed the names of 30 Shang kings and 14 rulers who preceded the establishment of the dynasty back to its mythical origins. They also named seven capitals, the last Yin, ruled by 12 Shang kings. Knowledge of Shang was dramatically increased by the discovery of oracle bones in the 1890s and the inception of archaeological research in 1928 at Yin, also known as ANYANG.

ORACLE BONES

The oracle bones are flat bones, preferably turtle shells or cattle ribs and shoulder blades, that were used by the Shang rulers for divining the future. Cracks formed through the application of heat to pits cut in the underside of the bone were regarded as oracular predictions. They were accompanied by INSCRIPTIONS that described the issue under consideration and the result of the divination. Advice was sought on whether to attack a given enemy, to go hunting, and how to appease the ancestors and thereby relieve the emperor of some ailment. Others were concerned with the weather, with particular reference to the agricultural round. Rain in the growing season, for example, was regarded as vital to the interests of the state.

When an oracle bone was no longer used, it was placed into a pit. Some archive pits at Anyang contained thousands of specimens, and their texts have significantly increased knowledge and understanding of the Shang civilization. Kings formerly known only through much later histories, such as that of Sima Qian, appear in the oracle texts in a vital part of their royal role, communication with the ancestors and planning of their policies. Specific instances of warfare and the results of such conflicts are recorded in these texts. The only intact royal tomb at Anyang contained the remains of a royal consort, FU HAO, whose name is recorded in oracle bones.

EXCAVATIONS OF CAPITAL CITIES

Excavations at three of the capitals described in the historic records have revealed the layout of urban centers. ZHENGZHOU was occupied during the middle Shang period and was probably the capital known as Ao, founded by Zhong Ding, the sixth king whose name is known. Located in Henan province at the confluence of two rivers, Zhengzhou was surrounded by massive walls made of stamped earth. These survive in part to this day in the modern city. These walls enclose an area of 335 hectares (838 acres); the entire urban complex, including its satellite cemeteries, occupation areas, and specialist workshops, extended over an area of 25 square kilometers (10 sq. mi.). The northeastern quarter of the walled precinct contains extensive raised platforms, also of the HANGTU, or stamped-earth construction, thought to have been part of a palace area. This part of the city also contained some elite graves, with fine jade and bronze vessels as mortuary offerings, as well as some fragments of the oracle bones that denoted royal activity. The city as a whole contained other such platforms, indicating a dense population, although the presence of a modern city makes extensive excavation difficult.

The extramural area included a bronze workshop. The clay-mold fragments indicate the local casting of vessels, daggers, knives, and arrowheads. Some of the bronzes attained monumental proportions. One cache found outside the city walls contained 13 fine bronze ritual vessels, including a *ting* that stood one meter (3.3 ft.) high and weighed 86.4 kilograms (190 lbs.). Large kilns were associated with the ceramic workshops at Zhengzhou, and bone workers produced ornaments and weapons.

In late 1999, a walled Shang city was found at Huanbei. The central part of the walled area included a very large palace and temple complex, covering an area of 10 hectares (25 acres). The stamped-earth foundations of more than 25 individual buildings were identified through excavations in 2001, one of which covered 170 by 95 meters. Roads have also been found, one still bearing the rut marks of wheeled vehicles. Liu Zhongfu has suggested that the site might have been the capital known as Xiang, founded by He Tan Jia, the 12th king of the dynasty.

Anyang is the name given to the Shang capital that probably replaced Huanbei. It was the last capital and was ruled by 12 successive kings. Unlike for its predecessors, no central walled city has been found. The remains of this site, described by the occupants as Shang, occupy an extensive area north and south of the Huan River. Toward the end of its occupation, it covered at least 24 square kilometers (9.6 sq. mi.). It was discovered when scholars attempted to trace the source of the oracle bones that were being used for medicinal purposes in Beijing. Excavations, which began in 1928, uncovered the foundations for a series of large buildings raised on stamped-earth foundations south of a bend in the Huan River. These form the royal core of Anyang and cluster in three groups. The northern group, at least 15 buildings, is thought to be the earliest. The expansion of this royal area then saw the construction of the 21 buildings of the central group, and, finally, the southern group completed the complex. The buildings of the last group were associated with many human and animal sacrificial burials. As it grew, so the palace area enclosed earlier royal tombs, including that of Fu Hao, a principal consort to King Wu Ding. The complex included the palace precinct, ancestral temples, and repositories for the oracle-bone records. Some pits also held complete chariots and the skeletons of the horses and charioteers.

Royal Tombs

In 1933, during the eighth season of research there, the team was informed of the discovery on the northern bank of the Huan River of some exceptionally large bronze vessels. Further inquiries led them to a subterranean tomb of massive size. Subsequently, an area of 8,000 square meters (3.2 sq. mi.) was opened, and four tomb chambers up to 13 meters (43 ft.) deep were excavated. Although long since looted, the disturbed fill of the graves still contained fine jades and some large bronze ritual vessels. Moreover, more than 400 smaller burials of sacrificial victims interred as part of the royal mortuary rituals were uncovered. In 1935 nearly 10,000 square meters was excavated, and three further royal graves were cleared together with 800 smaller burials.

The seven royal graves were dominated by a deep central pit that had contained the wooden tomb chamber. It was reached by four ramps that entered from each side. In the case of Burial HPKM 1004, the central pit reached a depth of 12.2 meters below the ground surface and measured 15.9 by 10.8 meters at the base. The southern and longest entrance corridor was 31.4 meters long. The base of the pit contained a wooden chamber entered from the south. The space between the tomb and the sides of the pit was filled with pounded earth. Lengthy rituals would have accompanied the interment of the body, including the sacrifice of those found in the smaller graves in the vicinity.

A small part of another grave had escaped looting, and the finds revealed the wealth of the Shang kings. Two huge bronze cauldrons were found in the central pit, at a level just two meters above the top of the wooden burial chamber. These overlay a deposit of bronze weapons, including 360 spearheads and 141 helmets. Jade figures of animals, including turtles, frogs, and monsters, were found in the looters' pits.

One of the most intriguing aspects of this royal necropolis is that the number of shaft graves matches the number of kings named in the Anyang oracle bones. The oracle bones state that humans and animals were sacrificed to the dead royal ancestors. Excavations have confirmed this. Extensive rows of graves in the vicinity of the royal tombs have been grouped into clusters, each representing a sacrificial event. Some contain the remains of complete human skeletons, others only skulls, and still others individuals who had been beheaded. Most were young men, but some victims were female. Children were found in a position suggesting that they had been bound and immolated while still alive. Animals were also slaughtered to appease the ancestors. Some pits contain multiple burials of horses; others include the remains of monkeys. The two largest pits, however, contain the skeletons of elephants, along with their keeper.

According to the oracle bones, the ruling elite of the Shang state were members of the Wang Zi, the royal segment of the Zi clan. Other clans of less exalted status made up the rest of Shang society, and some of them were encouraged to open new land to cultivation and establish town settlements. PANLONGCHENG is just such a foundation.

Tomb of Fu Hao

The location of the graves of their queens is not known. However, the discovery of intact Burial M5 in 1976, which housed the remains of FU HAO, has enlarged the understanding of the wealth of royal women's graves and their possible location at Anyang. This tomb, which belonged to a consort of King Wu Ding, contained considerable wealth, expressed in bronzes and jades of outstanding quality. The base of the pit was lined with wood to form a chamber, in which lay nested and lacquered wooden coffins. Sixteen individuals, a number that included men, WOMEN, and children, accompanied the primary burial. Some burials were placed in wall niches on each side of the tomb; others rested within the grave fill, which was composed of layers of stamped earth.

This tomb is most renowned for the wealth of the mortuary offerings for the dead person. Among them are 468 bronzes, including the most significant group of ritual wine and food vessels known from Shang contexts. Some of these were inscribed with the name of Fu Hao, thereby for the only time in the history of Shang studies illuminating the burial of a person specifically named in the oracle bones. The grave also contained about 7,000 cowry shells, 755 items of jade, hundreds of bone ornaments, and three rare ivory cups decorated with TURQUOISE inlay. The two largest bronze vessels weighed 120 kilograms (264 lbs.) each. Several other cemeteries at Anyang contained the graves of the population at large. These seem to have been structured along lineage lines, as the senior members had the largest and best furnished chambers.

Workshops

As at Zhengzhou, greater Anyang incorporated a series of specialist workshops. One of these at Miaopu, dedicated to the casting of ritual bronze vessels, covered one hectare (2.5 acres). Another bronze workshop specialized in casting tools and weapons. Bronze weapons were clearly a vital element in the maintenance of the Shang dynasty. They include dagger axes, spearheads, and arrowheads.

Shields were strengthened with bronze, and this metal was used in the components for chariots. There were also ceramic centers, bone workshops, and an area dedicated to making stone artifacts. One pit, for example, contained as many as 1,000 sickles, some of which were incomplete. Bone workshops produced a wide variety of items, including hairpins, awls, and arrowheads.

PROVINCIAL CITIES

The oracle bones often mention centers beyond the capital but under Shang control, and one example of such a site at Panlongcheng, in the middle Chang (Yangtze) Valley, has been examined. It had been occupied between about 1500 and 1200 B.C.E. As was Zhengzhou to the north, it was surrounded by stamped-earth walls, and much evidence of industrial activity was located beyond this central area. It is, however, much smaller, the walls enclosing an area of only 7.5 hectares (18.75 acres). The local ruler lived in a palace raised on a stamped-earth platform in the city, but again the extramural area included a bronze-casting area, complete with the remains of copper slag and broken crucible fragments. Many of the bronzes were placed in the cemetery that was evidently restricted to the elite members of the community; one such grave contained 63 bronzes, including ritual vessels, weapons, tools, many items of jade, and the skeletons of three sacrificial victims. There are two other cemeteries at this site, one containing moderately wealthy individuals, and the other poor graves with only a pottery vessel as a mortuary offering.

TAIXICUN is a second major provincial Shang site, located in Hebei province. It covered at least 10 hectares (25 acres), within which excavations have revealed houses of between one and three rooms constructed of stamped earth and unfired clay BRICK, in addition to the foundations of a much larger house. Sacrificial remains of humans and animals associated with the large residence suggest that it was occupied by an elite member of the community. The cemetery contains a small number of well-endowed, graves including fine bronze vessels, weapons, jades, gold ornaments, and oracle bones. One burial incorporated a ledge to retain sacrificed bodies. Other graves, however, were markedly poorer and contained only ceramic vessels and the occasional bronze. Pottery shards include scratched written graphs, and a particularly interesting find, an ax, was made from meteoric rather than smelted iron. Far to the north, a grave has been found at Pinggu in Beijing, where a second meteoric iron ax has been found together with Shang ritual bronze vessels. It is intriguing to note the presence of gold ornaments more typical of the LOWER XIAJIADIAN CULTURE than that of metropolitan Shang.

SUFUTUN is a further important site dated to the period of the Shang dynasty. It is located to the east of Anyang, in Shandong province. Four elite graves were excavated, and the wealth of mortuary offerings indicates the presence of a royal center. One of the four graves followed the layout well known at the Shang capital, having a central rectangular tomb chamber linked with a large main entrance ramp and three entrance passageways. The junction of the ramp and the tomb chamber was choked with the remains of human sacrificial victims, among which 47 individuals were counted. There were also five dog skeletons. More than 4,000 cowry shells were recovered, symbolizing wealth and fertility. The grave pit was surrounded by a podium in which three ancillary burials were placed. The northern wall of the podium contained two further pits for large ceremonial bronze axes. This grave in all probability was that of a regional king of the state of Bogu, which is mentioned in the oracle bones as a Shang ally.

RAW MATERIALS

The wide reach of the Shang kings involved not only dependent settlements, but also the control of sources of vital raw materials. Oracle-bone texts make it clear that the success of the millet and rice harvests was of paramount importance in providing the surpluses necessary to sustain the court, and the symbols used in the writing system include hoes, spades, and probably a plow. The king owned agricultural estates and sent royal labor gangs to open new land in his name. Officials were given instructions to develop new estates. The Shang landscape, however, appears to have been dotted with villages associated with millet fields. Cultivation of this crop was probably afflicted by natural pests and inclement weather conditions, if the oracle divinations are any guide. Domestic stock was also important, and the bone workshops of Anyang processed the remains of cattle, sheep, pigs, dogs, and horses. Some of the cattle shoulder blades and ribs were further used in divination. One oracle text described the provision of 50 pairs of ox scapulae for this purpose.

Supplies of copper and tin were of major strategic importance for providing the ritual vessels that were used in feasts to propitiate ancestors, as well as casting weapons and tools. Jade was an essential raw material for satisfying the elite; hundreds of jades were found in the tomb of Fu Hao. The nearest known source to Anyang was nearly 400 kilometers away. Cowry shells were a currency unit, and some of these had to be from warm tropical seas thousands of kilometers to the south. Turtle shells for use in divinations also had to be transported from the Chang Valley or farther south still. Hence the control of sources or, failing that, the trade routes was necessary to maintain these important links in the trade network.

DEITIES

In the royal capital, much energy was expended in the worship of a range of deities. Temples formed a major portion of the central precinct of Anyang. The gods fall into a number of categories beginning with DI, the high god, and those associated with natural forces, such as the sun, rain, thunder, and wind. Oracle-bone texts confirm di's control over nature. Thus, in one example, it was divined "di, in the fourth Moon, will order rain." He might also influence military matters by ordering war on an enemy state. Ultimately, the Zhou described how it was the di who enjoined them to attack and destroy the Shang themselves.

However, at Anyang after the reign of Wu Ding, di was less frequently cited as responsible for controlling the elements, while the ancestors increasingly assumed this role. The ancestors were a major group of divinities. Preference was given to the principal former kings in direct line of descent and their consorts who were mothers of a king. Their individual spirit tablets were located in temples where the ritual obligations were fulfilled. Wine was consumed, meat cooked, and humans and animals sacrificed. These were undertaken to seek the ancestors' benign influence in the provision of, for example, rain, success in war, safe deliverance of sons, and good harvests. These rituals were attended by senior members of the royal clan and were accompanied by feasting. A graph describes a ritual shows two men facing a large vessel. Again, the casting of huge wine and food containers of bronze was a key element in the Shang bronze repertoire.

The *Shiji* contains a graphic account of the end of the Shang dynasty. The last king was dissolute and licentious. He tortured his enemies, and leading ministers defected. King Wu of Zhou marshaled his forces to attack Shang and defeated them at the BATTLE OF MUYE in about 1045 C.E. The defeated king "put on his jade suit and jumped into a fire." A thousand years later, we learn that jade suits were worn by dead members of the royal family to ensure immortality. However, the last Shang ruler was decapitated by the Zhou king, who was then accorded the MANDATE OF HEAVEN.

Further reading: Chang, K.-C. *The Shang Civilization.* New Haven, Conn.: Yale University Press, 1980; Keightley, D. N. *Sources of Shang History: The Oracle Bones of Bronze Age China.* Berkeley: University of California Press, 1978; Loewe, M., and E. L. Shaugnessy, eds. *The Cambridge History of Ancient China.* Cambridge: Cambridge University Press, 1999.

Shang Yang (fourth century B.C.E.) *Shang Yang was one of the foremost statesmen of the* WARRING STATES *Period (475–221 B.C.E.) in China.*
SIMA QIAN in his great history of China, the *SHIJI,* devoted a biographical chapter to him but clearly had no sympathy for his policies and reviled his achievements. Shang Yang adopted a ruthless and totalitarian approach both to local administration and to war, when he took the field. Shang Yang was born in the small state of WEI and rose to

prominence in the royal household. When the leading minister fell ill, this minister advised the king to appoint Shang Yang his successor. The minister had recognized the qualities of Shang Yang, because he warned the king that if he did not appoint Shang Yang, he should have him killed to prevent him from crossing the border and serving another state. The advice went unheeded on both counts, and soon thereafter Shang Yang heard that the duke Xiao of QIN (r. 361–338 B.C.E.) was actively seeking men of talent to join his administration. He was presented to the duke on three occasions, but without being offered an appointment. On the fourth interview, the duke was taken by Shang Yang's advice on strengthening his administration and securing fame in his own lifetime. Shang Yang was appointed and set in train a series of reforms that were to change the very nature of the state and equip Qin with the social and physical means of dominating its rivals.

LEGAL REFORMS

The *Shiji* describes how Shang Yang first turned his attention to the legal system. To control the rural population, he created laws providing for the division of the population into groups of five to 10 households. Every member was required to watch and report on others. Punishment for those who failed to report a criminal was draconian: to be cut in half at the waist. But there were rewards for those who reported criminal activity. This marshaling of the populace was a prelude to a system of taxation that fostered production: If two adult men lived in the same household, their military tax would be doubled. This measure was designed to ensure that all men were encouraged to undertake agricultural production. Likewise, the families who worked hard to grow large quantities of grain or produce silk and cloth were exempt from the need to work for the state. The indolent would be conscripted as slaves and forced to work. At first, the laws were highly criticized, but in due course the absence of banditry and the clear path to rewards and honor for those who worked or achieved in battle led to widespread approval. Such rewards were carefully graded for those who fought in the Qin army. Promotion turned on battlefield success, measured in the number of enemy heads severed. The higher the rank, the greater the rewards, including land grants and property.

ADMINISTRATION

Shang Yang had the land of Qin divided by pathways into uniform blocks that could be cultivated by a single household and then imposed an extra poll tax on the families with more than one adult man living together. This encouraged the splitting of households and the departing male's to move to a new block of land to farm. Detailed population registers were maintained, and the establishment of a territorial subdivision known as a *xian* was instituted. It was the duty of the *xian* administrator to maintain the register and collect the poll or head tax. There were 41 such *xian* in the state of Qin, and each formed the basis for recruiting men for the army, all being registered from the age of 15. At the same time, Shang Yang discouraged merchants by sending them on extended garrison duties, forbidding them to wear silk clothes, and saddling them with higher taxes. A system of graded titles, which had benefits for those who showed valor and success in battle, was instituted. They were given land and the use of slave labor, often involving prisoners of war. The height of a person's burial mound and the number of trees planted on it were determined by rank.

MILITARY ACTION

Shang Yang was not only a political but also a military leader. He led victorious Qin forces against Wei at the Battle of Maling in 341 B.C.E. The following year, he showed a distinct Machiavellian touch when he persuaded the duke Xiao that the state of Wei should be the prime target for a military campaign because of its proximity and potential danger. The duke agreed and sent Shang Yang with an army to attack Wei. Shang Yang persuaded Ang, the Wei commander, to parley a truce. Having agreed to a covenant of peace, he then had his guards capture Ang and launched a successful onslaught against the Wei army. This led to their retreat, the abandonment of Anyi, and the ceding of land.

CAPITAL CITY

The establishment of a totalitarian state under the guiding hand of Shang Yang is also seen in the move to a new capital at Xianyang. This strategic location along the bank of the Wei River provided an opportunity for an entirely new approach to the tradition of first building an ancestral temple. He set in train the construction instead of the Jique Palace. This building program began with two ceremonial halls that were described by Sima Qian as Jique, or the gate towers on which official notices were posted. The palace itself was raised on three levels supported by an earth core, its size and height clearly projecting the power of the ruler. Its halls were decorated with painted scenes including four-horse chariots and elegant WOMEN.

SHANG YANG'S END

In 338 B.C.E., Duke Xiao died, to be succeeded by King Hui Wen. Shang Yang's fall from grace and death were graphically described by Sima Qian. First, he was accused of fomenting a rebellion, and hearing that troops had been dispatched to arrest him, he fled and sought shelter in an inn. There the inn owner reminded him that it was necessary for him to register his name under the laws of Shang Yang himself. He then went to the state of Wei, where the local administration, recalling his treachery, returned him to Qin. He then made his way to his own manor and there met his end when Qin troops arrived. King Hui ordered that he be torn to pieces by chariots and his entire household exterminated. His influence, memory, and writings, however, lived on. He was often quoted by Han historians, and his legal reforms laid the foundations for the rise to power of Qin and the establishment of a single Chinese state under the first emperor.

Shan-shan Shan-shan is the name of a state that was founded in the first century B.C.E. in the southern and eastern margins of the TARIM BASIN in western China. At its greatest extent, it encompassed the city of NIYA far to the west and progressing eastward the areas and cities of ENDERE, QIEMO (Cherchen), CHARKLIK, MIRAN, and LOU-LAN. The last site lies at the junction of the Kuruk Dar'ya and Lop-nor Lake, a highly strategic location on the SILK ROAD where the traveler could take either the northern or the southern route around the Taklamakan Desert. The latter would in theory involve the transit of the state of Shan-shan. This region was unsettled and continuously subject to warlike incursions of the XIONGNU.

The history of the Shan-shan kingdom was closely tied with that of China. During periods of central power in China, Shan-shan remained a client state, but when China was weak, as it was during the late second and early third centuries C.E., Shan-shan would have been virtually free of foreign domination. The documents recovered from Shan-shan sites, particularly those from Niya, provide much information on this state between about 230 and 335 C.E. The wealth of Shan-shan and its political vicissitudes were intimately related to the traffic of goods along the Silk Road. In Shan-shan the establishment of BUDDHISM can be appreciated through the many religious foundations that have been identified and investigated. The site of Miran is best known for the wall paintings collected and recorded by SIR AUREL STEIN. These include scenes of the Buddha and JAKATA TALES, sometimes with Western-looking figures. There can be no doubt that the third century was a period of strong Western influence in the kingdom of Shan-shan.

ORIGIN OF NAME

The name Shan-shan originated in 77 B.C.E. after conflict between the Han Chinese, who kept a close watch on this area, and the Xiongnu. Both the SHIJI (*Records of the Grand Historian*) and the *Han Shu* (*History of the Former Han*) describe how the Han official Zhang Qian visited this area and took home accounts of the walled cities there. He described the state of Lou-lan as having 1,570 households with 14,100 people, located 1,600 *li* from the Jade Gate, the official western border of the Han empire at that juncture. It was a region, he said, of sandy and salty soil and few agricultural fields but lay on the Han communication route westward along the vital Silk Road. In 77 B.C.E. a Han envoy visited the court of the king,

who had been installed as a puppet ruler by the Xiongnu. The *Hanshu* describes how everyone enjoyed a drunken dinner party and then the Chinese cut off the king's head and mounted it on the northern gate of the city.

The rebels replaced him with a nominee of their own, one Weitu Qi. This member of the local princely line had been living as a hostage in China, and he was given an official SEAL of office. However, the sons of his murdered predecessor were still at large, and the new king felt decidedly vulnerable to assassination. He therefore asked for and secured the establishment of a Han military garrison to protect him—thus developed a close paternal relationship between the Han and their client ruler, whose kingdom was now renamed Shan-shan. The location of the capital of Lou-lan before the name was changed is controversial. If the documentary records are accurate in detail, however, the site known as Lou-lan E is the most likely candidate, for it is the only one known with a northern gate. Air photographs reveal to this day the rectangular outline of a walled city in the sandy wastes, a city with no evidence for BUDDHISM and therefore of the appropriate time span. Nor is the capital of Shan-shan known; some think that it was Miran, but Stein preferred Charklik.

WRITTEN EVIDENCE

It is recorded that in 222 the ruler of Shan-shan sent tribute to the Chinese court, and during the reign of the Western JIN emperor WUDI (265–289 C.E.), a period of relative stability in China, the western routes were cleared. A remarkable collection of surviving documents on wooden slips, cloth, and paper provides insight into the state of the kingdom during the later third century. Most come from Lou-lan, others from NIYA. The vast majority date to the Western Jin dynasty, with a concentration in the years 266–270 C.E. The documents were issued by local officials. We learn of the presence of Chinese military commanders and those who supervised agriculture. The son of the king was sent as a hostage to the Western Jin court in 283 C.E. While most of the Lou-lan documents were written in Chinese, most of those from farther west at Niya and Endere appear in the KHAROSHTHI script. Kharoshthi documents on silk have also been found at Miran.

The documents were written in Niya or Krorän PRAKRIT, using the Kharoshthi script. It is possible that this resulted from influence by the KUSHANS, a notion supported by the long and elaborate titles used by the kings of Shan-shan in their documents. These include royal orders, messages, and issues of Buddhist administration. Since they include place names, it is possible to trace references to specific locations and learn the original names of certain centers: Krorän refers to Lou-lan, and Calmadana is now called Qiemo (Cherchen). Endere was then known as Saca, and Niya was Cadota. HOTAN's former name, Khotamna, is little changed. Some of the wooden documents have survived complete with their original sealings, and the corpus as a whole has made it possible to reconstruct with some degree of accuracy the names of the kings of Shan-shan and their approximate reign dates.

The sequence began with Tomgraka, followed by Tajaka, Pepiya, Amgvaka, Mahiri, Vasmana, and finally Sulica. The last name was recovered only in 1981, when a document for divorce bearing his name was found at Niya. Amgvaka probably reigned between 255/8 and 293/6 C.E., Mahiri from 292/5 to 320/3 C.E., and Vasmana from 321/324, but the duration of the latter's rule is not known. Their royal titles began as maharaja (great king), but this was to change to *maharaya*. During the reign of Amgvaka, his documents were also sealed with the title "The Chinese high commissioner for Shan-shan," which might well indicate a degree of Chinese influence in administration. The kingdom was a major center for Buddhism, and during his journey west in 399 C.E. the Chinese monk FAXIAN noted that the then ruler was a Buddhist, and the state included several thousand monks. In 442–445, Shan-shan was attacked by Chinese armies, and it succumbed to the northern Wei in 445. This was not the final foreign domination of Shan-shan. In due course, the HEPHTHALITE HUNS and in the sixth century the Turks controlled this region. Then the Chinese under the Tang returned in the mid-seventh century and permitted the local rulers a considerable degree of autonomy until 751 C.E., when the Tang were defeated by the Arabs.

Administration

The Kharoshthi documents are a key source for understanding the administration of this state in the third and fourth centuries C.E. The state was divided into districts known as *rajas*, each under the control of a *rajadaraja*, or royally appointed governor. One surviving text describes how the *rajadaraja* was required to detain the family of the leader of an embassy to Hotan until his return to Shan-shan. These provinces were further divided into a region known as a *nagara* or *avana*. Then there was a further division into *satas*, supposedly comprising about 100 households. The king was assisted in his rule by a number of court officials. There was an *ogu*, who seems to have been a highly ranked administrator. The legal system was under the control of the *kitsaitsa* and the *gusura*. Local affairs were run by a lesser official known as a *cojbho*. Taxation was paid at least in part in kind and was overseen by the *sothamga*. The assessment was based on the production of each *sata* and was assessed by *sothamga*s. The texts mention taxation levied on the production of butter, wine, sheep, carpets, cereal crops, and camels, a list that well describes the agricultural wealth of the oases and the industries that flourished. To maintain the records, there were scribes (*divira*), and messengers (*lekhaharaga*) and *dutiyae*. The title of *cojbho* and their duties are often found in the surviving documents. They helped to administer land ownership disputes, for example, and to fulfill royal decrees.

Much land was owned by the king, and high members of the nobility owned estates. It was possible for people to own and dispose of or buy land. The many Buddhist monasteries had their own landholdings. Some documents set out contracts for the purchase of slaves, people who might well have been taken in the many conflicts. Other texts record marriage and divorce. Although many of these documents have been described as administrative ephemera, they provide a virtually unparalleled glimpse of the inner workings of a state.

The wealth of detail contained in the Kharoshthi documents provides a remarkably rich picture of the administration of the state. On one occasion, the king ordered the dispatch of 10 camels to Calmadana, even mentioning the name of the camel driver, Lyipeya. Another text describes how the king bought a woman for 41 rolls of silk. The purpose of the sealed wedge-tablet was to order an official to inquire whether she was genuinely purchased. If this inquiry did not produce a clear conclusion, the matter was to be referred to the royal court.

EVIDENCE OF TRADE

Many examples of Chinese silks have been recovered from the graves in the kingdom, while the Chinese received jade from the Hotan source, Persian TURQUOISE, as well as Western LAPIS LAZULI, coral, pearls, glassware, and artifacts in gold and silver. Buddhist monks moved between the oases, and it was by this means that Buddhism penetrated beyond the TARIM BASIN and into China. Its spread east can be dated to at least the second century C.E., when Hotan was renowned as an early and vigorous center of Buddhism.

EVIDENCE OF BUDDHISM

The Buddhist establishments are found at the cities in the area of Lou-lan, Niya, Qiemo, Endere, and, particularly, Miran. The main center, which seems to have controlled other monasteries, was located at Lou-lan A. This site was discovered in 1901 by Sven Hedin. His recovery of a document in Kharoshthi sparked much interest, and this walled city was examined by Sir Aurel Stein five years later. The walls form a near square, each side measuring about 300 meters (990 ft.). Stein mapped a series of buildings within, which included a large stupa in the northeastern part of the site occupying a dominant elevated position. This monument was raised on a series of three square platforms of diminishing size, capped by the mound of the stupa proper. Even today, it rises to a height of 10 meters (33 ft.). Svedin also recovered a remarkable panel of wood, a meter long, which may have been a structural lintel. Only under the dry conditions of the Tarim could wood survive in such good condition; it was carved into the form of four successive niches, each containing an image of the Buddha.

The site of Miran was discovered fortuitously by Stein in 1906. It lies southwest of Lou-lan and northeast of Charklik amid an arid and desolate part of the Tarim Basin. Stein returned the following year to excavate and map the site, which lies between two dried-out river beds. He found traces of old canals and Buddhist monuments in sun-dried brick in a northern and a southern group. Most of these sites were small stupa shrines, but there were also walls of what was probably a monastery. The stupa forms in themselves are important in showing clear influence from the West.

Paintings of Miran

Stein had great difficulty at the time photographing the extraordinary paintings of Miran and removed some that are now to be found in the National Museum of India. When he returned to Miran in 1921 to photograph them again, they had been destroyed. The style of the paintings indicates a date in the third century C.E., the heyday of the Shan-shan kingdom. The paintings on the plastered walls of the shrines depict a wide range of scenes. Perhaps the most interesting from a social point of view is a prince leaving his palace on horseback as his wife and two children look down from a window. He is wearing a diadem, and the wall behind him is richly decorated. This has been identified as a scene from a Buddhist *jataka* story. A second example from Miran Structure V shows a young man of distinctly Western appearance, with a second person wearing a tall Phrygian-style peaked cap.

Semicircular panels contain images of clean-shaven men with short hair and wearing simple round-necked tunics. They sprout wings from their shoulders. Above, a young man is seen fighting a winged griffin. There is a painting from Structure III of a decidedly Western-looking Buddha followed by a group of six disciples. The Buddha has short hair and a mustache. The same structure was also decorated with a painting of two seated male figures who again suggest a court scene: One is splendidly dressed in a flowing robe, and another wears an elaborate hat identical to that seen on the prince leaving his palace. The name of at least one of the artists is given in an inscription in Kharoshthi script that reads, "This fresco is the work of Tita, who has received 3000 *bhamakas* for it." The name Tita, as Stein noted, matches Titus, which was popular in the Eastern Roman Empire. A second inscription describes one of the people in the *jataka* illustration as Isidata, the son of Bujhami.

Marylin Rhie has summarized the style and relations of these paintings both East and West. She finds parallels as far afield as a portrait of the Roman emperor Septimius Severus from Egypt and the art of Palmyra, Airtam, and TOPRAK KALA. Details of the armor on some paintings are closely matched in Gandharan images.

Sculptures

The monastery at Miran examined by Stein, known as Structure II, incorporated a row of huge seated Buddha statues, each measuring about two meters (6.6 ft.) across the knees. They were not complete, but some Buddha heads are of the same style and could have been from this row. Stylistically, the statues are later than the paintings and confirm that Buddhism flourished in Shan-shan into the fifth century C.E. as mentioned in historic records of visits by the monks Faxian and Dharmaksema.

Shaogao The *Shaogao*, "Shao announcement," is a surviving document that describes the foundation of a new city after the Chinese Zhou dynasty replaced the last king of the SHANG STATE after the BATTLE OF MUYE in 1045 B.C.E. It is an important source for the notion of the MANDATE OF HEAVEN as the legitimizing force underlying Chinese dynastic rule. In it, the duke Zhou, uncle of the young king, Cheng, describes the foundation of a new capital. It was first necessary to consult the oracles and make sacrifices. The duke then expounded on the need for the king to be virtuous and prudent in his rule, always ensuring prosperity and harmony with his subjects. He described how the Xia and Shang rulers had at first adhered to such moral precepts, but when later kings failed to observe proper decorum and became corrupt and depraved, the mandate was withdrawn.

See also XIA DYNASTY.

Shichishito The Shichishito is an iron sword with gold inlay that bears an INSCRIPTION. It has been stored for centuries in the Isonokami shrine, located in the Nara Basin of western Honshu Island, Japan. The inscription states that it was forged in 369 .C.E. in the Korean kingdom of PAEKCHE and presented to the king of the YAMATO kingdom. The sword is 75 centimeters (2.5 ft.) long. A passage in the NIHONGI historical text of the early eighth century C.E. described the presentation of such a sword to the Yamato king and the prediction by the Koreans that good relations between the two kingdoms would ensue.

Shiji The *Shiji* (*Records of the Grand Historian*) was the outstanding history of the Chinese people written by SIMA QIAN (c. 145–90 B.C.E.) and completed in about 100 B.C.E. Sima Qian was a scholar member of the court of the Han emperor WUDI. He succeeded his father, SIMA TAN, to the post of grand historian in 108 B.C.E. and, obeying his father's dying wish, continued to write the history. The work might never have been completed. Sima Qian offended the emperor by supporting a disgraced general and was condemned to suffer castration. As a matter of honor, the punishment required suicide. Sima Qian, however, determined to suffer the disgrace to complete his work. In his own words: "I submitted to the extreme penalty without rancor. When I have truly finished the work, I will deposit it in the Famous Mountain archives. If it may be handed down to men who will appreciate it, and penetrate to the villages and great cities, then though I shall suffer a thousand mutilations, what regret would I have?" Sima Qian's predictions have been amply borne out by history, for the *Shiji* not only is a unique source of historic information on Chinese history, but it also provided a precedent for all subsequent dynastic histories for two millennia. Moreover, it called on written sources that have subsequently been lost.

The volumes set out to describe the history of China from the earliest times down to the first reigns of the HAN DYNASTY (206 B.C.E.–220 C.E.). This was not an easy task, given the plethora of states that came and went, particularly during the Zhou dynasty, and the disparate and often conflicting sources. However, Sima Qian triumphed through a dedicated resolve to weave a consistent historic pattern. His description of the WARRING STATES PERIOD (475–221 B.C.E.) and the rise of the autocratic QIN dynasty remains a remarkable fount of information, while his text also incorporates biographies of many of the key historic figures over many centuries of Chinese history.

Under the Qin and Han dynasties, China embarked on an extraordinary imperial expansion that saw much land and many peoples incorporated into the empire. To the south Lingnan and northern Vietnam were conquered, and to the northeast the Han occupied Korea. These new lands were divided into provinces, or commanderies. Sima Qian took a considerable interest in the conquered peoples and incorporated descriptive chapters in his history.

Sima Qian provided his own comments on the virtues and vices of previous rulers, reserving particular venom for the first emperor, QIN SHIHUANGDI, whose military genius in concluding the Warring States period in favor of the state of Qin was not matched by the subsequent administrative and legal reforms that cemented repressive autocratic measures. In this context, it is paradoxical that he should suffer such indignity at the hands of a ruler who reintroduced Confucian ideals to the government of the Han empire.

See also CONFUCIUS.

Further reading: Nienhauser, W. H., ed. *The Grand Scribe's Records.* Vol. 1, *The Basic Annals of Pre-Han China,* by Ssu-ma Ch'ien. Bloomington and Indianapolis: Indiana University Press, 1994.

Shijia　Shijia is a city site on the right bank of the Huang (Yellow) River in Shandong province, central China. It was first occupied during the period of the late LONGSHAN CULTURE (2500–1800 B.C.E.), when a wall and moat enclosed an area of a little less than five hectares (12.5 acres). During the ensuing XIA DYNASTY (2100–1766 B.C.E.), the inhabitants used ORACLE BONES; the middle Shang period there witnessed early INSCRIPTIONS on cast bronzes.

Shijiahe　Shijiahe is a very large urban site located on the left bank of the Han River above its confluence with the Chang (Yangtze). It belongs to the central Chinese Qujialing (3300–2500 B.C.E.) and Shijiahe cultures (2500–2000 B.C.E.). This makes the site approximately the contemporary of similar early urban sites of the LONGSHAN CULTURE in the central plains and Shandong. The stamped-earth defensive walls form a square, in which lie residences, burials, and a jade workshop. A piece of bronze has also been found. For decades, the central plains to the north have been given precedence in terms of state formation in China. Shijiahe is one of several sites in the middle Chang Valley that reveal that similar trends to complexity also occurred in central China.

Shilla　The state of Shilla was one of the THREE KINGDOMS of Korea and was located in the southeastern part of the peninsula. It overcame its rivals KAYA, KOGURYO, and PAEKCHE during the sixth and seventh centuries, to rule Korea unchallenged. The unification of Korea was associated with deep-seated changes in government, centered on the growing authority of the king. The high aristocracy were given villages as rewards for meritorious service, and they were able to accumulate very great wealth as a result. The contents of the royal graves of Shilla reveal a rich and opulent society in which gold ornaments played a prominent part. The unification of Korea under Shilla control in 668 C.E. is the period known as Great Shilla. This unified state endured until 918, when the state of Koryo was founded. Great Shilla had its heyday in the eighth century and was in regular contact with the court of Tang China. Indeed, it is said that the capital, known as the city of gold, was modeled on the Chinese city of CHANG'AN and might have attained a population of more than a million people. BUDDHISM flourished under Great Shilla, and many temples with statues of the Buddha were spread across the landscape. The granite widely employed in sculpture encouraged the survival of complete works of art.

Mythical and much later historic records ascribe the origins of Shilla to a confederation of clans who in 37 B.C.E. resolved on an alliance against external dangers. Gradually this group developed into a powerful state that had regular conflict along its borders with Kogyuro to the north and Paekche to the west. In the early days, the king was entitled *kosogan,* or big man, but by the fourth century, vital in the full development of Korean states, he became the *maripkan,* or hereditary king. The rules of succession incorporated queens, and three are known to have succeeded. The early success of the Shilla state may well have been based on the rich iron ore deposits of Hwangsong-dong, which lie near the capital of Kyongju. Iron was among the most likely of Shilla exports to Japan.

RANKS IN SHILLA

The ranks of the Shilla state were determined by ancestry; *bone* was the term to denote status. Thus the supreme rank, *songgol,* or holy *bone,* designated the highest echelon with the right to rule. The *chingol*, or true *bone*, were ranked next before three further ranks and then the commoners. This last group was largely engaged in rice agriculture or worked in one of the 14 state departments specializing in the production of fine silk, leather goods, metal weapons and implements, woolen garments, tables, and wooden containers. Much of this output was used for trade, particularly with China. Unlike Koguryo and Paekche, Shilla preferred to retain its own shamanistic religious practices against the spread of Buddhism, which did not take hold until the early fifth century C.E.

TANG ALLIANCE

The Shilla kingdom had its capital in the Kyongju basin at PANWOL-SONG. The surrounding hills were peppered with hilltop defensive fortresses. The capital had scribes, for inscriptions in Chinese have been found, for example, at Naengsiri. These reveal the existence of seven grades of administrators and date to the early sixth century C.E. A second, from Bongpyong, relates how King Pobhung took a region into his kingdom in 524 C.E. King Chinhung (r. 540–576 C.E.) set BOUNDARY MARKERS inscribed in Chinese to demarcate his kingdom. These stretch from Maunnyong in the north to Pukhan Sansong in the west. Their need, however, was short lived. The two decades before 660 C.E. were politically tumultuous. In 642 C.E. King Uija (r. 641–660 C.E.) of Paekche attacked Shilla, capturing 40 strategic forts and forcing Shilla to withdraw from the frontier. King Muyong of Shilla immediately sought an alliance with Koguryo to repel this incursion, but the latter's demands for land were too high. Muyong therefore sought an alliance with the Tang emperor. When this was forthcoming, Paekche was subjected to a pincer attack: A Tang fleet landed in the west, while Shilla advanced and defeated the Paekche defensive forces at Yonsan. Both allies then advanced on the Paekche capital of Sabi, bringing this kingdom to its knees in 660 C.E. The allies then turned their attention to the kingdom of Koguryo. In 661 C.E. a Tang force was rebuffed at the mouth of the Taedong River. However, disaffection at the autocratic regime of King Yon Kaesomun and rivalry over the succession when he died weakened Koguryo resistance, and it succumbed to Shilla in 668 C.E. This brought the Three Kingdoms and the old Shilla period to an end and heralded in its place the United Shilla state, with authority throughout Korea south of the line from the Taedong River to the Gulf of Wonsan. To the north of this line, a Koguryo general named Tao Cho-yong founded the new kingdom of Parhae, with its capital far to the north at Sanggyong.

The Tang alliance was not, from the Chinese point of view, undertaken without an ulterior motive, and the true intentions soon became apparent. In the former kingdom of Paekche, the Chinese turned five old provinces into Chinese commanderies, or provinces, and appointed the son of the former Paekche king, Puyo Yung, to administer Ungjin commandery. For Shilla, the Chinese created the grand commandery of Kyerim under King Munmu. Farther north, they converted old Koguryo into nine commanderies and appointed a supreme governor for the peninsula, under the title protector-general to pacify the east, to reside in Pyongyang. The king of Shilla, however, refused to accept this undisguised attempt by China to absorb the Korean Peninsula. In a series of battles, mainly in the valley of the Han River, he drove back the Tang. In 671 C.E. Shilla captured the vital fortress of Sabi and thereby controlled all the former kingdom of Paekche. The protector-general and his office were moved back to Manchuria, and a unified Korea ejected the Chinese. This was a crucial period in the history of Korea, for had Shilla not triumphed, it is unlikely that the Chinese would ever have withdrawn.

KINGS OF SHILLA

The unification of Korea is best understood in the context of the rigid set of social ranks that prevailed. These distinguished among the royal line, aristocracy, and commoners. There were two royal lines, known as the holy *bone* and the true *bone* clans, whose members were accorded ranks 1–5. The aristocracy fell into ranks 6–27, and the three grades of commoners had no rank at all. These distinctions are manifest in the reign of King Hungkok, whose edict recorded in the SAMGUK SAGI noted: "There are superior and inferior people, and humble persons, in regard to social status." Until the death of Queen Chindok (r. 647–654 C.E.), the sovereign was drawn from the holy *bone* clan. A civil war then saw the accession of King Muyol (r. 661–681 C.E.), who had been responsible as Kim Ch'unch'u for inviting Tang China into Korean affairs. He was a member of the true *bone* clan, and he and his successors pursued a policy of strengthening kingly authority. King Sinmun (681–692 C.E.) had rivals and dissidents liquidated. He also faced the issue of ruling over conquered kingdoms of Paekche and Koguryo. Achieving this required that the former independent states were divided into provinces (*chu*). There were three each in Paekche, Kaya, and Koguryo. Each was further divided into prefectures (*kun*), which in turn were made up of a series of counties (*hyon*) and villages (*ch'on*). The administrators of the provinces were appointed from the capital at Kyongju, but the capital itself was now located far to the southeast of the new kingdom, and a move was considered but rejected. Rather, five new subcapitals were strategically placed, and members of the aristocracy were sent to live in them. They also housed the defeated rulers and their families. However, local administration below the province level incorporated regional magnates, whose loyalty was ensured through the *sangsuri* system, whereby they were periodically required to live in the capital as hostages to the local loyalty of their kinsmen.

ADMINISTRATION AND ARMY

The *New History of the Chinese Tang Dynasty* recorded, "Wealth flows constantly to the high officials, who possess as many as 3,000 slaves, and many weapons, cattle, horses and pigs." Grain from ascribed villages was also provided to members of the administration. It seems that the specialists who made the armaments and other necessities were attached to the aristocratic households in the manner of slaves. The villages, whose production underwrote the survival of the state, were subject to triennial census registers. A surviving document dating to 755 C.E. shows that the population was counted, together with the productive capacity of each village. The latter included the numbers of stock of various kinds, even the number of mulberry and nut trees, and the amount and quality of the land. Some of the villages were occupied by free families, but there were also many communities of conquered people or criminals, who were sent there as slaves to work the land for the state. However, the lives of the peasantry were at least spiritually alleviated by the rapid spread of a popular form of Buddhism, known as the Pure Land faith. Under its principal advocate, the monk Wonhyo, it asserted that everyone could expect rebirth into paradise.

The army underwent a major restructuring under King Sinmun, who recognized the need to control new territory. Nine divisions were stationed in the capital, each distinguished by the color of the collar on the uniform. Soldiers were drawn from all parts of the kingdom. The strategic province of Hanju was provided with two garrisons, while each of the remaining eight provinces was accorded one military garrison. The army was under the direct control of the king, a further index of the trend to centralization.

To establish a philosophy of government, Sinmun turned to Chinese precedents, and in 682 C.E. he founded a national academy as a medium to teach Confucian ethics. The *Samguk Sagi* recorded that the basic texts of instruction were the *Spring and Autumn Annals*, (CHUNQIU), the *Classic of Changes (Yijing)*, and the *Classic of Documents (Shujing)*. The period of learning lasted for nine years. Students were strictly graded, and those who excelled were given preference for government positions. Those who failed to achieve were expelled. This was a prelude to the long and peaceful reign of his second son, Songdok (702–737 C.E.). The government was organized around the *chipsabu*, an executive council who pursued royal policy. Under the *chungsi*, the head of the council of state, there were six ministries that covered taxation, justice, the legal code, war, defense, and intelligence.

BURIALS

The archaeological remains of Shilla before unification are dominated by burials. The earliest phases of state formation might well be represented at Choyangdong. Dating to the first to second centuries C.E. the pit graves from this site have furnished Han-style bronze mirrors and exotic glass beads from as far afield as the Mediterranean world. The burials from Kujongdong also include pits containing wooden coffins. Grave goods included iron spears and bronze swords. The six principal phases of Shilla mortuary remains date from 300 to 550 C.E. They are dominated by the royal graves at Kyongju, where 155 mounds survive of a total that formerly included many more. The construction technique made it difficult to loot and plunder the contents of the tombs, and fortunately several have survived intact. These are usually named after a particularly notable item of grave furniture.

The construction of the tombs began with a burial chamber constructed of wood. That uncovered at the TOMB OF THE HEAVENLY HORSE was 6.5 meters (21.5 ft.) long and 4.2 meters (13.9 ft.) wide. A lacquered wooden coffin was placed within, positioned so that the head pointed to the rising Sun. A wooden container was adjacent to the coffin for the storage of mortuary offerings. This was then covered by a massive tumulus of thousands of heavy river boulders, with no reentry passage. At the Heavenly Horse tomb, this cairn rose to a height of 7.5 meters (24.8 ft.), with a diameter of 47 meters (155 ft.). In turn, the stone mound was covered in earth to a height of nearly 13 meters (43 ft.). The lack of any passage or entrance into the tomb chamber made it very difficult to loot, but the natural decay of the wooden structure meant that in due course the weight of stone boulders above crushed and destroyed it.

Foremost in the royal tombs are the gold crowns, which took the form of treelike or antlerlike projections, possibly an echo of shamanistic beliefs. Jade and gold ornaments were attached to the trees, some in the form of leaves. Other gold attachments fell as tassels from the ring of the crown. The royal dead wore elaborate golden belts, the one from the Golden Crown tomb attaining a length of two meters. Again, they were embellished with gold dangling ornaments, including a model of a fish and a basket. The symbolism of these additions is not known. The Washing Vessel tomb, so-called on the basis of the bronze vessel found within, is dated by an inscription to 415 C.E. The burial also yielded a lacquered wooden mask embellished with blue eyes and a gold background. Gold finger and toe rings, bracelets, and heavily ornamented earrings are also regularly encountered. The kings and queens wore bronze shoes with gold attachments on the soles, an impractical form of footwear possibly signifying that they were regularly carried aloft on ceremonial occasions. Male burials included much armor. There were iron swords, arrowheads, helmets, as well as accoutrements for horse riding, such as saddles, harness, and stirrups. Many pottery vessels were placed as mortuary offerings, and these are interesting largely for the decoration. There are incised figures of animals, such as deer, boats, and warriors. Occasionally, human figurines are encountered.

OLD SHILLA ARCHITECTURE

The architectural remains of Old Shilla, is the period before it controlled the whole peninsula, are not great. Sites are dominated by fortresses, several of which were strategically placed around the capital of Kyongju. Panwol-Song is the most significant, because it housed the royal palace, as well as several other buildings whose stone foundations are still visible. A stone-walled fort also protected the important port of Pusan, where trade with Japan was undertaken and two warehouses were built. Buddhist temples were also constructed, one of which, built by Queen Sondok in 645 C.E., survives to this day. Investigations there have revealed the presence of Tang dynasty Chinese porcelain, confirming that trade contact with China was also pursued. The queen also had a nine-meter-high astronomical observatory built.

There is a ninth-century record that detailed the presence of 178,936 households in 1,360 residential quarters. The fabulous wealth of the ruling aristocracy was reflected in the presence of 35 mansions, whose owners had one residence for each of the four seasons. Endless rows of houses with tiled roofs, each set around a private courtyard, were described.

UNIFIED SHILLA REMAINS

Excavations at Kyongju have provided a rare glimpse of palace life; the great ornamental lake, known as the Anapchi Pond, once part of the royal compound, was investigated in 1975. After dredging, the original stone banks revealed a lake that formerly covered 1.5 hectares (3.75 acres). The eastern and northern banks were indented and formed into a map that resembles Korea, Japan, and the island of Taiwan, while the southern and western banks were straight and flanked by interconnected pavilions. The mud at the lake bottom has provided a rich array of artifacts relating to palace life, including wooden tablets bearing written records of administrative details. These are dated between 751 and 774 C.E., but the roof tiles were all dated in the two-year span of 679–80 C.E. Evidently the pavilions had been given a new roof at that period, or these years may have seen the completion of the lake, because it has been ascribed to King Munmu, who reigned from 661 to 681 C.E. A wooden die was inscribed with brief recommendations, one of which exhorted young men not to abandon an ugly woman partner. Four boats were also recovered, a set of gilt bronze scissors, and several gilt bronze images of the Buddha and BODHISATTVAS.

A fine example is from Mount P'algong, 60 kilometers northwest of Kyongju. The Buddha is seen in a cave, flanked by two bodhisattvas. Shilla craftspeople were also adept at casting bronze figures, as seen in the guardians, each standing about 22 centimeters (8.8 in.) in height, from the Kamun-sa temple and dating to the late seventh century C.E. Gold was also used as a medium for portraying the Buddha. Two fine examples are from the Hwang-bok-sa temple at Kyongju.

The specific Shilla style of architecture and associated sculpture developed by the eighth century; the most prominent example is the SOKKURAM cave temple at Mount Toham, near Kyongju. This famous site has three chambers constructed of granite blocks; the circular shrine room, with a diameter of eight meters (26.4 ft.), contains the finest Shilla Buddha sculpture, standing 3.3. meters (10.9 ft.) high. The Buddha sits serenely on a throne, accompanied by images of bodhisattvas and disciples located on the surrounding walls. The view of the Buddha from the antechamber was enhanced by the two large columns that supported the entrance arch at this point. One unusual aspect of later Shilla sculpture was the casting of images of the Buddha in iron, which was then gilt. Some Shilla specialists maintained this tradition after the rise of the Koryo state in 918 and the transfer of the center of power in Korea to Kaesong, north of Seoul.

See also KUMSONG.

Further reading: Barnes, G. *State Formation in Korea.* London: Curzon Press, 2001; Nelson, S. M. *The Archaeology of Korea.* Cambridge: Cambridge University Press, 1993; Portal, J. *Korea: Art and Archaeology.* London: British Museum, 2000.

Shimanosho Ishibutai Shimanosho Ishibutai is a large *kofun*, or burial mound, of the late YAMATO period, located in the southeast Nara Basin of western Honshu, Japan. It was built in the seventh century C.E., and therefore was close in date to the first local Japanese historical texts. It might have been the burial mound of a leader who lived at Shimanosho and died in 626 C.E. Unfortunately, the burial was looted centuries ago, and little remained in the central burial chamber in terms of mortuary offerings aside from fragments of pottery. However, archaeological investigations have revealed the massive nature of the internal tomb structure, constructed of granite slabs from three kilometers away. The larger of the two roof slabs is estimated to weigh 77 tons, and the smaller 64 tons. This tomb chamber was reached by a long stone passageway and had been built on top of a square platform supported by stone walls.

Shi Qiang (late 10th century B.C.E.) *Shi Qiang may be regarded as the first recorded person to attempt to write a history of China.*

In 1975, a chance discovery in Fufeng county, Shaanxi province, led to the recovery of an intact hoard of 103 bronzes that had been carefully secreted in a pit during the turbulent times that attended the end of WESTERN ZHOU DYNASTY (1045–771 B.C.E.) rule and the move east to LUOYANG. This hoard represents the bronze ritual vessels of a noble line of courtiers. The bronzes had been neatly stacked in three tiers, obviously with the intention of recovering them undamaged when calm returned, but this was not to be. The basal layer incorporated basins, wine flasks, and larger bells. Some of the smaller items had been carefully packed in larger ones. The middle and upper layers contained successively smaller items. Fortunately, many of the bronze vessels bore INSCRIPTIONS that reveal they belonged to successive generations of the Wei family including one of the first references to a state known as Chu.

The text on the Shi Qiang *pan* described a line of Zhou kings and their military exploits. King Wu (c. 1049–1043 B.C.E.) defeated and ruled over the people of Yin. King Cheng (r. 1042–1006 B.C.E.) defeated his enemies and strengthened the Zhou state. It is most fascinating to read that King Zhao (r. 977–957 B.C.E.) tamed Chu and opened the route to the south. Having extolled the virtues of the line of Zhou rulers, the text then describes how his own ancestors served the central court, before praying that his descendants might use this vessel for 10,000 years.

Shitenno-ji The Shitenno-ji in Osaka, Japan, was a Buddhist temple built by PRINCE SHOTOKU during the reign of Empress Suiko (r. 592–628 C.E.). It was thus one of the earliest Buddhist complexes in Japan and owes much to influence from the Korean state of PAEKCHE. The temple was built by following the standard unit of measurement used in the KOGURYO kingdom of Korea, the *koma-jaku*, approximately 35 centimeters (14 in.). There is a cloistered corridor built around a central pagoda. A *kondo*, or hall for images of the deities, was built in a central position in the court created by the cloisters. A lecture hall was built slightly later on the northern wall. Beyond this central area lie a bell tower and a hall to contain sacred manuscripts. The monks were housed in two dormitories on the northern edge of site.

Shit-thaung The Shit-thaung Pagoda is located at MRAUK-U, in the Rakhine (formerly ARAKAN) region of western Myanmar (Burma). The massive monuments there were built by King Min Bin in 1531, but the most important single item housed there is the Shit-thaung pillar, an INSCRIPTION in SANSKRIT that was added to by kings of the Rakhine (Arakan) Candra dynasty from the sixth century C.E. According to tradition, the pillar was regarded as a legitimizing force and was moved between successive capitals before reaching Mrauk-U. The most important and informative section of the inscription, the work of King Anandacandra, dates to 729 C.E. It details the names of 22 kings dating from the fourth century. It also describes his religious foundations and endowments and donations to monasteries as far afield as Sri Lanka.

Shizhaishan Shizhaishan is a late Iron Age royal cemetery located on a hill that dominates the southeastern margin of Lake Dian in Yunnan province, China. Excavations there in 1954–60 and again in 1998–99 uncovered graves of outstanding wealth, whose goods provide

insight into life and society. The site dates between the second century B.C.E. and the first century C.E. Chinese dynastic records refer to the powerful chiefdoms of Lingnan, the southern provinces of China, as the southern barbarians who were forcibly incorporated into the HAN DYNASTY during the last two centuries B.C.E. The DIAN CHIEFDOM grew in power and wealth in the face of this imperial expansion. According to Chinese historic sources, the people of Dian continued to resist Chinese rule well into the first century C.E.

The most wealthy burials were rectangular graves up to five meters (16.5 ft.) long and two (6.6 ft.) wide, the depth varying between one and almost three meters. The corpse was placed in a large wooden coffin over a layer of ash to insulate it against damp. Surviving fragments of wood reveal that the coffin was covered with lacquered decoration. The coffins were large enough to contain a wide variety of grave goods. These included exotic beads of TURQUOISE, agate, and jade, as well as bronze and iron weaponry, armor, bronze figures, and, perhaps most notable of all, bronze receptacles filled with cowry shells. These, which often take the form of drums, were embellished with scenes incorporating small figures taking part in rituals and battles. The cowry shells, symbolizing wealth, were obtained by exchange from the Indian Ocean and indicate far-reaching trade relations.

Burial 6 is particularly notable because it contained a golden SEAL inscribed, "the seal of the King of Dian," in Chinese characters. This is in all probability the seal given to the king of Dian by Han WUDI, the emperor, in 109 B.C.E. Other grave goods include an iron sword with a bronze hilt and gold scabbard, a bronze mirror, a group of bronze drums and cowry containers, and a bronze tomb guardian holding a ceremonial staff. There were also a set of bronze bells, a cattle figurine, horse and chariot fittings, a wine container, and a jade arm ring. One of the most important aspects of this grave was the recovery of the component parts of a jade suit, made of slats of jade that would have been stitched together with thread of gold or silver. Such suits were by imperial decree worn only by the highest royal members of the Han dynasty. Complete examples have been found at Mancheng and in the tomb of the emperor of Yue. The former incorporated gold thread, the latter silver. Unfortunately, the acidic soils prevented more than fragmentary human remains from surviving.

The scenes depicted on bronze cowry containers provide an unparalleled glimpse into the life of this rich chiefdom on the margins of the Han state. There are several battle scenes, in which the Dian leaders are depicted larger than others and covered in gold. The Dian warriors fought with swords, spears, and crossbows. There are also representations of rituals in which aristocratic WOMEN played a leading role and which involved human sacrifices. These are thought to have been dedicated to the agricultural seasons. Gilt images of high-status women are also seen receiving tribute. Graves of females usually contained artifacts for weaving. Models of houses raised on piles were also found. They depicted feasting activity. Court activities included hunting, bullfighting, and music and dance, but the most notable model shows a raised pavilion on which the paramount chief is meeting with subchiefs while a feast is being prepared.

Further reading: Higham, C. F. W. *The Bronze Age of Southeast Asia.* Cambridge: Cambridge University Press, 1996.

shoen A *shoen* was a manor or agricultural estate founded and managed in Japan from the period of the NARA STATE. Although land was in theory owned By the *TENNO,* or sovereign, from 711 C.E. it was decreed that virgin rice land could be developed at private expense. A later decision made it possible for such improved land to be passed to the descendants of the person who initiated the investment. Institutions were also able to invest in land in the same manner. Thus the authorities of the TODAIJI temple in HEIJO-KYO owned *shoen.* The introduction at the same period of copper COINAGE made it more practical to employ labor to work on the estates. Although labor was in theory under strict state controls and was not mobile, in practice it was possible to hire local farmers, who could supplement their income with cash payments.

The Nara state relied on surplus rice production for the maintenance of the ruling elite, and opening new land to cultivation in this way placed central finances on a firmer footing.

Shoku Nihongi The *Shoku Nihongi (Continued Chronicle of Japan)* is a historic document, completed in 797 C.E., that covers the principal events in the court centers of Japan between 697 and 791 C.E. Unlike its predecessor the NIHONGI, which incorporates much myth and legend, it is regarded as being historically accurate.

Shortughai Shortughai is a small settlement, covering about 2.5 hectares (6.25 acres), that lies near the confluence of the Amu Dar'ya and Kokcha Rivers in northern Afghanistan. This is an area renowned for its deposits of LAPIS LAZULI and rubies, and the excavations there have revealed that it was occupied during the period of the INDUS VALLEY CIVILIZATION (c. 2500–c. 1770 B.C.E.). The recovery of steatite SEALs of Indus type and structures built of mud brick indicate settlement from the south. Marine shell and the raw materials for the manufacture of ornaments from lapis lazuli, carnelian, and TURQUOISE leave no doubt as to the site's role in long-distance exchange. The economy was based on irrigation agriculture and the cultivation of flax.

Shotoku, Prince (d. 622 C.E.) *Prince Shotuku is the patron saint of Japanese Buddhism.*

He was appointed heir to Empress Suiko, who was enthroned in 592 C.E. and was one of the major early supporters of Buddhism in Japan. Much knowledge of the prince is from the NIHONGI, a historic tract dating to 720 C.E., but myth is combined with history in the accounts. Thus he is described as being able to talk at birth and to sit in judgment on 10 cases simultaneously. He became a Buddhist cult figure; some would say a Buddha himself. He had the Ikaruga Palace built for himself at Naniwa, south of the Yodo River as it approaches Osaka Bay. This palace was identified and examined archaeologically in 1939. He was also author of a constitution that advocated obedience to state requirements. These famous 17 injunctions, allegedly formulated in 604 C.E., reveal close adherence to Buddhism and Confucianism. One recommends conversion to Buddhism to be able to follow established

Prince Shotoku was the patron saint of Japanese Buddhism. He introduced Chinese ideals of government into Japan and wrote a constitution requiring obedience to the emperor. *(Art Resource, NY)*

teaching. Another requires absolute obedience to the emperor's wishes; others advise against jealousy and express the need to start work early and end late. He was thus a vital force in the introduction of Chinese political philosophy and the Buddhist religion to Japan. On his death, he was interred in a mounded tomb 57 meters (188 ft.) in diameter, entered through a stone-lined passage. It was evidently still intact in the 14th century, when a monk entered it and described three lacquered coffins. However, by the 19th century it had been looted, and only fragments of the lacquered coffin survived.

See also CONFUCIUS; SHITENNO-JI; YAMATO.

Shotorak Shotorak is a major Buddhist temple overlooking the Koh Daman Plain, five kilometers (3 mi.) distant from the capital of BEGRAM in northern Afghanistan. A main courtyard is dominated by a stupa, with a second stupa and court lying adjacent to it. It is well known for its reliefs that depict JATAKA TALES. The recovery of a coin of Vasudeva, linked with the art style, dates this site to the second to fourth centuries C.E. At Shotorak, the reliefs differ in style from those typical of Gandharan art. The portrayal of the Dipamkara Buddha, the last Buddha before Sakyamuni, shows flames rising from his shoulders, symbolizing divine power. This interest in flames may have derived from KUSHAN notions of the sacred fire.

See also BAMIYAN; KAPISI.

Shu The Chinese state of Shu was located in Sichuan province. This fertile region lies in southwestern China beyond the Chang (Yangtze) gorges. The history of Shu became inextricably tied to that of the states lying to the north and east. The homeland was early occupied by rice agriculturalists. One of the major recent discoveries in China has been the opening of the sacrificial pits at SANXINGDUI and the realization that here flourished a state contemporary with that of Shang in the central plains. The ritual and power evidenced by the bronzes, gold, and ivories of Sanxingdui provide compelling confirmation of the Shu people mentioned in the Shang oracle INSCRIPTIONS. Its relative remoteness meant that the Shu people were hardly mentioned in WESTERN ZHOU DYNASTY (1045–771 B.C.E.) records, and they escaped much of the turmoil of the WARRING STATES PERIOD (475–221 B.C.E.). However, the predatory power of the QIN put them in the mainstream of Chinese politics, wherein they played a key role during the HAN DYNASTY (206 B.C.E.–220 C.E.). Relatively remote, Shu culture might well extend as far as the remarkable walled city of Sanxingdui, a contemporary of the late SHANG STATE of the central plains, which has produced an outstanding assemblage of bronzes in a style unique in East Asia. Little is known of the development of Shu until the middle years of the first millennium B.C.E.; however, when it became the object of the predatory state of Qin, centered in the Wei Valley. In 441 B.C.E. Qin forces invaded Sichuan, but only after a struggle lasting at least a century did Shu become absorbed in the Qin realm. Thereafter, there are references to rebellions against foreign rule.

CHANGJIANG CIVILIZATION

The growing knowledge of the Shu state and finds from the lower reaches of the Chang River have led to the proposal that these areas made up the Changjiang civilization. The finds contrast in many basic ways with the better known Shang and Zhou states of the Huang (Yellow) and Wei River Valleys to the north. This civilization was also based on the intensive cultivation of rice, which as is now known, has a history in the area that extends back at least five millennia before the first states were formed.

MEANING OF SHU

The graph for Shu has a controversial origin and meaning. A first-century B.C.E. dictionary gave its meaning as *can*, "silkworm." This has vague support in the name Can Cong, the name of the first Shu king, and silk was certainly an important product of Sichuan, as is seen in the decoration on an early bronze showing people collecting mulberry leaves. However, this is only one of several possible explanations. There are references that probably allude to the Shu in the ORACLE-BONE archives of the Shang state and the Western Zhou dynasty. One Shang example questioned whether or not to send envoys to Shu; another referred to a body of 300 Shu archers. These oracle-bone inscriptions refer to the Shu with a graph not in the form of a silkworm, but of an eye with a curved projection below it. A much later text says that Cancong, a legendary king of the Shu, had vertical eyes. Clearly, eyes had some importance in Shu legends, and this is manifested also in the huge projections on the eyes of the bronze masks from Sanxingdui.

SHU AND SHANG CONFLICT

An important collection of Western Zhou oracle bones mention a military expedition against the Shu. This is not surprising: The late Shang and early Zhou records make it plain that it was a period of endemic strife between rival states and of a ferment of political alliances. The discoveries at Sanxingdui, Chengdu, and Yaan in the rich Sichuan basin are unanimous in disclosing the presence of a powerful state that commanded respect. Indeed, the *SHANG SHU* text lists eight states that combined to attack the Shang state, and Shu was one of them.

CONTACT WITH MAINSTREAM CHINA

Archaeologically far less is known of the Shu state than of virtually any other of the EASTERN ZHOU DYNASTY period (770–221 B.C.E.). There is also the problem that the Shu inscriptions are in a script that has not yet been deciphered. That there remained, as at Sanxingdui, a distinctive Sichuan BRONZE-CASTING tradition is evidenced in the styles of the many halberds and willow-leaf swords that have been found. But participation in the BATTLE OF MUYE in 1045 B.C.E. as a Zhou ally probably moved the people of Shu into the mainstream of Chinese politics and introduced them to new forms of weaponry and tactics. This is seen in weapons from the site of Shuiguanyin and a fine collection of ritual jade objects characteristics of the central plains repertoire, including ceremonial *cong* tubes, *fu* axes, and *yazhang* blades. A collection of halberds dating to the Western Zhou period from Shuiguanyin and the hoard from Zhuwajie alike show a preference for this weapon in war, whereas the chariot does not seem to have been adopted by the Shu.

Distinctiveness from the culture of the central plains in this southwestern part of China is also identified in the references to the people as having their own knotted hairstyle and local forms of dress. Nor does the state of Shu feature in the records of alliances and diplomatic contacts that survive from the period of Western Zhou, apart from a handful of equivocal references. One problem is the lack of indigenous written records, for what texts survive were written in a script that remains to be deciphered. With the Eastern Zhou dynasty, encompassing the Spring and Autumn period and the Warring States period, there are some vague literary references to Shu. A king Duyu, took the title of king and DI, implying semidivine status. Another reference noted that a certain Beiling from the state of CHU became king of Shu in the middle of the seventh century B.C.E. He allegedly founded a dynasty of 12 rulers. One of these, Lu Di, is said to have attacked the state of Qin, an unwise move as events unfolded, and interacted increasingly with the BA STATE people to the east.

NEW BURIAL CUSTOMS

The Ba move west from their bases in eastern Sichuan as a response to Chu pressure introduced new influences during the fifth and fourth centuries B.C.E. One of these probably produced a novel mortuary tradition in which the dead elite were interred in boat-shaped lacquered coffins. The best instance of this is in the tomb at Jiuliandun, dated to the early fourth century B.C.E. The burial chamber was cut into the ground with access by an eight-meter-long ramp. Within lay a severely plundered burial, the centerpiece of which was a boat-shaped coffin in a grave fully 10.5 meters (34.7 ft.) in length and almost as wide. Fortunately, one section for offerings remained unviolated and was found to contain sumptuary sets of five bronze vessels, including *ding* tripods. There were also bells and even a bronze saw still retaining its wooden handle and bindings for attachment. A similar boat coffin was found in the burial unearthed at the Chengdu Baihuatan middle school, this time in association with nearly 50 bronze tools, weapons, and vessels. Boat-shaped coffins continued to be in vogue in the area of the Shu state, centered at Chengdu, long after the conquest by Qin.

The boat coffins invariably contain weaponry, suggesting that they were reserved for fighting men. The spears, halberds, and battle axes often have Ba text inscriptions. Not all burials of this period, however, involved boats. The rich interment at Xindu was a series of chambers replicating an elite palace and is thought to have been the tomb of one of the later kings of the Kaiming dynasty. Trade with other states is evidenced by the presence of Chu vessels as grave goods and a mirror from the state of JIN. The weapons also show a number of innovations, such as the development of swords and crossbow in reaction to the increasingly dangerous political conditions.

ECONOMIC ADVANCES

This period of early Warring States was also marked by economic progress. Sericulture was a major industry, and rice cultivation was improved through the creation of IRRIGATION works. In one instance the Min River was diverted. SEALS were used, indicating an increase in trade, and these bore written symbols. A RITUAL BRONZE VESSEL from the Baihuatun grave in Chengdu bears decorative scenes that illustrate aspects of Shu life. There are people collecting mulberry leaves in baskets and cooking on the ground. Most of the scenes involve warfare, both on land and on water. The land warriors use a variety of weapons, including bows, arrows, and long spears tipped with halberds. One man is being decapitated; another falls dead with his head severed from his body. The boats had richly ornamented prows and sterns and were poled or rowed by oarsmen. A well-equipped and -organized army was essential in the troubles that lay ahead and that first manifested themselves in the Battle of Nanzheng in 387 B.C.E., which pitted Shu against its nemesis, Qin.

CONFLICT WITH QIN

The Warring States period drew into its maelstrom the powerful rulers of the central plains, Shandong, the northeast, and Qin, extending south to Chu in the Chang Valley. The Shu in their Sichuan fastness might have been expected to remain remote from the conflicts, but this was not to be. The Qin were interested not only in securing their southwestern flank, but also in seizing the rich agricultural and mineral wealth of Sichuan. The prelude to war between the two states involves a notable story steeped in legend. The Shu king Kaiming XII heard that his Qin counterpart owned five stone cattle that defecated gold. He asked for them as a gift, and King Hui of Qin agreed. A fine new road was built to enable the heavy sculptures to be transported to the Shu capital over the mountains. This provided access, and in 316 B.C.E. Qin invaded.

The Qin triumphed in the following battle. King Kaiming was captured and killed, and the Qin forces wheeled on Ba, their ally, and expanded over much of Sichuan. The state of Qin had adopted legalist principles in government. This involved a rigid central control over the populace on totalitarian lines. Already involved in the internecine strife that characterized the period of Warring States, Qin rulers saw that to succeed, they had to expand their power base. What better place than Sichuan, with its rich plains, mineral resources, stores of cattle and horses, and potential to produce rice surpluses, to give Qin the impetus to succeed in wars of annihilation? The ensuing century witnessed arguably the earliest case in world history of a totalitarian regime faced with the organizational problem of absorbing another state imbued with different people, unique customs, and long and independent traditions of its own.

Absorption of Shu into Qin

The resulting experiment in absorption began with the appointment of Kaiming XII's son, Yaotong, as a marquis rather than a king, subservient to the Qin court at Xianyang. At the same time, a Qin military governor and a minister were appointed, and many Qin families were encouraged to move south and settle in Sichuan. The land of the Shu thus became a dependent province, but in 311 King Hui of Qin died, and Zhang Ruo, his governor in Sichuan, saw his chance and murdered the marquis before declaring independence. This insurrection was put down by the dispatch of Qin armies, for Sichuan was too rich a prize to risk losing, and Zhang Ruo was executed. A new marquis was found, and steps were taken to fortify the capital Chengdu and other major centers. The former city now lay behind 23-meter (76-ft.)-high walls and covered an area of 250 hectares (62.5 acres). Marquis Hui suffered from a vicious family intrigue. Intent on ingratiating himself with the Qin court, he undertook appropriate sacrifices and had the special meat sent north to Xianyang. But his mother-in-law intercepted the caravan and had the meat laced with poison. On arrival, she suggested that the food be tested before being placed before the king. When the unfortunate taster died, the king ordered that Hui be required to commit suicide. So, in 300 B.C.E., a third marquis was found, but he also revolted against Qin dominance, perhaps as he saw his native patrimony being increasingly exploited through the new offices of salt and iron control and the regular dispatch of rice wagons north to Qin.

Economic Reforms in Shu

Economic reforms had a greater impact on Shu than the machinations of the ruling nucleus. A mint was established to promote trade and industry, and according to an important BAMBOO-SLIP text from Qinchuan in northern Sichuan, the Qin system of land division, involving strictly laid out plots on a grid pattern intersected by raised pathways, was applied. A further tomb text from Shuihudi in Hubei describes how Qin and other peoples from the north secured through conquest were route-marched to settle Sichuan, in a rush to the southwest to secure land and economic opportunities. Some of the newcomers branched out from agriculture to extract salt, smelt iron, or mine cinnabar. To enhance agricultural output linked with the newly parceled plots of land, the Qin conceived, or at least persisted with, the huge irrigation scheme based on the water of the Min River. Known as the Dujiangyan (capital river dam) project, it was directed by Li Bing, the governor of Shu appointed in 277 B.C.E. The Min River flows down from the mountains east of Chengdu and is prone to serious flooding. Li Bing, later locally deified for his efforts, divided the river into two channels. One continued on to its junction with the Chang, and the other, inner channel was directed along canals hacked through the surrounding upland and so onto the Chengdu Plain. There the water was reticulated to a vast area of rice fields.

The effect of the colonization of Sichuan was to greatly strengthen Qin, and in a domino effect the rival states fell one by one to its armies. By 221 B.C.E., Qin replaced Zhou as the ruling dynasty, but whereas Zhou had lasted for seven centuries, the Qin empire survived barely a decade. The death of the first emperor, QIN SHI-HUANGDI, fostered court intrigues and the rise of the Western Han dynasty. In 210 B.C.E., there was a compliant and orderly regime in Sichuan, while other areas of China had barely been brought under central control and still resented rule from anywhere but their own capital.

EMERGENCE OF HAN

At this juncture, Sichuan and the Han Valley took center stage in the impending power struggle to fill the vacuum left by the demise of Qin. It was a period of warlordism, with two principal protagonists, Liu JI, a man of humble origins but great leadership qualities, and Xiang Yu of the state of Chu. The former was first to take the Qin capital of Xianyang, but the latter, who adopted a highly destructive punitive policy, was more powerful. Liu Ji found himself placed as the king of Han, with charge over the Han Valley and the territory of Shu and Ba. This remote placement was designed to rid him from the central plains, the center of political power in China. Liu Ji bided his time. First, he ripped up the very road that had taken him to Sichuan, to indicate his decision not to return. Then he raised troops locally, from an area that had escaped the recent wars of attrition, and maintained a prosperous and productive economy. With a settled base, Liu Ji advanced again on Xianyang, took it for a second time, and from 206 until 202 B.C.E., engaged the forces of his rival in a war that still endures in Chinese memory as one of the greatest struggles in their long history. Throughout these years, the loyalty of Sichuan and the supplies transported over the mountains to sustain his army proved decisive. With final victory and his elevation to the position of first Han emperor GAOZU, Shu loyalty was not unrewarded.

Shu under Han Rule

The Han administrative system involved commanderies, or provinces, governed by central appointees and kingdoms established to reward loyal supporters of the emperor. Sichuan was divided into commanderies. Guanghan commandery lay in the northern part of the Shu homeland and Shu commandery to the south. Each was further divided into counties. With the establishment of Han, LEGALISM went into abeyance as Confucian thought returned to favor. A training school for imperial administrators was established at the capital, and under such governors as Wen Weng, appointed to Shu in 141 B.C.E., selected young men were sent to Chang'an for education. While Shu still provided a grain surplus, transporting it in quantity, even when much of the rest of China suffered famine, presented enormous difficulties. A scheme to cobble together a riverine route using the Bao and Xie Rivers failed. However, other products were lighter and more easily transported and provided the foundation for rising prosperity. Tea, for example, grew in the Shu territory and was exported by this period to other parts of China. The area was also noted for silk manufacture, metal, and lacquer products. LACQUER was manufactured at Chengdu and Guanghan and widely exported. This is seen on the inscriptions and seals on the finished products. A fine lacquered ladle from Tomb 1 at Mawangdui, for example, is inscribed with its origin in Chengdu. Even farther afield, a food bowl found in LELANG commandery, North Korea, originated in Sichuan. It was made, according to its inscription, in 69 C.E. A bowl from the tomb of Zhu Ran at Ma'anshan in Anhui province, dated to the late Eastern Han dynasty, was inscribed, "Strongly constructed in the Shu commandery." It must have been manufactured in Sichuan for export. Cinnabar, a material highly in demand for its alleged life-prolonging qualities, was mined. There were also large iron foundries employing thousands of people and major salt-producing enterprises. Sichuan enjoys a milder climate than the central plains, and many local delicacies were exported.

See also CONFUCIUS.

Further reading: Bagley, R. W. "A Shang City in Sichuan Province," *Orientations* 21 (1990): 52–67; Bagley, R. W. *Ancient Sichuan.* Seattle and Princeton: Seattle Art Museum, 2001; Gao Dalun. "Bronze Ritual Artefacts of the Shu Culture: A Preliminary Survey," *Orientations* 32 (2001): 45–51; Sage, S. F. *Ancient Sichuan and the Unification of China.* Albany, N.Y.: SUNY Press, 1992.

Shundi (Liu Bao; Submissive Emperor) (115–144 C.E.) *Shundi was the seventh emperor of the Eastern Han dynasty.* He was the only son of ANDI and acceded in 126 C.E. His reign was intriguing from a historic point of view, for a number of leading scholars had the temerity to criticize the central administration for corruption and nepotism. An earthquake at LUOYANG in 133 C.E., for example, motivated Zhang Heng, the inventor of the world's first SEISMOGRAPH, to urge on the court the restoration of power to the emperor, the "Son of Heaven," rather than see power continue to lie in the hands of royal cliques and eunuchs. There was also criticism of court extravagances, and a rebellion in the deep south was resolved through the dispatch of senior officials to restore order rather than the staging of a punitive military expedition.

Shunga dynasty The Shunga dynasty of India was founded by Pushyamitra, a Brahman who killed the last Mauryan king in about 180 B.C.E. The dynasty lasted for about a century.

See also MAURYA EMPIRE.

Shwe Zigon The Shwe Zigon stupa at PAGAN in Myanmar (Burma) was begun by King Anawrahta (1044–77) and completed by King KYANZITTHA (r. 1084–1111). It is said to house the clavicle, part of the skull, and a tooth of the Buddha. Its design set a precedent for many later Burmese stupas. The circular stupa is raised on three terraces each decorated with glazed plaques illustrating JATAKA TALE themes. Subsidiary temple buildings housing images of the Buddha are located on each side.

Siddhartha Gautama (b. c. 560 B.C.E.) *Siddhartha Gautama was the name of the Buddha before his enlightenment at the age of 35.*
His date of birth is controversial: He may have been born in about 560 B.C.E. of a royal family, at LUMBINI in Nepal, or up to 140 years later. Little is known of his early life, since the evidence is almost entirely from oral tradition rather than written records. The foundation of the Buddhist religion was to have a major impact on the states of Southeast Asia, many of which adopted his teachings.

See also BAYON; BOROBUDUR; BUDDHISM; JAYAVARMAN VII.

Further reading: Bhikkhu Nanamoli. *The Life of the Buddha: According to the Pali Canon.* Seattle: BPS Pariyatti Editions, 2001; Thich Nhat Hanh. *The Heart of the Buddha's Teaching: Transforming Suffering into Peace, Joy, and Liberation: The Four Noble Truths, the Noble Eightfold Path, and Other Basic Buddhist Teachings.* New York: Broadway Books, 1999.

Sidun Sidun is a major site of the LIANGZHU CULTURE, which dominated the lower Chang (Yangtze) Valley of China from about 3000 to 2000 B.C.E. It is located between the Chang River and Lake Taihu in Jiangsu province and was defended by a series of moats that enclosed an area of about 90 hectares (225 acres). A circular platform containing elite graves is the outstanding feature of this site. One young man, for example, was interred with 24 jade rings and 33 *cong*, a jade ritual artifact with a circular interior and square surface. These were very high-status items, and some were embellished with carved designs of animal masks and birds.

Sigiri　Sigiri is a remarkable complex located in central Sri Lanka, which dates probably to the late fifth century C.E. It is a palace and a fortified settlement and is renowned for its frescoes depicting female figures. Among the earliest surviving examples of Sri Lankan art, they are thought to represent princesses who resided on Mount Kailasa, home of the gods.

Sikri　Sikri is a site that has yielded many examples of Gandharan art. It was discovered in 1888 in the Mardan district of Pakistan. Although it claimed to be the first site of this school of art to have been properly investigated, its location is not known with certainty. The site is best known for the statue of the fasting Buddha, but many other examples of Gandharan art were also recovered. These reveal many aspects of the architecture of the day, including Corinthian and Persian columns, city gates guarded by soldiers, and a woman at a square well pulling up water. Scenes include the Buddha's first meditation and the JATAKA TALE of the Dipamkara Buddha. Thirty-five episodes in the Buddha's life are incorporated in the reliefs from the stupa bases.

After the excavations, a site plan was prepared, and the sculptures were lodged in the Lahore Museum. Foremost among these was the base of a subsidiary stupa liberally ornamented with 13 panels of reliefs. Eleven further panels, curved to fit around the drum base, probably are from the monastery's main stupa. The collection was divided with the partition of India and Pakistan in 1947, some to Chandigarh, most remaining in Lahore.

See also GANDHARA.

Silk Road　The Silk Road is a name given to the routes by which China was linked with India and the Roman Empire through the passage of trade goods. Exchange was also the medium by which information and ideas flowed in both directions, particularly in the spread of BUDDHISM from India to China, Korea, and Japan. The northern Silk Road had very early origins, in the prehistoric period. Knowledge of copper and tin smelting and BRONZE CASTING, reached China from the West along what was to become the Silk Road. At a slightly later date, the chariot was introduced to the rulers of the Chinese SHANG dynasty (1766–1045 B.C.E.) along the same route. By the first half of the first millennium B.C.E., knowledge of iron technology probably spread west into China. A century ago, parallels were noted between the art styles found in the area of the Black Sea of the seventh century C.E. and those in China.

Archaeological investigations into possible early links between China and the West have advanced rapidly over the past 20 years. These have been spurred by the increasing number of cemeteries in the TARIM BASIN that have provided compelling evidence for the presence of individuals with clothing of clear Western affinities, pre-served by the arid conditions there. These cemeteries have been linked with the survival into historic times of people who spoke the Indo-European Tocharian group of languages. The presence there of such groups by the third millennium B.C.E. documents the early passage of people, goods, and ideas over the vast distances of Central Asia.

Although the origin of the term is often traced to K. Richthofen, writing in 1878, the Silk Road was well known to the Romans, and the Roman historian Ammianus Marcellinus coined the term in his *History* dating to the fourth century C.E. In the early third century C.E. the division of the Han empire into three separate kingdoms barred the southern kingdom of Wu from access to the lucrative Silk Road, and in consequence the Wu emperor sought an alternative by dispatching representatives by sea to the south. One of these, Kang Dai, reported that he had encountered in a state called FUNAN (in modern Vietnam and Cambodia) clear evidence of trade between Southeast Asia and India, giving rise to the term "the maritime Silk Road."

By the HAN DYNASTY (206 B.C.E.–220 C.E.), the land route was regarded as vital to Chinese interests. It was said at the time that "messengers come and go every season of the month, foreign traders and merchants knock on the gates of the great wall every day." There were many branches and linkages along the 8,000-kilometer (4,800 mi.) journey from the Mediterranean to the gates of China. Moreover, few merchants would have traveled the entire length. Instead, goods were exchanged at the centers that flourished through trade. Moving west from China, the route followed the Gansu Corridor, noted for its expansive grasslands and fine horses. DUNHUANG was an important stepping-off point for the most perilous part of the entire journey that skirted the TAKLAMAKAN DESERT. This rich and important settlement was located close to the Buddhist sanctuaries at MOGAO. The northern route took the traveler through the oases of Turpan, Yanqi (Karashahr), and Kuqa. The southern passed through MIRAN, HOTAN, and NIYA, before both joined at KAXGAR. It then became rather easier with the passage through FERGHANA, noted for its heavenly horses, and on to PANJIKENT and Samarqand. Goods from India joined the Silk Road via BACTRIA and the valley of the Amu Dar'ya River. To the west lay the oasis of MERV (now Mary) and then the Caspian Sea. After the traveler had skirted the Caucasus range, the Black Sea beckoned and beyond lay the cities of the Roman Empire.

The importance of the Silk Road to Asian civilization is to be seen in many different fields. It was a conduit for ideas. The spread of Buddhism into Bactria, China, and ultimately Korea and Japan followed the traders of the Silk Road. There was a constant flow of innovative ideas in the arts and architecture in both directions. City-states developed along its labyrinth of routes. Armies followed its course, and sites such as BEGRAM display luxury items from many regions, valued by the KUSHANS during the first few centuries C.E.

Further reading; Grotenhuis, E. T. *Along the Silk Road.* Washington, D.C.: Arthur M. Sackler Gallery, Smithsonian Institution, 2002; Hopkirk, P. *Foreign Devils on the Silk Road: The Search for the Lost Cities and Treasures of Chinese Central Asia.* Boston: University of Massachusetts Press, 1984; Tucker, J. B. *The Silk Road; Art and History.* Chicago: Art Media Resources, 2003; Umesao, T., and T. Sugimura, eds. "Significance of the Silk Roads in the History of Human Civilizations." *Senri Ethnological Studies No. 32* (1992); Whitfield, R., S. Whitfield, and N. Agnew. *Cave Temples of Mogao: Art and History on the Silk Road.* Los Angeles: Getty Conservation Institute and the J. Getty Museum, 2000.

silk tomb offerings The frequency with which silks are found in tombs or described in the inventories of tomb contents, taken in conjunction with the skill of the silk weavers, makes it clear that silk fabrics were abundant during the WARRING STATES PERIOD and the HAN DYNASTY. This abundance carries with it important implications for understanding of the SILK ROAD that linked China with India and the Western world. The frozen tombs of nomads in the Altai region of Siberia have yielded Chinese silks embroidered with phoenixes, dated to the fifth century B.C.E. Silk must indeed have been exported in considerable quantities. Silk is the spun cocoon of the silkworm *Bombax mori*. The fine silk filaments are reeled off the cocoon and can then be woven into fabric. Silk was the foundation of considerable wealth for the Han Chinese (206 B.C.E.–220 C.E), when the trade link known as the Silk Road expanded across Central Asia. The silkworm feeds on the leaves of the *fusang* (mulberry) tree, and images of this tree in art of the SHANG STATE (1766–1045 B.C.E.) suggest that silk was already woven at that period. This is confirmed by the recovery of impressions of silk fabric on Shang bronzes from ANYANG. It seems that finely woven silks, embroidered with mythical animal designs, were used to wrap bronzes before interment in elite burials.

SILK IN THE WESTERN ZHOU PERIOD

Silk was used as a medium for inscriptions and paintings in China from at least the Warring States period (475–221 B.C.E.) Its fragility, however, means that few complete silks have survived. It is highly likely that silk wrappings and garments were in use at a far earlier date. When adjacent to bronze or iron, fabric is often present in the form of a pseudomorph or even as fragments of silk itself. Silk has been recovered from the Shang site of Taixi in Hebei province, attached to bronze vessels and weapons. The weavers were able to produce a marked variety of weaves reflecting a sophisticated industry with a long tradition behind it. A woman is seen working at her loom in a scene incised on a stone slab from Jiaxian, Shandong province. The quality of silk production is seen in the fine materials unearthed at the Western Zhou site of Rujiazhuang, where patterned weaves and rich red colors have survived. However, the material dating to and after the Spring and Autumn period (770–476 B.C.E.) is best known, as a result of particularly rich finds from sites belonging to the state of Chu. The production of silk during this period undoubtedly benefited from the invention of the spinning wheel, which replaced the laborious technique of hand spinning using a rod and whorl.

WARRING STATES PERIOD

Burial 44 at Zuojiatang, which dates to the Middle Warring States period, was found to contain a large quantity of silk garments in the coffin of the deceased. The quality is clearly seen in the range of weaves, the rich colors, and the patterned images of dragons, phoenixes, and geometric forms. There must have been highly specialized weavers; the brocade-weaves are very fine, with up to 120 strands of silk per square centimeter, and the remains of a stamp from a SEAL on one fragment might have been placed there by the weaving establishment responsible. Mazhuan is another Chu cemetery, where excavations in 1982 uncovered a remarkably complete set of silks dating to the period of Warring States. Tomb 1 held a coffin in a wooden chamber. The importance of silks in the mortuary rituals can be appreciated through the quantity of clothing and the variety of weaves, embroideries, and patterns. The skeleton of the tomb master was found under a silk quilt and a robe. Clothing included trousers, further robes, and a silk square over the face. All were tied with silk ribbons. Silk ribbons had also been tied around the thumbs and big toes. Apart from the clothing, there was a silk painting and bags for containing other mortuary furniture. Examination of the silks themselves revealed the outstanding quality of the weavers. There were brocades and gauzes as well as plain weaves and a variety of finishes, including one brocade with 170 filaments of silk to the square centimeter. Some of the clothes were embroidered with patterns that include images of phoenixes, tigers, dragons, plant designs, and human figures. The colors survived: red, yellow, green, blue, black, and brown.

There are two particularly interesting silk banners dating to the Warring States period (the third century B.C.E.): one from Chenjia dashan, the other from Zidanku, both in the vicinity of Changsha. The silk banner from Chenjia dashan was looted, but the robber allegedly found it on or in a suitcase adjacent to the corpse. The Zidanku painting had been placed on top of the coffin, facing upward. Both are thought to be *mingjing*, a name banner that played an important role in mortuary rituals and that bore a portrait of the dead person. That from Chenjia dashan shows an elegantly dressed woman standing on a crescent Moon under a phoenix. The bird seems to be rising up in anger against a snake. The man from Zidanku rides on a dragon boat. A crane has alighted on the dragon's tail, and a carp swims in the water below. Most interestingly, the sword the man wears matches that found in the tomb. Again, the man in the banner appears to be of middle age; the tomb master was known to be a middle-aged man. This particular silk painting also has a length of bamboo on the upper edge and a ribbon attached, just as on modern banners.

HAN DYNASTY SILKS

The most famous silk garments and paintings of the Han dynasty, including a further *mingjing* tomb banner, are from Tomb 1 at MAWANGDUI. The chamber of this burial was covered in layers of charcoal and clay and, effectively sealed from air and the damp, was exceptionally well preserved. It contained the remains of the wife of the marquis of dai, who was interred not long after her husband, who died in 168 B.C.E. The innermost of the four nested and lacquered coffins was covered with a painted silk banner of three pieces of fabric sewn together into a T-shape.

Mawangdui Silk Banner

The painting was intended to act as a guide for the spirit of the deceased woman to the next world. For the Chu, there were two spirits of the dead, one known as the HUN, the other as the *po*. At death, the former traveled to heaven; the latter remained in the ground and became a ghost, or *gui*. To satisfy the needs of the *po*, it was necessary to supply offerings that were useful or desirable; hence the many artifacts and personal effects listed on bamboo tomb inventories and placed with the dead.

The *hun*, however, had to undertake a dangerous journey on its route to celestial heaven. This remarkable banner was probably carried in the funerary procession. The painting can be divided into three linked representations of the journey to heaven. At the base, there is a scene of the underworld. Two entwined fish indicate the watery world below, while two large dragons emerge from the depths, and their bodies pass through a jade ring before they ascend into the middle part of the banner. Their tails are linked by a snake that lies on top of the fish, while a giant, also standing on the fish, holds aloft a floor that contains a remarkable scene: the body of the marchioness of Dai lying on her back surrounded by six mourners. Sacrificial vessels lie in front of the dais containing the body, wrapped in a silk shroud, and other vessels are set on a table beyond. A large jade pendant is suspended from the jade ring, and together they symbolize the link between the world of people and the heavens. Part of each dragon's sinuous body supports a leopard, which in turn supports a platform richly ornamented with lozenge patterns. The central figure of the banner stands on this platform: She is a richly dressed older woman holding a stick. Three servant women stand behind her, one dressed in white, one in red, and the third in blue. Two men kneel in front of her, each carrying a tray. This woman is the marchioness of Dai. She

wears an elegant patterned robe incorporating cloud patterns matched by the fabric on the platform below that bears her prostrate body.

A further platform hangs over this scene, supported by an owl. It bears two phoenixes, creatures waiting to escort the spirit to heaven. This celestial realm is depicted on the upper third of the banner, lying beyond two portals protected by leopards. The heavens contain numerous symbolic figures. The Sun is seen encircling the crow that represents it, both positioned over a *fusang* (mulberry) tree, through which smaller solar disks can be seen. This scene is full of symbolic meaning. The early texts refer to the *fusang* tree as the link between Earth and heaven. There were formerly 10 Suns, all of which are represented over and through the branches of this tree. The large disk over the tree incorporates the *jingwu* bird, the crow, which carries the solar disk across the heavens daily and rests over the tree at night. To the top left is the crescent Moon. Two more dragons occupy the middle of the scene, and there are deities on horseback who surround a bell. The most intriguing figure is a human head and torso with a serpent's tail. This probably represents the dead woman transformed into an ancestral deity. A similar male figure with a serpent's tail is found in the same location on the silk banner from Tomb 3 at Mawangdui.

Other Silk at Mawangdui

This unique banner was not the only remarkable silk painting from Mawangdui. Two other tombs were also uncovered; however, in neither case was the preservation of organic remains so perfect. One contained the remains of the marquis of Dai; their son is the person probably buried in Tomb 3. This last pit contained manuscripts written on silk. Silk was widely used as a medium for written documents during the Han dynasty, and those from Mawangdui must represent part of this aristocrat's library, for they include some well-known texts. The *Yijing*, for example, is a renowned book on divining. Another text covers medical remedies and includes pictures illustrating breathing exercises. There are also three remarkable maps showing the topography and location of military garrisons in the region of which Mawangdui was part. A second banner like that found in Tomb 1 was also recovered.

Silk was used as a medium for writing before the invention of paper, and it might also have played a role in the evolution of printing. A Chu tomb at Changsha was found to be stamped with the name of either the owner or the manufacturer. Similar designs imparted to the silk by means of a stamp were found on some of the Mawangdui fabrics.

Further reading: Klimburg-Salter, D. E. *The Silk Route and the Diamond Path.* Los Angeles: UCLA Art Council, 1982; Li Xueqin. *Eastern Zhou and Qin Civilizations.* New Haven, Conn.: Yale University Press, 1985;

Loewe, M., and Shaugnessy, E. L., eds. *The Cambridge History of Ancient China.* Cambridge: Cambridge University Press, 1999; Umesao, T., and T. Sugimura, eds. "Significance of the Silk Roads in the History of Human Civilizations." *Senri Ethnological Studies No. 32.* (1992).

sima   A *sima* is a term found in ninth- and 10th-century INSCRIPTIONS from Java in Indonesia to describe a charter issued by royal authority for the determination of taxation payments. The *sima* were recorded on stone and copper inscriptions and provide much information on the way in which taxes on rice field production could be diverted to the maintenance of temples or the provision of facilities such as aqueducts.

Sima Qian (145–85 B.C.E.) *Sima Qian was the grand astrologer to the Han court during the reign of Emperor Han Wudi.*

He succeeded his father, SIMA TAN, in this post in 108 B.C.E., having already spent several years in the court undertaking a variety of functions. In 111 B.C.E. he was sent to the newly won southwestern provinces on a tour of inspection. One of his first responsibilities after his appointment was to reform the Chinese calendar in 104 B.C.E., but his enduring importance rests on the *SHIJI* (*The Records of the Grand Historian*). His work set out to be the definitive history of the Chinese people; in his own words, "I have wanted to study everything that concerns heaven and man, to understand the evolution that has been proceeding from antiquity to our own times." The *Shiji* set a new standard for Chinese historic scholarship that not only is a valued source of information on Chinese history to this day, but also provided a model for the many subsequent dynastic histories over a period of two millennia. There are 130 chapters and five sections, known as the annals; the history of dynastic houses; biographies of leading individuals; the history of foreign peoples; and treatises. It was written under considerable duress, for Sima Qian infuriated the emperor by defending General Li Ling, who had suffered disgrace. He was charged with the offense of defaming the emperor and although he was reprieved from the death penalty, he suffered the punishment of castration in 98 B.C.E. Despite this punishment, he continued to serve in the imperial court, rising to the important post of *zhongshuling*, head of the secretariat.

SIMA QIAN'S SOURCES

Writing a history of China at that time was not straightforward. The unification of China under the first emperor, QIN SHIHUANGDI (259–210 B.C.E.), had replaced a series of independent states under the nominal rule of the ZHOU DYNASTY (1045–256 B.C.E.) with a centralized autocracy, and Sima Qian's sources were disparate and often contradictory. His work included an essay written by his father, Sima Tan, who was grand historian between about 140 and 110 B.C.E., on the six early traditions of political philosophy. This provides an invaluable insight into the reaction of a major historian to the tenets of such schools of thought as LEGALISM ("They are harsh and lack compassion"), the Confucians, and the Taoists. Sima Qian began his own great contribution by outlining the history of the dominant kingdom first at any given time and then within one chronological framework describing the development of each state. There follow detailed histories of each kingdom and a series of biographies of important individuals. These were used as vehicles for illustrating the pitfalls and opportunities presented by different approaches to the art of government.

The Han dynasty under Han Wudi was undergoing an unprecedented period of imperial expansion. To the south, the many chiefdoms of Lingnan and Vietnam were being absorbed in the empire, while to the north, Korea was occupied, and there was much warfare and expansion to the northwest. Sima Qian therefore incorporated as far as he could the available information on the peoples who lived beyond the border or were in danger of being absorbed in it.

His work, particularly as it concerned events close to his own life, when memories were still fresh, provides a remarkable insight into the turbulent end of the WARRING STATES PERIOD (475–221 B.C.E.), the advent of the brief-lived QIN dynasty (221–206 B.C.E.), and the inception of the HAN DYNASTY (206 B.C.E.–220 C.E.). At the same time, it must be stressed that he had every reason to criticize the autocracy of Qin Shihuangdi, the first emperor, to embellish the image of his own emperor. He was also critical of the faults and strengths of former regimes. There is a Confucian element to his comment: "One who succors the weak and aids the weary, as the ruler of a great kingdom is commanded to do, need never worry that he will not gain his way with the lands within the seas." By contrast, he says of Qin Shihuangdi: "The First Emperor trusted his own judgment, never consulting others, and hence his errors went uncorrected." The second emperor, HUHAI, "carried on in the same manner, never reforming, compounding his misfortune through violence and cruelty. . . . Is it not fitting that they perished?"

DEATH OF QIN SHIHUANGDI

Sima Qian provides a vivid picture of the life, death, and burial of the first emperor, who was interred beside the terra-cotta army at Xi'an. Qin Shihuangdi exercised an enormous influence on China for centuries after his death. Sima Qian wrote, "The First Emperor was greedy and short-sighted, never trusting his meritorious officials." He was violent and cruel, harsh and deceitful. Just before his death, he wrote that his son, Prince Fusu, should undertake the burial rituals and presumably succeed him. But palace officials destroyed the letter and forged another, requiring Fusu to commit suicide and declaring their own choice of successor. The emperor's body was returned secreted in a carriage accompanied by fish to disguise the odor of putrefaction, in case news of the death encouraged insurrections. The interment of the emperor in his tomb at Mount Li near Xi'an involved a huge investment of labor, including a bronze outer coffin and innumerable treasures. Crossbows were put in place to deter looters, the king's wives who had not borne a son were sacrificed, and the workers who knew of the interior layout of the tomb were immured alive.

See also CONFUCIUS; TAOISM.

Sima Tan (active 140–110 B.C.E.) *Sima Tan was the grand historian to the Han court in China.*
The unification of China under the QIN dynasty in 221 B.C.E. saw the replacement of many conflicting states by one centralized autocracy. This provided for the first time a sense of imperial unity given further impetus under the HAN DYNASTY (206 B.C.E.–220 C.E.), with its policy of imperial expansion. Sima Tan was therefore in a position to initiate the idea of a great history of China from its earliest dynasties. However, he died before he could complete the text. As recorded by his son, SIMA QIAN, Sima Tan described how their ancestors had for generations been historians to the Zhou emperors and exhorted his son to continue his work. Sima Qian did succeed his father as grand historian and completed the work in about 100 B.C.E. He incorporated the writings of his father on the six major traditions of political philosophy in the SHIJI (*Records of the Grand Historian*).

Simhapura *See* TRA KIEU.

Sindok (early 10th century C.E.) *Sindok was a Javanese king who ruled in the Brantas River Valley in east Java in Indonesia.*
The earliest INSCRIPTION to name Sindok as king is dated to 929 C.E. The Brantas River area was strategic both for rice cultivation and for international trade, particularly in spices.

Sirkap Sirkap is the local name for the second city at the site of TAXILA in northern Pakistan. Strategically situated to take advantage of major trade routes, Sirkap was occupied during the Indo-Greek and Scythian-Parthian periods, from the second century B.C.E. until the conquest by the KUSHANS in the late first century C.E. Excavations by SIR JOHN MARSHALL revealed a rigid grid plan to the city and the stone foundations of substantial domestic dwellings. Marshall also uncovered a palace structure and the northern gate, which formed part of a heavily fortified stone wall equipped with bastions.

Sirsukh Sirsukh is the local name for the third city of TAXILA in northern Pakistan. Founded by the KUSHANS in the late first century C.E., it was heavily defended by a stone wall incorporating regularly spaced bastions.

Sisupalgarh Sisupalgarh, ancient Tosali, is located to command the lower reaches of the Mahanadi River system in Orissa province, eastern coastal India. It is a large walled city covering an area of 130 hectares (325 acres), and excavations within the walls have revealed an occupation sequence to a depth of eight meters (26.4 ft.), with four major periods of occupation. The first has revealed little material culture and is not dated. The pottery, however, is probably earlier than 500 B.C.E. Period 2A lasted from about 500 to 200 B.C.E., but it was during the next period, 2B, that the fortifications were constructed. The fortifications date to between 200 B.C.E. and 200 C.E. and are a massive wall of mud, 10 to 12 meters wide at the base and rising to a height of at least eight meters.

The excavations of the western gateway revealed a large and impressive structure of cut laterite, including guardrooms, corridors, and steps to the upper rampart. This gateway was, according to an INSCRIPTION, severely damaged by a cyclone and later rebuilt, events confirmed by archaeology. The interior of the city was at this time laid out in a regular grid of streets, and substantial houses were constructed of laterite. Rut marks on the roads reveal the regular passage of wheeled vehicles. It was during this phase that an inscription was raised at Udayagiri Hill 10 kilometers (6 mi.) from the city that mentioned the reconstruction of a canal by King Kharavela, who reigned during the first century B.C.E., that carried water to the city. It is likely that this strongly defended fortress was his major center. It is well positioned to take advantage of maritime trade with Southeast Asia and with southern India, as the presence of rouletted ware confirms.

Siva Siva was one the great trinity of Hindu gods. He was commonly worshiped in the form of a LINGAM, or phallus. One of the earliest lingams in southern India is from a a second-century B.C.E. context at Gudimallam. Siva had many names, including Rudra, Mahadeva, Trinetra, and Sitikantha. He became very popular in Southeast Asia, adopted into the pantheon of gods worshiped in the kingdom of ANGKOR, in Cambodia and among the CHAMS. Many lingams were placed in the temples, and the name of Siva was linked with that of the ruling sovereign.

Siyelik Siyelik is a site of the HOTAN kingdom, China. It was discovered by SIR AUREL STEIN in 1906, during his expedition to the TARIM BASIN, lying south of the large Buddhist temple of Rawak. The area of Siyelik has several Buddhist temples and stupas, dating probably to the fourth century C.E.

Skandagupta (455–467 C.E.) *Skandagupta was the Gupta emperor in India who had to withstand the HEPHTHALITE incursions.*

The Junagadh INSCRIPTION describes him as "the chosen one of Sri Lakshmi, goddess of wealth." The GUPTA EMPIRE was known for its prosperity, which is reflected in the coin issues of the successive kings. Skandagupta's issues are no exception, and the themes show him with his divine queen, Lakshmi, and with the mythical Garuda after his victory over the Huns.

slavery   It is clear that Chinese emperors commanded huge pools of labor. In the case of the SHANG DYNASTY; however, the ORACLE BONES have not provided any instance of a word that means "slave." The two terms to describe people who work or undertake duties for the ruler, *zhong* and *ren,* do not imply a condition of slavery. Nor do the many burials associated with the royal tombs of ANYANG, which might just as well contain the remains of retainers with no implication of their being slaves.

The documentary sources for the period of the GUPTA EMPIRE in India reveal the presence of a form of slavery that was linked with the caste system. Thus members of the Brahmin cast could not be enslaved. If a free woman married a slave, she herself became one, but in the contrary case, a woman marrying a free man was freed from slavery. There are also allusions in Gupta dramas to unsuccessful gamblers becoming slaves to repay debts.

CAMBODIA

The issue of slavery in the history of states in Cambodia is not easy to resolve, because it is highly likely that the status of potential slaves changed over the course of 1,500 years. Many INSCRIPTIONS employ the KHMER word *knum* to designate slave. Although this word means "slave" in Khmer today, Michael Vickery has pointed out that in Old Mon, a language closely related to Old Khmer, the word means "child." Thus, early inscriptions might be referring to junior relatives of emerging leaders when employing this word. There is no doubt, even in the period of CHENLA, that many men and women worked for the temple. Again, however, this might have been a means of making merit rather than the result of coercion. An inscription from Wat Prei Val mentions King JAYAVARMAN I who ruled in the second half of the seventh century C.E. It specifies that he ordered that the great-nephew of the two founders of the sanctuary have the exclusive rights over the donations made by his great uncles, including the animals, slaves, forests, and fields. An inscription of the same reign noted that the king joined others in endowing a foundation with fields, gardens, cattle, many buffaloes, and slaves. The inscriptions of the first dynasty of ANGKOR (about 800–1000 C.E.) refer to elite aristocrats and their meritorious acts but also contain details of land ownership, field boundaries, and duties of the retainers. Again, there are many references to slaves, but it would wrong to regard this as a slave-based society. The rural populace donated part of their time and labor to maintain the local temple.

A text from the reign of JAYAVARMAN IV (928–942 C.E.) includes an order from the king to join two temples. The benefactor of the temple provided 117 male and female slaves for the dark fortnight when the moon is waning and 130 for the period of the waxing moon, each group with its person in charge. This important insight suggests that there was a rotation system in which workers were required to provide labor for half the month to the temple and presumably worked for themselves during the rest of the month. A text from Phnom Mrec, inscribed during the late 10th century C.E., describes how a certain Soma gave an endowment of land to a sanctuary of SIVA. He paid two pairs of buffaloes and four *jyan* of silver for a piece of land. For a second parcel, he paid two slaves, a measure of gold, a pair of buffaloes, and two cattle. The prices paid for slaves assigned to the temple of the goddess Bhagabati are set out in an inscription from Phum Mien. Several were exchanged for other slaves, and one was bought from a Vietnamese for silver. An inscription from Phnom Kanva, Battambang, describes how a worker named Viruna escaped from the estate where he was born and on his recapture had his eyes gouged out and his nose cut off. It was also customary in listing workers to include their children and even grandchildren. Writing of his visit to ANGKOR THOM in the late 13th century, ZHOU DAGUAN described how rich families would maintain more than 100 slaves; poorer families had only a handful or none at all. These slaves, while able to speak Khmer, were acquired from the forested uplands. Recaptured slaves who had attempted to escape were to be confined by an iron collar or anklet.

It thus seems likely that at least some form of tied or corvée labor predominated, at least in the kingdom of Angkor, for the inscriptions contain so many allusions to workers required to donate half their time to a temple foundation. The inscriptions from KOH KER (Lingapura), the capital of Jayavarman IV, also list numerous workers from various districts who labored on the construction of the temples and reservoir. The status of those listed as *knum* during the Chenla period, however, may have been that of junior kin of the social elite, whose work for the temple provided at least a measure of personal merit.

Sogdiana   Sogdiana lies in the basins of the Zerafshan and Kashka Dar'ya Rivers, between the Syr Dar'ya and Amu Dar'ya Rivers in Kazakhstan, south of the Aral Sea. Sogdian cities were flourishing centers for trade, agriculture, and the arts. The building technique involved construction in compressed loess and mud brick. Large town houses and palaces often had three stories. Interiors were decorated with vigorous and accomplished wall paintings, which illustrate the sumptuous way of life of aristocratic merchants and rulers. There are, for example, images of the receipt of ambassadors, feasting scenes, hunting, and travel in elegant boats into the reedy margins of lakes rich in waterfowl. Horse riding and images of warriors were popular, as were mythical events. Rich houses, too, included a hall with images of the deities. Wooden statues and reliefs have also survived; silversmiths were skilled in the production of ceremonial or feasting vessels, which elegantly depict camels and deer. The broad canvas of Sogdian trade and travel meant that many religions and scripts are represented: Christian and Buddhist texts have been found scratched on pottery vessels. The dead were excarnated and the bones placed in decorated ossuaries. A scene from one such ossuary shows two worshipers on their knees before a fire altar. In the sophisticated dress of the upper classes at cities like Panjikent, status was indicated through belts with golden plaques. This flourishing and sophisticated society finally succumbed in the eighth century to the eastward expansion of the Arabs.

Farther east than the rich agricultural land of KHWARIZM, Sogdiana was not so exposed to foreign domination, although it was described as the most easterly of the Seleucid satrapies. Its main center during the early historic period, also the most easterly known Greek city foundation, was Alexandria Eschate (modern Khojand). Sogdiana was a satrapy of the ACHAEMENID EMPIRE from the sixth century B.C.E. but was subdued during the eastern campaign of ALEXANDER THE GREAT in 329–327 B.C.E. and thereafter was incorporated in the independent state of BACTRIA-Sogdiana under Diodotus I in the middle of the third century B.C.E. Sogdiana itself assumed independence from Bactria, an event long assumed to have taken place after the death of King Euthydemus I in about 200 B.C.E. However, new numismatic evidence now places this event toward the end of that king's reign. Sogdiana was not fully incorporated into the KUSHAN empire but was briefly subdued by the HEPHTHALITE HUNS during the early sixth century C.E. Sogdiana thereafter is best known as a vital node in the SILK ROAD, controlling as it did the east-west caravans, and it was as well the source of furs from the north. *The History of the Tang Dynasty* noted: "They excel at commerce and love profits. . . . Men of Sogdiana have gone wherever profit is to be found."

SOGDIAN CITIES AND COLONIES

Thus there developed a series of major cities, whose wealth grew not only on the success of their merchant class, but also on the returns from extensively irrigated fields and the establishment of craft workshops to weave silk. The Sogdian language was eastern Iranian and became a lingua franca of the Silk Road. There was a Sogdian colony at distant DUNHUANG, and their letters home have survived in the archives of the ruler of PANJIKENT, Divashtich, dating to the early eighth century. Although Divashtich claimed sovereignty over all Sogdiana, there appear to have been local polities based in the major centers, of which AFRASIAB, modern Samarqand, was the largest with an area of about 220 hectares (550 acres). Other urban centers were Panjikent and VARAKSHA. Each such center was ruled by a local prince.

The Sogdians established trading settlements subject to their own laws, at strategic points along the Silk Road. In 1907 SIR AUREL STEIN was working at one such site near Dunhuang when he discovered a mailbag containing letters from the local Sogdian community for delivery to Samarqand. It never reached its destination; its contents are most revealing. One letter was written by a woman abandoned by her husband. Another, from the hand of a merchant named Nanai-vandak, provides a clear image of the political upheavals that beset China, and in its description of historical events it can be dated to June or July 313 C.E. It describes famine in the capital, LUOYANG, and war with the XIONGNU. It also lists some of the goods that were traded along the Silk Road, including gold and silver, linen and woolen fabrics, wheat, pepper, and camphor. Intriguingly, it does not mention silk.

Further reading: Marshak, B. I., and N. N. Negmatov, *Sogdiana*. In *History of Civilizations of Central Asia*, Vol. III, edited by B. A. Litvinsky. Paris: UNESCO, 1996; Marshak, B. I., V. A. Livshits, and W. A. Pini. *Legends, Tales, and Fables in the Art of Sogdiana*. New York: Bibliotheca Persica, 2002.

Sokkuram   Sokkuram is without doubt one of the most famous of all Buddhist shrines in Korea, if not the most famous. It is located at Mount Toham near Kyongju in the southeastern part of the peninsula and dates to the mid-eighth century C.E. By that juncture, the kingdom of SHILLA had overcome the other states of the Three Kingdoms period, PAEKCHE and KOGORYU, and ruled all Korea from the capital of Kyongju. BUDDHISM had taken hold in this area five centuries previously and was enthusiastically followed from the seventh century. The Sokkuram shrine incorporated first an antechamber, then a small vestibule, before entering the circular shrine room. It was constructed of large slabs of granite hewn from the neighboring rock and covered with a tumulus to resemble a rock-cut temple. A sculpture of the enthroned Buddha standing 3.3 meters (10.9 ft.) high dominates the shrine room and is rendered with matchless serenity and power. Behind, on the walls, are 11 figures of BODHISATTVAS, gods, and disciples. The most famous of these is the 11-headed Bodhisattva Avalokitesvara.

Song Yirang (early 20th century) *Song Yirang was a leading scholar and student of the Anyang oracle-bone texts.* In his 1917 publication *Chiwen Juli* (Examples of ORACLE-BONE inscriptions), he noted, "At last, I found some way to understand the meanings of these ancient documents."

The eighth-century shrine at Sokkuram, Korea, is one of the finest examples of Shilla architecture. The temple contains a notable stone image of the Buddha standing to a height of more than three meters (about 10 feet). (© Carmen Redondo/CORBIS)

Sonkh Sonkh is a major urban settlement located near the middle reaches of the Jamuna River in Uttar Pradesh state, India. As have many other cities of the MAURYA to GUPTA EMPIRES, it has a long sequence of preceding IRON AGE occupation, dating to between 800 to 400 B.C.E. There followed a Mauryan occupation during which houses were constructed of mud and roofed with wood and reeds. During the ensuing period of SUNGA rule (185–73 B.C.E.), mud-brick structures, houses having several rooms grouped around a courtyard, were recovered. There were a street system and public drains. Excavations in 1966–74 also encountered a temple building raised on a platform and dated to the first century B.C.E. It had undergone several rebuilding phases. Occupation continued through the KUSHAN period into the period of the Gupta empire, again with houses grouped along a street grid and equipped with bathrooms and latrines.

Sothi Sothi is a four-hectare (10-acre) settlement located in the former valley of the extinct Drishadvati River in northern India. Limited excavations in 1978 revealed two phases of occupation, the lower belonging to the SOTHI-SISWAL phase of the early Harappan culture, and the second to the fully developed INDUS VALLEY CIVILIZATION (c. 2500–c. 1770 B.C.E.).

Sothi-Siswal Sothi-Siswal is the name given to one of the four pre-Harappan phases of cultural development in India. The sites in question concentrate in the valley of the extinct rivers SARASVATI and Drishadvati. The name derives from two of the typical sites of the period; KALIBANGAN in its early phase and Banawali are the best-known settlements. In terms of size, the vast majority of the villages were less than five hectares (12.5 acres) in area and reveal evidence of ceramic industries, long-distance trade in marine shells and LAPIS LAZULI, and a knowledge of copper smelting. Some of the sites might have been occupied only on a temporary basis, for subsistence included animal herding as well as agriculture. A date in the third millennium B.C.E. is most likely, but the chronology of this phase remains equivocal.

See also INDUS VALLEY CIVILIZATION; SOTHI.

Spice Islands Spices were one of the major export commodities of Southeast Asia, and their cultivation and trade generated considerable wealth for the local rulers. CLOVES, NUTMEG, and mace were particularly favored and grew only in the Maluku (Moluccas, or Spice Islands in Indonesia). They include about 1,000 islands, many of which are small and uninhabited, east of Sulawesi and west of Papua New Guinea.

Spring and Autumn period See EASTERN ZHOU DYNASTY.

Sras Srang The Sras Srang, "royal bath," is a small BARAY (reservoir) measuring 700 by 300 meters (770 by 330 yds.) located south of the EASTERN BARAY at ANGKOR in Cambodia. It was constructed during the reign of RAJENDRAVARMAN (944–68 C.E.), and a contemporary INSCRIPTION decrees that tame elephants should not be permitted to bathe in it or damage its earth dykes. The *baray* was embellished under JAYAVARMAN VII (1181–1219), who added a laterite and sandstone platform, a large statue of GARUDA, and access stairs to the water. A chance discovery at the northwest corner of the Sras Srang uncovered three pottery jars containing cremated human remains associated with bronze Buddha images. The French archaeologist B.-P. Groslier subsequently excavated extensively and found further mortuary jars containing human ashes. Offerings included Chinese ceramic vessels, ceramic figures, bronze mirrors, iron weapons, ingots, and pieces of lead. A tin vessel was associated with one cremation, and one pot contained seven lead ingots. In one instance, a pair of bronze mirrors was found on an east-west orientation. The ivory handle survived on another mirror. Bronze images of the Buddha and Vishnu riding the eagle Garuda were also recovered.

Sravasti Sravasti was the capital of the MAHAJANAPADA of Kosala. It was designated one of the cities fit to receive the remains of the Buddha after his cremation and is located next to a former channel of the Rapti River, a tributary of the Ganges (Ganga) River in northern India. The city was visited by XUANZANG, a Chinese Buddhist monk, in the early seventh century C.E. He described the old palace city as lying in ruins but was still able to trace its boundaries as measuring about 12 kilometers (7.2 mi.). A disciple of the Buddha, Sudatta-Anathapindika, founded a monastery there for the use of the Buddha, and this is known as the Jetavana Vihara. This gift is recorded in a second-century B.C.E. INSCRIPTION on one of the railing pillars of the stupa there; the text describes how Anathapindika bought the Jetavana Park by covering it with coins and presenting it to the Buddhist community. This monastery forms the nucleus of Saheth, that part of Sravasti that was the focus of Buddhist pilgrimage and worship. It is enclosed by a wall. Xuanzang described this monastery as lying about three kilometers south of the city, but it too lay in ruins. He also saw two stone columns standing 20 meters (66 ft.) high, one topped with a wheel, the other with the carving of a lion. Both were erected, he said, by King ASOKA. Maheth, on the other hand, is the fortified city of Sravasti.

The Jetavana monastery was examined in detail by SIR ALEXANDER CUNNINGHAM in 1875–76. He found the site covered in jungle and used an elephant to move through the dense vegetation to identify walls and foundations. Excavations undertaken in 1959 identified three periods. Initial settlement took place during the period when NORTHERN BLACK POLISHED WARE was in vogue, dated to about 500–300 B.C.E. The mud ramparts, with a fired-brick addition, belong to Period 2, when punch-marked coins were used. This period belongs to the last three centuries B.C.E., and during the third period, occupation continued into the first centuries C.E. The monastic establishment continued for many centuries, for an inscription of the 12th century recorded a gift of land to the Jetavana monastery.

See also COINAGE.

Sreshthapura See WAT PHU.

Sri Ksetra The Chinese monk I CHING in the seventh century C.E. described a city probably located in the Irrawaddy Valley of Myanmar (Burma), which he named Sri Ksetra.

EXCAVATIONS AT SRI KSETRA

Reporting in 1926, Charles Duroiselle described his excavations at the Khinba mound. This site was identified after villagers found stone sculptures representing Vishnu, but the mound turned out to be the base of a Buddhist stupa. Many votive terra-cotta tablets were found; the prize was the intact relic chamber, sealed with a large stone. This slab bore a relief carving of a stupa, whose form matched that of the large stupa of Bawbawgyi. Removal of this stone revealed a brick-lined chamber in the center of which lay a miniature silver stupa surrounded by four Buddha figures each with an attendant. The stupa was inscribed in Pyu and PALI of a style characteristic of the sixth century C.E. Each text names the figure facing it as being one of Buddha's disciples. A Pyu text also names two individuals, Sri Prabhuvarma and Sri Prabhudevi, who are probably the founding king and the queen. Other items in this relic chamber provide some idea of the wealth that is missing from other such monuments as a result of widespread looting. They include a superb gold statue of the Buddha standing 15 centimeters (6 in.) high, seated on a throne. A second such gold statue was found, but without the throne. No fewer than 50 other Buddha statues were recovered, in gold, silver, and lead, varying in height from 2.5 to 12.5 centimeters (1 to 5 in.). There were 24 silver or gold plates with relief images of the Buddha, a glass image of the Buddha, silver plates bearing images of door guardians, many silver bowls, silver or gold caskets, and five gold trays. Forty-five silver coins were also found among the offerings, together with 20 inscribed gold leaves. Extraordinarily, these gold leaves were bound together with gold wire, which was threaded through two holes on each leaf. When the wire was cut, it was possible to unfold and read the texts. Each leaf incorporated three lines in Pali of sacred Buddhist texts. The DHARMA preached by the Buddha is one of the four objects of veneration that might be included in a stupa reliquary; the others are the actual remains of the Buddha, his personal belongings, or items from places the Buddha had visited. The catalogue of finds from this remarkable deposit continues with a large assemblage of beads in gold, quartz, carnelian, amethyst, chalcedony, glass, and jade and 12 jade figurines of elephants. One of these is only 12 millimeters (0.48 in.) long. There are silver and gold lotuses, gold and silver bells, gold and silver cups, butterflies, statuettes of deer in gold, and a silver duck. These finds, which could have originated only with a royal foundation, stress the extraordinary amount of information that has been lost to the widespread looting that had afflicted such monuments even a century ago.

Two years later Duroiselle continued his research at Sri Ksetra with the examination of a series of 34 stupas and burial mounds. One stupa foundation contained a brick-lined chamber just over one meter square, in which he found eight bronze images of the Buddha, each about 10 centimeters (4 in.) tall. This chamber lay over a second, which contained many terra-cotta votive tablets of 10th-century style, bearing SANSKRIT holy texts. Outside the city walls, he investigated a low mound also with a relic chamber and found a superb hollow gold image of the Buddha. It contained a tiny silver casket full of cremated ash. During this season, a villager took to Duroiselle a strip of gold about 20 centimeters (8 in.) long, on which an inscription in Pali set out a Buddhist sacred writing. Such gold plaques have also been found in the FUNAN sites of the Mekong Delta. A further archaeological discovery in the 1966–67 excavation season provided insight into the skill of the bronze casters and aspects of city life: a group of five figures each standing 110 centimeters (3.6 ft.) in height. Two are dancing, while the others play musical instruments. The elegant hairstyles and profusion of jewelry worn by these Pyu entertainers enhance the appreciation of life in this huge urban complex. A further bronze of Avalokitesvara had been found near the Bobogyi stupa in 1911.

XUANZANG, a Chinese pilgrim, described this Buddhist capital of a state in about 643 C.E. The large walled and moated city of Hmawza is widely considered to have been a major capital of this PYU CIVILIZATION. A SANSKRIT inscription dating on stylistic grounds to the seventh century C.E. describes two cities, each ruled by a separate dynasty. Sri Ksetra was probably one of these cities. Another inscription in Old Mon from the Shwehsandaw temple describes the mythical founding of Sri Ksetra in 544 B.C.E. It lies in the valley of the Nawin River just east of the modern city of Prome. Here the rivers flowing from the Pegu Yoma are a source of irrigation water in an area where rainfall itself is insufficient for the cultivation of rice.

Burmese tradition has it that Sri Ksetra was founded by King Duttabaung about 2,400 years ago. He captured Princess Panhtwar of BEIKTHANO and took her to his city.

This piece of oral history might well reflect warfare between rival Pyu centers: Both at Beikthano and at HALIN there is widespread evidence for destruction by fire. Sri Ksetra fell into a decline during the ninth century and was abandoned.

THE CITY PLAN

Sri Ksetra has an oval plan, demarcated by a massive BRICK wall and a moat enclosing an area of 1,880 hectares (4,700 acres). A rectangular enclosure just south of the city center, measuring 650 by 350 meters (715 by 385 yds.), was probably a palace precinct. There are also many other moated enclosures, both within and beyond the walls, which may have enclosed religious structures. The study of aerial photographs has also identified two large reservoirs within the city walls and the large eastern reservoir beyond the eastern walls. Janice Stargardt has further noted possible field systems that would have been fed by IRRIGATION water. Several stupas have survived, confirming the dominance of BUDDHISM in the Pyu state. The Bobogyi stupa, dating to the seventh or eighth century on the basis of its votive tablets, has a cylindrical form above five circular terraces and lies just south of the city wall. The Lemyethna temple, also outside the city wall, is of square form with four entrances. The foundations of a large hall have been uncovered by excavation near the Shedaga city gate. It was 30 meters (99 ft.) long and 20 (66 ft.) wide, and the superstructure was made of wood. The Payamagyi stupa lies north of the city wall, and an adjacent brick structure contained stone mortuary vessels inscribed with the names of three kings. These have been translated by Charles Blagden as follows: "A relative of Suryavikrama died in 673 C.E. Suryavikrama died in 688 C.E. at the age of 64. Harivikrama died in 695 C.E. at the age of 41, and Sihavikrama died in 718 C.E. at the age of 44 years." It is highly likely that these kings were members of a ruling dynasty. Other large stone urns have also been recovered and were in all probability the burial places of the elite. Finely decorated stone "thrones" have been recovered, confirming a megalithic aspect of the Pyu monumental carving.

Many brick mortuary structures lie outside the city walls, as at the related Pyu city of Beikthano. The brick temples and stupas were formerly covered in plaster and presumably decorated. Many of the plans and elevations anticipate those of PAGAN, and large stone images of the Buddha and Hindu deities, particularly Vishnu, make clear the religious leanings of the Pyu rulers. Small statues and precious artifacts in gold and silver have been found.

Sringaverapur Sringaverapur is a historic Indian city site located on the banks of the Ganges (Ganga) River. Already known as a major site mentioned in the RAMAYANA, it was excavated in 1977–85 under the direction of B. B. Lal. Late prehistoric settlement was revealed, followed by occupation during the MAURYA EMPIRE (324–c. 200 B.C.E.), when a remarkable tank was constructed to store floodwaters from the Ganges (Ganga) River. This was followed by KUSHAN occupation, during which houses were constructed.

Sri Thep Sri Thep is strategically located in the valley of the Pa Sak River in central Thailand. It is a large moated settlement covering 4.7 square kilometers (1.88 sq. mi.). As many DVARAVATI CIVILIZATION sites have, it has prehistoric origins; historic occupation began in the sixth century and lasted at least into the 13th century C.E. Several monuments lie within the moated precinct, most prominent of which is the Khao Klang Nai temple with its stucco friezes. One frieze depicts crouching dwarfs, some with the head of a lion or a cow. Further finds include part of a "wheel of the law" (DHARMACAKRA) and bronze images of the Buddha. Lying on the western margins of the kingdom of ANGKOR in Cambodia, the site was heavily influenced and probably incorporated into this state. Prang Song Phi Nong and Prang Sri Thep were built in the 11th to 12th centuries; images of SIVA, Vishnu, Surya, and Krishna have been found at or near Sri Thep.

Srivijaya Srivijaya was a kingdom centered on the island of Sumatra in Indonesia. Several inscriptions in Old Malay recovered from the vicinity of PALEMBANG reveal the presence of a king named Jayanasa, who followed BUDDHISM, created a public park for making merit, and expanded his domain through maritime and land-based military campaigns. According to the Chinese monk I CHING, there were then a walled capital and a population of more than 1,000 Buddhist monks versed in the sacred scriptures. According to his report, they had gold and silver images of the Buddha and gold ritual vessels in the form of lotus flowers. Palembang, the capital, was situated on the bank of the Musi River, which gave it direct access to the sea and international trading routes. The wealth and power of Srivijaya were largely based on this favorable location for participating in trade, which linked China with India and Persia. However, its continued prosperity also depended on controlling rival port states, and the INSCRIPTIONS and contemporary accounts suggest that Srivijaya incorporated potential rivals in its own polity.

Thus Palembang was first and foremost a port. It is located on the southeastern part of Sumatra, so as to control the Strait of Melaka to the north and the Sunda Strait that separates Sumatra and Java to the south. As Chinese trade began to bypass the Mekong Delta and go directly to Sumatra, the state of FUNAN declined, and Srivijaya expanded. Aerial pictures have revealed possible docking facilities at Palembang. An inscription dated to 683 C.E. describes a military expedition with a force of 2,000 against the rival port center of Jambi-Malayu. A second inscription from Nakhon Sri Thammarat on the east coast of peninsular Thailand illustrates this point, for it describes how in 775 C.E. a Buddhist king of Srivijaya founded a monastery there. Further archaeological evidence for Srivijayan presence in peninsular Thailand, and therefore control of the transisthmian trade routes, is from the sites of Chaiya, where the temples of Phra Boromathat and Wat Kaew were constructed, and from Yarang in the valley of the Pattani River on the east coast of the peninsula.

The Musi River is also rich in silt, and flooding would have laid down alluvia that encouraged rice production in the vicinity of Palembang. It would also have been possible to augment rice production through IRRIGATION based on tidal flows and therefore flooding on the margins of the lower river. This would have been vital in sustaining the large number of visitors and members of the Srivijayan merchant marine.

Further reading: SPAFA. *Consultative Workshop on Archaeological and Environmental Studies on Srivijaya (I-W2b), Jakarta, Padang, Prapat, and Medan, Indonesia, September 16–30, 1985 Final Report.* Bangkok: SPAFA, 1885; Wolters, O. W. *The Fall of Srivijaya in Malay History.* London: Lund Humphries, 1970.

steatite Steatite is a variety of talc that is soft and therefore easily carved and has a fine luster. It was widely used in India for beads, seals, boxes, and statuettes. Steatite was a vital part of the material culture of the INDUS VALLEY CIVILIZATION, particularly in the manufacture of SEALS. After detailed engraving or shaping, steatite can be heated to above 1100°C (2012°F) to harden it. Steatite paste can also be molded into shape and then finished by heating.

Stein, Sir Aurel (1862–1943) *Hungarian-born explorer-archaeologist who more than any other scholar brought the cultures of the Silk Road to prominence.*
Born in Budapest, Hungary, Aurel Stein studied Persian and Indian archaeology at the University of Tübingen in Germany before settling in England in 1884 to undertake further studies in classical and eastern archaeology at the University of Oxford. In 1888 he was appointed registrar of Punjab University at Lahore, Pakistan, and during his free time began archaeological explorations in Kashmir and the Northwest Frontier. Twelve years later, with the enthusiastic support of the viceroy of India, Lord (George) Curzon, he embarked on the first of his four major exploratory journeys to Inner Asia. These took him to the oasis cities of the TARIM BASIN in western China; the Han Chinese western *limes,* or frontier; and, most famously, to the MOGAO caves. There he secured a fabulous collection of Buddhist manuscripts that now reside in the British Museum. His Central Asian research, which he pursued with unflagging energy under the most arduous of circumstances, resulted in a series of massive reports on his findings. When political conditions ruled out proposed fieldwork in Central Asia, he turned his attention to the Roman Empire's eastern border with PARTHIA and the itinerary of Alexander's conquest of the Persian Empire. His long-term desire to undertake fieldwork in Afghanistan, continually thwarted by the authorities there, was finally permitted in 1943. However, he suffered a stroke and died only a few days after reaching Kabul, where he was buried.

See also CHERCHEN; DUNHUANG; ENDERE; GANDHARA; LOU-LAN; MIRAN; NIYA; SHAN-SHAN; SILK ROAD.

Sufutun Sufutun is an important site dated to the period of the SHANG STATE in Shandong province, China. In 1965 four large graves were excavated, and the wealth of finds, despite severe looting, indicated the presence of a royal center. One of the four graves followed the layout well known at the Shang capital of ANYANG in having a central rectangular tomb chamber linked with a large main entrance ramp and three entrance passageways forming a cruciform shape. The chamber itself measured 15 by 11 meters (49.5 by 36.3 ft.), and the longest access ramp, the only one to give direct access to the tomb, was 26 meters (85.8 ft.) long. The junction of the ramp and the tomb chamber was choked with the remains of human sacrificial victims, of whom 47 individuals were counted. There were also five dog skeletons. Despite the destruction of this burial by robbers, more than 4,000 cowry shells were recovered. Cowries symbolized wealth and fertility and could have been obtained only through long-distance trade with the south. The grave pit was surrounded by a podium in which three ancillary burials were placed. The northern wall of the podium contained two further pits for large ceremonial bronze axes. This grave, in all probability, was that of a regional king of the state of Bogu, which is mentioned in the ORACLE-BONE records as being an ally of the Shang.

Suixian *See* LEIGUDUN.

Sulamani temple The Sulamani temple at PAGAN in Myanmar (Burma), built during the reign of King Narapatisithu in 1181, is a colossal temple in a walled precinct.

The Sulamani temple at Pagan, Myanmar (Burma), was built under the reign of King Narapatisithu in 1181. It is one of the largest temples at this remarkable site. (© Luca I. Tettoni/CORBIS)

It has two floors surrounded by terraces bearing small stupas. It represents the last major phase of temple construction at this royal capital in central Myanmar (Burma).

Sunga The Sunga dynasty of India was founded when Pushyamitra Sunga killed Brihadratha, the last Mauryan king, in 185 B.C.E. He had inherited the considerable extent of the MAURYA EMPIRE and defended it against the BACTRIAN GREEK incursions in the west and those of King Kharavela of Orissa in the east. By degrees, however, much territory was lost, including the area of Sind, and the 10th and last king, Vasudeva, was himself killed in about 73 B.C.E.

Sunzi (c. fourth century B.C.E.) *Sunzi, or Master Sun, was the leading militarist thinker during the Spring and Autumn period (770–476 B.C.E.) in China.*
The tension at this time was but a prelude to the WARRING STATES PERIOD (475–221 B.C.E.). Many philosophers arose in this period of social ferment. On the one hand, CONFUCIUS and MENCIUS advocated righteousness, humanity, and old chivalric values. On the other, the legalists and militarists took a pragmatic view rooted in the principle of survival. While the legalists argued for autocratic central power, the militarists laid down a new ethic in battle, which ran counter to the long tradition of chivalry. He probably lived during the late Spring and Autumn period. A contemporary of Confucius, Sunzi advocated an entirely new and totalitarian approach to war. Sunzi stressed the vital importance of knowledge of every possible aspect of war: the terrain, the weather, the morale and psychology of the troops, the state of the enemy, and their tactics. As in a game of chess, he urged the importance of timing: "What is meant to be skilled is to be victorious over the easily defeated."

His words were written during the third century B.C.E. and have long been influential. Further texts relating to Sunzi have been found on BAMBOO SLIPS from Tomb 1 at Yinqueshan in Shandong province, dating to the second century B.C.E. These incorporate questions and answers on war between Sunzi and Wuzi. The Confucian school particularly resented his advocacy of deception as a military tactic. "When able," he said, "manifest inability. Attack when the enemy is unprepared." While recommending orthodox tactics such as not attacking when backed by water, or when there is no escape, he also identified the means to take advantage of the unusual or unorthodox. He was also incisive in setting out appropriate strategy, for example, when deep in enemy territory: "Throw the troops where they cannot leave, for facing death, they will not be routed."

Surkh-Kotal Surkh-Kotal was a temple set in a fortress built during the reign of KANISHKA I, the KUSHAN king who ruled from 100 to 126 C.E. Located near the headwaters of the Amu Dar'ya River in Afghanistan, it included a series of four platforms linked by stairways that culminate in a colonnaded temple probably dedicated to the Kushan ancestors. Its design shows strong Achaemenid Persian influence.

Surkhotada Field surveys undertaken in 1964–68 on the eastern margins of the Rann of Kachchh in Gujarat province, India, identified a series of sites ascribed to the INDUS VALLEY CIVILIZATION. This Rann is now much silted, but it was formerly an arm of the sea that facilitated maritime trade, and many Harappan sites are found along its shoreline. Surkhotada is one of these. It is a very small rural settlement when compared with the great cities farther west, covering only 1.4 hectares (3.5 acres). Nevertheless, the spatial layout incorporated, as in the main Indus cities, a citadel adjoining a residential quarter, both created in about 2300 B.C.E. The difference between this small site and the major cities of the Indus is that the so-called citadel and the residential area are of the same size. Mud-brick houses, baths, and drains were all laid out, and SEALS and the INDUS VALLEY CIVILIZATION SCRIPT on pottery vessels indicate literacy and trade. The finding of horse bones confirms the presence of this domestic animal in Indus sites.

The defenses are a particular feature of this site, being thick and fortified at the corners with bastions. Excavations along the line of the southern fortification wall have revealed two entrance gateways, giving access to each half of the site, while a third gateway links the two parts of the settlement internally. As at RANGPUR, the site continued to be occupied into the second millennium B.C.E. The fortifications were strengthened during this period, and houses with an average of five rooms were in use. Excavations by J. P. Joshi in 1971–72 revealed that the site was occupied during the mature Harappan phase; there were three subphases dating to 2500–1900 B.C.E. However, 300 meters (990 ft.) northwest of the walls, he found a cemetery demarcated by stone cairns with capstones over interments in oval or rectangular shallow graves. This method of disposing of the dead has not been found at other Harappan sites. The human remains were fragmentary, and one such grave contained none. However, the mortuary vessels were more akin to early Harappan styles.

Suryaparvata *See* PHNOM CHISOR.

Suryavarman I (r. c. 1002–1049 C.E.) *Suryavarman I (Protégé of the Sun) was the first king of a new dynasty who ruled at Angkor in Cambodia.*
His origins and legitimacy remain obscure, and some have traced his ancestry to a homeland in Malaysia. His outstanding achievement was arguably the construction of the WESTERN BARAY at Angkor, the largest reservoir (BARAY) of the Angkorian kingdom. Beyond the capital, he energeti-

cally ordered building works at Preah Vihear, PREAH KHAN OF KOMPONG SVAY, and Phnom Chisor and was responsible for the construction of roads and rest houses. Michael Vickery, on the basis of 13 lengthy INSCRIPTIONS that set out the dynastic histories of the great aristocratic families of the preceding two centuries, has suggested that Suryavarman was a member of the elite Saptadevakula lineage, whose members claimed descent from King INDRAVARMAN I (877–89). If so, under the flexible rules of succession, he and his faction could have claimed legitimacy. The surviving texts make it clear that years of civil war between Suryavarman and Jayaviravarman preceded the former's reign. Suryavarman's early inscriptions concentrate in eastern Cambodia, but after 1005 no more is heard of Jayaviravarman, and by 1010 Suryavarman appeared at Angkor. Shortly thereafter, his inscriptions, or those mentioning his name, are also found to the west of the capital.

In 1011 King Suryavarman I summoned his officials to swear an oath of allegiance. They offered their lives and unswerving devotion to the king in the presence of the sacred fire. The officials promised to safeguard the meritorious foundations of the country and urged the king to punish severely those who supported any rival. Further to consolidate his position, in 1018 he had inscriptions set in place at PREAH VIHEAR, PHNOM CHISOR, Wat Baset, and an unidentified location probably to the east of Angkor, in which LINGAMS named Suryavarmesvara were erected to identify the boundaries of his kingdom. Suryavarman was responsible for a burst of building activity at Angkor. He placed his palace north of the BAKHENG, within the bounds of the future ANGKOR THOM, and ordered the construction of the relatively small royal temple of the PHIMEANAKAS.

Suryavarman II (r. 1113–1150 C.E.) *Suryavarman II (Protégé of the Sun) was king of Angkor in Cambodia.*
His temple mausoleum, known today as ANGKOR WAT, is one of the world's outstanding buildings. A devotee of Vishnu, Suryavarman took power in a battle against his great-uncle. For the first time for any Angkorian king, it is possible to see his image, carved on the reliefs of Angkor Wat. He is portrayed in battle and in his court receiving high officials. He was also renowned as a warrior who fought against the Chams and pushed north and west into Thailand.

See also CHAM CIVILIZATION.

Sutkagen Dor Sutkagen Dor is the most westerly of all INDUS VALLEY CIVILIZATION sites. It lies on a rocky shore in western Pakistan and was discovered in 1875. SIR AUREL STEIN briefly worked there, and limited excavations were later undertaken by George Dales. The site is dominated by a rectangular stone-walled citadel measuring 335 by 200 meters (369 by 220 yds.), but the extent to which there was occupation outside the defensive walls remains to be determined. The walls are robust, to 7.5 meters (24.8 ft.) wide at the base. It is possible that this site owes its existence to the passage of Indus trade vessels to Near Eastern ports. The pottery recovered belongs to the mature Indus tradition of the later third millennium B.C.E.

svami (late fourth to the early third centuries B.C.E.) KAUTILYA, a chief minister to King Candragupta Maurya (325–297 B.C.E.) of the MAURYA EMPIRE in India, authored a treatise on statecraft known as the *Arthasastra*. He identified seven vital elements, of which the *svami*, or king, occupied the key position.

T

tai-fu Under the HAN DYNASTY (206 B.C.E.–220 C.E.) the *tai-fu* was the most senior member of the government. His official duty was to provide moral guidance to the emperor, and the title has been translated as "grand tutor." The office changed significantly between the Western and Eastern Han dynasties. During the Western Han there were only four such appointments, beginning with Wang Ling in 187 B.C.E. and ending with WANG MANG, the future usurper. As far as can be judged, the post was used mainly as a way of manipulating venerable but senior mandarins into a virtual sinecure. With the enthronement of GUANG WUDI in 25 C.E., however, the office was constantly filled, beginning with Zhuo Mao. Many of the grand tutors under the Eastern Han were also appointed to the important post of intendant of the Masters of writing and, with a large secretariat, were responsible for the proper flow of information to the emperor.

Taika Reforms The Taika Reforms were a vital part of the increasing centralization of imperial authority in Japan. In 645 C.E., the powerful Soga clan was eliminated from its position of power in the YAMATO court. For generations members of this clan had intermarried with the royal line and dominated the political scene. Two men, the future emperor TENJI and Fujiwara no Katamari, proceeded to introduce in the name of the emperor Kotoku a series of laws designed to weaken provincial resistance to the imperial court and establish an autocracy on the model of Tang China. The new regulations struck at the heart of the production system of Japan by reallocating land from nobles and designating it for the use of peasants. This was associated with a new system of taxation based on production. Such a system necessitated a census to establish the tax base.

The reforms provided state support for the Buddhist temples, a strong force in promoting the notion of imperial supremacy. The long tradition of employing lavish and ostentatious burial mounds (*kofuns*) to project the status of local elites was terminated by new regulations limiting the size of mounds and the number of people permitted to work on them. This change can be confirmed, archaeologically, with a sharp fall in their number and size at this juncture. The Taika Reforms were followed by further centralizing trends, particularly illustrated by the new set of penal and administrative laws established in 701 C.E. and the rigid grading of ranks that ultimately led to the autocratic NARA STATE centered at HEIJO-KYO.

Taixicun Taixicun is a major site of the SHANG STATE (1766–1045 B.C.E.), located near Shijiazhuang in Hebei province, China. There are three large mounds in an occupied area of at least 10 hectares (25 acres). Excavations have uncovered houses of between one and three rooms constructed of stamped earth and unfired clay BRICK, in addition to the foundations of a much larger house. Sacrificial remains of humans and animals associated with the large residence suggest that it was occupied by an elite member of the community. The presence of a social hierarchy is also evidenced in the cemetery, where 58 graves have been opened. A small number are particularly well endowed with mortuary offerings, including fine bronze vessels, weapons, jades, gold ornaments, and ORACLE BONES. One burial incorporated a ledge to retain sacrificed bodies. Other graves were markedly poorer and contained only ceramic vessels and the occasional bronze. Pottery shards include scratched written graphs, and a particularly interesting find, an ax, was made from meteoric rather than smelted iron.

Takamatsuzuka Takamatsuzuka is a late *kofun,* or burial mound, of the YAMATO state of Japan, located in the Nara Plain region of Honshu Island, Japan. It is significant because, although long since looted, the central burial chamber contained the remains of a lacquered coffin. The chamber walls were embellished with painted scenes of the celestial bodies, mythical creatures, and people dressed in the style of Korea. It dates to the late seventh century C.E. and, with a diameter of 15 meters (49.5 ft.) is a relatively small burial complex that might have housed a courtier of Korean origin.

Taksasila See TAXILA.

Tamluk Tamluk is the modern name of the port city at the mouth of the Rupnarayan River in India. It was mentioned by both Pliny (first century C.E.) and Ptolemy (second century C.E.) as Taluctae or Tamalities. Other recorded names are Tamralipta and Tamralipti. Excavations have identified a long sequence of occupation with deep prehistoric roots and the presence of a flourishing port during the Mauryan, SUNGA, and Gupta periods (325 B.C.E.–500 C.E.) Ceramics and intaglios evidence trade with the Roman Empire. Although the modern occupation has made extensive excavation difficult, it was a major center of BUDDHISM, according to the reports of the Chinese monks FAXIAN and XUANZANG. The latter emphasized the wealth of the inhabitants in the seventh century C.E.

See also GUPTA EMPIRE; MAURYA EMPIRE.

Tanjung Rawa Tanjung Rawa is a site located on an island at the mouth of the Selinsing River, on the west coast of Malaysia. It documents early trade contact with India, in the form of a gold ring with a Hindu motif and a seal of carnelian dated to the fourth or fifth century C.E. on the basis of a brief text in SANSKRIT. It also has imported Chinese glazed pottery; radiocarbon dates suggest a lengthy period of occupation between the third and eighth centuries C.E. The inhabitants interred the dead in wooden boat coffins.

Taoism Taoism represents one of the two major philosophical schools of thought on the organization and administration of the Chinese state; the other is Confucianism. Taoism stresses detachment from the affairs of the world, in contrast to Confucianism. The term *taoist* does not enter the Chinese literature until the early HAN DYNASTY, but preceding texts on the Taoist way are known as the *Huang Lao* (Teachings of the Yellow Emperor), or the Teaching of LAOZI. The date and career of Laozi, "old master," is not known. There may have been more than one author of the *Daodejing,* but there is no doubting its importance in subsequent Chinese theo-

ries of governance. In 1973 a remarkable discovery in a tomb at MAWANGDUI, dated to 168 B.C.E., included a version of the *Daodejing* written in silk.

In attempting to appreciate the subtleties and nuances of the *Daodejing,* it is necessary to understand the political ferment during the course of its compilation. This WARRING STATES PERIOD (475–221 B.C.E.) saw the replacement of the old feudal order of the Zhou dynasty by a period of constant warfare among a diminishing number of states, as QIN achieved military preeminence. QIN SHIHUANGDI, the first emperor of a forcibly united China, introduced a centralized autocracy rooted in repression and military power. His dynasty barely outlived his own life, however, and the ensuing Han rulers inherited a vast new empire without any established rules of conduct. Were they to follow in the autocratic footsteps of their predecessor or develop a new form of government that could still hold together the many divergent and formerly independent kingdoms that made up their empire?

In contrast to Confucianism, which was compiled during the Spring and Autumn period (770–476 B.C.E.) and advocated a direct, compassionate, and humanistic approach of the sovereign, Taoism adopted a mystical and almost metaphysical approach rooted in the concept of Tao. Taoism encourages acceptance of the concept of *wuwei,* a word not subject to simple translation. It involves the ruler's distancing himself in a remote and tranquil way from the lives of the people, through a harmonious and yielding acceptance of order eschewing warfare, ostentation, and vanity.

The *Daodejing* became particularly influential during the first six decades of the HAN DYNASTY. It comprises 81 chapters and is written partly in prose and partly in poetry. By employing a rich variety of metaphors, it explores the nature of the way:

> Thirty spokes conjoin in one hub;
> there being nothing in between,
> the cart is useful.
> clay is molded into a vessel;
> there being nothing inside,
> the vessel is useful.
> doors and windows are carved out to make a room:
> there being nothing within,
> the room is useful.
> thus, with something one gets advantage,
> while with nothing one gets usefulness.
> (de Bary and Bloom 1999)

Further reading: De Barry, W. T., and I. Bloom, eds. *Sources of Chinese Tradition.* New York: Columbia University Press, 1999; Kohn, D., ed. *Daoism Handbook.* Handbook of Oriental Studies, 14. Leiden: Brill, 2000; Miller, J. *Daoism: A Short Introduction.* Oxford: Oneworld Publications, 2003.

Taosi Taosi is a major site of the LONGSHAN CULTURE, located north of the Huang (Yellow) River in Shanxi province, China. The radiocarbon dates obtained during the excavations between 1978 and 1985 indicate that it was occupied during the last few centuries of the third millennium B.C.E. With an area of at least 300 hectares (750 acres), it is the largest Neolithic site known in China. The finds included the remains of houses, kilns for firing ceramic vessels, and storage pits, but it is best known for its cemetery, which covers three hectares (7.5 acres). Almost 1,000 graves have been uncovered. The most important aspect of the cemetery is the division of burials into three groups on the basis of their size and mortuary offerings. These three groups have been subdivided into a further seven types on the basis of size and grave furniture.

The nine elite graves were up to three meters (10 ft.) in length and were exclusive to adult males. They were richly endowed with grave goods, including fine ceramic vessels decorated with red painted designs. One such design reveals a coiled snake in red against a black background, its tongue fully extended and scales represented by alternating red and black forms. Wooden vessels also survived, some painted and others covered in LACQUER. The jades included adzes, knives, *cong* tubes, and *bi* disks that were in all probability used by the leaders of Taosi in rituals. The man buried in Tomb 3015 was accompanied by two wooden drums, painted and incorporating alligator-skin striking surfaces, as well as stone chimes and three dogs. These burials also included whole pig skeletons, large chime stones, and stone arrowheads.

The majority (87 percent) were small, barely large enough to take the body. There are two subgroups: those with no grave goods and those equipped only with such items as a bone pin, a pottery vessel, or part of a pig's jawbone.

Eighty graves (11.4 percent of the sample) belong to the medium group. These were large enough to take a wooden coffin and reached a length of 2.5 meters (8.25 ft.) and a width of up to 1.5 meters (4.95 ft.). One of these included a copper bell, indicating, as do other late Longshan settlements, that metallurgical skills had reached the central plains. The absence of any evidence at Taosi for smelting or casting makes it likely that this item was imported. The rich subset of this medium group were interred in a wooden coffin with cinnabar, a group of painted ceramic vessels, wooden bowls, and jade ornaments together with pigs' jawbones. A middle subgroup also contained cinnabar, but no pottery vessels and few pigs' jawbones and jades. The poorest graves in the medium sample were buried with one or two pigs' mandibles, a bone pin, and stone ornaments.

This site is one of the clearest indicators of social ranking before the development of the XIA DYNASTY based at ERLITOU.

taotie The *taotie* symbol is an image of an animal's head in frontal view, formed from two animals facing each other, found on early Chinese ritual bronzes. It probably had a much earlier ancestry before the development of casting decorated bronze vessels dating from the early SHANG STATE (1766–1045 B.C.E.) to the middle to late WESTERN ZHOU DYNASTY (1045–771 B.C.E.). The bronze frontlet with TURQUOISE inlay from a tomb belonging to Period 2 at ERLITOU (c. 1900–1800 B.C.E.) has a simple form of *taotie* mask. Possibly the earliest examples are to be seen on the pottery vessels of the LOWER XIAJIADIAN CULTURE at DADIANZI (2300–1600 B.C.E.). The actual term is documented first in the ZUOZHUAN (770–481 B.C.E.), where it was described as one of four evil animals given to gluttony, and indeed the depiction of the *taotie* usually incorporated a human or an animal in the creature's mouth. It is not known what the motif was called during the Shang dynasty. Its earliest form is virtually confined to a pair of eyes surrounded by abstract designs, but over time its rendition began to include more animal-face features without metamorphosing into a recognizable creature. Its use was widespread over time and space in China. It is found, for example, on a ritual ax from the Shang tomb of FU HAO and on a vessel from the early site of PANLONGCHENG (1500–1200 B.C.E.). Many examples are from the Western Zhou dynasty corpus of bronzes, such as the Zhifangtou tomb and the Zhuangbai hoard (771 B.C.E.). It is also, however, represented on bronzes

The Shang rulers of China had ritual vessels cast in bronze to feast the ancestors. This example was decorated with *taotie* mask images. *(© Asian Art & Archaeology, Inc./CORBIS)*

from SANXINGDUI in Sichuan (1400–1200 B.C.E.). A fine example of a jade *taotie* mask was found in the tomb of the second king of *yue*, dated to the second century B.C.E. This example held in its mouth a jade *bi* disk. The latter were regarded as auspicious symbols. While it is hard to be precise on the symbolic meaning of the *taotie* itself, its presence on bronzes designed to feast and honor the dead ancestors makes it probable that it represented death.

Ta Prohm   The temple of Ta Prohm, formerly known as Rajavihara, was built to honor the mother of JAYAVARMAN VII (1181–1219 C.E.) of ANGKOR in Cambodia. Set within a wall of laterite one kilometer long by 600 meters (1100 by 660 yds.) lie two courts enclosed by passageways, each containing many small single-chambered temples. The foundation stela was written by Sri Suryakumara (the Sun prince), one of the king's sons, and was set in place in 1186 C.E. The temple housed many statues of divinities. The principal image, said to be covered in gems, represented the king's mother in the form of the mother of Buddha. There were also many other images. Indrakumara mentions 260 in the shrines. Brief INSCRIPTIONS name the statues that once stood within, and they suggest that the complex incorporated not only the principal image of the king's mother, but also family shrines with images of the ancestors of members of his court. Thus the monument was a center for the worship of deified ancestors. The foundation inscription provides a glimpse of the temple in its heyday, revealing it as a symbol of royal and dynastic power and a generator of both religious and economic activity, around which a whole society in miniature operated. Eighteen high priests and 2,740 officials lived and worked there, together with 2,202 assistants, who included 615 female dancers; 12,640 people had the right to lodge there.

Feeding and clothing this multitude involved the provision of rice, honey, molasses, oil, fruit, sesame, millet, beans, butter, milk, salt, and vegetables, all the quantities scrupulously listed for appropriation from the royal foundations and warehouses. Clothing was also required, and even the number of mosquito nets is set down. In all, 79,365 men and WOMEN were assigned to supply the temple. The foundation's assets included gold and silver vessels, 35 diamonds, 40,620 pearls, 4,540 precious stones such as beryl, copper goblets, tin, lead, 512 silk beds, 876 veils from China, cushions, and 523 sunshades. There were musical instruments "to charm the spirit," and for nightfall or for rituals, there were 165,744 wax torches.

Tarim Basin   The Tarim Basin in western China occupies a strategic position west of the Gansu Corridor and east of TRANSOXIANA, on the SILK ROAD. It lies north of the Kunlun Shan range and south of the Tien Shan. The rivers flowing from these mountain ranges enter the low and flat basin and form oases before they dry up as they enter the arid Taklamakan Desert. These oases are potentially productive and attracted settlement from the prehistoric period. Indeed, there is now a consistent body of evidence to indicate that the favorable oases around the Tarim Basin were occupied from at least the second millennium to the dawn of the historical period. The people in question must have moved into the area from the west and almost certainly spoke an Indo-European language or languages ancestral to the historically recorded Tocharian. With the quickening of trade during the QIN and HAN dynasties, many small centers emerged under local rulers. They were, however, so widely distributed around the southern and northern margins of the basin that they formed independent polities. As such, they were not sufficiently powerful to withstand pressure from the people known as the XIONGNU, ancestors of the Huns who exerted considerable influence through the speed of their horses and their ability to concentrate forces. As the Han Chinese showed increasing interest in what they called the western regions during the second century B.C.E., so the states of the Tarim Basin fell under Chinese control, gaining independence only during periods of central Han weakness or preoccupation elsewhere. The *History of the Former Han* (HANSHU) and the SHIJI both provide historic accounts of the Han expansion to the northwest. They name 36 polities and provide both a census and the number of soldiers that each could deploy. Essentially, the Silk Road could follow two routes that passed through these little kingdoms. Both began at DUNHUANG in the east and terminated at KAXGAR (Kashgar) in the west. The northern route passed from east to west through LOU-LAN or Turpan, Yanqi, Kuqa (Kucha), and Yarkand. The southern route followed the oases lying on the southern fringe of the Kunlun range, through QIEMO, NIYA, and HOTAN.

CHINESE EXPANSION

During the disruptions caused by the end of the Qin and the establishment of the Western Han dynasty, the Tarim states were tributaries of the Xiongnu. Consolidation under Han WUDI (r. 141–87 B.C.E.), however, presented the opportunity for the Chinese to exert their influence in the Tarim Basin. The emperor dispatched Zhang Qian on a diplomatic mission in about 138 B.C.E. to secure intelligence on this area and attempt to forge alliances against the power of the Xiongnu. His journey is recorded in the *Shiji* of SIMA QIAN and provides one of the first eyewitness accounts of the Tarim Basin and beyond to BACTRIA and FERGHANA. Of the Lopnor region of the eastern Tarim Basin, he wrote, "The Loulan and Gushi peoples live in fortified cities along the Salt Swamp. The Salt Swamp is some 5,000 *li* from CHANG'AN."

A Chinese military expedition in 108 B.C.E. put the eastern settlements of the Tarim Basin under Han control, and a decade later the whole area was taken. This hegemony was disrupted during the WANG MANG interregnum (8–23 C.E.), but the trade along the Silk Road was too important to forgo, and by the mid-first century C.E., Eastern Han authority was reasserted. The passage of trade caravans to the west was then accompanied by the spread of BUDDHISM to the east.

EARLY INVESTIGATIONS

Both the description in Chinese accounts of walled cities and the known spread of Buddhism have attracted a number of scholars interested in the peoples of the area. Abel Rémusat (1788–1832) wrote the first history of the state of HOTAN. Early expeditions were undertaken largely by Russian explorers. Chokan Valikhanov (1835–65) identified evidence for Buddhism near Kuqa (Kucha); Nikolay Przhevalsky (1839–88) led a series of expeditions to the Tarim region and encountered the desiccated prehistoric burials of people with European features. Later archaeological expeditions to the Tarim Basin during the late 19th and early 20th centuries led to the discovery and exploration of some major sites. Between 1868 and 1872, Freidrich von Richthofen (1833–1905) recognized the now dry lakebed of Lopnor, the same salt swamp noted by Zhang Qian. Sven Hedin (1865–1952) undertook many major scientific expeditions and identified important archaeological sites that included the desiccated mummies of the Qāwrighul culture. Paul Pelliot (1878–1945) was a French Sinologist who visited and removed a considerable number of documents from the Buddhist caves of Dunhuang. SIR AUREL STEIN (1862–1943) was the most active archaeologist to explore the Tarim Basin in the early years of discovery. Beginning in 1900 he mounted four expeditions into Central Asia. The first took him to Hotan, a center in the southwestern margin of the Tarim Basin. He also inveigled himself into the good offices of the overseer at Dunhuang and managed to secure a huge collection of Buddhist manuscripts that are now housed in the British Museum in London.

RECENT EXCAVATIONS

In recent years archaeological research in the Tarim Basin has provided much vital and surprising information. The area is so dry that organic material has survived in sites often covered by drifting sand after their abandonment. It is evident that the oases were settled by farming communities originating in the West. Surviving documents have been found to be written in the Tocharian language, a member of the Indo-European family. Moreover, the desiccated mummies from Tarim burial sites have clear European rather than East Asian features. Their woolen clothes were also woven with patterns matched in western Europe.

Early Sites

Qāwrighul in China is the earliest cemetery site to furnish human remains with Western affinities. It is located in the Könchi River Valley in the northeastern fringe of the basin and dates between 2000 and 1500 B.C.E. The dead were interred under woolen blankets and were associated with sprigs of ephedra, a plant with medicinal qualities thought to have been a component of soma. Soma was drunk during rituals by the Indo-Iranian-speaking peoples and was mentioned in the Vedic texts of India. A well-preserved woman interred at this site had fair hair. The nearby site of Krorän has also furnished burials of the same period, the most notable that of a woman who died when aged about 45 years. She wore woolen clothing, a felt hat with two goose feathers, and leather boots. Her facial features were emphatically Western, and her hair was fair. These people took with them to the Tarim oases sheep and goats, wheat, and barley.

Later Sites

To the northeast of Qāwrighul, the cemetery of Qizilchoqa has been excavated and found to date to the early first millennium B.C.E. Again, Western features are characteristic of the dead, and the presence of barley and body tattoos also points to a westerly origin. In 1992 a cemetery was excavated at Subeshi on the northern margin of the basin. Several burials were uncovered, dating to about 400 B.C.E. One man wore a felt helmet, sheepskin coat, and leather leggings. He has been labeled a warrior, because he was accompanied by a bow and arrows made of bronze, iron, and bone. Perhaps the most extraordinary of the finds from this site were the remains of WOMEN interred with tall pointed hats resembling those associated with witches in European society. One of them was interred with a leather bag containing her cosmetic set, including a COMB.

Similar material has been found at Qaradöng, near the later center of Kuqa (Kucha). Excavations there revealed the remains of a settlement, in which the houses were made of wood and the inhabitants cultivated millet. The southern margins of the Tarim Basin also attracted early settlement. At Zaghunluq, a remarkable grave nine meters (29.7 ft.)deep was excavated in 1985. It contained the remains of a man and three women, who had been covered by layers of matting, animal skins, and wood. The clothing from this burial only extremely well preserved and abundant and was also important from the point of view of weaving techniques. One cap had been knitted, and a shirt was of woven wool. The man wore woolen trousers with a multicolored belt and high leather boots. The weaving technique here and in the site of Qizilchoqa employed a plaid twill with a tartan design whose closest parallels were founded in contemporary sites in western Europe.

CHINESE-DOMINATED SITES

The Han Chinese refer to the presence of the 36 city-states of the western region. Based on their fertile oases, these polities were in all probability occupied by the descendants of those found in the preceding prehistoric cemeteries. They were never powerful enough singly to withstand the power of the Xiongnu, nor were they able to coalesce into a larger political unit because of their isolation. Therefore, they were always subjected to either Xiongnu raids or Han Chinese expansion.

Niya

The best documented is the oasis state of Niya, on the southern margin of the basin. Here the remains of the ancient settlement line the dried-out bed of the Niya River over a distance of 25 by 10 kilometers (15 by 0.6 mi.). The remains of wooden house posts still stood over the drifting sand when the site was explored by Sir Aurel Stein, who also found the remains of a wooden bridge over the ancient river course. The houses had been constructed of wooden uprights bearing a wattle frame covered with mud daub. Each had a fireplace, and the mud of the living space floors contained wheat straw and cow dung. The inhabitants were most proficient in iron working, and the long prehistoric tradition of weaving continued, as is evidenced by the outstanding woolen, linen, and cotton garments recovered from the graves. Stein's record of his visit to Niya illustrates the extraordinary preservation of the remains of this settlement. He found, for example, wattle walls of tamarisk twigs that still stood to a height of about 60 centimeters (2 ft.). A second building was almost completely covered by sand, but on removing it Stein found pottery vessels and wooden artifacts. Beyond the houses, he encountered the remains of an ancient vineyard. It was enclosed by a fence covering an area of 230 by 135 meters (253 by 149 yds.), in which the posts that would have supported the trellises remained in serried rows about five or six meters apart. Even the vine stems survived against their supporting posts. Fruit trees also grew there: apricots, peaches, apples, and walnuts.

Krorän, Hotan, Kaxgar, Kuqa

Krorän, another city-state, is located at the eastern end of the Tarim Basin. Its stamped-earth walls cover an area of about 10 hectares (25 acres), and the interior of the city included the foundations of temples, residences, and official buildings. Hotan in the far west of China was one of the major city-states, located where several rivers flow into the piedmont from the mountains to the south. It has long been renowned as a source of jade, while its strategic position rendered it vulnerable to more powerful peoples. Kaxgar (Kashgar) in northwest China was one of the richest city-states of the Tarim, and there are many early sites in the area around the modern city. It was also notable for the early development of a silk industry. Kuqa (Kucha) in northwest China was the center of a flourishing city-state with a long history. There are many early settlements there, including the temples of Subeshi, where inscriptions in the Tocharian language have survived. These are but the major states of the Tarim, and they present many important issues needing further resolution, not least the degree to which the populace included the descendants of the Indo-European–speaking peoples who seem to have introduced Western agricultural crops, livestock, and weaving technology.

HAN DOMINANCE AND TRADE

The ensuing phase of Tarim Basin history saw the increasing dominance of the Han Chinese, as they established western provinces, sent garrison troops, and built their own military settlements. This led to an influx of Han objects and expansion of trade. Chinese silks were imported, often as gifts from the emperor to dependent rulers; cotton from India was also found. Vines were introduced from the west; mulberry trees and sericulture originated in the east. The city-states in the broad reach of the Han also used Chinese coins, which are abundantly found in the Tarim Basin, except in Hotan, where the coins were minted with the local king's name in the KHAROSHTHI script. Archaeologically, watchtowers are the most obvious remains of the Han period. These were designed to warn the local garrisons of an impending attack by the Xiongnu, and some still stand up to 10 meters (33 ft.) in height. These towers were integral units of small walled enclosures with a building within to accommodate the guards. The top of these beacons contained a facility for burning wood by night or emitting smoke by day. From Kuqa to the Jade Gate and then on to Dunhuang and China proper, it was possible to transmit warnings of the gathering of the Xiongnu to the capital of Chang'an within a day.

The garrisons themselves were established to control and ward off attack from the Xiongnu. They were supposed to supply themselves locally, and their IRRIGATION canals to carry water to the fields and the field ridges themselves are still visible on the margins of the Qizil River. The irrigation system of the Miran River area was particularly sophisticated, involving subterranean channels to carry water from melted snow to the fields. There were main and branch canals in a complex distribution system. Much information on these military colonies, which introduced a marked infusion of Chinese settlers into the western regions for the first time, can be gained from the written documents on wood that have survived in this arid environment. Colonists and their families from all regions of the Han empire settled and engaged in both agricultural and defense. The presence of Han soldiers also provided the peaceful conditions necessary for the operation of the trading caravans that plied the Silk Road. The walled cities acted as intermediaries or way stations in this exchange, as increasing quantities of Chinese silks were taken westward.

INTRODUCTION OF BUDDHISM

But such exchange also involved the spread of ideas that, in the Tarim Basin, saw the establishment of foreign enclaves in the walled cities and the introduction of Buddhism. Buddhist monuments and their precious archives of manuscripts, have survived from the third century C.E., and Sir Aurel Stein was responsible for discovering and opening several Buddhist sites of outstanding importance. On 8 December 1906, he encountered by chance the site of MIRAN. He returned to excavate it the following year and uncovered a series of extraordinary wall paintings and massive stucco images of the Buddha, documents dating to the fourth century C.E., and the foundations of stupas. The subsequent research on the material at this site has confirmed a flourishing community by the third century C.E., whose art shows strong parallels with that of western Central Asia.

The area of Kuqa also contains important evidence for the establishment of Buddhism from the west. Qizil and Qumtura incorporate shrines cut into the hillside. At the former, the temples contain wall paintings, one of which depicts benefactors wearing sumptuous long embroidered coats with long sleeves and trousers, with swords hanging from their belts. The women wore long flowing skirts and tightly fitting bodices, both with matching patterned decoration. One painting even shows the artist at work. These people were depicted with blond or red hair, and the graffiti on the cave walls contained instructions to the artists in the Tocharian language.

Niya has also furnished evidence of Buddhist worship. Stein found the remains of a stupa, and a large assemblage of documents written in Kharoshthi and Chinese dating to the third century C.E. These include permits issued by the Chinese to merchants traversing the Silk Road and indicate that during that period Niya was part of the kingdom of SHAN-SHAN. More recent research has led to the discovery of more documents and a double burial of a man and a woman dating to the third or fourth century C.E. It included a complete and elegant coat of silk embroidered with Chinese characters and fragments of paper.

Further reading: Barber, E. W. *The Mummies of Urumchi.* New York: W. W. Norton, 2000; Mallory, J. P. *In Search of the Indo-Europeans: Language, Archaeology, and Myth.* London: Thames and Hudson, 1991; ———., and Mair, V. H. *The Tarim Mummies: Ancient China and the Mystery of the Earliest Peoples from the West.* London: Thames & Hudson, 2000.

Taruma Four inscriptions in the style of the mid-fifth century C.E. have been identified in western Java in Indonesia. They mention a state called Taruma and its king, Purnavarman. These are the earliest evidence in Java for the formation of states ruled by kings who had adopted Indian names and Hindu religion, suggesting that as in the maritime state of FUNAN on the mainland, international trade was deeply affecting strategically placed island communities.

Tatetsuki Tatetsuki is a large mounded tomb located near Kurashiki on the northern shore of the Inland Sea in Japan. During the third century C.E., the YAMATO state developed in its heartland, the Nara Basin. It was characterized by *kofun*—dominating earthen mounds covering stone-lined mortuary chambers. These contained the dead aristocrats who formed the basis of Japan's first civilization. Some scholars have suggested that this development owes much to the intrusion of elite horse-riding warriors from the Korean Peninsula. However, Tatetsuki is a mounded tomb that some authorities date to the preceding late YAYOI period (300 B.C.E.–300 C.E.), although some doubt exists as to whether it should in fact be ascribed to the early Yamato period itself. It measures 70 meters (23 ft.) across at its maximal extent. The evidence from the tomb suggests the possibility that there were local precedents for the *kofun* so characteristic of the Yamato state.

Excavations in 1976 showed that the top of the mound had been deliberately leveled, and five large stones had been put in place. Three of these lined the edge of the central burial pit. The surviving parts of two projections from the circular main mound had been paved. The principal grave was a pit in which a wooden chamber had been constructed. This contained a wooden coffin two meters (6.6 ft.) long, the base of which was lined with as much as 30 kilograms (66 lbs.) of cinnabar. Grave goods included a necklace made of jade, agate, and jasper beads and an iron dagger. Jasper and glass beads lay beside the dagger. The burial chamber had been filled with soil and a layer of pebbles that included broken pottery vessels and parts of a stone statue. It is considered likely that these accumulated during feasting or mortuary rituals. A smaller burial was found on the mound, but it was poorly preserved and smaller than the main tomb. The exotic beads of jasper and the presence of cinnabar point to exchange with other parts of Japan for exotic goods. Contemporary Yayoi sites also included HANIWA, clay cylinders that recur regularly in Yamato contexts.

Taxila Taxila in modern Pakistan is one of the great cities of ancient India. It was first described by SIR ALEXANDER CUNNINGHAM, who discovered the ruins of Taxila during his 1863–64 field season. The successive cities there flourished for about 1,000 years, from the fifth century B.C.E. until the city was razed by the Huns. When the site was visited by the Chinese pilgrim XUANZANG in the seventh century C.E., it was deserted, but he commented on the fertile soils of the region, mild climate, many springs, and luxuriant vegetation. Taxila changed hands on many occasions, and three separate cities can be identified on the site: the BHIR MOUND, Sirkap, and Sirsukh. The initial foundation saw Taxila as the capital of GANDHARA, a province controlled by DARIUS THE GREAT, king of Persia, who invaded northeast India in 518 B.C.E. HERODOTUS OF HALICARNASSUS described this province as the richest in the Persian empire. After a short period of Greek control, the city was incorporated into the MAURYA EMPIRE under CANDRAGUPTA MAURYA (r. 325–297 B.C.E.). It thus became a regional or provincial center under the ultimate control of the Mauryan kings at Pataliputra. It was during this period that the city now known as the Bhir mound was constructed. With the collapse of the Mauryans, Taxila fell under the control of the Indo-Greek kingdom of BACTRIA, and until the first century B.C.E. the second city known as Sirkap was occupied. Brief periods under the Scythians, known in India as the SAKAS, and Parthians followed. In about 60–79 C.E. Taxila again changed hands and fell under the dominance of the KUSHANS under Kujula Kadphises. In the fourth century C.E., Taxila was conquered by the Sassanian king Shapur II, and a century later the Chinese pilgrim FAXIAN commented on the number of Buddhist shrines there. This was the prelude, however, to the destruction of the city by marauding White Huns between 390 and 460, and it never recovered.

The original name, Taksasila, the city of cut stone, is probably an allusion to the use of stone in the construction of the defenses and buildings within. It owed its wealth to its strategic location, for it lies near the left bank of the Indus and the eastern entrance to the Khyber Pass. It also has easy links across the Punjab to the Ganges (Ganga) Valley. It thus commanded a crossroads, with access to the SILK ROAD to the north, the rich communities of the Ganges (Ganga) to the east, and through the Khyber Pass to the Western world. MEGASTHENES, ambassador of SELEUCUS I NICATOR to the Mauryan court at PATALIPUTRA in about 300 B.C.E., described the royal road linking the capital with Taxila and then on to the west. This location, however, was also a liability because the same routes that carried trade gave access to invasions.

ACHAEMENID, GREEK, SAKA, AND PARTHIAN RULERS

Initially, the Achaemenid province was strictly controlled from Susa, the capital of the ACHAEMENID EMPIRE. But as the central power began to slacken under the reign of Artaxerxes II (404–359 B.C.E.), the rulers of Taxila began to exert independence. The city then fell to the conquering army of ALEXANDER THE GREAT of Macedon in 326 B.C.E., and the local ruler Ambhi allied himself with the Greek host. It is recorded that Ambhi cemented this alliance with gifts of elephants, bulls, and sheep. Lavish hospitality and the exchange of gifts followed, and Alexander then placed Philip, one of his generals, in charge of Taxila. Philip's control was short lived, for he was assassinated in 324 B.C.E., and Greek control rapidly dissolved. Greek written sources do not illuminate any aspect of the city but do mention some of the local customs, such as the burning of widows and exposing of the dead to be consumed by birds. The author Philostratus described the city's fortifications and the grid pattern of the roads. The Scythian conquest was achieved under a leader called Moga or Maues in Greek, whose name is recorded on a copper inscription at Taxila dated probably 70–80 B.C.E. He took the title *basileus* in Greek and *Maharaja* in the KHAROSHTHI texts seen in his COINAGE. The Scythians succumbed to the Parthians under King Gondophares in the early years of the first century C.E. This ruler is best known in the West on the basis of a record in the Apocrypha that Saint Thomas the apostle visited India and encountered him. A large earthquake afflicted the city during this period, and many buildings were destroyed. Rebuilding to a new and stronger design followed.

KUSHAN AND SASSANIAN DOMINATION

One notable result of the Kushan attack was that the inhabitants of Sirkap seem to have buried their valuables, recovered by SIR JOHN MARSHALL 2,000 years later. His excavations encountered two pottery vessels containing exquisite treasures. One had an image of Eros and Psyche five centimeters (2 in.) high in gold repoussé work. A pair of golden earrings was found in the same vessel. They are in the form of a crescent with pendants attached. There are three pendants of flowers and gold bangles. One of the most outstanding pieces is a necklace made of 43 individual plaques joined by two thin gold wires. The plaques incorporated oval insertions made of crystal, surrounded by tiny fish facing one another, each embellished with tiny pieces of inlaid shell. A gold belt with no fewer than 494 pieces threaded together is another tour de force of the gold worker's art. Nearly all the items in the vessel were made of gold; there were also items of silver, copper gilt, glass, chalcedony, and silver coins. One was issued by a king Sapedana, a ruler who acknowledged Pacores as overlord. Pacores succeeded King Gondophares, who ruled Taxila in the mid-first century C.E. This knowledge assists in the dating of these hoards.

A silver inscription dated to 78 C.E. discovered in a chapel at the Buddhist temple the DHARMARAJIKA refers to the king of Taxila as supreme king of kings, son of the gods, the Kushana. This probably refers to Vima Kadphises. His successor, the Kushan king KANISHKA I, founded the third city, known as Sirsukh. The Kushan kings were Buddhist, and they were responsible for many large religious monastic foundations, including the Kalawan, Giri, and Mohra Moradu.

As Kushan power declined, so that of Sassanian Persia grew. King Ardashir, who founded the Sassanian dynasty, expanded his kingdom into northwest India. An inscription from Persepolis in Persia records that the Sassanian king Shapur II in 356 C.E. occupied modern Kabul and instituted campaigns in the Punjab.

EXCAVATIONS

This rich textual record and the many allusions in Western and Indian sources to the wealth of Taxila present an intriguing challenge to archaeology. Taxila was discovered

Taxila was one of the centers of Gandharan art. This frieze, dating to the early centuries C.E., shows the Buddha and devotees. (*Art Resource, NY*)

in the late 19th century by Sir Alexander Cunningham and was the focus of major excavations by Sir John Marshall between 1913 and 1935; SIR MORTIMER WHEELER worked there in 1944–45.

Bhir Mound

Excavations by Marshall at the Bhir mound, the earliest city, reached the natural substrate at a depth of about 5.5 meters (18 ft.) and encountered the remains of four superimposed structures. The earliest, of which little is known because of its depth and destruction by later construction activity, dates to the fifth century B.C.E. at the latest. The second was in occupation during the fourth century B.C.E. and would have witnessed the arrival of Alexander the Great. The third phase corresponds to the period of Mauryan control, and the last probably belongs to the period after the decline of the Mauryas and the arrival of the BACTRIAN GREEKS in the second century B.C.E. The excavations revealed streets, lanes, and domestic houses. The quality of the stone masonry developed over time from fairly rough to a much more compact form, and the walls were covered in a mud plaster strengthened with straw.

Most of the available plans derive from the third period, the Mauryan city. The layout of the streets and houses is irregular. It is evident that the main street and various squares were retained throughout the life of the city, whereas houses were leveled and rebuilt on occasion, but on the same site and often following a plan similar to that used for their predecessors. Some lanes branching off the main streets are very narrow. The drains running along the main street were to take rainwater. There was no city sewage system, but each house was equipped with a deep pit to receive human waste. Such latrines were also placed in public squares. There were several types of latrines. They have in common a deep circular well-like hole extending up to seven meters (23 ft.) into the ground. Some were filled with broken pottery shards to

allow wastes to filter downward. Others were lined with ceramic rings: One of these held 14 such liners, each 65 centimeters (26 in.) wide. A third type was filled with large ceramic jars one on top of the other, each having the base removed to form one continuous tube. Large stone rubbish bins were also strategically placed in public areas, and excavations revealed broken pottery and animal bones. The houses were a series of large rooms grouped around a courtyard. Windows looking onto the street were tall but very narrow. Many rooms were small, and others had a street frontage and were probably shops. One appears to have been the business of a shell worker, since Marshall found much cut shell within.

As might be expected in the excavation of so large an area of an ancient city, many artifacts were recovered. Beads had many forms, with a preference for glass, carnelian, and agate. Other semiprecious stones included onyx, amethyst, beryl, and garnet. A remarkable hoard of 1,167 silver coins was discovered in the second city, including a silver Persian coin and two coins of Alexander the Great. Among the bronzes, particular attention is given to a third-century B.C.E. bowl made of an alloy containing 21.55 percent tin. This alloy and the shape of the vessel recall those found in the Thai cemetery of BAN DON TA PHET. Iron was used for weapons, particularly arrowheads, spears, and daggers; for tools such as chisels, adzes, and tongs; nails for construction purposes; and for hoes.

Sirkap

Sirkap, the second city, covers approximately 111 hectares (278 acres). The Bactrian Greeks who founded it early in the second century B.C.E. chose a location of relatively flat terrain immediately east of a small stream and incorporated in its walls a walled citadel. The outer wall is massive, varying between six and nine meters (20 and 30 ft.) wide, with regularly spaced bastions. Local limestone was used as the building material. Excavations of the northern gateway revealed a substantial structure that was probably more than one story high, which included guardrooms and a well. About 180,000 square meters (72,000 sq. mi.) of the northeastern quarter has been opened by excavation and seven phases of occupation recognized. This massive excavation encountered seven cultural phases with a maximal depth of 6.6 meters. The lowest, Layer 7, preceded the Greek foundation. The Greek city is found in Layers 5 and 6, the early Scythian or Saka city is Layer 4, the late Scythian and Parthian cities are represented by Layers 2 and 3, and there is some Kushan material on the surface, Layer 1. In the Greek city the regular grid pattern of streets and buildings followed the development of Greek city plans in the West, and some idea of a Greek dwelling can be derived from a house of 11 rooms around a court. One room included a large ceramic storage jar.

By far the greatest quantity of cultural material is from Layer 2, the Scythian-Parthian occupation. The regular grid pattern of the streets continued in use throughout, while the domestic buildings underwent modifications and rebuilding after a major earthquake. Marshall published a plan of the city as it would have appeared in about 40 C.E. under the rule of the Parthian Gondophares. New houses of stone were plastered and painted in a variety of colors: blue, red, green, and yellow, as well as white. Shops flanked the main thoroughfare, but the visitor entering the city from the north gate and walking down the main street would have noticed on the left the stupa of a temple and, after another two city blocks, the walled precinct of a Buddhist temple. The domestic houses lie behind the shops and have one or more courtyards as the focus of surrounding rooms. There are a few latrines in the form of deep circular pits, but far fewer than at the Bhir mound. Walls were of stone faced with plaster. This appears to have been a rich quarter of Taxila, for many opulent items of jewelry were recovered. A ceramic jar in House 3B, for example, held gold ear pendants, a gold necklace, gold bangles, a second gold necklace of 83 beads, two solid silver bangles, and a carnelian seal in a gold casing engraved with the figures of Eros and Psyche. Several other hoards of golden jewelry were found in other houses. Farther up the main street lies what Marshall described as a palace. It has many rooms linked by corridors, courts, and a stupa. This reconstruction of a substantial part of a city plan emphasizes the potential of such archaeology in other major urban center in the subcontinent. In the southeastern quarter, Marshall identified a large building with multiple courts and chambers that he described as the Mahal Palace.

Images of Daily Life
One of the most fascinating aspects of the excavation of Sirkap, however, were the intimate glimpses into the lives of the ordinary citizens provided by such extensive excavations. In the 1928–29 season Marshall uncovered the remains of 30 houses in an area of about one hectare. An ivory comb had on one side an incised portrait of a man and woman, perhaps the people who owned the house, and on the reverse side an energetic goose. The man had short hair and a mustache; the woman wore large ear pendants, and her hair was tied in an elegant bun at the back, with short bangs at the front. An adjacent house yielded a broken copper medallion showing a woman holding a flower in a design that Sir John Marshall found to be Greco-Roman. Anther house held a schist plaque showing a man and woman with elegant dress and hairstyles, holding cups that may well have contained wine. There was also a small iron vessel described as an inkpot. It still held the remains of black ink and brings to mind the writing found on birch bark scrolls dating to this period. Another inkpot was made of bronze and had a serpentine handle. A tiny figure carved in stone, standing no more than 10 centimeters (4 in.) tall, is of a woman holding a casket in both hands. She wears a tunic with sleeves, a necklace, bangles, and anklets. The pleasures of Sirkap, however, are nowhere better illustrated than on a circular stone plaque 16 centimeters (6.4 in.) in diameter on which a drinking scene has been carved. A man is seated on a bench with his left arm around his female companion as she offers him a glass of wine. A woman plays a lyre, and a young man the panpipes. To the right, two men tread on grapes in a large vat. In the left foreground, a man pours wine into a large container, while another samples it. Two further figures lie in front of the wine containers, blissfully oblivious of their surroundings.

Coinage
The coins from Sirkap are particularly instructive from a historical point of view, for they give the names of the Greek kings who ruled the city. The first dynasty included Demetrius, followed by Pantaleon, Agathocles, Apollodotus I, Menander, and Strato. A new line of rulers followed, with the names Heliocles, Lysias, Antialcidas, and Archebius, of the dynasty of Eucratides. The coins bore the name of the ruler in Greek and Kharoshthi scripts. Greek inspiration is also seen in some of the terra-cotta figurines. The names of the subsequent Scythian kings, such as Azilises, Azes I, and Azes II, are also known from their issue of coins.

Marshall's excavations at Sirkap, particularly those relating to the Scythian-Parthian phase in the upper layers, provide a remarkable image of life in this city. There were numerous Buddhist temples and stupas and opulent houses. Coins were in general circulation, and molds indicate a local mint. The successful wore elegant gold and silver jewelry and used mirrors, scent flasks, ear cleaners, hairpins, toothpicks, and combs. There is little evidence for the disposal of sewage. This may have accounted for a visitation of plague. Children played with toy carts and models of birds and animals. There is even toy furniture of bone and ivory.

Sirsukh

The third city, known as Sirsukh, was founded by the KUSHANS 1.5 kilometers to the northeast of Sirkap. It covered an area of 1,400 by 1,000 meters (1,540 by 1,100 yds.) and lay behind a large stone wall fortified with semicircular bastions. Little is known of the interior because of lack of excavation but Marshall did uncover part of a large stone building with rooms around a courtyard.

BUDDHIST SHRINES

A number of Buddhist monasteries were located beyond the confines of the three cities described, but the most intriguing of all the temples in the area of Taxila, albeit not within a city wall, is the Jandial. It is located 600 meters north of Sirkap, adjacent to the main road leading to the Indus River. It was a classical Greek temple with Ionic columns. It almost certainly belongs to the Bactrian

Greek period of occupation at Sirkap. The largest Buddhist stupa and associated monastery at Taxila are known as the Dharmarajika; possibly built by ASOKA (268–235 B.C.E.) of the Mauryan dynasty during his period as viceroy there.

Further reading: Allchin, F. R. ed. *The Archaeology of Early Historic South Asia.* Cambridge: Cambridge University Press, 1995; Dani, A. H. *The Historic City of Taxila.* Delhi: Unipub, 1987; Marshall, J. *Taxila, an Illustrated Account of the Archaeological Excavations.* Cambridge: Cambridge University Press, 1951.

Temmu (631?–686 C.E.) *Temmu was the 40th emperor of Japan, who ruled the state of Yamato between 672 and 686 C.E.*
He married his niece, who later became the empress JITO. As Prince Oama, he rebelled against the succession of his nephew in 672 as Emperor Kobun and fomented the civil war known as the JINSHIN DISTURBANCE. His victory led to his own succession and the move of the capital of Yamato to Asuka. From there, he instituted a series of fundamental reforms that led to the establishment of central imperial power over Japan. These involved the reduction in the power of regional noble families in favor of the imperial line. One means of achieving this objective was the sponsorship of the official history of Japan, which in due course appeared as the NIHONGI (720) and the KOJIKI (712). These gave recognition to the ancient and sacred origins of the royal lineage. He instituted land and social reforms to order the tax base. Land was taken from the noble families and vested in the emperor himself. He set in train the legal reforms that led to the Taiho Code of 701. His ruling principles were recalled centuries later in Japanese history.

Tenji (626–672 C.E.) *Tenji was the 38th TENNO, or sovereign, of Japan.*
The son of Emperor Jomei (593–641), he was known as Prince Naka no Oe. On his father's death, his mother, Empress Kogyoku, was enthroned, at a time when the Soga family was all-powerful in the YAMATO state. When aged 19, he conspired to overthrow this clan and then began to introduce reforms based on his knowledge of Tang Chinese administration, which favored a strong, centralized state founded on the sanctity of the ruling family. These are known as the TAIKA REFORMS. He acted as the powerful regent during the reign of his uncle, Kotoku, and again when his mother was again created the *tenno*. From this position, he had more ability to operate the levers of power than if he had been emperor. His reign officially began in 661, but he was not consecrated until 668, by which time he had relocated the capital of Yamato to Otsu. His foreign policy was not uniformly successful, for his support of PAEKCHE in its struggle with SHILLA and Tang China led to a major military defeat in 663. After his death, there was a bitter civil war, known as the JINSHIN DISTURBANCE, between his brother and his son, leading to the reign of the former, who became Emperor TEMMU.

Tenjinyama Tenjinyama is a large settlement of the middle YAYOI culture, located in eastern Honshu Island, Japan, facing west toward the Inland Sea. There are many sites in this region, representing the expansion of early rice cultivators from their original area of development in Kyushu. The Yayoi culture, dated from 300 B.C.E. to 300 C.E., was the seminal period in the evolution of Japanese civilization and owes much to the arrival of newcomers from southern Korea. After the long Jomon period of hunting and gathering (10,000–300 B.C.E.), the Yayoi culture was characterized by wet rice cultivation, metallurgy involving both iron and bronze, and expansion of maritime trade. Tenjinyama is one of the sites that provide evidence for a middle Yayoi settlement, with its house plans, storage pits, and a probable community building nearly seven meters (23 ft.) long in a ditched, defended enclosure. It is likely that the city's foundation took place as a result of a population spurt in the region as rice cultivation formed the basis of a regular food supply to sedentary village farmers. Two DOTAKU bells, both buried in the vicinity of the site, may have been used in a ritual activity.

tenno Tenno was a title taken by Japanese rulers of the late YAMATO and NARA STATES from the rule of Emperor TEMMU (631?–86 C.E.). It entered common usage under Empress JITO (645–702). During this period, there were many empresses, and the title, which means "heavenly sovereign," is equally applicable to male or female rulers. In the NIHONGI, completed in 720 C.E., sovereigns were retrospectively accorded the title in a deliberate policy to glorify the royal lineage.

Ter Ter is a major city located in the central Indian state of Maharashtra, equidistant between the east and west coasts of India. Commanding the Godavari River routes, it occupied a strategic position for trade and was described in the PERIPLUS OF THE ERYTHRAEAN SEA as Tagara, a place that produced muslin cloth and played an entrepreneurial role in the transmission of trade goods. Limited excavations have provided convincing evidence that the site was, in fact, a Satavahanan center during the first century C.E. Molds for producing figurines and ornaments reveal the presence of craft workshops. A large brick stupa was built during the following century, and it seems that it was fortified with a wooden palisade.
See also SATAVAHANA.

Termez Termez commands a strategic location on the upper reaches of the Amu Dar'ya River in Uzbekistan. It formed a nodal point on the SILK ROAD, linking Mary (MERV) with KAXGAR (Kashgar) to the east and BEGRAM to the south. Termez was a foundation of the BACTRIAN GREEKS, its name derived from its founder, King Demetrius. Little is known of the site in its earliest phase of occupation because the layers are buried deep below later cities. However, it has yielded many Bactrian Greek coins and Greek-style stone column bases. There is also substantial evidence for occupation during the KUSHAN period. By the early centuries C.E., the city walls enclosed 350 hectares (875 acres) and were surrounded by an extensive area under agriculture. It was visited in the mid-seventh century C.E. by the Chinese monk XUANZANG, who commented on the number of Buddhist stupas and monasteries there.

See also COINAGE.

Terrace of the Leper King   The Terrace of the Leper King is situated in the center of the city of ANGKOR THOM in northwest Cambodia. It faces a huge reviewing ground where the king provided tournaments. It is misnamed the terrace of the leper king because of a statue dating proba-

bly to the 14th century, representing the god of death. GEORGES CŒDÈS suggested that this terrace might have been the location for royal cremation ceremonies. The high reliefs that front the terrace portray many gods and demons, as well as numerous sacred *nagas* (snakes). A second wall immediately behind the front and hidden from view contains similar scenes.

Thap Mam   Thap Mam is an archaeological site in central Vietnam that has given its name to a late style of Cham art, dated from the end of the 11th to the beginning of the 14th century. It was during this period that the Cham navy attacked and sacked ANGKOR in Cambodia, and Emmanuel Guillon has noted certain Khmer influences in this style, seen for example in the GARUDA figure from Son Trieu in Vietnam. The sculptures concentrate on Hindu deities and ascetics. Some were very large indeed: A door guardian from Thap Mam had a head 60 centimeters (2 ft.) in height; most of the body is missing. There are also fine renditions of dancers. The individuality of Cham sculpture is seen in the fine statues of animals, such as the splendid lion-elephant that has

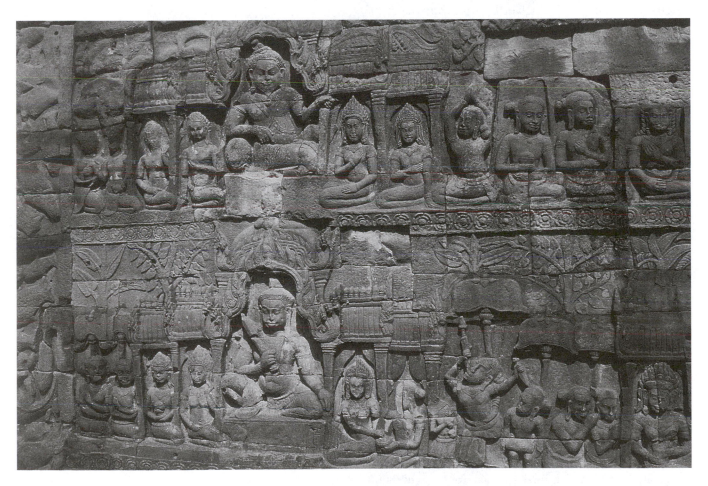

The Terrace of the Leper King at Angkor incorporates many reliefs showing gods and demons. It lies at the center of the city of Angkor Thom, adjacent to the royal palace. *(Charles Higham)*

survived intact and stands 2.15 meters (7.1 ft.) high. It has a raised trunk and tusks and a lion's paws.

See also CHAM CIVILIZATION.

Thatbyinnyu temple The Thatbyinnyu temple at PA-GAN in Myanmar (Burma) was built under the reign of King Alaungsithu (1113–60 C.E.). It represents a departure in design from that of the preceding temples dedicated to the Buddha in both size and form. The central spire of this temple rises to a height of 60 meters (198 ft.). It is also equipped with windows that render the interior much lighter than the dark recesses and corridors of earlier structures.

Thaton Thaton is the name of the capital city of a Mon state in southeastern Myanmar (Burma) known as Ramannadesa. It lies behind twin stone ramparts and a moat and has at its center a royal palace precinct. The strategic location at the western end of the Three Pagodas Pass would have facilitated trade contact with both India and the related Mon states of Dvaravati in central Thailand. It was a center of BUDDHISM, and there are several large Buddhist temples with foundations dating back to at least the fifth century C.E. The city was taken by King Anawrahta of PAGAN (1044–77 C.E.), and the artisans were removed to Pagan, thereby ensuring a strong Mon influence on the art and architecture of central Myanmar (Burma).

See also DVARAVATI CIVILIZATION.

Thaungthaman Thaungthaman is an Iron Age site located just above the Irrawaddy River floodplain south of Mandalay in Myanmar (Burma). Excavations there have uncovered inhumation burials dating to about 500–100 B.C.E. The dead were laid out on their backs and were accompanied by a range of offerings that include pots, beads, iron knives, short swords, and fishhooks. Some rich graves include round etched onyx beads as offerings, and these may well have originated in Indian workshops. There is evidence for a workshop for making stone tools and for houses raised on wooden posts. Clay-lined hearths have also produced rice remains. The site is important for illuminating the late prehistoric Iron Age culture from which the PYU CIVILIZATION developed during the first millennium C.E.

Theravada Buddhism After the death of the Buddha, there were two great councils to discuss the basic tenets of the religion. The first took place shortly after his death; the second occurred about a century later. By the time of the second council, a schism had developed between the so-called *mahasanghikas*, "members of the great order," and the Theravada Buddhists, who followed "the teaching of the elders." The former stressed the existence and values of BODHISATTVAS, that is, divine adherents who saw it as their duty to help humanity to attain nirvana. The

Theravada school strictly followed what it saw as the doctrine of the Buddha—that salvation from continuous cycles of rebirths and attendant sorrow resulted from the abandonment of individuality and the attainment of the state of nirvana. This word means the "blowing out," as of a light, and most followers saw its meaning as a state of transcendent bliss. The complete canon of Theravada BUDDHISM, known as the Tripitaka, has three sections that cover the proper rules of conduct for monks and nuns; discourses, some of which might have originated with the Buddha; and doctrines. It was preserved in Sri Lanka, a great stronghold of Theravada thought and practice, and was allegedly first written down during the reign of King Vattagamani (89–77 B.C.E.). Now absent from India, the Theravada branch of Buddhism is found in Myanmar (Burma), Thailand, Laos, and Cambodia.

Three Kingdoms The period of Three Kingdoms in Korea involved three states, known as SHILLA, KOGURYO, and PAEKCHE. During this vital period in Korean history, the three kingdoms played a part in the burgeoning trade network that linked China with the West, and several exotic items from China and farther west have been found in royal graves. Indeed, the royal graves, particularly of the Shilla kingdom, but also the intact grave of King Muryong of Paekche, have yielded remarkable assemblages of gold crowns, ornaments, and clothing. Shilla was also a major producer of iron, which was used for armor and weaponry as well as for export. BUDDHISM was adopted in Korea during the Three Kingdoms period and, after a slow start, particularly flourished in late Shilla contexts, in which many fine renditions of the Buddha and his followers were cast in bronze and iron or carved from granite. Temples were also constructed, linked with monasteries. The Three Kingdoms settlements were given strong defenses in view of the endemic warfare of the period, and the landscape was filled with many fortresses. Chinese writing was adopted, and INSCRIPTIONS were set up to mark boundaries or pronounce edicts. There was also a strongly defined class system, involving the royal elite, administrative officials, and commoners. The states were reliant on agriculture, with rice predominant in the warmer south, but there were also groups of specialist metalworkers, potters, weavers, and woodworkers.

According to the *SAMGUK SAGI*, the history of the period written by Kim Pu-Sik (1075–1151 C.E.), the three kingdoms were founded in 57, 37, and 18 B.C.E. Archaeological research has suggested otherwise: The inception of states in Korea was a phenomenon of the third and fourth centuries C.E. Koguryo dominated the northern half of the peninsula, Paekche the southwest, and Shilla the southeast. There were several other states, such as the components of KAYA, but they were always under threat from the big three and were absorbed over time. Ultimately Shilla defeated all rivals, and Korea became unified under Shilla control in the early seventh century C.E. The period ended when Shilla defeated its two rivals in 668 C.E.

Tianma-Qucun   Tianma-Qucun, near Houma in Shanxi province, China, was the capital of the WESTERN ZHOU DYNASTY state of JIN. Founded in the late 11th century B.C.E. by Tangshu Yu, the brother of King Cheng of Zhou, it developed into a powerful polity in its own right. Investigations there by Beijing University have identified the cemetery of the rulers of Jin during the ninth and eighth centuries B.C.E., including more than 600 tombs. Some of these not only were very richly endowed with grave offerings, but also showed remarkable preferences for jades and for placement of antique pieces with the dead. The burials took the form of deep pits containing a wooden coffin, with access by ramps. There were also pits containing chariots and horses. Burial 31 held an antique jade disk with a SHANG STATE inscription. The dead ruler's face had been covered by a jade mask made of 79 individual pieces that would probably have been sewn onto a fabric backing. Burial 8 incorporated either an original or a copy of an antique ritual jade *cong* tube of LIANGZHU CULTURE origin, as well as a pectoral of jade plaques, agate, and carnelian beads. A second pectoral from Burial 63 also included pieces of jade and agate in addition to FAIENCE. RITUAL BRONZE VESSELS displayed a series of local innovations; some were cast in imitation of older forms or even as MINGQI, representations of vessel forms that could have served no useful purpose.

Tianxingguan   Tianxingguan is a CHU state cemetery near Jiangling in Hupei province, China. In 1978 Tomb 1 was excavated. The BAMBOO SLIPS within identify this as the burial of Pan Cheng, lord of Diyang, who died in the mid-fourth century B.C.E. The grave took the form of a pit 12.2 meters (40.3 ft.) deep, at the base of which stood a wooden mortuary structure with a central burial chamber and side rooms to contain the offerings. Many of these offerings, according to the records found in the tomb, were gifts to the lord from friends and relatives. One of the ancillary chambers contained musical instruments, a second was an armory, and the third held LACQUER figures. One of the most extraordinary offerings was a lacquered tomb guardian in the form of a double-bodied creature with antlers. Standing 1.7 meters (5.6 ft.) high, this figure probably represents Tu Bo, named in the *CHUCI* (*The Songs of the South*) as god of the underworld. The collection of bamboo slips also record the turtle and MILFOIL divinations made on Pan Cheng's behalf. Would he obtain benefit over the ensuing year in serving the king? The answer was auspicious, but sacrifices to the spirits would be necessary.

Tianzimao   Tianzimao is a late prehistoric cemetery of the DIAN CHIEFDOM, located on the northeastern margin of Lake Dian in Yunnan province, China. Dating to the last two centuries B.C.E., it is particularly notable for the 44 burials uncovered and the insight provided into the social structure at a provincial rather than an elite royal level. The cemetery is dominated by one outstandingly large burial. Contained in a grave measuring 6.3 by four meters (20.8 by 13.2 ft.) and four meters deep, were many fine mortuary offerings. The lower part of the grave was lined with a wooden floor supporting a coffin that contained the remains of an adult and a child. Grave goods were found in the coffin, on the wooden platform, and in boxes or wrapped in silk. There was much bronze weaponry, including 18 swords, spearheads, axes, hundreds of arrowheads, shield ornaments, and armor. These were superbly decorated. A bronze situla was decorated with boats, birds, and cattle. There are a bronze headrest and thousands of malachite beads. In contrast, other graves are far less wealthy and fall into groups distinguished by the presence of either weapons or spindle whorls. These represent the men and WOMEN of a community that seems to have had a paramount leader. Such a situation conforms with what is known of the social organization at SHIZHAISHAN to the south of this site, where a scene on a bronze container depicts the king of Dian receiving subsidiary chiefs such as the individual portrayed in the rich grave of Tianzimao.

Tieyun Cangui   The six volumes of *Tieyun Cangui* written by Liu Taiyun in 1903 were the seminal publication on the texts of the Shang ORACLE BONES. During the first three decades of the 20th century until the excavations at ANYANG got under way, this publication stimulated many Chinese scholars to collect and safeguard this precious archival material.
    See also SHANG STATE.

Tillya Tepe   Tillya Tepe, "Golden Hill," is located in a commanding position south of the Amu Dar'ya River, in northern Afghanistan. Its wealth and long sequence of occupation are related to its strategic location for trade and the opportunities for agriculture afforded by the fertile Bactrian Plain. It was first occupied in the second millennium B.C.E., when a temple probably devoted to fire worship was built. During the period of Achaemenid dominance in the sixth to fourth centuries B.C.E., it was converted into a palace with the addition of a high BRICK rampart. However, it suffered a severe fire, probably at the hands of the invading Greeks in the fourth century B.C.E. The site is best known for the KUSHAN-period cemetery dating to the first century C.E. In 1970 an Afghan-Soviet team examined this mound, beginning when it was intact. At the end of the first season, much of the site was removed by contractors for road fill, but the archaeologists arrived just in time to save the small intact area. Their excavations revealed six graves about two meters

(6.6 ft.) in depth. No surface markers were apparent; the dead had been interred in wooden plank coffins reinforced with iron clamps. Five of the coffins had been covered in shrouds embellished with gold plaques, while the sixth was encased in black and brown leather. The six bodies had been interred fully clothed, with about 20,000 gold ornaments that were embellished with inlays of TURQUOISE, garnet, and mother-of-pearl. Some personal possessions lay beside the bodies. The disposition of the gold in an assemblage dominated by plaques that had been attached to at least three layers of clothing allowed the styles of dress to be reconstructed. These six graves belonged to a local Kushan princely family and have been assigned, on the basis of the associated coins, to the first century C.E.

BURIAL 1

Burial 1 was that of a woman aged between 25 and 35 years at death. Wearing a long robe, trousers, and shoes, she was interred in a grave measuring 2.5 by 1.3 meters (8.3 by 4.3 ft.). A cloak over her shoulders had been embellished with a gold ornament showing a man riding on the back of a dolphin. She wore a gold earring in the form of a boat and a hairpin of gold, pearls, and leaf-shaped attachments. Her ivory toilet box still contained a white face powder, and other cosmetics included antimony crystals and pieces of pink rouge. Even her tweezers with a wooden handle survived.

BURIAL 2

Burial 2 was found in a coffin of wooden planks secured by heavy iron clasps; the coffin had been covered in a shroud embroidered with gold and silver plaques. The woman, who died when aged between 30 and 40, was oriented with her dead pointing to the north and wore a remarkable array of ornaments, including a gold diadem and a gold torque. The beads of her necklace were made of gold and ivory, and ornaments of musicians, also in gold, lay beside each shoulder. A Chinese bronze mirror had been placed on her chest. Tiny models of feet, a fish, hands, and an ax were found at the wrists. Gold bangles were decorated with images of antelopes, and the surface wear shows that they would have been worn in life. She wore a long robe that had been held in place by a remarkable clasp depicting two identical dolphins being rode by cupids. The dolphin motif is of Greco-Roman inspiration, but features of this artifact, such as the bracelets and anklets on the cupids, reveal local input. One of the two rings on her left hand bears an image of Athena, together with the name Athena incised backward on the surface. This suggests that it had been used as a SEAL.

BURIAL 3

Burial 3 also held a female, aged between about 18 and 25 years at death. The coffin had been placed between two layers of animal hide, one painted black and the other brown. The coffin was oriented with the head to the north. This burial had been disturbed by rodent activity, but it was still evident that the head had been placed over a gold bowl. She wore at least three layers of clothing, as can be determined by three clasps one over the other on the chest. These lay near a Chinese silver mirror. A silver coin of the Parthian king Mithridates II (r. 123–88 B.C.E.) was found beside the hands, as if she had been holding it, and a golden coin of the Roman emperor Tiberius, minted in the French city of Lugudunum between 16 and 21 C.E., was found outside the coffin. The mass of gold ornaments included a large torque around the neck and a pendant in the form of two horses, inlaid with garnet and turquoise. The popular theme of cupids riding dolphins is also found in this burial in the form of a clasp. The intriguing point about these motifs is that the dolphin image was popular in Greek art, as seen depicted at AY KHANUM in northern Afghanistan, but the dolphins were transformed in Kushan art into local river fish. Greco-Roman influence is also illustrated by another clasp from this burial in the form of a warrior armed in Mediterranean style, the helmet closely paralleled in the portraits of Greco-Bactrian kings on their coin issues. This woman also wore a unique pair of shoes with gold soles, fastened by gold plaques. Her cosmetics were placed in the grave in ivory containers, together with an ivory comb.

BURIAL 4

A horse's skull was found in the fill of Burial 4, the coffin of which had been covered by a lattice of wooden laths, which had supported a mat. This would have prevented the fill of the grave from raining down on top of the coffin. The coffin contained the skeleton of a man judged to have stood nearly two meters tall. His head lay on a gold vessel associated with a tree fashioned from gold with fruit of pearls. A model of an ibex, of clear Bactrian Greek origin, had also been attached to this vessel. He wore weaponry: a sword and a dagger both in gold-plated scabbards and a second dagger with an ivory hilt. A quiver with a decorated silver lid was filled with iron arrowheads, and two bows lay nearby. The dagger with gold sheath also has a gold haft, decorated with fantastic animals that include a dragon embellished with turquoise inlay. A bear cub is seen on the pommel of this weapon, gripping a vine with grapes in its mouth. One coin was found in the grave. It depicts the wheel of the law (DHARMACAKRA) and a lion, with the inscription "as fearless as a lion." It is unique, but coins that are not dissimilar were minted at Ay Khanum in the reign of the Bactrian Greek king Agathocles. The style of dress represented by the surviving ornaments can be partially reconstructed and compared with known reliefs depicting Kushans. These show men wearing trousers tucked into short boots and a tunic fastened at the waist by a belt into which a scabbard is fixed.

BURIAL 5

Burial 5 had been interred in a log coffin wrapped in a shroud embellished with silver disks. The young woman was aged between 15 and 20 years at death, and it may be that her youth accounts for the less opulent set of grave goods. Nevertheless, she was interred with a silver wand or scepter, gold anklets, and a superb pectoral of gold, garnet, and turquoise. Her mirror was fashioned from silver and had been encased in fabric embroidered in gold thread and pearls.

BURIAL 6

The last burial was equipped with a wooden plank coffin, again covered by a wooden trellis that had supported mats to exclude the soil that backfilled the grave. It contained a woman who died when aged between 25 and 30 years. Her head lay on a silver bowl, and she wore a gold crown. A gold figurine of a winged goddess lay on her chest, and she held in her right hand a golden scepter. Her shoes had been adorned with gold disks. As with other women in this cemetery, personal cosmetics had been placed in the grave, together with iron tweezers and a Chinese mirror. A silver coin had been placed in her mouth, a Greek custom. Its Greek text attributes it to the Parthian king Phraates IV (r. 38–32 B.C.E.). A later stamped text belongs to the reign of an early Kushan leader named Sapaleisis. A unique gold Parthian coin was clutched in the left hand of the dead woman.

The treasure from these six royal burials reveals several sources. There are, for example, items of clear Bactrian Greek origin (300–145 B.C.E.), such as the gold figure of an ibex and an intaglio of a ruler wearing a Greek-style helmet. Chinese mirrors dating to the HAN DYNASTY (206 B.C.E.–200 C.E.) were found, together with what appear to be local imitations. There are also Roman and Parthian coins. The local goldsmiths, however, also took exotic motifs and reworked them within their own experience, most clearly seen in the figures riding dolphins, in which the sea mammal was depicted as a local river fish. Certain forms also hark back to the art of the steppes, as seen in the Scythian animal forms. It is evident that the early Kushan rulers of what was once a Greek kingdom relished costumes virtually covered in gold ornaments, and only by the narrowest of margins were the 20,000 golden items from Tillya-tepe saved from the bulldozer and grave robber.

See also BEGRAM; OXUS TREASURE.

Further reading: Sarianidi, V. I. *The Golden Hoard of Bactria: From the Tillya-tepe Excavations in Northern Afghanistan.* New York: H. N. Abrams; Leningrad: Aurora Art Publishers, 1985.

Tircul Tircul is the Mon name for the PYU CIVILIZATION of Myanmar (Burma).

titles Titles reflecting specific tasks and ranks in a hierarchy are a recurrent feature of early states, and their very presence is indicative of social complexity and the development of a central bureaucracy. Chinese histories describing the mythical earliest states begin with the *Shi ben* (Roots of the Generations), which was available to SIMA QIAN (145–85 B.C.E.) when he wrote his history of China but has since been lost. It refers to ancient heroes that include emperors and bureaucrats, an archivist, diviners, and those in charge of wedding rituals. This period probably corresponds archaeologically with the XIA DYNASTY. With the SHANG DYNASTY we have the records contained in ORACLE-BONES texts. These reveal that the title *di* was accorded kings, whose continuing influence on events after their death caused them to call regularly on the oracular ceremonials. The royal lineage incorporated a series of titles. *Zi*, for example, was the title accorded royal princes. Lesser male members of the royal line were given the titles *duo zi* or *duo zi zu*. The oracle bones also provide us with other titles. There were *quan*, or dog officers, charged with assisting in hunting; guards (*wei*); and officials who worked in the area of agriculture (*tian*). Cultivation of crops was recognized as a vital area for state intervention, so we read in one oracle text that "the king ordered many *yin* [officials] to open new fields in the west." Animal husbandry was also regulated by officials, such as the *duo quan* and *duo ma*, concerned with dogs and horses respectively.

Inscriptions on bronze vessels, which were often cast to celebrate the conferral of a royal appointment, are an important source of titles during the WESTERN ZHOU DYNASTY. These reflect a powerful central bureaucracy. There were court scribes, known as *shi*, who maintained records that refer to the three principal ministers. These were known as the *sima*, *situ*, and *si gong*. *Shanfu* were responsible for ensuring that royal commands were transmitted to the right authorities. Land disputes were mediated by judges, indicating the establishment of a legal system.

Titles took on increasing political meaning with the EASTERN ZHOU DYNASTY, during which a series of powerful states vied for dominance. *Ba* means the "senior one." Zhuan Gong of the state of Zheng, who died in 701 B.C.E., was foremost in protecting Ping, the first king of Eastern Zhou, after his move east at the end of the Western Zhou dynasty. He was the first *ba* who, in practice, was the leader of a coalition central plains states during the Spring and Autumn Period (770–481 B.C.E.). At the same time, the system of rule involving members of a royal kinship web, known as the *zongfa*, broke down, to be replaced by administration involving appointed officials. Land divisions during the seventh century B.C.E. came to be known as XIAN, administered by *yin*, or governors. Their staff included stewards and sheriffs (*zai* and *shou*).

The period of WARRING STATES (475–221 B.C.E.) saw the development of totalitarian rule. This was most evident in the state of QIN, whose senior administrator, SHANG YANG, instituted a system of graded titles. The height of a person's burial mound, and the number of trees planted upon it, were determined by rank. By the mid-fourth century B.C.E., Hui Hou, ruler of Wei, adopted the royal title of king, a move soon followed by other leaders of the major states. In 288 B.C.E. the leaders of the two emerging powers, Qin and Qi, declared themselves, respectively, the eastern and western *di*, a divine title not hitherto accorded any leader in China. This presumption was short-lived, but the followers of the king of Qin persuaded him to assume the title *huangdi*, or "emperor," when he finally defeated his rival states. The administration of the first emperor (*see* QIN SHIHUANGDI) involved many ranks and titles. He even gave the title of fifth-rank counselor to a tree, under which he had been sheltered from the rain.

The HAN governmental machine was headed by three senior statesmen, whose titles can be translated as "chancellor," "imperial counselor," and "commander of armed forces." Security in the capital city was under the control of an official with the title "bearer of the gilded mace." The commandant of waters and parks was an office created in 115 B.C.E. His officials were numerous and among other duties, ensured the maintenance of royal parks, the provision of food for the royal table, and building and maintaining the pavilions that dotted the extensive imperial pleasure gardens. The prefect of the stables ensured that the emperor's horses were well cared for. Ranks were instituted in the royal harem, where up to 14 different titles were accorded the women, from the "brilliant companion" at the top to the "pleasing maid" at the bottom. In 178 B.C.E., during a crisis in the harvest, it was decided that grain could be made into a negotiable commodity and used to purchase titles.

JAPAN AND KOREA

The use of titles also reflects the rise of the state in Japan. Fifth-century finds of inscribed swords, for example, reveal the existence of an official group of sword bearer guards of the royal palace. An example from EDAFUNAYAMA on west coast of Kyushu, included the word for king, *okimi*. In cementing control over their kingdom, these YAMATO kings controlled the *uji*, or clan, and the *be*, or specialist group. Both were under the control of the *kabane*, a title confessed by the king. There were several ranks of *kabane*, ranging from village headmen to high officials of state. The seventh-century Asuka enlightenment involved the creation of imperially appointed ranks based on merit and ability. There were 12 ranks, identified on the basis of the color of the feathers worn in a purple silk hat embellished with gold and silver. The senior rank bore the title "greater virtue," then descending through such terms as "greater propriety" and "greater justice" to the lowest of all, "lesser knowledge." These ranks of state officials replaced the former system of hereditary access to positions of influence.

In Korea, the ranks of the SHILLA state were determined by ancestry. Thus the highest rank, *songgol*, or "holy bone," involved only those with the right to rule. The *chingol*, or "true bone," were ranked next, before three further ranks and then the commoners.

INDIA

The lack of an accepted translation of the INDUS VALLEY CIVILIZATION SCRIPT rules out any investigation of the titles that almost certainly were in place, given that state's social complexity. However, the Vedic literature of early India refers to warrior nobles, or *kshatriyas*, and the leader, or *rajan*, who was elected from their number. With the development of the JANAPADAS, or early states, in the Ganges (Ganga) Valley during the sixth to the fourth centuries B.C.E., we encounter a set of highly significant titles. These include the *purohita*, or high priest; *senapati*, or army commander; and *gramani*, or village headman. The administrative machine of the MAURYA EMPIRE can be considered on the basis of the writings of KAUTILYA and MEGASTHENES and the inscriptions of ASOKA. The empire was divided into four provinces, each under the rule of a princely viceroy, known as a *kumara* or *aryaputra*. These, in turn, made up districts under the jurisdiction of *mahamatras*, officials who doubled as judges, or *nagara viyohalakas*. Lower-order officials included *yuktas*, *rajukas*, and *pradeshikas*. The fourth of Asoka's pillar inscriptions records that a *rajuka* had administration over many hundreds of thousands of people. The orders from the emperor were transmitted by *pulisani*.

In 402 C.E., the Chinese monk FAXIAN visited India during the reign of the GUPTA king CANDRAGUPTA. He noted that the court officials were all paid a salary, along the lines recommended much earlier in the writings of Kautilya. The emperor, who was now approaching divine status, was known as the *maharajadhiraja*, or "great king of kings." There was a new ministry of war and peace under a *sandhivigrahika*, while, as before, provinces were under the rule of royal princes. Subsidiary districts came under the control of *kumaramatyas* or *visayapatis*. There were also local or district boards made up of four officials, known as the guild president, the chief merchant, chief artisan, and chief scribe (*nagara-sresthin*, *sarthavaha*, *prathamakulika* and *prathamakayastha* respectively).

Northeast India and Pakistan were subject to a series of incursions by foreign peoples who either brought their own or adopted alien systems of titles. The KUSHAN king KANISHKA I (100–126 C.E.) took the title *devaputra*, or "son of god," as well as *maharajadhiraja*. Kushan provinces were controlled by *mahaksatrapas*, and other officials held the titles *mahadandanayakas* and *dandanayakas*.

CENTRAL ASIA

Many states that developed on the SILK ROAD developed their own system of graded titles, and the KHAROSHTHI documents of SHAN-SHAN provide a clear example of this polity in the third and fourth centuries C.E. It was divided into districts (*rajas*), each under the control of a governor, or *rajadaraja*. These provinces were divided first into *nagaras*, then *satas*, each composed of about 100 households. The king was assisted in his rule by a number of court officials. There was an *ogu*, who seems to have been a highly ranked administrator. The legal system was under the control of the *kitsaitsa* and the *gusura*. Local affairs were run by a lesser official known as a *cojbho*. Taxation was paid at least in part in kind and was overseen by the *sothamga*. The assessment was based on the production of each *sata* and was assessed by *sothamgas*. Scribes (*divira*) and messengers (*lekhaharaga* and *dutiyae*) ensured efficient communication.

CAMBODIA

The titles and duties of officials in the CHENLA and Angkorian kingdoms are contained in the contemporary INSCRIPTIONS. These provide a means of identifying the growth of the bureaucracy and the duties seen as relevant in maintaining the state.

Chenla Titles

The dominant honorific title in the early history of the Chenla kingdom was the PON. Always male, the title was inherited through the female line. *Pon* are seen as district chiefs, organizers of temple donations and transactions and water resources, until they disappear from the historical record in 719 C.E. The *mratan*, on the other hand, was a title that appears to have been approved by the sovereign for aristocrats given special functions and was not inherited. The growing numbers of the latter suggest increasing central control over regional administration. Under JAYAVARMAN I OF CHENLA, who ruled 635–80 C.E., there was a proliferation of titles. A certain Jnanacandra was described as an *amatya*, or official, of high birth. There is also mention of a *rajasabhapadi*, "president of the royal court." Officials were given the right to carry symbols of their status, and this president was honored with a white parasol and a golden vase. A family from Dharmapura held the priestly position of *hotar*. There were a *samantagajapadi* (chief of the elephants) and a *dhanyakarapati* (chief of the grain store). The king also had a *sabha*, or state council. All these titles suggest that Jayavarman I had a growing bureaucratic administration. Although his ancestors had been given the divine title *dhuli jen vrah kamraten an* (dust of the feet of the lord) after their death, Jayavarman was the first king to bear the title while still living.

Angkor Titles

The kingdom of ANGKOR in Cambodia saw a great proliferation of titles. *Vap*, for example, meaning "father," were first encountered in a retrospective inscription describing a land grant to a follower of JAYAVARMAN II (c. 770–834 C.E.). INDRAVARMAN I (877–99 C.E.) appointed Amarabhava as a chief of religious foundations, and YASHOVARMAN I (r. 889–910 C.E.) later gave him the title *acaryadhipati*, or

head *acarya*. Under Yashovarman, a *mratan* was given the title *vyapara* of the second rank and charged to determine land boundaries. His successor, Harshavarman I, issued an order to an official with the new title *rajakulamahamantrin* exempting the foundation from the tax on rice. RAJENDRAVARMAN (r. 944–968 C.E.) appointed one Ksetrajna as royal barber with the title *mahendropakalpa*. JAYAVARMAN V (r. 968–1001) commanded two officials with the title *khlon glan* (chief of the warehouse) of the second and third ranks to settle a land dispute. The dynasty founded by Jayavarman II, over its two centuries of development, incorporated many titles and grades. The *hotar* and *vrah guru* fulfilled religious duties. The *klon visaya* was concerned with land ownership, and even at the village level there were *klon sruk*.

After the long civil war that finally saw SURYAVARMAN I (r. c. 1002–49) enthroned, the king ordered all his officials to swear an oath of allegiance. Many *tamrvac* of the first to fourth ranks offered their lives and unswerving devotion to the king in the presence of the sacred fire. Some names were later erased, perhaps because they failed in their intention. The long family inscriptions inscribed at the same time list hereditary court functions, such as carrier of the royal fly whisk and chief of the fan carriers. These symbols of kingship and those charged with their employment reflect a court that incorporated a legion of grandees, many of whom were related to the royal line. The author of the SDOK KAK THOM inscription, Sadasiva, was successively given the exalted titles *kamsten an* Jayendrapandita and *dhuli jen vrah kamraten an* Jayendravarman. ZHOU DAGUAN noticed the graded titles at Angkor in 1296–97. He set down their titles: *Mratan* had gold handles for their parasols, while those of the *sresthin* were made of silver.

Todaiji The Todaiji was the centrally important Buddhist temple of the Nara capital, HEIJO-KYO, in Japan. This city was occupied between 710 and 784 C.E., with a brief period of five years when it was abandoned during a rebellion against Emperor Shomu. In 743 C.E., when the court was located 40 kilometers (24 mi.) to the north at Shigaraki, the emperor ordered the casting of a massive bronze of Buddha in his guise as Vairocana, source of creation. Known as the Daibutsu, it was to be covered in gold. On the court's return to Heijo-kyo in 745 C.E., the Todaiji was selected as the location of this statue. Shomu ordered a huge team of workers to level the area to the east of the Heijo-kyo, and all the copper supplies of the country were directed to the casting of the statue. When completed in 749, after at least two years of casting, it stood nearly 11 meters (36.3 ft.) tall, reaching almost double that height when its lotus pedestal is included. It was surrounded by a large hall that originally measured 52 by 47 meters (172 by 155 ft.) and stood to a height of 47 meters. It was rebuilt on a smaller scale in the 12th century, but, even so reduced, it remains the largest single wooden building in the world. Two pagodas, each about 100 meters (330 ft.) high, were added to this complex.

The construction of this structure, described as the largest state temple ever constructed in Japan, involved a huge deployment of resources. In March 1988, this process was illuminated by the discovery of 226 MOKKAN, wooden slips containing written records, just outside the hall for the bronze Buddha. These included shipment tags for the 400 tons of copper that went into the casting. One record notes the receipt by the palace of 7.6 tons of high-grade copper.

As the center of Nara BUDDHISM, this temple played a key role in the life of the state. It is also known that the authorities invested in agricultural estates known as *shoen*. That at Kuwabara was founded in 754 C.E. and included irrigable rice land, sluices, farm tools, and agricultural buildings. The profits were accumulated by the temple.

tomb models and reliefs   During the WARRING STATES PERIOD (475–221 B.C.E.) and the long life of the HAN DYNASTY (206 B.C.E.–220 C.E.) in China, rulers and wealthy nobles were interred with rich assemblages of mortuary offerings. These included wooden and ceramic models that provide compelling evidence for houses, boats, agricultural practices, and people. The available texts state that during this period the concept of MINGQI, which helps in the interpretation of the symbolism underlying these models, evolved. *Mingqi* describes articles of spiritual importance, which can be regarded as spirit articles. Thus a figurine may be taken to represent the person designated to serve the tomb occupant in the afterlife. In the state of CHU during the Warring States period, such figurines were made of a block of wood with movable arms affixed by dowels to the body. Quite the best example of the use of wooden figures where in former times sacrificial victims had been placed in the tomb is from Burial 1 at Changtaiguan in Henan province. There are seven chambers in a tomb measuring 10 by seven meters (33 by 23 ft.). The middle room contained the coffins in which the dead were interred with rich offerings of jade and gold. That representing a stable to the north included two figurines of drivers. Two cooks had been placed in the kitchen to the south. Behind the main chamber is the study, in which two figurines represent clerks. Their high status is reflected in the quality of their clothing. A guard was placed in the storage room, which contained large pottery vessels. Immediately behind the tomb chamber, another room included four figurines, one of which had a bamboo point impaling its chest, together with a mysterious antlered creature with a long protruding tongue and staring eyes.

At Zhangqui in Shandong, the models assumed miniature proportions. Modeled from clay, an ensemble of 36 figurines was recovered, of which 10 were dancers standing barely eight centimeters (3.2 in.) high. There are also musicians playing the zither, drums, and bells, and a further 10 people are thought to represent the audience.

QIN SHIHUANGDI TOMB FIGURES

The pits associated with the mortuary complex of QIN SHIHUANGDI (259–210 B.C.E.), the first emperor of China, are one of the foremost archaeological sites in the world. The complex is located near Xi'an. When digging a well in 1974, farmers encountered a jumbled mass of life-size clay soldiers, still bearing their original paint and holding bronze weaponry. They had stumbled on the silent army that had protected the tomb of Qin Shihuangdi, for two millennia.

Set in a rectangular walled precinct 2.25 by one kilometer (1.35 by 0.6 mi.), the tomb complex is known from two sources. The first is archaeology, and the second is the historical record as described by SIMA QIAN. Pit 1 contains rows of terra-cotta warriors in long, parallel chambers. A chariot and four horses stand out toward the front. The infantry soldiers stand erect, holding long-handled bronze spears or a quiver of arrows, the edges still sharp to the touch. The uniforms and body armor provide a remarkable insight into the appearance of the QIN army. A second pit nearby contains the cavalry division of more than 100 chariots and 100 war horses, while the third pit houses the army headquarters staff.

HAN DYNASTY MODELS OF PEOPLE

This practice of including models of people rather than sacrificial victims continued with the Han dynasty. Thousands of clay models of soldiers have been recovered from a pit adjacent to the tomb of a king of Chu at Shizishan in Jiangsu province. Infantry and cavalry were represented, but there were no chariots. The same mix of foot soldiers and cavalry is seen at a rich royal tomb at Yangjiawan in Shaanxi province of the same Western Han date. In contrast to the Qin army, which was represented by life-size figures, those from Yangjiawan stand about a half-meter (1.65 ft.) in height. There are 1,800 foot soldiers, 580 horse riders, and some model chariots. The infantry soldiers were arrayed in rows and columns, each person in full battle dress richly painted in red and black and holding a shield, likewise painted with identical red heraldic symbols on a black background. Tomb 1 at MAWANGDUI in Hunan, dated to about 168 B.C.E., included wooden figurines of ladies-in-waiting to the marchioness of Dai. Standing a half-meter tall, they wore costumes splendidly rendered in black and red designs. Perhaps the most extraordinary assemblage of figurines is that from the pits adjacent to the tomb of Han Jingdi (188–141 B.C.E.). These cover an area of almost 10 hectares (25 acres) and are said to contain at least 40,000 figurines at about a third life-size, each painted and clothed in silk or hemp garments.

HAN HOUSE MODELS AND RELIEFS

The clay models and reliefs of houses and agricultural activities provide much insight into the social conditions under the Han dynasty. A model of a fortified domestic residence of the Eastern Han dynasty from the far south, in Guangzhou, shows a series of buildings in a walled compound. The walls have watchtowers at each corner, and, although only 40 centimeters square (6.4 sq. in.), the model includes the lord of this estate, his servants, and armed guards. Just such an armed retainer for a local magnate is seen in a tomb from Sichuan. He wears a round cap and has a sword at his belt. A scene incised on a stone slab from Yinan in Shandong, dating to the end of the Eastern Han dynasty, shows the house of a relatively well-to-do person. It provides an intimate aerial view of the property, which had two ranges of buildings on one level, each surrounding a courtyard. Access to the house was through a large doorway decorated with a mask, beside which there stands a frame from which a gong or drum is suspended. Two tall watchtowers lie beyond the walls, and birds are flying over trees. One hen is feeding chicks on the ground. The residence includes rooms grouped around two courtyards. The first contains a circular well surrounded by a wooden fence, and a pulley and rope are suspended from a wooden frame. Two doors, one ajar, lead to the second court. These doors are embellished with face masks. A box, a large vessel, and possibly a table lie in this second court around which the living rooms are grouped. A second Han-period house was depicted on an impressed brick from Sichuan. This is a rather larger residence that incorporates four courts. Two men converse in an elegant columned room, while cranes disport themselves in the court in front of them. A servant is seen sweeping the ground of a second court, while a dog plays. There is also a tall storied tower with steps leading from the ground floor to the rooms above.

AGRICULTURAL MODELS AND RELIEFS

A grave of the Western Han dynasty at Shaogou in Henan province contained the model of a well almost a half-meter in height. There are even a pulley wheel and ceramic vessel for drawing water from a depth and a trough alongside for water storage. Such wells could have been used to irrigate field plots. Agricultural activities are themselves represented in a model of a person holding a hoe from Sichuan province, and a figure is seen in an Eastern Han burial from Laodaosi, Shaanxi province, holding a spade. Such iron spades had a considerable impact on farming during this period. The most informative of agricultural models, however, is from Shuangfuxiang in Sichuan. Dating to the Eastern Han dynasty, it is a flat plaque measuring 81 by 48 centimeters (32.4 by 19.2 in.). The surface is divided into two by a wall. On one side of the wall, two kneeling figures are seen in a field, transplanting rice. Behind them lie heaps of manure for spreading. The other scene shows a farmyard with a pond and aquatic animals: a duck, crab, water snail, and lotus plants. There is even a small boat. This model, from an area subject to monsoon rains, illustrates that the system of transplanting rice into small plots demarcated by low banks was already developed. Transplanting in this manner provides for higher yields than broadcasting, because it reduces competition for light and nutrients between the growing plants. It is the backbone of rice agriculture throughout the lowlands of Southeast Asia at present.

Rice Agriculture

Rice was a particularly important crop, because surpluses could be stored and used to support the many specialists and administrators who made up the upper reaches of Han society. Therefore, it is not surprising to find that advances in rice processing and storage are also prominent in the clay tomb models. One relief, also from Sichuan, shows a group of people harvesting with hand-held sickles; another shows people husking rice with a tilt hammer. This is a much more efficient procedure than use of an old-fashioned pestle and mortar. A model of a granary for storing rice from Hernan province shows the sophistication of such a structure, with its floor raised to prevent dampness from penetrating the storeroom above and a row of windows to provide ventilation. This granary also had a pitched roof, and the walls were decorated with red painted designs that include depictions of people working on the placing of the grain within. Pigs and chickens were raised on a large scale, and other clay models show a hen coop and a pig pen. The latter was attached to a latrine, depicting the use to this day in China of animal and human wastes to fertilize the fields. It was elevated above the level of the pigsty and reached by a flight of nine steps, presumably to provide room below for the collection of wastes.

Other Industrial Activities

There are also clay reliefs that portray other industrial activities undertaken during the Han dynasty. One shows a winery. There are rows of vessels for producing wine, a shop, a customer, and even a worker leaving to deliver a consignment. Another shows in great detail salt production in Sichuan. The brine was raised by bucket and pulley from its source and reticulated by a long pipe to the workshop, where it was boiled in a row of pottery vessels over an enclosed furnace. Meanwhile, in the background, two men are seen hunting with bow and arrows and their dogs. A market scene reveals a special walled precinct, in which people run their stalls and purchasers, who have entered by the East Market Gate, as indicated in an explanatory inscription, buy. There is also a tower from which a flag was flown when the market was open for business.

Such tomb models and scenes illustrate with impressive clarity aspects of life during the Qin and Han dynasties.

Further reading: Bagley, R. W. *Ancient Sichuan*. Seattle and Princeton: Seattle Art Museum 2001; Loewe, M. *Chinese Ideas of Life and Death*. London: Allen and Unwin, 1982; Loewe, M., and E. L. Shaugnessy, eds. *The

Cambridge History of Ancient China. Cambridge: Cambridge University Press, 1999.

Tonglushan Tonglushan is one of the largest and most impressive copper-mining sites in China. It is located about 140 kilometers south of Wuhan in Hubei province. The intensity of exploitation can be appreciated when it is considered that the deep mine shafts penetrated up to 60 meters (198 ft.) below the present ground surface and were then interlinked with tunnels to gain access to the malachite and cuprite ores. This great depth reached well below the water table, and long wooden troughs had to be installed to carry underground water to sumps, where it was raised to the surface in wooden buckets. There was also a system of closing off older shafts to direct air to that part of the mine being worked at a particular time. In earlier centuries, the pits and shafts were as narrow as 50 centimeters (1.65 ft.), but with the advent of more efficient iron tools, this span was more than doubled. The underground workings had to be reinforced with wooden supports and frames to guard against roof collapse, and in the airless lower reaches of the mine, these have survived. Other wooden items preserved in this manner include the wooden buckets used to raise water and the ore itself and the windlasses that aided both operations.

The word Tonglushan means "great smelting place," and as early as 18 C.E. contemporary records describe how the hill shone with verdigris flowers after heavy rain. The ancient mining complex was recognized when further exploitation began in 1965, and for a decade beginning in 1974, intensive excavations revealed the full extent of the early activity at the site and the extent of ore extracted. The slag resulting from a millennium of mining, which began toward the end of the second millennium B.C.E., covers 140 hectares (350 acres), and it has been estimated that the total weight is in the vicinity of nearly a half-million tons.

Bronze was a vital commodity in early Chinese civilization. Probably introduced from the West via the ancient SILK ROAD during the late third millennium B.C.E., it was employed in the casting of ritual vessels during the XIA DYNASTY (2100–1766 B.C.E.). During the SHANG STATE (1766–1045 B.C.E.) there was an extraordinary increase in the quantity and quality of such castings, and in addition bronze was used for chariot fittings and weaponry. The Shang bronze workers employed the piece-mold technique, and some of their castings weighed much more than 100 kilograms (220 lbs.). Bronze continued to be highly valued during the succeeding Zhou dynasty (1045–256 B.C.E.), and some of the finest of all bronzes are from the period of the Qin dynasty, in particular the horse-drawn chariots from the tomb complex of QIN SHIHUANGDI, the first emperor of China.

The need to secure regular supplies of copper was a preoccupation of major states. Copper was strengthened by the use of bronze for weaponry during the troubled times that characterized the period of the Zhou dynasty; a state without ready access to copper ore would have been seriously weakened. Tonglushan lies in the area controlled by the kings of the state of CHU. As may be seen in the Chu cemeteries such as XIASI, bronzes were abundant in aristocratic graves, and the Tonglushan mine must have contributed much wealth to the rulers. The complex is also of vital importance not only because wooden artifacts have been preserved in the underground workings, but because its use spanned the introduction of iron. Thus the impact of iron on mining technology can be gauged.

The ore was initially hacked out with bronze mattocks and pickaxes, but from at least the third century B.C.E. such bronze implements were replaced with iron tools, including hammers and spades designed specifically for this mining operation. On reaching the surface, the ore was hand sorted and then crushed by anvils and heavy stones. Several large enclosed furnaces have been excavated. Iron ore was used as a flux to assist smelting, and the resulting ingots contained up to 93 percent copper and 5 percent iron. The furnaces themselves had the refinement of two chambers, a lower one for tapping the molten copper and an upper one for firing the chamber.

The social dimension of the Tonglushan mine is little known, but it is self-evident that it employed many hundreds of miners in its heyday, as well as a specialized staff of copper processors on the surface. Part of the complex has been transformed into a museum.

Tonle Sap *See* GREAT LAKE.

Toprak-kala Toprak-kala is a walled city covering 250 hectares (625 acres), located on the right bank of the lower Amu Dar'ya River in ancient Khwarizm (Uzbekistan). Excavations that took place between 1945 and 1950 revealed evidence for three major phases of occupation. The city was founded during the first century C.E. and was to become a royal capital of the KUSHANS. It continued to be a royal center into the sixth to eighth centuries. The defensive walls incorporated vaulted corridors and were built of sun-dried brick. The top was crenellated, and the sides were equipped with loopholes. A moat lay in front of the walls, crossed by an entrance only at the southern side. The city had a rectangular form divided by a street system into a series of blocks. The southern half of the city contained the residential area; a citadel that dominated the lower city was visible from a great distance. It incorporated a massive palace with more than 100 rooms on the ground floor alone, and numerous sculptures and fine wall paintings have survived. Some of the sculptures are thought to depict members of the ruling royal families. An almost complete statue in unfired clay probably represents a queen. She wears an elegant robe of Hellenistic inspiration. There is also the head of a warrior wearing a headband. These had been placed in niches in one of the great halls. This part of the city also contained a large open area in which thick ash layers were encountered. It is thought to have been a fire temple for Zoroastrian worship. Excavations also revealed a workshop for manufacturing bows and written records in the Khwarizm language on wood and leather containing the accounts of the city.

Toro   Toro is one of the most important excavated sites of the Japanese YAYOI culture (300 B.C.E.–300 C.E.). This culture represents a major change in the prehistory of central and southern Japan, because it involved the widespread adoption of wet rice agriculture, metallurgy, maritime exchange, and the development of social elites. The technique of rice production was similar, if not identical, to that of mainland China at the same time, and it is beyond reasonable doubt that Yayoi farmers were indebted to the long tradition of rice cultivation in the Chang (Yangtze) Valley. All contributed to the rapid development of the early Japanese states. Few Yayoi sites have provided such complete evidence for the way of life of agricultural communities that stand at the origins of the Japanese civilization.

RICE CULTIVATION

Toro is located in the delta of the Aba River where it reaches the southern shore of central Honshu. This region was subjected to regular flooding, and the occupation, which spanned the latter part of middle Yayoi and the early years of the late period (about 50–150 C.E.) was more than once damaged by serious floods, the last of which sealed its end. These floods laid down deposits that have led to the preservation of organic remains in profusion as well as prehistoric rice fields. Rice cultivation involved the construction of low banks to control the flow of water across the landscape. At Toro these have survived and were retained in place by vertically placed posts. The individual plots were about 30 by 30 meters (100 by 100 ft.) square. Ditches that crossed the cultivated area, again revetted with wood, could have borne water to the rice fields when necessary, and one of these was equipped with a sluice gate to control water distribution. The large size of the Toro rice fields is unusual. Many other sites have revealed far smaller fields, even as small as four by seven meters (13 by 23 ft.) in extent. The survival of wooden clogs of virtually identical form to those in use today by workers transplanting rice suggests further parallels of rice cultivation with China.

FARM IMPLEMENTS

Wooden farm implements have survived. Large blades are thought to have been used for plowshares. Plowing itself represents a major advance in agricultural efficiency, since traction animals and a plow can put a much greater area under cultivation than human labor alone, and turn-ing and harrowing of the soil produce larger returns of rice. There were also spades, rakes, and hoes among the inventory of surviving wooden tools.

THE SETTLEMENT

In the settlement itself, which lay adjacent to the rice fields, the outlines of substantial wooden houses have been identified. The interiors were equipped with a central hearth and wooden benches around the periphery. The houses were probably roofed with a thatch of rice straw, some of which has survived. Matting was placed on the floor. Rice was stored in wooden structures and processed by using wooden pestles and mortars. Stone net sinkers and bone fishhooks were employed, and both freshwater and saltwater fish bones have survived. Domestic cattle were raised, and deer were hunted, presumably with the bow and arrow, as seen on Yayoi bronzes. Iron tools were used to fashion the many wooden artifacts, which included swords and scabbards, and trade carried exotic glass beads to the site.

Tosali   *See* SISUPALGARH.

T'osong-ni   T'osong-ni was the capital of the Chinese commandery of LELANG in North Korea. The expansion of the HAN DYNASTY in the late second century B.C.E. saw the establishment of commanderies, or provinces, in captured territory. In Korea, the commandery of Lelang was founded in 108 B.C.E. and endured for at least three centuries. T'osong-ni was probably the capital of this province. It is located on the southern bank of the Taedong River, opposite the modern capital of Pyongyang. Its walls enclosed an area of 31 hectares (77.5 acres) and fortified a hill that already afforded natural protection from attack. Excavations that began in 1936 revealed all the items of material culture typical of a Han colony. There were Chinese coins and the molds for local casting of currency. Bronze mirrors, eave tiles, and SEALS, one of which bore the title of the governor of Lelang, were recovered. Beyond and south of the walls, five cemeteries have been identified, containing more than 2,000 Han tombs. These were either subterranean pits containing chestnut wood chambers or surface tombs of BRICK covered by a mound. The grave offerings reflect the wealth of provincial society. They include fine bronzes, ceramic vessels containing food, LACQUER tables and plates, and personal ornaments of jade. Iron weaponry included typical Han crossbow mechanisms, swords, daggers, and halberds.

Tra Kieu   Tra Kieu is a walled city of the CHAM CIVILIZATION, located in the kingdom known as AMARAVATI in Vietnam. As with other Cham centers, it was located at a junction of two rivers. Tra Kieu has also given its name to a Cham art style current during the 10th century C.E., and the most famous example of this period is the pedestal found at Tra Kieu itself. The base, 1.75 meters square (2.1 sq. yds.), was embellished with superbly carved scenes of the life of Krishna as described in the *Bhagavad Purana*. The original name of Tra Kieu was Simhapura, and the first excavations were undertaken by J. Y. Claeys in 1927–28. He uncovered the foundations of a sanctuary structure and recovered much statuary and some INSCRIPTIONS, as well as evidence for settlement in the fifth and sixth centuries C.E., but most of the evidence, including 11th-century Chinese coins, is of later date. More recent excavations have encountered a stratigraphic sequence three meters (10 ft.) deep, and 18 radiocarbon dates indicate initial occupation in the last two or three centuries B.C.E. until at least the sixth or seventh century C.E. One fragment of Indian pottery from the lowest layer is similar in style to the ceramics from ARIKAMEDU in India, indicating the early existence of maritime trade. Later layers included a considerable quantity of locally made ceramics strongly influenced by Chinese wares, as well as tiles and bricks.

In Tra Kieu style, Indian influence pervades the design and even the clothing worn by the people carved on the reliefs of the pedestal from that site. One scene shows Krishna about to cure a female hunchback; another shows merchants bearing offerings to the god. The quality of the carving is outstanding, and details of the personal jewelry, clothes, and hairstyles are revealing of the upper ranks of Cham society. Indian influence is also evident on a second pedestal from Tra Kieu, named after the dancers and musicians portrayed on the sides. The pose of the dancers with the hands and fingers outstretched remains a widespread feature of this art in Southeast Asia to the present day. The role played by music in ritual and dance is at once evident from the vibrant renditions of the musicians on this same pedestal.

Transoxiana The region known as Transoxiana (in modern Uzbekistan and Kazakhstan) occupied a strategic position on the ancient SILK ROAD that linked the empires of China and Rome from 200 B.C.E. onward. It had been occupied by numerous peoples and received cultural influences from Achaemenid and Seleucid Persia, India, PARTHIA, the Scythians (SAKAS), and Greece. During the early first millennium, the KUSHANS and the SASSANIAN EMPIRE impinged on Transoxiana. It lies south of the Aral Sea and has the Amu Dar'ya River (Oxus) as the western border and the Syr Dar'ya River (Jaxartes) on the eastern flank. Three ancient regions lay within these two rivers: BACTRIA, SOGDIANA, and Khwarizm. From TERMEZ the Silk Road linked with a route leading south to BEGRAM, TAXILA, and MATHURA.

See also ACHAEMENID EMPIRE.

travan A *travan* was an artificial tank or pond. They are often mentioned in the CHENLA and Angkorian INSCRIPTIONS in Cambodia as demarcating land divisions. This is clearly illustrated in an inscription from Tuol An Tnot, dated to 681 C.E. King JAYAVARMAN I OF CHENLA united two foundations. The description of the land boundaries includes references to the *travan* of various PON (local leaders). Where a *travan* was dug to below the water table, it would have been a constant source of water during the dry season. Robert Acker has suggested that they were important in maintaining rural food production for this reason.

See also ANGKOR.

Tribhuvanadityavarman (r. 1165–1177) *King Tribhuvanadityavarman (protégé of the rising Sun of three worlds) of Angkor in Cambodia was a usurper who seized the throne in about 1165 C.E.*

It is said that this event led to JAYAVARMAN VII's returning from Champa. In the civil war that ensued, Jayavarman (r. 1181–1219) was victorious and became one of ANGKOR's greatest kings.

Tripuri Tripuri is an urban center on the bank of the upper Narmada River in Madhya Pradesh state, central India. Excavations were undertaken on the mound, which rises to a height of seven meters (23 ft.), between 1951 and 1959. Five periods of occupation were encountered, beginning in about 1000 B.C.E. with ceramic remains and a stone industry. During the second period, which began in about 400 B.C.E., Tripuri was probably a major center, if not the actual capital, of the MAHAJANAPADA of Cedi. The site by now incorporated mud-BRICK houses with terra-cotta tiles and punch-marked COINAGE. Exchange is seen in the presence of carnelian and agate beads, and there was an iron and glass industry. Late stone SEALS of this phase, which lasted for one or two centuries, belong to the period of the MAURYA EMPIRE. The site continued to flourish under the period of Mauryan dominance during the third phase, which lasted until 100 B.C.E. when SATAVAHANA influence is seen in the presence of their coinage. During the ensuing period, dated from 100 B.C.E. into the second century C.E., two Buddhist monasteries were constructed; the final phase yielded sealings that contain a sequence of royal names belonging to a local dynasty postdating the Satavahanas.

Turpan Basin The Turpan Basin lies to the northeast of the TARIM BASIN and occupies a strategic location on the ancient SILK ROAD that linked China with the West. Its eastern border gives access to the Gansu Corridor. It covers an area of 250 by 300 kilometers (275 by 330 yds.) and incorporates Lake Ayding, the second lowest location in the world. Environmentally, the basin is very dry, but water from the surrounding mountains feeds rivers that form oases, thus encouraging IRRIGATION and agricultural settlements. A series of states developed in the Turpan

Basin largely through their control of trade. Yarghul, founded in at least the third century B.C.E., was the main center, until it was superseded by Idiqut in the fifth century C.E. During the long struggle to control the Silk Road between the Han Chinese and the XIONGNU, Turpan occupied a vital strategic location because it provided access to the caravans for the Xiongnu. In 108 B.C.E., a Han army defeated the people of Turpan and opened up a route for the control of the so-called western regions.

Idiqut was a walled city, the defenses standing to a height of 11 meters (36.3 ft.). The area within incorporated a palace and residential and commercial precincts. The nearby cemetery of Astana has yielded a rich array of grave goods, which illustrate clearly the widespread trade links. There are silks and both Persian and Roman coins. The textiles were particularly well preserved and reveal a continuation of a long tradition of fine weaving evidenced in the prehistoric fabric remains from such sites as Zaghunluq and Subeshi.

See also HAN DYNASTY.

turquoise   Turquoise is a blue-green gemstone widely used in the ancient world in the manufacture of jewelry. The principal source is the region of Kyzyl Kum between the Amu Dar'ya and Syr Dar'ya Rivers in Uzbekistan. There are also sources in Iran and India. There is evidence for the manufacture of turquoise beads at the INDUS VALLEY CIVILIZATION site of Mundigak. Turquoise was widely used for jewelry and for decorative inlays in China, at least from the period of the LONGSHAN CULTURE (c. 2500–1800 B.C.E.).

U

Udayadityavarman II (r. 1050–1066 C.E.) *Udaya-dityavarman II was king of Angkor in Cambodia.*
He succeeded SURYAVARMAN I, but his relationship to his predecessor is not known. He was responsible for the BAPHUON, a splendid temple pyramid, and the WESTERN MEBON. His reign was punctuated with rebellions, which are recorded in a number of INSCRIPTIONS, one of which related how his general Sangrama defeated the rebel Kamvau and was then called on to head south to defeat a second uprising under Aravindhahrada.

Udozuka Udozuka is a *kofun,* or burial mound, over-looking the Nara Plain of western Honshu, Japan. It is one of about 20 in a group that was, according to early historic records, the burial ground of a powerful clan in this region during the sixth century C.E. Unfortunately, this tomb, which attained a length of 60 meters (198 ft.), had been pillaged in antiquity. A stone-lined passageway led to the central chamber, which contained the remains of a large stone coffin. A second and smaller stone coffin was found in the passageway, together with fragments of ceramic HANIWA figures representing houses and armor. What remained of grave goods after the looting included iron swords and halberds and horse trappings. The person had been interred with gold and bronze rings and glass beads. The size and wealth of such burials are eloquent testimony to the power of the YAMATO elite.

uji An *uji* was a social and political unit of the YAMATO state and beyond in Japan. The origin of the system probably lies in the PAEKCHE state of Korea. It included those related by blood as well as their tied laborers, who made up a unit known as a *be.* The leader of the *uji* was given a title, or *kabane,* by the Yamato sovereign. The rank of the *kabane* was determined by that individual's status and duties at court. This system allowed the ruler to exercise authority through the *uji* and obtain tax payments in kind from the sustaining territory. The most notable *uji* of the first half of the sixth century were the Soga, Imbe, Nakatomi, and Otomo lineages. The Soga were particularly powerful. After the centralizing TAIKA REFORMS of 645 C.E., the *uji* system was replaced by the ascription of fixed rank to permanent administrators, a system that by 685 C.E. recognized 48 grades. These people were drawn from the noble families.

Ujjain Ujjain lies on the east bank of the Sipra River in Madhya Pradesh province, India. It is one of India's seven holy cities and was also well known as a site of historical importance as early as 1834, when Edward Connelly observed that the town beggars would try to sell curios they had collected, such as glass and stone beads, SEALS, and ornaments, to Europeans. Excavations undertaken in 1955–58 identified a long sequence of occupation, beginning in the late prehistoric period when iron was already in use and a mud wall surrounded the settlement. The moat beyond was fed by the river. An iron spade and the impressions of wicker baskets in the dried mud indicate how the rampart was excavated and formed by digging out material from the moat. During the second phase of occupation, structures were made of mud BRICK and some fired brick. It was during the earlier part of this period that Ujjain was the probable capital of Avanti, one of the 16 MAHAJANAPADAS, or incipient states centered on the

Ganges (Ganga) Valley. But according to an INSCRIPTION of ASOKA, it became a vice-regal center during the MAURYA EMPIRE (c. 324–c. 200 B.C.E.), and the quickening of industrial skills can be seen in the excavation of a major facility for iron working and workshops for the production of bone arrowheads and stone beads. The iron industry produced a wide range of tools and weapons, including arrowheads, spearheads, spades, chisels, horse bits, and choppers. A road entering the city was constantly repaired and marked by the ruts of wheeled vehicles. Already by the second century B.C.E., the inhabitants were using ivory seals inscribed in the BRAHMI script.

The importance of trade during the third phase, which began in about 200 B.C.E., is seen in the reference to Ujjain as Ozene, a site noted for its trade with Rome, in the *PERIPLUS OF THE ERYTHAEAN SEA*. During the centuries to the middle of the first millennium C.E., Ujjain reveals SUNGA, KUSHAN, and GUPTA periods of occupation. An extremely rich material culture has been unearthed, including beads from a wide range of precious or semiprecious stones, glass, bone, and ivory; ivory COMBS; many animal figurines; and coins. It was also a center for the production of beads from chalcedony.

unicorn The unicorn, or *qilin*, along with the phoenix and dragon, was one of the mythical animals often portrayed in China, particularly during the HAN DYNASTY (206 B.C.E.–220 C.E.). It was held to be auspicious, and its appearance would predict the birth of a virtuous emperor and good government. Unicorns are depicted on tomb doors as a protection measure. A fine wooden specimen has been excavated from a Han tomb at Mocuizi in Gansu province. It is almost one meter in length and was painted with red and black designs. In a belligerent charging posture, the figure was chiseled from seven pieces of wood joined by dowels. A second example in bronze from Xiaheqing, also in Gansu, had been placed at the tomb entrance as a guardian against unwanted intrusion. The same protective position for a unicorn occurred at LEITAI.

Uriyudo Uriyudo is a large and important site of the YAYOI culture, located in the area of Osaka city in Japan. When occupied during the early and middle Yayoi periods (300 B.C.E.–100 C.E.), it commanded excellent low-lying and well-watered rice land but was also subject to regular and often catastrophic flooding. This would have been exacerbated by forest clearance with iron tools and a climatic warming that resulted in raised river levels. Thus the early Yayoi settlement was covered by a thick flood deposit, and the site was abandoned after further deep flooding at the end of the middle Yayoi period. Excavations have confirmed the importance of rice cultivation, not only in the presence of rice remains, but also in the wooden tools of cultivation: spades, hoes, and pestles for grinding in a mortar. There are also stone reaping knives. The settlement contains many postholes, defying any attempt to identify the distribution of houses and other structures, because of constant rebuilding of the foundations. However, the recovery of organic remains reveals that in addition to rice, people consumed melons, peaches, plums, and walnuts and cultivated wheat.

The dead in middle Yayoi times were interred either in jars or under mounds in wooden coffins. Neither type of grave contained grave goods, but the coffin mounds were associated with ceramic vessels distributed around the mounds, which may well represent offerings to elite individuals. The concentration of sites in the Kawachi Plain, linked with the abundance of stone arrowheads, suggests intercommunity conflict, a spur to the development of social elites that characterized late Yayoi culture.

Ushtur-Mulla The site of Ushtur-Mulla is a Buddhist monastery of the Kushan-Sassanian period (78–c. 651 C.E.), located in the upper reaches of the Amu Dar'ya River in Tajikistan. There are cells for monks, a stupa, and a large hall for meetings.

See also KUSHANS; SASSANIAN EMPIRE.

Ustrushana Ustrushana was a small polity east of SOGDIANA on the left bank of the Syr Dar'ya River in Kyrgyzstan. It was closely related linguistically and culturally to Sogdiana but had its own currency and capital at Kala-i Kahkaha (Bunjikat). Its prosperity was based on extensive irrigated agriculture, which supplied barley, wheat, cotton, and grapes. This area is also rich in minerals, and its strategic location on the SILK ROAD led to widespread foreign contacts and a wealthy merchant class. This success is reflected in the size and architectural sophistication seen in the city of Kala-i Kahkaha, where a three-storied palace dominated the settlement during the seventh and eighth centuries. This palace was built on a raised platform and incorporated a series of courts, staterooms, kitchens, halls, and a throne room. Fine mural paintings and wooden statues decorated the walls and halls of the palace. Motifs include the four-armed goddess Nana riding a lion and a series of demons. Wooden friezes reveal elegant floral and geometric patterns and the heads of deities. The capital also included a quarter for the specialist manufacture of ceramics and detached family homes.

U-Taphao U-Taphao is a Dvaravati city in central Thailand, the rampart, or wall, surrounding the site being up to 10 meters (33 ft.) high to this day. It has yielded a large sample of DVARAVATI CIVILIZATION (400–900 C.E.) coins stamped with the conch shell, fish, and *srivatsa* (mother goddess) motif. A stone rendition of the "wheel of the law" (*DHARMACAKRA*) contains an INSCRIPTION in PALI recording Buddhist doctrine, while large quantities of iron slag provide evidence for an industrial aspect to this settlement. The area of U-Taphao is known for the quality of its iron ore.

U-Thong The DVARAVATI CIVILIZATION (400–900 C.E.) center of U-Thong in Thailand was encircled by an oval moat covering an area of 1,690 by 840 meters (1,860 by 924 yds.). This moat was linked to a small stream. A copper INSCRIPTION recorded the accession of Harshavarman to the lion throne. Most structures are of Buddhist inspiration, and they are found in and beyond the moats. Excavations have revealed the foundation for a Buddhist assembly hall and three octagonal brick stupas. The fragments of stucco ornamentation for these buildings include plants, mythical GARUDAS (eagles), *makaras* (marine monsters), and *naga*s (sacred snakes) as well as lions. To judge from the description of the lion throne in the U-Thong copper tablet and the number of terra-cotta models of the lion discovered, this animal might have had some special significance to the occupants of this site. The lion was often used to symbolize the Buddha in the period before representing him as a person became acceptable.

Vaisali After the cremation of the Buddha, his ashes were distributed to seven places, of which Vaisali was one. The site is located north of the Ganges (Ganga) River in Bihar province, India. It is recorded that the Buddha visited Vaisali, already a major center, on several occasions. The excavation of a stupa between 1950 and 1962 indicated a long history, beginning with a clay mound with a diameter of about eight meters (26.4 ft.), which was subsequently increased. The first embellishment took place probably during the fourth or third century B.C.E., the second during the reign of ASOKA (268–235 B.C.E.). A relic casket was found to contain gold leaf, two glass beads, and a conch shell. The clay stupa is beyond doubt one of the earliest Buddhist structures known and might well be that constructed over the remains of the Buddha himself.

The original urban complex is seen today as a walled enclosure. It was visited in the early seventh century by the Chinese Buddhist monk XUANZANG, who found the city wall badly collapsed and the interior sparsely populated. He recorded that the king obtained bones of the Buddha after the cremation and had them preserved under a stupa. The monk went on to relate that King Asoka later opened the relic chamber and removed eight of the nine fragments of bone and described an Asokan column at the site with a lion at the top. Excavations there in the early years of the 20th century uncovered a large sample of SEALS dated to the GUPTA EMPIRE, but the site is considerably earlier.

Vaisnaism Vaisnaism is the cult of the god Vishnu the protector. He is referred to in the RIG-VEDA and is thus of considerable antiquity. He was known and worshiped in several incarnations, such as Rama and Krishna.

Varaksha Varaksha is a city in SOGDIANA (Uzbekistan) well known for its palace and mural paintings of the seventh century C.E. One vigorous series of wall decorations shows scenes of lions attacking riders on elephants.

Vardhamana Mahavira (599–527 B.C.E.) *Vardhamana Mahavira was the 24th tirthankara, or leader, of the Jain religion in India.*
JAINISM, one of the old religions of India, developed at the same time as BUDDHISM, during the period of JANAPADAS, when regional states in the Ganges (Ganga) Valley were striving for dominance during the sixth and fifth centuries B.C.E. He was from a noble family in the area of Vaisali and sought enlightenment during a 12-year period of wandering. He attracted thereafter a following of monks, who advocated peace, reflection, and righteousness and who wore no clothes. He died near Patna at the age of 72. Jainism, which takes its name from the title *jina*, or conqueror, accorded him at enlightenment, continues, with its two sects, to flourish in India.

varman Varman, "shield" or "protégé of," is a title taken by kings of the PALLAVA dynasty of the Andhra region of eastern India during the late third century C.E. This region of India, which had a strong Buddhist tradition, was engaged in trade with Southeast Asia. By the fifth century C.E., inscriptions in the lower Mekong Valley, central Thailand, and the island of Java in Indonesia were naming local kings who had themselves adopted *varman* as part of a royal name. The title was universally employed by the rulers of ANGKOR in Cambodia and was also conferred as an honorific title on highly ranked members of the aristocracy.

Varuna In the RIG-VEDA, Varuna was the god who controlled cosmic order. The Rig-Veda says that Varuna set the Sun on its daily path, oversaw regular rainfall, ensured that the ocean did not overflow, and tamed the water in the rivers so that they would not fill the oceans to overflowing. Varuna also ensured that human as well as cosmic law was upheld.

Veda A Veda is a sacred hymn chanted during religious ceremonies. Vedas originated in the culture of Indo-European speakers, and their language is archaic SANSKRIT. Transmitted verbally from a remote past, they illustrate many aspects of life and behavior before the development of writing in the BRAHMI or KHAROSHTHI script. The earliest Veda, the RIG-VEDA is said to date to about 1500 B.C.E. with invading peoples responsible for the destruction of the cities of the INDUS VALLEY CIVILIZATION. According to a second school of thought, the earliest Vedas are contemporary with the Indus civilization and were composed by the priests of the time. Since there are no means of dating their origin, this dialogue continues. The Vedas are full of references to the early gods who later formed the basic pantheon of Hinduism, such as Surya the Sun god, Agni the god of fire, and INDRA the god of war. In addition to the Rig-Veda, there is the rather later Yajur Veda, which was recited by the priest in charge of the sacred fire and contains much material derived from the Rig-Veda. The Sama Veda was chanted during sacrificial ceremonies. The Athar Veda is rather different in that it includes a considerable body of folklore.

Further reading: Arya, V. K. *The Book of the Vedas: Timeless Wisdom from Indian Tradition.* Rockport: Fair Winds Press, 2003; Doniger, W., ed. *The Rig Veda: An Anthology: One Hundred and Eight Hymns.* New York: Viking Press, 1982; Griffith, R. T. *Hymns of the Rigveda.* Columbia, Mo.: South Asia Books, 1999.

Vesali Vesali is a major city site and former royal capital located in Rakhine (formerly ARAKAN) in western Myanmar (Burma). The outer moat and brick walls enclose an oval area covering approximately 540 hectares (1,350 acres). A second walled precinct in the northern half of the city housed the palace complex. The city lay beside the Rann Chuang, a river that provides access to the Bay of Bengal and the trading opportunities that developed with the major maritime exchange routes. Vesali seems to have superseded DHANYAWADI as the capital of this area during the early sixth century C.E. Excavations in the 1980s revealed a number of Buddhist foundations, including monasteries, an ordination hall, and a cult building incorporating a statue of a bull. The last structure could indicate devotion to SIVA, whose sacred mount was the bull Nandi. BUDDHISM, however, dominated at Vesali, as is seen in the SHIT-THAUNG INSCRIPTION text ascribed to King Anandacandra. One

section of the stela dating to 729 C.E. describes how the king founded monasteries and donated slaves, fields, and buffaloes for their maintenance. He also sent gifts to the monastic communities of Sri Lanka. Trade and commerce centered at Vesali are reflected in the recovery of locally minted coins. One side has the image of a bull, symbol of the ruling family, and the other has the *srivatsa* (mother goddess) motif, as in the DVARAVATI CIVILIZATION COINAGE of central Thailand, which symbolizes prosperity. Some Vesali coins have been recovered from Bangladesh sites. Trade also took to Vesali an intaglio ornament that originated in the Mediterranean and gems bearing brief inscriptions in South Indian characters. In this respect, the site falls into a wide range of other port cities in Southeast Asia, including OC EO in Vietnam and KHUAN LUKPAD in Thailand.

Vichigrama *See* BHITA.

Vidisanagara *See* BESNAGAR.

Viet Khe Viet Khe is a cemetery site of the Dong Son culture, located in Haiphong province in northern Vietnam. It is dated to the last few centuries B.C.E. and is notable for the wealth of grave goods in one of the wooden boat coffins found there. Offerings include spears and axes of bronze as well as a wide range of bronze ceremonial vessels. One of these, a *thap,* is almost half a meter (1.65 ft.) high even in a broken condition and is ornamented with rows of plumed warriors and a massive warship also carrying warriors. This and other bronzes seem to have been used in ritual feasting, for there is also a ladle ornamented with a man playing a *khen,* a type of reed pipe still popular in the area today. Several bronzes are likely to have been imported from southern China. These include a tripod, ring-ended knives, and a bronze counterweight placed on the end of a spear. It is evident that the wealthy Dong Son chiefs were exchanging goods with their counterparts to the north.

Vijayapura *See* NAGARJUNAKONDA.

Vima Kadphises (r. 90–100 C.E.) *Vima Kadphises was the king of the Kushan empire, which his grandfather, Kujula Kadphises, had established.*
The empire extended into Afghanistan and northern India from its initial base north of the Hindu Kush range. Vima Kadphises minted outstanding gold coins, which bear his image. He is seen as a military leader, wearing a helmet, coat, and boots.
See also COINAGE; KUSHANS.

Vimayapura *See* PHIMAI.

visaya A *visaya* was a territorial subdivision, perhaps a province, of the kingdom of ANGKOR in Cambodia. First used during the Angkorian period, it is often cited as evidence that formerly independent kingdoms were falling under central administrative control.

Vo Canh Vo Canh, which is located near Nha Trang on the southern shore of Vietnam, is the find spot of the earliest known SANSKRIT inscription on the mainland of Southeast Asia. It is dated to the third or fourth century C.E. on stylistic grounds.

W

Wall, the Great The construction of long defensive walls in China originated during the EASTERN ZHOU DYNASTY (770–221 B.C.E.). With the unification of China in 221 C.E. under the first emperor, QIN SHIHUANGDI, defensive measures were instituted against a foreign adversary, the XIONGNU barbarians to the north. The emperor drafted hundreds of thousands of workers to construct the first major wall under the direction of his great general MENG TIAN. During the succeeding HAN DYNASTY (206 B.C.E.–220 C.E.), there was a constant tension between China and the Xiongnu, as periods of peace were punctuated by war. Moreover, the Han were keenly interested in promoting trade along the SILK ROAD that linked their empire with India and Rome. They therefore extended the wall in a westerly direction and resettled many communities there. The wall was extended to a length of about 10,000 kilometers (6,000 mi.), incorporating forts, watchtowers, and tall signal beacons to warn the center against imminent attack. Many of these compressed earth towers survive to this day. The length of wall most visited today, north of Beijing, was built much later, during the Ming dynasty. The first Ming emperor ruled from 1368 C.E., a time of danger from the Mongols.

Techniques for building city walls however, have a long history dating back to the LONGSHAN CULTURE in the third millennium B.C.E. The soft loess soil was compressed in a wooden framework in what is known as the *HANGTU* form of construction. Extensive city walls survive at many sites, such as ZHENGZHOU of the SHANG dynasty (1766–1045 B.C.E.). The political situation during the Eastern Zhou dynasty has been divided into the Spring and Autumn period (770–476 B.C.E.) and the WARRING STATES PERIOD (475–221 B.C.E.). It was a time of endemic conflict, during the course of which iron working was introduced into China. Capital cities were defended by high walls; to counter these attackers used so-called cloud ladders to gain entry into besieged centers. The states also adopted the measure of constructing long walls to mark their boundaries and aid in defense.

The Han Great Wall was regarded as a defensive mechanism as well as a symbolic divide between the Chinese and the Xiongnu mounted warriors beyond. The Han emperor WENDI sent a message to the Xiongnu leader in 162 B.C.E.: "The land north of the Great Wall, where men wield bow and arrow, is to receive its command from the Shanyu, while that within the wall, whose inhabitants dwell in houses and wear hats and girdles, is to be ruled by us."

Wangcheng Wangcheng, "royal city," was the seat of the Kings of the EASTERN ZHOU DYNASTY. It was located at the junction of the Luo and Jian Rivers and, according to archaeological investigations, was of approximately rectangular outline. Many tombs have been excavated within and beyond the city walls. These have been divided into seven phases, the last of which dates to the end of the Eastern Zhou dynasty in the third century B.C.E. Discoveries include a few rich pit burials with wooden chambers and coffins and fine bronze vessels. One, to judge from its INSCRIPTION, belonged to a bureaucrat in the service of the royal family. On the other hand, the majority of burials contained either a few ceramic vessels or nothing other than the dead person. Thus they reveal the spectrum of the population at this royal capital from wealthy administrators to the poorer section of the community.

The Great Wall of China was commenced by the first emperor, Qin Shihuangdi, in about 220 B.C.E. It followed in a tradition of defensive wall building over the previous three centuries and was added to and maintained for 2,000 years. *(Erich Lessing/Art Resource, NY)*

The city was demarcated by a large city wall and moat, the northern length of which attained a length of 2.4 kilometers (1.44 mi.). This was not as large as many other contemporary cities in China. The interior included specialist manufacturing areas for bone, ceramics, and stone. Ceramic pipes indicate a drainage system, and there are both literary reports and archaeological evidence for the royal palace. Its existence was threatened by the moving channels of these rivers in the 22nd year of the reign of King Lingwang, 550 B.C.E. The city continued after the fall of the dynasty and became a smaller walled regional center during the Western Han period.

Wangchenggang Wangchenggang is a LONGSHAN CULTURE walled site located in Henan province, China. The walls enclose an area of only one hectare (2.5 acres), making it more a fort than a settlement, but within the precinct there are 10 stamped-earth platforms and pits containing the remains of people who were probably sacrificed when the buildings were founded. There are traces of a second walled enclosure to the west. Some potsherds have written characters scratched on the surface, and the remains of a

bronze alloy of copper, tin, and lead have been found. This item is the only Longshan bronze that could be from a cast vessel. Very thin and elegant ceramic vessels from this site also suggest the presence of a specialized ceramic workshop. There is evidence for long-distance trade in exotic goods in the inclusion of one jade ring and some TURQUOISE. The walls date to about 2400 B.C.E.

Fang Yanming has described Wangchenggang as a central place in the local Longshan culture, emphasizing the fact that most of the settlements in the Ying River valley lacked the walls, jades, fine ceramics, and evidence for early writing.

See also QIN DYNASTY.

Wang Guowei (1877–1927) *Wang Guowei was one of the foremost early scholars of the Anyang oracle bones.*
In two articles published in 1917, he reported on the results of his research on the dynastic succession of the SHANG STATE (1766–1045 B.C.E.) kings. This was based on his piecing together oracle-bone texts concerned with sacrificial ceremonies to honor ancestral spirits. These mentioned the names of kings in such a manner as to

make it possible to order the names chronologically. He concluded that there were 31 Shang kings over a period of 17 generations. His research lasted for a decade until 1927, when he committed suicide by drowning in the lake of the Summer Palace in Beijing.

Wang Mang (45 B.C.E.–23 C.E.) *Wang Mang, formerly known under his title of the marquis of Xindu, was the founder and only emperor of the Xin (New) dynasty of China.*

Wang Mang revealed himself to be a man of considerable energy and resolve. His accession followed a long period of central weakness, during which a succession of young emperors were manipulated by their relatives. Corruption was rampant; the peasantry were near revolt as rich landlords increased their landholdings and turned the landless farmers into serfs. There were floods in a countryside filled with bands of brigands and thieves. One of the new emperor's first tasks was to tackle the problem of land tenure. His policy was sweeping in its intensity, for he resolved to nationalize all land, renaming it, "the king's fields." This was a prelude to redistributing it to the peasantry under the old well-field system. This hearkened back to the days before QIN absolutism, when eight families would be attached to a well unit, with sufficient land for them to sustain themselves and to give a proportion of the production to the state. No private sales of land were allowed, and SLAVERY was abolished. Since the implementation of this crushing edict lay in the hands of the very people who would most suffer from its consequences, the reaction can easily be imagined. Wang Mang alienated those on whom any emperor relied for support, and after only three years the edict was revoked.

Wang Mang took power after a long period in which court families vied for power through placing on the throne a succession of helpless infants. Thus Pingdi (9 B.C.E.–6 C.E.) was only eight years old when he became emperor, and his successor, Ruzi, was only two years when he succeeded Pingdi in 7 C.E. Wang Mang at least showed a humanitarian attitude when he decided not to have Ruzi killed but rather arranged for the boy to marry his granddaughter. Wang Mang's ascent to power provides in microcosm a classic example of how a family could rise through associations with the court.

RISING POWER OF WANG MANG

His ancestors were middle-range administrators until his aunt, Zheng Jun (71 B.C.E.–13 C.E.), was admitted as a concubine of Emperor XUANDI. She was later transferred to the harem of Emperor Yuandi when he was the heir apparent and bore him a son. This son was in due course to be chosen as emperor under the title Chengdi, and Zheng Jun became empress in 48 B.C.E. This led automatically to the ennoblement of her family. Her father became a marquis, and Wang Mang, marquis of Xindu, was given several court sinecures. His place at court seemed secure, since he was the emperor's cousin. In 8

B.C.E., he was appointed regent. However, the death of Chengdi the following year led to the appointment of Aidi as emperor, and Wang Mang was dismissed as regent and retired to his country estate. When Aidi died in 1 B.C.E., he was succeeded by another child, Pingdi, who was the last male heir of Yuandi. Wang Mang now returned as regent and betrothed his daughter to the young emperor. Despite the poor and biased reporting of his regency in the surviving texts, it is evident that he was a sensible and able administrator. He had a new road cut over the mountains to Sichuan and called conferences to discuss philosophical issues of the day. He also set about reforming provincial schools. But his regency was imperiled when his son-in-law, the emperor, suddenly died in 6 C.E. This precipitated a crisis. There were no more male descendants of Yuandi from whom to choose a successor. But returning a generation to the descendants of Xuandi, who had died half a century earlier, the choice extended to at least five kings and 50 marquises. Wang Mang engineered the appointment of a great-great-grandson of Xuandi, another infant, to the succession and had himself appointed acting emperor.

WANG MANG AS EMPEROR

The immediate aftermath of his appointment saw several uprisings against him, linked with accusations of his poisoning the young emperor. These were soon put down, and Wang Mang entered into a period of relative calm. In this period, from 6 to 8 C.E., a series of manufactured portents favored Wang Mang as the recipient of the MANDATE OF HEAVEN, and in 9 C.E. he announced that he was the emperor of the New, or Xin, dynasty with his capital at the old HAN DYNASTY center of CHANG'AN.

In the year after his accession, he reimposed and strengthened the establishment of state monopolies over many areas of production and trade, particularly in such vital commodities as iron, salt, and liquor. The marketing of basic commodities—foodstuffs and silk—was also deemed a state monopoly. Tax at the rate of 10 percent was imposed on incomes, and through a series of issues, the COINAGE was changed and in effect debased. At the same time, private holdings of gold were forcibly purchased for less than their face value, another measure designed to alienate those on whom any emperor depended.

On the frontiers, Wang Mang faced problems similar to those that confronted the rulers of both the former and later Han dynasties. There were rebellions among the tribal groups in the far south, in Yunnan. On the northern frontier, restlessness among the XIONGNU led to a major mobilization of more than a quarter-million troops. Punitive expeditions also had to be dispatched against rebellions as far west as the TARIM BASIN.

One of the problems in summarizing the reign of Wang Mang is that he was given a poor press by BAN GU (32–92 C.E.), who succeed his father as compiler of the

HANSHU (*History of the Former Han*). It has been argued that had Wang Mang and his new dynasty survived under the Mandate of Heaven, he would be remembered in official histories as a great reforming emperor. His failure indicated that he did not possess the Mandate of Heaven and was therefore no more than a usurper. In fact, Wang Mang's policies had many precedents among his major and successful Han predecessors. The imposition of state monopolies was not his innovation, and the reform of land tenure was widely seen as being timely and necessary. Other emperors had also attempted to reform the currency. The population of China during his reign shows a vast concentration of people in the valley of the Huang (Yellow) River. However, this river burst its banks and changed course several times with catastrophic results for the peasant farmers. This, and the rural insurrections that followed, could well have been the root cause of his downfall. The immediate reason for the fall of Wang Mang, however, was a revolt originating in Shandong by a group of rebellious peasants known as the RED EYEBROWS. The inhabitants of this peninsula were in a desperate condition after the flooding of the Huang River, and not even an army of central troops could quell their insurrection. The success of the Red Eyebrows encouraged the descendants of the Western Han emperors to rise up, and after several engagements the forces of Wang Mang were severely defeated at the Battle of Kunyang. The net then closed on Wang Mang, who was closeted in his palace at Chang'an. Rebellious forces entered the city on 4 October 23 C.E., and two days later he was decapitated.

Further reading: Gu Ban et al. *Wang Mang: A Translation of the Official Account of His Rise to Power.* China Studies: From Confucius to Mao Ser. New York: Hyperion Press, 1977; Loewe, M. *A Biographical Dictionary of the Qin, Former Han and Xin Periods (221 BC–AD 24).* Leiden: Brill, 2000; Thomsen, R. *Ambition and Confucianism: A Biography of Wang Mang.* Aarhus: Aarhus University Press, 1988; Twitchet, D., and M. Loewe, eds. *The Cambridge History of China.* Vol. I, *The Ch'in and Han Empires, 221 B.C.–A.D. 220.* Cambridge: Cambridge University Press, 1986.

Wangxian The city of Wangxian was the capital of the state of CHOSON in Korea, before the area was conquered by the Han Chinese and reorganized into a commandery, or province, in 108 B.C.E. After the Chinese conquest, Wangxian continued as the center of the new Lelang commandery. The walled site covered an area of 42 hectares (105 acres), and excavations in 1935 revealed the presence of streets lined with brick and the foundations of various structures. Not only Han coins but also the molds for casting coins indicate a developed Chinese settlement with a mint. Bronze and iron arrowheads were also recovered, but the extent of the site during the Choson period is not known.

See also COINAGE; HAN DYNASTY.

Wang Yiyong (fl. late 19th century) *Wang Yiyong was a scholar and dean of Hanlin College, north China, in the late 19th century.*

He was the first person to appreciate the importance of the inscribed tortoiseshells, or ORACLE BONES, which were the majority of the written records of the late SHANG STATE (1766–1045 B.C.E.). At that time, these irreplaceable records were dug up by villagers for sale to drug dealers. They were powdered and incorporated in medicines, thought to be effective to cure cuts and abrasions. When a member of Wang Yiyong's family sickened with malaria, the doctor prescribed a medication that included "decayed tortoiseshell." Wang examined this particular ingredient and found that the surface of the shell was inscribed with ancient Chinese written characters. He asked the pharmacy owner for the origin of the bones and was told that they were from a place called ANYANG and were very cheap. He forthwith purchased the entire stock of bones and those from other stores in Beijing and initiated the study of the archives of the Anyang kings.

Wang Yuanlu (late 19th–early 20th century) *Wang Yuanlu was a Taoist monk who settled in the Buddhist center of Mogao in western China in the late 19th century and began restoration of some of the cave shrines there.*

He was responsible for the discovery of a cave sealed during the troubled times that had accompanied the Arab expansion to the east in the early 11th century. It contained an archive of precious Buddhist manuscripts and paintings on silk. He informed the government, who ordered that the cave be sealed again. Seduced by SIR AUREL STEIN's persuasiveness, in 1907 he allowed a collection of thousands of manuscripts and paintings to be removed. These are now housed in the British Museum in London.

Wari-Bateshwar Wari-Bateshwar was a major trading site located in Bangladesh, on a former channel of the Brahmaputra River. There is no obvious settlement mound or defenses, but the site has been known for many decades for the number of punch-marked coins and hard stone beads and must formerly have been a major port.

Warring States period The period of Warring States, a vital period in the history of China, dates from 475 to 221 B.C.E. It corresponds to the last three centuries of the EASTERN ZHOU DYNASTY.

The Warring States period saw many developments in urban architecture, agriculture, art, and literature. Cities, for example, were provided with massive defensive walls. The projection of power through architecture and art by rival sovereigns led to a flowering of specialist skill in many fields, a move quickened further by the interment of rich personal possessions in elite aristocratic burials. They intricately decorated bronze vessels were not as in the past intended to honor the ancestors through rituals, but to enjoy in the present, to use while entertaining to a background of music and dance, and to project an image of opulence.

The fortunate survival of fabrics from a tomb at Mashan has revealed the complexity of weaves and rich design motifs of the silk weaver during this period. Jade, which had long been used for ritual objects, was now transformed into superb personal ornaments, including headdresses, pectorals, and pendants. One of the most compelling innovations of the Warring States period lay in the new free-flowing painting of scenes from daily life.

The changes in the form and decoration of bronzes, lacquerware, and personal ornaments carried through to the disposal of the dead. Traditionally the cemeteries were designed to house successive members of the same lineage. The individual graves would be set out in a formal order, often in proximity to one another. With the Warring States period, burials began to emphasize the person rather than the lineage. Emphasis was placed on aboveground structures that, like the palaces, were raised on high mounds known as *shanling*, or mountain mausolea.

MILITARY STRUGGLES

Politically, the Warring States was a period of tumultuous wars between a diminishing number of rival states; the most prominent being QIN in the west, CHU in the south, Yan in the far northeast, QI, ZHAO, HANN, and WEI. These major states progressively absorbed lesser polities, such as Lu, the home state of CONFUCIUS. Temporary alliances were punctuated by changing fortunes on the battlefield, a situation that bred increasingly totalitarian forms of government. This saw the rise of LEGALISM, a school of political thought that stressed the autocratic power of the ruler rather than the benevolence advocated by the school of Confucius. Technologically it was also the period when iron was brought into play, and weaponry saw a major leap in proficiency and deadliness. The crossbow, for example, was developed into a powerful addition to armory. Scaling ladders were also used, for the political situation stressed the provision of large defensive walls around cities, and long walls were constructed to demarcate state boundaries.

ORGANIZATIONAL CHANGES

The stresses of war led to major changes in the organization of the increasingly powerful states that grew up out of the fiefs granted to close kin by the early rulers of the WESTERN ZHOU DYNASTY. The dispersal of centers of authority dependent on the Zhou capital was replaced by multiple capitals of contending states, wherein authority lay with the monarch and his administrative appointees. Thus, in the state of Jin, the regional power centers of highly ranked lineages were progressively replaced by *xian*, districts administered by court appointees. Under these circumstances, the Eastern Zhou emperors resident in LUOYANG became ciphers whose power was symbolic rather than real.

These changes of policy toward realpolitik are best seen in the career of SHANG YANG, who rose to become the chief minister to Duke Xiao of Qin (r. 361–338 B.C.E.). Shang Yang first turned his attention to the legal system. To control the rural population, he put in place laws providing for the division of the population into groups of five to 10 households. Every member was required to watch and report on others at risk of severe capital punishment. He then imposed a system of taxation favoring production. Rewards for those who excelled in war turned on battlefield success, measured in the number of enemy heads severed. The higher the rank, the greater the rewards. His detailed population registers and foundation of 41 *xian* provided an efficient, centrally directed system of taxation. These administrative and legal reforms laid the foundations for the rise to power of Qin, which ultimately defeated all rivals. In 221 B.C.E., the king of Qin proclaimed himself QIN SHIHUANGDI, the august first emperor of China.

CHANGES IN ARCHITECTURE

The growth of cities assumed extra impetus as capitals changed hands and new centers were founded. It is, for example, recorded that the state of Chu established five new capitals in a half-century. Iron was applied not only to a new range of armaments, but also to agriculture and construction. With a ready supply of cheap iron tools, it became easier to install large-scale IRRIGATION works, to establish more efficient mining operations, and to construct large buildings or deep and impressive tombs. Military activity went hand in hand with increasing commercial ventures so that the new cities were far larger than their predecessors and supported unprecedented numbers and classes of people. At such foundations as LINZI and HANDAN, there was a separate royal enclosure for the palace and administration, and a larger adjacent walled area was for the populace at large. As the power of the king grew, the form of the palace assumed greater prominence. Earlier palaces were places of secrecy and mystery, built on, at best, a shallow platform and including successive courts and columned walkways. But with the Warring States period, rulers vied with one another to raise their palaces on top of huge *tai* platforms, to exhibit to the populace the grandeur of the ruling house. Some of these stand to this day up to 20 meters (66 ft.) tall. Scenes on contemporary bronzes show such palaces: Steps led up to the raised platforms on which people performed rituals that involved large, presumably bronze, vessels. The palace of the state of Wei was so large that a contemporary described it as a platform "reaching halfway to heaven." The Jique palace of the state of Qin at Xianyang has been excavated over many seasons. It was raised high on a *tai* platform, and the interior was decorated with fine wall paintings. There was a flourishing industry producing decorated ceramic tiles and bronze ornamental fittings.

BRONZE CASTING

One of the most spectacular burials from this period belonged to Zeng Hou Yi of Zeng (Hubei province), who died in about 433 B.C.E. His bronzes are among the finest ever cast. By employing the lost-wax casting technique, it was possible to smother the vessels in minutely intricate decoration, seen in its most impressive form in the set of two vessels, a *zun* and a *pan*, covered in tiny writhing dragons. A further innovation in the art of BRONZE CASTING was the production of human and animal figures, which were used as part of composite artifacts. One of the best examples, seen in the bell stands from Leigudun, includes human figures with swords at the waist. The tallest stands a meter (3.3 ft.) high and weighs 359 kilograms (790 lbs.). Some bronzes were also ornamented with gold and silver inlay to accentuate the decorative motifs. It is not surprising that this period also saw a proliferation in the casting of mirrors. These concentrate in the area of the Chu state but are found in lesser quantities in the north. They were embellished on the back with motifs, again highlighted by inlaid gold and silver threads, and glass, TURQUOISE, or jade insets. The same trend toward intricate ornamentation and elaboration of colors and designs is seen in the lacquerwares.

SILKS, PAINTINGS

One compartment in the tomb of Mashan contained figurines standing 60 centimeters (2 ft.) high wearing silk clothing. The woman herself was wrapped in successive layers of fabric tied into a tight bundle with nine brocade bands. She had been interred fully dressed in a skirt, robe, and gown. She was accompanied by many varieties of woven and embroidered fabric, embellished with dragons, phoenixes, and tigers. Clothing was also enhanced with belt hooks that were used as vehicles for inlaid designs highlighted in gold, silver, and semiprecious stones. One notable painting from BAOSHAN in Hubei province shows a nobleman on a chariot journey through a countryside populated by wild boars and cranes until he reaches his destination and alights. A LACQUER duck from LEIGUDUN illustrates a stand of bells being played. Palace walls, as at Xianyang, now bore painted mural scenes. Silk was also a medium for painted images. In an example from Zidanku, a silk painting had been placed on top of the coffin, facing upward. It showed the tomb master riding on a dragon boat. A crane has alighted on the dragon's tail, and a carp swims in the water below. A painting from Chenjia dashan shows an elegantly dressed woman standing on a crescent Moon under a phoenix. The bird seems to be rising up in anger against a snake.

BURIALS

The ultimate development in burials is seen in the mausoleum of Qin Shihuangdi, the first emperor, where his tomb lay below a colossal pyramid surrounded by an enclosing wall. Such funerary parks had developed during the preceding two centuries, as seen at Tomb 1 at Zhaoshan. Here the earliest architectural plans known from China survive to show the layout of the enclosure, with its five pavilions within.

This emphasis on the individual was reflected also in the subterranean part of the tomb. The traditional vertical pit was maintained, but it now contained a set of rooms to receive the tomb master's personal belongings needed for eternal life. Special care was taken to protect the tomb chamber by enveloping it in stones, clay, and charcoal. At Baoshan Tomb 2, surviving bamboo texts give clear insight into this procedure, for they describe the contents of each chamber and their future role. One room, for example, was set aside for items needed when traveling. Another was used to store food, a third for the goods used in the actual mortuary rituals. Nowhere is this trend more evident than in the tomb of the marquis of Zeng at Leigudun, with its sumptuous bronzes, lacquers, and tomb figures. Here three categories of mortuary goods were recognized: Those used in war, such as his armor and weaponry, were placed in a separate compartment. There was also provision for his ritual paraphernalia and his musical instruments.

The inclusion of MINGQI, symbolic goods especially manufactured for inclusion in the tomb, gained momentum during this period. Servants or retainers, for example, were represented by clay or wooden models, often carefully painted and clothed. Again, this trend reached its climax in the tomb of the first emperor.

Further reading: Lawton, T. *Chinese Art of the Warring States Period*. Bloomington: Indiana University Press, 1983; Li Xueqin. *Eastern Zhou and Qin Civilizations*. New Haven, Conn.: Yale University Press, 1985; Loewe, M., and E. L. Shaugnessy, eds. *The Cambridge History of Ancient China*. Cambridge: Cambridge University Press, 1999; Yu Weichao, ed. *Journey into China's Antiquity*, Vol. 2. Chicago: Art Media Resources, 1998.

Wat Ban Song Puay Wat Ban Song Puay, a site in northeast Thailand, has yielded an inscription that mentions a king Paravarasena and his capital center of Sankhapura. Dated stylistically to the seventh or eighth century C.E., it provides evidence for small regional polities or kingdoms during the period known as CHENLA (550–800 C.E.).

Wat Baset The temple of Wat Baset in the province of Battambang, Cambodia, was formerly known as Jayaksetrasiva. It was designated one of four temples by SURYAVARMAN I (r. c. 1002–49 C.E.) setting the limits of his kingdom. In the reign of JAYAVARMAN IV (r. 928–42 C.E.), Queen Indradevi had given an image of the god Jayarajamahesvara to the temple of Jayaksetrasiva.

See also ANGKOR.

Wat Phu   Five kilometers (3 mi.) to the west of Mount Lingaparvata in Laos lies the temple complex known as Wat Phu. This is one of the major temples of the kingdom of ANGKOR, in Cambodia, and the visible vestiges belong to the 11th and 12th centuries. However, it was occupied and venerated from at least the fifth century C.E. There is an inscription of the reign of YASHOVARMAN I (889–901), setting out the rules for the ashrama, or religious retreat, that he founded there. SURYAVARMAN I (r. c. 1002–49) visited the site during his quest for supreme rule over the kingdom of Angkor, and JAYAVARMAN VI (1080–1107) made donations to the temple. After the consecration of his descendant, King SURYAVARMAN II, in 1113 C.E., the high priest Divakarapandita embarked on a pilgrimage to make offerings at holy shrines. He began at Wat Phu, for the king had provided him with a script to be engraved on all the goods donated to temples. Divakarapandita donated valuables and ordered the construction of BARAYS (reservoirs). Two large *barays* survive to this day and link with a causeway that ultimately leads to a cleft in the base of the mountain, where there is a continuous supply of water. The causeway passes two stone buildings known, probably inaccurately, as palaces. A further causeway leads past a temple to Nandi, the sacred mount of SIVA, to a terrace that supports a cruciform building and then to a series of steps to the terrace on which stand six brick shrines. The main sanctuary is reached only by climbing another set of steep stairs. With PREAH VIHEAR and PHNOM CHISOR, Wat Phu was one of the foremost Angkorian temples outside Angkor.

Mount Lingaparvata lies about 60 kilometers (36 mi.) south of the junction of the Mekong and Mun Rivers in Laos, its peak taking the form of a LINGAM (phallus). Known as Lingaparvata and visible for miles, the mountain remains a place of pilgrimage and veneration to this day, and a series of springs at its foot, taken in conjunction with the natural lingam on the summit, attracted early attention during the period of state formation. An INSCRIPTION dated to the second half of the fifth century names a king DEVANIKA, meaning "celestial protection" or "divine inspiration." He ascended to rule there from afar as supreme king of kings, having gained victory over innumerable enemies. His celebratory rituals involved, he said, the donation of thousands of cattle. The site of this inscription incorporates the rectangular outline of an early city. The city lies on the bank of the Mekong River and contains a series of internal walls, one of which might represent the outline of the earliest urban foundation. There are also numerous mounds, now severely looted, that almost certainly represent temple foundations. It is possible that this city was formerly known as Sreshthapura, a site often mentioned in the Angkorian inscriptions as being seminal in the origins of the Cambodian people.

Wei   The state of Wei was formed from the breakup of JIN. The Jin state had been a dominant force during the Spring and Autumn period (770–476 B.C.E.) in China, but by 409 B.C.E. it was divided into three states: Wei, Hann, and Zhao. Wei dominated the Fen River Valley and part of the Huang (Yellow) River plains but was strategically stressed by the existence of powerful rivals on all sides, particularly QIN to the west. Less powerful than Qin, it had, according to contemporary records, 700 chariots and an infantry force of 360,000. These figures, however, are valuable only in a comparative sense; the corresponding figures for Qin are 1 million infantry and 1,000 chariots. This vulnerability might have underlain the Wei investment of much labor in the construction of a defensive wall along the Luo River. During the second half of the fourth century B.C.E., the problems posed by juxtaposition between powerful neighbors intensified, and Wei suffered a series of military defeats at the hands of the state of QI. The most serious of these took place in 353 and 341 B.C.E. These were followed by further disasters against Qin, which led in 322 B.C.E. to a virtual takeover of Wei by the king of Qin.

ROYAL TOMBS

The first capital of WEI was at Anyi, a large walled city with an inner palace precinct, but after its move to Daliang in 361 B.C.E. a further defensive wall was constructed there. A tomb of a Wei king has been investigated at Guweicun in Henan province: It includes three subterranean pits, each of which was covered with a funerary temple. Unfortunately, the site was extensively looted before proper archaeological investigations could take place. Swedish and Japanese collectors took away fragments of lacquered coffins and bronzes. Scientific examination of the remains between 1935 and 1951 revealed three massive tomb structures, the largest having a walled chamber measuring 18 by 17 meters (59.4 by 56.1 ft.). It had been entered by southern and northern ramps, the former more than 125 meters (412 ft.) in length. Wei state coins were found, as were the remains of a pit meant to contain two chariots. This tomb might have belonged to either King Huiwang or Xiangwang, both of whom reigned in the late fourth century B.C.E. Further Wei tombs have been excavated at Shanbiaozhen. One, known as the Jizhong tomb, was investigated as early as 279 C.E. It contained the BAMBOO SLIPS known as the *Zhushu Jinian*, or BAMBOO ANNALS. The latest entry on this vital set of documents was dated to the reign of King Xiangwang of Wei in 298 B.C.E. Further excavations in 1935 yielded a rich harvest of new finds. One tomb, measuring eight by seven meters (26.4 by 23.1 ft.), contained four sacrificial victims and nearly 1,500 bronzes. A remarkable battle scene had been cast onto one vessel, showing archers, spearmen, and soldiers wielding halberds and fighting from boats. There is also a wheeled scaling ladder to assault defensive walls. One panel depicts decapitated soldiers. A large and well-equipped army was vital to survival during those troubled times.

Weizhi   The state of Wei formed after the breakup of the Eastern HAN DYNASTY in China in 220 C.E. and endured for 45 years; this state was unrelated to the Wei of the first millennium B.C.E. The *Weizhi* (*History of the Wei Dynasty*) was compiled toward the end of the third century C.E. and contains passages that describe the life and customs of the Wa, the people of the Japanese archipelago. It is known that the Wa sent tribute missions to China in 57 and 107 C.E., and the *Weizhi* is a major source of information on Japan during the late YAYOI phase (300 B.C.E.–300 C.E., when the Wa inhabitants were on the brink of early state formation. The relevant passages begin with a description of early contact with China during the Han dynasty and the existence of more than 100 communities in Japan. Thirty, it proceeds, maintained such contact with the Wei court by dispatching envoys.

The account of the Wa people is highly informative about the social conditions of the third century C.E. and presents a challenge to archaeologists to find, test, and verify its findings. The people had body tattoos, which varied by region and class. The ruler was a woman shaman called Himiko, who lived secluded in a palace attended by 1,000 WOMEN and was rarely seen. When she died, she was interred under a mound 100 paces across, with 100 sacrificed victims. After the death of Himiko, there was much unrest until a young woman was found to replace her. There was a marked class system, whereby the lower orders would bow before aristocrats. The latter were also interred under mounds. War was conducted with halberds, shields, and bows and arrows, the latter made of bamboo with a stone or iron head. Before embarking on a major venture, the Wa would heat animal bones and divine the future through interpreting the resulting cracks. There were a legal and a taxation system, and the economy was based on cultivation of wet rice and of mulberry trees to raise silkworms. These records provide an important glimpse of the Wa people as they approached the transition to early states.

well-field system The well-field was a system of land division that was established in China as part of the expansion of the WESTERN ZHOU DYNASTY from the 10th century B.C.E. until it was abandoned during the EASTERN ZHOU DYNASTY (770–221 B.C.E.). The system was established at a time when the king in theory owned all land, which was enfeoffed to his senior relatives as new states were formed in outlying areas. The system, according to MENCIUS, involved nine plots of land assigned by the lord for the use of eight families of the same lineage. Each family was permitted to till its own block, but the families combined to farm the lord's central ninth block for his benefit. The word *well* is from the Chinese written symbol for a well, an important component of daily life in such a community. This essentially feudal and communal system broke down as regional states grew in strength during the Spring and Autumn period (770–476 B.C.E.) of Eastern Zhou. Under the new regimes, the state sought taxation revenue, which in turn promoted private owner-

ship and the establishment of large estates and more efficient agriculture aided by the new availability of iron implements and draft animals. This saw, in northern China, the rotation of large fields under millet and wheat, allowing the harvesting of three crops every two years. The well-field system during the HAN DYNASTY (206 B.C.E.–220 C.E.) remained in the consciousness as a utopian system, but it was never again seriously adopted.

Wendi (Liu Heng; Literary Emperor) (202–157 B.C.E.) *Wendi was the fifth son of Gaozu, the founding emperor of the Western Han dynasty.*
Wendi ruled longer than the sum of all his Han predecessors' reigns (r. 180–157 B.C.E.). He was blessed with a principal consort who preferred philosophy to political ambition and an heir who followed perforce in her footsteps. A lengthy period of relative peace and a stable succession combined to strengthen the legitimacy and power of the Han dynasty. This period produced important political changes in the structure of the empire. Although the foundation of kingdoms under the control of royal sons might have induced a measure of stability under Gaozu, with time the relationship between the center and the peripheral states became more distant. On his accession, Wendi controlled 19 commanderies and 11 kingdoms, but when an opportunity presented itself, he dissolved a kingdom and replaced it with commanderies or divided a kingdom into smaller units. This reduced the likelihood of powerful kings revolting. Thus in 174 B.C.E. the large kingdom of Huainan was replaced by commanderies, and the death of the king of QI with no heirs was followed by the creation of five smaller kingdoms with centrally appointed rulers. The need to have available a corps of administrators encouraged Wendi to approve the foundation of a civil service examination in 165 B.C.E. Competitive examinations tested knowledge of the Confucian ethics of government. Wendi died in 157 B.C.E. and was succeeded by his son, Jingdi.

BACKGROUND TO WENDI'S EMERGENCE

The years after the death of Wendi's father in 195 B.C.E. had been extremely difficult. The senior wife of Gaozu, Lu Hao, dominated the weak second emperor of the dynasty and, acting as regent, placed members of her own family in positions of power both at court and in the provinces. This caused considerable resentment, which was exacerbated by the structure of the empire after Gaozu's reforms. These had involved a twofold political system. The eastern parts of China were divided into kingdoms, the rulers of which were selected on the basis of loyalty to the emperor. The western tracts were commanderies under the governorship of political appointees. Many of the former kings of these commanderies were members of the royal family, who could under conditions of instability advance their own claims for the succession to the imperial title.

After the death of Lu Hao and the opportunity to rid the court of the members of her family, the empire was unstable. There were at least three regional kings who could claim succession rights. The kings of Dai and Huainan were sons of Gaozu by minor wives, while the king of Qi was a grandson of Gaozu, but of senior descent to his uncles. This last claimant had also led his armies to Xi'an to topple the regent and had lost considerable parts of his territory to land seizures by Lu Hao. However, the king of Qi suffered a major disadvantage: His mother was powerful and ambitious and might have followed the same path as the widely detested Lu Hao. The choice therefore fell on Liu Heng, the king of Dai, who became emperor in 180 B.C.E., with the regnal name WENDI.

See also CONFUCIUS.

Western Baray The Western BARAY is the largest such reservoir of the kingdom of ANGKOR. No inscriptions survive to date its construction, but since the southern dyke partially covers the temple of AK YUM, which was still functional in 1001 C.E., and its island temple was built in the style of UDAYADITYAVARMAN II, it has been ascribed to the reign of SURYAVARMAN I (r. c. 1002–49). Its massive earthen dykes enclose 17.6 square kilometers (7 sq. mi.), and it retains a considerable body of water. This has been augmented by recent modifications that now feed IRRIGATION water through a sluice gate into canals. Whether or not it was originally designed for irrigation is controversial. B.-P. Groslier maintains that Angkor was a hydraulic city dependent on irrigated rice for its survival. Others maintain that even when full, this *baray* could have contributed only a tiny fraction of total production through irrigation, nor is there any evidence for the existence of a canal distribution system during the period of the Angkorian kingdom. A temple known as the WESTERN MEBON lies in the center of the reservoir, and it formerly housed a colossal bronze statue of Vishnu. It is likely that the original purpose of the Western Baray lay in representing the sacred oceans surrounding MOUNT MERU, home of the gods.

Western Mebon The Western Mebon is the temple located on an island, in the center of the WESTERN BARAY at ANGKOR in Cambodia. It was built in the reign of King UDAYADITYAVARMAN II in the early 11th century C.E. The temple is ringed by a wall 100 meters square (40 sq. mi.), and a causeway gives access to the foundations of the central shrine. A shaft in the shrine contained the remains of a huge bronze statue of Vishnu.

western satraps Between the first and fourth centuries C.E. much of the territory now comprising Sind, Gujarat, and Rajasthan in western India and southern Pakistan was ruled by the so-called western satraps. A satrap is a viceroy; however, the rulers of the western satraps were independent rulers of SAKA origin. The old-est dynasty is known as Kshaharata, and its earliest kings were Bhumaka and Nahapana. The latter, who assumed the title raja, or king, was defeated by a long-standing rival, the SATAVAHANA dynasty under Gautamiputra Satakarni. The Kardamaka dynasty then took control of the western satraps, the most successful Kardamaka ruler being RUDRADAMAN. An inscription from Junagadh, dated to 150 C.E., described his military prowess and the wide extent of his domain. He turned the balance of power in his favor against that of the Satavahanas to the south. Such success encouraged him to assume the title Mahaksatrapa (Great Satrap). Internal rivalries as much as external threats then beset the later satraps, until their line was extinguished by CANDRAGUPTA II.

Western Zhou dynasty It is widely appreciated that the Western Zhou dynasty was a vital and formative period in Chinese history. Study of its characteristics is a rich and dynamic historical field, because of the growing number of contemporary documents being found through archaeological research. It links the still rather shadowy SHANG dynasty (1766–1045 B.C.E.) with the Spring and Autumn period (770–476 B.C.E.) of the EASTERN ZHOU DYNASTY and presents many cultural developments that were to be incorporated into Chinese culture. Literature and poetry flourished, there was clearly a vigorous musical tradition, and the techniques and products of the bronze foundries reflect changing cultural preferences. Considerable demands were placed on the supply of raw materials to feed the need for fine bronzes, ceramics, and lavish palaces and tombs, and

Bronze casting in China maintained a state of great skill. This wine vessel in the form of an elephant dates to the Western Zhou dynasty (1045–771 B.C.E.), during which many new forms developed. *(Nimatallah/Art Resource, NY)*

the organization of trade encouraged new administrative structures. Politically, the dynasty began with a policy of enfeoffing members of the royal clan with new states to ensure border stability and provide a protective shield. This system was in due course to engender the very opposite effect as regional rulers sought independence from the central court, which led to a weakening at the center and the final relocation of the capital to found the successor Eastern Zhou state in 770 B.C.E.

TEXT SOURCES FOR WESTERN ZHOU HISTORY

In contrast to the Shang dynasty, which the Western Zhou overthrew at the BATTLE OF MUYE in 1045 B.C.E., the Western Zhou dynasty is well documented in the historic as well as the archaeological record of China. The traditional historic sources include the basic Chinese historical texts known as the *Classic of Odes* (*Shijing*), the *Classic of Documents* (*Shujing*), and the *Classic of Changes* (*Yijing*). Some of the texts in the *Classic of Documents* contain sections that record the speeches of founding members of the dynasty, although the oldest surviving texts were written at a much later date. The *Classic of Odes* incorporates sacred hymns chanted during ceremonies at the ancestral Zhou temples. There is also much important information on the SHIJI (*Records of the Grand Historian*), which was completed during the Western HAN DYNASTY by SIMA QIAN in about 100 B.C.E. Sima Qian could call upon a much wider range of historical sources than are presently available. The BAMBOO ANNALS are a remarkable source of information. They include a narrative history of China up to 298 B.C.E., when they were placed in the tomb of King Xiang of WEI. More than five centuries later, in 279 C.E., the tomb was rifled and the precious BAMBOO SLIPS exhumed.

TEXTS ON BRONZE VESSELS AND ARCHAEOLOGICAL EVIDENCE

A second and growing source of documentary information on the Western Zhou dynasty are contemporary texts cast into bronze vessels. It was the practice of those who could afford the metal and had access to appropriate specialists to have vessels cast to commemorate a significant event in their life. These documents were often interred in the owner's tomb and provide an unparalleled source of contemporary events. Thus the text often includes reference to the date, ruling king, and important events, such as campaigns against named enemies or court rituals that involved the owner of the bronze in question. The social role of the investiture ceremonies that preceded the casting of a commemorative bronze has been reconstructed in some detail. The original term for the ceremony was *ceming,* "to give and record and order." The king would take his position in his great hall, looking down on his scribes, the recipient of the order, and court officials. Behind him there was a screen decorated with axes that symbolized his royal power. The king would read the order, and the recipient would proceed to

have a bronze cast to record this significant event in his career.

Thus vital historic details emerge from these bronzes, and as the total number known grows through further excavations, so these contribute to writing the history of Western Zhou. A vessel known as the Song *gui* was cast to commemorate an official position and responsibilities given to the owner by King Xuan (r. 827–782 B.C.E.). It records how the king in state commanded him to take charge of a new royal warehouse and gave him fine clothing and a horse's bridle. The accumulation of many such texts shows how an initial period when royal relatives were provided with important regional positions was replaced by one in which bureaucrats were appointed on the basis of their merit.

For the preceding Shang state, the dominant source of historic information are the divination texts incised on the ORACLE BONES. This practice continued into the early Western Zhou period, as is recorded in the historical documents and the bones themselves. However, the oracle bones are markedly less abundant and play a relatively minor role in the assessment of Zhou history. On the other hand, the growing evidence of archaeological excavations is the principal means whereby further knowledge can be gained. These have gathered pace since 1970, leading to the recovery of many inscriptions on bronze vessels placed with the dead. For example, in 1976 the LI GUI was discovered at Lintong in Shaanxi province. Its text described the victorious campaign of the Zhou in defeating the last Shang ruler. Archaeologists have investigated many hundreds of Zhou dynasty cemeteries, yielding a rich harvest of finds and information. In addition, research at settlement sites has added to knowledge of technological developments and the economy.

ORIGINS OF ZHOU

The origins of the Zhou have not been definitively settled. One source of information is the allusion to a polity named Zhou in the actual Shang oracle bones dated to the reigns of King Wu Ding and Zu Geng, late 12th century B.C.E. These name the Zhou as an enemy located in the valley of the Fen River some 160 kilometers (96 mi.) east of the Shang capital at ANYANG. Not long after these texts were inscribed, the Zhou seem to have moved farther west into the valley of the Wei River, at which point, being farther removed from Anyang, they cease to be mentioned in the oracle-bone archives. The Wei Valley is not only highly strategically placed, but also well endowed with fertile agricultural land. The soil is soft and easily worked, and the recovery of agricultural tools from excavations at the site of Zhangjiapo shows that the local shell and animal bone, as well as stone, were used to fashion spades, knives, and sickles. Bronze tools may also have been important but are probably underrepresented as a result of the ease with which bronze can be recast. The *Book of Odes* describes how the land was cleared of forest cover and opened to agriculture under the early Zhou rulers.

Battle of Muye and Its Aftermath

The Western Zhou dynasty encompassed 13 kings from the victory at Muye in 1045 until 771 B.C.E. It was thus one of the longest dynasties of China and was looked back on in later centuries as a golden age. It was a period when historic writing and poetry developed to a high pitch of excellence, and methods of government were established that were followed, at least in part, for centuries after its demise. Archaeological findings have shown that among the reasons for the Zhou success in war were innovative new armaments. The Zhou developed a new form of bronze halberd and cast swords of greater potency than that of the daggers of their Shang adversaries. It is recorded that chariots took part in the Battle of Muye, along with the so-called tiger-warrior infantry, 3,000 strong. The Zhou also developed a form of bronze armor that was more efficient and allowed greater flexibility than that of the Shang.

The Li *gui* text describes the battle itself, and several other bronze vessel inscriptions cover its aftermath. The Ho *zun,* for example, recounts how King Cheng (r. 1042–1006 B.C.E.) recalled the plan of his ancestor, King Wu, to move his capital from the Wei Valley to the land of the XIA DYNASTY, which together with his holding the MANDATE OF HEAVEN would have given him enhanced legitimacy. The postconquest policy in general witnessed the movement and redeployment of the experienced Shang scribes and other administrators. This is described in the text of the Shi Qiang *pan.* It was also necessary to send out the troops for mopping-up operations, in which, as contemporary sources describe, 750 states were defeated. In this context, a state was probably little more than a local community, but it is clear that pacification of the former Shang dependencies was necessary. This was followed by the development of a feudal policy, in which close relatives of the king, usually his sons or cousins, were enfeoffed with land on the borders of the Zhou domain to provide a loyal buffer against outside danger. As many as 71 such vassal states were ascribed to the initiatives of the duke of Zhou, who exercised regency powers between 1042 and 1036 B.C.E. The MAI ZUN text describes in detail the procedure that was involved when a leading follower of the sovereign was so authorized to command a border area. Under King Cheng (r. 1042/35–1006 B.C.E.), Xinghou Zhi was sent to take charge of a new colony 100 kilometers (60 mi.) north of Anyang. The king presented him with handsome gifts, including horse harnesses, fine clothing, soldiers, and 200 families to assist in the new settlement. This process was followed by King Kang (r. 1005/3–978 B.C.E.), who during a reign later characterized as peaceful sent his brothers to rule in new vassal states.

ZHOU EXPANSION

The degree to which this reign was in fact peaceful can be questioned on the basis of the texts on two bronze vessels cast by one Yu. The Da Yu *ding,* for example, describes how Yu, the grandson of a previous high official in the government, was appointed the supervisor of the armed forces. Yu's military success was recorded two years later on another vessel, which went into minute detail about not only the number of captives and amount of booty taken, but also the subsequent court ceremonials and celebrations. Two leaders of the Guifang people who lived north of the Zhou domain were taken, along with 13,055 of their soldiers. The text describes the capture of 30 chariots and their horses, cattle, and sheep. King Kang celebrated with the sacrifice of one of the Guifang to his ancestors, divinations, and a grand banquet.

During the reign of King Zhao (977/5–957 B.C.E.), there was an attempt to expand to the south. This put the Western Zhou state up against the Chu, who commanded the Han and Middle Chang (Yangtze) Valleys. Several bronze inscriptions record this southern adventure. The Ling *gui,* for example, which was looted from a site near LUOYANG in 1929, employs a so-called great event date "when the king was attacking the elder of Chu." A second vessel, the Yiyu *gui,* describes how Yiyu participated in the southern war. The attraction of a southern expansion of the Zhou realm probably lay in the wealth of its resources, which included gold, copper, and tin. The copper mine at TONGLUSHAN, for example, is one of the largest investigated in East Asia. Subsequent allusions to this campaign are oblique, but it appears that the campaign was a disaster for the Zhou. The king lost his life, allegedly by drowning when the bridge over the Han River collapsed, taking him with it.

CONFLICT WITH OUTLYING AREAS

With the reign of King Mu (956–918 B.C.E.), the Western Zhou dynasty reached its first century, and the dragons' teeth sown in the early years began to sprout. The basic problem was the enfeoffment of royal relatives to control the border regions. As long as there was mutual trust, this was a sensible arrangement often used in early states. However, with the passage of time blood ties slackened, and the outlying regions, instead of being supportive, began to seek independence. This naturally led to friction and strife. In the case of the Western Zhou, contemporary accounts describe an invasion of the capital by the Zhu Rong people, a confederation of rival states on the eastern border. Countering this threat, which had its first portents with the disastrous defeat at the hands of the Chu in the south, involved a reorganization of the military command structure, as seen in the text cast into the Li *fangyi.* This describes how Li was given control of armies and showered with gifts by the king. At the same time, the central bureaucracy was strengthened with new appointments to supervise departments of state. One of these involved landownership. As the Zhou realm contracted on the margins under the reign of King Gong (917/15–900 B.C.E.) and the population grew, there was evidently friction over land tenure, and disputes and the redistribution of property are encountered for the first time in the inscriptions.

The historical framework of the following three reigns, which involved the kings Yih (899–873 B.C.E.), his brother and probable usurper, Xiao (872–855 B.C.E.), and Yih's son, Yi (865–858 B.C.E.), are unclear. However, some texts and later accounts point to further problems with maintaining territorial integrity. The state of Qi on the eastern border was one of the major and earliest foundations that followed the Battle of Muye, but it is recorded that its king was captured during the reign of King Yi and killed by being boiled in a cauldron. At the same time, there is compelling evidence that the powerful Chu from the south invaded the Zhou heartland and, as seen in the Yu *gui* inscription, were repulsed only with difficulty.

King Yi was succeeded by King Li (857/53–842/28 B.C.E.). The *Shiji* (*Records of the Grand Historian*), written seven centuries later, recounted that the new ruler refused to take proper advice and through his reckless behavior gravely risked losing the Mandate of Heaven. Sima Qian wrote: "The king acted cruelly and extravagantly. The people in the capital spoke of the king's faults." When this was brought to King Li's notice, he appointed spies to report to him on such criticisms. Those identified were executed. The king was pleased with his success in putting an end to such sedition but was reminded that stopping people from talking was like trying to stop a river. When it burst its banks, it caused trouble. Rivers should be dredged and water would flow. People should be allowed to speak their minds, or there would be rebellion. The king would not listen to such advice, and the prediction was realized. After three further years, the people rose up in rebellion, and the king fled. Before fleeing, King Li had requisitioned the casting of a magnificent bronze vessel, known as the Hu *gui*. This offered his own version of events and sought a long life and sage counsel. It did not prevent his fleeing into exile in or about 842 B.C.E.

DECLINE OF WESTERN ZHOU

The government of the Western Zhou after the deposition of King Li was clarified by the text on the Shi X *gui*. The inscription makes it clear that in 841 B.C.E., because the rightful heir was an infant, a regency was established under Gong He. This lasted for 14 years, until King Li died, and his son, King Xuan (r. 827/5–782 B.C.E.), acceded to the throne. During both the regency and the reign of Xuan, the Zhou were under constant threat from the western barbarians known as the Xianyun. The Xi Jia *pan* text describes a victory against this adversary; Xi Jia himself was rewarded with a four-horse chariot. The inscription provides important information that the Zhou still controlled the trade and taxation revenue for eastern border states that had long assumed a strong measure of independence from the central court. There were further victories until 816 B.C.E. against the Xianyun, but there-

after the tide turned, and the Zhou found themselves under mounting pressure. On the king's death in 782 B.C.E. by assassination, when an arrow is said to have pierced his chest, the king was succeeded by his son, You, who reigned for a decade. However, there were three serious natural portents of disaster at the beginning of his reign: eclipses of both the Sun and the Moon and a severe earthquake. Along with his resolve to replace his legitimate heir with the son of his favorite concubine, further inroads from the west that ultimately sacked the capital Zongzhou, and the king lost both the Mandate of Heaven and his life. In 771 B.C.E. the Western Zhou dynasty came to an end, but this did not spell the end of the Zhou lineage. The rulers of the eastern states of JIN and Qin went to the aid of the Western Zhou aristocracy, moving them to the new eastern capital and installing as king Yi Jiu, the son of You and his legitimate successor. As King Ping, he reigned for 50 years until 720 B.C.E., now under the name of the Eastern Zhou dynasty.

ADMINISTRATION OF EMPIRE

The skeletal dynastic history, while stressing warfare and crises, nevertheless represents one of the longest periods of rule by any Chinese state. Having conquered the Shang, early Zhou rulers found themselves in charge of a far larger area than their ancestors were accustomed to, an area that expanded farther over time. Keeping control over such a domain was a problem that confronted many other early Asian states, and a widespread solution was to appoint members of the royal house to rule over dependent and compliant states. In the case of the Zhou, this has often been described as the feudal system, and many inscriptions from the RITUAL BRONZE VESSELS confirm the way it operated. Later Chinese writings also explain how the establishment of vassal states immediately followed the defeat of the Shang, a process known as *fengjian*. It is recorded in the writings of Xunzi that there were 71 vassal states after the implementation of this policy, of which 53 were placed under the control of members of the royal clan and the remainder given to those who had married into royalty. In the case of the foundation of the state of Jin, King Cheng appointed his brother, Prince Tangshu Yu, to proceed to a part of the kingdom and take control. Kangshu, one of King Wu's younger brothers, was sent to the new state of Wei. The appointee would take his own relatives and a large group of people to be resettled in the new area. Many texts describe the lavish gifts given to the new leader by the Zhou king, including weaponry, bronzes, chariots and horses, and fine clothing. These gifts were in effect the symbols of authority conferred on the ruler of the new state. They centered on the special chariot and fittings, ritual bronzes, pennants and scepters.

SUBSIDIARY STATES

With his entourage and followers, the ruler would form the administrative and social elite over the indigenous inhabitants. He would be expected to remain a vassal to the central court and provide for defense to shield the capital against outside aggression. The regional armies were likewise ordered on the basis of kinship. Once formed, the administrative structure in the vassal state became in microcosm a replica of the original. Junior kinsmen were sent out from secondary centers to found new settlements and construct their vital ancestral temples for worship. In this context, the role of the ceremonial bronzes with their inscriptions can be easily appreciated. They were to fulfill part of the rituals of ANCESTOR WORSHIP, rituals that linked the participants to a bonded lineage. The temples themselves, to judge from the surviving texts, were graded in terms of size. The royal temple had seven shrines each dedicated to one ancestor, while temples for feudal overlords had five, and those for a minister three. The temple was also used for investiture ceremonies often described in the bronze inscriptions.

A plethora of states was thus formed, and their definition was based first on the people rather than on a territory with fixed boundaries. Indeed, most of the states, estimates of whose numbers vary between 20 and 70, were relocated from one part of the Zhou kingdom to another. Under this zongfa system, the vassal princes had their own administrative officials in a descending hierarchy.

BURIAL PRACTICES

Jin, with its capital of Tianma-Qucun in Henan province, was one of the major states of the Western Zhou. Excavations there have unearthed more than 600 burials of varying degrees of wealth. Some later tombs incorporated remarkable images of faces fashioned from pieces of jade. There were also fine bronzes and pits for chariots and horses. Rich burials have been excavated in the cemetery of Xincun, which belonged to the state of Wei in Henan province. The richest of these took the form of deep mortuary pits, embellished with two access ramps on the northern and southern sides. Again, horses and chariots were part of the grave furniture. Farther east, small states were established in Shandong. To the north, the state of Yan was founded. Again, there is documentary evidence for a founding prince of very high status in the Zhou royal line, for texts on bronzes refer to Tai Bao, the title accorded Shao Gong, the half-brother of King Wu himself (r. 1049/45–1043 B.C.E.). The cemetery of Fangshan, located near Beijing, has been examined archaeologically and found to contain extremely rich burials. Bronze vessels of this state were of the highest quality, and there were also multiple chariot burials and horse interments.

SHANG BORROWINGS

One of the key points to emerge from recent archaeological research is the way in which the early Zhou adopted ritual and mortuary practices from the Shang. For example, typically Shang forms of bronze vessels were cast for use in banquets to feast the ancestors. Many such vessels had inscriptions that expressed the wish that they be used by the descendants of the original caster for generations lasting 10,000 years. During later times of danger, such vessels were accumulated and placed in underground hoards, such as the exceptionally rich one unearthed at Zhuangbai. The conjunction of bronzes covering decades and, on occasion, centuries of evolution indicates that they were indeed used over many generations of the same lineage. The interment of chariots, horses, and charioteers in pits associated with the nobility was also a practice adopted from the Shang, and the form of the chariots themselves was a clear link between the two dynasties. However, the Zhou expressed their own preferences in their bronzes, and there were marked regional styles over the extensive area they controlled.

ZHOU CITIES

While excavations in the cemeteries have yielded a rich harvest of information, archaeological research in the cities and other settlements is no less important in providing a complete picture of the Western Zhou state. The foundations of a palace, for example, have been uncovered at Fengchu in the so-called Zhouyuan, the plain of the Zhou. Raised on a stamped-earth foundation, this building had large wooden pillars that formed two enclosed courts. A large hall dominated the center between the two courtyards, which themselves were flanked by covered passageways providing access to subsidiary rooms. This site is notable for the discovery in the foundations of a set of inscribed oracle bones, suggesting that it was occupied by a high-ranking member of the royal family. More practically, the structure was drained by a complex system of ceramic pipes.

This site formed part of a much larger complex that included a further palace area. The most important result of the excavations there has been the opening of the foundations of a great hall measuring 22 by 14 meters (about 72 by 46 ft.). It is possible that this represents the sort of structure in which the vital investiture ceremonials took place. It incorporated substantial postholes one meter wide to accommodate the supporting columns and one particularly large one in the center, almost two meters across, to take the main weight of the roof. This site also included specialist ceramic workshops, bronze foundries, and locations where bone artifacts were manufactured.

BRONZE INDUSTRY

The location of bronze foundries in a major settlement with a palace precinct recalls the layout of earlier Shang cities such as Anyang. Indeed, the Zhou bronze industry was clearly related to that of the Shang, in terms of both the vessels and weapons cast and the techniques of manufacture. It is highly likely that the early Zhou rulers seized the opportunity to redeploy Shang specialists in their own workshops. Excavations at Luoyang have uncovered a bronze-working area that once covered at least 700 by 300 meters (2,310 by 990 ft.). Apart from the dwellings of the workers, it has produced many fragments of clay molds and furnaces used to heat molten bronze. The scale of production, which lasted from early in the dynasty until the second half of the 10th century B.C.E., was very great. The BRONZE-CASTING technique employed the Shang system of clay piece molds. These could be decorated or incised with texts before being fired and then pieced together with mortise-and-tenon joints over a central clay mold. As many as 10 separate pieces were necessary in the case of complex vessels. There is evidence in other foundry areas for specialized production, where vessels were cast by one group and chariot fittings or weapons by another. Such bronze workshops were established in the royal domain as well as in the vassal states, and hence the latter could produce their own important ritual vessels as well as weaponry that would in due course support competition and civil friction. Indeed, it is through the analysis of the cast bronzes that social change, described by Jessica Rawson as a "ritual revolution," can be traced.

EVOLUTION IN BRONZE VESSELS

This series of changes has been dated to a relatively brief period during the first half of the ninth century B.C.E. The changes are best documented in the mortuary record, the forms of the vessels being cast, the manner in which chariots were interred, and the increasing importance of jade grave goods. The principal evidence for change is taken from the ritual bronzes. Whereas formerly there had been a range of vessels to serve food or wine, now sets of virtually identical forms were cast with longer and similar or identical inscriptions. They were also much heavier than their predecessors. Wine containers and cups for serving were no longer found, and a series of new vessel forms was introduced, such as the *dou, xu,* and *yi.* Well-tried vessels, formerly rendered in clay, were now cast in bronze, and the individual rank of the owner could be detected in the number of virtually identical vessels owned. At the same time, sets of bells were cast. Bells had been virtually absent from the earlier Western Zhou tombs, but they were now adapted from southern prototypes and would have added an important musical element to ritual occasions. Moreover, these changes were not confined to the central power, for identical changes and sets of bronzes were found over the entire Zhou realm. The same multiple sets of identical vessels are also found in the hoards that were buried during this period of change. It would seem that the multiple sets of bronzes that could be augmented if resources permitted were a way to exhibit the status and achievements of particular lineages. The practice encouraged the mass production of virtually identical pieces and the commercialization of a bronze industry hitherto dedicated to the provision of specific items for court ritual purposes.

See also TONGLUSHAN.

Further reading: Hsu, Cho-yun, and K. M. Linduff. *Western Zhou Civilization.* New Haven, Conn.: Yale Uni-

versity Press, 1988; Rawson, J. "Statesmen or Barbarians? The Western Zhou as Seen Through Their Bronzes," *Proceedings of the British Academy* 75 (1989): 71–95.

Wheeler, Sir Mortimer (1890–1976) *Sir Mortimer Wheeler was one of the leading British archaeologists of the 20th century.*

Wheeler specialized in the Iron Age and Roman periods in Europe and was best known for his meticulous excavation technique and the promptitude with which he published his results. The excavations of Maiden Castle in Dorset and Verulamium, a large Roman city near Saint Albans in Hertfordshire, were among his best known achievements. In 1943, while serving with the British army in North Africa, he was invited to become the new director-general of the ARCHAEOLOGICAL SURVEY OF INDIA. On his arrival in India, he faced the enviable task of organizing a series of excavations that took him to the major historic and prehistoric sites in the subcontinent. His first choice fell on TAXILA, where excavations doubled as a training school for promising Indian students of archaeology. His research at the BHIR MOUND, TAXILA, recovered a hoard of Greek coins dated to about 300 B.C.E. in a layer overlying those containing NORTHERN BLACK POLISHED WARE (c. 550–100 B.C.E.). This led to the dating of this important and widespread style of pottery. Wheeler was responsible for major excavations of HARAPPA and MOHENJO DARO, among other sites in India and Pakistan and for his clarification of aspects of the INDUS VALLEY CIVILIZATION. His emphasis on precise archaeological techniques and record keeping shaped archaeological efforts in many parts of the world.

ROMAN TRADE WITH INDIA

In 1945 he turned his mind to the frequent recovery of Roman coins, particularly in southern India. This, he surmised, could well assist in identifying a site where trade had taken place and permit archaeological inquiries. A chance visit to the Madras Museum, then deserted after a Japanese airstrike, led to his recognizing a Roman amphora, a ceramic vessel employed to ship wine. Further inquiries identified its find spot as ARIKAMEDU, a site near Pondicherry 130 kilometers to the south. His immediate visit to Arikamedu took Wheeler to the local library, where a glass case revealed shards of bright red Arretine ware, a type of pottery manufactured in Italy from the first century B.C.E. until the first century C.E. The importance of the subsequent major excavation of this port is hard to overestimate, not only because it documented the Roman trade with India so clearly described in the *PERIPLUS OF THE ERYTHRAEAN SEA,* but also because datable Roman material might be found together with Indian artifacts of unknown age. On the 12th day of excavations, an Arretine-ware shard was discovered with a potter's stamp on the base that read VIBIE. This identified it as originating in the workshop of the Vibieni at Arezzo.

From Tuscany, this and other Roman exports reached Podouke Emporion, a trading port in distant India.

MAJOR SITES IN INDIA

In 1946 Wheeler turned north again to Harappa in Pakistan. Up to that point, it was thought that the cities of the Indus Valley civilization lay undefended in a pacific social atmosphere. Fresh from the battlefields of North Africa, Wheeler rapidly traced the path of a massive defensive wall around the site on a base 13 meters (143 ft.) wide. He proceeded to excavate a trench that sectioned the site against and below the defensive wall, thereby identifying the cultural remains that underlay it. He also sectioned between Cemeteries H and R37 to find their stratigraphic relationship.

After the independence of India and the formation of Pakistan in August 1947, Wheeler turned his attention to Mohenjo Daro, now located in the latter state. Here he uncovered a huge platform on the citadel that he interpreted as an ancient granary. These excavations resulted in a major collection of artifacts and prompted him to suggest that the Indus civilization sites were destroyed by invading Aryans, authors of the RIG-VEDA.

In 1958 Wheeler undertook his last major excavation at CHARSADA. This site, famed as a city that resisted the forces of ALEXANDER THE GREAT (356–323 B.C.E.) for 30 days, was little studied. Wheeler was able to piece together its sequence, again through the management of an excavation of audacious size, and published a full report a few years later after his time in India that had a profound impact on subsequent excavation procedures and achievements. His influence, however, extended east of India. A Chinese graduate student, XIA NAI, was one of his field workers at Maiden Castle in 1936 and learned there the techniques of trial trenching and a grid layout involving baulks between the excavation squares. Xia Nai was greatly affected by this, his first excavation after working on the royal tombs at ANYANG, and took back his enthusiasm to China. There he rapidly rose through the ranks of Chinese archaeologists, and the Wheeler system was and remains widely applied in China.

Wilkins, Sir Charles (1749–1836) *Sir Charles Wilkins was one of the foremost early Western pioneers in the study of Sanskrit languages in India.*
In 1781 he published the paper "A Royal Grant of Land Engraved on a Copper Plate Bearing Date Twenty-Three Years before Christ; and Discovered among the Ruins of Mongueer. Translated from the Original Sanskrit by Charles Wilkins." He went on to translate further inscriptions, including a notable text in BRAHMI from Nagarjuni.
See also JONES, SIR WILLIAM; PRINSEP, JAMES.

women

CHINA

The historic importance of women in the history of China can be traced back to the SHANG DYNASTY, although rich prehistoric graves of women indicate that their social prominence long preceded the foundation of early states. FU HAO, known in her cult temple as Mother Xin, is the clearest example of a prominent female member of the Shang court. During her life, she was mentioned in the ORACLE BONES of the emperor Wu Ding, for she was one of his three principal consorts. She was a wealthy landowner who undertook important court rituals to consult with the ancestors. She commanded troops in a number of military campaigns, and the king himself consulted the oracles to ensure her health and well-being during pregnancies. Her death was marked by long mortuary rituals, and she was laid to rest in a tomb of fabulous wealth. Her son, who died before he could become emperor, was worshiped under the name of Elder Brother Ji. The mortuary evidence for high status accorded some women is seen much later in the WESTERN HAN burial of Xin Zhui, wife of the marquis of Dai, at MAWANGDUI. Her tomb, found 17 meters (56 ft.) below ground, was encased in charcoal and clay to withstand the forces of decay. This led to the preservation of the hundreds of items that accompanied her in death, including a tomb banner that portrayed her attended by servants before her ascent to heaven. Her fine silk clothing, LACQUER ware, favorite recipes, and even her theater where she was entertained with fine music confirm her luxurious life as a high-ranking woman. Similar attention was given the royal consorts of the Han emperors, of which there were numerous grades. At its height, there were up to 3,000 women in the royal harem, and the ranks increased progressively from six to as many as 14, with salaries and living quarters commensurate with status. Empresses were often involved in court intrigues in favor of their sons against those of their rivals and, hence, wielded much power.

JAPAN

Women in Japan could achieve the same high social standing as men. The Chinese text known as the *Weizhi* (*History of the Kingdom of Wei*) describes female leaders in Japan who were interred in tumulus graves. One of them, Himiko, evidently lived in a heavily guarded palace. In the period of the YAMATO state, women had access to the most exalted title of TENNO, or sovereign. Empress SAIMEI, for example, was the 35th *tenno*. During her reign, she organized military expeditions to extend her kingdom or to assist her Korean ally, the state of Paekche. Jito (645–703) was the 41st *tenno*. Daughter of Emperor Tenji, she is particularly remembered for founding Fujiwara, the Nara capital. Jito was succeeded by her sister Genmei, the empress who ordered the construction of HEIJO-KYO. She was followed by her daughter Gensho (680–748 C.E.), and on Gensho's abdication in 724, her nephew Shomu (701–756 C.E.) was enthroned. He was succeeded by his daughter Koken (718–770 C.E.). The opulent life of a highly ranked female aristocrat is clearly seen in the excavations that have uncovered the private residence of Princess Kibi, wife of Prince Nagaya, at Heijo-kyo. Located close to the royal palace, the princess was an extensive landowner, and tribute came to the compound where she lived from all quarters of the Nara state.

INDIA

The social role of women in the early history of India is best assessed on the basis of the SAMHITAS, the sacred hymns of the Hindu. The oldest of these, the RIG VEDA, incorporates hymns that were composed by woman priestesses, known as *brahmavadinis*. The lives of women are also richly illustrated in the RAMAYANA and the MAHA-BHARATA. Here, we find women such as Anasuya, wife of the sage Atri, who through meditation and self-privation reached the heights of spiritual enlightenment. Low-caste women, too, such as Sramani Sabari, were able to reach a high spiritual plane through self denial. The most notable of all women in Indian literature, however, is Sita. Seized by the giant Ravana, Sita was held captive until freed by the hero Rama after the Battle of Lanka. Rama then required Sita to undergo an ordeal to test her purity before the couple returned for their coronation in Ayodhya. These ideals were tarnished with time, and in the notable *Manu Samhita,* (Laws of Manis) the author has much to say on the status of women. Since it has had a long and profound influence on Hindu conduct over the centuries, the contents are a vital source. Manu, while advocating the importance of women in the household, also stated that they should at all times be protected, whether by father, husband, or son, at various stages of their lives. Marriage, in which the father took a prominent part in securing a husband for his daughter, did not admit divorce. In one statement, Manu said that "women were not fit for freedom." However, PANINI, writing in the fourth century B.C.E., noted that the word for wife, *patni*, meant "one who shared religious ceremonies with her husband."

SOUTHEAST ASIA

As far back as the prehistoric period, women were accorded degrees of wealth similar to men's in mortuary rituals. While men were often interred with weaponry, both men and women wore rich and often exotic jewelry. NOEN U-LOKE, an Iron Age site in northeast Thailand, has furnished 126 graves, often clustered into what appear to be family groups. One woman was interred with gold, agate, bronze, and silver beads and bangles. Women continued to play a central role in early states. Indeed, the evidence from INSCRIPTIONS indicates a matrilineal system of inheritance whereby a man was succeeded by his sister's son. During the period of the CHENLA kingdoms (550–800 C.E.), there is compelling evidence of women's assuming positions of the highest possible status. An inscription dated to 639 C.E. from the Mekong Delta cites a woman with the title *kanhen vrah an lan gus*, which can be translated as queen or princess. A text of 803 C.E. was set up by a queen of Sambhupura, whose mother and grandmother also had the royal title *kanhen kamraten an*. JAYAVARMAN I OF CHENLA (c. 635–80 C.E.) was succeeded by his daughter, Jayadevi, who ruled in the region of ANGKOR in Cambodia. Her sister, Sobhajaya, bore the title *ge klon*, which was accorded high-status women, some of whom are recorded as donating meritorious gifts to temples. *Tan* is a title given to minor temple officiants, who were often women whose duties included the recording of holy days and offering of flowers and perfume to the gods. The Chenla inscriptions contain lists of those serving the temple in the capacity of perfume grinders and rice-field workers. Women are listed in considerable numbers. women continued to be assigned to temple duties during the Angkorian period, but the records also make it clear that some continued to wield considerable wealth, power, and influence. In the great stela of the PHIMEANAKAS, for example, Indradevi described the meritorious gifts and good works of her sister, Queen Jayarajadevi. The queen had given gold ritual vessels and statues to her husband's temple foundations and founded a safe haven for 100 girls abandoned by their mothers. In 1296–97, ZHOU DAGUAN visited Angkor and described many scenes involving women. He noted that they were active in the marketplace and returned to work only a day or two after giving birth. Beautiful girls were sent to the palace, he said, and his description of the court included many references to women retainers and even female armed guards.

Wu, King (d. c. 1043 B.C.E.) *King Wu was the first ruler of the Western Zhou dynasty.*
The LI GUI incorporates an important INSCRIPTION recording the victory of Wu over the last Shang emperor at the BATTLE OF MUYE in 1045 B.C.E. Wu had a reign of only three years. SIMA QIAN's account of this overthrow of the SHANG STATE contained in his *SHIJI* is graphic. The last Shang emperor had lost the MANDATE OF HEAVEN through his lustful and sadistic behavior. Leading members of the nobility who displeased him were roasted on a rack or cut into strips of meat. He ordered bacchanalian orgies that lasted deep into the night. Emperor Chow of Shang, dressed in his jade suit, was immolated when he jumped into a fire. Wu, son of King Wen of Zhou (r. 1099–1043 B.C.E.), bided his time before the final and successful attack on the Shang. His reign was brief. The *Shangshu* says that only two years after his conquest of Shang, the king became sick and uncomfortable. The duke of Zhou undertook divinations leading to an improvement, but then Wu died. A similar series of events is recorded in the second-century B.C.E. text known as the *Huainanzi*, stating that the king reigned for three years only.

Wucheng The importance of Wucheng and the associated XIN'GAN burial lies in documenting a major center of civilization contemporary with, but different from, that of the Shang in the central plains of the Huang (Yellow) River. Until sites such as SANXINGDUI in Sichuan and Wucheng were discovered, the SHANG STATE (1766–1045 B.C.E.) was seen as the sole center of early Chinese civilization. It is clear that the middle reaches of the Chang (Yangtze) River Valley sustained an equally impressive civilization based on the cultivation of rice.

Wucheng is a settlement site located near the Gan River in Jiangxi province, China. It was discovered in 1973. Excavations there have uncovered evidence for a sophisticated BRONZE-CASTING tradition involving the casting of tools and weapons in stone and ceramic molds. The typology of the artifacts dates this activity to the second half of the second millennium B.C.E. Ceramic vessels of the same period were inscribed with written symbols, but these cannot be deciphered. The middle-period ceramics from Wucheng are virtually identical to the vessels from the spectacular tomb of Xin'gan, located 20 kilometers (12 mi.) away, discovered in 1989. The Xin'gan burial, the second richest of its date in China, falls in the 13th century B.C.E., immediately before the establishment of ANYANG as the Shang capital.

Wudi (Liu Che; Martial Emperor) (157–87 B.C.E.) *Wudi was one of the greatest emperors of the Western Han dynasty of China.*
He was aged only 16 on the death of his father and was to rule China for 54 years. His reign witnessed a series of fundamental changes. With a long and relatively peaceful internal situation and the inheritance of a stable, prosperous agricultural system, Wudi's ministers embarked on a series of major territorial expansions. The major thrust was to the northwest, where the Gansu Corridor and land beyond to DUNHUANG and the Jade Gate were absorbed and new commanderies formed. This gave the Han easy access to the SILK ROAD, and with new state sponsored caravans-trade greatly expanded. To secure this frontier region, veterans were settled in new agricultural colonies, and many of the settlers were granted honorific titles. The records of these settlers have partially survived in the form of written documents. The GREAT WALL was extended as far as Dunhuang, and for a period the XIONGNU were held at bay. The emperor then dispatched his envoy ZHANG QIAN on two great journeys of discovery along the Silk Road as far as BACTRIA and SOGDIANA. Expansion also proceeded in a northeasterly direction into Korea, where four new commanderies were established. To the south, the strategic and mineral-rich land of Yunnan was taken, and the local leaders given honorific Chinese titles and seals. The Yuan (Red) River Delta up to the Truong Son foothills was likewise invaded by Han armies, and commanderies were established. The cost of imperial expansion, no less than the extravagances of the central court, took their toll. Internal conflicts increased in the years before Wudi's death.

ADMINISTRATION

This process of imperial expansion entailed the need to provide good administrators. In 136 B.C.E. official posts were established for academicians, and the major Confucian texts were identified as basic for the instruction of officials trainees. Twelve years later, 50 such trainees a year were sent to study Confucian notions of government before joining the bureaucracy. The role of provincial administrators in the 84 commanderies was complex and included the provision of written reports, implementation of government policy, and taking of censuses, for the military expansion and the maintenance of an army required new measures of taxation. There was a poll tax and imposts on market transactions and agricultural production. Where the iron and salt industries had been organized on the basis of private enterprise, Wudi nationalized them and appointed former entrepreneurs as government administrators. The issuing of currency also became a state monopoly, and he took control of the marketing of alcohol.

Local Rulers

Although 18 kingdoms continued to exist, their role decreased with the growth of newly created commanderies. After a rebellion, the kingdom of Huai Nan was dissolved. There were, however, many honorific ranks that were liberally used to reward loyalty, and many marquisates, the highest such rank, were created. The wealth and style of the local rulers are clearly reflected in the Mancheng tomb of Liu Sheng, whose mortuary suit had more than 2,000 jade tabs stitched together with gold. Wudi himself emerges from the contemporary records as a man who participated in civil ceremonials, but whose precise role in the administration might have been remote. He poured resources into the construction of magnificent palaces and pleasure gardens and became obsessed with the attainment of immortality. Diviners and magicians who satisfied him were given estates, gold, and even a royal daughter in marriage.

END OF WUDI'S REIGN

Increased taxation fostered rural discontent, and the long reign, involving many consorts and descendants, fostered rivalries over preferment and the succession. In 90 B.C.E. increasing banditry was recorded. In 91 B.C.E. these rivalries led to open conflict, and the Wei family, relatives of the empress, were virtually exterminated, and the empress herself was required to commit suicide. Three years later, there was an attempt to assassinate the emperor himself. The powerful Li family also practically died out after the loss of one of their number in a battle against the Xiongnu. In 87 B.C.E. Wudi fell into a terminal decline, and one of his leading councillors, Huo

Gang, took a leading role in determining the succession. One of the foremost considerations was to identify a son of the emperor who was not associated with any of the rival factions, and the choice fell on the eight-year-old Liu Fuling. Under the control of a powerful triumvirate who included Huo Gang, the new emperor, ZHAODI, succeeded in 87 B.C.E.

The emperor was interred, as befitted his exalted status and long reign, in a huge funerary complex at Maoling, near Xi'an. The mound covering his tomb measures 480 by 414 meters (528 by 455 yds.) and was surrounded by a wall six meters (19.8 ft.) thick. Written reports indicate that up to 5,000 people were permitted to live in the funerary park to tend the gardens and guard the tomb not only of the emperor, but also of the many aristocrats buried in his vicinity. The tomb itself, which has not been opened, may have suffered looting during the periods of unrest that followed the end of the HAN DYNASTY in the third century C.E..

Wu Guang (late third century B.C.E.) *Wu Guang was, according to the* SHIJI (Records of the Grand Historian) *and the* Hanshu (History of the Former Han), *one of two peasants who instigated a revolt against the second Qin emperor in 209 B.C.E.*
After the institution of a centralized repressive dictatorship by QIN SHIHUANGDI, thus forming the first Chinese Empire in 221 B.C.E., the common people were moved by imperial whim to different parts of the empire to undertake construction work as on the GREAT WALL or to fulfill garrison duties. Wu Guang and his fellow peasant CHEN SHE were assigned garrison duties but were delayed from arriving at their destination by heavy rain. Late arrival meant death, so they rose up and killed their commanding officers and fomented a successful revolt that ultimately led to the establishment of the HAN DYNASTY.

Wu state The state of Wu was located in the lower Chang (Yangtze) Valley of China and gained the attention of historians in the late sixth century when it was recorded that the Wu army attacked and defeated the forces of CHU in 506 B.C.E. The lower Chang Valley, rich in agricultural land and minerals, had been prominent in the prehistoric period because of the rich LIANGZHU CULTURE. The concentration of research in the central plains of the Huang (Yellow) River Valley by Chinese archaeologists has often ignored developments in the rice-growing areas to the south. However, from the SHU state of Sichuan through the state of Chu in the middle reaches of the Chang to the delta area dominated by Wu, there were powerful states strong enough to challenge their counterparts formed to the north with the establishment of the WESTERN ZHOU DYNASTY in the late 11th century B.C.E. The Wu had access to rich deposits of copper ore, but tin was scarce. The cast bronzes adopted individual forms,

while some earlier Western Zhou vessel types antedating the "ritual revolution" continued in favor. The lack of bronze was compensated for by adding lead to the castings; many Wu bronzes also contain a high proportion of iron. The ceramic industry, based on a long prehistoric heritage, was also highly proficient, but the hallmark of the Wu specialists lay in the field of weaponry. Wu bronze swords were highly prized and often inlaid with gold inscriptions. These record the names of Wu kings. The local industry was also at the fore in the application of iron to war and industry. Perhaps on the basis of their impressive output of swords and halberds, the Wu state achieved considerable political ascendance. After defeating the mighty state of Chu to the west in 506 B.C.E., Wu became the BA STATE in 482 B.C.E., but nine years later its southern rival, YUE, administered a major defeat while the Wu king was engaged in the north.

It is hardly surprising to find that the mortuary practices and the material culture of Wu, as far as it is currently understood, differed from those of metropolitan Zhou traditions. In contrast to the pit tombs of Zhou, the Wu preferred raising a tumulus over the dead, who were sometimes placed on a bed of stones or in a stone-lined chamber. A substantial mound-burial cemetery has been examined at Jianbi-Dagang on the southern bank of the Chang River in Jiangsu province. It covered the period from the ninth to fifth century B.C.E. and may have been a necropolis of the ruling royal group. Some later tombs are richly furnished, including chariot and horse pits. The major settlements also differ from those characteristic of the central plains. No longer are the beaten earth HANGTU foundations identified at such walled centers as Yancheng, an enigmatic site that incorporates three large tumuli but no obvious remains of occupation sites in the enclosures.

wu xing The notion of *wu xing* is a Chinese philosophical construct meaning "five phases." Five phases or elements are ascribed to the passage of time and the destiny of human beings and dynasties. The origin of this idea in Chinese historic tradition is not known with certainty, but it was a major element in the explanation of the cyclic rise and fall of cosmic and human affairs during the HAN DYNASTY (206 B.C.E.–220 C.E.). It was integrated with the ideas of yin and yang, in which each has a phase of dominance followed by retraction and succession of the other. Objects and animals were deemed to correspond to the five phases and the rise and fall of yin and yang. These began with the rising power of yang, corresponding to wood and a green dragon. There followed the apogee and phase of maturity, corresponding, respectively, to fire and a scarlet bird. The equilibrium between yang and yin was represented by earth, while the rise and apogee of yin were indicated by metal and water, a white tiger, and a turtle. Each phase saw one element supersede its predecessor in the sense that fire burns wood and creates ash or earth, from which metal is extracted in the form of liquid. These concepts are represented on the bronze mirrors placed with the dead in Han tombs as talismans that directed the HUN or spirit of the deceased on the route to the land of the eastern isles or the mother of the west.

See also BO.

Wuyang Wuyang, also known as Xiadu, was a major urban center of the YAN state of northern China. Yan was located north of the central plains, with its main center in the area of Beijing. Wuyang lies between the northern and southern branches of the Yi River in Hebei province. It was occupied from the WESTERN ZHOU DYNASTY (1045–771 B.C.E.) at least until the demise of Yan at the end of the WARRING STATES PERIOD in 222 B.C.E. Wuyang had three distinct enclosed areas that cover about 3,200 hectares (8,000 acres). Little is known of Beijing because of later urban development, but at Wuyang it has been ascertained through excavations that began in 1930 and continued in the 1950s that the two eastern enclosed areas, which are separated by an east-west wall, were earlier than the western city. The latter was probably added late in the Warring States period, and few remains have been identified there. On the other hand, the older city incorporates the foundations for palaces in association with decorated ceramic roof tiles and fine ceramic remains. There are also several cemeteries. One excavated tomb, although long since looted, still yielded many MINGQI pottery vessels imitating bronze forms, as well as the presence of seven *ding* tripods indicating that the deceased was a man of ministerial rank. His other grave offerings included a set of musical instruments, among them bells and chimestones. A second remarkable burial, dated to the late Warring States period, incorporated 22 badly mutilated skeletons associated with individual deposits of iron weapons and Yan state coins. This is thought to have been a war grave containing soldiers who died in battle.

The provision of the best available weaponry to the Yan army, essential during the period of Warring States, is demonstrated in the presence of iron foundries. There were also locations in the old city where bronze mirrors were cast, for the clay molds have been recovered in considerable numbers. The city also contained a mint and bone and ceramic workshops. One site yielded 108 bronze halberds that bore inscriptions naming Yan lords hitherto known only from documentary sources.

See also EASTERN ZHOU DYNASTY.

Xia dynasty The Xia has long been regarded as the first dynasty of China. Knowledge of this mythical state is in the main from the SHIJI (*Records of the Grand Historian*), a work written by the Han scholar SIMA QIAN and completed in 100 B.C.E. Sima Qian devoted considerable space to the Xia in his section on basic annals. The initial events revolved around Yu, the son of Gun, and his achievements. On occasion too fantastic to credit, they nevertheless touched on a series of issues central in the early formation of states. The story began with a serious problem over flooding in the basin of the Huang (Yellow) River. Gun was charged by the emperor to solve this problem, but, after trying for nine years, he failed and was sent into exile. Shun, the emperor, then selected Yu to take on this task on the advice of his vassals and advisers. Yu traveled widely over a period of 13 years, keenly aware that failure would be punished. He traveled in the hills, along rivers, over marshes, and to the seashore. Many of the places mentioned by Sima Qian can be identified on the ground today, from Mount Hukou near the Huang River in Shanxi province to Mount Chi, about 50 kilometers (30 mi.) north of Xi'an, and from Henan to Shandong, south to the mouths of the Chang (Yangtze) River and up the course of that river to Lake Poyang and the marshes of the river's floodplain. His strategy to control flooding involved the digging of channels to expedite the flow of floodwater to the sea, the drainage of marshland, and the creation of reservoirs. One of the most intriguing aspects of this section of the *Shiji* is the catalogue of land quality in each area and of the goods sent by river transport to the capital as tribute.

Shandong sent LACQUER and silk, while the coastal region there supplied salt. The area around Lake Daye in Shandong, which had been turned into a reservoir, fur-

nished soil of five colors for performing ritual sacrifices, along with pheasants, stone for chimes, pearls, and fish. The wet swampy land of the lower Chang sent jade, bamboo for arrow shafts, three kinds of metal thought to have been varieties of bronze, ivory, and animal hide. Joseph Needham has suggested that the hide was from rhinoceros and was destined for use as armor. From the communities of the middle Chang Valley came pheasant feathers, ivory, metals, cinnabar, and large turtles. While rivers were used for transport, Yu also had roads constructed. Once he had resolved the problems of flooding and converted swamps and wasteland to agricultural production, he turned his attention to the region of the capital, ensuring that the storehouses were always full and setting out the tribute requirements in the form of grain. He also divided the capital territories into defensive zones under local client leaders.

For these extraordinary achievements, he was given a black jade commemorative tablet. The emperor Shun recommended Yu as his successor and died 17 years later. While doubtless relying on oral history and many later documents, Sima Qian identified a number of key achievements that credibly were central to the early development of the state in China. These included the organization of defense, the provision of a central surplus to sustain the court, the classification of land, and the organization of taxation through tribute for the necessities to maintain the state.

XIA RULERS

Yu declined the imperial throne and left the capital. But the lords entreated him to return. This he did, and the name of his state was declared as Xia. Sima Qian then traced the line of Xia rulers. Yu had nominated Yi to succeed him, but the lords showed a preference for Yu's son, Qi. When the You-hu clan refused to accept his rule, Qi went to battle and defeated them at Gan, about 25 kilometers (15 mi.) southwest of Xi'an. Qi was succeeded by his son, Taikang. He was followed by his younger brother, Zhongkang, with a dynastic list of rulers from Zhong Kang to his son, Xiang, to his son, Shangkang, and successively to Dishu, Dihuai, Dimang, Dixie, Dibujiang, Dijiong, Diyinjia, and King Dikongjia. There followed a series of revolts against the capital, and the last Xia king, Dilügui, was deposed by Tang of Yin after a dynastic succession lasting more than 400 years (2100–1766 B.C.E.). According to the place names recorded in the *Shiji*, the Xia dynasty was located in western Henan and southern Shanxi provinces.

ARCHAEOLOGICAL EVIDENCE

This history presents an exciting challenge to archaeologists. The physical remains of cities ascribed to the SHANG STATE (1766–1045 B.C.E.) that succeeded Xia at Zhengzhou and ANYANG have been discovered. The question remains, Are there any known sites earlier than the Shang centers that could correspond to the degree of social complexity portrayed in the *Shiji* for the remote Xia dynasty? ERLITOU is a large and important archaeological site that was identified in 1957 during a fieldwork program specifically designed to find archaeological remains of Xia. It is located south of the Huang (Yellow) River in Henan province, and archaeological remains cover the large area of more than 300 hectares (750 acres). Excavations have revealed a buildup of cultural remains almost four meters (about 13 ft.) thick, which has been divided into four major phases of occupation dated in the first half of the second millennium B.C.E. The first two phases yielded remains that are widely matched in sites of the LONGSHAN CULTURE in the Huang River Valley: There are stamped-earth building foundations and rare bronze grave goods, including awls, knives, and bells. Some of the bronzes must have been locally cast, because crucibles were found. The dead were interred with pottery vessels and jade ornaments. Some, however, were cast unceremoniously into rubbish pits.

The third and fourth phases reveal a marked change. Among the most significant discoveries were the foundations of two palaces. The first was located in a walled enclosure 100 meters square (120 sq. yds.). It incorporated a central columned hall overlooking a large courtyard. The second palace followed a similar plan but was rather smaller. In the elite burials the dead were interred in painted wooden coffins, accompanied by a new range of locally cast bronzes. These included the first festive or ritual vessels in the form of a tripod jug, or *jue,* a form that stands at the head of a long sequence of similar forms over the ensuing centuries. These important vessels in the history of Chinese bronze industries were cast

Bronze *jue,* or wine jugs, are a vital component of the bronze industry identified in the later deposits at Erlitou. These are thought to represent the shadowy Xia dynasty. *(© Asian Art & Archaeology, Inc./CORBIS)*

by the piece-mold technique. A typical example stands 13.5 centimeters (5.4 in.) in height. There are also bronze dagger axes and a battle-ax. Jades, including a *yazhang* handled blade, a form that was widely distributed in China during the second half of the second millennium B.C.E., were found. There are also jade knives, dagger axes, and ritual *cong* cylinders. Excavators have recovered several examples of graffiti on pottery vessels that clearly anticipate later Chinese written characters. A sheep's shoulder blade had been used for divination by subjecting it to heat, then reading the portents expressed in the formation of the resulting cracks.

See also ORACLE BONES.

Further reading: Chang, K.-C. *The Shang Civilization.* New Haven, Conn.: Yale University Press, 1980; Fitzgerald-Huber, L. G. "Qijia and Erlitou: The Question of Contacts with Distant Cultures," *Early China* 20 (1995): 17–68; Loewe, M., and E. L. Shaugnessy, eds. *The Cambridge History of Ancient China.* Cambridge: Cambridge University Press, 1999.

Xiajin Xiajin is located in Shanxi province, China, and includes a cemetery of the LONGSHAN CULTURE dating to 2500–2000 B.C.E. As with the huge cemetery of TAOSI in the same region, excavations undertaken in 1997–98 have uncovered hundreds of graves, some of which reveal such marked mortuary wealth as to indicate the establishment of societies on the brink of statehood. There are, for example, individuals buried with ritual jades, large bracelets embellished with chips of TURQUOISE, and in each case a solitary but finely made ceramic vessel with red painted decoration.

xian A *xian* was an administrative subdivision of a Chinese state. The earliest record of such territorial units dates to the Spring and Autumn period (770–476 B.C.E.) of the EASTERN ZHOU DYNASTY, when *xian* were set up in newly conquered territory as a means of putting them under central control. After absorption into the kingdom, they could be given to loyal followers. One of the major states of the period, JIN, employed *xian* in this way. In 350 B.C.E. SHANG YANG instituted *xian* in the rising state of QIN. The entire country was divided into 41 units, each under a magistrate with a staff of administrators. These units were designed to permit tight control over the population. Shang Yang also devised a poll or head tax, which necessitated the creation of a register of the population. The *xian* were the unit from which troops were levied as the conflicts between the Warring States became increasingly totalitarian in nature. The *xian* continued as administrative units during the QIN dynasty (221–206 B.C.E.) and were employed during the HAN DYNASTY (206 B.C.E.–220 C.E.) in the commanderies, or provinces. Under direct central control through the appointment of their administrative staff, the *xian* differed fundamentally from the former system of privately owned noble estates.

Xia Nai (1910–1985) *Xia Nai was the leading archaeologist in China after the establishment of the People's Republic of China in 1949.*
He had studied at Qinghua University in Beijing before winning a scholarship to study overseas. Before proceeding to London, he gained fieldwork experience under LI JI at the SHANG dynasty royal tomb excavations at ANYANG. In London he enrolled in the Department of Egyptology of University College, London, and learned at first hand the latest field techniques under SIR MORTIMER WHEELER at the site of Maiden Castle during the season of 1936. He then gained fieldwork experience in Egypt, where he met Sir Flinders Petrie, arguably the father of modern archaeology. Back in China in 1943 and under the most difficult of circumstances, Xia Nai undertook fieldwork in Gansu, concentrating on Neolithic sites. Faced with the agonizing choice of following many colleagues with the Nationalists to Taiwan or not, he decided to remain, and in 1959 he joined the Communist Party. He conducted a wide range of excavations, including at the rich Ming dynasty (1368–1644) imperial tombs north of Beijing. He gave the first university course on archaeology in China in 1952 and inspired the exhibition "The Genius of China" that drew recent finds to the attention of the West. This generated official opprobrium for a gesture of friendship with the enemy, but he survived and set up the first

radiocarbon dating laboratory in China, a move that was to transform understanding of the past in his country as the first results appeared. He also survived to see the excavations of the tomb of FU HAO, the Shang princess, at ANYANG; the tomb of the second king of Nan Yue; and the opening of the terra-cotta army pits at Mount Li. His impact on Chinese archaeology is unrivaled.

Xiandi (Liu Xie; Dedicating Emperor) (181–234 C.E.) *Xiandi was the 12th and last emperor of the Eastern Han dynasty of China.*
He was the son of Emperor Lingdi and acceded to the throne in 189 C.E. Xiandi ascended the throne amid chaos and conflict with the help of General Dong Zhuo, but his power did not outlast the death of Dong Zhuo in 192. In 220 C.E. Xiandi abdicated. The choice of Xiandi, whose natal name was Liu Xie, was made in competition with his older brother, Liu Bian. At first the choice fell on Liu Bian, who was accorded the title *xiandi*. There followed a chaotic palace coup, during the course of which the eunuchs were surrounded in the northern palace at LUOYANG and exterminated. Their leader, Zhang Rang, managed to escape the carnage, taking with him the two young half brothers, the older of whom was the titular emperor Sundi. Dong Zhuo, a general of the army, now took a hand in determining events. Arriving in the capital and finding a shambles, with the eunuchs dead and the emperor missing, he set out in search of Sundi. He finally found the two boys and interrogated them about what had been happening. There follows a story engrained in Chinese folklore. The older boy, Sundi, in fear of Dong Zhuo and his army, fell silent. But Liu Xie explained that they had wandered aimlessly during the night and then taken refuge in a peasant's cart before meeting Dong Zhuo. The general returned the two to Luoyang and arranged for the younger of the two, Liu Xie, to replace his older brother as emperor with the title *xiandi*. He then took for himself the title minister of works and had the empress removed and killed.

Former high officials who had left Luoyang during the coup now began to marshal their forces against Dong Zhuo, but the latter held a trump card in the person of the emperor and control of the capital. He had the members of rival families exterminated, and the former emperor, Sundi, who could be used as a rallying cry for opposition groups, was murdered. In 190, Dong Zhuo resolved to send the emperor and his court back to the old HAN DYNASTY capital at CHANG'AN for reasons of security, and he had Luoyang, including the precious imperial library, destroyed. Dong Zhuo himself moved to Chang'an, but in 192 he was killed, and the only semblance of central authority based on the person of the emperor evaporated. Against a background of anarchy and chaos, Xiandi returned with his retinue and wife to Luoyang in 196 C.E. At this juncture, it is possible to recognize at least eight regional warlords in charge of different parts of the empire.

It was within the warlords' areas of influence that the Han dynasty was laid to rest, and its three successors would emerged. One of the warlords, Cao, had managed to secure the person of Xiandi, and his daughter was married to the young emperor.

Xianggang *See* ZHAO HU.

Xiasi Xiasi is an important cemetery of the CHU state of Henan province, China, which dates to the period between about 575 and 490 B.C.E. The excavations have revealed many important aspects of Chu political and social organization during the Spring and Autumn period (770–476 B.C.E.). For example, the principal graves, set out in a linear disposition and in a chronological sequence, contained the remains of high-ranking members of the Yuan lineage. The members of this line were of sufficiently high status to marry into the ruling families of dependent states of Chu. They referred to themselves as Chu Shuzhisun, meaning the descendants of a junior line of the Chu royal family. While some of the nine major tombs have been damaged by looting, sufficient remains to identify in Tomb 2 the burial of Yuan Zi Feng, who acted in the capacity of chief minister to the king of Chu in 552–548 B.C.E. His tomb furniture stands out because of the quantity and quality of offerings. It contains a lost-wax casting of an altar unique to this period both in the technique of manufacture and in the ornate nature of the ornamentation. A second innovation in BRONZE CASTING is seen in the use of metal inlay. This tomb incorporated 26 bells of graded sizes, suspended by lead ropes to their frame. It is a set of extraordinary musical sophistication that sounded more than five octaves. The bells were made for Wangsun Gao, the grandson of the Chu king, and their INSCRIPTION described his dedication to the then king and extolled his many virtues. The bells were described as "long-vibrating and sonorous, with a fine loud sound." They can still be played.

The ritual and sumptuary bronzes were also of a higher quality than those of the remainder of the burials and probably originated as gifts from the court during his period of royal service. His burial is surrounded by 15 graves containing the remains of sacrificial victims and three other tombs designated for his consorts. A further pit contained his chariots and horses.

See also CHARIOTS AND CHARIOT BURIALS.

Xibeigang Xibeigang, on the northern bank of the Huan River, is the site of the SHANG STATE (1766–1045 B.C.E.) royal graves of ANYANG. There are two sections, an eastern and a western. Excavation that began in 1933 uncovered seven graves in the western section, each equipped with four entrance ramps, and one square

unfinished tomb. One hundred thirty meters (429 ft.) to the east lay five further tombs, one with four entrance ramps, three with two ramps, and a single grave with one ramp. While all the graves have been long since looted, some corners that escaped destruction reveal the wealth that they would once have contained. A cache in Tomb 1004 incorporated 360 spear points and 141 bronze helmets.

Xin dynasty In 9 C.E., WANG MANG, formerly regent of the Western HAN DYNASTY and marquis of Xindu, pronounced himself emperor of China and first ruler of the Xin dynasty (New dynasty). Wang Mang was related to the Han royal line in that his father was the brother-in-law of the emperor YUANDI (49–33 B.C.E.). The dynastic name has not been recognized by subsequent historians, and indeed the period up to the death of Wang Mang in 23 C.E. is usually described as the interregnum between the Western and Eastern Han dynasties. Nevertheless, Wang Mang attempted serious reforms, particularly in the area of land tenure, by nationalizing land ownership and abolishing slavery. This policy was designed to reduce the power of the great landowning families and reinstate the old WELL-FIELD SYSTEM, in which peasants owned a block of land and paid a proportion of their produce to the state. He also adopted strict control over expenditure, thus accumulating a reputed 140,000 kilograms (308,000 lbs.) of gold, a policy that had a wide impact, even as far west as the Roman Empire. However, his reforms created many powerful enemies, and when he was murdered in 23 C.E., the Xin dynasty came to an end.

Xin'gan Xin'gan is a remarkable archaeological site located on the east side of the Gan River in Jiangxi province, China. This river flows north and empties into Lake Poyang. The discovery there in 1989 of an exceedingly rich and intact tomb dated to the same period as the SHANG capital at ANYANG (1200–1045 B.C.E.) has caused a radical reconsideration of the distribution of early Chinese states. The grave, which measured 10.6 by 3.6 meters (35 by 12 ft.), is slightly earlier than that of FU HAO at Anyang and is second only to that royal tomb in terms of the quantity and wealth of its mortuary offerings, including bronze vessels that show local features in form and decoration. The discovery of the Xin'gan tomb has revealed a powerful early polity south of the Chang (Yangtze) River that indicates that parallel developments toward early states took place in different parts of China and redresses the dominance long held by the central plains. The Shang looked south for the supplies of turtle plastrons to be used in ORACLE-BONE divinations. The rich resources of copper ore locally available here could well have underwritten the wealth evidenced at this site.

The grave shaft was stepped inward to provide space to house funerary offerings and contained hints of the existence of two lacquered coffins. No bones remained, but a jade necklace indicated where the body would probably have lain. It contains hundreds of ceramic vessels, 150 jades apart from the jade beads, and 475 bronzes. Of these, about half were weapons, while there were also 50 vessels and four bells. Three of these, the *nao* form, typify this southern region and add distinctiveness to its early bronze repertoire. The bronzes do not slavishly follow Shang forms but reveal distinctive local features, such as the casting of tigers onto the handles of bronze vessels. Tigers were popular features of this BRONZE-CASTING tradition. One bronze tiger, with open mouth and impressive canine teeth, stands to a height of 25 centimeters (9.6 in.), and was accompanied by a bird perched on its back. A horned bronze mask 53 centimeters (21.2 in.) high is not readily matched in northern contexts. In addition to their designs and decorative elements different from those of the Shang repertoire, the forms of the RITUAL BRONZE VESSELS present intriguing differences, with an emphasis on serving food rather than pouring wine. Some vessels reached impressive sizes, the tallest, a *yan* steamer, standing a little more than one meter in height. It differs from northern equivalents in having four legs rather than three, and its handles were embellished with male animals. The grave was equipped with a large assemblage of bronze weaponry, made up of spears, dagger-axes, knives, arrowheads, and a single heavy bronze helmet embellished with a raised mask. A small circular projection above would probably have held a plume of some sort.

The weight of research on the early dynasties of Chinese civilization has been in the central plains, with particular reference to the XIA and Shang states documented in early histories such as the *SHIJI*, and archaeologically verified by the discoveries at ERLITOU, ZHENGZHOU, and ANYANG. Any bronzes found beyond this core region have been considered Shang exports or peripheral settlements. At SANXINGDUI a large city containing sacrificial pits has documented a second early state center, characterized by bronzes and jades of local distinctiveness. The discovery of a city site at WUCHENG, about 20 kilometers (12 mi.) west of Xin'gan, in 1973 revealed a major center contemporary with the late Shang state. Xin'gan is in all probability the royal necropolis of this early state. In conjunction the two sites confirm the development of civilization south of the Chang (Yangtze) River.

Xintian Xintian is a huge urban complex located at the confluence of the Kuai and Fen Rivers in Shanxi province, China. It was founded by Duke Jinggong of the state of JIN in 585 B.C.E. and remained the capital until 369 B.C.E., when Duke Huangong was forcibly evicted by the forces of the states of Han and Zhou. The site, documented in early historic accounts, was discovered in 1956. It has been the object of major excavations over a lengthy period. Xintian includes a core of walled cities together with specialist industrial areas, extramural cemeteries, and ritual pits. The major walled area, known as Pingwang, formed a nearly square area covering about 100 hectares (250 acres). Raised *HANGTU* (stamped-earth) foundations within were probably the foundations for palace and temple structures, a feature of which was the trend toward raising the palace to provide a visible profile symbolizing the power of the overlord. One of the distinctive features of Xintian was the existence of such craft centers. Several were dedicated to BRONZE CASTING, and the clay molds for casting a wide range of RITUAL BRONZE VESSELS have been recovered. Many molds indicate the casting of swords and arrowheads, while chariot fittings were locally manufactured. One mold set had been made to cast a bronze axle. The concentration of mold fragments dedicated to one form of artifact shows that even in these workshops specialization prevailed: One area was concerned with casting of coins, another with belt buckles. The demand for copper, lead, and tin must have been considerable, and the output was a measure of the power and reach of the Jin rulers. The expertise of their specialists can be seen in such vessels as the *zheng* that was cast to commemorate the marriage of the daughter of Duke Pinggong in 537 B.C.E. Not only a fine bronze in its own right, it was further embellished with gold inlay. There were also specific areas for the manufacture of bone artifacts and ceramic vessels.

AREAS OUTSIDE THE MAJOR AREA

Taishen and Niacun are two further and slightly larger enclosures lying just to the south of Pingwang, thought to have been added to accommodate lesser families of the ruling group, and still more walled areas containing stamped-earth foundations were designated for members of ministerial families. The majority of the populace lived outside these reserved areas, and many of them would have been engaged in specialist workshops. At the Beiwu settlement, three vast granaries have been uncovered, as well as many foundations of domestic structures that incorporated ovens, drainage facilities, and underground storage pits.

CEMETERY AND SACRIFICIAL PITS

The cemetery of Shangmacun at Xintian has also been examined through archaeology and found to contain a wide range of burials in terms of wealth. One of the richest took the form of a deep pit containing a wooden chamber. Within lay the human remains in a lacquered coffin, together with 180 bronze vessels, jades, ceramic vessels, and bronze bells. The spears and halberds suggest that this interment, which dates to the late Spring and Autumn period, contained the remains of a man. Ritual practices associated with a massive temple building dedicated to the Jin ancestors included sacrificial pits containing the remains of horses, cattle, sheep, and, occasionally, humans. A further area was dedicated to the excavation of pits to incorporate animals sacrificed as part of a ceremony known as *zaishu*. This, according to surviving literary sources, involved sacrificing animals during the swearing of oaths of allegiance. Cattle, horses, sheep, and chickens were placed in pits up to six meters (19.8 ft.) deep, and the text of the oath, inscribed or painted on jade, was placed over them. The texts themselves provide an insight into historical events such as a dispute within the Zhao family that erupted in 497 B.C.E. Loyalty to the leader entailed an oath promising not to indulge in magic rites or communion with the rival group for fear of divine retribution. The research undertaken at Xintian has illuminated the size and grandeur of the capital of Jin during the EASTERN ZHOU DYNASTY (770–221 B.C.E.), before it was abandoned during the rule of Duke Huangong in 369 B.C.E.

Xinzheng Xinzheng was a major center of the state of ZHAO in China; after its defeat at the hands of the HAN DYNASTY in 375 B.C.E., it became the capital of the Han state. As is often the case with cities of the Western and Eastern Zhou, it lay between two rivers. It is a substantial city with two walled precincts. Stamped-earth walls survive up to a height of 18 meters (59.4 ft.). The old city, which lies to the west of the complex, incorporated a substantial palace and many house foundations. The later eastern addition was probably walled to afford protection to the specialist bronze, iron, ceramic, bone, and jade workshops that had formerly lain beyond the city walls. One part of the wall, for example, loops round a massive bronze foundry that covered 10 hectares (25 acres). It had been used to cast production tools. The WARRING STATES PERIOD ironworks, also found in the western area, covered almost half that area and had been used not only for production tools, but also for manufacture of iron swords and halberds.

See also EASTERN ZHOU DYNASTY; WESTERN ZHOU DYNASTY.

Xiongnu The Xiongnu were a tribal confederation of pastoralists who occupied the Mongolian grasslands to the northwest of the GREAT WALL of China. The name is Chinese and, pejoratively, means "fierce slave." Much information about them is from Chinese histories and archaeological discoveries. As long as they were divided into 24 competing tribes, the Xiongnu did not present a major threat to China. But toward the end of the third century B.C.E. the leader Touman began to form a confederacy, a trend consolidated by his son, MAODUN, who became the *shanyu* (great leader), in 209 B.C.E., after killing his father with a bow and arrow. Much has been learned about the Xiongnu through archaeological research. The graves reveal the wealth of the Xiongnu through the imported and local grave offerings. These include Chinese LACQUER; beads of malachite, amber, and glass; tiny pyrite crystals pierced for attachment to clothing; and fine bronze vessels.

ANCESTORS OF XIONGNU

The ancestors of the Xiongnu described in the HAN DYNASTY Chinese histories are archaeologically documented through the slab graves of Mongolia. These burials are so called because the dead were interred, usually with the head pointing to the rising Sun, within a wall of upright stone slabs. Sometimes a stone column decorated with animal motifs was also set on the grave. The graves, dating to the period 700–300 B.C.E., included many artifacts that reveal far-flung trade, including cowry shells and jades of Chinese origin. Ceramic vessels were also placed into graves, as well as animal bones that indicate the maintenance of domestic horses, cattle, and sheep. These people were essentially nomadic pastoralists who also cast fine bronzes and forged iron weapons.

XIONGNU CONSOLIDATION

The Xiongnu began to pose an immediate problem for the Chinese after the rise of Maodun, which led to the construction of the Great Wall of China under Emperor QIN SHIHUANGDI. In 214 B.C.E. this emperor also sent a large military force, said to number 100,000, against the Xiongnu under General Meng Tian. As with all later campaigns, the soldiers had to face vast distances, cold, problems of supply, and a mobile, well-organized enemy. The Xiongnu had developed their cavalry to a fine pitch of skill. They had hardy steppe horses from which they wielded large composite bows.

EXCAVATIONS OF BURIALS AND SETTLEMENTS

Four major cemeteries have been excavated, and hundreds of graves opened at Khunui-göl in the upper reaches of the Orchon River in central Mongolia near Cecerleg, at Noin-Ula, north of Ulaan baatar, and at Sudzhinsk and Derestui, south of Lake Baikal. The burial ground at Khunui-göl is thought to contain the grave of Maodun himself. One of the most important individual burials from Noin-Ula was excavated in 1924. It is very large, measuring 24.5 meters (80 ft.) on each side, and the wooden coffins, preserved in the dry and cold conditions, were decorated with painted lacquer. These had been placed on a fine felt carpet decorated with animal designs. This was the tomb of the *shanyu* Wuzhu lü, who died in the early first century C.E. One grave contained a bronze crown depicting the head of a wolf. There are felt carpets with fine animal and abstract designs, Chinese silks, and Western fabric showing the influence of Gandharan art. Archaeology has also shown how the development of a powerful steppe empire influenced settlement patterns, for several large fortified settlements have been found, as at Gua-Dov and Ivolgnisk east of Lake Baikal. Under the *shanyu* Zhi-zhi, a fort was built at Talas that is said to have been influenced by Roman mercenaries who had gravitated east after their defeat at Carrhae in 53 B.C.E. The Xiongnu also developed their own legal system and a script.

SIMA QIAN'S DESCRIPTION OF XIONGNU

It was natural that the Grand Han historian SIMA QIAN should devote a chapter of his history to these people who exercised such a profound influence on Han foreign policy. He described their nomadic way of life, in which they herded their cows and sheep and hunted with bows and arrows from horseback. He was struck by the way in which young boys learned to fire bows and arrows at hares and birds from a tender age, developing hunting and fighting skills as they grew up. After describing the long and difficult relations between the Chinese and the Xiongnu since the days of the remote XIA DYNASTY, he concentrated on the rise to power of the great leader Maodun, a *shanyu* who was to play a prominent part in the foreign relations of the early Han dynasty. Maodun's father, Touman, favoring his younger son for the succession, had sent Maodun as a hostage to the Yuezhi. Touman then attacked the Yuezhi, anticipating that they would murder Maodun in retribution. Maodun escaped and was placed in charge of 10,000 Xiongnu cavalry in recognition of his bravery. He developed a whistling arrow and trained his men to fire their own arrows at all his chosen targets on pain of death if they disobeyed. Many were killed when they hesitated to fire after Maodun first shot his arrow at a favorite horse and then at his major wife. Having trained the remainder in implicit obedience, he fired at and killed his father and then murdered the court nobility. It was this fiery spirit that the first Han emperor, GAOZU, had to contend with.

According to Sima Qian, just as Gaozu, the founder and first emperor of the Western Han dynasty, established himself after a period of upheaval, Maodun became the *shanyu* of the Xiongnu. The military expertise and unified following forged by Maodun created an immediate threat to the security of the Han empire, and a confrontation was inevitable. In 200 B.C.E. Gaozu led his army in person, and he was surrounded and defeated at the Battle of Pingcheng. The emperor managed to escape capture but thereafter changed his policy toward to the Xiongnu to one of diplomacy. A treaty was signed with four major provisions. The first was that a royal Han princess should be sent to the Xiongnu in a marriage alliance. She should be accompanied by expensive gifts of silk and food, and the two states should be recognized as equals. Finally it was agreed that their mutual border should be the Great Wall of China. This treaty, which in effect was a means of reducing the Xiongnu threat through gifts and bribery, was renewed on many occasions, always entailing an increased quantity of gifts from the Han, including pieces of gold. Maodun died in 174 B.C.E. and was succeeded by his son, Ji Zhu, who ruled until 160 B.C.E., and then by Jun Chen (r. 160–126 B.C.E.).

Until 134 B.C.E. the Xiongnu both accepted the gifts of the Han emperor and sent raids south of the Great Wall with relative impunity. However, the forceful emperor WUDI in 134 B.C.E. reversed this policy and sent his armies against the Xiongnu. Successful campaigns in 127, 121, and 119 B.C.E. saw the Han throw back the Xiongnu and establish new commanderies in the western regions. In the period between these setbacks and 52 B.C.E., military defeats were exacerbated by internal dissension. The Xiongnu splintered into rival groups, and at one stage there were as many as five claiming the title *shanyu*. At the same time, the magnificent and valued gifts from the Han court dried up, and there were problems with the Han succession, for under the system of primogeniture it was possible for very young boys to succeed. This might be possible under the Han court system with its entrenched regencies, but it was not adaptive for relations with the steppes. Many attempts to renew the marriage alliance system were rebuffed by the Han, because they insisted that the *shanyu* pay homage to the emperor and accept the status of a client state. However, the situation was reversed in 52–51 B.C.E. when the *shanyu* Huhanye decided to accept Chinese terms and traveled personally to Xi'an.

The terms involved sending Huhanye's son to the Han court as a hostage and paying homage to the emperor. He was treated with considerable respect and was not required to prostrate himself. On the contrary, he returned home laden with gifts, including five kilograms (11 lbs.) of gold, 77 suits of clothes, 8,000 bales of silk cloth, and 1,500 kilograms of silk floss. Attracted by such expensive gifts, he expressed a wish to repeat the ceremony two years later and was given even more in return. On each such occasion until the end of the dynasty, the gifts increased in quantity until in 1 B.C.E., 30,000 bales of silk cloth changed hands. These gifts, a serious drain on Han resources, served to maintain peace on the northwest frontier and enhance trade along the SILK ROAD. The situation changed dramatically for the Xiongnu with the WANG MANG interregnum and the political turmoil in China during the civil wars that preceded the establishment of the Eastern Han dynasty. From 18 to 48 C.E., Yu became the *shanyu* and not only spurned the new dynasty's attempts to revert to the client relationship, but had an alleged descendant of Emperor WUDI declared emperor in the northern region of China so that the puppet ruler could pay him homage. This episode was short lived, however. The Xiongnu were now divided into southern and northern groups.

In 50 C.E. the *shanyu* Bi, leader of the southern group, again paid homage to the Han emperor. The act of prostration was well rewarded, for he returned home with 36,000 cattle, 10,000 bales of silk cloth, rice, and an official gold SEAL. Thereafter, annual payments to the southern Xiongnu were regularized, reaching in 91 C.E. the sum of 100 million cash, according to the administrator

Yuan An. The nomads were also brought in to settle south of the Great Wall, alongside Chinese communities, in an attempt at assimilation. The Northern Xiongnu, however, were not recognized and were treated as a potential enemy.

Further reading: Loewe, M., and E. L. Shaugnessy, eds. *The Cambridge History of Ancient China*. Cambridge: Cambridge University Press, 1999; Psarras, S.-K. "Xiongnu Culture: Identification and Dating," *Central European Journal* 39 (1995): 102–136.

Xuandi (Liu Bingyi; Proclaimed Emperor) (74–49 B.C.E.)
Xuandi was a grandson of the Han dynasty emperor Wudi, who succeeded Zhaodi as emperor in 74 B.C.E.

In the aftermath of the expansionary policy of WUDI, Xuandi's reign was marked by retrenchment and remission of taxation. Thus the office in charge of music, founded under Wudi, was first reduced in scope in 70 B.C.E. The reins of power were in the hands of the minister Huo Gang and his family. Intent on maintaining its position, the family arranged that the pregnant empress be poisoned and replaced by one of its own. After the death of Huo Gang, knowledge of the plot to poison the empress leaked out, and the Huo family, formerly all-powerful, was virtually eliminated when it was discovered that it had planned treason.

The *History of the Former Han* (HANSHU) is a major source of information on this reign. It describes discussions on policy after the huge expansion under Wudi. It was resolved to maintain a hold on the new northwestern territories through agricultural settlement rather than military expeditions, and there was even a partial withdrawal from Korea. More old kingdoms were replaced by new commanderies or subdivided into small realms so that the political map now showed scattered islands of kingdoms in a broad sea of commanderies. These new policies, labeled "reformist," characterized the reign of Xuandi.

Xuanzang (602–664 C.E.) *Xuanzang was a Chinese Buddhist monk who traveled as a pilgrim to the holy places of India and Central Asia and translated the Buddhist texts from Sanskrit into Chinese.*

While living in Sichuan as a recent convert to BUDDHISM, he was concerned by contradictions in the texts available to him and decided to leave China in 629 C.E. to visit the major Indian monasteries. His route, devious because of the lack of a permit, took him along the SILK ROAD to Samarqand, then south to BACTRIA and northwest India. He took a boat to travel down the Ganges (Ganga) and visited MATHURA. His travels in India were extensive, but he spent most time at the Buddhist university center of NALANDA. He returned to the Chinese capital after an absence of 16 years accompanied by a large collection of manuscripts central to Buddhist thought and spent the balance of his life engaged in their translation. He also wrote an account of his travels, describing the countries, peoples, and customs of the places he visited, a vital source of information to this day.

XUANZANG'S EXPERIENCES
At Tokmak he had been the guest of the great khan of the Western Turks. He was treated as an honored guest, and after a banquet attended by 200 of the khan's bodyguards dressed in fine embroidered silks, he spoke to the assembled guests on Buddhist doctrine. In Tokharistan he described the Hephthalite script as being written from left to right, a reference to a script ultimately rooted in the BACTRIAN GREEK system of 500 years earlier. Of the Hephthalites themselves he noted that they controlled a considerable area, including walled cities, but that some also lived in felt tents and moved from place to place.

It is remarkable to have an eyewitness account of BALKH, one of the major centers of the Hephthalite empire, which he described as being strongly fortified, but with a low population. There were about 100 monasteries there and more than 3,000 Buddhist monks. At BAMIYAN he wondered at the colossal statues of the Buddha carved into the mountainside, now destroyed after the Taliban dynamited them, and noted 10 monasteries there supporting 1,000 monks. Of Kapisa he wrote: "It produces cereals of all sorts, and many kinds of fruit trees." There was a flourishing trade, for which the Kapisans used gold, silver, and copper coins. At Kuga he described the royal palace as shining in its decoration of gold and jade.

Some of his most interesting comments involved visits to particularly revered places, and his descriptions of ruined or deserted cities make him virtually the first person to engage in field archaeology in India. He found PATALIPUTRA, the old capital of the MAURYA EMPIRE, in a ruined condition with only the foundations of the former monasteries visible. He also made a pilgrimage to the site of the *bodhi* tree where the Buddha had found enlightenment. The brick walls surrounding the location were high and 500 paces in circumference, he said. There were a large monastery beyond the northern gate and a flower pool beside the southern entrance. The tree itself was still there but had suffered damage and was not as high as it had once been. Each year, on the anniversary of the enlightenment, kings and monks and a multitude of people irrigated the tree with perfumed water and made offerings.

On his return to China after an absence of 16 years, he had hundreds of precious documents and relics of the Buddha. A notable mural from MOGAO dating to the Tang dynasty shows him on his return journey, accompanied by a highly auspicious white elephant. Officially welcomed at DUNHUANG, he visited the Mogao caves and then carried on to the capital, CHANG'AN. For the remaining two decades of his life, he translated the texts he had returned with into Chinese, and these have become classics of Buddhist literature.

Further reading: Bernstein, R. *Ultimate Journey: Retracing the Path of an Ancient Buddhist Monk Who Crossed Asia in Search of Enlightenment.* New York: Knopf, 2001; Devahuti, D., ed. *The Unknown Hsuan-Tsang.* Oxford: Oxford University Press, 2001; Wriggins, S. H. *Xuanzang: A Buddhist Pilgrim on the Silk Road.* Boulder, Colo.: Westview Press, 1998.

Xue Xue was a small state located south of the state of Lu in Shandong, China. As virtually all the less powerful states of the EASTERN ZHOU DYNASTY (770–221 B.C.E.) were, it was subject to predatory attacks from larger neighbors, and Xue fell during the WARRING STATES PERIOD (475–221 B.C.E.) to QI. Intensive archaeological investigations have allowed a reconstruction of its capital city of Xue. These show that it was initially a LONGSHAN CULTURE (c. 2500–1800 B.C.E.) settlement that was greatly expanded during the WESTERN ZHOU DYNASTY (1045–771 B.C.E.). The city walls at this phase covered an area of 900 by 700 meters (990 by 770 yds.). A still larger city was then built during the Warring States period, which covered 1,750 hectares (4,375 acres), almost 30 times as large as its Western Zhou predecessor. This is a rare indication of the increase in the size of cities over time that culminated in the Warring States period, as the nature of the city moved from a palace-administrative center to one that incorporated industry and trade. With the rebuilding, the former Western Zhou center became a second inner precinct of the new foundation. Archaeological research has also unearthed a number of rich tombs within this city that cover the Spring and Autumn and Warring States periods of Eastern Zhou. The former were notable for their burial chambers and nested coffins, as well as the presence of sacrificial victims. Fortunately, some have survived unlooted and provide many fine jade ornaments and bronze vessels. The inscriptions on the bronzes reveal that the tombs belonged to members of the ruling elite lineage of Xue.

Xunzi (c. 310–215 B.C.E.) *Xunzi is the name given to the Chinese philosopher Xun Qing.*
Through a long life, he witnessed the final decades of the WARRING STATES PERIOD and ultimately the triumph of the kingdom of QIN. He spent much of his life as a teacher and member of the Jixia Academy in the state of QI but also traveled widely to CHU and Qin and witnessed in the latter a single-minded drive to military success that involved long and bloody battles. Such experiences probably influenced him toward a less optimistic view of the human condition than that of MENCIUS, and his ideas are discussed in a series of long essays. His philosophy was rooted in the belief that human beings are basically evil and that strict laws are required to tutor and control their behavior. He was a contributor to the legalist school so popular with the first emperor, QIN SHIHUANGDI. During his later life, he lived and taught in Shandong province, and his legacy beyond his writings is seen in the long list of his pupils who lived through the brief life of the Qin dynasty and into the Western HAN DYNASTY.

Y

Yakushi-ji The Yakushi-ji was a Buddhist temple that was first constructed at the city of FUJIWARA on the Nara Plain in Japan in 698 C.E. Fujiwara was a short-lived capital of the late YAMATO state, and soon after the consecration of the temple a new city was constructed 20 kilometers (12 mi.) to the north at HEIJO-KYO. A new temple with the same name was begun at Heijo in 718 C.E. and occupied a prominent position in the southwestern quarter of the city. The complex had an outer cloistered corridor with a square plan that enclosed the central *kondo*, or shrine hall, and two tall impressive pagodas. On the northern cloister, there was a lecture hall beyond which lay the monks' quarters, a refectory, bell tower, and library for storing sacred Buddhist texts.

The Yakushi-ji at Heijo-kyo in Japan was one of the major temples of that city. This image of the healing Buddha dates to the 19th century. *(Scala/Art Resource, NY)*

Yamatai The Chinese text known as the WEIZHI (*History of the Kingdom of Wei*) was compiled in the late third century C.E. by Chen Shou (233–297 C.E.). He became the official historian of the JIN dynasty. In 280 C.E. Jin reunited China after the Three Kingdoms period (beginning in 220 C.E., with the fall of Eastern Han), and Chen Shou began work on his *History of the Three Kingdoms* that had arisen from the HAN DYNASTY: WEI, WU, and SHU. One section of this highly regarded document, devoted to Wei, included a section on foreign peoples, including the kingdom of KOGURYO in Korea and the people of Wa in Japan. The section on the Wa described a journey from the vicinity of modern Seoul, Korea, to a place in Japan named Yamatai. There were eight stops en route, five of which have been identified with a reasonable degree of certainty; the last three, particularly the location of Yamatai, remain highly controversial. Archaeologists have, however, identified in Japan the late period of the YAYOI culture (late third century C.E.) as that corresponding to Yamatai. The relevant passage describes Yamatai as being ruled by a female shaman called Himiko, who lived secluded in a palace.

She sent embassies to the Chinese court and received in return gifts of swords, mirrors, and a gold SEAL with a purple sash. Yamatai had officials, markets, a taxation system, and much conflict. The lower orders bowed before highly ranked people. The latter were accorded fine tombs. All these aspects of Yamatai indicate that a complex society existed, perhaps even Japan's first state.

The *Weizhi* raises the question of whether any sites are sufficiently complex to correspond to the palaces, tombs, and markets described in the history. This question has not been conclusively answered, although some Late Yayoi sites, such as Yoshinogari on Kyushu Islands, attained a large area (up to 25 hectares [62.5 acres]) and were defended by a ditch and watchtowers. A large mounded tomb could well have been constructed for receiving elite members of this rice-farming community.

Yamato The kingdom of Yamato, centered in western Honshu in Japan, developed from the late YAYOI culture in the third century C.E. The Yamato state, over a period of four centuries, saw the development of an increasingly powerful civilization that grew in tandem with the THREE KINGDOMS of Korea and, finally, with Tang China. It received much influence in terms of ideas and goods from the continent but throughout displayed a specific Japanese ideology. Thus, although BUDDHISM was accepted, the local KAMI spirits continued in importance, as they do to this day. The rulers developed increasingly efficient forms of rice cultivation, the basic prop of the court centers, and disposed of sufficient wealth to deploy a naval fleet and armed force across the Tsushima Strait in support of their ally PAEKCHE in Korea. Huge royal and elite tombs, among the largest ever known, were constructed and filled with opulent grave goods. Heavily armed cavalry, another Korean import, were maintained. Large cities, palaces, and temples, again on continental models, were built. Writing was adopted from the Chinese script, and records of tax payments written on wood have survived. Japanese civilization can look back at Yamato as its seminal period of development that led directly to the NARA STATE, when the capital city on the model of Tang CHANG'AN was built at HEIJO-KYO.

Yamato was ruled by *okimi,* or great kings, whose tombs under large burial mounds were known as *kofun.* Hence Yamato is also known as the *kofun* period of Japanese history. The Yamato kingdom was rapidly forming by about 300 C.E., dated on the basis of imported Chinese mirrors from burial mounds, and lasted for about four centuries. Knowledge about the Yamato state has relied on three main sources. The first are two early historic accounts compiled by royal order in the early eighth century C.E. and known as the NIHONGI and KOJIKI. Next are INSCRIPTIONS, for example, on swords recovered from elite tombs, and finally there is the evidence of archaeology.

ORIGINS OF YAMATO

During the late Yayoi culture, population densities had grown as rice agriculture became more efficient. The remains of extensive IRRIGATION works have been identified during this period, and iron technology became more widespread, with applications in both agriculture and warfare. Within a broader frame, complex societies were evolving during this period both in Korea and in Japan. This trend was given stimulus by the previous foundation of Chinese provinces in the northern part of the Korean Peninsula, but with their demise, the development of the states of KOGURYO, Paekche, and SHILLA occurred. Yamato can be seen as a component of the same process.

EARLY YAMATO ROYAL BURIALS

Kofun burial mounds are widely found around the shores of the Inland Sea of Japan and match in many respects similar large and ostentatious burial mounds in Korea of the period. Perhaps by historical accident, particular stress in Japan has been given the huge mounded tombs found in the Nara Basin as representing the earliest phase of Yamato. This reflects the later political domination of this region during the compilation of the *Kojiki* and *Nihongi* historical texts in the early eighth century. In this interpretation, the then rulers sought local origins for their royal ancestry. The names of the early Yamato kings are thus recorded, and attempts have been made to match them with particular burials. In general, this early phase of Yamato was characterized by large tumuli in which the dead leaders were interred in wooden coffins sunk into the tops of the mounds. The elite were associated in death with exotic high-prestige goods, such as jasper and tuff jewelry, bronze mirrors, and iron weaponry, including body armor. The earliest dynasty, named after the alleged founder, Sujin, included five kings. Sujin himself is said to have reigned from 219 to 249 C.E., followed by Suinin, Keiko, Seimu, and Chuai, the last reigning from 343 to 346. Sujin, described as "he who ruled first," was closely involved in the worship of the *kami* of Mount Miwa in the southeastern flank of the Nara Plain and thereby sought sacred powers of legitimacy. Here at the foot of Mount Miwa six colossal *kofun* have been found and sequenced. The earliest is known as Hashihaka, followed by Nishitonozuka, Tobi Chausu-yama, Mesuri-yama, the Sujin tomb, and, finally, the Keiko tomb. They vary in length from 207 to 310 meters (683 to 1,023 ft.). Sujin is also described as a military leader who sent out princes to fight his enemies and took captives. This implies that there were rival polities around the Inland Sea and into Kyushu and that the period was one of competition and militarism documented in the widespread placement of iron weapons and armor in elite tombs.

SECOND DYNASTY OF YAMATO

The second dynasty of Yamato is named after its founder, Ojin, whose reign dates traditionally fall between 346 and

395. During his reign there is clear evidence for the introduction of literacy into Japan through the aegis of Korean tutors. The political center initially moved north in the Nara Basin to Saki, where a group of very large *kofun* mounded tombs are located. However, by 400 C.E., the power base had moved west, out of the Nara Basin and onto the Osaka Plains near the store of the Inland Sea. Six subsequent rulers are named in the early historical accounts, ending with Yuryaku, who reigned from 457 to 479. If these dates are accurate, Ojin would have been the ruler to whom the SHICHISHITO sword was presented by the ruler of the Korean kingdom of Paekche in 369. This gold inlaid ceremonial weapon, which is still kept in the Isonokami shrine in the Nara Basin, reflects the strong relations that existed between Paekche and Yamato, a relationship that drew much valued iron to Japan. The elite burials of this phase contained considerable quantities of iron weaponry and armor as well as tools. From 450, gold and silver ornaments of Korean inspiration were also found in elite burials.

The tombs were now surrounded by moats, and clay HANIWA, representations of houses, people, and animals, increased in numbers and complexity as part of the mortuary ritual. Tomb chambers were now lined in massive stones and coated with clay to counter dampness. Charcoal and pebble-based drains were also used for the same purpose.

The changes from tomb offerings that stressed ritual, such as bronze mirrors, to increasing quantities of weaponry and armor have been cited as evidence for an actual invasion by foreigners who introduced cavalry into warfare. This "horse-riding" invasion theory has been the object of considerable debate but has not been sustained by archaeological evidence. The alternative and more likely hypothesis is that the second dynasty developed from the first with a change in its political center, perhaps to take advantage of the power of local clans, in a context of increasing political contact with Korean counterparts. This trend involved territorial gains against former rivals to the west by the Yamato rulers, intent no doubt on securing maritime access to the Tsushima Strait and therefore to Korea. While it is clear that the Yamato kings of the fifth century commanded considerable military power and engaged in political relations with contemporary Korean states, little is known of the actual mechanisms whereby they conducted their administration. They must, for example, have been able to control a large force of labor to construct their massive tombs and excavate extensive irrigation works. Chronicles refer to a number of court positions, such as guards and sword and quiver bearers, and the close relations with Korea drew immigrant scribes. There were also specialist craft workers. The rulers, according to the early historical accounts of the period, were less concerned with rituals and spent more of their time in organizing secular activities: provision of irrigation works and suppression of regional dissent.

Production of Grave Gifts

Archaeological research has provided compelling evidence for the development of specialization in the manufacture of the high-prestige goods encountered in the rich burials of this period. At Furu on the Nara Plain, for example, excavations have uncovered a center for the production of iron blades dating 450–550 C.E. The wet conditions in part of the site led to the survival of wooden hilts, both complete and unfinished, of knives and swords. There were also the foundations of square buildings thought to have been storehouses. Soga Tamazukuri was a site that concentrated in the production of stone beads. The sources of the talc, jasper, and tuff are exotic to the Nara Plain and reveal the transportation of raw materials over considerable distances for processing there.

The move of the political center onto the Osaka Plains saw the construction of the largest tombs recorded in Japan and probably the largest mounded-earth tombs ever constructed. The Furuichi group contains the so-called Ojin tomb, which attained a length of 420 meters (462 yds.), while the Mozu group incorporated the Nintoku tomb 486 meters in length. The grave offerings in the tombs of this period included huge caches of weapons: One located near the Qin tomb contained 77 iron swords. These massive tombs also held assembled-chest coffins formed by joining large slabs of stone.

Inscribed swords provide evidence for the extension of Yamato control during the fifth century. That from INARIYAMA is dated to 471 C.E., during the reign of King Yuryaku (r. 457–479). It had belonged to a member of the official group of sword-bearer guards of the royal palace, who was an official of the court located more than 300 kilometers west of the tomb. A second inscribed sword dating to the same reign from the mound of EDA-FUNA-YAMA on the far west coast of Kyushu included the word *okimi*, "great king," and thus confirms central control over a region 550 kilometers to the west.

Clans and Specialist Groups

In cementing control over their kingdom, Yamato kings of the fifth century relied on two major social groupings, the *uji*, or clan, and the *be*, or specialist group. Both were under the control of the *kabane*, a title given to their hereditary head by the king. There were several ranks of *kabane*, ranging from village headmen to high officials of state. *Uji* formed the backbone of the agricultural system that sustained the central court; the *be* were specialists, living in specific locations, and provided goods or performed tasks needed by the central authority. Thus through the control of the *be* groups, some of whom were immigrants from Korea with special skills, the rulers could harness to their own purposes iron workers, makers of shields, irrigation engineers, horse trainers, and fletchers. Yamato's participation in the affairs of Korean states during the fifth century may well have drawn in some such immigrants against their will, but nevertheless as such groups occupied provincial areas of Japan, central rule was extended more widely.

Relations with Korea

Close relations with Korea also obtained for Yamato the developed iron tools that transformed agricultural efficiency. This particularly applied to the iron-tipped hoe and spade, which made it possible to move greater quantities of soil. Doubtless such implements expedited the construction of the massive royal tombs, but at a more fundamental level they meant that irrigation facilities, canals, and ponds could be completed more efficiently. The Furuichi Canal, for example, on the Osaka Plain was between 8.5 and 9.5 meters (28 and 31.4 ft.) wide and ran for at least 10 kilometers (6 mi.).

These changes, allied with increasing agricultural surpluses, permitted the Yamato kings to play a significant role in Korean affairs. This was doubtless fueled by their demands for iron and other strategic or luxury goods but was also stimulated by the internecine wars being conducted between the Korean kingdoms of Koguryo and Shilla against Paekche. The rulers of Paekche turned to Yamato for military alliances, sending high-ranking members of the royal family to Japan to demonstrate their good faith. This policy is well illustrated in a memorandum of 478 sent to the Song court of China by the Yamato king Yuryaku (r. 457–479). Having described the Yamato conquest of hundreds of kingdoms, the memorandum sought the Chinese emperor's mandate as supreme commander of an expedition against the forces of Koguryo, which, he complained, had been preventing him from having regular contact with the emperor. Yuryaku died in the following year, and in any case he was denied the title he sought, and the maritime expedition against Koguryo did not eventuate

LAST RULERS OF YAMATO

In 507 a new king, named Keitai (r. 507–531), ascended the throne. Some have seen this as a dynastic break, but Keitai had the same royal credentials as his predecessors, and there was no serious rupture in tradition. The court center and the royal tombs were now relocated back to the Mount Miwa area of the Nara Plain. Fifteen kings and three queens were to rule until the end of Yamato, after the death of Empress Genmei (r. 707–715). The signs of decline in power appeared during Keitai's reign. Yamato drew on Korean iron for its weapons industry, particularly from areas under its own control in the confederation of statelets known as KAYA. These were uncomfortably located between the might of Shilla to the east and that of Paekche to the west. During the course of Keitai's reign, Shilla moved into Kaya, taking territory traditionally loyal to Yamato. An expedition to halt this move fell apart as a result of an insurrection in Kyushu, where a local leader called Iwai refused to cooperate. This required a diversion of forces to cope with the disobedience and

severely delayed action in Kaya, reflective of rising independence in the provinces.

Late Tomb Architecture

The *Nihongi*, quoting an earlier source, described how Iwai had a tomb constructed for himself of grandiose proportions, with 60 stone sculptures of warriors and a shrine with statues of men and horses, together with stone reproductions of palaces and storehouses. Directed to the correct location by descriptions in the *Nihongi*, archaeologists identified this tomb complex and found that it conformed to the eighth-century description. Its size reflects a widespread phenomenon of the sixth century, namely, a proliferation of *kofun* burial mounds for clan use, equipped with entrance passages to allow sequential interments of clan members. This is further evidence of the growing status and power of provincial clans. Some regional clans owned considerable estates and exercised local authority, but royal estates were also created at this period, the surpluses from which, be they from agriculture or the sea, went directly to sustain the court. They became a means of exercising political control over distant provinces, for example, on the rich Kanto Plain, always a problem for developing states. This move was further strengthened with the registration of individual workers, which hearkens back to the autocratic regime of China's QIN dynasty eight centuries before. Indeed, registration implies a writing system, and there is no doubt, beyond the solid proof of inscriptions on swords and mirrors, that the Yamato court now employed scribes to maintain its records. These were available to those who compiled the first histories, such as the *Nihongi*, early in the eighth century.

Korean Contacts and Arrival of Buddhism

While the sixth century saw major land and administrative reforms at home, contact was maintained in the developing political situation in Korea, where Shilla was growing increasingly powerful at the expense of Paekche. Ongoing crossing of the Tsushima Strait by Korean goods and migrants emphasized the importance of maintaining central control over northern Kyushu. This, by the midsixth century, introduced the first currents of Buddhism and Buddhist thought into Japan, naturally accompanied by monks and sacred texts. Japan was strengthening its ties with the continent, as the new religion and the written word took hold.

Internal Conflicts

In 585, the rivalries between senior powerful clans reached the royal court itself, and civil war broke out over the succession with the death in that year of Emperor Bidatsu. The problem of the succession was exacerbated by the lack of a clear rule for primogeniture and therefore the proliferation of possible claimants. Two protégés of Soga no Imako were placed on the throne: Yomei for only two years before his death, and Sushun for five years before his assassination arranged by Soga, to be followed by the succession in 592 of the empress Suiko. With PRINCE SHOTOKU as her nominated successor, the empress reigned until 628, a remarkably long span for that period. However, it was Soga no Imako whose hands rested on the levers of power.

Chinese Influence in Yamato

Political conditions in Japan were now strongly influenced by events in China. After centuries of fragmentation, China was reunited in 589 under the Sui dynasty. Yamato and the three states of Korea in due course sent tribute missions to the Sui court and were impressed by the power exercised by the emperor. Not only did he have a massive new capital and palace constructed, but he laced the empire with a canal system, and through the Confucian ethic of obedience to whoever was graced with the MANDATE OF HEAVEN received the obligatory homage of his subjects. Registration of individuals and an efficient system of revenue collection added to the knowledge of a powerful state that returned to Japan with members of the official mission of 600. These currents of change contributed to what has been called the Asuka enlightenment in Japan, the name from the new court capital located in the Nara Basin.

Rise of Buddhism

This enlightenment involved not only the rapid entrenchment of writing based on the Chinese script and the construction of palace capitals on the Sui model, but, more significantly, the adoption of BUDDHISM. The struggle over the succession leading in 592 to the enthronement of Empress Suiko also divided the protagonists on the basis of their preferred religion, as Soga no Imako and Prince Shotoku favored the new BUDDHISM. Buddhist monks were then imbued with the charisma of divination and miracle working, and both men vowed that if successful they would promote the monks to the full. True to their promise, they had massive new temples constructed, employing immigrant craftspeople who included carpenters, painters, and ceramic workers, who were responsible for the manufacture of roof tiles. Soga sponsored the construction of Asuka, the new capital in the southern Nara Basin, of the ASUKA-DERA temple; Shotoku was responsible for the SHITENNO-JI temple in Osaka. Both broke new ground in the size and splendor of religious structures in Japan, although neither temple has survived to the present day. The former was badly damaged by fire in 1196, and the latter was destroyed by bombing during the Second World War and now exists only in the form of a concrete replica of the original.

Buddhism under royal patronage, particularly at the hands of Prince Shotoku, rapidly spread, and it is recorded that nobles vied with one another to construct temples. Their foundation saw the deposit of horse-riding equipment and gold and silver ornaments recalling the mortuary offerings made in the *kofun* and indeed continuing the tradition. A census taken in 623 recorded that by that year there were 46 temples, staffed by 816 monks and 569 nuns.

Contributions of Korea in Religion and Society

It is important to stress the role played by Korean immigrants in the Asuka enlightenment. Korean priests were prominent among the 816 monks recorded in 623, Korean horse gear in Japan supports the widespread evidence for armored cavalry of the period with Korean influence, and similar currents can be seen in the architecture of the grand new temples and burial goods found in elite tombs. At the same time, the enlightenment saw the establishment of imperially appointed ranks based on merit and ability. There were 12 ranks, identified on the basis of the color of feathers worn in a purple silk hat embellished with gold and silver. The role of Confucian ethics is seen in the titles, beginning at the top rank with the title "greater virtue" and descending through such titles as "greater propriety" and "greater justice" to the lowest of all, "lesser knowledge." These ranks of state officials replaced the former system of hereditary access to positions of influence. The 17 injunctions, said to have been formulated in 604 by Prince Shotoku, although this has been questioned, confirm a Confucian approach integrated with complete deference to the emperor's wishes. They range from the requirement that officials always obey the emperor, to an order not to disturb farmers at critical times of the agricultural round, such as planting and harvest. Officials are enjoined not to be jealous, to confer with others before making important decisions, and to work long hours.

Taika Reforms

Interest in Chinese unification, art, and culture was magnified through diplomatic missions sent by the empress to the Sui court, a practice that became more accentuated after the fall of the Sui and the establishment of the Tang dynasty under Emperor Gaozu in 618. However, there followed a period of factional politics in the court, because Prince Shotoku died in 622, and the empress Suiko died six years later. The obvious choice as successor was Shotoku's son, Prince Yamashiro, but his succession was opposed by the strong Soga clan. First the ineffectual emperor Jomei acceded, to be followed by his wife as empress Kogyokui (r. 642–45). Bloodletting followed. Yamashiro and his family were eliminated at the hands of Iruka, a leading member of the powerful Soga clan. In 645 Iruka himself was murdered in the royal audience hall, setting the stage for the appointment of Emperor Kotoku (r. 645–54). One of his first actions was to move the capital from Asuka to Naniwa on the coast, followed on New Year's Day, 646, by a series of major reforms that provided greater powers for the emperor and improvements to the tax system. These, known as the TAIKA REFORMS, reveal recurrent features in the development of early states.

There was a census, and the tax on agricultural production was set at 3 percent of the yield. In addition, cloth to be given in tax was set against the area of land owned. Other goods required included horses (one horse per 100 households), labor for work on government projects, weaponry and armor, and even an attractive woman to be sent to the court. The new edicts also prescribed the size of tombs relative to the rank of the deceased. Was this order followed? It seems so, given the dimensions of the burial mounds of the period measured by archaeologists. These reforms have been seen by some scholars as the turning point that saw Yamato develop into a full-fledged state on the Chinese model. Others, however, deny their relevance, claiming that the reforms were later. This issue was illuminated by the discovery in 1975 at the site of the Itabuki palace of a MOKKAN, or wooden tablet, that stated simply, "Shiragabe 50 households." Since the Taika Reforms specified that each administrative village was to include 50 households, this gave new documentary proof of the 646 date.

THREATS FROM KOREA AND CHINA

The defeat of first Paekche in 663, Yamato's ally in Korea, and then Koguryo in 668 by the combined forces of Tang China and Shilla had a profound effect on Yamato. Predatory enemies, in the form of either the might of the Tang empire or a unified Korea under Shilla domination, were now at Japan's doorstep. Defensive forts were constructed from Kyushu east into the heartland of Yamato. The capital at Asuka was abandoned in favor of the more easily defended position at Otsu. The strength of the ruling dynasty under the emperors TENJI (668–71) and TEMMU (673–86) increased at the expense of the powerful clans. The investment in charismatic authority of the emperor was manifested in the construction of magnificent palace-capitals along Tang lines, such as FUJIWARA and in 710 the capital of Nara, also known as HEIJO-KYO. These were associated with a series of edicts that established the legal basis of the imperial rule. The 14-year reign of Emperor Temmu saw the construction of the Kiyomihara Palace at Asuka, a portent of the royal capitals to come, and increased central control over the armed forces. Historical records charting the godly origins of the royal dynasty were designed as a legitimizing force, and Buddhism was encouraged as the state religion. The sutras favoring royal rule were widely read. Temmu was succeeded by his widow, the empress JITO, who resolved to construct a great new capital at FUJIWARA on the Nara Plain, a city she was able to occupy in 694, which required huge resources of materials and labor to construct. It was designed along the lines of the continental cities on a grid layout, with the royal palace at its heart. In 702 the Taiho Code, a set of laws cementing the aristocratically based Fujiwara regime, was issued. It is important to note that the succession to the throne was not restricted to the male line, and the empress was succeeded by her sister, Genmei. One of the new ruler's first decisions was to abandon Fujiwara after less than a decade of occupancy and move the capital to Heijo-kyo, only 20 kilometers (12 mi.) to the north. This move established the Nara state, although the transition from Yamato was seamless and involved the same dynasty.

Further reading: Barnes, G. *Prehistoric Yamato: Archaeology of the First Japanese State.* Ann Arbor: University of Michigan Press, 1988; Brown, D. M. *The Cambridge History of Japan.* Cambridge: Cambridge University Press, 1993; Pearson, R. J., ed. *Windows on the Japanese Past: Studies in Archaeology and Prehistory.* Ann Arbor: University of Michigan Press, 1986; Totman, C. *A History of Japan.* Oxford: Blackwell, 2000.

Yan The state of Yan was located in northeastern China, centered in the vicinity of modern Beijing. It occupied a strategic location between the sea and the Taihang mountain range, protecting the central plains from any attack from a northeastern direction. Yan, as had several other states that came to the fore politically during the Spring and Autumn period (770–476 B.C.E.), had its origins in the wars of succession that followed the death of King WU, the first ruler of the WESTERN ZHOU DYNASTY. The succession should have passed to his oldest son, Song, who under the name Cheng was to rule from about 1042 until 1006 B.C.E. However, a younger brother of King Wu, Zhou Gong Dan, declared himself regent instead, on the grounds that Song was too young to rule alone. This fomented a civil war between the forces of Zhou Gong Dan and Cheng on the one hand and those of Dan's brothers on the other. Zhou Gong Dan fought successful campaigns to the east of the capital and greatly expanded the area under Zhou control. In time-honored tradition, rulers for the new territories were found among the loyal members of the ruling lineage, and Shao Gong Shi, a half-brother of Zhou Gong, was granted the fief that developed into the state of Yan. While under the Western Zhou, such fiefs owed fealty to the emperor, they assumed independence with the end of the Western Zhou dynasty in 771 B.C.E. Yan thus became an independent state during the EASTERN ZHOU DYNASTY. It was the most northerly of these states, and one of the smallest, but the splendor of the bronzes found in the cemeteries of Fangshan and Liulihe shows beyond any doubt the wealth based on agriculture and trade of the ruling Zhou elite. Despite surviving through judicious alliances, Yan finally fell in the early third century B.C.E. to a powerful alliance led by the rival state of QI.

The Huang (Yellow) River formerly flowed through Yan, and it would have been well positioned for trade and agricultural production. Excavations at Fangshan near Beijing have uncovered rich royal graves that include multiple chariots and horses as well as fine bronze vessels. Some of the vessels bear inscriptions that name individuals previously documented only in literary sources such as the *Shang Shu,* including *tai bao,* a title given to Shao Gong Shi. The title *yan hou* is also found on bronzes unearthed at the necropolis of Fangshan, and further chariot burials have been found at Liulihe. The old literary name for Beijing was Yanjing, meaning the "Yan capital," and the outstanding bronzes found there tend to sustain this interpretation.

Wuyang or Xiadu, a secondary capital of Yan, was founded by King Zhaowang in the late WARRING STATES PERIOD (475–221 B.C.E.). It has been investigated archaeologically and includes large walled areas with a canal flowing north to south through the center, thus linking the northern and central branches of the Yi River. Both walled areas cover 3,200 hectares (8,000 acres), the eastern or inner city being further divided by an east-west wall. As did virtually all Warring States capitals, Xiadu incorporated specialized workshop areas. One was dedicated to the casting of bronze mirrors, a product that proliferated during the last few centuries of Eastern Zhou. Another was dedicated to iron casting and was perhaps responsible for the well-known iron helmet of Xiadu, which was made of separate plates that could be joined. Yet another area was given over to the casting of coins, while there were also bone and ceramic workshops. A hoard of *ge* halberds, most of which bear the inscribed names of Yan state lords, has been recovered. In the northwestern section of the inner city there is an extensive cemetery. One of the excavated graves included seven ceramic *ding* tripods and belonged to a minister.

The records dating to the Warring States period provide figures for the size of the armies that took part in the internecine strife of the period. Yan is at the bottom of the league table with only 100,000 infantry, a tenth of that estimated for the state of QIN. The same relative weakness is found in the number of chariots and cavalry and perhaps explains the ultimate demise of the state.

Yangputou   Yangputou is a major site of the DIAN CHIEFDOM of Yunnan province, southern China. Dian was one of the many such chiefdoms spread across southern China that flourished during the later WARRING STATES PERIOD (475–221 B.C.E.) and the early Western HAN DYNASTY (206 B.C.E.–9 C.E.). With the imperial policy of the Han, however, it was to absorbed as a commandery, or province, of the Han in the second century B.C.E. Two major sites reveal through the wealth of their grave offerings the presence of an aristocratic elite: SHIZHAISHAN and LIJIASHAN. Yangputou was excavated on a grand scale in 1998–99, when a total of 495 burials was uncovered in an area of just over a hectare (2.5 acres). Excavation was undertaken ahead of a construction program that covered the site. The most important result has been the documentation of social divisions in the cemetery; there were four large and opulent graves, 23 of considerable wealth, and the balance with few grave goods. The rich mortuary offerings included items of gold, jade, agate, and LACQUER. Swords were retained in gold scabbards, and lacquer bowls of

probable Sichuan origin were uncovered. Unique features of this site were the human-like phalluses of antler or lacquered wood incorporating carvings of animals, such as a rabbit, bird, or deer head. The graves were lined with wood, and some of the human skeletons have survived to provide a rare opportunity of examining the health and demographic character of a Dian community in which local leaders were apparently identified by their particularly fine mortuary rituals and offerings.

Yangshao culture   Yangshao is the name given to the many Neolithic cultures of north China. The sites date between approximately 5100 and 3000 B.C.E. and concentrate in the loess uplands traversed by the Huang (Yellow) River and its tributaries. Loess is a fine windblown dust that was deposited in vast quantities during the last Ice Age. Soft and easily worked, it encouraged the cultivation of millet. Typical sites, such as Banbo, were large villages with an open area in the middle and circular houses. The cemeteries were placed outside a surrounding ditch, and individuals were interred with animal bones and fine painted pottery vessels, which are the hallmark of this culture. There are many regional subdivisions; the most interesting from the point of view of early civilization are those to the northwest of the area of distribution in the province of Gansu. Here some late Yangshao sites of the variants known as Majiayao, Banshan, and Machang have yielded the earliest evidence for a knowledge of BRONZE CASTING. Since bronzes were such a vital aspect of the ritual life of early Chinese states, the origins and early history of metallurgy in China are issues of considerable importance. At first sight, it might seem surprising that the earliest bronzes were found in remote Gansu. However, this part of China is strategically placed to give access to the TARIM BASIN, the Dzungarian Gates, and so across the steppes to the West. In later periods this came to be known as the SILK ROAD, linking imperial China, India, Persia, and Rome. Recent research has shown that a knowledge of bronze working, which originated in the Near East, spread in an easterly direction before it appeared in China. As does that of later cultural phenomena that seem to have been transmitted in a similar fashion, including use of the chariot and knowledge of iron working, the origin of Chinese copper and tin metallurgy appears to lie in the West.

The village communities of the Majiayao phase of the Yangshao culture, which is dated in the vicinity of 3000 B.C.E., typically include houses sunk into the soft loess soil as a protection against the bitter winter cold. The inhabitants cultivated millet and maintained domestic stock. They fashioned and kiln-fired pottery vessels and used polished stone tools. The longevity of these stable villages led to the formation of large inhumation cemeteries. Their millet was stored in underground pits for winter consumption, and in one of these pits at the site of Linjia a bronze knife that was between 6 and 10 percent tin was found. It was cast in a double mold and represents one of the earliest bronzes, if not the earliest, from China. Other pits at the same site have yielded fragments of bronze as well, but the knife is the only actual bronze artifact from this extensively excavated site. It presents a problem of interpretation in that major excavations at sites of the succeeding Banshan phase (2700–2350 B.C.E.) of the late Yangshao in this region have revealed no other bronzes. This lack is particularly notable at Liuwan, where more than 1,000 graves have been opened. Of these, 257 belong to the Banshan phase, and 872 to the succeeding Machang phase (2400–2000 B.C.E.). Yet no items of bronze were recovered.

Toward the end of the Yangshao culture in the central plains, cultural changes that quickened in the succeeding LONGSHAN CULTURE took place; particularly important were the first rammed-earth walls encircling settlements such as Xishan, near ZHENGZHOU.

Yantie Lun The *Yantie Lun (Discourse on Salt and Iron),* is an important HAN DYNASTY text that explores the rationale for state control over vital industries. The discourse touched on many themes that continue to dominate economic policy, such as the relative advantages of state control against private enterprise. Its background involved the fiscal policies of the emperor WUDI (157–87 B.C.E.). Wudi, the "Martial Emperor," had embarked on a major policy of imperial expansion. His armies had taken large new tracts of land in the northwest, which extended the empire to the Jade Gates and DUNHUANG. This provided immediate access to the lucrative SILK ROAD but at the cost of training and equipping large numbers of soldiers and extending the GREAT WALL many kilometers to the west. To the northeast he took the land up to and including the Korean Peninsula, creating new administrative provinces, or commanderies. He also expanded his southern frontiers to include many of the warlike tribes of Yue from modern Yunnan east to Guangdong and Vietnam. This policy was very expensive in labor and materials, and he had to seek many new and unpopular means of raising revenue. These included the confiscation of privately owned land for the most specious reasons, the sale of titles, and the seizure of private assets and businesses concerned with trade in salt, iron, liquor, and the minting of currency. In essence, this policy was a reversion to the LEGALISM of the QIN dynasty, whereby a policy was justified if it enhanced the power of the state. In 81 B.C.E., soon after the death of Wudi and at a time of financial duress, a debate took place between legalists and Confucian followers, and the proceedings are known as the *Discourse on Salt and Iron*. The principal purpose of this meeting, called by the government ministers, was to inquire into popular discontent about the effects of this policy.

The arguments were tossed to and fro between the ministers (modernists) and Confucian scholars (reformists), at times descending to personal abuse and ridicule. One minister said of the scholars: "See them . . . in their coarse gowns and worn shoes they walk gravely along, sunk in meditation as though they have lost something. These are not men who can do great deeds and win fame." The debate, however, was lively. The ministers described the plight at the frontier, where brave troops had to withstand the attacks of the XIONGNU, and the benefits of the new trade along the Silk Road that imported a whole range of new goods: precious stones, furs, and new ideas. To this, the Confucians responded derisively that Han had no business in Central Asia; they should concentrate on the homeland. As for the trade, the exotic imports benefited only the rich, for poor people who actually produced the fine silks for export could not afford such luxuries. The Confucians stressed the distortions that followed state monopolies, in which goods were bought cheaply and retained until prices soared. Then they could be sold at a huge profit, encouraging racketeering. This likewise diminished the vital importance of agriculture and tempted farmers into quick profits through trade. But the modernists were insistent. State control over iron, for example, meant that high-quality iron implements could be manufactured and made widely available, thus improving agricultural efficiency rather than letting any profits remain in private hands.

See also CONFUCIUS.

Yaoshan Yaoshan is located between the southern edge of Lake Taihu and the Chang (Yangtze) River in eastern China. It is a necropolis of the LIANGZHU CULTURE, dated 3200–2000 B.C.E. The site was a raised mound almost 100 meters (330 ft.) long, within which were at least 12 tombs laid out in two rows. This mound was surrounded by a moat two meters wide and a U-shaped platform. There is no evidence for occupation. Such ritual-mortuary sites are found at other Liangzhu sites such as SIDUN and Fanshan and emphasize the high degree of social gradation that existed in the Liangzhu culture, where many ordinary graves lack the rich grave goods and double wooden coffins with space for the placement of mortuary offerings found at Yaoshan. A typical grave gift was a jade *cong* commonly ornamented with monster's mark or face, in the form of bulging eyes, a broad nose, and tusklike teeth.

As a result of rice cultivation that employed IRRIGATION and plowing for added efficiency, the people of Liangzhu had fine craft workshops for the production of jade, lacquerware, and ceramics. This is seen in the offerings placed with the dead at Yaoshan, including jade *cong*. The term *cong* was coined during the EASTERN ZHOU DYNASTY (770–221 B.C.E.) to describe these unusual artifacts. The *cong* has a circular interior in a square decorated exterior. Many were found surrounding the skeleton of a young man at the related site of Sidun, giving rise to the theory that they were used in shamanistic rituals. Such monster images are also found on a series of trapezoidal jade plaques from Yaoshan. One example shows the monster flanked by men wearing feathered headdresses. Another such plaque was found associated with jade beads to form a necklace. These jades were made in the Liangzhu cultural area, although the location of the source of the jade itself is not known.

Yarang Yarang is a moated settlement in the valley of the Pattani River on the east coast of peninsular Thailand. Excavations have revealed a long sequence of occupancy. During the early phase there was a small moated settlement. This was expanded during the eighth to 10th centuries C.E. and involved the construction of several temples. The site was involved in widespread trade and was under the control of the kingdom of SRIVIJAYA.

Yashodharapura King YASHOVARMANI (r. 889–910) founded his new city of Yashodharapura around his state temple on the top of a hill known as Phnom BAKHENG in Cambodia. If the moat visible to the southwest of the Bakheng formerly enclosed his city, then Yashodharapura would have been very large indeed. This has long been regarded as likely. However, it has now been shown that this enigmatic "moat" was beyond reasonable doubt a 12th-century construction designed to link the city of ANGKOR with a canal leading to the GREAT LAKE. Under these circumstances, although Victor Goloubew in 1933 identified the Bakheng as the center of Yashodharapura first on the basis of air photographs and then on investigation of archaeological features on the ground, there is no certainty as to its size or limits. There is no doubt that he discovered faint traces of roads flanked by water basins, while further excavations have uncovered roof tiles, suggesting that elite residences were located around the central temple. Given the lack of walls or moats, Christophe Pottier has suggested that this and all later Angkorian cities had an open plan until the construction of ANGKOR THOM under JAYAVARMAN VII.

Yashodharatataka *See* EASTERN BARAY.

Yashovarman I (r. 889–910 C.E.) *Yashovarman I (Protégé of Renown) succeeded his father, Indravarman I, as king of Angkor in Cambodia in 889 C.E.*
He moved his capital from HARIHARALAYA to a new capital named YASHODHARAPURA. His state temple, known as the BAKHENG, was built atop a sandstone hill that dominates the flat plain north of the GREAT LAKE. In addition to completing the INDRATATAKA, his father's reservoir (BARAY), and its island temple of LOLEI, Yashovarman had the massive Yashodharatataka (EASTERN BARAY), a reservoir of unprecedented size northeast of his capital, built. Temples were also constructed on top of the other hills in the

vicinity of ANGKOR during his reign, and the king also founded ASHRAMAS, retreats for ascetics.

Yayoi During the late 18th century a number of burials were investigated in the vicinity of Fukuoka on the northern shore of Honshu Island, Japan. They were associated with bronze objects of clear Chinese inspiration or origin, including mirrors, halberds, and daggers. Stone molds for casting such items were also recovered. Between 1781 and 1789 several bronze mirrors and iron swords were found in a burial urn at Ihara near Fukuoka. In 1822 the site of Mikimo on the northern shore of Kyushu facing Korea yielded bronze swords, spears, and halberds as well as 35 mirrors of a style attributable to the former HAN DYNASTY. There were also glass beads similar to specimens found in Korea. This site also contained prehistoric burial urns of a type now known to be typical of the Yayoi culture. The rediscovery of this site in 1974 led to the recovery of further bronzes and glass beads and posed the key issue of the relationship between the prehistoric people of Japan and the sophisticated states that existed to the west and north. The word *Yayoi* is taken from a suburb of Japan where characteristic pottery was first recognized in 1884. There are three major phases: early (300–100 B.C.E.), middle (100 B.C.E.–100 C.E.), and late (until 300 C.E.). In many respects, the Yayoi period remains controversial. The degree to which its origin resulted from a major movement of people into Japan from the mainland has clear implications for the origins of the Japanese themselves. Alternatively, was there minimal settlement but a strong current of diffusion of new ideas into islands long occupied by complex hunter-gatherers? During six or seven centuries of expansion and change, did the Yayoi people establish a state as complex as that described in the Chinese texts? These questions remain under review, but there can be no doubting the importance of the period in the establishment of the quintessential basis of Japanese statehood, the stable community of cultivators.

Yayoi is a vital phase in East Asia because it was during these six centuries that the foundations of Japanese civilization were created. These rested on the firm base of rice cultivation, linked with bronze and iron metallurgy and increasing contact with China and Korea. The issue of the origins of Yayoi have not been clearly resolved, even if the main points are evident: Rice farming in prepared fields, following the developed Chinese method, was established by about 300–200 B.C.E., along with local skills in BRONZE CASTING and iron working. During the middle Yayoi there was a marked expansion of agricultural settlement from Kyushu past the Inland Sea and into Honshu, while sharp social divisions and large regional polities were forming during the late Yayoi.

BEGINNINGS OF YAYOI CULTURE

At the inception of the Yayoi culture, however, Japan had for millennia been occupied by hunter-gatherer groups known collectively as Jomon. By the beginning of the first millennium B.C.E. knowledge and practice of rice cultivation were spreading into Korea, and it was only a matter of time before it crossed into the Japanese islands. The basic issue is whether rice farming was introduced along with bronze and iron metallurgy into northern Kyushu by a wave of immigrants or more gradually entered social contexts involving Jomon groups who in due course integrated rice farming into their long-established economy. At Itazuke, an important site in northern Kyushu, archaeologists have recovered early Yayoi style potsherds in association with Yusu ware. The Yusu ware has been assigned to the late Jomon culture, although there is a school of thought that assigns it to the Yayoi proper. Resolving this issue is relevant to the question of Yayoi origins, because the remains of wet-rice fields at Itazuke have been found in association with Yusu pottery alone. The recovery of rice fields in Kyushu with late Jomon material culture, however, should not occasion surprise; rather, it indicates contact with established rice-farming communities in Korea or even mainland China, a movement that must have involved the settlement of immigrant groups. This point does not rely only on the archaeological record of new subsistence activities and types of artifact. Although not abundant by any means, the remains of the actual people disclose that the Yayoi were taller than their Jomon counterparts, and their heads were of a different shape. Estimates of the population of Japan during the late Jomon period and that typical at the end of the Yayoi in terms of settlement sizes and numbers also indicate that there must have been a considerable degree of immigration.

Adoption of Rice Cultivation
The Yayoi rice fields represent from the beginning a sophisticated method of cultivation. It is known from Han tomb models in China that the construction of bunds around field plots to control the flow of water, linked with plowing and transplanting, underpinned the production of vital rice surpluses. This system appeared fully fledged in Japan, and it is hard not to see it as a wholesale adoption of an established system. The Yayoi people permanently occupied moated villages in proximity to their fields and maintained long-term cemeteries. Their tools of cultivation, as seen at the TORO site, were solidly constructed of wood. However, it is necessary to emphasize that there were other crops as well, some of which were better suited to dryland cultivation than to the marshy wetland cultivation suited to the rice plant. These included two varieties of millet, wheat, and barley. A range of fruits were consumed, and acorns and nuts collected. There is little evidence for the maintenance of domestic stock, but hunting and fishing were undertaken.

MIDDLE AND LATE YAYOI CULTURE
The establishment of intrusive rice-farming communities in Kyushu was followed by a progressive expansion to the northeast into Honshu, while the extreme climatic conditions of Hokkaido favored the continuation of hunter-gatherers whose descendants in all probability constitute the surviving Ainu people of northern Japan. The initial expansion was probably rapid, a widespread feature of agricultural expansions that is also documented in Southeast Asia and Europe. In Japan it is reflected in the widespread distribution east and west of the Inland Sea of a similar pottery style known as Ongagawa ware. This spread appears to have reached north even by the end of the early Yayoi, as evidenced by the presence of rice fields at Sunazawa in northern Honshu and slightly later fields at Tomizawa in northeastern Honshu. The growth in the number of settlements during the middle Yayoi phase and the expansion from low-lying coastal flats to elevated terrain overlooking river valleys are both contributory factors to the increase in evidence for friction and fighting. Sites were ringed by defensive ditches, and stone arrowheads proliferated.

Much tantalizing information on the late Yayoi period is found in a Chinese historical text known as the WEIZHI (History of the Kingdom of Wei), which dates to the late third century C.E. It describes the third-century C.E. Wa people of the Japanese islands as possessing a social hierarchy in which female shaman leaders were interred in large mounded graves. Himiko is named as the ruling shaman at that time. She lived in a heavily guarded palace. The journey to this place, named YAMATAI in the text, is described, but so vaguely that its location is not defined and remains highly controversial in some quarters of Japan. It also makes it clear that warfare was endemic, that there were legal and taxation systems, and that divination followed the Chinese model of interpreting cracks generated on animal bones by the application of heat. The people of Japan cultivated rice and raised silkworms. They had no domestic animals but maintained officially sanctioned and regulated markets. There was a taxation system, and warfare involved soldiers equipped with bows and arrows, the latter tipped with iron. Hiniko in 238 and 243 C.E. sent embassies to China. The former led to the emperor's recognizing her as the queen of Wa, an ally; he sent her a gold seal, two swords, 100 bronze mirrors, and beads of jade.

Such Chinese accounts of foreign people are not confined to Japan. At about the same time that the Wei emperor was in contact with the Wa, the southern Chinese Wu emperor sent a mission to Southeast Asia, leading to a similar account of the people of FUNAN. Both described what they saw or heard of through Chinese eyes, making their comments unreliable. However, some of the descriptive passages on Funan have been confirmed by archaeology, and the challenge to confirm the account of Yamatai likewise has led, for example, to recognition of possible parallels in sites such as Yoshinogari on Kyushu. Here excavations have revealed a settlement that covered 25 hectares (62.5 acres) by late Yayoi times. It was demarcated by a large defensive ditch supplemented with watchtowers. The finding of a large mounded tomb covering an area of 40 by 26 meters (132 by 86 ft.), associated with ritual pottery deposits, suggests the presence of an elite rank in the local society.

New Technology—Pottery, Bronze, Iron

The wholesale adoption of rice cultivation was matched in the area of technology. Pottery vessels had been a major aspect of Jomon material culture, but with Yayoi forms and decorative techniques changed, and manufacture of a set of cooking, serving, and storage vessels became the norm. These forms probably mirror the needs of rice farmers. The same can be said of stone tool forms, particularly the newly arrived stone reaping knives. Their form is widespread on the Chinese mainland, where they had been in use for millennia. Wear on the blades of these knives proves their use in rice harvesting. Weaving likewise had a long history in China, and with the Yayoi culture it was introduced into Japan, for many spindle whorls have been

Yayoi period bronze bells had a major ritual significance and also illustrate aspects of life at that period in Japan. Here we see a hunting scene and a raised house. *(© Sakamoto Photo Research Laboratory/CORBIS)*

found. Silk entered Kyushu from southern China. As for wooden tools, the waterlogged conditions at such sites as Toro reveal the use of hoes, spades, rakes, and forks.

The establishment of Chinese provinces in the northern Korean Peninsula conveyed knowledge of bronze and iron closer to the Japanese islands, and with Yayoi bronze spears, halberds, swords, mirrors, and bells appeared. In each case, the imported items were transformed by local bronze casters into forms more suited to local tastes and requirements. Thus the weapons were enlarged and broadened. The mirrors became smaller, and the bells greatly enlarged. The Yoyoi bell is a notable achievement of bronze casting, with its decorative scenes and, in the largest example, a height of 1.35 meters (4.5 ft.). Much if not all the metal cast in Japan appears to have originated in imported items that were recycled or copper ingots. Earlier bronzes employed Korean metal; later smiths preferred Chinese sources. The same applies to iron. There are rich iron-ore sources in southern Korea, and finished products were traded south into Kyushu and western Honshu. Iron tools and weapons are regularly found in Yayoi sites, but not in great quantities, and local smelting does not appear to have become commonplace until after the end of the Yayoi period. There is, however, no doubt that iron played a significant role in agriculture, to judge from the presence of iron sickles, particularly in late Yayoi contexts. The recycling of iron and the propensity of iron to rust away under damp conditions might well account for its rarity. Links with the continent through trade are documented through the presence not only of bronze, but also of such imported goods as glass beads. These are widely distributed in Yayoi sites even from the earliest period. They have, for example, been recovered from Yoshitake-Takagi in Fukuoka prefecture and Higashiyamada-Ipponsugi in Saga prefecture. The number of sites yielding glass beads, which would have reached Japan by the emerging sea lanes linking East Asia with India and the Mediterranean, increased markedly during the middle and late periods of Yayoi culture. Some late sites such as Tounokubi and Futatsukayama have yielded thousands from mortuary contexts.

See also LELANG.

Further reading: Barnes, G., ed. *Hoabinhian, Jomon, Yayoi, Early Korean States*. Oxford: Oxbow Books, 1990; Kiyotari, T., ed. *Recent Archaeological Discoveries in Japan*. Tokyo: The Centre for East Asian Cultural Studies, 1987; Pearson, R. J., ed. *Ancient Japan*. New York: G. Braziller, 1992; ———, ed. *Windows on the Japanese Past: Studies in Archaeology and Prehistory*. Ann Arbor: University of Michigan Press, 1986.

yazhang A *yazhang* was a jade blade. The earliest known examples are from LONGSHAN CULTURE (2500–1800 B.C.E.) sites in the Huang (Yellow) River Valley, such as Dafanzhuan, Shangwanjiazhuang, and Simatai on the Shandong Peninsula. These may have been from the jade manufactories on the Liaodong Peninsula. The image of a *yazhang* has been found carved on a jade disk at Anxi in the LIANGZHU CULTURE area of the lower Chang (Yangtze). *Yazhang* continued in use during the XIA and SHANG dynasties for ceremonial purposes. About 200 are known, their distribution extending from the central plains of the Huang River Valley to Hong Kong and northern Vietnam. Two sites in particular have yielded impressive samples: ERLITOU and SANXINGDUI, where more than 25 percent of all known examples have been recovered. The latter site has furnished a bronze model of a man holding such a blade in a position that suggests a ritual. *Yazhang* may have originated in a metal prototype, for a rare bronze from Erlitou has a similar shape. However, the bronze version must soon have fallen out of favor. Manufacturing such large jades was a testing procedure: An example from Erlitou dating to the first half of the second millennium B.C.E. was almost 0.5 meter (1.65 ft.) in length, and a massive specimen from Sanxingdui of a slightly later date was 1.5 meters. The hafts were bored from one side only, presumably to assist in hafting, and the area between the handle and blade was cut to form a series of decorative ridges. After consistent grinding and polishing, the blade bore a very sharp cutting edge. During the Zhou dynasty, these blades became rare and of inferior workmanship, before disappearing from the archaeological record.

Yelang Yelang was a powerful chiefdom based in the southern Chinese province of Guizhou. It developed considerable cultural complexity before being absorbed into the empire of the HAN DYNASTY (206 B.C.E.–220 C.E.). Its wealth and ranked social structure are best seen on the basis of excavations at the cemetery of Liujiagou undertaken in 1976–78. Thirty-nine of the 208 graves uncovered were distinguished by the location, size, and wealth of their grave furniture. One of these was 2.8 meters (9.2 ft.) deep and contained two chambers, 8.1 by 4.7 meters (26.7 by 15.6 ft.), entered by a ramp. Grave goods included imports from the Western Han state, dated to the last two centuries B.C.E., such as bronze mirrors and coins. There are also house models in clay, which reveal domestic dwellings raised on wooden piles. These have several rooms, a pitched roof, and a rice-processing area under the floor. Burial 21 had wooden compartments, and grave goods included bronze vessels, spearheads, a crossbow, chariot fittings, ceramic vessels, and even the ceramic frame used when building or lining a well. The relatively less opulent graves were smaller and appear to have been set out in rows.

Yellow Springs The Yellow Springs was the place below the Earth where, in Han Chinese thought (206 B.C.E.–220 C.E.), the dead congregated. The Chinese conceived that at death a person was divided between the HUN and the BO.

The former may be translated as the soul, which might migrate to the heavens or to the land of the Yellow Springs. The latter either remained with the body or migrated to the land of the Yellow Springs. If the *bo* found itself in this new land, it needed some means of identification. This explains why tombs often contained the dead person's SEAL and figurines of servants and retainers.

See also HAN DYNASTY.

Yellow Turbans The Yellow Turbans participated in a major insurrection against the Eastern Han emperor LINGDI and his administration. Lingdi (156–89 C.E.) was one of the few later emperors of the Eastern HAN DYNASTY who lived long enough to have a political impact. Early in his reign when he was still a boy, there was a power struggle between the old court families and the eunuchs. The latter prevailed, and until the end of the reign they dominated the central administration, favoring their relatives and opening administrative positions for sale. At the same time, new methods of taxation were devised, and the system of providing central aid to commanderies suffering crop failures began to break down. This led to serious disaffection in the countryside. There were many local insurrections, the most serious instigated by Zhang Que. He was the leader of a sect that claimed that every 60 years a new cycle of peace and prosperity began and that the next cycle, due to begin in 184 C.E., entailed the end of the Han dynasty. Through the organization of the Yellow Turbans, which would now be described as terrorist cells, Zhang Que fomented a simultaneous uprising across 16 commanderies that stretched the defenses of the court to the limit. Military defeat in one area did not bring the rebellion as a whole to an end, for although Zhang Que himself died in the year of the rebellion, the Yellow Turban movement continued to create disturbances in the provinces for many years. Some Chinese historians, influenced by the importance of peasant revolts, have identified the Yellow Turbans as the cause of the fall of the Eastern Han dynasty, but this claim is probably exaggerated.

Ying Ying was one of the capitals of the CHU state of central China. According to the SHIJI, it was the capital from about 690 B.C.E. until 278 B.C.E. Controversy surrounds its actual location, but it was probably in the valley of the Han River.

Yinjiacheng Yinjiacheng is a settlement site of the LONGSHAN CULTURE in Shandong province, China. This culture, dated to the third millennium B.C.E., is one of several that, through evidence for social ranking, anticipate the transition to early Chinese states, especially notable in poor burials associated with each rich grave located near a house. Pits probably used for sacrifices are also found. More than 2,000 square meters (2,400 sq. yds.) of this site has been opened by excavation, revealing a four-phase sequence, of which the third is best documented. The village then had houses associated with pits and burials to form discrete residential-mortuary contexts. Burials have been divided into five classes depending on their size and the wealth of associated grave offerings. The richest of five Class 1 burials in Phase 3 measured 5.8 by 4.4 meters (19 by 15 ft.) and reached a depth of 1.55 meters (5.1 ft.). Grave goods included 23 pottery vessels of high quality, 20 pigs' jawbones, and the scutes (bony plates on the skin) of an alligator. This last find is highly significant, for the scutes probably formed the striking surface of a drum. Such drums have been found at the contemporary Longshan site of TAOSI and were seen in China as symbols of royalty. Each rich grave was associated with a group of poorer ones.

The presence of 245 pits in the excavated area is intriguing, for at sites such as CHENGZI, also in the Shandong Peninsula, they are thought to have been used for making ritual offerings to the ancestors. Some of those at Yinjiacheng probably had the same purpose. Two contained turtle shells that became prominent for divination ceremonies under the SHANG STATE; another included a jade knife. Such pits are found in association with the richer graves and confirm that the mortuary behavior can best identify the intense social ranking that marked the genesis of the first civilizations in China.

Yoro Code

Yoro Code The Yoro Code was a set of regulations of 718 C.E. that provided the legal basis for the NARA STATE of Japan. The code covered a wide range of activities, starting with the structure of the bureaucracy, for which it named and defined the duties of the departments of state. Provisions for land allocation played a prominent part in the organization of labor. Arable land was provided for each individual above the age of six. For each male commoner, for example, 2,300 square meters (2,760 sq. yds.) was made available. Unallocated land was also given to nobles, officials, Buddhist temples, and those who provided meritorious service to the court. The code provided for a reallocation based on population numbers and need every six years, but this was difficult to undertake thoroughly because of the time it required. Temples were exempt from the land tax. For the rest, there was a tax on rice and production of goods, such as cloth. One male member of every three in a household had to serve in the military, and every commoner had to be registered against his place of residence. It was not permitted to move from the home area. While the Yoro Code set out to regulate in detail the life of individuals in the Nara state, there is recurrent evidence of difficulties in enforcement. Nevertheless, its existence illustrates the desire of the court to take control of the penal and legal systems.

Yue Yue is the name of a state that flourished in southern China during the period of the EASTERN ZHOU DYNASTY (770–221 B.C.E.) until it was incorporated into the Han state. This region is rich in agricultural land and minerals and was early settled by rice farming communities. The concentration of research in the central plains of the Huang (Yellow) River Valley by Chinese archaeologists has often ignored developments in the south. However, from the Shu state of Sichuan through the state of CHU in the middle reaches of the Chang (Yangtze) to the delta area dominated by the WU STATE, there were states powerful enough to challenge those formed to the north with the establishment of the WESTERN ZHOU DYNASTY in the late 11th century B.C.E. Yue is one such entity. It is recorded in the historical Chinese literature that it engaged in internecine conflict with its neighbor state of Wu over possession of the strategic lower Chang Valley. In 496 B.C.E. the Yue army killed the king of Wu, and in 473 B.C.E. it resoundingly defeated the forces of Wu to become effectively the last BA STATE before the advent of the WARRING STATES PERIOD. The Yue army was well equipped with weaponry, to judge from surviving swords made for their kings. Several rich Yue burials have been investigated, and they show that there was much intercourse with the Chu centers to the north. Typical of some rich burials are sets of four human-headed staffs, probably symbols of office.

Wealthy Yue communities were clearly profiting from trade with their mighty Chu neighbor to the north. For centuries the south had supplied northern Chinese states with exotica, including turtle shells for divination, rhinoceros horn, cowry shells for currency, pearls, and kingfisher feathers to decorate Chu wall hangings. The south was also rich in mineral resources, particularly copper. Awareness of iron reached this part of China, it seems, by the fourth century B.C.E.

Several swords have survived, most famously that from Tomb 1 at Wangshan. Inscribed swords have supplied the names of several of the Yue kings. At the end of the Warring States period in 221 B.C.E., QIN SHIHUANGDI, the first emperor, sent armies south to incorporate Yue into his empire. This empire was short lived, for rebellions that followed his death in 210 B.C.E. saw the rise of a number of kingdoms, one of which, that of Nan Yue, covered most of the modern provinces of Guangxi, Guangdong, and the Yuan (Hong, Red) River Delta. This state was founded by Zhao Tuo (r. 203–137 B.C.E., according to the available Chinese records), the former governor of the Nanhai commandery, who saw his opportunity in the chaos that accompanied the fall of the QIN dynasty to reach for independence. He was succeeded by his grandson, ZHAO HU, also known as Wen Di (r. 137–122 B.C.E.). His intact tomb has been found at Xianggang in Guangzhou. He was succeeded by his son, Ming Wang (r. 122–113 B.C.E.). In 111 B.C.E., the HAN DYNASTY under Emperor WUDI returned to the south and extinguished the kingdom of Nan Yue, replacing it with commanderies answerable to the Chinese court.

BURIALS

At Matouling, which dates to the late Spring and Autumn period, bells and vessels probably imported from the Chu state to the north were found in burials in association with bronzes of local inspiration. The latter include four bronze staffs with human heads, short swords, lances, and axes. A second grave from this site had many weapons, including 22 arrowheads. Four human-headed staffs were found in a large and opulent grave from Nanmendong, together with bells and bronze vessels. The single grave investigated at Niaodanshan measured 5.7 by 3.5 meters (18.8 by 11.6 ft.) and contained the remains of a wooden coffin. The grave goods were dominated by RITUAL BRONZE VESSELS and weapons. The four human-headed staffs had on this occasion been placed in each corner of the northern chamber of the grave, facing one another. They must represent some form of symbol of office. At Beifushan, four human-headed staffs recur in a large and richly furnished grave that included numerous weapons, vessels, and jades. The richest Yue burial in this region is found at Beilingsongshan. It stands apart from all the rest by virtue of its size (eight by 4.7 meters) and the opulence of the grave goods. More than 100 bronzes were found, among which vessels predominate. There are also two cast swords and a spearhead. The set of vessels includes some Chu imports, such as a decorated jar inlaid with silver ornaments. A set of four human-headed staffs was also present, while the coffin itself had been embellished with bronze sheets on the exterior. Other grave goods were made of jade and gold.

In the strategic Wushui Valley, there was a large cemetery at Dagongpingcun, dating from the late Spring and Autumn to the Warring States period. Later graves included bronze weapons and vessels as mortuary offerings. To the west, at Yangjia, northern vessel forms were associated with weaponry in the burials. The bronze staffs, however, were now embellished with animal rather than human heads. Moving away from the Zhu River Delta into Guangxi province, the burials become markedly poorer, further confirmation, if needed, for the importance of commanding resources and trade routes.

Iron Objects

None of the graves described yielded any iron artifacts, but at Yinshanling, a cemetery dating to the late Warring States period, some of the 108 excavated graves contained iron offerings. The importance of this site lies in the number of intact graves excavated, their spatial layout, and the complete inventory of mortuary offerings found in each. The graves themselves varied considerably in size, in the presence or absence of a waist pit at the base, and in the provision of a layer of pebbles and a covering tumulus. These, together with as many as 59 different categories of mortuary offerings, make it possible to obtain some information on the social structure of a Yue community during the Warring States period.

The range of grave goods includes 10 types of ceramic vessels, clay spindle whorls for manufacturing yarn, three types of bronze vessels, and bronze swords, arrowheads, spears, halberds, and battle axes. Bronze tools, such as axes, chisels, scrapers, drill points, and knives, were also abundant. Sumptuary bronzes included the familiar animal-headed staffs, ladles, and bells; iron was employed for spearheads, axes, adzes, knives, and scrapers. A statistical analysis of this assemblage of graves has revealed a large number of similar graves with a few special ones. No grave with a spindle whorl was also found to include weaponry, suggesting a division along gender lines, but this hypothesis cannot be confirmed independently because of the poor survival of human bones. Whereas the proposed female graves, those with spindle whorls, also possess iron spades and certain types of pottery vessels, only burials with weapons also have the animal-headed staffs. Furthermore, this second group also has a near-monopoly of rare and exotic Chu imports.

The emphasis on weaponry in this cemetery stresses that it was in use during a period of intense warfare. After the victory of the state of Qin in 221 B.C.E., it is recorded that Qin Shihuangdi, the first emperor, sent five armies south to conquer Yue and take the capital, Panyu. The *History of the Former Han* (HANSHU) describes Panyu as "an emporium that sent north pearls, ivory, rhinoceros skins, fruit and cloth." However, the area of Yue was incorporated into the Qin and Han states as a series of provinces or commanderies. It was during this period that the tomb of Zhao Hu, the second king of Yue under the Western Han, was constructed. Discovered in 1983 at Xianggang in Guangzhou province, the tomb was entered via a ramp and steps nine meters (29.7 ft.) long. Its layout incorporated three chambers toward the front, a main chamber for the coffin, and three ancillary rooms for the storage of mortuary offerings. One of these has been described as the banquet room because of the fine bronzes there; another was called the kitchen. Four wives and seven attendants had been buried alive in another room. The mortuary offerings were varied, with origins in many different areas. There were Chu-inspired bronzes, an Iranian silver box, and African ivory. One large bronze container looks similar to those found in the DONG SON culture to the south. It was decorated with a boat typical of the bronzes cast in the Yuan River Delta.

Further reading: Chao Hing-wa, ed. *Archaeological Discoveries of Ancient Yue People in South China Exhibition.* Hong Kong: Museum of History, 1993; Li Xueqin. *Eastern Zhou and Qin Civilizations.* New Haven, Conn.: Yale University Press, 1985; Swart, P. "The Tomb of the King of Nan Yue," *Orientations* 21 (1990): 56–66.

Yueliangwan   *See* SANXINGDUI.

Yutian   *See* HOTAN.

Z

Zar Tepe Zar Tepe is a city located in the valley of the Surkhan Dar'ya in Tajikistan. Atop KUSHAN foundation, the walled city enclosed a palace and residential areas demarcated by major roads and smaller thoroughfares at right angles to one another. The upper layers contain coins dated to the Kushan-Sassanian period.

Zeng Hou Yi (d. c. 433 B.C.E.) *Zeng Hou Yi was a ruler of the small polity of Zeng, a fief of the Chu state, located in the Yun River Valley of Hubei province, China.*
He was particularly notable for the extraordinary wealth of his tomb, which was discovered intact. It contained bronzes described as among the finest ever cast. These include a set of 64 bells that weigh a total of 2,500 kilograms (5,500 lbs.) and wine containers, the largest of which stands 1.3 meters (4.3 ft.) high. Most bronzes were inscribed with the text, "Hou Yi makes and holds onto the bronze, using it forever."

See also CHU; LEIGUDUN.

Zhangdi (Liu Da; Methodical Emperor) (57–88 C.E.) *Zhangdi, was the third emperor of the Eastern Han dynasty of China.*
He was the fifth son of his predecessor, MINGDI, and acceded to the throne in 75 C.E. His reign was brief and relatively uneventful but did effect improvements in transportation of goods within the empire, particularly in the more remote southern commanderies.

Zhangjiapo Zhangjiapo is a cemetery of the Xing Shu clan, a junior line of the royal lineage of the WESTERN ZHOU DYNASTY. It is located in the vicinity of XIAN in Shaanxi province, China, and contains tombs covering the middle Western Zhou period, dating approximately 975–875 B.C.E. The largest grave, Burial 157, was equipped with two entrance passages with a combined length of 35.5 meters (117 ft.); other tombs had either one such entrance or none. It is thought that such elaboration turned on the status of the individual buried. Wives were interred in graves adjacent to male leaders. The social information that could have been obtained from this site has been greatly reduced by looting. However, it is clear that the person interred in Burial 157 was richly equipped in death, for the components of six chariots were found in association with the tomb, while pits for the burial of horses were also located in the vicinity. Fragments of tents that would have been placed in the burial chambers have also been found. This burial was flanked by two graves for WOMEN, and, despite further looting, these still retained some fine bells and ritual bronze vessels for serving wine.

Zhang Qian (d. 114 B.C.E.) *Zhang Qian was an emissary of the Han dynasty emperor Wudi, who more than anyone else opened the western regions to the expanding Han empire.*
Zhang Qian's travels across the SILK ROAD were instrumental in opening the Chinese to the potential of trade with the West. After his death, the western regions were taken into the Han empire and strongly garrisoned. Watchtowers were built to warn of danger. Strong steppe horses were introduced into China, and as trade grew, BUDDHISM became strongly established.

The Silk Road had for millennia provided a conduit for goods and ideas, linking China with India and the West. Its eastern routes passed north and south of the TARIM BASIN before reaching the oasis center of DUNHUANG and on to the Gansu Corridor. Access to this lucrative route from China was effectively controlled by the XIONGNU, nomadic pastoralists ancestral to the historic Huns. It was against the threat of these powerful and mobile people that the GREAT WALL was constructed. When Xiongnu captives were taken to China and interrogated, they informed the Han that they had defeated a people known as the Yuezhi. The Yuezhi had been forced to move westward, where they entered history as the KUSHANS. Sensing the possibility of securing an ally against the Xiongnu, the emperor dispatched Zhang Qian to make contact with them. This resulted in an epic journey chronicled in the *SHIJI* of SIMA QIAN and in the *History of the Former Han (HANSHU)*.

ZHANG QIAN AND THE XIONGNU

With Ganfu, a Xiongnu captive, Zhang Qian, then a palace attendant, set forth. He was captured and detained by the Xiongnu ruler for a decade, during which time he married a local woman. But he was able to escape and continue his journey westward. After 30 days he reached FERGHANA and was welcomed by the local ruler before continuing on his journey to the land of the Yuezhi. The great king of the Yuezhi did not wish to become embroiled in a war with the Xiongnu. Zhang Qian then continued his journey to visit BACTRIA before returning to China, where he arrived after enduring a second period of capture and confinement by the Xiongnu.

ZHANG QIAN'S TRAVELS WESTWARD

The information contained in the historical accounts of this extraordinary journey was most useful to the Han administration and likewise to historians interested in the state of affairs in Central Asia during the second century B.C.E. Of Ferghana, Zhang Qian wrote: "The people are settled on the land, plowing the fields and growing rice and wheat. They also make wine out of grapes. The region has many fine horses. The people live in fortified cities, there being about seventy or more cities of varying sizes in the region. The people fight with bows and spears, and can shoot from horseback." He described the SAKAS, north of the Amu Dar'ya River, as living a mobile life following their herds. The Parthians still farther west, however, lived in walled cities, while the countryside was under wheat, rice, and vineyards. Merchants there traveled by cart or boat over considerable distances, and he particularly noted that their COINAGE bore the image of the ruler. When the king died, his coins were replaced by a set with the image of the new king's face. Writing was done in horizontal lines on strips of leather. Although he did not travel farther west than PARTHIA, he heard of Mesopotamia through Parthian accounts and described it as hot and damp. The people lived by cultivating rice, by which he must have meant wheat and barley, and there were huge birds there that laid eggs as large as pots. Ostriches are thought to have lived then in the Near East.

He also visited and described Daxia, or BACTRIA, as a land with cities but no state organization. Each city had its own chief. At the capital, Lanshi (Bactra), there was a huge market, and the people were great traders. All sorts of merchandise could be seen there. Most intriguingly, he recognized cloth from Sichuan for sale in Bactria, and when he asked the merchants how it was obtained, they replied that they had bought it in India. In India, he noted, the people go to war on elephants and live beside a great river. Given the difficulties he experienced along the Silk Road, he suggested that the route west out of Sichuan might be the safest and most reliable.

RETURN TO CHINA

The emperor was most interested by all this information of rich potential allies and trading partners to the west and instructed Zhang Qian to attempt to forge a trade route west from Sichuan. This proved virtually impossible because of the dangerous tribes who lived en route. The Kunming of Yunnan, for example, murdered all Chinese on sight.

His career after this epic journey was checkered. He was first created a marquis and sent as a guide and assistant on two Han expeditions against the Xiongnu. However, the defeat of the Han army was partially blamed on his late arrival at a rendezvous, and he was sentenced to death. Commuted from this penalty, he was demoted to a commoner. The emperor then consulted him again on the internal politics of the Xiongnu, and Zhang Qian told him of the people of Wusun, whose king, Kunmo, had declared independence from the Xiongnu. Again, Zhang Qian set out to the western regions with many followers and laden with gifts for Kunmo, in the hope that the ruler would accept them and an alliance with the Han. He then returned to China, where he was honored once again, but he died a year later.

Zhao   Zhao was one of the three states that emerged from the disarticulation of the state of JIN in northern China toward the end of the fifth century B.C.E. It was also the most northerly and thus had the advantage of isolation during the WARRING STATES PERIOD (475–221 B.C.E.). Before the development of total war involving a policy of exterminating all enemy forces, the rulers of Zhao exercised skilled diplomatic alliances with either QIN or QI. There was also a corps of skilled military leaders, which in 269 B.C.E. was able to defeat the army of the powerful state of Qin itself. The size and wealth evident in the archaeological remains are matched by contemporary records describing Zhao. However, the development of a policy of total war in the state of Qin under its redoubtable minister Fan Sui led to the downfall of Zhao. After defeating Qin in 269 B.C.E., the two states entered the decisive phase of war. The Qin under general Bo Qi and Zhao under Zhao Kuo engaged each other, and Zhao suffered terminal defeat.

There were three capitals, beginning with Jinyang. In 425 B.C.E. a move was made to Zhongmau in Henan and 39 years later to Handang at the junction of the Qin and Zhu Rivers in the southern part of the state. Investigations at Handan beginning in 1970 have revealed four major walled precincts. There are three at Zhaowangcheng, covering 500 hectares (1,250 acres). This area includes raised stamped-earth mounds of the royal palace area. The precinct, known as the Dragon Platform, covered eight hectares (20 acres), and the platform survives to a height of more than 16 meters (53 ft.). Such huge so-called *tai* platforms were a widespread feature of the Warring States period, and their construction was said at the time to exhaust the resources of the state. However, their size was seen as a clear symbol of royal power. To the northeast lies a 1,500-hectare area that included the craft workshops. A cemetery to the northwest of the city has also been investigated. The tombs were placed in vertical pits sunk into the ground, and many contained sacrificed victims.

Zhaodi (95–74 B.C.E.) *Zhaodi was the son of a minor consort of the Han dynasty emperor Wudi.*

The final years of Zhaodi's father's reign (141–87 B.C.E.) had been marked by dynastic strife among the families of the emperor's wives, and the choice of Zhaodi, who was only eight years old on his accession, as successor was at least in part influenced by the fact that his mother had already died, and there was no likelihood of the influence of a powerful dowager empress. His reign was dominated by a triumvirate that included the powerful minister Huo Gang. Huo Gang retained a position of dominance during the reign, withstanding several coup attempts that led to the death or suicide of the two other members of the original triumvirate. Emperor Zhaodi died in 74 B.C.E. of unknown causes, and his death was followed by a renewal of factional strife among the members of the rival court factions.

Zhao Gao (precise dates not known) *Zhao Gao was a prominent member of the administration of the state of Qin toward the end of the Warring States period (475–221 B.C.E.).*

A eunuch, Zhao Gao attracted the attention of the king of QIN in about 246 B.C.E. and rose to become the administrator of royal carriages, two of which are represented in bronze in the tomb of QIN SHIHUANGDI, the first emperor of China. This gave Zhao Gao access to the royal court on their progresses through the empire after the final military triumph of Qin in 221 B.C.E. When the emperor died in 210 B.C.E., Zhao Gao was one of a small group who kept the fact secret to allow them time to manipulate the succession. This he achieved by securing a vital letter appointing the emperor's son, Fusu, to take charge of the mortuary rituals and instead sending a forged letter over the emperor's seal requiring the heir to commit suicide. He then manipulated the weak Ying

HUHAI onto the imperial throne and proceeded to dominate the affairs of state himself. The intrigues continued against a background of insurrection and revolt in the formerly proud and independent kingdoms. Zhao Gao forced Huhai to commit suicide and installed Zi Ying on the throne with the title of king rather than emperor. Time, however, was running out for Zhao Gao as further revolts moved closer to the palace, and he himself was murdered in 207 B.C.E.

Zhao Gong (11th century B.C.E.) *Zhao Gong was the son of King Wen of Zhou, the ruler who instigated the overthrow of the Shang state in the 11th century B.C.E., but he did not live to see the final victory at the Battle of Muye (1045 B.C.E.).*

Zhao Gong was the younger brother of King WU, the first king of the WESTERN ZHOU DYNASTY after the overthrow of Shang, and although the dates of his life are not known, he was active in the center of Zhou government during the second half of the 11th century B.C.E. On the death of King Wu, the rightful heir was Wu's oldest son, Song, later known as King Cheng (r. 1042/35–1006 B.C.E.). However, Zhao Gong declared himself regent because of the immature age of the legitimate ruler. A major civil war ensued, which saw the factions supporting Zhao Gong, or Duke Zhao as he is widely known, triumph. This resulted in Zhao's ruling from the major strategic center of Chengzhou, while his relatives spread the area of Zhou control more widely than before, laying thereby the foundations of the later states that rose up during the EASTERN ZHOU DYNASTY. When, in 6 C.E. the usurper WANG MANG put an end to the dynasty of Western Han, he cited Zhao Gong's declarations on the nature of the MANDATE OF HEAVEN in support of his actions. Over a millennium, Zhao Gong's arguments, summarized and repeated in later classic Chinese documents, have maintained his historic image as a man of persuasive ideas. In sum, he argued that the Mandate of Heaven, the charter to rule, was given to the elite, particularly the ministers advising the sovereign. The counterargument proclaimed at the time when the Western Zhou were establishing their kingdom was that the king alone received the mandate. With the increasing authority vested in King Cheng, Duke Zhou retired from active politics, but his legacy lived on.

Zhao Hu (d. 122 B.C.E.) *Zhao Hu, also known as Zhao Mo, was the king of the southern Chinese state of Nan Yue, who acceded to the throne in 137 B.C.E.*

After his death, he was given the posthumous name of Wenwang. He is principally known for the survival of his intact tomb at Xianggang on the Zhu River Delta. The survival of this royal tomb, discovered in 1983, is an extremely important event. This stone palace complex was sought out by Sun Quan, who ruled the southern Chinese state of WU in the third century C.E. He had heard rumors of the treasures it contained and wished to have them. Fortunately, his men were unable to find it.

Among the rich tomb gifts was an outstanding and rare jade found in the king's tomb itself. It was a circular lidded bowl decorated with birds and petals. Its value as an item for the personal use of Zhao Mo may be judged from its association with the king's personal gold SEAL. Its INSCRIPTION reads, "Administrative seal of Emperor Wen." This is the largest gold seal of the Western Han dynasty found, measuring 3.1 centimeters square (0.5 sq. in.). The handle is a fine coiled dragon. The grand title, linked with the magnificence of the tomb, emphasizes the strategic position at the mouth of the Zhu River that Zhao Hu controlled. Panyu, the capital of Nan Yue, commanded a highly strategic location at the mouth of the Zhu River. The king was interred with many rich offerings from Han China and Vietnam, a silver box from Iran containing medicinal pills, and ivory from Africa. It thus provides clear evidence for the operation of a major southern maritime trade route during the second century B.C.E.

FOUNDING OF NAN YUE

Bai Yue, a series of states in southern China, was invaded in 214 B.C.E. by the forces of QIN SHIHUANGDI, the first emperor. Three new commanderies were created, subject to the QIN capital. On the first emperor's death, local leaders revolted against foreign domination and established a series of new states, one of which was known as Nan Yue. The commander of the former commandery of Nanhai, Zhao Tuo (r. 203–137 B.C.E.), founded the kingdom of Nan Yue. While nominally a vassal of the Han emperor, he exercised virtually complete autonomy, and on his death he was succeeded by his grandson, Zhao Hu, who in turn was succeeded by his son, Ming Wang (r. 122–113 B.C.E.).

PLAN OF TOMB

The tomb resembles those constructed for Liu Sheng and his consort at MANCHENG, with chambers cut into a hillside. The construction of the tomb itself called on the placement of huge stone slabs, 24 for the roof, each weighing between three and four tons. Its layout had three chambers toward the front, a main chamber for the coffin, and three ancillary rooms for the storage of mortuary offerings. Internal doors were of wood, but the main entrance and the portal leading to the tomb itself had stone doors with a self-locking device that could not be reopened once closed. The suite of rooms was built as a subterranean palace. The first room to be entered was an antechamber, the walls of which were painted with cloud designs. The remains of a carriage with bronze fittings lay within. The chamber contained some of the king's possessions wrapped in silk and placed in bamboo and LACQUER receptacles. It was flanked by a storeroom to the west and a ceremonial chamber to the east. The latter had been used for musical instruments, including a set of bronze

bells and zithers, as well as bronze and ceramic wine containers. They were still protected by official clay seals. The skeleton of a young man, perhaps a musician, was found here, together with two wooden models of humans.

One of the chambers within has been described as the banquet room, because of the fine bronzes located there; another was called the kitchen, because of the remains of oxen, fish, chickens, and pigs. Seven servants had been killed and buried in this room. To the right of the burial chamber there was a room containing the remains of four WOMEN. Entrance to it was barred by a lacquer screen with bronze bases, decorated with bronzes and feathers. One of the women within was interred with a seal giving her name as You Furen, lady to the right. The right-hand side was regarded as the more prestigious. She wore a jade pendant in the form of two dragons facing each other, part of a set of jade pendants that would probably have been suspended from the neck. Six other sets were found with the women interred near the king.

TOMB FURNISHINGS

The tomb chamber itself was protected by two guards, buried at the same time as the king. He had been interred in a double lacquer coffin with gilt bronze fittings, but it had long since decayed through flooding. He wore a splendid jade suit made of 2,291 individual wafers. Those covering the head, hands, and feet were sewn together with silk thread, but others adhered to a backing. The remains of his skull and teeth suggested that he died when aged between 35 and 45 years. He was accompanied by a dazzling array of grave goods. His military role is reflected in his suit of iron armor and 10 long iron swords. Two bronze tallies in the form of a tiger inlaid with gold would probably have been used to confirm his duties, for the inscription on them reads, "By the king's orders." The jades found with him were of the highest quality. A single jade disk with a dragon and a phoenix in combat was found at his head, but nine other jade *bi* disks, auspicious symbols, were also present. One was held in the mouth of a TAOTIE mask. There were rare jade drinking goblets with handles of gilt bronze and a drinking vessel in the shape of a horn, ornamented with incised designs.

There are many other offerings of outstanding interest. One is a bronze dish from which emerge three sinuous creatures with catlike faces, gripping in their mouths a jade disk supporting a jade cylinder. This is thought to have been a dew collector. Documentary records reveal that dew conferred immortality, and the HAN DYNASTY emperor WUDI would drink dew collected in such a vessel to obtain everlasting life. There is a set of eight bronze bells, the heaviest weighing 40 kilograms (88 lbs.). They are inscribed with the words, "Made by the music department in the ninth year of the reign of WENDI" (129 B.C.E.). That bronzes were locally cast is shown by the presence of pieces of clay mold associated with a rectangular stove still containing the spikes for roasting meat. A tall bronze situla, probably for serving wine, is also a local product. It was embellished with images of plumed warriors, some in a war canoe. One man, standing on top of the cabin, is brandishing a bow and arrow. Another holds a captive by the hair. Identical motifs were found in northern Vietnam in sites of the DONG SON culture and in the DIAN CHIEFDOM cemeteries of Yunnan.

The remarkable wealth of this tomb and the presence of exotic items such as a Persian box stress the importance of maritime trade during the last few centuries B.C.E. Nan Yue was renowned in the Han court for its pearls, kingfisher feathers, ivory, marine shells, and turtle shells.

Further reading: Swart, P. "The Tomb of the King of Nan Yue," *Orientations* 21 (1990): 56–66.

Zheng   Zheng is the name of a state that was founded in China toward the end of the WESTERN ZHOU DYNASTY in 806 B.C.E. The enfeoffed first ruler was Zheng Huan Gong (r. 806–771 B.C.E.), younger brother of King Xuan. This was the twilight period of the WESTERN ZHOU DYNASTY, and the last two kings were supported strongly by the rulers of Zheng. Because of the threat from the west, the capital of Zheng was moved to ZHENGZHOU in Henan province. During the first reigns of the new EASTERN ZHOU DYNASTY, the rulers of Zheng assumed high prominence as early leaders of the BA SYSTEM, whereby one of the several emerging states became politically dominant. However, the third ruler of Zheng, Zhuang Gong, grew too prominent and clashed with the Zhou king, Ping. There followed a battle in 707 B.C.E. in which the king was injured. Zhuang Gong died in 701, and the authority of Zheng then declined as it entered into a period of internal friction over the succession. Zheng was never large or powerful enough to withstand the rising might of QI, QIN, CHU, or JIN and was particularly vulnerable to the northward expansion of Chu. However, the mortuary remains from Zhengzhou and Tanghu attest to the wealth of the leaders of this state. The Zhengzhou tomb was among the first to be examined with a semblance of scientific precision, in 1923. It contained many fine bronze vessels, but the INSCRIPTIONS have not survived sufficiently for a full translation. It is thought that it was the tomb of Duke Chenggong, who died in 571 B.C.E.

Zhengzhou   Zhengzhou is a major historical city, best known for its importance during the middle period of the SHANG STATE, which continued to be occupied during the WARRING STATES PERIOD (475–221 B.C.E.) and the Han and Ming dynasties. It is occupied today and is the capital city of Henan province. It is best known as a major royal city of the Middle Shang period before the capital was established at ANYANG. Excavations in the northeastern quarter of this city, which had a rectangular shape, have uncovered stamped-earth foundations that formed a raised platform at least 60 meters (198 ft.) long. This incorporated large circular holes for receiving posts or columns for a building so large that it was probably a palace, surrounded by a moat. The bronzes of Zhengzhou are particularly interesting. They tend to be smaller and thinner than their counterparts at Anyang, and there are no obvious intaglio inscriptions on them. Their designs are less complex than those of Anyang, but their quality leaves no doubt as to the skill of the specialists at this site. The site is located on elevated ground near the confluence of the Jinshui and Xionger Rivers, a typical situation for a Shang city, and commands the strategic junction of the western loess uplands and the broad expanses of the Huang (Yellow) River Plain. Of the several alternatives, most think that this site was known then as Ao, founded by King Zhong Ding of the sixth generation of Shang kings. However, it might equally have been the site of Bo, the first capital of the Shang dynasty (1766–1045 B.C.E.), and in the absence of a documentary record, it is hard to see how either attribution can be confirmed.

ARCHITECTURAL REMAINS

It has proved difficult to open substantial areas of the site because it lies under a modern city and extends beyond the ancient walls to cover an area of 25 square kilometers (10 sq. mi.). The site was first recognized for its early date and historical importance in 1950, when investigations took place at a small mound known as Erligang near the southeastern outskirts of the city. This site has given its name to the middle phase of the sequence of the Shang dynasty. To the north lie the stamped-earth city walls that survive, in part up to nine meters (30 ft.) high and 36 meters (119 ft.) wide at the base. These walls enclose an area of about 335 hectares (837.5 acres). Excavations across and below these walls reveal that they were built during the so-called Erligang period, a finding supported by a radiocarbon determination in the vicinity of 1650 B.C.E. These walls overlay cultural material ascribed to the Luodamiao culture and therefore corresponding to the last two phases of the occupation of ERLITOU. They were constructed of stamped earth, a technique that involved stamping down layers of earth about 10 centimeters (4 in.) thick in a framework of wooden planks. The impressions of the planks and the depressions formed with the stamping of the surface with a blunt instrument have survived. Occasionally skeletons of workers employed on the construction have also been found.

SACRIFICES AND OFFERINGS

A ditch in the northeast area was filled with a dense cluster of human skulls, many of which had been cut in half. They were mainly those of young men. Other pits in the northern part of the city contained many dogs' skeletons:

One had the remains of 23 dogs. Dogs were often sacrificed as part of divination rituals at Anyang, and animals and people were also commonly slaughtered with the construction of new buildings. Other smaller stamped-earth foundations elsewhere in the city indicate a dense urban settlement. Some graves in the vicinity of the palace were equipped with rich mortuary offerings, including RITUAL BRONZE VESSELS and jade and bronze ornaments, the equipment associated with the aristocratic element of society. Some pits contained fragments of ORACLE BONES. There was also a piece of bovid rib with a series of written characters, one of which is probably the word *zhen*. This is a widely used form for ritual divination, which makes it likely that Zhengzhou was one of the Shang royal capitals.

WORKSHOPS

The area outside the city walls has also been investigated and found to contain the remains of specialist manufacture. A bronze workshop yielded not only the remains of houses, presumably for the specialists involved, but also ceramic molds for casting ceremonial vessels, knives, daggers, arrowheads, and bronze residue from the casting process. There were also a ceramic workshop equipped with large kilns and the wastes of pots not properly fired. Once again, stamped-earth houses indicate that the potters lived adjacent to their places of work. There was an atelier for the manufacture of bone ornaments and weapons, including arrowheads and hairpins. One cache found outside the city walls contained 13 fine bronze ritual vessels, including a *ting* that stood one meter high and weighed 86.4 kilograms (190 lbs). There are also at least four extramural cemeteries, in which grave goods included sacrificed dogs, bronzes, jades, and ceramic vessels.

Further reading: Chang, K.-C. *The Shang Civilization.* New Haven, Conn.: Yale University Press, 1980; Loewe, M., and E. L. Shaugnessy, eds. *The Cambridge History of Ancient China.* Cambridge: Cambridge University Press, 1999.

Zhidi (Liu Zuan; Upright Emperor) (138–146 C.E.) *Zhidi was the ninth e\mperor of the Eastern Han dynasty of China.* He was the great-great-grandson of Emperor ZHANGDI and acceded to the throne in 145 C.E. He was on the imperial throne for only 16 months before his death at the age of eight.

Zhongshan Zhongshan was a small state in China that survived for much of the EASTERN ZHOU DYNASTY until it succumbed to the state of Zhou in 296 B.C.E. It was located in the province of Hebei in northern China and was hemmed in to the east and west by two more powerful states, Yan and Zhao. A royal funerary park outside the capital city of Lingshou was constructed for King Cuo of Zhongshan, who died in about 308 B.C.E. The king himself was interred in the central tomb, one of the largest vertical mortuary pits discovered in early China. Archaeological investigations in 1974–78 encountered a looted burial chamber but recovered a remarkable bronze plaque containing a detailed plan of the mortuary park complete with INSCRIPTIONS describing its parts and a warning that those who did not complete it according to plan would be executed without mercy. It was not to be completed because, only a decade after King Cuo's death the state of Zhongshan was annihilated. The plan, however, revealed that each of the five major tombs in a row was covered by raised pavilions in an innovative move to project the power and magnificence of the deceased. One underground pit contained the royal chariots, four in all, with 12 horses, a tent, and weaponry. Another was filled with his hunting equipment, including two dogs wearing gold and silver collars. Five royal boats filled a third pit, into which water could flow through a special channel. Other chambers were fortunately not only found intact, but filled with a treasury of outstanding bronzes that evidence the skill of the royal bronze casters. There was, for example, a tree with lamps. Birds perched among the branches, and men at the base were feeding monkeys.

The founding population of Zhongshan were thought to have been the White Di, a formerly nomadic steppe group whose heritage might be seen in the later vigorous bronze castings that recall steppe prototypes. However, the population was heavily sinicized, particularly during a period between 406 and 378 B.C.E. when it was conquered by the state of WEI. Archaeological and literary evidence makes it clear that the people of Zhongshan were proficient at iron working, and it is recorded that they fought with iron armor and weaponry. They were also described as a state that could put 1,000 chariots into the field.

Archaeological research at Sanji in Hebei has identified the capital city of Lingshou. Its walls cover an area of about four by two kilometers (2.4 by 1.2 mi.) and contained habitation areas and workshops for the production of bronze, iron, bone, and ceramic artifacts dating to the WARRING STATES PERIOD (475–221 B.C.E.). A royal mausoleum in the southwestern part of the city has been identified, known as Tomb 6, and beyond the confines of the city walls a royal funerary park has been investigated in detail. It includes a double-walled precinct, the outer walls covering an area of 410 by 176 meters (451 by 194 yds.). Moreover, despite the looting and burning of the central chamber, excavators encountered a number of subterranean pits that contained offerings for the deceased ruler. In many respects, these anticipate the much larger funerary complex of QIN SHIHUANGDI, the first emperor of China, who was interred a century later.

The central and largest tomb for the king was associated with two mausolea on each side, thought to have been designated for his queens and principal concubines.

Five further small tombs north of the king's pit contained the remains of court WOMEN, richly endowed with grave goods, each with her head pointing in the direction of the king. A particular feature of the bronze industry was the use of gold or silver inlay, seen to perfection on a figure of a magnificent tiger consuming a deer. The inlay was placed to accentuate the natural musculature of the tiger. A second lamp was formed as a human figure with a head cast in silver, and there was also a fine bronze table richly inlaid with silver over a base of entwined dragons and phoenixes. Iron was also used in the manufacture of goods designated to accompany the king, and a *ding* food vessel with iron legs was found. Some of the bronzes contained long inscriptions, which supply information on the ruling dynasty and encounters with other states. King Cuo, for example, took part in the defeat of the state of Yan, but Zhongshan, never large enough to maintain its independence, was eliminated soon after his death.

Zhou Daguan (late 13th–early 14th century) *Zhou Daguan visited Angkor in Cambodia as a member of a Chinese diplomatic mission from August 1296 until July 1297.* He wrote a description of his impressions, and these are an unparalleled source of information on the daily life of the inhabitants of ANGKOR THOM during the reign of King INDRAVARMAN III (r. 1296–1308). As a diplomat, Zhou Daguan was given access to the royal palace, while his travels to and from the capital enabled him to appreciate life in the countryside. It is possible to identify the monuments he described and the locations he visited. The southern entrance to the city of Angkor Thom today is a massive gateway in front of a bridge over the moat. This bridge is bordered by giants and demons holding a sacred *naga* snake. Describing the 54 giants, Zhou Daguan said that they were holding the snake as if it was trying to escape. Within, he described the tower of gold, which must be the BAYON temple, which was then gilded. The tower of copper was the BAPHUON temple. Today the temples are a gray sandstone. He described the PHIMEANAKAS, the temple in the walled palace precinct, as being covered with metal. To the east of this precinct lay a gold bridge guarded by gilt lions, which gave way to a splendid pavilion that stood, unmistakably, on the modern ELEPHANT TERRACE.

From this vantage point, the king and members of the court could view the spectacles that took place in the open ground between the palace and the temples to the east. Zhou Daguan was taken by the size of the great BARAYS, describing the Northern Baray (Jayatataka), with the NEAK PEAN island temple and the eastern lake, the temple on its central island harboring a huge bronze statue of the Buddha. Here he seems to have lost his bearings, for he was probably describing the WESTERN BARAY, where a bronze statue of Vishnu has been recovered.

Zhou Daguan lived in a middle-class home near the northern gate for much of his stay. The floor was covered by matting, and there were no tables, chairs, or beds. Rice was husked on a mortar and cooked over a clay stove before being served on pottery or copper plates. Alcoholic drinks were made of honey, rice, leaves, and water. Social classes were distinguished by their houses, clothing, and drinking vessels, ranging from gold for the aristocracy through silver to tin and pottery. Latrines, excavated by a group of families, were in the ground and covered with leaves. When full, they were replaced. Slaves performed a wide range of tasks. Rich families might own more than 100, poor families few or none.

A wide range of specialists and traders lived within the city walls. Astronomers were very skilled and could predict eclipses. There was an inspector for the collection of live human gall, which was used to give courage to men and elephants. Many Chinese traders lived at Angkor Thom. They imported Chinese ceramics, LACQUER, cloth, iron, and copperware. Local WOMEN were active in the city market. Three groups of religious functionaries were present: Buddhists, Hindu Brahmans, and Sivaites. The city gates were closed every night. Dogs and criminals who had had their toes cut off were barred entry. Those guilty of serious crimes had their limbs crushed under heavy weights.

Perhaps the most graphic of all his descriptions was that of a royal procession, in which members of the court who rode on elephants preceded the king, who, surrounded by female bodyguards, was holding aloft the *preah khan,* or sacred state sword. An audience with the king also involved intense rituals. Music preceded the arrival of the king at a gilt window. Supplicants prostrated themselves with the forehead on the ground. King Indravarman III wore exquisite clothes made of woven floral patterns, a gold diadem, and gold and pearl jewelry.

Beyond the city gates, Zhou Daguan described 90 provinces, each with a regional capital. River and lake transport was important, but there were also roads and stone bridges, with rest houses at strategic intervals. Four harvests of rice a year were possible, each involving a different technique of cultivation. The peasants used plows, sickles, and hoes and cultivated a wide variety of vegetables, herbs, and fruit trees.

Zhuangbai In 1975 a remarkable hoard of 103 RITUAL BRONZE VESSELS and bells was found in a two-meter-long pit at Zhuangbai in Fufeng county, Shaanxi province, China. The inscribed vessels had been stacked neatly in a manner suggesting that their owners intended to recover them after a period of social unrest, probably that attending the end of the WESTERN ZHOU DYNASTY in 771 B.C.E. The texts indicate that the hoard belonged to the Wei family and included heirlooms extending back through five generations. One of the most important items was the SHI QIANG *pan,* because its INSCRIPTION recorded the history of the Western Zhou kings, together with descriptions of the male ancestors back to the foundation of the dynasty and the end of the SHANG. This is often cited as the first Chinese historical text. It states that the high ancestor of the WEI line was granted land in the Zhou Plain by King Wu of Zhou just after the BATTLE OF MUYE in 1045 B.C.E. His descendants were Yi, Xin, Duke Yi, and then Shi Qiang, who had the vessel cast. Some of the vessels hoarded were heirlooms cast by these named forebears, but 36 of the vessels were later cast by Shi Qiang's son, Xing, and even more later ones by his grandson, Bo Xianfu. This last individual was probably the one who had the vessels hidden during the invasion of the plain of Zhou by the Quan Rong people in the eighth century B.C.E. This hoard, representing as it does at least five but possibly more vessels cast by successive generations of the same family, provides unique insight into the developing bronze styles of the Western Zhou.

Zhufeng Zhufeng is a site of the LONGSHAN CULTURE in Shandong province, China. This culture preceded the transition to the first civilization of the Huang (Yellow) River Valley, and the excavations at Zhufeng in 1987–89 uncovered three outstandingly rich burials of the middle to late Longshan, dating in the mid-third millennium B.C.E. The graves and their contents assist in documenting and understanding the growing size and wealth of the communities responsible for the transition. Burial 1 included a series of wooden compartments in a grave that measured 4.4 by 2.5 meters (14.5 by 8.3 ft.). It contained the skeleton of a woman in the coffin chamber, associated with TURQUOISE and jade ornaments, six fine eggshell-thin pottery goblets in a chamber containing a total of 35 ceramic vessels, and pigs' jawbones. A second burial was larger and richer. It measured 6.7 meters (22 ft.) long and reached a depth of more than two meters, but its width could not be ascertained because of disturbance. The dead individual wore a jade headdress and was found with jade ritual axes and a knife. Side compartments contained ceramic vessels of high quality and crocodile scutes, the bony parts of the skin, which may well have been the striking surface of a drum as at the related site of TAOSI. Some of the scutes at Zhufeng bore red, black, and white paint. The third grave was equally large, 6.5 meters (21.5 ft.) long and 4.5 (14.9 ft.) wide. It too contained internal wooden divisions for the body and mortuary offerings that included jade and turquoise ornaments or ritual objects and 50 ceramic vessels. The presence of smaller and poorer graves at this site emphasizes the social divisions that were opening up during the course of the later Longshan culture.

Zhukaigou Zhukaigou, a Bronze Age settlement in southwestern Inner Mongolia, has given its name to a group of similar sites dated 2000–1500 B.C.E. The Zhukaigou culture is thus a contemporary of many settle-ments from Gansu to Liaoning provinces and down the course of the Huang (Yellow) River that reveal a marked trend to social complexity during the Chinese Early Bronze Age. The excavation of Zhukaigou between 1977 and 1984 revealed five phases of occupation. The earliest layers included house foundations, human burials associated with pottery vessels, and stone axes and knives; the inhabitants cultivated millet and maintained domestic sheep and cattle. The second and third phases of occupation incorporated a series of important changes: Bronze awls and needles were cast, and sickles were now used. As is the case across much of northern China at this juncture, polished animal scapulae were burned and used in divination rituals. Many more animals were now placed as sacrificial offerings with the dead, and human sacrifice also appeared. The ORACLE BONES during Phase IV were carefully drilled before being cracked, while mortuary rituals became more elaborate. This phase has produced two radiocarbon dates of 1735 and 1565 B.C.E., making this phase equivalent to the late occupation of the site of ERLITOU. Finally, the fifth phase saw a proliferation in elaborate bronze castings, some of which were undertaken on the site, as is seen in the presence of a mold for casting an ax. There are also halberds and ritual bronze vessels such as the *ding* and *jue*. Tomb 1040 furnished a long ax and a dagger, as well as a bronze knife. These artifacts are clearly related to the repertoire of bronzes from the Erligang phase of the SHANG STATE. However, burials also include daggers matched in assemblages to the west on the steppes. Initially, Zhukaigou and related sites in western Inner Mongolia subscribed to a broad tradition of early copper and bronze use, oracle-bone divination, and a mixed economy of stock raising and agriculture. In the final phase, the culture was influenced, probably through trade contacts, by the increasingly sophisticated Middle Shang civilization as well as by the bronze-using societies on steppes.

Zhushu Jinian *See* BAMBOO ANNALS.

Zidanku In 1942, looters seized a silk manuscript from a tomb at Zidanku in Changsha, Hunan province, China. It dates to about 300 B.C.E. and is one of several documents on silk from the kingdom of CHU. This particular example, which had been interred in a woven bamboo container, was about 25 centimeters (10 in.) wide and represented a divination board. The text was concerned with the divine origin of the calendar and was surrounded by images of 12 gods, each of whom represented one month.

See also EASTERN ZHOU DYNASTY; MAWANGDUI.

***Zuozhuan* (Tso Chuan)** The *Zuozhuan*, or Commentary of Zuo (Tso), is a work of unknown authorship dating to the Chinese historical period named after the *Spring and Autumn Annals* (CHUNQUI FANLU) of CONFUCIUS. It was probably compiled later during the WARRING STATES PERIOD (475–221 C.E.) and incorporates a series of discourses on the nature of kingship. One passage, for example, provides the record of a conversation between Duke Dao of JIN and his musician, Shi Kuang. The two discuss the fact that in 559 B.C.E. the duke Xiang of WEI was deposed. This is seen by Dao as disastrous, but Shi Kuang argues that a ruler must be benevolent and fair to his people, and if he ignores the advice of his ministers, then there should be no impediment to expelling him. A second episode concerned the duke Xiang of QI, who reigned from 553 to 548 B.C.E. It includes a description of divination by interpreting the patterned fall of MILFOIL stalks and tells of poor governance that resulted in the duke's being assassinated by an arrow while attempting to escape imprisonment. A further delightful section describes the result of a divination with turtle shell by the duke Wen of Zhu, who in 614 B.C.E. responded to a divination that moving to a new capital would benefit the people, but not the duke himself. Despite this warning, Duke Wen insisted that any move that benefited the people would be desirable for him as well. The capital was moved, but the duke soon died. The moral to this story is then made clear: The duke understood the meaning of destiny.

CHRONOLOGY

5000 B.C.E.	Yangshao culture developing in the Huang (Yellow) River Valley, China
	Mehrgarh occupied in Baluchistan; a long prehistoric sequence unfolding
4700	Hongshan culture developing in northern China
4000 B.C.E.	Foundation of Chengtoushan in the Chang (Yangtze) Valley
3300	Ravi phase of the Indus Valley civilization developing; earliest evidence for Indus Valley civilization script
3200	Amri-Nal phase of early Indus Valley civilization begins
	Liangzhu culture of lower Chang (Yangtze) Valley flourishing
3000 B.C.E.	Earliest evidence for copper metallurgy in China at Linjia
	Amri culture of lower Indus Valley begins
2900	End of the Hongshan culture in northern China
2800	End of the Ravi phase of the Indus civilization
2600	Indus civilization developing strongly
2500	Early oracle bones found at Chengziyai
2400	Lower Xiajiadian culture of Inner Mongolia developing
2300	Jhukar culture of Indus Valley
	Longshan culture of China beginning
2200	Early bronzes in Qijia culture of northwest China
2100	Sapallitepa in Bactria occupied
2000 B.C.E.	Mohenjo Daro, great Indus civilization city, abandoned
	Liangzhu culture of lower Chang (Yangtze) Valley on the wane
1900	End of the Longshan culture of China
	Settlement of Erlitou
	Beginning of the Xia dynasty of China
	Indus Valley civilization on the wane
1700	Foundation of the Shang dynasty in China
1600	Lower Xiajiadian culture of Inner Mongolia on the wane
1500	Walls of Sanxingdui constructed
1400	Huanbei, Shang dynasty capital city, founded
1100	Beginning of North Indian Grey Ware culture
1000 B.C.E.	End of the Shang dynasty of China
	Battle of Muye
	Commencement of the Western Zhou dynasty
800	End of the Western Zhou dynasty
	Start of the Eastern Zhou
700	Beginning of the Spring and Autumn period in China
	Luoyang, the capital of the Eastern Zhou dynasty, founded
500	Confucius's promotion of his political philosophy in China
	Birth of the Buddha
	Period of *mahajanapadas* in northern India
	Brahmi script in use in Sri Lanka
	Appearance of Northern Black Polished Ware in Ganges (Ganga) Valley
	End of the Spring and Autumn period in China; beginning of the Warring States period
	Rise to prominence of the Wu state in southern China
	Darius the Great's eastward expansion of Achaemenid empire
400	End of the state of Jin in China; foundation of the states of Wei, Hann, and Zhao
	Oxus treasure created
	Leigudun tomb of the marquis of Zeng in China
	Bhir Mound at Taxila founded
	Maurya empire developing in India
300	Lomasa Rishi, one of the earliest Buddhist rock-cut temples in India, created
	Rice cultivation adopted in Japan
	End of Achaemenid empire; Alexander the Great victorious at Gaugamela
	Alexander the Great's conquest in Indus Valley
	Foundation of Seleucid empire
	Ay Khanum, a Greek city in northern Afghanistan, founded
	Bactrian Greek kings beginning rule; Kharoshthi script being used

Arthasastra composed by Kautilya, minister to Candragupta Maurya

Megasthenes appointed ambassador to the court of Candragupta

King Seleucus I Nicator fails to regain Indian territory

City of Anuradhapura in Sri Lanka founded

Beginning of Yayoi culture of Japan

Asoka's rule of Maurya empire

Asoka's conquests of the state of Kalinga

State of Hotan southwest of the Tarim Basin developing

Sa Huynh culture, predecessor of the Cham state, developing in Vietnam

End of the Warring States period in China

Establishment of Qin dynasty, China; terra-cotta army of Qin Shihuangdi created

Work commences on the Great Wall of China

Foundation of the Han dynasty

200   Foundation of the Shunga dynasty in India; end of the Mauryan dynasty

Battle of Pingcheng between Han emperor Gaodi and Xiongnu under Maodun

Sirkap, the second city at Taxila, founded

Beikthano city founded in Myanmar (Burma)

Records of the Grand Historian (Shiji) compiled by Sima Qian in China

Rule of Maodun, greatest leader of the Xiongnu

Tombs of Mawangdui, China, constructed

Amaravati stupa constructed in India

Text of the *Ramayana* probably completed in India

100 B.C.E.   End of the Choson state in Korea, foundation of the Lelang commandery

Beginning of the Tarim Basin state of Shan-shan

Sunga dynasty reign in the lower Ganges (Ganga) Valley

Arikamedu, a Roman trading port in India, active

Foundation of the state of Paekche in Korea

Foundation of the state of Shilla in Korea

Red Eyebrow rebellion in China

Wang Mang's creation of the short-lived Xin dynasty of China

0   Ban Biao's writing of the *History of the Former Han (Hanshu)*

Kushan empire founded by Kujula Kadphises

100 C.E.   Kushan founding of Sirsukh, the third city at Taxila

King Kanishka's rule of Kushan empire

The gold burials of Tillya Tepe in Afghanistan

Tomb of Prince Liu Sheng in Mancheng, China

Construction of the massive Alisara Canal by King Vasabha of Anuradhapura

Yellow Turban rebellion against the Eastern Han

Beginning of the Funan state in the Mekong Delta

Founding of Pyu civilization in Myanmar (Burma)

Satavahana dynasty founded in the Deccan, India

Rise of the western satraps in western India

200   End of the Han dynasty

Sassanian empire founded in Persia

Ajanta temples begun

Kofun burial mounds built in Japan for emerging elite

Mathura art style

300   Rise of the Pallava state of central India

Koguryo state of northern Korea developing in power

Yamato state developing in Japan

Beginning of the Cham civilization in Vietnam

Kushan empire declining in power

Foundation of Bamiyan

Mogao Caves near Dunhuang occupied

Foundation of Funan state, Mekong Valley

End of Yayoi culture of Japan

Kidarite Huns invade Transoxiana

400   Chinese Buddhist monk Faxian's visit to India

Begram treasure

State of Taruma in western Java developing

Rise of the state of Dvaravati in central Thailand

My Son, a major Cham capital in Vietnam, founded

Rule of King Nintoku of Yamato in Japan, interment in the largest known *kofun* mounded tomb

500   Reign of King Muryong of Paekche

End of the Funan state in the Mekong Delta

Hephthalite Huns invade Sogdiana

Chenla states of Mekong Valley active

Fall of state of Kaya in Korea to Shilla forces

Rise of Candra dynasty in Rakhine (Arakan), Myanmar (Burma)

Latest additions to rock-cut temples of Ellora

Chinese pilgrim Xuanzang's visit Bamiyan

Construction of the Horyuji Buddhist monastery in Japan

Shilla state unification of the Korean Peninsula

Asuka, capital of Yamato Japan, founded

600 Rise of the maritime trading state of Srivijaya on Sumatra, Indonesia

Death of Prince Shotoku, patron saint of Japanese Buddhism

Mokkan (wooden tablets) used in Japan to record transactions

Taika Reforms begun in Japan

State of Paekche in Korea conquered by Shilla forces

700 State of Parhae founded in north Korea and Manchuria

Ritsuryo Code promulgated in Japan

Fujiwara inaugurated as the capital of Yamato

Nihongi, Japan's first history, composed

Nara state founded in Japan

Todaiji temple at Heijo-kyo completed

Rise of the Sailendra dynasty in Java, Indonesia

Foundation of Angkor civilization

800 *Shoku Nihongi* (*Continued Chronicle of Japan*) completed

Borobudur temple in Java constructed

Shit-taung inscription of Rakhine (Arakan)

Foundation of the state of Pagan in Myanmar (Burma)

900 End of the Korean state of Parhae

Construction of Prambanan temples in Java, Indonesia

1000 Foundation of the dynasty of the "sun kings" at Angkor

Airlangga ruling in east Java, Indonesia

Anawrahta of Pagan ruling in Myanmar (Burma)

Establishment of the Mahidharapura dynasty at Angkor

1100 *Samguk Sagi* (*History of the Three Kingdoms*) compiled in Korea

Building of Angkor Wat

King Kyanzittha's founding of Apeyatana temple at Pagan, Myanmar (Burma)

BIBLIOGRAPHY

Allchin, F. R., ed. *The Archaeology of Early Historic South Asia*. Cambridge: Cambridge University Press, 1995.

Aston, W. G. Nihongi. *Chronicles of Japan from the Earliest Times to A.D. 697*. Rutland, Vt., and Tokyo: Tuttle, 1995.

Aung Thaw. *Historical Sites in Burma*. Rangoon: Sarpay Beikman Press, 1972.

———. *Report on the Excavations at Beikthano*. Rangoon: Government of the Union of Myanmar, 1968.

Aung-Thwin, M. *Myth and History in the Historiography of Early Burma: Paradigms, Primary Sources, and Prejudices*. Singapore: Institute of Southeast Asian Studies, 1998.

Bader, A., V. Gaibov, and G. Koshelenko, "The Northern Periphery of the Merv Oasis," *Silk Road Art and Archaeology* III (1993–1994): 51–70.

Bagley, R. W. *Ancient Sichuan*. Seattle and Princeton: Seattle Art Museum, 2001.

———. "An Early Bronze Age Tomb in Jiangxi Province," *Orientations* 24 (1993): 20–36.

———. "P'an-lung-ch'eng: A Shang City in Hupei," *Artibus Asiae* 39 (1977): 165–219.

———. "A Shang City in Sichuan Province," *Orientations* 21 (1990): 52–67.

Bailey, H. *The Culture of the Sakas in Ancient Iranian Khotan*. Columbia Lecture Series on Iranian Studies No. 1. New York: Caravan Books, 1982.

———. "Saka-Studies: The Ancient Kingdom of Khotan," *Iran* 8 (1970): 65–72.

Barnard, N. "The Nature of the Ch'in 'Reform of the Script' as Reflected in Archaeological Documents Excavated under Conditions of Control." In *Ancient China: Studies in Early Civilization*, edited by D. T. Roy and Tsuen-hsuin Tsien. Hong Kong: Chinese University Press, 1978.

Barnes, G. *Prehistoric Yamato: Archaeology of the First Japanese State*. Ann Arbor: University of Michigan Press, 1988.

———. *State Formation in Korea*. London: Curzon Press, 2001.

———., ed. *Hoabinhian, Jomon, Yayoi, Early Korean States*. Oxford: Oxbow Books, 1990.

Barrett-Jones, A. M. *Early Tenth-Century Inscriptions from Java*. Dordrecht: Foris Publications, 1984.

Bechert, H., and R. Gombrich, eds. *The World of Buddhism*. London: Thames and Hudson, 1984.

Beckman, J. "Master Zhao's Grave: Staging an Eastern Zhou Burial," *Orientations* 34 (2002): 22–26.

Begley, V., ed. *The Ancient Port of Arikamedu: New Excavations and Researches 1989–1992*. Pondichéry: École Française d'Extrême-Orient. Memoires Archéologiques, No. 22, 1996.

Belenitksy, A. *Central Asia*. Cleveland: World Publishing Company, 1968.

Bernard, P. "Ai Khanum on the Oxus: A Hellenistic City in Central Asia," *Proceedings of the British Academy* 53 (1967): 71–95.

Bielenstein, H. *The Bureaucracy of Han Times*. Cambridge: Cambridge University Press, 1980.

———. "The Restoration of the Han Dynasty," *Bulletin of the Museum of Far Eastern Antiquities* 26 (1954): 9–20.

Blakely, B. "In Search of Danyang 1: Historical Geography and Archaeological Sites," *Early China* 13 (1988): 116–152.

———. "On the Location of the Chu Capital in Early Chunqui Times in Light of the Handong Incident," *Early China* 15 (1990): 49–70.

Boisselier, J. *La Statuaire khmere et son evolution*. Paris: Publications de l'École Française d'Extrême-Orient, 1955.

Bopearachchi, O. "The Euthydemus Imitations and the Date of Sogdian Independence," *Silk Road Art and Archaeology* II (1991–1992): 1–22.

Boulnois, L. *The Silk Road*. London: Allen and Unwin, 1966.

Boyer, M. A., et al. *Kharosti Inscriptions Discovered by Sir Aurel Stein in Chinese Turkestan*, Parts 1–3. Oxford: Oxford University Press, 1920–1929.

Briggs, L. P. *The Ancient Khmer Empire*, Bangkok: White Lotus, 1999.

Brown, D. M. *The Cambridge History of Japan*. Cambridge: Cambridge University Press, 1993.

Brown, R. L. *Studies in Asian Art and Archaeology*. Vol. 18, *The Dvaravati Wheels of the Law and Indianisation in Southeast Asia*. Leiden: Brill, 1996.

Bruguier, B. "Le Prasat Ak Yum, état des connaissances," In *Nouvèlles Récherches sur le Cambodge*, edited by F. Bizot. Paris: École Française d'Extrême-Orient, 1994.

Buck, D. D. "Archaeological Explorations at the Ancient Capital of Lu at Qufu in Shandong Province," *Chinese Sociology and Anthropology* 19 (1986): 3–76.

Burrow, T. *A Translation of the Kharosti Documents from Chinese Turkestan*. London: The Royal Asiatic Society, 1940.

Cannon, G. *The Collected Works of Sir William Jones*, Vol. 1. Surrey: Curzon Press, 1993.

Carswell, J. "The Excavation of Mantai." In *The Indian Ocean in Antiquity*, edited by J. Reade. London: Kegan Paul, 1996.

Chang, K.-C. *The Shang Civilization*. New Haven, Conn.: Yale University Press, 1980.

Chao Hing-wa, ed. *Archaeological Discoveries of Ancient Yue People in South China Exhibition*. Hong Kong: Museum of History, 1993.

Chen Xiandan. "On the Designation 'Money Tree,'" *Orientations* 28 (1997): 67–71.

Chihara, D. *Hindu-Buddhist Architecture in Southeast Asia.* Leiden: Brill, 1996.

Chopra, P. N., ed. *The Gazetteer of India.* Vol. 2, *History and Culture.* New Delhi: Department of Culture, Ministry of Education and Social Welfare, 1973.

Christie, J. W. "Trade and State formation in the Malay Peninsula and Sumatra, 300 BC–AD 700." In *The Southeast Asian Port and Polity: Rise and Demise,* edited by J. Kathirithamby-Wells and J. Villiers. Singapore: Singapore University Press, 1990.

———. "States without Cities: Demographic Trends in Early Java," *Indonesia* 52 (1991): 23–40.

Clunas, C. *Art in China.* Oxford: Oxford University Press, 1997.

Cœdès, G. *Angkor: An Introduction.* Hong Kong: Oxford University Press, 1966.

———. *The Indianized States of Southeast Asia.* Honolulu: University of Hawaii, 1968.

Coningham, R. A. E. "Dark Age or Continuum? An Archaeological Analysis of the Second Emergence of Urbanism in South Asia." In *The Archaeology of Early Historic South Asia,* edited by Raymond Allchin. Cambridge: Cambridge University Press, 1995.

Cook, C. A., and J. S. Major, eds. *Defining Chu: Image and Reality in Ancient China.* Honolulu: University of Hawaii Press, 1999.

Cribb, J. "The Sino-Kharosthi Coins of Khotan," *The Numismatic Chronicle* 144 (1984): 128–152.

———. "The Sino-Kharosthi Coins of Khotan," *The Numismatic Chronicle* 145 (1985): 136–149.

Cucarzi, M., and P. Zolese, "An Attempt to Inventory Khmer Monumental Remains through Geomagnetic Modelling: The Ancient City of Wat Phu." In *Southeast Asian Archaeology 1994,* edited by Pierre-Yves Manguin. Hull: Centre for Southeast Asian Studies, University of Hull, 1994.

Dales, G. F. "The Balakot Project: Summary of Four Years Excavation in Pakistan," *Man and Environment* 3 (1979): 45–53.

———. "The Mythical Massacre at Mohenjo Daro," *Expedition* 6 (1964): 36–43.

Dalton, O. M. *The Treasure of the Oxus.* London: British Museum Publications, 1964.

Dani, A. H., and V. M. Masson, eds. *History of Civilizations of Central Asia.* Vol. 1. *The Dawn of Civilization: Earliest Times to 700 B.C.* Paris: UNESCO, 1992.

Dao Linh Con. "The Oc Eo Burial Group Recently Excavated at Go Thap (Dong Thap Province, Viet Nam)." In *Southeast Asian Archaeology 1994,* edited by Pierre-Yves Manguin. Hull: Centre for Southeast Asian Studies, University of Hull, 1994.

de Bary, W. T., and I. Bloom, eds. *Sources of Chinese Tradition.* New York: Columbia University Press, 1999.

Dehejia, V. *Early Buddhist Rock Temples.* London: Thames and Hudson, 1972.

Dematte, P. "Longshan-Era Urbanism: The Role of Cities in Predynastic China," *Asian Perspectives* 38 (1999): 119–153.

de Silva, K. M. *A History of Sri Lanka.* London: Hurst, 1981.

Deydier, C. *Archaic Chinese Bronzes: Xin and Shang.* Paris: ARHIS, 1995.

Donovan, D. G., H. Kukui, and T. Itoh. "Perspective on the Pyu landscape," *Southeast Asian Studies* 36 (1998): 19–126.

Dumarçay, J., and P. Royère. *Cambodian Architecture, Eighth to Thirteenth Centuries.* Leiden: Brill, 2001.

Duncan, J. *The Origins of the Choson Dynasty.* Seattle: University of Washington Press, 2000.

Elisseef, D., and V. Elisseef. *New Discoveries in China.* Seacaucus, N.J.: Chartwell Books, 1983.

Erdosy, G. "City States of North India and Pakistan at the Time of the Buddha." In *The Archaeology of Early Historic South Asia,* edited by Raymond Allchin. Cambridge: Cambridge University Press, 1995.

———. "The Prelude to Urbanization: Ethnicity and the Rise of Late Vedic Chiefdoms." In *The Archaeology of Early Historic South Asia,* edited by Raymond Allchin. Cambridge: Cambridge University Press, 1995.

Errington, E., and J. Cribb, eds. *The Crossroads of Asia.* Cambridge: Ancient India and Iran Trust, 1992.

Fahr-Becker, G., ed. *The Art of East Asia.* Cologne: Könemann, 1999.

Fairservis, W. A. *The Harappan Civilization and Its Writing: A Model for the Decipherment of the Indus Script.* Leiden: Brill, 1992.

Farris, W. W. *Sacred Texts and Buried Treasures.* Honolulu: University of Hawaii Press, 1998.

Fitzgerald-Huber, L. G. "Qijia and Erlitou: The Question of Contacts with Distant Cultures," *Early China* 20 (1995): 17–68.

Flam, L. "Excavations at Ghazi Shah 1985–1987," *Pakistan Archaeology* 28 (1993): 131–158.

Flood, G. *An Introduction to Hinduism.* Cambridge: Cambridge University Press, 1996.

Foltz, R. C. *Religions of the Silk Road.* Basingstoke: Palgrave Macmillan, 2000.

Fontein, J., and J. Klokke, eds. *Narrative Sculpture and Literary Traditions in South and Southeast Asia.* Studies in Asian Art and Archaeology, No. 23. Leiden: Brill, 2000.

Frawley, D. *The Myth of the Aryan Invasion of India.* New Delhi: Voice of India, 1994.

Frumkin, G. *Archaeology in Soviet Central Asia.* Leiden: Brill, 1970.

Gao Dalun. "Bronze Ritual Artefacts of the Shu Culture: A Preliminary Survey," *Orientations* 32 (2001): 45–51.

Ghosh, A. *An Encyclopaedia of Indian Archaeology.* Leiden: Brill, 1990.

Ghurye, G. A. *Vedic India.* Bombay: Popular Prakashan, 1979.

Giteau, M. *Khmer Sculpture and the Angkor Civilisation.* London: Thames and Hudson, 1965.

Glover, I. C. *Early Trade between India and Southeast Asia: A Link in the Development of a World Trading System.*

Occasional Paper No. 16. Hull: The University of Hull Centre for Southeast Asian Studies, 1989.

Gomez, L. O., and H. W. Woodward, Jr. *Barabudur: History and Significance of a Buddhist Monument*. Berkeley, Calif.: Asian Humanities Press, 1981.

Griffith, R. T. *Hymns of the Rigveda*. Delhi: South Asia Books, 1999.

Groslier, B.-P. "Angkor et le Cambodge au XVIᵉ siècle d'après les source portugueses et espagnoles," *Annales du Musée Guimet* 63 (1958): 1–194.

———. "La Cité hydraulique angkorienne: Exploitation ou surexploitation du sol?" *Bulletin de l'École Française d'Extrême-Orient* 56 (1979): 161–202.

Guillon, E. *Cham Art*. London: Thames and Hudson, 2001.

Guo Da-shun. "Lower Xiajiadian Culture." In *The Archaeology of Northern China beyond the Great Wall*, edited by Sarah Nelson. London: Routledge, 1995.

Gupta, P. L. *Coins. India—the Land and the People*. New Delhi: National Book Trust, 1969.

Gupta, S., D. Williams, and D. Peacock. "Dressel 2-4 Amphorae and Roman Trade with India: The Evidence from Nevasa," *South Asian Studies* 17 (2001): 7–18.

Gutman, P. "The Ancient Coinage of Southeast Asia," *Journal of the Siam Society* 66 (1978): 8–21.

———. *Burma's Lost Kingdoms: Splendours of Arakan*. Bangkok: Orchid Press, 2001.

———. "Symbolism of Kingship in Arakan." In *Southeast Asia in the 9th to the 14th Centuries*, edited by D. Marr and A. C. Milner. Singapore: Institute of Southeast Asian Studies, 1981.

Hagesteijn, R. "The Angkor State: Rise, Fall and in Between." In *Early State Dynamics*, edited by H. J. M. Claessen and P. Van der Velde. Leiden: Brill, 1987.

Hall, K. "Khmer Commercial Developments and Foreign Contacts Under Suryavarman I," *Journal of Economic and Social History of the Orient* 18 (1975): 318–336.

———. *Maritime Trade and State Development in Early Southeast Asia*. Honolulu: University of Hawaii Press, 1985.

Hallade, M. *The Gandhara Style and the Evolution of Buddhist Art*. London: Thames and Hudson, 1968.

Harle, J. C. *The Art and Architecture of the Indian Subcontinent*. London: Penguin Books, 1986.

———. *Gupta Sculpture: Indian Sculpture of the Fourth to the Sixth Centuries AD*. Oxford: Clarendon Press, 1974.

Harmatta J., B. N. Puri, and G. F. Etemadi. *History of Civilizations of Central Asia*. Vol. 2. *The Development of Sedentary and Nomadic Civilizations*. Paris: UNESCO, 1994.

He Jiejun. "Excavations at Chengtoushan in Li County, Hunan Province, India," *Bulletin of the Indo-Pacific Prehistory Association* 18 (1999): 101–103.

Herrmann, G. *Monuments of Merv: Traditional Building of the Karakum*. London: Society of Antiquaries of London, 1999.

Higham, C. F. W. *The Civilization of Angkor*. London: Weidenfeld and Nicholson, 2001.

———., and Thosarat, R. *Prehistoric Thailand: From First Settlement to Sukhothai*. Bangkok: River Books, 1998.

Hsu, Cho-yun. *Han Agriculture: The Formation of Early Chinese Agrarian Economy*. Seattle: University of Washington Press, 1980.

———., and K. M. Linduff. *Western Zhou Civilization*. New Haven, Conn.: Yale University Press, 1988.

Hyung Il Pai. *Constructing Korean Origins*. Cambridge, Mass: Harvard University Press, 2000.

Huntington, S. L. *The Art of Ancient India*. New York: Weatherill, 1985.

Ilyasov, D., and T. Mkrtychev. "Bactrian Goddess from Dalverzin-tepe," *Silk Road Art and Archaeology* II (1991/1992): 107–127.

Ishjamts, N. "Nomads in Eastern Central Asia." In *History of the Civilizations of Central Asia*, Vol. 2, edited by J. Harmatta. Paris: UNESCO, 1994.

Jacob, J. M. "Pre-Angkor Cambodia: Evidence from the Inscriptions in Khmer Concerning the Common People and Their Environment." In *Early South East Asia*, edited by R. Smith and W. Watson. Kuala Lumpur: Oxford University Press, 1978.

Jacq-Hergoualc'h, M. "Un Cité-État de la péninsule malaise: Le Langkasuka," *Arts Asiatique* 50 (1995): 47–66.

———. "La Region de Nakhon Si Thammarat (Thaïlande Péninsulaire) du Vᵉ aux XIVᵉ siècle," *Journal Asiatique* 284 (1996): 361–435.

Jacques, C. *Angkor, Cities and Temples*. Bangkok: River Books, 1997.

———. "'Funan', 'Zhenla:' The Reality Concealed by These Chinese Views of Indochina." In *Early South East Asia*, edited by R. Smith and W. Watson. Kuala Lumpur: Oxford University Press, 1978.

———. "New Data on the VII–VIIIth Centuries in the Khmer Lands." In *Southeast Asian Archaeology 1986*, edited by I. C. Glover and E. Glover. Oxford: British Archaeological Reports (International Series) 561, 1986.

Jarrige, J.-F. "Excavations at Nausharo 1987–8," *Pakistan Archaeology* 24 (1989): 21–67.

Jay Xu. "Reconstructing Sanxingdui Imagery: Some Speculations," *Orientations* 32 (2001): 32–44.

Kamalakar, G. ed. *South Indian Archaeology*. Delhi: Bharatiya Kala Prakahan, 2000.

Keightley, D. N. *Sources of Shang History: The Oracle Bones of Bronze Age China*. Berkeley: University of California Press, 1978.

Kenoyer, J. M. *Ancient Cities of the Indus Civilization*. Oxford: Oxford University Press, 1998.

Khan, F. A. "Excavations at Kot Diji," *Pakistan Archaeology* 2 (1964): 11–85.

Kiyotari, T., ed. *Recent Archaeological Discoveries in Japan*. Tokyo: The Centre for East Asian Cultural Studies, 1987.

Klimburg, S. D. *The Kingdom of Bamiyan*. Naples/Rome: Buddhist Art and Culture of the Hindukush, 1987.

Klimburg-Salter, D. E. *The Silk Route and the Diamond Path*. Los Angeles: UCLA Art Council, 1982.

Knobloch, E. *Beyond the Oxus: Archaeology, Art and Architecture of Central Asia.* London: Ernest Benn, 1972.

Kohl, P. L. *The Bronze Age Civilization of Central Asia: Recent Soviet Discoveries.* Armank: M. E. Sharpe, 1981.

Koshelenko, G. A., and V. N. Pilipko. "Parthia." In *History of the Civilizations of Central Asia,* Vol. 2, edited by J. Harmatta. Paris: UNESCO, 1994.

Kulke, H. *The Devaraja Cult.* Data Paper No. 108 Southeast Asia Program. Ithaca, N.Y.: Department of Asian Studies, Cornell University, 1978.

————. "The Early and the Imperial Kingdoms in Southeast Asian History." In *Southeast Asia in the 9th to 14th Centuries,* edited by D. G. Marr and A. C. Milner. Singapore: Institute of Southeast Asian Studies; Canberra: Research School of Pacific Studies, Australian National University, 1986.

Lal, B. B. *The Earliest Civilization of South Asia.* New Delhi: Aryan Books, 1997.

Lawton, T. "A Group of Early Western Chou Period Bronze Vessels," *Ars Orientalis* 10 (1975): 11–21.

————, ed. *New Perspectives on Chu Culture in the Eastern Zhou Period.* Washington, D.C.: Smithsonian Institution, 1991.

Le Bonheur, A. *Of Gods, Kings and Men.* London: Serindia, 1995.

Legge, J. *The Chinese Classics.* Oxford: Oxford University Press, 1893.

Leshnik, L. S. "The Harappan 'Port' at Lothal: Another View," *American Anthropologist* 70 (1968): 911–922.

Li Houbo. "Han Dynasty Tomb Murals from the Luoyang Museum of Ancient Tomb Relics," *Orientations* 25 (1994): 40–50.

Li Xueqin. *Eastern Zhou and Qin Civilizations.* New Haven, Conn.: Yale University Press, 1985.

Litvinsky, B. A. "Cities and Urban Life in the Kushan Kingdom." In *History of the Civilizations of Central Asia,* Vol. 2, edited by J. Harmatta. Paris: UNESCO, 1994.

————. "The Hephthalite Empire." In *History of Civilizations of Central Asia,* Vol. III, edited by B. A. Litvinsky. Paris: UNESCO, 1996.

————. "The Rise of Sasanian Iran." In *History of the Civilizations of Central Asia,* Vol. 2, edited by J. Harmatta. Paris: UNESCO, 1994.

————, Zhang Guang-da, and R. Shabani Samghabadi, R., eds. *History of Civilizations of Central Asia,* Vol. 3. *The Crossroads of Civilizations: A.D. 250–750.* Paris: UNESCO, 1996.

Liu Li. "Ancestor Worship: An Archaeological Investigation of Ritual Activities in Neolithic North China," *Journal of East Asian Archaeology* 2 (2000): 129–164.

Loewe, M. *A Biographical Dictionary of the Qin, Former Han and Xin Periods (221 BC–AD 24).* Leiden: Brill, 2000.

————. *Chinese Ideas of Life and Death.* London: Allen and Unwin, 1982.

————. *Divination, Mythology and Monarchy in Han China.* Cambridge: Cambridge University Press, 1994.

————, ed. *Early Chinese Texts: A Bibliographical Guide.* Berkeley, Calif.: Society for the Study of Early China and the Institute of East Asian Studies, 1993.

————, and Shangnessy, G. L., eds. *The Cambridge History of Ancient China.* Cambridge: Cambridge University Press, 1999.

Luce, G. H. *Old Burma: Early Pagan.* New York: Augustin, 1970.

————. *Phases in Pre-Pagan Burma.* Oxford: Oxford University Press, 1985.

Mackay, E. J. H. *Chanhu-Daro Excavations.* New Haven, Conn.: American Oriental Society, 1942.

Malleret, L. *L'Archéologie du delta du Mékong.* Paris: École Française d'Extrême-Orient, 1959–1963.

Manguin, P.-Y. "Southeast Asian Shipping in the Indian Ocean during the First Millennium A.D." In *Tradition and Archaeology: Early Maritime Contacts in the Indian Ocean,* edited by H. P. Ray and S. F. Salles. New Delhi: Manohar, 1996.

————. "Les Cité-États de l'Asie du sud-est cotière," *Bulletin de l'École Française d'Extrême-Orient* 87 (2000): 151–182.

Mani, V. R., and R. Chakravarti. *A Sourcebook of Indian Civilization.* Hyderabad: Orient Longman, 2000.

Mannika, E. *Angkor Wat: Time, Space and Kingship.* St. Leonards: Allen and Unwin, 1996.

Margabandhu, C. *Archaeology of the Satavahana Kshatrapa Times.* Delhi: Sundeep Prakashan, 1985.

Marshak, B. I., and N. N. Negmatov. "Sogdiana." *History of Civilizations of Central Asia,* Vol. 3, edited by B. A. Litvinsky. Paris: UNESCO, 1996.

Marshall, J. "The Bronze Age in Khorasan and Transoxiana." In *History of the Civilizations of Central Asia,* Vol. 1, edited by A. H. Dani, and V. M. Masson. Paris: UNESCO, 1992.

————. "Excavations at Bhita," *Annual Report of the Archaeological Survey of India* 1912–1913 (1912): 29–94.

————. *Taxila, an Illustrated Account of the Archaeological Excavations.* Cambridge: Cambridge University Press, 1951.

Mattos, G. L. "Eastern Zhou Bronze Inscriptions." In *New Sources of Early Chinese History: An Introduction to the Reading of Inscriptions and Manuscripts,* edited by E. L. Shaughnessy. Berkeley: Society for the Study of Early China and Institute of East Asian Studies, University of California, 1997.

Mazzeo, D., and C. S. Antonini. *Monuments of Civilization: Ancient Cambodia.* New York: Grosset & Dunlap, 1978.

Meadow, R. H. *Harappa Excavations 1986–1990.* Monographs in World Archaeology No. 3. Madison, Wis.: Prehistory Press, 1991.

Moore, E., and S. Siribhadra. *Palaces of the Gods: Khmer Art and Architecture in Thailand.* Bangkok: River Books, 1992.

Mukhamedjanov, A. R. "Economy and Social Systems in Central Asia." In *History of the Civilizations of Central Asia,* Vol. 2, edited by J. Harmatta. Paris: UNESCO, 1994.

Nelson, S. M. *The Archaeology of Korea.* Cambridge: Cambridge University Press, 1993.

———. "Ritualized Pigs and the Origins of Complex Society: Hypotheses Regarding the Hongshan Culture," *Early China* 20 (1995): 1–16.

Nerazik, E. E., and P. G. Bulgakov. "Khwarizm." In *History of Civilizations of Central Asia*, Vol. III, edited by B. A. Litvinsky. Paris: UNESCO, 1996.

Nienhauser, W. H. ed. *The Grand Scribe's Records*. Vol. 1, *The Basic Annals of Pre-Han China by Ssu-ma Ch'ien*. Bloomington and Indianapolis: Indiana University Press, 1994.

Nikitin, A. B. "Parthian Bullae from Nisa," *Silk Road Art and Archaeology* 3 (1993–1994): 71–75.

Parmentier, H. *L'Art khmer primitif*. Paris: École Française d'Extrême-Orient, 1927.

Pearson, R. J., ed. *Windows on the Japanese Past: Studies in Archaeology and Prehistory*. Ann Arbor: University of Michigan Press, 1986.

Pearson, R., ed. *Ancient Japan*. New York: G. Braziller, 1992.

Pearson, R. J., Jong-wook Lee, Wonyoung Koh, and Underhill, A. "Social Ranking in the Kingdom of Old Silla, Korea: Analysis of Burials," *Journal of Anthropological Archaeology* 8 (1986): 1–50.

Peng Jinzhang. "New Archaeological Discoveries in the Northern Area of the Mogao Caves at Dunhuang," *Orientations* 32 (2001): 72–75.

Pigott, V. C., ed. *The Archaeometallurgy of the Asian Old World*. Masca Research Papers in Science and Archaeology, Vol. 16. Philadelphia: University Museum, University of Pennsylvania, 1999.

Portal, J. *Korea: Art and Archaeology*. London: British Museum, 2000.

Possehl, G. L. *Harappan Civilization: A Recent Perspective*. New Delhi: Oxford University Press, 1993.

———. *Indus Age: The Writing System*. Philadelphia: University of Pennsylvania Press, 1996.

———. "Meluhha." In *The Indian Ocean in Antiquity*, edited by J. Reade. London: Kegan Paul, 1996.

———. "Revolution in the Urban Revolution: The Emergence of Indus Urbanisation," *Annual Review of Anthropology* 19 (1990): 261–282.

Psarras, S.-K. "Rethinking the Non-Chinese Southwest." *Artibus Asiae* 40 (2000): 5–58.

———. "Xiongnu Culture: Identification and Dating." *Central European Journal* 39 (1995): 102–136.

Pugachenkova, G. A. "The Buddhist Monuments of Airtam," *Silk Road Art and Archaeology* 2 (1991/1992): 23–41.

Puri, B. N. "The Sakas and Indo-Parthians." In *History of the Civilizations of Central Asia* Vol. II, edited by J. Harmatta. Paris: UNESCO, 1994.

Rangarajan, L. N. *The Arthashastra*. New Delhi: Penguin, 1992.

Rawson, J. "Statesmen or Barbarians? The Western Zhou as Seen through Their Bronzes." *Proceedings of the British Academy* 75 (1989): 71–95.

———. *Western Zhou Ritual Bronzes from the Arthur M. Sackler Collection*. Cambridge, Mass.: Harvard University Press, 1990.

Rawson, J., ed. *The British Museum Book of Chinese Art*. London: Thames and Hudson, 1992.

———., ed. *Mysteries of Ancient China*. London: British Museum Press, 1996.

Rhie, M. M. *Later Han, Three Kingdoms and Western Chin in China and Bactria to Shan-shan*. Leiden: Brill, 1999.

Ricklefs, M. C. "Land and the Law in the Epigraphy of Tenth-Century Cambodia," *Journal of the Royal Asiatic Society* 26, no. 93 (1967): 411–420.

Roveda, V. *Khmer Mythology*. Bangkok: River Books, 1997.

Rudolph, R. C., and Wen You. *Han Tomb Art of West China*. Los Angeles: University of Los Angeles Press, 1991.

Sage, S. F. *Ancient Sichuan and the Unification of China*. Albany, N.Y.: SUNY Press, 1992.

Salomon, R. *Ancient Buddhist Scrolls from Gandhara*. Seattle: University of Washington Press, 1999.

———. *Indian Epigraphy: A Guide to the Study of Inscriptions in Sanskrit, Prakrit and the Other Indo-Aryan Languages*. New York: Oxford University Press, 1998.

Sarianidi, V. I. *The Golden Hoard of Bactria: From the Tillya-tepe Excavations in Northern Afghanistan*. New York: H. N. Abrams; Leningrad: Aurora Art Publishers, 1985.

Sedlar, J. *India and the Greek World*. Totowa, N.J.: Rowman & Littlefield, 1980.

Sedov, L. A. "Angkor: Society and State." In *The Early State*, edited by H. J. M. Claessen and P. Skalník. The Hague: Mouton, 1978.

Sharif, M., and B. K. Thapar. "Food Producing Communities in Pakistan and Northern India." In *History of the Civilizations of Central Asia*, Vol. 1, edited by A. H. Dani and V. M. Masson. Paris: UNESCO, 1992.

Shaughnessy, E. L. "Historical Perspectives on the Introduction of the Chariot into China," *Harvard Journal of Asiatic Studies* 48 (1988): 189–237.

———. "On the Authenticity of the *Bamboo Annals*," *Harvard Journal of Asiatic Studies* 46 (1986): 149–180.

———. *Sources of Western Zhou History*. Berkeley: University of California Press, 1991.

———. "Zhouyuan Oracle-Bone Inscriptions: Entering the Research Stage?" *Early China* 11–12 (1985–1987): 146–163.

———., ed. *China: The Land of the Heavenly Dragon*. London: Duncan Baird, 2000.

Shelach, G. "Early Bronze Age Cultures in North China," *Asian Perspectives* 33 (1994): 261–292.

Sima Qian. *Records of the Grand Historian: The Qin Dynasty*, translated by Burton Watson. New York: Columbia University Press, 1993.

———. *Records of the Grand Historian: The Han Dynasty* II, translated by Burton Watson. New York: Columbia University Press, 1993.

———. *Records of the Grand Historian: The Han Dynasty* I, translated by Burton Watson. New York: Columbia University Press, 1993.

Sims-Williams, N., and J. Cribb. "A New Bactrian Inscription of Kanishka the Great," *Silk Road Art and Archaeology* 4 (1998): 75–142.

Sivaramamurti, C. *The Art of India*. New York: Harry N. Abrams, 1977.

Stargardt, J. *The Ancient Pyu of Burma*. Vol. 1, *Early Pyu Cities in a Man-Made Landscape*. Cambridge: PACSEA Cambridge and ISEAS Singapore, 1990.

Stark, M. T., et al. "Results of the 1995–6 Archaeological Field Investigations at Angkor Borei, Cambodia," *Asian Perspectives* 38 (1) (1995–1996): 7–36.

Stein, A. *Ancient Khotan*. Oxford: Clarendon Press, 1907.

———. "Excavations at Sahri-Bahlol," *Archaeological Survey of India Annual Report 1911–12* (1998): 95–119.

Stott, P. "Angkor: Shifting the Hydraulic Paradigm." In *The Gift of Water*, edited by J. Rigg. London: SOAS, 1992.

Swart, P. "The Tomb of the King of Nan Yue," *Orientations* 21 (1990): 56–66.

Tambiah, S. J. "The Galactic Polity: The Structure of Traditional Kingdoms in Southeast Asia," *Annals of the New York Academy of Sciences* 293 (1977): 69–97.

Tang Changshou. "Shiziwan Cliff Tomb No. 1," *Orientations* 28 (1997): 72–77.

Thapar, B. K. "Kalibangan: A Harappan Metropolis beyond the Indus Valley," *Expedition* 17 (1975): 19–32.

Thapar, R. *From Lineage to State: Social Formations in the Mid-First Millennium BC in the Ganga Valley*. Delhi: Oxford University Press, 1984.

Thorpe, R. "The Sui Xian Tomb: Re-thinking the Fifth Century," *Artibus Asiae* 43 (1981–1982): 67–92.

Thote, A. "The Double Coffin of Leigudun Tomb No. 1: Iconographic Sources and Related Problems." In *New Perspectives on Chu Culture during the Eastern Zhou Period*, edited by T. Lawton. Washington, D.C.: Smithsonian Institution, 1991.

Tian An. "Archaeological Exploration of the Lu City of Qufu," *Chinese Sociology and Anthropology* 19 (1986): 9–34.

Tosi, M., M., Malek Shahmirzadi, and M. A. Joyenda. "The Bronze Age in Iran and Afghanistan." In *History of Civilizations of Central Asia*, Vol. I, edited by A. H. Dani and V. M. Masson. Paris: UNESCO, 1992.

Totman, C. *A History of Japan*. Oxford: Blackwell, 2000.

Trautmann, T. R. *Kautilya and the Arthasastra*. Leiden: Brill, 1971.

Twitchet, D., and M. Loewe, eds. *The Cambridge History of China*, Vol. I, *The Ch'in and Han Empires, 221 B.C.–A.D. 220*. Cambridge: Cambridge University Press, 1986.

Umesao, T., and T. Sugimura, eds. "Significance of the Silk Roads in the History of Human Civilizations." *Senri Ethnological Studies* 32 (1992).

Underhill, A. "Variation in Settlements during the Longshan Period of Northern China," *Asian Perspectives* 33 (1994): 197–228.

Vickery, M. *Society, Economics and Politics in Pre-Angkor Cambodia*. Tokyo: The Centre for East Asian Cultural Studies for UNESCO, 1998.

Vickery, M. "What and Where Was Chenla?" In *Récherches Nouvèlles sur le Cambodge*, edited by F. Bizot. Paris: École Française d'Extrême-Orient, 1994.

Wagner, D. *Iron and Steel in Ancient China*. Leiden: Brill, 1993.

Wang Yuquan. *Early Chinese Coinage*. New York: Sanford Durst, 1980.

Wang Zhongshu. *Han Civilization*. New Haven, Conn.: Yale University Press, 1982.

Watson, W. *The Art of China to AD 900*. New Haven, Conn.: Yale University Press, 1995.

Weber, C. D. *Chinese Pictorial Bronzes of the Late Chou Period*. Ascona: Artibus Asiae, 1968.

Wheatley, P. *Nagara and Commandery: Origins of the Southeast Asian Urban Traditions*. Research Paper 207–208. Chicago: University of Chicago, Department of Geography: 1983.

Wheeler, R. E. M. *Charsada, a Metropolis of the North-West Frontier*. London: British Academy, 1962.

———. *Early India and Pakistan*. London: Thames and Hudson, 1959.

Whitfield, R., and Wang Tao, eds. *Exploring China's Past*. London: Saffron Books, 1999.

White, W. C. *Tombs of Old Loyang*. Shanghai: Kelly and Walsh, 1934.

Wicks, R. "The Ancient Coinage of Southeast Asia," *Journal of Southeast Asian Studies* XVI (1985): 2.

Wu Hung. "All About the Eyes: Two Groups of Sculptures from the Sanxingdui Culture," *Orientations* 28 (1997): 58–66.

———. "Art in Its Ritual Context: Rethinking Mawangdui," *Early China* 17 (1992): 111–145.

———. "A Deity Without Form: The Earliest Representation of Laozi and the Concept of *Wei* in Chinese Ritual Art," *Orientations* 34 (2002): 38–45.

———. *Monumentality in Early Chinese Art and Architecture*. Stanford, Calif.: Stanford University Press, 1995.

———. *3,000 Years of Chinese Painting*. New Haven, Conn.: Yale University Press, 1997.

Xiaoneng Yang, ed. *The Golden Age of Chinese Archaeology*. New Haven, Conn.: Yale University Press, 1999.

Yatsenko, S. A. "The Costume of the Yuech-Chihs/Kushans and Its Analogies to the East and to the West," *Silk Road Archaeology* 7 (2001): 73–120.

Zeimal, E. V. "The Kidarite Kingdom of Central Asia." In *History of Civilizations of Central Asia*, Vol. 3, edited by B. A. Litvinsky. Paris: UNESCO, 1996.

Zhang Xuehai. "Discussion of the Periodization and Basic Groundplan of the Lu City at Qufu," *Chinese Sociology and Anthropology* 19 (1986): 35–48.

———, et al. "Conclusions from the Ancient City of the Lu State," *Chinese Sociology and Anthropology* 19 (1986): 49–65.

Zheng Zhenxiang. "The Royal Consort Fu Hao and Her Tomb." In *Mysteries of Ancient China*, edited by J. Rawson. New York: Braziller, 1996.

INDEX